HARDPRESS.NET
HOME OF HARD-TO-FIND BOOKS

The Political State of the British Empire, Containing a General View of the Domestic and Foreign Possessions of the Crown, the Laws, Commerce, Revenues, Offices and Other Establishements, Civil and Military

by John Adolphus

Address:
HardPress
8345 NW 66TH ST #2561
MIAMI FL 33166-2626
USA
Email: info@hardpress.net

:it.
603 a

Adolphus

THE

POLITICAL STATE

OF

THE BRITISH EMPIRE;

CONTAINING

A GENERAL VIEW

OF

THE DOMESTIC AND FOREIGN POSSESSIONS
OF THE CROWN;

THE LAWS, COMMERCE, REVENUES, OFFICES,
AND OTHER ESTABLISHMENTS,

CIVIL AND MILITARY.

By JOHN ADOLPHUS, Esq.

BARRISTER AT LAW, F.S.A.

AUTHOR OF "THE HISTORY OF ENGLAND, FROM THE ACCESSION OF
KING GEORGE III. TO THE PEACE OF 1783."

IN FOUR VOLUMES

VOL. II.

LONDON:
PRINTED FOR T. CADELL AND W. DAVIES,
IN THE STRAND.
1818.

Printed by A. Strahan,
Printers-Street, London.

CONTENTS

OF

THE SECOND VOLUME.

ENGLAND *continued.*

Improvements

CONTENTS.

CONTENTS.

Compofition

Ely

Serjeants

Punishment

CONTENTS.

Bribery

POLITICAL STATE

OF THE

BRITISH EMPIRE.

OFFICERS OF STATE.

THE general neceffity of employing agents of talent and credit to execute the bufinefs in the various departments of government is ftrongly felt in every country; but the affignment of each branch to a diftinct avowed minifter is peculiarly requifite in the Britifh fyftem. In other nations, the bounty and patronage of the crown, and the execution of all the weighty affairs of ftate may be committed to one perfon, diftinguifhed by the name of favourite, prime minifter, or premier, and his malverfations may be fheltered by the authority of the monarch; but, in Great Britain, the axiom, that the king can do no wrong, is prevented from becoming an engine for oppreffing the fubject, by the ftrict refponfibility annexed to the fituation of minifters, and the power of inquiry and impeachment tenacioufly referved, and vigoroufly exercifed by parliament.

In the following enumeration, the duties of the moft eminent minifters of ftate will be exhibited, and fome details afforded refpecting the offices or departments over which they prefide. They are given in the order of their precedence, with the addition of embaffadors and confuls in foreign lands.

1. The Lord High Steward. In ancient times the lord high fteward of England was the firft great officer of the crown. The title is of Saxon etymology, *ftede* fignifying room, or *ftead*, and *weard* a warden or keeper; and therefore to the lord high fteward of England belonged vice-regal power. As next under the king he fuperwifed and regulated the adminiftration of juftice, and all other affairs of the realm both civil and military.

 The

The office was of great antiquity, being established before the reign of Edward the Confessor. It was annexed to the lordship of Hinckley in Leicestershire, which, belonging to the family of Montfort earl of Leicester, the possessors of that title were, in right of their fief, hereditary lord high stewards of England. Simon de Montfort, the last earl of that family, being defeated in the rebellion which he raised against Henry III., and his estates becoming forfeit, the monarch prudently embraced the opportunity of retrenching the authorities of an office which, in the hands of a turbulent and ambitious man, had been found sufficient to disquiet the rule it was intended to enforce, and shake the throne it was destined to support. It still continued, though reduced in power, an office of inheritance, till Henry of Bolingbroke, who last possessed it in that form, usurped the throne by the title of Henry IV. From that period lord high stewards have been appointed *pro hac vice* only, generally to officiate at coronations, or at trials before the high court of parliament.

A lord high steward, appointed for a coronation, receives and decides on the bills and petitions of all persons, peers or others, claiming to hold estates by grand serjeanty, and, in virtue of that tenure, to do certain honourable services at the king's coronation. In these cases, he is obliged to judge according to the laws and customs of the realm, and is entitled to customary fees and allowances. At the coronation, he carries St. Edward's crown, and the office is never conferred on any but a peer of parliament. Mention has already been made of the duty and office of the lord high steward on the trial of impeachments; he is, on those occasions, attended from his own abode to the house of lords in great state by the judges and officers of arms, and, after reading his commission, the white wand is with much ceremony put into his hands, and from that time, during the sittings on the trial, he is styled *your grace*. This office being only occasional, does not affect the general government of the realm, but is noticed in this place on account of its dignity.

2. Lord High Chancellor. The situation of lord high chancellor is the most dignified of all those which are considered as permanent; it is not indeed absolutely necessary that there should always be a lord chancellor, since the great seal may be given to a lord keeper, or put in commission. The powers of lord chancellor and lord keeper are the same, and therefore since the statute, 5 Elizabeth, both cannot be appointed at the same time; formerly they could, for it is said Henry V. had a great seal of gold which he delivered to the bishop of Durham, making him lord chancellor; and one of silver, which he gave to the bishop of London, appointing him lord keeper. By stat.

1 W.

1 W. & M. c. 21., commissioners appointed to execute the office of lord chancellor may exercise all the authority, jurisdiction, and execution of laws, which the lord chancellor, or lord keeper, of right ought to use and execute. Since that period the great seal has, on various occasions, been in commission, either in times when the pretensions of different persons could not be adjusted without difficulty by the other members of the cabinet, or when no person sufficiently eminent to fill a station so exalted could be found to accept one from which he might be so suddenly removed.

The lord high chancellor or keeper is created by the mere delivery of the king's great seal into his custody; whereby he becomes, without writ or patent, an officer of the greatest weight and power of any now subsisting in the kingdom, and superior in point of precedency to every temporal lord: and the act of taking away this seal by the king, or of its being resigned or given up, determines the office. The name chancellor is said to be derived *a cancellando*, because all patents, commissions, and warrants coming from the king, are perused by him before they pass under the great seal, and he may cancel them if repugnant to law; which is the highest of his privileges. Others however derive the name from the place where he anciently sate in judgment, which was said to be, like the chancel of a church, inclosed between lattices, *inter cancellos*. It is an office of high antiquity, having been certainly known to the courts of the Roman emperors; where it originally seems to have signified a chief scribe or secretary, who was afterwards invested with several judicial powers, and a general superintendency over the rest of the officers of the prince. From the Roman empire it passed to the Roman church, ever emulous of imperial state; whence every bishop has, to this day, his chancellor, the principal judge of his consistory; and when the modern kingdoms of Europe were established on the ruins of the empire, almost every state preserved its chancellor, with different jurisdictions and dignities, according to their various constitutions. In England it is clear that the British and Saxon kings had their chancellors, and the principal circumstance denoting their office, was the delivery to them of the great seal, which was sometimes tied about their necks.

The chancellor is a privy counsellor by his office, and, according to lord chancellor Ellesmere, prolocutor of the house of lords by prescription. To him belongs the appointment of all justices of the peace throughout the kingdom. Being formerly usually an ecclesiastic, (for none else were then sufficiently conversant in writings to be capable of the office;) and presiding over the royal chapel, he became keeper of the king's conscience; visitor, in right of the king, of all hospitals and colleges of the king's foundation; and patron of all the king's livings under the value of twenty pounds per annum in the king's books. He is the general guardian of all infants, idiots, and lunatics; and has the general superintendence of all the charitable uses in the kingdom. And all this over and above the vast and extensive jurisdiction which he exercises in his judicial capacity in the court of chancery, which will be noticed in another division of this work. His oath of office engages him to observe the following particulars:

1. That he will well and truly serve our sovereign lord the king and his people in the office of chancellor (or lord keeper). 2. That he shall do right to all manner of people, poor and rich, after the laws and usages of the realm. 3. That he shall truly counsel the king, and his counsel he shall keep. 4. That he shall not know nor suffer the hurt or disheriting of the king, or that the rights of the crown be decreased by any means as far as he may hinder it. 5. And if he may prevent it, he shall make it clearly and expressly to be known to the king, with his true advice and counsel; and, 6. And that he shall do and purchase the king's profit in all that he reasonably may.

The emoluments of the office of chancellor are very considerable, derived as well from the court where he presides, as from fees for affixing the great seal to a great variety of public instruments, and those which are due to him as speaker of the house of lords; but as he only holds his situation during pleasure, and if a lawyer, as in modern times he invariably is, he cannot accept of any situation in Westminster hall, after having filled the superior one of chancellor; it is usual to reward those who retire with a considerable pension; and some, before they would, by assuming so precarious an office, sacrifice all their other prospects, have stipulated for a remuneratory pension, or for the reversion of some ample sinecure place.

3. Lord High Treasurer. The lord high treasurer receives his appointment from the king in person, who formerly was used to deliver to him a golden key of the treasury, but now only a wand. When appointed, he goes in state to the court of chancery, and takes an oath similar to that of the lord chancellor, and to the court of exchequer, where he takes his seat among the barons as chancellor of that court. He is a lord by his office, and governs the upper court of exchequer; has the custody of the king's treasure, and of foreign and domestic records there deposited. He has the appointment of all commissioners and other officers employed in collecting the revenues

of

of the crown; the nomination of all escheators, and dispofal of all places in any wise relating to the revenue of the kingdom; and power to let leases of the crown lands.

In modern times a lord treasurer has not been appointed, but the office has been executed by five lords commissioners, of whom the chief, called the first lord of the treasury, possesses most of the powers formerly held by the lord treasurer, and is generally, though not invariably, chancellor and under treasurer of the exchequer. It is not exactly true that the chancellor of the exchequer cannot sit on the bench of that court for the decision of law questions; he has done so even in modern times, but, as the consideration of that part of the jurisdiction of the exchequer belongs to another branch of the work, it will not be treated on in this place, but those matters only will be noticed which belong to the office of revenue in which the first lord of the treasury and chancellor of the exchequer ordinarily and properly presides. The salary of the first lord of the treasury is 4000*l.*; the other lords have 1600*l.* each.

At the treasury, besides the lords commissioners, are two joint secretaries, four chief clerks, six senior clerks, six junior clerks, a minute clerk, two copying clerks, one principal clerk, with six assistants for keeping and stating the accounts of the revenue department, a receiver of fees, a keeper of the papers, a solicitor, a chamber keeper, four exchequer messengers, and one custom house messenger, a ranger of books and bag bearer, a housekeeper, a housekeeper to the levee rooms, and a door keeper; besides which there are five extra clerks, and three extra messengers employed in the treasury.

The business of the *board of treasury* is to consider and determine upon all matters relative to his majesty's civil list or other revenues; to give directions for the conduct of all boards and persons entrusted with the receipt, management, or expenditure of the said revenues; to sign all warrants for the necessary payments thereout, and generally to superintend every branch of revenue belonging to his majesty or the public.

The duty of the *joint secretaries* is to attend the board, to receive their orders, see to the execution of the same, and generally to superintend the conduct of the business in every department of the office. The attendance of the joint secretaries is in general constant and unremitting, and that of the chief and other clerks daily from about ten in the morning till the business of the day is finished; excepting very few instances, in which their attendance has, for special reasons, been dispensed with. Each of the secretaries has a salary of 3229*l.* 17*s.*

The duty of the *chief clerks* is occasionally to attend the board, to to distribute the official business among the other clerks, to prepare themselves all instruments that are of a special nature, to examine all those which are prepared by others, to present them for signature to the board, or to the secretaries, as the case may require, and to deliver them over to one of the six senior clerks, among whom the official business of the treasury is divided, each having a department for which he is responsible, and being assisted therein by one of the junior clerks.

The duty of the six *senior clerks*, with their assistants, is to prepare all instruments whatever that arise in each of their said departments, and deliver them to one of the chief clerks to be presented for signature, and, when returned, to give them over to the receiver of the fees, whose duty is to deliver them to the respective parties upon the receipt of the fees payable thereon, with which he charges himself, and accounts weekly for the same to one of the chief clerks.

The duty of the principal and other *clerks* of the revenue department is, to make up books containing a state of the income and issues of the customs and other duties and revenues payable at the receipt of the exchequer; for this purpose they receive weekly certificates from the exchequer, checked by other certificates received from the customs, and other offices of the revenue, from which they make out weekly for the treasury board what is called a cash paper, shewing the balance of money remaining in the exchequer for the uses of the civil government, or for the public service of the current year: they likewise make out for his majesty a monthly statement of the civil list receipts, and payments, and keep such other books and accounts as are required by the board of treasury, or are necessary for the public service. Each of the chief clerks has a salary of 1080*l.*, the appointments of the inferiors are from 700*l.* to about 100*l.*

The duty of the *keeper of the papers* is to schedule and digest all papers of any import transmitted to his repository; to inspect the books of office, to range and dispose them in presses, and be ready to inform the secretaries and clerks of their respective contents, when necessary: this officer has a deputy.

The *solicitor* considers it as his duty to solicit, prosecute, defend, and manage all causes and affairs from time to time directed by the lords of the treasury, the principal secretaries of state, or attorney general; to peruse all papers and memorials referred to him from the treasury, and to make his report in writing to their lordships thereon. His attendance on this duty is generally daily, and at all hours; but naturally varies according to the degree of business that occurs. His fixed salary is 2000*l.*, but the business continually arising in all parts of the kingdom

kingdom renders his ſituation extremely laborious, and probably very lucrative.

The duty of the remaining offices is implied by their titles; and their attendance is daily during the office hours. Their emoluments are various; ſufficiently liberal, but not extravagant.

To the *chancellor of the exchequer* it peculiarly belongs to take care of the intereſt of the crown. He is always in commiſſion with the lord treaſurer for the letting of crown lands, &c. and has power, with others, to compound for forfeitures of lands upon penal ſtatutes. He has alſo great authority in managing the royal revenues; and it is generally underſtood to be his duty to propoſe in the houſe of commons the meaſures of ſupply, ways and means neceſſary for the ſervice of the current year. His ſalary is 1800*l.* per annum.

Under the chancellor of the exchequer are the ſeveral offices of the auditor, the clerk of the pells, the tellers, the chamberlains, the uſher of the receipt, and the paymaſter of the exchequer bills.

Auditor. The duty of this officer is to take the accounts from other public offices, who collect the national revenue. He files the tellers bills, and duly enters them, and gives the lords of the treaſury a certificate of the money received from the ſeveral branches of the revenue the week before; and gives in thoſe accounts from year to year to the parliament. He alſo makes out debentures to the reſpective tellers of the exchequer before they receive any money, and takes their accounts, and ſees the tellers money locked up in the royal treaſury. He is appointed for life, by a conſtitution under the hands and ſeals of the commiſſioners of the treaſury. All the exchequer bills, orders, debentures, patents, and other inſtruments which paſs this office, are ſigned by him. The official profits are not received by himſelf, but by his firſt clerk, who accounts with him for them every month. His emoluments were formerly very large; they are now fixed by ſtatute at 4000*l.* per annum.

In his office are a chief clerk, a keeper of the records, and clerk of the debentures, who have all large ſalaries; and various other perſons are employed in inferior departments.

Clerk of the Pells. The duty of this officer is to enter every teller's bill in a parchment roll, called *pellis acceptorum*, the roll of receipts, and to make another roll, called *pellis exituum*, a roll of the diſburſements. He is appointed for life, by a conſtitution under the hands and ſeals of the commiſſioners of the treaſury, to exerciſe his office either by himſelf or deputy. In conſequence of this privilege, it has not been uſual, for many years, for the clerk of the pells to execute any part of the buſineſs himſelf, the deputy tranſacts the whole, and receives and accounts with his principal for all the profits that belong to him. The clerk of the pells receives for himself, deputy, and twenty clerks 6840*l.* a year. Among the persons employed in his office are *clerks of the introitus* and *exitus*, of declarations, patents, and debentures; and branches of this office are those of annuities and tontines.

Tellers. The duty of these officers is to receive all money due to the king, and give a bill of it to be entered by the clerk of the pells. They also pay all monies payable from the king, and enter the amount in weekly and yearly books, to be delivered to the lords of the treasury. The teller's is one office in four divisions, each consisting of a teller, a deputy, and first clerk, two offices executed by the same person, a second clerk and three inferior clerks; in all twenty-four persons. The teller is appointed for life by letters patent, which empower him to perform the office by deputy; and in that manner the whole business has long been transacted, the teller himself executing no part; even the profits being received and accounted for to him by his deputy. The emoluments annexed to the situation of teller are estimated at 2700*l.* per annum. The deputy, as such, has no profit whatever; but, as first clerk, he has fees both on the receipt and issue. The fees on the receipt are called bill money, and are in consideration of his writing the bills.

Of the offices of *chamberlain*, *usher of the receipt*, and some dependant situations as *tally cutters*, it is not necessary here to treat, since, in consequence of the statute 23 Geo. III. c. 82., some of them are already abolished, and the others will be so at the death, surrender, forfeiture, or removal, of the present possessors.

Paymaster of the Exchequer Bills. This office is executed by three paymasters, a comptroller, an accountant, a cashier, and two clerks; to whom are added a housekeeper and messenger, and occasional assistant clerks. The paymaster, the comptroller, and the housekeeper, are appointed by the commissioners of the treasury by constitution during pleasure; the rest of the officers are nominated by the paymasters themselves. The officers, as well as clerks, are paid by salaries only; no fee or gratuity being taken by any of them, except a small annual fee of 2*l.* 7*s.* allowed the accomptant for making up his year's accompt. Each paymaster has a nett annual salary of 249*l.* 3*s.* 4*d.* The comptroller's salary is 308*l.* 10*s.* The salaries of the rest are paid, clear of deductions, out of the public funds.

4. Lord President of the Council. As, under the title lord treasurer, all the offices and duties connected with the treasury were in general enumerated; so, in this division, notice will

will be taken of all matters relating to his majesty's privy council. The lord president is the fourth great officer of state, and is recorded as having existed in the seventh year of King John. In the reign of Elizabeth the office was discontinued, but seems to have revived in that of James I.; under Charles II. it was permanently re-established, and has ever since continued. The office has been always granted by letters patent under the great seal *durante bene placito*; and this officer is to attend on the king, to propose business at the council table, and report to his majesty the transactions there; also he may associate the lord chancellor, treasurer, and privy seal, at naming of sheriffs; and all other acts limited by any statute to be done by them.

The privy council, according to Sir Edward Coke's description of it, is a noble, honourable, and reverend assembly of the king and such he wills to be of his privy council, in the king's court or palace. The king's will is the sole constituent of a privy counsellor; and this also regulates their number, which in ancient times was twelve or thereabouts. Afterward it increased to so large a number that it was found inconvenient for secrecy and dispatch; and, therefore, in 1679, Charles II. limited it to thirty, whereof fifteen were to be the principal officers of state, and those to be counsellors, *virtute officii*; and the other fifteen were composed of ten lords and five commoners of the king's choosing. But since that time the number has been much augmented, and now continues indefinite. From this circumstance, however, no inconvenience can arise, as those only attend who are specially summoned for that particular occasion upon which their advice and assistance are required. The *cabinet council*, as it is called, consists of those ministers of state who are more immediately honoured with his majesty's confidence, and who are summoned to consult on the important and arduous discharge of the executive authority: their number and selection depend only on the king's pleasure, and each member of that council receives a summons or message for every attendance.

Privy counsellors are made by the king's nomination, without either patent or grant; and, on taking the necessary oaths, they become immediately privy counsellors during the life of the king that chooses them, but subject to removal at his discretion. A privy counsellor, though but a private gentleman, is styled *right honourable*, and has precedence of all knights, baronets, and the younger sons of all barons and viscounts.

As to the qualifications of members to sit at this board, any natural born subject of England is capable of being a member of the privy council, taking the proper oaths for security of the government, and the test for the security of the church. But in order

order to prevent any persons under foreign attachments from insinuating themselves into this important trust, as happened in many instances in the reign of William III., it is provided by the act of settlement, that no person born out of the dominions of the crown of England, unless born of English parents, even though naturalized by parliament, shall be capable of sitting in the privy council.

The duty of a privy counsellor appears from the oath of office, which consists of seven articles: 1. To advise the king according to the best of his cunning and discretion. 2. To advise for the king's honour, and good of the public, without partiality through affection, love, meed, doubt, or dread. 3. To keep the king's council secret. 4. To avoid corruption. 5. To help and strengthen the execution of what shall be there resolved. 6. To withstand all persons who would attempt the contrary. And, lastly, in general, 7. To observe, keep, and do all that a good and true counsellor ought to do to his sovereign lord.

The power of the privy council is to inquire into all offences against the government, and to commit the offenders to safe custody, in order to take their trial in some of the courts of law. But their jurisdiction herein is only to inquire, and not to punish; and the persons committed by them are entitled to their *habeas corpus*, by statute 16 Car. I. c. 10. as much as if committed by an ordinary justice of the peace. And, by the same statute, the court of star-chamber, and the court of request, both of which consisted of privy counsellors, were dissolved; and it was declared illegal for them to take cognizance of any matter of property belonging to the subjects of this kingdom. But, in plantation or admiralty causes, which arise out of the jurisdiction of the kingdom; and in matters of lunacy or idiotcy, being a special flower of prerogative, with regard to these, although they may eventually involve questions of extensive property, the privy council continues to have cognizance, being the court of appeal in such cases; or, rather, the appeal lies to the king's majesty himself in council. Whenever also a question arises between two colonies or dependencies of the crown, as concerning the extent of their charter, and the like; the king in his council exercises original jurisdiction therein, upon the principles of feodal sovereignty. So likewise when any person claims an island, or a province, in the nature of a feodal principality, by grant from the king or his ancestors, the determination of that right belongs to his majesty in council; as was the case of the Earl of Derby with regard to the Isle of Man, in the reign of Queen Elizabeth, and the Earl of Cardigan, and others, as representatives of the Duke of Montague, with

with relation to the Iſland of St. Vincent, in 1764. But from all the dominions of the crown, excepting Great Britain and Ireland, an *appellate* juriſdiction, in the laſt reſort, is veſted in the ſame tribunal, which uſually exerciſes its judicial authority in a committee of the whole privy council, who hear the allegations and proofs, and make their report to his majeſty in council, by whom the judgment is finally given.

The privileges of privy counſellors, as ſuch abſtracted from their honorary precedency, conſiſt principally in the ſecurity which the law has given them againſt attempts and conſpiracies to deſtroy their lives. For, by ſtatute 3 Hen. VII. c. 14. if any of the king's ſervants of his houſehold conſpire or imagine to take away the life of a privy counſellor, it is felony, though nothing be done upon it. The reaſon of making this ſtatute, Sir Edward Coke tells us, was becauſe ſuch a conſpiracy was, juſt before this parliament, made by ſome of the king's houſehold ſervants, and great miſchief was like to have enſued thereupon. This extends only to the king's menial ſervants. But the ſtatute 9 Anne, c. 16. goes farther, and enacts, that any perſon who ſhall unlawfully attempt to kill, or ſhall unlawfully aſſault, and ſtrike, or wound, any privy counſellor in the execution of his office, ſhall be a felon without benefit of clergy. This ſtatute was made upon the daring attempt of the Sieur Guiſcard, who, when under examination for high crimes, in a committee of the privy council, ſtabbed Mr. Harley, afterwards Earl of Oxford, with a penknife.

The diſſolution of the privy council depends upon the king's pleaſure; and he may, whenever he thinks proper, diſcharge any particular member, or the whole of it, and appoint another. By the common law alſo it was diſſolved, *ipſo facto*, by the king's demiſe, as deriving all its authority from him; but now, to prevent the inconveniences of having no council in being at the acceſſion of a new prince, it is enacted, by ſtatute 6 Anne, c. 7. that the privy council ſhall continue for ſix months after the demiſe of the crown, unleſs ſooner determined by the ſucceſſor.

The court of privy council is of great antiquity. The government in England was originally by the king and privy council; though at preſent the king and privy council only intermeddle in matters of complaint on ſudden emergencies; their conſtant buſineſs being to conſult for the public good in affairs of ſtate.

The lords and commons aſſembled in parliament have often tranſmitted matters of high concern to the king and privy council; and acts of the privy council, whether orders or proclamations, were of great authority. Henry VIII. procured an act of parliament to be made, that with the advice of his privy council,

council, he might set forth proclamations, which should have the force of laws; but this most tyrannical and detestable statute was repealed in the reign of Edward VI.

Acts of the privy council continued of great authority until the reigns of Charles I. and II.: and by these were controversies sometimes determined touching lands and rights, as well as the suspension of penal statutes; but their authority in this respect was never considered consonant with law, and was formally abolished by statute.

The king, with advice of his council, publishes proclamations binding to the subject; but they are to be consonant to, and in execution of the laws of the land.

By statute 33 Hen. VIII. c. 23. persons examined by the privy council, on treasons, &c. done within or without the realm, may be tried before commissioners of oyer and terminer, appointed by the king, in any county of England. This statute, as far as it relates to treason committed within the kingdom, is repealed by statute 1 and 2 Philip and Mary, c. 10.; but if a person be killed beyond sea, out of the realm, the fact may be examined by the privy council, and the offender tried according to the aforesaid statute.

As many important acts, deeply affecting the king and realm, must emanate from this body, it is usual for those who give some species of advice, to sign their names to a paper containing their opinions, thus pledging themselves to be responsible for its legality or necessity.

To the privy council belong four clerks in ordinary, who have annual salaries of 1000*l.* each, five clerks extraordinary, four under clerks, and a keeper of the records.

Lords of Trade. The necessity of an establishment for the purpose of investigating matters essential to the commerce of the nation, and reporting to superior powers, was strongly felt as soon as England began to gain an ascendancy as a trading nation. In 1655, Cromwell appointed his son Richard, with many lords of his council, judges, and gentlemen, and about twenty merchants of London, York, Newcastle, Yarmouth, Dover, and other places, "to meet and consider by what "means the traffic and navigation of the republic might be best "promoted and regulated, and to report on the subject." How useful such an establishment might have been, even at that period, is demonstrated by the observation made by the Dutch, as recorded in Thurloe's state papers. "A committee for "trade," they said, "was some time since erected in England, "which we then feared would have proved very prejudicial to "our state; but we are glad to see that it was only nominal, "so that we hope in time, those of London will forget that

"ever

" ever they were merchants." At the restoration, Charles II. established a council for the same purposes, consisting of several high officers of state, and other persons; but this was no more effective than the former plan. In 1668, by persuasion of Lord Ashley, who was then chancellor of the exchequer, the king instituted a council of commerce, consisting of a president, salary 800 *l.*; vice president, 600 *l.*; and nine other counsellors, with each 500 *l.* salary; who, instead of the former method of referring all commercial matters to a fluctuating committee of the privy council, which was liable to several objections, were to apply themselves diligently to the advancement of the nation's commerce, colonies, manufactures, and shipping; but in a few years the king laid aside this beneficial institution, and commercial matters fell into their former way of a reference to a committee of the privy council. Another attempt was made by the same monarch in 1672, to establish the committee of trade, but, like the former efforts, it was formally announced, and speedily abandoned. Consequently all disputes and regulations relative to commerce and colonies were usually referred to committees of the privy council; but such occasional committees being a constantly varying set of members, and having besides no stated appointments for their trouble and attendance, it is by no means surprising that they acted but loosely and superficially. In this position stood the commercial concerns of the nation, till 1696, when, on the repeated complaints of the merchants of England, of great captures by the French, and that little regard or care had, for many years past, been taken of trade and commerce, King William erected a new and standing council for commerce and plantations, in their most comprehensive sense, commonly styled the lords commissioners for trade and plantations. In the list were contained all the great officers of state, together with eight other persons, among whom was the celebrated John Locke; and each of the eight commissioners, appointed during the king's pleasure, had a salary of 1000 *l.* To this board proposals were made by merchants and others, for the ease, improvement, and encouragement of our commerce, navigation, plantations, manufactures, fisheries, &c. for redressing all grievances and burthens on trade, which were there argued between one party and another, and generally by counsel. British consuls appointed to reside in foreign parts, for the benefit and protection of our commerce, received their instructions from this board, with whom they were obliged to hold constant correspondence; as were also the governors of the American plantations, for the improvement of their respective governments, who also transmitted to this board the journals of their councils and assemblies, the accounts of the collectors

tors of the customs, and of naval offices, &c. Reports were also made, from time to time, how Britain might be best supplied with naval stores from the colonies, what new productions might be raised, and old ones improved. Inquiries also came before this board, for regaining of lost branches of trade, as well as enlarging those we possessed, and establishing new ones; and how to employ the poor and idle to the best advantage. Hearings also between merchants, trading corporations, manufacturers, &c. at home, as well as of appeals from the plantations, were brought before this board; who, upon all such matters, and many others, as the general balance of trade between England and foreign nations, made reports, and gave their opinions to the king and his privy council. That such a board might be eminently useful, the outline of duty leaves no room to doubt; and that it was so, cannot well be questioned, when the great names who occasionally composed it are considered, and the extent of their labours is viewed, which were comprized in two thousand three hundred folio volumes. The members of this board being, however, removeable at pleasure, it was, during the American war, when notions of economy and diminution of the government patronage were carried to an extent which many judicious persons deemed unwarrantable, considered advisable to suppress the establishment altogether. Accordingly, in the year 1782, it was abolished by act of parliament, and its powers were consigned to a committee, regulated by a president and vice president, and composed of the great officers of state for the time being, and some other privy counsellors. By this reform the patronage of government was withdrawn from eight persons, who might otherwise have been rewarded to the clear amount of 800*l.* a year each; and the saving to the nation was, at the utmost, no more than 6400*l.* Perhaps the period when this board was abolished was the very moment when its active functions could have been most beneficially exerted; when commerce was about to receive a new impulse, and unprecedented extension; encouraged by circumstances never foreseen, yet embarrassed by litigations, involved in the discordant interests of rivals, and encumbered with questions both legal and political, respecting charters, monopoly, and paper credit, requiring the utmost calmness in investigation and firmness in decision.

In the office of the lords of trade, as at present constituted, are two secretaries, being also clerks of the council; a chief clerk, with subordinate clerks, and other officers.

5. Lord Privy Seal. The lord privy seal is an officer of great trust, honour, and antiquity, being mentioned in the statute, 2 Richard II. and then ranked among the chief persons of the

the realm. He is appointed by letters patent; is a privy counsellor by his office; takes place next after the lord president of the council, and before all dukes; and would be chief judge of the court of requests, were it revived. He is admitted into his place by taking the oath of office prescribed by law. He derives his name from having the custody of the privy seal, which he must not put to any grant, without good authority under the king's signet, nor to any warrant, if contrary to law and custom, or inconvenient, without first acquainting his majesty therewith. This seal is used by the king to all charters, grants, and pardons, signed by the king before they come to the great seal; but a warrant may be granted by the king, under the privy seal, to issue money out of the exchequer, and is sufficient, because a chattel in possession; it may also be affixed to other things that never pass the great seal, as, to cancel a recognizance made to the king, or to discharge a debt; but no writs can pass this seal which touch the common law. In the office of the lord privy seal are four clerks and two deputies.

6. Lord Great Chamberlain of England. The office of the lord great chamberlain is very ancient, and he was formerly a person of high importance. To him belong livery and lodging in the king's court, and certain fees due from each archbishop or bishop, when they do their homage or fealty to the king, and from all the peers of the realm at their creation, or doing their homage or fealty; and, at the coronation of every king, he is to have forty ells of crimson velvet for his own robes; and, on the coronation day, before the king rises, to bring his shirt, coif, and wearing cloaths; and after the king is by him apparelled, and gone forth, to have his bed, and all the furniture of his bed-chamber, for his fees; and all the king's night apparel; and to carry at the coronation the coif, gloves, and linen, to be used by the king on the occasion; also the sword and scabbard, and the gold to be offered by the king, and the robe-royal, and crown; and to undress and attire his majesty with the robes-royal; and to serve him on that day, before and after dinner, with water to wash his hands, and to have the bason and towels for his fees. To this officer also belongs the care of providing all things in the house of lords, in the time of parliament; and to that end he has an apartment in the vicinity; he has the government of the whole palace of Westminster, and he issues out his warrants for preparing, fitting, and furnishing Westminster Hall against coronations and trials of peers in parliament time. The gentleman usher of the black rod, the yeoman usher, and door-keepers, are under his command. He disposes of the sword of state to what lord he pleases, to be carried before the king when he comes to the parliament; and goes on the right hand

hand of the sword, next to the king's person, and the lord marshal on the left. Upon all solemn occasions, the keys of Westminster Hall, and the keys of the court of wards, and court of requests, are delivered to him.

This high office appertained, for many centuries, to the noble family of De Vere, Earl of Oxford, having been granted to them by Henry I. On the death of John De Vere, the sixteenth earl of Oxford, without heirs male, Mary, his sole daughter and heiress, married Peregrine Bertie, Lord Willoughby, of Eresby, who made claim to the earldom of Oxford, as also to the titles of Lord Bolbeck, of Bolbeck Castle, in the parish of Whitchurch, near Aylesbury, in the county of Buckingham, Sandford and Badlesmere, and to the office of lord great chamberlain of England. After much dispute, the house of lords gave judgment that he had made good his claim to the office of lord great chamberlain of England, but not to the other objects of his demand; and he was admitted into the house of lords with his staff, November 22, 1626. His descendants uninterruptedly enjoyed this post till the death of Robert Bertie, fourth duke of Ancaster and Kesteven, Marquis and Earl of Lindsey, and Lord Willoughby of Eresby, lord great chamberlain in July, 1779, who dying unmarried, was succeeded, as Duke of Ancaster and Kesteven, Marquis and Earl of Lindsey, by his uncle the Lord Brownlow Bertie; but for the great chamberlainship there were several claimants, viz. his grace Brownlow, Duke of Ancaster; Hugh, Earl Percy, eldest son of the Duke of Northumberland; Charlotte, Duchess Dowager of Athol, in her own right Lady Baroness Strange, of Knockyn; the Lady Priscilla Barbara Elizabeth Burrell, in her own right Baroness Willoughby, of Eresby; and the Lady Georgina Charlotte Bertie, sisters and co-heirs of Robert, fourth Duke of Ancaster, deceased: when, after hearing all the parties at full length, in support of their several claims, the house of peers desired the advice of the twelve judges, who gave their opinion, that the office devolved to the Lady Willoughby of Eresby, and her sister Lady Georgina Charlotte Bertie, as heirs to their brother Robert, Duke of Ancaster, deceased; and that they had powers to appoint a deputy to act for them, not under the degree of a knight, who, if his majesty approved of him, might officiate accordingly. And agreeably to this opinion, the house gave judgment. The office is executed by a deputy, who has 3000*l.* a year.

7. LORD HIGH CONSTABLE. This is one of the offices which in ancient times acquired so much power as to be dangerous to sovereignty, but is now only created occasionally to attend a coronation. The lord high constable presided jointly

with the earl marshal in the court of chivalry, and the office was transmitted by inheritance.

8. Earl Marshal. Of the duty and rank of this officer mention has already been made.

9. Lord High Admiral. In former times the post of lord high admiral was of great trust and honour, and usually conferred on a prince of the blood, or one of the highest class of nobility. He had the management of all maritime affairs, the government of the royal navy; with power of decision in all maritime cases, both civil and criminal. He judged of all transgressions done upon or beyond sea, in any part of the world, upon the coasts, in all ports or havens, and upon all rivers below the first bridge from the sea. By him all naval officers, from an admiral to a lieutenant, were commissioned; as were all deputies for particular coasts, and coroners for viewing dead bodies found on the sea shore or at sea. He also appointed judges for his court of admiralty. To the lord high admiral belonged by law and custom, all fines and forfeitures of all transgressions at sea, on the sea shore, in ports, and from the nearest bridge on rivers to the sea; also the goods of pirates and felons condemned or outlawed; and all waifs, stray goods, wrecks of sea, deodands; a share of all lawful prizes, ligan, jetsam, and flotsam, not previously granted or belonging to lords of manors adjoining the sea; all great fishes, as sea hogs, and others of extraordinary bigness called royal fishes, whales and sturgeons only excepted.

Since the Revolution, the office of lord high admiral has been constantly, as it had before been frequently, put into commission, and the commissioners are generally styled *lords of the admiralty*. A spacious building, situate near Whitehall and formerly called Wallingford House, is retained for their official use, and for the residence of some of the commissioners.

They are seven in number; the first lord having a salary of 4000*l.*, and a house in the admiralty office; each of the others receiving in salary and allowances 1000*l.* per annum, and the four senior having also houses in the admiralty.

The business of the board of admiralty is to consider and determine on all matters relative to his majesty's navy, and departments thereunto belonging; to give directions for the performance of all services that may be required, either in the civil or naval branch; to sign, by themselves or their secretaries, all orders necessary for carrying their directions into execution; and generally to superintend and direct the whole naval and marine establishments of Great Britain.

The establishment also consists of two secretaries, a chief clerk, and several established and extra clerks, a secretary to the first lord, two marine clerks, a translator of foreign papers, messengers, porters, watchmen, and other officers. There is likewise a separate establishment for the marine service, and a solicitor who also acts for the navy office.

The duty of the *secretaries* is to lay before the board all memorials, letters, and other papers transmitted to this office; to receive and minute down the orders of the lords commissioners, and to see to the official execution thereof; to countersign all instruments, where the same may be necessary; and generally to attend to the dispatch of all business arising in the naval or marine department. These officers being constantly resident and always in attendance, their office is extrmely laborious; the salary of the first secretary is 4000*l*., that of the second 2000*l*.

The duty of the *established clerks* is to prepare memorials, instructions, orders, letters, and other instruments, conformable to the minutes of the board, and the direction of the secretaries: each clerk, the junior excepted, has a separate branch of the business under his charge, and is assisted therein by one or more of the extra clerks, according to the degree of labour in the branch assigned to him. The *chief clerk*, besides the charge of one of these branches, has the general superintendence of the whole official business in the naval department. He likewise has the care of the maps, charts, and books of the office, and the payment of most of the contingent expences. The fourth of the established clerks, besides the duty of his branch, acts as receiver of fees and accountant to the office, and is employed to check the bills of the admiralty messengers. The junior clerk on the establishment, having no branch of the official business assigned to him, acts in the capacity of assistant to the chief clerk. Two of the extra clerks are appointed to assist the secretaries; one of them acts as French and Spanish translator; and they are all employed from time to time in other services, as occasion requires. The attendance of the clerks is daily from ten o'clock or earlier, till five or later if required. They also attend by rotation in the evening, to make up, for franking, and to dispatch the public letters; and the extra clerks, besides the like daily attendance, are also required to be at the office every evening by turns, to assist in the entry and dispatch of such letters. The chief clerk has for salary 800*l*. per annum, and an addition of 150*l*. during the war, and apartments in the house. The appointments of the other clerks vary from 500*l*. to 150*l*. each, and the extra clerks receive 90*l*. per annum. The secretary to the first lord receives 300*l*., and the translator 100*l*. a year.

The duty of the *first marine clerk* is to prepare all the memorials,

rials, instructions, drafts of orders, and commissions required for the marine corps; also to examine and check the tradesmen's bills for their cloathing, accoutrements, and contingencies; and his attendance is daily from between twelve and one to about four o'clock.

The duty of the *second marine clerk* is to write all letters relative to the corps, to enter and dispatch the same, as well as the several orders and instructions; also to prepare half yearly lists of the marine half pay officers, and to arrange and take care of the marine papers: and his attendance is daily from about eleven o'clock till past four. The salary of the first is 300*l.* and of the second 150*l.*, with an advance of one fifth in time of war.

The head *messenger*, besides the duty usually belonging to such a situation, has the superintendance of all the inferior departments of the office; and his attendance is constant. The duty of the remaining officers is implied by their titles; and they attend (the housekeeper excepted) whenever their services are required. The salary of the messenger is 120*l.*, those of the others very moderate.

For the purposes of information and utility, connected with naval affairs, the admiralty employ an *hydrographer*, who has an annual salary of 500*l.*; an *assistant hydrographer*; and a *printer* whose stated income is 120*l.*

To this class also may be referred the *telegraph*, which serves for the conveyance of orders to, and receipt of intelligence from, Deal and Portsmouth. The original invention of this mode of communication belongs to the French; but that used by the admiralty is more simple in use, durable, and easily repaired. It occasions a great saving in the expenditure which was formerly made for expresses, and insures the inestimable advantage in maritime affairs, of celerity in the transmission, and promptitude in the execution of orders. Both the Deal and Portsmouth stations are under the care of an inspector, who has a salary of 300*l.*

Beside the secretaries and two clerks in the marine department, there is an establishment annexed to the admiralty for the *pay of his Majesty's marine forces*. This establishment consists of a paymaster, an agent, and three deputy paymasters, one at each of the out ports.

The duty of these officers is, in conjunction with the treasurer of the navy, to conduct the payment of the marines; the treasurer of the navy paying such of the non-commissioned officers and privates as are on ship board; the paymaster of the marines paying the general and lieutenant-general of that corps; also the half-pay, the cloathing, the charge of recruiting in Ireland, the salaries of most of the civil officers, the allowances to widows, and feveral of the contingencies of this fervice; the agent of the marines paying the fubfiftence and arrears of all the officers on full pay (the general and lieutenant-general excepted) the charge of the recruiting fervice in Great Britain, and the contingencies in the different quarters; the deputy paymafters at the feveral divifions paying the fubfiftence of the non-commiffioned officers and privates, for which purpofe they draw bills on the agent, and iffue the faid fubfiftence to the fquad ferjeants once a week, to diftribute among the men.

When the marine corps was firft eftablifhed in 1755, under the direction of the board of admiralty, the offices of paymafter and agent were executed by one perfon, and continued fo nearly two years, when they were feparated, and an agent appointed for each divifion; which arrangement exifted until 1763, when the number was again reduced to one, and has remained fo ever fince, not only without any prejudice, but even with benefit to the fervice.

The paymafter of the marine forces is fupplied with money for carrying on the fervice in the following manner: once a month he prefents to the lords of the admiralty an account of his receipts and payments during the former, with an eftimate of the fum neceffary for the fucceeding month. The admiralty direct the navy board to impreft a certain fum into his hands, generally about the expenditure of the former month. The navy board direct the treafurer of the navy to iffue the money to him accordingly; out of which he advances a certain fum to the agent for carrying on the fervices under his direction, and applies the remainder to the fervices carried on by himfelf, as before mentioned. The agent delivers to the paymafter a monthly account of his receipts and payments, and once a year a general account of the whole, diftinguifhed under proper heads, with the vouchers; from which, and from his own difburfements, the paymafter makes up an annual account, which he prefents, with the vouchers, to the navy board for their examination and allowance, which clears him, and is final.

The detail of the paymafter's bufinefs is carried on by his firft clerk, fo as feldom to occafion his attendance; but the agent attends the bufinefs of his office both morning and evening without intermiffion, except for an hour or two in the day. The paymafter has in falary and emoluments about 900*l.* a year; out of which he pays certain falaries and allowances to his clerks, and other expences of his office, and retains the remainder for his own ufe.

The agent of marines has in falary and emoluments about 600*l.* a year; out of which he pays for clerks and other contingencies nearly 200*l.* a year. The falary of the *deputy pay-*

mafters

masters at the out ports is at the rate of 5*l.* for each company belonging to the division, and amounts to 125*l.* a year at Portsmouth, the same at Plymouth, and 100*l.* a year at Chatham, paid out of the marine poundage and stoppages.

In the admiralty are two other officers; the receiver and comptroller of his majesty's rights and perquisites.

The duty of the *receiver* is to recover and receive for his Majesty's use, all rights and perquisites of the admiralty seized and taken in the time of war, or otherwise; and, also, all such other sums of money as have been usually paid, or ordered by decree of court to be paid to the register for the time being; and to take all such measures as are necessary for this purpose, and observe such orders and directions as he shall from time to time receive from the lords commissioners of the admiralty: and he is to appoint agents at all such ports and places as he shall think necessary. He has a salary of 300*l.* a year nett, and an allowance of 50*l.* more for a clerk.

The duty of the *comptroller* is to take an account of all ships and goods condemned as perquisites of the admiralty, and to note the burthen of such ships, and the quantities and qualities of the goods, together with their tackle, apparel, and furniture; to take an account of all other perquisites of the admiralty, and to compare and examine them with the sums charged by the receiver; to peruse, examine, and controul the accounts of the receiver; and generally to execute such orders and instructions as he shall, from time to time, receive from the lords of the admiralty: and he is likewise to appoint agents at all such ports and places as he shall think necessary. He has in salary and fees 250*l.* a year.

10. SECRETARIES OF STATE. The secretaries of state have an extraordinary trust which renders them very considerable in the eyes both of the king and of the subject. Requests and petitions are for the most part lodged in their hands to be represented to his majesty, and they make dispatches thereupon, pursuant to his directions. They are privy counsellors, and a council is seldom, if ever, held without the presence of one of them; they wait by turns, and one always attends the court, and, by the king's warrant, prepares all bills or letters, not being matter of law, for him to sign. Until the reign of Queen Elizabeth, the secretaries of state were not members of the privy council, but only prepared business for the council board in a room adjoining; which done, they came in and stood one on each hand; and, till they had gone through their proposals, nothing was debated. There was but one secretary of state, till Henry VIII. toward the close of his reign increased the number to two of equal rank and authority. On the union with

 Scotland,

Scotland, Queen Anne added a ſecretary of ſtate for Scotch affairs; an appointment which was afterwards diſcontinued. In the reign of his preſent majeſty the number was again increaſed to three, by appointing one for the American department; but, in the year 1782, this office was aboliſhed by act of parliament.

The buſineſs of the ſecretary of ſtate's office conſiſts in receiving intelligence, conducting correſpondence, preparing and iſſuing warrants, and managing tranſactions relative to the executive government of the Britiſh empire. Such of this buſineſs as relates to the Britiſh dominions, and to the four ſtates of Barbary, is carried on in the home department, in which there is a ſubordinate office for the affairs of the colonies. Such, on the other hand, as relates to the foreign powers of Europe, and the United States of America, is carried on in the foreign department.

The eſtabliſhment of the ſecretary of ſtate's office in each department conſiſts of a principal ſecretary of ſtate, two under ſecretaries, a chief and other clerks, (ten in the home, and nine in the foreign department,) together with two chamber keepers, and a neceſſary woman.

The *office for plantation affairs*, conſiſts of an under ſecretary and three clerks. There are likewiſe attached generally to both departments, the offices of gazette writer, his deputy, a keeper of ſtate papers, a collector and tranſmitter of ſtate papers, two commiſſioners for methodizing and digeſting the ſtate papers, a ſecretary for the Latin language, two decypherers, and ſixteen meſſengers.

The duty of the *under ſecretaries* is to attend to the execution of ſuch orders, to prepare drafts of ſuch ſpecial letters and inſtructions, as occaſion may require; to tranſact themſelves, whatever is of the moſt confidential nature; and generally to ſuperintend the buſineſs of the office in all its branches.

The duty of the *chief clerk* is to diſtribute the ordinary official buſineſs among the clerks; to ſee that all warrants and other inſtruments are duly prepared, tranſmitted to the proper perſons for ſignature, and delivered to the reſpective parties, when application is made, and the regular fees paid for the ſame; likewiſe that the office books are properly kept, and the public diſpatches punctually tranſmitted. He further acts as the accountant of the office, in which capacity he receives and accounts for the ſecretary of ſtate's ſalary, all the fees and gratuities, together with ſuch other ſums as are iſſued for defraying the general expence of the office.

The remaining clerks, who are diſtinguiſhed by the rank of ſenior

ſenior and junior in the home department, though without any diſtinction in the foreign, obey ſuch orders as they receive from their ſuperiors in office, but have no particular branches of buſineſs aſſigned to them.

The attendance of the under ſecretaries is conſtant and unremitting; that of the chief clerk's is likewiſe conſtant; and the other clerks, though not always employed, are in daily attendance, and are expected to be ready for the execution of any buſineſs in which their ſuperiors may think neceſſary to employ them.

The duty of the other inferior officers is ſufficiently expreſſed by the titles of their offices, and is ſuch as to occaſion their conſtant attendance.

Each of the principal ſecretaries of ſtate has a ſalary of 6000*l*., and the ſecretary for plantation affairs 2000*l*. The profits of the under ſecretaries were ſtated, in 1786, to be nearly 1100*l*. per annum each. A law clerk has 300*l*., a precis writer, whoſe duty it is to make an abſtract of all diſpatches and other communications, has 300*l*., a librarian 200*l*., and the clerks and other officers have reſpectable but not extravagant ſalaries.

To the office of ſecretary for the home department, has been annexed, ſince the French revolution, a branch called the *alien office*, which is under the perpetual controul of the two under ſecretaries of ſtate, and a perſon eſpecially appointed for that purpoſe called the ſuperintendant of aliens. At this office all foreigners are obliged to preſent themſelves when required; to obtain permiſſion to reſide in England, which may be modified by ſuch terms as are deemed neceſſary, and if thoſe conditions are broken, or if any complaint or ſuſpicion ariſes, the party may be ſent out of the kingdom. In this office are a chief clerk, clerk of the paſſports, and three aſſiſtants; and agents are ſtationed at Dover, Graveſend, Harwich, and Falmouth.

There is alſo, ſince the union with Ireland, a department in the ſecretary of ſtate's office, peculiarly ſet apart for tranſacting the affairs of that part of the united kingdom.

The State Paper Office belongs alike to thoſe of both ſecretaries of ſtate. In it are a keeper of ſtate papers, with ſalary of 500*l*., a deputy; a gazette writer with 300*l*. a year; a collector and tranſmitter of ſtate papers, and decypherer of letters, each 500*l*. a year; a ſecretary of the Latin language with 280*l*. a year; and an interpreter of Oriental languages. Several of theſe places are ſinecures.

The meſſengers employed in theſe offices, thirty-four in number, belong to the eſtabliſhment of the lord chamberlain's office, and were all under the direction of the clerk of the cheque (an officer ſpecially appointed to put the meſſengers upon their respective waits, and to examine their bills of service,) until the year 1772, when sixteen of them were set apart from the rest, to be independent of the clerk of the cheque, and subject solely to the orders of principal secretaries of state. These sixteen are accordingly appointed by the recommendation of, and attend particularly upon, the secretaries of state; nevertheless, they continue on the lord chamberlain's list, and are paid at his office. The messengers attend in rotation, and undertake their journies in the same manner; the foreign journies are confined exclusively to the sixteen attached to these offices. Each messenger upon his appointment takes an oath before the clerk of the cheque, for the faithful discharge of his duty. They have each a salary of 45*l.* a year, reduced by deductions to 35*l.* 8*s.*, and seven shillings and sixpence per day, called board wages, while in waiting, and during home journies, but which ceases when they are dispatched upon foreign journies; also an allowance of 25*l.* a year for keeping a horse; and are paid besides for the expence of journies, foreign and domestic, according to certain fixed rates.

The secretary of state for the home department has the custody of the *privy signet*, because the king's private letters are signed with it. There are four clerks of the privy signet office, who write out such grants and letters patent as pass by bill signed, or bill superscribed by the sign manual, or under the king's hand; the transcript and sealing of these with the signet is a warrant to the privy seal, as the privy seal is to the great seal. A *ne exeat regno* may by command be under the privy signet, or the privy seal, as well as by the king's writ under the great seal, and the subject ought to obey it; but a warrant under the privy signet is not sufficient for the issue of any treasure, or the discharge of a debt, much less verbal order; for it ought to be under the great seal, or at least under the privy seal. The signet office is entirely under the direction of the secretaries of state, a clerk attending the court wherever it may happen to reside, to prepare such bills or letters for signature, as the king may direct, or as may be ordered by warrant from the secretaries of state, or lords of the council. All grants prepared by the clerks of the signet, or by the king's counsel learned in the law, for the king's hand, are returned into this office, when signed, and there transcribed again. The transcript is carried to one of the principal secretaries of state, and being sealed by him, it is called a signet, which is directed to the lord privy seal, and is his warrant for the issuing of a privy seal; but privy seals for money always begin in the treasury, whence the first warrant issues, counter-signed by the lord treasurer, or the lords commissioners.

11. MASTER

11. Master general of the Ordnance. The office of ordnance is in the tower of London, and has both a civil and a military branch. It supplies both the army and navy with all sorts of military stores. When to the latter, they are delivered on board the respective ships, to the gunner, who has under him an armourer and a gunsmith. Storekeepers are established at all the principal sea ports, where any of his Majesty's ships are stationed, both at home and abroad, who receive the stores, from the board of ordnance, where there are clerks and other officers, with salaries, for expediting the business of the army and navy.

The master general, is deemed the principal officer in the civil branch of the ordnance; in him is vested the sole power of storing all the military magazines in the king's dominions, with proper munitions of war; and likewise to supply the royal navy with what they may need in his department; the parliament granting liberal supplies for this purpose. He is colonel in chief of the royal regiment of artillery, and is invested with a peculiar jurisdiction over all engineers employed in the several fortifications in his Majesty's dominions; to him they are all accountable for their proceedings, and from him they receive their particular orders, according to the directions and commands given by the king in council. As master general of the ordnance, he has a salary of 1500*l.* per annum, and the appointment of almost all the inferior officers and servants. He has a secretary, who has a salary of 220*l.* a year, and under secretary, who has a salary of 180*l.* a year. There is a secretary to the board of ordnance, who has a salary of 200*l.* and a counsel to the board, who has an annual fee of 300*l.*

The residue of the establishment consists of a lieutenant general, a surveyor general, a clerk, a storekeeper, a clerk of the deliveries, and a treasurer, with a great number of inferior officers, employed in the tower of London, at Woolwich, and in almost all the forts, garrisons, and principal ports in the British dominions,

The Lieutenant General of the Ordnance receives all orders and warrants signed by the master general, and from the other principal officers, and sees them duly executed; issues orders as the occasions of the state require, and gives directions for discharging the artillery on solemn or joyful occasions. It is also his peculiar office to see the train of artillery, and all its equipage fitted for motion, when ordered to be drawn into the field, or sent on any particular service. As lieutenant general of the ordnance, he has a salary of 1100*l.* per annum. He is colonel *en second* of the royal regiment of artillery, and has a secretary, and several officers and clerks under him.

The

The Surveyor General inspects the stores and provisions of war, in the custody of the store keeper, and sees that they are ranged and placed in such order, as is most proper for their preservation. He allows all bills of debt, and keeps a check upon all labourers' and artificers' work; sees that the stores received are good and serviceable, duly proved and marked with the king's mark, taking to his assistance the rest of the officers and proof masters. He has a salary of 700*l.* per annum; and to assist in the business, he has under him, the proof master of England, and other inferior officers.

The Clerk of the Ordnance records all orders and instructions, given for the government of the office; all patents and grants; the names of all officers, clerks, artificers, gunners, labourers, &c. who enjoy those grants, or any other fee for the same; draws all estimates for provisions and supplies to be made, and all letters, instructions, commissions, deputations, and contracts for his Majesty's service; makes all bills of imprest, and debentures, for the payment and satisfaction of work done, and provisions received in the said office; all quarter books, for the salaries and allowances of all officers, clerks, &c. belonging to the office; and keeps journals and ledgers of the receipts and returns of his Majesty's stores, to serve as a check between the two accountants of the office, the one for money, and the other for stores. He has 500*l.* a year salary, and 100*l.* a year more for being a check on the store-keeper. In his office he has a number of clerks, under-clerks, and ledger-keepers, who have all fixed salaries.

The Store-keeper takes into his custody all his Majesty's ordnance, munitions, and stores belonging thereto, and indents and puts them in legal security, after they have been surveyed by the surveyor general, any part of which he must not deliver, without a warrant signed by the proper officers; nor must he receive back any stores formerly issued, till they have been reviewed by the surveyor, and registered by the clerk of the ordnance, in the book of remains; and he must take care that whatever is under his custody be kept safe, and in such readiness as to be fit for service on the most sudden demand. He has a salary of 400*l.* a year; and in his office are several clerks.

The Clerk of Deliveries draws all orders for delivery of stores, and sees them duly executed. He also charges by indenture the particular receiver of the stores delivered; and, in order to discharge the storekeeper, registers the copies of all warrants for the deliveries, as well as the proportions delivered. He has a salary of 400*l.* per annum, and has several clerks in his office at fixed salaries.

The Treasurer and Paymaster receives and pays all monies, both salaries and debentures, in and belonging to this office. He has a salary of 500*l.* per annum. In his office are several clerks, ordinary and extraordinary.

12. SECRETARY AT WAR. This officer may not improperly be styled the minister of the war department. He is, in fact, military secretary to the king, and conveys all his Majesty's orders, to all the generals, and military governors, at home and abroad, relative to the troops and garrisons, under their respective commands; and with him they correspond, and to him they make their returns and reports, (as well as to the commander in chief), and he lays the business before his Majesty, for his inspection, and directions. All orders for marching, quartering, encamping, and recruiting the army, are signed by him, by his Majesty's command; and all military commissions are made out at the war office, situate at the Horse Guards, Whitehall, and by him, or the commander in chief, carried to his Majesty to be signed. The trust reposed in this officer is very great, and the profits of his office are considerable; he is always a member of the privy council.

In the war office, are a deputy secretary and first clerk, four principal, and many subordinate clerks, a paymaster of widows' pensions, who has 1067*l.* per annum, and a deputy; an examiner of army accounts, with assistants, messengers, and other officers.

13. THE PAY MASTER GENERAL OF THE FORCES. This office was one of the most lucrative in his Majesty's gift, not so much from his salary, (which was only 3000*l.* a year), and the perquisites of office, as from the immense sums of public money which necessarily remained in his possession, for a long space of time; as all the money voted by parliament for the land forces passed through his hands, and the balance was not paid into the treasury until his accounts were settled. In the year 1782, this office underwent a reform, and the pay master general, deprived of this and all other extraneous sources of emolument, was allowed a fixed salary of 4000*l.* and his deputy of 1500*l.* per annum.

The pay master general, is constituted by letters patent, under the great seal, and is always of the privy council. It has not been unusual, of late years, to appoint two persons to this office, as joint paymasters, in which case the salary is not augmented but divided.

The principal persons in the pay office, besides the deputy or deputies, for this office too is divided, are the accountant general, who has 1200*l.* per annum, and an assistant; the cashier 1000*l.* an assistant ledger keeper 800*l.* an assistant cashier of half pay 700*l.* and computer of off-reckonings 600*l.* There are besides many clerks and other persons in subordinate employments.

14. POSTMASTER

14. Postmaster General. Before any account is given of the particular duties of this officer, it will be proper to notice the origin, and other circumstances attending the establishment, over which he presides.

The necessity and advantage of a speedy and secure conveyance of letters to all parts of a state, and to foreign countries, must at all times have been sensibly felt by every government, and when once the ruling power had contrived an establishment, calculated to produce those effects, it would inevitably follow, that, if the country were free and prosperous, the nobility, the men of property, and above all, the commercial part of the community, would obtain the same benefits, either by participation, or by rivalship. The conveyance of letters, either of business or kindness, by the tardy, insecure, and uncertain mode of ordinary or accidental travellers, or even of persons employed on purpose, unless adequate provision were made for their speed and protection, must from the early periods of civilization, have been felt as a serious inconvenience. In England it was remedied, at first by provisions expensive to government; subsequent improvements removed the defects of the first contrivance; a judicious establishment obviated uncertainty in the effect, and the danger arising from injudicious rivalship; experienced utility, procuring general favour, shewed a dawn of profit to the state, and finally, the vigilance of the financier, aided by the ingenuity of sagacious projectors, converted that which had been originally a burden, into a most fruitful, secure, and popular source of revenue.

To travel post (*currere equis positis*) must have been usual in England, from the time when the effect of her admirable laws began to render the roads secure, and to afford at once protection and encouragement to those, whom business or pleasure led to visit places distant from their own abodes; but the first recorded instance of an attempt to apply the benefits of such a mode of journeying to the conveyance of letters occurs in 1479, when Edward IV. introduced an establishment of riders, with post horses, to be changed every twenty miles; who by handing letters from one to another, in two days forwarded them two hundred miles, apparently the furthest extent of the plan; but this improved mode of conveyance, like that in France, from which it was copied, had no connexion with commerce or public accommodation, unless it may be considered as the first rudiment of the present establishment. In the reign of Henry VIII. anno 1543, it is recorded, that letters dispatched from London reached Edinburgh on the fourth day; a degree of speed nearly equal to that of modern times, but this was only effected by means of a temporary arrangement, made for the use of government.

A foreign

A foreign post was originally established by the alien merchants, residing in London, who claimed the right of electing a person, in whom they could confide, to direct the undertaking. As the business grew extensive, the election became a source of discord, which occasioning many feuds, the citizens of London, in 1568, requested queen Elizabeth to consign that duty to one of her English subjects. This petition does not seem to have been attended with immediate effect, for the first regular nomination of a post-master, on record, was made by James I. who conferred that title on Matthew de Quester, or de l'Equester; but this was only for foreign letters; and after that period, as well as before, the business occasionally fell into the hands of private undertakers. In 1631, Charles I. granted by patent the reversion of the foreign post office to William Frizell and Thomas Witherings, and strictly enjoined, that none but his foreign post masters should presume to exercise any part of that office. In 1635, the same monarch, observing that there had been no certain intercourse between the kingdoms of England and Scotland, issued a proclamation, commanding his post-master of England for foreign parts to settle a running post, or two, to run night and day between Edinburgh and London; to go and return in six days, and to take with them all such letters as should be directed to any post town in or near that road; and that bye-posts should be placed at several places out of the road, to bring in and carry out the letters from and to Lincoln, Hull, and other places. The like rule was also to be observed to West Chester, Holyhead, and thence to Ireland; also to Plymouth, Exeter, and other places on the west road: and as soon as possible the like conveyance to be settled for Oxford, Bristol, and other towns in that direction; also to Colchester, Norwich, and divers other places on that road. The same proclamation settled the price for conveyance of letters, and for the hire of horses for that purpose, and ordained that no other messengers, nor any foot posts should carry letters, except to places where the king's post did not go. This part of the edict being frequently evaded, new proclamations were issued to enforce it, and the undertaking was in a state of some prosperity before the commencement of the civil war, which terminated in the murder of Charles I. The well conducting of this post had already engaged the vigilance of government; Witherings was superseded for abuses in the execution of his office, which was confided to Peter Burlamachy, to be exercised under the controul of the secretary of state. The civil war, in course, impeded the operations of the post, but when that was terminated, the protector and parliament, in 1656, erected a new general post office, which was formed by the same person who held the contract during

during the life of the king. The prosperity of the plan probably incited the merchants of London to attempt one in opposition, but they were restrained by a vote of the house of commons; and the ordinance made during the republican government, states, that the establishing one general post office, besides the benefit to commerce, and the convenience of conveying public dispatches, "will be the best means to discover and prevent "many dangerous and wicked designs against the common-"wealth."

Such was the origin of this most important and beneficial establishment, the succeeding efforts of legislation being confined to the regulation of its operations, the extension of its utility, and the augmentation of its profits. Omitting the tedious and uninteresting details of intermediate attempts, it is highly necessary to notice the great amendment introduced in 1783, by adopting the plan of reform and improvement, invented by John Palmer Esq. and carried into effect by his great ability and persevering industry, so necessary in all reforms, which oppose the prejudices of long habit. From an undeviating adherence to an established system, and the accumulation of indulgences and abuses, the post office had fallen into a state of general mismanagement in itself, and the revenue was injured, while the public suffered many inconveniences from those causes, as well as from the incorrect and injudicious system practised in the inland department of the office. The plan of conveying and distributing letters, having been unvaried for upwards of a century, the post, instead of being the most safe and expeditious, was become the most insecure and tardy conveyance in the kingdom; the mails being intrusted to boys, who were mounted on bad horses, incapable of defending themselves, were often plundered. Hence it happened, that, in defiance of every law that could be devised for preventing it, many persons preferred sending, at a very advanced price, their letters by any of the numerous vehicles, which the improved state of the turnpike roads enabled to travel with expedition, and which were defended by guards constantly attending and well armed. Comparing the dispatch used by the vehicles called diligences, with that which could be effected by the mail, and which considerably exceeded the proportion of two to one, Mr. Palmer rationally dismissed every thought of cramping private enterprize by prohibitions, against which the necessities of every class in the community must have been perpetually struggling, and recommended, that government should take advantage of the facilities which the advanced state of the country presented, and make contracts with the proprietors of the diligences for conveying the government mails. The train of reasoning which he pursued on the whole of this subject was plain,

plain, rational, and convincing; he ſhewed the beſt mode of inſuring the punctual performance of the contracts, the preciſe obſervance of fixed times for arrivals, and the faithful eſcort of guards. His project embraced alſo the means of increaſing the revenue, and diminiſhing the expence of the new project, by exempting the mail carriages from payment of turnpikes; a heavy tax perhaps on the proprietors of the roads, but an extraordinary ſaving to the nation at large.

Beſides a propoſition for regulating the privilege of franking, which was adopted and extended, Mr. Palmer's plan embraced and accompliſhed a ſalutary reform throughout the interior of the office; a reform beneficial to the clerks and perſons employed, who previouſly ſuffered in their health from the nature of their duties, and highly advantageous to the public. Since the eſtabliſhment of Mr. Palmer's ſyſtem, expedition, ſecurity, punctuality, and facility in tranſacting buſineſs, have been the characteriſtics of the poſt-office of this kingdom. The time of making up the bags, ſeven in the evening, inſtead of midnight as it was before, has produced, perhaps, more than could be expected, a radical change in the arrangements of life; a long buſy morning, being now ſucceeded by a late dinner, and a convivial evening, inſtead of the ſyſtem which formerly prevailed, particularly on poſt nights, of making the moſt preſſing exertions at a late hour, to forward thoſe letters, which would elſe perhaps be delayed for ſeveral days.

The revenue of the poſt-office is at this time very conſiderable, and perhaps none is paid with greater pleaſure, or collected with leſs difficulty. In fact, the payment of poſtage is not a tax, but a moderate compenſation for an eſſential ſervice; it is the only one which remains of the numerous monopolies, formerly in the power of the crown. The amount of this revenue, always progreſſive, has been in the laſt few years exceedingly extended by judicious management, and by occaſional additions to the charge of poſtage. The progreſs of improvement ſince the firſt eſtabliſhment of the poſt-office cannot be clearly aſcertained, becauſe the records of the early expenditure are not preſerved, ſo as to afford means of calculating the net produce; and of late years, the increaſed commerce of the country has cauſed a prodigious augmentation in the expence of packets, which is charged on the groſs receipt of the poſt-office. Yet ſome eſtimate of its progreſs may be formed from the following ſtatement of the ſums rendered, either nett or groſs at different periods.

In 1652, the revenue was farmed at 10,000*l.* before which government paid to the poſt-maſter for a weekly conveyance of letters, 5000*l.* per annum.

In

In 1663, the office was farmed at 21,000*l.*

In 1685, the revenue was estimated at 65,000*l.*; but probably this was too high, since in four years long afterward, 1707-10, the average was but 58,052*l.*; the gross amount in 1710, being 111,462*l.*

In 1711, the rates being somewhat increased, the revenue was on an average of four years, 90,223*l.*

In 1722, the gross amount was 201,804*l.* the net produce 98,010*l.*

In 1755, the gross amount was 210,663*l.*

In 1765, regulations having been made with respect to franking, the gross amount increased to 281,535*l.*

In 1775, it was 345,321*l.*

In the years next noticed, the gross and and net produce are given, and each of them till 1803, is to be taken asending on the fifth of April.

	£.		£.
1783, gross produce	416,668	nett	159,858
1784, (postage being increased)	438,734	—	197,655
1790, ...	548,967	—	327,634
1795, (franking restricted) .	745,238	—	414,548
1796, (postage again increased)	811,539	—	479,487
1799, ...	1,012,731	—	657,388
1800, ...	1,083,950	—	720,981
1801, ...	1,144,900	—	755,299
1802, ...	1,289,197	—	880,069
1803, (year ending 5th Jan.)	1,319,118	—	947,010
1804, ...	1,320,585	—	924,839
1805, (partly by estimate) .	1,343,180	—	942,846

In these years it will be observed, that the revenue of the post-office has been continually progressive, even when the rates of postage were not increasing; the expences, however, have been occasionally augmented by inevitable circumstances, such as war, which occasioned the capture of packets, and an advance in the wages of sailors; and scarcity, which obliged government to enlarge the allowance to the masters of mail coaches, on account of the advance in the price of horse provender.

To produce this, almost incredible, augmentation of revenue, no real hardship has been imposed on the subject; on the contrary, postage is one of the few objects of long established emolument to the state, in which the necessities of succeeding times have not effected a great change. The first imposition of postage, in 1635, was rather injudicious than moderate. It was twopence for distances not reaching eighty miles; from eighty to a hundred and forty, the sum of fourpence; above one hundred and forty, without further discrimination, sixpence; in in England, and on the borders of, and in Scotland, eightpence. It appears that these charges were not considered moderate, since in 1656, they were reduced; letters not to be carried eighty miles, paying twopence; all beyond, without discrimination, threepence; and to Scotland, fourpence. This, too, was at a time, when the office was farmed, and the merchants considered that a rival establishment would be a promising speculation. In 1710, the rates were advanced by the addition of one penny, on the lower description of letters. In 1765, they were new modelled, in the hope of counteracting the disadvantages then attending post-office conveyance, by extraordinary cheapness; a letter then paid for one stage, one penny; for two stages, twopence; for any distance exceeding two stages, and within eighty miles, threepence; beyond eighty miles, if in England, fourpence; and to Edinburgh, sixpence. These rates were too low to afford any considerable revenue, except by a parsimony, destructive of the main objects of the service, and by a monopoly, which would leave the public abundant reason to regret, that they were not at liberty to purchase at a higher price, speed, punctuality, and security. The modern rates are considerably advanced; but the profit is obtained by deserting the absurd limitation of never charging beyond a certain sum, whatever might be the distance, and adding to the postage, as in reason ought to be added, progressively according to the distance. But assuming the distance which seems generally to have formed a medium, eighty miles; this was in 1635, charged fourpence; and in 1656, reduced to threepence; it is now eightpence. If the relative value of money alone were considered, eightpence in these times bears no proportion to the fourpence, or even the threepence, then imposed, and the charge of postage is at that distance, really much lighter than it was then; but comparing the present dispatch of a daily, with that which was then allowed, a weekly conveyance; taking into consideration the difference between the present expences, and that which was then incurred, of twopence halfpenny per mile, for boy and horse, and it must be obvious that the brilliant revenue above described, is owing to the increased commercial activity of the nation, and the judicious system of management alone, and not to any extortion or imposition on the people.

A small deduction from the profits of the post-office has always existed, in consequence of the privilege claimed by members of both houses of parliament, and granted to certain officers of state, of sending and receiving letters free of expence, or, as it is termed, *franking*. This privilege in members of parliament was, at first, rather a demand founded on the implied duties of their station, than a right established by any defined principle; and there were not wanting many independent minds, who contemned it altogether as a reservation unworthy of their exalted rank. When a bill was brought in, soon after the restoration, in December 1660, for the settlement of the post-office, Colonel Titus having reported it to the house of Commons with amendments, Sir Walter Earle delivered a proviso for the letters of all members of parliament to go free, *during their sitting*. Sir Heneage Finch said, *It was a poor mendicant proviso, and below the honour of the house*. Mr. Prynne spoke also against the proviso.—Mr. Bunckley, Mr. Boscawen, Sir George Downing, and Serjeant Charlton for it: the latter, saying, "The council's letters went free."—The question being called for, the Speaker, Sir Harbottle Grimstone, was unwilling to put it, saying, *he was ashamed of it*, nevertheless, the proviso was carried, and made part of the bill, which was ordered to be ingrossed. The lords, however, struck out the clause, and the lower house, in this, among other instances, passed a bill of supply as amended by the peers.

The privilege of franking consequently stood on its old foundation of assumed claim, but it was guaranteed by the King's promise of perpetual allowance, and accordingly a warrant was constantly issued to the Post Master General, directing the allowance to the extent of two ounces in weight for each letter, and without limitation as to number. The right was, however, considered to be so firmly established, that in March 1735, the house of commons passed a resolution, declaring that the privilege of franking letters by the knights, citizens, and burgesses, chosen to represent the commons in parliament, began with the erecting of a post-office within this kingdom, by act of parliament: and that all letters, not exceeding two ounces, signed by, or directed to, any member of the house, during the sitting of every session of parliament, and forty days before, and forty days after every summons or prorogation, ought to be carried and delivered freely, and from all parts of Great Britain and Ireland, without any charge of postage.

In process of time, this licence was abused to a most dangerous extent; for as nothing more than the name of a member at the corner of the cover was necessary, to pass a letter free of postage to any part of the country, to which the sender thought fit to address it, these signatures, given with inexcusable facility, at length became so numerous, as even to be publicly sold. The average amount of payment thus deducted from the revenue was stated at 170,000*l.* per annum. On this occasion, in 1764, the commons resolved, that certain regulations should be be adopted with regard to members of their house, and the lords forming a similar resolution, a bill was framed for the correction of abuses, and establishment of regulations. The right of franking having thus, by voluntary concession of both houses, become an object of statute law, has since been further restricted by various acts of parliament, so that no member can now frank more than ten, nor receive more than fifteen letters in one day, free of cost, and the weight is limited to one ounce each. Nor will any letter go free, unless the member shall write the whole of the superscription, and shall add his own name, and that of the post town from which the letter is intended to be sent, and the day of the month in words at length, besides the year, which may be in figures; and unless the letter shall be put into the post-office of the place, so that it may be sent on the day upon which it is dated. And no letter shall go free, directed to a member of either house, unless it is directed to him where he shall actually be at the delivery thereof; or to his residence in London, or to the lobby of his house of parliament. Certain officers of state have a power of franking, unlimited, either as to number or weight. Printed votes and proceedings of parliament, and newspapers, are allowed to be sent in open covers, signed by, or directed to, members of parliament, at the places whereof they give notice at the post-office. The non-commissioned officers, seamen, and private soldiers, actually on service in the navy, army, militia, fencibles, artillery, and marines, may send single letters, if signed on their back by their commanding officers, to any place, on paying one penny; and they may also receive their letters from any place, on paying the same low postage, and covers, open at the sides, inclosing patterns of cloths, silks, stuffs, &c. and containing no writing but the address of the sender, and the prices of the goods, are allowed to go for single postage.

A branch of duty and emolument connected with the situation of post master, is the establishment for conveyance of letters and parcels from one part of the metropolis to another, and to a distance not exceeding ten miles from London, formerly called the *penny post*; now the *twopenny post*. The origin of this undertaking is involved in some obscurity. It commenced about the year 1683, and is said to have been invented by an upholsterer, named Murray, who sold it to Mr. Dockwra, a gentleman of Hertfordshire, though some consider Mr. Dockwra to have been the original projector. Under him it was successfully conducted for several years, till it was claimed by government, as connected, and interfering with the revenue due to the crown from the post-office, to which it was therefore united, and as a compensation, a pension of 200*l.* was allowed to Mr.

Docwra for life; but even of this fact there are some doubts. Parliament did not take cognizance of it till 1711, when general regulations respecting the post-office were made; in subsequent sessions the price of letters delivered beyond the precincts of the metropolis, or, as it is usually termed, off the stones, was augmented, and in 1765, the post master general was empowered to make a similar establishment, in any town in the British dominions. As the office is now established, letters, and parcels, not exceeding in weight four ounces, are conveyed from any part of the metropolis to any other part for twopence, and to or from any part of the country to which the limits extend, for threepence, payable either by the party sending or receiving: great improvements have been effected with respect to speed and certainty, and the profits are added to the general post revenue.

Thus is the communication between persons in all parts of the kingdom secured and facilitated; for the detached settlements in all parts of the globe, and for foreign correspondence, packets are established, and departments are assigned in the post office for transacting these branches of business.

The law too has made provision for the security, and, as much as is consistent with the public safety, the secrecy of this conveyance; for although, by a warrant from one of the principal secretaries of state, letters may be detained and opened; yet any person employed in the post office wilfully detaining or opening a letter, without such authority, forfeits 20*l.* and is incapable of having any future employment in the office. By the statute, 7 Geo. III. c. 57. any person in the service of the post office embezzling or destroying any letter, containing any valuable paper, or picking out such valuable paper, is deemed guilty of felony, and condemned to suffer death without benefit of clergy. And the robbery of the mail, or of a post office, is subjected to the same penalty. It is also enacted, 34 Geo. III. sess. 2. c. 37, that if any person shall fraudulently counterfeit, or alter the superscription of any person entitled to frank letters, he shall be guilty of felony, and shall be transported for seven years. It is however to be observed as the consequence of repeated decisions in courts of law, that the post master is not, like a common carrier, responsible for any property which may be lost or stolen from letters put into the office.

On the present establishment of the general post office, the office of his Majesty's post master general is vested in, and executed by two persons, with a secretary and six clerks, a principal and resident surveyor, seven riding surveyors, a receiver general, accountant general, a surveyor and superintendant of mail coaches, with various clerks and assistants.

In

In the inland department, are a ſuperintending preſident, with inferior and vice preſidents, eighteen ſenior clerks, and eighteen aſſiſtants, twenty junior clerks, from whom are ſelected five inſpectors of franks, &c.; four eſtabliſhed, and fourteen ſupernumerary meſſengers, a houſekeeper and chamber keeper to the poſt maſter general, an inſpector of inland carriers, and two aſſiſtants; 110 eſtabliſhed, and ſixteen ſupernumerary letter carriers, and eighteen of the eſtabliſhed letter carriers act likewiſe as ſorters.

The foreign department has a comptroller, and his deputy, and various clerks, a meſſenger, and letter carriers.

There is alſo an accountant for bye and croſs road letters, with four clerks, and an office keeper. There are a comptroller, a collector and accountant for the twopenny poſt office, with various ſorters and office men, and upwards of two hundred and fifty town and country letter carriers, and ſeven ſupernumeraries.

There are agents for the packet boats at Harwich, Holyhead, Falmouth, Milford, Weymouth, Liſbon, Gottenburgh, and Cuxhaven, and upwards of ſeven hundred deputy poſt maſters, &c. at home and abroad.

Unlike to other boards of revenue, the poſt office is charged with the performance of moſt extenſive and complicated ſervices in the nature of a carrying trade, dependant for its profits on great advances and continual diſburſements.

Not leſs than 54 ſail of veſſels, from 180 tons, down to 50 tons burthen, are conſtantly employed in the ſervice, for the benefit of the commercial intereſt of the empire, and for the correſpondence of his Majeſty's government; and theſe packets are navigated with 1057 officers and ſeamen.

There are 61 mail coaches, which run upon an average 10,000 miles a day, and require at leaſt 4000 horſes, and 200 guards, to be kept for that ſervice. It is true, that the econonical principles on which the contracts for thoſe coaches are formed, leaving to the contractors the profit of paſſengers and parcels, do not require that all the horſes employed ſhould be bought and kept ſolely at the public expence.

The mails which are forwarded in carts and on horſeback, are conveyed upwards of 4,000 miles a day at the loweſt computation, and many men and horſes are occupied at the expence of the poſt office revenue in that part of the ſervice.

Upwards of 1000 perſons are employed as officers, ſorters, meſſengers, letter carriers, receivers of letters, and ſervants in the inland, foreign, and twopenny poſt departments of the office; and there are nearly four thouſand perſons engaged in Great Britain, in carrying on the immenſe buſineſs of the office,

office, in forwarding and receiving letters, and in collecting the amount of postage arising from them.

The duty of the *Post Master General* is to superintend and regulate inland posts in all parts of Great Britain, and to and from any part of his Majesty's plantations; to obey and perform all such rules, instructions, orders, and directions, in relation to the revenue of his office, as he shall receive under the King's sign manual; and touching the management, ordering, and government of the revenue in the office, he is to observe the orders and directions which the commissioners of the treasury think fit and necessary for the service. The salary of the joint post master general is 5000*l*.

The duty of the *Secretary* is, under the direction of the postmaster general, to superintend the whole business of the office, in all its complicated branches, to carry on the official correspondence, to attend the board, take minutes of the proceedings and to give directions for carrying into execution the orders of the postmaster general: his attendance is constant, and at all hours when required. The person who now executes this office, from his peculiar knowledge of all the posts of the kingdom, acquired by his active and extensive agency, under Mr. Palmer, at the outset, and in the progress of his admirable plan, also holds the office of resident surveyor, and in this capacity has to direct the management of the various post offices, and proper conveyance of the mails all over the kingdom, to correspond with, and give directions to the several riding surveyors, and deputy postmasters, and to all persons who are employed in the conveyance, sorting and delivery of letters; to receive and determine, with the approbation of the postmaster general, upon all representations or applications for establishing new posts, or alterations in those already established, to report to the board the advantages or disadvantages, that, in his opinion, might probably arise to correspondence, or the revenue, from such alterations or establishments; to consider and report upon all petitions from deputy postmasters for increase of salaries for office duty, or for allowances for riding work; to attend to and redress all complaints of irregularity in the persons employed in the several departments; to regulate the mode of conducting the business in general, and of stating the accounts of the deputy postmasters, both for their salary and riding work. His salary is 1200*l*. per annum, a house in the office, and the privilege of franking newspapers and periodical publications to the West Indies and America.

The duty of the *Chief Clerk* is, to assist the secretary in carrying on the general correspondence of the office; to prepare fair drafts of the board's minutes; to enter all remittances on account of the revenue, from the country poſtmaſters, or from the poſtmaſters and agents abroad, and in the abſence of the ſecretary to acknowledge the receipt of them to the parties, and to deliver ſuch remittances to the accountant or receiver general, and take their acknowledgment for the ſame; and generally to aſſiſt in all the buſineſs of the ſecretary's department. His attendance is conſtant and at all hours. His ſalary and emoluments are nearly 600l. per annum.

The duty of *Superintendant of Mail Coaches* is to contract for the conveyance of the mails all over Great Britain, to attend that they be properly guarded, and generally to ſuperintend all the duties relative to the mail coaches, to ſee that proper and correct way bills are provided for all the roads and branches, and to fix, as near as poſſible, the time neceſſary for the performance of each ſtage, &c. &c. His attendance is conſtant, and the performance of the duties of his office occupy his whole time. His ſalary is 700*l.*

The duty of the *Riding Surveyors* is, to inſpect into the management of the country poſt offices; and to inſtruct the ſeveral deputies how to ſort, tax, charge, and circulate, the letters received at their offices, to check and report to the board, any impropriety in their conduct; to endeavour to detect all coachmen, carriers and others, who ſhall collect, carry or deliver, any letters or packets contrary to law; and when any alteration is made in the courſe of the poſt, or new branches eſtabliſhed in their diſtricts, to direct and regulate the operations. Their attendance is as occaſion may require, in town or country. One of them has a ſalary of 400*l.* a year, and chaiſe hire; the others have each a ſalary of 150*l.* a year, and an allowance of 26*s.* per day when travelling.

The duty of the *Receiver General* is, to receive and pay all monies appertaining to the revenue of the poſt office, to keep accounts thereof and tranſmit an annual ſtatement of the ſame, atteſted by him, to the office of the commiſſioners for auditing public accounts, for their examination. He pays into the exchequer 3000*l.* every week, purſuant to act of parliament, and at the end of each week the balance remaining in his hands, reſerving, however, ſo much as may be neceſſary to anſwer incidental payments in conſequence of the poſtmaſter general's warrants. He gives ſecurity to the amount of 10,000*l.* himſelf in 5,000*l.* and two ſureties in 2,500*l.* each; he has a ſalary of 800*l.* and under him five clerks, the chief of whom has a ſalary of 500*l.* a year.

The duty of the *Accountant General* is, to attend that all accounts, relative to the revenue of the poſt office, are properly kept and ſtated in his office; to keep a weekly checque on the receiver general,

general, to examine, ſign, and tranſmit the deputy poſtmaſter's quarterly accounts; to examine and ſign tradeſmen's bills, the ſolicitors and other bills for ſervices performed, packet warrants, &c. to examine, ſign, and atteſt, the annual general account of this revenue, and the annual caſh account, and tranſmit both to the auditor's office. He has a ſalary of 700*l.* a year. His deputy aſſiſts in examining and ſtating all theſe accounts, and ſuperintends the buſineſs performed by the clerks; his ſalary is 500*l.* a year, and there are five clerks in this office.

The *Superintending Preſident* of the inland office, is to ſee that all the officers, clerks, ſorters, and letter carriers, attend at the proper hours for diſpatch of buſineſs, and to keep them to their duty; to receive the charge of every mail from the ſorters, to compare ſuch charge with that reported to him by the letter carriers, and deliver the ſame to the receiver general, that he may obtain the amount from each letter carrier.

There are in this office ſix clerks of the roads, namely, Weſt, Briſtol, Cheſter, North, Yarmouth, and Kent, each of whom has 300*l.* a year, and the privilege of franking newſpapers on their reſpective roads. Their aſſiſtants, ſorters, and other ſubordinate agents have moderate ſalaries, which increaſe as vacancies occur, till they may reach from 70*l.* to 300*l.*

The duty of the *Comptroller of the Foreign Office* is to ſuperintend the whole buſineſs of the office, and to ſee that every officer and letter carrier does his duty, in ſorting, taxing, and delivery of the letters by the foreign mails; to charge the window men and letter carriers with the amount of the letters given them for delivery; to tranſmit weekly a bill thereof, together with an account of the money received at the window on poſt nights, to the receiver general, and a copy thereof to the accountant general, to keep an account of letters ſent and received to and from the poſt offices abroad, to take care of letters which come regiſtered from abroad, and on which a fee is received; and to examine the quarterly and general accounts from Hamburgh and Bremen. His attendance is conſtant on account of the uncertainty of the arrival of the mails. He has no ſalary, but is paid for his public ſervices by the privilege of franking newſpapers to foreign parts.

The *Deputy Comptroller* is to aſſiſt the comptroller in the general buſineſs of the office; he attends the ſorting and diſpatch of the letters by the mails of the night; he has the care of regiſtering all packets of value ſent, and remains in the office until the mail is diſpatched, and the whole buſineſs finiſhed. His attendance is conſtant, being obliged to be always in waiting for the arrival of the mails when any are due. His ſalary is 250*l.* with a privilege of franking newſpapers to foreign

foreign parts. There are in this office fourteen clerks, with ſalaries from 70*l.* to 120*l.*, a meſſenger, an inſpector, and twenty letter carriers.

Subordinate to theſe general departments are the *dead and miſſent letter office*, the inſpector of which has a ſalary of 400*l.* together with an aſſiſtant and ſix clerks; the office of *accountant for bye and croſs roads letters*, with four clerks; the accountant's ſalary is 250*l.* There is alſo a *ſhip letter office* for letters ſent and received by private ſhips, with an inſpector, at a ſalary of 280*l.* and two clerks.

The ſolicitor, whoſe buſineſs it is to commence, carry on, and defend all actions that concern the revenue of the office, to conduct all criminal proſecutions, prepare bonds from every perſon appointed to offices under the poſt maſter general, and regiſter the names and reſidence of their ſureties, and in general to execute all law buſineſs relative to the poſt office, has an annual fee of 300*l.*; and there is an architect and ſurveyor, who receives annually 150*l.*

The *two penny poſt*, under a late regulation, is made in the abſtract to conform as nearly as poſſible to the general poſt office. It has in the metropolis two principal offices, one in Lombard-ſtreet, connected with the ſuperior eſtabliſhment, the other in Gerrard Street, Soho Square. The chief officers, as before obſerved, are the comptroller, accomptant, and collector.

The *Comptroller* ſuperintends the duties performed by the ſeveral officers, clerks, and letter carriers, in ſorting, telling, taxing, and delivering letters. His ſalary is 500*l.*

The duty of the *accountant* is to keep an account of the receipts at the ſeveral receiving houſes, which are checqued at the chief office, and at ſtated periods, he makes out tickets for the collector of the money received by each during that period, deducting from the amount one penny in every ten, which is the allowance to the receivers for their trouble, and ſtrikes the clear balance to be received from each, and delivers in the charge to the collector: He alſo makes out a yearly account of the whole, which is ſigned by him, and by which he checks the annual amount of the collector. His ſalary is 400*l.*

The duty of the *Collector* is to receive the money collected by the letter receivers, window men, and letter carriers in this department; to pay the ſalaries, wages, and other diſburſements appertaining to this office, paying the net balance every week to the receiver general, reſerving only in his hands a very ſmall part for current expences; at the end of the year he makes out a general account of his receipts and payments, and ſtrikes a balance, which account is examined and ſigned by him, and afterwards

afterwards authenticated by the ſignature of the poſt maſter general; the collector then atteſts the account, and delivers it with the vouchers into the office of the commiſſioners for auditing the public accounts. He gives ſecurity in the ſum of 2,000*l.* with two ſureties; his attendance is conſtant, and his ſalary is 150*l.* He has in this department two ſub-collectors, with ſalaries of 110*l.* and 100*l.*

There are alſo in the office four principal clerks, window men, ſorters, inſpectors of dead letters, and ſtampers.

The deputy poſt maſters at home and abroad are very numerous, being between 7 and 800.

The *packets* and other charges attending the conveyance of letters to the colonies and to foreign countries are alſo very heavy, but the ſervice is performed with great preciſion and diſpatch.

The agents eſtabliſhed are as follow:—

At *Dover*, to receive and forward the French and Flanders mails;

Harwich, to receive and forward the mails, and other public diſpatches, to and from Holland, and the northern parts of Europe; and

Falmouth, to receive and forward the public diſpatches to and from Liſbon, the Weſt India Iſlands, and America; to muſter the men on board the packets before they ſail, and on their arrival; to ſend copies of the muſters to the poſt maſter general; to keep a journal, and report daily to the board, a ſtate of the winds and weather, of the arrival and ſailing of each packet, the names and condition of thoſe in the harbour, and to tranſmit the ſame every poſt to the poſt maſter general; alſo of the number of mails at Falmouth; to keep an account of all money received for freight or paſſage; to pay the neceſſary diſburſements, ſend an account of the ſame to the poſt maſter general at the end of every quarter, atteſted on oath; and generally to ſuperintend and direct the commanders according to the orders he receives from the board.

15. The Treasurer of the Navy, is alſo a diſtinguiſhed officer of government, but as the buſineſs of the offices with which he is connected relates to the details of the naval ſervice, a deſcription of his duties is reſerved till the navy is expreſsly under conſideration.

Embassadors.—Although theſe perſons are not properly within the deſcription of officers, whoſe council is ſuppoſed to aſſiſt, or whoſe reſponſibility is engaged in the tranſactions of, the cabinet, ſtill the information they convey, and the correſpondence they maintain in various directions, form the grounds of many deciſions which they influence more effectually than they

they could by their votes. Of these officers it may be fit first to take notice, as they are established by the general law of all civilized people, and next, as they are particularly protected by the law of England. A brief account is also added of some other ministers of inferior degree, employed in the correspondence between nations.

It is necessary, that nations should hold intercourse together, in order to promote their interests, to avoid injuring each other, and to adjust and terminate their disputes. But nations, or sovereign states, do not treat together immediately; and their rulers or sovereigns cannot well come to a personal conference in order to treat of their affairs. Such interviews would often be impracticable; and, exclusive of delays, trouble, expence, and many other inconveniences, it is rarely, that any good effect could be expected from them. The only expedient, therefore, which remains for nations and sovereigns, is to communicate and negotiate by the agency of delegates charged with their commands, and vested with their powers, that is to say, public ministers. These, every sovereign state has a right to send and receive; nay, princes or communities not possessed of sovereign power, may enjoy the right by the constitution of the state, the concession of the sovereign, or by reservations which the subjects have made with him. For where the members of any general union have retained separate and independant rights of sovereignty, such as those of granting succours of troops, or contracting alliances, it seems necessarily to follow that they must also have the power of appointing and receiving embassadors, or other ministers, for the adjustment and maintenance of treaties on those important points. Sometimes, this power has been delegated to viceroys, or chief governors of extensive provinces; during an interregnum it reverts to the nation, or devolves on those whom the law has invested with the regency of the state; a sovereign who attemps to hinder another from receiving or sending public ministers, offends against the law of nations; and so essentially is this right interwoven with that of sovereignty *de facto*, that if the embassador of an usurper is received, the legal prince, if restored, has no right to complain of it as an injury or disrespect to himself. A sovereign cannot, with propriety, refuse to receive the minister of a friendly state, though he may, if he sees cause, object to his long residence in his dominions.

The embassador is a minister of the first rank, his appointment places him above all other ministers, who are not invested with the same character, and precludes their entering into competition with him. At present, there are embassadors *ordinary* and *extraordinary*; but this is no more than an accidental distinction,

diſtinction, merely relative to the ſubject of their miſſion. The peculiar honours paid to embaſſadors, depend entirely on cuſtom; but in general, they are entitled to thoſe civilities and diſtinctions, which the uſage and prevailing manners of the times have pointed out as proper expreſſions of the reſpect due to the repreſentative of the ſovereign; and when a practice is ſo eſtabliſhed, as to impart, according to the uſages and manners of the age, a real value and a ſettled ſignification to things in their own nature indifferent, it is neceſſary to act with reſpect to ſuch things, as if they really poſſeſſed all that value which the opinion of mankind has annexed to them. For inſtance, according to the general uſage of all Europe, it is the peculiar prerogative of an embaſſador to wear his hat in the preſence of the prince to whom he is ſent. This right expreſſes that he is acknowledged as the repreſentative of a ſovereign; to refuſe it therefore to the embaſſador of a ſtate, which is truly independent, would be doing an injury to that ſtate, and, in ſome meaſure, degrading it. The ceremonials of public deference muſt be regulated by this principle, for the honour of a nation would be ſenſibly wounded by a ſlight ſhewn to its embaſſador, and an offence ſo given would be a proof of wanton contumely, or inconſiderate raſhneſs.

The reſpect due to ſovereigns ſhould redound to their repreſentatives, and eſpecially to their embaſſadors. Whoever offends or inſults a public miniſter, endangers his country and his ſovereign, and ſhould therefore be puniſhed with ſeverity; and the ſtate, at the expence of the delinquent, ſhould give full ſatisfaction to the ſovereign who has been offended in the perſon of his miniſter. If the foreign miniſter is himſelf the aggreſſor, the citizen may oppoſe him, without departing from the reſpect due to his character, and may prefer a complaint to his own ſovereign, who will demand for him an adequate ſatisfaction from the miniſter's maſter; but he muſt not entertain thoſe thoughts of revenge which the point of honour might ſuggeſt, although they ſhould in other reſpects be deemed allowable. Even according to the maxims of the world, a gentleman is not diſgraced by an affront for which it is not in his own power to procure ſatisfaction.

The neceſſity and right of embaſſies being eſtabliſhed, the perfect ſecurity and inviolability of embaſſadors and other miniſters is a certain conſequence of it: for if their perſons be not protected from violence of every kind, the right of embaſſy becomes precarious, and the ſucceſs very uncertain. Whoever offers violence to any embaſſador, or to any other public miniſter, not only injures the ſovereign whom that miniſter repreſents, but alſo attacks the common ſafety and well-being well-being of nations: he becomes guilty of an atrocious crime againſt mankind in general. This ſafety is particularly due to the miniſter from the ſovereign to whom he is ſent, who by admitting and acknowledging him, engages for his protection and ſafety. This duty extends beyond the protection due to perſons in general, reſident within his dominions; an act of violence committed on one of them is an ordinary tranſgreſſion, which, according to circumſtances, the prince may pardon; but if done to a public miniſter, it is an offence againſt the law of nations, to be pardoned only by him who has been offended in the perſon of his repreſentative.

Although the miniſter's character is not diſplayed in its full extent, and does not thus enſure him the enjoyment of all his rights, till he is acknowledged and admitted by the ſovereign, to whom he delivers his credentials; yet, on his entering the country to which he is ſent, and making himſelf known, he is under the protection of the law of nations; until he has had his audience of the prince, he is, on his own word, to be conſidered as a miniſter; and beſides, excluſive of the notice of his miſſion uſually given by letter, the miniſter has, in caſe of doubt, his paſſports to produce, which will ſufficiently certify his character. Theſe paſſports ſometimes become neceſſary to him, in the countries through which he paſſes on his way to the place of his deſtination; and, in caſe of need, he ſhews them, in order to obtain the privileges to which he is entitled. It is true, indeed, that the prince alone to whom the miniſter is ſent, is under any obligation, or particular engagement to enſure him the enjoyment of all the rights annexed to his character; yet the others, through whoſe dominions he paſſes, are not to deny him thoſe regards to which the miniſter of a ſovereign is entitled, and which nations reciprocally owe to each other. In particular, they are bound to afford him perfect ſecurity. To inſult him would be injuring his maſter, and the whole nation to which he belongs; to arreſt or offer him violence, would be infringing the right of embaſſy which belongs to all ſovereigns.

Theſe obſervations however apply only to nations at peace with each other. On the breaking out of a war, we ceaſe to be under any obligation of leaving the enemy in the free enjoyment of his rights; on the contrary, we are juſtifiable in depriving him of them, for the purpoſe of weakening and reducing him to accept of equitable conditions. His people may alſo be attacked and ſeized wherever we have a right to commit acts of hoſtility. Not only, therefore, may we juſtly refuſe a paſſage to the miniſters whom our enemy ſends to other ſovereigns, we may even arreſt them if they attempt to paſs privately, and without permiſſion, through places belonging to our juriſdiction.

The

The inviolability of a public minifter, or the protection to which he has a more facred and particular claim than any other perfon, whether native or foreigner, is not the only privilege he enjoys; the univerfal practice of nations allows him an entire independence on the jurifdiction and authority of the ftate in which he refides. But this independency is not to be converted into licentioufnefs, it does not excufe him from conforming with the laws of the country in all his external actions; fo far as they are unconnected with the object of his miffion and character, he is independent, but he has not a right to do whatever he pleafes. Thus for inftance, if there exifts a general prohibition againft paffing in a carriage near a powder magazine, or over a bridge, againft walking round and examining the fortifications of a town, &c. the embaffador is bound to refpect fuch prohibitions. Should he forget his duty, fhould he grow infolent, and be guilty of irregularities and crimes, there are, according to the nature and importance of his offences, various modes of repreffing him. As to what concerns the prince to whom he is fent, the embaffador fhould remember that his miniftry is a miniftry of peace, and that it is on that footing he is received. This reafon forbids his engaging in any evil machinations: let him ferve his mafter without clandeftinely or treacheroufly injuring the prince who receives him.

Should an embaffador forget the duties of his ftation, fhould he render himfelf difagreeable and dangerous, fhould he form cabals and fchemes prejudicial to the peace of the citizens, or to the ftate or prince to whom he is fent, there are various modes of punifhing him, proportionate to the nature and degree of his offence. If he maltreats the fubjects of the ftate, if he commits any acts of injuftice or violence againft them, the injured fubjects are not to feek redrefs from the ordinary magiftrates, fince the embaffador is wholly independent of their jurifdiction; and for the fame reafon thofe magiftrates cannot proceed directly againft him, but they muft apply to their fovereign, who demands juftice from the embaffador's mafter, and in cafe of a refufal, may order the infolent minifter to quit his dominions. Should a foreign minifter offend the prince himfelf, fhould he fail in the refpect he owes him, or by his intrigues embroil the ftate and the court, the offended prince, from a wifh to keep meafures with the offender's fovereign, fometimes contents himfelf with fimply requiring his recal, or if the tranfgeffion be of a more ferious nature, forbids his appearance at court in the interval while his mafter's anfwer is expected; and in cafes of a heinous complexion, he even expels him from his territories. Every fovereign has an unqueftionable right to proceed in this manner, for being mafter in his own dominions, no foreigner can ſtay in his court or territories, without permiſſion. And though ſovereigns are generally obliged to liſten to the overtures of foreign powers, and to admit their miniſters, this obligation entirely ceaſes with regard to a miniſter, who, being himſelf deficient in the duties attached to his ſtation, becomes dangerous, or juſtly ſuſpected. Yet, in extreme caſes, the power of the ſovereign is not held to be limited to the mere expulſion of a criminal embaſſador; in open acts of hoſtility, either by joining an enemy, or a rebellious party of ſubjects, the embaſſador foregoes his ſacred pacific character to aſſume that of an enemy, and muſt be treated accordingly. In caſes of revolutionary conſpiracy, it has been thought that a ſtate might puniſh an embaſſador; but this is doubted, and perhaps, on the whole, it were better to refer every offence of ſuch perſons to their own ſtates, ſince the puniſhment of a guilty individual is of ſmall moment, compared with the dangers which ariſe from any laxity or uncertainty in the obſervance of a ſacred principle of public law. But if an embaſſador attempts to poiſon or aſſaſſinate the monarch at whoſe court he is received, it ſeems that he may be puniſhed as a treacherous enemy, guilty of poiſoning or aſſaſſination. Sometimes princes ſend to each other ſecret miniſters, whoſe character is not public. If a miniſter of this kind be inſulted by a perſon unacquainted with his character, ſuch inſult is no violation of the law of nations; but the prince who receives this embaſſador, and knows him to be a public miniſter, is bound by the ſame ties of duty towards him as towards one publicly acknowledged.

It is not lawful to maltreat an embaſſador by way of retaliation, for the prince who uſes violence againſt a public miniſter, is guilty of a crime; and we are not to take vengeance for his miſconduct, by copying his example.

Some ſubordinate rights of embaſſadors, which are not indiſpenſably connected with their public functions, are yet generally allowed, and the withholding of ſome of them where they have once been admitted would be an act of harſhneſs, at which the power ſending ſuch miniſter might reaſonably take umbrage, though, with reſpect to others, prudence and dignity would equally recommend forbearance. One of the greateſt of theſe rights, is the free exerciſe of their own religion, by the embaſſador and his retinue; a conceſſion generally made, but which, if claimed as a right, would be ſubject to many exceptions and limitations. The exemption of his baggage from impoſt, and from its neceſſary concomitant, detention and ſearch at the cuſtom houſe, is a compliment dependant on uſage, one which it would be mean and unprincely to alter, but of the alteration of which no potentate could reaſonably complain.

In

In civil cafes, it is held that an embaffador is not fubject to the jurifdiction of the country where he refides; but if he chufes to renounce a part of his independency, and fubject himfelf in civil affairs to the jurifdiction of the country, he is undoubtedly at liberty to do fo, provided it be done by his own mafter's confent. Without fuch confent, the embaffador has no right to renounce privileges, in which the dignity and fervice of his fovereign are concerned, which are founded on the mafter's rights, and inftituted for his advantage, not for that of the minifter. It is true, indeed, that the embaffador, without waiting for his fovereign's permiffion, acknowledges the jurifdiction of the country when he commences a fuit as plaintiff in a court of juftice; but the confequence, in that cafe, is inevitable. Befides, in a civil caufe, on a point of private intereft, no inconvenience attends it, fince the embaffador has it at all times in his power to avoid commencing a fuit; but he ought never to inftitute a profecution, on a criminal charge, his vindication in fuch matters belonging exclufively to the fovereign, and the public.

A foreign minifter is independent of the jurifdiction of the country: but his perfonal independence in civil cafes would be of little avail, unlefs it extended to every thing which enables him to live with dignity, and quietly to attend the difcharge of his functions. Every thing, therefore, which directly belongs to his perfon in the character of a public minifter, every thing which is intended for his ufe, or which ferves for his own maintenance, and that of his houfehold, partakes of his independency, and is abfolutely exempt from all jurifdiction in the country. Thofe things, together with the perfon to whom they belong, are confidered as being out of the country; but this exemption cannot extend to fuch property as evidently belongs to the embaffador, under any other relation than that of a minifter. What has no affinity with his functions and character, cannot partake of the privileges which are folely derived from his functions and characters. Should a minifter, therefore, (as it has often been the cafe) embark in any branch of commerce, all the effects, goods, money, and debts, active and paffive, which are connected with his mercantile concerns, and likewife all contefts and law fuits to which they may give rife, fall under the jurifdiction of the country; and although, in confequence of the minifter's independency, no legal procefs can, in thofe law fuits, be directly iffued againft his perfon, he is neverthelefs, by the feizure of the effects belonging to his commerce, indirectly compelled to plead in his own defence.

The independency of the embaffador would be very imperfect,

perfect, and his security very precarious, if the house in which he lives were not to enjoy a perfect immunity, and to be inaccessible to the ordinary officers of justice. He might be molested and insulted under a thousand pretexts; and his secrets might be discovered by searching his papers. In all civilised nations, therefore, an embassador's house is, equally with his person, considered as being out of the country; to insult it, is a crime both against the state and against all other nations; but this immunity cannot be extended beyond its real and just import; the dwelling of an embassador cannot be converted into an asylum for criminals or debtors, nor is a sovereign obliged to tolerate an abuse so pernicious to his state, and so detrimental to society. It is not politic however to investigate too strictly the motives for which occasional refuge is afforded by embassadors, as a government suffers little by these occasional connivances, but public faith would be extremely insecure were the houses of foreign ministers frequently invaded by the inferior officers of the law on any pretence, however well founded. The observations on an embassador's house apply to his carriages and equipages. They are independent of all subordinate authority, of guards, custom-house officers, magistrates and their agents, and must not be stopped or searched without a superior order. But in this instance, as in that of the embassador's house, the abuse is not confounded with the right. It would be absurd that a foreign minister should have the power of conveying off in his coach a criminal of consequence, a man, in the seizure of whose person the state was highly interested; and that he should do this under the very eyes of the sovereign, who would thus see himself defied in his own kingdom and court. The embassador's wife, family, and retinue, partake of his inviolability; his independency extends to every individual of his household: so intimate a connexion exists between him and all those persons, that they share the same fate with him; they immediately depend on him alone, and are exempt from the jurisdiction of the country, into which they would not have come without such reservation in their favour. The embassador is bound to protect them; and no insult can be offered to them, which is not at the same time an insult to himself. His private secretary is one of his domestics: but the secretary of the embassy holds his commission from the sovereign himself; which makes him a kind of public minister, enjoying in his own right the protection of the law of nations, and the immunities annexed to his office, independently of the embassador, to whose orders he is indeed but imperfectly subjected, sometimes not at all, and always in such degree only, as their common master has been pleased to ordain. Couriers sent or received by an embassador, his papers, letters, and dispatches, all essentially belong to the embassy, and are consequently to be held sacred; since, if they were not respected, the legitimate objects of the embassy could not be obtained, nor would the embassador be able to discharge his functions with the necessary degree of security.

The persons in a foreign minister's retinue being independent of the jurisdiction of the country, cannot be taken into custody or punished without his consent. It would nevertheless be highly improper that they should enjoy an absolute independence, and be at liberty to indulge in every kind of licentious disorder without controul or apprehension. The embassador must necessarily be supposed to possess whatever degree of authority is requisite for keeping them in order: and some writers make that authority include even a power over life and death. In general, however, it is to be presumed that the embassador is possessed only of a coercive power, sufficient to restrain his dependants by other punishments which are not of a capital or infamous nature. He may punish the faults committed against himself and against his master's service, or send the delinquents to their sovereign, in order to their being punished; but should any of his people commit crimes against society which deserve a severe punishment, the embassador ought to make a distinction between such of his domestics as belong to his own nation, and others who are subjects of the country where he resides. The shortest and most natural way with the latter is to dismiss them from his service, and deliver them up to justice. As to those of his own nation, if they have offended the sovereign of the country, or committed any of those atrocious crimes in the punishment of which all nations are interested, and whose perpetrators are, for that reason, usually surrendered by one state when demanded by another, he should give them up to the nation which calls for their punishment. If the transgression be of a different kind, he is to send them to his sovereign. Finally, if the case be of a doubtful nature, it is the embassador's duty to keep the offenders in irons, till he receives orders from his court; but if he passes a capital sentence on the criminal, he cannot have it executed in his own house; an execution of that nature being an act of territorial superiority, which belongs only to the sovereign of the country; and although the embassador, together with his house and household, be reputed out of the country, that is nothing more than a figurative mode of speech, intended to express his independency, and all the rights necessary to the lawful success of the embassy: nor can that fiction involve privileges which are reserved for the sovereign alone, which are of too delicate and important a nature to be communicated to a foreigner, and, moreover, not necessary to the embassador forthe due discharge of his functions.

Among the several characters established by custom, it rests with the sovereign to determine with what particular one he chuses to invest his minister; and he makes known the minister's character in the *credentials*, which he gives him for the sovereign to whom he sends him. Credentials are the instruments which authorise and establish the minister, in his character with the prince to whom they are addressed. If that prince receive the minister, he can receive him only in the quality attributed to him in his credentials. They are, as it were, his general letter of attorney, his *mandate patent, mandatum manifestum*.

The *instructions* given to the minister contain his master's *secret mandate*, the orders to which the minister must carefully conform, and which limit his powers.

When the commission of an embassador is at an end; when he has concluded the business for which he came, is recalled or dismissed; or obliged to depart on any account whatever, his functions cease, but his privileges and rights do not immediately expire; he retains them till his return to his sovereign, to whom he is to make a report of his embassy. Accordingly, when an embassador departs on account of a war arising between his master and the sovereign at whose court he was employed, he is allowed a sufficient time to quit the country in perfect security: and moreover, if he was returning home by sea, and happened to be taken on his passage, he would be released without a moment's hesitation, as not being subject to lawful capture.

For the same reasons the embassador's privileges still exist at those times when the activity of his ministry happens to be suspended, and he stands in need of fresh powers. Such a case occurs in consequence of the death of the prince whom the minister represents, or of the sovereign at whose court he resides, on either of which occasions he must be furnished with new credentials. The necessity, however, is less cogent in the latter than in the former case, especially if the successor of the deceased prince be the natural and necessary successor; because, while the authority whence the minister's power emanated, still subsists, it is fairly presumable that he retains his former character at the court of the new sovereign. But if his own master is no more, the minister's powers are at an end; and he must necessarily receive fresh credentials from the new prince, before he can be authorised to speak and act in his name. In the interim, however, he still continues to be the minister of his nation, and, as such, is entitled to enjoy all the rights and honours annexed to that character.

These are the privileges and immunities, as enumerated by a celebrated writer on the law of nations, which every embassador

 enjoys;

enjoys; the peculiar provisions made in England, are entirely calculated to give effect to those rights, so far as they relate to foreign ministers residing among us, and to intitle those who are deputed by the government of Great Britain to other states to all the respect and consideration which belong to their functions. In all Europe the opinions of jurists have been divided whether the immunity of the embassador extended to all cases, or was restricted to such alone as were *mala prohibita*, and not *mala per se*; but in many instances the partition between these is too thin, and the distinctions too much dependant on local customs and manners for them to form the general basis of decisions, and therefore, as already has been observed, governments act more wisely in allowing even gross criminals to escape in all cases except treason, and frequently even in that, than in inciting disputes which might put the entire well-being of the state in hazard. The last instance which occurred in England of the punishment of an embassador, was that of Don Pantaleon Sa, during the protectorate of Cromwell; and although eminent lawyers have justified the proceeding, the law, as well as the policy of it, may reasonably be doubted. With respect to personal privilege, the law of England was so little settled, that in 1708, the Russian embassador was actually arrested, and taken out of his carriage in the public streets. Peter the Great, exasperated at this indignity, demanded that the sheriff of Middlesex, and all others concerned in it should be punished with immediate death; the queen remonstrated that such an atonement was not in her power, as the constitution of England would not permit the infliction of a punishment, even on the meanest subject, unless warranted by the law of the land. The offenders, seventeen in number, were however committed to prison, prosecuted by the attorney general, and found guilty; and the parliament passed a law reciting the arrest which had been made, "in con-
"tempt of the protection granted by her majesty, contrary to
"the law of nations, and in prejudice of the rights and privi-
"leges, which embassadors and other public ministers have at
"all times been thereby possessed of, and ought to be kept sa-
"cred and inviolable;" and enacting that for the future all process whereby the person of any embassador, or of his domestic, or domestic servant, may be arrested, or his goods distrained or seized, shall be utterly null and void; and the persons prosecuting, soliciting, or executing such process, shall be deemed violators of the law of nations, and disturbers of the public repose; and shall suffer such penalties and corporal punishment, as the lord chancellor and the two chief justices, or any two of them, shall think fit. But it is expresly provided, that no trader within the description of the bankrupt laws, who shall be in the

service

service of any embassador, shall be privileged or protected by this act; nor shall any one be punished for arresting an embassador's servant, unless his name be registered with the secretary of state, and by him transmitted to the sheriffs of London and Middlesex. And in consequence of this statute, thus declaring and enforcing the law of nations, these privileges are now held to be part of the law of the land, and are constantly allowed in the courts. On receiving a copy of this statute elegantly engrossed and illuminated, with a soothing letter from the queen, the monarch of Muscovy was appeased. Perhaps a little ambiguity in the wording of the act helped to mitigate his choler; for he might conceive that the power of punishment vested in the judges extends to sentence of death; but that is not the fact, as no law exists by which the offence is declared capital. It is however to be observed, and not without regret, that, in compliment perhaps to the injured feelings of this outraged potentate, and of the whole diplomatic body, who made it a common cause, the offender is deprived of his trial by jury.

Embassadors from the British to foreign courts are expresly appointed by the king; their emoluments are paid out of the civil list, and for the expences of procuring intelligence which the nature of the situation requires, they are furnished with sums from a fund devoted to secret service. They correspond with the secretary of state, and for the sake of secrecy, frequently use arbitrary signs or cyphers. Their salaries are undetermined, but each receives at the time of his appointment, a service of plate, or its value in money, which is settled at 2000*l*.

Besides embassadors, it is necessary, in treating on the subject of foreign communication, to notice some other classes of agents, termed, envoys, residents, ministers, and consuls.

Envoys are not invested with the representative character, properly so called, or in the first degree. They are ministers of the second rank, on whom their master was willing to confer a degree of dignity and respectability, which, without being on a level with the character of an embassador, immediately follows it, and yields the pre-eminence to it alone. There are also *envoys ordinary*, and *extraordinary*; and it appears to be the intention of princes that the latter should be held in greater consideration. This likewise depends on custom.

The word *Resident* formerly related only to the continuance of the minister's stay; and it is frequent in history for embassadors in ordinary to be designated by the simple title of residents; but since the practice of employing different orders of ministers has been generally established, the name of resident has been confined to ministers of a third order, to whose character general custom has annexed a lesser degree of respectability. The resident does not represent the prince's person in his dignity, but only in his affairs. His representation is in reality of the same nature as that of envoy: wherefore he is often termed as well as the envoy, a minister of the second order, thus distinguishing only two classes of public ministers, the former consisting of embassadors who are invested with the representative character in pre-eminence, the latter comprising all other ministers not equally exalted. This is the most necessary distinction and indeed the only essential one.

A custom of still more recent origin has introduced a new kind of ministers without any particular determination of character. These are called simply *ministers*, to indicate that they are invested with the general quality of a sovereign's mandatories, without any particular assignment of rank and character. It was likewise the punctilio of ceremony which gave rise to this innovation. Use had established particular modes of treatment for the embassador, the envoy, and the resident. Disputes between ministers of the several princes often arose on this head, and especially about rank. In order to avoid contests on certain occasions, the expedient was adopted of sending ministers, not invested with any one of the three known characters, who are not subject to any settled ceremonial, and can pretend to no particular treatment. The minister represents his master in a vague and indeterminate manner, which cannot be equal to the first degree; consequently he makes no demur in yielding pre-eminence to the embassador. He is entitled to the general regard due to a confidential person intrusted by a sovereign with the management of his affairs; and he possesses all the rights essential to the character of a public minister. This indeterminate quality is such, that the sovereign may confer it on one of his servants, whom he would not chuse to invest with the character of embassador: and on the other hand, it may be accepted by a man of rank, who would be unwilling to undertake the office of resident, and to acquiesce in the treatment at present allotted to men in that station. There are also *ministers plenipotentiary*, who are of much greater distinction than simple ministers; but are also without any particular attribution of rank and character, although by custom they are now placed immediately after the embassador, or on a level with the envoy extraordinary.

Among the modern institutions for the advantage of commerce, one of the most useful is that of *consuls*, or persons residing in the large trading cities, and especially the sea ports, of foreign countries, with a privilege to watch over the rights and privileges of their nation, and to decide disputes between her merchants there. When a nation trades largely with a country,

country, it is requiſite to have there a perſon charged with ſuch a commiſſion: and as the ſtate which allows of this commerce muſt naturally favour it, for the ſame reaſon alſo, it muſt admit the conſul. But there being no abſolute and perfect obligation to this, the nation that wiſhes to have a conſul, muſt procure this right by the commercial treaty itſelf. The conſul being charged with the affairs of his ſovereign, and receiving his orders, continues his ſubject, and accountable to him for his actions; he is no public miniſter, and cannot pretend to the privileges annexed to ſuch character; yet, bearing his ſovereign's commiſſion, and being in this quality received by the prince in whoſe dominions he reſides, he is, in a certain degree, entitled to the protection of the law of nations. This ſovereign, by the very act of receiving him, tacitly engages to allow him all the liberty and ſafety neceſſary to the proper diſcharge of his functions, without which the admiſſion of the conſul would be nugatory and deluſive. The functions of a conſul require, in the firſt place, that he be not a ſubject of the ſtate where he reſides; as, in this caſe, he would be obliged in all things to conform to its orders, and not at liberty to acquit himſelf of the duties of his office? they ſeem even to require that the conſul ſhould be independent of the ordinary criminal juſtice of the place where he reſides, ſo as not to be moleſted or impriſoned, unleſs he himſelf violate the law of nations by ſome enormous crime. And though the importance of the conſular functions be not ſo great as to procure to the conſul's perſon the inviolability and abſolute independence enjoyed by public miniſters, yet, being under the particular protection of the ſovereign who employs him, and intruſted with the care of his concerns, if he commits any crime, the reſpect due to his maſter requires that he ſhould be ſent home to be puniſhed. Such are the modes purſued by ſtates that are inclined to preſerve a good underſtanding with each other; but the ſureſt way is, expreſsly to ſettle all theſe matters, as far as practicable, by a commercial treaty.

REVENUE.

In this part will be conſidered the progreſs made by the nation in the ſcience of finance, from the rudeſt times to the preſent; the national debt, with the ſtocks in which it is inveſted; the eſtabliſhments formed for the purpoſe of tranſacting the public buſineſs connected with the revenue; and the means of raiſing ſupplies both ordinary and extraordinary; the coinage of the nation, and ſuch other ſubjects connected with the public welfare as ariſe out of pecuniary tranſactions.

Every ſtate is ſubject to the neceſſity of providing a public fund to pay the current expences of adminiſtration, and the manner of providing this indiſpenſable reſource is among the chief characteriſtics by which a government is denominated free or ſlaviſh, ſtrong or feeble, wiſe or impolitic. In Great Britain the public purſe has long been tenaciouſly retained by the Houſe of Commons; but neither the poſſeſſion nor the adminiſtration of the national treaſure was ſo inalienably conſigned to them in early times as in theſe days. The revenue and the laws by which its expenditure is regulated, have grown up with the commercial and political progreſs of the country; and its hiſtory is among thoſe which are beſt intitled to the notice of the politician. Sir John Sinclair, from whoſe excellent work on the revenue the following ſtatement is principally derived, obſerves that "in attempting to give an hiſtorical "account of the finances of this country, the ſubject naturally "divides itſelf into two branches: the firſt relating to our "public revenue prior to the revolution in 1688: the ſecond, "to our ſyſtem of finance ſince that period. During the firſt "era, the expences of the ſtate were principally defrayed by "the ordinary revenue of the crown. It ſeldom happened that "any extraordinary tax was impoſed on the people; and even "then, it was only a temporary grant to the monarch on the "throne. The period ſince the revolution, is diſtinguiſhed by "different principles. The ſtate, aſſuming the appearance of "a great corporation, extends its views beyond immediate "events and momentary exigencies; forms ſyſtems of remote, "as well as of immediate profit; borrows money, to cultivate, "defend, or acquire diſtant poſſeſſions, in hopes that it will be "amply repaid by the advantages they may be brought to yield; "at one time it protects a nation whoſe trade it conſiders as "beneficial; at another, it engages in war, leſt the power of "a rival ſhould become too great: in ſhort, it propoſes to itſelf "a plan of perpetual accumulation and aggrandizement, which, "according as it is well or ill conducted, muſt either terminate "in the poſſeſſion of an extenſive and powerful empire, or in "total ruin."

Britons. In the earlieſt periods of Britiſh hiſtory, the government, commerce, and revenue of the country can be but little known. The nation was divided into petty tribes, each of which had its prince or leader, whoſe influence was proportioned to his ability and ſucceſs. His domain, or individual eſtate, augmented by accidental acceſſions gained in war or by confiſcation, formed the principal ſupport of his government; plunder

plunder in battle and the prerogative of coining were additional means of wealth; and the remaining supplies arose from the presents given by foreign sovereigns, and the voluntary contributions of his own subjects.

ROMANS. During the time of the Romans, Britain was, like the other conquests of that empire, subject to the most grievous exactions: the taxes were partly levied in kind, and partly in money: those who paid in kind, were obliged to furnish about a tenth part of the produce of their lands, and to carry the quantity they were rated at, to any distance however great, according to the supposed necessities of the state, or the caprice of those who were in power; the duty on cattle, in which Britain abounded, was peculiarly oppressive: heavy customs were imposed on goods both imported and exported; the proprietors of mines were obliged to pay a certain share of their profits, for the benefit of the state: a duty was laid upon commodities sold by auction, or in the public market, above a certain value: capitation taxes were rigorously executed; to which might be added, a variety of other imposts, on legacies, slaves, houses, pillars, hearths, air, artists, animals, and other articles too tedious to mention; and there was even a tax on the dead body before interment could be allowed. At first the income of this province did not pay the expences of the establishment, but in process of time it furnished large remittances to the imperial treasury, the revenue amounting, according to a calculation, which is however uncertain, to 2,000,000*l.* sterling.

SAXONS AND DANES. The dominion of the Saxons presents few materials for an account of the progress of taxation. In the heptarchy, the sovereigns, in course, possessed the greatest portion of the land in their respective kingdoms, and all these when united in one sovereign must have yielded a large revenue. The mulcts arising from the trial of causes, and the composition for certain offences were also a great source of emolument: the *trinoda necessitas*, a duty incumbent on every man, to repel the enemy, construct fortresses, and repair bridges, when commuted for money, produced revenues called *Heregeld*, *Burg-bote*, and *Brig-bote*; but the greatest and most permanent tax was that levied under the title of *Danegeld*, imposed at first to bribe those barbarians from invading the country, and continued under pretence of defending it against them. It commenced in 991, and consisted in the payment of one shilling or more for each hide of land, of which there were in England 243,600. This tax as imposed by Canute in 1018, amounted to 83,000 Saxon pounds, equivalent to two millions and a half of modern money; but it exceeded the powers of the people.

NORMAN LINE. William the Conqueror secured his acquisition

quisition of the English throne, and enriched himself, principally by the complete establishment of the feudal system; the survey made of the kingdom in general, and in particular of the value and extent of the royal domains; and the institution of a court of exchequer, after the model of a similar court in Normandy. The feudal system in itself was not new; the tenure of lands on condition of performing military services, existed in the Roman and other empires, and, under the Saxon government, proprietors of land were obliged to assist the sovereign in war; but under the Norman system, the lands were not hereditary, and the devices for continuing the possession in families, gave rise to wardships, reliefs, and the other profitable incidents in the feudal system. The whole kingdom was then divided into 60,215 knights' fees; the holder of each of which was not only bound to furnish a knight, or armed horseman, for the public defence, but he was likewise liable to a variety of impositions, at first light and easy, and apparently for the benefit of the vassal, but afterwards converted, by the subtle dexterity of the feudal lawyers, into a system fraught with every species of oppression. A survey of the kingdom was rendered necessary, by the dispersed situation of the lands belonging to the crown; one had been made by order of Alfred, which extended to little besides his own possessions; but the book called Doomsday, compiled by command of the Conqueror, was, except as to a few of the northern counties, a general record of the highest value and authority. The court of exchequer was erected for the better management of the royal income; it was formed on the Roman model, and designed to oppress the people under colour of law.

The revenue of William may be considered under four heads. The income of the royal domains; voluntary gifts; legal taxes; and tyrannical exactions. His domains, after all his gifts to his followers, were ample and productive; the voluntary donations of his subjects, especially in the early part of his reign, were very large, they resulted from his exertions to conciliate their affections; but his conduct soon altered to a most atrocious tyranny; the taxes were at first contingent, arising from his profits as Lord Paramount of all the land, but afterward, on pretence of defending the realm, he revived the Danegeld, which, in his reign, varied from one shilling, to six shillings, per hide; the tyrannical exactions are described in their very name; they consisted in making arbitrary demands of money from individuals, and, at length, in the plunder of monasteries and churches, where wealth was supposed to be deposited; and this plunder was not confined to the money, jewels, and plate of individuals, but extended even to the shrines and chalices,

chalices. By such means this monarch is said to have raised an annual revenue of 400,000*l.* equal, according to some, to ten millions in our days, though others estimate it at less than six; but in either case it was truly enormous, since it was not incumbered by any charge. This amount is disputed by some authors, but it is not deemed remote from truth, by those who consider the magnificence in which the Conqueror lived, and the vast treasure in money and effects which he left at his death.

The reign of William Rufus contains nothing new in the history of revenue, except the compulsion he practised on his subjects, in order to extort money under the name of *benevolences*, and the various acts of meanness and oppression which procured him the expressive name of the Red Dragon.

Henry I. possessing the crown by a disputable title, sought to ingratiate himself with the nation, by the grant of a charter, which, when his authority became secure, he did not scruple to violate; but its provisions were favourable to liberty and property, and formed the basis of Magna Charta. In finance, his reign was remarkable for an imposition on churches, for which the incumbent was made responsible; and still more for the commencement of the custom of receiving the rents of royal demesnes in money, instead of taking them in kind, a change which contributed much to the impoverishment of the crown.

Stephen, a manifest usurper, passed his reign in perpetual war, and civil bloodshed. He had promised to remit the Danegeld, which he was, however, by necessity compelled to inforce, and it was the only regular tax he imposed; for during the greatest part of his reign, the only means he had of supporting his troops, and maintaining his dignity, was by plunder and extortion. He is also accused of alienating the demesnes of the crown, debasing the coin, and selling to the highest bidder, honours, offices, dignities, and benefices in the church, the last pitiful resource of a profuse and indigent monarch. The nation is represented to have been in a state the most deplorable. Some forsook their native country, to avoid the miseries under which it groaned. A multitude of foreign mercenaries, brought over by Stephen to assist him in his usurpation, and to support his authority, spread horror and devastation wherever they went; many who had lived in opulence, were glad to shelter themselves in the meanest cottages, and to feed upon dogs and carrion; the fields lay fallow and neglected; commerce and industry were abandoned; towns of considerable note were deserted by their inhabitants; nor was any place, however sacred or remote, exempted from the general calamity.

House of Plantagenet. No imposition laid by the monarchs

monarchs of the Norman race appeared to originate from, or conduce to the prosperity of the people; avarice or necessity dictated every exaction, and even the pretext of defending the country, which was assigned for the levy of the Danegeld, was considered as absolutely fictitious. No wonder then that the British people, so long oppressed, should hail the line of Plantagenet as the restoration of their Saxon kings; the omen would be well received, though not entirely free from fiction, since Henry II. although connected with the Saxon line, was not by that descent, heir to the throne. His measures of finance shewed the first glimmering of a better day: he resumed the crown lands, improvidently and illegally granted by his predecessor, and this too with the consent of parliament, and he began the custom of receiving a duty called Scutage, from each knight as a composition for the service which the individual must otherwise have performed. This led to the establishment of a regular army, by enabling the monarch to pay perpetual soldiers, instead of depending on the casual and temporary service of knights, who considering their attendance a hardship, longed for its termination. This monarch too, aided by the general zeal in favour of the crusade against the infidels, collected from his subjects an imposition with which England had been hitherto unacquainted; a tax on personal property. It was levied in this manner: a chest was erected in the different churches, into which every man, after having taken an oath, and justly summed up the value of his effects, and the debts which he considered secure, was obliged to put in two-pence in the pound for the first year, and one penny in the pound for the four following years, under the penalty of excommunication; this assessment would not probably have been submitted to, had it been appropriated to a less popular purpose. The same zeal also enabled him to raise a tax, called Saladin tythe, being a tenth part of the personal property of all those who staid at home, and took no share in the expedition against that gallant mussulman. To this contribution, the English are said to have paid 70,000, the Jews 60,000 pounds, the aggregate being equal to two millions of modern money. Henry was also the first who raised the feudal aid, *pour fille marier*, but this was drawn only from tenants *in capite*; he is accused of pillaging the church, executing with rigour the forest laws, and reviving the obsolete Saxon impositions Burg-bote, Brig-bote, Heregeld, and Horngeld, but these charges do not appear to be well founded; he offended the church, which, as Romish churchmen were the only historians, was sufficient to tarnish his fame; but in his reign, either by connivance or express command, the odious Danegeld was finally extinguished. Henry at his death possessed a treasure which authors estimate differently, but it was most probably about 100,000 marks.

The reign of Cœur de Lion exhibited a perpetual picture of financial rapacity proceeding from the distress of the monarch; but the causes of that distress were so closely allied with feelings of national glory, that the annals of Richard I. have ever been quoted as conspicuously honourable to England. The romantic ardour with which he embraced the enterprize of the crusade, and the renown he acquired during its progress, made his subjects forget the dangerous and oppressive means he took to equip himself, and submit without a murmur to the further exactions which were rendered necessary by his captivity and his subsequent wars. In the beginning of this reign, the crown lands, and offices of the greatest trust and power, were disposed of, almost at any price. The feudal superiority of Scotland was sold for 10,000 marks. Arbitrary fines were levied from the officers of the crown, under pretence of delinquency; the rich, who had escaped other modes of extortion, were compelled to supply the king with money by way of loan, without any hope of being repaid; nay, under colour that the great seal was lost, former grants were held to be invalid; a new seal was made, and every person was obliged to purchase a renewal and confirmation of his patent. It is said, that, by these and other means of exaction equally odious, so much money was raised, and carried out of the kingdom, that a genuine coin of this monarch's stamp is hardly to be met with in the most valuable and curious collections. The exorbitant sum demanded for his ransom, 150,000 marks, being beyond the power of the military tenants of the crown to supply, a general tax was imposed, and voluntary contributions were carried to their utmost extent. On his return, the monarch was obliged through necessity to resume many of the improvident grants he had formerly made; to tax the clergy, to renew, under the name of Hydage, the tax called Danegeld, and through scarcity of coin, to receive the tax on wool in kind. The distress of the exchequer furnished the hint of raising money by means of licences: these were first imposed on persons entering the lists at jousts and tournaments: the rates were, for an earl, twenty marks of silver; a baron, ten marks; a knight having lands, four; and a knight having no land, two marks.

John was in all respects a disgrace to the English throne. An usurper and a tyrant, cruel, unjust, prodigal, and feeble, he knew no restraint on his passions, but what arose from fear, nor any limitation to his baseness when driven to the necessity of submission. Magna Charta is a blessing resulting from his reign, but without procuring him either gratitude or esteem; while the

the surrender of his crown to the pope's legate, although no evil results from it in modern days, is ever remembered with detestation and disgust. In finance his rapacity was unbounded, and his only invention, cruelty and extortion. In a reign of seventeen years only three passed without some grievous imposition on the subject. The means were the direct plunder of those who were known to be rich, and considered to be unresisting: the clergy were drained of immense sums, and the Jews were compelled, by every kind of torture, to yield up their property; yet the king lost on the continent the ancient patrimony of his family, and passed his time at home in misery, turbulence, and disgrace; leaving a name consecrated to contempt by the addition of *Sans-terre*, or Lackland. The great charter was however a barrier against the oppressions of future kings, in preventing the impositions of scutages or aids, without the consent of parliament, except for certain purposes, and restraining the extortions committed under the name of fines and amercements. In this reign it appears too that the customs were of some, though very slight consideration, since they are mentioned in Magna Charta, though they were farmed at so small a sum as 1000 marks.

The long reign of Henry III., a term of continual profusion and distress, exhibits only the usual course of scutages, aids, talliages, and similar devices for supplying the wants of the monarch. From the Jews this king extorted 400,000 marks; for 300,000 French livres, and lands worth 20,000 livres per annum, he sold his title to Normandy and Anjou; he was obliged to sell the very furniture of the palace; pawn the jewels of the crown, and even the shrine of Edward the Confessor. He is represented as wandering about the country, soliciting the charitable contributions of his subjects, and his attendants were reduced to such straits and difficulties, that they were compelled to confederate with gangs of robbers, in order, by their share of the booty, to secure a maintenance. In this reign the device was invented of compelling persons possessing a certain portion of land, to receive kinghthood or pay a fine; and in this reign the customs were so far advanced as to produce 6,000 *l.* per annum, though the raising this sum occasioned grievous complaints.

Far different from that of his predecessor was the government of Edward I., the English Justinian; for although necessity drove him to occasional acts of oppression, still his subjects saw with satisfaction, that the treasure he obtained was expended for the advantage and glory of the nation; they saw the clergy, by his vigour, compelled to contribute toward the general expences, not by the effect of momentary violence, but of a deliberate and regular system, and above all, they had the happiness to obtain

obtain the final confirmation of Magna Charta, with additional articles, and the invaluable statute *de tallagio non concedendo*, which remedied the defect in the great charter, and prevented the king from raising any aid or talliage whatever, without the consent of parliament. In this reign the customs were greatly improved and augmented, and began to assume a regular form, and produce a beneficial effect; they were divided into *the ancient customs*, consisting of duties laid on wool, skins, and leather; and *the new customs*, comprising those afterward called tunnage and poundage, and being certain duties on goods imported and exported by alien merchants. In this reign, after undergoing many cruel oppressions, the Jews were banished the realm, but the act, however harsh, was far from unpopular, so odious, for some cause, were those people become. At this period commerce having made considerable advance, the usual resource of the crown, military services, became less productive than formerly, and the taxation of cities, towns, and boroughs, by their representatives, a matter of the highest importance.

Edward II. was much unlike his illustrious parent, but his weakness was prevented from being the cause of oppression on his subjects, by the operation of the laws which had been passed in his father's reign. The parliament might rather be accused of a too considerate regard of the national purse, at the expence of the dignity of the crown, and the public welfare; yet, in the hope of conquering Scotland, they consented to an imposition by which every village, town, and city in the kingdom was obliged to furnish a certain number of men armed and equipped for sixty days, and a fifteenth part of the moveables of the laity.

The reign of Edward III. was distinguished by a series of parliamentary grants, under all the denominations usual in those days, of twentieths, fifteenths, and tenths, besides some extraordinary taxes in kind, as the ninth sheaf, the ninth lamb, and sometimes, a subsidy in wool. In the 45th year of Edward, a tax was laid of 50,000*l*. on the whole kingdom, to be raised by the parishes in their respective proportions, being the first record of the grant of a specific sum. The customs were greatly enhanced, and those imposed by the first Edward on aliens alone, were extended to native merchants; this monarch also had recourse to the pernicious measure of a poll-tax, being an assessment of four-pence on every person, male and female, beyond the age of fourteen, except beggars, and the clergy granted twelve-pence for every beneficed, and four-pence for every other person except mendicant friars. This tax was not collected without great murmurs and difficulty, but increasing necessities demanded greater efforts; the statute *de tallagio non concedendo* was occasionally

casionally violated; the effects of the Lombards, who succeeded the Jews in the trade of usurers, and who inherited with it their unpopularity, were seized and confiscated. Edward is accused of being the first who erected monopolies; of extorting loans; and of possessing himself by force, of goods belonging to his subjects, undertaking to pay them an inferior price at a distant day; yet with all the sums thus acquired and extorted, and with all the wealth which resulted from his conquests, and the ransom of captive kings, Edward was in the latter, as in the early years of his reign in the greatest pecuniary distress, and finally stripped of all his foreign conquests, in consequence of an attempt to raise from his continental dominions a very slight tax.

The first conspicuous act in the reign of Richard II. was the imposition, during his minority, of a tax called a subsidy, designed to spare the poor, and imposed principally on the rich: it was levied partly by a poll-tax, and partly by one on income: the dukes of Lancaster and Brittany paid ten marks each; every earl was charged four pounds; every baron forty shillings; but the great body of the people, merchants, artificers, and husbandmen, were assessed a greater or lesser sum, according to the value of their estates. This tax occasioning some discontent among those whom it most affected, the ministers of the young king next tried the opposite extreme, and the necessity of the state requiring 160,000 *l.*, they levied a poll-tax of twelvepence on every person above fifteen years of age, mere beggars excepted. Some distinction was to be made in favour of the indigent, but it could not be very considerable, as no person was to be charged above sixty groats, for himself and family. This most unjust and excessive imposition being farmed by contractors, who behaved with great insolence, the people flew to arms, and the rebellion headed by Wat Tyler, was the consequence. In quelling this threatening insurrection, the young king shewed a spirit and judgment which, had they prevailed in other parts of his life, would have made his reign such as became the son of the Black Prince; but far different was his conduct, far different was his fate. He procured, from a garbled parliament, the subsidy on wool, leather, and wool-fells exported, *for life*—the first instance of such a grant, and which was considered as a baneful precedent. He extorted considerable sums from his wealthiest subjects, by way of loan, which it was dangerous for them to refuse, and ruinous to pay; and under pretence, that several counties had engaged in rebellious practices (notwithstanding a general pardon had been granted by act of parliament), he threatened them with the severest marks of his displeasure, if they did not compound for their offences: and

and they were actually compelled to sign blank bonds, in those days called *ragmen*, which the king filled up in any manner, and with any sum he thought proper. After all, the money which he obtained, either from the bounty of his people, or by means of extortion, instead of being laid out for the glory and advantage of his kingdom, was either thrown away upon the minions of his court, or wasted in maintaining an enormous household, amounting, it is said, to 10,000 persons, of whom 300 were employed in the very kitchens of the palace.

With Richard II., ended the Saxon line, or House of Plantagenet, under which, it is observed, no inconsiderable progress was made in the knowledge of finance. The necessity of converting military services into pecuniary aids was discovered; taxes began to be laid on personal as well as real property; the customs came to be accounted a considerable and important branch of the revenue; and the clergy were compelled to furnish contributions for the public service; nor was the sanction of the pope any longer accounted necessary for that purpose. New modes of taxation also were attempted; and though some of them were ill contrived and unproductive, yet it proves the strong anxiety of those who were intrusted with the government of the country, to provide an effective revenue, adequate to that high and distinguished rank, which England was entitled to hold among the kingdoms of Europe.

House of Lancaster. Henry IV., a military usurper, however urged by his necessities or inclinations, was obliged, at the beginning of his reign, to recommend himself to popularity by appearances of moderation, and his demands for money were small; but his judgment leading him to promote the commercial interests of his people, the customs increased, and the parliament granted him as large a revenue out of them as had been enjoyed by his predecessor. In his reign a tax was laid on places, pensions, and grants from the crown, one year's amount of each being given to the king by the celebrated lack-learning parliament, or *parliamentum indoctum.* A subsidy too was imposed in this reign of such fearful amount, that great pains were taken to prevent it from being known; it is however discovered to have been a tax on real and personal property, amounting to twenty shillings on every knight's fee; twenty pence upon every twenty pounds a-year in lands; and one shilling in the pound on money, and goods. Attempts were also recommended both by the above mentioned parliament, and the king's military counsellors, to seize on the property of the clergy; but the turbulence of the times did not allow of an experiment which the proposed sufferers avowed their intention of resisting.

In order to magnify that which requires no aid from fiction, the conquest of France by Henry V., historians have taken too easily on credit a report of his being furnished but with very scanty supplies. It seems however that, besides his ordinary revenue of 76,643*l.* per annum, he received large grants from parliament, and the clergy, and the intire revenues of one hundred and ten monasteries dependant on others in Normandy, which were given up by the ecclesiastics, to avert the seizure of their whole property, which was again proposed. To this great and beloved monarch, parliament for the first time granted the customs on wool, and leather, and the duties of tunnage and poundage, for life.

During the minority of Henry VI., the income of the crown was neglected and squandered in a most unprincipled manner; yet as the factions which then contested for the rule of the nation were desirous of popularity, the burthens on the public were not large, and to the parsimonious supplies sent to the army, the loss of France has been ascribed. In this and subsequent periods of the reign, subsidies were granted; the duties of tunnage and poundage were settled on the king for life, and made to fall doubly heavy on aliens, who were also subjected to a severe poll-tax; benevolences were also required, and now, for the first time, demanded, not as matter of courtesy, but of right. The king, it was said, could by law compel all his subjects, at their own charges, to attend his wars; but he was willing to spare such as would contribute the value of two days personal service, according to their rank and quality. The miseries of this unfortunate reign extended to pecuniary matters; Henry being obliged in his twenty-ninth year to submit to a sort of guardianship as to his property, while parliament became in some degree responsible for his debts, which amounted to the enormous sum of 372,000*l.*

House of York. Ascending the throne after a long and sanguinary struggle, Edward IV., with the consent of his parliament, began his financial operations by resuming the grants of crown lands made during the preceding reign, and these possessions were much augmented by confiscations of property, from the adherents of the house of Lancaster. The grants of parliament were liberal, and in the usual mode of tenths and fifteenths, with additional imposts on each; specific sums for stated purposes, and a yearly subsidy on aliens and denizens; yet the necessities of the monarch drove him to the expedient of extorting benevolences, in procuring which he was so earnest, as even to turn his natural graces to account. An expedition against France, projected with vast ostentation, terminated in a compromise by which Lewis XI., was to pay to Edward

Edward 75,000 crowns, and an annuity of 50,000 crowns during their joint lives; this tranſaction was ſo diſguſting to the nation, that the king, no longer venturing to call on parliament for ſupplies, had recourſe to ſeveral means of extortion, which hiſtorians have not ventured to commemorate, and among others, to a ſevere inveſtigation of titles to lands, thus compelling many to pay large fines for confirmation of their grants, and obtaining great ſums from the clergy for reſtitution of temporalities. The neceſſities of this prince even drove him to the unworthy, though lucrative, reſource of embarking in commerce.

Paſſing over the reign of Edward V., which on this occaſion may be conſidered as merely nominal; the ſhort period in which Richard III. held the throne is to be conſidered. It is remarkable for an act procured by the king himſelf, aboliſhing the mode of exaction called benevolences; and although Richard afterward levied a contribution in this form, ſuch a violation of a new law, in thoſe times when need was urgent, and the ſcience of finance had made ſo little progreſs, was of ſmall importance.

Under the houſe of Plantagenet finance was little improved, but the principle, that no tax ſhould be impoſed without the conſent of parliament, became in practice perfectly eſtabliſhed, and the fetters of the feudal ſyſtem were conſiderably lightened.

House of Tudor. During the reign of Henry VII., the nation enjoyed repoſe from civil wars, commerce was favoured by the diſcoveries of Columbus and other adventurers, and by the diſpoſition of the king, who ſought to depreſs the nobles and elevate the commons, and the activity and enterpriſe of the nation received a new and beneficial impulſe. To this king, tunnage and poundage were granted for life, and from his time the cuſtoms were conſidered as a permanent branch of the royal income. Henry, whoſe great paſſion was avarice, obtained ſuch large grants from parliament as to occaſion inſurrections in various counties: he revived the practice of extorting benevolences, under pretence that the laws made in the time of Richard III. were void, he being an uſurper, but the benevolence was no longer demanded at the king's mere pleaſure, it received, like other taxes, the ſanction of parliament: aids were granted to the crown, to marry his daughter, and make his ſon a knight. Henry alſo received a very large portion with Catharine of Arragon, who was married firſt to Arthur his eldeſt, and afterward to Henry his ſecond ſon; and he increaſed his revenue by letting out his ſhips to hire, and by lending out money on intereſt. Yet all theſe reſources were in-

insufficient to allay his thirst of gold; he exerted in their utmost rigour all the means of feudal exaction, and with the aid of Empson and Dudley, two rapacious judges, pillaged his subjects by prosecutions under obsolete or forgotten penal laws. This king died in possession of 1,800,000*l.*, a sum equivalent to at least eight millions in these days, but in his last moments he displayed the agonies of remorse and terrors of guilt.

The ill-gotten treasure of Henry VII., was speedly dissipated by his prodigal successor; grants of the most enormous extent extorted from parliament, a poll tax rating every subject in the kingdom, from the lowest, who had attained the age of fifteen, and who paid four pence, to the duke, who was assessed at ten marks, and large sums raised by other means were insufficient for the king's expenditure. A commission was issued for exacting from the clergy four shillings, and from the laity three shillings and four pence in the pound; but when this attempt met with a resistance which portended rebellion, the king disclaimed the commission, and added it to general causes of Wolsey's unpopularity. From foreign potentates, the king obtained some supplies, particularly for the restitution of Tournay to France; and he concluded a treaty, by which, in consideration of 50,000 crowns per annum, to be paid to him and his successors for ever, he agreed to renounce all title to the crown of France. Pressed by necessity, he adopted the expedient of debasing the current coin, and by threats of prosecution and oppression, extorted large sums as benevolences, under the new name of amicable grants. Finally, after many intermediate acts of extortion on the ecclesiastical body, he seized all the revenues, lands, and effects belonging to the monasteries and other religious and charitable establishments, and some of the lands belonging to the bishopricks; these, with the first fruits and tenths, were insufficient to satisfy his perpetual demands, occasioned by continual prodigality; and, however odious might be the oppression which Henry VII., exercised under colour of law, that of Henry VIII., committed in defiance of it, was not more tolerable in its effects, although it permitted the formation of better hopes. Tyranny might expire with the tyrant, but a depraved system of jurisprudence might extend its operation to a period incalculably remote. It may be incidentally observed, that in this reign the profits of feudal sovereignty were abated by the devices of conveyancers; and although parliament endeavoured to restore them to their ancient extent, the statutes formed for that purpose became the means of a directly opposite end.

Edward VI. was prevented by his tender years from taking a great a great ſhare in the affairs of government: his miniſters, who were themſelves rapacious, and in ſome of their meaſures imprudent, increaſed the neceſſities of the ſtate, and ſupplied them by injudicious means. Among the leaſt commendable of their efforts were a poll-tax on ſheep, and a duty on woollen cloth, both which, after a ſhort trial, were repealed; they alſo debaſed the coin to an extent which proved highly prejudicial to induſtry and commerce. The trade of the kingdom was however benefited by the revocation of a charter granted by Henry III., to a body of foreign merchants, called the Corporation of the Steel-yard; the abuſes of juſtice were puniſhed by heavy fines on judges who acted corruptly, and 400,000 crowns were obtained from France for the reſtoration of Boulogne. The debt of 240,000*l.* left unpaid at the deceaſe of this monarch, aroſe from the rapacity of his miniſters, who miſappropriated the money raiſed to diſcharge it; but had his days been prolonged, the people of England confidently hoped for the moſt bleſſed effects from his great abilities and eminent virtues.

The crimes and errors which diſgraced the reign of the bigotted Mary, were alſo the cauſe of great pecuniary diſtreſs, which could only be palliated, for it was never remedied, by the moſt oppreſſive devices. Her principles were ſo generally obnoxious to her ſubjects, that when an application was made to parliament for a ſubſidy, it was rejected; and many members declared, that it was in vain to beſtow riches on a monarch, whoſe revenues were thus waſted. She was therefore obliged to have recourſe to tyrannical extortions to repleniſh her exchequer. By means of embargoes, compulſive loans, and exactions of a ſimiliar nature, ſhe raiſed about 240,000*l.*; and two years afterwards, contrived to fit out by the ſame methods an armament for the aſſiſtance of her huſband, Philip II. king of Spain; but finding it impoſſible to ſupply it with proviſions, ſhe ſeized, for that purpoſe, all the grain which the counties of Norfolk and Suffolk could furniſh, without making the owners any recompence. She imitated her brother's example, in endeavouring to borrow money on the continent; but her credit was ſo low, that though ſhe offered 14 per cent. intereſt to the town of Antwerp, for the loan of 30,000*l.* ſhe could not obtain it, until ſhe compelled the city of London to join in the ſecurity.

The long and glorious reign of Elizabeth, is remarkable for many admirable meaſures in finance, and tarniſhed by ſome equally impolitic and tyrannical. Her occaſions for money ſeldom originated in any vicious or even imprudent meaſure or deſign, and the means by which ſhe obtained ſupplies, were not the devices of her own invention, but powers legally veſted in the crown by the constitution as it then subsisted. The causes of expenditure in the time of Elizabeth were principally the national defence, especially against Spain; the government of Ireland, and contest with the rebels there; the maintenance of a party in Scotland; the assistance afforded to Holland in empancipating itself from Spain; the support of Henry IV. of France against his rebellious subjects; the debts contracted by her predecessors, and which she honourably discharged; and the regeneration of the debased coin; these measures were all grand and patriotic, though the last was not pursued without deviation; but the remaining cause of her expences, her bounties to favourites, was of a nature to leave some stain on her memory, especially as these were not the great and wise ministers who made her government prosperous and glorious, but those individuals who, by the graces and accomplishments of their persons, pleased her taste, or by their flattery soothed her vanity. This was indeed her conspicuous foible; to this may be referred the splendid exhibitions of her court, and the studied attire of her own person, which reached such an excess, that she is said to have left in her wardrobe more than 3000 suits of various fashions and colours.

Her resources were, the dismesne lands of the crown, which were much underlet, and which she frequently chose to incumber rather than apply to parliament for money; the feudal prerogatives, which she exacted with as much rigour as the times would admit, insisting particularly on the right of Purveyance *, which she carried to a great extent; the customs, which were more than doubled during her reign, being farmed by Sir Thomas Smith at 50,000*l.* per annum, who, besides, refunded some of the profits of his former contracts; and the first fruits, tenths, and church lands which Mary had alienated, but which were now resumed. To these must be added the grants of subsidies, and fifteenths by parliament; the extortion of presents from her dependents; the money paid to her by Catholics, and non-conformists, for dispensations from the penalties incurred by not attending the established church; her share of the plunder obtained in war; a large sum which she received in virtue of a treaty respecting Calais; and compulsory loans from her subjects. This latter measure was undoubtedly tyrannical, and would give great offence in modern times, but it was then the undisputed prerogative of the crown recognized by parliament; Elizabeth had for her justification the notorious fact, that when she or her predecessors had been so far degraded by necessity, as to require loans from

* See Vol. I. page, 165.

any foreign city, as Hamburgh, Cologne, or Antwerp, the interest was ten, twelve, or even fourteen per cent. and the security of the sovereign was deemed insufficient unless supported by the city of London, or sometimes by the counsellors of state in their individual capacity. But when the punctuality of the queen in paying the monies she borrowed, both from her subjects and foreigners, had established public credit; loans ceased to be compulsory, and the people were ready to pour forth their individual treasures to relieve the necessities of the crown. In fact, Elizabeth well deserved the confidence of her people, by the evident proofs she exhibited, that not her own advantage, but theirs, was the rule of her conduct, and that, in those points where she carried the doctrines of prerogative to the greatest height, the dignity of the throne, and not personal eagerness for dominion, was the cause. Her contemporary Henry IV. is much celebrated for his benevolent wish, that every peasant in his realm might have a fowl in the pot on a Sunday; the trait exhibited by Elizabeth when she refused a subsidy, saying, "it was the same thing whether the money was in the pockets of her subjects, or in her own exchequer;" is perhaps equally endearing, and certainly more practically benevolent. Nor was this a solitary instance of her patriotic self-denial: she refused, on another occasion, a benevolence offered by the commons, saying she had no need of the money. Such conduct, and such principles met with a merited return. When her crown was in danger, in consequence of the warlike preparations of Philip king of Spain, who fitted out, what he called, an Invincible Armada, for the conquest of England, and the capture of Elizabeth, the spirit and loyalty of the people are hardly to be conceived. The nobility and gentry fitted out forty-three ships at their own expence. London, and the other principal ports in England, voluntarily equipped double the number of vessels that was demanded. Formidable armies were collected without difficulty or murmur. Every direction given for the better security of the coast, met with a prompt and cheerful obedience; and each person, in proportion to his ability, furnished pecuniary assistance, and gloried in an opportunity of displaying his attachment to his sovereign, and his zeal to preserve the liberties and independence of his country.

One profitable prerogative Elizabeth carried to an alarming extent; that of granting or selling monopolies; or the exclusive privilege of trading in such articles as were specified in the patents. The number and importance of the commodities which were thus monopolized, is almost incredible. Among many others, historians mention salt, iron, powder, cards, calf-ſkins, fells, pouldavies, ox-ſhin-bones, train-oil, liſts of cloth, pot aſhes, aniſeeds, vinegar, ſea-coal, ſteel, aquavitæ, bruſhes, pots, bottles, ſaltpetre, lead, accidences, oil, calamine-ſtone, oil of blubber, glaſſes, paper, ſtarch, tin, ſulphur, new drapery, dried pilchards; tranſportation of iron ordnance, of beer, of horn, of leather; importation of Spaniſh wools, and of Iriſh yarn, with many others. We are told, that when this liſt was read over in the Houſe of Commons, a member (Mr. Hackwell) loudly exclaimed, "Is not bread in the number?" "Bread!" ſaid every one with aſtoniſhment. "Yes, I aſſure "you," he replied, "if affairs go on at this rate, we ſhall "have bread reduced to a monopoly before next parliament." It is eaſy to ſee the conſequences of ſuch a ſyſtem. Trade and induſtry were greatly depreſſed. "It bringeth (ſaid a member "in the houſe) general profit into private hands, and the end "is beggary and bondage." A ſingle patent, contrived for the advantage of four rapacious courtiers, occaſioned the utter ruin of ſeven or eight hundred induſtrious ſubjects. This abuſe, and the manner in which ſo deſtructive a prerogative was exerciſed, is one of the greateſt blots in the reign of Elizabeth. In vain did parliament interfere; the haughty ſovereign would not permit her prerogative to be called in queſtion. In a ſpeech from the throne, at the diſſolution of one, ſhe ſaid, "That with regard to the patents, ſhe hoped her "dutiful and loving ſubjects would not take away her prero-"gative, which is the chief flower in her garden, and the prin-"cipal and head pearl in her crown and diadem, but that "they would rather leave the matter to her diſpoſal." However, not long after, ſhe iſſued a proclamation for repealing ſome of the moſt obnoxious monopolies; particularly on ſalt, oil, ſtarch, &c. for which ſhe received the ſolemn thanks of her Commons. At her death Elizabeth left a debt of 400,000*l.*, but this is not to be attributed to any relaxation of her general rules of economy. There was a ſubſidy then due which produced to her ſucceſſor 350,000*l.*; the king of France owed her 450,000*l.*, and the States of Holland 800,000*l.*, a large portion of the former ſum was ungratefully withheld; the latter in great part liquidated.

The period in which the houſe of Tudor inherited the throne, is remarkable for the evident relaxation of the feudal ſyſtem; the progreſs of mercantile adventure; and the deſtruction of the powerful reſource which ſovereigns had ever found in the contributions of the church, which was for ever deſtroyed by the blind rapacity of Henry VIII., whoſe raſhneſs in ſeizing the monaſtic property occaſioned the emperor Charles V. to obſerve that he had killed the hen which laid him

him the golden eggs. This meaſure, with the ſubſequent diſſipation of the property the king had acquired, formed the baſis of the public ſecurity, by rendering the crown completely dependant on the Commons, and enabling theſe to withhold ſupply, until aſſured of the permanence of liberty and juſtice. Not leſs remarkable is this period for the foundation by Elizabeth of that public credit, which has ſince been ſo rigidly preſerved, and wonderfully augmented, which forms the beſt anchorage for the veſſel of ſtate, and on which the ſubjects of this realm as well as foreigners place ſuch implicit reliance.

House of Stuart. The firſt of the Stuarts who aſcended the Britiſh throne, brought with him the ineſtimable bleſſing of an union between England and Scotland. James I., although accuſtomed in his early years to reſtrain his expences within the compaſs of a ſlender income, was afterward ſomewhat profuſe in his expenditure, and not always juſt or wiſe in his means of ſupply. The king, the queen, and the prince of Wales had each a ſeparate court, and, exceeding the liberality of all preceding ſovereigns, James allowed his eldeſt ſon Henry, a revenue of 51,415*l.*, equal to at leaſt 150,000*l.* of money at this time; this was a great ſource of expence, and another was found in his ill-judged and diſgraceful bounty to favourites, who enriched themſelves and families at the public coſt. Leſs exceptionable cauſes of expenditure aroſe from the army in Ireland, the ſupport afforded to the elector Palatine, and the improvement of the navy.

In the procuring of ſupplies, James ſhewed that infatuated adherence to the higheſt notions of prerogative, which afterward coſt his family ſo dear. The demeſnes of the crown, ſtill valuable, though perpetually diminiſhing, were by judicious management made to produce 80,000*l.* per annum, inſtead of 32,000*l.*, but James encumbered or alienated them to the amount of 775,000*l.* The feudal aids were alſo demanded with ſucceſs, particularly thoſe for making his ſon a knight, and marrying his eldeſt daughter; the privilege of purveyance was carried to a moſt oppreſſive extent, the officers of the crown compelling the people to receive for their goods, leſs than a tenth part of their value. The cuſtoms were greatly improved in the time of James, amounting at the cloſe of his reign to 190,000*l.* per annum; but the attempt of the king to alter the rates without the conſent of parliament, occaſioned a diſpute between him and the Commons, which was not terminated in his days, but was among the cauſes which produced the woes of his ſucceſſor. Parliament alſo granted ſeveral aids and fifteenths, but in theſe acts they began to ſhew a zealous vigilance over the public purſe. An indirect mode of ſupply adopted ed by the king, was the sale of honours. The dignities of baron, viscount, and earl, were to be bought at the respective prices of ten, fifteen, and twenty thousand pounds; and the sums received for the creation of baronets amounted to nearly 100,000*l*. This procedure cannot be justified, but it is extenuated by observing that the purchase could not be made indiscriminately by all persons possessing wealth; the usual requisites of blood being still indispensable. Monopolies were granted in this reign, but the practice received a severe check from the vigour of parliament, who fined the attorney-general 15,000*l*. for drawing the patents, and punished by fines, confiscation, and imprisonment, those who had obtained them. At last, an act was passed, by which all monopolies were condemned as contrary to law and the known liberties of the people; an act which ought for ever to have put an end to so destructive a grievance. Forced loans were raised to a considerable amount, and James silenced the remonstrance of the Commons on the subject, by sounding the loftiest notes of prerogative; benevolences too were twice essayed, but not with equal success. From foreign states James drew some money, but it was principally that due to his predecessors: the Dutch paid him 450,000*l*., and France 60,000*l*.; the Hollanders also engaged to allow a sum annually for the privilege of fishing on the English coasts, but this was not productive till the ensuing reign. Fines from offenders in various degrees, which were imposed to a large amount, were remitted, or compounded for at an easy rate. A lottery was first established in the days of James, for payment of the charges incurred in establishing settlements in America, and a project was formed for supplying the crown, by abolishing the order of bishops and selling the church lands; but this resource was left to those who murdered James's successor. The acts of this monarch were essentially injurious to his own family, and for a time to royalty itself; but on the whole his reign was beneficial to the state, by inviting and encouraging those inquiries which afterwards established and purified the constitution. Queen Elizabeth, endowed with courage and wisdom more than belong to man, and surrounded by counsellors of the first ability, speaking the high language of prerogative, rather complimented than offended her subjects, who seeing her feared and respected abroad, and feeling for her the utmost love and veneration, connected her glory with their own, and would have resented rather than promoted a doubt affecting any claim which she advanced: King James, degraded by pusillanimity more abject than ought to characterize a woman, pedantically vain-glorious, yet pitifully feeble, environed by the contemptible minions who made him at once disliked and despised, advancing, both in speech and writing,

writing, pretenſions more gigantic than the illuſtrious Elizabeth had even intimated, provoked inquiry and generated that general diſpoſition to cavil at regal authority, which prevented many perſons from paying due regard to the virtues of his ſon, and facilitated the meaſures of thoſe gloomy fanatics who overturned the throne, and diſgraced the Britiſh annals by the record of judicial regicide.

The extraordinary expences of Charles I. aroſe from wars with the emperor of Germany, and with France, both which terminated ingloriouſly; from one which he waged with his own ſubjects in Scotland; from the charges he incurred in patriotic endeavours to augment the navy; and from his war with the parliament, which for him had ſo fatal a termination. In his private expences, though perſonally frugal, he affected much the ſtate and ſplendour of a king. He kept up twenty-four palaces, all completely furniſhed. His collection of pictures was among the moſt valuable in Europe, and he ſpared no expence, nay he rivalled Philip IV. of Spain, the maſter of the Indies, in endeavouring to engroſs the moſt valuable productions of the ableſt artiſts.

In ſpeaking of the means by which he raiſed or endeavoured to raiſe ſupplies, the cauſe of all the ills which afflicted the latter portion of his life is to be developed; it is not fit in this work to enter into large details on that ſubject; but it may be generally, and not uſeleſsly obſerved, that there was not one of the unpopular and unjuſt impoſitions which he endeavoured to lay on his ſubjects, which ſome great lawyer did not warrant by undeniable authorities founded on former practice; yet that the meaſures of Charles juſtified the firſt meaſures of oppoſition, few are hardy enough to deny; and that many of them would have been avoided, had he not liſtened too readily to ſome of his miniſters, no one can doubt. His misfortunes then were only ſuch as muſt be the lot of every prince who in times of great emergency, which require vigour, deciſion, intelligence, knowledge of the human heart, and powers to turn every contingency to advantage, employs miniſters who, in juſtification of every act of rigour and oppreſſion, recur to the file for precedents, and think they cannot err if they follow the path which others have beaten before them.

Charles derived part of his income from the demeſne lands of the crown; by compounding with thoſe who held any portion of them by defective titles; and by raiſing on them a loan of 300,000*l*. The grants of parliament during his whole reign were very ſparing, and the ſubſidy no longer retained its ancient value; for although it was a tax on income, and the national wealth was greatly increaſed, yet the aſſeſſors, conciliating favour

favour by lenity, and contriving every species of evasion, had greatly reduced its product; the clergy also granted eight subsidies, but those amounted only to 20,000*l.* each; the queen's portion was 400,000 French crowns tardily paid; and the Dutch gave 30,000*l.* per annum, for liberty to fish on the coast.

These were tributes to the monarch unquestioned and not unpopular, but of a different complexion were those which are next to be enumerated. Queen Elizabeth drew sums of money by secret compositions from the Catholics for dispensations, but Charles, although the jealousy of the nation, particularly the puritanical part of it, was strongly excited by the circumstance of the queen being a Catholic, openly granted a commission for receiving such compositions; a most unwise and impolitic measure. The duties of tunnage and poundage had been levied without intermission, since the accession of Henry IV., and often without any previous vote of parliament; Charles received them in the like manner, and would probably, like his predecessors, have obtained a grant of them for life; but the commons, anxiously alive to their duty as guardians of the public purse, required as a preliminary, that he should for once desist from levying the duties; the king, alarmed at the thought of conceding a point of prerogative, dissolved the parliament; the controversy was afterward renewed, and determined in a manner extremely unfavourable to the crown. The exaction of the duties was not totally abstained from, but they were granted only for two months; and the grant was renewed from time to time, for very short periods; care also was taken, to assert, in the strongest terms, the exclusive right of parliament to bestow the grant; and in the preamble to the bills that were passed, all pretensions that the crown could make, to levy the duties by its own authority, were for ever annulled. The levy of ship-money was founded on the precedent established by Elizabeth, when the Armada of Spain menaced the coast; then every maritime town was required to furnish its quota, not of money but of ships and men, and this demand was so moderate and the general enthusiasm so great, that the city of London doubled the proposed supply. Far different was the case when Charles, encouraged by Noy, his attorney-general, attempted to extend a similar requisition all over the realm; the disgraceful abolition of the levy, and the immortality which Hampden acquired by resisting it, are too well known to be here detailed. Of a similar texture, and similar in its suppression, was the attempt to oblige every county, without the authority of parliament, to raise and equip a certain number of soldiers. Another measure in which Charles was very ill advised, was the effort to counteract or evade the recent statute against monopolies,

polies, under pretext of granting patents for new inventions. Not only salt, soap, leather, and other useful articles, were put under harsh restrictions; but grants were made out for gauging red herrings, for marking butter casks, and for gathering rags. The king, afraid of the consequences, or ashamed of having adopted such ridiculous expedients for raising money, abolished about thirty of these destructive patents, when he undertook the first expedition against Scotland; but the people were not satisfied with a partial concession, and the long parliament had no sooner assembled, than it annulled all the remaining monopolies; and as a proof how much they detested so illegal a measure, expelled at once such of its members as were at all concerned in them. Loans of all kinds were extorted, and those who resisted the demands of the monarch were punished by imprisonment, or by the more ruinous method of having soldiers illegally quartered on them; and the ill-advised and ill-fated prince, went so far as to attempt raising money by commissioners appointed by himself, and independent of parliament. Although the spirit of the House of Commons obliged him to cancel this commission, yet many arbitrary measures were pursued; large fees were annexed to new invented offices; every county was obliged to maintain a muster-master, appointed by the crown, for exercising the militia. The vintners were driven, by the terrors of fines and prosecutions, to submit to an illegal imposition on all the wine they retailed; an ancient duty for furnishing the soldiery with coat and conduct money, which had long been abolished, was revived; it was intended to coin base money, and to circulate it by proclamation. Heavy fines were also imposed in the star-chamber, and high commission courts; Sir David Fowles was amerced in 5000*l.*, for dissuading a friend from compounding with the commissioners of knighthood; thirty thousand pounds were exacted from those who had trespassed on an obsolete law, against converting arable land into pasture; encroachments on the king's forests were punished in a similar manner; proclamations were issued, commanding the nobility and gentry to retire to their country seats, and not spend their time idly in London, and if convicted of transgressing this arbitrary regulation, they were severely mulcted in the star-chamber: it was contended, that proclamations had equal authority with laws; and such as ventured to disobey them, where heavily fined, and, in some instances, condemned to the pillory. Another expedient, though sanctioned by law and the practice of remote times, was not less, nor less justly, odious; it was that of compelling all who possessed 40*l.* a-year in land to receive knighthood, or pay a heavy composition. If no other reason could have been

alleged

alleged againſt this proceeding, the altered value of money ſince the reign of Henry VI. when the rate was fixed, would alone have made it an intolerable hardſhip on thoſe whoſe eſtates barely amounted to, or little exceeded 40*l*. a-year.

But all theſe meaſures, and all the evil intentions imputed to the unfortunate king, although they well juſtified a ſtrenuous parliamentary oppoſition, afforded no excuſes for the atrocious act which terminated his days. The principles of deſpotiſm came to him by direct inheritance, and his predeceſſors on the throne had avowed and acted on them to a greater extent, without the ſame or ſimilar motives. They had not to encounter in parliament a factious and obſtinate oppoſition, but found their beheſts received with proſtrate reverence: they were not fettered by the continual efforts of the legiſlature, to reſtrain the exerciſe of prerogative, but ſtatutes of moſt poſitive prohibition were diſpenſed with to gratify the wants, or deſires of the ſovereign. It was ſurely time that the repreſentatives of the nation ſhould be raiſed from this abject ſtate, but a vigorous parliamentary oppoſition would have been fully ſufficient to effect the purpoſe, eſpecially when the voice of the whole people, raiſed in behalf of their deareſt intereſt, could be brought to ſupport thoſe who made exertions in their favour. Parliament could not complain that they wanted ſufficient power, when they could procure the abolition of the court of chivalry and the ſtar-chamber, and could obtain the recognition of the famous petition of right, which declared that "no gift, loan, "benevolence, tax, or ſuch like charge ſhould be exacted with-"out common conſent by act of parliament." Nor was it neceſſary that the wants of the king ſhould remain unſupplied, unleſs he were at liberty to oppreſs the ſubject: an honeſt application to the true principles of finance would have indicated many means of raiſing money from the increaſing luxuries of the times, a ſpecimen of which was given in the tax now firſt impoſed on cards. And it ſhould not be forgotten in ſpeaking of this unhappy king, that his total income, including all that was produced by ſhip money, and other illegal means, did not in years of war amount to 900,000*l*., of which more than 200,000*l*. were raiſed by the devices which parliament ſo much reprobated, but which a decent liberality on their part would have rendered unneceſſary.

INTERREGNUM. The period termed the Interregnum, or Commonwealth, will be ever memorable in the annals of finance; in the firſt place, as having furniſhed moſt of the permanent modes of taxation now in uſe, and in the next, as diſproving, by irreſiſtible experience, the ſaying attributed to Milton, that the trappings of monarchy would defray all the charges

charges of an ordinary republic. The time in which the property of the people of England was subject to the disposal of an authority exclusive of the lords and of the crown, may be considered as commencing with the sessions of the long parliament: they voted six subsidies and a poll-tax, for the purpose of disbanding the armies; but the product was confided to the management of parliamentary commissioners, and not, as formerly, paid into the treasury. When hostilities against the king were considered necessary, voluntary contributions produced incredible sums; the plate of almost every inhabitant in London was brought in, to be coined for support of the army; no article, however mean, no ornament, however valuable, was spared; even the thimbles and bodkins of the women were not withheld.

When these ceased to be productive, the parliament levied assessments on personal and landed property. These assessments varied, according to the exigencies of the times, from 35,000*l.* to 120,000*l.* a month. They were found so productive, and in every respect so much superior to the ancient mode of subsidies, that under the denomination of a land-tax, they have since formed a considerable branch of the public revenue.

To recruit the armies, every person was obliged to retrench a meal in a week, and pay the amount into the treasury; and this strange tax produced for six years 100,000*l.* a-year.

To the long parliament we owe the establishment of the excise, the plan originating, as is supposed, with the famous Pym. It was at first laid on liquors only; and it was solemnly declared, that at the end of the war all excises should be abolished; but the contest continuing longer than was expected, this obnoxious mode of levying money was extended to bread, meat, salt, and many other necessary articles. The excise on bread and meat was afterward repealed.

In the time of the Commonwealth, considerable additions were made to the revenue of the customs by the duties on coals and currants. Four shillings a chaldron on coals levied at Newcastle, brought in about 50,000*l.* The customs and excise, notwithstanding the destruction with which civil wars are necessarily accompanied, had become so productive, that Cromwell, in 1657, was offered 1,100,000*l.* a-year for a lease of both the branches.

The post office, as already has been mentioned, began now to be a source of revenue; all the feudal prerogatives of the crown, except the odious one of purveyance, were exercised with rigour, licences for inns and ale-houses, the profits of which had been claimed by James I. as a monopoly, but wrested from him by parliament, were made a source of revenue;

the ſequeſtration of the income of ſome public offices yielded a large ſupply; the lands and chattels of the crown were ſold, though at a low rate; all eccleſiaſtical property including even glebe lands was in a ſimilar manner diſpoſed of; the tythes were ſequeſtered for the public uſe; the royaliſts were either put to death and their eſtates confiſcated, or obliged to pay heavy ranſoms, and even perſons ſuſpected of attachment to that party were termed *malignants;* and under colour of this crime, it is ſaid that one half of the real and perſonal property in the kingdom was ſold and ſequeſtrated. Under ſo military and tyrannical a government, a variety of oppreſſive exactions muſt neceſſarily have taken place. Among many others, that of free quarter was particularly complained of. The ſoldiers were billetted on private houſes; paid nothing for their maintenance; were ſpies on the actions of thoſe upon whom they were quartered; and though guilty of the moſt ſhocking abuſes, their crimes were only ſubject to the cognizance of their own officers; no civil court, or magiſtrate, daring to interfere. But when Cromwell aſſumed the government of the ſtate, a general ſyſtem of oppreſſion was for ſome time put in practice. The whole kingdom was divided into twelve diſtricts, each of which was intruſted to the care of a major general, who was empowered to levy any tax the Protector thought proper to impoſe. An edict was iſſued, commanding the exaction of the tenth penny from all the royal party; and this oppreſſive tax, known by the name of *decimation*, Cromwell's military ſubſtitutes very rigorouſly enforced. The whole country was expoſed to their extortions; hardly any diſtinction was made; nor were the firmeſt friends to the exiſting government always exempted.

By an authentic document it appears that in the period of nineteen years which elapſed from the meeting of the long parliament till the reſtoration, 83,331,198*l.* were raiſed, making an average of 4,385,850*l.* per annum. But ſuppoſing all that was poſſeſſed and ſold by government to be public property, and conſidering at what rate it was ſold, and how much was given away to gratify beggarly intriguers, and embezzled by unprincipled agents, it muſt be evident that the nation was plundered to an infinitely greater amount. It is not neceſſary nor deſirable here to particularize all the means uſed to convert to private advantage this immenſe revenue. The neceſſary and honourable expences of government, beſides the civil adminiſtration, were incurred in the ſuppreſſion of hoſtile movements in Ireland and Scotland, in the wars with Holland and Spain, to which may be added the ſums expended for ſecret intelligence, in which the Protector was moſt wiſely liberal. Large however as were the ſums extorted from the nation, the army

army and navy were in misery through the non-payment of arrears, and Cromwell died 2,274,290*l.* in debt. Such was the saving effected by a government, established on the ruins of one which cost at the utmost 900,000*l.* year.

Restoration. The restoration so ardently and reasonably desired by the people at large, was not suddenly productive of all the good effects which were expected. The national expences were considerably reduced, but still contentions were perpetually maintained between the wants of a thoughtless, extravagant monarch, and the jealousies of a parsimonious parliament. The reign of Charles II. first exhibited the formation of a regular peace establishment, or a provision, even in times of peace, for the national protection and defence: whence have arisen permanent naval, military, and ordnance expences. In Charles's reign, the navy required large sums annually expended to counterbalance the force maintained by Holland, and that which Lewis XIV. was so assiduously employed in creating; a regular army in time of peace was also now for the first time maintained, and although it never exceeded 8000 men, and was sometimes as low as 4000, the public felt much jealousy and alarm, and the House of Commons pronounced it contrary to law; the ordnance was also a charge on government, but very moderate in comparison with that of succeeding times. The civil list expences amounted to 462,115*l.*, and the geral expenditure was within 1,200,000*l.*, the sum which parliament had first voted, but which was never fully made up. There were besides many incidental expences, arising from the necessity of replacing the property of the crown alienated by the republicans, the debts contracted by the late king during the civil war, and by Charles II. during his residence on the continent: and a still larger debt was due to those loyal individuals who had sustained such cruel losses by their unexampled firmness in adhering to the royal cause, but this was never satisfactorily discharged. The disbanding of Cromwell's army was attended with much expence in paying their arrears, and Charles, who had learnt during his exile, the value of such a fine military body, yielded with regret to the prudent advice of Lord Clarendon, in omitting to retain it in his service. The garrison of Tangiers, the dowry received with Catharine of Portugal, was for some time a source of great expence; as were the wars which arose in the course of the reign. To these must be added the profuseness of Charles himself, a quality which obscured the excellent talents he was allowed to possess; and deprived his character of every pretence to virtue or patriotism. This propensity was checked during the latter part of his life, with a vigour which demonstrated that his previous errors had arisen only from a miſconception of his duties, and a miſcalculation of his reaſonable expectations.

In the project of ſupply, the Commons acted with ſufficient liberality when they allotted to the king 1,200,000 *l.* a year; it was far ſhort of the monies received by Cromwell, but the people of England, when they deſired freedom from the yoke of pretended liberty, aimed at the eſtabliſhment of a beneficial and conſtitutional rule, and not at the exchange of one tyranny for another. The parliaments, however, acted unwiſely, as well as unjuſtly, in not providing effectually for the ſupply of the ſum they had voted; they exhibited a mean jealouſy in ſuffering the fear of the king's independence to ſtep between their promiſe and its execution, and are intitled to no ſmall ſhare in the blame due to the king's ſubſequent want of conduct, ſince by rendering his income inadequate, they juſtified his incurring debts; and the extent of that pernicious reſource no individual or public body can calculate.

To the ſupport of government in this reign were allotted the cuſtoms, which were greatly improved; the feudal perogatives were finally and utterly aboliſhed, and in their ſtead, a permanent exciſe on beer, ale, and other liquors, and the profits of wine licences, were permanently ſettled on the crown; a tax of two ſhillings on every hearth in houſes paying to the church and poor was impoſed, and very much, though perhaps unreaſonably, decried. By theſe means leſs than 1,100,000*l.* was obtained as an ordinary revenue. Occaſional grants were made by parliament, the amount of which was raiſed in different ways; there were three unproductive and juſtly unpopular poll-taxes; the cuſtoms and exciſe were augmented, but diſputes between the king and parliament prevented this augmentation from being permanent. Subſidies were in this reign, for the laſt time, impoſed, and it was evidently become neceſſary to ſuperſede a mode of taxation, in which perſons whoſe eſtates were known to be worth 2000 *l.* or 3000 *l.* a year, did not pay above 16 *l.* for four ſubſidies. Land taxes ſupplied their place, being collected monthly under the name of aſſeſſments, and for one purpoſe an impoſition was laid on perſonal property, being fifteen ſhillings on every hundred pounds belonging to bankers; the ſame ſum on every hundred pounds lent to the king at above ſix per cent. intereſt; ſix ſhillings per cent. on all perſonal eſtates; two ſhillings in the pound on the ſalaries of all offices and places, to which was added a ſhilling in the pound on lands and mines. Stamp duties were alſo firſt impoſed in this reign, and never afterward entirely ſuperſeded, though, for a time, ſuffered to expire.

These were the regular means by which the king obtained ſupplies;

ſupplies; he alſo derived ſome aids from adventitious, and others from exceptionable ſources. He received, beſides Tangiers in Africa, and Bombay in India, 250,000*l.* in part of 500,000*l.* promiſed as the portion of his conſort; and royal domains were ſold to an uncertain amount, probably about 500,000*l.* In the diſgrace of ſelling Dunkirk to France, the parliament muſt ſhare with the king, as their jealouſy and parſimony obliged him to conclude a bargain, which, for 336,773*l.*, diveſted him of that dominion; but the infamy of receiving a penſion from France, and all the baſeneſs and duplicity to his allies which enſued from it, were peculiarly his own. The ſums which he thus obtained amounted to 950,000*l.*, and the ſhare which he retained of the prize-money and other advantages during the Dutch wars amounted to 640,000*l.* In 1672, by advice of Lord Clifford, he ſhut up the exchequer, and inſtead of paying the bankers and others who had advanced money on the credit of parliamentary votes, their principal, he obliged them to receive the intereſt only, at ſix per cent., a fraud which procured him 1,328,526*l.*, at the expence of ruining many of his too confiding ſubjects, and greatly injuring public credit. With ſuch an inſtance in view, it would be difficult to believe that Charles would have been reſtrained by principle from any illegal extortion, but the conſtitution was now too well underſtood to allow much ſucceſs in ſuch efforts; an arbitrary duty was laid on coals, under pretence of providing convoys during the war with Holland; and when the king, in conſequence of the imprudence and miſconduct of thoſe who demanded the excluſion of his brother from the crown, had obtained a complete victory over that formidable party, and, indeed, had become almoſt maſter of the liberties of the people, he compelled the different corporations to ſurrender their charters into his hands, and exacted conſiderable ſums previouſly to their reſtitution. By all theſe means, he gained an annual revenue of 1,800,000*l.*, a ſum which, if regularly granted and prudently applied, would have been ſufficient to anſwer all his purpoſes. With all the faults and vices of this reign, political liberty and finance received many improvements; ſome relating to the latter having been mentioned, and two others deſerve notice. The clergy were no longer left to tax themſelves as a ſeparate body, but being now repreſented in the Houſe of Commons by voting in the election of county members, were aſſeſſed like other ſubjects of the realm; and the ſupplies were no longer voted in a general way, but ſeparately appropriated by parliament to the various purpoſes they were intended to effect.

James II. began his reign as if predetermined to juſtify thoſe who had ſought to exclude him from the throne, and furniſh every possible motive to those who afterward expelled him from it. Although dissuaded by his council, he issued a proclamation, commanding the payment of the customs and other taxes as usual, without waiting for the assent of parliament; and in his first speech to that body, he made them understand that they were not to attempt securing frequent meetings by granting small supplies; "I must tell you plainly," he said, "that "such an expedient would be very improper to employ with "me; and the best way to engage me to meet you often, is "always to use me well." The parliament however granted this king 2,000,000*l.* per annum, a larger permanent income than had been allowed to any of his predecessors. Had James been at all master of himself, and sought the establishment of the religion to which he was so bigotted, and the tyranny, of which it is the best support, by slow and cautious means, it is much to be feared that success must have crowned his measures. His very virtues were calculated to give effect to such a project; his frugality would have exempted him from making frequent application to parliament, and this circumstance would have secured him the love and confidence of a large portion of the people; his zeal for the advancement of the navy was evidently wise and patriotic, and calculated to gain popularity; and the standing army of 30,000 men which he had established, might, with cautious management, have been made subservient to any purposes. The impatient temper and undisguised tyranny of James hastened the revolution, and rendered its accomplishment easy, by combining against him, in every class, a strong and firm party. The operations of finance in his short reign were not considerable: he received one supply of 400,000*l.* to suppress the rebellion of the Duke of Monmouth, and in 1685, one of 700,000*l.* was voted, but the king, apprehensive that the Commons would interfere in his pretended prerogative of dispensing with tests, dissolved the parliament before the bill passed.

State of Finance at the Revolution. From this period, it is not intended to notice the financial operations of each reign; for the system of funding, which took place soon after the revolution, totally changed the manner and purpose of supplies. It may, however, be proper to remark from the foregoing statement, that before the funding system had begun, the origin of almost every species of taxation was laid, and its great principle developed. The customs, excise, land-tax, subsidy or income-tax, post-office, stamps, licences, house-tax, and assessments on some particular luxuries, had all been brought into use. Modern improvement has done little more than extend their application to new objects, facilitate the collection, and prevent

prevent frauds in thofe who pay, and thofe who collect. Taxation is now wound about every object, and every act of life; and many are apt to confider the fituation of the country as far worfe than in ancient times, when fums nominally fmall formed the whole mafs of annual expenditure; but without entering into the wide field, to which the difcuffion of this topic would lead, it may be proper to mention, in the firft place, the advantage which has been acquired in the eftablifhment of the great conftitutional doctrine, that the fubject fhall not be affeffed, but with the confent of his reprefentatives; in the next, to repeat that the modes of taxation now in ufe, were for the moft part difcovered before debts were incurred: and laftly, to mention, for it will be too long to defcribe, fome of the moft degrading, burthenfome, and tyrannical modes of acquiring property from the people, which have vanifhed before the improved fyftem of modern times. Firft, was the property vefted in the fovereign, which in the days of Edward the Confeffor amounted to 1422 manors, befides other lands and quit-rents, but was afterward greatly augmented; the royal forefts, which although not productive of immediate rents, were by the foreft laws rendered fnares and engines of oppreffion to the people refiding near them; the king poffeffed at one time fixty-eight forefts, thirteen chafes, and feven hundred and eighty-one parks, in different parts of England; he had alfo the right to mines, including the entire property of all the metals, if they contained the leaft portion of gold or filver. Next were the feudal prerogatives, many of which did not veft in the king alone, but extended to others, who were lords of fiefs. The chief of thefe were included in the right of feignory, which fuppofed the king proprietor of all the land in the realm; and from this right branched out the profits of efcuage, quit-rents, aids, reliefs, wardfhip, or the property in the income of an heir's eftate till he attained the age of twenty-one, marriage, or the right of felling a ward in wedlock, fines of alienation, and efcheats. Befides thefe were the *bona vacantia*, as treafure-trove, waifs, and various other minuter objects. All the other prerogatives of the crown will be feen in the preceding pages to have been at different times fources of undifputed profit; the military prerogative, in plunder, tribute, and the redemption of perfons and places captured; the judicial, in fees both legal and extorted, from fuitors in courts; the political, in the fale of offices, charters, and titles; the inquifitorial, in the odious right of purveyance and pre-emption, which was founded on the fuppofition, that the king was making a progrefs through fome part of his dominions, to inquire into its condition; and the commercial, in the fees for the eftablifhment of marts, the profit of coining, and the granting of patents and monopolies. The king's right to the service of his subjects was converted into an engine of oppression, by employing those who would not supply compulsory loans on ruinous services; and his ecclesiastical prerogatives gave him a strong hold on the property of the church, by corodies, extra parochial tythes, and the profits of bishoprics during vacancy. From the oppressive effect of all these, the kingdom is now happily relieved; if any are nominally retained, they are in fact of so little importance as to be rarely felt, and generally unknown. Still more effectually are abolished those royal extortions, of which occasional mention has been made; of them not the slightest vestige remains. Among these were the oblations, or fines, without which no man could claim freedom in his most ordinary actions, or prosecute with success his most undoubted rights; amercements, which were arbitrarily imposed on individuals, or communities, for slight offences, or even acts in themselves indifferent; talliages levied at pleasure on the tenants of royal demesnes, in which all the great towns were ordinarily included; and the farming of counties, by which all the people of the kingdom were subject to rapacious exactions. To these should be added the extortions of popery; and a notion may be formed of the load of oppression from which the nation was gradually relieved. Even the modes of taxation have undergone such a reformation in principle, as makes a considerable deduction from the pressure occasioned by its present extensive amount. Voluntary contribution being no longer recurred to, neither the rage of government, nor the torture of public opinion, can be used in forcing a supply. Before gold and silver were plenty, taxes were frequently levied in kind, an operation peculiarly injurious, as the commodities were sold raw to foreigners, and the people were thus deprived of the very elements of industry. Among the most odious taxes, to which government in its less perfect state had recourse, were the poll tax and hearth money; the objection against the latter was, that it subjected the interior of a person's dwelling to the visitation of revenue officers; the objection was perhaps overstrained, but as it was generally received, the new government, after the revolution, acted wisely in abolishing the impost. Popular opinion is not, however, a safe criterion in matter of revenue, for many taxes which are both just and productive have been assailed by violent public clamour, while one of the most popular ever imposed was that which lay for so many years on the Jews, subjecting them to the extortion of a separate exchequer, and finally driving them from the realm.

Before the revolution, every mode which can be generally devised,

vised, for discharging the expences of government, had been essayed in England, and the inconveniences of each had been sensibly felt. Some monarchs, when provided with the means of supporting their government in ordinary times, had relied for supply in case of war, or other emergency, on an accumulated treasure; but besides the numerous objections which evidently present themselves against the subtraction of a large portion of money from circulation, a hoarding monarch is little calculated to be a favourite with a generous people. When the possession of money becomes an object of intense desire, the character of the prince who is influenced by that passion is blended with every act of his government, and always in an unfavourable manner, since the obtaining of money from the subject must frequently, in such cases, be accomplished by craft or violence, and either character will be a just object of popular odium. The rapacious and tyrannical Conqueror, who plundered without disguise or pretext, was not more, or more justly, detested than the crafty and cold blooded Henry VII. who robbed the people under colour of law; and in order to gratify his darling avarice, leagued with informers, and became the patron of pettyfoggers. How different from these, the noble minded Elizabeth, whose patriotic and disinterested saying has already been recorded. Yet Elizabeth was not less lofty in her notions of prerogative than any of her predecessors; but she, dying without an accumulated treasure, left to her successor the task of conciliating, or awing parliament, in order to obtain supplies, while the treasures of William, seized by his sons according to their convenience, enabled them to usurp the throne, and violate the order of succession; and that of Henry VII. falling into the hands of his intemperate successor, gave spurs to his ever violent passions, and energy to that tyrannical disposition, which, for want of being checked by early necessity, produced many acts disgraceful to the British annals.

The raising of supplies within the year appears, at first sight, to be the most eligible plan for a nation to pursue; but those who regard with attention the history of those periods, in which that system prevailed in England, will perceive with regret and shame, that the constant disputes between the sovereign and the commons must have rendered the nation contemptible in the eyes of foreign powers, and its government insecure and dependent. The glorious projects of Edward III. and Henry V. however popular, were delayed, and, but for events almost miraculous, must have been frustrated, through the parsimony of the commons. In fact, in such a system of government, the welfare of the nation must depend entirely on the estimation which happens to attend the sovereign, or his minister; and if the

the ſtate is free, the neceſſity of ſecuring popularity will much interfere with the magnanimous ſpirit, which is neceſſary to preſerve its honour, and its external advantages. The monies expended by government are not devoted to the mere aggrandizement of the monarch, but the general good of the people; but it would be extremely difficult, to engage the people in an expenſive conteſt, for ſupport of the national honour and proſperity, if the ſacrifice to be made muſt produce great immediate inconvenience to individuals, and occaſion greater privations in one year of war or difficulty, than had been ſuſtained in many of peace, however inſecure or inglorious. In fact, when it was profeſſed, that the ſupplies ſhould be raiſed within the year, it was ever found that the vote did not create the money, and therefore ſome anticipation, by means of credit, was neceſſary. The credit, when legal or conſtitutional, was limited to the amount of grants already provided; but need, combined with arbitrary power, occaſioned the forced loans which have already been ſo often mentioned, and a complaiſant or ſlaviſh parliament has been known to make a law, declaring the ſecurities given by the king to the ſubjects void, or in form giving and granting to the king the money which individuals had lent him under the moſt ſacred guarantees. It was alſo a mean of keeping many ſovereigns in a ſtate of difficulty and diſtreſs, for thoſe who afterward became ſhamefully indifferent about their own debts, were often ſuperſtitiouſly exact in paying thoſe of their predeceſſors; and thus incurred pecuniary difficulties from the very commencement of their reigns. Another effect of theſe temporary loans was, that the lenders became extravagant in their demands of intereſt, and inſolent in their requiſitions of ſecurity. In proportion to the wants of the ſovereign, theſe demands roſe, and while intereſt to the amount of 12 per cent. or more, was rendered for money, the extortionate lenders required the collateral ſecurity of the city of London, or of the houſes of parliament; nay, ſometimes the crown, robes, jewels, and other regalia, were pledged for money.

Origin of Funding. Under ſuch circumſtances, when loans have been neceſſary, it has not been unuſual to mortgage the produce of taxes; but as the loans were only temporary, the expedient rather gave a hint, than furniſhed a precedent of a permanent ſyſtem. During the reign of Charles II. a clauſe of credit was inſerted in many acts, empowering the officers of the exchequer to borrow money from all perſons, whether natives or foreigners, on the ſecurity of the ſubſidy that was granted; and a law was paſſed, entitled, "An act for aſſigning orders in the exchequer, without revocation," which enabled the king to borrow money on the credit *of any branch*

of

of the revenue, becauſe in the words of the ſtatute, "it had "been found by experience, that the powers of aſſigning orders "in the exchequer by former acts, without revocation, had "been of great uſe and advantage to the perſons concerned in "them, and to the trade of the kingdom." The ſhutting of the exchequer, in the year 1672, laid the foundation of a permanent debt; for the king having thus ſecured the undue poſſeſſion of 1,328,526*l.*, iſſued letters patent, charging his hereditary revenue with the intereſt at ſix per cent. amounting to nearly 80,000*l.* per annum. Even the payment of intereſt was afterward ſtayed, and the parties being driven to a legal proceſs, after a very long delay, obtained a compoſition, by which intereſt at three per cent. on the original debt was charged on the hereditary exciſe, but the principal was to be redeemed on payment of 664,263*l.*

This ſum was, in fact, the only part of the preſent national debt which was due at the revolution; but it muſt not be too haſtily inferred, although the opinion is advanced by ſome enemies of that glorious event, that the incurring of a debt was not matter of neceſſity, but a mere contrivance to ſecure the authority of the new ſovereign. The ſtate of the realm at that time, if candidly conſidered, furniſhes a ſufficient anſwer to ſuch an objection. The government was weak, and its affairs diſhoneſtly adminiſtered, becauſe faction prevailed in every department, and immenſe ſums were miſapplied, or embezzled. The houſe of commons were influenced by new and dangerous principles, in meaſures of ſupply. Thoſe who conſidered the government unſtable hoarded their money, and out of 16,000,000*l.*, at which the exiſting ſum in the nation was computed, from five to ſix millions are ſaid to have been hoarded. The coin itſelf was in ſo bad a ſtate, that 2,415,140*l.* was the loſs ſuſtained by the re-coinage. Every ſpecies of credit was at the loweſt ebb; bank notes were at 20 per cent., and tallies at 40, 50, nay 60 per cent. diſcount. The expences of the revolution itſelf were not inconſiderable. To the Dutch alone were voted 600,000*l.* for the armament they had fitted out, in order to bring about that event. The reduction of Ireland was attended with great charges: nor were the partizans of the dethroned monarch driven from Scotland, without ſome bloodſhed and expence. The money that was thus required to place William on the throne of the three kingdoms, would have fully defrayed the charges of at leaſt one, if not of two campaigns. The honourable and neceſſary wars, in which the deliverer of England engaged, were alſo extremely expenſive, owing not leſs to the great power of the common enemy, Lewis XIV. than the languid manner in which the common cauſe was ſupported

ported by ſome of the allies. Whoever conſiders, therefore, the ſtate of our revenue, the magnitude of our expences, and the various circumſtances, both foreign and domeſtic, above enumerated, muſt clearly perceive, that contracting a public debt was a matter, not of choice, but of neceſſity. Whether the funding ſyſtem has been beneficial or injurious to the nation, is among the problems which have occaſioned, and ever muſt create, great differences of opinion, and would require more detailed arguments than can be introduced into this work; but certainly many, if not moſt, of the inconveniences complained of as reſulting from the preſent national debt, ariſe from the inevitable inexperience of thoſe who, for many years after the ſyſtem of the funds was adopted, conducted a ſcheme ſo new and difficult.

First Loans. The government of William III. adopted at firſt the plan of Charles II. borrowing on the anticipated produce of grants voted by parliament, without eſtabliſhing a fund for payment of intereſt. In 1692, an attempt was made to borrow a million upon annuities for ninety-nine years, for which 10 per cent. was to be given until the 24th June, 1700; and 7 per cent. afterwards, with the benefit of ſurvivorſhip, for the lives of the nominees of thoſe who contributed. So low, however, was the credit of government at that time, that even on theſe terms only 881,493*l.* 12*s.* 2*d.* could be procured. In 1693, a million was raiſed on ſhort annuities, and as every ſubſcriber received 14 per cent. for ſixteen years, with the additional benefits of a lottery, ſo advantageous an offer was eagerly graſped at. Some money was alſo borrowed during this reign on annuities for lives; and 14 per cent. was granted for one life, 12 per cent. for two lives, and 10 per cent. for three. Such terms were in the higheſt degree extravagant, particularly as no attention was paid to difference of ages. In this reign, the Bank of England and the Eaſt India Company were eſtabliſhed: they paid to government the ſum of 3,200,000*l.* for which they received an intereſt of 8 per cent.; and as the taxes impoſed to defray that intereſt were to remain until the principal, and all the arrears of their reſpective annuities were diſcharged, and conſequently were unlimited in their duration, this naturally paved the way for thoſe perpetual annuities which afterwards took place.

Funding established. The ſucceſs with which the Bank of England was attended, had encouraged ſome individuals to form the project of a *land bank*, with a view, not only of raiſing a conſiderable ſum for the uſe of government, but alſo of lending money on land ſecurities, at low intereſt, a part of the ſcheme being to give 500,000*l.* on mortgage, at 3*l.* 10*s.* per cent.

cent. to be paid quarterly, or 4 per cent. payable half yearly; but the project did not succeed. The temptation, however, of mortgages at so easy a rate, induced the landed gentlemen to agree to the establishment of perpetual taxes, to defray the interest of the money intended to be raised. The statutes in the year 1695-6 furnish the first example in our history of this climax of financial invention.

Such were the proceedings of government up to the period when the system of borrowing money on the permanent security of the taxes, became thoroughly established. Volumes have been filled with discussions on the good or evil tendency of this plan, and every topic of encouragement and alarm has almost been exausted in its eulogy or censure. On one hand it has been asserted as a kind of political axiom, that national debt is, in England, but another term for national greatness; while on the other, prophecies have been repeated till they are to many become objects of ridicule, that at some period the load of debt will be too great for the government to struggle with, and that, at last, a general insolvency must close the account. Much of the ridicule attending these prophecies has been occasioned by the positive manner in which periods have been fixed for this completion of disaster; which have arrived and passed again, and again, still leaving the nation in a state of wealth and prosperity, of which no previous example had existed: yet the too sanguine assertions made on the other side cannot be admitted without qualification, when it is recollected, that of late, necessity has enforced the raising of a part of supply within the year; and that extraordinary measures have been adopted for the purpose of taking up a portion of floating stock, in order to prevent its too great depreciation. Among the advantages arising from the funds which have been least insisted on, is the cheap and certain security which they afford to persons in subordinate situations in life, for the produce of small savings, and the receipt of a certain interest without any danger to the capital. In former times, the individual in humble life, as an inferior farmer, or tradesman, a clerk, or other person employed in trade, or a servant in a family, when he had by economy, or by a legacy, or other accident, become possessed of a small sum, was obliged to hoard it, without hope of its producing profit; or to lend it, with all the risque attending loans to individuals, and the expence to be incurred on one side or the other, of a legal security. In these times, supposing the three per cents. to be at 60*l*., a person possessing no more than twenty pounds, may at the expence of two shillings and sixpence, secure an interest of twenty shillings a year, and add to his capital from time to time by any sums, however minute,

6 which

which he may accumulate; and if he is desirous to receive his principal, it is returned to him without delay, and without hurting the delicacy, or interfering with the prosperity of any one, as easily as it was lent. The greatest evil which is apprehended from the increase of the national debt, is the perpetual augmentation of taxes, which, while they enhance the price of the first materials of commerce, cause a proportionate advance in the price of labour; and must, although the government duties are allowed as a draw-back on exportation, enable foreigners to undersell the British merchants in the market. Although this apprehension has not yet been realized, it would be most unwarrantably presumptuous to say, that it never can; but it is materially impeded by the extensive capital, unrivalled ingenuity, and unblemished honour of British manufacturers and merchants; and will, it is trusted, as well as all other mischiefs to be apprehended from the national debt, be finally averted by the wise measures hereafter to be described under the title of Sinking Fund.

Loans. In times of peace, or when no extraordinary exigency obliges the state to demand from the public unusual supplies, it is understood, that the permanent and general taxes will be sufficient to defray all expences; but when war is either made or menaced, or in the first years of a peace, when all the outstanding accounts are not yet made up, it is usual for the minister to supply the deficiencies by a loan. The duty of the chancellor of the exchequer in explaining to the house of commons the nature of the supplies, ways and means, and the committees constantly formed for the investigation of them, have already been mentioned. The terms on which a minister can make a loan, depend on various circumstances; the facilities of raising money; the state of public opinion with respect to affairs in general; and the popularity of the individual, with whom the monied men are to negotiate, are those which produce the greatest effect. When the amount of the intended loan is communicated to the merchants and bankers of London, they form separate classes under the head of some known monied man, or company; and each leader of these bodies attends the minister at a given day, proposing in writing the terms on which he, for himself and friends, can make good the sum required. The form of this proposal generally supposes a certain stock, either three or four per cent. at a certain value; and terminable annuities, at another value; according to their calculations, the minister estimates the proportionate benefit or disadvantage which would accrue to the public from the acceptance of either proposal, and in course, closes with that which furnishes the required sum at the lowest rate of interest.

Such

Such is the modern way of raising supplies; others have been resorted to by various ministers; but this is found to be most popular, most just, and in the end most beneficial. It has been objected, that combinations may be formed to defraud the public; but, in fact, the rate of interest has never been exorbitantly advanced, nor has the nation any reason to complain of a measure so open and liberal; consistent at once with an enlarged system of commerce, and a government founded on freedom. In the reign of William III., when loans were first proposed, attempts were made to raise money at only 6 per cent. interest; but it was found necessary, the very same session, to offer 7 per cent.; and, from the year 1690, during the remainder of the war, 8 per cent. was uniformly paid. In the late, tremendously expensive, contest with France, the interest on one loan amounted to *6l. 4s. 9d.* per cent.; but this was deemed an alarming circumstance, and occasioned some measures for taking a portion of the floating stock out of the market, and raising the supplies within the year; but with all the difficulties in which the nation was occasionally involved, and under the operation of all the mistaken principles, which conspired to alienate and terrify a portion of the public, the national credit stood so high, that the average interest of ten loans, was only *4l. 15s. 6d.* per cent. Yet it is not to be supposed, that persons possessed of large capital can advance the incredible sums frequently required by government, without strong motives of personal advantage. There are other circumstances, unconnected with the general effect of a loan on the public, which constitute what is termed a *bonus* or benefit to the contractor. The bonus arises in part from the allowance in temporary annuities, which are considered as being sold by the minister somewhat too cheap, to make the loan acceptable; and from the periods of payment of the sums subscribed, which are so divided as to accommodate the purchaser, and render his portion of the loan saleable in the market. When the subscription is full, the list of names, with the sums allotted to each, is sent to the bank; and as soon as conveniently may be, after the subscription is closed, receipts are made out, and delivered to the subscribers, for the several sums by them subscribed: and for the conveniency of sale, every subscriber of a considerable sum has sundry receipts for different portions of his whole sum, that he may the more readily part with what share he thinks proper; and a form of assignment, which being signed and witnessed, transfers the property to any purchaser. Then if a person has subscribed in the list accepted by the minister, any given sum, and is desirous to be eased of a portion before any part of the principal is paid in, he tenders it at the market, and generally sells it for a moderate premium. The completion

completion of the loan is generally made by instalments at given distances; and when any of these are paid, a receipt issues to the individual, and if he sells any part of his share after that, he expects to be allowed for the instalments already paid, with a premium if the loan bears it, or making a deduction if the the public opinion renders that necessary; the interests disposed of in either of these are termed *scrip*, the whole undivided loan is called *omnium*. The interest of each loan, when funded, is to be met by taxes, which the minister proposes in the House of Commons, and his speech, or scheme, on this occasion, is called *the Budget*.

NATIONAL DEBT. These borrowings by successive ministers, having accumulated from the period when the funding system began to be adopted, form what is called the national debt. Without entering minutely into the various political circumstances, which have occasioned the growth of this incumbrance, it will be sufficient to exhibit in the following tables its amount at different periods.

Progress of the national debt from its commencement to March, 1801.

	Principal.	Interest.
National debt at the revolution -	664,263	39,855
Increase during the reign of king William - - - - - - - - -	15,730,439	1,271,087
Debt at the accession of queen Anne - - - - - - - - - -	16,394,702	1,310,942
Increase during the reign of queen Anne - - - - - - - - - -	37,750,661	2,040,416
Debt at the accession of George I.	54,145,363	3,351,358
Decrease during the reign of George I. - - - - - - - - -	2,053,128	1,133,807*

* The apparent disproportion between the capital saved and the interest as annexed to it, arises from the reduction in the rate of interest from 6 to 5 per cent., which took place in the reign of George I. "It appears," Sir John Sinclair observes, "that the capital of the national debt, in 1714, and in 1727, was nearly the same; particularly, if no addition is made to the principal, in the former period, on the supposition, that the temporary annuities ought to be valued at the price they would fetch in the market, and not at the sum that was originally paid. The reader, at the same time, will perceive how much the two periods differ in regard to the interest. In the reign of queen Anne, for the same capital of about fifty-two millions, was paid annually the sum of 3,351,358*l.*, which, at the death of George I., was reduced to 2,217,551*l.* The difference amounting to 1,133,807*l.*, is a full proof of the flourishing credit which this country enjoyed, and of what might have been done at that time, for retrieving our finances, by an able, decided, and public-spirited minister."

Debt

	Principal.	Interest.
Debt at the acceſſion of George II.	52,092,235	2,217,551
Decreaſe during the peace - -	5,137,612	253,526
Debt at the commencement of the Spaniſh war, 1739 - - - - -	46,954,623	1,964,025
Increaſe during the war - - -	31,338,589	1,096,979
Debt at the end of the Spaniſh war, 1748 - - - - - - - - - -	78,293,312	3,061,004
Decreaſe during the peace - -	3,721,472	664,287
Debt at the commencement of the war, 1755 - - - - - - - - -	74,571,840	2,396,717
Increaſe during the war - - -	72,111,004	2,444,104
Debt at the concluſion of the peace, 1762 - - - - - - - - - -	146,682,844	4,840,821
Decreaſe during the peace - - -	10,739,793	364,000
Debt at the commencement of the American war - - - - - -	135,943,051	4,476,821
Increaſe during the war - - - -	121,269,992	5,192,614
Debt at the concluſion of the American war - - - - - - - - -	257,213,043	9,669,435
Decreaſe during the peace - -	4,751,261	143,569
Debt at the commencement of the French revolutionary war - -	252,461,782	9,52[illegible],866
Increaſe during the war - - -	327,469,665	12,252,152
Total amount of the debt, An. 1801 - - - - - - - - - - -	579,931,447	21,778,018
Deduct paid by the ſinking fund, and redeemed by the land-tax -	68,365,458	1,696,996
	511,565,989	20,081,022
Deduct the capital of the temporary annuities - - - - - - - -	9,379,807	
Amount of the national debt funded and unfunded in March, 1801, with the intereſt and charges thereon - - - - - - - -	502,186,182	20,082,022

State

State of the national debt of Great Britain, deducting the diminution by ſtock transferred to the commiſſioners for the reduction of debt, and on account of land-tax redeemed.

	£.	s.	d.
Total created - - - - - - - -	582,131,385	1	3¾
Redeemed by the commiſſioners for the reduction of the public debt, up to the 1ſt of February, 1805 - -	89,003,759	00	00
The public funded debt of Great Britain, as the ſame ſtood on the firſt day of February, 1805, as laid before the Houſe of Commons, was - -	493,127,726	1	3¾
Total of the annual intereſt and expence of management, including the million for the redemption of the national debt, and other ſums appropriated for that purpoſe, is — - - -	24,928,336	16	7½
Payable annually to the commiſſioners for reduction of debt - - -	6,834,114	10	7
	18,094,222	6	0½
Management reared on ſtock purchaſed by the commiſſioners, and on expired annuities - - - - - - -	39,067	14	8¼
Total intereſt, charge of management, and for the debt unredeemed on the firſt of February, 1805 - - -	18,055,154	11	4¼
The unfunded debt, and demands outſtanding on the 5th of January, 1805, was - - - - - - - - - -	34,460,521	19	0¾
The public debt of Ireland funded in Great Britain, as the ſame ſtood on the 5th of January, 1805, was - -	31,562,901	00	00

Intereſt, annuities, and charges of management 976,303*l.* 10*s.* 1*d.*

The total amount of the public funded debt created in Great Britain, for account of the emperor of Germany,

as

	£.	s.	d.
as the same stood 1st February, 1805, was - - - - - - - - - - -	7,502,633	6	8
Redeemed by the commissioners for reduction of debt 550,228*l*. 00*s*. 00*d*.			
Annual interest on unredeemed debt - - - - - - - - - - - - -	208,572	3	3
Annuities for a term of years - -	230,000	0	0
Charges of management - - -	5716	1	8
Interest on stock bought - - -	16,506	16	9
Annuity at 1 per cent. 36,693*l*. redeemable, with the 1 per cent. or at par.			
Total of annual expence - - -	460,795	1	8

Stocks. This large debt is chiefly vested in various stocks or funds, in which the public may purchase and possess shares of the capital, but some portion is borrowed from large trading or monied companies who are benefitted by receiving the interest. These sums are; to the bank 11,686,800*l*., which, at three per cent., gives for interest 350,604*l*., and South Sea stock to the amount of 3,662,784*l*., bearing the like interest. These are to be reckoned among the permanent funded debts, and the others which rank under that description, are the annuities payable at the bank, and bearing interest respectively at the rate of 3*l*. 4, or 5 per cent.

Consols. Of the 3 per cents., the fund called consolidated annuities, or for shortness *Consols*, is the most considerable. When first consolidated in 1751, it amounted only to 9,137,821*l*., but it now considerably exceeds three hundred millions, having been swelled to that magnitude, partly by real loans, for which value was received; and partly by adding an artificial capital, for which no purchase money was given. Perhaps such a system could not have been intirely avoided, though it materially tends to render our public debts more confused, unmanageable, expensive, and alarming, than otherwise would have been the case.

Reduced. The three per cent. reduced annuities are of much inferior amount, not exceeding one third of the consols. As the interest on both is the same, the funds might have been united, but that the dividends become due at different periods; the consols being paid half yearly, on the 5th of January, and the 5th of July; the reduced on the 5th of April, and the

10th of October. This division renders it less necessary to collect such large sums of money at once into the bank, or the exchequer, as might otherwise be required. Had these funds indeed been payable at the same time, it might have proved on some occasions inconvenient to the general circulation of the country.

Other three per Cents. Another 3 per cent. fund, under the management of the bank, is known by the name of the 3 per cents. 1726, at which time they were first created. The loan was made in that year in order to discharge certain civil list debts contracted in the reign of George I.

Four per Cents. The four per cent. bank annuities have been created since the year 1776; and no bargain was entered into with the public creditors, which prevents either the repayment of the principal, or a reduction of interest, whenever the nation is enabled to carry into effect either of these measures.

Five per Cents. The funds bearing 5 per cent. interest, are at present of two descriptions: the first, called the 5 per cent. navy annuities, and the second, the 5 per cent. annuities of 1797, commonly known under the name of the loyalty loan. The navy 5 per cent. annuities amount to 28,125,582*l.* bearing an interest of 1,406,279*l.*, and requiring 12,650*l.* for the expence of management. By the original contract with the public creditors, to whom this fund belonged, it was made redeemable whenever 25,000,000*l.* of three or four per cent. stock had been purchased by the commissioners for paying off the national debt; and that event having long ago taken place, nothing but the want of means can prevent the reduction of this fund to a lower rate of interest.

Loyalty Loan. The origin of the loan so called was this: at the conclusion of the year 1796, the minister, apprehending great difficulty, and some injury to the national credit, if he persevered in raising supplies in the usual manner, communicated to the directors of the bank a project for obtaining from those who possessed certain incomes a large sum, payable in money or five per cent. stock at a liberal price, and with benefits to be augmented in proportion to the forbearance of the lenders. This plan, in its first outline, contained a hint of compelling individuals to advance their money; but long before it had been mentioned in parliament, that thought was abandoned, and a proposition was made for the voluntary subscription of 18,000,000*l.*; a measure so congenial to the general wish of the country, that in five days the books opened for that purpose were filled, and the required sum might have been doubled. Unfortunately, it is impossible to speculate with correctness on the

the operations of public ſpirit; the miniſter limited his demand, not by his occaſions, but by his ſuppoſed probabilities of ſucceſs, and he was therefore obliged, in addition to this firſt loan, to raiſe another of fourteen millions and a half, which, at the rate then prevailing in the money market, afforded the proprietors a large profit, and conſequently reduced thoſe who could not make good their ſubſcriptions to the firſt loan as faſt as they became due, to the neceſſity of parting with their ſcrip at a great diſadvantage. To protect them againſt this unmerited inconvenience, the miniſter propoſed in the Houſe of Commons to make a proviſion in their favour, which would place them in as good a ſituation as the ſubſcribers to the other loan; but to this propoſition many objections of form, and ſome of principle were made, and a queſtion on the ſubject having been loſt by a majority of one vote, the miniſter abandoned his plan of compenſation altogether. The loyalty loan originally amounted to 20,124,843*l.* 15*s.* of capital, there was afterward added, by 42 Geo. III. c. 8. a capital of 2,227,612*l.* 10*s.* ſo that the total now amounts to 22,352,456*l.* 5*s.* As the creditors will ſoon be entitled to demand their money, it is very improbable that this fund will long be entitled to remain in its preſent ſtate.

South Sea Stock. The annuities payable by the public, under the management of the South Sea company, bear uniformly the ſame intereſt, namely, three per cent. They are divided however into three branches: 1ſt. The old South Sea annuities, amounting to 11,907,470*l.* 2*s.* 7*d.* bearing an intereſt of 357,224*l.* 2*s.* payable half-yearly, on the 5th of April, and 10th of October; 2d. The new South Sea annuities, amounting to 8,494,830*l.* 2*s.* 10*d.*, and the intereſt thereon being 254,844*l.* 18*s.* 1*d.*, is payable on the 5th of January, and 5th of July; and 3d. The ſum of 1,919,600*l.* funded in the year 1751, the intereſt on which, amounting to 57,588*l.* is payable at the ſame time.

Deferred Stock. The capital of the deferred three per cent. annuities, amounts to 1,740,625*l.* the intereſt payable on which does not commence till the 5th of January, 1808, when they are to be made a part of the three per cent. conſolidated annuities. The allowance for management amounts to 783*l.* per annum. The idea of poſtponing the payment of the intereſt on public loans was borrowed from America, but the ſyſtem is not likely to be much reliſhed by the monied intereſt on this ſide of the Atlantic.

Imperial and Irish Loans. To theſe permanent burthens ſhould be added, the Auſtrian or Imperial loans, and the Iriſh loans, ſince the year 1797, both being guaranteed by the Britiſh government. In the years 1795, and 1796, the emperor of

Germany, for the purpose of carrying on hostilities against the common enemy, was obliged to raise in London, by permission of parliament, two loans, amounting to 7,502,633*l.* the annual interest of which is 497,735*l.* The Irish loans are raised and the dividends paid in London, a measure which became necessary, in consequence of the heavy expences occasioned by the late rebellion; but the money for discharge of the interest is regularly raised and remitted from that country.

TEMPORARY ANNUITIES. The temporary annuities are, 1st. Those granted for life. 2dly. For a definite term of years. They are payable either at the bank or the exchequer. In the years 1778, and 1779, certain annuities were granted for short periods, ending on the 5th of January, 1808: they amount in all to 418,333*l.* per annum. However agreeable the prospect may be, of getting soon free from such an incumbrance, there is reason to believe, that less value is paid for such annuities, than for those of a more permanent nature, 25,000*l.* per annum of short annuities, which expired on the 5th of April, 1787, instead of being extinguished, are placed to the account of the commissioners appointed for the reduction of the national debt. The most important branch of the temporary annuities, amounting to 1,063,702*l.* per annum, unfortunately continues till the 5th of January, 1860. The only sums payable at the exchequer are certain annuities, granted in the reigns of king William and queen Anne, which end at different periods, prior to or at Lady-day, 1808, also some life annuities payable at the same place; and certain tontine annuities, the whole of which amount only to 127,750*l.* per annum, and require 5,490*l.* per annum, for the expence of management.

SALE AND TRANSFER OF STOCK. All these funds and stocks are transferred at the bank of England, where the dividends or interest are paid as they become due; books for recording and authenticating the sales and purchases made by individuals, with proper forms of receipts and other requisites, are kept at each office; a clerk in which also makes out, at a very small expence, powers of attorney for those who wish their bankers, agents, or friends to receive their dividends, or, if necessary, to transfer their stock. Adjoining the transfer offices are large rooms, where the buyers and sellers meet and prepare their documents.

BROKERS. Any person may transact his own business in the buying or selling of stock, if he thinks fit, but the more usual mode is, to employ a broker; and although many objections have been made to the intervention of these persons, they will hardly be considered as effectual, when it is recollected that those who have little business to do in the funds, must be prevented

vented by diffidence and aukwardneſs from accompliſhing it to their own ſatisfaction, but may employ a broker at the moderate price of two ſhillings and ſix pence per cent.; and thoſe who have daily tranſactions in the funds to a large amount, and to whom experience muſt be ſuppoſed to give confidence, are known to prefer the eaſe and ſecurity, though attended with the expence already mentioned, which are derived from employing brokers. Theſe perſons are within the juriſdiction of the lord mayor and court of aldermen; it being a law of the city, that any perſon may act as a broker, on giving a bond for his good behaviour, which is executed by himſelf alone, and in the penalty of 500*l.* and another for payment of forty ſhillings per annum into the comptroller's office, which is executed by the individual and two houſe-keepers, in the penalty of 150*l.*

Stock Exchange. Although the final concluſion of buſineſs relating to the funds muſt, and its preliminaries may, be performed in the bank, the much greater portion is tranſacted in a place called the Stock Exchange. This was, in old times, at a coffee-houſe in Change Alley, called Jonathan's; it was then removed to a ſubſcription room, near the Royal Exchange, where it continued till May, 1801, when the brokers, by a private ſubſcription, purchaſed a large building in Capel Court near the bank, which they pulled down, and erected a new edifice for the tranſaction of their daily affairs, ſecuring it by prudent regulations from many of the irregularities which diſgraced their former abode. Still, however, by accuſtomed phraſe, the place where this buſineſs is negotiated, is called *the Alley*, and a man who has bought or ſold ſtock on ſpeculation, is ſaid to have been *in the Alley*.

Jobbing. The ordinary tranſactions in ſtock, where perſons ſell that which they actually poſſeſs, or buy with money paid at the moment, is like every other dealing in an open market, where no groſs advantage can be taken, but where the vigilant and cautious will have ſome ſuperiority over the negligent and unwary; and this benefit is rendered leſs, by the publicity of all tranſactions, and the daily publication of a printed liſt of prices. But for many years the ſale and transfer of real ſtock has formed an inconſiderable part of the buſineſs tranſacted in the Alley, where bargains for time, or ſpeculations on the judgment of individuals, reſpecting the riſe or fall of the funds, have formed a vaſt and intricate maze of gambling. In proportion as money is ſcarce or abundant, public confidence elevated or depreſſed, the price of the funds is increaſed or lowered: in peace it is far from ſtationary, but in war, it is

 ſubject

ſubject to continual fluctuation, dependent on every demand of government for money, every article of intelligence received or expected. This uncertainty preſenting to ſome the opportunity of gaining advantage, by the imprudences into which hope or fear immoderately entertained will lead others, has generated a traffic carried on daily to an incredible extent, called *Stock Jobbing*. It were uſeleſs to deſcribe the riſe and progreſs of this ſpecies of gambling, or to recite the many reflections which the ruin of numerous individuals and families has occaſioned: the legiſlature has done its part towards ſuppreſſing it, by a ſtatute 7 Geo. II. c. 8. intitled, "An act to prevent the infamous practice of ſtock jobbing;" but when perſonal intereſt and an opinion of ſuperior penetration combine to favour any ſpecies of adventure, and when the moſt opulent and reſpectable members of the community are known to embark in it with avidity, the reſtraints of law are interpoſed in vain; no diſgrace attends thoſe who are known to be in the daily habit of infringing this ſtatute; but a man who avails himſelf of its proviſoes to cancel a debt which he has incurred in the alley, is generally deteſted and deſpiſed. Some terms are uſed in deſcribing the different claſſes of adventurers in the alley, which it may be proper here to explain. He who buys any portion of government ſecurities in the way of ſpeculation, and without any intention to pay for it, but only to pay or receive the difference of price, at a certain fixed time called the *ſettling day*; or he who holds a larger portion of ſcrip than he can retain, is called *a Bull*. He who, on the contrary, has agreed to ſell a large portion of ſtock which he does not poſſeſs, at a certain day and price, is called *a Bear*. Both theſe perſons deal for many thouſand pounds in ſtock, beyond any capital they are ſuppoſed to poſſeſs, becauſe the terms of their bargains always are ſuch that the difference between the market price on the ſettling day, and the price at which they have agreed to buy or ſell, being paid, the other party to the contract has all the benefit he can expect. A bull is always anxious to hear and propagate ſuch news as will keep up the ſpirits of the nation, and cauſe the funds to produce a high price: while the bear derives his beſt hope from public diſaſter, and would be completely enriched by events which ſhould occaſion national deſpondency. Thoſe who through diſhoneſty will not, or through poverty cannot, make good the engagements they have formed in the alley, are ſtigmatized by the name of *Lame Ducks*, and, by a recent regulation, their names are exhibited on a black board as a perpetual caution to others to avoid all tranſactions with them.

TAXES. The taxes by which money is raifed to pay the intereft of the national debt already mentioned, and to fupply the exigencies of the ftate, are divided into two general claffes; temporary and permanent.

TEMPORARY. The temporary taxes are thofe on land and malt: the former indeed, fince the act for its redemption, may with greater propriety be confidered as permanent; but as it ftill is, in refpect to public offices, and penfions, temporary, it is continued in its old fituation.

LAND TAX. The land tax originated in thofe monthly affeffments, which were impofed in the time of the commonwealth, and were occafionally levied in the reign of Charles II.; it has been affeffed without intermiffion, fince the reign of William III. It was at firft intended as a rate on every fpecies of income or property, and in that fenfe was originally, and ftill continues to be laid, on the profits of public offices and on penfions. The affeffment was framed in the year 1692, when a new valuation of eftates was made throughout the kingdom: which, though by no means a perfect one, had this effect, that a fupply of rather lefs than 500,000*l.* was equal to one fhilling in the pound, of the value of the eftates given in. This tax, though annually voted, was never afterward entirely remitted; it was fometimes moderated to three fhillings; fometimes to two; and in 1732 and 1733, to one fhilling in the pound; but by the ftatute 38 Geo. III. it was, for the fake of being redeemed, rendered perpetual, and ftill adhering to the valuation formerly made, eftimated at 2,037,627*l.* 9*s.*, of which 47,954*l.* 1*s.* 2*d.* is the portion raifed in Scotland.

COMMISSIONERS. The method of levying this tax, is by charging a particular fum on each county, according to the valuation made in 1692: and this fum is affeffed and raifed on individuals (their perfonal eftates, as well as real, being liable) by commiffioners, who are annually renewed, and who cannot execute the office in any county, except thofe in Wales, under a penalty of 50*l.*, unlefs they have fome eftate or intereft in land within the county, of the clear yearly value of 100*l.*, and which was taxed for that fum at leaft a year before. This reftraint does not extend to commiffioners being inhabitants of cities, boroughs, towns corporate, or cinque-ports, or the Inns of Court or Chancery. The commiffioners are obliged to hold their meetings at the accuftomed place in each county, where they fubdivide themfelves, appointing three for each divifion, and nominating clerks, affeffors, collectors and other fubordinate officers; they alfo fign the affeffment and warrant to collect it; parties confidering themfelves aggrieved may appeal, but to the commiſſioners alone, and their deciſion is final. From this rule there is one exception, as it relates to the voting for knights of the ſhire. In order to exerciſe this franchiſe, it is neceſſary that the party ſhall be aſſeſſed to the land tax in his own name, or that of his tenant. If the aſſeſſor has neglected to aſſeſs him, he may prefer his claim to the commiſſioners, and if diſſatisfied with their deciſion, he may, on giving ten days notice, appeal to the juſtices at the next ſeſſions.

Officers. *A Receiver General* for each county is appointed by the king, and due notice given to the commiſſioners; and he, giving the like notice, may appoint a deputy: he is paid from the treaſury, a ſalary not exceeding two-pence in the pound on the monies collected.

Aſſeſſors are appointed by precept, under the hands of two or more commiſſioners, at their firſt meeting, directed to ſuch inhabitants, conſtables, or other officers as they think fit; and at their ſecond meeting, they deliver to each aſſeſſor a printed form of aſſeſſment, together with a charge, how and in what manner they ought to proceed in the execution of their duty; and the perſons nominated in the precepts to be aſſeſſors, not appearing when ſummoned, or refuſing to act, forfeit to the king, a ſum not exceeding 5*l*., nor leſs than forty ſhillings.

Collectors are appointed by warrants, under the hands of the commiſſioners; they have power to demand the ſums aſſeſſed, of the parties on the premiſes, or at their laſt place of abode; they may levy a diſtreſs on refuſal to pay, without any further warrant than that of their appointment, and may break open doors, in the day time, and cheſts wherein any goods or effects are ſecreted. The collector pays the money as it comes to his hands, to the receiver general, deducting from his laſt payment, three-pence in the pound as a compenſation for his trouble. For the faithful performance of their duty, the commiſſioners may oblige the collectors to give ſecurity to the full amount of the rate, in their reſpective diſtricts; and they, and all other officers, neglecting their duty, are liable to a fine of forty pounds, to be impoſed by the commiſſioners, and not remitted, but by the majority of thoſe who inflicted it.

Clerks are alſo appointed by the commiſſioners in every diviſion, who receive a compenſation not exceeding three-halfpence in the pound.

Deductions. The expence of all theſe officers for England, is 53,574*l*.; the portion of Scotland is paid into the Exchequer free of all charges. There is alſo a deduction of about 1200*l*. from the receivers in Wales, who complain of great difficulty in remitting the money to London. Before the land

land tax is paid into the Exchequer, a further defalcation is made for the expence of the militia, the apprehending of deserters from the army, and the bounties granted by ſtatute 21 Geo. III. c. 58, for encouraging the growth of hemp and flax; theſe together are calculated at 130,000*l*.

REDEMPTION OF THE LAND TAX. It has already been ſaid that the act for redeeming this aſſeſſment, occaſioned its being changed from a temporary to a permanent impoſition. The plan was firſt recommended to government, as it is ſaid, in an anonymous pamphlet; and at a period of the French revolutionary war, when the ſtocks were exceedingly depreſſed, the miniſter brought forward a plan for enabling perſons by paying certain ſums of money, to be laid out in ſtock, for the benefit of the public, to diſcharge their eſtates from all aſſeſſments then impoſed. As the neceſſity of laying an annual land tax was conſidered one of the great ſecurities for frequent meetings of parliament, the new duties on malt, ſugar, tobacco and ſnuff, which before were perpetual, and which greatly exceeded the amount of the land tax, were rendered temporary. The miniſter hoped to relieve the nation from the burthen of ſtock to the amount of 66,666,666*l*., but in five years after the paſſing of his firſt act, which was very voluminous, and explained or amended by eight additional acts, no more than 19,180,587*l*. had been redeemed, and ſome are of opinion that there is no proſpect of any great addition.

MALT TAX. The revolution had taken place ſome time, and the public had experienced the greateſt difficulties in raiſing the ſupplies, before parliament could be prevailed on to impoſe a duty on malt, together with a proportionable rate on cyder, perry, and other liquors, the uſe of which might diminiſh the conſumption of that article. It was firſt granted in 1697, and it was always ſuppoſed would be only a temporary impoſt. By the treaty of union with Scotland, it was agreed, that during the continuance of the duty on malt, which then exiſted in England, (but which expired on the 4th June 1707,) Scotland ſhould not be charged with it. Indeed that country was not included in the malt act, until the year 1713, and even then it was thought adviſable for government to aſſume a ſort of diſpenſing power, and to give directions that it ſhould not be levied. Nay, the Scots were ſo impreſſed with an idea, that they were in a manner for ever exempted from ſuch a duty, by the treaty of union, that in 1725, when the tax was firſt enforced in that country, it occaſioned conſiderable riots which were with difficulty ſuppreſſed.

The income of this tax for England alone, excluſively of Scotland, at the rate of ſixpence per buſhel, was originally calculated at 750,000*l.* a year, a ſum which was far from being exaggerated; for on the average of eight years, ending Midſummer 1724, it produced at the rate of 755,000*l.* per annum. It fell off, however, during the American war; and its amount during the year, ending 5th January, 1803, deducting the expences of management and collection, was only 702,893*l.*

Perpetual Taxes. For ſome years after the revolution, duties were only granted till the money borrowed on the faith of them ſhould be paid off; but about the year 1710, they began to be impoſed in perpetuity; to defray the intereſt of debts and the ſurplus to be at the diſpoſal of parliament. Theſe permanent taxes are divided into cuſtoms, exciſe, ſtamps, and miſcellaneous.

Customs. The cuſtoms are the duties, toll, tribute, or tariff, payable on merchandizes, exported and imported. The original grounds of this impoſition were; the licence which the king gave the ſubject to depart the realm, and carry his goods with him; and the obligation which, of common right, reſted on the king, to maintain and keep up the ports and havens, and protect the merchants from pirates; to theſe is added a third cauſe, the permiſſion given to foreign merchants to trade in the king's dominions. The cuſtoms on imported goods are very extenſive, including a vaſt variety of articles, from the moſt precious to the moſt minute which can be an object of commerce. To theſe there can be no reaſonable objection in general; the modification moſt to be deſired is that which ſhould exempt, or but ſlightly affect raw materials, while certain manufactured articles, and the luxuries drawn from the ſtates or colonies of foreigners, ſhould, unleſs protected by a commercial treaty affording reciprocal advantages, be aſſeſſed ſo highly as to become almoſt prohibited. The duties on exports muſt be regulated by the wants, or the liberality of foreign purchaſers, and the probability of rivals in their markets. If the goods to be exported, will, after all expences paid, produce to the ſeller a certain advance, there is no reaſon why the government ſhould not ſhare, and largely too, in the profit which ariſes from the induſtry and enterprize of its own ſubjects. If materials are exported raw, the duties are ſtill higher, and juſtly too, ſince from them the ſubjects of a foreign ſtate are to derive ſupport and an exerciſe for their induſtry. On this account raw articles, as lead, tin, and alum, or ſuch as are incapable of being manufactured, as coals, are loaded with heavy duties, and the exportation of wool is prohibited altogether. But, as in certain manufactured articles, the probability of rivalſhip, or the impoſſibility of obtaining more than a ſtated price, would render the ſale difficult in foreign countries, if the duties impoſed on home conſumption were

were continued, a rebate or deduction of duty is made, under the name of a drawback. Besides the duties on imports and exports, there are some on goods carried coast-ways, the policy of which is questionable; and a new, important, and judicious duty on ships arriving in British ports, called tonnage.

The Bonding System. A great objection to the system of customs in general was, the necessity it imposed on merchants of paying in advance large sums of money for duties, obliging them to confine their trade, or borrow, at a disadvantage, monies which they frequently could not obtain again from the consumer. These inconveniences, and the remedy for them were in the contemplation of Sir Robert Walpole, who had projected a plan for receiving the goods of merchants into warehouses, under the joint custody of the proprietor and of government, and not demanding the payment of duty till a sale was effected. This simple and rational plan was at that day prevented from taking effect by the prevalence of party, but in a more happy period it was re-introduced to the notice of parliament by Mr. Pitt, and carried into practice by his successor, Mr. Addington. If the plan is capable of extension, no means for attaining that end ought to be omitted; since it contains within itself every possible recommendation; it is equally beneficial to the state, to the merchant, and the consumer, and obviates at once the inconveniences and frauds attending the allowance of drawbacks. By the act which establishes this system, (43 Geo. III. c. 132.) goods may be landed and warehoused as follows: at the Isle of Dogs, in warehouses belonging to the West India Dock Company, without payment of customs, and on bond to the excise for the duties payable to that part of the revenue, certain specified articles, containing in gross, the whole produce of the West India Colonies; at the London Docks, the following articles, not being the produce either of the East or West Indies: rice, tobacco, wine, brandy, geneva, and other spirits; at places to be approved by the commissioners of the customs, and on bond with one sufficient surety, a great number of other articles, including most of the materials for ship-building, cork, brimstone, kelp, mahogany, skins, tallow, and oil; and in warehouses to be approved by the lords of the treasury, a long list of articles, too numerous to specify. The lords of the treasury, or the privy council, may also at any time add to the articles by publication in the London Gazette, and the like privileges may be extended to other ports in Great Britain, which from the nature and extent of the trade there carried on, the convenience of the situation, and the security of the revenue by the construction of docks and warehouses, properly adapted for the reception and safe custody of goods, may be entitled

titled to it. This act, it is justly observed, grants facility to the British merchants, and will convince those of foreign countries, that they may send their property to this island, either for security or a market, without restraint, or incurring other than ordinary charges; on the whole, it is similar to, or on the footing of, a free port, but superior to some, since there is no *ad valorem* duty paid.

CONSOLIDATION OF DUTIES. Another great improvement in the customs ought not to be unnoticed, it is the consolidation, or simplification of the duties, effected by Mr. Pitt in 1787. It would at first sight appear almost incredible, to what an extent the numerous rates imposed on different articles had proceeded, how complicated, how embarrassed with fractions, and subject to disputes almost every part of this revenue was become, from the accumulation of duties laid at different periods, and in various proportions. The subject had not escaped the attention of Lord North, but the weighty cares of his administration, and the perpetual opposition with which he was harassed, prevented him from paying the attention it required. Mr. Pitt brought forward, in time of peace, a series of regulations for removing this evil, which were included in three thousand separate resolutions; but so well and so effectually arranged, as to gain for the minister the cordial support, and warm eulogy of the most vehement opponents of his other measures. The system thus ably and auspiciously begun was brought to perfection by a general act, 43 Geo. III. c. 68.

CUSTOM HOUSE. Until the reign of Queen Elizabeth, great frauds were practised in this department of the revenue by the introduction and export of goods from small and obscure creeks or places where no custom house officer was attending, or by the corruption of those officers, or by other fraudulent and undue practices. In the first year of this illustrious princess, an act passed prohibiting the landing of any goods, except at such places as she by commission should appoint. In pursuance of this statute the lord treasurer, under treasurer, and chancellor of the exchequer, published her pleasure with respect to divers ports of the kingdom, and for London they drew up a declaration, determining what particular quays, wharfs, and stairs should be allowed for landing and discharging all manner of merchandizes, and made other regulations for securing the payment of duties. In the neighbourhood of these wharfs, on the south side and not far from the east end of Thames-street, a custom house had been erected as early as the year 1385, by John Churchman, sheriff of London; but its benefits were superseded by the irregular manner in which those duties had hitherto been paid. The advantage of the plan adopted by Elizabeth,

Elizabeth, was ſpeedily manifeſted in the augmentation of revenue, which in her reign advanced from 14,000*l.* to 50,000*l.* a year. She cauſed a new cuſtom houſe to be built on the former ſpot, which being conſumed by the fire in 1666, and that erected in its ſtead being deſtroyed by the ſame calamity in 1718, a new one was founded, which ſtill ſubſiſts. Of the building it is unneceſſary to ſpeak, convenience is its ſole recommendation; it is well ſituated for buſineſs, as before it, ſhips of three hundred and fifty tons can lie and diſcharge their freights. The buſineſs of the cuſtoms is principally tranſacted in the apartment called the *Long Room*, where numerous perſons are employed in receiving the proper payments and ſecurities, adminiſtering the oaths required by the revenue laws, and making out the various papers and certificates requiſite for the ſafety both of the public rights, and the property of individuals.

It will not be poſſible in this work to enumerate the various kinds of goods ſubjected to the cuſtoms, but a general outline of the manner in which the buſineſs is tranſacted, may be conſidered as poſſeſſing ſome utility and intereſt.

Entering Goods on Importation. When foreign goods are imported, the maſter of the veſſel, on his arrival, muſt go to the cuſtom houſe and report his cargo on oath. The merchant may enter and land his goods at any time within twenty days from the date of the maſter's report: to do which in the moſt advantageous manner, he muſt write and ſign five bills of entry, one muſt be in words at length, and is called the *warrant*, the other four may be in figures. Theſe five bills the merchant delivers to the collector, or his clerk, who aſcertains the duties, which muſt be diſcharged, or a bond entered into for the payment on delivery from the public warehouſes, before the goods can be landed. Theſe requiſites being complied with, the warrant is duly perfected, ſigned, and delivered to the land waiters appointed to attend the delivery, together with blue books, wherein an account of the delivery is to be entered. The goods are then landed, examined, and the quantities taken. If the merchant is found to have entered leſs than the quantity conſigned to him, he muſt paſs *poſt entries*, and pay the duties for the goods ſhort entered, in the ſame manner as was obſerved in paſſing the *prime entries;* but if, on delivery, an over entry appears, he may apply to the collector to have his entries altered, and the overplus duly repaid; which may be done, if he applies, before the collector and comptroller have poſted the entry in the king's books, upon his making ſatisfactory proof that no fraud was committed: but, if the entry be poſted before he applies, then the duty muſt

muſt be repaid by certificate of over entry. It ſometimes happens, that goods are ſent by merchants to ſell by commiſſion, and arrive before the invoice. In this, and ſimilar caſes, when the merchant cannot make any tolerable conjecture at the quantities, and perhaps knows not the ſpecies, or proper denomination of the goods, the law permits them to be landed by *bills of ſight* or *view*. The merchant makes a depoſit in the hands of the collector, of as much money as the duties are imagined to amount to, or rather more, then the bill of ſight is made out, and given to the proper officers; who muſt examine and take the quantity of the goods, and make their report to the collector the next day, or render themſelves liable to the penalty of one hundred pounds in caſe of failure. According to the report the entries are paſſed, and the duties paid, in the ſame manner as they would have been, had there been no occaſion for a bill of ſight. If the officers cannot go through the examination in one day, they muſt report their day's work to the collector, as being in part of the ſight; for which the merchant muſt paſs entries, and pay duty, and ſo proceed till the whole bill of ſight is completed. Goods not rated in the book of rates are often imported, in which caſe, the duties are to be charged according to the value of the goods upon oath, by which value is to be underſtood the value at the port of importation at that time, excluſive of the duty. The merchant is to obſerve, that if he undervalues his goods, the law empowers the officers to take and ſell them; and, after repaying him the duties, according to the value he ſat upon them, together with the ſaid value, and alſo ten per cent. thereon, the ſurplus, if any, is to be confiſcated to government.

The proceſs on board the ſhip, and on the quays is as follows: the tideſmen on board the ſhip, keep a tally account of the delivery in blue books; the land waiters on the quays, under the inſpection of the land ſurveyors, enter in their blue books not only the number and quality, but alſo the quantity of the goods delivered. The deſign of the delivery is to aſcertain the quality and quantity of the goods, which is chiefly incumbent on the land waiters; who are to take care that the goods delivered agree in theſe particulars with the entry. The qualities of goods are always known to the merchants; the officers in determining them, muſt rely on experience, and the deſcriptions in the books of rates. The quantities are to be determined either by number, weight, or meaſure, according as the goods are rated in the book of rates. To enable either merchants or officers to do this, they ſhould be well ſkilled in arithmetic, gauging, and menſuration. If it appears, on delivery, that goods

goods have received damage, the furveyor and land waiters make their report on the back of the warrant, and return it to the collector and principal officers; who chufe two indifferent and experienced merchants to view the goods, and upon oath to determine the quantum of the damage. Then the furveyor and land waiters, certifying that the goods viewed by the merchants are the fame for which duty was paid; a certificate of the whole proceeding is made out, and a proportional reftitution of duty is made to the merchant. If, on delivery of foreign goods, it appears that the merchant, through inadvertency or miftake, has entered and paid duty for a greater quantity than is really imported and delivered, the furveyor and land waiters muft certify the cafe on the warrant, and return it to the collector and principal officers; who thereupon call on the merchant, or his known agent, to ftate on oath the quantity received, and alfo the reafon of the over entry; and the truth being confirmed by the certificate of the delivering officers, the duty for the quantity over entered is repaid. If the goods imported are entitled to a premium after entry and delivery, the officers will examine whether they are cleanfed and garbled from all dirt, drofs, &c., and in good merchantable condition, and have all the other qualifications required by law. Then the true quantities, qualities, circumftances of importation, &c. are certified at large, by the proper officers, and the certificate delivered to the importer, who, producing it to the commiffioners, or proper officers, receives the premium. Portage is an allowance, or premium to mafters of fhips, for making a true report of their cargoes. To obtain it, as foon as the cargo is delivered, and the duties all paid, the mafter muft apply to the land furveyor, who will give him a certificate, that he has made a true report, and is duly intitled to portage; wherein will be alfo expreffed the amount of the branches of duty for the whole cargo, out of which portage is payable. This certificate the mafter carries to the collector and comptroller, who examine it, and compute the amount of the portage: then a portage bill is made out and figned, and the money is paid according to eftablifhed rates.

Drawbacks. If foreign goods and merchandizes be exported within three years from the importation, reckoning from the time of the mafter's report, the greateft part of the duties firft paid are drawn back. The manner of proceeding at the cuftom houfe in this cafe is, that a certificate muft be obtained of the payment of the duties inwards, from the collector and comptroller; and proof is to be made, that the goods to be exported are thofe mentioned in the certificate, by the oaths of the exporter, and the merchants through whofe hands they have

have paſſed. The exporter then enters the goods outwards, as in the common way of exportation. The cocket granted upon this occaſion is called a certificate cocket, and differs a little in form from common over ſea cockets. Notice of the time of ſhipping is to be given to the ſearcher, who attends the ſhipping, examines and aſcertains the quantity, and returns the cocket endorſed, to the officers who granted it: all other proceedings at clearing the veſſel are the ſame as in ordinary caſes. Some time after the departure of the veſſel, the merchant exporter may apply to the collector and comptroller for the drawback, who will thereupon make out a debenture, on a proper ſtamp, containing a diſtinct and clear narrative of the whole proceeding, with the merchant's oath, that the goods are really and truly exported to parts beyond the ſeas, and not re-landed, nor intended to be re-landed, or brought on ſhore again; and alſo the ſearcher's certificate of the quality and quantity of the goods, and the time of ſhipping underwritten. The debenture being thus duly made out, and ſworn to, the branches of duty to be repaid are indorſed, the merchant's receipt taken below, and the money due paid. Much of this buſineſs is rendered unneceſſary, as already has been ſtated, by the bonding ſyſtem.

Exportation. When it is intended to export goods, four bills of entry are written and delivered at the cuſtom houſe to the collector or his clerk, by whom the duties are calculated and received. On payment, a cocket, certifying the payment of the duty or regular entry of the goods, is made out, which, before they are ſhipped, the exporter delivers to the ſearcher, with notice of the time when they are to be embarked. The ſearcher will attend and examine, and count, weigh, or meaſure the goods; which done, they are put on board, and the ſearcher certifies the quantity ſhipped on the back of the cocket, which is then returned to the principal officers, with whom it remains till the maſter comes to clear. When the maſter comes, the cockets for all the goods on board are collected, and entered in what is called a report outwards, on the maſter's declaring the ſaid cockets to contain a true account of his whole cargo. To this report the maſter makes oath before the collector and comptroller, pays his clearing charge, his cockets are delivered, and he is at liberty to proceed on his voyage. When goods intitled to bounty are exported, the merchant (after entering them, and taking out a cocket as before directed) is to give bond for the exportation; and the officers ought to be more than ordinarily careful, and exact in taking the quantities, and examining whether the goods have all the legal requiſites to entitle them to bounty. When the ſhip is ſailed and clear of the coaſt, the exporter may apply to the collector and comptroller for the debenture; which being duly ſigned, the bounty will be paid him immediately at the port, if there is money on the proper branches, but if not, the debenture will be delivered to him, and he muſt apply for payment in London. Theſe are the principal circumſtances neceſſary to be obſerved on theſe points; they are ſubject to ſome local and occaſional variations, as in ſhipping coals, and ſometimes corn, malt, or flour; but theſe are too minute and practical to be here detailed.

MEDITERRANEAN PASSES. Ships trading to the Mediterranean, muſt be provided with peculiar paſſes from the admiralty. The ſteps neceſſary to be taken for obtaining them are theſe: the ſurveyor of the port where the ſhip lies muſt go on board, and examine and ſurvey her, and muſter the ſeamen; then he is obliged to certify under his hand, to the collector of the port, the burden and building of the veſſel, the number of men, diſtinguiſhing natives and foreigners, the number of guns, what ſort of veſſel ſhe is, and other particulars. The collector, having received this, prepares an affidavit, to be ſigned and ſworn to by the maſter, which contains all the foregoing particulars, and likewiſe the name of the veſſel, maſter, and port bound to, the time when, and place where ſhe was built; to which is added, that ſhe is of Britiſh property; that her laſt paſs was delivered up; and that the maſter has delivered up all the paſſes he ever had before. This affidavit is tranſmitted to the ſecretary of the admiralty, who thereupon ſends down a paſs, and a bond for delivering it up, after the voyage is performed. The bond, being duly executed, is returned to the admiralty, and the paſs is delivered to the maſter.

Ships are not permitted to trade to the Britiſh plantations, or colonies, until proof be made upon oath, by one or more of the owners, that ſhe is Britiſh built, and Britiſh property, and the maſter, and at leaſt three fourths of the mariners, Britiſh; and that no foreigner, directly or indirectly, has any intereſt therein. After this the ſhip is regiſtered, and a certificate delivered to the maſter. Bond is alſo given, with one ſufficient ſecurity, in the penalty of 1000*l.* if the veſſel be under 100 tons; or in 2000*l.* if above that burden; that, if any of the goods of the produce of the ſaid plantations, enumerated in ſeveral acts of parliament, be taken on board, they ſhall be brought by the ſaid ſhip to Great Britain, and there landed. This bond may be given either in Great Britain, or in the plantations, and a certificate of the delivery muſt be produced in eighteen months from the date of the bond.

OFFENCES. The laws for impoſing cuſtoms are frequently evaded, both by fraud in the poſſeſſors of merchandizes which are the objects of them, and by activity and violence in contraband dealers, commonly called *ſmugglers*. In fact, the temptation

tation to commit these frauds is almost irresistible: the high duties tempt many persons to adventure the seizure of their goods, as in a game of chance, against the probability of securing them and evading the payment of a heavy impost. Those who reside near the coasts are frequently supplied with these articles, which are delivered to them in small quantities, and almost without danger; and their success inspires others with an inclination to enjoy the same benefits. But it happens in this, as in every other traffic, that where extensive supplies are required, large capital and an accumulated stock become necessary; numbers being engaged, and the defence of property strongly incited, affrays and murders frequently ensue; and it would become all those who by any encouragement to illicit traffic have gratified their avarice or parsimony, to reflect, when they hear of the blood which in these contests is so frequently shed, whether they can, in conscience, stand intirely acquitted of being accessaries. Against every fraud which the ingenuity of the exporter or importer can devise for evading the revenue laws, provision has been made, by the requisition of oaths, which are perhaps taken too frequently to produce the desired effect; by penalties and forfeitures of great severity, which lay the delinquent at the mercy of any one who can detect him in his illicit practices; and by the appointment of numerous officers in every department, whose industry is guided by experience, and excited by the certainty of sharing in the property confiscated, or the penalties recovered by their means. Against smugglers too, and their abettors, the laws are justly severe, ascending, according to the circumstances of offence and resistance, from forfeiture and penalty, to transportation and death. It is also to be observed that the offences amounting to felony, may be tried at the discretion of the attorney-general in any county in England; and that if any officer or other person employed in the service of the revenue, is beaten, wounded, maimed, or killed, or the goods seized by him are rescued, the inhabitants of the rape, lathe, or hundred, unless the offender is convicted within six months, forfeit one hundred pounds to the executors or administrators of any officer, who is killed, and pay damages to any officer beaten, maimed or wounded, not exceeding forty pounds, and for any goods rescued, not exceeding two hundred pounds. A reward of five hundred pounds is given for apprehending any offender; a person wounded in apprehending him to have fifty pounds extraordinary.

OFFICERS. The duties of this extensive portion of the revenue are performed by a great variety of officers, placed, not only at the custom-house in Thames-Street, but in all the ports

ports in the kingdom, and its dependencies: To describe or even to enumerate them all would require a large treatise, the most considerable are the following:

COMMISSIONERS. To the commissioners, the general controul and management of the business at the custom-house is assigned. They are appointed, as their title imports, by commission under the great seal; are nine in number, and have for salary 1200*l.* a-year each. When a commission is issued, the two first named are sworn before the chancellor, or chief baron of the exchequer, or master of the rolls, for the true and faithful execution, to the best of their knowledge and power, of the trust committed to their charge and inspection, and that they will not take or receive any reward or gratuity, directly or indirectly, other than their salaries, and what shall be allowed them from the crown, or the regular fees established by law, for any service to be done, in the execution of their employment in the customs, on any account whatever. All the other commissioners take the same oath before the first two, and then any two of them can administer those which are required to all the subordinate officers in London: those in the country take the oaths before two justices of the peace; and in all cases a certificate is sent to the next sessions to be inrolled of record. These commissioners form what is termed the Board, to give directions in doubtful cases, carry into effect the orders of the treasury board with respect to the revenue, and to hear appeals and grant relief to individuals according to circumstances. They have a secretary, whose annual salary is 710*l.* with various clerks and other officers.

CASHIERS, PAYMASTERS AND COMPTROLLERS. These form a separate office in the customs, consisting of many persons, whose business is indicated by the name of their employments. The receiver and comptroller general have each a salary of 1000*l.*, and the rest are paid, some by salaries, others by fees.

In all other branches of the business, and on the wharfs, numerous officers are employed.

LAW OFFICERS. There are solicitors for managing the business arising out of various departments of this extensive branch of revenue, who have annual salaries exclusive of their fees.

The remaining officers, of whom some are employed both in the metropolis and the country, and others in the country only, may be comprized under the following heads.

SEARCHERS. It is the duty of searchers to see that no goods are imported or exported without payment of duty; they also keep entries of all cockets, &c. passed to them, and likewise of their own seizures, and account yearly for the truth of their transactions. The searcher of every head port, must have one able and sufficient deputy or servant at the least, to reside at all members and creeks, appointed by commissions out of the court of exchequer, for passing, shipping, clearing, &c. of ships and merchandizes.

SURVEYORS. The surveyors are a kind of inspectors and supervisors of the whole business of the customs without doors, as well by land as by water; they attend, at shipping and landing of goods, to and from foreign parts, and coastwise, to see that the proper officers regularly discharge their respective duties, and to adjust the tares of goods, &c. and they make, attest, and transmit proper accounts and certificates.

LAND-WAITERS. These persons attend at the landing of imported goods; they assist the searchers in the execution of all cockets for the shipping of goods to be exported: and in all cases where drawbacks or bounties are to be paid on exportation, they certify the shipping thereof on the debentures.

COAST-WAITERS. The coast-waiters, at their respective ports, are to attend at the landing and shipping of all goods coming from, or going to any other port within Great Britain, to take an account thereof, and see that they exactly agree in quality and quantity, with the sufferances granted for the landing or shipping; so that, under the colour of bringing or sending one sort of goods coastwise, others may not be fraudulently imported or exported.

TIDE-SURVEYORS. These persons are at all times, when his majesty's service requires it, to attend by water, to visit all ships from foreign parts, on their arrival into port, in order to put tide-waiters on board, and also in outward-bound ships which have goods on board intitled to a drawback or bounty; to see that they do their duty, and remove them when their presence is no longer necessary.

TIDE-WAITERS OR TIDESMEN. These officers are placed by the tide-surveyors, on board all ships laden with goods from foreign parts, to prevent the fraudulent landing or conveying of them away without payment of duties, which is to be signified to them by a note under the land-waiter's hands: and, when they have received such note, order, or warrant, from the land-waiters, for permitting any goods to be unladen, they are to take an account of the marks, numbers, and outward package, in a book to be given them for that purpose: but they may send all small parcels of goods liable to be carried away to the king's warehouse, for security of the duties, without any order, having first entered them in the said books. And during the time they are on board, they are to prevent wines from being filled up, or the package of any goods opened, and endeavour

to

to discover all goods concealed, as likewise any bulk tobacco, or other prohibited goods, and to seize the same. They are likewise to be placed on board outward-bound ships, whereon there have been laden any goods intitled to a drawback or bounty on exportation, to prevent the fraudulent relanding; and during the time they continue on board, they are to take care that the packages of any goods be not altered.

Boatmen or Watermen. In some ports, these persons are appointed only to row and attend the tide surveyor's boats; but in most ports they likewise, when occasion requires, officiate as tide-waiters.

Coal Meters. The duty of coal meters is, to attend at the delivery of all ships coming coastwise with coals, culm, or cinders; to mete, measure, or weigh the same, and take account of the full quantities delivered, in order that the duties may be paid.

Riding Officers. These persons are appointed to reside at, or near, some particular places on the sea coasts, and have certain districts allotted them, some part whereof they are to visit daily, in order to discover any vessels hovering on the coasts, with a design to land or take on board any prohibited or uncustomed goods, which they must by all means endeavour to prevent; and in case of the fraudulent landing or shipping of any goods, to seize the same, with the vessels, boats, &c. They are to enter each day's transactions and proceedings, with their motions from place to place, in a proper book to be kept for that purpose; whence at the end of each month, two journals are to be transcribed, and sent or delivered to the collector; one whereof to be preserved in the office, and the other to be transmitted to the commissioners, in order to be examined by the person appointed for that purpose. But, before these journals are thus transmitted, the collector is, on the back thereof, to make his observations how far the officers have performed their duty.

Masters of Revenue Cutters. These are commanders of vessels appointed to cruize on the coasts of Great Britain, and are diligently to attend on board, and to keep their vessels in constant motion within their respective districts or stations, unless in cases of necessity or pursuit of suspected vessels: and, in cruizing, they are to speak with all the ships or vessels they meet at sea; and, if they have any reason to suspect they have goods on board designed to be smuggled, they are diligently to watch their motions, and keep them company till they are clear of the coast within their respective districts, in order to prevent the fraudulent landing of any such goods, and they are likewise to endeavour to prevent the exportation of prohibited goods of this kingdom; and, in case they discover any such to have been shipped, or shipping for foreign parts, they are to seize the same, with the vessels, &c. For the due navigation of each of these vessels, there are appointed, beside the master, a mate, and a sufficient number of mariners, who are to be under the direction of the masters. They keep journals of their transactions, with their motions from place to place, to be delivered monthly to the collectors of their respective ports, in order to be transmitted to the commissioners. And by way of distinction, all smacks, yachts, or vessels, employed in the service of the customs, are to wear a jack and ensign, with the seal of office thereon, the mark on the ensign being twice as large as that in the jack; but not to wear a pendant.

All these persons have moderate salaries, or fees of small amount, in compensation for constant and frequently very laborious and dangerous service.

Expence. The expence of collecting this revenue is estimated at *5l. 12s. 4d.* per cent.

Excise. The next branch of permanent revenue to be considered is the excise, which is an inland imposition, paid sometimes on the consumption of the commodity, or frequently on the retail sale, which is the last stage before consumption. This is doubtless, impartially speaking, the most economical way of taxing the subject: the charges of levying, collecting, and managing the excise duties, being considerably less in proportion than in other branches of the revenue. It also renders the commodity cheaper to the consumer, than charging it with customs to the same amount would do; because generally paid in a much later stage of it; but, at the same time, the rigour and arbitrary proceedings under the excise laws, seem hardly compatible with the temper of a free nation. The frauds which might be committed in this branch of the revenue, unless a strict watch is kept, make it necessary, wherever it is established, to give the officers a power of entering and searching the houses of such as deal in exciseable commodities, at any hour of the day, and, in many cases, of the night; and the proceedings in case of transgressions are so summary and sudden, that a man may be convicted in two days time, in the penalty of many thousand pounds by two commissioners or justices of the peace; to the total exclusion of the trial by jury, and disregard of the common law. The time when the excise was first imposed has already been mentioned; it was projected during the reign of Charles I., but never assessed in a regular way till after his death; but the rebels and the royalists both had recourse to it as an expedient, though under an express protestation that it should be discontinued when the public peace was restored. Experience however proved it to be too valuable to resign, and before

before the republican government was abolished, the champions of liberty pronounced it, "the most easy and indifferent "levy that could be laid on the people." From that period it has never been remitted, but numerous articles have been brought within its sphere.

The objects of the excise laws are enumerated under the following heads: 1. Ale, beer, cyder, perry, mum, metheglin, and mead. 2. Things sold by auction. 3. Bricks and tiles. 4. Candles. 5. Coaches and coachmakers. 6. Coffee, tea, chocolate, and cocoa nuts. 7. Glass. 8. Hops. 9. Leather. 10. Linen cloth, silks, cottons, and callicoes. 11. Malt. 12. Paper. 13. Plate. 14. Salt. 15. Soap. 16. Spirituous liquors. 17. Starch, hair powder, and stone blue. 18. Sweets. 19. Tobacco and snuff. 20 Vinegar, and verjuice. 21. Wine. 22. Wire. It were too much to recapitulate, even in the most compendious abstract, the regulations affecting all these articles; they form the basis of many laws which are collected, apart from the general statutes, and sold for the information of the public; and a good practical abstract of them is found in Burn's Justice.

Office. By the statutes for establishing the excise, it is ordered that one principal head office shall be kept in London; that all places within the bills of mortality shall be under its immediate care and management, and all other offices in the kingdom subordinate and accountable to it. This office was formerly established in the Old Jewry, but afterward removed to the south side of Broad-Street, where a commodious and magnificent building has been erected for the purpose, on the site formerly occupied by Gresham College.

Commissioners. The commissioners of excise are nine in number, having each a salary of 1000*l*. The duties of their office are analogous to those of commissioners of the customs.

Other Officers. There is in the head office in its various departments, a great number of officers with different duties and salaries. The secretary has 825*l*.; the registrar 450*l*.; there are five commissioners of appeals; and examiners and other officers appointed to the superintendance of each branch of the revenue. The auditor has a salary of 1240*l*.; the comptroller general of 3290*l*., and various others are liberally paid.

For transaction of business in the country, the commissioners appoint under their hands and seals, such persons as they think needful in each market town, to be there on every market day, in some known and public place, for receiving entries and duties, and performing all other things touching the revenue of excise: and if such office shall not be so kept in each market

 town,

town, the commiſſioners or others neglecting or refuſing, ſhall for every market day forfeit ten pounds. And ſuch perſon as ſhall come to ſuch market town to make his entry or payment, and tender the ſame accordingly, and be able to prove ſuch tender by oath of one witneſs, ſhall not be liable to any penalty for ſuch weekly or monthly entries or payments, as ſhould have been made or paid on ſuch market day.

Collectors. The kingdom of England and Wales, (excluſive of the bills of mortality) is divided into about 50 collections; ſome called by names of particular counties; others by the names of great towns, where one county is divided into ſeveral collections, or where a collection comprehends the contiguous parts of ſeveral counties: every collection is entruſted to a collector, and ſubdivided into diſtricts, within each of which there is a ſupervisor; and each diſtrict is parcelled into outrides and foot walks, within each of which there is a gauger or ſurveying officer.

Gaugers. The commiſſioners, or ſub-commiſſioners in their reſpective circuits and diviſions, conſtitute under their hands and ſeals, ſuch and ſo many gaugers as they find needful. In order to which, he who would be made a gauger muſt procure a certificate, that he is above twenty-one, and under thirty years of age; that he underſtands the firſt four rules of arithmetic; that he is of the communion of the church of England; how he has been employed, or what buſineſs he has followed; that he is not incumbered with debts; whether ſingle or married; and if married, how many children he has, for if he has above two, he cannot (by the rules of the office) be admitted. He muſt alſo nominate two perſons to be his ſureties, and it muſt be certified that they are of ſufficient ability; and that the ſaid certificate is of his own hand-writing: the certificate muſt be ſigned by the ſupervisor of exciſe where the party applying lives, and at the bottom muſt be the affidavit of the party applying, that neither he, nor any one elſe to his knowledge, has, directly or indirectly, given or promiſed to give any treat, fee, gratuity, or reward, for his obtaining or endeavouring to obtain an order for his being inſtructed.

When an order for inſtruction is granted, it is directed to an experienced officer, who receives ſuch perſon as his pupil; and the like books as officers have, being delivered to ſuch pupil, he goes with, and attends the officer, who inſtructs him, and takes ſurveys, and in his own books makes the like entries, as if he was an officer, until the inſtructor certifies that he is fully acquainted with his duty. After he is thus certified for, and until he is employed, he is called an expectant, being to wait till a vacancy happens.

Officer's

Officer's Oath. No person is capable of intermeddling with any office relating to the excise, until he has, before two justices of the county where his employment shall be, or before a baron of the exchequer, taken the oaths of allegiance and supremacy, with another binding him truly and faithfully to execute his office, without favour or affection, and from time to time to make and deliver true account to persons duly appointed, and to take no fee or reward for the execution of his office, from any other person than his majesty shall appoint in that behalf. The justices certify the taking of such oath to the next quarter sessions, there to be recorded; and the officer enters a certificate thereof with the auditor of the excise: and, if any such person shall act before he has complied with these forms, he forfeits fifty pounds a month. He must also, within six months after his admission to the office, take the oaths and subscribe the declaration against transubstantiation, at the quarter sessions, in like manner as other persons admitted to offices.

Officer's general Duty. The business of the supervisor is, to be continually surveying the houses and places of the persons within his district liable to duties; and to observe and see whether the officers duly perform their surveys, and make due entries thereof in their books and in their specimen papers; and every supervisor is in his own book to enter what himself does, each day and part thereof; and also set down the behaviour, good or bad, the diligence, or negligence, of the several officers of his district; and at the end of every six weeks to draw out a diary of every day's business, and of the remarks made each day of the several officers in his district, and to transmit such diary at the end of every six weeks to the chief office. Each commissioner takes and peruses a portion of these diaries, and when he meets with any remarkable complaint against any officer, communicates it to the rest; who for small faults, admonish; for great ones, reprimand; for greater, reduce; and for the greatest, discharge the offender. The commissioner who peruses the diary, writes in the margin, admonish, reprimand, or as the case is. These diaries, after having been thus written upon, are delivered to the clerk of the diaries, who, in a book called the reprimand book, places the admonitions, reprimands, and the like, to each officer's account, and gives notice of it to the offender. The reprimand book is resorted to, on discovering new faults; and if it is found, that the officer has before been admonished and reprimanded so often, that there are no hopes of amendment, he is discharged. The same book is likewise resorted to, when application is made for advancing or preferring officers, as frequent admonitions or reprimands are, if recent, a bar to preferment, but if for three years last he stands nearly without

without censure, those of more remote date are not much regarded. Reduced officers are degraded to the next inferior rank; those once discharged may be received again, but a second dismission is final.

The collector's business is, every six weeks to go his rounds; he is to be assisting in prosecuting offenders before the justices; to peruse the supervisor's diaries, and where he finds an officer complained of, to examine him and the supervisor, and, having heard both, is in the margin to write his opinion of each fact; he is also to notice how the supervisors and officers of his collection perform their duties; and from the vouchers he transcribes into his book the charge on each particular person in his collection.

Offences. Of the offences against the excise laws it is not possible to treat in detail, but the reader may find sufficient information respecting them in the authorities before referred to; the proceedings against offenders are summary; two justices having generally power to decide, with no appeal except to the commissioners. Penalties are extremely severe, and the vigilance of the officers is excited by a large participation, both in the property confiscated, and the fine imposed on the delinquent. For the security and guidance of those who deal in, or wish to remove goods subject to the laws of excise, *permits* are issued, expressing the quantity, names of the buyer and seller, payment of duties, and such other particulars as are judged necessary to give satisfaction and prevent fraud. The officers are protected from violence by laws similar to those which have been described as applying to those of the customs.

Expence. The expence of collecting the excise duties is estimated at 3*l.* 14*s.* 6*d.* per cent.

Stamps. The mode of raising a revenue by affixing a stamp to certain judicial and public proceedings, and to deeds, and other papers of contract, promise, or permission, owes its origin, in modern Europe at least, to the Dutch, by whom it was adopted about the middle of the seventeenth century. The French soon followed their example, and stamps were first imposed in England in 1671, by statute 22 Charles II. c. 3. The scion of this exotic, which was then planted, is now become a mighty tree, striking its roots into the very foundation of financial prosperity, and extending its branches over every transaction of life, whether of law, commerce, contract, travelling, or amusement. During life, stamps are necessary in almost every act and occupation, and after death, no inconsiderable share of our property is claimed for stamps on probates, administrations and legacies. Yet the stamp duties are not in themselves a grievance, they give security to every species of

business

busineſs on which they attach, are eaſily collected, and not ſeverely felt. Their exceſs may occaſion ſome apprehenſions, but it would ſeem politic to abrogate a great many other taxes before any material alteration ſhould be propoſed in the ſtamp laws. A great inconvenience formerly attended them from the circumſtance of their parts being diſperſed through a vaſt number of ſtatutes, and each addition being ſeparately inſerted into every ſtamp, inſtead of conſolidating the whole into one general amount; but by ſtatute 44 Geo. III. c. 98. this moſt deſirable end has been attained, and all the objects of taxation by ſtamps are brought together under proper heads, and arranged in clear and copious ſchedules. To deſcribe even by a catalogue all the articles ſubject to ſtamps would occupy a very conſiderable ſpace, ſo numerous are they, and ſo widely diffuſed; but they may be found either by a reference to the act, to Burn's Juſtice, where they occupy thirty-ſix pages in the mere enumeration, or to various other publications on taxes. The variety of them may be imagined from this circumſtance, that they extend from three halfpence, the demand on certain quack medicines, to 6000*l.* the duty on the probate of a will where the property of the teſtator amounts to half a million; but ſhould a perſon bequeath that ſum to one who was not related to him within a certain degree, the legacy ſtamp would amount to 40,000*l.*

Offences. As the ſtamp laws are very ſimple, ſo the execution of them is entruſted to the magiſtrates, who have power to hear and determine all caſes ariſing out of them, and generally to mitigate the penalties to a certain degree; but the party convicted may appeal to the next ſeſſions. Forgery of ſtamps is puniſhed with death; and other frauds againſt this department of the revenue are puniſhable on conviction by indictment or information, at the diſcretion of the court where the party is tried.

Office. The ſtamp office was formerly in Lincoln's Inn; it is now in the eaſt corner of the ſouth ſide of the grand quadrangle in Somerſet houſe. The apartments are admirably fitted up and well conſtructed for buſineſs, in the courſe of which every precaution is adopted to facilitate its progreſs, and prevent every ſpecies of fraud, whether in the purchaſer or the officers themſelves.

Officers. In the ſtamp office are *five commiſſioners,* each of whom has 800*l.* a-year, and commodious apartments for his reſidence; the *ſecretary* has a ſeparate office with ſix clerks; the *receiver*'s ſalary is 800*l.*; the *comptroller* has 400*l.*; the deputy comptroller, and accountant general, 550*l.*; under them are ſeveral clerks, and in all the other branches of the office a great many perſons are neceſſarily employed but not extravagantly paid. The *ſolicitor* has an annual fee of 300*l*., beſide the profits on his buſineſs. In all parts of the country diſtributors of ſtamps are appointed, who are remunerated by a ſmall poundage.

EXPENCE. The expence of obtaining the ſtamp duty is calculated at 3*l*. 15*s*. per cent.

MISCELLANEOUS TAXES. As the general amount raiſed by theſe as well as the preceding taxes, will be given in a table, it is not intended to treat at length on every minute particular of which they are compoſed, but under ſeparate heads to notice the moſt peculiar circumſtances reſpecting them.

ASSESSED TAXES. In this general denomination are included the rates on windows, houſes, ſervants, carriages, horſes of various deſcriptions, dogs, horſe dealers, hair powder, and armorial bearings. In this diviſion a ſet of taxes is included, which preſſes on the ſubject with aggravated hardſhips in many reſpects; particularly as the payment is direct, or in money without any equivalent, and that as to ſome of them, the party cannot by the exerciſe of any ſelf denial or prudence diminiſh their preſſure, as he may with reſpect to all thoſe which were before enumerated.

COMMISSIONERS. The aſſeſſed taxes are under the management of five commiſſioners, who have ſalaries of 500*l*. and an office in Somerſet Houſe, and in the office there are many ſubordinate perſons employed in tranſacting buſineſs and ſuppreſſing frauds.

DISTRICT COMMISSIONERS. Theſe are ſubordinate to the principal commiſſioners, and appointed to act in certain diſtricts throughout the kingdom. Each of theſe perſons to act in London, or the circumjacent places, muſt ſwear that he poſſeſſes property to the amount of 5000*l*., clear of all incumbrances, and ſpecify in the body of his oath, the particulars in which it conſiſts. They muſt alſo, in all caſes, be inhabitants of the diſtricts where they are appointed to act, and take an oath for the faithful execution of their duty.

CLERKS. At a meeting to be held annually in each diſtrict, the commiſſioners have power to nominate a clerk, and, if neceſſary, an aſſiſtant, who are to act for one year, unleſs removed for juſt cauſe.

ASSESSORS. They may alſo appoint aſſeſſors or preſenters, to whom they muſt deliver a charge, and who are to make their aſſeſſment, on oath, of the particulars committed to them, and an omiſſion may be puniſhed by a fine not exceeding 20*l*., nor leſs than 5*l*. The returns made by the aſſeſſors, with three duplicates

duplicates prepared by the clerk, are ſigned by the commiſſioners to be tranſmitted to the tax-office, and for other uſes. The aſſeſſors are bound to fidelity and diligence by an oath.

Collectors. The commiſſioners alſo, in conſequence of returns made by the aſſeſſors, appoint collectors for each diſtrict, to whom they deliver one of the before-mentioned duplicates, with warrants for the execution of their duties. The commiſſioners ought to take ſecurity from the collectors, to the full amount of their collection; and if they have not done ſo, it is competent to the church-wardens, overſeers, or guardians of the poor, or any ſeven or more of a ſelect veſtry, where there are ſuch veſtries, to require the commiſſioners to take ſecurity, and to tender perſons willing to become collectors and give ſecurity, in which caſe, the commiſſioners are reſtrained from appointing others without ſecurity. Many proviſions are made for ſupplying deficiencies of collectors, in caſe of their not being duly appointed; and they are empowered, having a warrant from any two commiſſioners, to break open houſes for the purpoſe of levying a diſtreſs, and if no diſtreſs is found, the commiſſioners may commit the perſon to gaol, till payment is made. Theſe powers are the more neceſſary, as, in ſome caſes of default of payment, the pariſh is liable to make it good.

Inspectors or Surveyors. To rectify errors and detect frauds, inſpectors or ſurveyors to the number of three hundred, acting in various parts of the kingdom, are appointed at the office in Somerſet Houſe. Theſe perſons have power, on detection of any falſe returns made by individuals, to puniſh them by a *ſurcharge* or double aſſeſſment, on the particulars withheld or omitted; theſe however may appeal to the commiſſioners.

Assessment. The manner of preparing the aſſeſſment of each individual, as preſcribed by act of parliament, is this. The aſſeſſors, at certain times, fix on the doors of the church, chapel, or market-houſe, according to circumſtances, general notices, requiring all perſons reſident within that place, to make out and deliver, within fourteen days, liſts of the particulars for which they are liable to be aſſeſſed, excluſive of the houſe and window tax. They are beſides to leave at every dwelling houſe inhabited, or ſuppoſed to be inhabited, by perſons liable to aſſeſſment, notices for the keeper of the houſe, and for every lodger and inmate liable, who are thereupon bound to make out liſts of all the particulars for which they ought to be aſſeſſed, and return them to the aſſeſſors, on penalty of being aſſeſſed according to the diſcretion of the aſſeſſors, guided by the liſts laſt delivered, or the beſt information they can obtain. When the

the lists are returned, the inspectors may, before their allowance by the commissioners, amend them in particulars where the party appears to have mistaken, without aiming at fraud; or, in case of evident fraud or neglect, may punish him by a surcharge. For their better information in these matters, the commissioners, inspectors, assessors and other persons employed, may have recourse to, and make copies or extracts from the books of poor-rates or other assessments, within the parish, and the persons who ought to shew them are subject, if they withhold them, to a penalty not exceeding ten pounds for every offence.

EXPENCES. The lords of the Treasury have power to appoint salaries or allowances to the surveyors, inspectors, and other officers, and to discharge incidental expences. Every receiver general has an allowance of two-pence in the pound, for all monies paid by him into the Exchequer; every collector three-pence in the pound, for what he pays the receiver general, and the clerk to the commissioners has three-halfpence in the pound, on the same sum. These together make the calculated expence of getting in these taxes amount to 3*l.* 12*s.* 5*d.* per cent.

The preceding observations apply to the assessed taxes in the gross. Some in particular require a few observations.

WINDOWS AND HOUSES. As early as the conquest, mention is made in Domesday, of fumage or fuage, vulgarly called smoke farthings; which were paid by custom to the king for every chimney in the house. And we read that Edward the Black Prince (soon after his successes in France,) in imitation of the English custom, imposed a tax of a florin upon every hearth in his French dominions. The first parliamentary establishment of this tax in England, was by statute 13 and 14 Cha. II. c. 10. whereby an hereditary revenue of two shillings for every hearth, in all houses paying to church and poor, was granted to the king for ever. On the revolution, by statute 1 W. & M. st. 1. c. 10., hearth money was declared to be "not only a great "oppression to the poorer sort, but a badge of slavery on the "whole people, exposing every man's house to be entered into, "and searched at pleasure, by persons unknown to him; and "therefore, to erect a lasting monument of their majesties' "goodness in every house in the kingdom, the duty of hearth "money was taken away and abolished." This monument of goodness remains among us to this day: but the prospect was somewhat darkened, when in six years afterwards, by statute 7 W. III. c. 18., a tax was laid on all houses (except cottages) of two shillings per annum, and a tax also upon all windows, if they exceeded nine, in such house. These rates have been from

from time to time varied, and greatly extended; and power is given to surveyors, appointed by the crown, to inspect and survey houses, and windows.

The most remarkable circumstance attending the tax on windows, (for its progressive increase hardly merits notice, that being in the nature of every productive tax,) was the regulation called the *commutation act*. At the close of the American war, it was found, with respect to many articles, but particularly tea, that the high duties which had been imposed, far from benefiting the revenue to the extent which had been expected, formed an inviting encouragement to smugglers, and an irresistible temptation to many who would not else have incurred the risk of dealing with them. The duties on tea were in customs and excise 58*l.* 5*s.* per cent., besides a tax of five shillings and nine pence on every five pounds weight. Under these circumstances it was proposed in parliament, to free the commodity from all duties except one of 12¼ per cent. on the price paid by the purchaser at the public sales, and to raise the deficiency, which would thus be occasioned in the revenue, amounting to 600,000*l.* by an additional tax on windows. After long and ingenious discussions, this plan was adopted, and its benefits are experienced beyond the supposed extent, for as tea was the staple commodity of the smugglers, the destruction of their trade in that branch, has caused it to languish in every other.

The house tax imposed by 18 Geo. III. c. 26, was at first from sixpence to one shilling in the pound, on the rack rent, it is now one shilling and four-pence in the pound, on houses at five pounds a year, and under twenty pounds, and on those which exceed forty pounds a year, two shillings and six-pence in the pound. The tax on windows varies in its progress. Houses having less than six windows, and not renting for five pounds per annum, are rated at sums not exceeding six shillings; seven windows produce eight; thence to ten windows, the advance is alternately eight shillings and twelve shillings each, making the gross amount 2*l.* 10*s.* The next advance is fifteen shillings per window, making eleven pay 3*l.* 5*s.*, and this continues till they arrive at thirty nine, for which 24*l.* 5*s.* are paid. From this a new system takes place, each advance including five windows, and rating them at thirty, fifty, or forty shillings additional at each stage, up to one hundred and eighty, for which 83*l.* are paid, and an additional two and sixpence for every window beyond that number.

SERVANTS. The tax on male servants is two pounds for one servant, and progressively increases, though not in a certain ratio, on each servant up to eleven; and persons keeping that number

number or upwards pay six guineas per annum for each; bachelors pay an additional sum of 1*l.* 10*s.* for every servant. This tax extends, though with modifications, to persons hired for temporary services; travellers, clerks, shopmen, waiters, and stable keepers, employed respectively by merchants, tradesmen, and innkeepers; and to servants employed in husbandry.

CARRIAGES. This duty is progressive; persons keeping one four-wheel carriage, paying ten pounds per annum; and those keeping any number up to nine, at an increased rate for every one; for nine and upwards must be paid fifteen pounds each. Carriages with less than four wheels, pay, if drawn by one horse, 5*l.* 5*s.*; if by more, 7*l.* 7*s.* There are also duties on hired carriages and taxed carts, and a licence to be taken out by those who make carriages, or sell them, either in a shop or by auction, and a tax of one pound on every four-wheel, and ten shillings on every two-wheel carriage sold.

HORSES. The duty on horses, kept for riding or draught, is for one, two pounds per annum, and thence progressively, though not regularly, to twenty, which are rated at 4*l.* 5*s.* each. There are many variations in this tax, as on horses let to hire, those kept for racing, and those which are used by small farmers, or in husbandry, and in many other particulars, which can only be ascertained by reference to the acts. Horse dealers in London and the circumjacent district, pay twenty pounds annually; in all other parts of the kingdom, ten pounds.

DOGS. A person keeping one dog, not being a greyhound, hound, setting dog, spaniel, lurcher, or terrier, pays six shillings, per annum; and those who keep one of any of those classes, or more than one of whatever description, pay ten shillings per annum for each. Packs of hounds may be compounded for at thirty pounds.

HAIR POWDER. Persons wearing this ornament, pay one guinea per annum.

ARMORIAL BEARINGS. Persons keeping any coach or other carriage, pay if they wear armorial bearings, two guineas per annum; those who do not keep a carriage, but are chargeable to the duties on windows, one guinea; all others ten shillings and six-pence.

Such is the outline of the assessed taxes; but to the general system, and to each in particular, appertain many exemptions, exceptions, limitations, distinctions, regulations, powers and authorities, more than can here be in the slightest manner mentioned. Some of these taxes, as those on houses and windows, seem grievous from their amount; others, as hair powder, dogs, and armorial bearings, rather insignificant; but to the others no objections can be made, unless they tend by excess, of which there

there is yet no probability, to restrain the use of the objects to which they apply.

Among the other miscellaneous taxes, two deserve particular notice; those on hackney coaches, and hawkers and pedlars.

Hackney Coaches. In 1662, four hundred hackney coaches were licensed in the cities of London and Westminster; but the sum exacted from them was then appropriated to the repairing of highways and sewers, and paving and cleansing streets in the metropolis; nor was it discovered, until 1694, that this might become a branch of the public revenue. By the first act passed for that purpose, permission was given to license a number not exceeding seven hundred hackney coaches; each licence to continue for twenty-one years, on payment of the fine of fifty pounds, and giving security for the additional sum of four pounds per annum; and a board of commissioners was appointed for granting licences, and for executing the different powers contained in the act. The number was increased in the reign of queen Anne, to eight hundred coaches; and the commissioners were also invested with authority to license hackney chairs, not exceeding two hundred, at the rate of ten shillings per annum, which number was increased first to three hundred, and afterwards to four hundred. In 1770, a thousand hackney coaches were permitted to be licensed, and the sum of five shillings per week, or thirteen pounds per annum, was imposed on them. That duty has since been doubled, consequently they now pay twenty-six pounds each per annum, and their number is augmented to twelve hundred; two hundred of these are hackney chariots, and of these the commissioners have power, if they think it necessary, to license two hundred more. Their fares are exactly the same as those of the coaches; but they carry no more than three persons, while the coaches carry four, with privilege to add another shilling to their demand, for every person beyond that number.

Regulations. Besides the regulations respecting the fares of hackney coachmen, many strict laws are enacted for protection of the public against the fraud, insolence, and neglect which they might experience from these people, if unrestrained; some of which it may not be improper to mention. Every coach must have its number on each side; and for altering it, the penalty is five pounds, half to the informer, the other to the king: the like penalty attaches on any one driving a coach for hire without a licence. The commissioners may appoint inspectors, to see that licensed persons provide safe and clean coaches, and sufficient horses; and they may suspend the licence of any perſon whoſe coach or horſes ſhall be defective, and may continue ſuch ſuſpenſion until the ſame be rectified: and if any perſon ſhall refuſe his coach and horſes to be inſpected, his licence ſhall be void. Every horſe uſed in a hackney coach, muſt be at leaſt fourteen hands high. Hackney coachmen are to provide and place in a convenient part of their coaches, check ſtrings or wire; and if they ply without, to forfeit five ſhillings. Every coachman plying is obliged, at all times, to go any where within London or Weſtminſter, or to a diſtance not exceeding ten miles; if he refuſes to go at, or exacts more than his fare, he is to forfeit not more than three pounds, nor leſs than ten ſhillings; all agreements to pay more than the proper fare are not binding, and any overcharge, if paid, may be recovered back, with a penalty, not exceeding five pounds. Every hackney coachman, where coaches are ſtanding, is compellable to go with any perſon when deſired, and on refuſal, (unleſs he prove being previouſly hired,) is liable to the like penalties. And if any perſon who drives a coach, or carries a chair for hire, acting under a perſon licenſed, is guilty of miſbehaviour, by demanding more than his fare, or giving abuſive language, or other rude behaviour; he ſhall, on conviction on oath, forfeit not exceeding ten pounds: and if he is not able, or refuſes to pay, he ſhall be committed to Bridewell, or ſome other houſe of correction, to be kept to hard labour not exceeding two months; or the commiſſioners may revoke the licence.

If any perſon refuſes to pay the fare, or defaces any coach or chair, any juſtice may grant his warrant to bring him before him; and on proof on oath, may award ſatisfaction to the party, and on refuſal to pay, bind him over to the next ſeſſions, who may determine the ſame.

Commissioners. The commiſſioners are five; their office is in Eſſex Street in the Strand. In all matters relating to complaint and puniſhment, the power of magiſtrates is equal with theirs, but thoſe peculiar authorities which conſiſt in the granting, revoking, and ſuſpending of licences, give the commiſſioners great additional power. They have, beſides, a right to make bye-laws, which, when ratified by the lord chancellor, or lord commiſſioners of the great ſeal, two chief juſtices, and chief baron, or any three of them, bind all perſons licenſed, and all renters of licences.

Hawkers and Pedlars. Itinerant retailers, known under the name of hawkers, pedlars, or petty chapmen, have long been an object of taxation, partly for the ſake of revenue, but perhaps principally for the purpoſes of police. In 1697, a licence duty was firſt impoſed on them, which has ſince undergone

undergone ſeveral variations. By 50 Geo. III. c. 4. every hawker, pedlar, petty chapman, or other trading perſon, going from town to town, or to other men's houſes, and travelling either on foot, or with horſe, horſes, or otherwiſe, in England, Wales, or Berwick-upon-Tweed, carrying to ſell, or expoſing to ſale, any goods, muſt pay a duty of four pounds for each year. And for every horſe, or other beaſt bearing or drawing burthen, the additional ſum of four pounds yearly. They cannot obtain a licence without a certificate ſigned by one clergyman and two reputable inhabitants atteſting their character and reputation; and they are under many ſevere and rigorous regulations, being reſtrained from vending many ſorts of goods, as tea, and ſpirituous liquors; prohibited from ſelling by auction in places where they are not reſident houſeholders, under a penalty of fifty pounds; obliged to have the words *Licenſed Hawker*, with the number of their licence printed conſpicuouſly on all their packs, incloſures, and conveyances; if they deal in ſmuggled goods, they forfeit their licences; if they trade contrary to their licences, or do not produce them when lawfully required, they forfeit ten pounds; for uſing a forged licence, the penalty is three hundred pounds; perſons lending or hiring out a licence forfeit forty pounds; and the like ſum is the penalty of trading without a licence. The act does not extend to perſons ſelling fiſh, fruit, or victuals, nor to the makers or workers of any goods, and their ſervants, carrying about their own manufactures, nor to tinkers, coopers, glaziers, plumbers, or harneſs makers, travelling and carrying with them their own tools. Penalties above twenty pounds, are recoverable by action at Weſtminſter; under that ſum, by information before one juſtice, who on default of payment, may commit, not exceeding three months: there is an appeal to the next ſeſſion.

Commissioners. The duties under this act are performed by the commiſſioners for hackney-coaches; but they cannot convict or levy penalties for offences againſt this act, as they can under the other branch of their juriſdiction.

Auditors. For the ſecurity and ſatisfaction of the public, in reſpect to the receipt and appropriation of the monies raiſed by many of the before-mentioned taxes, an office for auditing public accounts is eſtabliſhed in Somerſet Place. It conſiſts of five commiſſioners, two inſpectors general, with four ſubordinate inſpectors, clerks, and other officers. There is alſo a ſeparate office, in Palace Yard, for auditing the accounts of land revenue, land tax, and window tax, in which the auditors have ſalaries amounting to upwards of two thouſand pounds.

Lottery. Among the resources of the state which cannot be termed permanent, but which are so far from occasional as to be regularly expected, may be mentioned the lottery. This plan was, on its first introduction into England, sparingly used, and frequently intermitted: it afterward involved comparatively little of hope or fear to what it does at present; the capital prizes being smaller, and a portion of the money adventured being returned on a certain number of blanks. The general face of the scheme was changed when the duke of Grafton became minister; the capital prizes being greatly augmented in amount, and the returns on blanks being generally discontinued. But the tickets were formerly considered, less as productive of profit to government, than as a bonus or allowance to those who subscribed the loans. Modern finance, however, has so improved this resource, that it now sometimes augments the revenue by nearly half a million a-year; independently of the stamps on shares of tickets, and the licences taken out by the proprietors of offices, which amount to fifty pounds each. These persons are empowered to sell tickets entire, or divided into shares for the accommodation of those who wish not to encounter a large venture. The complicated interest which these office-keepers have, as subscribers to a general scheme, and as individuals pressing separate claims to public notice, with a view to emolument, occasion some very curious contrivances with respect to the retention or sale of tickets, and some very extraordinary essays in the art of puffing.

The mode of making a lottery is similar to that of raising a loan: the minister announces his intention to the monied men, and they bid for the tickets such prices as they think they can afford; the minister closes with the highest, and the purchasers are at liberty to form a scheme for distribution of the prizes. Lottery tickets then become, like other stocks or subscriptions, an object of active speculation, in which there are bulls and bears, differences paid instead of the actual purchase and transfer of tickets, and all the eagerness and dexterity are displayed, which characterize other transactions in the alley.

Commissioners. The lotteries are managed by commissioners, who superintend all transactions relative to the putting the numbers, and the corresponding blanks and prizes, into the wheels from which they are to be drawn; and attend daily in rotation, during the drawing, to ascertain the transactions of every day. They have under them, a convenient number of clerks and messengers, and the annual value of their situations is said to be 200*l*. each.

Drawing. The mode of drawing a lottery is this: two large coffers or boxes are prepared, which, from their being circular

circular and turning on an axis, are called wheels. Into one is put a series of numbers from one to the highest total of tickets mentioned in the scheme or plan of the lottery; they are written on papers of equal sizes and folded exactly alike. Into the other wheel are put similar pieces, marked with the prizes from the highest to the lowest proposed; and blank papers exactly similar making up the residue of numbers contained in the numerical wheel. On the day appointed for the beginning of the drawing, two boys from the school of Christ's Hospital, called the Blue-coat-School, attend, and one being placed before each wheel, they put in their hands at the same time, and each draws forth one paper: that containing the number is first proclaimed by the commissioner, and taken down in writing by clerks employed for the purpose; the word contained in the other, is then similarly proclaimed and written against the number. If a prize, the holder of the ticket becomes entitled to the sum mentioned; if a blank his stake is utterly lost. The same process is observed with respect to every ticket; and it is now usual to declare the drawing terminated when all the prizes are drawn, and sometimes without putting into the wheel any blanks; the numbers remaining after the drawing of the prizes, being, blanks in course. The former mode is more popular, and perhaps more justly satisfactory, and therefore most frequently pursued.

Laws relating to the Lottery. It is to be apprehended that in the present state of finance, and indeed of society in general, reflections on the morality of a national system of gambling would be of little avail. The desire of becoming suddenly and immoderately rich, diffused among all classes of society, produces many beneficial and glorious exertions: but it cannot be expected that such a desire, connected with the spirit of adventure, should be uniformly confined to such transactions as a sound political moralist can seriously approve; and therefore, it is not surprising that, in an age when every one seems to resign himself, in some degree, to the influence of fortune, lotteries have been almost constantly resorted to. As a tax, indeed, a lottery is most unexceptionable; for no individual is compelled to bear any portion of the burthen, but voluntarily brings in his sacrifice, in hopes of propitiating fortune: nor would it avail any thing to demonstrate to any one who is disposed to become an adventurer how much too dear he pays for his ticket, and how numerous the chances are against him; a sanguine confidence, not to be repressed by disappointment, hurries him on, and year after year lotteries are proposed, and tickets still sold at increasing prices.

Illegal Insurances. From this legal ſyſtem of gambling, another inconvenience has been found to ariſe; that it gives a ſtrong impulſe to thoſe who are inclined to prey on the public, and particularly on the lower claſs, by connecting with the ſtate lottery, another popular, but more deſtructive mode of adventure, commonly denominated inſuring. This is performed in the uſual manner of ſimilar tranſactions in commerce; the party deſirous to inſure, fixes on a number, pays a premium, and according to its amount, receives, if the number is drawn on the given day, a larger ſum in return. Were this adventure conducted on the faireſt principles, it would be liable to this objection, that the events being ſo frequently decided, the minds of thoſe engaged are kept in a moſt dangerous ferment, and all the paſſions which enter into the character of a gameſter are goaded to their utmoſt fury. The inſurance of lottery tickets by their real proprietors againſt the contingencies that a ſingle day may produce, is as reaſonable as any other of the various inſurances which form an appendage to commerce: but after the eſtabliſhment of lotteries, it was ſoon found that the practice of inſuring by thoſe who, poſſeſſing no tickets, fixed on numbers as a mode of gambling, was ſo common, as to occaſion general vice and miſery; and that ſhares, chances, or policies, regulated by the events of the lottery, but producing gain only to the projectors, were multiplied, in ſuch a manner as greatly to deprave the public morals, and to reduce the profits which government had a right to expect from the ſelling of tickets and ſhares. Againſt theſe practices a long ſeries of legiſlative edicts has been directed; and at length the ſyſtem adopted for ſuppreſſing illegal adventures in lotteries, is carried to a very great extent. By the laws now in force, all lotteries, whether dependent on tickets, cards, dice, or any other contrivance, unauthorized by parliament, are declared to be nuiſances; and all gaming in them, whether for lands, goods, money, or other beneficial event, is forbidden under heavy penalties. With reſpect to ſtate lotteries, it is enacted, that every perſon who ſhall publicly or privately ſet up, or keep, by himſelf or any other, any office or place for buying, ſelling or dealing in lottery tickets, or ſhares, without being licenſed; or ſhall ſell the chance of any ſuch ticket, or ſhare, for a day or part of a day, or leſs time than the whole time of drawing in ſuch lottery then to come; or inſure, for or againſt the drawing of any ſuch ticket; or ſhall receive any money or goods in conſideration of any agreement, or promiſe to repay any money, or to deliver the ſame, or any plate, jewels, or other goods whatſoever, if auy ſuch ticket ſhall prove fortunate or unfortunate; or upon any other chance, event, or contingency relative to the drawing any

any ſuch tickets, whether as to the time of their being drawn, or otherwiſe; ſhall be deemed a rogue and vagabond, and ſhall be puniſhed accordingly. Theſe offenders are alſo liable to a penalty of 500*l.* for every offence, for which they may be held to bail in any of the courts at Weſtminſter. And on proof made of the offence, if they have not before been ſued for it, they muſt be ſent to the houſe of correction until the next ſeſſions: and the juſtices at ſuch ſeſſions muſt examine the cauſe and proceed therein, as by law directed. On complaint upon oath before one juſtice, of any offence committed againſt the act for ſuppreſſing unlawful lotteries, in any houſe or place within the juriſdiction of ſuch juſtice, whereby any offenders may be liable to be puniſhed as rogues and vagabonds, ſuch juſtice, by warrant, may empower any perſon, employed by the commiſſioners of the ſtamp duties in the execution of the acts for regulating lotteries, by day or by night, (but if in the night in the preſence of a conſtable, who is required to be aiding and aſſiſting therein,) to break open the doors of any part of ſuch houſe, or place, where ſuch offence ſhall have been committed, and to enter and ſeize all ſuch offenders or other perſons, who ſhall have knowingly aſſiſted or been in any wiſe concerned in committing ſuch offence, and convey them before any juſtice of the county, city, or place wherein ſuch perſon ſhall be ſo apprehended, to be dealt with according to law; and all perſons who ſhall have been diſcovered in ſuch houſe or place, knowingly aiding, aſſiſting, or any ways concerned with ſuch offenders in carrying on any ſuch tranſactions, ſhall be deemed rogues and vagabonds, and puniſhed accordingly: and the officer having the execution of ſuch warrant, or perſon acting in his aid or aſſiſtance, may arreſt any ſuch perſons ſo diſcovered in ſuch houſe or place, and convey them before a juſtice as aforeſaid. And if any perſon ſhall forcibly obſtruct or hinder any ſuch officer, or others acting in his aid or aſſiſtance, in the execution of their duty herein, he ſhall be deemed an offender againſt law, and the court before whom he ſhall be tried and convicted may order him to be fined, impriſoned, and publicly whipped, as in their diſcretion ſhall be thought fit. And all perſons, although not diſcovered in ſuch houſe or place as aforeſaid, who ſhall employ any perſon in carrying on any of the tranſactions aforeſaid, or be aiding or aſſiſting therein, ſhall be deemed rogues and vagabonds, and puniſhed accordingly. And if any perſon ſhall be brought before any two juſtices, and ſhall be convicted of any offence againſt the ſaid act, whereby he ſhall be adjudged a rogue and vagabond, ſuch juſtices may order him to be ſent to the houſe of correction for any time not exceeding ſix, nor leſs than one calendar

 month.

month, and until the final period of the drawing of the lottery, in respect whereof such offence shall be committed; and such proceedings shall not be subject to appeal, nor removable by *certiorari*. Almost every new lottery act contains clauses of additional penalty, calculated to defeat some new contrivance in the agents of fraud, or to facilitate and render effectual the proceedings against them.

Restrictions so severe would extirpate, if it could be effected by force, the practice against which they are directed; but the desire of gaining by insurance in the lottery is so firmly rooted in the minds of the lower class, especially in the metropolis, that the severity of law has not altogether produced the desired effect, and for some time increased the virulence, if it has limited the extent, of the evil. The system of illegal insurance in lotteries was carried on in the manner of a powerful association against the regulations of society. Certain men of large property were at the head of the establishment; under them numerous desperadoes were appointed, who by all sorts of clandestine means, obtained money from those who were disposed to adventure, and brought it to the principals, who undertook for the event, and allowed their subordinates a considerable profit on the premium. With respect to the penalties, these illegal traders secured themselves by strength of purse; the means of detecting and bringing to justice the persons taking illegal insurances were in the hands of a few men, generally known as common informers, and these acted in subordination to certain chieftains, whom the illegal insurers largely bribed in the course of every lottery, and thus not only protected themselves against the attacks of these leading informers, but also gained the advantage of their powerful succour, if they or any of their agents were attacked by the subordinate conductors of penal prosecution. Thus although it was notorious that in every lottery, insurances were taken to a large amount, yet the courts of law rarely witnessed a prosecution; the institution of them being altogether prevented, or those which were commenced being illegally compounded; and the whole force of these tremendously penal statutes spent itself on a few wretches, who having established their illegal schemes without the sanction of the wealthy governors, or having been too unguarded in their conduct to hope for protection, were sent to Bridewell or the house of correction for a few weeks. Thus the acts of parliament did not extirpate this practice, but altered the nature and manner of it. Before they were passed, insurances were taken, almost publicly, by persons who were decent in their manners, and little different from other clerks to brokers or lottery office keepers; from

from them, therefore, the persons who insured, contracted no vice beyond that which was connected with the very act about which they were employed: afterward, none would accept the task of collecting insurances except the most abject and degraded of mankind, persons whose whole lives were spent in illegal and infamous pursuits; the underlings at gaming tables, and servants at brothels, pickpockets, passers of false money, and all the tribe who prefer the slavery of illegal enterprise to the labours of honest industry; from these every syllable was contamination, and the servant or mechanic, whom the desire of gain led to associate with them, could not escape the infection of their principles, manners, and conduct. Another effect of these laws was, that, as none but persons of a particular character and connection could pursue this iniquitous system, it grew into a sort of monopoly, the whole business being ingrossed by a few individuals, who fixed what premiums they pleased on insurances, plundered the unfortunate votaries of their practice at discretion, and accelerated with mighty steps all its ruinous consequences. These persons, besides the large fees they paid to informers, allowed the collectors of illegal insurances 7½ per cent. on the money they brought: to afford this, they calculated their premiums, so that the smallest reservation in their favour was thirty per cent., but in many instances it was much greater; and by such means they were enabled to purchase estates, and live luxuriously on the spoils of unfortunate wretches, whom they drove to want, guilt, despair, and suicide or the gallows. Of late, this evil has been much better provided against, by taking the penalties out of the hands of common informers, and permitting them only to be sued for by the attorney-general; and by the vigilance and care of the Stamp Office, in prosecuting as rogues and vagabonds all offenders, without distinction.

LITTLE GOES. When no state lotteries are being drawn, adventures are offered in a fictitious species of lottery, called a *Little Go*, where, without any voucher or security for fidelity or fairness, a certain number of tickets is drawn, or supposed to be drawn, for a series of days, not for the purpose of distributing prizes, or deciding any event, generally connected with the lottery, but merely for that of collecting premiums for insurances. These too are declared public nuisances; and it is enacted, that no person shall keep or suffer to be kept in his house, any office or place for any game or lottery called a *Little Go*, or for any other lottery whatsoever, not authorized by parliament, on pain of five hundred pounds for each offence, recoverable in the exchequer by the attorney-general to the use of the king; and such person, whether he transacts such business himself or employs

ploys others, ſhall be deemed a rogue and a vagabond. Juſtices are likewiſe empowered to break open doors, and purſue the ſame meaſures as againſt thoſe who take illegal inſurances in the ſtate lotteries.

In concluding this part of the ſubject it may be fit to mention that the legiſlature has frequently authorized the drawing of lotteries for the purpoſe of ſelling eſtates, muſeums, collections of pictures, and other things for which purchaſers could not otherwiſe have been found: with reſpect to eſtates, at leaſt, there are many reaſons why this indulgence ſhould not be too eaſily granted.

The Property-tax being now repealed, and the Convoy-duty having, in courſe, terminated with the war, it is neceſſary to make only ſlight mention of them. During the war which began in 1793, Mr. Pitt brought forward, under the name of an Income-tax, an aſſeſſment on the annual revenue of every individual in the kingdom, amounting, on thoſe above 200*l.* a year, to ten per cent. But as the intereſt of money in the funds was untouched, and the ſum of income which was aſſeſſed ſlightly or not all, was ſo conſiderable, evaſion was practiſed to a conſiderable extent, and the tax on the whole, was not ſo productive as might have been expected. This tax was repealed at the peace in 1802; ſome arrears charged upon it being provided for by an increaſe of the aſſeſſed taxes. On the renewal of hoſtilities, the miniſtry, of which Mr. Addington (Lord Sidmouth) was the chief, introduced the property-tax, ſubjecting the dividends on the public funds to its immediate operation, and allowing very few abatements or exceptions. The aſſeſſment was five per cent.; in the laſt adminiſtration of Mr. Pitt, it was raiſed to ſix and a half; and by the next miniſters, Lord Grenville and Mr. Fox, it was carried to ten per cent.; at which point it continued till the end of the war, when in conſequence of petitions from all parts of the kingdom, it was repealed. The convoy duty was impoſed in 1798, as a tonnage on ſhips for every paſſage out and home, varying, according to the ports of deſtination, from ſixpence to three ſhillings per ton. It brought a large revenue, and was not deemed injurious to commerce.

The following tables exhibit a general view of the income and expenditure of the United Kingdom for the year ending the 5th of January 1817, and for ſome portion of that which was then elapſing: they are given in the Fourth Report of the Select Committee of Finance to the Houſe of Commons, in the Seſſion of 1817. The document from which this extract is made furniſhes the moſt authentic and uſeful information on the ſubject.

Income of Great Britain.

1. *Consolidated Fund.*

			£.
The income of this fund, ending 5th January 1817, amounted to - - - - -			39,083,558

2. *Ways and Means granted by Parliament for the Supply of the Year.*

Annual duties upon malt, sugar, &c. - - -	3,000,000		
Excise duties, continued to 5th July, 1821 -	3,500,000		
Profits of lotteries, after reserving ⅓, the proportion for Ireland - -	168,459		
Old naval stores, after reserving 79,988*l.* the proportion for Ireland -	599,916		
		7,268,375	
Unclaimed dividends (after abating 206,175*l.* repaid to the Bank in respect of dividends afterwards claimed), interest on land-tax redeemed by money, and unclaimed money in the hands of the tellers of the exchequer -	239,871		
The surplus of the supply of the year 1815, granted as part of the ways and means for the year 1816, was 5,663,755*l.* of which, however, 959,090*l.* was applied to the reduction of the navy debt, leaving applicable to defray the supply voted for 1816, only - - -	4,704,665		
		4,944,536	
Total ways and means - -			12,212,911
And the total income, ordinary and extraordinary, exclusive of income arising from any loan funded, or from any addition to the unfunded debt, was			51,296,469

EXPEN-

Expenditure of Great Britain.

Consolidated Fund.

		£.
Charge upon the Consolidated Fund for the year ended 5th January 1817 - - -		39,693,430

Supply for the Service of the Year 1816:

The total amount of supply granted, and of expences incurred, on the joint account of Great Britain and Ireland, for the year 1816, was 26,342,422*l.*; of which, 15–17ths, the proportion of Great Britain, was - -	23,243,314	
The supply granted, or expences defrayed, on the separate account of Great Britain, including 1,265,232*l.* applied to the reduction of debt, was	3,921,150	
Making the total supply -		27,164,464
And the total expenditure for the year 1816, on account of Great Britain - - -		66,857,894

Income of Ireland for 1816.

The net amount received into the exchequer from the customs, excise, stamp-duties, and every other branch of revenue and income, was -	4,561,353
There was also paid into the exchequer of Ireland, or remaining to be remitted on account of the loan contracted for in England, in the year 1815	2,622,640
Making a total receipt of - -	£ 7,183,993

Expen-

Expenditure.		
The charge upon the Conſolidated Fund, in reſpect of the public funded debt of Ireland, in Ireland and Great Britain, including 2,438,124*l.* payable to the commiſſioners for the reduction of the ſaid debt, was - -	£6,446,826	
For the civil liſt, and other permanent parliamentary charges - -	539,138	
Making the total of permanent charges - -		6,985,964
The expenditure on account of the ſervices of the laſt or former years, actually paid within the above period, was - - -		3,075,561
		10,061,525
And there was remitted to England, and paid into the exchequer, towards making good the proportion of Ireland of 2–17ths of the joint expenditure		1,184,009
Making the total iſſues - -		11,245,534
Income.		
The total revenue and income of Ireland was, in the year ended the 6th of January 1817, as above ſtated - - - -		4,561,353
Expenditure.		
The total permanent charge upon the conſolidated fund of Ireland, for the year ended 5th January 1817, was, as before ſtated - - -		6,285,964
The total amount of the ſupply granted, and of the expences incurred, on the joint account of Great Britain and Ireland for the year 1816, was 26,342,423*l.*; of which, 2–17ths, the proportion of Ireland, was -	3,099,108	
The ſupply granted or expence defrayed on the ſeparate account of Ireland, was - - - -	193,978	
Making the total ſupply - -		3,293,086
And the total expenditure for the year 1816, on account of Ireland - - -		£10,279,050

The

The result of these statements is, that the total revenue and income of Ireland for the year 1816, amounted to 4,561,353*l.*; that the charges of her debt, and other payments of a permanent nature, amounted to 6,985,964*l.*; that the supply for that year to be defrayed by Ireland, as above stated, was 3,293,086*l.*; making a total expenditure of 10,279,050*l.*; of which the sum of 2,438,124*l.* was issued to the commissioners for the reduction of the national debt of Ireland.

The exchequer of the two countries having, from the 5th of January last, become united, and being now administered by one authority, it is proposed to take a view of the combined receipt and expenditure of the United Kingdom, as more particularly applicable to the year ended 5th January 1817.

INCOME.

The total income of Great Britain, applicable to the permanent charges of that year, and to the supplies granted for that period, was, as before stated - - -	£51,296,469	
And of Ireland - - -	4,561,353	
Making a total income of - -		55,857,822

EXPENDITURE.

The total charge upon the consolidated fund in England was - -	39,693,430	
The charge of the debt of Ireland, and other payments of a permanent nature, was - - - -	6,985,964	
Making the total permanent charge of the United Kingdom - - -		46,689,394
The total supply of the two countries, including the separate charges of each, which have from the 5th of January last become joint charges, was - - - - - -		30,457,550
Making a total expenditure of - -		£77,146,944

Of which 15,078,772*l.* was on account of reduction of debt existing before the 5th of January 1816.*

* Great Britain - - - -	£12,640,648
Ireland - - - - - -	2,438,124
	£15,078,772

Abstract

Abſtract of the Nett Produce of Great Britain, in the years ending 10th October 1816, and 10th October 1817; and alſo, the total produce of the Conſolidated Fund, the Annual Duties, and the War Taxes.

	Year ending Oct. 10, 1816.	Year ending Oct. 10, 1817.
	£	£
Cuſtoms - - -	4,789,892	5,748,728
Exciſe - - -	18,326,328	16,160,220
Stamps - - -	6,024,775	6,232,213
Poſt Office - - -	1,450,000	1,349,000
Aſſeſſed Taxes - -	6,170,181	6,001,996
Land Taxes - - -	1,123,402	1,197,848
Miſcellaneous - -	335,179	293,639
Unappropriated War Duties	- -	1,429,879
Total Conſolidated Fund	38,219,757	38,413,523
Annual duties to pay off Bills —		
Cuſtoms - - -	2,105,455	3,183,339
Exciſe - - - -	541,547	558,787
Penſions, &c. - -	16	4,016
Total Annual Duties	2,647,018	3,746,142
Permanent and Annual Duties	40,866,775	42,159,665
War Taxes —		
Cuſtoms - - -	1,777,310	525
Exciſe - - - -	5,504,715	3,109,814
Property - - -	11,990,063	2,171,615
Total War Taxes	19,272,088	5,281,954
Total Net Revenue	£60,138,863	£47,441,619

The

The Irish and Portuguese payments for the interest on their respective debts, payable in England, are excluded from this statement; and the war taxes appropriated to the interest of loans charged on them, are not included in the consolidated fund, but under the head of War Taxes, to the quarter ended 5th July 1816, inclusive; from which period certain war duties of customs being made perpetual by act 56 Geo. III. cap. 29, are included under the head Consolidated Fund.

The total of the permanent and annual duties for the last four quarters exceeds the total of the four preceding quarters by above 1,200,000*l.*, *viz.*:

Total of 1816. - - - -	£40,866,775
1817. - - - -	42,159,665
Balance in favour of 1817	1,292,890
The total consolidated fund for the same period is, for 1816. - - -	£38,219,757
1817. - - -	38,413,523
Leaving an excess in favour of 1817, of	193,766
The total war taxes for 1816. were -	£19,272,088
1817. - -	5,281,954
Against 1817	13,990,134

But this falling off is occasioned by the repeal of the war excise duty on malt, and the property tax.

Thus the difference between the whole produce of the Revenue for the year is as follows:

It was in 1816. - - - -	£60,138,863
1817. - - - -	47,441,619
Difference	12,697,244

or 483,895*l.* more than the difference (*viz.* 12,213,349*l.*) between the produce of the war excise duty and the property tax in 1816 and 1817.

OTHER

Other Taxes. However enormous this load of taxation may appear, it is far from the whole sum that is drawn from the people; poor rates, turnpikes, tolls, and the assessments for paving, watching, lighting and cleansing towns, with other charges which will be noticed in the progress of this work, give amounts more than equal to the revenue of many sovereign princes, even at this time, when many small potentates have been swallowed up in the gulph of the French revolution.

Sinking Fund. It is not to be supposed that such enormous burthens, however judiciously placed or patriotically borne, can be for ever increased without final ruin to a nation. Those whose love of their country has made them too sensitive on this account, have at least this countenance for the foundation of their fears, that at a very early period of the funding system, those statesmen whose glorious exertions contributed most to establish the constitution, foresaw the necessity of restricting the amount of the national burthens, and of providing a fund for their final reduction, or perhaps annihilation. Of the first sinking fund, its progress, benefits, alienation, and final extinction, it is not necessary here to treat *, nor would the mention have been required, but as it formed a precedent for the establishment of another, and a caution against the mischiefs which would ensue, should any minister, urged by financial distress, or deluded by sophistical reasonings or erroneous calculations, destroy this strong mound against the irruption of national ruin. Some time after the American war, when the finances of the country had derived great benefit from judicious regulations, when the debt created during that war was almost entirely funded, and the national burthens adapted to the national powers; it was determined to make a certain, permanent and unalienable provision for the necessary purpose of reducing the national debt, which then amounted to about 240,000,000*l*. The fund devoted to this object was to consist of an annual million to be paid quarterly, and of all the annuities for lives, or for limited terms of years, as they should expire, the taxes appropriated for the payment of them still continuing to be levied upon the people. And the sinking fund, thus secured, was vested in six commissioners of high rank and character, for the purpose of paying off any branch of the debt, which might be above par—(parliament previously taking the necessary steps to enable them,) and buying from those who offered

* For a clear and masterly account of this fund, see Coxe's Memoirs of Sir Robert Walpole, c. 40.

them for sale, any branches of it, which were below par*, or should they fail, and no provision be made by parliament, such funds as they might think most eligible, though above par. All dividends arising from such purchases are also to be immediately invested in the same manner; the commissioners are directed to make their purchases, in sums nearly equal, on every day of the week except Monday and Saturday. They may subscribe a sum, not exceeding their annual income, in any new loan bearing interest at the same rate with some of the existing branches of the funds. And, lastly, whenever the annual income, including the annual million, as well as the dividends arising from the purchases, shall amount altogether to four millions, "The dividends due on such part of the principal or "capital stock, as shall thenceforth be paid off by the said commissioners, and the monies payable on such annuities for "lives, or years, as may afterwards cease and determine, shall "no longer be issued at the receipt of his majesty's exchequer, "but shall be considered as redeemed by parliament, and shall "remain to be disposed of as parliament shall direct." It is evident that a fund, possessing so many copious sources of accumulation, and having no outlet of expenditure†, must soon increase to a prodigious amount; and indeed, the measure has been of very important service, not only to the public in a corporate capacity, but also to the vast number of individuals, who have property in the public funds, and to such landholders as have occasion to bring their estates to market, and by keeping the interest to be obtained by buying into the public funds from rising to a very extravagant height, it is also of great benefit to the commercial world. Some political writers have amplified the advantages flowing from this permanent sinking fund to an incalculable extent; but its merits need no exaggeration.

By the operation of this sinking fund, it has been observed, that the reduction of the debt existing before the war which began in 1793, would attain what is termed its maximum, or an interest of four millions a-year, probably in 1808, but in no case later than 1811, and consequently that debt which was, in familiar language, termed a mill-stone about the neck of the nation, would be completely annihilated in January, 1846: this was on a supposition that the three per cents. should be at the average price of eighty five, but as they have been for a long time far below that average, the redemption must have

* 100*l.* is the par price of an annuity of 5*l.* It has also been stated as the par price of one of 3*l.* by most writers on the finances.

† There is a trifling expence of about 1,800*l.* a-year for the secretary, broker, &c. but it does not appear to be borne by the fund, the amount of all the various branches of income being exactly balanced by the purchases made in the year.

have been greatly accelerated, and the term of patriotic hope proportionately abridged. The exact period at which the redemption of this debt will be effected, at every suppoſeable average price, may be ſeen by the following table; and as the dividends due on ſuch parts of the old debt, as ſhall be paid off after the ſinking fund ſhall have attained its maximum, and the annuities which ſhall afterwards fall in, will be at the diſpoſal of parliament; the period of repealing taxes annually, to an amount equal thereto, cannot be very long delayed.

An account of the ſeveral dates when the old ſinking fund will have increaſed to its greateſt amount, 4,000,000*l.* a-year, (adding thereto the 200,000*l.* annually voted by parliament:) alſo the dates when the whole amount of the debts incurred before the year 1793, will be redeemed, by the operation of the ſinking fund, according to the ſeveral average prices at which the three per cents. funds may hereafter be purchaſed.

Average Prices of the 3 per cent. Funds from the 1ſt Feb. 1799.	Dates when the Sinking Fund will have increaſed to 4,000,000*l.* its greateſt Amount.		Dates when the whole of the debt incurred before the Year 1793, will be cancelled.	
55	November,	1808	October,	1832
60	Auguſt,	1809	October,	1835
65	April,	1810	September,	1838
70	February,	1811	Auguſt,	1841
75	February *,	1808	June,	1842
80	February,	1808	April,	1844
85	February,	1808	January,	1846
90	February,	1808	January,	1848
100	February,	1808	May,	1852

Exceſs above 4,200,000*l.*, in the firſt year after the old ſinking fund ſhall attain its maximum, according to the prices of ſtocks as under.

75*l.* - -	23,600*l.*	85*l.* - -	376,800*l.*
80*l.* - -	203,300*l.*	90*l.* - -	488,400*l.*
100*l.* - - -	643,900*l.*		

* It is obvious that, in ſome caſes, the ſinking fund will increaſe to its greateſt amount ſooner with the ſtocks at a high price than at a lower one, by the redemption of the 5 per cents. or 4 per cents.

REDEMPTION OF LOANS. The sinking fund established in 1786, had already been productive beyond expectation, insomuch that on the fifth of April, 1792, when its operation for six years was complete, the commissioners had bought in 9,441,850*l.* of the capital of the national debt. It was now, however, thought proper, that, besides that general provision for buying up the national debt, there should be a particular provision made for the gradual extinction of any future debts to be created. For that purpose Mr. Pitt wisely availed himself of the plan proposed many years before by Doctor Price, by establishing, along with the funds necessary for paying the interest of any debt to be created, an additional annual fund of one hundredth part of the capital created. This plan was sanctioned by the authority of parliament, the funds appropriated for it being placed under the management of the same commissioners who have the charge of the annual million, the proceeds to be improved in the same manner. And it was enacted, that when the income of the fund should arise to three millions annually, exclusive of the sums paid in from the exchequer, the dividends should no longer be issued, and the capital to that amount should be considered redeemed. This is by far the most judicious, and the most powerful, dissolver of the national debt ever yet invented, and it has the peculiar advantage of bringing the remedy along with the disease. This sinking fund, and that established in the year 1786, have made a silent but a rapid progress in reducing the debt in the fairest possible way by buying, at the current price, from those who are desirous of selling. There need no longer be any of the tumult, vexation, and distress, which have been produced by the violent, not to say cruel and unjust, measure of compelling any of the national creditors to receive payment, or to submit to a reduction of their income. It is also a great beauty of this plan, that the higher the interest of money is, or, in other words, the lower the prices of the funds are, the quicker is the progress made in extinguishing the national debt, or of transferring the dividends from the sellers to the national purse, for the purpose of annihilating, in time, a portion of the taxes which press so hard upon the community. And a great advantage to all proprietors of the national debt is, that the constant and large purchases made by the commissioners, keep the value of their property considerably higher than it could be, if such large sums were not thus taken entirely out of the market: hence also the nation, corporately considered, derives a great advantage, from thus keeping up the price of the funds, in negotiating new loans on more favourable terms than could otherwise be obtained. By buying only from those creditors who are desirous of selling their

their ſtock, no one is diſtreſſed by being compelled, as in ſome other nations, to accept an annual payment of one or two per cent., which being too trifling to be reinveſted or employed to any uſeful purpoſe, ſerves only to wither away the capital in the hands of the creditor, and perhaps to work his ruin; this admirable plan has the great advantage of reconciling the intereſts of all parties.

As the operation of this truly grand principle of finance is perpetual, the following table will fully diſplay its effects under all probable and almoſt all poſſible circumſtances.

Account of the ſeveral periods of time in which each capital of public debt, bearing intereſt at 3, 4, and 5 per cent. per annum reſpectively, will be redeemed by an annual fund of one per cent., applied by quarterly iſſues, in purchaſing the ſaid capitals at the ſeveral average prices at which the 3 per cent. funds may be redeemable, as ſtated underneath.

	Periods of redeeming by a Sinking Fund of one per cent. per annum, iſſued by quarterly payments, a capital of Debt bearing intereſt.					
Average prices of the 3 per cent. Funds.	At 3 per cent. per annum.		At 4 per cent. per annum.		At 5 per cent. per annum.	
	Years.	Months.	Years.	Months.	Years.	Months.
50	23	3¾	27	0¼	30	1
55	25	7	29	8¼	33	0¾
60	27	10¾	32	4¾	36	0¾
65	30	2½	35	0¾	39	0½
70	32	6¼	37	9	42	0¼
75	34	10	40	5¾	45	0¼
80	37	1¾	43	1½	48	0
85	39	5½	45	9½	50	11¾
90	41	9¼	48	5¾	53	11¾
95	44	3¾	51	2	56	11½
100	46	4½	53	10¾	59	11¾

On the 31ſt of October, 1805, the ſum of national debt which had been redeemed, excluſive of the ſum purchaſed by ſale of the land tax, was 101,203,940*l.* which coſt in money 62,866,335*l.* 15*s.* 10*d.*

THE BANK. It has already been mentioned that the business relative to the funds is transacted at the bank of England. This establishment is, on all accounts, so important to the nation, and its transactions so closely connected with the highest interests of the country, that an account of it with some length of detail will not be improper.

ORIGIN. Many attempts were made to bring such an institution to bear, before the present bank was established. Soon after the restoration it was proposed to erect *an office of credit* for the reception of goods and merchandize; for the appraised value of which, notes were to be issued, which it was imagined the merchant would find less difficulty in negotiating than attended the borrowing of money on the goods themselves: and such a plan might be attended with considerable advantage to commerce, if commodities were to be warehoused in public repositories, a proper receipt given by an officer appointed for that purpose, and the property of goods transferred by indorsements upon such receipts. In 1678, Doctor Lewis, an eminent clergyman, published his model of a bank, with some observations on the great advantages that would accrue from it, to the crown and to the people; but who could venture in the reign of Charles II., to trust his property in any place to which the king could find access? The same circumstance prevented the establishment of a bank in 1683. By letters patent from the crown, a company had been erected, called the Royal Fishery of England, instituted for the purpose of carrying on that branch of commerce with advantage to this country, and, indeed, with the hopes of depriving the Dutch of the profits they acquired by fishing on our coasts. Upon this company, it appears, that a general bank of credit was engrafted: but though the plan was supported by persons of considerable character and property, neither the state of the government, nor the temper of the times, was calculated for such an institution; and consequently it was soon discontinued.

ESTABLISHMENT. The present bank of England was established in 1694. It was suggested by William Patterson, a Scotchman of great abilities, who was afterward one of the original directors, and the plan rendered practical by the exertions of Michael Godfrey, a gentleman of considerable influence in the city, who was appointed the first deputy governor. Nothing can more clearly prove the low state of public credit, and the great scarcity of specie at that time, than the terms which parliament found itself under the necessity of granting. For the sake of receiving 1,200,000*l*., government agreed to pay not only interest at eight per cent., and 4000*l*. for the expence of management; but the subscribers were also erected into a corporate

rate body for the purpose of carrying on the lucrative trade of banking. It was expected, however, that the circulation of their notes, and the establishment of paper credit, would greatly facilitate the raising of supplies, and prove a general ease and accommodation to the public in all pecuniary transactions. There were in Europe, at this time, but four very considerable banks, those of Amsterdam, Venice, Genoa, and Hamburgh; of which all but that of Genoa were solely for the convenience of merchants. At Amsterdam, Venice, and Hamburgh, all bills of exchange and other large payments were usually made at their banks, which saved much trouble to merchants. There were banks in other parts of Europe, not only for the conveniency of commerce, but also for the emolument of their proprietors, who had originally advanced money to the state, for which they had a perpetual fund of interest; and they obtained also the privilege of being cash-keepers for merchants and others. Such were the banks of Genoa, Naples, and Bologna; there being two such in the latter city, in one of which, though only ten per cent. was ever paid in, they were said to make a dividend on the whole nominal capital; and to lend money at one per cent. per annum, proceeding from the great sums with which they were entrusted without interest; and after this second sort of bank was the bank of England modelled.

The project was not suddenly popular; government was at that time reduced to great difficulties in raising the annual supplies, to support an expensive war against a potent foreign enemy, while the public measures were clogged and distressed by a violently disaffected faction, who alleged, that banks could thrive no where but in a republic, and yet would, at other times, argue, that such a bank as was proposed would make the king absolute. The projector found great difficulty in obtaining for his plan the sanction of the privy council, previous to its being brought into parliament; it was long debated with great pertinacity in presence of queen Mary, the king being absent in Flanders; many were of opinion that a bank would not succeed, as only eight per cent. interest was to be paid on the 1,200,000*l* to be advanced by the proposers of this bank. The disaffected were all hostile to it, alleging that it would ingross the money, stock, and riches of the kingdom. The monied men also opposed it, lest it should diminish (as it certainly soon afterward did) their exorbitant gains from the public distresses; for even eight per cent. on the land tax, beside additional premiums, though payable within the year, did not satisfy them. Other anticipations of the public revenues were much higher, the interest, premiums, and discounts on them rising to twenty, thirty, and forty per cent. And sad it was to consider, that contracts for things sold to government were made at forty, fifty, or even one hundred per cent. above their current value. So great was the difficulty of raising the annual supplies, that the ministry were obliged to stoop to solicit the London common council in order to borrow only one or two hundred thousand pounds at a time, on the first payments of the land-tax, as particular common-council-men did to the private inhabitants in their respective wards, going from house to house for the loan of money.

At length, the parliament having passed an act, 5, 6 William and Mary, c. 20. for granting several rates and duties on tonnage of ships, and on beer, ale, and other liquors, for securing certain recompences, &c. to such persons as should voluntarily advance 1,500,000*l.*, it was thereby enacted, that their majesties might grant a commission to take particular subscriptions for 1,200,000*l.*, part of the said 1,500,000*l.* of any persons, natives or foreigners, whom their majesties were empowered to incorporate, with a yearly allowance of 100,000*l.*, being 96,000*l.* or eight per cent. for interest, till redeemed, and 4000*l.* for charges of management; the corporation to have the name of *the Governor and Company of the Bank of England*; their fund to be redeemable, on a year's notice after the first of August, 1705, and payment of the principal; and then the corporation to cease. The company were enabled to purchase lands and other property without limitation; and to enjoy the other usual powers of corporations; and their stock to be transferable. They were not to borrow or give security under their common seal, by bill, bond, covenant, or agreement; nor owe at any one time more than 1,200,000*l.*, except by future acts of parliament, upon funds to be agreed on in parliament; and in case of their borrowing any greater sum than 1,200,000*l.* under their common seal, then every private member, and their heirs, executors, and administrators, were to be proportionably chargeable therewith, or for the repayment thereof. This corporation must not employ or trade with any of their stock, monies, or effects, in buying or selling any goods or merchandize whatever, on forfeiture of treble the value of the commodity. They might deal in bills of exchange, and in buying and selling bullion, gold, or silver, and in selling any goods or merchandize, pledged to them for money lent, and not redeemed at the time agreed on, or within three months after; and might also sell the produce of lands which they had purchased. Provided always, that all bills obligatory under the seal of the corporation might be assignable by indorsement; which should absolutely vest the property in the assignees. And that if the governor, deputy governor, directors, managers, or other members should, on the account of the corporation, purchase any

any crown lands or revenues, or advance to the crown any money by way of loan or anticipation on any branch of the revenue, other than on ſuch branches on which a credit of loan ſhould be granted by parliament, they ſhould forfeit treble the value lent; and no letters of ſignet, privy ſeal, or great ſeal, of the crown, could pardon or remit any fine or amerciament charged on this corporation, on account of any ſuit brought againſt them; but ſuch fine muſt be deducted out of their annual fund. The reſt of this long act relates to annuities for one, two, or three, lives, for 300,000*l.* principal money; the reſidue of the 1,500,000*l.* to be granted by the king.

If the adverſaries of the bank had been aſſiduous in exciting prejudices againſt it, thoſe who favoured the plan were not leſs induſtrious; they even ſanctified the meaſure, by preſſing into their ſervice the words of holy writ, Luke xix. 23. "Wherefore, then, gaveſt not thou my money into the *bank*, that at my coming I might have required my own with uſury?" However current ſuch a quotation might be with the inconſiderate, other arguments were neceſſary to produce a more general effect; it was therefore repreſented, that, by the new plan, the rich might have their perſonal property ſecured from every riſk, and might enjoy, at the ſame time, great pecuniary advantages. The landed gentleman, who formerly could not borrow four thouſand pounds on an eſtate of one thouſand pounds a-year, without additional perſonal ſecurity, might now, (it was ſaid,) borrow four thouſand pounds, on three hundred pounds per annum. The merchant who brought a cargo to England worth three thouſand pounds, might have money to that amount at the bank, without the ſmalleſt difficulty, and might thus carry on his traffick to additional advantage: and, to ſum up all in a few words, "It would render the ſovereign great, the gentry rich, the farmer flouriſhing: our commerce would increaſe, our ſhips multiply, our ſeamen would never want employment; new manufactures would be ſet up, and the whole greatly encouraged."

The public, by ſuch arguments as theſe, being impreſſed with a favourable idea of the meaſure, on the 16th June, 1694, a commiſſion was iſſued under the great ſeal, for taking ſubſcriptions. On the 21ſt of June, the commiſſioners attended for the firſt time, at Mercers' Chapel. Nearly 300,000*l.* were ſubſcribed the firſt day; 200,000*l.* the ſecond, and as much on the third; and before the ſecond of July, the whole ſum was made up. This event was beyond expectation; for it had been thought neceſſary to make proviſions in the bill, on the ſuppoſition that only 600,000*l.* might be ſubſcribed.

Charter. This great ſucceſs ſecured to the company their charter,

charter, which, after the act of parliament above recited, was considered a mere form: it directs that there be a governor, deputy governor, and twenty-four directors, of whom thirteen or more shall constitute a court, the governor or deputy governor to be always one. Five hundred pounds stock to be the lowest qualification for a vote in general courts; and no proprietor, how much soever his stock may be, to have more than one vote. The governor's qualification stock to be at least four thousand pounds; the deputy governor's three thousand pounds; and each director's two thousand pounds; and all these are to be natural-born subjects, or naturalized. Lessening their qualification stock, vacates their offices, which are only annual. They take the state oaths, that of office, and another of stock qualification. Voters also in general courts take the qualification and state oaths. No dividend can be made but by consent of a general court, and only out of the interest, profit, or produce, arising by such dealing, buying, and selling, as the act of parliament allows. General courts may make bye laws, &c. agreeable to the act of parliament and the general laws of the kingdom; impose fines on delinquents; appoint salaries to governors, directors, &c. Stock was to be diviseable by will, to be attested by three or more witnesses; but this was altered by an act of the 8th and 9th king William, which made bank stock a personal estate, and to descend accordingly. Lastly, neither the governor, nor the deputy governor in his absence, is to have any vote, either in general courts or in courts of directors, save where there shall appear to be an equality or equal number of votes.

PROGRESS. Although by their charter and the act of parliament, the bank had power to lend money on pledges, and although they once announced by advertisement their intention to do so, they never made extensive use of that power, but contented themselves with banking only, including therein the dealing in bullion, gold, and silver, discounting bills of exchange, advancing money to the public on the credit of acts of parliament, and circulating their own sealed bills, which bore interest, (though since laid aside,) and their cash notes on demand, bearing no interest; as also circulating exchequer bills for the government on a stated allowance.

Very soon after its establishment, the affairs of the bank were greatly embarrassed; a land-bank which had been for a short time attempted without success, the deficient funds for the annual supplies, the bad state of the silver coin, more especially in the years 1695, and 1696, and the ill humours occasioned by these circumstances, and by disaffection to the government, had brought the infant bank of England into such difficulty and distress,

distress, that in 1697, their cash notes were at a discount of fifteen to twenty per cent. their credit being so low that they were necessitated to pay those notes by instalments of ten per cent. once in a fortnight, and, at length, to pay only three per cent. once in three months. This distress was in a great degree occasioned by the bank having taken the clipped and diminished silver money, at the legal or par value by tale, and guineas at thirty shillings, for which they issued their notes payable on demand, and not having received from the mint, a sufficient quantity of the new silver coins, to answer the daily demands on them for their outstanding notes. The directors were thereupon obliged to make two different calls, of twenty per cent. each, on their members in the year 1696, and to issue bank sealed bills, at six per cent. interest, in exchange for bank cash notes; and to advertise, for the conveniency of trade, whilst the silver was recoining, that any person might keep an account with the bank, and transfer any sum under five pounds, from his own to another man's account; which was getting into the method of the bank of Amsterdam; yet, such was the distress of the times, that, on the 6th of May, 1697, the bank advertised in the Gazette for the defaulters of the last call of twenty per cent., which ought to have been paid by the 10th of November, 1696, and also those indebted to the bank on mortgages, pawns, notes, bills, or other securities, to pay in the said twenty per cent., and the principal and interest of those securities by the first of June next. Even so late as June, 1697, bank notes were at a discount of thirteen and fourteen per cent. A committee of the House of Commons had been appointed to inspect their books, and to examine certain accounts with regard to their situation which they had given into the house, and the report of this committee contained several curious particulars. It appeared that 893,800*l*. were issued in sealed bank bills, which bore an interest of six per cent.; 68,669*l*. in specie notes, on which, when exceeding twenty pounds, was paid an interest at the same rate: and that the notes bearing no interest amounted to 695,527*l*., but they were at a very great discount. It farther appears, that a balance of 300,000*l*. was due to the states of Holland for money advanced by them, and as this debt is called balance, it must have been originally more considerable. It is uncertain whether this sum was borrowed by the bank in order to carry on the original purposes of its establishment, or arose from the credit which the company gave to the king, to enable him to procure money on the continent for prosecuting the war. Only 42,160*l*. were issued on private loans and mortgages. In consequence of this enquiry, and in order to clear the market of part of a load then so much in disrepute; not

not without hopes also, by such means, of restoring the credit of the nation, then at the lowest ebb; an act was passed for enlarging the capital of the bank of England by ingrafting on its stock new subscriptions, four-fifths of which were to consist in exchequer tallies, and the remaining fifth in bank notes; and government agreed to allow interest, at the rate of eight per cent., on such tallies till they were paid off. The term which had been granted to the bank was also prolonged to the first of August, 1710; and during the continuance of the corporation, *no other bank or fellowship of that nature was to be erected, suffered, or countenanced, by act of parliament.* It was expected that 3,600,000*l.* would have been ingrafted; instead of which, the subscriptions amounted only to 1,001,171*l.* 10*s.* But even this operation, though on a smaller scale, was attended with considerable advantage; for about 200,000*l.* in bank notes, and 800,000*l.* in tallies, being thus sunk by the new subscriptions, the credit both of the bank and of the public began to revive. Notes without interest came to be on a par with specie; money began to circulate on moderate terms; and the exchange with the continent, from being very unfavourable, was soon brought to an equality. Thus the exclusive right of banking as a corporation was first acquired by the company, and its capital stock was thus increased to the sum of 2,201,171*l.* 10*s.* But so productive was the fund upon which the ingrafted tallies were placed, that they were all paid off in the course of a few years; and though the capital stock on which the proprietors divided, remained at the above sum, the money due by government was reduced to 1,200,000*l.* before the next prolongation.

From this period the charter of the bank has been frequently renewed or prolonged, and on different terms. In 1708, they advanced to government 400,000*l.* at six per cent., and received a prolongation of their privilege till August, 1732; in 1713, they purchased an additional term of ten years, by agreeing to circulate exchequer bills to the amount of 1,200,000*l.* for which they were to receive three per cent. per annum, and a further yearly sum of 8000*l.* payable quarterly, under the denomination of premiums for the expence of circulation, in addition to an interest of two pence per cent. a-day, payable to the bearer. In 1742, their expiring charter was extended for the further term of twenty-two years, in consideration of which, they advanced to government 1,600,000*l.* without interest; that is, they added that sum to their former debt of the same amount, both paying only three per cent., instead of six. At the time this bargain was made, the nation was involved in war, and therefore it is supposed the bank obtained favourable terms; but in 1763, the price of a renewal for twenty-one years was less

less moderate: the company agreed to pay 1,110,000*l*. to be disposed of by parliament, without allowance of interest, or repayment of principal; and to circulate a million in exchequer bills, undemandable for two years, at only three per cent. interest, though exchequer bills bearing four per cent. were then at a discount. In 1781, the charter was again prolonged by the addition of twenty-seven years to the former term, or till August, 1812; for this indulgence, the government received as an advantage, the circulation of two millions of exchequer bills not to be demanded for two years, and bearing no greater interest than three per cent. The last prolongation was confirmed by an act passed in 1800. Though the charter of the bank had several years to run, yet it was thought expedient to renew it at so early a period, with a view of strengthening the credit of the bank, and enabling it to give every possible assistance to government. The bank became bound to advance three millions for the service of the year 1800, on exchequer bills, payable without interest, out of the supplies to be granted for the year 1806, in consideration of which, the term of their charter was continued till the end of twelve months notice, after the first of August, 1833.

UTILITY OF THE BANK. The benefits derived by the public from the existence of the bank, are not however to be considered as limited to the receipt of the monies already mentioned; the taking up of exchequer bills and other government securities, when the market was overstocked, was a service of considerable importance, and, on great occasions, the bank has, by its capital and credit, opposed an effectual barrier against the fears and alarms which would have proved most ruinous to the nation. Thus in 1722, when the failure of the South Sea scheme had produced such dangerous effects on public credit, the bank contributed to allay the general inquietude, by purchasing four millions of the South Sea capital; and their aid and subscription have ever been ready in forwarding, so far as was proper, all public spirited and patriotic undertakings.

ITS DISASTERS. Nor has the prosperity of the bank been without some interruption, though the foundation of its credit has ever been unimpaired. The disasters attending the first years of its establishment have been mentioned. In November, 1700, the general terror occasioned by the claim which Lewis XIV., advanced to the crown of Spain in favour of his grandson, materially affected, for a time, the credit of the bank; and in 1704, the value of all securities was so much reduced, that they were again obliged to issue, to a large amount, sealed notes bearing interest. In 1708, the fear of an invasion of Scotland in support of the Pretender, occasioned what is called a *run* on the

the bank, but the credit of the corporation being now consider-ed inseparably connected with that of the exchequer, the lord treasurer, Godolphin, signified to the directors, that the queen would, for six months, allow an interest of six per cent. on their sealed bills, which, till then, bore only three per cent. Moreover, his lordship, and the dukes of Marlborough, Newcastle, and Somerset, and sundry other lords, offered to advance to the bank considerable sums of money: by which encouragement, and their making a call of twenty per cent. on their capital, the bank was enabled to weather that storm, and to preserve its credit. In 1711, the change of the ministry occasioned a similar run, but its bad effects were parried by the address and contrivance of the minister, in diverting the public attention to other objects. The apprehension of queen Anne's death, in 1714, occasioned again a depreciation of national securities, and a run on the bank, but the alarm speedily subsided, and the confidence of the country was restored; but in 1745, the crisis was more menacing. In that year, in consequence of the alarm raised in the metropolis by the progress of the Pretender's son, there was a great run on the bank in the month of September. The directors, to make their cash hold out as long as possible, paid in silver, and chiefly in sixpences; an expedient which could not have availed them long. An infinitely more effectual, as well as more honourable relief, was administered by a meeting of merchants, bankers, and traders, on the 26th of that month, when those gentlemen drew up a paper, declaring their resolution to support the credit of the bank by receiving their notes in all payments, and using their utmost endeavours to pay them away to all persons receiving monies from them. The resolution was soon signed by above eleven hundred individuals, and had the happy effect of quieting apprehension, restoring confidence, and putting an immediate end to the run upon the bank. From this period for fifty years, the bank continued to enjoy uninterrupted success and unlimited confidence; but in 1795, they found it necessary, from the nature of circumstances in the commercial world, to publish a resolution for limiting their accommodations by discount, though in fact, it is said, they did not, in the ensuing year, discount to a smaller amount than in that which preceded.

All these were however of inconsiderable importance compared with the great stoppage which occurred in 1797, an event which demonstrated, that, even in a commercial country, anxiously alive to its pecuniary interests, it is easy for a strong and popular administration to quiet apprehension, and restore confidence, amid circumstances the most unpromising, by the use

of

of temperate exertions enforced by convincing arguments, and supported by facts.

The great and continued drains of bullion, in consequence of the enormously expensive operations of the war, the loans to the emperor of Germany, and other subsidies to foreign princes, and also the large sums payable for cargoes and freights of neutral ships taken, which the foreign owners required to be paid in bullion, had raised the price of gold (8th of October, 1795,) to four guineas per ounce: and our gold coin being only 3*l.* 17*s.* 10½*d.* per ounce, it was evident that the current money of this country, consisting almost wholly of gold, would be carried abroad to a very alarming amount. Even since December 1794, the directors had repeatedly expressed to the chancellor of the exchequer, their uneasiness on account of the magnitude of the sums drawn from the bank for the service of government, and anxiously required payment, or at least a considerable reduction of the debt. They even resolved to limit their advances on treasury bills to the sum of 500,000*l.*; and requested Mr. Pitt to make his arrangements so as not to have occasion to draw on them for any sum beyond that limitation. And at last they acquainted him (30th of July, 1795,) that they were determined to give orders to their cashiers to refuse payment of any treasury bills, which would carry the advance beyond that amount. Nevertheless the chancellor of the exchequer obtained further advances from them, which were granted with extreme reluctance on their part, on his pressing solicitations, and statements that serious embarrassments would arise to the public service if refused.

It would be tedious to enumerate all the applications of the governors of the bank to the prime minister, urging a speedy diminution of the debt, and deprecating further demands; suffice it to say, that on the 10th of February, 1797, the government was indebted to the bank, according to a statement delivered to Mr. Pitt, as follows:

			£.
Arrears of advance on land and malt-taxes,		1794	337,000
ditto	ditto	1795	491,000
ditto	ditto	1796	2,392,000
Exchequer bills on vote of credit			968,800
——— on consolidated fund, 1796			1,323,000
Treasury bills paid at the bank			1,674,645
			7,186,445
Besides arrears of interest due, &c.			400,000
			£. 7,586,445

The

The directors of the bank represented to the minister, that, if the loan of 1,500,000*l.* to be raised in this country for Ireland, which was then in contemplation, should proceed, the greatest part of it must be remitted in hard cash, which would bring ruin on the bank, and probably compel them to shut their doors; that, at any rate, they must diminish their advances to the treasury, and lessen the customary accommodation to the merchants in the way of discount.

About this time there was much talk of an invasion from France: and it was supposed that many people in all parts of the country were desirous of securing as much as possible of their property in gold coin in their own possession. Certain it is, that very heavy demands were made on the country banks, and that two in Newcastle were obliged to stop paying in cash. The country banks were thereupon obliged to make large demands for money on the bankers in London, who were their correspondents, which consequently compelled them to drain very large sums in cash from the bank. This run had been progressively increasing; but particularly in the week beginning with Monday the 20th of February, it exceeded that of any foregoing week; and the demands on the Friday, and Saturday, were larger than the four preceding days taken together.

On Friday (24th) the committee of the whole court of directors, alarmed at the rapid diminution of the cash in their coffers, desired the deputy-governor, and Mr. Bosanquet, to wait on Mr. Pitt, to represent to him the dreadful drain of their specie, and to ask him, how far he thought the bank might go on paying cash, and when he would think it necessary to interfere, before their money was so reduced, as might be detrimental to the immediate service of the state?

In this crisis, the king was requested to come to town to assist at a meeting of the privy council; and on Sunday (26th) a council was accordingly held at St. James's, the result of which, and of another meeting immediately after it in Downing Street, between the members of the administration, and the governor, deputy-governor, Mr. Thornton, Mr. Bosanquet, and other directors of the bank, after a warm conference, was, an order of privy council declaring it indispensably necessary for the public service, that the directors of the bank of England should forbear issuing any cash in payment, until the sense of parliament could be taken on that subject, and the proper measures adopted for maintaining the means of circulation, and supporting the public and commercial credit of the kingdom.

The governors and directors immediately published the order of council, with an advertifement of their own, declaring that their general concerns were in an affluent and flourifhing fituation, and that they fhould continue their ufual difcount for the accommodation of the commercial intereft, paying the amount in bank notes; and the dividend warrants would be paid in the fame manner. The actual arrival of an event, which, by all perfons who had ever contemplated a probability of its happening, had been dreaded as the death-blow to the commercial profperity of the country, produced a confiderable alarm, but it was far fhort of what might have been expected. The principal merchants and bankers immediately met at the Manfion Houfe, the Lord Mayor prefiding, and unanimoufly adopted and fubfcribed a refolution that they would not refufe to receive bank notes for any fum of money to be paid to them; and would ufe the utmoft endeavours to make all their payments in the fame manner. In a few days, this refolution was fubfcribed by above three thoufand principal merchants, bankers, and traders; on the 28th of February a paper, nearly fimilar, was figned and publifhed by the lords of the privy council; and immediately tranfactions of every kind went on, as if nothing had happened. A number of papers tending to account for the fcarcity of money were prefented to parliament, from which, and the investigation to which they gave rife, it fully appeared, that the affairs of the bank were, by no means, in a fituation to give any real caufe of alarm to their creditors, and that the company were fully able to make good all demands of every kind. It was made evident, that, after deducting all claims againft them, they had a clear balance of property to the amount of 15,513,690*l.* and confequently, as fo large a capital could not be forced into cafh without great lofs, it was the intereft of all proprietors, as well as of all who regarded the welfare of the country, to unite in fupport of the eftablifhment by which alone it could be rendered valuable.

Issue of small Notes and Dollars. In a few days after the ftoppage of iffuing cafh from the bank, the directors began to iffue notes for one pound and two pounds, which have continued ever fince in general currency. As a further fubftitute for Britifh coinage they circulated Spanifh dollars, with a miniature impreffion of his Britannic Majefty's head ftamped upon them, at four fhillings and nine-pence. They continued in circulation till the 31ft of October, 1797, during which time a great many dollars had been iffued by unprincipled individuals with counterfeited ftamps. The King's head on the dollar was fo very fmall, not larger in circumference than a pear of moderate fize, that to counterfeit it was a very eafy operation.

operation. Tools for the purpose made of steel, imparted the figure to silver by means of a smart stroke with a hammer, and as the piece of silver afforded a handsome profit, the fraud was carried on to a great extent. The bank, when this sort of specie was called in, finding that much contention and much misery to poor persons would ensue from rejecting the spurious coinage received as genuine all that was produced to them, and submitted to the loss.

Other Dollars and tokens. In 1804, the current silver coin having been much reduced in value, a miserable spurious trash introduced, and even of that a great portion withdrawn from circulation, the bank again issued a number of Spanish dollars at five shillings each, which were afterward raised to five shillings and six-pence. In this emission, they totally changed the appearance of the coin; all traces of the Spanish monarch and his arms being struck out, and the King's head on one side, and some words on the reverse being produced at one blow by force of a steam engine. Other tokens were afterward issued at three shillings and eighteen pence each; but government having, in 1816, sent forth a copious supply of silver coin from the mint, these tokens have also been called in. Notwithstanding the pains which were taken to prevent these tokens from being easily counterfeited, they were no sooner issued than the hand of fraud was in full activity. Spurious dollars and tokens were issued in base metal, and some even in silver, when the price of bullion declined; in vain were strong statutes passed denouncing capital penalties, transportation and imprisonment against those who made, uttered, or unlawfully possessed these deceptive fabrications; they were supplied by the guilty makers at so low a price as to form an irresistible temptation to poverty or avarice, and innumerable prosecutions and convictions were not found to deter new adventurers from engaging in this wicked traffic.

Bank Indemnity and Restriction. Government aided the useful efforts of the bank by statutes indemnifying the governors as to all acts which might be irregular. On the third of May an act was passed reciting a minute of the company forbidding the issue of cash in payments, and legalizing and continuing that restriction for a limited time, and they were indemnified as to suits that might be brought against them for refusing to give cash for their notes. These restrictions have been by subsequent acts continued with little variation to the present time. By these wise and provident measures, all the apprehensions that were entertained have vanished; the credit of the bank is as high, both at home and abroad, as it ever was; and not the slightest inconvenience is or has been experienced from its not paying in cash.

Bank Stock and Dividends. In the preceding account mention has been made of monies advanced by the bank to government, the following table exhibits a general view of the progress of the capital and dividends of the Bank of England, from its establishment to the present time.

	Year.		Capital. £.	s.	d.		Dividend.
	1694,	-	1,200,000	0	0	-	8 per cent.
	1697,	-	2,201,171	10	0	-	9 per cent.
	1708,	-	4,402,343	0	0	-	9 per cent.
	1709,	-	5,058,547	1	9	}	varying from
	1710,	-	5,559,995	14	8	}	9 to 6 per
	1722,	-	8,959,995	14	0	}	cent.
25th March -	1730,	-	- - - -	-	-	-	6 per cent.
29th September	1730,	-	- - - -	-	-	-	5½ per cent.
25th March -	1731,	-	- - - -	-	-	-	6 per cent.
29th September	1731,	-	- - - -	-	-	-	5½ per cent.
25th March -	1732,	-	- - - -	-	-	-	6 per cent.
29th September	1732,	-	- - - -	-	-	-	5¼ per cent.
	1742,	-	9,800,000	0	0	-	5½ per cent.
29th September	1742,	-	- - - -	-	-	-	5⅓ per cent.
	1746,	-	10,780,000	0	0	-	5 per cent.
25th March -	1747,	-	- - - -	-	-	-	5 per cent.
5th April -	1753,	-	- - - -	-	-	-	4½ per cent.
10th October	1764,	-	- - - -	-	-	-	5 per cent.
10th October	1767,	-	- - - -	-	-	-	5½ per cent.
10th October	1781,	-	- - - -	-	-	-	6 per cent.
	1782,	-	11,642,400	0	0	-	6 per cent.
5th April -	1788,	-	- - - -	-	-	-	7 per cent.

Consequently the present capital on which the bank divides, amounts to 11,642,400*l.*, which at an interest of 7 per cent. is 814,968*l.* per annum. But this is not the exact sum due by the public to the company, and far less is the dividend above mentioned the sum annually paid by the bank to its proprietors. The sums which the bank has lent on permanent securities, no portion of which the public is under any necessity of repaying, until its privileges expire, amount to 11,686,800*l.*, being 44,400*l.* more than that on which the bank pays its dividends. The interest paid by the public is but 352,502*l.* 3*s.* 6*d.*; whereas the bank, in consequence of the profits of its business, is able to make a regular annual dividend, besides occasional ones, at the rate of 814,968*l.* per annum, or 462,465*l.* 16*s.* 6*d.* more than it receives. In addition to the above interest, the sum of 5,898*l.* 3*s.* 5*d.* is annually allowed for the charges of management; of which 4,000*l.* were given at the original establishment of the bank, and the remainder in 1742, when four millions were purchased from the South Sea company.

Besides these regular dividends, the bank has occasionally given to the proprietors of stock, extraordinary allowances under the name of bonuses; amounting in all to upwards of two millions. The capital stock of the bank is exempted from taxes; accounted a personal estate, assignable over and not subject to forfeiture. The dividends are paid at Ladyday and Michaelmas, old style.

BUSINESS OF THE BANK. The bank is to be considered as uniting three distinct classes of transactions; it is a place of deposit for monies, issuing its notes in return; it is an office for discounting the bills of merchants, bankers, and private tradesmen; and since the year 1747, the management of government securities has been transferred from the exchequer to the bank. The profit on the two former branches of commerce is uncertain, depending on prudence and fortune, but its average must be very considerable; the allowance on the management of government securities is 450*l.* per million of stock, or tenpence and four fifths of a penny per cent., in consideration of which government is freed from every charge for accountants, clerks, books, and the numerous other particulars requisite in the management of so great a concern as the national debt. From this management an indirect profit arose to the bank from sums which were left in their hands through mistake or indolence, and were called *unclaimed dividends*. In 1791, these dividends had accumulated to 660,000*l.*; and on the principle that a sum which the creditor neglects to call for, must remain with the debtor, and not with his agent or banker, Mr. Pitt proposed, that 500,000*l.* of that dormant money should be applied to the public service. The motion was opposed by the directors of the bank, as dangerous to public credit; and the matter was compromised by the nation accepting that sum as a loan from the bank without interest, on condition that a balance of the public money not less than 600,000*l.* (reckoning this loan of 500,000*l.* as part of it) should at all times remain in the hands of the bank, and that the annual allowance to the bank for the management of the public debt should continue at the accustomed rate of 450*l.* per million. Besides this profit, government pays to the bank, for receiving subscriptions on loans 205*l.* 15*s* 10*d.* per million, and for making out, issuing, and paying the tickets in each lottery, 1000*l.*

BANK NOTES. Mention has already been made of the first notes issued from the bank, but interest on them has long been discontinued. Until 1759, twenty pounds was the amount of the smallest: in that year notes for fifteen pounds, and ten pounds began to be circulated; in 1793 those of five [illegible] pounds [illegible] pounds were given, and in 1797, the bank gave notes of two and one pounds. All these notes are printed on a transparent but strong paper; the composition of which is so contrived as to exhibit in all parts a wavy appearance, each piece is surrounded with flourishes, and at the bottom, in Roman capital letters are the words "Bank of England." These characteristics cannot be discerned unless the note is held between the eye and the light. The more visible part consists of an engraved promise to pay to the principal cashier of the bank by name, or bearer, the given sum, which is again inserted in the lower corner on the left of the note, in white letters on a black ground. The notes are numbered progressively, the date of their being issued twice inserted, and the names of one clerk who promises to pay the money in the name of governor and company, and of another who attests the entry in the book, are subscribed; the numbers, dates, and signatures are in course written, the name of the general payee is engraved, but in a character more like an ordinary hand writing than the residue of the note. Besides these notes there are bank post bills, which differ principally in being made payable to some other person than the chief cashier of the bank, or order, and incapable of circulation without an indorsement. Considerable gains must undoubtedly accrue to the bank from the issue of their paper, not only by the use of money left with them at interest, while their notes bear none, but by the frequent, and almost continual loss of bank notes as well through carelessness as fire and other accidents. Yet the bank occasionally suffers by paying undetected forgeries, and the expence of preparing, filling up, signing, and entering the notes is so far considerable, that after some time the company issued again those for one pound and two pounds which came to them after having been in circulation: their general practice is not to reissue, but cancel all notes returning to them. The amount of bank notes in circulation in February 1797, was 8,640,250*l.*; in November 1803, it had increased to 17,931,930*l.*; but the property of the bank is more than adequate to a much larger issue for the purpose of extending discounts and facilitating commerce; and perhaps the reproach against them is not ill founded, that frequently they have had cash and bullion hoarded up, nearly equal in amount to all their notes in circulation.

Laws peculiarly relating to the Bank. Independently of the statutes made for the establishment and internal regulation of this great national concern, there are several laws for restraining offences by which their property or credit might be endangered. By 15th Geo. II. c. 13. any officer or servant of the governor and company, who embezzles, secretes, or runs away with any note, bill, dividend-warrant, bond, deed, or other security; money or other effects belonging to the said company, or belonging to any other person and deposited with the governor and company, or with him as their officer or servant, shall be deemed guilty of felony without benefit of clergy. By the same statute any person forging the seal of the bank, or forging or altering bank notes, or tendering such forged or altered notes in payment, or demanding to have them exchanged, or forging the name of any cashier of the bank, is guilty in the same degree. By 13th Geo. III. c. 79. Persons not authorized by the bank, making or using moulds for the making of paper, with the words *Bank of England*, visible in the substance, or having such moulds in their possession, are guilty of felony without benefit of clergy: and persons issuing notes and bills engraved to resemble those of the bank, or having the sum expressed in white characters on a black ground, may be punished by imprisonment, not exceeding six months; but innocent persons possessed of such notes carrying them for payment are not affected. By a late statute 41st Geo. III. c. 39. the penalties of this act are extended to persons who have in their possession any paper made from such moulds, or resembling that whereon the notes of the Bank of England are generally printed. It is also to be observed that persons dealing in, or being proprietors of bank stock are not by that dealing within the statutes respecting bankrupts, and such stock is not only exempt from tax, but protected against attachments.

Buildings and Offices. The business of this corporation was originally transacted at Grocers' Hall in the Poultry. In 1732 the first stone of the present building was laid, on the site of the house and garden of Sir John Houblon, the first governor; it then only comprised what now forms the centre, with the court yard, the hall, and the bullion court. The east wing was added in 1770; and the western wing, with the Lothbury front, were begun in 1789. The building is a stone edifice, situated a little to the north of Cornhill. The front is composed of a centre, eighty feet in length, of the Ionic order, on a rustic base; and two wings, ornamented with a colonnade. The back of the building, which is in Lothbury, is a high and heavy wall of stone, with a gateway for carriages into the bullion court. The principal entrance into the bank is from Threadneedle Street. The wings were designed by Sir Robert Taylor, and for the purpose of erecting them, several houses were taken down, and the church of St. Christopher le Stocks, to the great injury and disturbance of the ashes and memorials of the dead. On the east side of the great entrance is a passage leading to a spacious apartment, called the rotunda, where the stock ftock brokers, and other perfons, meet for the purpofes of tranfacting bufinefs in the public funds. Branching out of the rotunda are the various offices appropriated to the management of each particular ftock; in all thefe offices, under the feveral letters of the alphabet, are arranged the books in which the amount of every individual's intereft in fuch a fund is regiftered. The rotunda is a great fcene of pecuniary negotiation, and the clamour is fometimes fo exceffive, that the beadle or porter of the bank is obliged to obtain filence in the following manner. Dreffed in his robe of office, a fcarlet gown and gold laced hat, he mounts a kind of pulpit, holding in one hand a filver headed ftaff; in the other he has a common watchman's rattle, which he exercifes over the heads of the crowd, with a clattering noife that overpowers the ftouteft lungs, and he does not defift from enforcing this ftreporous kind of admonition till it produces the defired effect. The rotunda has a large dome, which admits light through the cupola, and has in the centre a wind dial. Befide the rotunda, and the various ftock offices, there are other apartments of the bank deferving of notice. The hall in which bank notes are iffued and exchanged, is a noble room, feventy nine feet by forty, and contains a marble ftatue of William III. the founder of the bank; an admired piece of fculpture, the production of Cheere. The vaft and increafing bufinefs carried on in this edifice requires the perpetual aid of the architect in making additions and alterations.

Officers. The bank is under the management of a governor, and twenty-four directors, none of whom muft be directors of the Eaft India Company. They are chofen by the owners of bank ftock, annually, the firft whole week in April. Formerly no court of directors could be held unlefs the governor or deputy governor was prefent, but this inconvenient regulation has been fuperfeded; their qualifications in ftock have already been fpecified. It were needlefs to detail the other perfons employed, as their occupations are expreffed by the names of their offices; they are eftimated at feven hundred, befides beadles, porters, and menial fervants.

Coin. Connected with the fubject of revenue in general that of the national coinage claims attention in this place. "The money or coin of a country," Lord Liverpool obferves, "is the ftandard meafure, by which the value of things, "bought and fold, is regulated and afcertained; and is itfelf, "at the fame time, the value or equivalent for which goods "are exchanged, and in which contracts are generally made "payable. In this laft refpect, money, as a meafure, differs "from all others; and to the combination of the two qualities

" before defined, which constitute the essence of money, the " principal difficulties, that attend it, in speculation and practice, both as a measure and an equivalent, are to be ascribed. " These two qualities can never be brought perfectly to unite " and agree; for if money were a measure alone, and made " like all other measures of a material of little or no value, it " would not answer the purpose of an equivalent. And if it " is made, in order to answer the purpose of an equivalent, of " a material value, subject to frequent variations, according to " the price at which such material sells at the market, it fails " on that account in the quality, or standard, or measure, and " will not continue to be perfectly uniform and at all times " the same. In all civilized nations money has been made " either of gold, or silver, or copper, frequently of all three, " and sometimes of a metal composed of silver and copper in " certain proportions, commonly called billon. It has been " found by long experience, and by the concurrent opinion of " civilized nations in all ages, that these metals, and particularly gold and silver, are the fittest materials of which money " can be made. Gold and silver are perfectly homogeneous " in themselves, for no physical difference can be found in any " pound of pure gold, or of pure silver, whether the production " of Europe, Asia, Africa, or America. They are divisible with " the greatest accuracy into exact proportions or parts. From " their value they are not too bulky for the common purposes " of exchange, and in all these respects they serve better than " any other material, as an equivalent. And, lastly, they are " less consumable or subject to decay, than most other commodities. Certain portions of these metals, with an impression struck upon them, by order of the sovereign, as a " guarantee of their purity and weight, serve as coin."

The King's Prerogative. The coins of every kingdom or state are the measure of property and commerce within every such kingdom or state, according to the nominal value declared and authorized by the sovereign. So far as they are made legal tender in exchanges with foreign countries, and in payments made to them, the intrinsic value of the metal of which the coin is made, is the only measure of property and commerce; because the authority of sovereigns cannot extend to regulate payments made in foreign countries, where they have no power or jurisdiction. There is no doubt, that the sovereigns of most of the kingdoms and states of Europe have enjoyed and exercised, from time immemorial, the right of declaring at what rate or value the coins of every denomination, permitted to be current in their respective dominions, shall pass and become, in that respect, lawful coins, or legal tender. In this kingdom, the sovereigns have always enjoyed and exercised this right. Sir Mathew Hale reckons it *inter Jura Majestatis*, and says, it is an unquestionable prerogative of the crown. This prerogative was sometimes invaded by powerful barons, who stamped monies of their own; but this practice was suppressed in the days of Henry II. In times less ancient, kings have occasionally conferred the right of making money on ecclesiastical corporations, but they did not grant the power of instituting either the alloy, the denomination, or the stamp; the dies were usually issued by the treasurer and barons of the exchequer, by the king's command under his great seal; and the masters or chief officers employed in these mints, were sworn to the king for the just execution of their trusts. The prerogative of setting a rate or nominal value on current coins is exercised either by a clause inserted in the mint indentures, or by proclamation; and it seems to be the better, though not the uncontroverted opinion, that the king may, by virtue of his prerogative, legitimate or make current base coin, or such as is below the standard of sterling. He may also raise any coin already in currency to a higher denomination or extrinsic value; decry any money already current, that is, either reject it wholly out of circulation, or make it pass at a less rate or value, than that at which it has hitherto been received, and make foreign coin current at a determined rate or value, and this by a proclamation alone; but, says Lord Liverpool, although this high prerogative is unquestionable, it is certainly advisable, that in the exercise of it, whenever any great change is intended to be made, the king should avail himself of the wisdom and support of his parliament.

Debasement of Coin. There are three ways of debasing the current coin; first, by diminishing the quantity or weight of the metal of a certain standard, of which any coin of a given denomination is made. Secondly, by raising the nominal value of coins of a given weight, and made of a metal of a certain standard; that is, by making them current, or legal tender, at a higher rate than that at which they passed before. Thirdly, by lowering the standard or fineness of the metal, of which coins of a given weight and denomination are made; that is, by diminishing the quantity of pure metal, and proportionally increasing that of alloy. Each of these modes has been practised at different times by the monarchs of this country before the revolution, and debasement of coin has already been mentioned as one of the extraordinary sources from which they endeavoured to draw emolument; the history of each specific act would be too long for this work.

Standard. The weight by which gold and silver are estimated

mated in this realm is the pound troy; in ancient times, there was a weight used at the mint said to be derived from the Saxons, called the Tower pound, or moneyer's pound; lighter than the pound troy, by three quarters of an ounce; but this weight has been discontinued since the eighteenth year of Henry VIII. The standard of silver was anciently eleven ounces two penny-weights fine, and eighteen penny-weights alloy; and this is now, and since the reign of Edward I. always has been, the standard of English silver coin, except during a short period, when Henry VIII. reduced it, in the thirty-fourth year of his reign, to ten ounces fine and two ounces alloy; a mischief which was remedied in the second year of Queen Elizabeth. Gold was anciently twenty carats three grains and a half fine, to half a grain of alloy, till the eighteenth of Henry VIII., when a new standard was introduced of twenty-two carats fine to two alloy; both standards were used till the fifteenth Charles II., but since that time, the new one alone has prevailed, and by a proclamation in 1732, coins of the old standard were forbidden to be any longer current.

Silver Coin. Silver money has, in point of antiquity, precedence over every other. The coins made in this realm before the conquest are little known, except to antiquaries, and even among them, subjects of much dispute; but William certainly instituted a coinage of silver, in which the denomination pound was used to express so much in actual weight, and the coin, called a penny, weighed twenty four grains, or the twentieth part of an ounce. Henry I. introduced half-pennies and farthings, both of silver, and having their just relative proportion to the penny and the pound. These continued to be the sole denominations of coin, till Edward I. introduced groats, which had the inconvenience of being uncertain in value; for groat, though now ordinarily taken to signify four-pence, has, in fact, no precise meaning, and those made by Edward I. weighed from ninety-four, to one hundred and thirty-nine grains, which as the weight of the penny was then reduced to twenty three grains and a half, equalled four-pence, in the smaller, or almost sixpence in the greater size. Henry VIII., in the course of his reign coined all the before-mentioned pieces, besides crowns, and testons, which are called shillings, but as he adulterated the metal, sometimes by introducing one half, sometimes two thirds of alloy, the value of these pieces is uncertain. For the same reason, the crowns and half crowns, shillings, six-pences, three-pences, and rose-pennies in the next two reigns cannot be relied on, since the example of Henry VIII., continued to prevail, until adulteration was carried to the extent of three fourths alloy. Queen Elizabeth, restoring the

the ancient ſtandard, gave to ſhillings and ſix-pences nearly their preſent value; for in her time the coin retaining old denominations had been ſo much reduced in weight, that a pound of ſilver was repreſented by three pounds in money, of ſterling fineneſs. In this reign various pieces were coined beſides ſhillings and ſix-pences, which all had reference to nearly the ſame proportionate value between a pound weight, and a nominal pound in money; theſe were groats, half groats, three-pences, three-half-penny pieces, three-farthing pieces, crowns and half-crowns; porcullis crowns or dollars, which weighed ſeventeen penny weights eleven grains; half dollars, quarter dollars and rials or teſters; ſome of theſe pieces fell into diſuſe; and in the reign of James I. two-pences, pence, and half-pence were coined in ſilver; to which Charles I. added ten-ſhilling and twenty-ſhilling pieces, and many obſidional monies coined in different places, and at various periods of the civil war. Of all theſe pieces there now remain in circulation only crowns, half-crowns, ſhillings, and ſix-pences; four-penny, three-penny, and penny pieces in ſilver being occaſionally produced, but rarely uſed as coins. During ſcarcities of ſilver, Spaniſh dollars have twice been brought into circulation, but, although marked with the king's head, they cannot properly be conſidered as coins, but as tokens.

Gold Coin. It was generally believed till the year 1732, that Edward III. was the firſt of the Engliſh kings who iſſued from their mints any gold coins: but, by a manuſcript preſerved in the archieves of the city of London, it was then diſcovered, that Henry III., in the latter part of his reign, that is, in his forty-firſt year, made what was called a penny of fine gold, weighing two ſterlings, or the one hundred and twentieth part of the Tower pound; which gold penny was to paſs for twenty ſterlings or ſilver pennies in tale. This information has been indiſputably confirmed, but it is probable that theſe coins were not in general circulation. Foreign gold coins muſt have been introduced before that time, and received in payment according to their value in proportion to ſilver; frequent mention is made of byzants of gold, ſo called from thoſe ſtruck by the Greek emperors at Conſtantinople; and of florins, ſo denominated from their being firſt coined at Florence. Theſe florins furniſhed the models on which Edward III. in the eighteenth year of his reign made coin of the ſame denomination, weighing four penny weights nineteen grains, or the fiftieth part of a Tower pound of gold; they paſſed for ſix ſhillings, and were intrinſically worth about nineteen ſhillings of our preſent money; he alſo coined half and quarter florins; nobles at ſix ſhillings and eight-pence each, and half and quarter nobles. The florins were estimated at rather more than twelve times and a half the value of silver of equal weight; but this being considered as exceeding the just proportion, they were only to be taken by consent, and the other coins, issued at little more than eleven to one, served as a new currency when the florins and the fractions of them were returned to the mint. The nobles and their fractions continued at the same nominal and nearly the same intrinsic value, till Edward IV. made some which passed for eight shillings and four-pence, and subsequently others weighing only five penny-weights eight grains which were current at ten shillings; and had also the name of rials, and were divided into halves and quarters; he also made a coin called an angel, weighing three penny-weights thirteen grains and a half, which took the place of the old noble, being circulated at six shillings and eight-pence, and its diminutive called an angelet, or half angel. In the reign of Henry VII., sovereigns and half sovereigns were coined at twenty shillings and ten shillings; these were enhanced by Henry VIII., to twenty two shillings and six-pence, and the half sovereign was also called a rial; pieces called angels were in value seven shillings and six-pence, and the George noble brought that coin to its ancient rate of six shillings and eight-pence. Henry also, after the establishment of the new standard, coined crowns at five shillings, and half crowns; in succeeding reigns, as silver bore a smaller relative value to gold, the sovereign advanced to thirty shillings, and the angel to ten shillings. Elizabeth gave the name of noble to a coin worth fifteen shillings and of double noble to one of thirty shillings, sinking the sovereign to twenty shillings. James I. continued it at the same value, and gave it the name of unites; he issued also double crowns at ten shillings, and Britain crowns at five shillings; he raised the unites to twenty two shillings, without increasing the weight, but afterwards decreased the weight and reduced the value to twenty shillings, giving them the additional name of laurels; he also coined rose rials of thirty shillings, spur rials of fifteen shillings, double crowns at eleven shillings, Britain crowns at five shillings and six-pence, and thistle crowns at four shillings and four-pence three farthings. Charles I. issued in the time of the civil war, several gold as well as silver coins. In the time of the interregnum the twenty shilling coins were called broad pieces, and Cromwell coined some of fifty shillings. Charles II. had a coinage called guineas, at twenty shillings each, their weight being five penny-weights nine grains and a half, with half guineas, double guineas, and five pound pieces, which last weighed twenty six penny-weights twenty three grains and a half. Guineas have continued to be the circulating coin ever ſince, their value having been once raiſed by proclamation to twenty-two ſhillings, but by common conſent diminiſhed to twenty-one ſhillings and ſix-pence, and afterwards by proclamation to twenty-one ſhillings; in the reign of George I. quarter guineas were coined, but they are now out of uſe, though of late years a gold coin has come into circulation, in value one third of a guinea, and generally called a ſeven ſhilling-piece.

OBSERVATIONS ON GOLD COIN. In this kingdom the gold coins only have been for many years paſt, and are now, in the practice and opinion of the people, the principal meaſure of property and inſtrument of commerce. The integer, or pound ſterling, which at the acceſſion of William I. was a pound weight of ſilver, and which by ſucceſſive debaſements was reduced, in the forty-third year of Elizabeth, to $\frac{20}{62}$ parts of a pound troy of ſtandard ſilver, is now become, by the courſe of events, and by the general conſent of the people, $\frac{20}{21}$ parts of a guinea, or of five penny weights nine grains and a half of ſtandard gold. This change in the baſis of calculation has been viſibly effected ever ſince Henry VII. iſſued the coins called ſovereigns, intended to repreſent the integer or pound ſterling; and gold coin is now the meaſure of almoſt all contracts and bargains; and by it, as a meaſure, the price of all commodities bought and ſold is adjuſted and aſcertained. For theſe reaſons the gold coin ſhould be made as perfect and be kept as pure as poſſible. With reſpect to the quantity of gold coin now in circulation, it cannot be reduced to a poſitive certainty, and in the calculation a wide difference of opinion prevails between two perſons enjoying the beſt means of obtaining information, and the greateſt ability to draw from it the moſt correct inferences. Mr. Roſe eſtimates it at 43,950,042*l.*; Lord Liverpool at only 30,000,000*l.*; Mr. Roſe does not however form any ſpecific calculation, but merely recapitulates, with occaſional deductions, the ſums coined during the preſent reign; while the Earl of Liverpool gives very cogent reaſons for thinking that the eſtimate he has made is by no means too low.

OBSERVATIONS ON SILVER COIN. The ſilver coins are the ſecond in rank, and next in value to thoſe made of gold. The quantity of legal ſilver coins now in currency is certainly far too ſmall for the purpoſes of commerce, particularly of the retail trade, and for the convenience of the people. Their deficiency in weight is at preſent even greater than before the general recoinage of the ſilver coins in the reign of William III. It is impoſſible to form any eſtimate or reaſonable conjecture of the nominal value of the legal ſilver coins now in circulation; and

and coined in the mints of this kingdom: it is possible however to ascertain the value which they cannot exceed. The nominal value of the silver monies which were coined at the general recoinage in the reign of William III., and those which have been occasionally issued since that period, amounts to 8,076,092*l.* Of these the crown pieces, amounting in value to 1,553,047*l.*, have almost wholly disappeared; their value therefore must be deducted from the total above mentioned. It may fairly be estimated, that one moiety of the half crown pieces has in like manner disappeared; half of their value, being 1,164,785*l.*, must therefore be deducted, which leaves the like sum of 1,164,785*l.*, being the value of the remainder.

What may be the nominal value of the legal shillings and sixpences, and silver coins of smaller denominations remaining in circulation, it would be idle to attempt ascertaining, except on the ground of probable surmise; their number has certainly very much diminished; deducting therefore, for the sake of conjecture, one third, the nominal value of those that remain will be 2,795,650*l.* The total value of all the legal silver coins now in circulation cannot, therefore, according to this estimate, exceed 3,960,435*l.*, it is probably much less. There are certainly many counterfeits in daily use, but fewer perhaps than is generally imagined. It is not very difficult to discover them; and the officers of the mint can very readily distinguish them from the legal silver coins by the quality of the metal. The present deficiency in weight of the legal silver coins, according to their several denominations, has been ascertained by the two following experiments; the one made in December, 1787; the other, in July, 1798, by the officers of the mint.

In 1787, it was found that

$12\frac{8}{10}$ crowns	were requisite	$12\frac{4}{10}$	crowns	As issu-
27 halfcrowns	to make up	$24\frac{8}{10}$	half crowns	ed from
$78\frac{1}{10}$ shillings	a pound Troy,	62	shillings	the
$194\frac{6}{8}$ six-pences	instead of	124	six-pences	mint.

In 1798, it was found that

$12\frac{13}{40}$ crowns	were requisite	$12\frac{16}{10}$	crowns	As issu-
$27\frac{23}{40}$ half crowns	to make up	$24\frac{32}{40}$	half crowns	ed from
$82\frac{9}{40}$ shillings	a pound Troy,	62	shillings	the
$200\frac{17}{40}$ six-pences	instead of	124	six-pences	mint.

And if we compare the deficiency in weight of these several denominations of silver coins, according to the last experiment, with

with what they ought to weigh by the mint indenture, the deficiency will amount in the

Crowns to	3 162/511	per cent.
Half crowns	9 991/110 r	per cent.
Shillings	24 1064/3126	per cent.
Six-pences	38 2294/5037	per cent.

Copper Coin. Before the Union of the two kingdoms under James I., there was not any braſs or copper money coined for the uſe of England, though the French had it in 1575, as moſt of the neighbouring kingdoms and ſtates had ſome time before. Queen Elizabeth, it ſeems, had it under conſideration before her death, and the queſtion was ſtated to Martin, warden of the mint, about coining farthings, whether to make them of ſilver or ſilver debaſed, or copper; and his report recommended that they ſhould be copper, and of one penny weight each, or two hundred and forty in a pound weight, which ſhould be current for five ſhillings. There was even, as is ſuppoſed, a die, or mould made, but the project was not carried into execution. Probably this prudent and politic ſovereign intended an experiment on the utility of the meaſure, when, in the forty-third year of her reign, ſhe allowed pence and half-pence of copper to be made for Ireland, and it is conjectured that they were alſo current, though not formally introduced in England, as a ſort of licenſed copper token had, for ſome time, been uſed in the city and vicinity of Briſtol. In the reign of James I., the neceſſity of coining copper money appeared by the prodigious quantity of private tokens of lead and braſs, which every tradeſman made and paid for half-pence. Sir Robert Cotton reckoned that there were above three thouſand retailers of victuals and ſmall wares, in and about London, who uſed their own tokens; which, one with another, ſtood them in nearly five pounds a piece, whereof the tenth remained not to them at the year's end; and when they renewed their ſtore, it amounted to fifteen thouſand pounds, beſides what was in the other parts of the kingdom. He therefore propoſed the coining of tokens by the king's authority, whereby the advantage made by the retailers might accrue to the crown. The king approving this propoſition, farthing tokens, as they were then ſtyled, were ſtruck with an engine, and on iſſuing them, a method of rechange was ſettled, whereby the ſubject had the uſe without loſs, and the ſame were generally current throughout England, Ireland, and Wales. The genuine copper coin iſſued from the mint, conſiſted only in half-pence and farthings, both very handſome; queen Anne's farthings are conſidered highly curious from their ſcarcity, and there is an half-

half-penny of the year 1770, in which, by a mistake, a letter is left out, the name of his majesty standing Georius instead of Georgius; which is seldom to be met with.

It is more difficult to form any judgment of the value of the copper coins now in circulation, than of those made of gold or silver: in 1787, the officers of the mint were of opinion, that the lawful copper coins issued from the mint, and remaining in circulation, were equal in weight to nearly 1500 tons, and in nominal value to 322,000*l*. sterling: no copper coins are known to have been issued, since that time, from the mint. Mr. Bolton coined in 1801, by his Majesty's order, 1815 tons of copper in two-penny pieces, penny pieces, half-pence, and farthings, amounting in nominal value to 282,075*l*. 5*s*. 8*d* *. The principle adopted in making these coins was, that the nominal value of each piece should be equal to that of the metal which it contained, and the price of the workmanship employed in making it: these new coins therefore were of much more intrinsic value than any others of that metal. It was also the wish of the lords of the committee to have made the new copper coins serve the purposes of weights, as this circumstance would have been of great convenience to all persons concerned in the retail trade. They so far attained their object, that each two-penny piece, made and issued in consequence of their advice, was of the weight of two ounces avoirdupoise, and each penny-piece of one ounce avoirdupoise. But from the rise in the price of copper, it was found impossible to conform to this principle in the halfpence and farthings, which were afterwards issued.

Tokens. Having noticed the tokens circulated in the reigns of Elizabeth and James I., it may be fit to mention that of late years many pieces of that description have been issued in England. Whether the deficiency of copper coin, or the prodigious quantity of counterfeit money which, circulating in all directions, occasioned general mistrust, occasioned the production of these substitutes it is not material to determine. They began to be issued in the year 1787, by the Anglesea copper company, in pieces of two-pence, one penny, and an halfpenny each, which were valuable and beautiful. The example was followed by numerous masters of manufactories and other individuals in trade, but as the pieces greatly degenerated both in size and beauty, and as their great number occasioned confusion, they became generally decried, except perhaps in the immediate

	£.	s.	d.
* Two penny pieces	6,019	15	8
Penny pieces	183,177	18	0
Half-pence	88,506	18	4
Farthings	4,370	13	2

neighbourhood

neighbourhood of thoſe who iſſued them. The Angleſea tokens could never occaſion loſs to their poſſeſſors, as the intrinſic value of the copper was greater, after a ſhort time, than the nominal price at which they were circulated. The emiſſion of dollars by the bank is alſo to be conſidered as a circulation of tokens, though of ſilver: they are not coin, although impreſſed with the effigy of the king, having never been recognized by royal authority. The firſt that were iſſued at four ſhillings and nine pence, having only a ſmall impreſſion of the king's head, were largely counterfeited, and the bank ſuſtained a conſiderable loſs; thoſe which were ſtamped in 1803, at five ſhillings, are impreſſed on both ſides all over the ſurface, in ſo ſtrong a manner by the machinery of Mr. Boulton, that no fear is entertained of their being imitated for profit.

THE MINT. The kings of this realm had frequently mints of their own, not only in London, but in Southwark, Calais, Briſtol, Hull, Dublin, and many other cities and towns of England and Ireland: theſe were all royal mints, and under the immediate management and direction of the king's officers. But as great inconvenience was found to ariſe from this diſperſion, Queen Elizabeth eſtabliſhed one general mint at the Tower, where alone the buſineſs of coinage has been tranſacted ever ſince, except when Charles I. was obliged, during the civil wars, to make money at Oxford, York, and Newark-upon-Trent, and the period of the recoinage after the revolution, when William III., for the ſake of expedition, erected mints at Exeter, Briſtol, York, and Wincheſter.

OFFICERS. The mint is managed by divers officers, formed into a corporation; which conſiſts of a warden, maſter-worker, comptroller, maſter of the aſſay, auditor, ſurveyor, clerk of the irons, engraver, melters, blanchers, provoſt, moneyers, and ſome others.

The *Warden* receives the ſilver and gold from the goldſmiths, and pays for it; and overſees all the reſt that belong to this office. His ſalary is 450*l*.

The *Maſter-Worker* receives the metal from the warden, orders it to be melted, delivers it to the moniers, and receives it back from them again. His ſalary is 3000*l*.

The *Comptroller* ſees that the money is made of a juſt aſſize; overſees the officers, and controuls them, if the money does not prove as it ought to be. His ſalary is 300*l*.

The *Maſter of the Aſſay* weighs the bullion, and takes care that it is according to ſtandard. His ſalary is 142*l*. 16*s*.

The *Auditor* takes the accounts and makes them up.

The *Surveyor of the Melting* is to ſee the bullion caſt out, and that the metal be not altered after the assay-master has made trial of it, and it is delivered to the melter.

The *Clerk of the Irons* sees that the working irons are kept clean, and fit for work. These two offices are executed by one person, who receives 132*l.* 10*s.* per annum.

The *Engraver* makes the stamps for the money; the *Melters* melt the bullion before it comes to coining; the *Blanchers* anneal, boil, and cleanse the money; the *Provost* of the mint provides for all the moneyers, and oversees them; the *Moneyers* are they who sheer the money and forge it; some beat it broad, others round it, and some stamp or coin it.

Mode of Coining. The manner of stamping is all the public are permitted to see; and this is very quickly performed by an engine used by three men. This engine works by a spindle like that of a printing press, to the point of which the head of the die is fixed with a screw; and in a little kind of a cup, which receives it, is placed the reverse. Between these two parts, the metal to be stamped, being already cut to the size, and exactly weighed, is placed; and, by once pulling down the spindle with a jerk, is completely stamped. The whole process is performed with an amazing dexterity; for, as fast as the men, who work the engine, can turn the spindle, so fast does another with his finger and thumb put in a piece unstamped, and twitch out with his middle finger that which has been stamped. The manner of stamping all metals is the same; but a little more care is taken in one than in the other, according to their value, to prevent waste. The silver and gold thus stamped are delivered to be milled round the edges, by a method which no person is permitted to see performed.

Assay. Previously to the making of any coin, mint indentures are executed between the king and the corporation, declaring at what rate or nominal value the coins, therein ordered to be made, shall be current. To ascertain whether this contract has been faithfully performed, the process called assaying is applied both to the gold and silver coin; for as each has some portion of alloy, it is necessary to determine whether the quantity allowed has been exceeded, and also to judge of other particulars relating to the weight and fashion of the coins. The pieces of coin on which the assay is to be made are taken promiscuously and thrown into a box or chest, called in the old term a pix, and the facts concerning it are tried by members of the goldsmiths' company impanneled and sworn as a jury, whence this process is denominated *the trial of the pix*.

The art of assaying is carried to a very high degree of perfection; it has been improving from the days of Charles II. to the

the present time. In the reign of Charles II. the defect in the fineness of our gold coins is stated to have been 9*s*. 10*d*. $\frac{2}{11}$ per cent. At present the metal of which our gold coins are made is declared to be perfect standard *. This perfection in the fineness of the gold of which our coins are made is greatly to be attributed to the skill of that excellent officer of the public, the late Mr. Alchorne. In several experiments or trials of the pix made by the goldsmiths' company on twenty eight millions of gold coin, sent into circulation, there has been recorded no deviation of fineness. By the mint indentures, if the gold coin does not vary more than forty grains in fineness, or in weight in the pound, or both together, which is called the remedy, such gold coin is allowed to pass as standard; or, in other words, it is to be considered as perfect as the officers of the mint are under any legal obligations to coin it. In the trials of the pix by the goldsmiths' company, there has been no deviation in fineness; and in the same trial there has not been recorded more than an error of four grains in weight. The officers of the mint therefore might have varied in weight or fineness thirty six grains more in each pound, or as much as thirteen shillings and seven-pence three farthings per cent. without incurring any blame or penalty on that account, provided such error was not committed by design. It is clear from hence, that the remedy allowed in coining gold, by the mint indentures, is too great, and it produces this ill effect, that our gold coins are estimated in foreign mints at less than their intrinsic value. The alloy put into these gold coins is in its quality as proper as can be devised. From the great quantity of gold coins, which have been returned through deficiency in weight to the mint, since the general recoinage, a suspicion had been entertained, that the nature of the alloy put into these coins rendered them too hard and brittle, and subject to abrasion and speedy diminution, by friction. To ascertain this fact, Mr. Hatchett, an excellent chemist, was employed, under the inspection of that very eminent philosopher, Mr. Henry Caven-

* Previous to the recoinage of the gold in 1774, experiments were made of the fineness of the gold coin issued in the reigns of our several princes from Charles II. to the present time, by melting guineas of each reign into ingots of fifteen pounds each; and from the contrary ends of each ingot assays were made, by which it appeared, that in former reigns the gold coins were worse than standard in the following proportions:

			s.	*d.*	
Charles II. -	26	grs. troy worse than standard,	9	10 2-11	per cent.
James II. -	30	- - - - - - - - -	11	4 4-11	per cent.
William - -	13	- - - - - - - - -	4	11 1-11	per cent.
Anne - - -	7	- - - - - - - - -	2	7 9-11	per cent.
George I. -	6	- - - - - - - - -	2	3 3-11	per cent.
George II. -	5	- - - - - - - - -	1	11 7-11	per cent.
George III. -	standard.				

dish, to make experiments, for the purpose of shewing how far this evil was produced by the nature of the alloy put into our gold coins; and whether it could not be remedied by making an alteration in the alloy. The gentlemen before mentioned employed a considerable time in making experiments on the quality of different metals. They exerted great ability as well as industry to ascertain the point referred to them; and in a report, made by Mr. Hatchett, it appears to be the result of their opinion, that gold coins are not so likely to wear by abrasion and friction, if they are alloyed by silver and copper mixed; but that the difference between them and coin alloyed with copper alone, provided the copper be very pure, is so little, that there is no sufficient reason for altering the present alloy in our gold coins, consisting alone of pure copper. These observations apply with equal force to the silver coin.

General Observations. The author, from whose excellent work the foregoing remarks, and many of the preceding facts, are extracted, makes the following observations on the general business of the mint. "The subsisting regulations for "receiving bullion of any description into the mint; for transferring it from one department to another; for preserving "it in security while it continues in the custody of the different officers; and lastly, for returning it in the shape of "coins to those to whom it belongs, are wise, and require no "alteration: these regulations are very ancient, and probably "of Norman origin. Some old statutes made in the reigns of "Edward III. and Henry V. refer to these regulations; but "they do not appear to have introduced any new ones; they "contain only strict injunctious for carrying into execution "such as had long subsisted." This is certainly, the Earl of Liverpool proceeds, no slight commendation: but the mint is defective in the lower departments, that is, in the operative or mechanical parts; it is in want of that new and improved machinery, which has of late years been invented, and from which every branch of British manufactures has profited in so great a degree. Coins were originally struck with a hammer only: in the reigns of Queen Elizabeth and Charles I. coins were occasionally made by what is now called the mill and screw; but this instrument was never introduced into constant practice at the English mint, till the year 1662, when letters and grainings were first placed on the edges of the coins. From that time to the present this mode of making coins has continued to be practised in the mint; but the new machinery now employed in the manufacture of every sort of metal, in which the mechanics of this country far surpass those of any other, has not in general been admitted into the mint. It is an an acknowledged principle, that machines which act with a given force, can work with more truth and accuracy than the arm of man, the force of which necessarily varies occasionally from several causes. Another practice has been invented; that of striking coins in a steel collar, so as to make them perfectly round, and all precisely of the same diameter; an improvement which certainly contributes at least to the beauty of the coin. New modes of putting what is called the graining on the edges of coins have also been invented; which at the same time that they protect the coins from being filed equally with the present mode, do not occasion those rough points or edges, which expose them to wear by abrasion or friction. For these, and many other valuable inventions, the public are indebted to the ingenuity of Mr. Boulton, of Soho, near Birmingham. It is singular, that though the manufacturers of England have greatly profited by these inventions, the officers of the mint have never, or at least not sufficiently, availed themselves of them: the mints of foreign countries are in search of them; and their governments in more than one instance have employed Mr. Boulton in erecting mints on his new principles; and parliament has authorised the same. One government (I need not name it) has, as I have learned from good authority, sent persons at different times, under pretence of treating with Mr. Boulton, in the course of his business, to obtain by artifice the knowledge of his inventions, for the benefit of the countries under its sway. But it is not only in the fashion and beauty of the coins, that the mint would profit by adopting these new inventions; there are other considerations, which strongly recommend their introduction into the mint: the coins of the realm will thereby be made with much more expedition, and with less charge to the public. By an account which I have seen, Mr. Boulton can coin at least ten times as many pieces, in a given time, as can be coined at the mint by the method now practised; and though, as I have already observed, the security of the precious metals, while in the custody of the officers of the mint, is at present very great, it will certainly be increased when fewer persons are employed in the operation. If a new silver coinage should be undertaken, expedition * is certainly of great importance; and I could wish that the whole might be performed at one mint in the Tower, rather than at several mints in different parts of the kingdom, as practised in the reign of King William, and at other preceding

* It would be easy to coin 60,000,000 of shillings, or 3,000,000*l* sterling, in a year, with the aid of the improved machinery; or even double, if the nature of the business should require it.

periods:

periods: it is certainly more eafy to find artifts of proper talents and abilities, fufficient in number to occupy the refpective departments in one mint than in many.

OFFENCES RELATING TO COIN. By the ftatute 25th Edw. III. "If a man counterfeit the king's money; and if a man "bring falfe money into the realm counterfeit to the money of "England, knowing the money to be falfe, to merchandize and "make payment withal, or if the king's own minters alter the "ftandard or alloy eftablifhed by law, it is treafon." But gold and filver money only are held to be within the ftatute. Thefe were the original laws; but they not being found fufficient to reftrain the evil practices of coiners and falfe moneyers, other ftatutes have been fince made for that purpofe. By ftatute 5 Eliz. c. 11. clipping, wafhing, rounding, or filing, for wicked gain's fake, any of the money of this realm, or other money, fuffered to be current here, fhall be adjudged high treafon; and by ftatute 18 Eliz. c. 1. the fame fpecies of offence is defcribed in other more general words; viz. impairing, diminifhing, falfifying, fcaling, and lightening; and made liable to the fame penalties. By ftatute 8 and 9 William III. c. 26. made perpetual by 7 Ann, c. 25. whoever, without proper authority, fhall knowingly make or mend, or affift in fo doing, or fhall buy, fell, conceal, hide, or knowingly have in his poffeffion, any implements of coinage fpecified in the act, or other tools or inftruments proper only for the coinage of money; or fhall convey the fame out of the king's mint; he, together with his counfellors, procurers, aiders, and abettors, fhall be guilty of high treafon: which is by much the fevereft branch of the coinage law. The ftatute goes on farther, and enacts, that to mark any coin on the edges with letters, or otherwife, in imitation of thofe ufed in the mint; or to colour, gild, or cafe over any coin refembling the current coin, or even round blanks of bafe metal; fhall be conftrued high treafon. But all profecutions on this act are to be commenced within three months after the commiffion of the offence: except thofe for making or mending any coining tool or inftrument, or for marking money round the edges; which are directed to be commenced within fix months after the offence is committed. And, laftly, by ftatute 15 and 16 Geo. II. c. 28. if any perfon colours or alters any fhilling or fixpence, either lawful or counterfeit, to make them refpectively refemble a guinea or half guinea; or any half-penny or farthing, to make them refpectively refemble a fhilling or fixpence; this is alfo high treafon: but the offender fhall be pardoned, in cafe (being out of prifon) he difcovers and convicts two other offenders of the fame kind. In other acts of parliament,

liament, offences of inferior enormity are noticed. By statute 27 Edw. I. c. 3. none shall bring pollards and crockards, which were foreign coins of base metal, into the realm, on pain of forfeiture of life and goods. By 9 Edw. III. st. 2. no sterling money shall be melted down, upon pain of forfeiture thereof. By statute 17 Edw. III. none shall be so hardy to bring false and ill money into the realm, on pain of forfeiture of life and member by the persons importing, and the searchers permitting such importation. By 3 Hen. V. st. 1. to make, coin, buy, or bring into the realm any gally half-pence, suskins, or dotkins, in order to utter them, is felony; and knowingly to receive or pay either them, or blanks, is forfeiture of an hundred shillings. By 14 Eliz. c. 3. such as forge any foreign coin, although it be not made current here by proclamation, shall (with their aiders and abettors) be guilty of misprison of treason. By 13 and 14 Chas. II. c. 31. the offence of melting down any current silver money shall be punished with forfeiture of the same, and also the double value: and the offender, if a freeman of any town, shall be disfranchised, if not, shall suffer six months imprisonment. By 6 and 7 William III. c. 17. if any person buys or sells, or knowingly has in his custody, any clippings or filings of the coin, he shall forfeit the same and 500*l.*; one moiety to the king, and the other to the informer; and be branded in the cheek with the letter R. By 8 and 9 William III. c. 26. if any person shall blanch, or whiten, copper for sale, (which makes it resemble silver,) or buy or sell, or offer to sale any malleable composition, which shall be heavier than silver, and look, touch, and wear like gold, but be beneath the standard; or if any person shall receive or pay at a less rate than it imports to be of (which demonstrates a consciousness of its baseness, and a fraudulent design) any counterfeit or diminished milled money of this kingdom, not being cut in pieces; an operation which is expressly directed to be performed when any such money shall be produced in evidence, and which any person, to whom any gold or silver money is tendered, is empowered by statutes 9 and 10 William III. c. 21. 13 Geo. III. c. 71. and 14 Geo. III. c. 70. to perform at his own hazard, and the officers of the exchequer, and receiver general of the taxes are particularly required to perform: all such persons shall be guilty of felony; and may be prosecuted for the same at any time within three months after the offence committed. But these precautions not being found sufficient to prevent the uttering of false or diminished money, which was only a misdemeanor at common law, it is enacted by 15 and 16 Geo. II. c. 28. that if any person shall utter or tender in payment any counterfeit coin, knowing it so to be, he shall for the first offence be imprisoned six months, and find

find ſureties for his good behaviour for ſix months more: for the ſecond offence, ſhall be impriſoned two years, and find ſureties for two years longer: and, for the third offence, ſhall be guilty of felony without benefit of clergy. Alſo if a perſon knowingly tenders in payment any counterfeit money, and at the ſame time has more in his cuſtody; or ſhall, within ten days after, knowingly tender other falſe money; he ſhall be deemed a common utterer of counterfeit money, and ſhall for the firſt offence be impriſoned one year, and find ſureties for his good behaviour for two years longer; and for the ſecond, be guilty of felony without benefit of clergy. By the ſame ſtatute it is alſo enacted, that if any perſon counterfeits the copper coin, he ſhall ſuffer two years impriſonment, and find ſureties for two years more. By ſtatute 11 Geo. III. c. 40. perſons counterfeiting copper half-pence or farthings, with their abettors; or buying, ſelling, receiving, or putting off any counterfeit copper money (not being cut in pieces or melted down) at a leſs value than it imports to be of; ſhall be guilty of ſingle felony. And by a temporary ſtatute, (14 Geo. III. c. 42.) if any quantity of money, exceeding the ſum of five pounds, being or purporting to be the ſilver coin of this realm, but below the ſtandard of the mint in weight or fineneſs, ſhall be imported into Great Britain or Ireland, the ſame ſhall be forfeited in equal moieties to the crown and proſecutor.

Paper Currency. On this moſt important and truly delicate ſubject, the conſiderations to be preſented to the reader are extracted entirely from the Earl of Liverpool's Treatiſe on the Coins of the Realm, the order of the paragraphs being only a little varied, and the forms omitted which are appropriately uſed by his lordſhip in an addreſs to the ſovereign.

"The ſtate of the paper currency of this country, in its "manner and extent taken together, is without example in the "hiſtory of mankind. The trade or profeſſion of banking "has been exerciſed in all countries and in all ages: it exiſted "in the republics of Greece, and in ancient Rome: there "were in all theſe ſtates men who received money as a de-"poſit, repaid it upon the drafts of thoſe who had entruſted "them with it, and derived their profits from having this "money in their cuſtody; but it does not appear that they "ever iſſued notes, ſuch as are now called paper currency. In "the middle ages the traffic of money was exerciſed ſolely by "the Jews; for Chriſtian men, as they were then called, from "a miſtaken principle of religion, would not engage in it: but "the Jews, who interpreted the law of Moſes in a different "ſenſe from the Chriſtians, thought that they might lawfully "carry it on with ſtrangers; and to them every man was a

"ſtranger

" stranger who was not a Jew. The wealth of these Jews, " and the extortions and cruelties to which they were exposed " on this account, contrary to the principles of humanity and " justice, are well known to every one. When commerce was " first revived in the republics of Italy, banking companies and " private bankers appeared in numbers, and carried on trade in " money, and particularly bills of exchange, to a very great ex- " tent. The origin and history of the banks of Venice and " Genoa need not be here inserted: the wealth of these " banks was very great; and many of the principal families in " Italy derive their origin and ample fortunes from persons who " once exercised the trade of banking. I cannot however dis- " cover from history, that either the Jews before-mentioned, " or the banking companies established in Italy, or any of the " private bankers, ever issued what is now called paper cur- " rency, that is to say, bills, or notes, payable or convertible in- " to cash on demand by the person who issued the same, at the " will of the holder. It is certain at least that they did not " issue it in so great a degree, as to drive the coins out of the " country; for it is asserted by historians of undoubted credit, " that Italy at that time had drawn to itself almost the whole of " the gold of Europe. After the example of what had been " thus practised in Italy, banking companies were gradually " established in many of the principal cities of Europe, parti- " cularly at Hamburgh, Nuremberg, and Amsterdam: many " of these corporate banks issued paper currency for the pay- " ment of foreign, and sometimes inland, bills of exchange: " but this privilege was always exercised under certain regula- " tions and restrictions, sanctioned by the governments of these " places, for the security of the individuals who trusted them, " and for the preservation of public credit. It is singular, that " it was found necessary to require, that the notes of these " banks should be accepted and employed exclusively in certain " payments: but the privilege thus given never included any " payments for which a single piece of coin, or, as I believe, " any small number of them, was sufficient, so as to interfere " with the retail trade of the country. The reasons for esta- " blishing this paper currency have been fully explained, in a " former part of this letter; and I have never heard that pri- " vate bankers issued paper currency in any European country, " to the extent in which it is now practised in the British " dominions: if it has prevailed any where to excess, it has " been in the United Provinces of America. The practice " of issuing paper currency within his majesty's dominions " first began in Scotland: it was natural that this device should " originate in a country where there was a great want of coins " and capital: the evils it produced were felt so early as the

" year

" year 1765, when a wife law was paffed by the legiflature, " to reftrain and regulate it within that part of the united " kingdom. This law did not extend to England, for the evil " at that time had not been felt here: the Englifh however " foon followed the example of their northern brethren; and " in the year 1775, the mifchiefs arifing from the iffue of fmall " paper notes were fo feverely felt, that a law was paffed for " regulating and reftraining it; but it was afterwards found " that this law did not remedy the evil, and a fecond law, ftill " more reftrictive, was paffed in 1777. It was neceffary how- " ever for a temporary purpofe, to enact a fhort fufpenfion of " thefe laws, in confequence of the difficulties, to which pub- " lic credit was expofed, in the year 1797. At the fame time, " the bank of England was difcharged by the legiflature from " the obligation of paying in cafh: but, contrary to expecta- " tion, thefe fufpenfions have been continued to the prefent " day; and from that period the bank of England have iffued " notes for fmaller fums, and to a greater extent, than they " ever did before; and the number of private bankers fpread " over every part of the country, during that interval, has been " more than doubled *."

" This currency," his lordfhip obferves, " is carried to fo great " an extent, that it is become highly inconvenient to his majef- " ty's fubjects, and may prove in its confequences, if no " remedy is applied, dangerous to the credit of the kingdom. " It is certain, that the fmaller notes of the bank of England, " and thofe iffued by country bankers, have fupplanted the gold " coins, ufurped their functions, and driven a great part of " them out of circulation: in fome parts of Great Britain, and " efpecially in the fouthern parts of Ireland, fmall notes have " been iffued to fupply the place of filver coins, of which there " is certainly a great deficiency. If this practice is fuffered to " continue, as at prefent, without any limitation, there can be " neither ufe nor advantage in converting bullion of either of " the precious metals into coins, except fo far as it may ferve " for the convenience of the people in their moft private con- " cerns; that is, no greater quantity than many of the writers, " who have of late fpeculated on this fubject, will allow to " continue in currency: the bullion, of which thefe coins are " made, had better be exported in its natural ftate, like any " other unmanufactured commodity, for the ufe of which the " trade of the country has no occafion. The coins of this realm,

* It is ftated in the fummary of the report of the fecret committee of the Houfe of Lords in 1797, that the number of country bankers, which had, in 1792, amounted to 280, had, in 1797, been reduced to 230. It appears by the lift of country bankers now publifhed, that they amount to 517.

" when

" when carried into foreign countries, will only be valued
" as bullion; and the precious metals, whether exported in
" coins or in bullion, will equally ſerve the purpoſe of a com-
" mercial capital; and it is uſeleſs and abſurd to impoſe upon
" the public the expence of making coins, merely for the pur-
" poſe of ſending them out of the kingdom. It has been a com-
" mon artifice, practiſed by thoſe who have written on paper
" currency, to confound paper credit with paper currency,
" and even the higher ſorts of paper currency with the inferior
" ſorts, ſuch as immediately interfere with the uſe of the coins
" of the realm. Paper credit is not only highly convenient
" and beneficial, but is even abſolutely neceſſary, in carrying
" on the trade of a great commercial kingdom. Paper cur-
" rency is a very undefined term, as uſed by ſpeculative writers.
" To find arguments in its ſupport, at leaſt to the extent to
" which it is at preſent carried, they have been obliged to
" connect it with paper credit; ſo that the principles, on
" which the uſe of paper credit is truly founded, may be
" brought in ſupport of a great emiſſion of paper currency:
" I do not mean to ſay, that even the higher orders of paper
" currency may not be very convenient, in carrying on many
" branches of the trade of a country ſo wealthy as Great Bri-
" tain: the ſort of paper currency to which I principally
" object, is that which interferes with the uſe of the coins of
" the realm, more eſpecially in the payment of labourers and
" artificers, of the ſailor and ſoldier, and in the ſmaller
" branches of the retail trade of the kingdom. Many words
" are not neceſſary to point out the evils to which his majeſty's
" ſubjects are expoſed, by the practice which now prevails,
" of iſſuing the lower ſort of paper currency by country
" bankers; the complaints on this head are univerſal. The
" notes of theſe country bankers have credit only within a
" certain extent or diſtrict: if a traveller paſſes from one diſ-
" trict to another, he muſt provide himſelf with the notes of
" other bankers, which have credit within the diſtrict on which
" he is entering; and an inconvenience to which travellers
" have hitherto been ſubject, in paſſing from one ſmall inde-
" pendent ſtate on the continent to another, is experienced by
" thoſe who travel through the kingdom, in paſſing from one
" diſtrict to another; ſo that the circulating medium of the
" different parts is various; an evil which I believe never ex-
" iſted before in one great united kingdom. But I have not
" hitherto deſcribed the principal evils reſulting from this
" paper currency. It was natural to ſuppoſe, that the precious
" metals, being no longer wanted in the ſame degree, for the
" purpoſe of being converted into coins, the price of them
" would

"would fall in the British market: on the contrary, for a considerable time, bullion, both of gold and silver, has not been generally sold, but at a price above the rate at which each of them is valued at the mint. It would not be proper for me at present to assign the probable cause of this apparent contradiction: in such a state of things, whatever may be the cause, no bullion, either of gold or silver, will be brought to the mint to be coined; for it cannot be coined without a loss to the person who brings it; and if it were converted into coins, the moment they were issued they would be thrown into the melting pot, and reconverted into bullion, because it would be of more value in the shape of bullion than in that of coins. Till some remedy is applied to this evil, no new system of coinage can be adopted, with any reasonable hope of success. When the situation of the bank of England was under the consideration of the two houses of Parliament, in the year 1797, it was my opinion, and that of many others, that the extent to which paper currency had then been carried, was the first and principal, though not the sole cause of the many difficulties, to which that corporate body was then, and had of late years, from time to time, been exposed, in supplying the cash occasionally necessary to the commerce of the kingdom; for the bank of England being at the head of all circulation, and the great repository of unemployed cash, it necessarily happens, that whenever a sudden increased supply of coins becomes indispensable, in consequence of private failures or general discredit, by which notes of the before-mentioned description are driven out of circulation, the bank of England can alone furnish the coins which are required to make up this deficiency; and this corporate body is thereby rendered responsible, not only for the value of its own notes which it may issue, but, in a certain degree, for such as may be issued by every private banker in the kingdom, let the substance, credit, or discretion of such a banker be what it may: and if the price of both the precious metals in bullion then be above that at which they are rated at the mint, the bank of England have it not in their power to supply this deficiency, but at a great loss to its proprietors; and even if they were to submit to this loss, and issue new coins in consequence, it would only be, as has been already observed, in order that they might be thrown into the melting pot and converted into bullion; so that till some remedy is applied to this evil the bank of England cannot, I think, return to the first principles of its institution, under which it has so long and greatly flourished, and re-assume, without any restriction, its payments in cash."

INTEREST AND USURY. These subjects, though not immediately connected with the public revenue, are placed in this division, as naturally incident to the possession and use of money. *Interest* and *Usury*, though now used in senses as opposite as those which can be applied to the same act, in order to denominate it honest or unjust, seem in ancient times to have been synonymous, or at least convertible terms. When money was lent on a contract to receive not only the principal sum again, but also an increase, by way of compensation for the use; it was generally called *interest* by those who thought it lawful, and *usury* by those who did not so. In modern times, the application of these terms does not depend on the principles or opinions of him who uses them, but are defined notions of law; interest meaning the return made by the borrower according to law and custom for the loan, advance, or forbearance of money; usury the sum extorted by the person lending, beyond what the law allows, from the wants, hopes, or weakness of the borrower. An inconvenience resulting from an absurd notion entertained in ancient times, that all profit received for the loan of money was unlawful, and even damnable, was, that none would practise the trade of lending, but those who were indifferent to character, and hopeless of esteem; nor could the legislature frame laws for limiting those contracts which they altogether condemned, though they despaired of preventing them. More enlightened times brought forth a better understanding, and the statute 37 Hen. VIII. prohibited the payment of interest exceeding ten per cent. In the reign of his successor, religious zeal again prevailed so far as to prohibit all interest; but the statute of Henry VIII. was revived by the 13th of Elizabeth, cap. 8.; and ten per cent. continued to be the legal rate of interest till the 21st James I. when it was restricted to eight per cent. It was reduced to six per cent. soon after the restoration, and by the 12th of queen Anne to five per cent. All these different statutory regulations seem to have been made with great propriety. They seem to have followed and not to have gone before the market rate of interest, or the rate at which people of good credit usually borrowed. Since the time of queen Anne, five per cent. seems to have been rather above than below the market rate. Before the American war, the government borrowed at three per cent.; and people of good credit in the capital, and in many other parts of the kingdom, at three and a half, four, and four and a half. The statute of Anne against usury is as strong and operative as words can devise, so much so that Lord Mansfield declared that the wit of man could not evade it; it provides that no person on any

any contract, shall, directly or indirectly, take for the loan of any money, wares, &c., above the value of five pounds for the forbearance of one hundred pounds for a year; and all bonds and assurances for payment of any money to be lent upon usury, whereupon or whereby there shall be reserved or taken above five in the hundred, shall be void; and every person who shall receive, by means of any corrupt bargain, loan, exchange, chevizance, shift, or interest of any wares, merchandizes, or other things, or by any deceitful way, for the forbearing or giving day of payment for one year, for their money or other things, above five pounds for one hundred pounds for a year, shall forfeit treble the value of the monies or other things lent. The wholesome severity of this law cannot in all cases prevent a practice to which avarice presents strong incitements, and necessity, inconsiderateness, and hope, offer ready votaries; but it is of general use in restricting the speculations of unprincipled men; and as the securities given are void, in whose hands, or on what consideration soever, they may be, the danger of such transactions, and the odium applied to those who engage in them, are greatly enhanced. The law however is not so strict as to prevent the extension of compensation where the risque, trouble, or inevitable expence of the lender fairly require it. Thus in the contracts known by the names of *bottomry* and *respondentia*, which depend on the arrival and safety of ships, and in annuities for lives, the receipt of interest far exceeding five per cent. is allowed, on account of the danger to which the lenders submit of a total loss of their capital. *Pawnbrokers* receive for the loan of money twenty per cent. although without any risque, but as a compensation for their care and trouble in registering and securing the pledges deposited with them, and the various other restrictions imposed on their business. There is also one ordinary transaction in which, by force of custom allowed as law, the receipt of more than five per cent. is permitted; it is in the *discount* of bills or notes of hand. In those cases the lender, deducting the interest from the whole sum specified, and advancing only the remainder, receives, in fact, a greater interest than the law supposes to be just. For instance, if a bill were drawn for one hundred pounds to be due in twelve months, the person discounting it would give but ninety-five; at the end of the year he would be paid five pounds, not for the loan or forbearance of one hundred pounds, but for the loan of ninety-five pounds, being at least at the rate of five pounds five shillings per cent.

Some have doubted whether the laws should in any ways restrain the rate of interest, and recommended that money, like other articles in a market, ſhould find its own level; but it ſhould be conſidered that the laws againſt uſury have always been remedial, the grievance of extortion has been ſeverely felt before the legiſlature interpoſed, and the reſtrictions have been productive of general benefit, and increaſed general confidence; the wiſh to take advantage of individual diſtreſs having been ſuperſeded by the more honourable and beneficial deſire of contributing to general proſperity: the former would yield benefits to the temporary ſpeculiſt, the latter alone can promote the honourable views of the whole moneyed or commercial community. Nor is it true that extravagant intereſt facilitates loans; millions are lent at and under five per cent., where it would be difficult with leſs approved ſecurity to raiſe even a ſmall portion of the ſums; and it is invariably found that negotiations for loans on Weſt India, or even Iriſh ſecurities, where the intereſt is eight or ſix per cent. are extremely difficult, until the redundancy of money in the market has made Engliſh ſecurities attainable only at a much inferior rate.

ARMED FORCE.

It has already been ſtated, as a high prerogative of the Britiſh monarch, that he alone has the right of declaring war and making peace; but as a check againſt the abuſe of that power, parliament has retained the privilege of limiting the number of perſons to be employed, and the ſtill more eſſential authorities of iſſuing monies for paying, and framing laws for regulating them. In this diviſion of the work, the navy and the army will be ſeparately conſidered, and ſome few ſubjects of regulation added which are common to both. In treating of the navy, the royal or warlike ſhips will chiefly be conſidered, but ſome points affecting commercial veſſels will occaſionally be found inſeparably connected; and ſome notice muſt be taken of the offices and inſtitutions formed on ſhore for the benefit of the navy, and the local and perſonal regulations, as well as the general laws affecting thoſe who follow the maritime profeſſion, as well as thoſe who by conſanguinity or property become connected with them. The army will include every department of land force, as regulars, militia, and volunteers; with ſimilar additions, as to offices and inſtitutions. The topics common to both are principally ſome general laws relating to mutiny and deſertion, and the form of trial by court martial.

THE NAVY.

Establishment and Progress. The insular situation of the British dominions pointed out, at an early period, the necessity of maintaining the security of the people by the equipment of a powerful navy; for while the riches of the country invited invasion, its want of external protection afforded every facility to those Northern plunderers who possessed the advantage of a superior fleet; and the annals of England, at a remote period, are stained with the perpetual narratives of the depredations and enormities of those barbarians. Alfred, who so well deserved the name of Great, succeeding to his throne at a period when his people were in the highest degree depressed by Danish tyranny and extortion, first rescued them by the union of valour and policy from the galling weight of a foreign yoke, and then planned their future security by the establishment and support of a powerful and well-appointed navy. The bravest and best disciplined army, he found, could be of but little avail against an enemy, who by his naval superiority could choose and vary his points of attack at pleasure. He therefore determined to meet the invaders on their own element; and the very earliest of his naval efforts were crowned with success. His superior genius did not merely imitate the vessels of the Danes or Frisons, but conceived an improved model of construction. His gallies were almost twice as long as those of the enemy, and carried sixty oars, some of them even more; and they were in all respects better fitted both for progress and hostility. By an unremitting and successful attention to his fleet, this great prince acquired the glorious title of Father of the British Navy. The marine force maintained by Edgar, the successor of Alfred, is stated to have amounted to upwards of three thousand ships, but this is generally considered as a gross exaggeration. Ethelred, his son and successor, was obliged for want of a navy to purchase the forbearance of a Danish invader; and in subsequent reigns, the want of the great national bulwark left the kingdom exposed to the insults and spoliation of every lawless ravager. In the reign of Edward the Confessor the English recovered their military and naval character; chiefly under the conduct of his brother-in-law Harold, who, on the death of Edward without issue, became king, to the injury of Edgar Atheling. Harold appears to have been, after Alfred, the greatest of the Saxon princes; and like him he was sensible that a well-appointed navy was the safeguard of England. As soon as he became king, he was threatened with an invasion with William Duke of Normandy; and, knowing the great power and military talents of of the duke, he provided above feven hundred fhips, which he ftationed on the coaft oppofite to France. Unfortunately a part of it was called off by the unexpected naval attack of Harold Hardrad, king of Norway, whofe life paid the forfeit of his unprovoked hoftility. William landing on the fouth coaft, almoft at the fame time, faw his enterprife crowned with unexpected fuccefs; but the utility of a fleet was evident, as that of the Conqueror was, even after the death of Harold, blocked up in the ports of Pevenfey and Haftings; as fovereign of the land, however, he was allowed to be the mafter of the navy, which inftead of oppofing augmented his power.

During the reign of the Conqueror and feveral of his fucceffors little occurred to mark the advance of naval character; few invafions of England were attempted, and thofe eafily fruftrated; but the recovery of the Holy Land from the infidels, which fo much engaged the attention of all Chriftian fovereigns, drew forth alfo the emulation of the Englifh monarchs, and after feveral inferior attempts, the gallant Richard Cœur de Lion, in 1190, equipped a fleet of extraordinary force, both in refpect to the number and fize of the veffels. According to authors of good credit, there were thirteen veffels larger than the reft, called buffes, or dromones, which failed with a triple fpread of fails, about fifty armed galleys, and one hundred tranfports or veffels of burthen. Befides thefe, one hundred and fix veffels, which had affembled at Lifbon, coafted round Spain as far as Marfeilles, and thence took a departure for Syria, without touching at any other land. All thefe veffels rowed and alfo failed. The policy or fuccefs of the holy war is foreign from the prefent fubject, except as it ferved to increafe the navy by exciting the fpirit of enterprife, and furnifhed a motive for the equipment of large fhips and the undertaking of diftant voyages. At this time the courage and fkill of the Englifh mariners had become diftinguifhed, and Richard, in his voyage from Cyprus to Paleftine, captured a fhip of uncommon magnitude, having on board eight hundred men intended to relieve the garrifon of Acon.

In the reign of Henry III. the hoftilities between England and France occafioned a grand naval engagement, in which Britifh prowefs and fkill were difplayed to great advantage. The fleet, compofed of forty fhips, was fitted out by the Cinque Ports to protect the kingdom againft an invafion threatened by France, and placed under the command of Hubert de Burgh, captain of Dover caftle, Philip D'Albany and John Marfhall. They met the enemy's armament, confifting of eighty large, befides fmaller veffels, on the 24th of Auguft 1217, but not daring, with a force fo inferior, to affail them in front, tacked about, and getting to windward, bore down upon them, and sunk several of their ships, by running forcibly against them with the iron bows or beaks of their vessels. The archers likewise made great slaughter; but the victory was completed by means of a great quantity of quick lime in powder, they had on board, which being cast into the air, and blown by the wind into the eyes of the enemy, blinded them. The English either took or sunk a great part of the fleet, and the event terminated the hope of invading England. This action is only mentioned to shew the manner of fighting at sea in those rude times; and until the use of powder became thoroughly established, little further improvement was made, the shock of ships, the throwing of darts, the exertion of personal strength, and particularly in boarding, were the chief ordinary means; auxiliary to these were the use of dangerous and offensive missiles, the dispersion of quick lime, and the employment of burning arrows and combustibles for the purpose of setting ships on fire. "In sea engagements," says an author describing those in the days of Richard I. "they still preserved the ancient semicircular line of "battle, stationing the strongest vessels in the wings or points "with a view to inclose the enemy as in a net. The soldiers, "stationed on the upper deck; (or on the raised platform or "forecastle,) made a close bulwark of their shields; and, to give "them free room to fight, the rowers sat together below. "When the hostile fleets approached, the sound of the trumpets "and the shouts of the men gave the signal for the engagement, "which commenced by a discharge of missile weapons on both "sides: the sharp beaks, or spurs, were forcibly dashed against "the enemies sides: the oars were entangled: and the hostile "vessels being grappled together, a close fight ensued, while the "engineers endeavoured to burn their enemy's ships with the "Greek fire which was now in common use with the Turks and "Saracens, as well as the Christians."

Guns introduced. The earliest account of the use of cannon in naval engagements, is in 1372, when, by means of them, the Castilians gained a great victory over the English before Rochelle, burning, sinking, and destroying most of their vessels. From that period, however, the English commanders began to employ their genius and judgment in the improvement of the means of naval warfare which they have brought to a degree of perfection which renders the British fleet the pride and defence of the country, as well as the envy and terror of its enemies.

Sovereignty of the Sea. From the earliest times, the monarchs of England claimed the sovereignty of the British seas, some having even taken the title of *Basileus quatuor marium*, or emperor

emperor of the four seas. This right has been recognized in the most solemn manner, in repeated treaties, by foreign nations; and the acts of concession and acknowledgment which proved its being admitted, have been generally continued without interruption, until of late times, when the practice of requiring them has been discontinued. Of the extent and nature of this claim, however, it may be fit to give a short account.

The four seas over which Great Britain claims dominion are denominated from the cardinal points of the compass. Toward the east is the German Ocean, generally called the North, but by the Danes, Swedes, and other northern regions, named the West Sea: and the boundaries on this side are the shores of those countries opposite to Great Britain that way, as the Netherlands, Germany, Denmark, and Norway. Southward is the British Ocean so called by Ptolemy; one part of which is commonly denominated the Channel, or, by the French, La Manche, which divides England from France. This way the boundaries extend to the opposite shores of France, to those of Spain, as far as Cape Finisterre, and to an imaginary line, drawn from that cape, in the same parallel of latitude to their boundary on the west, thus taking in that part of the British seas which consists of the Channel, the Bay of Biscay, and part of the Atlantic Ocean. On the west is that sea anciently called the Vergivian Ocean, which, where it washes the coast of Scotland, is from thence called the Deucaledonian Sea. That part of it which flows between England and Ireland, is sometimes called the Irish Sea, anciently the Scythian vale, but now St. George's Channel, and the rest, the Western or Atlantic Ocean. Northward is the sea anciently known by the several names of the Hyperborean, Deucaledonian, and Caledonian Ocean, now the Scotch Sea; in which are situated the Orcades, Thule, and other islands. The proper boundaries of the British seas for the west and north, on those quarters, are generally reckoned a line drawn from the beforementioned imaginary line, extending from cape Finisterre, in the longitude of 23 degrees west from London, to the latitude of 63 degrees, and thence another line drawn, in that parallel of latitude, to the middle point of the land Van Staten in Norway; thereby taking in, to the west, that portion of them which consists of part of the Atlantic Ocean, and the Irish Sea or St. George's Channel.

The sovereignty or dominion of the British seas consists in an exclusive property over them, as well with regard to passage, as fishing. The recognition of this sovereignty consisted in what was termed the duty of the flag, which was, that all ships or vessels met by British men of war on those seas, do strike their flag, and lower their topsail; or where they have no flag, that they lower their top-ſail only, in deference to his majeſty's ſovereignty, and an implied acknowledgment that the prince grants a general licence for the ſhips of his friends to paſs in thoſe ſeas, paying him that duty.

OF THE KING'S FLEET. When England firſt found it neceſſary to oppoſe her enemies on the ocean, the navy equipped by Alfred was properly his own, but for a long period after his time, no fleet, and ſcarcely a ſingle ſhip could be termed royal. Some indiſtinct occaſional accounts are preſerved of oars purchaſed for the king's gallies, mention is made in 1208 of a royal ſhip, and Richard I. certainly purchaſed ſome veſſels for the cruſade, but all theſe circumſtances do not ſhew any thing like a naval eſtabliſhment. In fact, the equipments fitted out for war were merely the whole mercantile ſhipping of the kingdom, preſſed into the ſervice: ſo that in thoſe times the owners could never call their veſſels their own. By theſe means the kings occaſionally collected very large fleets, as Henry III. for inſtance, who obtained from all the realm above one thouſand, of which three hundred were large ſhips, to be employed againſt his malcontent barons in Gaſcoigne. This monarch ſeems alſo to have had ſome ſhips which could properly be called his own, as mention is made of the king's gallies, in Ireland, and at Bourdeaux, and of a large ſhip called the Queen, which he let for hire to a merchant.

Beſides the ſeizure of merchant veſſels, it was a part of the royal prerogative to call on the towns and cities throughout the kingdom, as well as the Cinque Ports, to furniſh ſhips in a certain proportion for defence of the realm, or invaſion of the enemy. In this manner Edward III. in 1346, obtained upward of 700 ſhips, and near 15,000 ſeamen for the ſiege of Calais. The liſt is preſerved, and, among many other remarkable circumſtances, ſhews that London only ſupplied 25 ſhips and 662 ſeamen, while Fowey produced 47 veſſels and 770 mariners, and Yarmouth 43 ſhips, and 1095 men. Several of theſe were diſtinguiſhed as ſhips of war, but whether they were built and kept for that expreſs purpoſe, or were merely larger and more fit for martial purpoſes than the reſt of the fleet is not aſcertained. Of the king's own property there were 25 veſſels with 419 mariners, and for the purpoſe of building and equipping them, the king exerciſed the prerogative of demanding from his ſubjects foreſt trees, and from the ſheriffs of cities the materials for his anchors and other ſupplies. The mode of obtaining a naval force by requiſition from the different diſtricts in the realm was practiſed without queſtion or doubt during many enſuing reigns, until the unfortunate attempt of Charles I. to revive and commute

it

it for a tax, under the name of ſhip-money, occaſioned diſcuſſions, in the reſult of which it was declared illegal.

The progreſs of ſcience having occaſioned great improvements in maritime affairs, and the diſcovery of America having concurred with other cauſes in animating adventure and enterprize, the ſovereigns of Europe became more anxious than they had been to poſſeſs the advantages of a regular marine eſtabliſhment, and our king, Henry VIII. having entered into a league of mutual defence with the king of Spain, did, in 1512, by indenture with his admiral, Sir Edward Howard, covenant for the maintenance of eighteen ſhips, the largeſt of which, the Regent, was of one thouſand tons burhen, and the ſmalleſt only of ſeventy. They were manned with 1750 ſoldiers and 1252 mariners, making, together with their eighteen captains, 3000 men, who were all victualled at the king's expence, but by the indenture, the admiral was, in conſideration of a certain monthly ſtipend, to pay and clothe them, and the king was to receive half the value of prizes captured by ſea or land, and all priſoners, being chieftains. This fleet was to guard the ſeas from the channel to the ſtraights of Gibraltar, the king of Spain undertaking to protect the Mediterranean. In this reign the navy was conſolidated, and means taken, by the eſtabliſhment of offices, to ſecure its permanence; a ſervice ſufficient, notwithſtanding his many enormous faults, to procure for Henry VIII. a title to the gratitude of his country. In his time, the building of ſhips became more ſcientific, the ſtores were accumulated in a regular and plentiful manner, the veſſels were rated by the number of guns as well as quantity of tonnage, and, on the loſs of his great ſhip, the Regent, he cauſed another of dimenſions before unequalled in England to be built, which he called Henry Grace de Dieu. Edward VI. at the beginning of his reign found provided by his father's care upward of ſixty ſhips, part of which he might ſtrictly term his own, the reſidue being permanently hired from the proprietors, the ports and harbours of the realm improved, the mouth of the Thames fortified by batteries at Graveſend and Tilbury, magazines, ſtore-houſes, and docks ſyſtematically provided, and offices for maritime affairs duly conſtituted and ably filled.

The illuſtrious Elizabeth, provident in all things for the good and glory of her country, made great exertions to perfect the eſtabliſhments commenced by her father for the advancement of the navy; filling her magazines with ammunition, military and naval ſtores, introducing into England the manufacture of gunpowder, and cauſing braſs and iron ordnance to be caſt. She alſo built a conſiderable number of ſhips for war, forming the moſt reſpectable fleet England had ever ſeen; erected Upnor caſtle on the river Medway; increaſed the pay of her naval officers and ſeamen; and gained from foreigners the title of reſtorer of naval glory, and queen of the northern ſeas. In imitation of the queen, the opulent ſubjects alſo built ſhips of force; the national navy, including the royal and private ſhips, was able to carry twenty thouſand fighting men; and England no longer depended on Hamburgh, Lubeck, Dantzick, Genoa and Venice, for a fleet in time of war. In 1573, Elizabeth poſſeſſed a fleet of fifty-nine ſhips, of forty guns and upwards, one of which carried one hundred guns, and eighty-ſeven ſhips of inferior force; of theſe only thirteen belonged to her, the reſidue being hired, out in 1588, ſhe had at ſea 156 ſhips of ſuperior deſcription, of which forty were her own. This increaſe, however, muſt have ariſen after the defeat of the armada, proudly termed invincible, ſince, at that period, the Britiſh fleet conſiſted of only 76 ſhips paid by the queen, and 38 by the city of London; beſides 83 coaſters, &c. ſent by ſeveral other ſea ports; in all 197 veſſels great and ſmall, beſides thoſe of Holland and Zealand, carrying in burthen 29,744 tons, and having 15,785 men. The force intended for invaſion was compoſed of 132 ſhips of ſuperior deſcription, the burthen being 59,120 tons, and the number of men on board 30,621, with 2630 cannon; beſides which there were numerous galleons, galeaſſes, hulks, and other veſſels. Of the fate of this armament it is not neceſſary here to treat, further than by obſerving that its ſignal defeat and deſtruction, by which Spain loſt eighty one ſhips and thirteen thouſand five hundred ſailors and ſoldiers, beſides a vaſt treaſure, confirmed the policy of maintaining a powerful royal marine force, rendered all inſtitutions for its eſtabliſhment popular, and inſeparably connected achievements at ſea with the ſafety and glory of the nation. France firſt began under Henry IV. to aim at the creation of a navy. The aſſaſſination of that great monarch ſuſpended the project, but it was ſoon revived by cardinal Richelieu, who inſcribed on the ſterns of the new ſhips, in alluſion to the fleur de lis, the enſign of France, the elegant and appropriate motto "*Florent quoque lilia ponto.*" From this eſtabliſhment, which increaſed as the power of Spain declined, moſt of the labours of the Britiſh navy have ariſen, but thoſe labours are accompanied with ſo much glory, and have ſo abſolutely confirmed the aſcendancy of Great Britain both in arms and commerce at ſea, that they form the brighteſt portions in her hiſtorical annals. It is not intended to trace with regular details the progreſs of the navy; for general information the following tables will ſuffice, as they exhibit its ſtate at the end of every reign, with the particulars of its eſtabliſhment at the preſent period.

A. D. 1547.

			Tons.
A. D.	1547.	Henry VIII.	12,455.
	1553.	Edward VI.	11,065.
	1558.	Mary	7,110.
	1603.	Elizabeth	17,110.
	1625.	James I. }	uncertain.
	1649.	Charles I. }	uncertain.
	1660.	Reſtoration	57,463.
	1685.	Charles II.	103,558.
	1688.	James II.	101,892.
	1702.	William	159,017.
	1714.	Anne	167,171.
	1727.	George I.	170,862.
	1760.	George II.	321,104.

In the firſt year of his preſent majeſty's reign, when a war was conducted with the greateſt glory and proſperity, the royal navy was thus compoſed.

2	Ships of the firſt rate, carrying	96 to	110 guns.
11	2d rate	84	90
60	3d rate	64	80
43	4th rate	48	60
71	5th rate	26	44
40	6th rate	16	24
68	Sloops	8	14

12 bomb veſſels; | 39 hired armed veſſels;
10 fire ſhips; | 7 royal yachts;
4 ſtore ſhips; | 5 ſmall yachts.

Total, 372 veſſels of all kinds.

In 1806, which was likewiſe a period of war, maintained againſt an enemy formidable by means of unreſiſted power on the continent, the greater part of which was either ſubdued by, or in alliance with him, the British fleet conſiſted of the following ſhips.

	Line.	50 to 44.	Frigates.	Sloops, &c.	Gun-brigs and under.
In commiſſion	128	15	155	176	247
In ordinary and building	88	19	68	41	31
Total	216	34	223	217	278

Making a grand total of 968 armed veſſels.

The importance of the above force will be more juftly eftimated by comparing it with that of the other nations of Europe, of which at the end of 1805, the following was confidered a correct abftract.

	Line, including fifties.	Frigates.
Ruffia	60	100
Spain	57	44
Sweden	26	13
Denmark	23	23
Turkey	20	4
France	19	43
Batavian Republic	16	15
Portugal	10	5
Naples and Sicily	6	9
Etruria	2	4
Ragufa	0	12
Ecclefiaftical State	0	5
Total	239	277

The immenfe preponderance of the naval force of Britain over that of her probable enemies, becomes more ftriking when we take into confideration the fkill, courage, and enterprize of the feamen and officers, the confidence refulting from continual victory, and the emulation infpired by the glory of the greateft names which the annals of Britifh hiftory can produce, men in fpeaking of whom, terms of praife are exhaufted without doing juftice to their merit, and on whom honours and emoluments are fhowered while living, and honorary memorials accumulated when dead, without fatisfying the public that fufficient homage has been paid to their valour, or fufficient tributes rendered to their merit.

Establishment in time of Peace. This formidable force is not however always maintained. In time of peace, the fhips in ordinary at each port are formed into divifions, to each of which is appointed a mafter to fuperintend, from the fenior part of the lift. Each fhip has a boatfwain, a gunner, a carpenter, and a cook, with their fervants to remain on board; alfo a purfer, who, under an order in council dated September, 1803, has permiffion to refide at a prefcribed diftance from the port, in order to be ready when called on: for which purpofe he is to fend quarterly, to the clerk of the cheque, at the port at which the fhip is in ordinary, or building, a certificate from the minifter of the parifh that he is alive and a refident: this alfo enables his

his agent to receive his pay; but he is not obliged, as heretofore, to place or continue a deputy or servant. The following number of seamen is allowed for each class of ships, who have been rated able, for six calendar months: one hundred guns and upwards, 36 men; ninety-eight or ninety, 32; eighty, 30; seventy-four or seventy, 26; sixty-four, 20; fifty-four, 16; fifty, 14; forty-four, 12; thirty-eight or twenty-eight, 10; twenty-four or twenty, 8; sloops, 6; cutters, brigs, &c. in proportion to their size.

Rate of Ships. For the general understanding of this subject, the following particulars should be noticed. There are several denominations of ships or vessels of war.

1st. The largest down to sixty-fours, inclusive, are ships of the line of battle.

2d. Fifties and fifty fours, which form a class of themselves, are never placed in line of battle but in cases of great emergency.

3d. Forties to twenties inclusive, which are, without exception, frigates.

The foregoing classes are commanded by post captains, and they mount long guns or carronades on their quarter decks and forecastles. All are pierced for and mount more pieces of cannon than by the rules of the navy they are registered for on the books. If any are wanted for services that do not require complete equipment as men of war, and do not take on board the full number of guns and men, they are, in that case, commanded by officers of inferior rank to post captains.

Yachts rank with third rates, except the king's particular yacht, which ranks as a second rate. Fire ships and hospital ships rank with 5th rates.

4th. Eighteen to sixteen guns inclusive are sloops of war. Fire ships and bombs, being commanded by commanders, are also reckoned under this denomination. Merchant vessels purchased by government and fitted as sloops, are registered as the latter.

5th. Gun-brigs, and vessels fitted as gun-vessels, stand next in rank above schooners; next cutters; and lastly, tenders, with other small craft. The establishment of rates and men is as follows:

1st rate,	100 guns and upward,		875	men to	850
2d,	98 to 90	- -	750	-	700
3d,	80 to 64	- -	650	-	500
4th,	60 to 50	- -	420	-	320
5th,	40 to 32	- -	300	-	220
6th,	28 to 20	- -	200	-	140
Sloops,	18 to 16	- -	125	-	90
Gun-brigs, Cutters, &c.	14 to 6	- -	50	-	25

When

When an admiral's flag is hoisted on board a first rate, her complement of men is increased to 875. When a vice-admiral's, to 870. When a rear-admirals to 865.

Ships of the line, fifties, frigates, and royal yachts, are commanded by post captains; sloops of war, bombs, fire ships, armed ships, store ships, and *armées en flute*, under fifty guns, by commanders. Schooners, cutters, and other small armed vessels, by lieutenants. Sloops fitted for the conveyance of stores are occasionally commanded by masters, and small craft by midshipmen who have passed for lieutenants.

Upon the official register of the navy there are no sixty-eights or fifty-sixes; nor any frigates classed higher than forties.

First and second rates have three complete decks or tiers of guns fore and aft. Third and fourth rates, two complete decks or tiers of guns fore and aft. Fifth and sixth rates, which include sloops of war and all under, are some of them rigged with three masts, as ships, some with two masts, as brigs, &c.

Mode of providing Ships. In ancient times, as already has been shewn, the king, by virtue of his prerogative, could call on the subject to supply vessels for defence of the realm or attack of the enemy; the sea ports, and subsequently the whole kingdom, were obliged to contribute to the formation of the navy; a mixed fleet was then formed, partly of ships belonging to the crown and partly of those which were hired from private proprietors; but as the want of a navy became more sensibly felt, the care of government was more strongly directed to it, and public docks and arsenals were established for the building, repairing, and equipping of vessels for the public service. It has also been usual, in late years, to contract for the construction of ships at the dock yards of the mercantile ship builders.

Dock Yards. There are six principal dock-yards in the kingdom; at Deptford, Woolwich, Chatham, Sheerness, Portsmouth, and Plymouth.

Deptford was first raised into consideration by Henry VIII. who erected a storehouse, and, by a charter dated in the 4th of his reign, established a guild, or corporation, for the increase and better conducting of the royal navy, known by the name of the Trinity House. Camden, who takes no notice of Woolwich, mentions Deptford, as being, at the time he wrote (1607), a noted dock. The area of the yard has been since more than doubled. A wet dock of two acres for ships, and another of one acre and half for masts, have been added. It was at this place that Peter the Great of Muscovy studied ship building; and in this yard, the little ship, in which Sir Francis Drake sailed round the world, in the year 1580, was laid up by order of queen Elizabeth in remembrance of the voyage.

Woolwich. This dock precedes all in point of antiquity; ships of war had been built here before the reign of Henry VIII; but that prince added to the celebrity of this yard, by building, in the fourth year of his reign, his famous ship of more than one thousand tons burthen, named *Henry Grace de Dieu*, but more commonly called the Great Harry. At this dock likewise were built the Prince Royal of fourteen hundred tons, in the 8th of James I. and the Sovereign Royal, a ship of the first rate, in the 13th of Charles I.; also three famous first rate ships of war, called the Charles, the James, and the Saint Andrew, in the reign of Charles II.

Chatham yard owes its origin to queen Elizabeth, who, in in the second year of her reign, built a dock at a great expence on the spot beneath the church, which, in the next reign was assigned to the office of ordnance; and a more extensive yard was constructed, in 1622, on the adjoining bank, where it is now situated. Gillingham road, on the Medway, just below Chatham, had early been a principal station for ships, and is mentioned as such by Hollingshed. It was on that account that Upnor castle was built in the reign of Henry VIII.

Sheerness had no extence till Charles II. constructed a fort by means of piles on a sand bank, at this point of the isle of Sheppey, as a more convenient barrier against the approach of the enemy than Queenborough castle. An alluvium of soil being soon after collected on the south side around several hulks which were run ashore there, it was deemed a proper place for the establishment of a yard on a small scale, as an appendage to that at Chatham, for the occasional repair and refitting of ships, without their going up the Medway, and for the construction of ships of lower rates. The forts were taken and dismantled by the Dutch in 1667, but were soon restored, and Sheerness is now a place of considerable strength, and celebrated for its well, planned and executed a few years since by Sir Thomas Page, to supply what had been its chief defect, the want of fresh water. The principal inconvenience attending the yard is, that it is a thoroughfare to all persons coming into or going out of the fort; though this is less felt than it would otherwise be, from the whole place being the property of the crown.

Portsmouth had been long celebrated for its harbour, and noted as a fortified place, before any dook was established there. The walls were originally of timber and mud; but two towers of freestone at the mouth of the harbour were begun by Edward IV. continued by Richard III. and completed by Henry VII.; and fortifications of freestone were added by queen Elizabeth. Southsea castle, and the block-house, were built by Henry VIII. who made this one of the principal rendezvous for his navy. The

dock

dock begun in that century (though inconſiderable at firſt) has been gradually improved and extended, till it has become the moſt complete naval arſenal in the kingdom; and, with the advantage of the fortifications, the harbour and the roads at Spithead and St. Helens, forms a moſt eligible ſtation for the royal navy. On the third of July 1768, a dreadful fire broke out at midnight, in the dock-yard, and raged with great fury. It rained very hard all that night, and it was thought the ſtores caught fire by the lightning. In the warehouſes that were conſumed were depoſited one thouſand and fifty tons of hemp, five hundred tons of cordage, and about ſeven hundred ſails, beſides many hundred barrels of tar and oil. A ſtill more dreadful conflagration happened in the dock-yard on the 27th July, 1770; it was firſt diſcovered by the centinels on duty about 5 o'clock in the morning, when the drums beat to arms, and, in a few minutes after the dock-yard was all in a flame. The houſe where the pitch and tar were lodged was ſoon reduced to an heap of rubbiſh, and in a few minutes it broke out in four different parts, and burnt with ſuch violence, as to threaten the whole place. The inhabitants were filled with the greateſt conſternation; but by the wind ſhifting about, and the aſſiſtance of the marines and ſailors its progreſs was ſtopped before ſeven in the evening. The rope houſe was again deſtroyed, December the ſeventh, 1776, when the damage was eſtimated at ſixty thouſand pounds. For this act an incendiary named James Aitkin, but called John the Painter, was found guilty and executed.

Plymouth, though originally a ſmall fiſhing town, grew into conſequence from the excellence of the havens at the mouths of the Plym and the Tamer, the former of which is mentioned by the hiſtorians of the ſixteenth century, as being, in their time, walled on each ſide of the entrance, and chained acroſs in time of neceſſity, and as having a blockhouſe on a rocky hill on the ſouth ſide. At the period of intended invaſion by the Spaniſh armada, it was one of the ſtations of the Engliſh fleet; but the dock-yard is of later date than any of the others, having been eſtabliſhed by William III, who began in 1691, and finiſhed in 1693, a wet and dry dock, both of conſiderable magnitude. The yard is ſince greatly increaſed, and forms a ſmall town, with a ſeparate chapel, and has every appendage that can render it a complete naval arſenal.

There is a naval ſtorehouſe at Harwich, and ſhips have been occaſionally built there, but it has no pretenſions to the title of a dock-yard, and is only calculated for refitting any of the king's ſhips, which happen to touch there, for which purpoſe there is a ſtorehouſe with offices belonging to it.

Deal and Leith in Great Britain, and Kinſale in Ireland, are in the

the same predicament, as are likewise Gibraltar, Antigua, and Greenwich in Jamaica, at each of which there are storekeepers, and at the last, master shipwrights; but at Halifax, in Nova Scotia, there is a regular dock-yard, though on a small scale, established in the reign of George II., and superintended by a resident commissioner, with proper officers in the different branches.

Government. The dock-yards are all under the general controul and direction of the commissioners of the navy: those at Deptford and Woolwich are under the immediate inspection of the navy board, and are visited weekly by the comptroller and surveyor of the navy. The yards at Chatham, Portsmouth, and Plymouth, are respectively superintended by a resident commissioner, who conducts the business under the direction of the admiralty and navy boards, of which latter the resident commissioners are members: the yard at Sheerness is under the charge of the commissioner resident at Chatham.

Officers. The establishment of each of the dock-yards consists of the five following principal officers. A master, or master's attendant, a master shipwright, a clerk of the cheque, a storekeeper, and a clerk of the survey; each of whom, as well as the commissioners resident at three of the yards, have a certain number of clerks employed under them. There are likewise at each yard, a surgeon, a boatswain, and a master porter, and at all the yards, except Sheerness, a purveyor; likewise at all except Sheerness, and Deptford, a clerk of the rope yard, and a master rope-maker.

The *Commissioner*, at the yards where one is resident, superintends all the works carrying on, and the due performance of the duties incumbent on the officers and workmen; he controuls the payment of the ships afloat, and those made at the pay-office on shore; superintends the sale of old, and purchase of new stores when necessary; examines and proves the entry of seamen, and the discharge of those unfit for service, also the entry of artificers, labourers, &c. for the yard. He causes the standing orders for the good government of the yard to be read to the officers and workmen quarterly, sees that the proper precautions are taken for the security of the yard, administers the oath for qualifying commission and warrant officers; and for receiving widows pensions; inspects and transmits to the navy board the accounts of the officers of the yard, and corresponds with the admiralty and navy boards on all matters relating to the ships in port or dock, and on all occurences in his particular department.

The *Master Attendant* assists at the survey of all boatswain's stores brought into the yards, and inspects the works going

going on in the ſail-loft and rigging houſe; examines the ſtate of ſhips arriving from ſea; viſits occaſionally thoſe laid up in ordinary; muſters the ordinary; and makes a proper diſtribution of the men for the ſervices on ſhore, and on board the ſhips in harbour; attends the launching, docking and undocking of all ſhips of war in the yard, the launching of king's ſhips built in merchants' yards, and the ſurvey, valuing, and approving of ſuch ſhips as are tendered to government for purchaſe or hire, as tranſports or ſtore ſhips, and reports his opinion thereon, jointly with the maſter-ſhipwright, and clerk of the ſurvey.

The *Maſter Shipwright* aſſiſts in ſurveying the quality of all ſhipwrights' ſtores received into the yard, and certifies the ſame; inſpects all the ſhipwrights' work going on in the yard or elſewhere when required; attends the ſurvey, valuation and approval of ſhips tendered for ſervice or hire, and reports his opinion thereon, jointly with the clerk of the ſurvey and maſter attendant.

The *Clerk of the Cheque* keeps liſts of all the ſhipwrights, artificers, and labourers belonging to the yard, of all the officers, ſhip-keepers, and ſeamen belonging to the ordinary, and of all the officers and ſeamen belonging to the ſhips in commiſſion at the ports; muſters the yards daily; the ordinary weekly on board, and monthly on ſhore; and the ſhips in commiſſion once or twice a week; makes out quarterly pay-books for the yard and ordinary; and tranſmits to the navy board copies of the muſters of the ſhips in commiſſion on their leaving the port, and ſends to the admiralty and navy boards weekly accounts of them during their ſtay. When there are any hired tranſports or veſſels at the port, he muſters them daily, and ſends accounts to the navy board; he ſurveys the quantity and quality of all ſtores received, and inſpects and meaſures all works performed by contract in the yard; and, on application, makes out bills for the ſame: he receives for the treaſurer of the navy the money ariſing from the ſale of old ſtores, pays the contingent expences of the yard, of which he makes up a quarterly account.

The *Storekeeper* inſpects, jointly with the other principal officers, all ſtores ſerved into the yard, and upon finding them of proper quality, receives and depoſits them in the proper place: he ſigns bills for all he receives, and iſſues none without a warrant ſigned by two of the principal officers: he keeps an exact account of the receipt, iſſues, and remains of every article, and ſends monthly accounts to the navy board.

The *Clerk of the Survey* grants warrants, jointly with the maſter attendant and maſter ſhipwright, for the iſſue of all ſtores to boatſwains and carpenters of ſhips of war, and keeps a charge

charge on them for the ſtores received; adjuſts and balances their reſpective accounts, and tranſmits fair copies to the navy board. He ſurveys all rigging, ſails, ground tackle, and ſtores of every kind in the boatſwains' and carpenters' charge; joins the proper officers in the yard in making timely requiſitions to the navy board for ſupplies; alſo in taking ſurveys of all ſtores and materials ſerved into the yard, and of all works performed by contract; and in forming eſtimates for the enſuing year, under the heads of extra, wear and tear, and ordinary; and he tranſmits quarterly to the navy board accounts of the actual expence under each of theſe heads. He keeps ſuch further charges and accounts as are neceſſary to aſcertain the quantity of ſtores in hand, and their uſe and value; and aſſiſts the maſter attendant and maſter ſhipwright in the ſurvey, valuation, and approval of tranſports, and other veſſels tendered for purchaſe or hire.

Navy Bills. From the account here given of the ſeveral principal officers, it appears that there are certain occaſions on which they act collectively, ſuch as ſurveying and certifying ſtores delivered into the yard, and ſigning bills for the amount; the proceſs on which occaſions is as follows: copies of all contracts made by the board for ſtores are tranſmitted to the officers of the yard where the ſtores are to be delivered: upon the delivery of ſuch ſtores, it is the duty of the maſter attendant for ſtores in his line, and of the maſter ſhipwright in his line, to attend the clerk of the checque, ſtore-keeper, and clerk of the ſurvey, to examine their quality and quantity, their agreement or diſagreement with the terms of the contract, and to enter the ſame in a book. On receipt of the articles into ſtore, the ſtore-keeper charges himſelf with them, the clerk of the ſurvey keeps a checque charge upon him for them, and the clerk of the checque makes out a bill for the amount, according to the contract which he and the ſtore-keeper ſign; and the maſter attendant, or maſter ſhipwright, according to the deſcription of ſtores, together with the clerk of the ſurvey, certifies on the back of ſuch bill, that the ſtores were good, fit for the ſervice, and agreeable to contract, or to the warrants by which they were received; the commiſſioner of the yard ſigns his name on the front of the bill to the amount, which is written in words at length; this bill ſo ſigned and certified, is ſent to the navy board, where it is ſigned by two other commiſſioners, and when delivered to the party, entitles him, or his aſſigns, to receive the amount in due courſe. Such is the progreſs of a navy bill.

Further Duties of Officers. The attendance of the reſident commiſſioners is conſtant; they have all houſes in their

their respective yards, and are never absent without leave from the admiralty. All the other officers and clerks in the yards are efficient and perform their duty in person. The commissioners of the dock-yards have not any instructions for their government; but the following officers have very full and particular instructions from the navy board; viz. master attendant, master shipwright and his assistants, clerk of the checque, storekeeper, clerk of the survey, clerk of the rope yard, master rope maker, boatswain, and porter.

Emoluments. Besides the established salaries, wages, and allowances of each, the principal officers have certain emoluments, but not of very great value. The principal officers have a house unfurnished (except with certain articles of ship furniture which are allowed to be issued for them from the stores); with a few other perquisites peculiar to other offices. All the chief officers of the yard, including the master, shipwrights, assistants, and the surgeon, boatswain, and porter, have houses in the yard. Some officers have apprentices, and the number allowed to each, is as follows: master shipwright five, his assistants, each three, master caulker three, master mast maker two, master boat builder two, purveyor one, master rope maker four. The wages for these apprentices are small at first, but increase every year. The chief receipt of the master porter arises from a tap, which he is allowed to keep for the convenience of the yard, and his own advantage.

A considerable abuse formerly arose in the several yards from indulging the artificers and workmen with permission, every day at noon, to take away a bundle of chips; the quantity originally allowed was as much as each could carry under his arm; but they had gradually raised them to their shoulders, and carried double the portion originally allowed. They used to leave off work, perhaps half an hour before bell ringing, for the purpose of gathering together these chips, and, even during working hours, sometimes they clandestinely cut up useful timber to complete their bundles; and opportunities were found for secreting valuable stores, such as copper, brass, &c. The suppression of this abuse was long recommended, and often attempted, but the effort occasioned conspiracies and mutinies among the men; until, at length, in 1802, it was, if not totally suppressed, at least so far reduced, as to be no longer a grievance of any great importance.

Inspector General's Office. For the preservation of regularity, and encouragement of improvement in all matters relating to the construction of ships, an office is established at the admiralty, with an inspector general of his majesty's naval works, whose duty it is, to consider of all improvements in relation

lation to the building, fitting out, arming, navigating and victualling ſhips of war, and other veſſels employed in his Majeſty's ſervice, as well as in relation to the docks, ſhips, baſons and other articles, appertaining to his Majeſty's eſtabliſhment. The inſpector has a ſalary of 1250*l.* and under him are officers with ſalaries as follow. An architect, 400*l.*, a mechaniſt 400*l.*, a chemiſt 400*l.*, a ſecretary 300*l.*, a metal maſter 200*l.*, a draftſman 200*l.*; a firſt clerk 150*l.*, and a ſecond clerk 100*l.*

Improvements in the Navy. The preſent ſtate of the navy, ſo glorious and advantageous to the country, is the reſult of great attention, or fortunate circumſtances, and of a continual application of the genius, wealth and induſtry of the nation to all objects connected with the building, ſecuring, and management of ſhipping. Warlike veſſels, of large ſize, were ever conſidered deſirable, but in this particular, England was long behind Spain, for although Henry VIII. had built his famous Grace de Dieu, veſſels of great magnitude were ſo little encouraged in England, that the Engliſh fleet was conſidered unable to cope with the armada, not leſs on account of the ſuperior number than the ſuperior ſize of the Spaniſh ſhips. Even in the reign of James I., in 1610, a ſhip of 64 guns, and 1400 tons burthen, called the Prince, was deemed ſuperior to any veſſel before ſeen in England. Since that time, however, the Britiſh navy has been furniſhed with ſhips of ſuch dimenſions, that the 64 is the ſmalleſt regularly admitted into the line of battle. France and Spain ſtill build larger ſhips, but the conſtruction is not conſidered ſufficiently advantageous to induce the Britiſh government to rival them, and the ſucceſs of Britiſh fleets leaves no reaſon for calling this judgment in queſtion.

Fire Ships. It was long before the ancient ſemicircular line of battle fell into diſuſe; it was preſerved in the combat with the Spaniſh armada; but as, at that time, fire ſhips began to be employed, it is probable that the mode of fighting underwent, from that circumſtance, a neceſſary alteration. This deſtructive artifice, now no longer formidable, becauſe no longer operating by ſurprize, was conſidered at the time a moſt extraordinary invention; and certainly it is no deduction from the praiſe due to the brave commanders of the Engliſh fleet to ſhew that traces of ſuch a diſcovery are found in more ancient hiſtory, ſince there is no probability that they derived information from any work, or were ſupplied with the means of execution from any ſource but their own judgment.

The Compass. In ſpeaking of improvements in nautical affairs, it is impoſſible to omit noticing the grand diſcovery which has always been found ſufficient to give ſecurity to enterprizes otherwise hopeless, by enabling fleets or single ships to traverse the trackless level of the ocean with unerring certainty, and at all times to ascertain the point to which the course of the vessel ought to be directed. This discovery is, in fact, the basis of all naval grandeur, for it would be a useless and even unnatural effort to build ships of a large size, when the impossibility of making long voyages would keep them always near shore, where the chief recommendation of the vessel would be to draw little water, and when there would be no necessity for stores of various kinds to be accumulated in such quantities as are required by numerous crews for long adventures. An account at some length, of this most valuable instrument, cannot be deemed improper in this place, especially as many errors respecting it have been currently received. The magnet or loadstone was known to the ancient philosophers of Greece for its quality of attracting iron, and in later ages, produced admiration, without being considered of use; but it does not appear that until about the end of the twelfth century, any discovery had been made of its more valuable property, its polarity, or that power by which one point of it, or even of a needle or bar of iron or steel touched with it, turns to the North Pole, and the opposite point to the South. Toward the conclusion of the twelfth century, a notice on this subject appears in the poetical works of Hugues de Berry, called also Guiot de Provins, who says, "This (polar) star does not move. They (the seamen) "have an art, which cannot deceive, by virtue of the *manete*, "an ill looking, brownish, stone, to which iron spontaneously "adheres. They search for the right point, and when they "have touched a needle on it, and fixed it on a bit of straw, "they lay it on the water, and the straw keeps it afloat. Then "the point infallibly turns towards the star; and when the "night is dark and gloomy, and neither star nor moon is visible, they set a light beside the needle, and they then can "be assured, that the star is opposite to the point; and *thereby* "*the mariner is directed in his course.*" This rude description of this most important instrument is confirmed by other authors, and yet, in defiance of these unquestionable authorities, the Italian writers claim the honour of inventing the compass for John Gioia or *Flavio* Gioia, a citizen of the commercial city of Amalfi, who, they say, first used it in the year 1302, or 1320: and as a proof, they adduce a line of Anthony of Palermo, a Sicilian poet, "*Prima dedit nautis usum magnetis Amalfi.*" From the simple contrivance of laying the magnetic needle on a floating straw, as described by Guiot, navigators, by gradual improvements, in the course of time, came to add the use of a circular card affixed to the needle, and traversing with it, on which

which were drawn lines reprefenting the various winds. It is probable that Gioia of Amalfi was the firft, who thought of ufing a card, and that only eight winds, or points, were drawn upon it. The French, the Venetians, the Germans, and the Scandinavians (or people of Norway and Denmark) have all difputed with thofe of Amalfi, and with each other, the honour of difcovering this moft noble inftrument. Some praife may perhaps be due to every one of them, and, as is generally allowed, alfo to the Englifh, for improvements made upon the original invention. In 1263 the compafs, fitted into a box as now, though probably without a card, was in common ufe among the Norwegians, who had fo juft an idea of its great importance, that they made it a device of an order of knighthood; and it is mentioned as well known in Scotland, by Barber, a writer of that country in the fourteenth century. It is probable that the Englifh, as well as all the fouthern maritime nations, were acquainted with it before it was ufed in Norway and Scotland.

In procefs of time, navigators, or experimental philofophers, difcovered that the polarity of the magnetic needle was not perfectly true, and that it diverged, or varied, fomewhat from the real north point. Succeeding experiments fhowed, that the variation was not every where the fame; that there was a line on the furface of the globe, on which there was no variation; that on one fide of that line the north point of the compafs varied to the eaftward, and on the other to the weftward, of the true north; and that the quantity of the variation increafed in an unknown proportion to the diftance from the line of no variation. This irregularity was known in, or before, the year 1269, when Peter Adfiger wrote on the various properties of the magnet, the conftruction of the Azimuth compafs, and the variation of the magnetic needle. The difcovery of the variation has, however, been attributed by fome to Chriftopher Columbus in 1492, and by others to Sebaftian Cabot in 1500, who may have obtained this reputation becaufe, in their voyages, wherein they made more difference of longitude than former navigators, they had more ample opportunities of making experiments on the variation.

It was afterwards difcovered, that the variation not only differed as it receded eaft or weft from the line of no variation, but that that line itfelf, which was found to be an oblique waving curve, had alfo in the northern hemifphere fhifted to the eaftward of its former ftation. The nice obfervations of the eighteenth century have demonftrated, that the variation is in a progreffive and perpetual ftate of alteration; and alfo, that it is fo far affected by heat and cold, as to differ confiderably in summer and winter, and even in the course of the same day. Another property of the magnet is the *dip*, or inclination of the north end of the needle toward the horizon, as if heavier than the south end, which is therefore in fact made a little heavier in order to counterpoise the dip. By the use of the magnet, and the application of its wonderful powers, man has become acquainted with the whole globe which was given him to inhabit, and been enabled to make prodigious improvements in the important sciences of geography and natural history. The compass has given birth to a new era in the history of commerce, and rendered navigation expeditious and comparatively safe. By the use of this noble instrument the whole world has become one vast commercial commonwealth; the most distant inhabitants of the earth are brought together for their mutual advantage: ancient prejudices are obliterated, and mankind are civilized and enlightened. And, by the compass, Great Britain has acquired that naval pre-eminence, which she confessedly possesses over all the maritime nations of the world.

OTHER IMPROVEMENTS. Without noticing the quadrant, the various telescopes both for night and day, the chain pump, the log, and many other philosophical and mechanical instruments and contrivances connected with nautical affairs, some may be mentioned in a general way, as from their constant use they present themselves to continual observation, and as they have been the objects of fame or pecuniary remuneration.

SHEATHING was first practised in 1553, on a ship fitted out for a voyage of discovery, and considered a most ingenious invention, calculated to preserve the vessel from the worm, and many other injuries. It was at first performed with thin plates of lead. A supposed improvement on sheathing was the object of a patent in the reign of Charles I., under the name of a cement to dress ships, to prevent their being burnt in sea fights, and to preserve them from the worm or bernacle; but this is mentioned only as one of many inventions for the benefit of the navy for which patents have been obtained, but which have not been generally adopted. A method of preserving the bottom of ships from the worm, and from the adhesion of weeds, had been some years before 1761 submitted to the society for the encouragement of arts and manufactures; and some experiments made in various climates, with wood prepared according to the directions of the inventor, were found satisfactory; so that this new method was supposed to be of infinite service to all kinds of shipping: but it was soon superseded by another, and apparently a more effectual preservative, consisting of thin sheets or plates of smooth copper, which no worm or animal

animal of any kind will touch, and no vegetable will adhere to; circumſtances equally favourable to the duration of ſhips, and to their ſwift ſailing; it is neat, much lighter than lead, or even the thinneſt ſheathing of boards, and laſts almoſt as long as the ſhip can be kept afloat. The firſt trial was made on the Alarm, one of the king's ſhips at Woolwich; and it ſoon came into general uſe, not only in the navy but alſo in the merchants' ſervice.

Sliding Keels. In 1790 a very conſiderable improvement, which unites the oppoſite advantages of flat and ſharp built veſſels, was introduced by Captain Schank of the royal navy. It conſiſts in making three wells, or water-tight openings, from the bottom up to the deck in the middle of the veſſel, wherein frames of plank, fitted to act as moveable partial keels, are let down under the bottom as occaſion requires. When the veſſel is on a wind, all the three are let down; and they may be lowered more or leſs according to the judgment of the commander, in order to aſſiſt the helm or gain the wind; when ſhe is tacking or lying to, only the headmoſt is let down; when wearing, or ſcudding in a gale of wind, only the after one; and they are all hove cloſe up, when ſhe goes before the wind, or has occaſion to go over a ſhoal. Theſe keels are of eminent uſe in going about, as the veſſel loſes no way: and ſhe may be ſteered by them very correctly without the uſe of the rudder; a matter of prodigious importance, when the rudder happens to be carried away. Captain Schank having tried the principle of his ſliding, or dropping, keels, upon boats in the year 1774 at Boſton in New England, and in 1789 at Depford, a cutter of twelve guns was built under his direction, which was found fully to poſſeſs all the advantages expected from it; and many veſſels have ſince been built for government on the ſame principle. It is the opinion of good judges, that the ſame principle, if applied in building veſſels for the merchants' ſervice, would be of very great utility, eſpecially to coaſters, which have occaſion to be much in ſhallow water, and to go over ſhoals, and alſo to veſſels carrying grain and other cargoes liable to ſhift. Such veſſels would alſo be of great ſervice in navigating the deeper canals, which extend from ſea to ſea.

Gun Boats. The ſame officer in 1798 produced a plan for enabling every boat belonging to a merchant veſſel, every river-lighter, barge, ſcow, and keel, to carry one great gun, to be fired in every direction by means of a ſlide reaching from ſtem to ſtern of the boat. In caſe of a number of merchant veſſels being attacked by a privateer in light winds or a calm, the fleet of boats, armed in this manner, which they could fit out againſt her in twenty minutes, would have a great

 advantage

advantage in moving more rapidly with their light oars than she could with her heavy sweeps, and could choose their point of attack with such effect as to make her glad to escape from such a swarm of unexpectedly powerful antagonists.

Discovery of the Longitude. In 1714, on the petition of Mr. Whiston and Mr. Ditton, the British parliament passed an act for providing a public reward for the discovery of the longitude at sea. The preamble observes, "It is well known by "all that are acquainted with navigation, that nothing is so much "wanted and desired at sea as the discovery of the longitude, "for the safety and quickness of voyages, the preservation of "ships and lives of men; and whereas in the judgment of "able mathematicians and navigators, several methods have "been discovered, true in theory, though very difficult in "practice, some of which, there is reason to expect, may be "capable of improvement, some already discovered may be "proposed to the public, and others may be invented here-"after. And whereas such discovery would be of particular "advantage to the trade of Great Britain, and very much for "the honour of this kingdom; but, besides the great difficulty "of the thing itself, partly for the want of some public reward "as an encouragement, and partly for want of money, necessary "for trials and experiments, no such inventions or proposals, "hitherto made, have been brought to perfection." It was therefore enacted, that the lord high admiral, the speaker of the House of Commons, and sundry other great officers, by virtue of their offices, and several other persons, should be commissioners for trying and judging of all proposals, experiments and improvements, relating to the longitude; who, being satisfied of the probability of such discovery, should certify it to the commissioners of the navy, who were empowered to issue a bill for any sum, not exceeding 2000*l*., which the commissioners for the longitude should think necessary for making the experiments. And the ultimate reward offered to the discoverer of the longitude, if he determines it to one degree, or sixty geographical miles, was 10,000*l*., if to two thirds of a degree, 15,000*l*., and if to half a degree 20,000*l*. Five hundred pounds, part of the sum of 2,000*l*., had been paid by the commissioners to Mr. William Whiston, for surveying and determining the longitude and latitude of the chief ports and headlands on the coasts of Great Britain and Ireland, and 1250*l*. to Mr. John Harrison, for certain experiments, warranted by the commissioners, when, in 1753, an act was passed empowering them to disburse the further sum of 2000*l*., and adding to the former list of commissioners, the governor of Greenwich hospital, the judge of the admiralty court, the secretaries of the treasury, the ſecretary of the admiralty board, and the comptroller of the navy. The perfection of a diſcovery ſo difficult could not however be expected but from experiments of a nature too expenſive for mere men of letters, unaided by public bounty, to engage in, and therefore, in 1762, a new ſtatute enabled the commiſſioners to beſtow a ſum not exceeding 2000*l.* to any perſon, whoſe propoſal they ſhould think worthy of a trial.

Chronometers. The greateſt effort toward completing the required diſcovery was made by Mr. John Harriſon, the inventor of the chronometer, of which, and the longitude itſelf, the following account is given. The many improvements of the inſtruments uſed for taking the altitude of the ſun, had made it perfectly eaſy for navigators to aſcertain their latitude very exactly, every day that the ſun is viſible; but for the longitude they were obliged to depend on the accuracy of the courſe ſteered, and the menſuration of the ſhip's velocity by an inſtrument called the log. Theſe are both liable to much uncertainty; from the indeterminate allowance for currents and lee-way, which muſt depend on the judgment or conjecture of the navigator; from an erroneous conſtruction of the compaſs; from erroneous meaſurement of the log line, erroneous quantity of ſand in the half-minute glaſs, inexperience of the perſon heaving the log, ſwell of the ſea, variation of the ſhip's rate of going between the ſtated times of heaving the log, and various other cauſes. Hence a method of aſcertaining the longitude, with the ſame degree of accuracy which is attainable in the latitude, had for ages been the grand deſideratum in navigation; and ſince the year 1714, when the parliament offered a reward of 20,000*l.* for the beſt method of aſcertaining the longitude at ſea, many ſchemes had been deviſed, but all to little or no purpoſe, as going generally upon wrong principles, till Mr. John Harriſon aroſe. It is evident, that as the globe revolves round its axis in twenty-four hours, every one of the 360 degrees of longitude muſt be equal to four minutes of time; and conſequently, that if a ſhip has ſailed from any given point, where the ſun was in the zenith, (or in his meridional altitude,) and next day, when the ſun is in the zenith, it is found by a watch, which goes exactly true, that it is four minutes after twelve, the ſhip has made one degree of difference of longitude to the weſtward; or, if the watch wants four minutes of twelve, one degree of eaſt longitude; and ſo in proportion for any greater or leſs difference: hence nothing more is required to make us ſure of the longitude than a watch perfectly true. But watches, like all other productions of human art, are liable to error, and are, moreover, in a conſiderable degree affected by the changes of atmoſphere. To the correction of theſe defects Mr. Harriſon devoted the aſſiduous ſtudies of a long life; and he produced, what is probably, in principle, the neareſt approach that ever will be made by human ingenuity to the great object of the wiſhes of navigators and philoſophers, a *chronometer* or time-keeper, which in two voyages made by his ſon to the Weſt Indies, under the direction of the commiſſioners, was found to determine the longitude at ſea with an accuracy beyond the niceſt exactneſs required by the act of parliament, as appeared by certificates from the captain and officers of the ſhip, which was appointed to attend him on the trial, and alſo from the governor of Jamaica. The board of longitude thereupon paid Mr. Harriſon 1500*l.*, and parliament, the next year, ordered 5000*l.* to be paid to him, on condition that he ſhould lay open to the public the principles on which his time-keeper was conſtructed: and they promiſed to pay him the remainder of the 20,000*l.*, if on further trials, in the courſe of four years, it ſhould ſtill be found to aſcertain the longitude within the required limits of exactneſs; during which period no other artiſt ſhould be permitted to enter into competition with him in the ſame line of diſcovery. At different times afterward, Mr. Harriſon obtained payment of the remainder of the 20,000*l.* Time-keepers have ever ſince been made on his principles with great ſucceſs, and alſo with improvements by ſeveral watchmakers. The general uſe of them on board the navy, the Eaſt India ſhips, and many private merchant ſhips, has been productive of this important advantage to navigation, that many in the preſent race of navigators are much better acquainted with the principles on which the ſcience is founded, than their predeceſſors generally were, many of whom knew nothing more than merely how to uſe the inſtruments, apply the rules, and extract numbers from the tables, which men of ſcience had conſtructed for their uſe, without ever inquiring why thoſe inſtruments, rules and tables, were ſo conſtructed. To the uſe of time-keepers in the hands of men of ſcience we are alſo indebted for the great improvements lately made in the knowledge of currents in the ocean, whereof we may ſoon expect accurate charts deſcribing their courſe and velocity as correctly as the ſoundings and ſet of the tide are marked in the preſent charts of harbours and bays. Thus does Harriſon's invention conſtitute a new and ſplendid era in the hiſtory of navigation.

Other Premiums. Many other premiums have been given by the board of longitude, as one of 500*l.* in 1762, to Dr. Irwin, for the invention of a *marine chair*, which would enable the navigator to take obſervations of the heavenly bodies during a ſtorm, and for *lunar tables* conſtructed by him on the principles of Sir Iſaac Newton; one of 1000*l.* in the ſame year to Mr. Witchell for a *marine table* to facilitate the calculation of longitude

gitude by the *lunar method*. This mode of obſervation was carried to perfection in 1775, by Meſſrs. Turnbull and Latimer, who invented an inſtrument for aſcertaining the longitude, by meaſuring the diſtance of the moon from the ſun, by the aid of which the longitude may be determined at ſea at all times when the obſervation can be made. Many acts of parliament were framed for continuing the authorities of this board, and extending their diſcretionary power of offering rewards, until the year 1790, when the legiſlature empowered the commiſſioners of the navy to give rewards not exceeding 5000*l.* to ſuch as the board of longitude ſhould at any time certify to have made any uſeful diſcovery in the ſcience of the longitude, or any other improvement in navigation.

Making sea water fresh. Among the projects for the benefit of the navy which parliament judged worthy of reward, was one for this purpoſe by Dr. Charles Irving, for which in 1772 he received 5000*l.*

Victualling the Navy. In the early period of naval eſtabliſhment, this important branch was, like almoſt every other, managed by temporary arrangements, or by the ſudden exerciſe of an undefined prerogative. In the indenture already noticed between Henry VIII. and Sir Edward Howard, it was expreſsly provided that the king ſhould victual the fleet at his own coſt; in the reign of James I. 1622, a regular contract was entered into for ſupply of the navy, the daily allowances to each man being ſpecified, the facilities allowed to the contractors, and the ſum paid for the proviſion of each man, which was, in harbour ſeven-pence halfpenny, and at ſea eight-pence a day.

Victualling Office. In thoſe times, when the fleet was upon a ſmall ſcale, the commiſſioners of the navy, in addition to other weighty concerns, managed alſo thoſe of the victualling; but, in the year 1683, the latter department ſeems to have been ſeparated from the navy board, and conſtituted a diſtinct but ſubordinate eſtabliſhment; one of the members of that board being ſtyled comptroller of the victualling accounts. At that period the board of victualling conſiſted of four commiſſioners, who were diſmiſſed in 1689, and five others appointed in their place. In 1704, two commiſſioners were added to the number. Inſtructions were given to them for their conduct at different times. Each commiſſioner, according to theſe regulations, took the chair in rotation, there having been no precedence fixed, either according to their appointment, or to their offices, until the third of November, 1784, when the lords of the admiralty directed that the commiſſioner who ſuperintends the branch of accomptant for caſh, ſhall preſide at the board: and that the other members ſhall take precedence from their reſpective

ſpective departments in the following order, viz. department of accomptant for caſh, of accomptant for ſtores, hoy-taker, brew-houſe, cutting-houſe, bake-houſe, cooperage. The commiſſioners are appointed by letters patent, and receive inſtructions from the admiralty for the ſuperintendance of the departments committed to their care, and for the regulation of their general conduct as members of the board.

The buſineſs of the victualling office is, to provide, either by contract or otherwiſe, all the proviſions, and alſo certain ſtores required for his Majeſty's navy; arranging and diſtributing the whole to the ſeveral ports at home and abroad, as the ſervice may require; to take care that the different proviſions and ſtores, when ſo iſſued, be properly charged to the agents, ſtore-keepers, purſers, maſters of tranſports, or others to whom they were iſſued; and to compel the reſpective parties to paſs timely and regular accounts; alſo to take care that all offal ariſing from articles manufactured, be properly diſpoſed of, all old ſtores ſold to the beſt advantage, and the proceeds duly accounted for; to attend to the various checks and regulations which have been inſtituted for the ſecurity of the public; with many other important objects.

The eſtabliſhed articles of victualling uſed in the navy, are biſcuit, beer, beef, pork, peas, oatmeal, butter, cheeſe, vinegar and bags, or the materials, ſuch as wheat, malt, hops, oats, oxen, hogs, ſtaves, and hoops; from which biſcuit, beer, oatmeal, ſalt beef, ſalt pork, and caſks are manufactured in the ſtore-houſes at Deptford, and in other places. In time of war, large quantities of each ſpecies of proviſions are ſent abroad, as alſo ſome extra articles, ſuch as ſour crout, eſſence of malt, molaſſes, and pot barley. For the performance of ſuch extenſive and important ſervices, it has been found neceſſary to conſtitute permanent eſtabliſhments at Deptford, Chatham, Dover, Portſmouth, Plymouth and Gibraltar; at each of which places there are regular and ſubordinate offices. Agents are alſo appointed occaſionally for the like purpoſes, upon various parts of the coaſts of Great Britain and Ireland, and alſo at foreign ſtations in the Weſt Indies, America, India, &c.; but notwithſtanding the appointments juſt mentioned, recourſe is frequently had to contracts for the victualling of his Majeſty's ſhips on different ſtations, both at home and abroad; and the commanding officers of ſquadrons on detached ſervices deem it neceſſary to appoint agents for ſecuring ſupplies of proviſions and victualling ſtores; ſuch ſupplies are alſo often provided by purſers of ſingle ſhips, touching at ports where there is neither a contractor nor agent.

For the purpoſe of enabling the board of victualling to execute the comprehenſive and important duties which have been already ſtated,

stated, store houses and other conveniences were attached to the office on Tower hill, and similar receptacles also provided in other situations, not only for containing such provision and stores as had been already manufactured, but also for the manufacturing of such articles as might be found necessary, from the materials purchased by the board. The advantages resulting from those establishments have been so considerable as to render buildings on a much larger scale necessary; and accordingly other erections have been constructed at Deptford; and a canal into the centre of them has been proposed. The stores at Deptford are connected with and make part of the victualling office of London; and the commissioners attend at Deptford from time to time, for the purpose of superintending the business of their respective departments; a considerable portion of which must be transacted at that place. The entire system of victualling accounts with all its numerous and subordinate branchesand connexions, as well foreign as domestic, after passing through many previous checks and forms, finally centres in London in the two departments of the accomptant for cash, and the accomptant for stores, where all vouchers, certificates, bills, accounts and affidavits, undergo further checks, and are submitted to every degree of examination which the nature of the case will admit: every part also of the business transacted in the separate departments of the other commissioners must be brought ultimately to those offices; consequently the accomptant for cash can, at all times, furnish particulars of monies received and paid, and what sums are due to and from the crown, under separate and distinct heads; and the accomptant for stores can furnish particulars of provisions and stores received, issued, and which remain; together with the names of the several parties who originally delivered the same, according to contract or otherwise; and also of those officers or persons who are respectively charged or discharged for the provisions and stores in question. And it is from those materials, furnished to the accomptant for cash, with the assistance of other documents in his possession, that he is enabled to form the estimates for victualling the fleet.

All officers and chief clerks are appointed by warrant from the admiralty, and the inferior clerks by the commissioner who superintends the respective branch; the officers in general are furnished with instructions for the regulation of their conduct in the department to which they belong.

In every branch of the victualling, where money is impressed to pay salaries, wages or contingencies, or where money is received by any officer for the sale of provisions, old stores, &c. the accounts are not only confirmed by regular vouchers and certificates,

certificates, but likewise by the oath of the party; purporting that the money has been duly expended or accounted for, agreeably to the statement of particulars which he has exhibited. Security is required from many, although not from all, the officers, employed under the board.

The following is an outline of the principal duties belonging to each officer.

The *First Commissioner* has under his superintendance the department of accomptant for cash, where a daily register is kept of all the victualling bills; and where accounts undergo an examination, and bills are made out, when vouchers and explanations are satisfactory: also the departments for examining and stating of imprest accounts, for keeping a charge on the treasurer, and for paying short allowance money, which three departments, though each under the direction of a separate chief clerk, are nevertheless branches of the department of the accomptant, for cash, to whom consequently they are subordinate. The same commissioner also superintends the offices of the surveyor, and clerk of the cheque, the first of which is for drawing plans, and forming estimates, and reporting on the materials and rates of work done; and the latter is for mustering the workmen of the yard, and attending the receipts and surveys of provisions and stores.

Under the *Second Commissioner* are comprehended the department of secretary, where, besides the ordinary duties, the important one of receiving tenders and drawing up contracts is transacted, and the department of accomptant for stores, where various books are kept, which shew, at any period, the state of provisions, &c. in store, and the expenditure for the same: also the department for keeping a charge on pursers, and of clerks of the issues, the duties of which are implied by their respective titles.

The *Third Commissioner* has under his direction the department of Hoy-taker, whose duty it is to examine, in conjunction with other principal officers employed by the board, the tonnage and condition of vessels tendered upon freight, or otherwise, and to report upon every particular respecting them previous to their being hired; to attend the loading and unloading of provisions, and other things issued for, or returning from ships, transports, and victuallers, and to keep accounts thereof, and to superintend the hoys and craft belonging to the victualling service.

The other commissioners superintend respectively; the fourth, the brewing house; the fifth the cutting-house; the sixth the bake-house; and the seventh the cooperage; which departments need no description further than to state that great variety of checks are adopted in each to secure the due performance of contracts,

to

to prevent any waste or embezzlement of the articles in hand, to insure the regular adjustment of accounts, and generally to prevent the abuses, to which such departments would be liable from the nature of their business.

THE OFFICE. The business of the victualling office, so far as relates to orders, warrants and instructions, is now transacted in apartments devoted to that purpose in Somerset House. The old victualling office is on Tower hill. The site was formerly occupied by an abbey church, consecrated by Edward III. in the 25th year of his reign, to St. Mary of the Graces, and inhabited by monks of the Cistertian order, who obtained large possessions in various counties. After the reformation, the monastery was pulled down, and slaughter houses, store houses, and other conveniences erected for the express purpose of supplying his majesty's navy, and for those purposes it is still used by the contractors, proper offices being established by government for the requisite works and attendants.

DUTY AT OUT PORTS. Most of the branches on the establishment at *Deptford* are different from the victualling offices at Portsmouth, Plymouth, Chatham, and Dover; being considered as appendages to the special duty of the commissioners in London; and the chief officers communicate with those commissioners individually, with respect to such affairs as relate to their respective departments. At Deptford, however, are stationed an agent victualler, with three established clerks under him, and a storekeeper, with one extra clerk. The office of the *agent victualler* at Deptford, although without the extensive controul or trust which is reposed in similar offices at the out-ports, is nevertheless of great importance, arising from the very superior extent and magnitude of the transactions at this place.

Next to Deptford, in point of importance, is *Portsmouth*. The articles purchased at this port are wheat, malt, coals, candles, and sundry species of small stores; and contracts are frequently made by order of the board, for wheat and malt to be delivered at Plymouth. The articles received from Deptford are principally, salt beef and pork, peas, oatmeal, butter, cheese, vinegar, and hops; some of which, such as wheat, malt, and hops, are afterwards manufactured in the same manner as at Deptford. The contract for fresh beef for use at Portsmouth, is always made with persons in London, but the oxen are slaughtered at Portsmouth at the charge of the contractor, who delivers the four quarters, when cold, for which he is paid by weight, the tongue being given in, and every other part of the offal belonging to the contractor. Some of the tongues are distributed among the admirals and captains, according to a regulated proportion; the remainder are sold, and the money arising from such sale carried

ried to the credit of the offal account. In the ſame account is alſo included the money received for bran, grains, yeaſt, decayed proviſions, old ſtaves, hoops, and all ſtores ſold, and which is regularly paid to the treaſurer of the navy, purſuant to the inſtructions received from the board for that purpoſe.

At each of the three out-ports there is an agent victualler, a ſtore-keeper, and a clerk of the cheque, with clerks and other inferior perſons. At Plymouth and Portſmouth, there are likewiſe a maſter cooper and a maſter brewer; and at the latter place a maſter miller; but the ſame eſtabliſhment is unneceſſary at Chatham, on account of its vicinity to Deptford.

Making out and passing Accounts. The agent victualler, ſtore-keeper and clerk of the cheque or perſons deputed from their reſpective departments, muſt all join, in order to carry through any tranſaction whatever; ſo that they are mutual checks on each other, like the principal officers of a dock-yard. Every article of proviſion, and ſtores, received by the officers at the ſeveral out-ports, is charged againſt them in accounts kept at London by the accountant for ſtores; and all proviſions and ſtores iſſued by ſuch officers, are placed to their credit reſpectively in the ſame account. Thoſe accounts are afterwards checked, and examined in the office of the chief clerk for bringing up the accounts of ſtores in arrear. The bills made out by the agent victualler at the out ports, and certified by him, the ſtore-keeper, and the clerk of the cheque, are received by the accountant for caſh, and afterwards paſs through the ſame forms as bills which are made out in London. Every agent victualler keeps one general account of caſh; another ſtating all monies received for proviſions, &c. ſold; both which are ſent to and examined by the accountant for caſh. A third account, ſtating money impreſſed to ſuch agent victualler, is alſo tranſmitted to and examined by the chief clerk for examining and ſtating of impreſt accounts. The pay-liſts for wages are received by the clerk of the cheque, and thoſe for ſhort allowance money in the office of that name. All the above accounts are tranſmitted to London once in every three months, upon oath, and being corroborated by other documents, they collectively form a complete ſyſtem of connexion between the board of victualling in London, and the ſeveral ſubordinate eſtabliſhments at the out-ports, under every check and ſecurity which the public ſervice can render neceſſary; provided that the execution of the complicated duties of that extenſive department, as well in the ſuperintendance as the detail, be performed with fidelity and preciſion by the perſons intruſted.

Expence of Victualling. The expence of victualling his majeſty's fleet is provided for in the following manner; out of the

the ſum per month of twenty-eight days, which is voted by parliament to each man for the ſervice of the navy, a certain portion per month is appropriated to the victualling; a further ſum is likewiſe voted, under the head of harbour victuals, which is intended to defray the expence of victualling the ſhips in ordinary, and the officers and ſervants employed therein, alſo thoſe employed in navy tranſports, ſmall yachts, &c. The amount of thoſe ſums collectively is never adequate to the whole expence of the victualling eſtabliſhment; extra ſervices conſtantly occur, and old balances are frequently demanded, and paid, although not provided for in the eſtimate which is laid before parliament; and an additional charge likewiſe falls on this department, in conſequence of the high prices paid for proviſions or ſtores upon foreign ſtations, with other incidental expences, which are more or leſs conſiderable, according to circumſtances, and cannot be enumerated. Beſides the fund ariſing from the money voted by parliament, another fund is formed of monies produced from the ſale of offal, decayed proviſions, old ſtores, &c. to which are added, ſums repaid to clear impreſts, debts remaining due to government upon balancing the accounts with purſers, &c. and in general all monies whatſoever which are received by the board of victualling, except what is received directly from the exchequer.

Manning the Navy. In ancient times, as already has been ſhewn, the ſovereign by his prerogative enforced the ſervice both of ſhips and men when requiſite, and ſubſequently both were ſupplied by the kingdom at large on the king's demand. The principle on which this prerogative was founded probably gave birth to the practice which has been at all times reſorted to by government as a great mean of procuring men for the navy, that of inforcing ſeamen to ſerve, or, as it is generally termed impreſſing, or preſſing them.

The Impress Service. The unpopularity which muſt ever attend a ſyſtem where abſolute force is employed on perſons guilty of no offence to make them perform ſervices to which they have an utter repugnance, and which are alſo perhaps prejudicial to their intereſts, has occaſioned many warm diſcuſſions, on the legality of the practice of preſſing ſeamen. Thoſe who oppoſe it reaſon chiefly on general principles, and from them, arguments of great force and cogency are derived; but on the other ſide, every lawyer, hiſtorian, and antiquary, who has well inveſtigated the origin and progreſs of the Britiſh navy, agrees in the legality of the prerogative, according to the uſages of the moſt ancient times. Nor will they who duly conſider the neceſſity of adopting ſudden and vigorous meaſures for rendering available the great national defence in times of war, be too ready,

ready, even in argument, to rely on principles which can never be reduced to practice, and against which the writings of all lawyers, and the declarations of all statesmen may be almost uniformly cited. Among the former may be reckoned Sir Michael Foster, Lord Mansfield and Mr. Justice Blackstone, and as a splendid instance of the latter, the earl of Chatham, who, while he opposed government, declared, in 1770, his firm conviction that this mode of obtaining men for the navy was legal, and that those who opposed it, were actuated by faction, and guilty of an endeavour to cut off the right hand of the community. Edward III. in 1337, expressly empowered his admirals to chuse as many men as they thought necessary for manning the fleet, and to seize and imprison those who might be unwilling to go on board; the statute 2d Richard II. c. 4. speaks of mariners being arrested and retained for the king's service, as of a thing well known and practised without dispute; and provides a remedy against their running away; and in 1481, Edward IV. preparing a navy against Scotland, empowered eleven commanders to press mariners for manning their vessels.

Regulations. This most unpleasant and difficult, though indispensable, service is reduced to regularity and method by the division of the united kingdom into twenty-six stations, to the officers at which the press warrants are directed. At each station is a captain, and generally two (but on some more, and on one or two fewer) lieutenants, who have under them bodies of seamen, called gangs, or generally press-gangs. In some places; in the city of London in particular, their warrants cannot be executed until sanctioned by the indorsed permission of the civil magistrates, whose signature is called backing the warrant, and the attendance of a peace officer. The officers and men on this duty have an extraordinary pay. The lieutenants attend with the gangs, and place the men whom they impress on board a vessel prepared for the purpose, and called a tender, where they undergo an examination before the regulating captain, and unless they can shew sufficient reason to obtain a release, they are consigned to such of the king's ships as are in want of hands, and compelled to serve during the residue of the war, or until discharged. The accounts of every lieutenant on the impress service are audited monthly at the admiralty: they contain the sums expended on the men impressed, and their number; also the amount of the pay and incidental expences of himself and gang. The regulating captain of each lieutenant makes oath as to the validity of his account, and passes it at the admiralty.

Exemptions and Regulations. A striking hardship which attends the practice of pressing is apparent in the situation of those seamen, who, after making long voyages in the service of merchants,

merchants, are, the moment they come in ſight of ſhore, compelled to renew their labours on board a king's ſhip. Another evil is, that ſometimes it is found neceſſary to impreſs landſmen as well as ſailors, and in theſe caſes ſerious affrays have ariſen, in which even lives have been loſt. In order to prevent theſe calamities, the legiſlature has framed ſome proviſions, and occaſional attempts have been made to ſubſtitute means leſs harſh, for ſupplying the navy with hands. By ſeveral ſtatutes, any waterman, who uſes the river Thames, hiding himſelf during the execution of any commiſſion of preſſing for the king's ſervice, is liable to heavy penalties; no fiſherman ſhall be taken by royal commiſſion to ſerve as a mariner, but the commiſſion ſhall be firſt brought to two juſtices of the peace, inhabiting near the ſea coaſt where the mariners are to be taken, to the intent that the juſtices may chuſe out, and return for ſervice, the number of able-bodied men mentioned in the commiſſion; eſpecial protections are allowed to ſeamen in particular circumſtances to prevent them from being impreſſed; and ferrymen are ſaid to be privileged by the common law. Theſe protections are however occaſionally ſuperſeded in caſes of urgent neceſſity, by acts of parliament, and diſcretionary protections granted by the admiralty, are revoked without notice to the parties.

Other means of manning the Navy. One of the means tried for ſuperſeding preſſing was a ſcheme in the middle of king William's reign, for regiſtering 30,000 men for a conſtant and regular ſupply of the king's fleet; with great privileges to the regiſtered men, and, on the other hand, heavy penalties in caſe of their non-appearance when called for: but this regiſtry, being judged to be ineffectual as well as oppreſſive, was aboliſhed by ſtatute 9th Anne, c. 21. In 1795 acts were paſſed requiring the ſeveral counties in England and Wales to furniſh men in ſtated proportions, amounting in the whole to 9859, and thoſe in Scotland to 1814, the number being levied on each according to the valued rent, and the men raiſed by a tax ſimilar to a poor rate, but this experiment was never renewed. In the ſame year, an embargo was laid on all Britiſh ſhipping in the ports of Great Britain, and a requiſition made from the owners of all veſſels, excepting thoſe belonging to the king and the royal family, and craft uſed only in rivers and canals, to furniſh able-bodied men for the navy, (one able ſeaman being accepted as equivalent to two able-bodied men) in certain proportions—amounting in the whole to 19,867 men. This laſt operation was, indeed, little different from preſſing, except that it allowed the maſters of ſhips to ſelect from their own crews the men they were leaſt inclined to keep; and the following meaſure was in fact a land preſs, with the reſervation only, that the perſons exposed to it must be guilty, or at least reasonably suspected of being injurious to society. The justices of peace and magistrates of cities and towns, were authorised and required to send on board the navy, all able-bodied idle and disorderly persons, exercising no lawful employment, and not having some substance sufficient for their support and maintenance, all offenders, coming under the description of rogues and vagabonds, smugglers, and embezzlers of naval stores, between the ages of sixteen and sixty, unless they were intitled to vote for the election of members of parliament.

A mode more eligible than any of these, and which, it is to be regretted, is not always sufficiently productive, is that pursued in every war, of giving bounties to volunteer seamen, and that established by act of parliament, of allowing them certain advantages in pay and prize money, over those whose reluctance is only overcome by force. As an encouragement to foreign seamen to enter into the British service, they are declared, after being two years on board any man of war, merchantman, or privateer, to become *ipso facto* naturalized. Parishes, too, may bind out poor boys apprentices to masters of merchantmen, who shall be protected from impressing for the first three years; and if they are impressed afterwards, the master shall be allowed their wages.

Navigation Act. A law which has contributed more than any other to the superiority of the British navy, although at first designed only for the promotion of commerce, is that known under the name of the Navigation Act, for as it always provides employ for a great number of British seamen, it facilitates, in course, the manning of the royal navy. The act now in force owes its origin to Cromwell, and hence some continental politicians, hostile to England, have been led to describe it as the offspring of injustice, bred in the mind of a gloomy and fanatical usurper. It may however be proper to observe, that the undoubted public right vested in the sovereign power, of determining in what manner the commerce of a nation shall be carried on, was not first exercised in England in the days of Cromwell, but its early traces are found in the regulations of a legitimate sovereign, whose court was, during his prosperity, singularly brilliant, and whose mildness and carelessness were among the chief causes of his melancholy fate. Richard II. in the fifth year of his reign, enacted, that none of his subjects should ship any merchandise, outward or homeward, except in ships of the king's allegiance, on penalty of forfeiture of vessel and cargo; and this was the first navigation act passed by the parliament of England. Acts of the same import, but less general in the prohibition, were framed in succeeding reigns, even to that of Charles I. and almost every statute contained a recital of the decay of commerce, the disuse of British shipping, and the want of mariners occasioned by the incroachments of foreigners on the carrying trade. The statute passed by the Rump Parliament in 1651, was revived and improved nine years afterward, on the restoration of Charles II. but as it chiefly relates to commercial affairs, its substance will be stated in another page, although in this place it was necessary to mention its effect on the navy.

NAVAL ACADEMY. Nor does the supply of the fleet rest on temporary exertion or casual inclination alone, an establishment being formed at Portsmouth under the name of an academy, for the express purpose of instructing youth in all the branches of science requisite for the education of a good seaman. The scene of their instruction affords them every practical advantage, excellent masters are provided, and a ship for practice is kept within the premises.

MARINE SOCIETY. Another source from which the navy derives considerable supplies arises from the union of patriotism with charity, in an institution called the Marine Society. This admirable establishment was projected in 1756, by Jonas Hanway, a man whose name is never pronounced in England but with associated ideas of philanthropy and active benevolence. The plan was of extreme simplicity; it consisted in a subscription for feeding, cloathing, preparing and fitting out for the sea service, poor and destitute boys. Liberal donations and bequests perfected the establishment, and at an early period, Mr. Hickes, a merchant in Hamburgh, bequeathed a legacy of 20,000*l.*, being his whole fortune. In 1773, the marine society, the benefit of which had been fully ascertained, was incorporated by act of parliament. The boys placed out as apprentices by them were exempted from being impressed while under eighteen years of age, and privileged to excercise any trade in any part of Great Britain or Ireland. The officers of the society are a president and six vice-presidents. Annual subscribers of two guineas, or donors of twenty, are stiled governors. There are also belonging to the society, a chaplain, a surgeon, an apothecary, a secretary, and a messenger. The office is in Bishopsgate Street, London.

GOVERNMENT OF THE NAVY. In ancient times, when ships were collected in a hasty manner, or furnished by different ports, they were subject to no general regulation, but having once fallen into the possession of fighting men, were considered as the means of predatory adventure, or, according to the passions or prejudices of those who furnished or happened to command them, employed in enterprizes of civil warfare. Thus in the 13th century, the mariners of the Cinque Ports carried on, in defiance of royal authority, a piratical warfare against all the world, and in the middle of the same century, the people of Winchelsea, enraged that those of Yarmouth had excelled them in building a superb ship, attacked the vessel, and murdered several of the crew; nor were these single, or even rare instances of such piratical and barbarous enterprizes. The first appearance of a better naval system occurs in the reign of Edward I., who preparing, in 1292, for his intended war against France, divided his navy into three fleets, and appointed three admirals, viz. John of Botetourt admiral of the fleet of Yarmouth, and the east coast; William of Leybourn, of the Portsmouth division; and an officer (not named) of Irish birth commanded the ships of the west coast and Ireland. This is believed to be the earliest appearance in England of the title of admiral, which had been some time before adopted, in imitation of the Saracens, by the maritime states of Italy, for the commander of a fleet. It can hardly be supposed that a nation once acquainted with the benefit of order will desist from enforcing it if possible; accordingly from that period the navy of England continued improving in its internal regulations, until it has become as complete as human judgment can devise in the appointment and perfection of its officers, and the discipline of the men.

Admirals. The fleet consists of three squadrons distinguished by the colours of their several flags; and the principal commanders bear each the title of admiral of his squadron; but the first admiral of the red commands in chief the whole fleet, and is called admiral of the fleet. Under the admirals are vice-admirals and rear-admirals. The style of admiral of the red had been for many years disused, but was restored in 1805, and in 1806 there were in the British fleet, of the red, twenty-two admirals, including the admiral of the fleet, seventeen vice and eighteen rear-admirals; of the white, fifteen admirals, fifteen vice and nineteen rear-admirals; the blue had eighteen admirals, eighteen vice and twenty rear-admirals.

Their Duty. The flag officer, or commander in chief of a fleet or squadron, is to inform the secretary of the admiralty of his proceedings; and the other public offices of all matters relating to them. He is to exercise his squadron frequently; and to visit the ships under his command. In directing naval officers abroad, he is to conform as much as possible to the standing rules of the navy. He is not to be concerned in purchasing stores or provisions abroad, without an absolute necessity, and then not to have any private interest in it.

Pay. Flag officers commence pay from the date of their commissions, or orders to repair to their squadrons; and continue in in pay to the day they ſtrike their flag by order. Their ſtipend is,

	Pay. £.	s.	d.	Half-pay. £.	s.	d.
Admiral and commander in chief of the fleet - per day	5	0	0	3	0	0
An admiral - - -	3	10	0	2	0	0
A vice-admiral - - -	2	10	0	1	10	0
A rear-admiral - - -	1	15	0	1	2	6

Admirals and vice-admirals commanding in chief, are alſo allowed for table-money twenty ſhillings per day.

Each flag officer is allowed to have a *ſecretary*, with a clerk under him, an appointment of which the utility is too obvious to require explanation. The pay of theſe perſons is as follows:

	Per annum. £.	s.	d.
Secretary of an admiral of the fleet -	500	0	0
Secretary of an admiral of the white, or blue, being commander in chief - -	400	0	0
Secretary of a vice or rear-admiral, being commander in chief, and of a commodore having a captain under him - -	300	0	0
Secretary to a flag officer, and to a commodore, with captains under them, not commanding in chief - - -	150	0	0
Each clerk to a ſecretary - - -	50	0	0

Commodore. This title, although frequently uſed in converſation and in print, does not indicate any eſtabliſhed rank in the navy, the perſon ſo diſtinguiſhed being only a temporary commander without a commiſſion, but proceeding on the cuſtom of the navy, by which the ſenior commander of a ſquadron is ſtyled commodore, leader or commander in chief, and is thereby intitled to ſome honours, and ſometimes to more pay than a private captain.

Captains. The rank in fact next to rear admiral, is that of captain, in which there are ſeveral degrees, according to the rate of the ſhip conſigned to their command, thoſe who are recently advanced from the rank of lieutenant, not being at firſt intruſted with the government of a ſhip of large ſize, but employed in thoſe of an inferior rate; and in ſtrictneſs termed only *maſters and commanders*. In this ſituation, they are not intitled to half pay. When promoted to a ſuperior veſſel they are rated as *poſt captains*, and become poſſeſſed of all the privileges and emoluments due to their rank.

DUTY. The duties of a captain are numerous and active, requiring a found and clear underftanding, and a fteady undeviating attention. Some of the principal are comprized in the following articles. To vifit the fhip he is appointed to command. To fend accounts weekly, or oftener if neceffary, to the admiralty and navy offices, of the progrefs made in fitting her out, and her circumftances. Not to lye out of the fhip without leave from the admiralty, or his commander in chief. To be prefent when ftores come on board, of which his clerk is to take account. To be a cheque on his officers and audit their accounts. To enter none but able men, and not to exceed his complement. To mufter the fhip's company, once a week, in ports, and to do the fame at fea, without ufing any fraud in his mufters. To take care of the fhip's ftores, and fuffer none to be mifapplied or wafted. To make no alteration in any part of his fhip. To fet up his rigging at feafonable times, and to be very careful to favour his mafts. Before any rigging or ftores are caft, he is to order a regular furvey thereof to be taken. To fee the fhip kept clean, and the air let into the hold, as frequently as may be. Before the fhip proceeds to fea, to examine and rate the fhip's company, impartially and without favour; as likewife to make a regulation for quartering the officers and men, and diftributing them to the great guns, fmall arms, rigging, &c.; and to difcipline the fhip's company frequently, in the exercife of the great guns and fmall arms. To inform the fecretary of the admiralty of the officers abfent, when the fhip is under failing orders, and the caufe of their abfence. To keep a journal, according to a form prefcribed, and to fend a copy of it, at ftated times, to the fecretary of the admiralty; and at the expiration of the voyage, to the admiralty and navy offices. To inform the fecretary of the admiralty of his proceedings, and the condition of his fhip; and to correfpond with the proper offices, in whatfoever refpectively concerns them. Not to go into any other port, than fuch as his orders direct him, unlefs by unavoidable neceffity, and then to make no unneceffary ftay. To demand Englifh feamen out of foreign fhips. Upon the death of any officer to feal up his books and papers, as well public as private, in prefence of at leaft two figning officers. Upon the death, fufpenfion, or removal of any officer, having ftores or provifions under his cuftody, he is to caufe an exact furvey and inventory to be taken, of the remains of fuch ftores and provifions. When removed himfelf, he fhall fhew his original orders which remain unexecuted, to his fucceffor, and leave him attefted copies of the fame; as likewife leave a complete mufter book, and fend all his other books and accounts, to the offices they refpectively relate to. When removed by commiffion from one fhip ſhip to another, he is allowed to carry with him the following number of men including his ſervants; viz. from a firſt rate, eighty, a ſecond rate, ſixty-five; a third rate, fifty; a fourth rate forty; a fifth rate, twenty; and a ſixth rate, ten. In caſe of ſhipwreck, or other diſaſter, by which his ſhip may periſh; he, with his officers and men, are to ſtay with the remains, as long as may be, and endeavour to ſave all that is poſſible. When the ſhip returns to the port, where ſhe is to be laid up, the captain is to give an exact account of her qualities, to the commiſſioner of the navy, at the port, and ſend a duplicate of it to the navy board; and he is then likewiſe to make up his pay-book, and with his officers, to attend the payment. He is anſwerable for the conduct of every one in the ſhip, and for all errors of his clerk; to receive no wages without proper certificates; and to be anſwerable for all damages occaſioned by his neglect or irregularity.

Pay. The pay of a captain is as follows. Firſt rate, 1*l.* Second rate 16*s.* Third rate, 13*s.* Fourth rate, 10*s.* Fifth rate, 10*s.* Sixth rates, 8*s.* per day Fire ſhips, hoſpital ſhips, and priſon ſhips, are paid as fifth rates: ſloops, bombs, yachts, &c. are paid as ſixth rates. The firſt captain to an admiral, and commander in chief of the fleet has the pay of a rear admiral. The ſecond captain to the ſame admiral, and captains to other admirals, have the pay of a captain of a firſt rate. The captains to vice-admirals have the pay of a ſecond rate; and the captains to rear-admirals the pay of a third rate. But if a vice or rear-admiral ſerve in a firſt or ſecond rate, the captain has the proper pay of that rate. Captains commence pay from the date of their commiſſions, unleſs they are appointed in the place of an officer removed, who is to enjoy his pay till relieved by his ſucceſſor. *Captain's half pay.* Fifty of the oldeſt, 12*s.*; the next ſeventy-five, 10*s.* and the reſt 8*s.* per day. Commanders. Fifty of the oldeſt 8*s.*; the next one hundred 7*s.*; and the reſt 6*s.* 6*d.* per day. Officers on half pay make oath half-yearly, that they hold no employment in the public ſervice at the time: but no oath is required of officers on the ſuperannuated or penſion liſts.

Lieutenants and Midshipmen. Young gentlemen entering into the navy, are generally rated as midſhipmen, and, after they have ſerved a proper period in this ſtation, they are, if they can paſs the ordeal of a very ſtrict and ſcientific examination, paſſed for lieutenants. This ſtage is, in fact, if the term may be uſed, the practical apprenticeſhip of an officer, and perhaps, from the regularity with which it is obſerved, as much as from any other cauſe, has ariſen the pre-eminence of the Britiſh navy. The neceſſary time of ſervice, previous to paſſing for lieutenant, is six years in all, viz. four years as landman, or able volunteer, and two years as midshipman or master's mate. By this regulation no man can aspire, even to subordinate command, who has not learnt his duty by personal service, and the evidence he must give of his ability consists, not merely in having been a certain number of years at sea, or in having learnt by rote a certain series of problems, but in the acquaintance with practice and a judicious intelligence in matters of theory. From this no individual in the navy is exempt; interest, influence, or rank, even that nearest allied to the throne, have never yet infringed, nor probably ever will infringe, this most valuable and essential regulation. Lieutenants are appointed by the board of admiralty, midshipmen generally by the captain.

On the first Wednesday in every month, gentlemen are examined to pass for lieutenants at the navy office; where journals, certificates of service, and registers of age, should be previously left.

Duty. The principal duties of a lieutenant are, generally, to obey his commander's orders. To muster the watch, and see good order kept in it. Not to change the course of the ship without orders. The lieutenant of the watch is to be informed when boats come, or go off; is to be on the deck in his watch, and is to inform the captain of all irregularities; to see the men at their proper quarters, and that they do their duty, in time of action. To keep a journal, sea-book, &c. and at the end of a voyage, to deliver copies to the admiralty and navy offices. The youngest lieutenant is to exercise the seamen, to be chiefly with them in time of action; and to see the small arms kept in order. The station of some midshipmen is on the quarter deck, of others on the poop; their duty is to mind the braces, to look out, and give about the word of command, from the captain and other superior officers, they also assist on all occasions, both in sailing the ship, and in storing and rummaging the hold.

Pay. The pay of lieutenants is, when under an admiral, 5*s*. 6*d*.; all others 5*s*. per day, except those commanding prison ships, who have 6*s*. Their pay commences from the date of their commissions, unless appointed in the place of an officer removed, who enjoys his pay till relieved by his successor. A lieutenant, succeeding to the command of a ship, on the death of the captain in foreign parts, receives the pay and allowance of a captain, until he is superseded. They are also allowed sixpence per mile for travelling expences, but only on their first appointment during a war. *Lieutenant's half-pay.* Two hundred of the oldest 5*s*. per day; the three hundred next oldest, 4*s*. 6*d*.; the next five hundred, 4*s*.; the rest 3*s*. 6*d*. *Sub-lieutenants* full pay 4*s*. per day, of this 3*s*. 6*d*. per day is drawn quarterly, the other sixpence

ſixpence is receivable at the end of every twelve months, by the delivery of a log book; no half-pay; travelling expences allowed as to lieutenants. Midſhipmen have pay, per month, in a firſt rate 2*l.* 10*s.* 6*d.*; ſecond rate 2*l.* 5*s.* 6*d.*; third rate 2*l.* 3*s.*; fourth rate, 1*l.* 19*s.* 3*d.*; fifth and ſixth rates, 1*l.* 15*s.* 6*d.*

Beſides theſe there are ſubordinate officers, of whom ſome account is neceſſary.

Masters. No perſon can ſerve in this ſtation, unleſs he has, before his appointment, paſſed an examination at the Trinity-houſe. Candidates for paſſing are required to be above twenty-one years of age; to have been ſeven years at ſea, and to have been two years as midſhipman, maſter's mate, ſecond maſter, or acting maſter; and to produce certificates from the commanders under whom they have ſerved of ſobriety, diligence, and attention to their duty. Such as have not ſerved in the navy muſt be of the age and time at ſea as above, and have been two years as mate, and one year as maſter, or one year as mate, and two years as maſter of a ſquare rigged veſſel, in the merchant ſervice, and produce certificates of ſobriety, &c., from the reſpective owners or commanders. By his majeſty's order in council, of the fifteenth of Auguſt, 1805, ſuch perſons as ſhall have acted as maſters, and ſecond maſters, and pilots, may be conſidered as eligible to lieutenancies, from meritorious conduct or other cauſes, although the perſons who ſhall ſo diſtinguiſh themſelves, may not have been rated as mate or midſhipman, provided they have ſerved ſix years in the royal navy.

Duty. The duty of a maſter is, to repair on board, and obey his commander's orders. To inſpect the ſtores and proviſions ſent on board; and when not good to inform the captain or chief officer on board. To take care of the ballaſt; and to ſtow the hold carefully. To ſee the rigging and ſtores duly preſerved. To navigate the ſhip, under the directions of his ſuperior officer. To obſerve the coaſts, ſhoals, &c. When the ſhip is at anchor, to be watchful that the hawſe be kept clear. To be provided with proper inſtruments, &c.; and to keep an exact and perfect journal, and other books, to be delivered, when the ſhip is laid up, to the navy office. To be careful in not ſigning any accounts, books, liſts or tickets, before he has a thorough information of the truth of them. Commanders in chief, having a captain of the fleet on board, have a maſter under them, independent of the maſter of the ſhip, who is to be called the *firſt maſter*, and whoſe duty is to attend to the navigation of the fleet. He muſt be qualified for, and receives the pay of a firſt rate.

Pay.

Pay. The full pay per month is; first rate 12*l.* 12*s.* Second rate 11*l.* 11*s.* Third rate 10*l.* 10*s.* Fourth rate 9*l.* 9*s.* Fifth rate 8*l.* 8*s.* Sixth rate 7*l.* 7*s.* Of brigs and cutters, with complement of more than fifty men, 6*l.* 6*s.* Second master and pilots of gun brigs, &c. 5*l.* 5*s.* The foregoing are allowed a servant, or as compensation for one, 11*l.* 8*s.* 2*d.* per annum. Ships of the line have a second master at 5*l.* 5*s.* but no servant or compensation. *Half Pilotage* is universally allowed to masters for taking the sole charge of a ship or vessel; the commander being satisfied as to their capacity. A master, to be intitled to half pay, must have been in actual service five years, either as master, or, for the first two years, as midshipman, master's mate, second master, or acting master. The first fifty (qualified for first and second rates) 5*s.* per day. The next fifty (qualified for first and second rates) 4*s.* 6*d.* The next one hundred (qualified for third rates) 4*s.* per day. The next one hundred (qualified for fourth and fifth rates) 3*s.* 6*d.* per day; those for sixth have 3*s.* No master is permitted in time of war, on any account whatever, to receive half pay during such time as he shall be employed in the merchant service, or in any other occupation, unless absolutely incapable, from infirmity, of serving in the royal navy.

Purser. To this officer are committed the charge and inspection of the victual and water, and it is also his duty to provide the ship with necessaries, as coals, wood, turnery ware, and candles; he is allowed to sell tobacco, and some other things to the men, and his office branches out into a vast variety of petty cares and subordinate attentions.

Food. Provisions of a good quality are issued to the crew by the purser daily, according to a stated order applying to each day in the week; and in the modern regulation of king's ships many articles are included which are not so absolutely necessary to subsistence, as conducive to health; as vegetables, fresh and pickled, tea, wine, spirits, rice, and many other articles.

Short Allowance. Commanders have it in their discretion to shorten the stated allowance, when the service requires it, but must take care, that the men be punctually paid for it; and no officer is suffered to be at whole allowance, when the men are shortened. In such cases, the captain is to make out short allowance lists. In foreign parts the short allowance money is to be paid, every three months, by money taken up by the purser, on bills of exchange for that end. Commanders in chief, or captains when alone, are to attest those bills, and to controul the payment; and the surplus of any such money

is

is to go to the next payment. Purſers are to ſend the liſts home. The ſhip's company is to be paid according to ſterling money, and to have the benefit of the exchange. The buying of ſhort allowance money is ſtrictly forbidden.

COOK. The cook too, is mentioned among the officers, and his duty, beſides that expreſſed in the title of his place, extends to the preſervation of the tubs and other things connected with his duty.

OTHER OFFICERS. There are ſeveral other officers, whoſe duties are expreſſed by their names, or too minute for deſcription, as the boatſwain and his mates ; the chaplain ; the gunners ; the ſchoolmaſter who inſtructs the volunteérs, and other youth of the ſhip, in reading, writing, arithmetic, and the ſtudy of navigation ; the maſters at arms and the carpenters ; theſe are appointed by the admiralty. There are alſo ſail-makers, and caulkers, who are appointed by the navy board ; armourers, armourers mates, and gunſmiths, who receive their appointments from the board of ordnance.

PHYSICIANS AND SURGEONS. The care of the ſick and wounded on board ſhip, occupies the moſt ſerious attention of government. The duty of the phyſician is to reſide in the hoſpital ſhip, where there is any, or ſuch other as the commander in chief ſhall appoint. To viſit the ſick in the ſhips of the ſquadron. To inſpect the cheſts of the ſurgeons ; to obſerve the admiral's orders, and demand no fees from his patients. By an order in council, dated January 23, 1805, every perſon appointed phyſician to a fleet or hoſpital, muſt have ſerved as ſurgeon at leaſt five years.

PAY. On firſt appointment, 21*s.* per day ; half pay 10*s.* 6*d.* Having ſerved three years as phyſician, pay 2*l.* 2*s.* per day ; half pay 1*l.* 1*s.* Lodging money when a reſidence is not appointed, per week 1*l.* 1*s.*

SURGEONS are appointed after a rigid examination, both in ſurgery and phyſic, at Surgeons Hall, Lincoln's Inn Fields, London ; and before the commiſſioners of ſick and hurt, from whom they receive their warrants. The diſtinction of *ſurgeon's mate* is annulled, but there are on board ſhips *aſſiſtant ſurgeons* ; and in the hoſpital department, the aſſiſtants and aſſiſtant diſpenſers, are called *hoſpital mates.* The number of aſſiſtant ſurgeons, in firſt and ſecond rates, is three ; in third and fourth rates, two ; hoſpital ſhips, three ; all other ſhips formerly bearing a ſurgeon's mate, one. No perſon is to be appointed an aſſiſtant ſurgeon who is not qualified to ſerve as ſurgeon or firſt aſſiſtant.

DUTY. The duty of the ſurgeon is, to provide himſelf with inſtruments, and a cheſt of medicines, and to have the ſame viewed

viewed and approved; as it muſt be, in like manner, when recruited. To keep ſick tickets. To examine the neceſſaries ſent on board for the uſe of the ſick, and to iſſue them out for relief. Carefully to attend the men under his care, and, in difficult caſes, to adviſe with the phyſician of the ſquadron, where there is any. To inform the captain, every day, of the ſtate of the ſick. When patients are ſent to the hoſpitals, he is to tranſmit an account with them of their diſtempers, and all other proper circumſtances; to take all due and immediate care of the wounded men in an engagement; to keep a day book of his practice, and to deliver journals of it, at the end of the voyage, that it may be examined into.

Pay and other Circumstances. Surgeons not having actually ſerved ſix years, per day, 10*s.* half pay 5*s.* Thoſe of ſhips, having ſerved ſix years in actual ſervice, *pay* 11*s.*; half pay 6*s.* Having ſerved ten years, *pay* 14*s.*; half pay 6*s.* Surgeons of receiving, ſlop, convaleſcent, priſon, and all other except hoſpital, ſhips, employed only in harbour duty, per day 10*s.*; half pay according to the time of ſervice. Of hoſpital ſhips, unleſs intitled by term of ſervice to a ſuperior rate, pay 15*s.*; half pay as other ſurgeons. Surgeons, excepting thoſe of receiving and ſome other ſhips, employed only in harbour duty, after twenty years ſervice on full pay, receive as full pay 18*s.* per day. All ſurgeons, having ſerved twenty years on full pay, have the privilege of retiring on a half pay of 6*s.* per day, unleſs their retirement is occaſioned by ill health contracted in the ſervice; in which caſe, they are intitled to 10*s.* All ſurgeons, after thirty years ſervice on full pay, are allowed an unqualified right to retire on 15*s.* per day, but in theſe periods of time, not more than three years as hoſpital mate or aſſiſtant ſurgeon are allowed. The pay of aſſiſtant ſurgeon is per day, 6*s.* 6*d.*, with the ſhip's proviſion; half pay, when reduced, 2*s.*, provided they have ſerved two years ſubſequent to January 23, 1805, and 3*s.* having ſo ſerved for three years. Aſſiſtant ſurgeons are to be promoted according to ſeniority, and to furniſh themſelves with ſuch inſtruments as the commiſſioners ſhall direct. Of thoſe in actual ſervice, not having obtained the qualification required, ſuch as ſerve as firſt or ſecond mates, or aſſiſtants, are allowed 5*s.* per day; third mates or aſſiſtants 4*s.* Theſe claſſes are not, however, required to provide inſtruments, nor allowed half pay. Surgeons of hoſpitals receive per day, on firſt appointment 15*s.*; having ſerved ten years in hoſpitals 20*s.* Half pay as to ſurgeons of ſhips. Lodging money, if not provided with a reſidence within the hoſpital, per week 15*s.* The time of ſervice is to be added to, and calculated with, the time ſerved on board ſhip. Surgeons of naval hoſpitals, dock yards, and marine infirmaries, derive the ſame advantages, from the terms of twenty and thirty years ſervice, as thoſe who have ſerved on board: but, as ſome of theſe ſurgeons may not have ſerved on board, the advantage of this regulation extends only to thoſe already appointed, whoſe pay, half pay, and retirement, ſhall be regulated by the time they have ſerved, as the reſt. Diſpenſers in hoſpitals, receive per day, 5*s*. When a reſidence is not provided, lodging money per week, 12*s*. Hoſpital mates in all departments have, at home, per day 6*s*. 6*d*.; on foreign ſtations 7*s*. 6*d*. Half pay, per day 2*s*. if they have ſerved two years on full pay, ſubſequent to January 23, 1805. If not accommodated within the hoſpital, lodging money, per week, 10*s*. 6*d*. Hoſpital mates removing from one department to another, are to prove themſelves qualified by an examination.

Regulations for the Benefit of the Sick and Hurt. A convenient place is to be ſet apart, in every ſhip, for ſick and hurt men. Proper perſons are to be appointed to attend them, night and day, by turns. Conveniences, as cradles, &c., are to be made and freſh fiſh to be caught for them. They are not to be ſent into hoſpitals attending the fleet, or aſhore, unleſs it be inconvenient to have them on board their own ſhips. They are to be ſent aſhore by ticket, together with their cloaths and bedding, and the captains may order them ſlops if needful. Care is to be taken in the landing them, that they be duly attended, and furniſhed with proper carriages and neceſſaries. A commiſſioned officer is to go, twice a week, to the hoſpital to receive recovered men; and may receive thoſe of other ſhips, when they are at a diſtance, and it is required by the agent. Captains are to correſpond with the office for ſick and hurt, about his ſick men. Commanders in chief, and the commiſſioner of the navy, are to viſit the hoſpitals at the ports, and to hear and redreſs complaints and grievances. Captains are to take care of their ſick and wounded men, in foreign parts. In *hoſpital ſhips*, the gun deck is to be fitted up for the reception of the ſick men, with proper conveniences. The hoſpital ſhip is to have ſupernumerary to her complement, a phyſician, an able and experienced ſurgeon, four mates, and ſix men aſſiſtants, a ſervant to the ſurgeon, a baker and four waſhermen. The captain is to ſubſiſt the men under cure, with the beſt and neweſt proviſions in the ſhip, and freſh meat as often as may be. Captains are to ſend boats for their recovered men.

Servants allowed to Officers. The admiral and commander in chief of the fleet, is allowed fifty; admirals, thirty; vice admirals, twenty; and rear admirals, fifteen. Of which may be borne on the ſhips books, as ſervants; to the admiral and commander in chief of the fleet, ſixteen; to admirals, twelve; to vice

and

and rear admirals, ten. Captains are allowed four ſervants in every hundred men of their complement. The lieutenant, maſter, ſecond maſter, purſer, ſurgeon, chaplain, and cook, in all ſhips down to ſixty men incluſive, each one ſervant. The boatſwain, gunner and carpenter, in all ſhips down to a hundred men, incluſive, each two ſervants; and from a hundred to ſixty men, one ſervant. ſervants to flag officers are to be reckoned over and above the complement of the ſhip; but the ſervants of captains and all other officers, are to be included in it. No ſervants to be allowed on the ſhip's books, under thirteen years of age, unleſs the ſon of an officer, and then not under eleven.

Superannuation. All the petty officers above mentioned are intitled, after various terms of ſervice, to retire as ſuperannuated, on certain penſions or allowances, in order to the acquiſition of which, the parties muſt apply with proper certificates, firſt to the admiralty, and afterward at ſurgeons' hall, where they are duly examined.

Widows. The widows of officers are intitled to penſions as follows. Thoſe of Captains three years poſt, 80*l.* per annum; of poſt captains of leſs than three years ſtanding, 70*l.*; of a commander, 50*l.*; of a ſuperannuated lieutenant with the rank of commander, 45*l.*; of a lieutenant, a maſter and ſurgeon, 40*l.*; of a purſer 30*l.*; of a boatſwain, gunner, carpenter, ſecond maſter of a yacht, or maſter of a naval veſſel, warranted by the navy board, 25*l.* The children of the latter, with the widows and children of all thoſe who die on half pay, to have ſuch allowances as the lords of the admiralty ſhall think fit. The widows of each claſs are obliged, every year, to make oath that they are not married. The widows of officers who die on their half pay, and having employed no regular agent, are, upon application to the admiralty, furniſhed with printed forms, and every information relating to the penſions. In order to obtain the pay due at the time of deceaſe, nothing more is required than to produce a certificate of death and adminiſtration.

Seamen. The duty of private ſailors extends to every operation both of navigation and war, and in deſcribing the command and regulation affecting officers, the ſtate of ſeamen as affected by their exertions or orders, has been in great part diſcloſed. Yet there are many particulars, relating to this claſs of men, both while at ſea and on ſhore, which ought to be conſidered and underſtood.

Government and Discipline. The method of ordering ſeamen, and keeping up a regular diſcipline in the royal fleet, is directed by certain expreſs rules, articles, and orders, firſt enacted by the authority of parliament ſoon after the reſtoration;

tion; but since new modelled and altered, after the peace of Aix la Chapelle, to remedy some defects which were of fatal consequence in conducting the preceding war. In these articles of the navy almost every possible offence is set down, and the punishment annexed: in which respect the seamen have much the advantage over their brethren in the land service; whose articles of war are not enacted by parliament, but framed from time to time at the pleasure of the crown. None under the captain are allowed to inflict punishment. Articles of war are to be set up in some public place of the ship, and to be read to the ship's company once a month.

Rights and Privileges of Seamen. No seaman can be taken out of his majesty's service by any process other than for some criminal matter, unless affidavit be first made, that the debt or damage amounts to 20*l.*; but in order to prevent the practice of obtaining the liberation of seamen by means of improperly suing out civil or criminal process, it is enacted, that petty officers or seamen arrested by sheriffs or by other officers, shall be kept in custody after being intitled to a discharge from any process, and conveyed to the commander in chief, or some commissioned officers, to serve on board his majesty's fleet. And the sheriff, gaoler, or other officer, shall be paid, by the treasurer of the navy, on producing a certificate, for conducting such seaman, at the rate of two shillings per mile. Seamen who have been employed in the king's service, and not deserted, may set up and exercise their trades, in any town or place of Great Britain or Ireland, without molestation, (except in Oxford or Cambridge,) and if any person is sued thereupon, and the plaintiff is cast, such persons shall have double costs. A seaman, instead of being committed to the house of correction, for default of paying the penalty for swearing, shall be put in the stocks for one hour for every single offence, and for any number of offences of which he shall be convicted at one and the same time, two hours. The treasurer, comptroller, surveyor, clerk of the acts, or any of the commissioners of the navy may punish seamen and others, making disturbances in the yards or offices, and may bind them to their good behaviour, and to appear at the next assizes, or general quarter sessions, to be prosecuted for such offence. Seamen are also intitled to send letters from their ships under the hand of the commanding officer on board, and to receive letters wherever they may happen to be on actual service, free of postage; and their receipts for wages, pay, and provisions are exempt from the stamp duty.

Wages. With respect to their wages, several protective and beneficial statutes have been made. Whosoever willingly and knowingly shall personate or falsely assume the name or character

racter of any officer, seaman, or other person, intitled, or supposed to be intitled, to any wages, pay, or other allowances of money, or prize money, for service done on board any of his majesty's ships, or vessels; or willingly and knowingly shall personate or falsely assume the name or character of the executor or administrator, wife, relation, or creditor, of any such officer, or seaman, or other person, in order to receive any wages, pay, or other allowances of money, or prize money as aforesaid; or shall forge or counterfeit, or procure to be forged or counterfeited, or utter or publish as true, knowing the same to be false, forged, or counterfeited, any letter of attorney, bill, ticket, certificate, assignment, last will, or any other power or authority, in order to receive any such wages, pay or other allowances of money or prize money as aforesaid; or shall willingly and knowingly take a false oath, or procure any other person to take a false oath, to obtain the probate of any will or letter of administration, in order to receive the payment of any wages, pay, or other allowances of money or prize money due, or that were supposed to be due, to any such officer, seaman, or other person as aforesaid, who has really served, or was supposed to have served, on board any of his majesty's ships or vessels; every such person so offending shall be guilty of felony without benefit of clergy. And for the more effectual bringing the offenders to justice, the treasurer, comptroller, surveyor, clerk of the acts, or any commissioner of the navy, may act as justices, in causing any person charged with forging or counterfeiting, or procuring to be forged or counterfeited, any letter of attorney, bill, ticket, certificate, assignment, last will, or other power, or authority, or with uttering or publishing the same as true, in order to receive any wages, pay, or other allowance, due to any officer, seaman, or other person in his majesty's service, or with taking or procuring to be taken, for any of the purposes aforesaid; or to obtain a probate of any will, or letter of administration, in order to receive such wages, pay, or allowance, to be apprehended, committed and prosecuted for the same, and the constables, gaolers, and other officers, shall obey their warrants accordingly.

By a most excellent and benevolent series of acts framed by the right honourable Henry Dundas, afterward Lord Melville; after 1st May, 1795, every petty officer, and seaman, or landman, non-commissioned officer of marines, and marines serving or entering on board any vessel of his majesty, may allot a certain part of his monthly pay for the maintenance of his wife and children, or mother. And by 37 G. III. c. 53, an increase of wages is made to such persons, and they are allowed to allot a part of such pay, to be calculated as nearly as may be, to equal one

one half thereof. All petty officers, able seamen, ordinary seamen, landmen, and marines, who may hereafter be wounded in action with the enemy, shall receive their full wages and allowances, until their wounds are healed; or until (being declared incurable) they shall receive a pension from the chest, or be admitted into Greenwich Hospital. If any seaman or landman shall voluntarily enter himself with any regulating officer, and shall at the same time declare his name and place of abode, and that he is married, and the name of his wife, and her place of residence, and if he has children, how many, and how many are boys; and if he has a mother then living, the place of her residence; and that he is willing to allot a part of his wages for their support; then, in case his wife or mother reside in London, the same shall be paid by the treasurer of the navy; if at Portsmouth, Plymouth, or Chatham, or within five miles thereof respectively, by the clerk of the cheque, at those places; elsewhere, by the receiver-general of the land-tax of the county or city, or collector of the customs or excise nearest the residence of such wife or mother. And such regulating officer shall make out three declarations of allotment, and three orders of payment, to be triplicates of each other in a prescribed form, which being numbered and dated, and the blanks filled up, such seaman or landman shall sign the same, and such regulating officer shall also sign as a witness: and if such wife or mother shall then attend in person, such officer shall deliver to her one of the triplicate orders, and send the other two to the commissioners of the navy; but if the wife or mother shall not attend, the officer shall send all the said triplicates to the said commissioners, and shall specify and mention, opposite to the name of every man so entered, whether he has allotted any part of his pay as aforesaid, and to what amount, together with the date of such order. And as often as the commander of any such vessel shall read over the muster of his ship's company, if any such petty officer or person aforesaid shall declare, by word of mouth, or deliver in writing, the name and place of abode of his wife, and number of his children, if he have any, and how many are boys, or that he has a mother living, and the place of her residence, and shall desire that a part of his wages may be paid for their support, the same shall be paid in like manner as aforesaid. And the commissioners of the navy shall examine such declarations and orders, with the lists transmitted by such regulating officer, or commanding officer of any such vessel, and if found right, shall be filled up and signed by three commissioners, specifying the date; and they shall transmit one of the said declarations and orders to such wife or mother, and another to such receiver-general, collector of the customs or excise, or clerk of the cheque, to whom such order shall be directed, and the third shall be delivered to the treasurer of the navy. And at the end of twenty-eight days or more, after the date of such declaration and order, the same, together with such certificate as is mentioned therein from the minister and churchwarden of the parish where such wife or mother shall reside, shall be presented to the treasurer of the navy, or other public officer to whom the same is addressed, who shall examine into the truth thereof (upon the oath of such wife or mother, if necessary); and upon his being satisfied, he shall immediately pay to such wife or mother the sum so allotted, without fee or deduction, taking her receipt for the same, and shall sign his name as witness thereto, and shall mark such receipt with the same number as that of her husband's declaration and order, and shall also mark thereon the sum paid, and the date, and the time from whence, and up to what time the same so became due, and shall deliver back such declaration and order to such wife or mother; and shall also mark such triplicate in like manner; and at the end of every twenty-eight days afterwards, upon similar application, a like payment shall be made in the same manner. If the wife of any such person shall die and leave a child or children under fourteen, the minister and church-warden where such wife resided at the time of her death, shall certify to the commissioners of the navy the day of her death; and if children are left, the ages of those under fourteen, as nearly as they can, and how many are boys; and shall also certify their intention of appointing a fit person, resident within such parish, to receive that part of the father's wages allotted for the maintenance of his children, in case of his wife's death; and along with such certificate shall also transmit the triplicate of the declaration and order, which was in her possession at the time of her death; and if the commissioners of the navy are satisfied of the truth thereof, and that the father is still alive, and in the service of his majesty, they shall make out three certificates and orders, which shall be triplicates of each other, in a prescribed form, and shall send them to the minister or churchwarden of the parish where the wife died, who shall fill up the blanks, and sign them, and having procured two justices of the county, wherein such parish lies, to attest the same, shall return the said three triplicates to the commissioners of the navy. Certain forms of caution are then to be fulfilled, and at the end of twenty-eight days more, from the last payment made to the wife who died, or from the date of the original declaration and order, in case she has received no payment thereon, the person so appointed may apply to such public officer, to whom the same is addressed, for payment of what may be due thereon, and shall then produce the original declaration and

 order,

order, and the certificate of the minister and churchwarden, and attestation by the justices, and allowance by three commissioners, as aforesaid; and shall also deliver a certificate from the minister and churchwarden, specifying that there is a child, or the number of children, under fourteen, then living in their parish, distinguishing how many are boys, and their ages as near as they can; and shall in all things proceed in the same manner as before directed; and such payment shall be continued so long as all, or any one of such children shall remain under fourteen, or the father shall live and continue in the king's service; except as afterwards excepted, where no demand shall have been made within six months. And if any such seaman, landman, or marine, shall be promoted, he may increase the allowance out of his pay to his wife, children, or mother, to the amount allowed to his rank as aforesaid; and the same rules and regulations shall be observed as before are directed and prescribed. Many clauses are introduced into this truly wise and benevolent law, for the prevention of fraud and delay; and it is enacted, that if any such wife as aforesaid shall desert, or otherwise neglect and leave unsupported and unmaintained any such child under fourteen, and who shall for one month become chargeable to any parish, the minister and churchwarden of such parish may certify the fact to the commissioners of the navy, and also their intention to appoint a proper person to receive, and apply to the use of such child, the pay so allowed for the support of her and such child; and if such commissioners be satisfied therewith, they shall proceed to appoint a proper person to receive such pay in the same manner as if such wife had died. All allotments of wages to be paid in pursuance of this act shall be fully paid, without deduction, although a part thereof be in fractions of the smallest denomination; and every person withholding any part thereof under any pretence whatever, shall forfeit 20*l*. And if any person shall make, forge, or counterfeit any such declaration or order, or any certificate or receipt herein before described or mentioned, or publish the same, in order to enable any person to obtain any such wages so allotted as aforesaid, he shall be guilty of felony without benefit of clergy.

Marines. Beside the regular seamen employed on board his majesty's ships, there are bodies of marines, or soldiers, raised for the sea service, and trained to fight either in a naval engagement or in an action ashore. These useful corps were first raised in 1755, and their utility was frequently manifested in the seven years war, particularly at the siege of Belleisle, where they acquired a great character although they were then but little exercised in military discipline. At sea they are incorporated with the ship's crew, of which they make a part: and many of them learn in a ſhort time to be excellent ſeamen, to which their officers are ordered by the admiralty to encourage them, although no ſea officer is to order them to go aloft againſt their inclination. In a ſea fight their ſmall arms are of very great advantage in ſcouring the decks of the enemy, and they are of great uſe in preventing attempts to board. The ſole direction of the corps of marines is veſted in the lords commiſſioners of the admiralty; and in the admiralty is a diſtinct apartment for this purpoſe. The ſecretary to the admiralty, is likewiſe ſecretary to the marines, and he has under him ſeveral clerks for the management of this department. The marine forces of Great Britain in the time of peace are ſtationed in three diviſions; one of which is quartered at Chatham, one at Portſmouth, and another at Plymouth. By a late regulation, they are ordered to do duty at the ſeveral dock-yards of thoſe ports, to prevent embezzlement of the king's ſtores, for which a captain's guard mounts every day. The marine corps are under the command of their own field officers, who diſcipline them, and regulate their different duties. In 1760, George II. formed a new eſtabliſhment of marine officers, entitled, the general, lieutenant-general, and three colonels of marines (one of each diviſion), to be taken from officers in the royal navy. The firſt two are always enjoyed by flag officers, the laſt by poſt captains only. This eſtabliſhment was formed to reward diſtinguiſhed officers.

GOVERNMENT. When at ſea, the marines are under the general naval regulations, and there are annual acts for the better governing his majeſty's royal marine forces whilſt on ſhore, which are in moſt reſpects the ſame with the regulations concerning the land forces; only with ſome neceſſary variations, on account of thoſe forces being ſubject to the juriſdiction of the admiralty. Thus, the lord high admiral, or three commiſſioners of the admiralty, are to form articles of war, and grant commiſſions for holding courts martial. The juſtice's certificate for enliſting is to ſet forth, that the ſecond and third ſections of the articles of war, for the better government of his majeſty's royal marine forces, while on ſhore in Great Britain or Ireland, were read to the perſon inliſted, and that he had taken the oath of fidelity mentioned in the twelfth ſection of the ſaid articles of war. Notice of a deſerter being apprehended, is to be ſent to the ſecretary of the admiralty. The billeting and carriages are to be in purſuance of orders from the admiralty.

ESTABLISHMENT.—The preſent eſtabliſhment of the marines, conſiſts of 173 companies, beſides four of artillery; and their head quarters are, at Chatham 48 companies, at Portſmouth and Plymouth 49 companies each, and at Woolwich 31 companies.

PAY.

PAY. The establishment for the pay of his majesty's marine forces, has already been described at page 19 of this volume.

PRIVATEERS. A privateer is a kind of private man of war; the use of such ships is not very ancient, and some persons account those but one degree removed from pirates, who without any respect to the cause, or having any immediate injury done them, or not being so much as hired for the service, plunder men and goods, and ruin innocent traders, making a traffic of it amidst the calamities of war. That privateers in general are lawful when under right conduct, there is no room to question; all ways of bringing an enemy to reason, which are not repugnant to the laws of nations, are allowed; and it is of no consequence whether a person so commissioned is paid from the public fund, or content to pay himself, out of the spoils of the enemy; or if he acts for no pay at all, but out of love to his country, and loyalty to his prince. It has therefore been customary, since the trade of Europe has been so extensive, for princes and states, in times of war, to issue commissions to private men to equip ships and the persons concerned in privateers administer at their own costs a part of a war, by providing vessels of force, and all other military utensils, to damage the enemy; and they have, instead of pay, leave granted to keep what they can take, allowing the admiral his share. Besides the common commissions, mention is made of special commissions, granted to persons that take pay, who are under discipline; and if they do not obey orders, may be punished with death. And the wars in later ages have generally given occasion for the issuing commissions to annoy the enemies in their commerce, and hinder such supplies as might strengthen them, or lengthen out the war; and likewise to prevent the separation of ships of greater force from their fleet. By a law made in the sixth year of the reign of queen Anne, the lord high admiral, or commissioners of the admiralty, during the war, were empowered to grant commissions to commanders of British ships (on their giving security as usual, upon granting such commissions, except for payment of the tenths to the lord admiral) for the seizing and taking ships and goods belonging to enemies, in any sea or river; and persons serving on board privateers are not to be impressed by any ship of war, under 20*l.* penalty. Privateers may not attempt any thing against the law of nations; as to assault an enemy in a port or haven, under the protection of any prince or republic, be the friend, ally, or neuter; for the peace of such place must be kept inviolably. When these private commissions are granted, great care is always to be taken, to preserve the leagues of allies, neuters, and friends, according to their several treaties.

The owners of privateers are not to convert any part of their captures to their own uſe, until they are condemned as prize: and whether a ſhip ſhall be prize or not, is tried in the admiralty, and no prohibition can be granted.

Letters of Marque and Reprisal. Letters of marque are extraordinary commiſſions granted by authority for reparation to merchants, taken and deſpoiled by ſtrangers at ſea; and repriſal is the retaking of that which has been captured, or the taking of an equivalent. The goods of others may be taken upon the ſea, by letters of marque and jus repriſaliarum; but not by any private authority, only by the power of that prince or ſtate, whoſe ſubject the injured perſon is.

In modern times, the actual fact of caption by an enemy and a refuſal of reſtitution is not required in order to the iſſuing of letters of marque and repriſal; they form part of the general ſyſtem of warfare, and are of uſe only as vouchers for certifying to the ſhips of our own nation, or to the officers of friendly and neutral countries, the quality of the armed ſhip which is furniſhed with them. In ancient times, however, they were formally required and regularly iſſued. The earlieſt notice on Engliſh record of letters of marque, occurs in 1295, when they were granted by Edward I. to one of his Gaſcon ſubjects, to indemnify him for an injury ſuſtained from the king of Portugal. Afterward they were granted to a private merchant for recovery of a debt; but by later treaties, proviſion has been made that they ſhall not be iſſued raſhly, nor are they now allowed in any other caſe than that of a war between two countries. Before any letters of marque or repriſals are iſſued, it is enjoined, that ſecurity be given, in the high court of admiralty, before the judge, in the ſum of three thouſand pounds, if the ſhip carry above one hundred and fifty men, and, if a leſs number, fifteen hundred pounds, to make good any damages that ſhall be done, contrary to the intent and true meaning of their inſtructions, and (in caſe the whole of the prizes is not given to the captors) to cauſe to be paid to his majeſty, or to ſuch perſon as ſhall be authoriſed to receive the ſame, the full tenth part of the prizes, goods, and merchandizes, according to the price at which the ſame ſhall be appraiſed, as alſo the cuſtoms due to the crown.

Prizes. The right of taking prizes is among the moſt ancient and eſtabliſhed cuſtoms of war. It was formerly carried to a much greater extent than modern policy allows. The ſyſtem at preſent obſerved in England and the Britiſh dependencies, with reſpect to captures at ſea, is perfectly correſpondent with the pureſt principles of the law of nations. No prize can be appropriated until legally condemned; the proprietors are allowed

lowed all poſſible means of defence in the admiralty court, and if diſſatisfied with the deciſion, they are at liberty to appeal to a tribunal inſtituted on purpoſe; and the deciſions are not formed on the narrow principles which avowed hoſtility might be expected to create, but on ſuch as are founded on general law, locally adminiſtered, but in its mode of adminiſtration convertible into a precedent, and ſubject to the animadverſion of thoſe nations with which Great Britain is at peace.

Distribution of Prizes. The diſtribution of the value of prizes taken by privateers has already been mentioned. The property in all other captures, is by prerogative veſted in the crown; but as an incitement to, and reward of valour, it is uſual for the king by proclamation to apportion the value of all prizes among the captors and in the diſtribution is included the value of the ſhip, if retained for the public ſervice, and a ſuppoſed ranſom of the crew, called head money. The proportions in which this benefit is diſtributed, vary according to the diſcretion of the miniſtry, but that which has been moſt in uſe is as follows. To the flag-officer, when there is any ſuch concerned in the capture, $\frac{1}{8}$ part of the whole, and to the captain $\frac{2}{8}$; but if there be not any flag-officer, who has a right to a ſhare, then the captain is to have $\frac{3}{8}$. To the marine captain if any, lieutenants of the ſhip, and maſter $\frac{1}{8}$. To the marine lieutenants, if any, boatſwain, gunner, carpenter, maſters mates, ſurgeon, and chaplain $\frac{1}{8}$. To the midſhipmen, carpenter's mates, boatſwain's mates, gunner's mates, corporal, yeoman of the ſheets, coxſwain, quarter maſtor, mates, aſſiſtant ſurgeons, yeomen of the powder room, and the ſerjeant of the marines $\frac{1}{8}$. To the trumpeters, quarter gunners, carpenter's crew, ſteward, cook, armourer, ſteward's mate; cook's mate, gunſmith, coopers, ſwabbers, ordinary trumpeters, able ſeamen, ordinary ſeamen, volunteers by warrant, and marine ſoldiers, if any, $\frac{2}{8}$. And where there are no marine officers or ſoldiers on board, the officers and ſoldiers of land companies, if any, have the like allowance as is appointed for them; but in caſe any officers are abſent, in time of capture, their ſhares are to be caſt into the laſt article.

Embargoes. It has been uſual in all nations at the time of going to war, to ſeize and detain all ſhips in their ports belonging to the enemy, even although they were trading there under the faith of treaties, and incapable of doing injury or violence.

Perhaps this practice is better vindicated by allegations of its antiquity and generality, than by arguments of its juſtice. As it is always mutual it is ſo far not unfair; and were the right abandoned by all nations, it would be difficult to define what voyage a ſhip ſhould perform, or under what guaranty ſhe ſhould ſail,

ſail, ſo as to effect her own ſecurity without doing injury to the nation whoſe ports ſhe quitted, or conveying aſſiſtance or intelligence to the enemy. The veſſels thus ſecured have ever been condemned as lawful prize; but as no admiral or other perſon is intitled to the benefit, the produce remains purely the property of the crown. It is generally applied by his majeſty's direction, and with the conſent of parliament, in proſecuting ſome of the objects of the war, or in relief of the public burthens.

NAVY AGENTS. All matters relating to the intereſts of individuals in the navy, both in pay and prize money, are tranſacted by navy agents. Theſe perſons are not appointed by government, or limited in number; they recommend themſelves by diligence and integrity, and are paid by a moderate poundage out of the ſums they receive.

The general buſineſs of the navy connected with government is tranſacted at the following offices:

NAVY PAY OFFICE, OR TREASURER OF THE NAVY'S OFFICE. The treaſurer of the navy was formerly included in all commiſſions, as a member of the navy board; but having generally had other duties, as a privy counſellor and confidential officer of government, the duty of preſiding at the board has been left to the comptroller; and, by the new commiſſions, he is no longer a member of the board, but allowed to be preſent at their deliberations, if he thinks proper.

His emoluments aroſe from a poundage out of the payments made by him, which, with the advantages derived from monies left in his hands, became in time enormous, and the whole ſyſtem was altered by increaſing the treaſurer of the navy's ſalary, and debarring him from the uſe of the public money, which by the regulations of the act of 25th Geo. III. c. 31. commencing 1ſt of July, 1785, is not to be applied for out of the exchequer, till the current payments require, and muſt then be placed in the Bank of England, and drawn from thence as wanted, for each head of ſervice to which it is appropriated. He has at preſent a ſalary of 4000*l.* a year net, in lieu of all other emoluments whatever, ſtationary for his own uſe, and a houſe, excepted. Former treaſurers had unlimited allowances of coals and candles, which are not now received.

The chief eſtabliſhment of the treaſurer of the navy's office conſiſts of a treaſurer, a paymaſter, five chief officers at the head of as many different branches, an aſſiſtant in the inſpector's branch, with clerks and other inferior officers.

The treaſurer does not execute the duties of his office in perſon, but delegates powers for that purpoſe to the *pay-maſter*, who accordingly conducts the buſineſs. The treaſurer, however,

ever, is responsible for his conduct, and for all the money issued from the exchequer, or that shall come into his hands by any other means; his salary is 800*l.* a year.

The business of the five branches of which the office at present consists is briefly as follows.

The *Pay Branch*, to pay seamen's wages and the yards. The chief person empoyed in this branch, has a salary of 660*l.*, and is called deputy-paymaster. The residue of the business is committed to the officers next mentioned, and with their places their salaries are specified. Superintendant of the payments at Deptford and Woolwich Dock yards, 495*l.*; at Portsmouth two, one having 440*l.*, the other 330*l.*; at Plymouth two who are similarly paid; at Sheerness one, 330*l.*; at Chatham one 440*l.* In the office in London, the first clerk, who superintends the making up of accounts, has 495*l.*; and there are several other clerks, with salaries from 275*l.* to 101*l.*

The *Navy Branch*, to pay bills assigned by the navy, and sick and hurt boards. The chief person in this department is the cashier of the navy for paying navy bills, whose salary is 660*l.*; and under him are various clerks, with salaries from 330*l.* to 101*l.*

The *Victualling Branch*, to pay bills assigned by the victualling board. In this division the cashier has 660*l.*, and the other clerks salaries as in the navy branch.

The *Accomptant's Branch*, to bring-up the accounts of the ex-treasurers, and to carry on and make up the account of the treasurer in office. The salary of the accomptant is 660*l.* and the clerks as above.

The *Inspector's Branch*, to inspect and examine all wills and powers of attorney, and to see that they are duly executed, according to act of parliament, and to grant certificates as an authority for the payment of wages due to the parties.

There is also a branch for *paying seamen's tickets*, the chief cashier in which receives the same salary as those at the head of the preceding departments, and the inferior clerks are paid in the same proportion. Two clerks for *prize matters* receive respectively 200*l.* and 100*l.* a year, and there are several *extra clerks* with salaries of 78*l.* 5*s.*

The chief of the officers, called *conductors*, receives and packs the money to the out ports; and the other three conductors attend at each port to count out at the pay-table on shore, or to convey on board ship the money for payments at each port. And the officer called keeper of ships' books, attends in like manner the payments in London; the first of these persons has 330*l.* a year; the next three, stationed at Portsmouth, Plymouth, and Chatham, 150*l.* each; and the last 140*l.*

OFFICE.

OFFICE. The navy pay office is in Somerfet Place.

NAVY OFFICE. The first eftablifhment of a royal navy office was in the reign of Henry VIII. who appointed perfons, under the title of principal officers of his navy, to manage the civil branches thereof, under the lord high admiral; but thofe officers had no pofitive inftructions for their guidance in the execution of their duty, until the reign of Edward VI. when certain ordinances were iffued for the conduct of the officers intrufted with the management of marine affairs; which ordinances form the bafis of all the fubfequent inftructions given for the conduct of the officers to whom the management of the civil branch of the navy has been committed. The officers at that time appointed to this duty were, the vice-admiral of the fleet, the mafter of the ordnance, the furveyor of marine caufes, the treafurer, the comptroller, the general furveyor of the victualling, the clerk of the fhips, and the clerk of the ftores; who were directed to meet once a week at the office on Tower Hill, to confult together for the good order of the navy, and to report their proceedings once a month to the high-admiral: particular duties are alfo allotted to each member. The affairs of the navy appear to have continued under the management of fuch officers, until the time of James I. who, in the fixteenth year of his reign, iffued a commiffion, under the great feal, to Sir Thomas Smith and others, to inquire into frauds and abufes, with power to remedy the fame, and to manage, fettle, and put the affairs of the navy into a right courfe. This commiffion was determined on the demife of James I. in 1625, and feveral new ones were iffued with various effect until the reftoration, when Charles II. conftituted a navy board by commiffion under the great feal, confifting of the treafurer, comptroller, furveyor, and clerk of the navy, who were ftyled principal officers. To them on the 4th July, 1660, three commiffioners were added, to affift in the management of the affairs of the navy. In January, 1661, the Duke of York, then lord high admiral, eftablifhed certain inftructions now in ufe for the conduct of the four principal officers; the other three, being commiffioners at large, had no particular line of duty allotted them, until the year 1666, when one of them was directed to take upon him fo much of the comptroller's duty as related to the examination and controul of the treafurer's accounts; another that part which related to the victualling accounts; and in the year 1671, the third commiffioner had that part of the comptrollers' duty which related to the examination and controul of the ftore-keeper's accounts, affigned to him; which, with the addition of one commiffioner at large, is the prefent arrangement of the navy board. Thus it appears that the conftitution of this board, and the relative duties

duties of its members, have undergone very little alteration (except the occasional variation of the number of commissioners) for upwards of a century, notwithstanding the great increase of the navy; and that the duty then prescribed to the principal officers and commissioners remains nearly the same at this day.

Establishment. The establishment of the navy office consists of eleven commissioners (exclusive of the treasurer); an assistant to the clerk of the acts; five assistants to the surveyor; a store keeper of slops; with a great number of clerks and other inferior officers. The treasurer is not included in the patents granted to the navy board, but provision is made therein for his acting as a member of the board, when he thinks fit to attend. Of the eleven commissioners, seven are resident in London; the other four are specially appointed to reside individually at the dock yards at Chatham, Portsmouth, Plymouth, and Halifax in North America.

Duty. The duty of the navy board is, under the directions of the Lords of the Admiralty, to consult together how to transact, to the best advantage, all affairs tending to the well being and regulation of the civil establishment of the navy, and all its subordinate instruments, wherein they are to proceed by common council, and agreement of most voices; to make contracts for and attend to the proper distribution of naval stores of every kind; to prepare all estimates of expences; to direct all monies for naval services into the treasurer's hands, and to examine and certify his accounts of expenditure.

The seven commissioners resident in London, who properly compose the navy board, are, the comptroller, the surveyor, the clerk of the acts, the comptroller of the treasurer's accounts, the comptroller of the victualling accounts, the comptroller of the store keepers' accounts, and one extra commissioner.

Besides the general duty of these officers, as members of the navy board, they have each, as their titles import (except the extra commissioner), special duties, of which an abridged account is here given.

The *Comptroller* is to preside at, and prepare matter for the discussion of the navy board; to conduct the general business that comes before it; to superintend the offices particularly committed to his charge, viz. the office for bills and accounts, domestic and foreign, and that of the payment of seamen's wages; to controul the payment of half pay at the navy pay office, the payment of artificers and labourers at Deptford and Woolwich yards, and of the ships paid off at those places; besides visits to the yards, attendance at the admiralty and other offices in town, and general superintendance of all the branches of the navy

navy office. The comptroller's duty originally extended to the treaſurer's accounts, both naval and victualling, the ſtore keepers' accounts, the ticket office, and the payment of all wages, till ſeparate comptrollers for theſe branches were appointed in 1666 and 1671. The comptroller of the navy has under his charge two offices, one for bills and accounts, and the other for ſeamen's wages. In the former all accounts are examined, and bills made out relative to the following heads, viz. the yards, manning of the navy, contracts for ſtores and ſervices, tranſports, diſburſements of admirals, and other naval commanders at home and abroad, contingencies of admiralty, and various other articles of the like nature; alſo for the pay of the whole civil eſtabliſhment of the navy. In the ſeamen's wages office, a check is kept on the wages due to all officers and men belonging to ſhips and veſſels in ſea pay; quarterly eſtimates are made out; clerks are deputed to attend the payments; and to aſſiſt in making up ſhip and yard books, half pay liſts, &c. The accounts of men borne in each ſhip, and of the officers and ſervants allowed to each, and of ſick men on ſhore, are examined and adjuſted: ſundry liſts, ſuch as of officers' annual pay, half pay, arrears, claims, defalcations, &c. are kept here; entries are made out of the clerk of the cheque's muſters; a hurt book is kept of the penſioners at Chatham, and their particular injury, alſo books of the payment of ſuch penſioners; and a check is kept on the navy pay office of all abatements made upon ſhip and yard books for the uſe of the ſaid cheſt.

The *Surveyor* is to ſurvey or examine reports of ſurveys taken of ſhips, to attend to their repairs, or the building of new ſhips, and providing them with ſtores; to examine all demands for ſtores at home, or accounts of ſtores purchaſed abroad; with other articles of buſineſs of a ſimilar nature. His two aſſiſtants ſuperintend the repair and building of ſhips by contract in the merchants' yards, and draw up reports, returns, and eſtimates, on all buſineſs in the ſurveyor's department carried on there, or in the ſeveral dock yards.

The *Clerk of the Acts* is to conduct the correſpondence of the board; forward all orders to dock yards; take care of the papers, journals, and log books, prepare contracts and ſecurities, accept bills drawn on the board; make out impreſt bills, widows' and orphans' bounty bills, warrant officers' appointments, navy officers' certificates; with other duties of a ſimilar nature. He is, in ſhort, regiſter and accountant to the navy office; and his aſſiſtant acts as ſecretary to the navy board, and has of late been known by that appellation.

The *Comptroller of Treaſurer's Accounts* is to check the treaſurer's accounts for naval and ſick and hurt ſervices; to examine the

the accounts ſent by the treaſurer half monthly, and prepare a monthly account current, ſhewing the balance in his hands on each head of ſervice; to prepare the annual eſtimates for the ordinary of the navy, and account of navy debt: to check ſub-accountants; to make out daily liſts of bills aſſigned on the treaſurer, and to prepare aſſignments. It is alſo a part of his duty to ſuperintend the ticket office, where the accounts of the number of ſeamen and mariners are made up, and the various payments made by liſts and ſigned tickets are adjuſted; where likewiſe bond tickets are prepared to ſupply the loſs of originals, and certificates of various kinds when requiſite, are granted to officers and men. He has likewiſe the joint ſuperintendance of the ſlop office, where the ſlops received from the contractors are inſpected, and certificates for them granted, if approved; and where ſtore-keepers' and purſers' accounts are examined, and all other matters relative to this branch of buſineſs are tranſacted.

The *Comptroller of Victualling Accounts* has the ſame duty with reſpect to the treaſurer's victualling accounts, as the preceding commiſſioner has with reſpect to the naval and ſick and hurt accounts. Beſides which he attends in his turn the payment of ſhips and recals in London, and of the yards at Deptford and Woolwich.

The *Comptroller of Store-keeper's Accounts* is to ſee that the accounts of ſtores in the different yards are properly kept; to check the receipt and iſſue of them, and be able to give information, when called upon, of the quantity in hand of all the different kinds of ſtores, which conſiſt of the various articles and materials neceſſary for the conſtruction and equipment of ſhips. Beſides which, he takes his turn of attending payments in London, and in the neighbouring yards.

The *Extra Commiſſioner* has no particular branch of buſineſs allotted to him, but his uſual employment has been to examine journals, certificates, log books, caſes of run men, muſters, returns, reports, and accounts of cordage; alſo to attend examinations of midſhipmen for lieutenancies; and, in his turn, the payments in London and in the neighbouring yards.

The attendance of comptroller of the navy is conſtant and unremitting, as is alſo that of the aſſiſtant to the clerk of the acts, who officiates as ſecretary to the board. The other commiſſioners of the navy attend, in general, daily, as do likewiſe the aſſiſtants to the ſurveyor of the navy, as well as the ſtore-keeper of the ſlop office.

From the great increaſe of buſineſs ſince the original inſtitution of the navy board, ſeveral parts of the perſonal ſervices allotted to the commiſſioners are unavoidably left to be conducted by the chief and other clerks in each department; the voluminous and extended correſpondence, together with the direction of the whole, and the execution of a part of the buſineſs occupying the whole time of the principals.

Emoluments. The ſalaries and emoluments of the commiſſioners are calculated at 1200*l*. a year each. In their various branches clerks are liberally but not extravagantly remunerated.

Ships afloat. There are alſo commiſſioners at Portſmouth, Sheerneſs, and Plymouth, who have each a guinea per day, for ſuperintending the payment of ſhips afloat at the out ports.

Sick and wounded Sailors. The methods adopted on board ſhips of war and hoſpital ſhips for the relief of thoſe whom the hand of providence or the chance of war has diſabled from continuing their exertions to ſerve the country, have already been noticed, and it will be found that on ſhore, the ſame benevolent exertions are made in their favour, that when ſuperannuated and helpleſs, they are not deſtitute of a comfortable and honourable aſylum, and that their widows and orphans have alſo a ſupport, from public inſtitution or private benevolence.

Sick and Hurt Office. A commiſſion, from which this office appears to have originated, exiſted in the reign of William III., but in 1692, it was diſſolved, and from that time, until of late years, the office was in a ſtate of fluctuation, overburthened with duties or uncertain of their extent, the number of commiſſioners unſettled, and the accounts incapable of being reduced to regular and ſatisfactory order. The duty is now perfectly well adjuſted and underſtood, and tranſacted with the greateſt uniformity and ſucceſs.

The buſineſs of this office is to provide hoſpitals, ſick quarters, medical aſſiſtance, medicines, and neceſſaries for ſick and wounded ſeamen belonging to his majeſty's ſervice; to pay all expences attending ſuch ſervices; and examine and paſs the accounts of all perſons employed in the execution thereof. The preſent eſtabliſhment conſiſts of four commiſſioners, a ſecretary with chief clerks, junior clerks, and other inferior officers; beſides which there are medical aſſiſtants, and agents, employed at different ports and places, at home and abroad.

Commissioners. The commiſſioners are four in number; of whom three are phyſicians; their duty is, to ſuperintend the whole buſineſs, under the direction of the lords of the admiralty; to appoint proper perſons for executing it; to contract for, or otherwiſe provide, hoſpitals, ſick quarters, proviſions, medicines, bedding, ſlops, and other neceſſaries; to viſit the

ſeveral

ſeveral hoſpitals, occaſionally, to ſee that no abuſes are committed, and that the ſtanding regulations for their good government are properly attended to, and to hear and redreſs complaints; to examine, and, if approved, to allow, all accounts relative to this ſervice, and to aſſign bills upon the treaſurer of the navy for payment of charges and expences. Their attendance is two days in a week, or oftener if the buſineſs requires it. Their ſalaries are 500*l.* each, the ſenior commiſſioner having an additional allowance of 65*l.* for houſe rent.

OTHER OFFICERS. The buſineſs of the office is divided into branches, each chief having under him a proper number of ſubordinate perſons, and the name of the office generally denoting its duty. The ſecretary has a ſalary of 500*l.*; there are home and foreign departments for ſeamen, the chief clerk in each of which has 400*l.*; a ſuperintendant of the London hoſpitals, with a ſalary of 150*l.* There is alſo a department for ſick priſoners of war, and formerly all their concerns fell under the inſpection of the commiſſioners.

HOSPITALS. For the reception of the ſick and hurt, hoſpitals are provided at the moſt convenient ports in Great Britain and its dependencies. The principal eſtabliſhments in England are at *Haſlar* near Goſport, at *Stonehouſe* near Plymouth, and at *Deal.* They are under the direction of governors, lieutenants, and other officers, who have liberal, though not extravagant appointments; phyſicians and ſurgeons are regularly appointed and ſufficiently paid; and there is a due portion of ſubordinate officers, and a chaplain. Two phyſicians are alſo appointed *general inſpectors of naval and priſon hoſpitals*, with ſalaries of 500*l.* each.

On foreign ſtations, hoſpitals are eſtabliſhed at Madras, Jamaica, Antigua, Halifax and Gibraltar.

Theſe are the means of relief ſupplied by public bounty out of the national purſe, for thoſe who have ſuch juſt and irreſiſtible claims to protection and gratitude: it remains to notice other eſtabliſhments for the ſolace of age, the relief of widowhood, and the protection and care of orphans, which have originated in, or are ſupported by, royal or private munificence.

GREENWICH HOSPITAL. The greateſt and moſt conſpicuous of theſe eſtabliſhments is Greenwich hoſpital. Of a royal reſidence at this ſpot, traces occur as early as the year 1300, and thence conſtantly to 1433, when it was the property of Humphry, commonly called the *good* Duke of Glouceſter, who received a royal licence to embattle his manor houſe, and to make a park of 200 acres. Soon after this, the duke rebuilt the palace, calling it *Placentia*, or the manor de Pleaſaunce; he incloſed

closed the park also, and erected within it a tower on the spot where the observatory now stands. On the Duke of Gloucester's death, in 1447, this manor reverted to the crown, and continued upward of two centuries a celebrated royal residence, the birth place of many princes, and among others the illustrious and ever memorable queen Elizabeth, who also made it her summer residence. During the protectorate it shared the fate of other royal and public property, parts being sold to defray the expences of the republican government, but these portions were recovered at the restoration; and Charles II. having pulled down the decayed edifice begun by Humphry Duke of Gloucester, commenced a new erection on the spot, on a most magnificent scale, but completed only one wing. In this state the palace remained until after the revolution, when, at the suggestion of Queen Mary, a project was formed for providing an asylum for seamen, disabled by age, or maimed in the service of their country. Among various places recommended for its site, Sir Christopher Wren proposed that the palace at Greenwich should be converted to this use, and enlarged with new buildings; and in pursuance of his advice, the king and queen, by letters patent in 1694, granted that, with other buildings and certain parcels of ground adjoining, to trustees, "to be converted and "employed to and for the use and service of a hospital, to be "there founded for the relief and support of seamen of the "Royal Navy, who, by reason of wounds or other disabilities "should be incapable of farther service at sea, and unable to "maintain themselves; and for the sustentation of widows, "and the education of children of such seamen as should be "slain or disabled in the King's service." The following year, the king (Queen Mary being dead) appointed commissioners for the purpose of considering, with the assistance of the surveyor general and other artists, what part of king Charles's palace, and the other buildings granted, would be fit for the intended hospital, and how they might be best prepared for that use; of procuring models for such new buildings as might be required; of preparing, with the assistance of the attorney and solicitor general, a charter of foundation, with statutes and orders for the management of the hospital; and for other purposes. The king also granted 2000*l.* yearly, towards carrying this noble work into effect. The commissioners having ascertained that king Charles's unfinished palace might, by the addition of a building on the west side, be made capable of receiving, conveniently, between three and four hundred seamen, the preamble of a subscription-roll was drawn up, but the sum received did not amount to 8000*l.* Sir Christopher Wren, who was appointed the architect, generously contributed his time, labour,

labour, and ſkill, and ſuperintended the progreſs of the work for ſeveral years without any emolument or reward. The foundation of the firſt new building was laid on the third of June, 1696, from which time the hoſpital has been gradually enlarged and improved, till it has attained to its preſent ſplendour and magnificence.

DESCRIPTION. Greenwich Hoſpital, in its preſent ſtate, conſiſts of four piles of building, diſtinguiſhed by the names of King Charles's, Queen Anne's, King William's, and Queen Mary's. King Charles's and Queen Anne's are thoſe next the river: between them is the grand ſquare, 270 feet wide; and in front by the river's ſide a terrace 865 feet in length. The view, from the north gate, which opens to the terrace in the midway between the two buildings, preſents an aſſemblage of objects uncommonly grand and ſtriking. Beyond the ſquare are ſeen the hall and chapel, with their beautiful domes, and the two colonnades, which form a kind of avenue, terminated by the ranger's lodge in the park; on an eminence of which appears the royal obſervatory amidſt a grove of trees. King Charles's building ſtands on the weſt ſide of the great ſquare; the eaſtern part of it, which is of Portland ſtone, was erected in 1664, by Webb, after a deſign of his late father-in-law, Inigo Jones. The front toward the eaſt has in the centre a portico, ſupported by four Corinthian columns; and at each end a pavilion formed by four columns of the ſame order. In this range of buildings is the council room, with an antichamber. The north front of King Charles's building, which is towards the river, contains the apartments of the governor and lieutenant governor. This and the ſouth front have each two pavilions ſimilar to thoſe in the eaſt front. The weſt ſide of this building, comprehending the north weſt and ſouth weſt pavilions, was originally all of brick. It was the firſt addition to King Charles's palace, being called the *baſs building*. The foundation was laid in 1696, and it was nearly completed in 1698. The whole of what is now called King Charles's building, contains fourteen wards, in which are 301 beds.

Queen Anne's building, on the eaſt ſide of the great ſquare, nearly correſponds with King Charles's, on the oppoſite ſide. The foundation of this building was laid in 1698: the greater part of it was raiſed and covered in before 1728. In this building are ſeveral of the officers' apartments; and twenty-four wards, in which are 437 beds.

King William's building ſtands to the ſouth weſt of the great ſquare. It contains the great hall, veſtibule, and dome, deſigned and erected by Sir Chriſtopher Wren, between 1698 and 1703: to the eaſt of theſe adjoins a colonnade 347 feet in length, ſup-

 ported

ported by columns and pilasters of the Doric order, twenty feet in height. In the vestibule of the hall is a model of an antique ship, found in the Villa Mattea (given by Lord Anson). The great hall is 106 feet in length, 56 in width, and 50 in height. In the frize is the following inscription. "*Pietas augusta ut* "*habitent securè et publicè alantur qui publicæ securitati invigi-* "*larunt regia Grenovici Mariæ auspiciis sublevandis nautis desti-* "*nata regnantibus Gulielmo et Mariâ*, 1694. The painting of this hall was undertaken by Sir James Thornhill in 1708, and finished in 1727. It cost 6685*l.* being after the rate of 3*l.* per yard for the ceiling, and 1*l.* for the sides. This price the directors agreed to pay, after consulting some of the most eminent artists, who declared the performance to be equal in merit to any thing of the kind in England, and superior in the number of figures and ornaments. On the ceiling are portraits of the royal founders William and Mary, surrounded by the Cardinal Virtues, the four Seasons, the English Rivers, the four Elements, the arts and sciences relating to navigation; and other emblematical figures, among which are introduced, portraits of Flamstead, the astronomer royal, and his pupil Mr. Thomas Weston. The sides are adorned with fluted pilasters, trophies, &c. The ceiling of the upper hall represents Queen Anne and Prince George of Denmark, accompanied by various emblematical figures; the four quarters of the globe, &c. The subjects on the sides are, the landing of the prince of Orange at Harwich; and of George I. at Greenwich. At the upper end of the hall are portraits of George I. and his family, with many emblematical figures; among which Sir James Thornhill has introduced his own portrait. The west front of King William's building, which is of brick, was finished by Sir John Vanburgh about the year 1726. This building contains eleven wards, in which are 552 beds. The foundation of the eastern colonnade (whch is similar to that on the west side) was laid in 1699; but the chapel, and other parts of Queen Mary's building which adjoin to it, were not finished till 1752. This building, which corresponds to that called King William's, contains thirteen wards, in which are 1092 beds.

On the 2d of January, 1779, a dreadful fire happened in the building, which destroyed the chapel with its dome, part of the colonnade, and as many of the adjoining wards as contained 500 beds. The whole has been since rebuilt. The former chapel, which was destroyed, was designed by Ripley; the present, by the late James Stuart, well known by his interesting publications on the antiquities of Athens. It is 111 feet in length, and 52 in width: the portal is extremely rich; and the interior fitted up in the most elegant style of Grecian architecture. On the sides

ſides are galleries for the officers and their families, and beneath, ſeats for the penſioners, nurſes, and boys.

The two pavilions at the extremities of the terrace were erected in 1778, and dedicated to their Majeſties. The eaſt and weſt entrances into the hoſpital are formed by two piers of ruſtic work. On theſe at the weſt entrance are placed two large ſtone globes, each ſix feet in diameter.

THE INFIRMARY. In 1763, it having been determined to erect an infirmary without the walls of the hoſpital for ſick penſioners, Mr. Stuart gave a deſign for the building, which was immediately completed by Mr. Robinſon, then clerk of the works. It is a quadrangular brick building, 198 feet in length, and 175 in breadth, containing 64 rooms, each formed ſo as to accommodate four patients; every room having a chimney place and ventilator. This building contains alſo a chapel, hall, and kitchen; apartments for the phyſician, ſurgeon, apothecary, matron, &c. Within the walls are hot and cold baths.

SCHOOL HOUSE AND DORMITORY. In 1783, a ſchool houſe, with a dormitory for the boys, was built without the walls of the hoſpital; the wards which the boys formerly occupied being appropriated to the reception of an additional number of penſioners. This building is 146 feet in length and 42 in breadth, excluſive of a Tuſcan colonnade in front, which is 180 feet long, and twenty broad. The ſchool room, 100 feet by 25, is capable of containing 200 boys. In the upper ſtories are two dormitories of the ſame length, furniſhed with hammocks. There are apartments alſo for the guardian, nurſes, and other attendants; and, at a ſmall diſtance, a houſe for the ſchool maſter. Among other out-buildings belonging to the hoſpital are, a large brewery, and ſtables for the uſe of the officers.

QUALIFICATIONS OF THE PENSIONERS. The penſioners who are the objects of this noble charity, muſt be ſeamen diſabled by age, or maimed either in the king's ſervice, or in the merchants' ſervice, if the wounds were received in defending or taking any ſhip, or in fight againſt a pirate. Foreigners who have ſerved two years in the Britiſh navy, become entitled to receive the benefits of this charity in the ſame manner as natives. The widows of ſeamen, purſuant to the intention of the royal founder, are provided for in this eſtabliſhment, enjoying the excluſive privilege of being appointed nurſes in the hoſpital. In the month of January, 1705, the hoſpital was firſt opened for the reception of penſioners, when forty-two ſeamen, qualified as above mentioned, were admitted. Their number has ſince been gradually increaſed to nearly 3000. They are provided with clothes, diet, and lodging; and have a ſmall allowance for pocket money; that of the common ſailors being a ſhilling a week; the boatswains two shillings and sixpence; and the boatswain's mates one shilling and sixpence. The nurses, who must be widows of seamen, and under forty-five years at the time of their admission, are allowed 8*l.* per annum as wages, and provided with clothing, diet, and lodging.

Out-Pensioners. In 1763, in consequence of an application from the commissioners of Greenwich hospital, assembled at a general-court, an act of parliament passed, enabling them, after defraying the necessary expences of the hospital, to grant pensions to such poor seamen, worn out and become decrepid in the king's service, as could not be received, for want of room, in the hospital. In pursuance of this act 1400 out-pensioners were appointed to receive 7*l.* per annum: their numbers having gradually decreased, by death, or admission, 500 more were appointed in 1782. For the protection of these persons in the enjoyment of the provision made for them, it is enacted, in the same statute, that whoever shall personate or falsely assume the name and character of an out-pensioner of Greenwich hospital, in order to receive the money due to him, or procure any other to do so, shall be guilty of felony without benefit of clergy. And in order to receive the pension half yearly as it becomes due, each pensioner must, together with the printed bill delivered to him by the commissioners, produce a certificate under the hand of the minister and church-wardens where he resides, that the person is, to the best of their knowledge and belief, the person named in such bill.

Education of Seamen's Sons. From the beginning of the institution, in compliance with the royal founder's intention, a certain number of seamen's sons have been educated in the hospital; at first, ten only; in 1731, they were increased to sixty; and afterward to 150. The boys must be, at the time of their admission, between eleven and thirteen years of age; objects of charity; of sound mind, and able to read. They are lodged, clothed and maintained three years; during which time they are instructed in the principles of religion by the chaplains; and in writing, arithmetic, navigation, (and drawing if they shew any genius for it,) by the school-master. Each boy has a bible and prayer book given him on his entrance, and is supplied, during his stay, with all necessary books and instruments; which he is allowed to take with him on leaving the school, to be bound out for seven years to the sea service. About 3000 boys have thus received the blessing of an useful education. The master, who is appointed by the directors, has a salary of 150*l.*, and a house.

Revenue of the Hospital. The funds which have sufficed to raise the magnificent buildings of this hospital, and

to

to increase, from time to time, the establishment to its present extent, have been derived from the following sources: the sum of 2000*l.* per annum granted by the king, in 1695. About 8000*l.* subscribed as before mentioned. A duty of sixpence per month, paid by every mariner, either in the king's or merchant's service; granted by parliament in 1696, and in 1712 *. The sum of 19,500*l.*, being fines paid by certain merchants for smuggling, given by the king, in 1699. The sum of 600*l.*, being the produce of a lottery, (anno 1699,) from which much greater gain was expected. The profits of the market at Greenwich, given by Henry Earl of Romney, in 1700. The sum of 6472*l.* 1*s.* being the effects of Kid, a pirate, given by Queen Anne, in 1705. The moiety of a large estate bequeathed by Robert Olbaldeston Esq. in 1707, (valued at 20,000*l.*) and the profits of his unexpired grant of the North and South Foreland light-houses (since renewed for ninety-nine years to the hospital). Forfeited and unclaimed shares of prize money, granted by Queen Anne, in 1708. Six thousand pounds per annum, granted by Queen Anne, in 1710, out of the duty on coals, and continued for a longer term by George I. The wages and allowance of the chaplains of Deptford and Woolwich dock yards, granted to the hospital in 1714; an increase of salary having been given in lieu to the chaplains. The half pay of all the officers belonging to the hospital, from the year 1728, when salaries were assigned them in lieu. Ten thousand pounds granted annually by parliament in 1728, and for several years following. An estate given by Mr. William Clapham, of Eltham, (1730,) consisting of wharfs and warehouses, near London bridge (after the death of his sister without issue.) The estates forfeited by the Earl of Derwentwater, given by act of parliament in 1735, with certain monies received on account of the said estates, and then remaining in the exchequer; but in 1788, on a petition from the Earl of Newburgh, an act of parliament passed, granting to him and his heirs male, a rent charge of 2500*l.* per annum, to be paid by the treasurer of the hospital. Benefactions of private persons at various times, (subsequent to the subscription already mentioned,) amounting in the whole to about 9400*l.* The present revenue of the hospital arises from such of the grants and benefactions above mentioned as were of a permanent nature, and from fines for fishing

* At first the benefit of the institution was confined entirely to seamen in the king's service; but, in 1712, all seamen having been made liable to the duty of sixpence per month, imposed before only on seamen in the king's service, the benefits of this charity, in aid of which the duty was granted, were extended as above mentioned.

with unlawful nets, and other offences committed on the river Thames.

FUNDS OF THE SCHOOL. The expences of the ſchool are not paid out of this revenue, but it is ſupported ſolely by the following incidental funds, viz. money received for ſhewing the hall, chapel, and other parts of the building; mulcts, abſences, checques, &c. of the penſioners and the nurſes; profits on the proviſions purchaſed of the penſioners; ſale of old houſehold ſtores; and unclaimed property of deceaſed penſioners and nurſes. Theſe funds have proved adequate to the expences of the eſtabliſhment: and have produced a balance of ſavings inveſted in the ſtocks.

CONSTITUTION AND GOVERNMENT OF THE HOSPITAL. Two commiſſions relating to Greenwich hoſpital were iſſued by William, and in 1703 a third by Queen Anne, which directed that ſeven commiſſioners ſhould form a general court, whereof the lord high admiral, the lord treaſurer, or any two privy counſellors ſhould be a *quorum*; general courts were to be held quarterly; the governor and treaſurer of the hoſpital to be appointed by the crown, all the other officers by the lord high admiral, having been recommended to him by the general court: the ſame commiſſion appoints twenty-five directors to be a ſtanding committee, to meet every fortnight; it veſts the internal regulation of the hoſpital in the governor, and ſuch a council of the officers as the lord high admiral ſhall appoint. Such has been the conſtitution of the hoſpital to the preſent day, warrants having been iſſued from time to time by the admiralty for forming new councils, as the increaſe of officers or other circumſtances rendered it neceſſary. New commiſſions of the ſame nature as that of Queen Anne were granted by George I. and George II; but it was not till the year 1775, that the commiſſioners became a body corporate by a charter of George III., who granted powers to finiſh the building; to provide for ſeamen, either within or out of the hoſpital; to make bye laws, and for other purpoſes. It is provided by the charter, that all the officers of the hoſpital ſhall be ſeafaring men; the office of the directors is defined to be, to inſpect the carrying on of the buildings, to ſtate the accounts, and to make contracts; and to place the boys out as apprentices. The internal regulation of the hoſpital to be in the governor and council, as before mentioned. This charter was followed by an act of parliament, which veſted in the commiſſioners thus incorporated, all the eſtates held in truſt for the benefit of the Hoſpital.

PRINCIPAL OFFICERS. The principal officers of Greenwich hoſpital,

hospital, with their salaries, are as follow: a governor, 1000*l.*; lieutenant-governor, 400*l.*; four captains, 230*l.* each; eight lieutenants, 115*l.* each; a treasurer, 200*l.*; secretary, 160*l.*; auditor, 100*l.*; two chaplains, 130*l.* each; a physician, 182*l.* 10*s.*; surgeon, 150*l.*; steward, 160*l.*; clerk of the checque, 160*l.*; surveyor, 200*l.*; clerk of the works, 91*l.* 5*s.*; besides assistants and a great number of inferior officers. The officers are allowed, in addition to their salaries, a certain quantity of coals and candles, and fourteen pence a day in lieu of diet.

THE CEMETERY. In 1707, a piece of ground, lying on the east side of Greenwich park, 660 feet in length, and 132 in breadth, was given by Prince George of Denmark, to the hospital for the burial ground. In has been long disused; another parcel of ground, containing about two acres and a half, having been appropriated for that purpose in 1749.

CHEST. The explanation of this institution is already given in describing the deduction of sixpence per month from the pay of each mariner, which is made by authority of parliament for the support of those who are past service. This admirable institution originated in 1588, on the suggestion of Sir Francis Drake, Sir John Hawkins, and some other public spirited commanders. The establishment, or chest, was kept at first at Chatham, and is most generally known by that description, but it has been removed to Greenwich. The duties relating to it are executed by supervisors, consisting of the first lord of the admiralty for the time being, the comptroller of the navy, and the governor and auditor of Greenwich hospital; to whom are added five directors, with a secretary, accountant, and other officers.

OTHER CHARITABLE ESTABLISHMENTS. Besides this great national fund for relief, there are many less public establishments for the benefit of the navy. *Alms-houses* are provided in various parts of the kingdom to afford them retreats; a *society* was formed, in 1793, *for relief of the widows of sailors and soldiers;* in 1804, another arose under the care and patronage of their royal highnesses the Prince of Wales, the Duke of Clarence, and several other members of the royal family, called the *naval asylum for the maintenance and education of the orphans of sailors and marines;* and there is an establishment called the *naval knights of Windsor*, of which the following account is given. Agreeably to the will of S. Travers, Esq. in the year 1724, seven old and infirm lieutenants, single and without children, were to be chosen naval knights of Windsor, each to have an apartment near the castle, and 60*l.* per annum, exclusive of the half pay, and the senior lieutenant to have 12*l.* per annum extra. They are not entitled to superannuation. The whole to be paid out of two estates in Essex. The above bequest took effect November 27th, 1795, being the day his majesty signed the warrants, and seven gentlemen were appointed. When there are vacancies, lieutenants wishing to fill them must apply, with a testimonial of their qualifications, to the navy board, that one may be recommended to the admiralty. By the above will, thirty-seven sons of naval officers, from seven to twelve years of age, are admitted into the mathematical school of Christ's hospital, London. Sons of commissioned officers are preferred to those of warrant officers. The application is by petition to the governors.

Transport Service. Returning to some further duties in which portions of the navy are occasionally engaged, it is necessary to mention the transport service, or the duty of supplying vessels and accommodations for troops ordered abroad on garrison or colony duty, or on expeditions. As ships for this express service cannot always be maintained by government, they are frequently hired by contract from merchants or other proprietors, and, sailing under the protection of king's ships, are called transports. They are laden with troops, both cavalry and infantry, with their horses, artillery, baggage, field equipage, and all other requisites for the service about which they are to be employed.

Transport Office. This business is managed by four commissioners who have each 1000*l*. per annum, and under them are accountants, clerks, and other inferior officers, and they have agents stationed at most of the principal ports in Great Britain and abroad.

Prisoners. One great department in this office is the superintendance, custody, and care of prisoners of war, which has been tranferred to them from the sick and hurt office. The duty of this branch is to provide proper places of confinement, provisions, bedding and necessaries, for prisoners of war; to negotiate their exchange, carry the same into effect, by transporting them to the dominions of their respective sovereigns, and to bring back British prisoners in return; to pay all expences attending such services; and examine and pass the accounts of all persons employed in the execution thereof. They are also occasionally to visit the several prisons, to see that no abuses are committed, and the standing regulations properly attended to; to hear and redress grievances, and examine and pass accounts relative to this and the other parts of the service. Agents for prisoners are also established in all proper places.

Office. The transport office is in Dorset-square, Westminster.

Convoy. The right of a sovereign to prevent any of his subjects

ſubjects from incurring the danger of being captured by an enemy, even though deſire of gain, or want of judgment, ſhould render them unmindful of the peril, is evident, and the only effectual way of inſuring this end at ſea, is by the appointment of ſhips of force to accompany mercantile ſquadrons, for their protection. So long ago as the year 1336, Edward I. ordered that the merchant veſſels ſhould proceed on their voyages in large bodies for mutual ſafeguard, and on ſeveral ſubſequent occaſions, he appointed armed convoys. In ſucceeding ages, this wholeſome practice was continued and improved; but ſtill the hope of extraordinary gain, from an opportune arrival and an expeditious voyage, rendered many indifferent to danger, and it was common in time of war to *run it*, as it was called, the profit forming a great allurement, and the ſhip being ſtill inſurable, though at an advanced premium. In 1798, parliament thinking it neceſſary to aboliſh this practice, prohibited ſhips from ſailing without convoy, except in certain caſes. The commander of every veſſel ſailing under the protection of a convoy is required to uſe his beſt endeavours to continue with the convoy; and if he ſails without, or wilfully ſeparates from the protecting ſhip during the paſſage, without leave obtained from the commanding officer of the convoy, he ſhall forfeit 1000*l*., or, if naval ſtores form any part of his cargo, 1500*l*.; but the courts are authorized to mitigate theſe penalties in their diſcretion, ſo as not to bring them below 50*l*. Moreover, all policies of inſurance, wherein the commander ſailing without convoy, or deſerting convoy, or any perſon intereſted in the veſſel directing, or being inſtrumental in, ſuch deſertion of convoy, is concerned, are declared null and void; and every underwriter making any ſettlement on ſuch a policy forfeits 200*l*. The officers of the cuſtoms are alſo directed not to clear out any veſſel, till the commander give bond with proper ſecurity not to ſail without, nor to deſert, his convoy at ſea Veſſels not required to be regiſtered, thoſe licenſed by the admiralty to ſail without convoy, or proceeding with due diligence to join a convoy, or bound to or from Ireland, or from any one port to another within Great Britain, thoſe in the ſervice of the Eaſt India company, the Hudſon's Bay company, and in ballaſt, are exempted from the obligations and penalties of this act. Neither are ſhips, coming from foreign parts, where no convoy may have been appointed, liable to trouble or cenſure for ſailing without one. Every commander of a merchant veſſel is required to provide proper flags, vanes, and other articles neceſſary for making ſignals; to have a board ſtuck up in a convenient place on board, containing that part of the act, 33 Geo. III. c. 66, for manning the navy, &c. which makes cap-

taina

tains of merchant ships under convoy liable to be articled in the high court of admiralty, for disobeying signals or deserting convoy; and, in case of being boarded by an enemy, to destroy all instructions relating to the convoy. It was in consideration of this additional protection, that the tax already mentioned, called convoy duty, was imposed.

DUTY OF THE SHIPS CONVOYING. Commanders are to give instructions to their convoy; and to send a list of them to the secretary of the admiralty before they sail. They are to receive no gratification; to keep in sight of, and protect the ships; to inform against masters who misbehave, and to wear a top-light. The commander in chief may order his signals to be repeated by other ships under his command, if he thinks fit. Different convoys are to keep company, as long as their courses lie together; and, on those occasions, the eldest commander of a convoy is superior. Commanders of different convoys are to wear lights, and repeat signals, as flag officers. Convoys are to sail like divisions: and signals are to be made at separation. Commanders of convoys are to take under their care ships of his majesty's allies or friends.

TRINITY HOUSE. Several establishments and regulations of the utmost importance to the navy are under the guardianship of the corporation of the Trinity House, of which, and its dependent charities, the following is an account. The society of the Trinity House was founded at Deptford in 1515, by Sir Thomas Spert, knight, commander of the great ship Henry Grace de Dieu, and comptroller of the navy to Henry VIII. for the regulation of seamen, and the convenience of ships and mariners on the coast, and incorporated by the above-mentioned prince, who confirmed to them, not only the rights and privileges of the company of mariners of England, but their several possessions at Deptford, which, together with the grants of queen Elizabeth and Charles II. were also confirmed by letters patent of the first of James II. in the year 1685, by the name of "the master, "wardens, and assistants of the guild or fraternity of the most "glorious and undivided Trinity, and of St. Clements in the "parish of Deptford Strond, in the county of Kent." This corporation is governed by a master, four wardens, eight assistants, and eighteen elder brothers; but the inferior members of the fraternity, named younger brethren, are of an unlimited number; for every master or mate, expert in navigation, may be admitted as such; and these serve as a continual nursery to supply the vacancies among the elder brethren when removed by death or otherwise. The master, wardens, assistants, and elder brethren, are by charter invested with the following powers: that of examining the mathematical children of Christ's Hospital;

pital; the examining of the masters of his majesty's ships; the appointing pilots to conduct ships into and out of the river Thames: and the amercing all such as shall presume to act as masters of ships of war, or pilots, without their approbation, in a pecuniary mulct of twenty shillings; settling the several rates of pilotage, and erecting light-houses and other sea-marks, on the several coasts of the kingdom, for the security of navigation, to which light-houses all ships pay one halfpenny a ton; granting licences to poor seamen, not free of the city, to row on the river Thames for their support, in the intervals of sea-service, or when past going to sea; the preventing of aliens from serving on board English ships, without their licence, upon the penalty of five pounds for each offence; punishing of seamen for desertion or mutiny in the merchants' service; and the hearing and determining the complaints of officers and seamen in the same employ, but subject to an appeal to the lords of the admiralty, or the judge of the court of admiralty. To this company belongs the *ballast office*, for clearing and deepening the Thames, by taking up a sufficient quantity of ballast, for the supply of all ships that sail out of the river; in which service sixty barges, with two men each, are constantly employed, and all ships that take in ballast, pay them one shilling a ton, for which it is brought to the ship's sides. In consideration of the increase of the poor of this fraternity, they are by their charter empowered to purchase in mortmain, lands, tenements, &c. to the amount of 500*l.* per annum; and also to receive charitable benefactions of well-disposed persons to the amount of 500*l.* per annum, clear of reprizes. There are annually relieved by this company about 3000 poor seamen, their widows and orphans, at the expence of 6000*l.* The ancient hall at Deptford, where their meetings were formerly held, was pulled down about the year 1787, and an elegant building erected for that purpose, in London near the Tower. The arms of this corporation are, Arg. a cross G. between four ships of three masts in full sail proper.

Trinity Hospitals. There are two hospitals at Deptford belonging to the corporation of the Trinity-House. The old one was built in the reign of Henry VIII. It consisted originally of twenty-one apartments; but being pulled down and rebuilt in 1788, the number was increased to twenty-five. This hospital adjoins to the church-yard. The other, which is in Church-street, was built about the latter end of the 17th century. Sir Richard Browne, in 1672, gave the ground, after the expiration of a short term; and captain William Maples, in 1680, gave 13,000*l.* towards the building. This hospital consists of fifty-six apartments, forming a spacious quadrangle; in the

the centre of which is placed a ſtatue of Captain Maples. On the eaſt ſide oppoſite the entrance, is a plain building, which ſerves both for a chapel and a hall. Here the brethren of the Trinity-houſe meet annually on Trinity-Monday, and afterwards go to Saint Nicholas's church, where they hear divine ſervice and a ſermon. The penſioners, in both hoſpitals, conſiſt of decayed pilots and maſters of ſhips, or their widows. The ſingle men and widows receive about 18*l.* per annum; the married men about 28*l.*

Light Houses and Sea Marks. Although by charter, the Trinity Houſe poſſeſſes the controul of theſe moſt uſeful and important eſtabliſhments, the erection of them, and of beacons for alarming the country on the approach of an enemy, is the undoubted prerogative of the crown. For this purpoſe the king has the excluſive power, by commiſſion, under his great ſeal, to cauſe them to be erected in fit and convenient places, as well upon the lands of the ſubject, as upon the demeſnes of the crown: which power is uſually veſted by letters patent in the office of lord high admiral. And by ſtatute 8 Eliz. c. 13. the corporation of the Trinity Houſe are impowered to ſet up any beacons or ſea-marks wherever they ſhall think them neceſſary; and if the owner of the land or any other perſon ſhall deſtroy them, or ſhall take down any ſteeple, tree, or other known ſea-mark, he ſhall forfeit 100*l.* or in caſe of inability to pay it, ſhall be *ipſo facto* outlawed. Of ſea-marks it is not neceſſary here to treat, ſince they are often caſual, and in themſelves unimportant, or deſigned for other uſes, as protuberances of ſoil, trees, ruins, churches, and almoſt every other conſpicuous fixed object, that can be imagined. On light-houſes, the munificence of government, and the ingenuity of architects have been inceſſantly employed, and ſome are conſpicuous monuments of ſkill, conducted to ſucceſs by perſeverance. They are placed in all ſituations on the coaſt where it is ſuppoſed they can conduce to ſafety; and the eſtabliſhments in them all are framed on a plan combining utility with economy.

Pilots. A pilot, in ancient times, was an officer permanently eſtabliſhed on board every ſhip, and who alone on all occaſions managed the helm, having, in fact, the government of the veſſel under the maſter; but this claſſical ſenſe is no longer applicable to practice, as pilots are now only taken on board for temporary ſervice, as when the ſhip has any dangerous place to paſs through, or is ſo near the ſhore that a more than ordinary ſkill is requiſite to bring her ſafe off; but otherwiſe, ſuch of the other mariners as are moſt capable of the function, are appointed to do it by turns. By various ſtatutes paſſed in the reigns

reigns of George I. and George II. persons are prohibited from acting as pilots in the Thames or Medway, or on several parts of the coast, unless examined by the master and wardens of the society of Trinity House, and approved and admitted into the said society, at a court of load manage, by the lord warden of the Cinque Ports, or his deputy, and the said master and wardens, under the penalty for the first offence of 10*l*.; for the second 20*l*.; and for every other offence 40*l*.; to be sued for and recovered by any one in the court of admiralty for the Cinque Ports, if the offending pilot live within the jurisdiction of that court, or else by action in any of the courts at Westminster; one moiety to go to the informer, and the other to the master and wardens of the Trinity House, to be distributed among their superannuated pilots, and widows of pilots. And the master, and such wardens are appointed to examine into the skill and ability of any person, on his being admitted as a pilot, take an oath, given them by the register of the said court of load manage, or his deputy, binding themselves impartially to examine the qualifications of the candidate, and to make a true return. The names, ages, and places of abode of pilots are to be yearly affixed in some public place, at the custom houses at London, and Dover or Deal, to which all persons may have recourse; and for not returning lists, the master and wardens forfeit 10*l*. But these acts do not prevent the master or mate of any ship or vessel, or any part owner, residing at Dover or Deal, or the Isle of Thanet, from piloting his own ship from any of the said places up the said rivers, nor subject any person, though not of that society, to the penalties before mentioned, who shall be employed by any master to pilot his vessel from the places aforesaid, when none of the Trinity-House pilots shall, within one hour after the arrival of the ship, be ready to pilot her; and masters of merchant ships may chuse their pilots; and for preventing exorbitant demands, fees are established according to her draught of water. The lord warden of the Cinque Ports is also empowered to nominate three persons there, to adjust differences between the master of any ship and others, where ships by bad weather are forced from their anchors and cables, for saving and bringing them ashore; and any person, though he is not a pilot, may assist a ship in distress. The pilots so admitted and licensed, are subject to the government of the Trinity-House, provided such regulations do not make the pilots keep terms or settle the rates of payment for their services; and pilots shall, within ten days after the receipt of their fees, pay the ancient dues, not exceeding one shilling in the pound, out of their hire, for the use of the poor of the corporation. And if pilots refuse to take the charge of any of his majesty's ships,

ſhips, when duly appointed, miſbehave themſelves in the conduct of any ſhips, or other part of their duty, or if they refuſe to obey any ſummons or orders of the corporation, then the general court, on examination, are required to recal the warrants granted to ſuch pilots; and if, after notice, they act as pilots, they ſhall be ſubject to the penalties inflicted on unlicenſed pilots.

It is to be obſerved that there are alſo Trinity-Houſes belonging to Dover, Deal, and the Iſle of Thanet, and to Kingſton upon Hull, and Newcaſtle upon Tyne, whoſe privileges are expreſsly protected againſt the operation of theſe ſtatutes, as are alſo thoſe of the Lord Mayor, commonalty, and citizens of London, and the juriſdiction of the admiralty.

Shipwreck. The dreadful calamity againſt which pilots are appointed as a protection, has been the ſubject of many laws calculated to reſtrain rapacity, and enſure for the wretched ſufferers the poſſeſſion of the reſidue of their effects. It has already been mentioned, (Vol. I. page 165,) that the property in wrecks is one of the rights of the crown. It was declared ſo by the prerogative ſtatute, 17 Edw. II. c. 11. and was ſo, long before, at the common law. It is worthy obſervation, how greatly the law of wrecks has been altered, and the rigour of it gradually ſoftened in favour of the diſtreſſed proprietors. Wreck by the antient common law was where any ſhip was loſt at ſea, and the goods or cargo were thrown upon the land; in which caſe theſe goods, ſo wrecked, were adjudged to belong to the king; for it was held, that, by the loſs of the ſhip, all property was gone out of the original owner; but it was firſt ordained by Henry I. that if any perſon eſcaped alive out of the ſhip, it ſhould be no wreck; and afterwards Henry II. by his charter, declared, that if on the coaſts of either England, Poictou, Oleron, or Gaſcony, any ſhip ſhould be diſtreſſed, and either man or beaſt ſhould eſcape or be found therein alive, the goods ſhould remain to the owners, if they claimed them within three months; otherwiſe they were to be eſteemed a wreck, and belong to the king, or other lord of the franchiſe. This law was again confirmed with improvements by Richard I.; who, in the ſecond year of his reign, not only eſtabliſhed theſe conceſſions, by ordaining, that the owner, if he was ſhip wrecked and eſcaped, ſhould enjoy all his effects, free and unmoleſted; but alſo that if he periſhed, his children, or, in default of them, his brethren and ſiſters ſhould retain the property; and, in default of brother or ſiſter, then the goods ſhould remain to the king. The law, as laid down by Bracton in the reign of Henry III. ſeems ſtill to have improved in its equity; for then, if not only a dog (for inſtance,) eſcaped by which the owner might be diſcovered, but if if any certain mark was set on the goods by which they might be known again, it was held to be no wreck; a regulation agreeable to reason; the rational claim of the king being only founded on this, that the true owner cannot be ascertained. Afterwards, in the statute of Westminster the first, the time of limitation of claims, given by the charter of Henry II. is extended to a year and a day, according to the usage of Normandy: and it enacts, that if a man, a dog, or a cat, escape alive, the vessel shall not be adjudged a wreck. These animals, as in Bracton, are only put for examples, for it is now held, that not only if any live thing escape, but if proof can be made of the property of any of the goods or lading which come to shore, they shall not be forfeited as wreck. The statute further ordains, that the sheriff of the county shall be bound to keep the goods a year and a day, (as in France for one year, agreeably to the maritime laws of Oleron, and in Holland for a year and a half,) that if any man can prove a property in them, either in his own right or by right of representation, they shall be restored to him without delay; but if no such property be proved within that time, they then shall be the king's. If the goods are of a perishable nature, the sheriff may sell them, and the money shall be liable in their stead. This revenue of wrecks is frequently granted out to lords of manors as a royal franchise: and if any one be thus entitled to wrecks on his own land, and the king's goods are wrecked thereon, the king may claim them at any time, even after the year and day. Wrecks, in their legal acceptation, are at present not very frequent; for if any goods come to land, it rarely happens, since the improvement of commerce, navigation, and correspondence, that the owner is not able to assert his property within the year and day limited by law. And in order to preserve this property entire for him, and, if possible, to prevent wrecks at all, our statutes have made many very humane regulations, in a spirit quite opposite to those savage laws, which formerly prevailed in all the northern regions of Europe, and a few years ago were still said to subsist on the coasts of the Baltic Sea, permitting the inhabitants to seize on whatever they could get as lawful prize; or as an author of their own expresses it, "*in naufragorum miseria et calamitate tanquam vultures ad predam currere.*" By the statute 27 Edw. III. c. 13, if any ship be lost on the shore, and the goods come to land (which cannot, says the statute, be called wreck) they shall presently be delivered to the merchants, paying only a reasonable reward to those that saved and preserved them, which is intitled *salvage*. Also by the common law, if any persons (other than the sheriff) take any goods so cast on shore, which are not legal wreck, the owners might have a commission to inquire and find them out, and compel them to make restitution.

restitution. And by statute 12 Anne, st. 2. c. 18. confirmed by the 4 Geo. I. c. 12, in order to assist the distressed, and to prevent the scandalous illegal practices on some of our sea-coasts, (too similar to those on the Baltic,) it is enacted, that all head officers and others of towns near the sea, shall, upon application made to them, summon as many hands as are necessary, and send them to the relief of any ship in distress, on forfeiture of 100*l.* and in case of assistance given, salvage shall be paid by the owners, to be assessed by three neighbouring justices. All persons that secrete any goods, shall forfeit their treble value; and if they wilfully do any act whereby the ship is lost or destroyed, by making holes in her, stealing her pumps, or otherwise, they are guilty of felony, without benefit of clergy. Lastly, by the statute 26 Geo. II. c. 19, plundering any vessel either in distress, or wrecked, and whether any living creature be on board, or not; such plundering, or preventing the escape of any person that endeavours to save his life, or wounding him with intent to destroy him, or putting out false lights, in order to bring any vessel into danger, are all declared to be capital felonies; in like manner as the destroying of trees, steeples, or other stated sea-marks, is punished by the statute 8 Eliz. c. 13, with a forfeiture of 100*l.* or outlawry. Moreover by the statute of George II. pilfering any goods cast on shore is declared to be petty larceny; and many other salutary regulations are made, for the more effectually preserving ships of any nation in distress. Voluntary shipwreck by captains or masters of ships, whether for the purpose of injuring the owners, or defrauding the underwriters, is felony, without benefit of clergy; and by a statute made in 1772, the same penalty is denounced against those who shall burn or destroy ships of war or naval stores.

INVENTIONS. In speaking of shipwreck it would be improper to omit noticing two inventions calculated to diminish the distresses attendant on those disasters, by facilitating the restoration of property and the preservation of life. The first of these inventions is the *diving bell*, of which a hint is to be found in the works of Roger Bacon in the thirteenth century; in 1680, a machine was used in the West Indies, which enabled Sir William Phipps to recover in a place where a Spanish fleet had been lost, nearly 200,000*l.* in pieces of eight; but in 1776, Mr. Spalding completed the diving bell, in which the divers can lower themselves down, without fear of being overturned by rocks, or other impediments at the bottom, and can re-ascend to the surface at pleasure: and they can also, when at the bottom, move to a considerable distance from the spot on which they lighted. Some improvements have since been made; but, on the whole, the reputation of the plan is annexed to the memory of Mr. Spalding, who unfortunately fell a victim to his own art in Ireland in 1783. The other invention above alluded to, is called the *life-boat*. A project of a boat which could not be sunk or overset was tried in France in 1771; but in 1789, Mr. Greathead of South Shields formed one which has proved so generally useful, and so perfect in its construction, that it is, after the most satisfactory testimonies of its utility, now generally adopted, and one is kept at most of the harbours in the kingdom.

Ports and Harbours. From the most ancient times, the king has possessed the prerogative of appointing *ports* and *havens*, or such places only, for persons and merchandize to pass into and out of the realm, as he in his wisdom sees proper. By the feudal law, all navigable rivers and havens were computed among the *regalia*, and were subject to the sovereign of the state, and in England it has always been holden, that the king is lord of the whole shore, and particularly is the guardian of the ports and havens which are the inlets and gates of the realm; and therefore so early as the reign of king John, we find ships seized by the king's officers for putting into a place that was not a legal port. But though the king had a power of granting the franchise of havens and ports, yet he had not the right of resumption, or of narrowing and confining their limits when once established; but any person might load or discharge his merchandize in any part of the haven; whereby the revenue of the customs was much impaired and diminished by fraudulent landings in obscure and private corners. This occasioned the statutes of 1. Eliz. c. 11. and 13 and 14 Chas. II. c. 11. § 14. which enable the crown by commission to ascertain the limits of all ports, and to assign proper wharfs and quays in each, for the exclusive landing and loading of merchandize. Although the royal prerogative in the appointment of ports is undoubted, still it is fettered like all other prerogatives, by the privilege of parliament over the national purse; and hence it is to be observed, that although in late times, the establishment, enlargement and improvement of ports and havens, have been very frequent, yet those measures have never been effected by the king alone, but on every occasion an act of parliament has passed for the purpose. To every port a court is appendant for the adjudication of matters arising within its jurisdiction, the presiding officer in which was anciently called the port-reeve, but in more modern times a mayor and bailiffs have been generally substituted.

Members and Creeks. These are inferior descriptions, and places subordinate to and dependant on ports. In this sense ports are places to which the officers of the customs are appropriated,

priated, and which include all the privileges and guidance of all members and creeks thereunto allotted. Members are places where anciently a custom-house has been kept, and officers or deputies attending, and are lawful places of exportation or importation. Creeks are places where commonly officers are or have been placed, by way of prevention only, and are not lawful places of exportation or importation, without particular licence from the port or member under which they are placed. Thus Gravesend is a creek, belonging to the port of London; Plymouth is a port, of which Falmouth is a member, and Saint Mawes a creek.

Cinque Ports. The term cinque ports has already occurred several times in treating of naval affairs, and although, in modern times, these places are not exclusively devoted to any maritime use, but are merely regarded as portions of the realm enjoying some peculiar privileges, yet in consideration of their ancient state, and the frequent mention of them in all matters of maritime history, it is judged most proper to give some account of them here. The cinque ports are ancient trading towns lying to the sea coast, and as they were instituted for the defence and safety of the kingdom, several liberties and privileges were granted them. At first, the privileged ports were but three, Dover, Sandwich, and Romney; but Hastings and Hithe were added by William the Conqueror, to which Winchelsea and Rye were subsequently adjoined. Each of them now sends representatives to parliament; and though seven in number, are still called cinque ports. The charters of these ports are indisputably traced to the time of Edward the Confessor, and they were confirmed by the Conqueror, and by several subsequent kings. An ancient record or custumal of Hythe, mentions the state and duties of the cinque ports, when they were but five, in these terms. *Hastings* shall find one and twenty ships, and in every ship, one and twenty men and a boy. The members of this port are the sea-shore in Seaforth, Pevensey, Hodeney, Winchelsea, Rye, Ihame, Bekesbourne, Grenge, Northie and Bulwerheth. *Romney* finds five ships, men as Hastings; members, Promhell, Lede, Eastwestone, Dengemerys, and Old Romney. *Hithe*, ships and men as Romney; member, Westhithe. *Dover*, ships and men as Hastings; members, Folkstone, Feversham, and St. Margaret's; not for the land, but the goods and chattels. *Sandwich*, ships and men as Romney and Hithe; members, Fordwich, Reculver, Serre, and Deal, not for the soil, but for the goods. Sum of ships 57, men 1187, and 57 boys. This service the barons of the cinque ports do acknowledge to owe to the king, upon summons yearly, (if it happens,) for the space of fifteen days together, at their own costs and charges, to to be reckoned from the firſt day they ſpread their ſails to depart for the place the king ordered; and to ſerve after the fifteen days at the king's pleaſure, he paying them. In proceſs of time the cinque ports grew ſo powerful, and by the poſſeſſion of a warlike fleet ſo audacious, that they made piratical excurſions in defiance of all public faith, and to the injury of Britiſh as well as foreign commerce; nay on ſome occaſions, they made war and formed confederacies, as ſeparate independent ſtates, but theſe irregularities were ſoon ſuppreſſed when government was ſtrong, and ſufficiently confident to exert its powers. So long as the mode of raiſing a navy by contributions from different towns continued, the cinque ports afforded an ample ſupply; but ſince that time their privileges have been preſerved, but their ſeparate or peculiar ſervices diſpenſed with.

The Lord Warden. William the Conqueror, conſidering Dover caſtle the key of England, gave the charge of the adjacent coaſt, with the ſhipping belonging to it, to the conſtable of Dover caſtle, with the title of *Warden of the Cinque Ports*; an office reſembling that of count of the Saxon coaſt, (*comes littoris Saxonici*) in the decline of the Roman power in this iſland. The lord warden has the authority of admiral in the cinque ports and their dependencies, with power to hold a court of admiralty; he has authority to hold courts both of law and equity, which will be noticed in a ſubſequent page; he is the general returning officer of all the ports, parliamentary writs being directed to him, on which he iſſues his precepts, and in many reſpects he was veſted with powers ſimilar to thoſe poſſeſſed by the heads of counties palatine. At preſent the efficient authority, charge or patronage of the lord warden is not very great, the ſituation is however conſidered very honorable, and the ſalary is 3000*l*. He has under him a lieutenant and ſome ſubordinate officers, and there are captains at Deal, Walmer, and Sandgate caſtles, Archcliff fort, and Moat's Bulwark.

Laws affecting the navy. As it is not intended in this diviſion of the work to treat on the admiralty court, nor to mention courts martial till thoſe affecting officers of the army can at the ſame time be conſidered it is only neceſſary here to mention one crime, and one regulation peculiarly affecting naval affairs, namely, piracy and quarantine.

Piracy. The crime of piracy, or robbery and depredation on the high ſeas, is an offence againſt the univerſal law of ſociety; a pirate being, according to Sir Edward Coke, an enemy of the human race. As therefore he has renounced all the benefits of ſociety and government, and has reduced himſelf afreſh to the ſavage ſtate of nature, by declaring war againſt all mankind, all mankind muſt declare war againſt him: ſo that every community

nity has a right by the rule of ſelf-defence, to inflict that puniſhment upon him which every individual in a ſtate of nature would have been otherwiſe entitled to do, for any invaſion of his perſon or perſonal property. By the ancient common law, piracy, if committed by a ſubject, was deemed a ſpecies of treaſon, being contrary to his natural allegiance; and by an alien to be felony only: but now ſince the ſtatute of treaſons, 25 Edward III. c. 2. it is held to be only felony in a ſubject. Formerly it was only cognizable by the admiralty courts; which proceed by the rules of the civil law; but it being inconſiſtent with the liberties of the nation, that any man's life ſhould be taken away, unleſs by the judgment of his peers, or the common law of the land, the ſtatute 28 Hen. VIII. c. 15. eſtabliſhed a new juriſdiction for this purpoſe; which proceeds according to the courſe of the common law. The offence of piracy, by common law, conſiſts in committing thoſe acts of robbery and depredation on the high ſeas, which if committed on land, would have amounted to felony there. But, by ſtatute, ſome other offences are made piracy alſo; as by 11 and 12 W. III. c. 7. if any natural born ſubject commits any act of hoſtility upon the high ſeas, againſt others of his majeſty's ſubjects, under colour of a commiſſion from any foreign power; this, though it would only be an act of war in an alien, ſhall be conſtrued piracy in a ſubject; and further, any commander, or other ſeafaring perſon, betraying his truſt, and running away with any ſhip, boat, ordnance, ammunition, or goods; or yielding them voluntarily to a pirate; or conſpiring to do theſe acts; or any perſon aſſaulting the commander of a veſſel to hinder him from fighting in defence of his ſhip, or confining him, or making or endeavouring to make a revolt on board; ſhall, for each of theſe offences be adjudged a pirate, felon, and robber, and ſhall ſuffer death, whether he be principal, or merely acceſſary by ſetting forth ſuch pirates, or abetting them before the fact, or receiving or concealing them or their goods after it; and the ſtatute 4 Geo. I. c. 11. expreſſly excludes the principals from the benefit of clergy. By the ſtatute 8 Geo. I. c. 24. the trading with known pirates, or furniſhing them with ſtores or ammunition, or fitting out any veſſel for that purpoſe, or in any wiſe conſulting, combining, confederating, or correſponding with them; or the forcibly boarding any merchant veſſel, though without ſeizing or carrying her off, and deſtroying or throwing any of the goods overboard, ſhall be deemed piracy: and ſuch acceſſaries to piracy as are deſcribed by the ſtatute of William, are declared to be principal pirates, and all pirates convicted by virtue of this act, are made felons without benefit of clergy. By the ſame ſtatutes alſo, (to encourage the defence of of merchant veſſels againſt pirates,) the commanders or ſeamen wounded, and the widows of ſuch ſeamen as are ſlain, in any engagement with a pirate, ſhall be entitled to a bounty, to be divided among them, not exceeding one fiftieth part of the value of the cargo on board, and ſuch wounded ſeamen ſhall be entitled to the penſion of Greenwich Hoſpital; which no other ſeamen are, except only ſuch as have ſerved in a ſhip of war. And if the commander ſhall behave cowardly, by not defending the ſhip, if ſhe carries guns or arms, or ſhall diſcharge the mariners from fighting, ſo that the ſhip falls into the hands of pirates, ſuch commander ſhall forfeit all his wages, and ſuffer ſix months impriſonment; laſtly by ſtatute 18 Geo. II. c. 30. any natural born ſubject, or denizen, who in the time of war ſhall comit hoſtilities at ſea againſt any of his fellow ſubjects, or ſhall aſſiſt an enemy on that element, is liable to be tried and convicted as a pirate.

QUARANTINE. The derivation of this word refers it to the term of forty days, which was preſcribed in law for other purpoſes as well as that of keeping perſons who might be infected with the plague apart from the ſociety. Many regulations had been made by ancient ſtatutes for preſerving the public health from the ill effects which might have ariſen, if thoſe who arrived from places where that dreadful malady prevails, had been ſuffered without precaution to mingle with ſociety; but theſe being found contradictory and inſufficient, an act was paſſed in 1800, repealing all former ſtatutes, and forming a new code on the ſubject. By this it is enacted, that all veſſels, perſons, and merchandizes, coming into any place in Great Britain, or the iſles of Guernſey, Jerſey, Alderney, Sark, or Man, from any place whence his majeſty may judge the plague may be brought, ſhall perform quarantine in ſuch manner as his majeſty, by his order in council, and notified by proclamation, or publiſhed in the London Gazette, ſhall direct; and until ſuch veſſel, perſon, and merchandize, ſhall have performed quarantine, no perſon or goods ſhall come or be brought on ſhore unleſs licenſed by his majeſty. And the commander of every veſſel liable to quarantine, who ſhall meet with any other veſſel at ſea, or within four leagues of the coaſt of Great Britain, or the ſaid iſles, ſhall hoiſt a ſignal to denote that his veſſel is liable to quarantine; and on failure thereof, ſuch commander or perſon having charge of ſuch veſſel ſhall forfeit 200*l.* The penalty on maſters of veſſels not liable to perform quarantine hoiſting ſuch ſignals is 50*l.*; and pilots conducting veſſels liable to quarantine into places not appointed, forfeit 100*l.* For the purpoſe of aſcertaining whether any ſuſpected veſſel has on board perſons liable to perform quarantine or not, the

 principal

principal officer of the cuſtoms, or perſon authoriſed to ſee quarantine duly performed, ſhall go off to ſuch veſſel, and at a convenient diſtance from the ſame, demand of the commander, or perſon having charge thereof, to give an anſwer in writing or otherwiſe, and upon oath or not, as he ſhall be required, to all ſuch queſtions as ſhall be put unto him in purſuance of any order of council; and upon refuſal the maſter, &c. ſhall forfeit 200*l*. for every ſuch offence. If the veſſel is liable to perform quarantine, the officers of any ſhips of war, or forts, or garriſons, or other officers whom it may concern, ſhall upon notice, compel ſuch veſſel to go to the appointed place; and the maſter of every ſuch veſſel, coming from any place viſited with the plague, or having any infected perſon on board, and concealing the ſame, ſhall be guilty of felony without benefit of clergy. The maſter is alſo obliged under a penalty of 500*l*. to deliver to the chief officer appointed to ſee quarantine performed, certain documents, and a ſchedule of his cargo, and if he afterward fail to produce any of the articles ſpecified, he forfeits not more than 500*l*. nor leſs than 100*l*. And if the maſter of any veſſel liable to perform quarantine ſhall himſelf quit, or knowingly permit any ſeaman or paſſenger to quit ſuch veſſel before ſuch quarantine ſhall be performed, unleſs by a proper licence, or ſhall not, within a convenient time after notice, cauſe ſuch veſſel and lading to be conveyed into the place appointed to perform quarantine, he ſhall forfeit 500*l*.; and if any perſon ſhall ſo quit ſuch ſhip contrary to the true meaning of this act, any perſon whatſoever, by any neceſſary force, may compel ſuch perſon to return on board, who ſhall be impriſoned for ſix months, and ſhall alſo forfeit 200*l*. Veſſels having performed quarantine in foreign parts, are not to land goods liable to infection, without directions from the privy council, under penalty of 200*l*. And all perſons liable to perform quarantine ſhall be ſubject to the orders of the officers authorized to direct the performance thereof, who may inforce obedience thereto, and in caſe of neceſſity call in others to aſſiſt, who are required to aſſiſt accordingly; and may compel all perſons liable to perform quarantine to repair, and to convey all goods comprized in any order made as aforeſaid, to the lazaret, or place appointed in that behalf; and if any perſon ſhall neglect to duly repair to the place ſo appointed, or ſhall eſcape therefrom, he ſhall be deemed guilty of felony without benefit of clergy. And if any officer of the cuſtoms, or other perſon employed concerning quarantine ſhall be guilty of any wilful breach or neglect of duty, he ſhall forfeit his office, and alſo 100*l*.; and if he ſhall deſert from his duty, or knowingly permit any perſon, veſſel, or goods to depart or be conveyed out of the lazaret, ſhip, or place appointed, unleſs by by an order of council, or ſhall give a falſe certificate, he ſhall be guilty of felony without benefit of clergy; and if any ſuch officer ſhall wilfully damage any goods performing quarantine under his direction, he ſhall be liable to treble damages and coſts of ſuit. And if any ſound perſon ſhall enter any lazaret, he ſhall perform quarantine; and if he ſhall return from thence (unleſs duly licenſed), or ſhall eſcape, or attempt to eſcape, he ſhall be guilty of felony without benefit of clergy. After the quarantine has been duly performed, and certified, the veſſel is under no further conſtraint.

THE ARMY.

Prerogative. The king as generaliſſimo of the whole kingdom has the ſole power of raiſing and regulating armies, as well as fleets. This prerogative indeed was diſputed and claimed, contrary to all reaſon and precedent, by the long parliament of Charles I. but, on the reſtoration of his ſon, was ſolemnly declared by the ſtatute 13 Chas. II. c. 6. to be in the king alone: for that the ſole ſupreme government and command of the militia within all his majeſty's realm and dominions, and of all forces by ſea and land, and of all forces and places of ſtrength, ever was and is the undoubted right of his majeſty, and his royal predeceſſors, kings and queens of England; and that both or either houſe of parliament cannot, nor ought to, pretend to the ſame. This ſtatute, it is obvious to obſerve, extends not only to fleets and armies, but alſo to forts, and other places of ſtrength, within the realm; the ſole prerogative as well of erecting, as manning and governing of which, belongs to the king in his capacity of general of the kingdom: and all lands were formerly ſubject to a tax, for building caſtles, wherever the king thought proper. This was one of the three things, from contributing to the performance of which no hands were exempted; and therefore called by our Saxon anceſtors the *trinoda neceſſitas: ſc. pontis reparatio, arcis conſtructio, et expeditio contra hoſtem.* And this they were called upon to do ſo often, that, as Sir Edward Coke from M. Paris aſſures us, there were in the time of Henry II. 1115 caſtles ſubſiſting in England. The inconveniences of which, when granted out to private ſubjects, the lordly barons of thoſe times, were ſeverely felt by the whole kingdom; for as William of Newburgh remarks in the reign of king Stephen, "*erant in Angliæ quodammodo tot reges vel potius tyranni, quot domini caſtellorum;*" but it was felt by none more ſenſibly than by the two ſucceeding princes, John and Henry III. And therefore the greateſt part of them being demoliſhed in the barons' wars, the kings of after times have been very cautious of suffering them to be rebuilt in a fortified manner: and Sir Edward Coke lays it down, that no subject can build a castle, or house of strength embattled, without the licence of the king; because of the danger which might ensue, if every man at his pleasure might do it. In this precaution indeed the public liberty is most materially interested; a nation familiarised to the sight of military strong holds, and unused to travel, but under the regulations of garrison towns, is subdued without power to struggle: that which a lord can do is not forbidden to the king; and it is said to have been among the compendious hints which a subtle courtier gave to an English monarch, for the complete establishment of tyranny, that he should make all the roads in the kingdom pass through or begin and end at garrison towns. On the other hand, that safety against foreign irruption, or local violence may not be precarious, the statute called the bill of rights has provided that all the subjects of the realm may have arms for their defence suitable to their condition and degree, and such as are allowed by law.

General progress of the Army. In a land of liberty it is extremely dangerous to make a distinct order of the profession of arms. In absolute monarchies it is necessary for the safety of the prince, and arises from the main principle of their constitution, which is that of governing by fear: but in free states, the profession of a soldier, and taken singly merely as a profession, is justly an object of jealousy. In these no man should take up arms, but with a view to defend his country and its laws: he puts not off the citizen when he enters the camp; but it is because he is a citizen, and would wish to continue so, that he makes himself for a while a soldier. The laws, therefore, and constitution of these kingdoms, know no such state as that of a perpetual standing soldier, bred up to no other profession than that of war: and it was not till the reign of Henry VII. that the kings of England had so much as a guard about their persons, and then the establishment consisted only of fifty yeomen of the guards, whom the king appointed in 1486.

In the time of our Saxon ancestors, as appears from Edward the Confessor's laws, the military force of this kingdom was in the hands of the dukes or heretochs, who were constituted through every province and county; being taken out of the principal nobility, and such as were most remarkable for being wise, loyal, and valiant. Their duty was to lead and regulate the English armies, with a very unlimited power, as to them should seem fitting, for the honour of the crown, and welfare of the realm. And because of this great power they were elected by the people in their full assembly, or folkmote. This large share

ſhare of power, thus conferred by the people, though intended to preſerve the liberty of the ſubject, was perhaps unreaſonably detrimental to the prerogative of the crown: and accordingly we find a very ill uſe made of it by Edric duke of Mercia, in the reign of king Edmund Ironſide; who, by his office of duke or heretoch, was entitled to a large command in the king's army, and by his repeated treacheries at laſt transferred the crown to Canute the Dane.

It ſeems univerſally agreed by all hiſtorians that king Alfred firſt ſettled a national militia in this kingdom, and by his prudent diſcipline made all the ſubjects of his dominion ſoldiers: but we are unfortunately left in the dark as to the particulars of this his ſo celebrated regulation; though, from what was laſt obſerved, the dukes ſeem to have been left in poſſeſſion of too large and independent a power: which enabled duke Harold on the death of Edward the Confeſſor, though a ſtranger to the royal blood, to mount the throne in prejudice of Edgar Atheling, the rightful heir.

On the Norman conqueſt, the feudal law was introduced in all its rigour, the whole of which is built on a military plan; all the lands in the kingdom were divided into what were called knight's fees, in number 60,215; and for every knight's fee, a knight or ſoldier, *miles*, was bound to attend the king in his wars, for forty days in a year; in which ſpace of time, before war was reduced to a ſcience, the campaign was generally finiſhed, and a kingdom either conquered or victorious. By theſe means the king had, without any expence, an army of ſixty thouſand men, always ready at his command. This perſonal ſervice in proceſs of time degenerated into pecuniary commutations or aids, and the laſt traces of the military part of the feudal ſyſtem were aboliſhed at the reſtoration, by ſtatute 12 Chas. II. c. 24.

In the mean time the kingdom was not left wholly without defence in caſe of domeſtic inſurrections, or the proſpect of foreign invaſion. Beſides thoſe who by their military tenures were bound to perform forty days ſervice in the field, firſt the aſſize of arms, enacted 27 Hen. II. and afterwards the ſtatute of Wincheſter, under Edward I. obliged every man, according to his eſtate and degree, to provide a determinate quantity of ſuch arms as were then in uſe, in order to keep the peace; and conſtables were appointed in all hundreds by the latter ſtatute, to ſee that ſuch arms were provided. Theſe weapons were changed by the ſtatute 4 and 5 Ph. and Mary, c. 2. into others of more modern ſervice; but both this and the former proviſions were repealed in the reign of James I. While theſe continued in force, it was uſual from time to time,

for

for our princes to iſſue commiſſions of array, and ſend into every county, officers in whom they could confide, to muſter and array (or ſet in military order) the inhabitants of every diſtrict; and the form of the commiſſion of array was ſettled in parliament in the 5th of Hen. IV. ſo as to prevent the inſertion of any new penal cauſes; but it was alſo provided that no man ſhould be compelled to go out of the kingdom at any rate, nor out of his ſhire but in caſes of urgent neceſſity; nor ſhould provide ſoldiers unleſs by conſent of parliament. About the reign of Henry VIII. or his children, lieutenants began to be introduced as ſtanding repreſentatives of the crown; to keep the counties in military order; for we find them mentioned as known officers in the ſtatute 4 and 5 Ph. and M. c. 3. though they had not been then long in uſe, for Camden ſpeaks of them in the time of queen Elizabeth, as extraordinary magiſtrates conſtituted only in times of difficulty and danger; but the introduction of theſe commiſſions of lieutenancy, which contained in ſubſtance the ſame powers as the old commiſſions of array, cauſed the latter to fall into diſuſe.

In this ſtate things continued, till the repeal of the ſtatutes of armour in the reign of James I. after which, when Charles I. had, during his northern expeditions, iſſued commiſſions of lieutenancy, and exerted ſome military powers, which, having been long exerciſed, were thought to belong to the crown, it became a queſtion in the long parliament, how far the power of the militia did inherently reſide in the king; being now unſupported by any ſtatute, and founded only on immemorial uſage. This queſtion, long agitated with great heat and reſentment on both ſides, became at length the immediate cauſe of the fatal rupture between the king and his parliament; the two houſes not only denying this prerogative of the crown, the legality of which perhaps might be ſomewhat doubtful; but alſo ſeizing into their own hands, the entire power of the militia, the illegality of which ſtep could never be any doubt at all.

Soon after the reſtoration of Charles II. when the military tenures were aboliſhed, it was thought proper to recognize the ſole right of the crown to govern and command the militia, and to put the whole into a more regular method of military ſubordination: and the order, in which the militia now ſtands by law, and which will ſoon claim particular attention, is principally built on the ſtatutes which were then enacted.

When the nation was engaged in war, more veteran troops and more regular diſcipline were eſteemed to be neceſſary, than could be expected from a mere militia; and therefore at ſuch times more rigorous methods were put in uſe for the raiſing of armies, and the due regulation and diſcipline of the ſoldiery: which

which are to be looked upon only as temporary excrefcences bred out of the diftemper of the ftate, and not as any part of the permanent and perpetual laws of the kingdom. For martial law, which is built upon no fettled principles, but is entirely arbitrary in its decifions, is, as Sir Matthew Hale obferves, in truth and reality no law, but fomething indulged rather than allowed as a law. The neceffity of order and difcipline in an army is the only thing which can give it countenance; and therefore it ought not to be permitted in time of peace, when the king's courts are open for all perfons to receive juftice according to the laws of the land. The petition of right moreover enacts, that no foldier fhall be quartered on the fubject without his own confent; and that no commiffion fhall iffue to proceed within this land according to martial law. And whereas after the reftoration, Charles II. kept up about five thoufand regular troops, by his own authority, for guards and garrifons; which James II. by degrees increafed to no lefs than thirty thoufand, all paid from his own civil lift; it was made one of the articles of the bill of rights, that the raifing or keeping a ftanding army within the kingdom in time of peace, unlefs it be with confent of parliament, is againft law. But, as the fafhion of keeping ftanding armies, which was firft introduced by Charles VII. in France, in 1445, has of late years univerfally prevailed over Europe, it has alfo, for many years paft, been annually judged neceffary by our legiflature, for the fafety of the kingdom and the defence of its poffeffions, to maintain even in time of peace a ftanding body of troops, under the command of the crown; who are however *ipfo facto* difbanded at the expiration of every year, unlefs continued by parliament.

In fact, the indifpenfable duty of obferving and regulating our conduct by the events which are daily paffing around us, requires that the rigour of the principle againft ftanding armies fhould be relaxed, or perhaps that the axiom itfelf fhould receive from practice a new conftruction. It may fafely be affirmed that it is illegal for the monarch by his own prerogative, or out of any monies which he may poffefs in his own right, or with which he may be fupplied by any other means than by the authority of parliament, to keep up a ftanding army; but that which parliament declares to be law, is legal, and the popular fafety now requires that the popular jealoufy fhould no longer be directed againft a regular and well trained military force, maintained even in time of peace in very confiderable numbers, and attended with all the means of giving perfection to fuch an eftablifhment, as places for the exercife of artillery, fchools and colleges for the inftruction of youth intended for the military profeffion, and all other requifites for the attainment of knowledge and inforcement

of

of discipline. The safety of the realm demands that a military body of sufficient magnitude and perfectly taught, should always be ready for our protection against sudden or premeditated design, but the safety of the subject also requires that the checks on the power of the crown with respect to military bodies, should be most tenaciously maintained. The right of parliament to fix the number and issue the sums required for pay, the annual mutiny act, the prohibition to extend martial law beyond its proper bounds, and the strict observance of all laws which tend to prevent the soldier from being effectually separated from the citizen, will ever afford ample security against the incroachments of prerogative, while the valour and loyalty of the military body will be sufficient to protect the realm, and divert into other quarters the fury of hostile operations. Ever since the revolution the standing military force has been augmenting, and, far from producing any evil, war has never been undertaken, but regrets have been expressed that its extent was not greater, and schemes are perpetually imagined for rendering it more ample and efficient. In the reign of William III. the standing force in peace was 25,000 men; Queen Anne, after the peace of Utrecht, was obliged, in order to garrison her conquests, and in conformity with general practice, to maintain a still larger force; after the peace of Aix-la-chapelle in 1748, the troops on the English and Irish establishments, exclusive of those on foreign stations, amounted to 26,000; after the peace in 1763, domestic and foreign duty demanded 40,000; on the peace in 1783 the force was fixed at 50,000, and in 1787 advanced to 60,000. After the great struggle against France in the war begun in 1793, and on the conclusion of peace at Amiens, in 1802, arrangements to reduce the war establishment were made; but the reduction was very trifling. The second battalions of those regiments that received drafts from the militia, were, according to agreement, discharged; the fencibles were disbanded; and the militia disembodied.—Most of the foreign corps were discharged; the invalid companies were disbanded; and in their stead seven battalions, from the invalids and out-pensioners, incorporated. These new regulations being thus arranged, the standing army of Great Britain rested at thirty five regiments of horse and dragoons; eight battalions of artillery besides their followers; seven battalions of foot guards; 96 regiments of infantry of 102 battalions; nine West India regiments; seven garrison battalions; and the regiment called the Queen's Germans, that so highly distinguished itself in Egypt; the whole amounting to about 75,000 men.

War Establishment. Thus far, following in general, the

steps of the learned commentator on the laws of England, the army has been viewed as affecting the internal policy of the realm, and as connected in time of peace with the general state and government of the kingdom. As a war establishment, it is necessary to analyze its various parts, and to consider its formation, regulations, pay and allowances, and official establishments.

FORMATION. The general or gross division of the military force, is into regulars and irregulars, the former composed of troops inlisted for life or during his Majesty's pleasure, to be employed on all services, and paid out of funds assigned for that purpose by parliament; the latter of militia, volunteers, fencibles, and other troops varying in some essential particulars from the regulars. Each of these bodies is again composed of cavalry, or men on horseback, and infantry or soldiers on foot; besides which there are regiments of artillery, and corps of engineers. The regular cavalry are divided into life guards, of which there are two regiments; royal horse guards, one regiment; dragoon guards, seven regiments; and dragoons, heavy and light, twenty four regiments: of foot guards there are three regiments; and of foot soldiers exclusive of guards, one hundred regiments, besides eight West India regiments; three garrison battalions; nine royal veteran battalions; four regiments of foreign fencible cavalry, and several miscellaneous corps, as new South Wales and Royal Africans; and the foreign regiments, as the King's German legion, the regiments of De Rolle, Dillon, Chasseurs Britanniques, and Corsican rangers, and of artillery and engineers each a regiment. Of these forces, it is not possible to state the exact amount, but it is calculated to exceed 260,000 men. The militia, and other irregular forces are supposed to carry the number of men armed for the defence of the country and its possessions, exclusive of the navy and marines, beyond 800,000 men.

RANK. The degrees of rank of commissioned officers in the army are; in the first division, called that of general officers, field marshals, generals, and lieutenant and major generals; in the division of field officers, colonels not being general officers, lieutenant colonels, and majors; captains not having higher rank in the army form a class by themselves, and under them is the division called subaltern officers, consisting of lieutenants, cornets of horse and ensigns of foot. The general duties of officers consist in exercising, and submitting to command, according to their stations, and in attending with scrupulous exactness to all the regulations of discipline and all the rules of social propriety; their failure in any of the former, as, being absent without leave, and many other instances, would subject them to be superseded, and with respect to the latter, the ſyſtem of honour is carried to the higheſt degree of ſtrictneſs; a ſyſtem which is abſolutely neceſſary to preſerve that exactneſs of behaviour which makes every one free and equal, without danger of encroachment, and properly reſpectful without ſuſpicion of fear, or any other unworthy motive. The ſeparate duty of each individual officer is not eaſily diſcriminated, and the recital would lead to explanations too technical for this work. There are alſo in the regiments, both of cavalry and infantry, officers of an inferior deſcription, called non-commiſſioned, as ſerjeants and corporals.

Comparative Rank. The Comparative rank of officers in the navy and army is as follows:

Navy.		*Army.*
Admiral of the fleet	-	equal with Field-marſhal.
Admirals	- -	equal with Generals.
Vice-admirals	-	equal with Lieutenant-generals.
Rear Admirals	-	equal with Major-generals.
Commodores, and firſt captains to commanders in chief		equal with Brigadier-generals.
Captains of three years poſt		equal with Colonels.
Other poſt Captains	-	equal with Lieutenant-colonels.
Commanders	-	equal with Majors, and
Lieutenants	-	equal with Captains.

Privates. In treating of the ſituation of private ſoldiers, it will be neceſſary, in many points, to conſider the mode of recruiting the army, and the particular regulations to which its members are ſubject.

Recruiting. For augmenting or ſupplying the ranks of the regular army, no compulſory means, like thoſe uſed to ſailors, can be reſorted to; but parties, under the command of commiſſioned officers, are employed in the various portions of the kingdom, called recruiting diſtricts, for the purpoſe of engaging men to ſerve, by the offer of ſuch bounty as the government thinks proper to allow.

Paymasters of recruiting districts. For each recruiting diſtrict, there is a *paymaſter* appointed by ſpecial military commiſſion, under the ſign manual, and not removeable, except by command of the king, or by ſentence of a court-martial. He is amenable in the ordinary courſe, to martial law, for every part of his conduct; but he is not liable to receive orders touching the manner of making up his pay liſts and accompts, unleſs under a ſpecial inſtruction in writing, from the commander in chief of the forces, the ſecretary at war, or the inſpector-general of the recruiting ſervice. His allowance is ſimilar to that of a captain, but he has no military rank.

Recruiting Officers. For the purpofe of obtaining recruits, active non-commiffioned officers are employed, under the name of recruiting-ferjeants; and in many places crafty perfons are difperfed, who, by every pretence and every artifice, allure the unwary to embrace the military life, and for this a compenfation is allowed. Thefe perfons, in vulgar phrafe, are called crimps. Houfes are alfo opened in towns and cities, under the title of recruiting-offices, where the fame arts are employed, and with which the perfons, called crimps, have daily communication.

Inlisting. To prevent thofe, who in an incautious moment, may have made an engagement of which they afterward repent, from being permanently fettered, againft their better judgment, the law has provided, that when any perfon fhall be inlifted, he fhall, in four days, but not fooner than twenty-four hours, be carried before the next juftice, or chief magiftrate of a town corporate (not being an officer in the army), and before him fhall be at liberty to declare his diffent to fuch inlifting; and on fuch declaration, and returning the inlifting-money, and paying 20*s.* for the charges expended on him, he fhall be forthwith difcharged, in prefence of fuch magiftrate: but if he fhall refufe or neglect, in twenty-four hours, to return, and pay fuch money as aforefaid, he fhall be confidered as inlifted. If he declares that he voluntarily inlifted himfelf, the juftice, or chief magiftrate, reads over, or in his prefence caufes to be read, a certain portion of the articles of war, and lets him take the oath of fidelity, and another, declaring his age, and place of birth, and his freedom from rupture, fits, and fome other diforders, and that he is not an apprentice, nor belongs to any other regiment, regulars, or militia. But if any perfon fhall receive the inlifting-money, knowing it to be fuch, and fhall abfcond, or fhall refufe to go before a magiftrate, he fhall be deemed inlifted, as if he had taken the oath. And when any corps beyond feas is relieved, in order to return home, fuch of the men as chufe it may be inlifted, and incorporated with thofe appointed to remain; the occafion of quitting fuch former corps to be recited in the inlifting certificate, in order to protect fuch foldier from fufpicion of defertion.

Muster. The recruit, having been attefted before a magiftrate, is to be muftered by a commiffary, or mufter-mafter, previous to his being received into a regiment. For the prevention of frauds in this part of the fervice, it is directed, that every commiffary or mufter-mafter, upon any mufter to be made, fhall, on penalty of 50*l.* and the lofs of his office, give convenient notice to the mayor, or other chief officer, of the place where the foldiers are quartered; (except Weftminfter ſter and Southwark, where it muſt be two magiſtrates, neither of whom is an officer in the army;) and the mayor, or other chief officer ſhall be preſent, and give his utmoſt aſſiſtance for the diſcovering of any falſe muſter; and no muſter-roll ſhall be allowed, unleſs ſigned by ſuch mayor, or other officer: but, if he ſhall not attend, or refuſe to ſign, without giving ſufficient reaſon; then the commiſſary may proceed, and ſuch muſter-roll ſhall be allowed, though not ſigned, provided that oath be made, and the muſter-roll produced before, and ſigned by a juſtice in 48 hours afterward; he certifying that there appears no ſufficient objection to it. And if any perſon ſhall give a falſe certificate, to excuſe any ſoldier from muſter, or ſervice, on pretence that he is employed on ſome other duty of the regiment, or of ſickneſs, being in priſon, or on furlough, he ſhall forfeit 50*l.* and be caſhiered, and diſabled to hold any military office. No certificate ſhall excuſe the abſence of any ſoldier, but for the reaſons abovementioned, or one of them; and the commiſſary ſhall ſet down on the roll, at the time of taking the muſter, the reaſon of ſuch abſence, and by whom certified: and not to ſet down any ſuch excuſe, without view of ſuch certificate. Every officer that ſhall make any falſe muſter of man or horſe, and every commiſſary, muſter-maſter, or other officer, who ſhall wittingly allow, or ſign the muſter-roll wherein any ſuch falſe muſter is contained, or ſhall take any reward for muſtering, or ſigning muſter-rolls, ſhall be caſhiered, and diſabled. If any perſon ſhould be falſely muſtered, or offer himſelf to be falſely muſtered; he ſhall on proof be committed to the houſe of correction for ten days; and if any perſon ſhall wittingly furniſh a horſe to be muſtered, he ſhall, if the property of the perſon furniſhing, be forfeited to the informer; otherwiſe, the offender ſhall forfeit to the informer 20*l.* or, for want of ſufficient diſtreſs, be committed to the common jail for three months, or be publickly whipped; and the informer, if a ſoldier, ſhall be diſcharged, if he demands it. But fictitious names, allowed by his majeſty's order upon the muſter-rolls for the maintenance of widows of officers who loſt their lives in the late war, or during the late rebellion, ſhall not be conſtrued a falſe muſter.

Recruiting Staff. The army depot for recruits was formerly at Chatham: it is now in the Iſle of Wight, and a ſtaff for this branch of ſervice is eſtabliſhed, conſiſting of an inſpector-general, with an aſſiſtant, and aid-de-camp; a brigade-major, adjutant, quarter-maſter and paymaſter, a phyſician, and inſpector of hoſpitals, with a deputy, and a ſurgeon, with aſſiſtants and mates.

Billetting. It has already been mentioned as one of the op-

oppreſſions practiſed while the government of England was unſettled, that ſoldiers were ſent to live at free quarters on thoſe whoſe conduct or principles gave offence to government. Againſt this abuſe, it was enacted, by ſtatute 31 Ch. II. c. 1, that no officer, military or civil, nor any other perſon whatſoever, ſhall preſume to place, quarter, or billet any ſoldier on any ſubject or inhabitant of this realm, of any degree, quality, or profeſſion whatſoever, without his conſent; and every ſuch ſubject or inhabitant may refuſe to ſojourn or quarter any ſoldier, notwithſtanding any command, order, warrant, or billeting whatever. But by the mutiny act, which is renewed annually, and generally with little or no alteration, the conſtables, and other chief officers and magiſtrates of cities, towns, and villages, and other places, and in their default or abſence, any one juſtice inhabiting in, or near ſuch place, and no other, ſhall and may quarter and billet the officers and ſoldiers in inns, livery-ſtables, ale-houſes, victualling-houſes, and the houſes of ſellers of wine by retail to be drunk in their own houſes, or places thereunto belonging (other than perſons who keep taverns only, being free of the Vintners' company in London), and all houſes of perſons ſelling brandy, ſtrong waters, cyder, or metheglin, by retail, to be drunk in their houſes, and no other, and in no private houſes whatſoever; nor ſhall any more billets be ordered than there are effective ſoldiers; and if any conſtable, or ſuch like officer, or magiſtrate, ſhall preſume to quarter or billet any officer or ſoldier in any private houſe, without conſent, the owner or occupier ſhall have his remedy at law againſt ſuch officer or magiſtrate for damages; and if any military officer ſhall take upon him to quarter ſoldiers otherwiſe than by this act, or ſhall offer any menace or compulſion to any mayor, conſtable, or other civil officer, tending to deter and diſcourage any of them from doing their duty, he ſhall, on conviction before any two of the next juſtices, by the oath of two witneſſes, be *ipſo facto* caſhiered and diſabled to hold any military employment; provided the conviction be affirmed at the next quarter ſeſſions, and a certificate tranſmitted to the judge advocate, who ſhall certify it to the next court-martial. And if any perſon ſhall be aggrieved by having more ſoldiers billeted than in proportion to his neighbours, and complain to one juſtice, or if the perſon ſo billeting them be a juſtice, then if he complain to two juſtices, they may relieve him. The king's regiments of foot guards are to be in like manner billeted in Weſtminſter, or other parts of Middleſex, except the city of London, and Surry, including the borough of Southwark, and places adjacent to Weſtminſter; but this clauſe is conſtrued as not confining the foot-guards to theſe places, but only directing that if quartered there, the ſame rules muſt be obſerved as in other parts of the kingdom. If any conſtable, or other officer, neglect his duty in billeting for the ſpace of two hours, provided ſufficient notice has been given before of the arrival of the forces; or if he takes any reward to excuſe any one; or if any perſon liable refuſes to receive any ſoldiers, or to furniſh them, as required by this act, they incur a penalty, not exceeding 5*l.* nor leſs than forty ſhillings. And if any military officer takes money of any perſon for excuſing the quartering of ſoldiers, he ſhall be caſhiered, and incapacitated. Officers and ſoldiers, duly billeted, are to be received, and furniſhed with diet and ſmall beer, paying for the ſame, at a certain fixed, but very inadequate price. But if any perſon ſhall chuſe rather to furniſh them with candles, vinegar, and ſalt, and with either ſmall beer, or cyder, not exceeding five pints a day, *gratis*, and allow them the uſe of fire, and the neceſſary utenſils for the dreſſing and eating their meat, and ſhall give notice thereof to the commanding officer, and ſhall furniſh the ſame accordingly; in ſuch caſe, they ſhall provide their own victuals, and the officers ſhall pay the ſums out of the ſubſiſtence-money for diet and ſmall beer to ſuch ſoldiers, and not to the perſons on whom they are quartered; except on a march, or recruiting. In all places, where horſe or dragoons ſhall be quartered, the men and their horſes ſhall be billeted in one and the ſame houſe (except in caſe of neceſſity); and in no caſe there ſhall be leſs than one man billeted, where there ſhall be one or two horſes, nor leſs than two men where there ſhall be four horſes, and ſo in proportion; and each man ſhall be billeted as near his horſe as poſſible. Officers may remove, or exchange men or horſes with others quartered in the ſame town; provided the numbers ſo exchanged are equal: and the conſtables, or other officers, ſhall billet them accordingly.

Barracks. Such are the principal features of the regulation for billeting or quartering of ſoldiers, which has ever been deemed a grievous hardſhip on innkeepers, and no inconſiderable cauſe of diſorder and inſubordination among the troops. Yet, as an ancient cuſtom, it had many advocates, eſpecially among thoſe who looked with extreme jealouſy at any ſyſtem which appeared to ſeparate the ſoldiery from the people. In late years, however, the plan of building barracks for the reſidence of ſoldiers, has very much prevailed. Of this ſyſtem, the oppoſition to it, and the advantages derived from it, the following account was given by Mr. Roſe: "Another department, that of providing barracks for the troops, created a few years ago, has been the ſubject of repeated diſcuſſion in parliament, and of frequent obſervation without doors: every effort was uſed that ingenuity could deviſe to render the meaſure unpopular, and to impreſs on the public mind a perſuaſion, that immenſe ſums of money

money were lavished, without any apparent use or necessity. In a measure intimately connected with the safety and defence of the country, economy alone is not to be attended to: we are persuaded, however, the arrangement is to be justified, even on this ground, and that on an attentive consideration of the subject, it will be found there is a saving to the public during war of about 400,000*l.* a year by the system (after deducting the expences attending it), without taking into the calculation the great saving by the preservation of horses. In this, as in other instances, we must not lose sight of the nature of the war in which we are engaged; whatever reliance we may justly have on our navy, the glorious achievements of which have been above all praise, as well as beyond all example, and on the powerful aid of our yeomanry, incited by an unparalleled enthusiasm in the cause of their country, we should not neglect the attention due to our brave army and militia, at the same time we employ their services in the stations best calculated for our defence. In many parts of the country the troops could not have been kept on the coast in the winter, if barracks had not been provided; but what is most interesting to our feelings, and important to the state, is, the saving of the lives of the soldiers, by their being comfortably lodged in barracks instead of being exposed to the consequences of encampments, particularly, late in the year. The advantages accruing to the discipline and good conduct of the army, are obvious, even to common observers." To prove the benefits already derived from the plan, he subjoined to his work (edition 1799) the following table:

Statement of the comparative Expence of keeping Troops in Camp, in Quarters, and in Barracks.

Considering the present establishment of the army, the regiments of cavalry may be stated at 675, officers and men, each; and the infantry at 726; at which numbers it may be proper to take them: for, although there are many regiments on much higher establishments, yet, on the whole, the above appears to be a just average.

	£.	s.	d.
A regiment of cavalry of 675 men and officers, in camp for 160 days (the usual time for encampment) will cost -	11,200	0	0
The same in barracks for the same period -	4,123	0	0
Saving -	7,077	0	0
A regiment of infantry of 726 men, for 160 days, will cost in camp -	3,516	0	0
The same in barracks for the same period	1,000	0	0
Saving -	2,516	0	0

 There

There are in Great Britain; Guernſey, and Jerſey, &c. barracks for 107,359 men, and for 10,419 horſes; of which, ſufficient to contain 102,161 men and 8,218 horſes, are ſituated where camps muſt otherwiſe have been formed: it may therefore be ſtated, that if thoſe barracks had not been provided, the troops muſt have been placed in camp for 160 days.

	£.	s.	d.
Taking, conſequently, 8212 men and horſes, which will compoſe twelve regiments of cavalry, the ſaving, at 7,076*l.* 19*s.* 8*d.* each regiment, will be - -	84,923	0	0
And deducting the above cavalry from 120,161 men, there will remain 93,943 infantry, which will compoſe 128 regiments, at 2,515*l.* each, making -	321,920	0	0
Total ſaving in 160 days	406,843	0	0

The comparative expence of keeping troops in barracks and in quarters on the publicans, is 4*l.* 7*s.* 11¾*d.* for each horſe, and 3*s.* 0¾*d.* for each man per annum, leſs in the former caſe than in the latter, which, taken on the number before ſtated, of 10,419 horſes, and 107,359 men, will be 61,278*l.* 6*s.* 9*d.* per annum; from which ſhould be deducted the fair wear and tear of different articles. But as this calculation is made on the full iſſue of all the articles allowed in the barracks, and as there is a conſiderable ſaving made, in conſequence of the power veſted in the barrack-maſter-general, to give only what may be ſufficient, according to the conſtruction of the different barracks; and as there are other ſavings to the amount nearly of 10,000*l.* per annum, the whole may ſafely be taken at leaſt at 30,000*l.* per annum, and will leave the above ſum clear.

	£.	s.	d.
The annual ſaving therefore, between keeping men in quarters, and in barracks, will be in favour of the latter -	61,278	6	9
And adding thereto the ſaving of encampments - - - - - -	406,843	0	0
	468,121	6	9
Total expence of the barrack eſtabliſhment	30,712	0	0
The total ſaving by barracks annually will be	437,409	6	9

The above ſtatement is independent of the original coſt of the buildings and ſupply of ſtores; but it muſt appear, that

6 the

the paſt ſavings have gone very far towards defraying the ſame.

The following, according to the lateſt publiſhed account, is a Liſt of Barracks in Great Britain, with the number of men which can be received in each.

BARRACKS.		Cavalry. Officers & men.	Cavalry. Horſes.	Infantry. Officers & men.	Infantry. Horſes.
Aberdeen	N. B.	—	—	579	4
Alderney		—	—	434	—
Alwick Green, Bognor		—	—	758	—
Arundel		342	340	—	—
Aſhford		—	—	2188	40
Ayr	N. B.	—	—	464	4
Barnſtaple		62	63	—	—
Barn Rock		—	—	84	—
Battle		—	—	943	120
Belhaven		326	320	—	—
Bellericay		—	—	206	—
Berryhead		—	—	1050	20
Berwick		—	—	642	—
Bexhill		—	—	939	50
Birmingham		188	188	—	—
Blackneſs	N. B.	—	—	51	—
Blatchington		234	219	724	—
Bogner, (ſee Alwick)		—	—	—	—
Bopeep, (ſee Haſtings)		—	—	—	—
Braybourn Lees		185	170	2265	—
Bridport		62	63	—	—
Brighton		705	715	752	—
Canterbury		1154	1089	2600	—
Carliſle		—	—	144	—
Chatham		—	—	2148	—
Chelmsford		—	—	4040	—
Cheſter		—	—	54	—
Chicheſter		350	340	982	—
Chriſtchurch		62	63	—	—
Colcheſter		480	450	6785	—
Coventry		216	193	—	—
Croydon		384	372	—	—
Cuckmere Haven		—	—	124	4
Danbury		—	—	831	—

BARRACKS.	Cavalry. Officers & men.	Cavalry. Horses.	Infantry. Officers & men.	Infantry. Horses.
Dalkeith	—	—	160	—
Deal	149	141	2260	—
Dorchester	395	400	—	—
Dover	—	—	215	—
Dunbar N. B.	—	—	1128	—
Dunbarton N. B.	—	—	163	—
Dungeness	—	—	512	33
Dundee N. B.	—	—	538	4
Eastbourn	183	63	668	—
Edinburgh N. B.	—	—	1858	—
Exeter	416	412	—	—
Eyemouth N. B.	—	—	75	—
Feversham and Ospring	280	280	2100	—
Fort Augustus N. B.	—	—	297	2
—— Charlotte N. B.	—	—	272	—
—— Cumberland	—	—	1350	—
—— George N. B.	—	—	1840	—
—— Monkton	—	—	503	—
—— William N. B.	—	—	481	—
Forton	—	—	700	—
Fulwell	—	—	460	—
Glasgow N. B.	—	—	1040	—
Gosport	—	—	694	—
Guernsey	—	—	4696	59
Guilford	501	537	—	—
Haddington N. B.	326	310	1128	—
Haylsham	—	—	982	—
Hamilton N. B.	189	202	—	—
Hampton Court	139	171	—	—
Harwich	—	—	1586	—
Haslar	—	—	821	—
Hastings and Bopeep	187	170	554	—
Herring House	—	—	68	—
Hilsea	—	—	1515	—
Honiton	81	85	—	—
Horsham	—	—	2440	—
Hounslow	316	329	—	—
Hull	—	—	2138	—
Hurst Castle	—	—	68	—
Hyde Park	290	385	—	—
Hythe	262	262	3378	145

Ipswich

BARRACKS.		Cavalry. Officers & men.	Cavalry. Horses	Infantry. Officers & men.	Infantry. Horses.
Ipswich		1108	1156	5911	—
Jersey		—	—	5771	22
Kensington		46	52	—	—
Kew		—	—	67	—
Kingsbridge		—	—	531	—
King Street		39	384	—	—
Knightsbridge		—	—	502	4
Langney Point		—	—	278	—
Languard Port		—	—	416	—
Leith	N. B.	—	—	136	—
Lewes		512	510	2218	—
Littlehampton		—	—	379	—
Liverpool		—	—	104	—
Lymington		—	—	934	—
Maidstone		679	148	2100	—
Maldon		187	180	1206	—
Manchester		349	353	—	—
Maker		—	—	343	—
Margate and Westgate		—	—	400	—
Medina Mill		—	—	500	—
Modbury		65	63	—	—
Musselburgh	N. B.	—	—	1728	—
Newcastle and vicinity		—	—	2500	—
Newport, Isle of Wight		—	—	22	—
Norman Cross		—	—	1266	—
Norwich		252	266	750	—
Northampton		126	124	—	—
Nottingham		189	186	—	—
Ospring, (see Feversham)		—	—	—	—
Ottery		—	—	605	—
Out Posts, Isle of Wight		—	—	118	5
Pendennis and St. Mawes		—	—	1125	—
Parkhurst, Isle of Wight		—	—	1705	—
Perth	N. B.	189	188	159	—
Pevensey		—	—	757	—
Piquets, Essex		113	21	—	—
Piers Hill	N. B.	357	368	—	—
Pleydon (see Rye)		—	—	—	—
Plymouth		221	210	7790	—
Port Patrick	N. B.	—	—	24	—
—— Chester		—	—	1074	—

BARRACKS.	Cavalry. Officers & men.	Cavalry. Horses.	Infantry. Officers & men.	Infantry. Horses.
Port Seaton	—	—	300	—
Portman Street	—	—	571	—
Portsmouth and Portsea	—	—	2059	—
Preston (see Port Seaton)	—	—	—	—
Queensbury House	—	—	800	—
Radipole	430	340	—	—
Ramsgate	169	161	829	—
Riding Street	—	—	940	12
Ringmer	—	—	140	136
Romford	364	378	—	—
Romney	187	172	—	—
Rye and Pleydon	187	172	—	—
Sandhurst	—	—	102	—
Sandown, Isle of Wight	—	—	435	13
Savoy	—	—	50	—
Scarborough	—	—	118	—
Scilly	—	—	108	—
Seaton Sluice and House	—	—	—	—
Selsea	—	—	304	—
Silver Hill	—	—	2132	—
Sheerness	—	—	585	—
Sheffield	175	182	—	—
Shoreham	187	170	616	—
Southampton	62	63	10	—
St. Mawes, (see Pendennis)	—	—	—	—
Steyning	—	—	984	—
Stirling N. B.	—	—	927	—
Stonar	157	160	—	—
Sunderland	—	—	156	—
Taunton	62	63	—	—
Tilbury Fort	—	—	198	—
Tontine, (see Queensbury)	—	—	—	—
Totness	62	63	—	—
Tower	—	—	455	—
Trowbridge	62	63	—	—
Truro	215	310	—	—
Tynemouth	—	—	483	—
Upnor	—	—	93	—
Wareham	62	63	—	—
Weely	374	360	3925	—
Westgate, (see Margate)	—	—	—	—

Weymouth

BARRACKS.	Cavalry. Officers & men.	Cavalry. Horses.	Infantry. Officers & men.	Infantry. Horses.
Weymouth - - - -	—	—	377	—
Whitburn (see Fulwell) -	—	—	—	—
Windsor - - -	222	220	642	—
Winchelsea - - -	—	—	150	—
Winchester - - -	—	—	3533	—
Woodbridge - - -	724	720	4165	—
Woolwich - - -	—	—	215	—
Worthing - - -	—	—	158	—
Yealm - - - -	—	—	190	—
Yarmouth - - -	—	—	1020	—
——— Isle of Wight -	—	—	286	6
York - - - -	261	266	—	—
	16854	16467	138410	897

Barrack Office. The barrack department was originally formed in May, 1793, and gradually increased until it was erected into an establishment completely distinct from all others, by a warrant from the king, the 24th of March, 1794, and was enlarged in 1796 and 1797. It is under the following officers.

Barrack Master General, 40*s*. per day, 40*s*. extra, and travelling expenses.

Deputy Barrack Master General, 20*s*. per day, 20*s*. extra, and travelling expenses.

Assistant Barrack Masters General, one at 15*s*. per day, and travelling expenses: three at 10*s*. per day each, and travelling expenses.

Assistant Barrack Master General, for supplies, 300*l*. per annum, and 5*s*. per day extra.

Accountant, 374*l*. per annum, and 100*l*. per annum extra.

Assistant Barrack Master General for North Britain, 300*l*. per annum, 50*l*. rent, with coals, candles, and travelling expenses.

Assistants to ditto, two at 10*s*. per day each, and travelling expenses.

The officers in the building department are:

Assistant barrack Master General, 10*s*. per day, and travelling expenses.

Checking Clerk, 200*l*. per annum.

Archi-

ARCHITECTS AND SURVEYORS, 20s. per day, 20s. extra, and travelling expenses, when in the country.

ASSISTANTS TO DITTO, one at 10s. ditto, 10s. ditto, another at 100l. per annum.

AGENT, 530l. per annum, for self and clerks.

OFFICE. The office is in Spring Gardens.

BARRACK MASTERS. Every one of the barracks above-mentioned is under the controul of an officer, called the Barrack-master, for whose regulation in the performance of his duties, his majesty by warrant, dated 24th March, 1795, directed that officers commanding in barracks, and the barrack-master, in all matters relative to the accommodation, disposition, and supply of the troops stationed therein, shall be under the direction of the *barrack master general*, to whom all applications and requisitions are to be made. Every barrack master shall, upon notice from the barrack master general, or on production of the route by which troops are ordered to march, attend the arrival of such regiment or detachment, as is ordered to quarter in any barrack within his district; and having, with the commanding officer, or with such officer as he may appoint, viewed the condition of the said barrack, and of every room and part thereof, and of the furniture and utensils thereto belonging, shall deliver the same to such officer, with an inventory under his hand, stating its particular condition; two copies of which inventory are to be signed by the commanding officer, and returned to the barrack master, one of which he will forthwith transmit to the barrack master general. And, from the time of such delivery, the commanding officer shall stand charged with the said barrack furniture and utensils, according to the inventory, until such regiment or detachment is relieved, or ordered away; and the like method shall be observed both by officers and barrack masters, on every relief, or removal. And after delivery made, and receipts taken, the barrack masters are not to exchange any articles, unless it be certified by the commanding officer that they have been rendered useless by fair wear. These certificates to be transmitted with the barrack master's accounts, as also receipts for the subsequent delivery.

Each barrack master is to make frequent inspections of the barracks under his care, and of the appurtenances, and report the state to the barrack master general: and on the removal of troops, report what new furniture is necessary, that due means may be taken to supply it. But in case inspection is not made in due time, or the demand is not brought by the barrack master, immediately after inspection, the damage must be made good by himself.

Every barrack master, when a regiment, or detachment, marches

marches in or out of a barrack, is to make a return to the barrack master general, by the next post, specifying the particular regiment, or detachment, the commanding officer's name, number, and other particulars; and on every quarter day, transmit to the barrack master general a return of the state of the barracks and furniture, and how the apartments of the barrack have been occupied for the three months preceding; which returns are to be countersigned by the commanding officers, who are personally and diligently to inspect the same.

The barrack master general takes care that sufficient firing, candles, and other stores, be provided for each barrack. And they are to be delivered out to the troops by the barrack masters, in due times and proportions, and the deliveries must be minutely vouched. The barrack masters must also transmit to the barrack master general, a weekly return of the number of officers and men to whom barrack stores have been issued for the preceding week: and half yearly accounts of expenditures with vouchers.

In case of neglect of duty in the barrack master, the commanding officer is to report it to the barrack master general; and, if on inquiry it shall appear that he has neglected to pay due obedience to orders, an inspector is to be sent down at his expence to take possession of the barracks, until every cause of complaint be removed; the barrack-master general takes cognizance of all matters relative to accommodation, disposition, and supply of troops in barracks, reporting thereon, when requisite, to the secretary at war. And all officers, and barrack masters are to obey such orders and directions as the barrack master general finds necessary to be given thereon.

On the arrival of a regiment in barracks, the soldiers are supplied by the barrack master with one pair of clean sheets to each bed, for which 3*d*. per pair is paid for a double, and 2*d*. for a single bed; the same every month when they are changed, for washing: they are also supplied with one round towel per week, fixed on a roller, the washing of which costs one penny: the rooms besides are furnished with every necessary article for the convenience and comfort of the soldiers.

Barrack stores are only allowed from the day on which the issue takes place. And all barrack masters are strictly enjoined not to allow any commutation either in money or otherwise for the same.

The rooms for the quarter-masters and serjeants of cavalry, and the serjeant major, and the quarter master serjeant, are furnished in the same manner as those of the soldiers; those of the officers have a few additional conveniences.

When there is a sufficient number of rooms in a barrack, subalterns fubalterns of infantry may have one each, and the full allowance of coals and candles.

The officers, commanding in each of the cavalry barracks, where *forage* is iffued, tranfmit to the barrack mafter general a weekly return of the number of horfes for which it has been delivered, and alfo the name and rank of each officer, with the number of horfes for which he has received rations of forage; and when required a general ftatement of the quantity of forage received, and actually iffued to the troops.

The rations of forage to be iffued to the horfes of officers and foldiers, actually effective in the barracks, are as follow:

	Rations.		Rations.
Field officers, each	4	Quarter mafters, non-commiffioned officers and privates, each	1
Captains, each - -	3		
Subalterns, and ftaff officers, each	2		

For each of thefe rations 8½*d*. per day is ftopped.

Each ftable is furnifhed with the neceffary utenfils. Many other regulations are prefcribed for the comfort of the troops, the enforcement of regularity and the prevention of fraud, but of a nature too minute to be here inferted.

PAY. It has appeared proper to place in one view the pay allotted to officers and privates in the army, with the general regulations affecting them. Whenever money is wanted for the fervice of the army, the *pay-mafter general*, by a memorial delivered to the treafury, ftates the particular fums required, and prays that they may be iffued to the governor and company of the Bank of England on his account. On receiving this memorial, the lords of the treafury direct the auditor of the exchequer to iffue the money as requefted, which is placed to an account kept in the books of the bank, in the name of the paymafter of the forces; fo that no money is paid immediately from the exchequer into his hands, but he, or his deputy, draws for it as wanted upon the bank, and inferts in his draft the heads of fervice to which the fums are to be applied. In the firft memorial of each month to the treafury, the pay-mafter general fpecifies the balance of public money then lying in the bank on his account; which balance, on his death or removal, vefts in his fucceffor. He alfo makes up an annual account, to the 24th of December, of the ordinary and extraordinary fervices of the army, figned and attefted by every pay-mafter-general who may have paid or difcharged any part of the faid account. This account is tranfmitted, together with proper vouchers, to the auditor

auditor of the impreſt, who within ſix months examines, and, if ſatisfactory, preſents it to the proper officer for declaration; after which an acquittance in the uſual form is given to the pay-maſter.

Regimental Pay-masters. Pay-maſters in the corps of the line cannot hold any other commiſſion; they rank as captains in their reſpective regiments, have baggage and forage money the ſame, and chuſe rooms in barracks or quarters according to the dates of their commiſſions; but they have no military command. They give ſecurity to the ſecretary at war; themſelves in 2000*l.* and two ſureties in 1000*l.* each. In the militia, the ſecurity is, the principal 1000*l.* and the ſureties 500*l.* each. The above ſums become forfeit on proof of malefaction, neglect of duty, or conſideration directly or indirectly given to obtain the appointment. In regiments of the line their pay is 15*s.* per day; in the militia they are allowed to hold another commiſſion, and their pay made up to the above ſum; they hold their ſituation by a commiſſion from his majeſty, and are not removeable but by his command, or the ſentence of a general court-martial. When there is a vacancy in any regiment, of a paymaſter, the accounts are to be taken by the major, or, if he is abſent, the commanding officer, and the next two officers in ſeniority, are to act as a committee, to make up and tranſmit the pay-liſts and other accounts to the agent, for which trouble, on ſpecial application to the ſecretary at war, they are remunerated. When a pay-maſter is appointed to a regiment on foreign ſervice. he is only allowed 5*s.* per day till he joins: the remainder going to thoſe who do the duty in his abſence; a clerk is allowed to the pay-maſter who is not borne in addition to the number of the corps, for which an allowance of 1*s.* 6¼*d.* is made per day. The pay-maſter has an allowance of 20*l.* per annum for poſtage and ſtationary.

For the regulation of regimental pay-maſters, rules are laid down tending at once to render their duty eaſy and certain, and to prevent fraud. Their office alſo includes that of muſter maſter. They are amenable, in the ordinary courſe, to martial law for every part of their conduct relating to military diſcipline, or ſubordination; but they are not liable to receive orders touching the manner of making up their pay-liſts and accounts, unleſs under a ſpecial inſtruction, in writing, from the officer commanding in chief on the ſtation, if abroad; or, if at home, from the king, through the commander in chief of the forces, or the ſecretary at war. In caſe of imputed miſdemeanour in the execution of office, it is in the power of the commanding officer in chief on the ſtation if abroad, (but of no other), to ſuſpend them from duty, until proper inquiry can be made into the

the charges alleged, and to provide, in fuch manner as the commander in chief fhall think fit, for the temporary fupply of the department. In cafe of a pay-mafter's death, or incapacity from accident, his papers of accounts are taken into the poffeffion of the major, if prefent; if not, of the commanding officer, and the two officers next in feniority, who act as a committee of pay-mafterfhip, and make up and tranfmit the feveral pay lifts and accounts, at the fame periods and under the like regulations as are prefcribed for pay-mafters, until further provifions. Their pay is 15*s.* per day, with an allowance of 20*l.* a year for ftationary and poftage.

The following Table exhibits a view of the daily Pay of the commiffioned and non-commiffioned Officers, and Privates, in the regular forces.

	Life Guards. Subsist. £	s.	d.	Life Guards. Full Pay. £	s.	d.	Horse Guards. Subsist. £	s.	d.	Horse Guards. Full Pay. £	s.	d.	Foot Guards. Subsist. £	s.	d.	Foot Guards. Full Pay. £	s.	d.
Colonel	1	7	0	1	10	0	1	11	0	2	1	0	1	10	0	1	12	10
Colonel (en 2d)	-	-	-	-	-	-	-	-	-	-	-	-	-	-	-	-	-	-
Lieutenant Colonel	1	3	[illegible]	[illegible]	1	0	1	2	6	1	9	6	1	1	6	1	8	6
Second ditto	-	-	-		-	-	-	-	-	-	-	-	-	-	-	-	-	-
Major	0	19	6	1	6	0	1	1	6	1	7	0	0	18	6	1	4	0
Second ditto	[illegible]	18	0	1	4	0	-	-	-	-	-	-	-	-	-	-	-	-
Captain	0	12	0	0	[illegible]	0	0	16	6	1	1	6	0	12	6	0	16	6
Lieutenant	0	5	3	0	11	0	0	11	6	0	13	0	0	6	0	0	7	10
Second ditto	-	-	-	-	-	-	-	-	-	-	-	-	-	-	-	-	-	-
Cornet	0	7	3	0	8	6	0	11	6	0	14	0	-	-	-	-	-	-
Ensign	-	-	-	-	-	-	-	-	-	-	-	-	0	4	6	0	5	10
Adjutant	0	8	3	0	11	0	0	11	6	-	-	-	0	3	0	-	-	-
Quarter Master	0	4	0	0	6	0	0	6	6	0	8	[illegible]	0	5	8	-	-	-
Pay Master	-	-	-	-	-	-	0	15	0	-	-	-	-	-	-	-	-	-
Senior Surgeon		-	-	-	-	-	-	-	-	-	-	-	0	12	6	0	17	0
Surgeon	0	9	0	0	12	0	0	[illegible]	0	0	12	0	0	7	6	0	11	4
Assistant ditto	-	-	-	-	-	-	0	7	6	-	-	-	0	7	6	-	-	-
Veterinary ditto	0	8	0	[illegible]	10	6	0	8	0	0	[illegible]	6	-	-	-	-	-	-
Solicitor	-	-	-	-	-	-	-	-	-	-	-	-	0	[illegible]	0	[illegible]	4	0
Serjeant Major	-	-	-	-	-	-	-	-	-	-	-	-	-	-	-	-	-	-
Serjeant	-	-	-	-	-	-	-	-	-	-	-	-	0	1	[illegible]	-	-	-
Corporal	0	3	[illegible]	-	-	-	0	3	[illegible]	-	-	-	0	1	[illegible]	-	-	-
Kettle Drummer	0	2	6	-	-	-	0	2	6	-	-	-	-	-	-	-	-	-
Private	[illegible]	[illegible]	[illegible]	-	-	-	0	2	[illegible]	-	-	-	0	1	1	-	-	-

	Dragoons. £	s.	d.	Foot Artillery. £	s.	d.	Horse Artillery. £	s.	d.	Infantry. £	s.	d.
Colonel	[illegible]	12	10	2	5	6	[illegible]	[illegible]	[illegible]	1	2	6
Colonel (en 2d)	-	-	-	1	3	9	1	9	8	-	-	-
Lieutenant Colonel	1	3	0	0	19	9	1	5	8	0	15	11
Second ditto	-	-	-	0	16	10	-	-	-	0	15	11
Major	0	19	3	0	14	[illegible]	1	0	0	0	14	1
Second ditto	-	-	-	-	-	-	-	-	-	0	14	1
Captain	0	14	7	0	9	11	0	15	4	0	9	5
Lieutenant	0	9	0	0	6	0	0	9	0	0	5	8
Second ditto	-	-	-	0	5	0	0	8	0	0	4	8
Cornet	0	8	0	-	-	-	-	-	-	-	-	-
Ensign		-	-	-	-	-	-	-	-	0	4	8
Adjutant	0	10	0	0	5	0	-	-	-	0	8	[illegible]
Quarter Master	0	[illegible]	6	0	6	0	0	8	0	0	5	8
Pay Master	0	15	0	0	15	0	0	15	0	0	15	0
Senior Surgeon	-	-	-	-	-	-		-	-	-	-	-
Surgeon	0	11	[illegible]	[illegible]	9	11	0	11	10	0	11	4
Assistant ditto	0	5	6	[illegible]	5	[illegible]	0	6	0	0	7	6
Veterinary ditto	0	[illegible]	0	-	-	-	0	8	0	-	-	-
Solicitor	-	-	-	-	-	-	-	-	-	-	-	-
Serjeant Major	[illegible]	[illegible]	11	-	-	-	[illegible]	[illegible]	4	0	2	[illegible]
Serjeant	[illegible]	2	11	0	[illegible]	[illegible]	0	2	[illegible]	0	1	[illegible]
Corporal	0	2	[illegible]	0	[illegible]	[illegible]	0	[illegible]	[illegible]	0	1	[illegible]
Kettle Drummer	-	-	-	-	-	-	-	-	-	-	-	-
Private	0	2	0	-	-	-	-	-	-	0	1	[illegible]

Besides

Besides the particulars contained in the table, there are a few circumstances to be mentioned respecting each division.

Life Guards. To these two regiments there is one marshal, with a salary of 25*l.* per annum; and a stoppage of 1*s.* 3*d.* is made for each horse, from the non-commissioned officers and privates. In the *Horse* and *Dragoon Guards* and *Dragoons*, the same stoppage is made.

Foot Guards. The drum-major has 1*s.*; the drummer 1*s.* 2¼*d.*, the deputy marshal 9*d.* and the hautbois 1*s.* per day subsistence.

Foot Artillery. The men are divided into three classes; *bombadiers*, whose daily pay is 1*s.* 10¼*d.*; first gunners, 1*s.* 7*d.*: and second gunners, 1*s.* 3¼*d.*

Horse Artillery. In these regiments, are *bombadiers*, with the daily pay of 2*s.* 0¼*d.*; gunners, 1*s.* 5¼*d.*; gunner drivers, 1*s.* 3¼*d.* farriers and smiths, 3*s.* 4¾*d.*, and collar makers and wheelers, 2*s.* 0¾*d.*

Infantry. In these regiments, the adjutant has an extra allowance of 2*s.* per day for a horse, and the surgeon is also obliged to keep one.

Engineers. The pay and persons employed about this service differ so widely from those in other regiments, that it is necessary to state them separately, as well as some other heads incident to the service.

Pay of the Royal Engineers. First colonel commandant, 2*l.* 4*s.*; second ditto, 2*l.* 4*s.*; first colonel, 1*l.* 4*s.*; second ditto 1*l.*; first lieutenant colonel, 17*s.*; second ditto, 15*s.*; captain 10*s.*; captain lieutenant, 7*s.*; first lieutenant, 6*s.*; second ditto, 5*s.*; brigade major, 10*s.*

Pay of the *Military Surveyors and Draughtsmen.* Chief surveyor and draughtsman, 15*s.*; first assistant ditto, 12*s.*; second ditto, 10*s.*; first class of surveyors and draughtsmen, 7*s.* 6*d.*; second ditto, 5*s.*; third ditto, 4*s.*; cadet ditto, 2*s.*

Pay of the *Military Artificers.* Serjeant major, 2*s.* 9¾*d.*; serjeant, 2*s.* 3¼*d.*; corporal, 2*s.* 0¼*d.*; artificer and drummer, 1*s.* 2½*d.*; labourer, 1*s.*

Pay of the *Royal Waggon Train.* Lieutenant colonel commandant, 18*s.*; major, 14*s.* 1*d.* and allowance for a horse, 2*s.*; captain, 9*s.* 5*d.* and allowance for a horse, 2*s.*; cornet, 4*s.* 8*d.* and allowance for a horse, 2*s.*; adjutant, 5*s.*; surgeon, 11*s.* 4*d.*; veterinary surgeon, 8*s.*; quarter master, 3*s.*; serjeant, 2*s.* 2*d.*; corporal, 1*s.* 7½*d.*; drummer, 1*s.* 3*d.*; collarmaker, 3*s.*; wheelwright, 3*s.*; smith, 3*s.*; farrier, 3*s.*; driver, 1*s.*

Pay of the *Quarter Master General's Department.* Quarter master general in time of war, 3*l.* per day; deputy quarter master general, 2*l.*; assistant quarter master general, 15*s.*

In

In time of war, field officers, resident in the different districts, are employed as assistants to the quarter master general: they receive pay according to their rank; during which time their regimental pay ceases. Lieutenant colonel, (including 1*s.* 6*d.* per day, in lieu of a servant), 1*l.* 4*s.* 6*d.*; major, ditto, 1*l.* 0*s.* 9*d.*

Pay of the *General Hospital Staff.* Physician 1*l.*; purveyor (including 5*s.* for a clerk) 1*l.* 5*s.*; deputy purveyor, 10*s.*; surgeon 15*s.*; ditto of a recruiting district, 10*s.*; apothecary, 10*s.*; hospital mate, 6*s.* 6*d.*; ditto on foreign service, 7*s.* 6*d.*; military superintendant, (beside regimental pay), 5*s.*; superintendant quarter master serjeant 2*s.* 0½*d.*

Pay of the *Recruiting Staff.* The inspecting field officers are generally taken from the half pay; each is allowed 10*s.* per day for this service, in addition to the full pay of his regimental rank, which is made up to him yearly. They are also allowed the actual expence of postage and stationary.

The adjutant is allowed 3*s.* per day for this service, in addition to the full pay of his regimental rank, which is made up to him also yearly if he is on half pay.

Two serjeants (one to act as serjeant major, and the other as clerk) to the district are allowed, each an additional pay of sixpence per day. The surgeon is allowed 10*s.* per day, and the paymaster 15*s.*

Officers of cavalry chosen for these situations, receive the full pay of their regimental ranks as infantry.

The paymaster is allowed 20*l.* per annum for stationary; also 8*s.* per week for lodging, and a serjeant, whose additional pay is 6*d.* per day.

Pay of the General Officers, and others, on the Staff; shewing also the nett Amount, after Deductions for Poundage, Civil List, and Hospital.

	Per day.			Per annum.			Per annum nett.		
	£.	s.	d.	£.	s.	d.	£.	s.	d.
General - -	6	0	0	2190	0	0	2019	15	0
Lieutenant general	4	0	0	1460	0	0	1346	10	0
Major general -	2	0	0	730	0	0	673	5	0
* Brigadier general	1	10	0	547	10	0	504	18	9
Brigade major - } Aid-de-camp - }	0	10	0	182	10	0	168	6	3

No deductions are made for poundage, civil list, or hospital, on foreign service.

The following tables will be found of great utility in estimating the strength and expence of armies.

Pay of a Regiment of Cavalry for 1, 31, and 365 Days, according to the Strength eſtabliſhed by the War Office, June, 1802.

		For 1 day.			For 31 days			For 365 days		
		£.	s.	d.	£.	s.	d.	£.	s.	d.
1	Colonel -	1	12	10	50	17	10	599	4	2
2	Lieutenant colonels	2	6	0	71	6	0	839	10	0
2	Majors -	1	18	6	59	13	6	702	12	6
8	Captains -	5	16	8	180	16	8	2129	3	4
8	Lieutenants -	3	12	0	111	12	0	1314	0	0
8	Cornets -	3	4	0	99	4	0	1168	0	0
1	Adjutant -	0	10	0	15	10	0	182	10	0
1	Paymaſter -	0	15	0	23	5	0	273	15	0
1	Surgeon -	0	11	4	17	11	4	206	16	8
1	Aſſiſtant ditto	0	8	6	13	13	6	155	2	6
1	Veterinary ditto	0	8	0	12	8	0	146	0	0
8	Quarter-maſters	2	4	0	68	4	0	803	0	0
1	Serjeant major	0	3	11	6	1	5	79	9	7
1	Paymaſter ſerjeant	0	2	11	4	10	5	53	4	7
1	Armourer ditto	0	2	11	4	10	5	53	4	7
1	Sadler as ſerjeant	0	2	11	4	10	5	53	4	7
24	Serjeants -	3	10	0	108	10	0	1277	10	0
24	Corporals -	2	17	0	88	7	0	1040	5	0
8	Trumpeters -	0	18	8	28	18	8	340	13	4
376	Privates -	37	12	0	1165	12	0	13724	0	0
80	Ditto diſmounted	5	0	0	155	0	0	1825	0	0
558	Nett pay	73	17	2	2289	12	2	26958	5	10

Excluſive of other expences, &c.

Pay of a Regiment of Infantry for 1, 31, and 365 Days, according to the Strength eſtabliſhed by the War Office, June, 1802.

		For 1 day.			For 31 days.			For 365 days		
		£.	s.	d	£.	s.	d.	£.	s.	d.
1	Colonel -	1	2	6	34	17	6	410	12	6
2	Lieutenant colonels	1	11	10	49	6	10	580	19	2
2	Majors -	1	8	2	43	13	2	514	0	10
10	Captains -	4	14	2	145	19	2	1718	10	10
12	Lieutenants -	3	8	0	105	8	0	1241	0	0
27	Carried over	13	4	8	379	4	8	4465	3	4

8 Enſigns

	For 1 day.			For 31 days.			For 365 days.		
	£.	s.	d.	£.	s.	d.	£.	s.	d.
27 Brought over -	13	4	8	379	4	8	4465	3	4
8 Ensigns -	1	17	4	57	17	4	681	6	8
1 Adjutant -	0	10	0	15	10	0	182	10	0
1 Quarter-master	0	5	8	8	15	8	103	8	4
1 Paymaster	0	15	0	23	5	0	273	15	0
1 Surgeon -	0	11	4	17	11	4	206	16	8
2 Assistant ditto	0	15	0	23	5	0	273	15	0
1 Serjeant major	0	2	0¾	3	3	11¼	37	12	9¾
1 Quarter-master serjeant -	0	2	0¾	3	3	11¼	37	12	9¾
1 Pay serjeant	0	1	6¾	2	8	5¼	28	10	3¾
1 Armourer serjeant -	0	1	6¾	2	8	5¼	28	10	1¾
30 Serjeants	2	6	10½	72	13	1½	855	9	4½
40 Corporals	2	7	6	73	12	6	866	17	6
22 Drummers	1	5	2½	39	1	5½	460	1	0½
710 Privates -	35	10	0	1100	10	0	12957	10	0
847 Nett pay	58	15	10	1822	10	10	21458	19	2

Exclusive of clothing, appointments, contingencies, barracks, bedding, fuel, forage, marching, and other expences, and allowance in the different situations and departments, &c.

HALF PAY, AND PENSIONS. The following Tables shew the half-pay allowed to officers, and the pensions to their widows.

Half-pay of the Army.

Rank.	Cavalry.						Infantry.					
	Per day.			Per annum.			Per day.			Per annum.		
	£.	s.	d.	£.	s.	d.	£.	s.	d.	£.	s.	d.
Colonel -	0	13	0	237	5	0	0	12	*0	219	0	0
Lieutenant colonel	0	10	0	182	10	0	0	8	6	155	2	6
Major -	0	8	0	146	0	0	0	7	6	136	17	6
Captain -	0	5	6	100	7	6	0	5	0	91	5	0
Lieutenant -	0	3	0	54	15	0	0	2	4	42	11	8
Cornet, Ensign	0	2	0	45	12	6	0	1	10	33	9	2
Adjutant -	0	2	0	36	10	0	0	2	0	36	10	0
Quarter Master	0	2	0	36	10	0	0	2	4	42	11	8
Pay-master -	0	7	6	136	17	6	0	7	6	136	17	6
Surgeon -	0	6	0	109	10	0	0	6	0	109	10	0

* This half pay on the Irish establishment is 12s. 6d. per day; £228. 2s 6d. per annum.

Rank.	Cavalry.						Infantry.					
	Per day.			Per annum			Per day.			Per annum.		
	£.	s.	d.	£.	s.	d.	£.	s.	d.	£.	s.	d.
Affiftant ditto	0	3	0	54	15	0	0	3	0	54	10	0
Surgeon to a recruiting diftrict	-	-	-	-	-	-	0	5	0	91	5	0
Infpector of hofpitals	-	-	-	-	-	-	1	0	0	365	0	0
Deputy ditto -	-	-	-	-	-	-	0	12	6	228	2	6
Hofpital mate	-	-	-	-	-	-	0	2	0	36	10	0
Apothecary -	-	-	-	-	-	-	0	5	0	91	5	0
Commiffary -	0	15	0	273	15	0	-	-	-	-	-	-

The deduction made from an officer on the Britifh eftablifhment is 2¼ per cent. and if he is not on the fpot to receive it himfelf, he gives 2½ per cent. more to his agent: it is always paid half yearly; two months, or fooner, after it became due.

Penfions to the Widows of commiffioned Officers.

Colonel - - - - - - -	£80
Lieutenant colonel - - - -	50
Major - - - - - - -	40
Captain, phyfician, purveyor - -	30
Lieutenant, furgeon, apothecary, pay-mafter	26
2d lieutenant, cornet, enfign, quarter-mafter, adjutant, affiftant furgeon, veterinary furgeon - - - - -	20
Deputy purveyor, hofpital mate - -	16
Quarter-mafter of dragoons - - -	16

The widows of officers on half pay of the Britifh eftablifhment, are not intitled to the penfion: in Ireland they receive it. The quarter-mafter's widow is not intitled to this penfion, farther than his majefty's gracious confideration.

Clothing. The power of fixing and altering the uniform, both in the land and fea-fervice, belongs to the king, and is exercifed by orders from the commander in chief. On the elegance and utility of dreffing whole military bodies in the fame apparel, it is unneceffary here to make any obfervations. The origin of the practice has occafioned fome difpute; the French writers claim it for Lewis XIV. and perhaps juftly as to whole armies, for, as before his time, the feudal practice of arming, on the requifition of the fovereign, was not altogether difcontinued, it is not probable but that every perfon coming in fo fudden ſudden a manner into the field, dreſſed himſelf in ſuch cloaths as he could eaſily obtain; but long before the days of Lewis XIV. large bodies of troops in royal pay, both in England and in other countries, received from the ſovereign who engaged them uniform dreſſes. Henry VII. for example, gave his yeomen of the guard an uniform which continues to this day; and, on another occaſion, an order was iſſued for apparelling a troop of 1000 in clothing all alike. It is not intended here to deſcribe the uniform of officers in the different regiments; every one is allowed to be at once ſplendid and commodious, and in point of appearance, the military have no rivals; the only diviſion of opinion they create, being to which particular variation of dreſs the preference is due. The regulations reſpecting clothing iſſued by his majeſty, are as follow:

Cavalry. In a regiment of *Dragoon Guards*, or *heavy Dragoons*, each ſerjeant, corporal, trumpeter, and private, has for clothing, one hat and one pair of gloves annually. One coat, one waiſtcoat, and one pair of breeches, once in every two years.

In a regiment of *Light Dragoons*, each ſerjeant, corporal, trumpeter, and private has, for clothing, one pair of gloves annually; one upper and one under jacket, one flannel waiſtcoat, and one pair of leather breeches, once in two years. One helmet once in three years; and one watering cap once in four years.

In the *Royal Waggon Train*, each ſerjeant has for clothing, a leather cap, laced with ſilver, when actually required; a blue jacket with ſilver lace, a blue waiſtcoat with ſleeves, and a pair of blue pluſh breeches, once in two years. Each corporal has for clothing, a plain leather cap, when actually required; a blue jacket, ſilver lace on cuff and collar; a blue waiſtcoat with ſleeves, and a pair of blue pluſh breeches once in two years. Each private has for clothing, a plain leather cap, when actually required; a plain blue jacket, a blue waiſtcoat with ſleeves, and a pair of blue pluſh breeches, once in two years.

Infantry. In a regiment of *Foot Guards*, each ſerjeant has for clothing, a coat, the ſleeves unlined; a waiſtcoat with ſleeves, a pair of breeches, made of materials of the ſame quality as the coat, and lined, a pair of military ſhoes, a pair of gaiters, and a pair of doe-ſkin gloves, annually. A lackered felt cap, with a cockade and tuft, once in two years. Each corporal, drummer, and private, has for clothing, a coat, the ſleeves unlined, a waiſtcoat with ſleeves of milled ſerge, a pair of breeches, made of materials of the ſame quality as the coat, a pair of military ſhoes, a pair of gaiters, and a pair of mitts, annually. A cap, as above, once in every two years.

In a regiment of *Infantry of the Line* ſerving in Europe, North America, or New South Wales (Highland corps excepted) each ſerjeant ſhall have for clothing, a coat, the ſleeves unlined, a pair of breeches, made of materials of the ſame quality as the coat, a cloth waiſtcoat, lined, with ſleeves of milled ſerge, and a pair of military ſhoes, annually. A cap, as above, once in two years. Each corporal, drummer, and private, has a coat, the ſleeves unlined, a pair of breeches, of materials like the coat, a kerſey waiſtcoat, with ſerge ſleeves, and a pair of military ſhoes, annually; a cap once in two years.

In a Highland corps on the above ſtations, each ſerjeant has a jacket, the ſleeves unlined, a cloth waiſtcoat, with ſerge ſleeves, and a pair of military ſhoes annually. Each corporal, drummer, and private, a jacket, the ſleeves unlined; a kerſey waiſtcoat, with ſerge ſleeves, and a pair of military ſhoes annually. The colonel is to be at the charge of Highland appointments, viz. bonnet, feathers, plaid, and purſe.

In a regiment of *Infantry ſerving in the Weſt Indies* (except the 5th battalion of the 60th regiment, and the regiments compoſed of people of colour), each ſerjeant has a coat, partly lined; a ſerge waiſtcoat with ſleeves; two pair of Ruſſia linen trowſers; a pair of flannel drawers, and a pair of military ſhoes, annually; and a cap once in two years. Each corporal, drummer, and private, has a coat, partly lined; a ſerge waiſtcoat, with ſleeves, cuffs and collar, the colour of the facing; a pair of Ruſſia linen trowſers; a pair of military ſhoes, and a foraging cap, annually; and a cap once in two years. In the fifth battalion of the 60th regiment, and the 95th regiment of foot (rifle corps), each ſerjeant has a jacket, the ſleeves unlined; a waiſtcoat, with ſerge ſleeves; a pair of pantaloons, and a pair of military ſhoes, annually; and a cap once in two years. Each corporal, drummer, and private, has a jacket lined, but not laced, the ſleeves unlined; a kerſey waiſtcoat, with ſerge ſleeves; a pair of blue pantaloons, made of ſuch cloth as the jacket, and a pair of military ſhoes, annually; and a cap once in two years. The men are to pay the extraordinary charge of 2*s.* 3*d.* on this clothing, in conſequence of receiving pantaloons inſtead of breeches.

In the *regiments compoſed of people of colour*, ſerving in the Weſt Indies, each ſerjeant has for clothing, a jacket, the ſleeves unlined; a ſerge waiſtcoat, with ſleeves; two pair of Ruſſia linen trowſers, and a pair of military ſhoes, annually; and a cap, and a grey coat, diſtinguiſhed from thoſe of the privates by cuffs, collar, and buttons (conformable to the facings, &c. of the regiment), once in two years. Serjeants, being Europeans, have alſo one pair of flannel drawers annually. Each corporal, drummer, and private, has a round jacket, partly lined; two pair of Ruſſia linen trowſers, and a pair of military ſhoes, annually; and a cap, and a grey great coat, once in two years.

In

In a regiment of *Infantry serving in the East Indies*, each serjeant has a coat, partly lined, and two pair of military shoes, annually. A cap, once in two years. In lieu of other articles, clothing adapted to the climate is to be supplied at the discretion of the commanding officer, to the amount of 18*s*. 8*d*. per annum, which becomes an annual charge against the colonel. Each corporal, drummer, and private, has a coat, partly lined, and two pair of military shoes, annually; and a cap once in two years. In lieu of other articles, clothing adapted to the climate is supplied, at the discretion of the commanding officer, to the amount of 6*s*. 7½*d*. per annum, which becomes an annual charge against the colonel.

In the *Staff Corps*, each serjeant, corporal, drummer, and private, has a coat, waistcoat, pair of blue cloth pantaloons, and a pair of half boots, annually; and a cap once in two years. And further, in consideration of the laborious nature of their service, each serjeant, corporal, drummer, and private, has a Russia duck waistcoat, with sleeves, and a pair of Russia duck pantaloons, annually. And to these a great coat once in three years is added.

For clothing regiments on *foreign stations*, materials are not furnished; but the things required are sent out made up; except in instances where a special dispensation is granted by the king, through the commander in chief, or secretary at war.

With respect to the receipt of *clothing at stated times and broken periods and compensations* in certain cases, the following are the rules. Non-commissioned officers and soldiers, dying, or discharged before the completion of the period for which the clothing is assigned to last, reckoned from the usual day of delivering the same, have no demand whatever on account thereof. If a serjeant is reduced to the ranks, his clothing is to be received for the use of his successor, and he will receive private clothing equally worn. A recruit who comes into the regiment after the proper time for the delivery of clothing (if not raised for an augmentation, in which case he is to be furnished with new clothing complete) shall be immediately intitled to clothing as good as that in wear by the rest of the regiment: and he shall be entitled to new clothing at the next period of general delivery to the regiment. It is the duty of the colonels, and of those employed by them, to take especial care that the clothing be forwarded and delivered to their respective corps at the exact period when it is due; and few cases ought to arise, in which it should become a question whether an allowance in money might not be substituted by the colonels in lieu of delivering in kind the articles which by the regulations they are required to furnish: but if from any extraordinary circumstances of the service, such an instance should be supposed to have occurred in any regiment or detachment serving abroad, the grounds on which a commutation in money is proposed, shall be fully stated to the commander in chief, or if there is none, to our secretary at war, in order that his majesty's pleasure may be previously known. If the king approves the measure, the following sums, being the estimated amount of what the colonels would have paid to their clothiers, after a reasonable deduction for incidental charges to which they are liable, is to be given to the men.

In the Dragoon Guards and Dragoons.	£. s. d.	*In the Infantry.*	£. s. d.
To each serjeant, in lieu of clothing complete -	6 4 0	To each serjeant, in lieu of clothing complete - -	3 12 0
To each corporal, trumpeter, and private, ditto -	3 9 0	To each corporal, drummer, and private, ditto -	1 16 6

The date from which the annual, biennial, and other rights to clothing are to be computed, is fixed on the 25th December, 1803.

Necessaries and Appointments. For necessaries a stoppage is made in the pay of cavalry of 2*s.* 7½*d.*; and of infantry 1*s.* 6*d.* per week. Exclusive of clothing and necessaries, the cavalry have certain articles, denominated appointments. These are described as follows:

To the *Dragoon Guards and Heavy Dragoons*; boots, and cloaks with sleeves. *Sadlery.* Saddle with pannel and pad in one; a web girth, with six roller buckles; pair of strap flaps; martingale, breast-plate, with roller buckles, leather surcingles, with roller buckles; pair of stirrup leathers, with roller buckles; pair of stirrup irons; bit and bridoon complete, with head reins and nose band; pair of double and single forage straps; pair of cloak straps and single ditto; pair of holster and a firelock strap with roller buckles; holster and shoecase; carbine bucket with picket ring; carbine bucket strap; cover for holsters; leather cloak cover; horse collar with iron chain. *Buff accoutrements.* Pouch curved for thirty rounds; pocket behind ditto, and roller buckles; carbine belt, three inches wide, and buckles with two brass tongues and tip; pair of straps for the pouch to hang by; brass slider and swivel; sword waist belt, 2½ inches wide; brass plate and slide with a bar and double tongue; bayonet frog of buff leather, and leather sword knot.

To the *Light Dragoons.* Cloak with sleeves, and boots. *Sadlery.* Saddle complete as for the above. *Buff accoutrements.* Pouch curved for thirty rounds, pocket behind ditto, and roller buckles;

buckles; carbine belt, 2½ inches wide; buckles with two braſs tongues and tips; pair of ſtraps for the pouch to hang by, braſs ſlider and ſwivel; ſword waiſt belt, 1¼ inch wide; ſword carriage; bayonet frog, of buff leather, and leather ſword knot.

To the *Royal Waggon Train*. Cloak, and boots, &c.

The duration of theſe appointments is thus limited: Saddles, holſter pipes, buckets, ſtirrup leathers and irons, 16 years; bits and cloaks twelve years; headſtalls, reins, breaſt plates, cruppers, girths, ſurcingles, ſtraps and boots, ſix years, and buff accoutrements twenty years.

Articles of Neceſſaries paid for by the Cavalry. An extra pair of breeches of the ſame quality, to be in wear with thoſe furniſhed by the colonel; a ſtable jacket, trowſers and foraging cap; a noſe bag, watering bridle, and log; three ſhirts, a night cap and black ſtock; three pair of worſted ſtockings: one pair of long black gaiters; two pair of ſhoes, combs, razors, &c.; one clothes and three ſhoe bruſhes; mane comb, ſponge, curry comb and bruſh, worm and picker; horſe picker and ſciſſars; emery, oil, pipe clay, whiting, and blacking; button ſtick, hook, carbine lock caſe, and a pair of ſaddle bags; the actual expenditure for horſe cloths, and ſurcingles, not exceeding 1*s*. 8*d*. per annum for each man, is defrayed by the public.

Articles of Neceſſaries paid for by the Infantry. One pair of ſhoes, and three ſhirts; one pair of long gaiters, three pair of ſocks, and mitts during the winter; one black ſtock, foraging cap, and knapſack; one clothes and three ſhoe bruſhes; black-ball, hair ribbon, combs and ſtraps for carrying the great coat; a yearly allowance of 2*s*. 9*d*. is made for effectives each, in regiments at home, for the ſupply of turnſcrew, bruſh, worm, oil, emery and duſt. For Highland and other regiments wearing peculiar clothing, peculiar regulations are made.

Off reckonings. Out of the off reckonings (6*d*. per day from each ſerjeant, 4*d*. from each corporal, and 2*d*. from each private) allowed to colonels, the clothing, accoutrements, &c. are furniſhed: it alſo affords poundage to the pay-office of 1*s*., one day's pay from the whole regiment to Chelſea hoſpital, and 2*d*. in the pound for the agent.—The remainder is nett off reckonings.

Allowances. When the army is ordered to take the field, an allowance, for the firſt year only, is iſſued to the officers, under the following denominations:

Officers.	Baggage.	Forage.	Total.
	£. s. d.	£. s. d.	£. s. d.
Colonel - -	7 10 0	28 15 0	36 5 0
Lieutenant-colonel	7 10 0	22 10 0	30 0 0
Major - -	7 10 0	17 10 0	25 0 0

Captain

Officers.	Baggage.	Forage.	Total.
	£. s. d.	£. s. d.	£. s. d.
Captain - Pay-master - Surgeon - Adjutant -	7 10 0	12 10 0	20 0 0
Lieutenant - Ensign - Quarter-master Assistant-surgeon	7 10 0	5 0 0	12 10 0

Field officers and captains are allowed each, for a horse, 18*l.* 18*s.* The same allowauce is made to every two subalterns and staff.

Regiments of cavalry taking the field have none of the above allowances made them, except the field officers and captains; they have an allowance of 18*l.* 18*s.* to purchase a horse, and the subaltern and staff the same between every two.

Each regiment is also allowed six horses, at 18*l.* 18*s.* each, for the following purposes: For the carriage of ammunition, two; for camp kettles, two; for intrenching tools, one; for the medicine chest, one. Officers, in camp, are allowed a certain proportion of forage, out of the first year's allowance, to provide themselves with marquees and tents; the field officers and captains have each a separate one: the subalterns have a tent between two. In militia regiments, the paymasters and assistant surgeons have captain's allowances made them, provided they hold, with their staff appointment, subaltern commissions. Officers returing from India to Europe, on leave of absence, are accommodated with their passage on board the Company's ships, for which an allowance is made to the commanders, for each colonel, 150*l.*; lieutenant-colonel, 120*l.*; major, captain, 100*l.*; subaltern, staff, &c. 80*l.* The bills for passage are signed by the commanding officers of regiments, also by the commander in chief, or, under his order, by the quarter-master-general.

Officers sent home on the recruiting service are allowed each, from North America, West Indies, or Africa, 12*l.* 10*s.* Gibraltar, &c. 5*l.* 5*s.* According to circumstances this allowance is sometimes increased.

Officers and privates sent on the recruiting service, have an allowance for passage, each, to and from

	Officers.	Privates.
	£. s. d.	£. s. d.
Port Patrick to Donaghadee -	0 10 6	0 5 0
Liverpool to Belfast, or Dublin -	1 11 6	0 5 0

Holyhead

	Officers. £.	s.	d.	Privates. £.	s.	d.
Holyhead to Dublin	1	11	6	0	5	0
Bristol to Dublin, Belfast	2	2	0	0	6	6
Bristol to Cork, Waterford	1	11	6	0	5	0
Bristol to Limerick	2	2	0	0	10	6
Milford Haven to Waterford	1	11	6	0	5	0
Isle of Wight to Cork, Waterford	2	2	0	0	10	6
Isle of Wight to Limerick	3	3	0	0	10	6

A further allowance of 9*d*. per mile is made to officers going to or returning from their ſtations, for the land carriage of their baggage; theſe extras come into the accounts of the paymaſter of the diſtrict in which the officer is ſtationed.

Contingent Allowances to Captains of Troops and Companies.

Cavalry.

No. of men in a troop.	Non-effect. per ann. £.	Contin. per ann. £.	Riding houſes. £. s.	Total per ann. £. s.
When leſs than 40	20	10	18 1	48 1
When leſs than 50	20	10	23 6	53 6
When leſs than 60	20	20	23 6	63 6
When leſs than 70	20	20	23 6	63 6
70 and upward.	20	30	23 6	73 6

The colonel is allowed 2*s*. 8*d*. per day for each troop.

Infantry.

No. of men in a company.	Non-effect. per ann.	Contingencies. Men at 6*d*. per day.	Contingencies. Amount per ann.	Total per ann.
	£.		£. s. d.	£. s. d.
Under 50	20	Two -	18 5 0	38 5 0
Under 76	20	Three -	27 7 6	47 7 6
And upwards	20	Four -	36 10 0	56 10 0

The colonel is allowed 6*d*. per day for each company; the contingencies are given to the ſubaltern who pays them.

The non-effective money is ſtill continued to the field-officers, who

who have loſt their troops or companies by the late regulation.

There is a yearly allowance of 2*s.* 9*d.* to each ſoldier, under the head of ordnance money, for keeping his arms bright: alſo 2*s.* 6*d.* for altering each man's clothing; but theſe do not extend to regiments on foreign ſtations.

Officers, non-commiſſioned officers, and privates employed in the public works, have the following allowances: ſubalterns, in addition to their daily pay, 4*s.*; non-commiſſioned officers, as overſeers, ditto, 4*s.*; ditto, or privates as artificers, 1*s.* 8*d.*; ditto, in winter, 1*s.* 4*d.* Privates as labourers, 10*d.*; ditto, in winter, 8*d.*

Allowances of Rations to every Six Soldiers on board Tranſports, &c. equal to the Quantity iſſued to Four Seamen.

	lb weight of biſcuit.	Pints of peaſe.	lb weight of pork.	ozs. of butter.	ozs. of cheeſe.	Pints of meal.	lb weight of beef.	lb weight of flour.	ozs. of plums.	Pints of ſpirits.
Sunday -	4	2	4	0	0	0	0	0	0	2*
Monday -	4	0	0	6	9	2	0	0	0	2
Tueſday -	4	0	0	0	0	0	4	3	8	2
Wedneſday	4	2	0	6	9	2	0	0	0	2
Thurſday -	4	2	4	0	0	0	0	0	0	2
Friday -	4	2	0	6	9	2	0	0	0	2
Saturday -	4	0	0	0	0	0	4	3	8	2

Allowances in ſtationary Quarters. Each ſoldier, in barrack or quarter, is allowed to make uſe of 1lb. of bread, and three quarters of a pound of meat per day. When the price of meat exceeds 6*d.* per pound, and bread 1½*d.* ſuch exceſs beyond the ſtated prices is defrayed at the public expence.

Allowances on a March. Soldiers on a march are allowed 11*d.* per day, each, in addition to his pay. Of this conſolidated ſum 1*s.* 4*d.* goes to the innkeepers on whom they are billetted. Innkeepers furniſh ſoldiers billetted on them, as ſtationary, with candles, vinegar, ſalt, pepper, and muſtard, for which they receive ½*d.* per day from each; and for each horſe belonging to officers billetted on them, 1*s.* 2*d.* per night for hay and ſtraw.

Men permitted to find their own lodgings, have each, in lieu of beer, 2*d.* per day allowed them, if in billet, 1½*d.* a halfpenny

* When ſpirits are not uſed, double that quantity of wine is iſſued in its place. Vinegar is iſſued as occaſion and the preſervation of health require it.

of

of which goes to the landlord, for the articles ſtated above: and if in barrack, 1*d.* per day.

Allowances to Waggoners for the carriage of baggage, &c. For a waggon with five horſes, 1*s.* per mile; ditto with four horſes, or 15 cwt. 9*d.* per mile: leſs than four horſes, or under 15cwt. 6*d.* per mile.

Additional rates may, if reaſon ſhould demand it, be fixed by magiſtrates, at the general ſeſſions, not exceeding 4*d.* 3*d.* 2*d.* in proportion to the firſt.

Allowances to men for life, who become blind or wounded in ſervice. Serjeants, 1*s.* 6*d.*; corporals, 1*s.* 2*d.*; and privates, 1*s.* per day. When a wound occaſions the loſs of an eye or a limb to an officer, he is, by his majeſty's warrant, entitled to a gratuity in money equal to one year's pay of the rank he holds; further, he is allowed the expence attending his cure, if not performed at the public charge. The *widow and orphans* of an officer killed in action, are allowed according to his regimental rank, viz. The widow, one year's pay; each child under age, or not married, one third of what is allowed to the widow. All perſons dying of their wounds within ſix months, are deemed ſlain in battle. Officers commanding regiments are to certify the time, place, and event: a duplicate of which is to be ſent with the monthly return.

Allowances to diſcharged Men *not recommended.*

In England	to any part of ———	14	days pay.
	to any part of Scotland	21	
	to any part of Ireland	28	

Regulations relative to the Commiſſary Department in Home Encampments.

Bread. Each ſoldier is to receive as his allowance for four days, a loaf, weighing ſix pounds, made of wheat flour, for which he is to be charged five-pence, to be paid by the regimental paymaſter, at every ſettlement, to the contractor, or to ſuch other perſon as the commiſſary-general may appoint. Servants not being ſoldiers, in the proportion of two per troop or company, and waſher-women for each troop or company, in the proportion of one for every twenty men, are permitted to receive bread at the ſame price, to be paid alſo by the paymaſter. Each ſoldier is allowed wood or coal at the rate of 3lb. weight per day; and 27lb. weight of ſtraw for every 32 days: the ſame is iſſued at certain periods. The batmen of each troop, or company, are allowed 72lb. and the waſher-women 108lb. weight of ſtraw for every ſixteen days: iſſued in like manner. Each troop, or company, is allowed 1080lb. weight of ſtraw for thatching the huts. Soldiers of regiments

not

not having paillhaffes, are allowed one third ftraw in addition. Hofpitals, &c. are fupplied with both; as the furgeons deem it neceffary. Officers are allowed wood or coal in rations of 3lb. weight each, per day; viz. commander in chief, without limitation; general, 100; lieutenant-general, 70; major, adjutant, quarter-mafter, barrack-mafter, and commiffary-general, each 50; brigadier general, 40; deputies adjutant, quarter-mafter, and commiffary general, each 12; infpector-general of hofpitals, 10; colonel (or officer commanding a regiment) and the officers of each troop or company, 8; affiftants, adjutant, quarter-mafter, commiffary-general, majors of brigade, and infpector of hofpitals, each, engineer and provoft marfhal, 6; refident commiffary, furgeon, apothecary, purveyor, aid de camp, and field officers, each 4; deputy-purveyor, affiftant provoft marfhal, and hofpital mate, 2.

Forage is daily iffued in rations of 10lb. weight of oats, 14lb. hay, and 6lb. ftraw, each, for the effective horfes in camp, belonging to officers, not exceeding the following numbers: commander in chief, 30; general 16; lieutenant-general, 12; major-general, 10; brigadier, adjutant, quarter-mafter, barrack-mafter generals each, and colonel of cavalry, 8; colonel of infantry, and lieutenant colonel of cavalry, each 7; commiffary general, lieutenant colonel of infantry, and major of cavalry, 6; deputies adjutant, quarter-mafter, and barrack-mafter generals each, fecretary to the commander in chief, and major of infantry, 5; affiftants, adjutants, and quarter-mafter generals, each, deputy commiffary, infpector-general of hofpitals, aid de camp to the commander in chief, and captains of cavalry, each 4; phyfician purveyor, aid de camp, major of brigade, affiftants commiffary and infpector of hofpitals each, captains and adjutants of infantry, and fubalterns of cavalry, each 3; provoft marfhal, furgeon, apothecary, deputy purveyor, pay-mafter, adjutant of infantry, and futlers, 2; affiftant provoft marfhal and furgeons, each, quarter-mafters of horfe and foot, veterinary, and furgeons of both, 1. Rations of ftraw iffued to cavalry and artillery horfes are but 4 lb. weight each.

Returns are to be tranfmitted to the refident commiffary, figned by each officer, on the day preceding the morning of delivery. Officers having brevet rank, draw forage according to their regimental rank; and thofe having two commiffions draw but for one. The field officers and captains of cavalry pay fixpence per ration for the forage. The pay-mafter pays 8½*d*. for the troop horfes: all other officers receive theirs without payment. After four deliveries of bread, wood, and forage, and one of ftraw, making a period of fixteen days, a fettlement is made by the pay-mafter, and bills on the agents, given to the contractors, in the prefence of the refident commiffary. The fettlement for the general and ftaff officers is to take place

 at

at each period of thirty-two days. The aid de camps ſign receipts for the latter; a commiſſioned officer of cavalry, and quarter-maſter of infantry for the former; and phyſicians or ſurgeons for the general or regimental hoſpitals.

By another regulation officers commanding diſtricts have the following yearly allowance of forage for taking the field.

	Number of Rations for 100 days.	Amount at 6d. per Ration.
General - - -	40 - -	£200
Lieutenant general -	30 - -	150
Major general - -	24 - -	120
Brigadier general - -	20 - -	100
Aid-de-camp, &c. -	4 - -	20

From the above, a deduction of one ſhilling in the pound is made at the war office, and ſixpence at the pay office. In general, the forage allowances to officers on foreign ſtations, wherein they differ materially, are greater than thoſe at home; they are regulated by the commanders in chief there, and iſſued by their warrants accordingly.

Indemnifications for Loſſes ſuſtained by Officers on Service.

Infantry.

	Baggage.	Camp Equipage.		Horſes,	
	£.	£.	s.	£.	s.
Colonel -	120 -	80	0 -	31	10
Field Officer	100 -	60	0 -	31	10
Captain -	80 -	35	0 -	18	18
Sub. ſtaff	60 -	17	10 -	18	18
Adjutant	60 -	17	10 -	31	10

Horſes ordered to be ſhot for the glanders, killed, or taken by the enemy, come under the head of loſſes. Should a part only of baggage be loſt, it is eſtimated at $\frac{1}{4}$, $\frac{1}{2}$, or $\frac{1}{3}$, without entering into the particulars, according to which they receive in proportion, upon certificates ſtating the circumſtances and cauſes, ſigned by themſelves, and authenticated by the officers commanding their regiments.

Cavalry.

	Baggage.			Camp Equipage.			Horſes.		
	£.	s.	d.	£.	s.	d.	£.	s.	d.
Colonel -	140	0	0	90	0	0	31	10	0
Field officer -	120	0	0	90	0	0	31	10	0
Captain -	90	0	0	45	0	0	31	10	0
Sub. -	70	0	0	45	0	0	31	10	0

Quarter-

	Baggage.			Camp Equipage.			Horses.		
	£.	s.	d.	£.	s.	d.	£.	s.	d.
Quarter-master	40	0	0	00	0	0	29	8	0
Staff officers whose situations require their keeping good horses							31	10	0
General officer's first charger							47	5	0
Ditto - second ditto							31	10	0
Heavy dragoon's first charger							47	0	0
Light dragoon's first ditto							36	15	0
Batt-horses both for cavalry and infantry							18	18	0

Claims, as preferred in these cases, are to be submitted to the consideration of the general officers commanding in chief on foreign stations, who are authorised to order payments accordingly.

Indemnification for Loss of Necessaries, &c. sustained by Non-commissioned Officers and Privates on Service.

	Cavalry.			Infantry.		
	£.	s.	d.	£.	s.	d.
Serjeant	2	15	0	2	10	0
Corporal, trumpeter, private	2	10	0	2	2	0
A servant, not being a soldier in either cavalry or infantry	3	8	0	0	0	0

Certificates of the above to be signed by the captains of troops or companies, also by the officers commanding regiments.

Officers embarking with their regiments for foreign service, or ordered out with recruits, are allowed each; lieutenant colonel, 30*l*.; major, 25*l*. captain, subaltern, and staff, 20*l*.

Prize Money. In 1803 a board of general officers was convened for the purpose of regulating the future distribution of prize money; who, having agreed, submitted the following plan for his majesty's consideration, which being approved of, is now the standing regulation.

In all captures, made in conjunct expeditions, the navy and army to share equally, according to their corresponding ranks.

The total amount, being separately received by the agents respectively appointed by each, to be divided similarly to the present mode practised in the navy, according to the following proportions.

	Shares.
Private, drummer, driver, artificer, servant, each	1
Corporal, bombadier, and foreman of artificers, each	1½
Serjeant, conductor of stores, and master artificer, ditto	5
Staff serjeant	8

	Shares.
Quarter-maſter of dragoons - - - -	12
2d lieutenant, cornet, enſign, ſurgeon, hoſpital mate, clerk of the ſtores, and of works, overſeers and draughtſmen, each - - - - - -	16
Lieutenant, baggage and waggon maſters, provoſt marſhal, deputy purveyor, aſſiſtant adjutants, quarter maſter, commiſſaries and paymaſters general, and draughtſmen, each - - - - - -	20
Captain, paymaſter, ſurgeon, major of brigade, aid-de-camp, judge advocate, phyſician, purveyor, field inſpector, apothecary, commiſſaries, ſurveyor, and draughtſmen, each, and ſecretary to the commander in chief - - - - -	50
Major, inſpector of hoſpitals, (not at the head of the department,) deputy commiſſaries, and deputies, adjutant, and quarter maſter, inſpectors, and aſſiſtant inſpector general, each - - - - -	80
Lieutenant-colonel, deputy paymaſter-general, deputies, adjutant, quarter-maſter, and commiſſary general (at the head of the departments,) and director, ſuperintendant, and inſpector general (not at the head of the departments), each - - -	100
Colonel, adjutant, quarter-maſter, and director general, and ſuperintendant and inſpector general at the head of the department, each - - -	150
Brigadier generals, and commiſſary general, in an army commanded by a major general, each -	300
Major-generals, and commiſſary general -	450
Lieutenant-generals, each - -	800
Generals, each - - -	1200
Field-marſhal - - - -	2000

The officer in command may have for his choice one ſixteenth of the whole prize, or the number of ſhares of the rank above that which he holds in the army. Officers having brevet rank ſhare according to it; and thoſe having two commiſſions receive but for one. Only thoſe who were preſent at the attack, or having formed a part of the army at the time, have claim: but thoſe who have remained behind, or been ſent another way; though formerly forming a part of the army, are excluded. The board alſo recommended the appointment of prize agents, to be under the direction of the ſecretary at war.

Staff. The ſtaff of the Britiſh army is compoſed of the following perſons. The commander in chief and his military ſecretary; ſecretary at war; deputy ditto; adjutant general; deputy ditto; quarter maſter general; deputy ditto; barrack-maſters general; deputy ditto; inſpector general; deputy ditto;

ditto; commissary general of musters; deputy ditto; commissary general of stores; deputy ditto; inspector general of army accounts; physician general; surgeon ditto; apothecary ditto; military superintendant and inspector of hospitals; two paymasters general; judge martial and advocate general; veterinary surgeon general.

COMMANDER IN CHIEF'S OFFICE. This office is held at the Horse Guards, Whitehall, for the purpose of receiving information and transacting business relative to the details of military affairs. In it are the commander in chief, a public secretary, a private secretary, with aids-de-camp, assistants and clerks.

WAR OFFICE. This office is also held at Whitehall. Of the rank and duties of the secretary at war, some account has been given in this volume, page 27; his deputy secretary prepares the correspondence, and (under the orders or authority of the secretary at war) directs the whole business of the department, the accountant's branch excepted.

The *first clerk* is responsible for the execution of the detail of the business, and superintends the conduct of all the clerks, messengers, tradesmen, &c.

The *principal clerk* is employed in conducting the current business of the office, under the directions of the first clerk. There are other clerks, who prepare and are responsible for the estimates and establishments of the army; they also transact the business relating to the payment of the staff, garrisons, &c. are employed in the current business of the office, and in particular attendance on the secretary, and deputy secretary at war, enter all commissions of officers, prepare the army lists, and make out the warrants for holding courts martial, receive and pay the charges for subsistence and escort of deserters from British regiments, taken up in Ireland, and from Irish regiments taken up in Great Britain; and transact all the business relative to the pensions of the widows of officers.

In the *Accountant's department* are persons who superintend the examination and settlement of all the accounts of the army, that come under the cognizance of the war-office. This branch is not considered as subject to the directions of the deputy secretary, but only of the secretary at war himself. The principal assists in examining the army accounts, and in proposing the sums to be issued from time to time on account, for various services not borne on the regimental establishment; such as recruiting, extra feed, innkeepers allowances, &c.; he also prepares the beating orders, and copies thereof; and two assistants make out from the muster rolls, abstract statements of the numbers, rank, and pay of the officers and men borne thereon; by

a [illegible]

a comparison with which, the corresponding charges in the regimental accounts are to be verified.

Adjutant General's Office. This office is held in Crown Court, Westminster, but considered a branch of the commander in chief's office. In it are the adjutant general, deputy adjutant general, quarter master general and his assistants.

Paymaster General, and the Barrack Department, have already been described; the former at page 27 of this volume, the latter at page 290.

Army Agents. The colonels of regiments appoint their own agents. These persons give security to government for the several sums of money intrusted to their care, and act between the paymaster general, secretary at war, and the paymasters of regiments. Agents are subject to the articles of war: should they withhold the pay of officers or soldiers for one month, on proof before a court martial, they are liable to be dismissed from their situation, and to forfeit 100*l.* for every such offence. In the cavalry, agents are allowed one warrant man per day (at 1*s.* 2*d.*) for each troop; and in the infantry one (at 6*d.*) for each company. They are also allowed 2d. in the pound on the full pay of regiments. According to the strength established by the war office, the allowances to agents are, for paying a regiment of cavalry, 433*l.* 13*s.* per annum, and for paying a regiment of infantry, 270*l.* 1*s.* 6*d.*

Garrisons. Some forts and fortresses are necessarily maintained in various parts of the British dominions, for protection, and in these, garrisons are placed in the proper and genuine sense of the word; but in military colleges and hospitals, and in some towns where garrison duty is necessarily performed, the government is in the hands of military officers, and they are also in general denominated garrisons. Those in the united kingdom, of both species, are included in the following list, some being under the command of governors with subordinate officers, others of town majors: Alderney, Belfast, Berwick, Blackness Castle, Calshot, Carlisle, Carrickfergus, Charlemont, Chelsea Hospital, Chester, Cinque Ports, Cork, Dartmouth, Dunbarton, Dublin, Duncannon Fort, Edinburgh, Galway, Gravesend and Tilbury, Guernsey, Hull, Hurst Castle, Jersey, near Inverness, Kinsale, Landguard, Limerick, Londonderry and Culmore, Londonderry, St. Mawes, Royal Military College, Royal Military Asylum, Pendennis Castle, Plymouth, Portland Castle, Portsmouth, Ross Castle, Scarborough Castle, Scilly Island, Sheerness, South Sea Castle, Stirling Castle, Tynmouth and Cliff Fort, Tower of London, Upnor Castle, the Isle of Wight, Fort William, Windsor, and North Yarmouth.

Among the garrisons above mentioned, the Military College,

 Chelsea

Chelsea Hospital, and the Military Asylum, will be noticed in a subsequent page; and the Tower of London, in treating of the metropolis.

MILITIA. Of the origin and use of this portion of the military force some account has already been given; the following are the details respecting it, drawn from the statute 42 Geo. III. c. 90, and some subsequent regulating acts; but it is to be observed, they do not apply to the city of London, the Tower Hamlets, the Stannaries or the Cinque Ports.

LORD LIEUTENANTS OF COUNTIES. These officers are appointed by the king, and are intrusted by parliament with full power and authority to call together, arm, and array the militia, and cause them to be trained and exercised once in every year. They may appoint twenty or more persons duly qualified, and living within their respective counties, ridings, and places, to be their deputy lieutenants; and may also appoint a proper number of colonels, lieutenant colonels, majors, and other officers duly qualified, to train, discipline, and command the militia. But the names of the deputy lieutenants, and persons for whom commissions are intended, are to be laid before the king, and if he expresses disapprobation within fourteen days, the commissions are not to issue. And if the lieutenant is out of the kingdom or the situation vacant, the king may empower three deputy lieutenants to nominate officers, who, when appointed, rank with the officers of the regular forces as youngest of their rank.

QUALIFICATIONS. *Deputy Lieutenant* must have 200*l.* a year in land, freehold, copyhold, or customary, or in estates for long terms of years determinable on one or more life or lives, held in his own right, or in right of his wife; or he must be heir apparent to some person possessed in like manner of 400*l.* a year. *Colonel*, 1000*l.* a year, or heir apparent to 2000*l.* *Lieutenant-colonel*, 600*l.* a year, or heir apparent to 1200*l.* *Major*, 400*l.* or heir apparent to 800*l.* *Captain*, 200*l.* or heir apparent to 400*l.* or younger son of a person who is, or at the time of his death was, possessed of 600*l.* a year. *Lieutenant*, a similar estate of 50*l.* per annum, or 1000*l.* in personal estate, or in real and personal together 2000*l.* or son of a person who is, or who died possessed of an estate of 100*l.* per year, or of personal property in value 2000*l.* or real and personal together 3000*l.* *Ensign*, 20*l.* a year, or in personal estate 500*l.* or in real and personal together, 1000*l.* or son of a person who has, or had, 50*l.* a year, 1000*l.* in personal, or in real and personal together 1500*l.* one moiety of the qualifications to be situate within the county or place for which the commission is granted: reversions to be estimated at one third of their actual produce; that is, an estate of 300*l.* a year in reversion, to be esteemed equal to one in possession of 100*l.* and so in proportion; and beneficial leaseholds

holds where the original term exceeded twenty years, to be considered as full qualifications to the extent of their annual value.

In the counties of *Cumberland*, *Huntingdon*, *Monmouth*, *Westmoreland*, and *Rutland*, and in every county and place in *Wales*, the estates requisite for the qualification of the deputy lieutenants and officers are smaller. For a *deputy lieutenant* 150*l*. a year, or heir apparent to 300*l*. *Colonel*, 600*l*. or heir apparent to 1200*l*. *Lieutenant-colonel* or *major commandant*, 400*l*. or heir apparent to 800*l*. *Major*, 200*l*. or heir apparent, 400*l*. *Captain*, 150*l*. or son of a person who has or had at his death 300*l*. *Lieutenant*, 30*l*. a year, or personal estate 600*l*. or or real and personal together 1200*l*. or son of a person who is, or died, worth 60*l*. a year, or with a personal estate of 1200*l*. or real and personal 2400*l*. *Ensign*, 20*l*. a year, or personal estate in value 300*l*. or real and personal together 600*l*.; or son of a person who is, or died, worth 30*l*. a year, or in personal estate 600*l*. or real and personal mixed 1200*l*.

In the *Isle of Ely* the qualifications are nearly similar, but in some respects rather lower, a *Captain* being required to possess no greater estate than 100*l*. a year, or to be heir apparent to double that sum, or younger son of one a proprietor of 300*l*. per annum. In the lieutenant and ensign there is no difference from those in the last mentioned counties.

In *cities or towns which are counties within themselves*, and have been used to raise and train a separate militia within their liberties; the lieutenant of every such city or town, or where there is none appointed, the chief magistrate nominates the deputy lieutenants and officers of militia, whose number and rank must be proportionable to the number of militia-men which such city or town is to raise as their quota; and all powers and provisions made with respect to counties at large take place in them. The qualification for a *deputy lieutenant* is 150*l*. a year as aforesaid, or a personal estate alone, or real and personal estate together, to the amount or value of 3000*l*. *Field officer*, 300*l*.; or personal estate alone, or real and personal together, to the value of 5000*l*. *Captain*, 150*l*. a year; or personal estate alone, or real and personal together, to the value of 2500*l*. *Lieutenant*, 30*l*. a year, or personal estate of 750*l*. *Ensign* 20*l*. a year, or personal estate of 400*l*. One half of the real estates (except those for lieutenants and ensigns) must be within such city or town, or within the county to which it is united.

No person can be admitted a deputy lieutenant, or to any rank in a regiment of militia higher than that of *lieutenant*, until he delivers to the clerk of the peace or his deputy, a specific description in writing, signed by himself, of his qualifica-

 tion;

tion; stating the parish in which it is situate; of which the clerk of the peace transmits to the lord lieutenant a copy; and no commission for a higher rank than that of lieutenant is valid, unless it be declared in it that such officer has delivered in his qualification as directed. The clerk of the peace is also to enter the qualifications on a roll, to publish the commissions granted, and in whose room, in the London Gazette, and, every January, transmit to the secretary of state a complete account of qualifications left with him, to be laid before parliament; and the officers must, within six months at some general or quarter session, or in one of the courts of record at Westminster, take the oaths appointed by law. Every deputy lieutenant and officer down to major, acting without having delivered in his qualification, to forfeit 200*l.* and every captain 100*l.* half to the informer, and the proof of qualification to rest on the party sued; but the necessity of delivering in a qualification does not rest on peers or their heirs apparent, whether they be lords lieutenant, or commissioned officers.

Number. The number of private men to be raised (exclusive of the places excepted) is as follows:

For the county of Bedford	317
Berks	561
Bucks	599
Cambridge	481
Chester, with the city and county of the city of Chester	885
Cornwall	647
Cumberland	615
Derby	939
Devon, with the city and county of the city of Exeter	1512
Dorset, with the town and county of the town of Poole	411
Durham	492
Essex	1244
Gloucester, with the city and county of Gloucester, and the city and county of Bristol	1163
Hereford	520
Hertford	480
Huntingdon	159
Kent, with the city and county of the city of Canterbury	1296
Lancaster	2439
Leicester	643
Lincoln, with the city and county of the city of Lincoln	1368
Middlesex (exclusive of the Tower Hamlets)	3038
Monmouth	280
Norfolk, with the city and county of the city of Norwich	1209
Northampton	724

Northum-

Northumberland, with the town and county of the town of Newcastle, and town of Berwick	649
Nottingham, with the town and county of the town of Nottingham	564
Oxford	603
Rutland	83
Salop	991
Somerset	1556
Southampton, with the town and county of the town of Southampton	859
Stafford, with the city and county of the city of Litchfield	1133
Suffolk	1048
Surry	1336
Sussex	803
Warwick, with the city and county of the city of Coventry	853
Westmoreland	243
Worcester, with the city and county of the city of Worcester	616
Wilts	917
York, West Riding, with the city and county of the city of York	2429
——, North Riding	911
——, East Riding, with the town and county of Kingston upon Hull	564
Anglesea	128
Brecknock	204
Cardigan	244
Caermarthen, with the county borough of Caermarthen	405
Caernarvon	128
Denbigh	344
Flint	205
Glamorgan	403
Merioneth	121
Montgomery	279
Pembroke, with town and county of the town of Haverford West	201
Radnor	140
Total	39,573

This quota was to remain in force till the 25th of June 1805, and at that time, and afterward, at the expiration of every period of ten years, the privy council is empowered to fix and settle such quotas as they shall think fit, but as nearly as possible in the same proportion, sending the amount of each quota to the lord lieutenant whom it shall concern, and publishing the whole in the London Gazette. If the number thus required shall

ſhall exceed that before provided, the lord lieutenant, with three or more deputy lieutenants, at a general meeting to be holden for that purpoſe, muſt appoint what number of militia-men ſhall ſerve for each reſpective hundred, rape, lathe, wapentake, or other diviſion within ſuch county or place; and ſuch additional men are to be provided or choſen in the ſame manner as other militia-men. If the number required is leſs than that which is eſtabliſhed, the general meeting may diſmiſs the ſupernumeraries by ballot; but every one of them muſt appear and ſerve again if his preſence is rendered neceſſary by vacancies in the regiment or any other cauſe.

Supplementary Militia. In caſe of invaſion, or of imminent danger, and alſo in caſe of rebellion, the king may (the occaſion being firſt communicated to parliament if ſitting, or declared in council and notified by proclamation, if there be no parliament ſitting) by his proclamation, order and direct an additional number of militia men, not exceeding one-half of the aggregate number of the ordinary militia, to be raiſed and enrolled. The form of apportioning them, and their duties when embodied, are exactly the ſame as thoſe of other militia men, and the ballot is to be taken out of the old liſts. If at the time when the ſupplementary militia is called out the parliament is ſeparated or prorogued for a term which will not expire in fourteen days, the king is to iſſue a proclamation for aſſembling them within that time; and if his majeſty thinks it expedient to reduce the whole or any part of the ſupplementary militia, he may do it by proclamation; but the men ſo diſbanded remain liable, in caſe of vacancy, to ſerve for the pariſh or place for which they were originally ballotted.

Making Lists and Ballotting. The firſt meaſure taken to raiſe the militia, is by a *general meeting of the lieutenancy* of every county, riding, and place, holden in ſome principal town; to conſiſt of the lieutenant, together with two deputy lieutenants at the leaſt, or on the death or removal, or in the abſence of the lieutenant, then of three deputy lieutenants at the leaſt; and one ſuch general meeting is held annually, the laſt Tueſday before the 10th of October, or earlier if required; and other general meetings may be ſummoned on giving notice in the London Gazette; and alſo in any weekly newſpaper uſually circulated in ſuch county, riding, or place, fourteen days at leaſt before the days appointed for holding them. If the number of deputy lieutenants who attend is not ſufficient to proceed to buſineſs, any deputy lieutenant preſent, or the clerk, may adjourn them to any other time and place. At theſe general meetings, *ſubdiviſion meetings* are appointed, conſiſting of two deputy lieutenants, or one and a magiſtrate, of which meetings the clerk of the general meet-

ings

ings is to give notice to every deputy lieutenant residing in the sub-division, and also to the commander of the regiment, battalion, or corps of militia, with an account of the days fixed for receiving the lists, and ballotting for and enrolling the men; and another list specifying the names, trades, and usual places of abode of all such militia men as are enrolled; and, where there are substitutes, the names, trades, and places of abode of the persons in the room of whom such substitutes were enrolled.

At the general meeting, orders are to be issued to the chief constables, or other officers of the several hundreds, rapes, lathes, wapentakes, or other divisions within their respective counties, ridings, and places, requiring them to issue orders under their hands to all constables, tythingmen, headboroughs, or other officers of every parish, tything, or place within their divisions, to return to the deputy lieutenants within their respective sub-divisions, fair and true lists in writing of the names of all the men usually, and at that time, dwelling within their respective parishes, tythings, and places, between the ages of 18 and 45 years. Such constables and other officers are then, within fourteen days after any such returns shall be required, to give or leave notice in writing to or for every occupier of a dwelling-house where any person shall reside, within the limits of the places for which they act, at his or her dwelling house, or where such dwelling house shall be divided into different apartments, and occupied distinctly by several persons, then to or for the occupier of each, to prepare and produce, within fourteen days, a list in writing, to the best of his or her belief, of the Christian and surname of every man resident therein, between the ages of 18 and 45, distinguishing every person claiming to be exempt from serving; and every such notice is to mention the time and place appointed for hearing appeals; and every occupier must make out the list, and sign and deliver it to the constable or other officer under penalty, in case of neglect or falsity, of a sum not exceeding 5*l*. If the officer who ought to demand these lists happens to be a *Quaker*, two justices may appoint a deputy to act for him, and if the householder is of that sect, the officer may make the list for him; but in both cases the religion of the party must be proved by the written attestation of two respectable individuals of his persuasion. The constables and other parish officers are, after they have obtained these returns, to make out and fix on the church doors, or other public place annually, a general list of persons whom they consider liable to serve, with a notice of the latest or only day of appeals. Copies of these lists are then to be returned to the deputy lieutenants, who may, if they think proper, add together any two or more of them as if but one list; the constables whose duties applied to these

theſe liſts are to act conjointly; and in all caſes the deputy lieutenants may determine differences between theſe officers with reſpect to the limits of their juriſdictions. The act extends to all extra-parochial places, and in them the officers of the circumjacent diſtrict are to act. Perſons endeavouring by menaces or promiſes to procure their names to be omitted or eraſed from a return forfeit 50*l*., and thoſe who refuſe to diſcloſe their names, 10*l*.

The conſtables, if required, are to attend the ſubdiviſion meetings, and if convicted of neglect or partiality, to be committed to the common jail for one month, or fined not exceeding 20*l*. nor leſs than 40*s*. They may amend their liſts according to facts which may appear, or make out new, in caſe of any being caſually loſt or deſtroyed, and they muſt verify them on oath. Perſons who conſider themſelves aggrieved may appeal to the ſubdiviſion meeting appointed, but the deciſion of the majority of deputy lieutenants there is final. The clerks of the ſubdiviſion meetings are to tranſmit to the clerk of the general meeting copies of the rolls of perſons liable to ſerve, as ſigned at the ſubdiviſion meeting, and theſe, properly made out and arranged, are ſent to the privy council. Clerks of ſubdiviſion meetings neglecting their duty in theſe particulars forfeit 20*l*., thoſe of general meetings 100*l*.

From theſe liſts the lord lieutenant, and three deputies, or, on his death or removal, five deputies, at a general meeting, fix or alter the ſubdiviſions in their county, riding, or place, and the allotments in each reſpective hundred, rape, lathe, wapentake, or other diviſion. At a ſecond ſubdiviſion meeting the deputy lieutenants appoint the number of men to ſerve for each pariſh, tything, and place; in proportion to the number appointed to ſerve for each hundred, rape, lathe, wapentake, or other diviſion; and appoint another meeting to be holden within three weeks. And they iſſue an order to the chief conſtable or other officer of the hundreds, or other diviſions, requiring them to give notice to the conſtable or other proper officer of every pariſh, tything, or place, of the men appointed to ſerve for ſuch pariſh or place, and of the time and place of the next ſubdiviſion meeting.

The deputy lieutenants, or any two or more of them, in conſequence of ſuch appointment, cauſe the number of men appointed to ſerve to be choſen by ballot out of the liſt returned for every pariſh or place. They alſo, at the ſame or ſubſequent meetings, ballot for men to fill up vacancies which may ariſe from any of the following cauſes: miſtake or neglect in the conſtables, the perſon ballotted being infirm in health, or under five feet four inches in height, and not having property to the amount of 100*l*., death, or diſcharge, or promotion of any

any private to the rank of serjeant, corporal, or drummer, the fact being certified by the commanding officer, and the persons ballotted deserting or not appearing within a month.

The persons ballotted for are liable to serve, although they remove from the place where they resided when the list was made. When a parish is situated in two counties, the persons ballotted belong to the militia of that wherein the parish church stands.

Churchwardens and overseers, with the consent of the parish, obtained at a vestry called for the purpose, and of which three days notice must be given, may provide substitutes for the whole number or any portion of it which their parish ought to raise; and if they hire the men at a price not exceeding *6l.* each, they may make a rate for the purpose of reimbursing themselves. In this case the same appeals may be made as against a poor rate.

For the purpose of swearing and enrolling the men, the deputy lieutenants and justices appoint another meeting to be holden within three weeks in the same subdivision; and they issue an order to the chief constables, to direct the constables or other officers of each parish or place to give notice to every man so chosen to appear at such meeting; which notice must be given to him or left at his place of abode at least seven days before the meeting.

Exemptions. The following persons are entirely exempt from service in the militia. Peers of the realm, commissioned officers in his majesty's other forces, or in any castle or fort, officers on the half pay of the navy, army, or marines; officers or private men in any other forces, or officers serving or having served four years in the militia; resident members of either of the universities; clergymen, licensed teachers of separate congregations, whose places of meeting are duly registered; constables, and other peace officers; articled clerks, apprentices, seamen, or seafaring men, persons mustered, trained, or doing duty, or employed in any of his majesty's docks or dock-yards, in the Tower of London, Woolwich Warren, gun-wharfs at Portsmouth, the powder mills, powder magazines, or other storehouses under the direction of the board of ordnance; persons being free of the company of watermen of the river Thames; any poor men having more than one child born in wedlock; persons serving or having found a substitute in the army of reserve; and effective volunteers. And no person having served personally or by substitute can be obliged to serve again until by rotation it comes to his turn; but no person who has served only as a substitute or volunteer in the militia, is by such service exempted from serving again, if chosen by ballot. On these exemptions it is only necessary to observe, that although an articled clerk is protected, an attorney is not; and if the deputy lieutenants and justices at any subdivision meeting receive information, or suspect, that any person inserted in any list described as an apprentice, has been fraudulently bound in order to avoid serving, they may inquire into such binding, and summon witnesses, and examine them on oath: and if such fraud appears, they may appoint the person to serve immediately if there be a vacancy; if not, then on the first vacancy that shall happen: and the person to whom the apprentice was fraudulently bound, forfeits 10*l.*

Swearing and Enrolling. At the meeting appointed for the purpose of swearing and enrolling militia-men, the constables attend and swear to the service of notices, and the individuals chosen by ballot must appear. The parties are examined on oath, as to their families, residence, age, and state of health, to which last they are also corporally examined by skilful surgeons attending for the purpose. The militia man, if approved, takes an oath that he will serve faithfully, and his name is written in a roll provided for the purpose, the term of his service being five years. If the persons ballotted refuse to appear, they incur a penalty of 10*l.* and are liable to serve again at the expiration of five years. Persons refusing to be examined as to their fitness to serve, may be imprisoned a week, and still are liable.

Substitutes. If any person chosen by lot, shall produce for his substitute, a man of the same county or riding, or of some adjoining county or riding, able and fit for service, who shall have not more than one child born in wedlock, and who shall be examined and approved, such substitute shall be enrolled to serve for five years; and also for such further time as the militia shall remain embodied, if within the space of five years his majesty shall order such militia to be drawn out and embodied. The substitute undergoes the same examinations, and takes the same oath as the ballotted man; but he must be at least five feet two inches in height, and not a seaman or seafaring man. If a substitute, after receiving any portion of his money, refuses to appear and be sworn, he must return the money, with a penal addition not exceeding 40*s.* nor less than 20*s.* or be committed for fourteen days to the house of correction. When substitutes are engaged, if the militia is not embodied, two deputy lieutenants or one justice may order the money agreed for to be paid to the substitute; but if the militia is embodied, a sum not exceeding one half is to be paid to the substitute; the residue to the clerk of the subdivision meeting, to be by him forwarded to the paymaster or regimental clerk, who will pay it to the substitute on his joining the regiment:

ment: and if the ſubdiviſion clerk neglects to remit it for one week, he is to forfeit 20*l*. for every offence.

If a Quaker is ballotted, and refuſes to ſerve or to find a ſubſtitute, two deputy lieutenants may provide one on as reaſonable terms as poſſible, and defray the expence by a diſtreſs on his effects; but if he ſhall not have ſufficient goods to diſtrain, and yet be able to pay 10*l*. he is to be committed to the common jail for three months; and if Quakers refuſe to pay a parochial rate for finding ſubſtitutes, a diſtreſs may be levied, and the juſtices may allow coſts.

Servants enrolled in the militia do not vacate their contracts unleſs embodied, and then are to receive their wages up to the day.

Any high conſtable, or chief or other conſtable, or any adjutant, quarter maſter, or ſerjeant in the militia, inſuring or taking any money for the inſurance of, or being in any way concerned in any company, ſociety, partnerſhip, or office for the inſurance of perſons, for the providing ſubſtitutes or volunteers, or for the paying or returning any money for the providing ſubſtitutes or volunteers in the militia, for any perſon ballotted, forfeits 50*l*.

Classes. The deputy lieutenants in their ſeveral ſubdiviſions, as ſoon as they ſhall have enrolled the number of men required, divide them into the following claſſes, *viz*. in the firſt claſs, all the men under thirty years of age, and having no child living; in the ſecond, all the men above thirty, having no child living; in the third, all the men not having any child living under the age of fourteen years; in the fourth claſs, all the men having only one child under fourteen years; and in the laſt claſs, all the men not included in any of the former deſcriptions. They then make out a liſt of ſuch claſſes, and within three days, the clerk of ſuch ſubdiviſion muſt tranſmit to the clerk of the general meetings a true copy, to be entered in a book kept for the purpoſe.

Regulars entering. For preventing the men enrolled in militia regiments from inliſting in other forces, it is enacted, that no recruiting officer ſhall knowingly receive them; but if by falſe ſtatements any man procures himſelf to be received, he is to be committed to jail for ſix months, then to return to his militia regiment, and after his term of ſervice there is expired, to be paſſed over to that in which he had ſo fraudulently entered. If any perſon ſerving in the regulars offers himſelf as a ſubſtitute in the militia, he forfeits 10*l*. or is to be impriſoned, not exceeding three months. Any perſon ordering another to beat up for volunteers to ſerve in the militia forfeits 20*l*.; and if the ſerjeant or drummer refuſes to declare who gave

gave him his orders, he is to be imprisoned, not exceeding three months.

Seamen. And as, at the beginning of a war, it may probably happen that many persons serving in the militia may be seamen, it is provided that if they will agree to enter the royal navy they may be discharged from their regiments, and be delivered over to naval officers; but such change must not be made so precipitately as to diminish the ranks of the regiment in a greater proportion than one in ten. For every man so changing his service, the commanding officer is entitled to demand from the receiver of the land-tax of his county in England, or the receiver general in Scotland, ten guineas, to be applied toward providing a substitute; and when he thus obtains new men, he is to continue discharging all seamen desirous of serving in the navy, and supplying their places by new drafts for money, and new bounties to substitutes. If militia-men happen to be serving in the navy, they are not to be discharged, but their place is to be supplied by substitutes. Militia-men entering into the navy and deserting, or sailors not duly discharged entering into the militia, are to be apprehended and lodged in the common jail, and dealt with as deserters; persons apprehending them are entitled to twenty shillings to be paid on a justice's warrant by the collectors of land-tax within the parish; and persons harbouring them forfeit 10*l.* or on failure of payment, are imprisoned three months.

Of forming Regiments and appointing Officers. The militia of the several counties, ridings, and places, are formed into companies, consisting of not more than 120, nor of less than 60 privates. To each company there are one captain, one lieutenant, and one ensign; and where the number of men raised for any county, riding, or place, is sufficient, the militia is formed into one or more regiments, consisting of not more than twelve, nor of less than eight such companies; and where the number is not sufficient to form a regiment, it is formed into a battalion, consisting of not more than seven nor less than four companies; and where the number is not sufficient to form a battalion, it makes a corps of not less than three companies. The field officers of these regiments, battalions, and corps, must in no case exceed the respective numbers and ranks following; that is to say, in every regiment of not less than 800 privates, one colonel, one lieutenant colonel, and two majors; in every regiment of not less than 480 privates, one lieutenant colonel and one major; and in every corps consisting of three companies, one lieutenant colonel or major, and no other field officer; but no colonel, or field officer in the militia can be a captain of a company. Every battalion of five compa-

nies

nies or upwards may have one company of grenadiers or light infantry, to which two lieutenants are appointed instead of one lieutenant and one ensign; and every such regiment may have one company of grenadiers, and one of light infantry, to each of which companies two lieutenants shall be appointed instead of one lieutenant and one ensign. The King may, if he thinks fit, direct that any proportion of the militia shall be trained and exercised to the service of the artillery attached to any regiment or battalion, and that a supernumerary officer or officers of the regiment or battalion, of such rank as he shall order, and being duly qualified, shall be appointed to and for the men so directed to be trained and exercised. The law also provides for the formation of independent companies, and for the proportion of officers to be appointed where the number of militia is not sufficient to form a regiment: that is, when there are enough to form a battalion of less than 480, but not less than 360 men, the lord lieutenant may appoint a colonel, lieutenant colonel, and major, but with no higher pay than if they were appointed lieutenant colonel, major, and captain respectively. And where the number is sufficient to form three, but not four companies, of 60 privates at the least, he may appoint two persons with the rank of lieutenant colonel and major, but only one of them shall be entitled to any higher pay than that of captain. And where the number is not sufficient to form more than two companies of 60 privates at least, the eldest captain shall serve with the rank of major, but shall only be entitled to the pay of captain.

The king may also, if necessary, augment the number of officers, but the additional field officers must not exceed the following proportions: to a regiment of at least 1000 rank and file, one colonel, two lieutenant colonels, and two majors: to a regiment or battalion of 750 rank and file, one colonel, one lieutenant colonel, and two majors. And no field officer should be added to any corps consisting of less than 750 rank and file, except in temporary cases.

If officers duly qualified as to property cannot be found, his majesty may, after two months from the militia being embodied, appoint officers of the army or marines, whether on full or half pay, to militia regiments, although they may not be qualified; but such officers must have no higher rank than they held in the regulars, nor can the lords lieutenants promote them beyond the rank of captains. Also if persons duly qualified cannot be found within the proper limits to accept commissions, the lord lieutenant, with his majesty's approbation, may appoint

point others duly qualified from any part of England or Wales. Officers rank according to the date of their commissions.

In certain cases of non-appointment of a commanding officer, the lord lieutenant may lead the militia of his own county or place; or if the commanding officer is absent from England, the next in rank takes the command, until the proper officer notifies his return to the clerk of the peace.

SUBALTERNS AND NON COMMISSIONED OFFICERS. The king may appoint a person, who has served in the regulars or in the militia, for at least five years, to be an *adjutant* in each regiment, battalion, or corps. The adjutant, if appointed of the king's other forces, shall, during his service in the militia, preserve his rank in the army; and although not qualified as to property, he may have the rank of captain, but not precede or command any captain in the militia. He must never be absent from the town or place to which his militia regiment belongs without leave, for more than three months in one year, except in case of sickness; and during his absence, the serjeants, corporals, and drummers are to be under the command of the battalion clerk, if a commissioned officer, or of the serjeant major, or some other serjeant appointed for that purpose by the adjutant, with the commanding officer's approbation, or of the senior serjeant, in case the corps has no adjutant or serjeant major.

SECOND ADJUTANT. In all cases where it may be found necessary to appoint a second adjutant, the lord lieutenant may grant him (unless the king disapprove of it) the rank of lieutenant by brevet.

SERJEANTS AND OTHERS. All serjeants, corporals, and drummers must constantly be resident within the city, town, or place, where the arms are kept, and be under the command of the adjutant, or, in his absence, of his substitutes as already mentioned; the adjutant or deputy makes monthly returns of the true state of the serjeants, corporals, and drummers, to the secretary of state, the lieutenant of the county, and the colonel or other commandant of the corps, or in default is subject to punishment by a court martial. No serjeant, corporal, or drummer is to be absent without a regular furlough or licence in writing, signed by his colonel or other commandant; and during such absence they receive the pay following; serjeant, one shilling; corporal, eightpence, and drummer sixpence per day. These officers are appointed in the following proportions, when not in actual service; one serjeant and one corporal to every 20 privates; and when drawn out, an addition is made, so that there is one serjeant and one corporal to every 20 privates; and when not in actual service, there is is one drummer to every company with the addition of one drummer for each flank company of regiments or battalions consisting of five or more companies; and when drawn out into actual service an addition of one drummer to every company. They take the oath of allegiance and of faithful service. Serjeant-majors and drum-majors may also be appointed; but no publican, or dealer in liquors by retail, can be a subaltern officer.

Surgeons. In corps, not less than two companies of 60 men each, the lord lieutenant may, with the king's approbation, appoint a surgeon, who has obtained a certificate of due examination from Surgeons'-hall, who while the militia is disembodied, receives ten shillings for every day of his actual attendance during exercise, and his fair charge for medicines and necessaries; but when the militia is embodied, he receives pay, and is subject to regulation, like an army surgeon, and he cannot hold any other commission in the militia.

Quarter Master. When a regiment amounts to 360 privates, a quarter master may be in like manner appointed; he must previously have served in the regulars or the militia; ranks, though not qualified, as to property, with lieutenant or ensign, and cannot receive pay in virtue of any other commission in the militia at the same time.

Regimental Clerk. In regiments consisting of three companies, and not in actual service, the colonel or commandant may appoint a regimental or battalion clerk, who executes the office of paymaster; but where the number of men is not sufficient to form three companies of 60 privates no clerk is allowed, but the money for the use of the regiment is remitted to the commanding officer, who accounts for it like a regimental or battalion clerk. No adjutant, surgeon, regimental or battalion clerk, or quarter-master, is capable of being appointed captain of a company; nor can any captain of a company be appointed to those places; and no officer who is intitled to half pay, during the time he serves as lieutenant, ensign, adjutant, regimental or battalion clerk, quarter master, or surgeon in the militia, is to forego such half pay; but instead of the oath usually required of half pay officers, they swear they have no place or employment of profit, except that which they enjoy in the militia regiment.

Training and Exercise. The militia are called out twenty eight days in every year, for the purpose of being trained and exercised; and in places where the whole militia is not trained or exercised at the same time, the respective parts are taken successively, until all have completed their twenty eight days. The times, proportions, and places are then appointed, with the approbation of his majesty, by the lieutenants, or deputy lieutenants, at, or occasionally without, a general meeting. They cannot order less than two companies of sixty private men at the least, with officers and serjeants, corporals and drummers in proportion, to be trained and exercised together, unless the militia of the county, riding, or place do not amount to so many. The place of assembling may be altered at a general meeting of lieutenancy; but the clerk must take proper means for distributing notices, which are finally fixed on the doors of the churches or chapels for general information; and the constables give notice in writing to each militia man severally, at his place of abode. If a regiment or corps has been disembodied, his majesty may order it to be trained or exercised for any time not exceeding a year. During the time of exercise, the mutiny act and articles of war are in force, and offenders may be tried by courts martial, duly constituted, but which can have no power over life or limb. On these occasions, the officers and men become intitled to receive pay, but calculated only from the day on which they join their regiment or corps. If a militia man in his way to the place of exercise falls sick, any justice, or mayor of a town, may order for him proper relief, which the officers of the parish must give, and the account being afterward verified before and allowed by a magistrate, the parish officer is reimbursed by the treasurer. At such times, too, the officers and privates may be billeted, like those of the regular troops; and at all times the serjeants, corporals, and drummers may be billeted, and provided with lodging, fire, and candle. For the conveyance of the arms and necessaries to the place of training, justices must, on the requisition of the lord lieutenant, deputy lieutenants, or commanding officer of the regiment, obtain from the parishes and places through which they are required to pass, sufficient carriages and able drivers. For these carriages the proprietors receive, if drawn by five horses, six oxen, or four oxen and two horses, one shilling per mile; if four horses, ninepence, and so in proportion; these sums are paid by the commanding officer to the chief constable of every parish and other place, and he has power to compel the proprietors to let their vehicles for one day's journey, but no more. If the charge inevitably exceeds the allowance above mentioned, the treasurer of the county where the excess is incurred must pay it on demand.

The law also directs that stoppages, at the rate of four pence per day, from the pay of each private shall be made for linen and repairs of arms; that the colonel or commanding officer shall in fourteen days, or seven days if all do not meet

meet at once, make a return of the true ſtate of his corps to the lord lieutenant, with a duplicate to the clerk of general meetings; that captains ſhall make a correct and accurate return of the ſtate of the claſſes of men belonging to their companies, and deliver it to the adjutant, or if none, to the commanding officer, who is to forward to the clerks of ſub-diviſion meetings proper abſtracts to inſtruct them in correcting their books of inrolment, and to the clerk of general meetings, who, within two months after the time of exerciſe is expired, tranſmits correct abſtracts to the ſecretary of ſtate. And every perſon failing to make any of theſe returns, forfeits for each offence 50*l.*

Men not attending theſe times and places of exerciſe, unleſs prevented by illneſs, are conſidered as deſerters, and if not taken till the time is over, forfeit 20*l.*; the ſame penalty is inflicted on thoſe who attend and afterward deſert, and if they are unable to pay, they are to be committed to the houſe of correction to hard labour, or to the common jail, for ſix months. When a deſerter has been abſent four months, a new man muſt be ballotted for; but if the deſerter is afterward found, he muſt ſerve out his time.

If the Iriſh militia are ſo inclined, they may volunteer to ſerve in Great Britain, and his majeſty may accept their offer to the number of 10,000, but the offer muſt be purely voluntary; the defalcations in ſuch regiments are not to be filled by new ballots in Ireland during their abſence; but the offer once made and accepted is binding and cannot be retracted.

Arms and Accoutrements. All muſkets delivered for the ſervice of the militia are marked with the letter M, and the name of the place to which they belong; and if any militia-man ſells, pawns, or loſes any of his arms, clothes, accoutrements, or ammunition, or neglects or refuſes to return them in good order to his captain, or the perſon appointed to receive them, he forfeits for every offence a ſum not exceeding 3*l.* or for default of immediate payment, is committed to the houſe of correction, to hard labour, for any time not exceeding three months. And if any perſon knowingly buys, takes in exchange, conceals, or otherwiſe receives any militia arms, clothes, or accoutrements, or any ſuch articles belonging to any militia-man as are generally deemed regimental neceſſaries, or any public ſtores or ammunition whatever delivered for the militia, he forfeits for every offence 10*l.*; or muſt be committed to jail for ſix months, or be publickly or privately whipped at the diſcretion of the juſtice.

The arms, accoutrements, clothing, and other ſtores belonging to every regiment, or corps of militia, when not em-

 bodied,

bodied, are kept in ſuch convenient place, as the colonel or other commandant ſhall direct, with the approbation of the lieutenant of the county or place; and the general meeting of the lieutenancy may direct a fit place to be provided, or, if neceſſary, built for the purpoſe; the hire or coſt to be paid by the treaſurer of the county, out of the county rates.

Clothing, Pay, and Allowances. The pay of militia when embodied is exactly the ſame as that of other infantry. When they are unembodied, it is regulated by annual acts. The laſt paſſed for this purpoſe directs, that in every place where the militia is raiſed, the receiver-general of the land tax ſhall iſſue and pay the whole ſums required, in the manner and for the uſes following: for the pay of the militia for four calendar months in advance, at the rate of 6*s.* a day for each adjutant, where an adjutant is appointed; 3*s.* a day for each quarter-maſter, where appointed; of 1*s.* 6*d.* a day for each ſerjeant, reſident at the head quarters, with the addition of 2*s.* 6*d.* a week for each ſerjeant-major, where appointed; 1*s.* 2*d.* a day for each corporal; and 1*s.* a day for each drummer, with the addition of 6*d.* a day for each drum-major, where appointed; and alſo at the rate of 4*d.* per month, for each private man and drummer, for defraying contingent expences; half of which is to be applied in aid of the ſtoppage fund of each regiment, or corps, for providing the men while abſent from home, with neceſſaries, under the direction of the colonel, or other commandant; and alſo for half a year's ſalary for the clerk of each regiment, or corps, at the rate of 50*l.* a year; and alſo for the allowances to the clerks of the general and ſubdiviſion meetings; the clerk of the general meetings having 5*l.* 5*s.*, and the ſeveral clerks of the ſubdiviſion meetings, 1*l.* 1*s.* for each meeting; and alſo for clothing, after the rate of 3*l.* 10*s.* for each ſerjeant, and 2*l.* for each corporal or drummer, with the addition of 1*l.* for each ſerjeant-major and drum-major, provided theſe perſons have not been clothed within two years; and with reſpect to the privates, at the rate of 1*l.* 12*s.* for each. But any ſerjeant, corporal, or drummer, abſent on furlough or licence, receives for that period as follows: ſerjeant, 1*s.*; corporal, 8*d.*; and drummer, 6*d.* per day. Serjeants being on the eſtabliſhment, or out-penſioners at Chelſea Hoſpital, may receive their militia pay beſides their allowances; and an additional remuneration is made to the clerks of ſubdiviſion meetings, for their various ſervices. The payments for the regiments are made at the ſtated periods, by the receiver-general of the land tax, to the clerks of the regiments or battalions, who for the uſe of the ſubalterns, pays proper ſums in advance into the hands of the adjutants, and for the privates into the hands of the captains, who are reſpectively

ively obliged to make out accounts, and pay over the ſurplus. The regimental or battalion clerk alſo pays out of the money iſſued to him, for the repair, carriage, and removal of arms, and in aid of the ſtoppage fund, if required by the commanding officer; he makes up his accounts three times in a year, and the balance in his hands, if any, forms a regimental ſtock purſe, in aid of which all penalties, levied for offences, not otherwiſe diſpoſed of, are applied.

During the twenty-eight days of exerciſe, pay is iſſued by the receiver-general, to the regimental and battalion clerks, at the rates following: 9*s.* 8*d.* per day for each field officer, and for the captain of each company; 5*s.* 5*d.* for each lieutenant; 4*s.* 8*d.* for each enſign; 10*s.* for each ſurgeon; 2*s.* per day (additional) for each adjutant; 2*s.* 8*d.* (additional) for each quarter-maſter; and 1*s.* for each private. There is alſo a further allowance of beer money, at the rate of one penny per day, for each private, ſerjeant-major, drum-major, ſerjeant, corporal, and drummer, but when the men are billeted, theſe ſums are paid to the publicans, in the ſame manner, and on the ſame conditions, as in the caſe of regular infantry.

Proper regulations are eſtabliſhed for making up, verifying and checking accounts; when the militia are embodied, the pay from the receivers general ceaſes; the regimental or ballot clerks give ſecurity for duly accounting for the monies in their hands; and if they fail, the receiver general muſt put the bonds in ſuit, and if he recover he ha a poundage of 5*l.* per cent.; and for the better encouragement of militia-men, who may be attached to the ſervice of the artillery, his majeſty may raiſe their pay to the ſame amount as is given men in the royal artillery.

ALLOWANCES TO SUBALTERNS. Any adjutant of militia, having ſerved thirty years in the whole in the militia or regulars, but having been fifteen of thoſe years an adjutant of militia, and becoming incapable of further ſervice through age or infirmity, having no other office or employment of profit, civil or military, except as regimental, or battalion clerk, may, on producing the neceſſary certificates of ſervice, demand from the receiver general 6*s*, per day.

Surgeons in the like ſituation, having ſerved thirty years in the militia, are intitled to 3*s.* per day.

When the militia is diſembodied, the receiver general is to pay to every *reduced adjutant* 3*s.* a day, and to every *reduced ſerjeant major* 1*s.* per day, with an addition of 2*s.* 6*d.* per week. The term from which theſe allowances commence, is aſcertained by certificates from the commanding officer, indorſed by the miniſter and churchwardens where the adjutant or ſerjeant-major reſides; and on production of them, the collector of the

 land

land tax for the place, muſt pay the money under penalty of 10*l.* Regulations are adopted, to prevent frauds and miſtakes in caſe of removal, by proper certificates of reſidence; the parties are liable to be called out into ſervice, when required by the commanding officer; and from that time, they become entitled to their original pay, and the allowance ceaſes, and ſo it does if they are promoted to a better rank, or if they neglect to ſend proper certificates of their reſidence, or refuſe to join when required, unleſs prevented by ſickneſs or other ſufficient cauſe.

Actual Service. In caſe of actual invaſion, or imminent danger, or of rebellion, or inſurrection, the king may, on notice to parliament, if ſitting, or if not, on proclamation, order the lords lieutenants, or deputy lieutenants, with all convenient ſpeed, to draw out and embody all the militia, or ſo many as he ſhall judge neceſſary, and in the manner beſt adapted to the circumſtances of the danger, and to put them under the command of ſuch general officers as he ſhall appoint, and direct them to be led by their reſpective officers, into any part of Great Britain, but not out of it. From the time of their being embodied until their return to their own county, riding, or place, and being diſembodied by his majeſty's order, they are all ſubject to the mutiny act, and the articles of war. The king muſt however aſſemble the parliament, within fourteen days after calling out the militia.

On theſe occaſions, the lord lieutenant, or the deputy lieutenants, direct the chief conſtables and other officers, in every place, to give notice in writing to the ſeveral militia-men, and if they do not appear, and march according to the order, they are treated like deſerters from the regulars, and any perſon harbouring them incurs a penalty of 100*l.*; but as ſome of the men, who live at a diſtance from the place where they may be ordered to, could not travel ſo far without aſſiſtance, the ſubdiviſion clerk advances to every one ſo many days pay, as will ſupport him till he reaches the place appointed, counting that he marches not leſs than ten miles per day, with a proper number of halting days; and the money ſo advanced is repaid by the receiver general of the land-tax. Beſides this, the receivers of the aſſeſſed taxes pay into the hands of every captain, or other commanding officer of militia, one guinea for each man under his command, which the officer muſt give to the private, or lay it out for his benefit, in ſuch way as he ſhall think fit, accounting for it to the privates by the 24th day of the enſuing month.

And when the militia is drawn out, if any perſon not poſſeſſing land, goods, or money, of the clear value of 500*l.* is balloted, and ſerves, or finds a ſubſtitute, the church-wardens or overſeers of the pariſh, on receiving an order, under the hands of two deputy lieutenants, muſt pay him ſuch ſum as the deputy lieutenants ſhall judge to be half the current price paid for a ſubſtitute, under penalty of 10*l*.

When regiments are abſent from the place to which they belong, the commanding officers muſt apply to every man, whoſe term of ſervice is within four months of expiring, and who is ſtill fit to ſerve, and inquire whether he is willing to continue in the ſervice for a new term, and at what price, and on the firſt day of January, and every other alternate month, the officer is to tranſmit to the clerk of the general meetings a liſt of ſuch men as are willing to continue, ſpecifying certain neceſſary particulars, and ſubſcribed by them, which ſubſcription binds them to ſerve. The clerk of the general meetings ſends extracts of theſe liſts to the clerk of the ſubdiviſion meetings, and the deputy lieutenants may decide whether they will aſſent to the inrolment of ſuch men; and if they approve it, may order the church-wardens and overſeers of the place to which the militia men belong to remit the bounties to the paymaſter of the regiment; the receiver general of aſſeſſed taxes alſo pays for every ſuch man, a guinea in the manner already mentioned to be paid on their marching.

When the whole militia are ordered to be embodied, vacancies occaſioned by default, or deſertion, are filled by a ballot. When only part of the militia is embodied, notices are given by the conſtables ſo as to obtain a general muſter, and the deputy lieutenants having ſelected, by choice or ballot, the required number, the men anſwer to their names on being called over; the deputy lieutenants publicly declare who of them are to be embodied; it then becomes their duty to march immediately, and the reſt are for the time diſcharged from further attendance, being firſt paid one ſhilling per day for the time they are abſent, but not exceeding three days. Theſe ſelections are not however purely arbitrary; for when the number required amounts to all that are contained in the firſt, or firſt and ſecond claſſes, formed as before mentioned, thoſe men are to be taken in preference, and ſo on, deſcending through all the claſſes, not touching the lower, till the higher is exhauſted. The deputy lieutenants too may reform the liſts of claſſes, according to the circumſtances which may have ariſen ſince their laſt meeting. In caſe of vacancies in theſe partial embodyings, by default, or deſertion, or in any other manner, a freſh ballot is to be made in the proper ſubdiviſion, according the rule before declared. Volunteers may be taken on theſe occaſions, if under thirty-five, and unincumbered with children under fourteen years of age. The king may, at his pleaſure, embody the reſidue of the militia of any county or place, or any part of it; and he may, in like manner disembody them, either in part, or in the whole; but the men are still subject to the same regulations as before they were drawn out.

Relief of Families when the Militia is drawn out. If any non-commissioned officer, or drummer, ballotted man or substitute, shall, when embodied, and called out into actual service, leave a family unable to support themselves, the overseers of the parish, tything, or township, where the family dwells, must, by order of one justice, pay to them out of the poor rates, a weekly allowance, not exceeding the price of one day's labour in husbandry, nor less than one shilling for every child, under the age of ten years; and for the wife the same sum; and if the rates are insufficient, a new one may be made for the purpose. This rate of allowance may be ascertained by the justices, at the Michaelmas general quarter sessions, and will be binding on all other magistrates.

From the benefit of this allowance, the families of the following persons are excluded: those who have not joined, or do not continue with their regiments; women who quit their abode without licence from magistrates or overseers, unless for the purpose of residing with their husbands; the family of any man who, at the time of enrolment, fraudulently declared that he had neither wife nor family, or that he had not, when in fact he had, more than one child; unless however the militia-man, to the satisfaction of the justice to whom application for relief is made, undertakes to support all his family, except his wife and one child; the family of every non-commissioned officer, or drummer, reduced to the ranks for misconduct; and the families of substitutes who, after enrolment, have married without the consent of their colonel or commanding officer. The families of persons in the last mentioned situations, must, if in distress, be relieved as ordinary casual poor, but others are not to be so treated, nor to be sent to the workhouse, nor deprived of their legal settlements elsewhere; nor do the men forego the right of voting for members of parliament. The allowances so paid by the overseers of the parish, where the families happen to reside, are refunded by the treasurer of the county to which the militiamen belong, and by them demanded again from the parishes for which the men serve, having been first allowed at a general quarter session. The payments made by overseers are allowed in their accounts; but if they refuse, or neglect to pay, under any order, they incur a penalty of *5l.*

Disobedience and Desertion. Every adjutant, serjeant-major, and drummer of the militia, is subject to the acts for punishing mutiny and desertion, and for the better payment of the army and their quarters, and to the articles of war, under the command

command of the colonel or commanding officer, who may direct courts martial to be held for their trial, for any offence committed during the time the regiment or battalion was not embodied; but so that no punishment shall extend to life or limb; and if a sufficient number of officers belonging to the regiment cannot be found to form a court-martial, the commanding officer may order officers of militia regiments, residing within ten miles, to assist as members, but their sentence cannot be put into execution, till confirmed by the commanding officer, by whose order the court was assembled. Serjeants, corporals, and drummers, may by order of a court-martial, be reduced to the ranks, there to serve for fifteen months.

A serjeant, corporal, or drummer absenting himself from the place where the arms are deposited without a furlough, forfeits all pay during the period, and is liable to be treated as a deserter. A private not appearing, or not abiding the orders of the deputy lieutenants, is in the same predicament. Substitutes not joining when the militia is embodied, may be apprehended and punished as deserters, or may, by sentence of court-martial, be ordered to serve for a further limited time in the militia, or without limitation in the regulars. Deserters may be apprehended by means of a certificate, signed by their commanding officer, and transmitted to the adjutant, or serjeant major of the battalion, or corps, serving near where they are residing; and they are passed under a guard, from one militia regiment to another, till they reach their own, and justices being informed or knowing of deserters, may order them to prison for safe custody, till a sufficient party is sent to convey them away. If the king publishes a proclamation for pardoning deserters on their joining their regiments, the commanding officers of militia, after the day mentioned in the proclamation is expired, shall make lists of defaulters, deserters and absentees, and give them to the subdivision clerks, to be published in proper newspapers, for the expence of which the receiver general shall supply money; and all justices, magistrates, constables, and peace officers, may seize such persons and lodge them in prison, till a court-martial can be held, which on their being identified, shall sentence them to serve in the regulars: the persons apprehending them are entitled to a reward of 20*s.* above any reward given by the mutiny act, to be paid by the clerk of the regiment or battalion to which the deserter belongs, on warrant from the justice before whom the deserter was committed.

Privileges of the Militia. For one year ending the 25th March 1805, certain allowances were directed to be made to officers who were not qualified by the possession of property, to hold a captain's commission; that is to say, to a lieutenant or surgeon,

ſurgeon, 25*l.* 18*s.* 6*d.*, and to an enſign, 21*l.* 7*s.*; theſe could not extend to more than ten ſenior lieutenants in any regiment, but were limited to ſmaller corps, in proportion to the number of companies. The permanent privileges are, that a half-pay officer in the regulars having a commiſſion in the militia, not higher than that of lieutenant, does not forego his half-pay; a commiſſion is not conſidered a place of profit, ſo as to vacate a ſeat in parliament; an officer in the militia cannot be compelled to ſerve as ſheriff; no officer, or private, is liable to penalty or puniſhment for his abſence, while going to vote for the election of a member of parliament; they are exempt from pariſh offices, and highway duty; men who have ſerved in the militia when drawn out in actual ſervice, may, if married, ſet up and exerciſe any trade in any town in Great Britain, without moleſtation, and not be ſubject to removal, until actually chargeable to the pariſh. Chelſea penſioners do not renounce the benefits of that ſituation by ſerving in the militia; ſerjeants, corporals, and drummers, after ſerving twenty years, are entitled to be placed on that eſtabliſhment, and ſo are non-commiſſioned officers and privates, if maimed or wounded in actual ſervice.

Further Particulars. Regulations are alſo made for levying and apportioning a penalty of 10*l.* for every man, who ought to be raiſed in any county or place, but is not; for generally enforcing the execution of the law, and adminiſtering the oaths. The lords lieutenants and deputy lieutenants are indemniſied for acts done in execution of their office, in the ſame manner as juſtices of the peace. Fines, exceeding 20*l.* are to be recovered by action in any of the courts at Weſtminſter; but ſmaller fines by proof on oath before one juſtice, to be levied by diſtreſs, and applied, where not otherwiſe particularly directed, to increaſe the public ſtock of the regiment, in which they ariſe. No order or conviction is removeable by certiorari; and perſons ſued for acts done in execution of their duty, if they gain a verdict, recover treble coſts.

General Exceptions. The city of *London* and the *Tower hamlets*, as to their militia, are regulated by particular acts of parliament; in the *Stannaries*, the lord warden arrays, aſſeſſes, and muſters the tinners, according to immemorial privilege and cuſtom; in the *Cinque-ports*, the lord-warden alſo exerciſes the powers generally committed to the lords lieutenants of counties; in *Suſſex* and *Kent*, the churchwardens and overſeers execute the powers elſewhere given to conſtables; the *Iſle of Wight* furniſhes its quota to the militia of Southampton, the powers for that purpoſe being veſted in the governor, who appoints five deputies to attend him, the men remain for the internal defence of the iſland till the king directs otherwiſe; *Berwick upon Tweed* is ſimilarly circumſtanced

circumstanced with respect to the county of Northumberland; the chief magistrate of the town, acting as lord lieutenant, and appointing under him five deputies. It is also declared that the constablery of *Craike* which belongs to Durham, but is surrounded by the North Riding of Yorkshire, shall be deemed within that Riding; part of the parish of *Maker* is deemed within Cornwall; the parish of *Wockingham* in Berkshire; the parish of *Filey*, in the East Riding of Yorkshire; *Threapwood* is considered part of the parish of Worthenbury in the county of Flint; and *Stamford Baron* in the county of Lincoln.

REDUCTION OF THE MILITIA. The statute 44th Geo. III. c. 56, commonly called the additional defence act, directs that the militia raised up to that time, shall be reduced to the specified quotas, then to serve exclusively of any supplementary militia. From the passing of that act, no ballot was to take place in any county where the number of men actually serving should exceed or amount to the original quota; and when it should be necessary to reduce the number of officers, the reduction was to begin from the youngest, but the officer reduced is competent to succeed to any vacancy of an equal rank with that which he filled at the time such reduction took place, or may fall back again into the post he quitted on his promotion, at his option, preserving his rank in the general line of the militia.

ADDITIONAL FORCE. The statute last mentioned was framed to supersede one, for forming an army of reserve and for the purpose of establishing a permanent additional force, instead of permitting the undefined increase of those bodies which were merely occasional or temporary. It fixed a number of men to be raised in every county, empowered the justices in session to apportion the number among the parishes, and directed the manner in which the parish officers were to raise, examine, and pass the men, which they were to do, under a penalty of 20*l.* for every man deficient. A detailed statement of this subject had been prepared, but as it was probable that the act would be repealed, it was thought expedient to omit it, and give in the way of an appendix, if possible, some account of the measure to be substituted.

GENERAL LEVY. At the beginning of war with France, in 1803, as the ruler of that country made loud and boastful threats of invasion, the ministry brought in a bill, reciting that it was expedient to enable his majesty to exercise his prerogative of requiring the military service of all his subjects, in case of invasion, and requiring the lieutenants, deputy lieutenants, and justices of the peace, constables, tything men, headboroughs, churchwardens, overseers of the poor, and other officers, to carry the act into execution.

Meetings. It ordered that a general meeting of lieutenancy should be held in each county, within ten days after the passing of the act, when the lieutenants, deputy lieutenants, or other officers, should issue orders to the chief constables of the several hundreds and districts, within their counties, requiring each of them to issue an order to all constables, tythingmen, headboroughs, or other parochial officers, to return to the deputy lieutenants, when and where they should point out, fair and true lists of the names of all the men, at that time dwelling within such parishes, between the ages of 17 and 55 years. They were also to appoint the first subdivision meeting, and a day for a second general meeting, if necessary; and during the month of October in every year, or oftener if necessary, a like meeting is to be held in every county, for the purpose of carrying the act into execution.

Lists to be required. The lieutenants and deputy lieutenants, in obedience to his majesty's orders, are to procure returns of all boats, barges, waggons, carts, cars, horses, and other cattle and sheep, and of all hay, straw, corn, meal, flour, and other provisions, and of all mills and ovens, and other things which may be useful to an enemy, or applicable to the public service, within their respective counties and places; and which of such boats, carriages and horses, the owners thereof are willing to furnish, in case of emergency, for the public service, either gratuitously or for hire, and with what number of boatmen, drivers, and other necessary attendants, and upon what terms and conditions, and of all such other particulars as shall be required, for enabling his majesty to give the necessary orders for removing, in case of danger, all who are incapable of removing themselves, and also for removing all boats, carriages, horses, sheep, corn, and other provisions and things, or for employing the same in the king's service, as the case may require; and generally to give such directions, as may be deemed most likely to defeat the views of the enemy, and most advantageous for the public service. The lieutenants or deputy lieutenants of counties, also the deputy lieutenants, within their respective subdivisions, may (when they think proper) appoint from the fourth class of persons, to be enrolled for military service under this act, such number as may be willing to act as special constables in the execution thereof, whose names must be transmitted to the chief constable, or other proper officer of the district; and such special constables may perform all the functions of other constables, in the execution of any of the purposes of the act, and shall not be liable to military service, while they act in that capacity. Some exceptions from the duties of constables, are made in favour of Quakers, and members of the society called *Unitas Fratrum*.

Duties

Duties of Constables in making out Lists. Nearly in the manner prescribed for the militia, the constables are to give notice, and to demand from the occupiers of, and lodgers in, every dwelling house, lists of every man resident therein, and distinguishing whether he is married or unmarried, whether he has any child or children under the age of ten years, and whether he is willing to engage himself as a volunteer, under the act, and also distinguishing therein other particulars, according to a prescribed form; and these lists are to be made out, under penalty in case of neglect of 10*l*., or on refusal of 20*l*.

Classes. Within ten days after delivering such notices, the constables, or other officers, shall make out annually, a list of the names of all the men at that time dwelling within their respective parishes, between the ages of 17 and 55 years, distinguishing their ranks and occupations, and those who have made returns to such notices, from those who have neglected; and dividing the several persons returned, according to their respective ages, situations, and descriptions, into the following classes, viz. in the *first* class, all the men of the age of 17, and under 30 years, unmarried, and having no child living under ten years; in the *second*, all the men of the age of 30, and under 50 years, unmarried, and having no child living under 10 years; in the *third* class, all the men of the age of 17 and under 30 years, who are, or have been married, and have not more than two children under 10 years; and in the *fourth* class, all the men not included in any of the former classes; and also distinguishing in such lists, which of the persons so returned labour under any infirmity, likely to incapacitate them from military service, and which of them are willing to engage to serve as volunteers under the act; which of them are clergymen, licensed dissenting ministers, Quakers, people of the congregation of *Unitas Fratrum*, or medical practitioners, being house-holders, or persons serving as officers or otherwise in the army, navy, marines, militia, sea fencibles, or volunteers; and which of them are constables, or other peace officers, acting in the execution of the present act. Copies of these lists are to be affixed on the doors of churches, or in some other conspicuous situation, with notice of the time of hearing appeals; and all ministers, and churchwardens, and other parish officers are required to assist in making out the lists, and in classing the men. These lists are to be perfected after the hearing of appeals by the deputy lieutenants, who have, in that case, a final jurisdiction, and entered on subdivision rolls; the subdivision clerks then send copies of the rolls to the clerk of general meetings, and these forward true abstracts to the secretary of state.

Penalties. The penalties are: on ſubdiviſion clerks making falſe entries on the rolls, 20*l.*; on clerks of general meetings neglecting their duty, or making falſe returns, 100*l.*; on perſons attempting to induce parochial officers to make falſe returns, or eraſe or omit names, 50*l.*; on refuſing to tell, or falſely telling the chriſtian or ſurname of himſelf, or any lodger, 10*l.*; on a conſtable or other officer refuſing to attend, or diſobeying the orders of the deputy lieutenant, one month's impriſonment, or fine, not more than 20*l.* nor leſs than 40*s.*; perſons obſtructing a conſtable, or other officer from acting, not leſs than 5*l.* or more than 100*l.* or to be impriſoned not exceeding three months.

Persons exempted. The lord chancellor, the keeper of the great ſeal, chief juſtice of the court of king's bench, maſter of the rolls, chief juſtice of the court of common pleas, chief baron of the exchequer, the puiſne judges of the court of king's bench or common pleas, and the barons of the court of exchequer; all perſons labouring under any infirmity rendering them incapable of military ſervice, clergymen, licenſed diſſenting miniſters, not carrying on any trade, and exerciſing no other occupation for their livelihood, except that of a ſchoolmaſter; Quakers, and people called *Unitas Fratrum*; medical men actually practiſing as ſuch, and being houſekeepers, perſons actually ſerving as officers, non-commiſſioned officers, drummers, or private ſoldiers, in his majeſty's army, or in the marines or the militia, or enrolled and ſerving in any corps of ſea fencibles, or volunteers whoſe ſervices are accepted by his majeſty, perſons actually ſerving as officers or ſeamen in his majeſty's navy, lieutenants, or deputy lieutenants of counties, conſtables, or other peace officers; and all perſons leaving the kingdom.

Arms. His majeſty may, from time to time, direct that any pariſhes ſhall be provided with arms and accoutrements, in order to the inſtruction of the men enrolled for military ſervice, under ſuch regulations as ſhall be communicated by his majeſty's order to the lord lieutenant, or deputy lieutenants. Theſe arms and accoutrements are to be kept in the church or chancel, or any other ſafe place in the pariſh, as the lord lieutenant, or deputy lieutenants ſhall appoint, under the cuſtody of the churchwardens, conſtables, and other parochial officers, who are to obey the directions of the lord lieutenant, or deputy lieutenants, reſpecting their cuſtody or removal. The expence which may be incurred in keeping them in order is to be borne by the pariſh, or united pariſhes, or extra parochial places, for which the ſame ſhall be provided; and two or more deputy lieutenants of the ſubdiviſion are, once at leaſt in every year, to view them, for the purpoſe of aſcertaining their ſtate and condition; and they, or any other deputy lieutenant, and one juſtice, may make orders

orders for the payment of such expences, and if necessary, may direct a rate to be made for the purpose, and levied like a poor rate.

All muskets, delivered for the purpose of training and exercising the men, are to be marked distinctly, with the letters G. R.; and in case any man shall not re-deliver, or duly replace the arms after exercise, or shall sell, pawn, lose, or wilfully damage any arms or accoutrements delivered to him, he shall forfeit not exceeding forty shillings, or be committed to jail not exceeding a month. And if any person knowingly and wilfully buy, take in exchange, or conceal, any such arms or accoutrements, he forfeits 10*l*. and in default of payment is committed for three months.

Training and Exercise. The king may order the lieutenant, or deputy lieutenants of any county, to cause the persons comprised in the first, second, and third classes, or any of them, to be trained and exercised; and on receipt of such order, the lieutenant or deputy lieutenants shall direct the deputy lieutenants of the respective subdivisions to regulate the times and places of exercise for such parishes respectively; and such deputy lieutenants shall cause the men to be trained and exercised, two hours at least, on every Sunday, either before or after divine service, or on some other convenient day in the week, between the 25th of March, and the twenty-fifth day of December in every year, and cause public notice of such times and places of exercise and training to be given in the churches or chapels of the respective parishes during divine service, and to be affixed on the doors there, and in the market places, or on some other convenient and conspicuous place; and such deputy lieutenants may, if they deem it expedient, order such men to be exercised on any other additional day or days in the week, taking care to interfere as little as possible with their occupations. Before the return of the subdivision rolls, his majesty may signify what number of men, to be comprised in the first three classes, shall be trained and exercised in any county or subdivision; if the number signified shall, upon the return of the subdivision rolls, be found to equal, or exceed the whole number comprised in those classes, then the whole number of men, comprised in such classes respectively, is to be trained and exercised; if less than the whole are required, then such proportion only of the classes is to be trained and exercised as shall equal the number signified by his majesty; and the deputy lieutenants of subdivisions are within seven days to fix the number; and the men to be trained and exercised are to be chosen by ballot.

Officers. The lord lieutenant, or, in his absence, three deputies, may appoint proper officers, and non-commissioned officers,

cers, from among the men residing in any parish, to train and discipline the privates, in the proportion of one captain, two lieutenants, one ensign, three serjeants, three corporals, and one drummer, for every 120 men; these officers may be displaced by the king's order, and rank with the youngest similar officers of militia. Captains of companies may appoint non-commissioned officers, in the proportion of six serjeants, six corporals and two drummers to every 120 men. The deputy lieutenants of subdivisions, or the captains and other commanding officers of companies may employ any serjeant, or other person, being an out-pensioner of Chelsea or Kilmainham hospital, or any other fit person, having served in the regulars, marines, militia, or fencibles, or in any volunteer corps, for the purpose of instructing the men in the use of arms, and may allow him any sum not exceeding 2*s.* 6*d.* per day, to be paid by the overseers, out of the poor rate, upon an order signed by a deputy lieutenant, or by one justice of the peace; and any overseer, refusing to pay such allowances, forfeits double the amount.

Musters. A constable or other officer is to attend every day at the exercising of the corps, and if he behaves properly, he will at the end of the year, on a certificate of two deputy lieutenants be entitled to a sum not exceeding 5*l.*; but if he fails in his duty he incurs a penalty of ten shillings for every day. On the days of training, muster rolls are to be called, and the commanding officer, or in his absence the constable, is to mark down the persons present, and the absentees, and sign and certify the correctness of the roll. Persons having religious scruples may, on making oath they have no other reason for desiring to absent themselves from training, be dispensed with on Sunday, but must attend some other day; and the captain, or other officer of any company, may grant a certificate to persons, who by diligent attendance, for twelve calendar months at least, shall have attained a due degree of proficiency in the use of arms, which being allowed by any deputy lieutenant, they shall thenceforth be wholly excused from all further attendance, and discharged from all fines for non-attendance. The king may order extraordinary musters, but on those occasions, every man present, if it be in the ordinary times of labour, may receive one shilling on production of the roll, to be paid him by the overseer of the poor, who is at the end of the month to be repaid by the receiver-general.

Fines. Persons whose place of residence is not more than four miles from the place of exercise, are fined for neglecting to attend, five shillings; but if they are excused from paying the poor rates, the fine is reduced to one shilling; but those who neglect to attend three successive days, pay every time instead of of five ſhillings, forty ſhillings, and inſtead of one ſhilling, five ſhillings. Thoſe who, during the times of training, conduct themſelves in an indecent or diſorderly manner, or diſobey command, are to be fined five ſhillings, or on non-payment impriſoned a week. All theſe fines, if not otherwiſe paid, may be levied by diſtreſs. Some cauſes of inevitable abſence, as reſidence in another pariſh, if the party has been trained elſewhere in the time; or travelling by land or ſea, are allowed as excuſes from paying the fines.

Drawing out and embodying. In caſe of actual invaſion, or appearance of the enemy in force upon the coaſt, his majeſty may give orders for embodying all, or any part of the men ſo trained and exerciſed, and cauſe them to be placed in any exiſting regiment, whether regulars, militia, or fencibles, appointed to ſerve in Great Britain, or to be formed into ſuch new regiments, battalions, or corps, as he ſhall judge neceſſary, and to be put under the command of ſuch officers as he may appoint, and led into any part of Great Britain for repelling and preventing invaſion, or ſuppreſſing rebellion or inſurrection; and from the time of any men being ſo drawn out, and embodied, until they return to their own counties, and be diſembodied by his majeſty's order, the officers of every deſcription ſhall be ſubject to the mutiny act and the articles of war. But, whenever his majeſty deems it expedient to take this ſtep, the occaſion of iſſuing the order muſt as early as poſſible be communicated to parliament, if ſitting; and if not, then the occaſion muſt be declared in council, and notified by proclamation; but no perſon drawn out, or embodied, is compellable to ſerve out of Great Britain. The mode of embodying is by precept from the lord or deputy lieutenants, to the head conſtables, and from them through the ordinary conſtables to the parties, in manner nearly ſimilar to the militia; and although no invaſion may have taken place, or any enemy have appeared, the king may give proviſional orders in relation to the drawing out, aſſembling, and embodying theſe forces.

Other Regulations. There are alſo proviſions for giving proper notices of meeting, and ſignals of alarm, and for arranging ballots, if only a part of the force is called out. And it is provided, that whenever in any county, diſtrict, or pariſh, the number of volunteers who ſhall have agreed to march to any part of Great Britain, in caſe of actual invaſion, or the appearance of an enemy in force on the coaſt, or for the ſuppreſſion of any inſurrection or rebellion then ariſing or exiſting, ſhall appear ſatisfactory to his majeſty, he may ſuſpend, as to ſuch places, the operation of the act for a general levy; but every ſuch volunteer corps, and all perſons engaged to ſerve as volunteers, will be liable to march to any part of Great Britain, on actual

 invaſion,

invasion, or the appearance of an enemy in force on the coast, or to suppress any rebellion or insurrection arising or existing, whenever summoned by the lords lieutenants, or upon any general signals of alarm. All persons serving as volunteers under this act are liable to be embodied, and commanded, and to serve for the same period, and in the same manner, as other persons liable to military service under the defence acts; but persons serving as effective members of volunteer corps, will not be liable to be placed in any regiment, battalion, or corps of regulars, militia, or fencibles. And all persons, whether members of volunteer corps, or volunteers under this act, who shall refuse to march, on such summons or signal, shall be deemed deserters, and subject to the mutiny act and articles of war. Persons called out are to take an oath of allegiance.

Removal of Persons and Things. In case of actual or apprehended invasion, the king may, by order under his sign manual, authorize and empower the lieutenants and deputy lieutenants, on any emergency, and on requisition of the officer commanding within the district, or of such other persons as his majesty shall especially empower to make such requisition, to give the necessary orders, for removing any boats, barges, waggons, or other carriages, horses, cattle, sheep, hay, corn, or other provisions, or things, which may be of advantage to an enemy, or useful to the public service, and to take the same if necessary for the public service; and also to give the necessary orders for removing the inhabitants of any house, hamlet, or place, and especially such as shall be incapable of removing themselves in case of danger; and also, in case of necessity, to destroy any such boats, barges, waggons, or other carriages, horses, cattle, corn, or other provisions or things, and to remove, destroy, or render useless, any house, mill, bridge, or other building, and generally to act in the premises, as the public service and particular exigencies shall require.

Pay and Allowances. When these forces are embodied they are paid like regiments of infantry, or militia, and are similarly entitled to Chelsea Hospital; they are, on being called out, to have from the receiver general, two guineas each for necessaries, and after the defeat or expulsion of the enemy, one guinea each over and above their pay, to enable them to return home; and their wives and children are entitled to relief in the same manner as those of militia men. But the persons so raised, and trained, are not exempt from being balloted for the militia.

Purchase of Land. Provision is also made for taking land wanted for the public service, and paying the proprietor a proper rent or purchase, either by agreement or by verdict of a jury, which can only be impanneled on a certificate from two deputy

deputy lieutenants that the land in queſtion is really wanted; and a party diſſatisfied may ſtill appeal to the court of exchequer. The ſtatute alſo makes the proper exceptions to favour the privileges of the Stannaries, the Tower hamlets, the Cinque ports, and the City of London.

FINES. The fines, penalties and forfeitures go in aid of the poor rates in the pariſh where they accrue; one juſtice may convict, and no objection is to be taken for want of form, nor is any conviction to be removed by *certiorari*.

VOLUNTEERS. In the act for the general levy, mention was made of volunteers; and ſuch was the ardour of the people, at the beginning of the war in 1803, to preſs forward in defence of the country, that a greater number of volunteers offered their ſervices than ever had been known on any former occaſion; greater than government, reaſoning from the experience of the paſt, could reaſonably expect; greater than on the ſudden could be ſupplied with arms; and ſufficient to prevent altogether the neceſſity of training and diſciplining under the ſtatute for a general levy. The law then made for regulating theſe patriotic troops, was however by a ſucceeding adminiſtration repealed, and a new one paſſed, of which the following are the outlines.

ACCEPTANCE OF SERVICES. The king may accept the ſervices of volunteer corps, and diſband or continue them at pleaſure; and every volunteer muſt take the oath of allegiance.

EXEMPTIONS. The commanding officer of any corps, at the time of returning every muſter roll of his corps, ſhall (if required) give to every effective volunteer, reſident, or liable to be ballotted for the militia, or any other additional force, in any other county, than that in which ſuch muſter rolls ſhall be returned, a certificate, which, on being delivered to the clerks of general meetings of lieutenancy for the county where ſuch volunteer reſides, will entitle him to exemption from ſervice, as effectually as if he had been returned in a muſter roll under this act. And every perſon enrolled, and ſerving as an effective member of any corps of yeomanry or volunteers, and certified as ſuch, is exempt from being liable to ſerve perſonally, or to provide a ſubſtitute in the militia, or additional force, and remains exempted ſo long as he continues an effective member, unleſs in the offer or acceptance of ſervice, it has been ſpecified, that ſuch exemptions ſhould not be claimed; nor will exemptions be allowed to more than the eſtabliſhed number of the corps. The term *effective* is explained to require four days attendance, if cavalry, and eight, if infantry, in the courſe of four months preceding each return made by the commanding officer, or, at leaſt the proper number of days within the year; each being, if ſupplied, properly armed and accoutred, and if cavalry, mounted. The ballots for militia are made complete by de-

 ducting

ducting the number of volunteers from the number of persons liable to be drawn; but no volunteer is exempt from ballot, and if drawn, and afterward discharged from his volunteer corps, for misconduct, he becomes immediately liable to serve in the militia; but if such volunteer has served during the war, and at the end of it his corps is disbanded, he is not then liable to serve in the militia, in consequence of that ballot. Cavalry volunteers are exempt too from the tax accruing on one horse, and both classes of volunteers, while effective, from that on wearing hair-powder; they are also while on duty, and in uniform, free from toll at turnpikes.

Arms. The commanding officer of any corps receiving arms and accoutrements supplied at the public expence, or by subscription, may appoint a proper place in or near the parish, where his corps is formed, for depositing and safe keeping them, and employ proper persons to repair and keep them in good condition; and such sum as his majesty shall direct to be paid on that account may be demanded from the receiver general. Arms delivered out of the public stores are marked with the letter V, and initial of the county to which the corps belongs. There are penalties on selling, or pawning, and on purchasing them, and on purchasing stores or ammunition, accoutrements, or clothing given to volunteers; and persons having any such, or any musical instruments in their custody, and refusing to deliver them up, forfeit for every offence 10*l*. and double the value of the things, or are committed to jail for two months.

Rank of Officers. The officers rank with those of regulars and militia, as youngest of their rank; they sit in courts martial on the trial of members of their own body, but not on any others, nor can the regulars, or militia, sit in courts martial on them.

Powers of Officers. The commanding officer may, when the corps is not on actual service, dismiss any private for disobedience, breach of discipline, neglect of attendance and duty, or other, in his judgment, sufficient cause, and strike his name out of the muster roll; but the person so dismissed still remains liable to pay all arrears of subscription, or fines which he had previously incurred, or may then incur by not delivering up his arms, accoutrements, and clothing; but such dismissions are subject to the declaration of his majesty's pleasure. In cases of misconduct under arms, not expressly provided for, the commanding officer may deprive the person misbehaving of the benefit of that day's attendance, and he may order such person into custody during the time of exercise.

Exercise. If any volunteer cavalry shall signify in writing, through their commander in chief, to the lord lieutenant of the county,

county, their desire to assemble under the command of their own officers, at any convenient place within the same county, for the purpose of being trained and exercised for any time not exceeding fourteen days, either successively or at intervals, within the space of twelve months, either in separate corps, or together with other corps of yeomanry or volunteer cavalry, or with regular cavalry, if his majesty shall think it proper; the lord lieutenant, or, in his absence, deputy lieutenants, may, with the king's approbation, signified through the secretary of state, direct an order to any justice of the county where such corps of yeomanry or volunteer cavalry are appointed to assemble, specifying the place at which, and the time during which, such corps, are to continue so assembled; and the justice shall issue his precept to the constable or other peace officer of that place, for quartering and billeting the non-commissioned officers, trumpeters, or buglemen, and privates, in the same manner as regulars; and the same rules are generally to be observed, except that the corps is not subject to the mutiny act, or articles of war. At these times the secretary at war, or his deputy, is, if required by the lord lieutenant, to issue for every private 2*s.* per day, and for every horse 1*s.* 4*d.* per day for any term not exceeding fourteen days. In all other cases, when corps are assembled on military duty, they are subject to military discipline, the mutiny act, and articles of war. All adjutants, serjeant-majors, drill serjeants, and serjeants of yeomanry or volunteers, receiving the constant pay of their rank, and all trumpeters, buglemen, and drummers receiving any pay as such therein, are subject to the mutiny act, and articles of war, and liable to be tried for any crime committed against such act, or articles of war, by any general or detachment, or regimental court-martial, according to the nature and degree of the offence, in like manner, and under the like regulations, as adjutants, serjeant majors, serjeants, corporals, or drummers of his majesty's military forces; provided that every such court martial be composed wholly of officers of the yeomanry or volunteer establishment: and no punishment awarded by such court martial is to extend to life or limb, except when such corps are called out in cases of invasion, or appearance of an enemy in force upon the coast.

RETURNS. The commanding officers of corps are to make certified returns on the first days of April, August, and December, to the clerks of general meetings of lieutenancy, of the number of men on the establishment and the supernumeraries in their corps, distinguishing the effective from non-effective, and stating the names of all such as have been admitted into, and joined the corps since the last return, the names of all persons absent on leave, and all who have been discharged from, or quitted the corps since the last return; and also in all cases where exemptions are allowed, distinguishing the persons entitled, from such as are not entitled to them; and in all cases where any arms required by any corps, at the expence of his majesty, shall not have been supplied, stating such circumstance specially at the foot of the return. Accurate returns are also to be made to the secretary of state, and the general officer commanding the district, specifying the numbers of effective and non-effective men, as nearly as may be, in the form in which monthly military returns are usually made. Copies and abstracts of these returns are to be made by the clerks of general meetings, and forwarded to the clerks of subdivision meetings, under penalty of 50*l*. and a commanding officer making a false return, forfeits 200*l*.

Resignations. Doubts having arisen respecting the right of volunteers to resign, it was enacted, 44 Geo. III. c. 54. that, except when summoned, or assembled upon actual service, in case of invasion or appearance of the enemy in force upon the coast, or voluntarily assembled for the purpose of doing military duty, under any of the provisions, or in any of the cases specified in the act, any volunteer may quit such corps, and he shall accordingly be struck out of the muster roll. But he must give fourteen days notice of his intention to the commanding officer, give up all arms, accoutrements, clothing, and appointments, furnished to him at the public expence, or by any subscription, in good order and condition, and pay all subscriptions and fines. Persons entering into his majesty's service are however instantly discharged from that of a volunteer corps; but those who are dismissed for misconduct are liable to serve in the militia, and deprived of all their privileges and exemptions. Persons aggrieved in any of these particulars, may appeal to two deputy lieutenants, or a deputy lieutenant and a justice.

Actual Service. In all cases of actual invasion, or appearance of any enemy in force on the coast of Great Britain, or of rebellion or insurrection, on the appearance of any enemy, or during any invasion, all corps of yeomanry and volunteers must, whenever summoned by the lieutenants of the counties, vice-lieutenants, or deputy lieutenants, or upon the making of any general signals of alarm, forthwith assemble within their respective districts, and be liable to march according to the terms and conditions of their respective services, whether general or limited, on pain of being treated as deserters; and from that time they are subject to all the laws and articles of war. Their commanding officers are, on these occasions, entitled to demand from the receiver general, two guineas per man for their

their use; and the treasury may direct one guinea for every volunteer to be paid to the commanding officer by the receivers general; and the money shall be laid out in providing necessaries; and the commanding officer shall, within one month after the receipt, account to the parties entitled, for the application of it; but the commanding officer is not to draw money for any person who is not desirous to receive it. While on actual service, volunteers are to receive pay, and be billeted as other forces; and after the defeat and expulsion of an invading army, to be returned to their respective homes, and paid one guinea each toward their expences.

FAMILIES. While thus embodied, the wives and families of volunteers are entitled to the same relief, and under the same conditions exactly, as those of militia-men under the same circumstances.

PRIVILEGES. Commissioned officers disabled in actual service are entitled to half pay according to their ranks; non-commissioned, drummers, and privates, to Chelsea Hospital; and widows of those killed in service to the same compensations, as widows of regulars. Officers on half pay do not forego it by filling any stations in volunteer corps, nor do members of parliament vacate their seats by accepting commissions.

MONEY. The commanding officer of every corps is to keep an account of all monies paid to him on account, during their exercise; and within ten days after its termination, deliver the account signed, and pay the balance (if any) to such person as the secretary at war, or his deputy, shall direct. And all money subscribed by or for the use of any corps, and all arms, stores, ammunition, drums, fifes, or musical instruments, or other articles whatever, belonging to, or used by any such corps, not being the property of any particular individual, are vested in the commanding officer, for all purposes of indictment or action; and no proceedings are discontinued or abated by the death, resignation, or removal of any commanding officer, but may be proceeded in by his successor. On non-payment of subscriptions or fines by members of corps, any commanding or field officer, or serjeant major by their order, may make application to magistrates, who may direct double the sum to be recovered by way of penalty, and if not paid, to be levied by distress on the defaulter's goods and chattels, and to be applied to the general fund of the corps; or the justice may mitigate the penalties to one half.

FURTHER REGULATIONS. These are the principal regulations relating to these troops; the statute 44th of the king already mentioned, has further provided, that in future, no rules or regulations relating to any corps shall be valid, unless transmitted

mitted to the lieutenant of the county, and by him to the secretary of state; and if after twenty-eight days they are not disallowed by the king, they are considered as allowed and confirmed. And the king may also annul at any time any rules or regulations of any volunteer corps whatever.

Agency Office. For transacting all matters relative to the pay and allowances of these corps, an agency office, under the direction of the secretary at war, is established in Spring Garden; in it are a general agent, with a chief, two subordinate, and several extra clerks.

Artillery Company. Besides the troops already mentioned, there are in some places peculiar corps, of which it is not necessary to give a detailed account, but the artillery company is of the most ancient establishment, and highest consideration among them. This association had its origin about 1585, when London being wearied with continual musters, a number of its gallant citizens, who had served abroad with credit, voluntarily exercised themselves, and trained others to the ready use of arms. The ground they used was at the north-east extremity of the city, nigh Bishopsgate, and had before been occupied by the "fraternity of artillery," or gunners of the Tower. Within two years there were near three hundred merchants and others sufficiently skilled to train common soldiers; and in 1588, some of them had commissions in the camp at Tilbury; but this association soon after fell to decay. From the company's register, the only book they saved in the civil wars, it appears, that the association was revived in 1611, by warrant from the privy council; and the volunteers soon amounted to six thousand. Three years after this, they made a general muster, when, according to contemporary authority, the men were better armed than disciplined. In 1622, they erected an armoury, towards which the chamber of London gave 300*l.*; it was furnished with five hundred sets of arms of extraordinary beauty, which were all lost in the civil wars. Their captain, during a part of those affrighted times, was Mr. Manby, who irrecoverably detained for his own purposes, the arms, plate, money, books, and other goods of the company. The protector was in vain solicited to enforce their being restored. In 1640, they quitted their old field of discipline, and entered on a spot of ground in Bunhill-fields, leased to them by the city. This company at present forms a regular battalion of infantry, consisting of a grenadier, light infantry, and battalion divisions; together with the matross division, for the use of two field pieces, presented in the year 1780, by the city. There is also kept up a division of the archers; archery being the art cultivated by the company, in days when the bow was an instrument of war. The command of of the battalion is veſted in officers who are annually elected. This municipal corps is authoriſed and privileged by many royal patents and warrants; and particularly by one of his preſent majeſty, under the ſign manual, wherein his royal highneſs the prince of Wales is declared captain general. It conſiſts of gentlemen of character and property, bound by a ſolemn declaration and obligation of attachment and fidelity to the king and conſtitution, and of readineſs to join in ſupporting the civil authority, and defending the metropolis. It is regulated by a court of aſſiſtants, conſiſting of a preſident, vice-preſident, treaſurer, the field officers; the lord mayor, aldermen, and ſheriffs for the time being, and twenty-four elective members.

Sea Fencibles. The force called ſea fencibles may alſo be reckoned among the aſſociations purely for the defence of the realm. It comprizes all fiſhermen and other perſons employed in the ports and on the coaſt, who from their occupation are not liable to be impreſſed, and they act either on ſhore or afloat. On actual ſervice their daily pay is as follows: ſenior poſt-captains, 1*l.* 10*s.* and 5*s.* for contingencies; junior poſt-captains, 1*l.* 10*s.*; commanders, 1*l.* 1*s.* and 10*s.* 6*d.* per week for contingencies; lieutenants, 8*s.* 6*d.* per day. The ſenior poſt-captain of every diſtrict of ſea fencibles has command of the armed boats, compoſing the armed flotilla for the fencibles of the diſtrict; and he regulates alſo all the ſignal poſts within his diſtrict, at each of which there is a lieutenant. There are from three to ſix lieutenants at each diſtrict, according to the number of fencibles enrolled.

The diſtricts of the united kingdom comprehended in their line of defence, with the general rendezvous of each, are as follows:

Diſtrict.	*General Rendezvous.*
At Chatham, Rocheſter, &c. to Sheerneſs	Chatham
From Emſworth to Beachy-Head -	Shoreham
From Beachy-Head to Dungeneſs	Haſtings
From Dungeneſs to Sandgate -	New Romney
From Sandgate to Sandown -	Dover
From Sandown to the North Foreland	Ramſgate
From the North Foreland to Eaſt Swale	Margate
From the Lower Hope to Blackwater	South End
From Blackwater to the Stour -	Harwich
From the Stour to Southwold -	Aldborough
From Southwold to Cromer -	Yarmouth
From Cromer to Forſdyke-waſh -	Lynn
From Forſdyke-waſh to the mouth of the Humber	Boſton

From

District.	*General Rendezvous.*
From the mouth of the Humber to the river Ouze - - -	Barton
From the river Ouze to Flamborough Head - - - -	Hull
From Flamborough Head to the river Tees - - -	Whitby
From the river Tees to North Shields	Hartle-Poole
From North Shields to St. Abb's Head	Berwick
The Frith of Forth - - -	Leith
Coast of Argyleshire - -	Dundee
Isle of Wight - - -	Brading
From Emsworth to Calshot-Castle -	Stokes Bay
From Calshot Castle to St. Alban's Head	Poole
From St. Alban's Head to Puncknole	Weymouth
From Puncknole to Teignmouth -	Exmouth
From Plymouth to the Ram-Head	Plymouth
From Teignmouth to the Ram-Head	Dartmouth
From the Ram-Head to the Dodman	Fowey
From the Dodman to the Land's End	Falmouth
Scilly Islands - - - -	St. Mary's
From Land's End to Hartland Point	Padstow
From Hartland Point to Kingroad	Minehead
From Bristol to Gloucester, and Gloucester to Chepstow - -	Bristol
From Chepstow to the mouth of the British Channel - -	Swansea
From Kidwelly to Cardigan -	Haverfordwest
Isle of Anglesea, &c. - -	Holyhead
Coast of Lancashire, &c. - -	Liverpool.

Kingdom of Ireland.

From Malin-head to Hoon-head -	Buonevana
From Hoon-head to Teeling-head	Rutland
From Teeling-head to Donnegal -	Killybegs
From Ballyshannon to Killala -	Killala
From Killala to Blacksod-bay -	Broadhaven
From Blacksod-bay to Killery harbour	West Port
From Killery harbour to Greatman's Bay	Birterbin
From Greatman's Bay to Blackhead	Galway
From Loop-head to Kerry-head -	Tarbert
From Kerry-head to Blacket island	Tralee
From Blacket-Island to Valentia -	Dingle
From Valentia to Durfey-Island -	Sneem-harbour
From Dursey Island to Sheep's Head	Beerhaven

From

Diſtrict.	*General Rendezvous.*
From Sheep's Head to Gulley-Head	Caſtle-Townſhend
From Gulley-Head to Cork-Head -	Kinſale
From Cork-Head to Youghall -	Cove
From Youghall to Waterford -	Paſſage
From Hooktower to Arklow -	Wexford
From Arklow to Dublin - -	Wicklow
From Donaghadee to Larne - -	Carrickfergus
From Howth to Balbriggen -	Malaheide.

Military Districts. In order to render the operation of the land force equally eaſy, certain, and conſiſtent, the kingdom is alſo divided into military diſtricts, each having a proper proportion of troops, and a ſtaff attached to it. Theſe diſtricts are as follows: the *Home*, which contains the whole of the counties of Middleſex and Surry; and places in Eſſex, within any plan of defence for the capital; Kent, to the river Cray and Holwood Hill incluſive; Hertfordſhire and Berkſhire. The head-quarters are at St. James's palace. The *Southern* diſtrict contains, Kent eaſt of the river Cray and Holwood Hill; Suſſex, and Tilbury Fort in Eſſex. Head-quarters are at Canterbury. It has a cavalry depot at Maidſtone. The *South-inland* diſtrict extends over the counties of Bedford, Northampton, Oxford, and Buckingham. Head-quarters, Oxford. The *South-weſt* diſtrict contains Hampſhire, Wilts, and Dorſet. Head-quarters, Wincheſter. In it is included the grand army depot at the Iſle of Wight. In the *Eaſtern* diſtrict are compriſed Norfolk, Suffolk, Cambridge, Huntingdon, excluſive of the hundreds of Beacontree and Waltham, and Tilbury Fort. Head-quarters, Colcheſter. In the *Weſtern*, are Devonſhire, Cornwall, and Somerſet, excluſive of the vicinity of Briſtol, viz. Bath, Troubridge, Bradford, Wells, and Axbridge, and any other place occupied by detachments from Briſtol. Head-quarters, Exeter. The *Severn* diſtrict includes Glouceſterſhire, and vicinity of Briſtol in Somerſet, the counties of Worceſter, Hereford, Monmouth, and South Wales. Head-quarters, Bath. The *Northern* contains Northumberland, Cumberland, Weſtmoreland, and Durham. Head-quarters, Newcaſtle. The *North-inland*, the counties of Derby, Nottingham, Stafford, Leiceſter, Warwick, and Rutland. Head-quarters, Litchfield. The *York* diſtrict is formed by York-ſhire and Lancaſhire, the head-quarters being at Beverley; and the *Northweſt* by Cheſhire, Shropſhire, Lancaſhire, North Wales, and the Iſle of Man. Head-quarters, Liverpool. North Britain, Jerſey, and Guernſey, form ſeparate diſtricts.

Instruction. The eſtabliſhments for inſtruction in military affairs

affairs have not been numerous; and perhaps, while the opinion of the illegality of a ſtanding army is tenaciouſly maintained, they will not be duly popular. The experience of late years has however been ſufficient to convince the Britiſh nation, that officers of the moſt finiſhed deſcription are no leſs neceſſary in the military, than in the naval ſervice.

Academy at Woolwich. The moſt ancient and beſt known place for inſtruction in military affairs, is the Royal Academy eſtabliſhed at Woolwich, under the board of ordnance, for the purpoſe of qualifying of young gentlemen, intended as candidates for the office of engineer, in the military branch of that office; theſe are called *cadets*, and are appointed by that board. They are taught the principles and art of fortification, and every branch of military ſcience relating thereto, with the French and Latin languages, writing, fencing, and drawing. They are under the immediate direction of a governor, lieutenant governor, and maſters in each reſpective branch of literature.

The models of fortification preſerved in this ſeminary are ſpoken of in high terms of commendation; and it is no ſmall advantage to the ſtudents, that they are placed near the *Warren*, where artillery of all kinds and dimenſions are caſt, and frequently proved before the principal engineers and officers of the board of ordnance, at which many of the nobility and gentry often attend. The gunpowder purchaſed by contract is here proved, as to its ſtrength and goodneſs. Here is alſo a laboratory, where the matroſſes are employed in the compoſition of fire works and cartridges, and in charging bombs, carcaſes, grenades, &c. for public ſervice.

College at High Wycombe and Marlow. This eſtabliſhment (for, although locally divided, it is but one) owes its origin to Major General Le Marchant, who began it in 1799. In 1801, his majeſty, looking beyond the mere occaſions of the day, and contemplating the abſolute neceſſity there was, in the preſent ſtate of Europe, for a ſchool in Great Britain, where a certain number of young perſons might be regularly trained up in military ſcience, informed parliament, by a meſſage, that ſuch an eſtabliſhment had been formed under his direction; and conſidering that it muſt conduce to the improvement of that ſkill and diſcipline, which, combined with the valour of the Britiſh troops, had ſo often maintained the rights, and aſſerted the honour of the nation, he recommended to the commons, the making of an adequate proviſion, for enabling him to accompliſh an object of ſuch great national importance. The meſſage being referred to a committee, Mr. Yorke, ſecretary at war, explained

plained the plan in the following terms: "The proposition "applies to the institution of a royal college or seminary for "military instruction, comprehending as well the education of "such young men as are from early life intended for the army, "in the rudiments of military science, previous to their attain-"ing the age which enables them to hold a commission, as the "perfecting and forming a certain number of officers of matu-"rer years, and riper experience in the more arduous, difficult, "and important duties of their *profession; I mean those which* "belong to the general staff *of the army, and in particular* to "the quarter-master general's department in the field. It is "intended to consist of a senior, and a junior department; "the first and most important of which will be occupied in "the education of officers for the staff, and will include thirty "officers, selected from the service, and recommended by their "zeal and intelligence, grounded at least in the rudiments of "their profession, and of an age capable of reflection. It is to "this class more particularly that the chief military director "and superintendant will devote their time, and apply their "personal instructions. The plan of instruction for this class "appears to have been conceived on the justest practical mili-"tary principles; adapting itself particularly to the nature of "ground actually under examination at the time; to the choice "of camps and positions; to the best mode of occupying, at-"tacking, or defending them with a given force; to the proper "combination of all the component parts of an army; to its "movements from place to place, either in advancing or retreat-"ing; and among other essential acquirements, to the most "ready and effectual means of affording assistance to the com-"manding general, in making his dispositions, by military plans "rapidly designed, by the habitual accuracy of the eye, cor-"rected by the scientific preparation and judgment of the mind. "This plan of instruction, so described in its nature and de-"tails, has been already acted upon, and brought to maturity, "by the very able and skilful general officer, whose services in "this line this country has at present the advantage of possessing; "(I mean general Jarry;) first in the Prussian service, under the "inspection, and with the approbation of Frederick the Great; "and latterly in this country, at High Wycombe, (with the "assistance of a very able and intelligent officer of our own, "colonel Le Marchant), though on a very limited scale, in a "manner the most useful and advantageous to the service. I "must also observe, that this institution is nearly of the same "sort and description, with that which is now in use, for the "formation of staff-officers, in the Austrian, Prussian, and "French armies; and that it has the advantages of having

"been

"been examined and recommended by his royal highness "the commander in chief, assisted by the quarter-master and "adjutant-generals, and by a board of general officers of the "highest reputation in the British army."

"The second, or junior department, is intended to receive "300 young men, from the age of fourteen to sixteen; 100, "the sons of noblemen and gentlemen intended for the pro-"fession of arms; 50, cadets of the East India company; "100, the sons of officers actually in his majesty's service; and "50, the sons of officers who have died or been disabled in the "service, leaving families in distressed circumstances. For "these, masters and professors of all the arts, sciences, and ac-"complishments relating to the military profession will be pro-"vided. It is further proposed, that as the establishment is "intended to be entirely of a military nature, it shall be govern-"ed and regulated as a military body, by the rules and ordinan-"ces prescribed for the discipline of his majesty's service; with "such additional regulations and restrictions as may be found "necessary for the conduct of youth, and the good order of the "institution."

On the plan thus ably and clearly delineated, and which met the approbation of all parties in parliament, an united establishment composed of two branches has proceeded; the senior department being continued at High Wycombe, the junior at Great Marlow; but it is intended to remove both, when the building about to be erected for their reception at Sandhurst, in Berkshire, shall be completed.

The regulation of this establishment is confided to commissioners who are all general officers, and at their head the commander in chief; and there are a governor, and a lieutenant governor: both the departments have proper officers, and the most exact discipline is observed. All necessaries are supplied by contracts entered into in pursuance of a public advertisement.

Charitable Establishments. Of foundations formed by private benevolence, for the relief and comfort of maimed and superannuated soldiers, it is not intended here to treat; but two great national establishments demand attention.

Chelsea Hospital. This receptacle for soldiers no longer able to exert themselves in the service of their country, is generally called by the softer name of Chelsea College, and, in fact, its first institution corresponded with that title. Toward the beginning of the seventeenth century, Dr. Sutcliffe, dean of Exeter, set on foot a project for establishing a college of polemical divines, to be employed in opposing the doctrines of papists and sectaries. At first the undertaking seemed attended with good

good omens; prince Henry was a zealous friend to it; the king consented to be deemed the founder, called the college after his own name, endowed it with the reversion of certain lands at Chelsea, which were fixed upon for its site, laid the first stone of the building, gave timber out of Windsor Forest, issued his royal letters to encourage his subjects throughout the kingdom to contribute towards the completion of the structure, and as a permanent endowment, procured an act of parliament to enable the college to raise an annual rent, by supplying the city of London with water from the river Lee. Under these encouraging circumstances the building was begun and carried to a considerable extent; but although Dr. Sutcliffe's will would have added considerably to its resources had the work not been interrupted, it was soon at a stand for want of supplies. With a limited establishment, and in frequent danger of being applied to purposes widely different from those originally intended, the college subsisted till the murder of Charles I.; during the interregnum it was used for various purposes, some of them so disgraceful that it would appear as if the triumphant sectaries wreaked on it some portion of the spleen excited in their minds by the intentions of those who had founded it. After the restoration it was once a prison for Dutch seamen; afterward it was granted to the Royal Society, but it was re-purchased for the crown by Sir Stephen Fox, and a plan suggested, it is said by him, was immediately carried into effect for erecting an hospital for maimed and superannuated soldiers*. In March, 1682, the king went to Chelsea, attended by many of the nobility, to lay the first stone of a fabric, which promises to be a monument of national honour to far distant ages. Sir Christopher Wren was the architect of the new structure, which was not completed till the year 1690: the whole charge of it was computed at 150,000*l*. Sir Stephen Fox contributed largely towards the building, and archbishop Sancroft gave 1000*l*.

This noble edifice is situated about a mile westward from St. James's Park, at a small distance from the northern bank of the river Thames. The approach to the north front from the road, is through a handsome gate-way, opening into a spacious court divided into avenues, and planted with lime and horse chesnut trees. The whole building is of brick, excepting the pillars, pediments, coins and cornices, which are of freestone.

* A tradition prevails at Chelsea, that the famous Nell Gwyn first projected the scheme of building an hospital for superannuated soldiers, and persuaded the king to become the founder. The sign board of a public house, not far from the college, is still decorated with her portrait, underneath which is an inscription, ascribing the foundation to her desire Whether this celebrated lady has any claim to dispute the palm with Sir Stephen Fox, it would be difficult perhaps to determine.

It consists of three quadrangular courts, the largest of which is in the centre, and is open to the south, as the two side courts are to the east and west. The south front, which extends 790 feet, is composed of a principal building, and two inferior wings. In the centre, under a pediment supported by four three-quarter Doric columns, and crowned by a turret surmounted by a vane, is the grand entrance, which leads through a large octagonal vestibule into the principal court, in the centre of which is placed a pedestrian statue in bronze, of the founder, Charles II. in a Roman habit, the gift of Mr. Tobias Rustat. The vestibule communicates on the right with the great hall, and on the left with the chapel. At the upper or west end of the hall, which is the dining room of the pensioners, is a large painting of Charles II. on horseback, designed by Verrio, and finished by Henry Cooke, the gift of Richard earl of Ranelagh, paymaster general of the forces. The chapel has few decorations; it is paved with black and white marble, and wainscotted with Dutch oak. The altar-piece, by Sebastian Ricci, represents the ascension of our Saviour. The service of gilt plate, consisting of a pair of massy candlesticks, several large chalices and flagons, and a perforated spoon, was given by James II. and the organ by major Ingram. The centre of the south front is distinguished by a handsome Doric portico, on each side of which is a colonnade, continued to the wings, bearing the following inscription on the frieze: "*In subsidium et levamen, emeritorum senio, belloque,* "*fractorum, condidit Carolus Secundus, auxit Jacobus Secundus,* "*perfecere Gulielmus et Maria, rex et regina,* 1690." The two wings which project from the south front, are each 365 feet in length, and separate the principal from the two inferior courts. They are chiefly occupied by the pensioners' wards; but the ends next the garden contain the residence of the governor, and principal officers of the hospital. The centre of each wing is decorated by a pediment, supported by four Doric pilasters. In the governor's house is the state room, a fine apartment, in which are portraits of Charles I. and II. William and Mary, George II. their present majesties, and others. The buildings on the north and south quadrangles consist of offices, apartments for the inferor officers, and the infirmaries, which are well supplied with cold, hot, and vapour baths. The garden is separated from the hospital by a handsome balustrade, and extends to the river, where it is terminated by iron gates leading to a descent of stone steps, between two square brick pavilions, ornamented with stone coins. It is very neatly laid out in the Dutch taste, in regular walks, with two canals bordered with rows of clipt trees, after the prevailing mode of the times when the hospital was built. There is a very fine walk, from

from the water gate to the creek, at the weſt end, planted with a row of lofty trees, that affords a delightful view of the river Thames and its oppoſite bank. From the garden, the ſouth front of the hoſpital appears to great advantage. A little to the eaſt of the buildings is a ſpacious cemetry, wherein may be found ſome intereſting memorials of the longevity of Britiſh veterans. The whole extent of theſe premiſes contains about 50 acres.

The eſtabliſhment conſiſts of a governor, with a ſalary, beſides other advantages, of 500*l.*; a lieutenant governor, with 400*l.*; a major, who has 250*l.*; an adjutant, 100*l.*; two chaplains, who have 100*l.* each; an organiſt, a phyſician, ſurgeon, apothecary, ſecretary, ſteward, treaſurer, comptroller, clerk of the works, and various ſubordinate officers. The number of ordinary penſioners is 336; theſe men muſt have been twenty years in his majeſty's ſervice; ſuch as have been maimed or diſabled may be admitted at any period; but except under very particular circumſtances, no perſon is received into the houſe under ſixty years of age; by which means the benefit of the charity is appropriated with much greater certainty to thoſe who are its moſt proper objects. The penſioners who live in the houſe, commonly called the in-penſioners, are provided with clothes, (an uniform of red lined with blue) lodging, and diet; beſide which they have an allowance of eight-pence per week; they mount guard, and perform other garriſon duty; and are divided into eight companies, each of which has its proper complement of officers, ſerjeants, corporals, and drummers. The officers who have the nominal rank of captain, lieutenant, and enſign, are choſen from the moſt meritorious old ſerjeants in the army, and have an allowance of three ſhillings and ſixpence per week; the ſerjeants two ſhillings; the corporals and drummers tenpence. Two ſerjeants, four corporals, and fifty-two of the moſt able privates, are appointed by the king's ſign manual, to act as a patrol on the road from Chelſea to Pimlico, for which duty they have an additional allowance. The actual patrol conſiſts of half the number here mentioned, the duty being taken alternately. There is likewiſe in the college a ſmall corps called the light-horſemen, thirty-four in number, who are allowed two ſhillings per week, and are choſen indiſcriminately out of any of the regiments of cavalry. The various ſervants of the college, among whom are twenty-ſix nurſes, make the whole number of its inhabitants about five hundred and fifty. There are alſo belonging to the eſtabliſhment, four hundred ſerjeants who are out-penſioners. The number of private out-penſioners is unlimited; and has been much increaſed ſince the commencement of the militia ſyſtem; they are diſperſed all over the united kingdom,

kingdom, at their various occupations, being liable to be called on to perform garrison duty, as invalid companies, in time of war. There are three degrees of out-pensioners; the first having annually 18*l.* 5*s.*; the second, 13*l.* 13*s.* 9*d.*; and the third, 7*l.* 12*s.* 6*d.* The expences of this noble institution (excepting about 7000*l.* which arises from the poundage of the household troops, and is applied towards the payment of the out-pensioners) are defrayed by an annual sum voted by parliament. The yearly expence of the house establishment, including the salaries of the officers, repairs, and other incidental charges, varies from 25,000*l.* to 28,000*l.* The internal affairs of the hospital are regulated by commissioners appointed by the crown, and consisting of the governor, lieutenant governor, and some of the principal officers of state, who hold a board, as occasion requires, for the paying of out-pensioners, and other business.

The following are the chief benefactions by which private individuals have endeavoured to extend the sphere of this useful charity. In 1695, the earl of Ranelagh vested 3250*l.* in trustees for the use of the hospital, to be disposed of as he should afterward appoint; and by a deed poll, dated 1707, he directed that the interest should be laid out, in purchasing great coats for the pensioners, once in three years; a mode of distribution which was confirmed by a degree in chancery. In 1706, John Delafontaine, Esq. bequeathed the sum of 2000*l.* for the use of the hospital, subject to the direction of the governor and treasurer. Some time afterwards, 800*l.* having in the mean while accrued for interest, the whole was laid out by order of the court of chancery in the purchase of bank annuities. Out of this benefaction the sum of 60*l.* 10*s.* is distributed among the pensioners annually on the 29th of May. In 1729, lady Catherine Jones, (daughter of the earl of Ranelagh), lady Elizabeth Hastings, Lady Anne Coventry, and other benevolent persons, founded a school at Chelsea for the education of poor girls, whose fathers were, or had been pensioners in the college. The funds of this school, arising from an endowment of 14*l.* per annum paid out of the estates of Lady Elizabeth Hastings, and the interest of 1262*l.* 15*s.* 3 per cent. consols, are vested in three trustees, who are enabled to clothe and educate twenty girls.

Military Asylum. An establishment under the name of a military asylum, had some time been established at Chelsea, for the reception and education of 500 children of soldiers, when in 1801, parliament granted, on the motion of Mr. Yorke, the necessary supplies for extending the benefits of the institution to 1000 children, and it was provided that the whole expense should

ſhould be defrayed by the public, without raiſing any part of it by deduction from the pay of the military.

MUTINY ACT. To keep the troops in order, an annual act of parliament paſſes, " to puniſh mutiny and deſertion, and for " the better payment of the army and their quarters." This act, which has frequently been mentioned and alluded to in preceding pages, regulates the manner in which they are to be diſperſed among the ſeveral innkeepers and victuallers throughout the kingdom; and eſtabliſhes a law martial for their government: by this, among other things, it is enacted, that if any officer or ſoldier ſhall excite, or join any mutiny, or knowing of it ſhall not give notice to the commanding officer; or ſhall deſert or enliſt in any other regiment, or ſleep upon his poſt, or leave it before he is relieved, or hold correſpondence with a rebel or enemy, or ſtrike or uſe violence to his ſuperior officer, or ſhall diſobey his lawful commands: ſuch offender ſhall ſuffer puniſhment as a court martial ſhall inflict, though it extend even to death.

REGULATIONS RESPECTING DESERTERS. When a perſon is apprehended on ſuſpicion of being a deſerter, the ſtation of the corps to which he belongs muſt be officially reſorted to: if the party accuſed is taken up in Ireland, and belongs to a regiment there, the war-office in Dublin makes the neceſſary inquiry at the head-quarters of the regiment: but if the corps is in Great Britain, or abroad, and the apprehenſion happens in Ireland, the particulars are ſent from Dublin to the ſecretary at war in London, who inveſtigates the caſe, and communicates the reſult to the Iriſh war office. The like proceedings are had, when perſons charged with deſertion from regiments in Ireland are apprehended in Great Britain; and the removal under eſcort, or releaſe of the perſon accuſed, depends upon the iſſue of thoſe proceedings, and the orders are given accordingly, by the war-office in London or in Dublin.

Inſpection. In order to avoid unneceſſary expenſes, when a deſerter under eſcort arrives at any place in the united kingdom, where a ſtaff ſurgeon is ſtationed, he there undergoes a medical examination; and, if found unfit, either from age or infirmity, an immediate report is tranſmitted by the commanding officer to the ſecretary at war, who (in Great Britain, with the concurrence of the commander in chief, and in Ireland, with that of the commander of the forces there) cauſes the man to be diſmiſſed; unleſs in particular caſes, where circumſtances appear to make it adviſable, for the ſake of diſcipline, to forward men, even of this deſcription, to the head-quarters of their reſpective corps. Each man ſo diſmiſſed is to have a reaſonable proportion of pay to carry him back to his laſt place of reſidence, at the rate of ſixpence per day, and ſuch additional allowance as may be made for deserters in confinement by any special regulation then in force: the pay and extra allowance, if any, to be charged on the back of the route, to which is to be annexed a certificate from the commanding officer, that the man has been dismissed by order.

Escort. When an order is received by the commanding officer of any corps, or detachment, for a party to take charge of a deserter, and convey him to any place, he advances so much money on account of pay for the deserter, as is sufficient to defray his arrears, during the time of his confinement, and the expense, if any, of medicines and attendance. He likewise causes such necessaries as the man may stand in need of to be provided and paid for, which are not to exceed one shirt, one pair of shoes, and one pair of stockings; the sums so defrayed, and advanced, must appear distinctly on the back of the route, as likewise the particular and actual charge of the necessaries, signed by the commanding officer himself, or by the adjutant or paymaster, by his direction. The commanding officer also causes to be advanced a further sum, sufficient to subsist the deserter to the next quarter on the road; on arrival at which, the officer commanding there repays the non-commissioned officer of the escort the money disbursed at the first quarter, and so much of the sum advanced for subsistence, as appears expended, and properly accounted for on the route; and also advances the sum necessary to subsist the deserter to the next quarter on his route; the total of the sum disbursed at the second quarter, and so much of the sum advanced there for subsistence, as appears expended, and properly accounted for on the route, are in like manner repaid by the officer commanding at the third quarter; and so on, from quarter to quarter, until the deserter arrives at his final destination.

The jailor, and the non-commissioned officer who takes charge of the deserter, must likewise sign to the sums respectively received by them.

When a deserter is delivered over from one party to another, the commanding officer of the corps, to which the latter party belongs, or the adjutant or paymaster, by his direction, must carefully inspect the route, and see that the money received is there properly accounted for; if upon such inspection of the route, any improper charges are found, they are crossed out, and the amount only of what had been advanced, exclusive of such improper charges, returned by the regiment receiving the deserter; the non-commissioned officer under whom such improper charges were incurred, is required by his commanding officer to make good the amount, and on failure is to be put under stoppages.

No

No pay can be advanced, nor neceſſaries provided, but by order of the commanding officer, adjutant, or paymaſter, who ſigns the charge; and no more pay will be advanced than the time and diſtance may require. At thoſe ſtations where the eſcort is relieved by a detachment under the command of a quarter-maſter, or of a non-commiſſioned officer, ſuch officer is to ſign for the expenditure; who, in that caſe, is to ſubjoin to his ſignature, the following words; *No ſuperior officer at the ſtation.*

Neceſſaries are ſupplied but once for any march; if deſtroyed, or made away with, the officer commanding at the next quarter muſt order a detachment court martial to try the priſoner, non-commiſſioned officer, or any of the eſcort who appear to be in fault, in order that an immediate example may be made of the offender; after which, ſhould the puniſhment inflicted render him unable to proceed, the ſame muſt be reported; in Great Britain, to the commander in chief; and in Ireland, to the commander of the forces.

No horſe or carriage hire is allowed, except in caſe of a deſerter being taken ſo ill between one ſtage and another, as to be incapable of proceeding on foot; on ſuch occurrence happening, the neceſſity that occaſioned the extra charge muſt be certified on the back of the route by the commanding officer, and a ſurgeon at the next town; and ſhould the deſerter ſtill be unable to proceed on foot, a report is to be made to the war-office for further inſtructions.

No fees are allowed at jails; the mutiny act having expreſsly provided for the admiſſion of deſerters on the road, as at the places where they are firſt committed; therefore all non-commiſſioned officers, commanding eſcorts with deſerters, endeavour, as much as poſſible, to march in ſuch a manner as to lie in towns or villages having public places of confinement, or where troops are ſtationed, as they muſt otherwiſe be reſponſible for the ſecurity of the deſerters in their own quarters.

Expenſe. The agent of the regiment to which a deſerter belongs, or the paymaſter, repays the money advanced, as above mentioned, provided it is properly accounted for on the route, and charges the ſame againſt the public; if in regular regiments, as recruiting diſburſements, under the following heads, *viz.* the ſubſiſtence at 6*d.* per day for each deſerter, whether from the cavalry or the infantry, during the period of his confinement, and on the march; the extra allowance for the ſame time liable to variation or diſcontinuance, according to the price of proviſions; neceſſaries not exceeding the limits preſcribed by the inſtructions; and handcuffs; medicines, and other neceſſary expences in conſequence of ſickneſs;

subject to the approval of the inspector of regimental hospitals.

The deserter is not to be replaced on the strength of his regiment, until the day he joins it.

The route by which deserters are marched must, in no case, include men belonging to different regiments. Each route is to be carefully preserved, and deposited with the agent or paymaster, who reimburses the expenses, in order to its being transmitted with their public accounts, as vouchers for the charges.

NAVY AND ARMY.

It was stated that besides the peculiar circumstances characteristic of each service, there were some common to both, which it would be proper to include in one division. These particulars relate principally to offences and benefits.

VAGRANCY. The law was formerly very severe against idle soldiers and mariners wandering about the realm, or persons pretending so to be, and abusing the name of that honourable profession. Such a person not having a testimonial, or pass, from a justice of the peace, limiting the time of his passage; or exceeding the time limited by fourteen days, unless he fell sick; or forging such testimonial; was by statute 39 Eliz. c. 17, made guilty of felony without benefit of clergy. This sanguinary law, which though in practice deservedly antiquated, long remained a disgrace to the statute book, was yet attended with this mitigation, that the offender might be delivered, if any honest freeholder or other person of substance would take him into his service, and he remained in the same for one year; unless licensed to depart by his employer, who in such case was to forfeit ten pounds. By the effect of subsequent acts of parliament, soldiers and mariners in this predicament are put on the same footing with other vagrants, but with some special exceptions in their favour; for every soldier, marine, or sailor, on carrying his discharge within three days, to the nearest magistrate, may receive a certificate of his place of settlement, on production of which, being in his route, he is not to be deemed a vagabond for asking relief. But this certificate can only be made use of in the direct route of the possessor, from the place where it was given, to that of his legal settlement; and it must contain a fixed time for its expiration, not exceeding the rate of ten days for every one hundred miles, and must express the sums of money, if any, which were paid to the party when it was given: wives of non-commissioned officers or soldiers gone abroad, on making proof of not being permitted

permitted to embark with their husbands, receive from the nearest chief magistrate a like certificate of their place of settlement, which entitles them to ask for relief while in their route, and such persons asking relief, with the limitations before expressed, are not subject to the laws against vagrants. In case of accident or sickness duly proved, which shall prevent the person having such certificate from proceeding on his or her journey, according to the terms prescribed, the chief magistrate of any other city, town, port, or corporate place where such person shall be or arrive, may grant a new certificate, stating the true reasons for granting it, and containing the like provisions with the former, to which it is to be annexed. Certificates or passes granted as usual from the office of admiralty or war-office to discharged sailors, soldiers, or marines, or to the families of sailors, soldiers, or marines, serving abroad, or lately deceased, to carry them to their respective homes, have the same effect and force as the certificates of magistrates, and may be, according to circumstances, renewed or extended by them.

Desertion. To what has already been said on this subject it may be proper to add, that desertion from the king's armies in time of war, whether by land or sea, in England, or in parts beyond the seas, is by the standing laws of the land (exclusive of the annual acts of parliament to punish mutiny and desertion,) and particularly by statute 18 Hen. VI. c. 19. and 5 Eliz. c. 5. made felony, but not without benefit of clergy. But by the statute 2 and 3 Edw. VI. c. 2. clergy is taken away from such deserters, and the offence is made triable by the justices of every shire. The same statutes punish other inferior military offences with fines, imprisonment, and other penalties.

Courts Martial. For the investigation and punishment of every kind of offence committed by persons serving in the army or navy, while on actual duty, the tribunal called a court-martial is established. The origin of these courts is said to be found in the court of chivalry, but perhaps it may be with less hazard of error ascribed to the necessity of speedy judgment, and peremptory regulation, in a state where force must be exercised with unhesitating unanimity, where general deliberation cannot exist without common ruin, and where mutual confidence and good opinion must be preserved by the most rigid adherence to the laws of honour and rules of propriety. Therefore, although the law of the land punishes mutiny and desertion as already has been mentioned, still the nature of military service will not admit of the delays and formalities which would be necessary in appealing to ordinary courts; although most of the crimes of which the court-martial takes cognizance would be punished by a jury, yet the delinquent must rather escape with impunity, than the public service be delayed by the necessary absence of parties and witnesses from a ship or a regiment; and although most misdemeanors would render the person offending amenable to a civil tribunal, yet it is found inconsistent with the high and ardent sensibility which is the very life of honourable service, that pecuniary compensation should be sought, when an appeal to the opinion of those who are equally interested with the person who complains in the maintenance of his honour, will be productive of a more satisfactory and not less just determination. It was not, however, till the reign of Charles II. that a regular court for the administration of martial law in the army or navy, was established: but the decline of the court of chivalry, to which such cases might have been referred, then rendered the measure necessary, and the system has been pursued with various improvements to the present time. It is observed that in the naval articles, contained in the act 22 Geo. II. almost every possible offence is set down, and the punishment annexed; in which respect the seamen have much the advantage over their brethren in the land service, whose articles of war are not enacted by parliament, but framed from time to time, at the pleasure of the crown; which, with regard to military offences, has a sole, and almost absolute legislative power. For, by the mutiny act, his majesty may form, make, and establish articles of war, and constitute courts-martial, with power to try any crime by such articles, and inflict penalties by sentence or judgment of the same; which articles must be judicially taken notice of by all judges, and in all courts whatever; but it is at the same time provided, "that no officer "or soldier shall, by such articles of war, be subjected to any "punishment extending to life or limb, for any crime which "is not expressed to be so punishable by the mutiny act." This, Sir William Blackstone observes, is a vast and important trust; an unlimited power to create crimes, and annex to them any punishments, not extending to life or limb! It cannot however escape the reader's observation, that the annual consent of parliament is requisite to pass the mutiny act, and that consequently no permanent evil can result from the exercise of royal authority.

A power is given to the lords of the admiralty over the marines, by an annual act passed "for the regulation of his ma-"jesty's marine forces while on shore," similar to that given to the crown by the annual mutiny act. And officers of marines may be associated with officers of the land forces, for the purpose of holding courts-martial, as often as it shall be expedient, and particularly in certain cases, wherein the marine forces may be be interefted; taking rank according to the feniority of their commiffions in either fervice. The king is likewife empowered by parliament to frame and eftablifh articles of war, for the regulation and government of the troops in the fervice of the Eaft India Company; and it is declared, by the mutiny act, that, as often as there may be occafion, officers of his majefty's land forces and thofe in the Eaft India Company's fervice may fit in conjunction at courts-martial, and proceed on the trial of any officer or foldier, as if fuch court were compofed of officers of either fervice only; and on the trial of any officer or foldier belonging to the Eaft India Company, regard muft be had to the regulations made in 27th year of George II. for punifhing mutiny and defertion of officers and foldiers in that fervice. By thefe tribunals alfo may be tried artillery officers, and thofe ferving in the royal corps of engineers, and perfons ferving and hired to be employed in them, officers and perfons ferving in the corps of royal military artificers and labourers, mafter gunners and gunners under the ordnance, and in the corps of royal engineers, and officers and perfons ferving in the corps of royal military furveyors and draftfmen. For differences arifing among themfelves, or in matters relating folely to their own corps, the courts martial on perfons belonging to the artillery may be compofed of their own officers; but where a fufficient number cannot be affembled, or in matters wherein other corps are interefted, the officers of artillery fit in courts martial with the officers of other corps, taking rank according to the dates of their refpective commiffions. All troops raifed in any of the Britifh provinces of America, by authority of the governors or governments, are, while acting in conjunction with his majefty's Britifh forces, under the command of an officer having a commiffion immediately from his majefty, liable to martial law and difcipline, like other troops, and fubject to the fame trials and punifhments by courts-martial. The fubjection of the militia to military law has already been mentioned, and its extenfion to volunteer and yeomanry corps, while in actual fervice; and the courts-martial on each muft be compofed of officers of their own clafs; that is, an offender in the militia muft be tried by the militia, and not by regular or volunteer officers; and fo in every cafe.

Extent of Military Law. Military law, as exercifed by the authority of parliament, and the mutiny act annually paffed, together with the articles of war framed by his majefty, and the printed regulations from time to time iffued for the regulation of his majefty's troops, has often been confounded by able lawyers and writers, with a different branch of the royal prerogative, denominated *martial law*, and which is only reforted ed to on an emergency of invaſion, rebellion, or inſurrection. The diſtinction was ably defined by the late earl of Roſslyn, while lord chief juſtice of the common pleas, in the caſe of ſerjeant Grant, who moved for a prohibition againſt the ſentence of a general court-martial, by which he was adjudged to receive a thouſand laſhes, for the being inſtrumental in inliſting, for the ſervice of the Eaſt India Company, two drummers, knowing them to belong to the foot guards. His lordſhip, in delivering the opinion of the court, ſaid, "Martial law, ſuch as "it is deſcribed by Hale, and ſuch alſo as it is marked by Sir "William Blackſtone, does not exiſt in England at all. Where "martial law is eſtabliſhed, and prevails in any country, it is "of a totally different nature from that which, by inaccuracy, "is called martial law, merely becauſe the deciſion is by a court-"martial; but which bears no affinity to that which was for-"merly attempted to be exerciſed in this kingdom, which was "contrary to the conſtitution, and has been for a century "totally exploded. Where martial law prevails, the authority "under which it is exerciſed claims a juriſdiction over all "military perſons, in all circumſtances: even their debts are "ſubject to inquiry, by a military authority. Every ſpecies "of offence, committed by any perſon who appertains to the "army, is tried not by a civil judicature, but by the judicature "of the regiment or corps to which he belongs. It extends "alſo to a great variety of caſes, not relating to the diſcipline "of the army in thoſe ſtates which ſubſiſt by military power. "Plots againſt the ſovereign, intelligence to the enemy, and "the like, are all conſidered as caſes within the cognizance of the "military authority. In the reign of king William, there was "a conſpiracy againſt his perſon in Holland; and the perſons "guilty of that conſpiracy were tried by a council of officers. "There was alſo a conſpiracy againſt his perſon in England; "but the conſpirators were tried by the common law. Within "a very recent period, the incendiaries, attempting to ſet fire "to the docks at Portſmouth, were tried by the common law. "In this country, the delinquencies of ſoldiers are not triable, "as in moſt countries in Europe, by martial law: but where "there are ordinary offences againſt the civil peace, they are "tried by the common law courts. Therefore, it is totally "inaccurate, to ſtate martial law as having any place whatever "within the realm of Great Britain. But there is, by the pro-"vidence and wiſdom of the legiſlature, an army eſtabliſhed in "this country, of which it is neceſſary to keep up the eſtabliſh-"ment. The army being fixed by the authority of the legiſ-"lature, it is an indiſpenſable requiſite of that eſtabliſhment, "that there ſhould be order and diſcipline kept up in it; and

"that

"that persons who compose the army, for all offences in their military capacity, should be subject to a trial by their officers. This has induced the absolute necessity of a mutiny act accompanying the army. It has happened indeed, at different periods of the government, that there has been a strong opposition to the establishment of the army; but the army being established and voted, that led to the establishment of a mutiny act. It is one object of that act to provide for the army; but there is a much greater cause for the existence of a mutiny act, and that is, the preservation of the peace and safety of the kingdom; for there is nothing so dangerous to the civil establishment of a state, as a licentious and undisciplined army. The object of the mutiny act, therefore, is, to create a court invested with authority to try those who are a part of the army, in all their different descriptions of officers and soldiers; and the object of the trial is limited to breaches of military duty. Even, by that extensive power granted by the legislature to his majesty, to make articles of war, those articles are to be 'for the better government of his forces;' and they can extend no further than they are thought necessary for the regularity and due discipline of the army. Breaches of military duty are, in many instances, strictly defined; they are so in all cases, where a capital punishment is to be inflicted. In other instances, where the degree of offence may vary exceedingly, it may be necessary to give a discretion with regard to the punishment; and in some cases, it is impossible more strictly to mark the crime, than to call it a neglect of discipline."

The military law is, in fact, subordinate to the civil and municipal laws of the kingdom, and does not in any way supersede those laws, but they materially aid and co-operate with each other for the good order and discipline of the army in particular, and for the benefit of the community in general. Thus it is declared by the mutiny act, that "nothing in that statute shall extend, or be construed to exempt any officer or soldier whatsoever, from being proceeded against by the ordinary course of law." And that if any officer, soldier, &c. shall be accused of any capital crime, or any offence against the person, estate or property, of any of his majesty's subjects, which is punishable by the known laws of the land, the commanding officers of all regiments, troops, or parties, are required to use their utmost endeavour to deliver over such accused person to the civil magistrate, and to assist the officers of justice in apprehending such offender; and this, under the penalty of being *ipso facto* cashiered, and declared incapable of holding any civil or military office, within the united kingdom of Great

Britain

Britain and Ireland, or in his majeſty's ſervice. But this ſentence is not put in execution till the conviction has been affirmed at the following quarter ſeſſion, and a certificate tranſmitted to the judge advocate in London, or Dublin, according to the country where it took place; and the judge advocate is to certify the fact to the next general court martial, which court is by the articles of war bound to caſhier the offender. Martial law is proclaimed by authority of parliament, and prevails generally or partially in a kingdom for a limited time. The authority under which martial law is exerciſed, when it prevails in its full extent, claims a juriſdiction in ſummary trials by courts martial, not only over all military perſons in all circumſtances; but it alſo extends to a great variety of caſes, not relating to the diſcipline of the army, but relative to that ſtate which ſubſiſts by military power; as plots againſt the ſovereign; intelligence to the enemy; which are all conſidered as caſes within the cognizance of the military authority. The ſtatute, for putting in execution martial law, uſually gives a power to arreſt or detain in cuſtody, all ſuſpected perſons, and to cauſe them to be brought to trial in a ſummary manner by courts martial, and to execute the ſentence of all ſuch courts, whether of death or otherwiſe; and declares, moreover, that no act done in conſequence of thoſe powers ſhall be queſtioned in any of the king's ordinary courts of law; and that all who act under the authority of ſuch ſtatute, ſhall be reſponſible for their conduct in the ſame only to ſuch courts martial.

By ſection 26 of the mutiny act it is provided, that no officer or ſoldier ſhall, by the articles of war, be ſubjected to any puniſhment extending to life or limb, for any crime which is not expreſſed to be ſo puniſhable by that act, nor for ſuch crimes as are expreſſed to be ſo puniſhable in any manner, or under any regulations which ſhall not accord with the proviſions of the act. But his majeſty having the power at all times, to make and iſſue regulations for the army, thoſe regulations embrace all the inferior offences for which a court martial may inflict correſponding puniſhments, not extending to life or limb. That the laws may not be infringed through ignorance, it is provided that the articles of war for the navy ſhall be printed, and hung up, or affixed in the moſt conſpicuous parts of every ſhip; and for the army, that all the rules and articles are to be read and publiſhed, once in every two months, at the head of every regiment, troop or company, muſtered or to be muſtered in the ſervice.

Crimes cognizable. The crimes cognizable by naval or military courts martial, may be divided into felonies and miſdemeanors; or, more properly, into capital offences, and offences only

only criminal and not capital. Thoſe which are comprehended and ſpecified in the naval as well as military articles of war, may, for the ſake of perſpicuity, be claſſed under the following general heads: 1ſt, Thoſe that are immediately againſt God and religion: 2dly, Such as affect the executive power of the ſtate, or infer a criminal neglect of the eſtabliſhed articles and rules of diſcipline, in his majeſty's ſervice. 3dly, Such as violate or tranſgreſs the rights and duties, which are owing to individuals: and 4thly, Offences in themſelves ſtrictly military, and ſuch as are peculiarly the object of martial law.

1ſt. *Againſt God and Religion.* In this diviſion are claſſed the offences contained in the firſt and ſecond of the naval articles, viz. neglecting public worſhip, and being guilty of profane oaths, curſing, execrations, drunkenneſs, uncleanneſs, or other ſcandalous actions; the puniſhment of which is left to the diſcretion of the court martial. And although the higher offence of blaſphemy is not particulariſed in theſe articles, yet it is unqueſtionably implied, by the words profane oaths, curſings, and execrations. By the military code, all officers and ſoldiers, not having juſt impediment, ſhall diligently frequent divine ſervice, and ſermon, in the places appointed for the aſſembling of the regiment, troop, or company to which they belong; ſuch as wilfully abſent themſelves, or being preſent behave indecently or irreverently, ſhall if commiſſioned officers, be brought before a court martial, there to be publicly and ſeverely reprimanded by the preſident; if non-commiſſioned officers or ſoldiers, every perſon ſo offending, ſhall for his firſt offence forfeit twelve-pence, to be deducted out of his next pay; for his ſecond offence he ſhall not only forfeit twelve-pence, but be laid in irons for twelve hours; and for every like offence ſhall ſuffer and pay in like manner; which money ſo forfeited, ſhall be applied to the uſe of the ſick ſoldiers of the troop or company to which the offender belongs. It is alſo ordained, "that no "officer or ſoldier ſhall uſe any unlawful oath or execration, "under the penalty expreſſed in the firſt article. Whatſoever "officer, non-commiſſioned officer, or ſoldier, ſhall preſume to "ſpeak againſt any known article of the Chriſtian faith, ſhall "be delivered over to the civil magiſtrate to be proceeded "againſt according to law: whatſoever officer, non-commiſ-"ſioned officer, or ſoldier, ſhall profane any place dedicated "to divine worſhip, or ſhall offer violence to a chaplain of the "army, or to any other miniſter of God's word, ſhall be liable "to ſuch puniſhment, as by a general court martial ſhall be "awarded. No chaplain who is commiſſioned to a regiment "or garriſon ſhall abſent himſelf, except in caſe of ſickneſs, or "leave of abſence, upon pain of being brought to a court

"martial,

"martial, and punished as their judgment and the circum-
"stances of his offence may require. And whatsoever chaplain to
"a regiment, or garrison, shall be guilty of drunkenness, or of
"other scandalous or vicious behaviour, derogating from the
"sacred character with which he is invested, shall, upon due
"proof before a court martial, be discharged from his office."

2d. *Crimes which affect the executive power of the king and his government.* In the naval code these crimes are defined in the following terms. Holding intelligence with an enemy or rebel; concealing letters or messages from, or relieving an enemy or rebel; deserting to an enemy; running away with ship's stores, or yielding the same to an enemy; desertion from the service, or entertaining deserters; waste or embezzlement of stores; mutinous assemblies; seditious or mutinous words; concealing any traitorous or mutinous designs, &c.; striking, quarrelling with, or disobeying the orders of a superior officer; sleeping upon the watch, neglecting duty, or forsaking a station allotted, and knowingly signing false muster books.

In the military articles of war they are described as follows: traitorous or disrepectful words against the king, or any of the royal family; contemptuous or disrespectful behaviour towards the general, or other commander in chief; mutiny or sedition, not endeavouring to suppress the same; or coming to the knowledge of any mutiny, or intended mutiny, and not without delay giving information thereof; striking or drawing any weapon against a superior officer, or disobeying orders; not making due musters and returns as by law directed; desertion; receiving and entertaining deserters; inlisting in another regiment, &c.; absenting from a troop or company. Provoking speeches or gestures; giving or sending a challenge; suffering any person to go forth to fight a duel; upbraiding another for refusing a challenge. Selling or embezzling military stores; and holding correspondence with, or giving intelligence to the enemy, either directly or indirectly. Many of these offences are capitally punished by the general law of the land, but the whole article is not quite so general as that of the navy, which makes no distinction between an enemy and a rebel. By the mutiny act it is ordained, that officers or soldiers, who shall mutiny, or stir up sedition, or shall desert his majesty's service, shall suffer death, or such other punishment, as a court martial shall award. It is also declared, that a non-commissioned officer or soldier, inlisted or in pay in any regiment, troop, or company, who shall, without having first obtained a regular discharge therefrom, inlist himself in any other regiment, &c. shall be deemed to have deserted his majesty's service, and shall in like manner suffer death, or such other punishment as by a court martial shall be

 awarded,

awarded, and may be puniſhed as a deſerter in the corps in which he had inliſted. Acceſſaries to this offence are deemed almoſt equally guilty with the principals, it being declared that in caſe any officer ſhall knowingly receive and entertain ſuch non-commiſſioned officer or ſoldier, or ſhall not, after his being diſcovered to be a deſerter, immediately confine him, and give notice thereof to the corps in which he laſt ſerved, the officer ſo offending ſhall, on being convicted thereof before a general court martial, be caſhiered. It is further enacted that, in the caſe of any non-commiſſioned officer or ſoldier, tried and convicted of deſertion, where the court ſhall not think the offence deſerving of capital puniſhment, they may, inſtead of awarding a corporal puniſhment, adjudge the offender to be tranſported as a felon for life, or for a certain term of years, and if he return without proper authority, before the expiration of the term limited, he ſhall ſuffer death as a felon, without benefit of clergy. The military articles of war declare, that "whatſoever "officer, non-commiſſioned officer, or ſoldier, ſhall be convicted of having adviſed or perſuaded any other officer or ſoldier "to deſert, ſhall ſuffer ſuch puniſhment as by the ſentence of "a general court martial ſhall be awarded." By the mutiny act it is further declared, "that any perſon who ſhall knowingly detain, buy, or exchange, or otherwiſe receive from a "ſoldier or deſerter, or any other perſon, any arms, clothes, "caps, or other furniture belonging to the king, or cauſe the "colour of any ſuch clothes to be changed; the perſon ſo offending ſhall, upon conviction before a juſtice of the peace, "by the oath of one credible witneſs, forfeit 5*l.* to be levied "by diſtreſs, and in caſe of no ſufficient diſtreſs, he ſhall be "committed to the common jail for three months; or be publickly whipped at the diſcretion of the juſtice." The crimes of harbouring ſoldiers, being deſerters, purchaſing their arms, clothes, caps, or other furniture belonging to the king, are puniſhable, in virtue of the mutiny act, either by a military or civil tribunal. If the offender be a perſon ſubject to military juriſdiction, he will of courſe be tried by a general court martial; but if in the civil line of life, and not amenable to martial law, the remedy and puniſhment are left to a civil tribunal. The offences relating to mutinous aſſemblies, ſedition, &c. are puniſhed by the articles of war with death, or otherwiſe, as a court martial ſhall think fit. By ſtatute 22 Geo. II. cap. 33. ſect. 19. ſentences of death by naval courts martial, in caſes of mutiny, may be put in execution, within the narrow ſeas or on foreign ſtations, without reporting the proceedings of the court martial, either to the lords commiſſioners of the admiralty, or to the commander in chief abroad, where ſuch ſentence was paſſed.

paſſed. But no ſentence of death, for other crimes ſpecified in the articles of war, can be put in execution till after report of the proceedings made to the lords of the admiralty, or to the commander of the fleet or ſquadron in which the ſentence was paſſed, and their or his directions ſhall have been given therein. By the military articles of war it is declared, that any officer, non-commiſſioned officer, or ſoldier, who, being preſent at any mutiny or ſedition, ſhall not uſe his utmoſt endeavour to ſuppreſs the ſame, or, coming to the knowledge of any mutiny or intended mutiny, ſhall not without delay give information thereof to his commanding officer, ſhall ſuffer death, or ſuch other puniſhment as by a general court martial ſhall be awarded. The naval articles declare, that, "if any officer, mariner, ſoldier, " or other perſon in the fleet, ſhall ſtrike any of his ſuperior " officers, or draw, or offer to draw, or lift up any weapon " againſt him, being in the execution of his office, on any " pretence whatſoever, every ſuch perſon being ſo convicted " of any ſuch offence, by the ſentence of a court martial, ſhall " ſuffer death."

3d. *Crimes which violate and tranſgreſs the rights and duties, which men owe to their fellow ſubjects.* Under this head may be claſſed murder, and robbery, rapes, and crimes againſt nature. There are no ſpecific articles in the military code for the puniſhment by courts martial of the crimes juſt noticed; but it is provided, that nothing contained in the mutiny act ſhall exempt any officer or ſoldier from being proceeded againſt by the ordinary courſe of law. In the naval articles 28, 29, and 30, murder and the crimes againſt nature are puniſhable with death, by ſentence of a court martial, and robbery with death, or otherwiſe according to circumſtances. Under the deſcription of robbery may be included the illegal taking of effects out of prizes, and ſtripping or pillaging of perſons on board them. Perhaps the true reaſon, for the diſtinction between the naval and military codes in this point, may be the different circumſtances of the ſoldier and the ſailor. The former paſſing the greater part of his life on ſhore, if he commits capital offences, generally does it ſo to the prejudice of his majeſty's ſubjects, who are not included in the military code, and conſequently can neither be partial, nor ſtrictly amenable to, a military tribunal. Sailors, on the contrary, are always, when objects of a court martial, ſo circumſtanced, that either ſailors or ſoldiers muſt be the parties injured by theſe offences, and the deciſion of no other tribunal is attainable.

4th. *Offences ſtrictly military, and as ſuch peculiar to martial law.* In the naval code theſe crimes are contained in the following articles. Every flag officer, captain, and commander in the

the fleet, who upon signal or order of fight, or sight of any ship or ships which it may be his duty to engage, or who upon likelihood of an engagement, shall not make the necessary preparations for fight, and shall not in his own person, and according to his place, encourage the inferior officers and men to fight courageously, shall suffer death, or such other punishment as from the nature and degree of the offence, a court-martial shall deem him to deserve; and if any person in the fleet shall treacherously or cowardly yield, or cry for quarter, every person so offending, and being convicted thereof by sentence of a court martial, shall suffer death. Every person in the fleet, who shall not duly observe the orders of the admiral, flag officer, commander of any squadron, or division, or other his superior officer, for assailing, joining battle with, or making defence against any fleet, squadron, or ship; or shall not obey the orders of his superior officer as aforesaid, in time of action, to the best of his power; or shall not use all possible endeavours to put the same effectually into execution: every such person so offending, and being convicted thereof by the sentence of a court-martial, shall suffer death, or such other punishment, as from the nature and degree of the offence, the court-martial shall deem him to deserve. Every person in the fleet, who through cowardice, negligence, or disaffection, shall in time of action withdraw or keep back, or not come into the fight or engagement; or shall not do his utmost to take or destroy every ship, which it shall be his duty to engage; and to assist and relieve all, and every of his majesty's ships or those of his allies, which it shall be his duty to assist and relieve; every such person so offending, and being convicted thereof by the sentence of a court-martial, shall suffer death. Every person in the fleet who through cowardice, negligence, or disaffection, shall forbear to pursue the chace of an enemy, pirate, or rebel, beaten or flying; or shall not assist and relieve a known friend in view, to the utmost of his power, being convicted of any such offence by the sentence of a court-martial, shall suffer death. The peremptory denunciation of death in the last two cases being, however, found too severe in its operation, it was by statute 19 Geo. III. c. 17. declared lawful for a court-martial to pronounce sentence of death, or to inflict such other punishment, as the nature and degree of the offence therein recited, should be found to deserve. The other naval articles applying to this division are, if when action, or any service shall be commanded, any person in the fleet shall presume to delay or discourage the said action or service, upon pretence of arrears of wages, or upon any pretence whatsoever; every person so offending, being convicted thereof by the sentence of a court-martial, shall suffer death, or such other punishment, as from the nature and degree of the offence, a court-martial shall deem him to deserve. The officers and seamen of all ships, appointed for convoys and guard of merchant ships, or of any other, shall diligently attend upon that charge, without delay, according to their instructions in that behalf; and whosoever shall be faulty therein, and shall not faithfully perform their duty, and defend the ships and goods in their convoy, without either diverting to other parts or occasions, or refusing or neglecting to fight in their defence if they are assailed; or running away cowardly, and submitting the ships in their convoy to peril and hazard; or shall demand or exact any money or other reward from any merchant or master, for convoying of any ships or vessels intrusted to their care, or shall misuse the masters or mariners thereof, shall be condemned to make reparation of the damage to the merchants, owners, and others, as the court of admiralty shall adjudge; and also be punished criminally according to the quality of their offences, be it by pain of death, or other punishment, as shall be adjudged fit by the court-martial.

The abstract of the duties and offences belonging to this division, which are contained in the military code, is as follows. The regulations relative to the suttling, and conniving at others selling provisions to soldiers at exorbitant rates, &c. Commanding officers quartering more than the number of effective men, and not redressing all abuses or disorders in quarters, garrisons, or on a march. Commanding officers to pay for carriages on the march, and not to suffer the persons attending them to be abused. Officers, non-commissioned officers, or soldiers to redress wrongs; not to embezzle military stores; waste ammunition delivered out for the service; spoil arms, accoutrements or regimental necessaries. Commissioned officers not to embezzle or misapply regimental money; and non-commissioned officers not to misapply or embezzle the pay of the men. Officers and soldiers to behave themselves orderly in quarters and on their march. Non-commissioned officers and soldiers not to absent themselves one mile from the camp; not to lie out of quarters, garrison, or camp, without leave; to retire to quarters on the beating of the retreat; repair at the time fixed to the parade of exercise, or other rendezvous; not to quit guard before regular dismissal. Also the following offences; hiring another to do his duty. Officers conniving at soldiers doing so. Officer or soldier quitting his platoon or division, without leave of his superior officer. Found drunk on guard. Centinel found sleeping on his post, or quitting it before he is relieved. Doing violence to any person, who brings provisions or other necessaries to camp, garrison, or quarters. Forcing a safeguard. Making known

known the watch-word, or giving a falſe one. Making falſe alarms in camp or quarters. Not ſecuring public ſtores taken from the enemy. Leaving poſt or colours in ſearch of plunder. Caſting away arms or ammunition. Miſbehaving before the enemy, or ſhamefully abandoning or delivering up any garriſon, fortreſs, poſt, or guard, committed to his charge. Compelling others to do the ſame. Menacing words, geſtures, or diſturbances, before a military court-martial. Releaſing priſoners to be tried by a court-martial without proper authority. Officer breaking his arreſt, or leaving his confinement; or behaving in a ſcandalous, infamous manner, ſuch as is unbecoming an officer and a gentleman. Not tranſmitting regimental accounts agreeably to regulations.

Courts of Inquiry. Although no articles of war, or acts of parliament, authoriſe courts of inquiry, either in the army or navy, yet, from various precedents and cuſtoms long eſtabliſhed, they have become an eſſential branch of military and naval juriſdiction. They bear no ſlight analogy to the functions of a grand jury, as the reſult of their inveſtigation is a report to the power veſting them with authority to inquire, whether or not there be ſufficient grounds for bringing the perſon or perſons, whoſe conduct has been the ſubject of inquiry, to a court-martial, in order that if judicially found guilty, a puniſhment correſponding to the offence may be inflicted. A court of inquiry, fairly and impartially conducted, may be regarded rather as a royal mark of lenity than ſeverity; more particularly conſidering the prerogative of the crown to diſmiſs officers from the ſervice, without giving them any chance of trial. The king, or any commander to whom the power of aſſembling courts-martial is delegated, may appoint courts of inquiry for examining the conduct of officers in the army, and the lords of the admiralty have the power of appointing courts of inquiry in the navy, as being immediately derived from the crown; but neither the king nor the admiralty have power to inflict any corporal puniſhment for offences, unleſs by ſentence of a court-martial. In many inſtances, however, the crown has exerciſed its prerogative, in diſmiſſing officers of rank from the ſervice, even after having undergone a trial by a court-martial, and being acquitted of the charges exhibited againſt them. A court of inquiry, by examining the evidence produced on both ſides in a ſummary manner, *viva voce*, avoids the procraſtination incident to a court-martial, and is leſs inconvenient to the ſervice, by having fewer members. Three are generally deemed ſufficient, but where the matter is important it is uſual to have five. No oath is adminiſtered to the members or witneſſes, and many have queſtioned even the legality of any witneſs being obliged to give teſtimony, or of the perſon, whoſe conduct is the ſubject of inquiry, being bound to plead; becauſe it might be more favourable to reſerve his caſe and evidence for a court capable of pronouncing definitive judgment. Theſe courts are, however, uſeful in adjuſting diſputes between officers. Theſe often are of ſuch a nature that nothing criminal can be imputed to either party, ſo as to give juriſdiction to a court-martial; but a court of inquiry prevents much unneceſſary trouble, and does not materially retard or obſtruct the ſervice.

Composition of a Naval Court-Martial. By ſtat. 22 Geo. II. c. 33. no court martial to be held or appointed, ſhall conſiſt of more than thirteen, or leſs than five perſons, to be compoſed of ſuch flag-officers, captains, or commanders preſent, as are next in ſeniority to the officer who preſides at the court martial. It is alſo declared that the lord high admiral, or lords of the admiralty, or any officers empowered to hold courts-martial, ſhall not direct or aſcertain the particular number of perſons of which any court-martial ſhall conſiſt.

Of a Military Court-Martial. By the 17th ſection of the mutiny act (1804) it is enacted, that no general court-martial ſhall conſiſt of a leſs number than thirteen commiſſioned officers, except in Africa, or in New South Wales; where five will ſuffice, but none muſt be under the degree of a commiſſioned officer: nor can the preſident of any general court-martial be the commander in chief, or governor of the garriſon where the offender is tried; nor under the degree of a field officer, unleſs where a field officer cannot be had, nor in any caſe whatever under the degree of a captain.

General Courts-Martial. Military courts-martial are either *general*, for the trial of crimes of magnitude; or *regimental* or *garriſon* courts, for the cognizance of ſmaller offences. A general court-martial is held either by direct authority from his majeſty, under ſign manual, or by a delegation of the royal authority to a general officer having the chief command of a body of forces, within any particular part of the king's dominions. In the former caſe, the warrant for holding the general court-martial, uſually contains the name of the preſident and all the members who compoſe the court; and ſuch warrant is directed to the judge advocate general, or his deputy. In the caſe, where the court is aſſembled by a general officer commanding in chief, who has the royal authority delegated to him, an order or warrant is directed by him to the preſident alone; and orders are iſſued, by the ſame authority, for certain regiments to furniſh each a certain quota of officers,

of

of a rank therein specified, to be members of the court, and to return their names to the office of the adjutant general.

Regimental Courts. Regimental courts-martial are held by virtue of the articles of war, sect. 16. under the head of *administration of justice*; which provide that the commissioned officers of every regiment may, by the appointment of their colonel or commanding officer, without any special warrant from his majesty, hold regimental courts-martial for inquiry into such disputes or criminal matters as may come before them, and for inflicting corporal or other punishments for small offences, and shall give judgment by the majority of voices, but no sentence to be executed until confirmed by the commanding officer, not being a member of the court-martial; and it is likewise declared, that no regimental court-martial shall consist of less than five officers, except in cases where that number cannot be conveniently assembled, when three may be sufficient, who are likewise to determine upon the sentence by the majority of voices. Where a sufficient number of officers of the same corps or regiment cannot be had, the commanding officer, or the governor of the garrison, fort, castle, or barracks, may appoint officers, from different corps, to compose the regimental court martial; and the same power is given to the commanding officer in any town or place, with detachments of different corps. The usual practice of constituting a regimental court-martial, is to appoint one officer of the rank of captain as president, and the other four members, subalterns, if they can be conveniently assembled; if not, a captain and two subalterns will be sufficient to constitute the court.

Detachment Courts. By the articles of war, his majesty has laid down regulations for constituting another species of military courts, called *detachment* courts-martial. These are for trying officers not commissioned by his majesty, or by any general officers having authority to grant commissions, but appointed by warrant under the signature of the colonels or commandants of the corps to which they belong; hence they are distinguished by the appellation of warrant officers. It is thereby declared and directed, that, in all cases where the offence charged against any warrant officer may not be of so heinous a nature as to require investigation by a general court-martial, such officer may and shall be tried by a detachment court-martial, to be appointed by the general officer commanding his majesty's forces in the district where the corps shall be situated, if in Great Britain, Ireland, Jersey, Guernsey, Alderney, Sark, or Man, and if in any of his majesty's dominions beyond the seas, or in foreign parts, by the general commanding in chief on the station; which detachment courts-martial are to be held, and to proceed in the nature of regimental courts-martial. Provided that ſuch detachment court-martial ſhall not, in any caſe, conſiſt of leſs than five commiſſioned officers, of whom not more than two ſhall be taken from the regiment, in which the warrant officer to be tried is ſerving; that the preſident of ſuch court-martial ſhall not be under the degree of a field officer; that not more than two of the other members ſhall be under the degree of a captain; and that no ſentence of ſuch court-martial ſhall be put in execution, if the trial ſhall have taken place in Great Britain, Jerſey, Guernſey, Alderney, Sark, or Man, until after a report ſhall have been made to his majeſty, and directions ſhall have been ſignified thereupon through the commander in chief of his majeſty's forces, or (in his abſence) through the ſecretary at war; or if in Ireland, or in any of his majeſty's dominions beyond the ſeas, or in foreign parts, until ſuch ſentence ſhall have been confirmed by the general officer commanding in chief on the ſtation, who is thereby authoriſed to cauſe ſuch ſentence to be put into execution, or to ſuſpend, mitigate, or remit the ſame, as he ſhall judge beſt, and moſt conducive to the good of his majeſty's ſervice, without waiting for further orders: Provided alſo, that no court-martial ſhall have authority by their ſentence to award corporal puniſhment, in any caſe of a warrant officer; nor ſhall a warrant officer be liable to be reduced, by the ſentence of either a general or detachment court-martial, to ſerve in an inferior ſituation, unleſs he ſhall have been originally inliſted as a private ſoldier, and ſhall have continued in the ſervice until his appointment to be an officer by warrant.

Proceedings in Regimental and Detachment Courts. The members of a regimental, garriſon, or detachment court-martial have not, as in trials before a general court martial, the aſſiſtance of a judge advocate, or his deputy; neither were the members or witneſſes ſworn, as thoſe of a general court-martial; but, by a late act of parliament, every member compoſing ſuch courts takes an oath, that he will well and truly try and determine the matter ſubmitted, and adminiſter juſtice according to the articles of war and the mutiny act, without partiality or affection. The proceedings are regularly committed to writing, either by the preſident, or by any of the members of the court named by him. The ſentence is ſigned by the preſident alone; but at naval courts-martial, by the preſident and every member compoſing the court. As ſentences of military courts-martial are not put into execution until approved of by his majeſty, or the commander empowered to convene them, the court, in the event of diſapproval, may be directed to reviſe the ſentence, and reconſider the proceedings: but this power is very properly reſtricted; for it is declared by the mutiny act, that no ſentence ſhall be more than once liable to a reviſion.

Appeal

APPEAL FROM THEM. The articles of war have provided that any party thinking himfelf aggrieved by the decifion of a regimental or detachment court-martial, may appeal to a general court-martial; but if, upon a fecond hearing, the appeal fhall appear to be vexatious and groundlefs, the perfon fo appealing fhall be punifhed, at the difcretion of the general court. It is underftood, however, that this right of appeal only exifts in cafes where the original caufe has been a fuppofed wrong fuftained by fome inferior, or non-commiffioned officer, or private, from his fuperior.

OFFENCES COGNIZABLE IN EACH. The jurifdiction of each of thefe courts is limited to a feparate clafs of offences, but fome few crimes are liable to be tried before either court.

GENERAL COURT-MARTIAL. The offences cognizable in a general court are, profaning churches, or offering violence to chaplains. Traitorous or difrefpectful words by officers. Officers behaving with difrefpect to the general or commanding officer. Mutiny. Not fuppreffing mutiny, or countenancing it. Striking, or drawing a weapon againft a fuperior officer. Officers figning falfe certificates. Officers making falfe mufters. Commiffary or mufter-mafter taking money on a mufter. Officers making falfe returns. Not tranfmitting monthly returns to the commander in chief and fecretary at war. Officers entertaining, and not confining deferters. Perfuading one to defert. Refifting officers in quelling frays and diforders. Officers making improper exactions from futtlers, &c.; conniving at others felling provifions at exorbitant rates; refufing or neglecting to make up accounts. Officers refufing to fee juftice done, if any perfon fhall be abufed or wronged by a foldier. Offences relative to carriage on the march. Crimes punifhable by law. Commanding officer, ftorekeeper, or commiffary, felling military ftores without orders. Warrant officers embezzling or mifapplying regimental money. Officers conniving at the hiring of duty. Sleeping upon poft. Violence to any one who brings provifions to camp or quarters; punifhment *death*, without any alternative. Forcing a fafeguard; punifhment *death*. Making known the watch-word, or giving a falfe one. Making falfe alarms in camp or quarters. Holding correfpondence with an enemy. Relieving or harbouring an enemy. Going in fearch of plunder. Cafting away arms or ammunition. Mifbehaving before the enemy. Compelling others to mifbehave before the enemy. Officer breaking his arreft; and a commiffioned officer cannot be cafhiered but by a general court-martial.

Offences cognizable by a general, or regimental, or garrifon court-martial. Non-commiffioned officer or foldier uttering traitorous or diſreſpectful words. Soldiers abſenting themſelves from their troop or company. Demanding billets for quartering more men than the effective number. Non-commiſſioned officers or ſoldiers waſting ammunition, delivered out for ſervice. Selling or ſpoiling arms. Non-commiſſioned officers embezzling money. Spoiling the property of individuals. Soldiers abſenting themſelves a mile from camp. Lying all night out of camp or quarters. Not retiring to quarters, at the beating of the retreat. Not repairing at the time fixed to the parade of exerciſe, &c. Quitting platoon or diviſion without leave. Drunkenneſs.

REGIMENTAL COURTS. Regimental, garriſon, and detachment courts, are regulated by ſeparate ſections in the articles of war, and are a great reſource to inferiors thinking themſelves aggrieved by their commanding officers. They alſo take cognizance of ſoldiers hiring their duty; and the following offences are cognizable by a court martial, without declaring whether it muſt be general, or may be regimental. Abſenting from divine ſervice, and irreverent behaviour. Swearing or curſing. Chaplain abſenting himſelf from the regiment, guilty of drunkenneſs, or ſending a challenge.

NAVAL COURTS MARTIAL. The juriſdiction of naval courts martial extends to the trial of all offences, ſpecified in the articles of war, which may be committed on the main ſea, or in great rivers only, beneath the bridges of the ſaid rivers, nigh to the ſea, or in the haven, river, or creek within the juriſdiction of the admiralty; and which ſhall be committed by perſons then in actual ſervice, and full pay in the fleets or ſhips of war of his majeſty. Likewiſe, to the trial of all ſpies, and of all perſons whatſoever, who ſhall come and be found, in the nature of ſpies, to bring or deliver any ſeducing letters or meſſages from any enemy or rebel, or endeavour to corrupt any captain, officer, mariner, or other in the fleet, to betray his truſt, &c. as ſpecified in the fifth article of war. The juriſdiction alſo extends to the trial of every perſon who ſhall be guilty of mutiny, deſertion, or diſobedience to any lawful commands, in any part of his majeſty's dominions on ſhore, when in actual ſervice, relative to the fleet, and for crimes committed on ſhore by ſuch perſons, in any places out of his majeſty's dominions, as are more fully ſpecified in the thirty-fourth or thirty-fifth naval articles of war. Naval courts-martial cannot take cognizance of murders, except in caſes where the ſtroke or poiſon is given on board ſhip, and the perſon die in conſequence thereof on board. Hence, if a ſeaman be ſtricken or wounded by another on ſhore, and ſhould in conſequence die on board ſhip, the aggreſſor muſt be delivered up to the civil magiſtrate of the diſtrict

to

to be dealt with according to law; upon proper application being made to the commanding officer of the ship, where such wounded man died. If the stroke or wound were given on board ship or alongside, and the wounded man afterwards sent on shore, to an hospital or other place, where death ensued, the offender must also be delivered up to the civil magistrates, to take his trial at the next jail delivery for the county where such death happened. In order to prevent any failure of justice, and for taking away all doubts touching the trial of murders, in the cases herein-after mentioned, it is enacted by statute 2d Geo. II. c. 21, "that where any person shall be feloniously "stricken or poisoned upon the sea, or at any place out of that "part of Great Britain called England, and shall die of the "same stroke or poisoning, within that part of Great Britain "called England; or where any person shall be feloniously "stricken or poisoned at any place within that part of Great "Britain called England, and shall die of the same stroke or "poisoning upon the sea, or at any place out of that part of Great "Britain called England; in either case an indictment thereof, "found by the jurors of that part of Great Britain called Eng-"land, in which such stroke or poisoning shall happen respect-"ively as aforesaid, whether it shall be found before the coro-"ner upon the view of such dead body, or before the justice "of the peace, or other justices or commissioners, who shall "have authority to inquire of murders, shall be as good and "as effectual in law, as well against the principals, as the ac-"cessaries, as if such felonious stroke and death, or poisoning "and death thereby ensuing, and the offence of such accessaries, "had happened in the same county where such indictment "shall be found, and also any superior court, in case such in-"dictment shall be removed, shall and may proceed upon the "same in all points, as they might or ought to do in case such "felonies, stroke and death, or poisoning and death, and the "offence of such accessaries, had happened in the same "county where such indictment shall be found. And every "such offender shall answer upon their arraignments, and have "the like defences, advantages, and exceptions, (except chal-"lenges for the hundred,) and shall receive the like trial, judg-"ment, order, and execution, as if their respective offences "had happened in the same county where such indictment "shall be found." Where one standing on the shore, shot at another standing in the sea, who afterwards died on board a ship, all the judges held, that the trial must be in the admiralty court, and not at common law.

But courts-martial cannot take cognizance of offences committed by masters, mates, or seamen belonging to navy transports; for

for they are perſons not ſubject to naval diſcipline. They are entitled to be diſcharged in time of peace or war, on their own application. The articles of war, and abſtract of the act of parliament, are never ſtuck up or read on board of navy tranſports; and although the officers and men receive their wages quarterly at the yards, in the ſame manner as the officers and men of his majeſty's ſhips in ordinary, yet there is a broad line to be drawn between them. The ſtanding warrant officers of ſhips in ordinary, viz. purſers, gunners, boatſwains, and carpenters, are appointed by the admiralty, and the cooks by the navy board; and, as already noticed, they are amenable to courts-martial. The maſters of navy tranſports are appointed by the navy board, and the mates are recommended by the maſter, and appointed by the maſter attendant of the dock yard, with the approbation of the board, or of the commiſſioners reſident at the port: the ſeamen make application to the maſter attendant, who approves and certifies the ſame to the commiſſioner reſident at the port; and if it likewiſe meet with his approbation, he ſigns the certificate, which is an authority to the clerk of the cheque to enter him. And they being regularly diſcharged in time of war or peace on their application, conſequently are perſons not ſubject to naval diſcipline. Naval-courts martial can alſo take cognizance of crimes committed by the officers and men belonging to the Eaſt India Company's ſhips, having letters of marque in time of war; as well as thoſe committed by the officers and men belonging to privateers. The acts of parliament which ſubject to courts-martial the officers and men ſerving on board privateers, or merchant ſhips having letters of marque, enact, "that all offences, committed on board of privateers, or "merchant ſhips having letters of marque, are to be tried and "puniſhed in the ſame manner as ſuch offences are tried and "puniſhed, when committed on board king's ſhips. Every offender, however, who is accuſed of ſuch crimes as are cognizable by a court-martial, ſhall be confined on board the privateer or merchant ſhip having a letter of marque, until the "veſſel arrive at ſome port in Great Britain, or Ireland, or "can meet with ſuch a number of his majeſty's ſhips of war "abroad, as are competent to conſtitute a court-martial. And "upon application made by the commander of ſuch privateer, "or letter of marque, to the lord high admiral, or to the commiſſioners for executing that office, or to the commander in "chief or ſenior officer of his majeſty's ſhips of war abroad, "the ſaid lord high admiral, or any three or more of ſuch commiſſioners, or ſuch commander in chief, or ſenior officer, "are authoriſed and required to call a court-martial, for trying "and puniſhing ſuch offences."

Or

Of Degradation in the Navy. No tribunal inferior to a general court-martial can be reſorted to in the navy; but a captain has the power of inflicting puniſhment upon a ſeaman in a ſummary manner, for any faults or offences committed contrary to the eſtabliſhed rules of diſcipline and obedience. This power the framers of our naval articles and orders, wiſely conſidered preferable to eſtabliſhing inferior courts-martial for trying trivial offences, as calculated leſs to obſtruct his majeſty's ſervice at ſea, and as carrying more promptly into execution the rules and articles laid down for its regulation. In ſtrictneſs, this puniſhment cannot exceed a dozen laſhes on the bare back, with a cat-o'-nine-tails; but as one charge may involve different offences, the puniſhment is frequently made cumulative, as when drunkenneſs is attended, as it frequently muſt be, with diſobedience of orders, and quarrelling or fighting, the offender is puniſhed at once for the three offences. There is alſo a power exerciſed by captains and commanders, by their own authority, and merely reſulting from uſage, that has often been a topic of animadverſion in the ſervice, that is, the power of degrading a petty, or non-commiſſioned officer, to the ſituation of an ordinary ſeaman, or ſwabber of decks, after he may have been rated on the books maſter's mate, midſhipman, quarter-maſter, corporal, gunner's mate, or boatſwain's mate, &c. Although this power be not ſpecially recognized by the articles of war, or general printed inſtructions, yet, it having been the uſage from time immemorial for captains to exerciſe it, on proper occaſions, with due diſcretion, the juſtice and policy of the authority may perhaps be admitted. The captain being authoriſed to rate his ſhip's company according to their capacities and merits, and for whoſe diſcipline he is reſponſible, it is but juſt, that on conferring on any one a rank which, by bad conduct or demerits, the non-commiſſioned officer afterwards forfeits, he that gave ſuch rank ſhould have the power of taking it away. During the adminiſtration of earl St. Vincent, a regulation was adopted by which the lords of the admiralty appoint a certain number of midſhipmen, who are called admiralty midſhipmen, and it is much doubted whether theſe can be degraded by the captains.

Degradation in the Army. By the military articles of war, and long uſage in the army, a ſimilar power of degrading a non-commiſſioned officer, and reducing him to the ranks, is veſted at all times in the colonel of the regiment. The 18th article of ſection 16th, under the head of adminiſtration of juſtice, declares that, "no commiſſioned officer ſhall be caſhiered "or diſmiſſed from the ſervice, excepting by an order from "the king, or by the ſentence of a general court-martial, ap-

"proved

" proved by him, or by some person having authority from under the king's sign manual; but non-commissioned officers may be discharged as private soldiers, and, by the order of the colonel of the regiment, or by the sentence of a regimental court-martial, be reduced to private centinels. A commanding officer of marines may also, with the sanction of the captain of the ship in which his party is embarked, degrade a serjeant or corporal for misconduct; but in such case it will be necessary afterwards, and by the first opportunity, to assign cogent reasons to the commanding officer of the division to which the party belongs, that such degradation may be approved and confirmed."

Rules respecting Courts-Martial. All naval courts-martial are to be held, and offences tried, in the forenoon, and in the most public part of the ship, where all who will may be present; and the captains of all his majesty's ships in company which take post, have a right to assist thereat. In the army, courts-martial are also conducted publicly, and are not by law allowed to sit longer than seven hours a day; and no court can be assembled before eight o'clock in the morning, or sit later than three o'clock in the afternoon, unless in cases which require an immediate example.

All complaints at sea, or in foreign parts, upon which the summoning of a court-martial is to be grounded, are made in writing to the commander in chief (unless where he of himself sees cause to call a court); in which are to be set forth the particular facts, with the place, time, and in what manner they were committed: and, if any captain, who is entitled by his rank to sit in the court, be personally concerned in the matter to be tried, he shall not be admitted to sit at the trial. It appears to be an established doctrine, that neither the lords commissioners of the admiralty, nor a commander in chief abroad, vested with a power of assembling courts-martial, can exercise a discretionary power in rejecting charges or articles of accusation, preferred against any officer, properly drawn up, and specifically pointed.

The commander in chief is to order the judge advocate to send, at a sufficient interval before the trial, an attested copy of the charge or accusation to the party accused, that he may prepare for his defence. The judge advocate should also inform himself of all the circumstances of the case; and by what evidence the articles of accusation are to be proved against the prisoner. He ought to require from the prisoner a list of those witnesses, whom he wishes to be summoned in his exculpation; and the witnesses on both sides should be summoned in due time, to give their attendance at the trial.

The

The proceedings of a court-martial are not to be delayed by the absence or death of any of its members, when a sufficient number remains to compose the court; which is required to sit from day to day (Sundays excepted) until the sentence is given. And no member can absent himself from the court, during the whole course of the trial, upon pain of being cashiered; except in cases of sickness, or other extraordinary and indispensable occasion, to be judged of by the court: but as no general court-martial can consist of less than thirteen officers, unless it is held in Africa, or New South Wales, it is usual to appoint more than the required number, to guard against the death or illness of any one of them.

The members are sworn, pursuant to the form prescribed in the act, to administer justice according to the articles and orders established, without partiality, favour, or affection; and, if any case shall arise, which is not particularly mentioned in the said articles and orders, to administer justice according to their consciences, to the best of their understanding, and to the custom of the navy in the like cases. In order that the minds of the younger members may not be influenced by the opinion of their seniors, the youngest member votes first, proceeding upwards in order to the president, who votes last; and the determination of the court is settled according to the majority of voices. But, should there be an equal number of votes on each side, and the several members of the court, upon reconsidering the point at issue, adhere to the first opinion, the question remains undecided.

At all courts-martial, it is customary to have, if possible, the number of members odd, or unequal; but it may happen, by the death or sickness of a member, originally making the number of a court-martial unequal, that it might be reduced to even or equal numbers, and that there might be an equality of votes. In similar predicaments, it is the usage of army courts-martial to allow the president to have a double or casting vote, where the court is equally divided.

By the act 22d Geo. II. no member of any court-martial, after the trial commenced, could go on shore, or leave the ship, in which the court should first assemble, until sentence was given; but it was found that this restraint and confinement had been attended with great inconvenience, and prejudice to the health of the members, and it was so severelly felt by those who sat on admiral Keppel's long trial, that they represented the hardship to the lords of the admiralty. And soon after, the clause of the act alluded to was repealed, and all the members are now at liberty to retire upon every adjournment.

Military courts-martial once assembled, remain in existence till

till they are diſſolved by the ſame authority by which they are held or conſtituted; and although the members may have terminated the whole buſineſs brought before them at any trial, and pronounced ſentence therein, yet they are not at liberty to return to their ordinary duty, or leave the place where the court is aſſembled, without ſpecial leave from the commander in chief, until he ſignify that the court is finally diſſolved. This diſtinction is neceſſary in military courts-martial; as the ſentence may be ordered to be reviſed, or the members may be directed to intimate publicly, in court, to the perſon tried, his majeſty's pleaſure, or that of the commander in chief.

It is to be regretted that a difference of opinion has often ariſen, and ſtill prevails among naval and military men, with reſpect to the extent of the authority, with which commanding officers in the navy are inveſted, for puniſhing ſoldiers of every deſcription, according to the rules and articles eſtabliſhed for the diſcipline of his majeſty's ſhips of war; or for trying officers or ſoldiers of the land forces, by naval courts-martial, for any offences committed while ſerving on board king's ſhips.

The privileges of parliament do not protect a member, belonging to the army or navy, from being amenable to a court-martial for offences committed in his naval or military capacity; but previous to the arreſt of any member, in order to try him for a military crime, it is uſual to give notice to the houſe to which he belongs, with a requeſt, for the ſake of public juſtice, that the houſe will allow his being put under arreſt for trial.

In the navy, as well as in the army, officers ſuſpended, who, in that interval, commit any offence ſpecified in the articles of war, are ſubject to be tried by courts-martial.

It has been the uſage to afford captains in the navy the means of juſtification, by granting them a public inquiry into their conduct, when ſuperſeded or diveſted of the command of their ſhips for ſuppoſed miſconduct; but this is merely of grace, not of right, and, however harſh the inſtances may occaſionally appear, there may often be abundant reaſons for withholding ſuch an inquiry, however ardently deſired.

Several inſtances having recently occurred in the military ſervice of officers ſent home, by commanders in chief on foreign ſtations, with articles of accuſation againſt them, but not duly inveſtigated, the duke of York, conceiving the diſcipline of the army, and the intereſt of the ſervice to be materially affected, was of opinion that this practice, except in caſes of the moſt urgent neceſſity, ought to be avoided: becauſe, though it might relieve the commander on the ſpot from ſome embarraſſments,

the

the meaſure ſeldom failed to transfer them to head-quarters with increaſed difficulties. And his royal highneſs judged it further expedient to expreſs in general orders of the 1ſt of February 1804, his diſapprobation of the erroneous opinion which had prevailed in the army, that an officer who has been put under arreſt, had a right, as it is termed, to demand a court-martial upon himſelf, and to perſiſt in conſidering himſelf as ſtill under the reſtraint of ſuch arreſt, although expreſsly releaſed by the ſuperior officer who impoſed it; whereas, in fact, a ſuperior officer is inveſted with a diſcretionary power of liberating, as well as of arreſting, and of requiring the officer ſo liberated, to return to his duty as before; nor can an officer inſiſt upon a trial, unleſs on a charge preferred againſt him. It by no means follows, however, that an officer, conceiving himſelf to have been wrongfully put in arreſt, or otherwiſe aggrieved, is without remedy. A complaint is afterwards open to him, if preferred in a proper manner, for which proviſion is made by a ſpecial article of war.

Military and naval courts-martial are ſubject to the controul and juriſdiction of the ſupreme courts of king's bench and common pleas; and the members are liable to puniſhment, for any wanton abuſe of power, or illegal proceedings.

Judge Advocate. The judge advocate may be ſaid to be the *primum mobile* of a court-martial, as not only impelling it to action, but as being the perſon on whom, in a great meaſure, depends that harmony of motion, ſo neceſſary to conſtitute a regular court. He is impowered by the printed inſtruction to adviſe the court of the proper forms, when there ſhall be occaſion, and to deliver his opinion in any doubts or difficulties which may ariſe in the courſe of the trial. He examines the witneſſes on oath, takes down their depoſitions in writing, and makes minutes of the proceedings to which the court may refer. The act of parliament directs, that, in the abſence of the judge advocate, or his deputy, a court-martial has power and authority to appoint any perſon to execute the office. And although it is uſual and neceſſary for the preſident, ſome days before the trial, to appoint, by warrant, a perſon to officiate as judge advocate, in order that he may timely ſend to the party accuſed an atteſted copy of the articles of charge, give him information of the time and place of trial, furniſh him with a liſt of the witneſſes to be adduced againſt him, and require a ſimilar liſt from him; alſo, to ſummon the witneſſes, and all perſons concerned; yet the warrant ought to expreſs the appointment to be by the court, according to the conſtruction of the ſtatute; and a majority of the members, when the court is aſſembled, ſhould concur in the appointment.

In military courts-martial, the judge advocate general, or some person deputed by him, is impowered to prosecute; and in all trials of offenders by general courts-martial he is to administer the oaths in the forms prescribed. The judge advocate general is appointed by warrant, under the king's sign manual. The commander in chief on a foreign station, by virtue of the power and authority vested in him by his majesty, appoints by warrant any eligible officer, deputy judge advocate. Though a judge advocate may be considered in the light of a prosecutor for the crown, it does not follow that he is to deny every reasonable assistance to the prisoner, in his defence, either in point of law or of justice. It is his duty, that the proof, both on the part of the crown and the prisoner, should be properly laid before the court; where any doubtful point may arise, he should incline on the part of the prisoner; and nothing should induce him to omit any circumstances, in the minutes of proceedings, that might have a tendency to palliate the charges exhibited. In the deliberations and debates of a court-martial, the judge advocate may offer his sentiments and opinion, if required; or, if he observe any error in point of law, or doubts arise, he ought to offer his judgment on the point, for the information of the court; and he should communicate every matter or thing, which may conduce to a legal decision of the points in question.

A deputy or officiating judge advocate in the navy, is paid by certificate, at the rate of four pounds for each trial, in conformity to the standing regulation of the admiralty, made in the year 1780. Although the trial may end in one day, it is usual to insert in the certificate, ten days employed in summoning witnesses, attending the trial, and transmitting a copy of the minutes, &c. Where trials have lasted longer, twelve days have been allowed, at the rate of eight shillings per day. A deputy judge advocate in the army, is usually allowed a constant salary; and the officiating judge advocate has ten shillings per day, for a given number of days, whether the trial last so long or not; but, if its duration exceed that number of days, he is paid at the rate mentioned until the trial is ended, besides an allowance for stationary.

Evidence. All persons subject to military law are bound by their duty to attend and give their testimony at military courts martial, whenever summoned for that purpose; and, should some of the witnesses be persons in a civil capacity, and not bound to obey the citation of such a court-martial, their attendance may be enforced, by an application to the court of king's bench. But there is no act of parliament, compelling persons in civil capacities to attend as witnesses at a naval

 court-

court-martial. Witneſſes attending are privileged from arreſt, and in the army, but not in the navy, it is uſual to make an allowance to ſubalterns for their expences.

On important trials at naval courts-martial, it is cuſtomary for the judge-advocate to take preparatory affidavits from the witneſſes in ſupport of the charge, which he is to communicate to the commander in chief, and to the preſident of the court-martial, but not to the ſeveral other members ſummoned, until they are properly laid, in a judicial manner, before the court. Neither is it proper that copies of theſe affidavits ſhould be delivered, or ſhewn to the perſon accuſed, previous to his trial. Should the trial laſt longer than one day, it is his duty, at the cloſe of each day, to prepare a fair copy of the proceedings ſo far as they go, and he continues ſo to do, until the concluſion of the trial, when the whole ſhould be diſtinctly read over by him to the court, before the members proceed to deliberate on the ſentence to be pronounced, and afterward approved by them. The preſident is the proper perſon to put all the interrogatories to the witneſſes: and, ſhould the preſident think proper to decline allowing the judge-advocate to put a queſtion propoſed by any of the junior members, it is the practice to clear the court, and it is to be determined by a majority of votes, whether the queſtion ſhould be put or not. The judge advocate as proſecutor in behalf of the crown, and being ſuppoſed by law to be able to judge what are proper, has therefore a right to aſk all fit queſtions.

Opening the Court. When a naval court-martial is aſſembled for trial, the judge-advocate, by direction of the preſident, reads with an audible voice, ſtanding up, the order for aſſembling the court, and likewiſe the order or warrant of his own appointment. It then becomes his duty to adminiſter to the reſpective members the oath preſcribed by act of parliament; and which is uſually done by the preſident, and each member holding his right hand on the evangeliſts, and, according to ſeniority, repeating his name, and the words of the oath audibly, after the judge-advocate. The ſubſtance of the oath is, duly to adminiſter juſtice, according to the ſtatute, without partiality; or in caſes where the act does not give direction, according to conſcience and the uſage of the navy. And further not to diſcloſe or diſcover the vote or opinion of any particular member of the court, unleſs thereunto required by act of parliament. A ſimilar oath of ſecreſy is alſo taken by the judge-advocate, or perſon officiating as ſuch.

In the army it is uſual, at general courts-martial, for the judge-advocate to adminiſter the oath as directed by the mutiny act and military articles, firſt to the preſident alone, and after-

 wards

wards to the other members of the court. The oaths are, to try the case and determine according to evidence, duly to administer justice according to the articles of war and the mutiny act; or if any doubt arises, which they do not solve, according to conscience and the custom of war. They further swear not to divulge the sentence of the court, until approved by his majesty, or by some person duly authorised by him; nor upon any account at any time to disclose or discover the vote or opinion of any particular member, unless required to give evidence thereof, as a witness by a court of justice, in a due course of law. The president also administers to the judge-advocate a similar oath of secresy, as to the opinions of members of the court. The variance between the oaths required at the different courts is not satisfactorily explained.

The prisoner, it is said, may challenge or object to be tried by any member of the court, if for so doing he can assign a valid reason; but he is not intitled to that which, in criminal law proceedings, is called a peremptory challenge; nor is it very clear what causes of objection would be deemed sufficient.

Arrest of Offenders. Previous to any complaint or accusation to the commanding officer of the ship, it is supposed the offender is under arrest, or in custody. Although neither the naval articles of war, nor the statutes specify the form or nature of arrests previous to trial, yet the mode is well understood by the immemorial usage of the service. It depends upon the rank of the accused, and the degree or measure of the crime with which he stands charged. Should an officer be accused of a capital crime, or an offence of such a nature as might affect his life, or of which the punishment might bear so heavy upon him as to tempt him to elude justice by escaping; it is the custom to detain him in close confinement; but if the offence is of a more trivial nature, he is allowed to be in arrest at large, that is, to walk the deck without interfering in the duty on board; or he may be even allowed to go on shore without his sword, on his word of honour to wait the issue of a trial, or until his enlargement. The master at arms, who acts as provost-marshal in the fleet, takes charge of every prisoner, and keeps him in safe custody until duly authorised to release him. Previous to the day of trial he receives his warrant to officiate as provost-marshal, for which he is paid at the rate of four shillings a day during the time he may have such prisoner in his charge.

In the army, a prosecution may be brought in a court-martial at the instance of a person who is himself not subject to military jurisdiction, provided the offence be of a military nature, and committed by a person under military law; in the naval

service,

ſervice, the commander in chief may appoint a proſecutor, and the perſon injured would be admitted as a witneſs on the trial.

Accusations. In the articles of accuſation, the preciſe formalities which have been deemed neceſſary in indictments, are in ſome degree diſpenſed with, yet the more ſubſtantial requiſites to juſtice muſt be obſerved. The particular facts charged, and in what manner committed, with the time and place, are directed to be clearly ſpecified. The time may be very material, where there is any limitation in point of time aſſigned for the proſecution of offenders, as in the caſe of naval courts-martial, by ſtatute 22 Geo. II. cap. 33. ſect. 23. which enacts, that no perſons, not flying from juſtice, ſhall be tried or puniſhed by any court-martial for any offence, unleſs the complaint of ſuch offence be made in writing, or unleſs a court-martial, to try ſuch offender, ſhall be ordered within three years after the offence committed, or within one year after the return of the ſhip into any of the ports of Great Britain or Ireland. The offence itſelf ought to be ſet forth with clearneſs, preciſion, and certainty; thus in caſes of mutiny, the facts muſt be ſaid to be done "in a *mutinous* or *ſeditious* manner." In an accuſation of murder, it is neceſſary to ſay, that the party accuſed "*murdered,*" not killed, &c. It is alſo neceſſary in all accuſations, that the name, ſurname, rank, or ſtation, and the ſhip or regiment to which the offender belongs, ſhould be clearly ſpecified. But when miſnomers have been made, it has been uſual to keep the priſoner under arreſt; and, after the charges have been preferred anew with his name correctly ſpecified, a court-martial may aſſemble for his trial, on the ſpecific charges originally brought againſt him. Not only the crime alleged, but the attendant circumſtances ſhould be diſtinctly ſpecified; for example, it is not ſufficient to ſay that an officer behaved in a ſcandalous, infamous, cruel, oppreſſive, and fraudulent manner, unbecoming the character of an officer, unleſs the particular circumſtances of ſuch behaviour were clearly defined, and the time and place diſtinctly ſpecified.

Formation of the Court. In Great Britain or Ireland, any complaint or accuſation in the navy is to be tranſmitted by the commander in chief, or ſenior officer, to the lords of the admiralty, who thereupon iſſue an order or commiſſion for aſſembling a court-martial to try the party accuſed; and the order may be directed to the firſt, ſecond, or third in command, as may be found moſt expedient, and for the good of the ſervice; and ſuch flag officer or captain ſo directed, ſhall preſide at ſuch court-martial. In time of actual ſervice, the lords of the admiralty have even found it expedient to tranſmit blank orders

 to

to the commander in chief at any of the ports, empowering him to fill up the blanks in the order, with the date, and addrefs of the officer who fhould happen to be fecond in command; or if the exigency of the fervice required it, he might fill it up in the name of the third in command, inftead of the fecond; and having fo done, he was inftructed to inform the admiralty, that the books of the office might be made to correfpond with the orders fo filled up. But if in foreign parts, and the commander in chief, or fenior officer, fhould be under the neceffity of prefiding, the order for affembling a court-martial differs a little in the form from that iffued by the admiralty at home, or by a commander in chief to the fecond or third in command on foreign fervice.

By fection 16, art. 1, of the military articles, (1804,) it is directed, that a general court-martial, in the united kingdom of Great Britain and Ireland, fhall not confift of lefs than thirteen commiffioned officers, and the prefident fhall not be the commander in chief, or governor of the garrifon where the offender fhall be tried, nor be under the degree of a field officer. By article 2, a general court-martial, held at Gibraltar, or other places beyond the feas, fhall not confift of lefs than thirteen commiffioned officers, of whom five at leaft, befides the prefident, fhall not be under the degree of a field officer, unlefs where a field officer cannot be had; nor fhall the prefident, in any cafe whatever, be the commander in chief or governor of the garrifon, nor under the degree of a captain.

For preventing difputes which may arife between officers of the life-guards or horfe-guards, and officers of the foot-guards, in relation to their holding of courts-martial, and upon other points of duty, it is declared, by fection 16, art. 3, that when it fhall be found neceffary to bring any officer or foldier, belonging to the life or horfe-guards, before a general court-martial, for differences arifing purely among themfelves, or for crimes relating to difcipline or breach of orders, the courts fhall be compofed of officers ferving in any or all of thofe corps (as they may then happen to lie for their being moft conveniently affembled), wherein the officers are to take poft according to the dates and degrees of rank granted them in their refpective commiffions, without regard to the feniority of corps, or other formerly pretended privileges.

In like manner, alfo, the officers of the three regiments of foot-guards, for differences arifing purely among themfelves, or for crimes relating to difcipline, or breach of orders, fhall of themfelves compofe courts-martial, and take rank according to their commiffions; but for all difputes or differences which may happen between officers or foldiers belonging to the life

or

or horſe-guards, and thoſe belonging to the foot-guards, or between officers or ſoldiers belonging to either of thoſe corps of life, horſe, or foot-guards, and thoſe of any other of his majeſty's forces, or among officers or ſoldiers of any other troops, but belonging to different corps, the courts-martial are to be equally compoſed of officers belonging to the corps, in which the parties complaining and complained of then ſerve; and the preſident ſhall be taken by turns as nearly as the ſervice will with convenience admit, beginning firſt by an officer of life-guards, and ſo on in courſe out of the other corps, according to the ſeniority in rank of the corps.

No officer ſerving in the militia can ſit in a court-martial, or be tried in ſuch court by any perſon ſerving in any other forces.

The members both of general and regimental courts-martial, when belonging to different corps, take the ſame rank which they hold in the army, but when courts-martial are compoſed of officers of one corps, they take their ranks according to the dates of the commiſſions by which they are muſtered in that corps.

The proviſions of the mutiny act extending both to the land forces and marines, it is declared, that in matters wherein marines are intereſted, the officers of that body ſhall be aſſociated with the officers of the land forces, for the purpoſe of holding courts-martial: and the members of the court ſo compoſed take their rank according to the ſeniority of their commiſſions in either ſervice. It is likewiſe provided, that when any of the land forces are employed in the Eaſt Indies, courts-martial may be there aſſembled, compoſed jointly of the officers in the ſervice of the Eaſt India Company, and of the king's forces, with this diſtinction, that when the perſon tried belongs to the king's forces, regard ſhall be had to the regulations of the Britiſh mutiny act; and when he belongs to the Company, to the regulations made in purſuance of the act, 27 Geo. II. for the puniſhment of offences committed by officers or ſoldiers in their ſervice. Artillery officers, and thoſe ſerving in the royal corps of engineers, and officers in the corps of royal military artificers and labourers, and all maſter gunners and gunners in the ſervice of the ordnance, are amenable to courts-martial; and artillery officers may ſit in courts-martial with officers of other corps, taking rank according to the dates of their commiſſions.

In the abſence of the judge-advocate for the fleet, or his deputy, it is uſual for the officer, who is directed to aſſemble the court-martial, in this ſtage of the procedure, to nominate ſome perſon to officiate as judge-advocate on the occaſion;

 and

and in which appointment, according to the conftruction of the ftatute already mentioned, a majority of the members, when the court is affembled, fhould concur. The prefident likewife appoints a perfon to officiate as provoft-marfhal on the occafion, who is to take the party accufed into cuftody, to produce him at the time of trial, and to keep him until he fhall be delivered by due courfe of law. The commander in chief iffues memorandums of notice or fummonfes to the refpective flag-officers and captains of the fhips of the fquadron prefent, announcing a court-martial to be held on board a particular fhip, on a ftated day; at the fame time he directs the prefident to affemble the court at the place and time accordingly, and to give notice to the refpective flag-officers and captains, that they may attend in like manner. He iffues likewife a memorandum to the captain of the fhip, on board of which the court is to be affembled, that he may make the eftablifhed fignal for a court-martial, at the given hour of the day appointed.

Should the prefident be taken ill in the intervening time, and fhould it be neceffary, on that account, to poftpone the trial, the judge-advocate muft announce the circumftance to the profecutor and party accufed, that directions may be given to the witneffes on both fides, to attend the court on the new day appointed, inftead of that in the former fummons.

Proceedings. When all the officers, who are to conftitute the court, are affembled at the time and place appointed; and if any member has abfented himfelf through ill health, the fame is to be minutely certified to the court; and the furgeon of the fhip, which fuch member commands, muft attend, that he may atteft, upon oath, if required, the truth of his inability to attend. Should he decline fo doing, and the other teftimonials be deemed inadmiffible, the members affembled may immediately break up, as not being authorifed to form a court, or to difpenfe with the non-attendance of a member not legally excufed; and the reafons are to be ftated in a letter to the admiralty, figned by all the members who did attend. On the other hand, when the teftimonials are admitted, the court may be formed, and the judge-advocate takes the fact down in the minutes, immediately after the names of the members prefent, in the forms prefcribed.

The preambles to the minutes of courts-martial vary a little in form from the circumftances that may arife at the affembling of fuch courts, and ought to be carefully recorded by the judge-advocate. The preamble to the minutes of a court-martial, affembled by a fenior officer, meeting with five or more fhips abroad, differs materially from others, in like manner

manner as his order, as already noticed, for assembling the court. The members being to the right and left of the president, according to seniority, and the judge-advocate facing him at the bottom of the table, the president is to cause the party accused to be brought into court, attended by the provost-marshal; all the witnesses, as well in support of the charge, as in the prisoner's defence, and every other person who shall choose, being admitted, the judge-advocate, standing up, reads audibly the order for assembling the court, and likewise the order or warrant of his own appointment; he then calls over the names of the president and members who have arranged themselves alternately on the right and left hand of the president, and administers to the respective members the oath prescribed.

The judge-advocate then reads the letter of accusation, or charge against the prisoner, and he is required to plead guilty or not guilty. If he stands mute or pleads guilty, sentence passes in course; if he pleads in bar, as a former trial for, or pardon of, the same offence, or that the court is not competent to take cognizance of it, he may have the benefit of such plea; and if, as is most generally the case, he pleads not guilty, the witnesses are ordered to leave the court and the trial proceeds. If the prisoner is a foreigner, he may have the aid of an interpreter, and so may any witness or any member of the court-martial. Trials may be put off on affidavits of the absence of a material witness, but this is purely in the discretion of the court. A trial may also be put off, on an affidavit, either on the part of the prosecutor or of the prisoner, stating that printed pamphlets or papers have been published and circulated, without the procurement or knowledge of the party applying, whereby the public mind has been prejudiced.

The witnesses being sworn, it is the practice of courts-martial for the prosecutor to put all proper questions to them; or the president of the court may, in the first instance, desire them to relate what they know respecting the charge against the prisoner: and afterwards the members, with the approbation of the president, put such interrogatories as they may think proper and necessary, for investigating the truth.

Although the mutiny act does not authorise military courts-martial to inflict a summary punishment for perjury, yet there is no doubt that offenders, subject to military authority, may be proceeded against by indictment, or punished by the sentence of a general court-martial, to be assembled for that purpose. But all persons, who commit, or suborn another to commit wilful perjury, in any evidence or examination at a court-

 martial,

martial, may be profecuted in the court of King's Bench, by information or indictment, fetting forth only the offence charged upon fuch perfon, without mentioning the commiffion for holding the court-martial, or the particular matter tried, or to be tried before fuch court.

The court, having gone through the examination of all the witneffes in fupport of the charge, and allowed the prifoner to crofs-queftion them feverally, he is then put on his defence; which, if already prepared, he is allowed to read to the court, or he may dictate it to the judge-advocate, in order to its infertion in the minutes. But fhould the trial be of importance, and a variety of circumftances have been brought forward, upon which the prifoner was unprepared, he may, upon foliciting the court, be indulged with an adjournment until a fubfequent day, for the purpofe of the better preparing himfelf for his defence, and the examination of witneffes in fupport of what he may have occafion to affirm. The prifoner may fubmit his defence to the court, either verbally or in writing; and a profecutor has no right to reply. The prifoner having made his defence, the witneffes in fupport of it are to be feparately called into court, fworn and examined, the prifoner firft of all afking them fuch queftions as he may deem proper or material; whether to invalidate the profecutor's evidence, or to eftablifh his general character and good behaviour. And he is allowed to produce written documents, either in his exculpation, or as to character and good behaviour. The examination of the prifoner's witneffes is conducted in a fimilar manner to that of the evidence for the profecution. When the prifoner's interrogatories are ended, the members of the court, or judge-advocate, may put fuch queftions as appear to them proper for difclofing truth. The profecutor is generally allowed to crofs-examine the witneffes upon the points adduced by the prifoner, but he is by no means to introduce new or extraneous matter; and, after that, the prifoner may again put any additional interrogatories to his witneffes; and the prifoner having clofed his evidence, and having nothing further to offer in his defence, the court is cleared, that the members may proceed to deliberate on the judgment to be pronounced.

The proceedings at military courts-martial differ in fome degree from thofe of naval. 1. The profecutor addreffes the court in explanation of the charges, and details what he intends to prove. 2. His witneffes are adduced, who are fworn, examined by the profecutor or court, and afterward crofs-examined. 3. The prifoner makes his defence, in which he anfwers the profecutor's addrefs, comments on his evidence, and enters into a detail of the exculpatory evidence he means to bring forward. 4. As this evidence may prove stronger or weaker than the prisoner expected, he is allowed to address the court a second time, when the defence is closed. And, 5. The prosecutor is allowed to reply; and sometimes, by special permission of the court, he may explain by evidence some collateral circumstances omitted.

Judgment. The court being cleared, the members proceed to deliberate on the question guilty or not guilty; and if guilty, to pronounce that judgment which the articles of war, or laws of the land, have annexed to the crime or offence. In discriminating the degrees of guilt with which a prisoner stands charged, it frequently happens at courts-martial, that he may appear not guilty of the identical crime laid to his charge, but of an offence of less magnitude, though of the same species or nature, and nearly connected with it. In this case, it is customary for the court to acquit him of the greater, and finding him guilty of the offence of inferior magnitude, to inflict a corresponding punishment. Although there may appear strong suspicions of a prisoner's guilt of some other crime or offence, not set forth in the charge, yet, in acquitting him of the one he is tried for, the court cannot legally find him guilty of any distinct offence. Neither can a prisoner be found guilty of what may be an *ex post facto* offence, or misdemeanour; that is, one committed after he had been confined, or even indulged as a prisoner at large: but in all such cases he may be ordered into confinement, and brought to a new trial, for the distinct crime or offence appearing against him. In this place it may be proper to remark, that if a prisoner be tried for a crime, said to have been committed on a particular day of the month; and in the course of trial, it is proved to have happened on a day different from what the indictment or accusation sets forth, it is incumbent on the court-martial to acquit him; and he is not liable to be tried a second time for the same offence.

Sentence. The members having deliberated on the evidence produced for and against the prisoner, and taken into mature consideration the palliating circumstances, either offered in his defence, or that have arisen in the investigation of facts; the judge-advocate states the question respecting the prisoner's guilt, and which at naval courts-martial is put to each member separately, beginning with the junior, and ending with the president, and is usually couched in the following words: "Are you of opinion, that the charge against the prisoner is proved or not proved?" Or thus, "Is he guilty or not guilty of the crime laid to his charge?" Should the majority of of members be of opinion that the charge is proved, thoſe members conſequently, are to aſſign the puniſhment to be inflicted.

At general courts-martial in the army, it is neceſſary, in judgment of death, that nine members out of thirteen; or if the number is greater, that two thirds, ſhould concur. The aſſent of two thirds, in every capital ſentence, is likewiſe requiſite in courts-martial, held in Africa or in New South Wales, conſiſting of a leſſer number than thirteen.

Although the members of a naval court-martial may not be unanimous in their determinations upon the matters before them, yet as the ſentence drawn up receives its force and validity from the judgment of the majority, all the members preſent ought to ſign ſuch ſentence, and which is always counterſigned by the judge-advocate. At army courts-martial, the preſident alone ſigns the ſentence, which is alſo counterſigned by the judge-advocate, who is directed by the mutiny act, ſect. 22, to tranſmit the original proceedings and ſentence to the judge-advocate-general in London, or, if held in Ireland, to the judge-advocate in Dublin; to the end that all perſons entitled may be enabled to obtain copies. Proviſions equally beneficial are made for parties out of Great Britain, but in Europe, but no ſuch privilege is reſerved for the navy. It is proper at all trials, that the judge-advocate, or his deputy, or the perſon empowered to officiate for him, ſhould carefully preſerve the original minutes of the proceedings, as recorded by him during the courſe of any trial; and he ſhould alſo keep in his poſſeſſion diſtinct notes of the opinions and votes of the ſeveral members, on deliberating upon the articles of accuſation, and pronouncing judgment; in order that he may be fully prepared to anſwer any queſtions or diſcuſſions that may be afterwards moved in parliament, or in the ordinary courts of law, relative to the trial, in the event of his being called upon to give evidence.

ACQUITTAL. When accuſations are made and not ſubſtantiated by proofs, courts ſometimes declare their judgments of acquittal, in terms which convey cenſure on the proſecutor, by pronouncing the charges *malicious, vexatious, and without any foundation*.

PUNISHMENTS. In ſeveral caſes, both in the army and navy, the puniſhment is not *diſcretionary*, but ſentence of death muſt be pronounced; in many others, however, the penalty is left to the diſcretion of the court, and ſometimes puniſhments of different degrees of rigour are inflicted. When the court has determined, or the law has fixed the penalty, the judge-advocate draws up the ſentence; the priſoner and audience are admitted; and

and judgment is pronounced in open court. Neither the naval nor military articles prefcribe the mode of inflicting the punifhment of *death*. It is ufual in the navy to adjudge an admiral, or officer of rank, to be fhot for a capital offence. There are fome inftances of fentences dooming captains and lieutenants to be fhot, and others ordering them to be hanged. In the army it is the general practice to adjudge officers or foldiers found guilty of capital offences, to be fhot; but for deferting to the enemy, or for theft, a foldier is ufually hanged, as the moft ignominious mode of punifhment.

In cafes where no ftatute orders fentence of death, it is in the power of courts both naval and military, to inflict, according to the nature and degree of the offences, various fentences from the higheft order to the loweft: namely, corporal punifhment from twelve to one thoufand lafhes on the bare back, with a cat-o'-nine-tails; running the gauntlet; degradation of rank, and being ignominioufly towed from a fhip to the fhore, with a halter round the offender's neck; degradation of rank, and to ferve on board any fhip in a fubordinate fituation, or as a common feaman; imprifonment; difmiffal from his majefty's fervice, and for ever rendered incapable of ferving in any military or civil capacity; difmiffal without expreffing incapacity of ferving again; difmiffal from the fhip to which the offender (if an officer) belonged, fometimes with the addition of being degraded, and put on the bottom of the lift of officers in which he ranks; the mulct of pay; fufpenfion of rank and pay for a limited time; fevere or moderate reprimand and admonition, which are the loweft fhades of punifhment. In the navy there are very few inftances of commiffioned officers being degraded in rank, and reduced by the fentence of a court-martial to ferve in inferior fituations; but warrant officers have repeatedly not only been degraded and reduced to ferve in fubordinate fituations, but alfo adjudged to receive corporal punifhment. The naval lift of punifhments includes thofe of keel-hauling, ducking, maft-heading, and feizing the offender by his arms and legs to the fhrouds, and there leaving him for hours, as is vulgarly called like a fpread eagle.

Of *imprifonment*. It may be neceffary to obferve, that by ftatute, no perfon convicted of any offence can be imprifoned for a longer term than two years, by the fentence of any naval court-martial. Prior to this act, which was 22 Geo. II. courts-martial have adjudged perfons to be imprifoned for ten or fifteen years, and fometimes even for life.

The *gauntlope*, pronounced gauntlet, is a military punifhment for felony, or fome other heinous offence, known to moft nations in Europe. In the navy, it is ufually inflicted on incorrigible delinquents,

delinquents, detected in robberies, pilfering or other scandalous practices. The punishment is inflicted in the following manner: the whole ship's crew is ranged in two rows, standing face to face on both sides of the deck, so as to form a line whereby to go forward on one side and return aft on the other; each person being furnished with a small twisted cord, or spun yarn, called a knittle, having two or three knots upon it. The delinquent is then stripped naked, above the waist, and compelled to march forward in ordinary or quick time, between the two rows of men, and aft on the other side, a certain number of times, rarely exceeding three, during which, every person gives him a stripe with his knittle as he passes along. Although the punishment is termed *running* the gauntlet, yet in the navy the delinquent is never permitted to run between the ranks of his executioners, but is compelled to march in ordinary or quick time, preceded by the master at arms with a drawn sword pointed in the rear towards him, while the corporal follows him behind with another drawn sword; or, instead of the corporal, it is sometimes usual to cause the boatswain's mate to follow him, furnished with a cat-o'-nine-tails, but he never applies the lash of it, in the march, unless the offender makes a retrograde movement. In the army, when a soldier is sentenced to run the gauntlet, the regiment is drawn up in two ranks facing each other; each soldier, having a switch in his hand, lashes the criminal as he runs along naked from the waist upwards. While he runs, the drums beat at each end of the ranks. Sometimes he runs three, five, or seven times, according to the nature of the offence. The major is on horseback, and takes care that each soldier does his duty. Of late years, however, this punishment has been disused in the army, nor is there in the navy more than one instance of its being inflicted by order of a court-martial.

Neither the punishment of *flogging*, nor that of running the gauntlet, is so severe in the army as in the navy. One dozen of lashes applied to the bare back by a boatswain's mate, furnished with a naval cat-o'-nine tails, is equivalent at least to fifty lashes laid on by a drummer with a military cat. This arises, not so much from the expertness of one executioner, over another, in the mode of laying on his lashes, as from the greater thickness, hardness, and severity of the one instrument of punishment than the other.

Keel-hauling is never ordered by a court-martial, and rarely inflicted by commanders. It was frequently resorted to in the fleet, as well as in the merchant service at the early periods after the revolution, and it appears to have been borrowed from the Dutch navy, where it is still practised. It is executed by plunging the delinquent

repeat-

repeatedly under the ship's bottom on one side, and hoisting him up at the other, after having passed under the keel. The blocks or pullies by which he is suspended, are fastened to the opposite extremities of the main-yard, and a weight of lead or iron is hung upon his legs, to sink him to a competent depth. By this apparatus he is drawn close up to the yard-arm, and thence let fall suddenly into the sea; where passing under the ship's bottom he is hoisted up on the opposite side of the ship. And this, after sufficient intervals of breathing, is repeated two or three times.

Ducking is a marine punishment, now seldom used, for uncleanness, blasphemy, or scandalous actions. The French inflict it on those who have been convicted of desertion, or exciting sedition. The criminal is placed astride on a short thick batten, fastened to the end of a rope, which passes through a block hanging at one of the yard arms. Thus fixed, he is hoisted suddenly up to the yard, and the rope being slackened at once, he is allowed to fall into the sea. This chastisement is repeated several times, and by having double-headed shot fastened to his feet during the punishment, he sinks a considerable depth before he is hoisted up again.

The punishment of *mast-heading* is frequently inflicted on young midshipmen, at the discretion of the captain or commanding officer, for misconduct, neglect of duty, or trivial offences.

Execution of corporal Punishment. In carrying the sentences of naval courts-martial for corporal punishment into execution, the admiral, or commanding officer of the ships and vessels for the time being, issues orders to the captain of the flag, or other particular ship, to make the signal for the boats of the squadron to assemble, manned and armed, on the day appointed to attend the punishment; and likewise directs the other captains to send a lieutenant with a boat manned and armed from their respective ships to attend and assist. An order is at the same time issued, to the captain or commander of the ship to which the prisoner belongs, (accompanied with a copy of the sentence) directing him to cause the punishment to be inflicted alongside of the different ships, in the manner, and in such proportions, as therein specified. It is usual to include in this order, directions to the captain to cause the surgeon of the ship to attend in the boat with the lieutenant, as well as one of his mates in the long boat with the prisoner, for the purpose of judging of his ability to bear all his punishment; which the surgeon may put a stop to, when he conceives him unable to bear any more with safety. The provost-marshal is ordered to attend, and read publicly the sentence of the court-martial alongside of each ship.

On

OF DEATH. When the king approves of a ſentence of death, the warrant for execution is tranſmitted by the admiralty to the officer commanding the ſhips and veſſels at the place for the time being, who iſſues the neceſſary orders, agreeably to the forms of the ſervice; and in purſuance of them, preparations are made. When the fatal morning arrives, the ſignal of death is diſplayed, the aſſemblage of boats, manned and armed, ſurrounds the ſhip appointed for the execution. The crews of the reſpective ſhips are arranged on deck, and after hearing the articles of war read, await in ſilence the awful moment. At length a gun is fired (the ſignal to rouſe attention), and at the ſame inſtant, the victim is run up by the neck to the yard arm.

Military executions are attended with ſtill more parade and ſolemnity. In no ſervice or country is the ceremony ſo awful and impreſſive. The ſentence of death being approved by the king, the warrant is iſſued under the ſign manual; and on foreign ſtations the commander in chief iſſues his warrant to the ſecond in command, and appoints the time and place for carrying the ſentence of death into execution. General orders are in conſequence iſſued from the adjutant general's office, arranging the regiments and corps allotted for parade, guards, and execution parties. Five execution parties, each conſiſting of a ſerjeant and twelve rank and file, are appointed, of whom the provoſt-marſhal takes the command on their arrival at the guard. All the guards of the garriſon and advanced poſts leave their centries at their reſpective ſtations, and repair themſelves to the provoſt-marſhal's guard, at the hour appointed, for the purpoſe of eſcorting the priſoner to the place of execution. All theſe guards, as well as the execution parties, under the immediate direction of the provoſt-marſhal, are commanded by the field officer of the day. The ſeveral corps of the line, at the appointed hour and place, parade three deep, and are prepared to draw up ſo as to form the three ſides of a ſquare. The execution parties in diviſions, preceded by a band of muſic, and a corps of drummers, with the provoſt-marſhal on horſeback at their head, march in ordinary time at the front of the priſoner. The muſic plays the dead march in Saul. The guards formed in diviſions, march at the ſame time in rear of the priſoner. The main-guard, commanded by the captain of the day, leads. The others follow in ſucceſſion, according to the rank of their regiments. The proceſſion comes into the ſquare from the rear by the right, and the muſic and drums of each corps play and beat to the ſlow march in Saul, as the proceſſion paſſes along its front. The execution parties march along the front of the whole line, and as far as the coffin placed in the centre, where the firſt three diviſions halt, and wheel back on their right pivots

pivots in line. The fourth and fifth divisions continue to advance until they can form opposite to the first three, by wheeling back into line on their left pivots. The dreadful moment now approaches,—the music ceases,—an awful silence ensues—the warrant and sentence of death are audibly read,—the signal is given,—and the fire of the execution parties puts an immediate end to the prisoner's existence.

PARDON. In courts-martial, as in other cases, the benevolence of the English law has lodged in the hands of the sovereign the power of pardon, either total, or by remitting or mitigating the sentence, or by reprieving the prisoner. He may also, if he disapproves the sentence, order the court to sit again, and revise their proceedings.

AUDITORS OF PUBLIC ACCOUNTS. In former times the duty of revising certain branches of public expenditure was confided to two officers appointed by patent, and called auditors of the imprest: but the commissioners of public accounts having, in their twelfth report, dated the 8th of June, 1784, represented that no solid advantage was derived to the public from their establishment, as it was then constituted; and having urged the propriety and necessity of introducing into this office, regulations similar to those they had recommended for other offices, an act was passed in the following year (25 Geo. III. c. 52.), which, after a preamble, stating the importance of providing a more effectual method for examining the public accounts of the kingdom, proceeds to vacate the patents of lord Sondes, and lord viscount Mountstuart, the two auditors of the imprests (on a compensation of 7000*l*. each per annum being made to them for their interest in the same) abolishes the receipt of all fees, gratuities and perquisites; and directs certain fixed annual salaries to be paid to the officers and clerks employed in the department for auditing the public accounts. The act then enables his majesty to appoint five commissioners for auditing the public accounts (two of them to be the comptrollers of army accounts for the time being), and to grant fixed salaries to each, not exceeding, on the whole, 4000*l*. clear of all deductions. Such commissioners to hold their offices during good behaviour. It then vests the appointment of the officers and clerks, and the power of allowing sums for stationary, coals, and contingencies, in the board of treasury, and limits the expence to 6000*l*. The rest of the act contains directions for the whole proceeding in auditing the accounts, gives the power of examining upon oath, and makes written vouchers necessary for every article in the accounts. By virtue of the powers in this act, his majesty issued a commission under the great seal in June 1785, appointing the two comptrollers of army accounts, and three other gentlemen, to be commissioners for auditing the public accounts. To the

 comp-

comptrollers, in addition to their exifting falaries, which with fees exceeded 700*l.* an annual fum of 500*l.* was given, and to the other three commiffioners 1000*l.* each. The office is in Somerfet Houfe. In 1805, Mr. Pitt, finding that thefe commiffioners could not fulfil their duties to the full extent, took meafures for appointing a new fet of commiffioners with further powers, and an eftablifhment of clerks and affiftants, fufficient, as it was expected, to complete the neceffary and important tafk confided to them. The death of that minifter prevented his completing the plan, but it was purfued and extended by his fucceffors.

Patriotic Fund. Some account has already been given of the modes devifed by the public care, and royal and individual munificence, for the relief of thofe who are wounded, or become helplefs in the public caufe, and for the benefit of their widows and orphans. Still it has ever been found, that, on extraordinary occafions, the number of claimants in various degrees of affinity with the fufferers, exceeded the powers of relief which could be made confiftent with the juft diftribution of public money. It had therefore become cuftomary, when any hard-fought battle, or fudden calamity involved great numbers in diftrefs, to open fubfcriptions, the amount of which was diftributed by a committee, for the benefit of thofe who were wounded, made widows or orphans, or otherwife reduced to diftrefs, by the calamities attending the fea or land fervice. Thefe fubfcriptions were generally, but not always, commenced in confequence of fome diftinguifhed engagement, but other occafions produced fimilar efforts of public benevolence; as the finking of the Royal George in 1782, and the fubfcription for fupplying the army in Holland with warm clothing in 1794. Great fums were frequently collected by thefe patriotic exertions, but ftill they did not anfwer every purpofe. Their deftination was limited to the exprefs object for which the fubfcription was propofed, and hence it happened that many meritorious fervices, and grievous calamities were unrewarded and unrelieved, becaufe the actions from which they arofe were not fufficiently grand to claim general attention; nor did thefe fubfcriptions afford the means of rewarding, or expreffing approbation of bravery and merit, in any other mode than the fupport of thofe whom the fate of war had reduced to mifery.

Experience of thefe inconveniences, and a defire to eftablifh at once a fund which fhould be permanently beneficial, and the amount of which might be expended in every mode of relief and reward which the gratitude and juftice of the country might require, impelled the merchants of London, at the beginning of the war in 1803, to propofe a fubfcription on a new plan.

plan. On the 20th of July, 1803, the merchants, underwriters, and other subscribers to Lloyd's Coffee House, met at that place for the purpose of setting on foot a general subscription, on an extended scale, for the encouragement and relief of those who might be engaged in the defence of the country, and who might suffer in the common cause, and of those who might signalize themselves during the present most important contest.

This patriotic and public-spirited body adopted, at their first meeting, resolutions in these terms.

"That, in a conjuncture when the vital interests of our "country, when the peculiar blessings which, under our beloved "sovereign and happy constitution, endear our social state, are "involved in the issue of the present contest; when we are "menaced by an enemy, whose haughty presumption is grounded "only on the present unfortunate position of the continental "powers; and when we seem to be placed for the moment, "as the last barrier against the total subjugation of Europe, by "the overbearing influence of France, it behoves us to meet "our situation as men, as freemen, but above all, as *Britons*. "On this alone, with the divine aid, depends our exemption "from the yoke of Gallic despotism; on this alone depends, "under the same protecting power, whether this empire shall "remain, what it has for ages been, the strenuous supporter of "religion and morals, the asserter of its own, and the guardian "of the liberties of mankind, the nurse of industry, the protector of the arts and sciences, the example and admiration "of the world; or, whether it shall become an obsequious tributary, an enslaved, a plundered, and degraded department "of a foreign nation.

"That, to give more effect and energy to the measures adopted "by government for the defence of our liberties, our lives, "and property; to add weight to those personal exertions which "we are all readily disposed to contribute, it behoves us to hold "out every encouragment to our fellow subjects, who may be in "any way instrumental in repelling or annoying our implacable "foe; and to prove to them, that we are ready to drain "both our purses and our veins, in the *great cause* which imperiously "calls on us to unite the duties of loyalty and patriotism "with the strongest efforts of zealous exertions.

"That, to animate the efforts of our defenders by sea and "land, it is expedient to raise, by the patriotism of the community "at large, a suitable fund for their comfort and relief; "for the purpose of assuaging the anguish of their wounds, or "palliating in some degree the more weighty misfortune of "the loss of limbs; of alleviating the distresses of the widow "and orphan; of smoothing the brow of sorrow, for the fall

of

"of dearest relatives, the props of unhappy indigence or helpless age; and of granting pecuniary rewards, or honourable badges of distinction, for successful exertions of valour or merit.

"That a subscription, embracing all the objects in the foregoing resolution, be now opened; and, to set an example to the public bodies throughout the United Kingdom and its dependencies, and to our fellow subjects of every class and denomination, that, independently of our individual contributions, the sum of *twenty thousand pounds*, 3 *per cent. consolidated annuities*, part of the funded property of this society, shall be appropriated to this purpose."

They further resolved; "that such part of the fund as shall not be used for the purposes now intended, be returned in proportion to the sums subscribed. And that all sums, however small, which shall be offered by the patriotism of the poorer classes of our fellow subjects, shall be accepted; the cause affecting equally the liberties and lives of persons of every description."

At their next meeting, on the 29th of July, the first fifty persons who had subscribed 100*l*. and upward, were formed into a committee, with power to add to their number, which they subsequently did. The subscription, which was speedily very prosperous, received the name of the *Patriotic Fund*, and seven members were appointed a committee of treasury, and three were nominated trustees for the purchase and sale of stock, or other government securities, for the purposes of the institution.

The benevolence of the public did not disappoint the expectation of those who proposed the plan; the subscription was rapidly and extensively successful. The rich and the poor were equally zealous in contributing; some individuals gave 1000*l*. and those who could only offer a few shillings, found their tribute received with kindness; public bodies gave portions of their funds, and convivial societies contributed from their stock purses; the officers, non-commissioned officers, and privates of several regiments carried in a share of their pay; and the theatres in the metropolis, and in various parts of the country, aided the general design by benefit plays, which produced considerable sums. As the war was not at first distinguished by many achievements which occasioned calls on the fund, it acquired a great amount and solid consistency. On such occasions as first occurred, the committee felt that it was sometimes necessary to grant annuities for lives, instead of sums for temporary relief, and they humanely ordered, that in all such cases a year should be paid in advance.

On

On the firft of March, 1804, the committee, for the fatisfaction of the fubfcribers, publifhed a report of their proceedings, by which it appeared that no act of fignal bravery had paffed unnoticed, and that no fpecies of diftrefs occafioned by calamitous incidents in the war had been left unrelieved. Sums of money, pieces of plate, fwords, and other honorary memorials, had been given to thofe who difplayed confpicuous merit; the wounded obtained fums of money, according to their neceffities, which were not paid till they produced certificates of convalefcence; and on the furviving relatives of thofe who were flain annuities were fettled of various amounts.

The mode of donation was not more judicious, than the progrefs of the collection was gratifying. The amount of the fubfcription was, in 3*l.* per cent. ftock, 21,200*l.* and in money, which had then been laid out in government fecurities, and was bearing intereft, 154,455*l.* 18*s.* 5*d.*; and the dividends then actually received amounted to 3768*l.*

In this manner the Patriotic Fund continued to be augmented and applied, till the latter part of the year 1805, when the glorious and difaftrous battle off Trafalgar, filled the nation at once with pride, gratitude, and affliction. The committee, on this occafion, felt the neceffity of diftributing large fums of money, and they appealed to the characteriftic humanity of the nation to prevent their powers of doing good in future from being impaired by the prefent exertion. The appeal was attended with the happieft effect; the clergy, to their infinite honour, aided the caufe of humanity and patriotifm, by preaching fermons in honour of the departed Nelfon, and at the fame time animating the public generally in favour of thofe who were fufferers by partaking in his glory. The fubfcription was revived with general ardour, and the donations of individuals, affifted by the collections made in churches and chapels, added more than 120,000*l.* to the fund.

To this truly noble and patriotic eftablifhment, the wounded failor and foldier may look with confidence for a fupply which fhall enable him to defy want and purfue honeft induftry; the widow may find her heart relieved from thofe pangs which are occafioned by the profpect of immediate want, and by anxiety for unprotected orphans; and the public may contemplate with fatisfaction the numbers fnatched from vice and infamy, by timely aid, and rendered, inftead of the difgrace and fcourge, the honour and the fupport of the country. Above all, in times when union in fentiment and exertion are moft effential to the nation, the poor have a vifible, fubftantial, and beneficial proof of the liberal gratitude with which the rich and the powerful confider their fervices, and pour forth a portion of their wealth

 to

to encourage and reward those who have struggled for the general good, and fought for freedom and for safety.

THE LAW.

In this division of the work, it is not presumed that information will be afforded respecting the law of England in general, or any particular head or description of law, sufficient to supersede the necessity of further research; but the end generally aimed at will be to convey a clear notion of the law itself, of the various courts in which it is administered, and the principal persons engaged in regulating and fixing the course of justice.

Law in general. Law, by a common, but too diffuse, interpretation, is termed a rule of action, and applied indiscriminately to all kinds of action, whether animate or inanimate, rational or irrational, to motion, gravitation, optics, mechanics, and many other subjects, as well as the government of man, the regulation of his conduct, and the preservation of his rights. On this general definition it is well observed, that when the word law is applied to motion, gravitation, or mechanics, it will be found, in every case, that with equal or greater propriety and perspicuity, might have been used the words quality, property, or peculiarity. The use of the word in speaking of inanimate objects is only sanctioned by custom; and an extension of its application, beyond the precise points to which it has been limited by usage, would be considered an instance of affectation or pedantry, or perhaps censured as altogether improper. These remarks would seem superfluous on the present occasion, had not most writers who treat on law as a science begun with such an explanation; Mr. Christian, in his edition of Blackstone, furnishes the argument against its propriety.

In a more correct and limited, though yet sufficiently extensive sense, municipal law is described to be a rule of civil conduct, prescribed by the supreme power in a state. Perhaps this may not, as a definition, stand exempt from censure in the minds of those who speculate with great refinement on the nature and modes of government; still it enjoys the advantage of being known, explained, and enforced by respectable authority, it is sufficiently abstract, for all practical purposes, and sufficiently easy to be received into every understanding.

The Law of England. By the act of settlement, the laws of England are declared to be the birth-right of the people; and,

and, according to an ancient maxim of the common law, this our birth-right in the laws is to be esteemed our most valuable inheritance, superior to every other denomination of property. *Major hæreditas unicuique venit à jure et legibus quam à parentibus.* Lord Coke says, it "is the best birth-right the subject "hath; for thereby his goods, lands, wife, children, his body, "life, honour, and estimation, are protected from injury and "wrong."

The municipal law of England, by which these great purposes are better effected than in any other known community, is divided into two kinds: the *lex non scripta*, the unwritten, or common law; and the *lex scripta*, the written, or statute law. The unwritten law includes not only *general customs*, or the common law properly so called; but also the *particular customs* of certain parts of the kingdom; and likewise those *particular laws*, that are by custom observed only in certain courts and jurisdictions.

Unwritten Law. This law, although described as not written, is not at this time purely *oral*, or communicated from former ages to the present solely by word of mouth. It is true indeed that, in the profound ignorance of letters which formerly overspread the whole western world, all laws were entirely traditional, because the nations, among which they prevailed, had but little idea of writing. But, with us, at present, the monuments and evidences of our legal customs are contained in the records of the several courts of justice, in books of reports and judicial decisions, and in the treatises of learned sages of the profession, preserved and handed down to us from the times of highest antiquity. They are termed unwritten, because their original institution and authority are not set down in writing, as acts of parliament are; but they receive their binding power, and the force of laws, by long and immemorial usage, and by their universal reception throughout the kingdom. This unwritten, or common law, is properly distinguishable into three kinds: 1. General customs; which are the universal rule of the whole kingdom, and form the common law, in its stricter and more usual signification. 2. Particular customs; which, for the most part, affect only the inhabitants of particular districts. 3. Certain particular laws; which by custom are adopted and used by some particular courts of pretty general and extensive jurisdiction.

General Maxims. The general maxims, or common law properly so called, form that system by which proceedings and determinations in the king's ordinary courts of justice are guided and directed. This, for the most part, settles the course by which lands descend by inheritance; the manner and

 form

form of acquiring and transferring property; the solemnities and obligations of contracts; the rules of expounding wills, deeds, and acts of parliament; the respective remedies of civil injuries; the several species of temporal offences, with the manner and degree of punishment; and an infinite number of minuter particulars, which diffuse themselves as extensively as the ordinary distribution of common justice requires. These customs and maxims are known, and their validity determined by the judges in the several courts of justice, who are the depositaries of the laws, the living oracles, who must decide in all cases of doubt, and who are bound by an oath to decide according to the law of the land. Their knowledge of that law is derived from experience and study; and each of them is sworn to determine, not according to his own private judgment, but according to the known laws and customs of the land; not delegated to pronounce a new law, but to maintain and expound the old one. Yet this rule admits of exception, where the former determination is most evidently contrary to reason; even in such cases the subsequent judges do not pretend to make a new law, but to vindicate the old one from misrepresentation. For if it be found that the former decision is manifestly absurd or unjust, it is declared, not that such a sentence was *bad law*, but that it was *not law*; that is, that it is not the established custom of the realm, as has been erroneously determined.

The judgment of the judges, and all the proceedings previous thereto, are carefully registered and preserved, under the name of *records*, in public repositories set apart for that particular purpose; and to them frequent recourse is had, when any critical case arises, in the determination of which former precedents may give light or assistance. They are also handed out to public view in the numerous volumes of *reports*, which furnish the lawyer's library. These reports are histories of the several cases, with a short summary of the proceedings, which are preserved at large in the record, the arguments on both sides, and the reasons the court gave for its judgment, taken down in short notes by persons present at the determination; and these serve as indexes to, and also to explain, the records; which always, in matters of consequence and nicety, the judges direct to be searched. The reports are extant in a tolerably regular series from the reign of Edward the second inclusive. Besides these reporters, there are also other authors, to whom great veneration and respect are paid by the students, and by the judges, as works of the very highest authority in the law.

PARTICULAR CUSTOMS. The particular customs or laws, which

which affect only the inhabitants of particular districts are, without doubt, the remains of that multitude of local customs out of which the common law, as it now stands, was collected, at first by Alfred, and afterwards by Edgar and Edward the Confessor; each district mutually sacrificing some of its own special usages, in order that the whole kingdom might enjoy the benefit of one uniform and universal system of laws. But for reasons that have been now long forgotten, particular counties, cities, towns, manors, and lordships, were very early indulged with the privilege of abiding by their own customs, in contradistinction to the rest of the nation at large; which privilege is confirmed to them by several acts of parliament. Such is the custom of *gavelkind* in Kent, and some other parts of the kingdom, which ordains, among other things, that not the eldest son only of the father shall succeed to his inheritance, but all the sons alike: and that, though the ancestor be attainted and hanged, yet the heir shall succeed to his estate, without any escheat to the lord. Such is the custom that prevails in divers ancient boroughs, and therefore called *borough-English*, that the youngest son shall inherit the estate, in preference to all his elder brothers. Such is the custom in other boroughs, that a widow shall be intitled, for her dower, to all her husband's land; whereas at the common law she shall be endowed with one third part only. Such also are the special and particular customs of manors, of which every one has more or less, and which bind all the copyhold and customary tenants that hold of the said manors. Such likewise is the custom of holding divers inferior courts, with power of trying causes, in cities and trading towns; the right of holding which, when no royal grant can be shewn, depends entirely upon immemorial and established usage. Such, lastly, are many particular customs within the city of London, with regard to trade, apprentices, widows, orphans, and a variety of other matters. All these are contrary to the general law of the land, and are good only by special usage; though the customs of London are also confirmed by act of parliament. To this head may most properly be referred a particular system of customs used only among one set of the king's subjects, called the custom of merchants, or *lex mercatoria*: which, however different from the general rules of the common law, is yet ingrafted into it, and made a part of it; being allowed, for the benefit of trade, to be of the utmost validity in all commercial transactions.

Of these particular customs, some are acknowledged by the law, as gavelkind, and borough-English; some are to be proved before a jury, and not by the judges, except the same particular custom has been before tried, determined, and recorded ed in the same court; and the customs of London are certified to the court wherein they are in question in a prescribed form from the Lord Mayor and aldermen, by the mouth of the recorder.

A custom must be *legal*, or it may be abolished; it must be so *ancient* that the memory of man runneth not to the contrary; for if its commencement can be proved within any time since the first year of Richard I. it is not good; it must have been *continued*, for an interruption of the right will destroy it, though a mere interruption of the possession will not; it must have been *peaceable*, or acquiesced in without contention or dispute; it must be *reasonable*, or, at least, not unreasonable; it must be *certain*, or, at least, capable of being rendered so; *compulsory*, and not left to option; and, lastly, customs must be *consistent* with each other, for opposite customs relating to the same object cannot be of equal antiquity. In the allowance of customs, those which are in derogation of the common law are taken in the utmost strictness, and none can prevail against the king's prerogative. Thus by the custom of gavelkind, a person aged fifteen may, by deed of feoffment, convey away his lands, in fee simple for ever; but he cannot, at that age, convey them by any other deed, or even make a lease for seven years; also if the king purchases lands of the nature of gavelkind, where all the sons inherit equally; yet, upon his demise, his eldest son alone shall succeed to those lands.

Civil and Canon Laws. By the peculiar laws, which by custom are adopted and used only in certain peculiar courts and jurisdictions, are meant the civil and canon laws. These laws are reduced to writing and set forth by authority, but are ranked among the *leges non scriptæ*, because they are not of any force in England, except in some particular cases and courts, where they have been admitted and received by immemorial usage and custom; or else, because they are, in some other cases, introduced by consent of parliament, and then they owe their validity to the *leges scriptæ*, or statute law.

By the civil law, absolutely taken, is generally understood the civil or municipal law of the Roman empire, as comprized in the institutes, the code, and the digest of the emperor Justinian, and the novel constitutions of himself and some of his successors. The Roman law (founded first upon the regal constitutions of their ancient kings, next upon the twelve tables of the decemviri, then upon the laws or statutes, enacted by the senate or people, the edicts of the prætor, and the *responsa prudentum*, or opinions of learned lawyers, and, lastly, upon the imperial decrees, or constitutions of successive emperors) had grown

grown to so great a bulk that, by an author who preceded Justinian, they were computed to be many camels', load. This was in part remedied by the collections of three private lawyers, Gregorius, Hermogenes, and Papirius; and then by the emperor Theodosius the Younger, by whose orders a code was compiled, A. D. 438, being a methodical collection of all the imperial constitutions then in force: which Theodosian code was the only book of civil law received as authentic in the western part of Europe, till many centuries after; and to this it is probable that the Franks and Goths might frequently pay some regard, in framing legal constitutions for their newly erected kingdoms. For Justinian commanded only in the eastern remains of the empire; and it was under his auspices, that the present body of civil law was compiled and finished by Tribonian and other lawyers, about the year 533. This consists of, 1. The institutes, which contain the elements or first principles of the Roman law, in four books. 2. The digests, or pandects, in fifty books; containing the opinions and writings of eminent lawyers, digested in a systematical method. 3. A new code, or collection of imperial constitutions, in twelve books; the lapse of a whole century having rendered the former code of Theodosius imperfect. 4. The novels, or new constitutions, posterior in time to the other books, and amounting to a supplement to the code; containing new decrees of successive emperors, as new questions happened to arise. These form the body of Roman law, or *corpus juris civilis*, as published about the time of Justinian; which however soon fell into neglect and oblivion, till about the year 1130, when a copy of the digests was found at Amalfi in Italy; which accident, concurring with the policy of the Roman ecclesiastics, suddenly gave new vogue and authority to the civil law, introduced it into several nations, and occasioned that mighty inundation of voluminous comments with which this system of law, more than any other, is now loaded.

The *canon law* is a body of Roman ecclesiastical law, relative to such matters as that church either has, or pretends to have, the proper jurisdiction over. This is compiled from the opinions of the ancient Latin fathers, the decrees of general councils, and the decretal epistles and bulles of the holy see. All which lay in the same disorder and confusion as the Roman civil law, till about the year 1151, when one Gratian, an Italian monk, animated with the discovery of Justinian's pandects, reduced the ecclesiastical constitutions also into some method, in three books; which he entitled *Concordia Discordantium Canonum*, but which are generally known by the name

name of *Decretum Gratiani*. These reached as low as the time of Pope Alexander III. The subsequent papal decrees, to the pontificate of Gregory IX. were published in much the same method under the auspices of that pope, about the year 1230, in five books; entitled *Decretalia Gregorii Noni*. A sixth book was added by Boniface VIII. about the year 1298, which is called *Sextus Decretalium*. The Clementine constitutions, or decrees of Clement V. were in like manner authenticated in 1317, by his successor John XXII; who also published twenty constitutions of his own, called the *Extravagantes Joannis*; all which in some measure answer to the novels of the civil law. To these have been since added some decrees of later popes, in five books, called *Extravagantes Communes*. And all these together, Gratian's decrees, Gregory's decretals, the sixth decretal, the Clementine constitutions, and the extravagants of John and his successors, form the *corpus juris canonici*, or body of the Roman canon laws. Besides these pontifical collections, which during the times of popery were received as authentic in this island, as well as in other parts of christendom, there is also a kind of national canon law, composed of *legatine* and *provincial* constitutions, and adapted only to the exigencies of this church and kingdom. The *legatine* constitutions were ecclesiastical laws, enacted in national synods, held under the cardinals Otho and Othobon, legates from pope Gregory IX. and pope Clement IV. in the reign of Henry III. about the years 1220 and 1268; the provincial synods, held under divers archbishops of Canterbury, from Stephen Langton, in the reign of Henry III. to Henry Chichele, in the reign of Henry V. and adopted also by the province of York, in the reign of Henry VI. At the dawn of the reformation, in the reign of Henry VIII. it was enacted in parliament, that a review should be had of the canon law; and till such review should be made, all canons, constitutions, ordinances, and synodals provincial, being then already made, and not repugnant to the law of the land or the king's prerogative, should still be used and executed. And, as no such review has yet been perfected, upon this statute now depends the authority of the canon law in England. As for the canons enacted by the clergy under James I. in the year 1603, and never confirmed in parliament, it has been solemnly adjudged upon the principles of law and the constitution, that where they are not merely declaratory of the ancient canon law, but are introductory of new regulations, they do not bind the laity, whatever regard the clergy may think proper to pay them.

There are four species of courts, in which the civil and canon laws are permitted (under different restrictions) to be used.

ufed. 1. The courts of the archbifhops and bifhops, and their derivative officers, ufually called in our law, courts chriftian, *curiæ chriftianitatis*, or the ecclefiaftical courts. 2. The military courts. 3. The courts of admiralty. 4. The courts of the two univerfities. In all, their reception in general, and the different degrees of that reception, are grounded entirely upon cuftom; corroborated in the latter inftance by act of parliament, ratifying thofe charters which confirm the cuftomary law of the univerfities. But in thefe courts, thefe laws cannot be exercifed to any greater extent than is warranted by cuftom or by ftatute, and any incroachment is prevented by thefe means: 1. The courts of common law have the fuperintendency over thefe courts; to keep them within their jurifdictions, to determine wherein they exceed them, to reftrain and prohibit fuch excefs, and (in cafe of contumacy) to punifh the officer who executes, and in fome cafes, the judge who enforces the fentence fo declared illegal. 2. The common law has referved to itfelf the expofition of all fuch acts of parliament, as concern either the extent of thefe courts, or the matters depending before them. Therefore, if thefe courts either refufe to allow thefe acts of parliament, or will expound them in any other fenfe than what the common law puts upon them, the king's court at Weftminfter will grant prohibitions to reftrain and controul them. 3. An appeal lies from all thefe courts to the king, in the laft refort; which proves that the jurifdiction exercifed in them is derived from the crown of England, and not from any foreign potentate, or intrinfic authority of their own.

WRITTEN LAWS. The written laws of the kingdom are ftatutes, acts, or edicts, made by the king's majefty, by and with the advice and confent of the lords fpiritual and temporal and commons in parliament affembled. The oldeft of thefe now extant, and printed in our ftatute books, is the famous *magna charta* as confirmed in parliament 9 Hen. III.: though doubtlefs there were many acts before that time, the records of which are now loft, and the determinations of them perhaps at prefent currently received for the maxims of the old common law.

The method of making thefe ftatutes has already been explained; they are either *general* or *fpecial*, *public* or *private*; the diftinction between which has already been ftated, vol. i. p. 271.

Statutes alfo are either *declaratory* of the common law, or *remedial* of fome of its defects. *Declaratory*, where the old cuftom of the kingdom is almoft fallen into difufe, or become difputable; in which cafe, the parliament has thought proper, *in perpetuum rei teftimonium*, and for avoiding all doubts and difficul-

difficulties, to declare what the common law is, and ever has been. *Remedial* ftatutes are thofe which are made to fupply fuch defects, and abridge fuch fuperfluities in the common law, as arife either from the general imperfection of all human laws, from change of time and circumftances, from the miftakes and unadvifed determinations of unlearned (or even learned) judges, or from any other caufe whatfoever. And this being done either by enlarging the common law, where it was too narrow and circumfcribed, or by reftraining it, where it was too lax and luxuriant, has occafioned another fubordinate divifion of remedial acts of parliament, into *enlarging* and *reftraining* ftatutes.

An *enlarging* or an *enabling* ftatute is one which increafes the power of action; thus the 32 Hen. VIII. c. 28. which gave bifhops, and all other fole ecclefiaftical corporations, except parfons and vicars, a power of making leafes, which they did not poffefs before, is always called an enabling ftatute. The 13 Eliz. c. 10. which afterward limited that power, is, on the contrary, ftyled a reftraining or difabling ftatute.

Courts. In order to put the laws in execution, the king is confidered as the fountain of juftice, the general confervator of the peace of this kingdom. He has alone the right of erecting courts of judicature; their jurifdictions are, either mediately, or immediately, derived from the crown, and their proceedings are generally in the king's name; they pafs under his feal, and are executed by his officers. It is probable, and almoft certain, that in very early times, before the conftitution arrived at its full perfection, the kings in perfon often heard and determined caufes; but now, by long and uniform ufage, they have delegated their whole judicial power to the judges of their feveral courts, whofe jurifdiction is fo well defined, and fo clearly eftablifhed, that the king can no longer refume his ancient authority, and cannot alter that of the judges without an act of parliament; and were he even to fit, perfonally, in the court of King's Bench, where by fiction of law, he is prefumed to be always prefent, juftice muft be adminiftered by the judges. Of thefe feveral courts, therefore, a brief defcription will be given, with a fummary account of the officers belonging to them, and the general limits of their jurifdiction.

A court is defined to be a place wherein juftice is judicially adminiftered. For the more fpeedy, univerfal, and impartial adminiftration of juftice, the law has appointed a prodigious variety of courts, fome with a more limited, others with a more extenfive jurifdiction; fome conftituted to inquire only, others to hear and determine; fome to determine in the firft inftance, others upon appeal, and by way of review. One diftinction, runs throughout them all; *viz.* that fome are *courts of record*, others

others *not of record*. A court of record is that where the acts and judicial proceedings are inrolled in parchment, for a perpetual memorial and testimony: which rolls are called the records of the court, aud are of such high and supereminent authority, that their truth is not to be called in question. But if there appear any mistake of the clerk in making up such record, the court will direct him to amend it. All courts of record are the king's courts, in right of his crown and regal dignity, and therefore no other court has authority to fine or imprison; so that the very erection of a new jurisdiction with power of fine or imprisonment, makes it instantly a court of record. A court not of record, is the court of a private man; whom the law will not intrust with any discretionary power over the fortune or liberty of his fellow subjects. Such are the courts-baron incident to every manor, and other inferior jurisdictions; where the proceedings are not inrolled or recorded; but as well their existence, as the truth of the matters therein contained, must, if disputed, be tried and determined by a jury. These courts can hold no plea of matters cognizable by the common law, unless under the value of forty shillings, nor of any forcible injury whatsoever, not having any process to arrest the person of the defendant.

Ecclesiastical Courts. In giving an account of the various courts established throughout the realm, for trial and regulation of all matters whatsoever, it is thought expedient to begin with those which are called ecclesiastical, or christian.

Their Origin. For the first three hundred years after Christ, the distinction of ecclesiastical or spiritual causes, in point of jurisdiction, did not begin; at that time no such distinction was heard of in the christian world; for the causes of testaments, matrimony, bastardy, adultery, and the rest, which are called ecclesiastical or spiritual causes, were merely civil, and determined by the rules of the civil law, and subject only to the jurisdiction of the civil magistrate. But after the emperors were become christian, out of a zeal and desire they had to grace and honour the learned and godly bishops of that time, they were pleased to single out certain special causes, wherein they granted jurisdiction to bishops; namely, in cases of tithes, because paid to men of the church; in causes of matrimony, because matrimony was for the most part solemnized in the church; in causes testamentary, because testaments were many times made *in extremis*, when churchmen were present, giving spiritual comfort to the testator, and therefore they were thought the fittest persons to take the probates of such testaments: and so of the rest. Yet these bishops did not then proceed in these causes, according to the canons and decrees of the church, (for the

the canon law was not then made) but according to the rules of the imperial law, and as the civil magiſtrate proceeded in other cauſes. Accordingly in this kingdom, in the Saxon times before the Norman conqueſt, there was no diſtinction of juriſdictions; but all matters, as well ſpiritual, as temporal, were determined in the county-court, called the ſheriff's tourn, where the biſhop and earl (or in his abſence the ſheriff) ſat together; or elſe in the hundred-court, which was held in like manner before the lord of the hundred and the eccleſiaſtical judge. In thoſe days the eccleſiaſtical officers took their limits of juriſdiction, from a like extent of the civil powers. Moſt of the old Saxon biſhopricks were of equal bounds with the diſtinct kingdoms: the archdeaconries, when firſt ſettled into local diſtricts, were commonly fitted to the reſpective counties; and rural deaneries, before the conqueſt, were correſpondent to the political tithings. Their ſpiritual courts were held, with a like reference to the adminiſtration of civil juſtice. The ſynods of each province and dioceſe were held at the diſcretion of the metropolitan and the biſhop, as great councils at the pleaſure of the prince. The viſitations were firſt united to the civil inquiſitions in each county; and afterwards, when the courts of the earl and biſhop were ſeparated, yet ſtill the viſitations were held like the ſheriff's tourns twice a year, and, like them too, after Eaſter and Michaelmas; and ſtill with nearer likeneſs, the greater of them was at Eaſter. The rural chapters were alſo held, like the inferior courts of the hundred, every three weeks; then, and like them too, they were changed into monthly, and at laſt into quarterly meetings. Nay, and a prime invitation was held commonly, like the prime folkmote, or ſheriff's tourn, on the very calends of May. The biſhop and the earl ſat together in one court, and heard jointly the cauſes of church and commonwealth, and, in all other matters, the eccleſiaſtical government bore an exact affinity with the temporal.

A plan ſo rational and moderate was wholly inconſiſtent with thoſe views of ambition, that were then forming by the court of Rome. It ſoon became an eſtabliſhed maxim in the papal ſyſtem of policy, that all eccleſiaſtical perſons, and all eccleſiaſtical cauſes, ſhould be ſolely and entirely ſubject to eccleſiaſtical juriſdiction, which juriſdiction was ſuppoſed to be lodged, in the firſt place and immediately in the pope, by divine and indefeaſible right and inveſtiture from Chriſt himſelf; and derived from the pope to all inferior tribunals. Hence the canon law lays it down as a rule, that *Sacerdotes a regibus honorandi ſunt, non judicandi*; and places an emphatical reliance on a fabulous tale which it tells of the emperor Conſtantine: that when ſome petitions were brought to him, imploring the aid of his authority

authority against certain of his bishops, accused of oppression and injustice, he caused the petitions to be burnt in their presence, dismissing them with this valediction; go, and discuss your own causes among yourselves; for it would be very unfit for us to sit in judgment on the Gods.

It was not, however, till after the Norman conquest, that this doctrine was received in England; when William I. (whose title was warmly espoused by the monasteries which he liberally endowed, and by the foreign clergy, whom he brought over in shoals from France and Italy, and planted in the best preferments of the English church) was prevailed on to establish this fatal incroachment, and separate the ecclesiastical court from the civil: whether he was actuated by principles of bigotry, or by those of a more refined policy, in order to discountenance the laws of Edward, abounding with the spirit of Saxon liberty, is not altogether certain. But the latter, if not the cause, was undoubtedly the consequence of this separation; for the Saxon laws were soon overborne by the Norman justiciaries, when the county court fell into disregard by the bishop's withdrawing his presence, in obedience to the charter of the Conqueror, which prohibited any spiritual cause from being tried in the secular courts, and commanded the suitors to appear before the bishop only, whose decisions were directed to conform to the canon law. These courts, when once established, usurped considerable powers, and the priesthood long, but ineffectually, contended not merely for the exercise of the civil and canon law, but for its advancement above, or rather substitution instead of, the common law. At present, however, the authority of these courts is restrained within very narrow bounds, they are not courts of record, but evidence must be given of their sentences; they can neither fine, imprison, nor amerce; and their sole power of punishment lies in penance, which may be commuted or dispensed with for money, and in costs.

Their jurisdiction being derived from the crown of England, the last devolution is to the king, by way of appeal. Although the canon or civil law is allowed as the direction or rule of proceedings; yet that is not as if either of those laws had any original obligation in England, either as they are the laws of emperors, popes, or general councils, but only by virtue of their admission here; which is evident, for that those canons, or imperial constitutions which have not been received here do not bind; and also, for that by several contrary customs and usages in this realm, many of those civil and canon laws were restrained and controlled. Although those laws are admitted in some cases in the ecclesiastical court, yet they are but *leges sub graviori lege*;

lege; and the common laws of this kingdom have ever obtained and retained the ſuperintendency over them.

The cauſes belonging to eccleſiaſtical courts are, blaſphemy, apoſtacy from chriſtianity, hereſy, and ſchiſm, (but of theſe two, they have not been permitted to take cognizance for many years), ordinations, inſtitution of clerks to benefices, celebration of divine ſervice, rights of matrimony, divorces, general baſtardy, tythes, oblations, obventions, mortuaries, dilapidations, reparation of churches, probate of wills, adminiſtration, ſimony, inceſt, fornication, adulteries, ſolicitations of chaſtity, penſions, procurations, &c. the cognizance whereof belongs not to the common law of England.

In the enumeration of the eccleſiaſtical courts it is judged convenient to begin with the loweſt, and proceed to the higheſt, noticing ſome of thoſe which are aboliſhed or diſuſed.

The Archdeacon's Court. This court is holden by the archdeacon, in places where, either by preſcription, or compoſition, he has juriſdiction in ſpiritual cauſes within his archdeaconry; he is called *oculus epiſcopi*, and exerciſes an eccleſiaſtical juriſdiction, either concurrently with the biſhop, or excluſively. In the archdeacon's abſence, the court is held before a judge appointed by himſelf, and called his *official*. From hence however, by ſtatute 24 Hen. VIII. c. 12. an appeal lies to the court of the biſhop.

The Consistory Court. The conſiſtory is the court chriſtian, or ſpiritual court, held formerly in the nave of the cathedral church, or in ſome chapel, iſle, or portico belonging to it; in which the biſhop preſided, and had ſome of his clergy for aſſeſſors and aſſiſtants; but this court is now held by the biſhop's chancellor or commiſſary, and by archdeacons or their officials, either in the cathedral church or other convenient place of the dioceſe, for the hearing and determining of matters and cauſes of eccleſiaſtical cognizance, happening within that dioceſe. From the conſiſtory, the appeal is to the archbiſhop of the province.

The Court of Arches. This is a court of appeal belonging to the archbiſhop of Canterbury; whereof the judge is called the *dean of the arches*; becauſe he anciently held his court in the church of Saint Mary le Bow, (*Sancta Maria de arcubus*). This court is very ancient, and ſubſiſted long before the time of king Henry II.; for Alexander III. then pope, did, by his edict, abrogate the then ancient ſtatutes of this court, and ſet up others in their ſtead; and it was there ſaid, that thoſe ancient ſtatutes were then, by length of time, become not legible. The proper juriſdiction of the dean is only over the thirteen peculiar

peculiar parifhes belonging to the archbifhop in London; but the office of dean of the arches, having been for a long time united with that of the archbifhop's principal official, he now, in right of the laft mentioned office, (as does alfo the official principal of the archbifhop of York,) receives and determines appeals from the fentences of all inferior ecclefiaftical courts within the province. And from him, by ftat. 25 Hen. VIII. c. 19, an appeal lies to the king in chancery, (that is, to a court of delegates appointed under the king's great feal) he being fupreme head of the Englifh church, inftead of the bifhop of Rome, who formerly exercifed this jurifdiction.

This court (as alfo the court of peculiars, the admiralty court, the prerogative court, and the court of delegates for the moft part) is now held in the hall belonging to the college of civilians, commonly called Doctors' Commons.

Officers. Befides the judge, there belong to the court of arches, an *Actuary*, whofe duty is to attend the court, fet down the judge's degrees, regifter the acts of the court, and fend them in books to the regiftry; a *Regifter*, who is, by himfelf or deputy, to attend the court, receive all libels or bills, allegations, and exhibits of witneffes, file all fentences, and keep the records of the court; and a *Beadle*, who attends the court, carries a mace before the judge, and calls the perfon cited to appear. Thefe, and all other offices belonging to the court, are in the gift of the archbifhop of Canterbury.

Practice. All procefs is iffued in the name of the judge, and was formerly returnable before him at Bow church, but now in the common hall at Doctors' Commons. The perfons practifing are in this, as in the other courts at Doctors' Commons, doctors of the civil law, and proctors, of whom fome account will be given in a fubfequent page.

The Court of Peculiars. Peculiars are exempt jurifdictions, fo called, not becaufe they are under no ordinary, but becaufe they are not under the ordinary of the diocefe, but have one of their own. They are of feveral forts; as *royal peculiars*; which are the king's free chapels, and are exempt from any jurifdiction but the king's, and therefore fuch may be refigned into the king's hands as their proper ordinary, either by ancient privilege or inherent right. *Peculiars of the archbifhops*, exclufive of the bifhops and archdeacons; which fprung from a privilege they had, to enjoy jurifdiction in fuch places where their feats and poffeffions were. *Peculiars of bifhops*, exclufive of the jurifdiction of the bifhop of the diocefe, in which they are fituated; *peculiars of bifhops in their own diocefe*, exclufive of archidiaconal jurifdiction. *Peculiars of deans, deans and chapters, prebendaries*, and the like; which are places wherein, by by ancient compositions, the bishops have parted with their jurisdiction as ordinaries to those societies. There are also peculiars belonging to monasteries, but the statute 31 Hen. VIII. c. 13. placed them within the jurisdiction and visitation of the ordinary, within whose diocese they are situate, or within the jurisdiction and visitation of such persons, as the king should limit and appoint.

As the persons, entitled to peculiar jurisdiction, have no known or certain registers, or public place to keep their records in, and wills are therefore liable to be lost; they are ordered by canon 126, once in every year, upon pain of being suspended from the exercise of their jurisdiction, to exhibit into the public registry of the bishop of the diocese, or of the dean and chapter, under whose jurisdiction the peculiars are, every original testament of every person in that time deceased, and by them proved, or a true copy of every such testament, examined, subscribed, and sealed by the peculiar judge and his notary.

The court of peculiars is a branch of, and annexed to, the court of arches. It has a jurisdiction over all those parishes dispersed through the province of Canterbury in the midst of other dioceses, which are exempt from the ordinary jurisdiction, and subject to the metropolitan only. These are seventy-five in number. All ecclesiastical causes, arising within these peculiar or exempt jurisdictions, are, originally, cognizable by this court; from which an appeal lay formerly to the pope, but now by the statute 25 Hen. VIII. c. 19. to the king in chancery.

The Prerogative Court. The prerogative court is established for the trial of all testamentary causes, where the deceased has left *bona notabilia* within different dioceses; in which case the probate of wills belongs to the archbishop of the province, by way of special prerogative. All causes relating to the wills, administrations, or legacies of such persons, are originally cognizable here, before a judge appointed by the archbishop, called the judge of the prerogative court; from whom an appeal lies, by statute 25 Hen. VIII. c. 19. to the king in chancery, instead of the pope as formerly. If the party dying has property only in one diocese, his will may be proved, or letters of administration may be taken in the court of the bishop of that diocese; but the probate of every bishop's testament, or granting of administration of his goods, although he has not goods but within his own jurisdiction, belongs to the archbishop.

The Court of Delegates. This is a great court of appeal erected by virtue of the king's commission, which issues out of chancery upon an appeal or petition directed to him, complaining

plaining of ſome grievance or injury the party has ſuffered by the ſentence or proceedings of the eccleſiaſtical court. Such a commiſſion may be granted at the inſtance of a perſon intereſted, though not an original party in the cauſe. The grounds of petition are: 1. When a ſentence is given in any eccleſiaſtical cauſe by the archbiſhop or his official. 2. When any ſentence is given in any eccleſiaſtical cauſe in places exempt. 3. When a ſentence is given in the admiral's court in ſuits civil and marine, by the order of the civil law. The commiſſioners are uſually ſome of the lords ſpiritual and temporal, or both, and commonly one or more of the twelve judges, and one or more doctors of the civil law. They are commonly called *delegates* (according to the language of the civil and canon law), on account of the ſpecial commiſſion or delegation they receive from the king, for the hearing and determining every particular cauſe; and accordingly their proceedings conform to the rules of the civil and the eccleſiaſtical laws; and on that account it has been particularly adjudged, that a ſuit there does not abate by the death of the parties: ſuch being the courſe in the eccleſiaſtical courts; alſo prohibitions go to them, as to an eccleſiaſtical court.

The Court of Commission of Review. A commiſſion of *review* is ſometimes granted, in extraordinary caſes, to reviſe the ſentence of the court of delegates, when it is apprehended they have been led into a material error. This commiſſion the king may grant, although the ſtatutes 24 and 25 Hen. VIII. declare the ſentence of the delegates definitive: becauſe the pope, as ſupreme head by the canon law, uſed to grant ſuch commiſſions of review; and ſuch authority as the pope heretofore exerted, is now annexed to the crown by ſtatutes 26 Hen. VIII. c. 1. and 1 Eliz. c. 1. But it is not matter of right, which the ſubject may demand *ex debito juſticiæ*; but merely a matter of favour, and which therefore is often denied.

The High Commission Court. At a leſs happy period of the conſtitution than the preſent, exiſted a moſt formidable juriſdiction, but now deſervedly annihilated, *viz.* the court of the king's *high commiſſion* in cauſes eccleſiaſtical. This court was erected and united to the regal power by virtue of the ſtatute 1 Eliz. c. 1. inſtead of a larger juriſdiction, which had before been exerciſed under the pope's authority. It was intended to vindicate the dignity and peace of the church, by reforming, ordering, and correcting the eccleſiaſtical ſtate and perſons, and all manner of errors, hereſies, ſchiſms, abuſes, offences, contempts, and enormities. Under the ſhelter of theſe very general words, means were found in that and the two ſucceeding reigns, to veſt in the high commiſſioners extraordinary

and

and almost despotic powers of fining and imprisoning; which they exerted much beyond the degree of the offence itself, and frequently over offences by no means of spiritual cognizance. For these reasons this court was justly abolished by statute 16 Car. I. c. 2.; and the weak and illegal attempt that was made to revive it, during the reign of James II. served only to hasten that infatuated prince's ruin.

The Convocation. The high commission court has been expressly abolished by act of parliament, while the convocation, although not formally abrogated, has, by long intermission, fallen so completely into disuse, and even into oblivion, that no attempt to revive it is now to be expected. The convocation is of two kinds; the one a general assembly of the clergy in every diocese, by order and under sanction of the bishop, to consider of spiritual affairs locally interesting them; the other an assembly held in each province, under the superintendance of the archbishops. The former is considered equally ancient with the establishment of christianity in Britain, the latter arising out of more recent policy, but yet of very high antiquity, and generally exclusively considered when the term convocation is used. This convocation is commonly called a national synod, convened by the king's writ, directed to the archbishops of Canterbury and York, requiring them to summon every bishop, dean, and archdeacon, a proctor for the chapter, and two proctors for the clergy of each diocese in the province of Canterbury; but in York, two proctors for each archdeaconry; otherwise the number would be so small, as scarcely to deserve the name of a provincial synod. By these means the parochial clergy have as great an interest in convocation there, as the cathedral clergy, whereas in the province of Canterbury, the lower house of convocation consists of twenty-two deans, including Westminster and Windsor, twenty-four proctors of the chapters, and fifty-three archdeacons, in the whole, ninety-nine of the cathedral clergy; and there are, at the same time, only forty-four proctors for the parochial clergy. Anciently the lower clergy sat in the same house with the bishops; and in the province of York, the bishops and other clergy still sit in the same house; but in the province of Canterbury, they consist of two houses; the upper being composed of the archbishop and bishops; and the lower of the rest of the clergy. And as there are two houses of convocation, so there are two prolocutors; one of the bishops of the higher house, chosen by that house; another of the lower house, and presented to the bishops for their prolocutor. Their jurisdiction is in matters of heresy, schisms, and other mere spiritual and ecclesiastical causes, but they cannot meddle with any matters relating to the laws of the

the land, or the king's crown or dignity; and in thoſe in which they have a juriſdiction, they are to proceed *juxta legem divinam et canones ſanctæ eccleſiæ*. Such was always the law with reſpect to the convocation; but in conſequence of the incroachments of the popiſh religion, it was found neceſſary to declare by ſtatute 25 Hen. VIII. c. 19. that no canon, conſtitution, or ordinance, ſhould be made or put in execution within this realm, by authority of convocation of the clergy, which were contrariant or repugnant to the king's prerogative royal, or the cuſtoms, laws, or ſtatutes of this realm. In the making of new canons, the convocation was to have the king's licence, and his aſſent for carrying them into execution; but the old canons, if not repugnant to law, or to the king's prerogative, were allowed to continue in force.

Privilege. The clerks of the convocation, their ſervants and families, had ſuch privilege in coming, tarrying, and going, as the commons called to parliament.

The Court of Audience. The archbiſhop of Canterbury had formerly his court of audience; in which at firſt were diſpatched all ſuch matters, whether of voluntary or contentious juriſdiction, as the archbiſhop thought fit to reſerve for his own hearing. They who prepared evidence, and other materials to lay before the archbiſhop, in order to his deciſions, were called auditors. Afterwards this court was removed from the archbiſhop's palace, and the juriſdiction of it was exerciſed by the maſter official of the audience, who held his court in the conſiſtory place of St. Paul's. But now the three great offices of official principal of the archbiſhop, dean, or judge of the peculiars, and official of the audience, are, and have been for a long time paſt, united in one perſon, under the general name of dean of the arches; who keeps his court in the hall of Doctors' Commons. The archbiſhop of York has, in like manner, his court of audience.

The Faculty Court. The Faculty court belongs to the archbiſhop of Canterbury; and his officer is called maſter of the faculties. His power is, to grant diſpenſations, as to marry, to eat fleſh on days prohibited, to hold two or more benefices incompatible, and ſuch like.

Jurisdiction. In all theſe courts, the juriſdiction which was or is exerciſed, is called *contentious* or *voluntary*; but ſome of the courts uſe both.

Voluntary juriſdiction is exerciſed in matters which require no judicial proceeding, as in granting probates of wills, letters of adminiſtration, ſequeſtration of vacant benefices, inſtitution, and ſuch like. *Contentious* juriſdiction is, where there is an action or judicial procefs, and confifts in the hearing and determining of caufes between party and party.

Officers. The principal officers, and others exercifing authority or tranfacting bufinefs in thefe courts, are as follows.

Archdeacons. Of thefe an account is given in Vol. I. page 352.

Chancellor, Official-Principal, Vicar-General, Commissary, and Official. The proper office of a chancellor as fuch, was, to be keeper of the feals of the archbifhop or bifhop. This office, as it is now underftood, includes in it two others, which are diftinguifhed in the commiffion by the titles of *official-principal* and *vicar-general*. The proper duty of an *official* is, to hear caufes between party and party, concerning wills, legacies, mariages, and the like, which are matters of temporal cognizance, but have been granted to the ecclefiaftical courts by the conceffions of princes. The proper tafk of a *vicar-general* is, the exercife and adminiftration of jurifdiction purely fpiritual, by the authority and under the direction of the bifhop, as vifitation, correction of manners, granting inftitutions, and the like, with a general infpection of men and things, in order to the preferving of difcipline and good government in the church. *Commiffary* is he that is limited by the bifhop to fome certain place of the diocefe, to affift him; and in moft cafes has the authority of official-principal and vicar-general within his limits. The chancellor is not confined to any place of the diocefe, nor limited to certain caufes of jurifdiction; but every where throughout the whole diocefe he fupplies the bifhop's abfence, in all matters and caufes ecclefiaftical; but the authority of commiffaries, as it is confined to certain places of the diocefe, is alfo reftrained to certain caufes of jurifdiction, limited to them by the bifhops: for which reafon the law calls them *officiales foranei*, as reftrained *cuidam foro* only of the diocefe. And what is faid of commiffaries may alfo be applied to the *officials* of fuch archdeacons as have a concurrent jurifdiction with the bifhop.

Surrogate. The Surrogate is the deputy to the ecclefiaftical judge, and concerning fuch deputies the canons have eftablifhed the following principles. No chancellor, commiffary, archdeacon, official, or any other perfon ufing ecclefiaftical jurifdiction, fhall fubftitute, in their abfence, any to keep court for them, except he be either a grave minifter and a graduate, or a licenfed public preacher, and a beneficed man near the place where the courts are kept, or a bachelor of law, or a mafter of arts at leaft, who has fome fkill in the civil and ecclefiaftical law, and is a favourer of true religion, and a man of modeft modeſt and honeſt converſation; under pain of ſuſpenſion, for every time that they offend therein, from the execution of their offices for the ſpace of three months *toties quoties:* and he likewiſe that is deputed, being not qualified as is before expreſſed, and yet ſhall preſume to be a ſubſtitute to any judge, and ſhall keep any court as aforeſaid, ſhall undergo the ſame cenſure. And by the ſtatute 26th Geo. II. c. 33. no ſurrogate deputy of any eccleſiaſtical judge, who has power to grant licences of marriage, ſhall grant any ſuch licence, before he has taken an oath before the ſaid judge, faithfully to execute his office according to law, to the beſt of his knowledge; and has given ſecurity by his bond in the ſum of 100*l.* to the biſhop of his dioceſe, for the due and faithful execution of his office.

Advocate. None are allowed to be advocates and plead in theſe courts, but doctors of the civil law in one of the univerſities of England; who, upon their petition to the archbiſhop of Canterbury, and his fiat obtained, are admitted by the judge of the court, upon condition not to practiſe for one whole year after ſuch admittance. The manner of their admittance is this: The two ſenior advocates, in their ſcarlet robes, with the mace before them, conduct the new advocate up to the court, with three low reverences, and preſent him with a ſhort Latin ſpeech, and the reſcript of the archbiſhop; then the oaths of allegiance, ſupremacy, and ſome other preſcribed in the ſtatute of arches, being taken, he is admitted by the judges, and a place and ſeat in the court aſſigned to him, either *à dextris*, or *ſiniſtris*, which he is always to keep when he pleads. The judge, and all the advocates in this court, always wear their ſcarlet robes, with hoods lined with taffety, if they are of Oxford, or white miniver fur, if of Cambridge, and round black velvet caps; and the proctors wear, or ought to wear, hoods lined with lambs-ſkin, if not graduates; but if graduates, hoods proper to their degree. For the furtherance and increaſe of learning, and the advancement of civil and canon law, it is ordained, that no proctor, exerciſing in any of the archbiſhop's courts, ſhall entertain any cauſe whatſoever, and keep and retain the ſame for two court days, without the counſel and advice of an advocate, under pain of a year's ſuſpenſion from his practice: neither ſhall the judge have power to releaſe or mitigate the ſaid penalty without expreſs mandate and authority from the archbiſhop. No judge in any of theſe courts may admit any libel or any other matter, without the advice of an advocate admitted to practiſe in the court, or without his ſubſcription; neither can any proctor conclude any cauſe depending, without the knowledge of the advocate retained and feed in the cauſe: which if any proctor does, or procures to be done, or if, by any colour whatsoever, he defrauds the advocate of his duty or fee, or is negligent in repairing to the advocate, and requiring his advice what course is to be taken in the cause; he is to be irrevocably suspended from all practice for the space of six months.

REGISTER. The general duty of the register has already been mentioned in treating of the court of arches. No chancellor, commissary, archdeacon, official, or any other person using ecclesiastical jurisdiction, can speed any judicial act, either of contentious or voluntary jurisdiction, except he is the ordinary register of that court, or his lawful deputy; or if he or they will not or cannot be present, then it is to be done by such persons as by law are allowed in that behalf to write or expedite the same, under pain of suspension *ipso facto*. If any register, or his deputy or substitute, receives any certificate without the knowledge and consent of the judge of the court; or willingly omits to cause any person cited to appear upon any court day to be called; or unduly puts off and defers the examination of witnesses to be examined by a day set and assigned by the judge; or does not obey and observe the judicial and lawful monition of the said judge; or omits to write or cause to be written such citations and decrees as are to be put in execution and set forth before the next court day; or does not cause all testaments exhibited into his office to be registered within a convenient time; or sets down or enacts, as decreed by the judge, any thing false or conceited by himself, not so ordered or decreed by the judge; or if, in the transmission of processes to the judge *ad quem*, he adds or inserts any falsehood or untruth, or omits any thing, either by cunning or by gross negligence; or in causes of instance, or promoted of office, receives any reward in favour of either party; or is of counsel directly or indirectly with either of the parties in suit, or in the execution of their office; or does aught else maliciously, or fraudulently, whereby the ecclesiastical judge or his proceedings may be slandered or defamed: the said register, or his deputy or substitute, offending in all or any of the premises, is by the bishop of the diocese to be suspended from the exercise of his office for the space of one, two, or three months or more, according to the quality of his offence; and the said bishop may assign some other public notary to execute and discharge all things pertaining to his office, during the time of his suspension.

NOTARY PUBLIC. A notary was anciently a scribe, that only took notes or minutes, and made short drafts of writings and other instruments, both public and private; but at this day, he he is called a notary public, who confirms and attests the truth of any deeds or writings, in order to render the same authentic. The law books give to a notary several names or appellations; as, *actuarius, registrarius, scriniarius,* and such like, all which words are put to signify one and the same person; but in England, the word *registrarius* is confined to the officer of some court, who has the custody of the records and archives, and is oftentimes distinguished from the *actuary* thereof; but a register ought always to be a notary public; for that seems to be a necessary qualification of his office. A notary public is appointed to his office by the archbishop of Canterbury; who in the instrument of appointment decrees, that "full faith be given, as well in as out of judgment, to "the instruments by him to be made;" which appointment is also to be registered and subscribed by the clerk of his majesty for faculties in chancery. A notary on his appointment must swear "that he will faithfully exercise the office of notary public; that he will faithfully make contracts, wherein the consent of parties is required, by adding or diminishing nothing, without the will of the parties, that may alter the substance of the fact; that if in making any instrument the will of one party only is required, he will in such case add or diminish nothing that may alter the substance of the fact, against the will of such party; that he will not make instruments of any contract, in which he shall know there is a violence or fraud; that he will reduce contracts into an instrument or register; and after he shall have so reduced the same, that he will not maliciously delay to make a public instrument thereupon, against the will of him or them, on whose behalf such contract is to be so drawn: saving to himself his just and accustomed fees. The business of a notary is however extended beyond the limits of the ecclesiastical courts to many mercantile and public transactions; and as the frequency of these, and the allurement of fees easily to be obtained, induced many to get themselves admitted who had neither knowledge nor experience to recommend them, the legislature has found it necessary to enact, that in future no one shall be admitted a notary who has not served to some other notary a clerkship under articles for five years; and to make every one who practises take out an annual licence on a stamp of ten pounds.

Proctor. Proctors are officers established to represent in judgment the parties who empower them, by warrant under their hands called a *proxy,* to appear for them, to explain their rights, to manage and instruct their cause, and to demand judgment. No proctor in any court can be a justice of the peace, during such time as he continues in practice; and during

during that time he also takes out an annual licence of ten pounds.

Apparitor. Apparitors, so called from that principal branch in their office which consists in summoning persons to appear, are appointed to execute the proper orders and decrees of the court, and are chosen by the ecclesiastical judges respectively, who may suspend them for misbehaviour, but may not remove them at discretion, as most of them hold their offices by patent. The proper business and employment of an apparitor is, to attend in court; to receive the commands issued by the judge; to convene and cite the defendants into court; to admonish or cite the parties in the production of witnesses and the like; and to make due return of the process by him executed. The process of courts is not to be sent by those who obtain them, nor by their messenger; but the judge is to send it by his own faithful messenger, at the moderate expence of the person suing it out; or at least the citation must be directed to the dean of the deanery where the party to be cited dwells, who, at the judge's command, must faithfully execute the same by himself, or his certain and trusty messenger.

Doctors Commons. Doctors' Commons is the college of civilians in London, which was purchased by Dr. Harvey, dean of the arches, for the professors of the civil law. It is situated in the parish of Saint Benedict, Paul's-wharf, London, the principal entrance being to the south-west of Saint Paul's Cathedral. It appears, that the fee simple was not obtained till the year 1783, when the dean and chapter of Saint Paul's, to whom the site originally belonged, vested the freehold in the doctors, in consideration of 105*l.* per annum, clear of all taxes. Here commonly reside the judge of the arches court of Canterbury, the judge of the admiralty, and the judge of the prerogative court of Canterbury, with divers other eminent civilians; who there living in a collegiate manner, and commoning together, it is known by the name of Doctors' Commons. It was burnt down in the fire of London, and rebuilt at the charge of the profession.

Courts Military. No court of this kind is permanent, except

The Court of Chivalry; of which an account is given, Vol. I. page 492.

Maritime Courts. Maritime courts are such as have the power and jurisdiction to determine all maritime injuries, arising upon the seas, or in parts out of the reach of the common law; they are only the court of admiralty and its courts of appeal.

The Court of Admiralty. This court takes cognizance

zance of all maritime causes or matters arising upon the high sea; and its jurisdiction is derived from the king, who protects his subjects from piracy and all other injuries, and who has a dominion over all the British seas; this jurisdiction he exercises by the lord-high-admiral, or those lawfully deputed for that purpose. The jurisdiction of the admiralty is two-fold, and holden before distinct tribunals: the one is the ordinary court for deciding controversies relating to contracts made at sea, and is called the *instance court*; the other determines the right to maritime captures and seizures, and is called the *prize court*. The jurisdiction in both is exercised by the same person, who is appointed judge of the admiralty, by a commission under the great seal, which enumerates particularly, as well as generally, every object of his jurisdiction, but makes no mention of prize. To constitute that authority, or to call it forth, in every war, a commission, under the great seal, issues to the lord high admiral, to will and require and authorise the court of admiralty, and the lieutenant and judge of the said court, his surrogate or surrogates, to proceed upon all manner of captures, seizures, prizes, and reprisals of ships and goods, that are or shall be taken; and to hear and determine, according to the course of the admiralty, and the law of nations; and a warrant issues to the judge accordingly.

Jurisdiction. It is laid down as a general rule, in the common law books, that the admiral's jurisdiction is confined to matters arising on the high seas only, and that he cannot take cognizance of contracts, &c. made or done in any river, haven, or creek, within any county; and that all matters arising within these are triable by the common law. But it has been resolved, that between the high and low water mark the common law and admiralty have a divided authority; that is to say, the one when it is not, and the other when it is, covered with water; and that the soil, upon which the sea flows and reflows, may be parcel of a manor. The admiralty court has jurisdiction, where a ship founders or is split at sea, over the goods which become *flotsam, jetsam,* or *ligan*; and a suit for these must be in that court; but goods wrecked must be claimed by action at common law. But it has no jurisdiction as to contracts made at land, whether such contracts be made here or in foreign parts. Mariners may sue in the admiralty court for their wages, although the hiring was by the master on land; and this is allowed of in favour of navigation, for here they may all join in the same libel; also, by the admiralty law they have remedy against the ship and owners, as well as against the master; and it would be a great discourage-

ment

ment to ſeafaring men, to oblige them to bring ſeparate actions, and thoſe againſt a maſter, who may happen to be inſolvent.

PROCEEDINGS. All maritime affairs are regulated chiefly by the civil law, the *Rhodian* laws, the laws of *Oleron*, or by certain peculiar municipal laws and conſtitutions appropriated to certain cities, towns and counties bordering on the ſea. As the proceedings in the admiralty are, according to the method of the civil law, like thoſe of the eccleſiaſtical courts, it is uſually held at the ſame place with the ſuperior eccleſiaſtical courts, at Doctors' Commons in London. It is no court of record, any more than the ſpiritual courts.

APPEALS. From the ſentences of the admiralty judge an appeal always lay, in ordinary courſe, to the king in chancery, as may be collected from the ſtatute 25 Hen. VIII. c. 19. which directs the appeal from the archbiſhop's courts to be determined by perſons named in the king's commiſſion, "like "as in caſe of appeal from the admiral court." This is alſo expreſsly declared, by ſtatute 8 Eliz. c. 5. which enacts, that upon appeal made to chancery, the ſentence definitive of the delegates appointed by commiſſion ſhall be final. Appeals from the vice-admiralty courts in America, and our other plantations and ſettlements, may be brought before the courts of admiralty in England, as being a branch of the admiral's juriſdiction, though they may alſo be brought before the king in council; but in caſe of prize veſſels, taken in time of war, in any part of the world, and condemned in any courts of admiralty or vice-admiralty as lawful prize, the appeal lies to certain commiſſioners of appeals, conſiſting chiefly of members of the privy council, and not to judges delegates. And this by virtue of divers treaties with foreign nations, by which particular courts are eſtabliſhed in all the maritime countries of Europe for the deciſion of the queſtion, whether lawful prize or not: for this being a queſtion between ſubjects of different ſtates, it belongs entirely to the law of nations, and not to the municipal laws of either country, to determine it. The original court, to which this queſtion is ſubmitted in England, is the court of admiralty; and the court of appeal is in effect the king's privy council, the members of which are, in conſequence of treaties, commiſſioned under the great ſeal for this purpoſe.

OFFICERS. In the admiralty court is a judge, whoſe ſalary is 2500*l.* a-year. There are alſo a *king's advocate-general*, and an *advocate-general for the admiralty*; a *ſolicitor* to the admiralty and navy; a *king's proctor*, and an *admiralty proctor*. To the court belong a *regiſter* with *deputies*, a *marſhal* and *deputy*. There is alſo a *judge-advocate* of the fleet, who has

has ten shillings per day, and his *deputy* eight shillings. At Halifax, a judge of the vice-admiralty court is established, with an annual salary of 2000*l*.

Courts of Special Jurisdiction. The courts already mentioned, although not courts of record, are considered as of general jurisdiction, tending to redress all possible injuries, so far as their powers extend; but there are other courts, which it will be fit to mention before the highest are treated of, whose jurisdiction is private and special, confined to particular spots, or instituted only to redress particular injuries. These courts are numerous, and divided into several branches, each having a certain portion of dignity or utility, and of each it will be necessary to give some account.

Forest Courts. A forest is described to be a certain territory of woody grounds, and fruitful pastures, privileged for wild beasts and fowls of forest, chase, and warren, to arrest and abide there in the safe protection of the king, for his delight and pleasure, which territory of ground so privileged, is meted and bounded with unremoveable marks, meets, and boundaries, either known by matter of record, or by prescription, and also replenished with wild beasts of venary or chase, and with great coverts of vert for the succour of the said beasts there to abide; for the preservation and continuance of which place, together with the vert and venison, there are particular officers, laws, and privileges belonging to the same, requisite for that purpose, and proper only to a forest, and to no other place. Before the statute of *charta de foresta*, the king used to convert the open and woody grounds of his subjects into forests; but though at this day he may make a forest, yet he cannot afforest any of his subjects' land. All the forests which were made after the conquest, except New Forest in Hampshire, created by William the Conqueror, were disafforested by the *charta de foresta*. The forest of Hampton Court was established by the authority of parliament in the reign of Henry VIII. The courts of the forest are those of attachments or woodmote; of regards, of swainmote, and of justice seat.

Court of Attachments. The court of *attachments, woodmote*, or *forty-days* court, is to be held before the verderors of the forest once in every forty days; and is instituted to inquire into all offenders against vert and venison; who may be attached by their bodies, if taken with the mainour, (or *mainœuvre, a manu;*) that is in the very act of killing venison or stealing wood, or preparing so to do, or by fresh and immediate pursuit after the act is done; else they must be attached by their goods. In this forty days court, the foresters or keepers are to bring in their attachments, or presentments *de viridi et venatione*; and the verderors are to receive the same, and to enrol and certify them

them under the seals to the court of justice seat, or swainmote: for this court can only inquire of, but not convict offenders.

Court of Regards. The court of *regard*, or survey of dogs, is to be holden every third year, for the lawing or expeditation of mastiffs, which is done by the cutting off the claws and ball (or pelote) of the fore-feet, to prevent them from running after deer. No other dogs but mastiffs are to be thus lawed or expeditated, for none other were permitted to be kept within the precincts of the forest; it being supposed that the keeping of these, and these only, was necessary for the defence of a man's house.

Court of Swainmote. The Swainmote is holden before the verderors as judges by the steward of the swainmote, thrice in every year, the swains or freeholders within the forest composing the jury. The principal jurisdiction of this court is, first, to inquire into the oppressions and grievances committed by the officers of the forest; *de superoneratione forestariorum, et aliorum ministeriorum forestæ: et de eorum oppressionibus populo regis illatis*. And, secondly, to receive and try presentments certified from the court of attachments, against offences in vert and venison. This court may not only inquire, but also convict, which conviction must be certified to the court of justice seat under the seals of the jury; for this court cannot proceed to judgment.

Court of Justice Seat. This court is so incident to a forest, that there cannot be a forest without it, but it cannot be holden oftener than every third year. It must be summoned at least forty days before sitting, and one writ of summons must be directed to the sheriff of the county in which the forest is situate, the other to the keeper of the forest or his deputy, to convoke all officers, &c. and all persons that claim liberties within the forest, to shew how they claim them. This court may inquire, hear, and determine all trespasses within the forest, according to the law of the forest, and all claims of franchises, &c. within the forest. The proceedings are *de hora in horam*, and therefore the defendant must plead to an indictment instantly. A felony committed within the forest must be inquired of and tried before the judges of the common law, for it belongs not to the cognizance of the chief justice of the forest.

Officers. To these courts there belong several officers, of which the principal are as follow:

Justices in Eyre. In mentioning the justices in eyre of the forest, it is necessary to premise that in ancient times there were other officers who bore that title. They were said to be constituted by the parliament of Northampton, in the twenty-second year of Henry II. in 1176, but it is rather considered that they had been previously established, and only then had new circuits

circuits appointed. They were invested with a delegated power from the king's great court, or *aula regia*, being looked upon as members thereof: and they afterwards made their circuit round the kingdom once in seven years, for the purpose of trying causes. They were afterwards directed by *magna charta*, c. 12. to be sent into every county once a year, to take (or receive the verdict of the jurors or recognitors in certain actions, then called) recognitions or assizes; the most difficult of which they are directed to adjourn into the court of common pleas, to be there determined. These itinerant justices were sometimes mere justices of the assize, or of dower, or of gaol delivery, and the like; and they had sometimes a more general commission, to determine all manner of causes, being constituted *justiciarii ad omnia placita*. They were constituted, at first, by writ in the nature of a commission, but afterward in pursuance of a statute, 27 Henry VIII. c. 24. by letters patent under the great seal; their authority was at one period very transcendant, but they are now superseded by the justices of assize.

The justices in eyre of the forest still continue according to the original institution. They are appointed by the king's commission, one to exercise his authority south, the other north of the Trent. The places are considered as sinecures; the salary of the chief justice south of the Trent is 3466*l.* 13*s.* 4*d.* and the chief justice north of Trent has 2450*l.*

Verderor. In every forest there are usually four verderors, so named *a viridi*, or *vert*. The verderor is a judicial officer of the forest, chosen by force of the king's writ in full county, and sworn to maintain the laws of the forest, and to view, receive, and enrol the attachments, and presentments of all trespasses within the forest, of vert and venison.

Regarder. The regarder or ranger, is a ministerial officer of the forest, sworn to make regard there as usual, to view and inquire of all offences within the forest in *vert* or venison, and of concealments, or defaults of the foresters, or other officers of the forest. And he is made by the king's patent, or by the chief justice in eyre, or upon a writ to the sheriff to make a regard of the forest; he is also chosen in the county court.

Forester. The forester is an officer sworn to preserve the vert and venison within his walk, to guard the vert and venison there, not to conceal but to attach all offenders, and to present the offences and attachments at the next court of attachments, or swainmote; to ride with the king, and conduct him in his hunting; and to take care of the lawing of the dogs. The forester may arrest any man who kills or chases any deer within the forest, if he be taken with the mainour within the forest, or be indicted before the swainmote, and may detain him till he

6 find

find pledges to appear before the justice in eyre; but if he offer sufficient pledges, he ought not to be imprisoned.

WOODWARD. A subject, who has land within a forest, according to usage, ought to have a woodward; and if he does not appear at the justice seat, the wood may be seized into the king's hands, till he make fine, and replevy it; and if he do not replevy it within a year, it shall remain in the king's hands for ever. If wood, part of the king's demesne within a forest, be demised to another for years, the lessee must find a woodward; and if he does not appear, the wood and office may be seized. And after seizure, no claim of the owner can be heard till he replevy the woods.

AGISTOR. The agistor is an officer whose duty is to present trespasses made by beasts in the forest.

If all these officers continue to be appointed, it must be observed that their employments are become of little consideration in the eye of the law. The last court of justice-seat of any note, was that holden in the reign of Charles I. before the earl of Holland, being one of the expedients devised by that unhappy prince to obtain a revenue independent of parliament. After the restoration another was held *pro forma* only, before the earl of Oxford; but since the era of the revolution in 1688, the forest laws have fallen into total disuse, to the great advantage of the subject.

COURT OF COMMISSIONERS OF SEWERS. Another species of restricted courts is that of commissioners of sewers. By the common law, the king used to grant commissions under the great seal for inquiring into the want of reparations of sea walls, ditches, gutters, sewers, &c. but these matters are now regulated according to several acts of parliament. These temporary tribunals are erected at the discretion and nomination of the lord chancellor, lord treasurer, and chief justices, pursuant to the statute 23 Hen. VIII. c. 5. Their jurisdiction is to overlook the repairs of sea-banks and sea-walls; and the cleansing of rivers, public streams, ditches, and other conduits, whereby any waters are carried off: and is confined to such county, or particular district, as the commission shall expresly name. The commissioners are a court of record, and may fine and imprison for contempts; and in the execution of their duty may proceed by jury, or upon their own view, and may take order for the removal of any annoyances, or the safeguard and conservation of the sewers within their commission, either according to the laws and customs of Romney-marsh*, or otherwise at their own discretion. They

* Romney-marsh in the county of Kent, a tract containing 24,000 acres, is governed by certain ancient and equitable laws of sewers, composed by Henry de Bathe, a venerable judge in the reign of Henry III.; from which laws all commissioners of sewers in England may receive light and direction.

2 may

may alſo aſſeſs ſuch rates or ſcots upon the owners of lands within their diſtrict, as they ſhall judge neceſſary: and if any perſon refuſes to pay them, the commiſſioners may levy the ſame by diſtreſs of his goods and chattels: or they may, by ſtatute 23 Hen. VIII. c. 5. ſell his freehold lands (and by the 7 Anne, c. 10. his copyhold alſo,) in order to pay ſuch ſcots or aſſeſſments. But their conduct is under the controul of the court of King's Bench, which will prevent or puniſh any illegal or tyrannical proceedings. In the reign of James I. indeed, the privy council endeavoured to abridge the authority of the court of King's Bench in this reſpect, and one of the reaſons for diſcharging Sir Edward Coke from his office of lord chief juſtice, was the countenance he gave to thoſe who appealed to the court of law. The privy council vindicated their proceeding by alleging the neceſſity of unlimited powers in works of evident utility to the public, "the ſupreme reaſon above all "reaſons, which is the ſalvation of the king's lands and people." But now it is clearly held, that this (as well as all other inferior juriſdictions) is ſubject to the diſcretionary coercion of the court of king's bench.

The Court of Policies of Insurance. This court, when ſubſiſting, is erected in purſuance of the ſtatute 43 Eliz. c. 12. which recites the immemorial uſage of policies of inſurance, "by means whereof it cometh to paſs, upon the loſs or "periſhing of any ſhip, there followeth not the undoing of "any man, but the loſs lighteth rather eaſily upon many than "heavy upon few, and rather upon them that adventure not, "than upon thoſe that do adventure: whereby all merchants, "eſpecially thoſe of the younger ſort, are allured to venture "more willingly, and more freely: and that heretofore ſuch "aſſurers had uſed to ſtand ſo juſtly and preciſely upon "their credits, as few or no controverſies had ariſen there-"upon; and if any had grown, the ſame had from time "to time been ended and ordered by certain grave and diſcreet "merchants, appointed by the lord-mayor of the city of "London; as men, by reaſon of their experience, fitteſt to un-"derſtand and ſpeedily decide thoſe cauſes:" but that of late years divers perſons had withdrawn themſelves from that courſe of arbitration, and had driven the aſſured to bring ſeparate actions at law againſt each aſſurer: it therefore enables the lord chancellor yearly to grant a ſtanding commiſſion to the judge of the admiralty, the recorder of London, two doctors of the civil law, two common lawyers, and eight merchants; any three of whom, one being a civilian or a barriſter, are thereby, and by the ſtatute 13 and 14 Chas. II. c. 23., empowered to determine in a ſummary way all cauſes concerning policies of assurance in London, with an appeal (by way of bill) to the court of chancery. But the jurisdiction being somewhat defective, as extending only to London, and to no other assurances but those on merchandize, and to suits brought by the assured only, and not by the insurers, no such commission has of late years issued: but insurance causes are now usually determined by the verdict of a jury of merchants, and the opinion of the judges in case of any legal doubts; whereby the decision is more speedy, satisfactory, and final: though, as Mr. Justice Blackstone, from whose commentaries these particulars are derived, observes, it is much to be wished that some of the parliamentary powers invested in these commissioners, especially for the examination of witnesses, either beyond the seas, or speedily going out of the kingdom, could at present be adopted by the courts of Westminster hall, without requiring the consent of parties.

The Marshalsea and Palace Court. The court of the Marshalsea, and Palace-court at Westminster, though two distinct courts, are frequently confounded together. The former was originally holden before the steward, and marshal of the king's house, and was instituted to administer justice between the king's domestic servants, that they might not be drawn into other courts, and thereby the king lose their service. It was formerly held in, though not a part of, the *aula regis*; and, when that was subdivided, remained a distinct jurisdiction, holding plea of all trespasses committed within the verge of the court, where only one of the parties was in the king's domestic service, in which case the inquest was to be taken by a jury of the country; and of all debts, contracts, and covenants, where both the contracting parties belonged to the royal household; and then the inquest was composed of men of the household only. By the statute 13 Rich. II. st. 1. c. 3. (in affirmance of the common law) the verge of the court in this respect extends twelve miles round the king's place of residence; and as this tribunal was never subject to the jurisdiction of the chief justiciary, no writ of error lay from it (though a court of record) to the King's Bench, but only to parliament, till the statutes of 5 Edw. III. c. 2. and 10 Edw. III. st. 2. c. 3. which allowed such writ of error before the king in his place. But this court being ambulatory, and obliged to follow the king in all his progresses, so that, by removal of the household, actions were frequently discontinued, and doubts having arisen as to the extent of its jurisdiction, Charles I. in the sixth year of his reign, by letters-patent, erected a new court of record, called *curia palatii*, or the *palace court*, to be held before the steward of the household and knight marshal, and the steward of the court or

his

his deputy; with jurisdiction to hold plea of all manner of personal actions whatsoever, which should arise between any parties within twelve miles of his majesty's palace at Whitehall. The court is now held once a week, together with the ancient court of Marshalsea, in the borough of Southwark; and a writ of error lies from thence to the court of King's Bench. If the cause is of any considerable consequence, it is usually removed on its first commencement, together with the custody of the defendant, either into the king's bench or common pleas, by a writ of *habeas corpus cum causa.* Actions in this court are generally bought in the following cases: first when the debt or damages to be recovered are not thought sufficiently considerable to warrant the party in incurring the expence of bringing them in the superior courts, as in actions not amounting to five pounds. Secondly, where the plaintiff wishes to avoid delay, particularly during the vacations of the superior courts; for here the continuances are from week to week without any vacations, and judgment is generally had in three or four weeks. Thirdly, in actions of trespass or assault, where the plaintiff wishes to avoid the risk of paying costs, as in this court he is intitled to his costs upon obtaining a verdict even for the smallest sum, as the statute 22 and 23 Chas. II. c. 9., which takes away costs in those actions unless the jury shall give forty shillings damages, does not extend to inferior courts, and was enacted for the purpose of confining those small actions to the inferior courts. Fourthly, when it is apprehended that several other writs may have been issued against a defendant, which, altogether, he may not be able to pay or bail, as a defendant arrested by process from this court, may be discharged on paying or bailing the debt for which he is arrested, without being subject to other detainers.

Officers. The judges who preside in this court are, the *lord steward* of the household, the *knight-marshal* and his *deputy*, the *steward of the court* and his *deputy*, which last is generally a barrister or serjeant at law, and in fact presides in court. The chief processes are issued from the office of a *prothonotary* of the court, in Clifford's Inn, who transacts the business by a deputy. There are in the court four counsel, whose appointments are held by patent, and transferred by purchase; other counsel may be brought into the court to plead, but in every cause an advocate regularly belonging to the court must be engaged on each side, and they take the business by rotation. The causes are conducted before they come into court by six attorneys, who alone are allowed to practise, and the process is executed by officers who are appointed by, and give security to, the knight-marshal for the time being.

COURTS OF THE PRINCIPALITY OF WALES. Another species of private courts of a limited, though extensive jurisdiction, are those of the principality of Wales: which, upon its thorough reduction, and the settling of its polity in the reign of Henry VIII. were erected all over the country; principally by statute 34 and 35 Hen. VIII. c. 26. though much had before been done, and the way prepared by the statute of Wales, 12 Edw. I. and other acts. By that of Henry VIII. before mentioned, courts-baron, hundred, and county-courts, are there established, as in England. A session is also to be held twice in every year, in each county, by judges appointed by the king, to be called the great sessions of the several counties in Wales: in which all pleas of real and personal actions shall be held, with the same form of process, and in as ample a manner, as in the court of common pleas at Westminster: and writs of error lie from judgments therein (it being a court of record) to the court of King's Bench at Westminster. But the ordinary original writs of process of the king's courts at Westminster do not run into the principality of Wales; though process of execution does; as do also prerogative writs, as writs of *certiorari, quo minus, mandamus,* and the like. And even in causes between subject and subject, to prevent injustice through family factions or prejudices, it is held lawful (in causes of freehold at least, and it is usual in all others) to bring an action in the English courts, and try it in the next English county adjoining to that part of Wales where the cause arises, and wherein the venue is laid. But, on the other hand, to prevent trifling and frivolous suits, it is enacted by statute 13 Geo. III. c. 51. that in *personal* actions, tried in any English county, where the cause of action arose, and the defendant resides in Wales, if the plaintiff shall not recover a verdict for ten pounds, he shall be nonsuited, and pay the defendant's costs, unless it be certified by the judge, that the freehold or title came principally in question, or that the cause was proper to be tried in such English county. And if any transitory action, the cause whereof arose and the defendant is resident in Wales, is brought in any English county, and the plaintiff does not recover a verdict for ten pounds, the plaintiff will be non-suited, and pay the defendant's costs, deducting thereout the sum recovered by the verdict.

JUDGES. The principality is divided into four sessions, in each of which preside a chief justice and a second judge. The sessions include the counties in the following order. 1. The *Chester circuit*, including Chester, Montgomery, Denbigh, and Flint. 2. The *North Wales circuit*; Anglesea, Caernarvon, and Merioneth. 3. The *South Wales circuit*; Caermarthen, Pembroke,

Pembroke, and Cardigan. 4. The *Brecon circuit*; Brecon, Radnor, and Glamorgan.

Court of the Duchy of Lancaster. The court of the duchy-chamber of Lancaster, is another special jurisdiction, held before the chancellor of the duchy, or his deputy, concerning all matters of equity relating to lands holden of the king in right of the duchy of Lancaster: which is a thing very distinct from the county palatine, (which has also its separate chancery for sealing of writs, and the like,) and comprizes much territory, which lies at a vast distance from it; as particularly a large district surrounded by the city of Westminster. The proceedings in this court are the same as on the equity side in the courts of exchequer and chancery; so that it seems not to be a court of record: and indeed it has been holden that those courts have a concurrent jurisdiction with the duchy court, and may take cognizance of the same causes.

Rise and Progress of its Jurisdiction. As the existence of this court is connected with some interesting periods of the British history, and its origin and progress are little known, the following account is offered.

The honour of Lancaster was of the most remote antiquity. It was composed of a number of honours, long before it was raised to an earldom, as it was subsequently to a dukedom.

The first possessor whom it is material to mention was Roger of Poitou, who was deprived for disloyalty, which he probably inherited from his father Roger de Montgomery, who got Arundel, Chichester, and the county of Salop, from William I. and rebelled against William II.

William earl of Montaigne Surry and Warren, third son of king Stephen, was next appointed lord of the honour of Lancaster, and put in possession of other considerable estates by his father; but Henry II. resumed what this royal earl held of the crown, and left him what came from his father before his father was king.

The third possessor was John, surnamed Sans-terre, afterward king of England. His brother Richard I. not weighing, as his father did, prudence against generosity, rendered him, who from ambition was too desirous of dominion, powerful by territories. After king John, the honour of Lancaster was raised to an earldom. Peter of Savoy, uncle to queen Eleonora, wife of Henry III. was created by that king earl of Lancaster. John his predecessor was indeed, in the enumeration of his titles, called earl of Lancaster, as a king's son, they being by the ancient laws of the crown, as is reported, earls of course, without any particular creation or investiture. Sir William Fleetwood, in his

his manuſcript hiſtory of the duchy, ſays, there is a natural and an artificial earl. A king's ſon was of the firſt ſort. Selden further defines this title to be local and perſonal. Part of the territories belonging to this earldom lay near the New Temple in London. It was called a Vavaſorie; here the ſaid earl Peter built a houſe, and named it from his own country, "Savoy." His ſon being deemed an alien, the earldom eſcheated to the crown, and Henry III. conferred it on his ſon Edmond, called "Crouchback," probably from his wearing a crouch or croſs on his back, as was often done by votaries to pilgrimage. From this prince is deſcended the royal houſe of Lancaſter, rival to that of York.

Edmond was ſucceeded by Thomas, his eldeſt ſon, who was ſheriff of Lancaſter by inheritance. He was made chief of Edward II.'s privy council, but after many mutual diſguſts and reconciliations, he took up arms againſt him, or rather againſt the Spencers, was defeated at Borough-bridge, and beheaded at Pontefract, after he had undergone the ſcoffs of the royaliſts for taking, as it was pretended he did, in a letter to the Scotch, the title of king Arthur. Never from the conqueſt to that time was the nation ſtained with more blood from the ſcaffold, than what flowed on his defeat. It was ſoon revenged; the Spencers and the king himſelf fell. The earl was defamed by his adverſaries, as an adulterer, a perverter of juſtice, and cruel. By the populace, and many clergy, he was canonized. The contradiction might ariſe from his having been an enemy to favourites, and a friend to the church. His perſon was contemptuouſly treated, but his picture was worſhipped at Saint Paul's. His miracles were ſuppreſſed; but his attainder was reverſed in the 1ſt of Hen. IV. he having been condemned without the form of a trial by his peers. He married Alice, daughter of Henry de Lacy earl of Lincoln, and added in her right the eſtates of Lincoln and Saliſbury to his immenſe patrimony; but ſhe, perfect in figure, was afterwards claimed by a deformed dwarf, Richard Saint Martin, who, by her confeſſion of the infamous connexion, and by court encouragement and ſupport (this Saint Martin being a retainer to the earl of Surry), demanded, ſome authors ſay obtained, the earldoms of Lincoln and Saliſbury, to the great diminution of the earl's power and fortune. The affront indubitably inflamed his diſaffection.

His brother Henry became intitled to ſuch parts only of his poſſeſſions and honours, as had been ſettled on him by the king, in caſe the laſt earl ſhould die without iſſue, which he did; and though the king afterwards conſiderably increaſed his eſtates by grant, yet he kept the greater ſhare of the property of the late earl,

earl, which had been forfeited by his attainder. Henry further increased his estate by a large fortune with his wife Maud, heiress to her father Sir Patrick Chaworth, and to other relations; by which acquisitions the earls of Lancaster grew very considerable in Wales.

His son Henry, who had been created earl of Derby and Lincoln in his father's lifetime, succeeded to his estates and honours. He added dignity to his illustrious family. He was the first duke of Lancaster and the second of our nobility raised to the ducal title. The duke of Cornwall stood before him. By his patent of creation in the 25th of Edward III. the king erected the county of Lancaster into a palatinate, and granted the duke *jura regalia* in that county, and many other privileges. The grant by this charter was only for his life; so all these distinctions, with his dukedom, ceased at his death in 1361. In the twenty-fifth year of his reign, the duke obtained, in exchange for Richmondshire, divers large domains in the counties of York, Durham, Nottingham, Derby, Sussex, and Norfolk. But shortly before his death, which happened the 23d of March, 1361, he surrendered many of his liberties and privileges to the crown, which were afterwards granted to John of Gaunt.

John of Gaunt married Blanch, daughter of the preceding nobleman, and made the house of Lancaster more royal. Maud, her eldest sister, dying without issue, all the Lancaster estates devolved to this prince, who was first created earl, and afterwards duke of Lancaster, by his father Edward III.; which king, the 28th February, in the fifty-first year of his reign, instituted, for the higher dignity of his son, a chancery, justices for the pleas of the crown, as well as for common law, *jura regalia*, and power of execution of writs and offices, and all other powers which were exerted by the earl of Chester in his county palatine. In the 13th of Richard II. duke John petitioned the king and parliament at Gloucester, that the late king's grant to him might be extended to his heirs male; and the king by charter, with the assent of parliament, extended it according to the prayer of the petition. He also obtained from Richard a grant and release of all the forfeited estates which came to the crown by the attainder of Thomas, earl of Lancaster. This duke had his council in Lancashire before the grant to him of *jura regula*, and in the grants and leases from the duke it is stiled the "Thrice noble council of the "thrice noble duke of Lancaster, &c." His council also took cognizance of title of land there, before the last foundation or confirmation of the palatinate. He married, after the death of Blanch, Constantia daughter of Peter king of Castille, and took his father-in-law's title, but ceded it afterward by contract, and was, by act of parliament, created duke of Aquitaine. His recited titles are, son of the king, duke of Aquitaine and Lancaster, earl of Derby, Lincoln, and Leicester. His estates were greatly augmented by his father, who, in the fiftieth year of his reign, granted to him and his heirs large domains in Hertfordshire, and at Calais in France. As his royal alliances and estates exceeded those of any other subject, so perhaps, in many respects, did his merits. He was temperate and courageous; neither too negligent nor too ambitious of glory. He was, however, in 1381, so much the object of popular odium, though he differed from an unpopular king, that Jack Straw burnt his castle, the Savoy. His benefactions to the church did not procure him the favour of the clergy; they thought he wanted zeal; some suspected his orthodoxy; and the citizens of London, inflamed by bigots, assaulted him with violence for his moderation to Wycliffe.

On his death, his son Henry de Bolinbroke, duke of Hereford, returned just as it was pronounced by a packed parliament that his banishment should be perpetual. At first, he only claimed his legal inheritance; but finding a weak government, and a strong torrent of popularity, his ambition burst forth, and filled every sail. He dethroned Richard II. by arms, but without a battle, and wore his crown by the name of Henry IV. but by act of parliament, he severed the duchy from the crown. This act, or charter, is intitled, "*Charta* "*Regis Henrici Quarti de Separatione Ducatus Lancastriæ a Corona.*" It recites all the titles and prerogatives of the duchy, and decrees that it shall be governed by its own officers, which were at that time a chancellor, an attorney-general, a receiver or treasurer, a clerk of the court, six assessors, twenty-three receivers, and three supervisors. But this is not the first institution of the duchy-court, as has been erroneously imagined. The same was granted to Henry, the first duke of Lancaster, and repeated in the charter or rescript of Edward III. by which that title was conferred on John of Gaunt, and also in the charter of the thirteenth of Richard II. for extending the title and estates to his heirs male. The court has indeed been preserved from this reign with little variation to the present time. Henry IV. was so jealous of his dukedom, and so zealous to preserve it, that he settled it on his son to save the title from being absorded in that of king.

Henry V. with the assent of parliament, enlarged the dukedom by his mother's estates. She was daughter and heiress of Humphry

phry de Bohun, earl of Hereford, whofe eftates were of great extent and value, and were fituate chiefly in the counties of Effex, Middlefex, Hertford, Cambridge, Norfolk, Lincoln, Bucks, Wilts, Berks, Suffolk, Surry, Gloucefter, Dorfet, and Hereford, and in the city of London, and the marches of Wales. In this reign, an act of parliament paffed, declaring that all grants of offices and eftates in the duchy fhould pafs under the duchy feal, or be void.

His fucceffor, Henry VI. did nothing of himfelf, and was made to do nothing worthy notice relating to the duchy.

After the dethronement and murder of this prince and his fon, the right to the dukedom defcended to John Beaufort, earl of Somerfet, fon of Catherine Swinford, third wife of John of Gaunt, duke of Lancafter, whofe children by her, before her marriage, were legitimated in the twentieth of Richard II. by act of parliament. But Edward IV. deemed the title and eftate forfeited by the attainder of Henry VI.; and by act of parliament united the eftates, ("appropriated" is the expreffion in the act,) to the crown, yet decreed at the fame time that the office fhould remain on its former eftablifhment. Until this period the office of chancellor of the county palatine was diftinct from that of the chancellor of the duchy, though often held by the fame perfon; neverthelefs the chancellor of the county palatine was always fubfervient to the chancellor of the duchy, by whom all grants of offices and lands, as well in the county palatine, as in the duchy at large, were made; and if the county palatine feal was neceffary to complete the grant, the chancellor of the county affixed it by virtue of a warrant from the chancellor of the duchy. By this act, the county palatine was annexed to the duchy, and the chancellor of the duchy has ever fince held the office of chancellor of the county palatine, executing the latter by his deputy or vice-chancellor.

In the twelfth year of this king an act of parliament paffed for vefting a very confiderable portion of the duchy eftates in truftees for the ufe of the king's will, and the king directed the fame by his will to be appropriated to divers charitable and fuperftitious ufes. But this truft was deftroyed by an act of the firft of Henry VII. and the eftates were refumed and re-united to the duchy.

Edward V. was not of an age to make any alterations during the fhort time he was called king.

Richard III. though he made fome excellent laws, with regard to the nation, left the duchy as he found it; but,

Henry VII. whofe right to it came from his mother Margaret,

garet, the countess of Richmond and Derby, daughter to John Beaufort, duke of Somerset, who was son to the earl of Somerset just mentioned, broke Edward IV.'s act and entail, separated the duchy again from the crown, and entailed both the crown and duchy on himself and his heirs for ever; and so it has continued distinct, though in the crown, (the time of the usurpation excepted,) to this day; yet it is not observed that any of our kings or princes have borne the title of duke of Lancaster since Henry V. who, by his father's express disposition, inserted it among his other titles when prince of Wales.

Henry VII. in 1509, began to found the hospital, called "Savoy," upon the site of the old palace there, being parcel of the duchy estate; but dying before it was finished, Henry VIII. assigned the building, with all the lands adjoining, to the executors of his father's will, by whom the hospital was completed.

It consisted of a master and four chaplains, who were to provide for one hundred poor out of its revenues, and to pray for the souls of Henry VII. and his mother.

The site of this hospital was part of the manor of the Savoy, which extends through the parishes of Saint Clement Danes and Saint Mary in the Strand. It reverted to Edward VI. by the voluntary surrender of the master and chaplains.

Philip and Mary, regarding the duchy of Lancaster as one of the stateliest pieces of her majesty's inheritance, re-founded the hospital, and re-instated the duchy in its rights and privileges; and annexed several estates to it, in lieu of what had been alienated.

Elizabeth, and afterwards William III. on complaints, visited this hospital by commission; and both, at the different periods, found such neglect and abuses of the charity, as required punishment and reformation. The master and chaplains still seemed incorrigible. Sir Nathan Wright, who, as keeper of the great seal, was visitor of all charities established by royal foundation, (though his right to visit this hospital has been questioned as being of duchy foundation,) perceiving that the original intent of the charity was totally perverted, declared it to be dissolved in 1702, and the lord high treasurer Godolphin thereupon appointed a receiver, to bring the profits of all its endowments into the exchequer. From hence arose a suit between the exchequer and the duchy for the jurisdiction, the rights, and revenues of so much of the possessions of the hospital as originally belonged to the duchy.

This contest commenced in 1718, and long remained undetermined.

termined. In the year 1743 and 1750, iſſues were joined for trials; but they were ſtopped both times on the conſideration that it appeared unbecoming adverſely to diſpute a point at the king's ſole expence, where the right was inconteſtably veſted in his majeſty only, to aſcertain whether that right emerged from the crown or the duchy.

The argument of decency continued in force, during the preſent, though not ſo ſtrongly as in former reigns; becauſe the queſtion, in fact, was become, whether the rents and revenues belonged to the public, under the civil liſt act of the firſt of George III. which appropriates the land revenues of the crown to the uſe of the public; or to the king in right of his duchy?

The exchequer derived its claim from the ſtatutes of diſſolution of the 32 and 37 of Henry VIII. whereby the poſſeſſions of diſſolved religious houſes were put under the ſurvey of the court of augmentations, and which court, with all its juriſdictions, were ſince annexed to the court of exchequer.

The duchy officers inſiſted that the hoſpital did not fall within the predicament of any of the ſtatutes of diſſolution; but on its being ſurrendered to Edward VI. came under the diſpoſition of the common law, and reverted to the donor or his heirs in the ſame right wherein he had granted it. That therefore Edward VI. took it in right of the duchy, which is evinced by the circumſtance of Philip and Mary re-granting it under the duchy ſeal; that their charter of re-foundation, paſſing both the great ſeal and duchy ſeal, was neceſſary to the erecting of the corporate body; and that the hoſpital in like manner reverted to Anne in right of her duchy upon the diſſolution. This diſpute was terminated in 1772 by an act of parliament, which declared that the king, his heirs and ſucceſſors, ſhould poſſeſs, in right of the crown, the two places of worſhip called the High German church, and the Low German church, in the Savoy precinct, with their church-yards and appurtenances, and alſo the barracks, with the priſons and ſuttling houſes belonging to them, with the two houſes near a place in the Savoy called the Friary, generally occupied by officers commanding the ſoldiers there; and theſe, with their rents and profits, were placed under the order, ſurvey, and governance of the exchequer. The reſidue of the Savoy precinct was declared to be parcel of the duchy of Lancaſter, and under the ſurvey, receipt, and governance of the chancellor, council, and officers of that duchy. And all grants, leaſes, and letters patent of theſe premiſes, are to be made by the king, his heirs and ſucceſſors, under the ſeal of the duchy, and no other.

To

To return from the digression respecting the Savoy hospital. The wide-speading inheritance of the duchy of Lancaster was greatly increased by the several acts of Henry VIII. for the dissolution of monasteries, and for erecting the court of augmentation; and by the act of Edward VI. for the dissolution of colleges and chanteries; and by a charter of Philip and Mary, made in pursuance of an act of parliament, whereby very large estates in the counties of Hertford, Essex, Bucks, Suffolk, Sussex, and York, were united to the duchy; and so great a regard was paid by this queen to the future preservation of this her patrimonial inheritance, that she got a clause inserted in this act, declaring that all such estates as had been since the first of Edward VI. or should be at any time afterward, granted from the duchy, and had or should revert, or be forfeited to, the crown, should return to the survey of the duchy court.

This favourite succession, thus formed and augmented, came to James I. (notwithstanding many grants in fee were given by those sovereigns) in such good condition as to raise in the beginning of his reign a very large annual income, and to make a considerable part of the civil establishment, over and above some extensive and valuable domains, which he granted, together with divers crown lands, to trustees, to maintain his sons Henry prince of Wales and prince Charles.

The king's necessities afterward requiring extraordinary sums to be raised from his landed property, he first began with taking large fines for leases of duchy estates, upon contract for sixty years; but finding money came in slowly from this scheme, he proceeded to make grants in fee, to all who would become purchasers on his terms; so that when Charles I. succeeded to the throne, he found the duchy possessions reduced to little more than the estates comprized in his own settlement, and in the leases for sixty years.

Charles's exigencies drove him to follow the example of his father in selling his duchy inheritance, by which he raised money to a considerable amount. No part of it was preserved, except some few forests and parks, and the estates which went to his queen Henrietta in jointure, and those which were comprized in the leases for sixty years, granted by his father, and even many of those were sold in reversion for small sums; but upon almost all the grants in fee, there were reserved to the crown fee-farm rents, which were in the whole of a large amount.

In 1649, a commission was appointed, by an act of the commons, for the sale of the crown and duchy lands. The restoration cancelled all transactions in consequence of that act.

Charles II. soon after his accession, made several very extensive five grants in fee of duchy estates to persons instrumental in his restoration, particularly to the duke of Albemarle, and the earl of Sandwich; and he also made many leases for terms of ninety-nine years in reversion, at very small rents, some of which are still subsisting. In 1665, he settled divers fee-farm rents, and very near all the landed estate of the duchy (which was not in jointure upon his mother Henrietta,) upon queen Catherine for her life; and Henrietta dying in 1671, the king added the estates comprized in her settlement to Catherine's jointure, so that the remaining revenue from the duchy to the crown sunk to a state of insignificance.

In 1670 and 1672, this king had two acts to sell all the fee-farm rents, as well those of the crown as of the duchy, and they were accordingly sold; and such as were in settlement on queen Catherine where either surrendered by her, and an equivalent granted to her by change on the hereditary excise, or were sold in reversion expectant on her death.

James II. though a prince of more order and business, did not attempt to save this ducal part of his patrimony from ruin; and such was the reduction of its income, that, in 1686, the officers of the duchy agreed to reduce their own salaries, to make them better tally with the small production from the duchy estate.

William III. accelerated the decline. He granted for ninety-nine years, after the demise of queen Catherine in 1705, most of the estates comprized in her jointure, which were all that remained unsold, except what is not worth mentioning.

Such is the history of this royal patrimony to the present period; but it is still believed, that if proper advantage is made of the leases when they expire, the public may derive from it a considerable revenue.

Officers. The officers in the duchy court, are a chancellor, an attorney general, king's serjeant, king's counsel, receiver general, two auditors, a clerk of the council and register, a secretary and clerks.

Office. The office of this court is in Somerset Place.

Courts Palatinate. The palatinate courts are superior courts of record, which exercise a jurisdiction within their own precincts in as ample a manner as the higher courts do at Westminster. Into them the king's ordinary writs do not run; and although they have *jura regalia*, yet they derive their authority from the crown; but at this day no palatinate jurisdiction can be erected, without an act of parliament. When the privileges of these counties palatine and franchises were abridged by statute 27 Hen. VIII. c. 24. it was also enacted, that all writs and process should be made in the king's name,

but

but ſhould be *teſte'd* or witneſſed in the name of the owner of the franchiſe. Wherefore all writs, whereon actions are founded, and which have current authority in counties palatine, muſt be under the ſeal of the reſpective franchiſes. And the judges of aſſize, who ſit therein, ſit by virtue of a ſpecial commiſſion from the owners of the franchiſes, and under their ſeal; and not by the uſual commiſſion, under the great ſeal of England. The palatinate courts are at this day three, *viz.* Cheſter, Durham, and Lancaſter.

Chester. This is a county palatine by preſcription, and, according to lord Coke, the moſt ancient and honourable remaining at this day. Within this county palatine, and the county of the city of Cheſter, there is, and anciently has been, a principal officer called the chamberlain of Cheſter, who has, and time out of mind has had, the juriſdiction of a chancellor; and the court of exchequer at Cheſter is, and time out of mind has been, the chancery court for the county palatine, whereof the chamberlain is judge in equity: he is alſo judge of matters at the common law within the county, for, like the court of chancery at Weſtminſter, this is a mixed court. There is alſo within this county palatine, a juſtice for matters of the common pleas, and pleas of the crown, to be heard and determined there, commonly called the chief juſtice of Cheſter. All pleas of lands or tenements, and all other contracts, cauſes, and matters ariſing and growing within this county palatine, are pleadable, and ought to be pleaded, heard, and judicially determined, within the county, and not elſewhere; and if any be pleaded, heard, or judged out of the county, the act is void, and *coram non judice*, except it be in caſe of treaſon, error, foreign plea, or foreign voucher.

Officers. The juſtices of Cheſter include in their duty, and compriſe under their authority, three counties in Wales. There is beſides an attorney general of Cheſter.

Durham. This is alſo a county palatine by preſcription, and ſaid to have been erected ſoon after the conqueſt, and is parcel of the biſhoprick of Durham. The juriſdiction of the biſhop of Durham extends to all places between the rivers Tine and Tees. In this county palatine there is a court of chancery, which is a mixed court both of law and equity, as the chancery at Weſtminſter. If an erroneous judgment be given, either in the chancery upon a judgment there, according to the common law, or before the juſtices of the biſhop, a writ of error muſt be brought before the biſhop himſelf; and if he gives an erroneous judgment, a writ of error may be ſued out returnable in the court of king's bench.

Lancaster. This county palatine is merged in the crown, but

but still the general rules respecting such counties are observed in it, and writs are directed to the chancellor, and not, as in other places, to the sheriff.

ELY. Ely is not a county palatine, but a royal franchise, granted by Henry I. to the bishop of Ely, and his successors, of hearing and determining as well civil as criminal pleas. The franchise is however of much earlier date than the time of Henry I. The bishoprick was founded by that prince in the tenth year of his reign, in 1109, and immediately afterward the grant here alluded to was made; but the franchise itself may be traced back to the seventh century; and Henry's charter, referring to preceding grants, declares that the church of Ely shall *continue* to have the same privileges and liberties as it had *die qua Edwardus vivus et mortuus fuit*. The jurisdiction of the bishop is now exercised by his justices by prescription, grounded on the said grant, and the judge of the Isle of Ely holds a circuit separate from the other judges.

COURTS OF THE CINQUE PORTS. There are several courts within the Cinque Ports; one before the constable of the castle at Dover; others within the ports of themselves, before the mayors and jurats; another, which is called *the court of the Cinque Ports*, at Shepway. There is a court of chancery in the Cinque Ports; from which no original writs issue, but it serves only to decide matters of equity. It is said the great use of their chancery is to relieve against errors in proceedings at law, which they used to endorse upon the bill. The lord-warden has two jurisdictions, the authority of an admiral, to hold plea by bill concerning the guard of the castle, &c. according to the course of the common law; and that exempt from the admiralty of England; which jurisdiction is saved to him in several acts of parliament. The mayors and jurats of the several Cinque Ports have power to hold plea, &c. and upon their judgment, no writ of error lies in the king's bench; but they are examinable by bill in nature of a writ of error, before the lord warden of the Cinque Ports, in his court at Shepway. The jurisdiction of the Cinque Ports is general, as well as to personal, as real and mixed actions.

A writ of error, it is to be observed, lies from all the other jurisdictions to the same supreme court of judicature, as an ensign of superiority reserved to the crown, at the original creation of the franchises; and all prerogative writs, as those of *habeas corpus*, *prohibition*, *certiorari*, and *mandamus*, may issue for the same reason to all these exempt jurisdictions; because the privilege, that the king's writ runs not, must be intended between party and party, for there can be no such privilege against the king.

COURTS

Courts of the Stannaries. The ſtannary courts in Devonſhire and Cornwall, for the adminiſtration of juſtice among the tinners, are alſo courts of record, but of the ſame private and excluſive nature. They are held before the lord warden and his ſubſtitutes, in virtue of a privilege granted to the workers in the tin-mines, to ſue and be ſued only in their own courts, that they may not be drawn from their buſineſs, which is highly profitable to the public, by attending their law-ſuits in other courts. The privileges of the tinners are confirmed by a charter, 33 Edw. I. and fully expounded by a private ſtatute, 50 Edw. III. which has ſince been explained by a public act, 16 Chas. I. c. 15. All tinners and labourers, in and about the ſtannaries, are, during the time of their working therein *bona fide*, privileged from ſuits of other courts, and can only be impleaded in the ſtannary court in all matters, excepting pleas of land, life, and member. No writ of error lies from hence to any court in Weſtminſter-hall, as was agreed by all the judges in 4 James I.; but an appeal lies from the ſteward of the court to the under-warden, and from him to the lord-warden; and thence to the privy council of the prince of Wales as duke of Cornwall, when he has had livery or inveſtiture of the ſame. And from thence the appeal lies to the king himſelf, in the laſt reſort.

Courts of the Universities. The univerſities of Oxford and Cambridge enjoy the ſole juriſdiction, in excluſion of the king's courts, over all civil actions and ſuits whatſoever, when a ſcholar or privileged perſon is one of the parties; excepting in ſuch caſes where the right of freehold is concerned. And theſe, by the univerſity charter, they are at liberty to try and determine, either according to the common law of the land, or according to their own local cuſtoms, at their diſcretion; which has generally led them to carry on their proceſs in a courſe much conformed to the civil law. Theſe privileges were granted, that the ſtudents might not be diſtracted from their ſtudies by legal proceſs from diſtant courts, and other forenſic avocations; and privileges of this kind are of very high antiquity, being generally enjoyed by all foreign univerſities as well as our own, in conſequence of a conſtitution of the emperor Frederick, in 1158. As to England in particular, the oldeſt charter, containing this grant to the univerſity of Oxford, was made in the 28 Hen. III. 1244; and the ſame privileges were confirmed and enlarged by almoſt every ſucceeding prince, down to Henry VIII.; in the fourteenth year of whoſe reign, the largeſt and moſt extenſive charter of all was granted. A ſimilar franchiſe was afterwards granted to Cambridge, in the third year of queen Elizabeth. The privileges granted by theſe charters of proceeding in a courſe different from the law of the land, were of ſo high a nature, that they were held to be invalid; for although the king might erect new courts, yet he could not alter the courſe of law by his letters patent; and therefore, in the reign of Elizabeth, an act of parliament was obtained, confirming *all* the charters of the two univerſities, and thoſe of the 14th of Henry VIII. and 3d Elizabeth by name. This *bleſſed act*, as Sir Edward Coke intitles it, eſtabliſhed this high immunity without any doubt or oppoſition. This privilege, ſo far as it relates to civil cauſes, is exerciſed in the chancellor's court; the judge of which is the vice-chancellor, his deputy or aſſeſſor. From his ſentence an appeal lies to delegates appointed by the congregation; from them to other delegates of the houſe of convocation; and if they all three concur in the ſame ſentence, it is final at leaſt by the ſtatutes of the univerſities, according to the rule of the civil law. But if there be any diſcordance or variation in any of the three ſentences, an appeal lies in the laſt reſort to judges delegates, appointed by the crown under the great ſeal in chancery.

Courts in the City of London. There are ſeveral courts within the city of London, which exerciſe authority according to their own ſtated rules and forms, but yet are ſubject to the controul and correction of the king's courts at Weſtminſter, whenever they exceed their juriſdiction. The chief of them are the following:

Court of Aldermen. The court of lord-mayor and aldermen is a court of record, wherein is lodged a great part of the executive power of the city; by it all leaſes and other inſtruments that paſs the city ſeal are executed, the aſſize of bread aſcertained, conteſts relating to water-courſes, lights, and party walls, adjuſted, and the city officers ſuſpended and puniſhed according to their ſeveral offences. This court has not only a power of electing annually eleven overſeers, or rulers of the fraternity of watermen; but likewiſe a right of fixing their ſeveral taxes, with the approbation of the privy council; and alſo a right of diſpoſing of moſt of the places belonging to the city officers.

Court of Common Council. This court conſiſts of the lord-mayor, aldermen, and repreſentatives of the ſeveral wards; who being the city legiſlature, make bye laws for its good government. They aſſemble in Guildhall, as often as the lord mayor by his ſummons thinks proper to convene them: they annually ſelect from among themſelves, a committee of ſix aldermen, and twelve commoners, for letting the city lands, to which end they uſually meet at Guildhall on Wedneſdays. They likewiſe appoint another committee of four aldermen and eight commoners, for tranfacting the affairs belonging to the benefactions of Sir Thomas Grefham, who generally meet at Mercers' hall at the appointment of the lord-mayor, who is always one of the number. They alfo, by virtue of a royal grant, yearly appoint a governor, deputy, and affiftants, for managing the city lands in Ireland. They have alfo a right of difpofing of the offices of town clerk, common ferjeant, judges of the fheriff's court, common crier, coroner, bailiff of the borough of Southwark, and city garbler.

THE COURT OF HUSTINGS. This is the higheft and moft ancient court of record within the city of London, and is always held at Guildhall, before the lord-mayor and fheriffs of London for the time being; but when any matter is to be argued and determined in this court, the recorder fits as judge with the lord-mayor and fheriffs, and gives rules and judgment therein. This court has jurifdiction of all pleas, real, perfonal, and mixed; and for this purpofe it is diftinguifhed into two courts, as the judges fit one week on real actions, and the other on thofe which are perfonal and mixed. In this court, deeds may be enrolled, recoveries paffed, wills proved, and replevins, writs of error, writs of right patent, writs of wafte, writs of partition, and writs of dower, determined for any matters within the city of London, and its liberties. Real actions are now, it is to be obferved, grown out of ufe. Judgment of outlawry in the huftings is not given by the mayor, who is coroner, or his deputy, but by the recorder, by the cuftom of the city. In this court, the lord-mayor for the enfuing year, the fheriffs, chamberlain, and bridge-mafter are chofen.

THE MAYOR'S COURT. The mayor's court is a court of record, held before the mayor and aldermen for all actions arifing within the liberties of London; in which the recorder is judge, but the mayor and aldermen may join with him when they pleafe. So, in this court, all matters of equity within London, may be determined upon bill and anfwer, upon which the recorder is alfo judge. This equitable jurifdiction is founded on the cuftom of London, by virtue of which, if a man be impleaded before the fheriffs, upon a fuggeftion, the mayor may bring the parties and record before him, and examine them upon their pleas; and if he finds that the plaintiff is fatisfied, order that the plaintiff be barred. But by the cuftom, the mayor cannot examine the parties after judgment. This court is held every day, except Sundays and Holidays, feffions at the Old Bailey, and in Southwark, and fittings of the common council and courts of confervancy. It takes cognizance of actions of debt and trefpafs, appeals from inferior courts, and foreign attachments, apprenticefhip, penal actions, and others arifing arising within the city and liberties. An action may be removed, by *habeas corpus*, or *certiorari*, into a superior court, if the debt be above five pounds, but if under ten pounds it cannot be allowed, until bail be put in before the register of this court. Affidavits of execution of deeds and other instruments are also exemplified under the mayoralty seal, by the attorneys of this court. The juries are returned by their several wards, at their wardmote inquests.

OFFICERS. The judges of this court have already been mentioned; they are assisted by the common serjeant, and the court is attended by a register and his assistant. The business is conducted by four appointed counsel, and there are belonging to the court, four attorneys, who have an office over the Royal Exchange.

THE SHERIFF'S COURTS. The sheriffs have two courts which are of record for trial of debt, case, trespass, account, covenant, attachment, and sequestration, held on Thursdays and Saturdays for the Poultry; and on Wednesdays and Fridays for Giltspur Street. An action may be moved by *habeas corpus*, into a superior court at Westminster, if the debt be above five pounds, but if under ten, it then cannot be allowed, until bail be put in before a judge of this court. Actions may also be removed as already mentioned into the lord-mayor's court, or the court of hustings, by a process called a *levatur*.

OFFICERS. In these courts the sheriffs sit as judges, aided by their respective under-sheriffs, and by two judges, who are barristers at law. The causes are conducted by the same counsel who practise in the lord-mayor's court; and there are eight attorneys, two secondaries, two clerks of the papers, who return all writs, and copy declarations; eight clerks sitters who enter actions, and take bail in their weeks successively; thirty-six serjeants at mace for both compters, and thirty-six yeomen.

THE CHAMBERLAIN'S COURT. This is an office kept in the Guildhall of London, by the chamberlain of the city, who is annually chosen by the liverymen of the respective companies on Midsummer day. This practice may however be considered a mere custom, for there is no instance of a chamberlain being turned out, unless found guilty of mal-practices. This place of chamberlain being one of great trust, he is obliged when chosen to give security for his fidelity. He receives and pays all the city's cash, and with him are deposited all public securities, for which he annually accounts to the proper auditors. This officer attends every morning for enrolling and turning over apprentices, admits all persons duly qualified to the freedom of the city, and decides all differences that arise between masters and apprentices.

COURT OF THE CORONER. The lord-mayor being perpetual coroner of the city, this court is held before him, or his deputy, who is to enquire into the cause of the death of any person, who, upon sight of the body, is supposed to have come to an untimely end, as he is likewise into the escape of the murderer; and also concerning found treasure, deodands, and wrecks at sea.

COURT OF THE ESCHEATOR. The lord-mayor of London being perpetual escheator within the city, this court is also held before him or his deputy, to whom all original writs of *Diem clausit extremum, mandamus, devenerunt, melius inquirend. &c.* are directed to find an office for the king, after the death of his tenant, who held by knights service. The escheator may also find an office for treason and felony.

COURT OF REQUESTS. The first of these courts was established in London, so early as the reign of Henry VIII. by an act of their common council; which however was certainly insufficient for that purpose, and illegal, till confirmed by statute 3 James I. c. 15. which has since been explained and amended by 14 Geo. II. c. 10. The constitution is this: two aldermen, and four commoners sit twice a week to hear all causes of debt not exceeding the value of forty shillings; which they examine in a summary way, by the oath of the parties or other witnesses, and make such order therein as is consonant to equity and good conscience. The time and expence of obtaining this summary redress being very inconsiderable, several trading towns and other districts have obtained acts of parliament, for establishing in them courts of conscience, upon nearly the same plan as that in the city of London.

THE COURT OF ORPHANS. This court is occasionally held by the lord-mayor and aldermen, who are guardians to children under the age of twenty-one years, at the decease of their fathers; and who take upon them, not only the management of their goods and chattels, but likewise that of their persons, by committing them to careful tutors, to prevent their disposing of themselves during minority, without their approbation. The common serjeant is authorized by the court, to take exact accounts and inventories of all deceased freemen's estates; and the youngest attorney of the mayor's court, being clerk to that of the orphans, is appointed to take securities for their several portions, in the name of the chamberlain of London, who is a sole corporation of himself, for the service of the orphans; and to whom a recognizance or bond, made on account of an orphan, by the custom of London, descends to his successor; which is hardly known elsewhere. When a freeman of London dies, and leaves children in their minority, the clerks of their several parishes give in their names to the common crier, who is is thereupon immediately to summon the widow, or executor, to appear before the court of lord mayor and aldermen, to bring in an inventory of, and give security for, the testator's estate; for which, two months time is commonly allowed: and in case of non-appearance, or refusal of security, the lord-mayor may commit the contumacious executor to Newgate.

THE WARDMOTE. The court of wardmote is held for every ward in the city: for each ward is of the nature of an hundred in a county. By inquisition of twelve men, the wardmote inquires of defaults in paving the streets, and similar matters. The wardmote is convened by precept annually, on Saint Thomas's day, on which occasion the aldermen and the householders of the ward proceed to elect their proper officers, and the precept, which is very long and minute, serves as instructions to the inquest in the performance of their duty.

FOLKMOTE. The folkmote or hall-mote belongs to the several companies of citizens, by whom it is occasionally held in their respective halls, and wherein the affairs belonging to each corporation are respectively transacted.

COURT OF CONSERVANCY. This court is yearly held eight times before the lord mayor, at such places and times as he appoints within the respective counties of Middlesex, Essex, Kent, and Surry; in which several counties he has a power of summoning juries, who, for the better preservation of the fishery of the river Thames, and regulation of the fishermen who fish therein, are, upon oath, to make inquisition of all offences committed in and upon the river from Staines bridge in the West, to Yenfleet in the East; and to present all persons found guilty of a breach of the articles prescribed for regulation in such matters. And for the more effectual preservation of the navigation, and fish in the river Thames, the lord-mayor, as conservator, has his assistant or deputy the *water-bailiff*; who, together with his substitutes, detect and bring to justice persons destroying either the current or fish.

THE TOWER COURT. This is a court of record, held by prescription, within the verge of the city, on Great Tower Hill, by a steward appointed by the constable of the Tower of London, by whom are tried actions of debt (for any sum,) damage and trespass.

COURT OF SAINT MARTIN'S LE GRAND. This court, though within the city, is yet without its jurisdiction, as being in and belonging to the liberty of that name, which is subject to the dean and chapter of Westminster: it is a court of record, held weekly on Wednesdays, for the trial of all personal actions whatsoever; the principal process whereof is a capias against the body, or an attachment against the goods; so that a man's

 effects

effects may be ſeized in his own houſe, upon the firſt proceſs, if his perſon is not ſecured before; which is according to the practice of all ancient liberties or franchiſes.

COMMON LAW COURTS. The numerous courts formed for the diſtribution of juſtice in the capital are ſo diſtinctly mentioned, as they may ſerve by analogy to illuſtrate the manner in which juſtice is, or may be adminiſtered in all other cities, boroughs, or corporate juriſdictions within the realm; for all, by grant or preſcription, may have courts for matters within their precincts. In every caſe, where power is given to any to hear and determine, they have judicial authority, and act as judges; and authority to fine and impriſon conſtitutes a court of record. It is to be obſerved that theſe eſtabliſhments, whether of public and general, or only of private and ſpecial juriſdiction, are not to be deemed innovations, but are, on the contrary, ſtrictly congenial with the ſpirit of the conſtitution. The policy of that conſtitution, as regulated and eſtabliſhed by the great Alfred, was to bring juſtice home to every man's door, by forming as many courts of judicature as there are manors and townſhips in the kingdom; wherein injuries were redreſſed in an eaſy and expeditious manner, by the ſuffrage of neighbours and friends. Theſe little courts, however, communicated with others of a larger juriſdiction, and thoſe with others of a ſtill greater power; aſcending gradually from the loweſt, to the ſupreme courts, which were reſpectively conſtituted to correct the errors of the inferior ones, and to determine ſuch cauſes as, by reaſon of their weight and difficulty, demanded a more ſolemn diſcuſſion. The courſe of juſtice flowing in large ſtreams from the king, as the fountain, to his ſuperior courts of record; and being then ſubdivided into ſmaller channels, till the whole and every part of the kingdom were plentifully watered and refreſhed.

The order obſerved by Sir William Blackſtone, whoſe courſe is followed on the preſent occaſion, in treating on theſe ſeveral courts, conſtituted for the redreſs of *civil* injuries, reſerving thoſe of a juriſdiction merely *criminal*, is by beginning with the loweſt, and thoſe whoſe juriſdiction, though public and generally diſperſed throughout the kingdom, is yet, with regard to each particular court, confined to very narrow limits; and ſo aſcending gradually to thoſe of the moſt extenſive and tranſcendent power.

COURT OF PIEPOUDRE. The loweſt, and at the ſame time the moſt expeditious court of juſtice known to the law of England, is the court of *piepoudre*, *curia pedis pulverizati*, ſo called from the duſty feet of the ſuitors; or, according to Sir Edward Coke, becauſe juſtice is there done as ſpeedily as duſt can fall from the foot. But the etymology given by Barrington, in his observations on the penal statutes, is much more ingenious and satisfactory; it being derived, according to him, from *pied poudreux* (a pedlar in old French,) and therefore signifying the court of such petty chapmen as resort to fairs or markets. It is a court of record, incident to every fair and market; of which the steward of him who owns or has the toll of the market is the judge; and its jurisdiction extends to administer justice for all commercial injuries done in that very fair or market, and not in any preceding one. So that the injury must be done, complained of, heard, and determined within the compass of one and the same day, unless the fair continues longer. The court has cognizance of all matters of contract that can possibly arise within the precinct of that fair or market; and the plaintiff must make oath that the cause of action arose there. From this court a writ of error lies, in the nature of an appeal, to the courts at Westminster; which are also bound by the statute 19 Geo. III. c. 70. to issue writs of execution, in aid of its process, after judgment, where the person or effects of the defendant are not within the limits of this inferior jurisdiction.

Court Baron. The court baron is a court incident to every manor in the kingdom, to be holden by the steward within the manor. The court baron is of two natures: the one is a customary court, appertaining entirely to the copyholders, in which their estates are transferred by surrender and admittance, and other matters transacted, relative to their terms only. The other is a court of common law, and it is the court of the barons, by which name the freeholders were sometimes anciently called, or rather, perhaps, it was so called as the court of the baron or lord of the manor, to which his freeholders owed suit and service. These courts, though in their nature distinct, are frequently confounded together. The court now under consideration, *viz.* the freeholders' court, was composed of the lord's tenants, who were the *pares* of each other, and were bound by their feudal tenure to assist their lord in the dispensation of domestic justice. This was formerly held every three weeks; and its most important business is to determine, by writ of right, all controversies relating to the right of lands within the manor. It may also hold plea of any personal actions, of debt, trespass on the case, or the like, where the debt or damages do not amount to forty shillings. But the proceedings on a writ of right may be removed into the county court, by a precept from the sheriff; and the proceedings in all other actions may be removed into the superior courts by the king's writs. After judgment given, a writ also of false judgment lies to the courts at Westminster to rehear and review the cause, and not a writ of error, for this is not a court of record.

HUNDRED COURT. A hundred court is only a larger court baron, being held for all the inhabitants for a particular hundred instead of a manor. The free suitors are here also the judges, and the steward the registrar, as in a court baron. It is likewise no court of record; resembling the former in all respects, except that in point of territory it is of a greater jurisdiction. This hundred court was denominated *hæreda* in the Gothic constitution; but as causes are equally liable to removal from hence, as from the common court baron, and by the same writs, and may also be removed by writ of false judgment, the court is fallen into equal disuse with regard to the trial of actions.

COUNTY COURT. The county court is a court incident to the jurisdiction of the sheriff. It is not a court of record, but may hold pleas of debts or damages under the value of forty shillings; over some of which causes these inferior courts have, by the express words of the statute of Gloucester, a jurisdiction totally exclusive of the king's superior courts. The county court may also hold plea of many real actions, and of all personal actions to any amount, by virtue of a special writ, called a *justicies*, which is a writ impowering the sheriff, for the sake of dispatch, to do the same justice in his county court, as might otherwise be had at Westminster. The freeholders of the county are the real judges in their court, and the sheriff is the ministerial officer. The great conflux of freeholders, supposed always to attend at the county court, is the reason why all acts of parliament, at the end of every session, were wont to be there published by the sheriff; why all outlawries of absconding offenders are there proclaimed; and why all popular elections, which the freeholders are to make; as formerly of sheriffs and conservators of the peace, and still of coroners, verderors, and knights of the shire, must ever be made *in pleno comitatu*, or, in full county court. By the statute 2 Ed. IV. c. 25. no county court can be adjourned longer than for one month, consisting of twenty-eight days. And this was also the ancient usage, as appears from the laws of Edward the elder. In those times the county court was one of great dignity and splendour; the bishop and the ealdorman (or earl), with the principal men of the shire, sitting to administer justice both in lay and ecclesiastical causes. Its dignity was much impaired, when the bishop was prohibited, and the earl neglected to attend; and, in modern times, as proceedings are removeable into the king's superior courts, by writ of *pone* or *recordari*, in the same manner as from

from hundred courts, and courts baron; and as the same writ of false judgment may be had, in nature of a writ of error, actions in the county court are fallen into disuse.

These are the several species of common law courts, which, though dispersed universally throughout the realm, are nevertheless of a partial jurisdiction, and confined to particular districts: yet communicating with, and, as it were, members of, the superior courts of a more extended and general nature; which are calculated for the administration of redress, not in any one lordship, hundred, or county only, but throughout the whole kingdom at large.

Court of Common Pleas. By the Saxon constitution, there was only one superior court of justice in the kingdom, and that had cognizance both of civil and spiritual causes, *viz.* the wittena-gemot, or general council, which assembled annually, or oftener, wherever the king kept his Easter, Christmas, or Whitsuntide, as well to do private justice as to consult on publick business. But after the conquest, the ecclesiastical jurisdiction was diverted into another channel; and the conqueror, fearing danger from these annual parliaments, contrived also to separate their ministerial power, as judges, from their deliberative, as counsellors to the crown. He therefore established a constant court in his own hall, made up of the officers of his palace, who transacted the business, both criminal and civil, as well as matters of the revenue. When they sat in the hall, they were called a court criminal, when up stairs a court of revenue; the civil pleas they held in either court. This court was called, by Bracton and other authors, *aula regia*, or *aula regis*. These high officers were assisted by certain persons learned in the laws, who were called the king's *justiciars* or justices, and by the greater barons of parliament, all of whom had a seat in the *aula regia*, and formed a kind of court of appeal, or rather of advice, in matters of great moment and difficulty. These, in their several departments, transacted all secular business, both criminal and civil, and likewise matters of the revenue: and over all presided one special magistrate, called the chief *justiciar*, or *capitalis justiciarius totius Angliæ*; who was also principal minister of state, the second man in the kingdom, and, by virtue of his office, guardian of the realm in the king's absence. And this officer it was, who principally determined all the vast variety of causes that arose in this extensive jurisdiction; and, from the plenitude of his power, grew, at length, both obnoxious to the people and dangerous to the government which employed him. This great universal court being bound to follow the king's household in all its progresses and expeditions, the trial

trial of common causes was found very burthensome to the subject. Wherefore John, who dreaded also the power of the *justiciar*, very readily consented to that article, which now forms the eleventh chapter of magna charta, and enacts "that common pleas shall not follow our court, but shall be holden in some place certain." This certain place was established in Westminster-hall, the place where the *aula regis* originally sat, when the king resided in that city; and there it has ever since continued. The court being thus rendered fixed and stationary, the judges became so too, and a chief, and other justices of the common pleas, were thereupon appointed, with jurisdiction, to hear and determine all pleas of land, and injuries merely civil, between subject and subject; which critical establishment of this principal court of common law, at that particular juncture, and that particular place, gave rise to the inns of court in its neighbourhood; and thereby collecting together the whole body of the common lawyers, enabled the law itself to withstand the attacks of the canonists and civilians, who laboured to extirpate and destroy it. The *aula regia* being thus stripped of so considerable a branch of its jurisdiction, and the power of the chief *justiciar* being also curbed by many articles in the great charter, the authority of both began to decline apace under the long and troublesome reign of Henry III.; and, in further pursuance of this example, the other several officers of the chief *justiciar* were, under Edward I. who new-modelled the whole frame of our judicial polity, subverted and broken into distinct courts of judicature. The distribution of common justice, between man and man, was thrown into so provident an order, that the great judicial officers were made to form a cheque upon each other; the court of chancery issuing all original writs under the great seal to the other courts; the common pleas being allowed to determine all causes between private subjects, the exchequer managing the king's revenue; and the court of king's bench retaining all the jurisdiction which was not cantoned out to other courts, and particularly the superintendance of all the rest by way of appeal; and the sole cognizance of the pleas of the crown, or criminal causes: for pleas or suits are regularly divided into two sorts; *pleas of the crown*, which comprehend all crimes and misdemeanors, wherein the king, on behalf of the public, is plaintiff; and *common pleas*, which include all civil actions depending between subject and subject. The former of these were the proper object of the jurisdiction of the court of king's bench; the latter of the court of common pleas, which is a court of record, and is styled, by Sir Edward Coke, "the lock-and-key of the common law," for herein only can

can real actions, that is, actions which concern the right of freehold or the realty, be originally brought: and all other, or personal pleas between man and man, are here determined; though, in the latter, the king's bench and exchequer have also a concurrent authority.

JURISDICTION. This court without any writ may, upon suggestion, grant prohibitions, to keep, as well temporal as ecclesiastical courts within their bounds and jurisdiction, without any original or plea depending; for the common law, which in these cases is a prohibition of itself, stands instead of an original. Actions are also removed into this court out of inferior courts, whether of record or not, by proper writs. In term time, it may award a *habeas corpus* by the common law for any person committed for any cause under treason or felony, and thereupon discharge him, if it shall clearly appear by the return, that the commitment was against law, as being made by one who had no jurisdiction of the cause, or for a matter for which, by law, no man ought to be punished. And now it is clear, that this court has a general jurisdiction to grant writs of *habeas corpus*, in all cases. It also has jurisdiction for the punishment of its own officers and ministers, and all other persons guilty of contempt against the rules and orders of the court. Its jurisdiction is general, and extends throughout England; and as inferior courts, which are not of record, cannot hold plea of debt, &c. or damages, but under forty shillings, so the superior courts, that are of record, cannot hold plea of debt, &c. or damages regularly, unless the same amount to forty shillings, or above.

OFFICERS. The officers of the court of common pleas are very numerous; and the duties of some of them apply solely to the jurisdiction which this court exclusively holds over the alienation of real estates. In the enumeration which follows, it is to be observed that those officers alone are mentioned whose appointment is peculiar to this court; the duties and appointments of judges and some other persons will be mentioned in a subsequent page.

CUSTOS BREVIUM. The custos brevium is the first or principal officer of this court, and holds his place by the king's letters patent. His office is to receive and keep all the writs, and put them on files, every return by itself; and, at the end of every term, to receive of the prothonotaries all the records of nisi prius, called the *postea*. The custos brevium also makes entry of the writs of covenant, and the concord upon every fine, and makes out exemplifications and copies of all writs and records in his office, and of all fines levied; and his duty extends to some other particulars respecting fines.

PROTHO-

Prothonotaries. There are three prothonotaries of this court, who hold their offices for life, and are admitted by the chief justice of the court for the time being; but the second prothonotary is admitted on the nomination of the *custos brevium*, who, in right of his office, has that appointment. In term time, they attend the sitting of the court at Westminster, for the dispatch of such matters as arise from causes entered in the office; and to inform the court of the state of such causes, and certify to them in matters of practice when required. They also attend at their office in Tanfield-court, in the Inner Temple, to tax costs, receive declarations, and pass officially many other matters in the progress of a suit at law.

Secondaries. There are also three secondaries, one belonging to, and nominated by, each prothonotary. In term time they attend the court and judges in the treasury, to read all the records, writings, affidavits, petitions, papers, and exhibits; take minutes of all rules and orders, and draw up the same, and take recognizances in court; have the custody of the court books, in which are entered the names of all causes on demurrer, special verdicts, and other matters that are to be argued in court, and of causes that are to be tried at bar; enter all commitments of prisoners, discontinuances, and satisfactions acknowledged upon record, and amend records by order of the court; they also attend trials at bar, and have some other duties.

Clerk of the Judgments. This officer draws up final judgments, enters satisfaction on judgments, and has several other duties relating to the judgment rolls.

Other Officers. From the specimen already afforded, it will be perceived that a description of the duty of every officer would only lead to a technical division of the various circumstances arising in the progress of a suit, without conveying any clear information; it is therefore considered sufficient merely to name several of the other officers in the court, and to describe only those whose duties are of more general extent. There are in the common pleas, a clerk of the dockets, clerk of the reversals, clerk of the treasury, clerk of the jurats, treasury keeper, clerk of the warrants, clerk of the essoigns, clerk of the juries, exigenter, clerk of the outlawries, and clerk of the errors.

Filacers. The filacer is an officer, so called, because he files those writs whereon he makes out process. There are thirteen filacers, among whom the several counties of England are divided, beside one for the counties palatine of Chester, Lancaster, and Durham. These officers make out all process before appearance in actions, wherein process of out-

outlawry lies, until the exigent is awarded; and many relating to the recovery of real eſtates. They alſo take ſpecial bail in common caſes; appearances are to be entered with them; they procure the original to be ſued forth and filed on proceſs to outlawry; take affidavits of debts, in order to hold to bail; affidavits of the ſervice of proceſs; file bills brought againſt perſons entitled to privilege of parliament, and make out the ſubſequent proceſs thereon, before appearance.

Fines and Recoveries. The offices peculiarly ſet apart to the tranſaction of this mode of transferring real eſtates are:

Return Office. The return office and office of inrolment of writs for fines and recoveries is in the nomination of the three puiſne judges, by virtue of an act of parliament made in the twenty third year of Elizabeth. The clerk of inrolment or his deputy returns all writs of covenant, entry, ſummons, and ſeiſin, in the names of the ſheriffs of the ſeveral counties and cities in England; and makes regular entries in books, provided at his own charge for that purpoſe.

King's Silver. The clerk of the king's ſilver claims it to be his duty, to inſpect and ſee that all fines, brought to his office, have regularly paſſed through the ſeveral offices conformably to the uſage of the court; to enter the whole of all fines, together with the poſt fine paid thereon, into books which remain in the office as records: he is alſo to ſtop all ſuch fines, againſt the paſſing of which caveats are entered, and file ſuch *caveats* with all rules of court, judges' orders, and affidavits of the cogniſors, being alive, where captions have been brought to this office. All caveats, and orders for ſtopping any fines, muſt be renewed every term, and copies left with the clerk of the king's ſilver, for which he is to demand only his ancient fee of 3*s.* 4*d.* the term; and in default thereof all caveats not ſo renewed, loſe their force and effect.

Chirographer. The chirographer draws up and makes out, from all parts of the fine, the final concord, and ingroſſes a record thereof. The office is held by letters patent from the crown. There is a regiſter and record-keeper belonging to the office, and the chirographer appoints certain clerks for the ſeveral counties in England.

Beſides theſe, there are other officers of the court, whoſe duties are dependent on particular circumſtances, and their appointments on certain individuals.

Judges' Clerks. The judges' clerks are verbally appointed by the reſpective judges, to continue during pleaſure. The clerks of the lord chief juſtice make out commiſſions for taking affidavits and ſpecial bails, and file the approbations ſigned ed by one of the puiſne judges, in order for ſuch commiſſions, and enter the name of the commiſſioners ſo appointed, in a book kept for that purpoſe.

ASSOCIATE MARSHAL, AND CRYER AT NISI PRIUS. Theſe offices are all in the gift of the chief juſtice, and he beſtows them by parol appointment, during pleaſure.

PROCLAMATOR. The office of chief proclamator is hereditary, and the holder of it had power to appoint another perſon and his heirs for ever, marſhal proclamator, and barrier of the court. There are four perſons who act as cryers to the court; one of them is alſo court keeper, and another porter of the court; which cryer, court-keeper, and porter, are deputies to the chief proclamator. Their duty is to attend this court, and make proclamations, &c.

CLERK OF THE PAPERS OF THE FLEET. The Fleet being the priſon of the court of common pleas, a clerk of the papers is appointed by the warden, who receives and records all commitments and diſcharges, and all papers in cauſes in this court, for which any priſoner is detained.

TIPSTAFFS. There are two tipſtaffs attendant on this court, who are admitted by deputation from the warden of the Fleet: they attend the judges while ſitting in a court, and, in the afternoon at their chambers; and out of term, they attend there morning and afternoon. One of them alſo attends the lord chief juſtice at the ſittings of *Niſi prius* for Weſtminſter, London, and on the circuits.

COURT OF KING'S BENCH. The court of King's Bench (ſo called becauſe the king uſed formerly to ſit there in perſon, the ſtile of the court ſtill being *coram ipſo rege**) is the ſupreme court of common law in the kingdom; conſiſting of a chief juſtice and three *puiſne* juſtices, who are, by their office, ſovereign conſervators of the peace, and ſupreme coroners of the land. Yet, though the king himſelf uſed to ſit in this court, and ſtill is ſuppoſed ſo to do; he did not, neither by law is he empowered to, determine any cauſe or motion, but by the mouth of his judges, to whom he has committed his whole judicial authority. This court, which is the remnant of the *aula regia*, is not, nor can be, from the very nature and conſtitution of it, fixed to any certain place, but may follow the king's perſon wherever he goes; for which reaſon, all proceſs iſſuing out of this court in the king's name is returnable "wherever we ſhall be in England." It has indeed, for ſome centuries paſt, uſually ſate at Weſtminſter-hall, but

* This court is called the queen's bench in the reign of a queen, and during the protectorate of Cromwell it was ſtiled the upper bench.

might

might remove with the king to York or Exeter, if he thought proper to command it; and, after Edward I. had conquerred Scotland, it actually did sit at Roxburgh. It is termed the *custos morum* of all the realm, and by the plenitude of its power, wherever it meets with an offence, contrary to the first principles of justice, and of dangerous consequences if not restrained, adapts a proper punishment to it.

JURISDICTION. The jurisdiction of this court is very high and transcendant. It keeps all inferior jurisdictions within the bounds of their authority; and may either remove their proceedings to be determined before its own judges, or prohibit their progress below; it superintends all civil corporations in the kingdom: commands magistrates and others to do what their duty requires in every case, where there is no specific remedy: protects the liberty of the subject, by speedy and summary interposition: takes cognizance both of criminal and civil causes; the former, in what is called the crown side or crown office; the latter, in the plea side of the court. The jurisdiction of the crown side is not intended to be here treated of, but on the plea side it has an original jurisdiction, and cognizance of all actions of trespass, or other injury alleged to be committed *vi et armis*; of actions for forgery of deeds, maintenanee, conspiracy, deceit, and actions on the case, which allege any falsity or fraud; all which savour of a criminal nature, although the action is brought for a civil remedy, and make the defendant liable, in strictness, to pay a fine to the king, as well as damages to the injured party. The same doctrine is also extended to all actions on the case whatsoever, except real actions, and has continued to be so for ages; it being surmised that the defendant is arrested for a supposed trespass, which he never has in reality committed; and being in the custody of the marshal of this court, the plaintiff is at liberty to proceed against him for any other personal injury; which surmise the defendant is not at liberty to dispute. These fictions of law are highly beneficial and useful, especially as this maxim is ever invariably observed, that no fiction shall extend to work an injury; its proper operation being to prevent a mischief, or remedy an inconvenience, that might result from the general rule of law. The king's bench is a court of appeal, into which may be removed, by writ of error, all determinations of the court of common pleas, and of all inferior courts of record in England; yet even this court is not the dernier resort of the subject: for, if he be not satisfied with any determination here, he may remove it by writ of error into the court of exchequer-chamber, if the proceedings are by bill,

bill, or into the houſe of lords if by original. This court grants an *habeas corpus* to relieve perſons wrongfully imprisoned; and upon return of the cauſe, they may be bailed or diſcharged as the court ſhall think fit: alſo writs of *mandamus* to inferior courts, to oblige them to do their duty, prohibitions to keep them within their proper juriſdiction, and may puniſh an inferior magiſtrate, or officer of juſtice, for wilful or corrupt abuſe of his authority.

OFFICERS. The officers on the crown ſide of this court are as follow:

MASTER OF THE CROWN OFFICE. The king's coroner and attorney, commonly called the clerk of the crown, or maſter of the crown office, taxes coſts, nominates all ſpecial juries on the crown ſide, takes recognizances, inquiſitions upon the death of any priſoner dying in the king's bench, &c.

SECONDARY. The ſecondary draws up the paper books, and makes up an eſtreat of all fines, &c. forfeited to the crown.

CLERK OF THE RULES. The clerk of the rules draws up all the rules of the court, and attends the court to take minutes thereof.

OTHER OFFICERS. There are alſo two other officers; the *examiner*, and *calendar keeper*; and eight *clerks in court*.

PLEA SIDE. The officers on this ſide are not ſo numerous as thoſe in the common pleas; but the duties they have to perform, except as to actions real, are nearly the ſame, and therefore their titles alone are mentioned. The chief clerks, ſecondary or maſter, their deputy, marſhal, clerk of the rules, clerk of the papers, clerk of the day-rules, clerk of the dockets, clerk of the declarations, clerk of the bails, poſteas, and eſtreats, ſigner of writs, ſigner of the bills of Middleſex, cuſtos brevium, clerk of the upper treaſury, filacer, exigenter, and clerk of the outlawries, clerk of the errors, deputy-marſhal, marſhal, and aſſociate to the chief juſtice, train-bearer, clerk of the niſi prius in London and Middleſex, clerks of the niſi prius to the different counties appointed by the cuſtos brevium, crier at niſi prius in London and Middleſex, receiver-general of the ſeal office; criers, uſhers, and tipſtaffs.

SEALER OF THE WRITS. On one of the officers mentioned in this liſt, it may be fit to obſerve that his duties apply equally to this court and that of common pleas. The office of ſealer of the writs is hereditary in the family of the duke of Grafton, but always executed by deputy, or receiver-general.

COURT OF EXCHEQUER. The court of exchequer is inferior in rank both to the king's bench, and common pleas; but is conſidered in this order in its double capacity, having juriſdiction both

both in equity. It is a very ancient court of record, eſtabliſhed by William the Conqueror, as a part of the *aula regia*, though reformed and reduced to its preſent order by Edward II. and intended principally to regulate the revenues of the crown, and to recover the king's debts and duties. It is called the exchequer, *ſcaccarium*, from the chequered cloth, reſembling a cheſs-board, which covers the table there; and on which, when certain of the king's accounts are made up, the ſums are marked and ſcored with counters. It conſiſts of two diviſions: the receipt of the exchequer, which manages the royal revenue, and of which an account has already been given; and the judicial part, which is ſubdivided into a court of equity, and a court of common law. In all its departments, both of revenue and juriſprudence, the exchequer is divided into ſeven courts: 1. The court of pleas. 2. The court of accounts. 3. The court of receipt. 4. The court of exchequer chamber, being the aſſembly of all the judges in England, for matters of law. 5. The court of exchequer chamber, for errors in the court of exchequer. 6. The court of exchequer chamber, for errors in the king's bench; and, 7. The court of equity in the exchequer chamber. Of theſe it is moſt material here to deſcribe in general the courts of equity and common law.

The court of equity is held in the Exchequer chamber before the lord treaſurer, the chancellor of the exchequer, the chief baron, and three *puiſné* ones. Theſe are conjectured to have been anciently made out of ſuch as were barons of the kingdom, or parliamentary barons; and thence to have derived their name. The primary and original buſineſs of this court is to call the king's debtors to account by bill filed by the attorney general; and to recover any lands, chattels, or profits belonging to the crown. So that, by their original conſtitution, the juriſdiction of the courts of common pleas, king's bench, and exchequer, was entirely ſeparate and diſtinct: the common pleas being intended to decide all controverſies between ſubject and ſubject; the king's bench, to correct all crimes and miſdeſmenors amounting to a breach of the peace, the king being then plaintiff; and the exchequer to adjuſt and recover his revenue, wherein the king alſo is plaintiff. But, as by a fiction almoſt all ſorts of civil actions are now allowed to be brought in the king's bench, in like manner, by another fiction, all kinds of perſonal ſuits may be proſecuted in the court of exchequer. For as all the officers and miniſters of this have, like thoſe of the other ſuperior tribunals, the privilege of ſuing and being ſued only in their own court, ſo alſo the king's debtors and farmers, and all accomptants of the exchequer, are privileged to ſue and implead all manner of perſons in the ſame court of equity that they themſelves are called into. They have likewiſe privilege to ſue and implead one another, or any ſtranger, in the ſame kind of common law actions (where the perſonalty only is concerned) as are proſecuted in the court of common pleas.

This gives origin to the *common law* juriſdiction of the exchequer, which was eſtabliſhed merely for the benefit of the king's accountants, and is exerciſed by the barons only of that court, and not the treaſurer or chancellor. The writ, upon which all proceedings here are grounded is called a *quo minus*, becauſe the plaintiff, fictitiouſly ſtates himſelf to be a debtor and accountant to the king, and alleges that the defendant withholds from him that which is his due, *quo minus ſufficiens exiſtit, &c.* that is, by which he is the leſs able to pay the king his debt or rent. Suits in the exchequer are expreſsly directed to be confined to ſuch matters only as ſpecially concern the king or his miniſters of the exchequer; and the *articuli ſuper cartas* enact that no common pleas be thenceforth holden there, contrary to the form of the great charter; but by the ſuggeſtion of privilege any perſon may be admitted to ſue in the exchequer, as well as the king's accountant. The ſurmiſe, of being debtor to the king, is mere matter of form, and the court is open to all the nation equally. On *the equity ſide* too, any perſon may file a bill on a ſuggeſtion never controverted, that he is the king's accountant.

An appeal from the equity ſide of this court is immediately to the houſe of peers; but from the common law ſide, in purſuance of the ſtatute 31 Edw. III. c. 12. a writ of error muſt be firſt brought into the court of exchequer chamber; from the determination in which, there lies, in the *dernier reſort*, a writ of error to the houſe of lords.

The court of exchequer chamber has no original juriſdiction, but is only a court of appeal, to correct the errors of other juriſdictions; it was firſt erected by ſtatute 31 Edw. III. c. 12. to determine cauſes upon writs of error from the common law ſide of the court of exchequer. It conſiſts of the lord chancellor, and lord treaſurer, taking unto him the juſtices of the king's bench and common pleas. In imitation of this, a ſecond court of exchequer chamber was erected by ſtatute 27 Eliz. c. 8. conſiſting of the juſtices of the common pleas, and the barons of the exchequer; before whom writs of error may be brought to reverſe judgments in certain ſuits originally begun in the king's bench. Into the court alſo of the exchequer chamber, (which then conſiſts of all the judges of the three ſuperior courts, and now and then the lord chancellor alſo) are ſometimes adjourned from the other courts ſuch cauſes, as the judges upon argument find to be of great weight and

and difficulty, before any judgment is given on them in the court below. From all the branches of this court of exchequer chamber, a writ of error lies to the houſe of lords.

Officers. Under the barons of the exchequer is an officer called the

Examiner. He is a commiſſioner for taking affidavits in the court in London, and within ten miles of the metropolis, in the abſence of the barons; he is alſo empowered to attend and ſwear thoſe who from impriſonment, or other unſurmountable impediments, cannot appear before a baron.

There are beſides, a *curſitor baron*, a *marſhal and aſſociate* to the chief baron; *tipſtaffs*, *uſhers*, *cryer*, *court-keeper*, and *meſſengers*.

Remembrancers. There are three remembrancers, one of the king, another of the treaſurer, and one of the firſt fruits. They hold their places by patent. The firſt two are only to be mentioned here.

King's Remembrancer. The king's remembrancer is a principal officer on the equity ſide of the court. It is his duty to make proceſs againſt collectors of the cuſtoms, &c. enter in his office recognizances acknowledged before the barons, take bonds for the king's debts, &c. and make proceſs upon them, make proceſs upon all informations upon penal ſtatutes (which are entered in his office,) and bills of compoſition upon them, enter the ſtallment of debts, keep all conveyances of lands, &c. granted to the king; and all proceedings by Engliſh bill are entered there. He alſo taxes all bills of coſts ariſing in the equity ſide of the exchequer. His office is executed by deputy, and under him are two *Secondaries*.

Clerks in Court. The buſineſs of the ſuitors paſſes through the king's remembrancer's office, in which are ſix *ſworn clerks* and twenty *ſide clerks*; to them ſolicitors apply for office copies of all proceedings, and by their intervention all the buſineſs ariſing in cauſes is tranſacted. No perſon can be either a ſworn or ſide clerk, who has not *bona fide* ſerved a clerkſhip in the office for five years. The office is in the Inner Temple.

Treasurer's Remembrancer. The treaſurer's remembrancer makes proceſs by *fieri facias*, and extent for the king's debts, &c. enters upon record if accountants pay their proffers, &c. He has a *deputy*, a *ſecondary* and *filacer*, three *ſworn clerks* and a *bag bearer*. His office is in Somerſet-place.

There are alſo a *clerk of the errors in the exchequer chamber*, and his *deputy*. To the courts belong an hereditary *chief uſher*, and a *marſhal*, with their *deputies*.

Foreign Opposer. There is an officer with this title, who opposes all sheriffs, &c. in their accounts of the green wax, *viz.* of all fines, issues, amerciaments, recognizances, &c. for which process is sent to the sheriff sealed with green wax.

Clerk of the Estreats. The clerk of the estreats provides that summons for all fines, &c. estreated into the exchequer be issued. He has under him two deputies, and a surveyor of the green wax.

Clerk of the Nichils. The clerk of the nichils makes a roll of the sums in process, for which the sheriff returns nichil, and delivers it to the treasurer's remembrancer.

Plea Side. The officers on the plea side are, *a clerk of the pleas, his deputy*, and four *sworn attorneys*. Under each attorney are four *side clerks*, who act in their respective names and divisions. The office is in Lincoln's Inn Old Square.

Court of Chancery. The high court of chancery derives its name, *cancellaria*, from the judge who presides in it, called in Latin *cancellarius*, and of whose functions, exclusive of those exercised in the court, some account is given at page 2 of this volume.

In the court of chancery, as in the exchequer, there are two distinct tribunals; the one ordinary, being a court of common law; the other extraordinary, being a court of equity.

The ordinary legal court is much more ancient than the court of equity. Its jurisdiction is to hold plea on *scire facias;* to repeal and cancel the king's letters patent, when made against law, or upon untrue suggestions; and to hold plea of petitions, *monstrans de droits*, traverses of offices, and the like, when the king has been advised to do any act, or is put in possession of any lands or goods, in prejudice of a subject's right. On proof of which, as the king can never be supposed intentionally to do any wrong, the law questions not but he will immediately redress the injury; and refers that conscientious task to the chancellor, the keeper of his conscience. It also appertains to this court to hold plea of all personal actions, where any officer or minister of the court is a party. It might likewise hold plea (by *scire facias*) of partitions of lands in coparcenary, and of dower, where any ward of the crown was concerned in interest, so long as the military tenures subsisted: as it now may also do of the tithes of forest land, where granted by the king, and claimed by a stranger, against the grantee of the crown; and of executions or statutes, or recognizances in nature thereof, by the statute 23 Hen. VIII. c. 6. But if any cause comes to issue in this court, that is, if any fact be disputed between the parties, the chancellor cannot try it, having no power to summon a jury; but must deliver the record *propria manu* into the court of king's bench,

bench, where it ſhall be tried by the country, and judgment given there. When judgment is given in chancery upon demurrer, or the like, a writ of error, in nature of an appeal, lies out of this ordinary court into the court of king's bench: though ſo little is uſually done on the common law ſide of the court, that no traces are found of any writ of error being actually brought ſince the fourteenth year of queen Elizabeth, A. D. 1572. In this ordinary, or legal court, is alſo kept the *officina juſtitiæ*: out of which iſſue all original writs that paſs under the great ſeal, all commiſſions of charitable uſes, ſewers, bankruptcy, idiotcy, lunacy, and the like; and for which it is always open to the ſubject, who may there at any time demand and have, *ex debito juſtitiæ*, any writ his occaſions may call for. Theſe writs (relating to the buſineſs of the ſubject) and the returns to them, were, according to the ſimplicity of ancient times, originally kept in a hamper, *in hanaperio*; and the others (relating to ſuch matters wherein the crown is immediately or mediately concerned) were preſerved in a little ſack or bag, *in parva baga*; thence has ariſen the diſtinction of the *hanaper* office, and *petty bag* office, which both belong to the common law court in chancery.

But the extraordinary court, or court of equity, is now become of the greateſt judicial conſequence; in which the juriſdiction of the chancellor is exerciſed in its fulleſt extent. This authority of the chancellor, it is ſaid, was plainly derived from the nature of his employment in the king's houſehold, and from the miniſterial powers over the kingdom, with which he thence became inveſted. By being the king's ſecretary and chaplain, he enjoyed the peculiar confidence of his maſter; and had the ſole charge of writing his letters; and afterwards of iſſuing writs in the name of the crown. As it became cuſtomary that every vaſſal ſhould hold his fief by a charter from the ſuperior, the power of granting thoſe deeds, throughout the royal demeſnes, became the ſource of great influence; and, after the Norman conqueſt, when the nobility were all reduced to vaſſals of the crown, raiſed the chancellor to be a principal officer of ſtate.

When the deeds iſſuing from the crown became numerous, the care of expediting many of them devolved on inferior perſons; and to aſcertain their authenticity, the ſubſcription of the chancellor, and afterwards a public ſeal, of which he obtained the cuſtody, was adhibited. At what time ſignatures became cuſtomary in England to deeds proceeding from the crown, is uncertain. It is probable they were known to the Anglo-Saxons; but did not become frequent, until the ſettlement of the Norman princes. From this period the chancellor was conſidered as having a title to keep the great ſeal; but,

 from

from the caprice of the monarch, there occurred ſome inſtances in which it was intruſted to a different perſon, ſtyled the lord keeper. In this manner all important writings, iſſued by the king, either came through the medium of the chancellor, or lord keeper, or were ſubjected to his inſpection. Before he affixed the great ſeal to any deed, he was bound to examine its nature; and, if it proceeded upon a falſe repreſentation, or contained any thing erroneous or illegal, to repeal and cancel it. So early were laid the foundations of a maxim, which, in after days, has been gradually extended, that the ſervants of the crown are juſtly reſponſible for meaſures which cannot be executed without their concurrence. As the exerciſe of theſe powers required a previous examination and cognizance, it gave riſe to an ordinary juriſdiction; which, although of great importance, has occaſioned no controverſy, and appears to have excited little attention.

The extraordinary juriſdiction of the chancellor aroſe more indirectly from his character and ſituation. When the king's baron court, confining itſelf within the rules of common law, had been laid under the neceſſity of giving a deciſion, which in its application to particular caſes was found hard and oppreſſive, the party aggrieved was accuſtomed to petition the king for relief. Applications of this nature were brought before the privy council; and the conſideration of them was naturally referred to the chancellor; who, as the ſecretary of the king, being employed to regiſter the decrees and to keep the records of his baron court, was rendered peculiarly converſant and intelligent in all judicial diſcuſſions. A juriſdiction of this nature appears to have been acquired by the ſame officer in ſeveral, if not in the greater part, of the kingdoms of Europe. Such, in particular, was that of the chancellor in France; who, under the kings of the firſt and ſecond race, had the cuſtody of their ſeal, and was diſtinguiſhed by the appellation of the *grand referandaire*.

In England, it ſhould ſeem that, before the end of the Saxon government, the chancellor was employed in giving redreſs againſt the hard ſentences pronounced by the judges, of the king's demeſne. As thoſe judges, however, had then a very limited authority, his interpoſitions were proportionably of little importance; but, after the acceſſion of William the Conqueror, when the *aula regis* became the king's ordinary baron court, and drew to itſelf almoſt the whole judicial buſineſs of the nation, the exerciſe of ſuch extraordinary juriſdiction began to appear in a more conſpicuous light. From this period, the multiplication of law ſuits, before the grand juſticiary,

ciary, produced more various inſtances of imperfections in the rules of common law; and, from greater experience and refinement, the neceſſity of relaxing in the obſervance of theſe rules, by the admiſſion of numerous exceptions, was more ſenſibly felt.

As applications for this purpoſe became frequent, proviſion was made in order to facilitate their progreſs; and the tribunal, to which they were directed, grew up into a regular form. A committee of the privy council had, in each caſe, been originally appointed along with the chancellor to determine the points in queſtion. But, as theſe counſellors paid little or no attention to buſineſs of this nature, of which they had ſeldom any knowledge, their number, which had been arbitrary, was therefore gradually diminiſhed; and, at laſt, their appointment having come to be regarded as a mere ceremony, was entirely diſcontinued. Subordinate officers were, on the other hand, found requiſite in various departments, to aſſiſt the chancellor in preparing his deciſions, and in diſcharging the other branches of his duty. The authority, however, which was thus exerciſed by this great magiſtrate, in order to correct and to ſupply the moſt remarkable errors and defects in the ancient rules of law, appears to have ſtill proceeded upon references from the king, or from the privy council. His interpoſitions depended upon the deciſions given by other courts; and were of too ſingular a nature to be eaſily reduced into a ſyſtem, or to be viewed in the light of a common remedy. It was at a later period, that the chancery became an original court, for determining cauſes beyond the reach of the ordinary tribunals. This inſtitution, ariſing from circumſtances more accidental than thoſe which produced the juriſdiction above mentioned, does not ſeem to have pervaded the other European nations, but is, in a great meaſure, peculiar to England.

According to the feudal policy in the Weſtern part of Europe, all juriſdiction was inſeparably connected with landed property; and actions of every ſort proceeded upon a mandate, or commiſſion, from that particular ſuperior, within whoſe territory the cauſe was to be tried. If an action was intended before a court deriving its juriſdiction from the king, the plaintiff made application to the crown, ſtating the injuſtice of which he complained; in anſwer to which, the ſovereign ordered the adverſe party to appear before a particular court, in order that the cauſe might be argued and determined. The writ, or brief, iſſued for this purpoſe by the king, ſerved not only to ſummon the defendant into court, but alſo, in that particular queſtion, to authorize the inveſtigation of the magiſtrate. The different barons, in their reſpective demeſnes, iſſued briefs, in like manner, for bringing any law-ſuit under the cognizance of their ſeveral courts.

In England this mode of litigation was uniformly obſerved in proceedings before the *aula regis*; and was afterwards adopted in the three courts of common law, among which the powers of the grand juſticiary were divided. The primitive writs, upon which any action was commenced, being accommodated to the few ſimple claims that were anciently inforced in a court of juſtice, were probably conceived in ſuch terms, as might occur without much reflection. But complaints, upon the ſame principle of law, being frequently repeated, the ſame terms naturally continued; ſo that, by long uſage, a particular form of writ was rendered invariable and permanent in every ſpecies of action. This preſervation of uniformity, although perhaps the effect of that propenſity, ſo obſervable in all mankind, to be governed on every occaſion by analogy, proved, at the ſame time, of great advantage, by aſcertaining and limiting the authority of the judge. From the advancement of property, however, and from the multiplied connexions of ſociety, there aroſe new claims, which had never been the ſubject of diſcuſſion. Theſe required a new form of writ; the invention of which, in conſiſtency with the eſtabliſhed rules of law, and ſo calculated as to maintain good order and regularity in the ſyſtem of judicial procedure, became daily a matter of greater nicety and importance.

Applications in ſuch caſes was made to the chancellor; who, from a ſcrupulous regard to precedents, was frequently unwilling to interpoſe, but referred the parties to the next meeting of parliament. Theſe references, however, as might be expected, ſoon became burdenſome to that aſſembly; and, by a ſtatute in the reign of Edward I. it was provided, that, "Whenſoever, from thenceforth, it ſhall fortune in chancery "that, in one caſe a writ is found, and in like caſe, falling "under like law, and requiring like remedy, is found none, "the clerks in chancery ſhall agree in making the writ, or "ſhall adjourn the plaintiffs to the next parliament, where a "writ ſhall be framed, by conſent of the learned in the law; "leſt it might happen for the future, that the court of "our lord the king ſhould long fail in doing juſtice to the "ſuitors."

The new writs, deviſed in conſequence of this law, were, for ſome time, directed to ſuch of the ordinary courts as from the nature of the caſe, appeared to have the moſt proper juriſdiction. At length, however, there occurred certain claims

claims, in which, though seeming to require the interposition of a judge, it was thought the common law would not interferere. In these, the chancellor, willing to grant a remedy, and, perhaps, not adverse to the extension of his own authority, adventured to call the parties before himself, and to determine their difference. This innovation is said to have been introduced about the time of Richard II. and for the purpose of supporting a contrivance to elude the statute of *mortmain*, by the appointment of trustees to hold a landed estate, for the benefit of those religious corporations to which it could not be directly bequeathed. The courts of common law could give no countenance to a stratagem so palpably intended to disappoint the will of the legislature; but the chancellor, as a clergyman, was led by a fellow feeling with his own order, to support this evasion; and, pretending to consider it as a matter of conscience, that the trustees should be bound to a faithful discharge of their trust, took upon him to inforce the will of a testator, in opposition to the law of the land.

Having succesfully assumed the cognizance of one case, in which he was particularly interested, the chancellor found little difficulty in extending his jurisdiction to others. In these he appears to have acted more from a general regard to justice; and, in consequence of the limited views entertained by the ordinary courts, his interposition seemed immediately necessary. His authority thus grew up imperceptibly: what was begun in usurpation, by acquiring the sanction of long usage, became a legal establishment; and, when it afterwards excited the jealousy of the courts of common law, its abolition was regarded as impolitic and dangerous. After the direction of the chancery had long been possessed by clergymen, who, from their situation, were intent upon the increase of its jurisdiction, it was, upon some occasions, committed to lawyers by profession; by whom its procedure was more digested into a regular system.

From what has been observed, concerning the extraordinary jurisdiction of the court of chancery, there can be no doubt that it was originally distinguished from that of the other courts of Westminster-hall, by the same limits which mark the distinction between common, or strict law, and equity. Its primitive interpositions were intended to decide according to conscience upon those occasions, when the decisions of other courts, from an adherence to ancient rules, were found hard and oppressive. It was afterwards led to interpose in original actions, in order to make effectual those new claims which the ordinary courts accounted beyond the limits

of

of their jurisdiction. This first branch of this authority in the court of chancery was therefore designed to correct the injustice, the other to supply the defects, of the other tribunals.

This accordingly seems to have been the universally received idea of that court, which is called a court of equity by every author who has had occasion to mention it. In this view it is considered by lord Bacon, who himself held the office of chancellor, and who, among all his contemporaries, appears to have been best qualified to understand its nature. The same opinion of this court was held by the learned Selden. "Equity," says that author, "is a roguish thing; for law we have a measure; know what we trust to. Equity is according to the conscience of him that is chancellor; and, as that is larger or narrower, so is equity. It is all one, as if they should make the standard for measure a chancellor's foot. What an uncertain measure would this be! One chancellor has a long foot; another a short foot; a third an indifferent foot. 'Tis the same thing in the chancellor's conscience."

The ingenious and acute author of "The Principles of Equity" has adopted this notion concerning the nature of the court of chancery; and disputes with lord Bacon, whether it is more expedient that the equitable jurisdiction, and the jurisdiction according to strict law, should be united in the same court, as in ancient Rome, or divided between different courts, as in England?

In opposition to these authorities, justice Blackstone, a writer who, in a practical point of this nature, can hardly be supposed mistaken, affirms that there is no such distinction between the chancery and the other courts of Westminster; and maintains that the latter are possessed of equitable jurisdiction; while the former, to which however, like other writers, he gives the appellation of a court of equity, is accustomed to decide according to the rules of strict law.

To reconcile these different opinions, it seems necessary to suppose that they refer to different periods; and that both the chancery, and the other courts in question, have, since their first establishment, been subjected to great alterations. This is what, from the nature of things, might reasonably be expected. Lord Bacon and Mr. Selden speak of the court of chancery as it stood in a remote period: Blackstone to one more modern.

The distinction between strict law and equity is never in any country a permanent distinction. It varies according to the state of property, the improvement of arts, the experience of judges, the refinement of a people.

In

In a rude age, the obſervation of mankind is directed to particular objects; and ſeldom leads to the formation of general concluſions. The firſt deciſions of judges, agreeable to the ſtate of their knowledge, were ſuch as aroſe, in each caſe, from immediate feelings; that is, from conſiderations of equity. Theſe judges, however, in the courſe of their employment, had afterwards occaſion to meet with many ſimilar caſes; upon which, from the ſame impreſſions of juſtice, as well as in order to avoid the appearance of partiality, they were led to pronounce a ſimilar deciſion. A number of precedents was thus introduced, and from the force of cuſtom, acquired reſpect and authority. Different caſes were decided, from the view of certain great and leading circumſtances in which they reſembled each other: and the various deciſions, pronounced by the courts of law, were gradually reduced into order, and diſtributed into certain claſſes, according to the ſeveral grounds and principles upon which they proceeded. The utility of eſtabliſhing general rules for the determination of every law, became alſo an object of attention. By limiting and circumſcribing the power of a judge, they contributed to prevent his partiality in particular ſituations; and by marking out the preciſe line of conduct required from every individual, they beſtowed upon the people at large, the ſecurity and ſatisfaction ariſing from the knowledge of their ſeveral duties and rights.

But although the ſimplification of deciſions, by reducing them to general principles, was attended with manifeſt advantage, it was, in ſome caſes, productive of inconvenience and hardſhip. It is difficult, upon any ſubject, to eſtabliſh a rule which is not liable to exceptions. But the primitive rules of law, introduced by inexperienced and ignorant judges, were even far from attaining that perfection which was practicable. They were frequently too narrow; and frequently too broad. They gave riſe to deciſions, which, in many inſtances, fell extremely ſhort of the mark; and which, in many others, went far beyond it. In caſes of this nature, it became a queſtion, whether it was more expedient, by a ſcrupulous obſervance of rules, to avoid the poſſibility of arbitrary practice, or, by a particular deviation from them, to prevent an unjuſt determination? In order to prevent groſs injuſtice under the ſanction of legal authority, an evil of the moſt alarming nature, it was thought adviſable, upon extraordinary occaſions, to depart from eſtabliſhed maxims, and, from a complex view of every circumſtance, to decide according to the feelings of juſtice. The diſtinction between ſtrict law and equity was thus introduced; the former comprehending the eſtabliſhed rules; the latter the exceptions made to thoſe rules in particular caſes.

But

But when questions of equity became numerous, they too were often found to resemble one another; and requiring a similar decision, were by degrees arranged and classed according to their principles. After a contract, for example, had been enforced by a general rule, it might happen, on different occasions, that an individual had given a promise, from the undue influence of threats and violence, from his being cheated by the other party, or from advantage being taken of his ignorance and incapacity. On every occasion of this nature, an equitable decision was given; and, by an exception to the common rule of law, the promiser was relieved from performance. But, the remedy given in such cases being reduced into a regular system, could no longer be viewed in the light of a singular interposition; and, by the ordinary operation of law, every contract extorted by force, elicited by fraud, or procured in consequence of error and incapacity, was rendered ineffectual. Every primitive rule of justice was productive of numerous exceptions; and each of these was afterwards reduced under general principles; to which, in a subsequent period, new exceptions became necessary.

Law and equity are thus in continual progression; and the former is constantly gaining ground upon the latter. Every new and extraordinary interposition is, by length of time, converted into an old rule. A great part of what is now strict law was formerly considered as equity; and the equitable decisions of this age will unavoidably be ranked under the strict law of the next.

Although the chancellor, therefore, was originally intrusted with the mere province of equity, the revolutions of time have unavoidably changed the nature of his jurisdiction. He continues to exert an authority in all such claims as were anciently taken under his protection; but his interpositions concerning them are now directed by general principles, to which various exceptions, according to equity, have since been introduced. He continues, likewise, those modes of procedure which were suitable to his primitive situation, and adapted to such investigations as the purpose of his establishment required.

The ordinary courts of Westminster-hall have, on the other hand, extended their jurisdiction beyond its ancient limits. Though they originally did not venture to deviate from the rules of strict law, the improvements of a later age have inspired them with a more liberal spirit; and have rendered their decisions more agreeable to the natural dictates of justice.

Thus the court of chancery has been gradually divesting itself of its original character, and assuming that of the courts of of common law; while those tribunals have been, in the same proportion, enlarging their powers, and advancing within the precincts of equity.

According to Blackstone, the essential difference at present, between the chancery and the courts of common law, consists in the modes of administering justice peculiar to each. It may deserve to be remarked, that these differences are such as would naturally arise between courts originally distinguished by having the separate departments of strict law and equity.

1. From the mode of proof adopted by chancery, all questions which require a reference to the oath of a party are appropriated to that court. This peculiarity arose from an opinion, entertained by early judges, that it was a hardship to compel any person to furnish evidence against himself. But the view suggested by equity was more liberal and refined. It appeared unjust that a defendant should refuse to satisfy a claim, which he knew to be well founded; and, unless he was conscious of having fraudulently withheld performance, he could suffer no damage by his judicial declaration.

2. The chancery alone is competent for taking proofs by commission, when witnesses are abroad, or shortly to leave the kingdom, or hindered by age or infirmity from attending. In the courts of common law, the method of trial by a jury was universally established; and as this form required that the witnesses should be examined in court, the interposition of equity was indispensable to authorize their examination in absence.

3. Instead of awarding damages for neglecting to fulfil a contract, the court of chancery has power to order specific performance. From the narrow principles embraced, in early times, by the courts of strict law, no complaint was regarded, unless the plaintiff had suffered in his pecuniary interest; and consequently, upon the breach of contract, nothing further could be claimed than reparation of the damage incurred. In a more equitable view, it appeared that every innocent and reasonable purpose of the contractors ought to be enforced; although, perhaps, the loss arising from the failure of performance could not be estimated in money. A court of equity, therefore, was accustomed to enjoin, that a contract should be expressly fulfilled.

4. Two other branches of power are mentioned as peculiar to the court of chancery: the one to interpret securities for money lent. This arose from the prohibition, introduced by the canon law, of taking interest for the loan of money; which occasioned an evasion, by means of what is called a *double bond*. The true construction of this deed, according to the intention of the parties, and in opposition to the words, was beyond the jurisdiction

jurisdiction of the ordinary courts. The other branch of power alluded to, was that of enforcing a *trust*. This, as formerly observed, was intended to evade the statute of *mortmain*; and afforded the chancellor the first ground for assuming his extraordinary authority in original actions.

Considering the origin of the court of chancery, there was no reason to expect that its jurisdiction would be separated from that of the ordinary courts by any scientific mode of arrangement. It was the offspring of accidental emergency; being merely a temporary expedient for granting an immediate relief to those who had suffered from legal injustice. Supposing that, after it became a permanent and regular tribunal, it had remained upon its original footing, the advantages likely to have resulted from it may reasonably be called in question. That one court should have a jurisdiction according to strict law, and another according to equity; that the former should be obliged, with eyes open, to pronounce an unjust sentence, in conformity to an old rule, leaving parties to procure relief by application to the latter; that, in a word, the common law tribunal should be empowered to view the law-suit only upon one side, and the court of equity upon a different one; such a regulation appears in itself no less absurd and ridiculous, than its consequences would be hurtful, by producing a waste of time, and an accumulation of expences; not to mention the uncertainty and fluctuation of conduct arising from the inaccurate and variable boundaries, by which equity and strict law must ever be distinguished. Even according to the later form which the chancery has assumed, and by which it has appropriated causes of a very peculiar description, or such as require a singular mode of procedure, its line of partition from the ordinary civil courts may be thought rather arbitrary and whimsical. But, however the present distribution of the judicial powers may be deficient in speculative propriety, it seems in practice to be attended with no inconvenience. The province belonging to each of the courts of Westminster-hall appears now to be settled with an exactness which prevents all interference or embarrassment; and there is, perhaps, no country in the world where equity and strict law are more properly tempered with each other, or where the administration of justice, both in civil and criminal matters, has a freer and more uniform course.

From this court of equity in chancery, as from the other superior courts, an appeal lies to the house of peers. But there are these differences between appeals from a court of equity, and writs of error from a court of law: 1. That the former may be brought upon any interlocutory matter; the latter upon nothing,

nothing, but only a definitive judgment. 2. That on writs of error, the house of lords pronounces the judgment; on appeals it gives direction to the court below to rectify its own decrees.

The court of chancery sits in term in Westminster-hall; in vacation, in the hall of Lincoln's Inn.

OFFICERS. The principal officers belonging to the court of chancery are the following:

MASTER OF THE ROLLS. The master of the rolls, anciently called *Guardein des Rolles*, *Clericus Rotulorum*, or clerk of the rolls, and now stiled in his patent, *Clericus parvæ Bagæ et custos rotulorum*, &c. is chief of the twelve masters in chancery, chief clerk of the petty bag office, and a very ancient judicial officer. His appointment is grantable by letters patent, formerly at the king's pleasure, but now always for life: it has been filled by spiritual persons. By a patent of Edward III. the master, when a clergyman, was appointed and installed in the house of the rolls in Chancery-lane, by the lord chancellor. In his judicial capacity, besides what he does as assistant to, or associate with, the lord chancellor when present, or as deputy to him when absent, many causes are set down before him to hear and decree, which he usually does on certain days appointed, commonly in the presence of one or more masters in chancery, and sometimes in their absence, and either in court, at his own house, or the chapel of the rolls; and all such orders and decrees as are made by him, are drawn up and entered as made by the court, but they cannot be enrolled, till signed by the lord chancellor, who has also the power to discharge or alter them. He is also the keeper of all records, judgments, sentences, and decrees given in chancery. It appears by the statute 14 Hen. VIII. c. 8. that the master of the rolls has the giving of the offices of the six clerks in chancery; he has also the appointment of the clerks of the petty bag office, the two chief examiners, the usher of the court of chancery, and some others. And he has divers prerogatives by statute, commission, and prescription. The emoluments of the office consist in 1200*l*. a year annexed to it by statute 23 Geo. II. c. 25. in the occupation of the house belonging to his office in Roll's yard, Chancery-lane; and in the rents of a circumjacent estate, amounting together, it is supposed, to somewhat less than 4000*l*. per annum. The officers under the master of the rolls are, a chief and under secretary, a train-bearer, usher of the court, deputy usher, tipstaff, and porter.

MASTERS IN CHANCERY. These officers are twelve in number, including the master of the rolls, who is their chief, and the accountant general. They are assistants or associates to the chancellor and master of the rolls, sit with them in court by turns, usually two at a time; and references touching accounts, matters of practice, &c. are directed to them, upon which they make their reports; they also administer oaths to those who swear to answer, take affidavits, and acknowledgments of deeds, recognizances, &c. They were formerly stiled *clerici de prima forma*; and were to be grave and ancient clerks, skilful and of long experience in the practice of the court; for they had equal authority with the chancellor in forming the *brevia magistralia*, in which, unless they all agreed, they were to go to parliament. They were anciently members of the king's court, allowed robes out of the royal wardrobe, and dieted as part of the household, for whom special purveyance was made; and in this quality, they attend the house of lords, and have a right to assist at coronations. By statute 13 Chas. II. a public office is to be kept near the rolls, for the masters in chancery, in which they, or some or one of them, shall constantly attend for the dispatch of all matters incident to their office, (references upon accounts, and insufficient answers only excepted,) from seven o'clock in the morning, till twelve at noon, and from two in the afternoon till six at night; by this act there are fees appointed; and tables of the fees are to be put up in their office, which is now held at an elegant building erected for that and other purposes in Southampton-buildings, Chancery-lane. Each master has a clerk; a salary of 200*l*. per annum issues from the bank for each master; but their further emoluments depend on the portion of business referred to them.

Masters Extraordinary. These are merely persons empowered by the court to take affidavits in the country, and they are appointed by commissions, which are obtained without difficulty, and at a small expence.

Accountant General. In former times each master in chancery was accustomed to keep in his hands the monies paid into court in the causes which were referred to him; but some losses and many inconveniences having arisen to the suitors, the accountant general was appointed in pursuance of an act of parliament. He does all such matters and things, relating to the delivery of the suitor's money and effects, into the bank, and taking them out, and keeping accounts with the bank, as by the orders of the court were to be done by the masters and usher; who, on the passing of the act, were to make up their accounts with the accountant general, and pay into the bank all monies remaining in their hands, to be placed to his account; and to transfer and assign to him all the securities for money which they held in trust for the suitors of the court. The accountant general cannot, however, meddle with the actual receipt and custody of the suitors money or effects, but only keeps the account with the bank; the governor and company of which are answerable for all money received by them, and not the accountant general. He holds his office subject to the further regulation, and during the pleasure of the court, which is generally for life. Forging the name of the accountant-general to any certificate, in order to the receiving any of the suitors money, is by the statute made felony. The office is in Chancery-lane.

Six Clerks. These officers are of ancient establishment, and they were heretofore spiritual persons, and they have been specially assigned, amongst other officers, to attend at the king's coronation. They are principally concerned in matters of equity; and transact and file all proceedings by bill and answer; and also issue some patents that pass the great seal, as pardons of men for chance medley, patents for embassadors, sheriffs' patents, and some others; all which matters are transacted by their under clerks, or others by them appointed. They likewise sign all office copies in order to be read in court, and also certificates, and attend the court in term, by two at a time, at Westminster, to read the pleadings. The business of the office is done by their under clerks, each of whom has a seat in the office, and whereof every six clerk has a certain number, usually about ten, besides two waiting clerks in each division, who are all accountable to their respective six clerks for the business they transact. At this day they employ deputies in their absence (usually a sworn clerk, or a waiting clerk of their own division) to file the proceedings, and sign office copies and certificates.

Sworn and waiting Clerks. In order to be qualified for clerks in court, a person must be articled to a sworn clerk, and serve him five years in the six clerks office, and at the expiration of their clerkships, they are to be examined by the master of the rolls, and, if approved of, they are admitted and sworn before him, to the faithful execution of their office, which constitutes them sworn clerks. All suitors in the court must employ one of the sworn, or one of the waiting clerks, to act as clerk in court. They make out all writs both special and common, and all process (except *subpœnas*) in all causes, depending on the equity side, wherein they are respectively employed. They claim a right to, and, as occasion requires, have, the custody of all records relating to causes there, of which they make copies for their clients. They also ingross bills, answers, &c. (if not done by their clients or solicitors), attend the court and masters in chancery as occasion requires, draw and enroll the decrees of the court, make copies of all depositions taken by by commiſſion in the country, &c.; and they attend, by themſelves or agents, not only in term time, but alſo in the vacation.

REGISTER. The regiſter holds his place by letters patent, and has ſeveral deputies under him, who ſit in court by turns, to take notes of all orders and decrees, in purſuance of which they draw up the orders, which are alſo entered in the office: having been firſt duly paſſed by a deputy regiſter. The office of regiſter alſo embraces ſome other duties. The buſineſs is tranſacted under the ſame roof with the ſix clerks. Office in Chancery-lane.

MASTER OF THE SUBPOENA OFFICE. In this office are made out all writs of ſubpœna, both ſpecial and common. The office is granted by letters patent: and the buſineſs is tranſacted by deputies. It is in Chancery-lane.

REGISTER OF AFFIDAVITS. This officer files, regiſters, and makes copies of affidavits, which copies are ſigned by himſelf or his deputy; and no counſel, clerk, &c. can give any affidavit in evidence that is not filed and regiſtered in the affidavit office. It is granted by letters patent, and ſituate in Southampton-buildings, Chancery-lane.

EXAMINERS. There are two examiners, who have under them ſeveral deputies, and copying clerks: they, by themſelves or deputies, examine witneſſes produced on either ſide (being firſt ſworn by a maſter on interrogatories), take their depoſitions, and make out copies of them, and of the interrogatories, where not by commiſſion in the country. And all depoſitions are to be kept private in the office till publication is paſſed. The examiners' office is in Roll's-yard, Chancery-lane.

CURSITORS. Theſe officers are of a very ancient inſtitution; they are in number twenty-four, and were incorporated by queen Elizabeth. They make out all original writs in chancery, returnable in the common pleas, &c., and amongſt theſe the buſineſs of the ſeveral counties is ſeverally diſtributed. Their office is in Chancery-lane.

PETTY BAG. The principal clerks of the petty bag are three in number, (of whom the maſter of the rolls is chief,) and have ſeveral clerks under them. They tranſact a great variety of buſineſs, which requires knowledge and experience in the practice of the law; and have the making out of writs of ſummons to parliament; and commiſſions directed to commiſſioners of every ſhire for aſſeſſing ſubſidies and taxes, *Conges d'élire* for biſhops, patents of cuſtomers, gaugers, controllers, and alnegers, *liberates* upon extent of ſtatute ſtaples, and recovery of recognizances forfeited, and all *elegits* upon them. All offices found *poſt mortem* are brought to the petty bag office to be filed. Here are entered all pleadings in chancery concern-

ing

ing the validity of any patent, or other thing which paſſes the great ſeal; which pleadings are according to the courſe of the common law. And if any queſtion ariſe about the acknowledgment of any deed before the lord chancellor, or any other officer of the court, it is to be here proſecuted; and all ſtatutes and recognizances taken before any officers of the court to that purpoſe deputed, are tranſmitted hither. Alſo all ſuits for or againſt any privileged perſon in the court, are brought and proceeded on only in this office. There are alſo various other duties. The petty bag office is in the Roll's-yard, in Chancery-lane.

Clerk of the Crown. The clerk of the crown in chancery is, by himſelf or deputy, continually to attend the lord chancellor or lord keeper; to write and prepare for the great ſeal of England ſpecial matters of ſtate, by commiſſion, or the like, either immediately from his majeſty, or by order of his council, as well ordinary as extraordinary, as commiſſions of lieutenancy, of juſtices itinerant, and of aſſize of *oyer* and *terminer*, of gaol delivery, and of the peace, with their writs of aſſociation. Alſo, all general pardons. He ſits in the lords' houſe in parliament time; and into his office, the writs of parliament, made by the clerks of the petty bag, with the names of the knights and burgeſſes elected thereupon, are returned and filed. He has alſo the making of all ſpecial pardons and writs of execution upon bonds of ſtatute ſtaple forfeited. This office is alſo in the Rolls-yard.

Clerk of the Hanaper. The function of this ancient officer is to receive all the monies due to the king, for the ſeals of charters, patents, commiſſions, and writs; as alſo fees due to the officers for enrolling and examining them. He is obliged to attend the lord chancellor daily in the term, and at all times of ſealing, having with him a leather bag, wherein are put all charters, &c. after they are ſealed, which bags being cloſed with the lord chancellor's private ſeal, are delivered to the controller of the hanaper.

Beſide theſe, there are many officers belonging to this court, whoſe duties are deſignated by their names; as the *clerk of enrolling letters patent; the clerk of the faculties for diſpenſations, licences, &c.; clerk of the preſentations for benefices of the crown in the chancellor's gift; clerk of appeals*, on appeals from the courts of the archbiſhop to the court of chancery; and there are others who are conſtituted by the chancellor's commiſſion or letter, and attend him for particular purpoſes, and on particular occaſions; ſuch as the ſealer of writs, &c. Others are conſtituted by patent from the king; as the clerks for writing licences of alienation,

ation, writs of licences of protection, and many others of like nature; and some are ordained by parliament to be nominated and constituted by the king's letters patent; such as the writer and enroller of confirmations of all licences and dispensations, as shall be brought into chancery under the archbishop of Canterbury's seal, &c.

The following officers are in immediate attendance on the person of the chancellor; his principal secretary, purse-bearer, deputy purse-bearer, secretary of bankrupts, deputy-secretary, clerks, secretary of the presentations, secretary of the commissions of the peace, secretary of lunatics, receiver of the fines, secretary of the decrees and injunctions, secretary of the briefs, usher of the court, deputy-serjeant at arms, deputy messenger or pursuivant, deputy gentlemen of the chamber, usher of the hall, clerk of the court, court-keeper, tipstaff, and running porter.

Bankrupts. The jurisdiction of the court of chancery in matters of bankruptcy is not specified in this place; it will be noticed in another division of the work.

In these four last mentioned courts, of common pleas, king's bench, exchequer, and chancery, the business is transacted, except as to the verbal statement of the merits to the court itself, by attorneys or solicitors, and the pleading or statement of the cause is confided to advocates, who are either barristers or serjeants at law.

Attorneys or Solicitors. An attorney is one who is appointed to do any thing in the *turn*, stead, or place of another. In chancery and in the exchequer, those who do the business of attorneys are termed solicitors. No person can act as an attorney or solicitor, unless he shall have been bound for five years. The articles are on a stamp of 100*l.* and every person articled to serve as a clerk to any attorney or solicitor, must within three months cause an affidavit to be made of the actual execution of the contract which is to be filed in the court where the attorney or solicitor is enrolled. The clerk must, during the whole time specified in the articles, be actually employed by his master or his agent, in the business of an attorney or solicitor; and before he is admitted, must cause an affidavit of himself, or of the attorney or solicitor to whom he was bound, to be made and filed like the other, that he has actually and really served and been so employed. One of the judges in the courts of law, and the master of the rolls, or two masters in chancery, and a judge of the other courts of equity respectively, are directed to examine any person touching his fitness and capacity to be an attorney or solicitor: if approved of, he is ſworn in open court, to demean himſelf honeſtly in his practice; and he alſo takes the oaths of allegiance, ſupremacy, and abjuration.

Privilege. The chief privilege of an attorney is, that he cannot be arreſted on any proceſs for the purpoſe of being held to bail; this indulgence is granted on a ſuppoſition that he muſt always be preſent in court, tranſacting the buſineſs of his clients, and therefore, in the allowance of it, the judges always take care to apply that cauſe to their deciſion. They will not diſcharge an attorney who is arreſted, or allow his plea of privilege, unleſs he was, at the time when the action was commenced, *bona fide* a practiſing attorney, and had duly taken out his annual licence, which is on a ſtamp of 10*l*. in London, and 6*l*. in the country. An attorney, in reſpect of his attendance at the court, cannot be preſſed for a ſoldier; but he is not privileged from ſerving in the militia, or finding a ſubſtitute. He cannot be made conſtable though there be a cuſtom that every inhabitant ſhall be choſen in his turn; and, in general, it is ſaid that he is not to be elected into any other office againſt his will; as to the office of overſeer of the poor, or churchwarden, or any office within a borough.

On the other hand, when proceedings are againſt an attorney by bill, the party ſuing him can obtain judgment much ſooner than where he proceeds by ordinary proceſs; and an attorney cannot bring an action for his bill of coſts for buſineſs in any court, until a month after he has delivered it to his debtor, ſigned with his name. Attorneys are alſo under the ſummary juriſdiction of the courts wherein they practiſe, and ſubject to be ſtruck off the rolls for mal-practice, or for groſs ignorance; and if their clients ſuffer by their ignorance or neglect, they may recover from them damages to the amount. And no attorney in confinement for debt, or any other cauſe, can commence or proſecute any ſuit for any other perſon; though it is held that he may proceed in thoſe which he had previouſly commenced; and he may ſue for any debt due to himſelf.

Special Pleaders, Draftsmen in Equity and Conveyancers. Under theſe ſeveral denominations many gentleman practiſe, who are neither attorneys, nor at the bar; but many gentlemen at the bar exerciſe alſo theſe branches of the profeſſion. *Special pleaders* are they who prepare drafts of all the pleadings in a cauſe at law, from its commencement to its cloſe; and they are accurately acquainted with all the deciſions of the courts relative to points of practice, and to thoſe queſtions which are likely to ariſe in the trial of cauſes. Their aſſiſtance therefore is eminently ſerviceable to attorneys, and their offices are conſidered the beſt ſchools in which ſtudents can acquire

 an

an accurate knowledge of the common law. *Draftsmen in equity* are the same with respect to the equity courts which special pleaders are to those of common law: and *conveyancers* are employed in the preparation of every species of deed, contract, and will, and in perusing drafts laid before them, in order to ascertain whether the title, securities, and terms of obligation are sufficient. All these, by a late act of parliament, are obliged to take out an annual certificate on a 10*l*. stamp.

STUDENTS. Before any person can be admitted to practise as an advocate, he must be regularly entered in, and be a member of, one of the inns of court five years, and must have kept his commons in such inn twelve terms. In favour of those who have taken a degree of M. A. or LL.B. at an English university, three years are allowed as sufficient to be a member of the inn, but the twelve terms must be duly kept. The fee on admission to an inn is about 37*l*. of which a great part is a stamp duty; and those students who have not taken a degree deposit 106*l*. to pay their fees on being called to the bar; but this sum, should they ever renounce their original intention, they are at liberty to draw out again. Those who have taken a degree are excused from making the deposit at first; but their fees, on being called, are of the same amount; and each member of an inn of court enters into a bond, with two housekeepers, or one member of the same society, for the due payment of his fees, and observance of the rules of the inn. Anciently, there were many ceremonies, and certainly not altogether unprofitable ones, of readings, mootings, and other exercises, preparatory to a call to the bar; but as these are now discontinued, or, if nominally observed in some inns, considered as mere matter of sport, it is not necessary to dwell on them. Instead of any public demonstration of ability, the student is now to rely on his industry for future support, and on his exertions after he is become an advocate for fame; in the mean time his hopes must depend on the use he makes of his time in his private study, his attendance in the courts, and in the office of the special pleader, the draftsman, or the conveyancer.

INNS OF COURT. As the Inns of Court are objects of much curiosity, some account of them in this place will not be improper.

It has been before observed, that previous to, and immediately after, the Norman conquest, the knowledge of the laws of England, as well as the administration of them, was chiefly confined to ecclesiastical persons, the unsettled state of the kingdom obliging the nobility and gentry, rather to addict themselves to the practice of arms, than the attainment of literature; and in consequence it most probably happened, that

that the decifion of controverfies in civil cafes was then fo frequently by combat, and in criminal ones by fire and water ordeal. On this account likewife, many of the juftices of the king's courts, as well as thofe called itinerant, before the time of Henry III. were bifhops, abbots, deans, canons in cathedral churches, archdeacons, &c.; and the chancellorfhip was exercifed by clergymen even fo late as the reign of Henry VII. But when by magna charta it was ordained, that "common pleas fhould not thenceforth follow the court, but "be held in fome certain place," and that certain place was fixed at Weftminfter-hall; this eftablifhment, gave rife to the inns of court, where the whole body of common lawyers was collected, as ftations moft proper for their ftudies, conference, and practice. Thefe colleges of common law foon attracted the attention and gained the approbation of government: the ftudy of the law was ordered to be carried on in them alone; and means were taken for placing them under the regulation of the judges.

Thefe inns, or *hoftels*, as they were anciently called, were from their firft inftitution divided into two forts, denominated *inns of court*, and *inns of chancery*. The former were fo named from the ftudents in them being to ferve the courts of judicature; or becaufe thefe houfes anciently received the fons of noblemen and the better fort of gentlemen, "who (fays Fortefcue) "did there not only ftudy the laws, to ferve the courts "of juftice and profit their country, but did further learn to dance, "to fing, to play on inftruments, on the ferial days, and to "ftudy divinity on the feftival, ufing fuch exercifes as they did "who were brought up in the king's court:" fo that thefe hoftels being nurferies or feminaries of the court, taking their denomination from the end wherefore they were inftituted, were called inns of court. The expences were very confiderable, and the gentility of the ftudents was proved by the declaration of their paternal ftock, and the emblazonment of their arms; cuftoms which are ftill continued. The inns of chancery were fo called, probably becaufe they were appropriated to fuch clerks as chiefly ftudied the forming of writs, which was the province of the curfitors, and fuch as belong to the courts of common pleas and king's bench. Thefe formerly were alfo a kind of preparatory houfes for younger ftudents, where many were entered before they were admitted to the inns of court.

The Inner Temple. The Temple is well known to have taken its name from that gallant, religious, military order, the Knights Templars, who came into England in the reign of Stephen. Their firft houfe was in Holborn, near the fite of the prefent Southampton-ftreet, and was called the Old Temple;

ple; but in the fucceeding reign they began the foundation of a nobler ftructure, oppofite the end of Chancery-lane, then called New-ftreet, which, to diftinguifh it from the former, was called the New Temple. This occupied all that fpace of ground from the monaftery of the Carmelites, or White Friars, in Fleet-ftreet, weftward to Effex houfe, without Temple Bar, where Effex-ftreet now ftands, and fome part of that too, as appears by the firft grant of it to Sir William Paget, by Henry VIII. That the Templars then feated themfelves at the New Temple, is evident from the dedication of their church, in the year 1185; and they continued till the fuppreffion of their order, in 1310. Between thefe two periods the church was again dedicated, viz. in 1240, probably on account of the greater part being re-edified. On the diffolution, the eftates, together with the houfe in London, devolving upon the crown, Edward II. in 1313, beftowed the latter on Thomas earl of Lancafter. After that nobleman's attainder, a grant was made to Adomar, or Aimer de Valence, earl of Pembroke, by the fame monarch, of "the whole place "and houfes called the New Temple, at London, with the "ground called Fiquet's Croft, and all the tenements and rents "with the appurtenances that belong to the Templars in the "city of London and fuburbs thereof, with the land called "Flete Croft, part of the poffeffions of the faid New Tem-"ple." From Aimer de Valence this ftructure came into the poffeffion of Hugh le de Spencer the younger; and on his execution, in the firft year of Edward III. the right once more reverted to the crown. Here it would probably have continued; but by a decree, which beftowed generally the lands of the Templars on the hofpitals of St. John of Jerufalem, the above monarch granted this manfion to the knights of that order in England. Thefe poffeffed it in the eighteenth year of his reign, when they were forced to repair the Temple bridge; but they foon after demifed it for the rent of ten pounds per annum, to certain ftudents of the common law, who are fuppofed to have removed from Thaive's-inn, in Holborn. While the Temple was a monaftic inftitution, fuch was its rank and importance, that not only parliaments and general councils frequently affembled there, but it was a fort of general depofitory or treafury for the greateft perfons in the nation, as well as the place where many of the crown jewels were kept. Soon after the damage committed by Wat Tyler, but at what particular period is not known, the ftudents in this feminary fo far increafed in number as to occafion their divifion into two feparate bodies, called the Society of the Inner Temple, and the Society of the Middle Temple, who had

two

two halls, &c.; but continued to hold their houses as tenants to the knights hospitallers, till the general suppression, in the reign of Henry VIII. and, after this event, for some time, of the crown by lease. In the sixth year of the reign of James I. all the buildings of the two Temples were granted by letters patent, bearing date at Westminster, 13th August, by the name of the inns and capital messuages, commonly known by the names of the Inner Temple and Middle Temple, otherwise the New Temple, London, to Sir Julius Cæsar, knight, then chancellor and under treasurer of the exchequer, Sir Henry Montague, knight, recorder of London, William Towse and Richard Daston, esqrs. treasurers of the said inns of court, and Sir John Boyse, knight, Andrew Grey, Thomas Farmer, Ralf Radcliff, and others, esqrs. then benchers of these houses; to have and to hold the said mansions, with the gardens and appurtenances, unto the said grantees, their heirs and assigns, for ever, for lodgings, reception and education of the professors and students of the laws of this realm; yielding and paying to the said king, his heirs and successors, for each mansion, the sum of ten pounds yearly.

INNER TEMPLE HALL. The Hall is supposed by Dugdale, from the form of the windows, to have been built near the age of Edward III. The south front was however erected about the year 1740, the old front having been recently destroyed by a great fire, which does not appear to have reached the north side, nor the roof of the building. A semi-hexagonal window, in the south front, has been new cased with stone on the outside, but has escaped the ravages of the flames within, and retains its original form. The contracted space on which the hall stands, admitted of no great exertion of skill on the part of the architect: there is consequently little either to censure or approve. The inside of the hall retains but a small portion of its antiquity. The most prominent features are the very small, and truly Gothic windows on the north side. They have the character of a very early style of building, most probably as ancient as that of Edward III. The room is very well proportioned, though small: the ceiling has a Gothic curve, and is supported by six ribs in the same bend; these spring (which is somewhat singular) irregularly from the new piers on the north side, as well as from the south or old front. The ribs are ornamented with grotesque figures, and the spaces between, in the ceiling, are filled up with large uncouth forms of roses, in chiaro oscuro. At the lower end of the room is a neat screen supported by four pillars of the Tuscan order. On the right of the passage, at the grand entrance, are two very ancient apartments,

ments, that appear to have been out-offices; they are ceiled with groined arches, and the Gothic windows are in part blocked up: they denote the full extent of the ancient buildings belonging to this hall. Between the two ancient windows at the upper end of the hall, within a Gothic compartment, is a large allegorical picture, painted by Sir James Thornhill; who has introduced the story of Pegasus, in compliment to the crest of the society. It appears to be one of his best productions. Beneath are whole lengths of William and Mary, queen Anne, Coke, and Lyttleton, in their robes. At the upper end of the hall is an entrance to a handsome spacious parlour lined with oak, and decorated around, on the upper part of the wainscot, with the arms of the various readers of the society, emblazoned in small compartments, from the time of Henry VI. to the present period. This room is called the parliament chamber: in it, the Treasurer and benchers of the society meet to transact their business, which from hence is called parliamentary. Through this room is the way to several handsome apartments appropriated to the purposes of a library, which, by several donations, is furnished with books of great value. This repository is open to students and others, on application to the librarian, from ten in the morning till one; and in the afternoon from two till six. It contains also a large and curious collection of manuscripts.

Many of the courts and buildings in the Inner Temple are spacious and elegant; the garden commands a beautiful view of the Thames, and is a favourite walk. In ancient times, Christmas, and some other festivals and grand occasions, were celebrated with masques and revels; but these have been long discontinued.

ARMS. The armorial bearing of the Inner Temple, assumed about the time of James I. is Pegasus.

THE MIDDLE TEMPLE. The history of the Middle Temple is included in that of the Inner Temple, the constitutions of the two were, however, somewhat different.

HALL. The Hall of the Middle Temple is justly celebrated. Of the outside it is observed, that its effect is lost for want of space, and that it is disgraced by some incongruous modern additions; but on entering the building the eye receives every gratification from an assemblage of the best disposed parts in the Gothic style of building, that could have been selected, and which are preserved with a degree of care and attention highly creditable to the members of the society. The length of this noble room, including the passage, is about one hundred feet, the width about forty. The height of the roof, which is of oak highly wrought, is well proportioned to the general dimensions of the building, and perfectly satisfies the eye of the

the critical obſerver. The roof conſiſts of eight principal rafters, projecting from the ſide walls to ſupport it; they reach the ſummit by three different curves, are richly carved and moulded, and have at the extremity of each curve a bold pendant ornament. There are alſo Gothic ribs, which, ſpringing from each of the principal rafters, give a richneſs to the whole deſign. The ſpacious windows riſing between each rafter, are decorated with coats of arms, in ſtained glaſs, of the various noblemen and gentlemen who have been members of the ſociety. The hall having fallen to decay, the rebuilding was begun in 1562, when the celebrated Plowden was conſtituted treaſurer for the work: it was finiſhed in 1572, four years after he quitted that office, but he voluntarily conſented to ſuperintend it, till completed. At the weſt end is a ſpacious Gothic window, decorated in the ſame ſtyle with the others, beneath which are ſeveral whole length portraits in oil, as large as life, viz. in the centre, Charles I. on horſeback, with his page holding his helmet, Charles II. and queen Anne on his right, and William III. and George I. on his left. Over the paſſage entrance, is a handſome muſic gallery, but its uſe has long been diſcontinued. It is equal in width to the hall, and about nine feet deep; decorated with various pieces of armour, conſiſting of breaſt-plates, helmets, &c. which, though evidently not more ancient than the time of Charles II., have been by ſome inconſiderately deſcribed as belonging to the Knights Templars. The ſcreen beneath this gallery was erected in the ſeventeenth year of queen Elizabeth. It is very richly carved in oak, with no regularity of order or ſtyle, but is in a kind of degenerate Gothic, and ſupported by ſix Doric fluted pillars, an order very much in uſe at that period. Beneath the windows on each ſide of the hall, are ranged, in ſmall compartments in oak, the arms and names of the various readers, from Richard Swaine, in 1597, to the preſent period; they are ſtill annually elected, and the place is preſerved, but the lectures have long ſince been diſcontinued.

Gate. The Middle Temple gate was erected on a ſingular occaſion. About the year 1501, Sir Amias Powlet thought fit to put Cardinal Wolſey, then parſon of Lymington, into the ſtocks. In 1515, being ſent for to London by the cardinal, on account of that ancient grudge, he was commanded not to quit town till further orders. In conſequence he lodged five or ſix years in this gateway, which he rebuilt; and, to pacify his eminence, adorned the front with the cardinal's cap, badges, cognizance, and other devices.

Library. The library was erected, as appears from the date over the door of the ſtair-caſe, in 1625. It contains a ſmall

ſmall number of ancient books, which were the bequeſt of Sir Robert Aſhley, in the year 1641, and ſome manuſcripts. It contains two globes, curious on account of their antiquity, being made in the reign of Elizabeth.

Societies. The ſociety of the Middle Temple, as well as the Inner Temple, conſiſts of benchers, or ſuch as have been readers, anciently called *apprentices* of the law, members, barriſters, and ſtudents; formerly denominated *utter* barriſters and *inner* barriſters, being ſtudents under ſeven years, and all of whom had their commons in the hall. The government of the ſociety is veſted in the benchers, whoſe general meetings to tranſact buſineſs are, and anciently were, dignified with the name of *parliaments*. The mode of holding them is deſcribed as follows: firſt, the benchers only who have been readers meet in the parliament chamber, which is at the lower end of the hall, and take their places according to ſeniority. Then the treaſurer, for the time being, ſits at the table bare-headed, and reads petitions, or propoſes ſuch other ſubjects as are to be diſcuſſed; the under treaſurer ſtanding by as an attendant. If a difference of opinion occurs, the votes are taken ſeparately, beginning at the youngeſt, and the majority determines it. Formerly, none who had been called to the bench to read attended theſe parliaments till they had filled the office of reader; but that objection was afterwards diſpenſed with. All new laws paſſed by the parliament are notified to ſuch inferior members of the houſe as are in commons, by the treaſurer; and ſuch members, by the orders of the ſociety, are bound to attend the laſt Friday of each term (which is called a parliament of attendance), and all abſentees are ſubject to a forfeit of 3*s*. 4*d*. *pro non conſultando*.

The officers and ſervants are, a treaſurer, ſub-treaſurer, ſteward, chief butler, three under butlers, upper and under cook, a panier-man, a gardener, two porters, two waſh-pots, and watchmen: anciently there were four under butlers, who wore gowns, and four waſh-pots, beſides a turn-broach, two ſcullions, &c.; who all, except the porter and gardener, had their diet in the houſe, beſides wages and other perquiſites belonging to their offices.

Arms. The arms of the Middle Temple are, argent on a plain croſs, gules, the holy lamb, the ſtaff or flag, argent, with a red croſs.

Church. The Temple church, a very beautiful ſpecimen of the early Gothic architecture, belongs in common to the two ſocieties: it has three aiſles running eaſt and weſt, and two croſs aiſles. The windows are lancet-ſhaped, very antique, and the weſtern entrance, which anſwers to the nave in other churches, is is a ſpacious round tower in imitation of the church of the Holy Sepulchre (a peculiarity which diſtinguiſhes all the churches of the Knight's Templars.) This is ſeparated from the choir, not by cloſe walls, but by a handſome ſcreen, which however has the defect of obſtructing the ſight. It is ſupported by ſix pointed arches, each reſting on four round pillars, bound together by a *faſcia*. Above each arch is a window with a rounded top, with a gallery, and rich Saxon arches interſecting each other. On the outſide of the pillars is a conſiderable ſpace preſerving the circular form. On the lower part of the wall are ſmall pilaſters meeting in pointed arches at top, and over each pillar a groteſque head. The choir is a large ſquare building, evidently erected at another time. The roof is ſupported by ſlight pillars of what is uſually called Suſſex marble; and the windows on each ſide, which are three in number, are adorned with ſmall columns of the ſame. On the outſide is a buttreſs between each. The entire floor is of flags of black and white marble. The length of the choir is eighty-three feet, the breadth ſixty, and the height thirty-four; it is unincumbered with galleries. The height of the inſide of the tower is forty-eight feet; its diameter on the floor fifty-one; and the circumference one hundred and ſixty. The pillars of this tower (ſix in number) are wainſcotted with oak to the height of eight feet, and ſome have monuments placed againſt them, which injure the uniformity of the plan. It is ſingular that the ſmall pillars, and the heads which ornament them, are not of ſtone, but a compoſition reſembling coarſe mortar, which is very rotten, and from neglect and damp, threatens (unleſs repaired) a ſpeedy demolition. The Temple church is principally remarkable (excepting the faſhion of the edifice itſelf, which has a very uncommon and noble aſpect) for the tombs of eleven of the Knights Templars. Eight of theſe have the monumental effigies of armed knights; the reſt are coped with grey marble. The figures conſiſt of two groups, out of which five are croſs-legged; the remainder lie ſtraight: each group is environed by a ſpacious iron grate. In the firſt are four knights, each of them croſs-legged, and three in complete mail, in plain helmets, flatted at top, and with very long ſhields. One of theſe is known to have been Geoffry de Magnaville, created earl of Eſſex in 1148: the other figures cannot be identified, either in this or the ſecond group; but three of them are conjectured by Camden to commemorate William earl of Pembroke, who died in 1219, and his ſons William and Gilbert, likewiſe earls of Pembroke and marſhals of England. One of the ſtone coffins alſo, of a ridged ſhape, is ſuppoſed by the ſame antiquary to be the tomb of William Plantagenet, fifth ſon of Henry III. The dreſs

dress and accoutrements of these knights are extremely singular: no two are alike, though all are armed in mail. Their position, likewise, is varied, and there is still sufficient expression in the faces to shew that personal resemblance was aimed at, and in some degree successfully. One figure is in a spirited attitude, drawing a broad dagger; one leg rests on the tail of a cockatrice, the other is in the action of being drawn up, with the head of the monster beneath. Another is bare-headed and bald, his legs armed, his hands mailed, his mantle long; and round his neck a cowl, as if, according to the common superstition of those days, he had desired to be buried in the dress of a monk, lest the evil spirit should take possession of his body. On his shield is a *fleur de lys*. The earl of Pembroke bears a *lion* on his shield, the arms of that great family. The helmets of all the knights are much alike, but two of them are mailed. The Temple church contains some few other ancient monuments, chiefly to the memory of eminent lawyers, as Plowden, Selden, Sir John Vaughan, &c. and one of a bishop in his episcopal dress, a mitre, and a crosier, well executed in stone. The superior clergyman of the Temple church, since the reign of Henry VIII. is called master (or *custos*) of the Temple, and is constituted by the king's letters patent, without institution or induction; there are, besides, a reader and lecturer. In Stowe's time it had four stipendiary priests, with a clerk, who had stipends allowed them out of the possessions of the dissolved monastery of St. John of Jerusalem; but the establishment was still greater in the Romish times, when the several priests had a hall and lodgings assigned them within the house. The charges of the present church are jointly paid by both societies, who have each their side at divine worship. The tone of the organ has long been remarked as the finest in the kingdom.

The inns of chancery belonging to the Inner and Middle Temple, are four.

CLIFFORD'S INN. Clifford's Inn, a member of the Inner Temple, is situated on the north side of Fleet-street, adjoining St. Dunstan's church, and is of considerable antiquity. It derives its name from the honourable family of the barons Clifford, ancestors of the earl of Cumberland, who had a residence there many ages since, which was called, according to the custom of the time, "Clifford's Inn." It was granted to Robert de Clifford, by the crown, in the third of Edward II., and the widow of Robert let it to the students of the law, at a yearly rent of 10*l*.; it afterward fell again to the crown, and again reverted to the Clifford family; but ever since the first demise by lease from Robert de Clifford's widow, which was in the 18th of Edward III., it has been held by the students of the law, having

having been afterward granted in fee-farm to Nicholas Sulyard, esq. principal of the houſe, and a bencher of Lincoln's Inn, in the reign of Henry VI. Nicholas Guybon, Robert Clinche, and others, the then ſeniors of it, in conſideration of 600*l*. and the rent of 4*l*. per annum.

SOCIETY. The ſociety was governed by a principal and twelve rulers. The gentlemen were to be in commons a fortnight in every term, or to pay about four ſhillings a week; they formerly had mootings. The chambers are ſold for one life.

ARMS. Their armorial enſigns are, chequy *or* and *azure*, a feſs gules, within a border of the third.

HALL. The hall is in ſome meaſure built in the Gothic taſte; it is about thirty feet long, and twenty-four wide, being proportionably lofty to its dimenſions. To the left of the entrance is hanging up an old oak caſe, opening with folding doors, within which the ancient inſtitutions of the ſociety are preſerved: they are written on vellum, and conſiſt of forty-ſeven items, but, except the capital letters, which were formerly emblazoned in gold, the writing is ſcarcely legible; they are headed by a pen and ink drawing of the arms of England, carefully executed, as they appeared in the reign of Henry VIII. Two angels are ſupporters of the ſhield, behind whom appear on either ſide a lion erect, bearing in his paws a ſmall banner, on which is drawn a ſingle *fleur de lys*. This curious piece of antiquity is about two feet and a quarter high, by one and a quarter wide. In this hall Sir Matthew Hale and the principal judges ſat, after the great fire of London, to ſettle the differences that occurred between landlord and tenant, and to aſcertain the ſeveral diviſions of property; which difficult and important buſineſs was performed by them ſo much to the ſatisfaction of the city, that the mayor and commonalty, in gratitude for ſo ſignal a ſervice, ordered their portraits to be painted, and hung in the Guildhall, where they ſtill remain.

LYON'S INN. Lyon's Inn is ſituate between Holywell-ſtreet and Wych-ſtreet, and is an appendage of the Inner Temple. It is known to be a place of conſiderable antiquity, from the old books of the ſteward's accounts, which contain entries made in the time of Henry V. How long before that period it was an inn of chancery is uncertain.

SOCIETY. Its government was formerly veſted in a treaſurer and twelve ancients. The gentlemen of the houſe were in commons three weeks in Michaelmas term, in other terms, two. They ſold their chambers for one or two lives, and had mootings once in four terms.

HALL. The hall ſtands in the ſouth-weſt corner of the court, and was formerly, when properly kept, a commodious handſome

handsome room; but it is now, with the rest of the inn, much neglected. The exterior is decorated with a handsome doorway, to which there is an ascent by a flight of stone steps and ballustrades: the roof terminates in a pointed pediment, in the midst of which is the armorial bearing of the society; a lion in *alto relievo;* indifferently sculptured.

CLEMENT'S INN. Clement's Inn appears to have derived its name from the church near which it stands, and a celebrated holy well adjoining; both which were dedicated to the Roman pontiff St. Clement. A house, or inn of chancery, for the education of students at law, was situated on this site in the time of Edward IV. To whom the inheritance anciently belonged is not known. In the year 1486, (2 Henry VII.) Sir John Cantlowe, knight, by a lease, bearing date the 20th of December, in consideration of eleven marks fine, and *4l. 6s. 8d.* yearly rent, demised it for eighty years to William Elyot and John Elyot, (in trust, as may be presumed, for the students of the law.) About the year 1528 (20th Henry VIII.) Cantlowe's right and interest passed to William Holles, citizen of London, afterwards knight, and lord-mayor of that city, and ancestor of the dukes of Newcastle, one of whom, John earl of Clare, son and successor of Sir John Holles, the first earl, and whose residence was on the site of the present Clare-market, demised it to the then principal and fellows. The buildings of the present inn are all modern, and occupy three small courts; through which there is a thoroughfare in the day time to Clare-market, and into New Inn.

HALL AND ARMS. The hall fills one side of the middle square or court, and is a well proportioned and elegant room. It contains a good portrait of Sir Matthew Hale, and five other pictures of no importance. On the outside, the front of which has a respectable and handsome appearance, are placed the arms of the society, argent, an anchor (without a stock) in pale proper, and a C sable passing through the middle.

In the centre of the garden, which adjoins that of New Inn, and is kept with particular neatness, is a sun-dial, supported by a figure of considerable merit kneeling, (a naked Moor or African,) which was brought from Italy by lord Clare, and presented to the society: it attracts much attention.

SOCIETY. St. Clement's Inn is an appendage of the Inner Temple. The society consists of a principal and twelve ancients; the principal being removed every three years, and his place supplied by election from among the ancients. The business of the society is transacted by the steward, and there are two porters.

NEW INN. Since the destruction of Strand Inn, which was demolished

demolished by the protector Somerset to make room for his palace called Somerset-house, New Inn is the only inn of chancery remaining in the possession of the Middle Temple. It stands contiguous to Clement's Inn, on the west, and has little to interest, being built of brick and entirely modern.

The site, about 1485, was occupied as a common inn, or hostery for travellers and others, and was called, from its sign of the Virgin Mary, "Our Lady Inn."

HALL. The hall is a high, square brick building, and stands towards the south-east corner of the square: the front is adorned with a large clock. It has nothing within side remarkable, but is a spacious and good room.

SOCIETY. The society is governed by a treasurer and twelve ancients. The members are to be in commons, in their gowns and caps, one week in every term, or pay absent commons. They had also anciently mootings once or twice a term.

ARMS. Their armorial ensigns are, *vert*, a *flower-pot* argent.

LINCOLN'S INN. This principal inn of court occupies a large plot of ground on the west side of Chancery-lane, formerly called Chancellor's-lane. Its government and rules for receiving of students, and calling them to the bar, vary in slight, but in no important particulars from those already mentioned in the Temple. Like that inn too, Lincoln's Inn had its ancient festivities, its masks, its revels, and all the strange pomp of aukward gaiety, which distinguished the learned and unpolished merry-makings of our ancestors.

Lincoln's Inn was founded partly on the ruins of the monastery of the "Blackfriars," who resided here previous to their removal to the quarter which now bears their name, and a mansion formerly belonging to Ralph Nevil, bishop of Chichester and chancellor of England in the reign of Henry III. In 1245, Richard de Wihtz, afterward called Saint Richard, became bishop of Chichester, and held the house near Holborn, as successor to bishop Neville. About that period both that mansion, and the contiguous house of the Blackfriars, which was deserted by them, became appropriated to the study of the law; but in what particular way does not appear. Tradition reports, that Henry Lacy, the great earl of Lincoln, who in the next age had a grant by patent from Edward I. of "the old "friary-house near Holborn, being a person well studied in the "law," assigned to the professors of it this residence; but whether by gift or purchase is not said. From this nobleman, however, it derived its name of Lincoln's Inn. Several temporary demises were afterward made of the spot in question, and additional lands granted, until the 12th of November, in the twelfth year

 of

of Elizabeth, when Edward Sulyard, in whom the estate of inheritance had become vested, did, in consideration of 520*l.* convey to Richard Kingsmill, and the rest of the then benchers, all the premises in fee; and a fine was levied accordingly.

GATE. Among the most striking parts of Lincoln's Inn, is the gate from Chancery-lane. This venerable structure consists of two wings or square towers, with a handsome stone arch in the centre, in the Gothic style. The building is of black or dark grey bricks, intersecting each other at right angles. Over the gateway are three circular compartments, containing in the centre the arms of England, encircled with the motto: "*Honi* "*soit qui mal y pense.*" The arms on the dexter side, are those of Lacy, earl of Lincoln; and on the sinister, those of Sir Thomas Lovel, knight of the garter. On a label beneath, in Arabic characters, is inscribed "*Anno Dom.* 1518." Over this entrance Oliver Cromwell is reported to have had chambers.

CHAPEL. On entering the grand arch, the venerable buildings of the hall and chapel cannot fail to strike the attention of the antiquary; although it must be confessed, they are both deficient in those elegancies and enrichments, that constitute the grandeur of the most admired Gothic structures. The chapel is from a design of Inigo Jones: it appears from the register of the inn, that on the 22d June, in the eighth of James, it was ordered that the whole chapel, being then in a ruinous state, and not sufficiently large for the society, should be pulled down, and a new one erected in the same court. Seven years afterward, measures were taken for carrying this order into execution; a plan was formed by Inigo Jones, and the requisite sum was raised, partly by voluntary contributions, and partly by an assessment on the members of the society. This chapel has recently undergone a thorough repair, but is still defective in point of ornament. The parapet wall is very ponderous, and the necessity for raising the ground above the base of this building, has, by lowering the height of the cloyster, destroyed, in a great measure, the effect of its most beautiful part. The cloysters are regularly divided, and consist of six Gothic groined arches, which, though rather a flat curve, appear elegant; they are highly enriched with Gothic ribs, closely intersecting each other, and at these intersections are embellished with roses, shields, and various clustered decorations. The space between the bands which spring from the piers, is enriched with Gothic tracery, which adds much to the general effect. Within this cloyster was interred Thurloe, secretary of state to Oliver Cromwell.

HALL. Lincoln's Inn hall was finished in the twenty-second year of Henry VIII. The principal part of the outside is cased with stone, particularly the coigns; the roof is sharp and cumbrous; the turrets above are of timber and covered with lead; the smaller one appears to be coeval with the more ancient parts of the building, and was, according to the register of the Inn, described; as "the loover or lanthorn set up in the sixth "of Edward VI." The arms on the lead are those of Lacy, earl of Lincoln, with Quincy, and the earl of Chester. The date 1682, the period when the whole underwent a thorough repair. In the interior, the roof appears of an elliptical form, with pointed groined intersections springing from the piers, inclosing an elliptical arch over the three centre windows. At the extremities are complete Gothic arched windows, in recesses evidently as ancient as its foundation. In the front of these recesses are moulded ribs, springing from heads of the grotesque kind, in the style of architecture of the period at which it was erected. The windows are decorated with coats of arms, in stained glass, of the many dignified characters who have belonged to, and by their abilities conferred honour on, the society. Viewing the hall from the justice seat, the screen at the lower end, which was added in the sixth of Elizabeth, has every characteristic feature of the buildings of that period; and, except its eccentric decorations and massiveness, it has not any thing striking to arrest attention. Over the justice seat, where the lord chancellor sits in vacation, is a picture by Hogarth, more celebrated than admired, representing Paul before Felix; as the forte of this truly great painter was the comic style, this serious attempt has been most severely criticised, and on the whole more censured than it deserves; though no one will attempt to prove that it is entitled to the highest praise.

Library. The library, which is situated in the stone buildings, contains, besides a good collection of books, many very fine and curious manuscripts. These were removed in 1787 from the old library to the present, which is a handsome, spacious, and commodious apartment, being made out of the three sets of chambers. The manuscripts are in close presses at one end of the library, where fires are daily kept in winter.

The building is very substantial, with stone staircases, and solid party walls. The keys of the presses are kept by the master of the library, who is chosen annually by the benchers from their own body, and the manuscripts cannot be viewed without a special order from one or two of the masters of the bench. The first formation of the library was in the time of Henry VII.; and in the early part of the reign of Elizabeth, the building was erected; but the books accumulated so slowly, that, in the sixth of James I., a tax was laid on the benchers and barristers for the purpose of augmenting it. The greater part of the

the valuable manufcripts was bequeathed by Sir Matthew Hale, and they have been accurately claffed and explained in the return made to the felect commitee for examining into the public records. The collection is very large and valuable, and continually augmenting.

The old buildings in this inn have a venerable appearance; while the new fquare and ftone buildings are models of elegance and convenience. The garden is handfomely laid out, and commands from its terrace a view of Lincoln's Inn Fields; the largeft, and, for building and plantation, among the fineft of the fquares in the metropolis.

To Lincoln's Inn belong two inns of chancery, of which one is no longer effectually, though ftill nominally to be confidered as an inn.

Thavie's Inn. This place is at leaft as old as the time of Edward III. It took its name from one John Thaive, or Tavie, whofe houfe it then was, and who directed, that after the decease of his wife Alice, his eftates, and the *hoftel* in which apprentices to the law were ufed to inhabit, fhould be fold, in order to maintain a chaplain, who was to pray for his foul and that of his fpoufe. In the reign of Edward VI. Gregory Nichols, citizen and mercer of London, being poffeffed by inheritance of the property of this manfion, granted it to the benchers of Lincoln's Inn for the ufe of ftudents; which fociety foon afterwards conftituted it one of their inns of chancery, and vefted the government in a principal and fellows, who were to pay as an acknowledgment to the mother houfe the annual rent of 3*l.* 6*s.* 4*d.* By the ancient orders of this fociety the members of Thavie's Inn were to be ten days in commons in iffuable terms, and in the reft of the terms a week, and were allowed the fame privileges for the admiffion of ftudents into Lincoln's Inn, as were enjoyed by the members of Furnival's Inn. But this inn having been burnt down, is now converted into a private court, compofed of ordinary dwelling houfes, not divided into chambers, but enclofed, and feparated from the ftreet by an iron gate.

Arms. The arms are, azure, two garbs or, bands guelfe; on a chief fable a letter, T argent.

Furnival's Inn. This inn of chancery is fituated in Holborn, between Brook-ftreet and Leather-lane: it occupies a confiderable plot of ground, and is divided into two fquares or courts. The firft, towards Holborn, is of a good width, but fhallow, and built round on the four fides. The fecond or inner court extends the depth of great part of Brook-ftreet, and has chambers on one fide only: the buildings of both are in a ftate of decay, and appear to be much neglected. It is

2 firft

first noticed as a law seminary in its steward's account book, written about the ninth of Henry IV. and derives its name from its original occupants, the lords Furnival. This noble family was extinct in the male line in 6 Richard II.; some time before which period this inn was demised to the students of the law; but the precise date of its establishment as a school of legal education is involved in obscurity. In the first of Edward VI. Francis earl of Shrewsbury sold it to Edward Gryffin, esq. then solicitor-general to the king, William Ropere, and Richard Heydone, esqrs. and their heirs, to the use of the society of Lincoln's Inn, for 120*l.* which sum was paid out of the treasury of that society. The principal and fellows of Furnival's Inn, to whom a lease was granted by the society of Lincoln's Inn, were to pay yearly 3*l.* 6*s.* 4*d.* and were allowed several privileges. The street front is an uncommonly fine specimen of brick-work, being adorned with pilasters, mouldings, and various other ornaments, and extends a considerable length. It contains a range of good chambers, and beneath, a handsome arched gateway leading to the interior parts of the Inn. It appears to have been erected about the time of Charles II. No other part of the inn deserves much notice.

Society. The society is governed by a principal and twelve ancients.

Arms. Their arms are, argent, a bend, between six martlets gules, within a border of the second.

Gray's Inn. The society in this, as well as in the other three inns of court, has the power of calling to the bar, and exercises it in the same manner. It may here be fit to observe a difference which prevails in these inns with respect to the admission of members. In the Middle Temple, and in Lincoln's Inn, no attorney or solicitor can be a member; but if any one previously admitted, embraces that branch of the profession, he is discharged from the society. In the Inner Temple and Gray's Inn, on the contrary, attorneys are members, and may eat in commons with the students, but cannot be benchers, they being invariably chosen from among the barristers.

Gray's Inn is situated on the north side of Holborn, nearly opposite the end of Chancery-lane, from which it extends, but enveloped by houses, to Gray's-inn-lane, a considerable distance eastward.

It derives its name from the lords Gray of Wilton, whose residence it originally was. The premises became the property of the prior and convent of Shene, by whom they were demised to the students of the law for the annual rent of 6*l.* 13*s.* 4*d.* at which rent they were held of that monastery till the dissolution, when becoming the property of the crown, a grant was made by the king in fee farm, and the property ſtill continues veſted in the crown. The orders for learning and government are in this ſociety very ſimilar to thoſe of the other inns. It has a miniſter, a reader, a ſteward, four butlers, two cooks, and other inferiors, making ſeventy perſons in all.

ARMS. Gray's Inn anciently bore arms derived from thoſe of lord Gray of Wilton; but in more modern times, they aſſumed azure, an Indian griffin proper ſegreant, with the laudable inſcription environing the ſame.

The ancient buildings of Gray's inn are ſpoken of by a contemporary writer as poſſeſſing very little beauty or uniformity, being erected by different perſons; and the ſtructure of the more ancient not only very mean, but of ſo ſlender capacity, ſays he, that even the ancients of the houſe were neceſſitated to lodge double. They are now however much improved, and the great court, called Gray's inn ſquare, is compoſed of elegant and commodious chambers.

HALL. The hall has no claim to attention except its antiquity. From its cumbrous roof, contracted windows, and general maſſiveneſs of deſign, it preſents, in every part, a heavy and gloomy appearance; nor is there reaſon to change this opinion, on a ſurvey of the interior. The roof is of oak, and is divided into ſix bays or compartments, by ſeven arched and moulded Gothic ribs, or principals. The ſpandles or ſpaces are divided by upright timbers, with a horizontal cornice in the centre. At the extremity of the projecting ſpandles, is a carved pendent ornament, in ſome degree partaking of the nature of an entablature. The eaſt and weſt windows, like thoſe on the ſide, are too low for their width; ſome ſpecimens of coats of arms are ſtill remaining in them. The ſcreen of the hall is ſupported by ſix pillars, of the Tuſcan order, with cariatides ſupporting the cornice. The roof has a ſolemn grandeur, which, in ſome degree, reſcues the whole building from obſcurity. It was erected in the reign of Philip and Mary, and every fellow of the houſe, having chambers, was aſſeſſed towards the expence.

CHAPEL. The chapel has, within a few years, been newly caſed with ſtone; and, except the Gothic windows, completely modernized. The inſide is on a very narrow ſcale, and can boaſt of no embelliſhment. The altar conſiſts of four Doric columns, and ſurmounted with a ſcroll pediment, in the centre of which are ſingularly reſplendent radii, iſſuing from a dove.

GARDENS. The gardens are ſpacious and commodious; and

and the public, from the free use of them, have derived great pleasure and advantage. The first mention made of them is in the fortieth of Elizabeth; when Mr. Bacon, afterwards Sir Francis Bacon lord Verulam, was allowed the sum *7l. 15s. 4d.* for planting elm trees; and it was ordered that a new rail and quick-set hedges should be set on the upper long walk, at the discretion of the same Mr. Bacon and Mr. Wilbraham, which amounted to *60l. 6s. 8d.* On this terrace, Mr. Bacon likewise erected a summer house, on a small mount; but as Hamstead and Highgate are no longer visible from this spot, the society have very judiciously taken down the prospect house.

There are two inns of chancery belonging to Gray's Inn.

Staple Inn. Staple Inn stands on the south side of Holborn, nearly opposite Gray's-inn-lane. It consists of two large courts surrounded with buildings. Great part of the second court was rebuilt in the early part of the eighteenth century, and contains a small garden, pleasantly laid out. The first court adjoining Holborn, and particularly the street front, is of a much greater age; it was probably erected about the time of queen Elizabeth, but possibly much earlier. The inn derives its name, according to tradition, from the merchants who dealt in wool, having had their meetings in it, when it was called Staple Hall.

Hall. The hall, though not large, is well proportioned. The roof is supported by five principal beams, framed with Gothic ribs of oak, and enriched with grotesque ornaments; and the ends of the posts are carved and moulded with drops, in the same style. On the lower short beams of the spandrils of the roof are placed upright ornaments of a grotesque and zig-zag character, differing from any even of the most unmeaning decorations of the most tasteless period. A modern plaister ceiling and cornice appear to have been added on the under side of the rafters; which, it may be presumed, were originally of oak and open to the view. The windows are decorated with stained glass, containing the royal arms, those of some of the judges of the king's bench, the principals of the inn, and others of eminence in the profession. There are also some pictures, and casts of the twelve Cæsars.

Society. Staple Inn is under the direction of thirteen ancients, which include a principal and pensioner; the first is elected every three years by the junior members, the other holds his office at his own discretion.

Arms. The armorial bearings of this inn is vert, a wool-pack, argent.

Bernard's Inn. Bernard's Inn is situated at a small distance from Staple Inn, in the same street, consisting also of two courts surrounded by handsome and convenient chambers, but inferior in size. Bernard's Inn was anciently called Mackworth Inn: it it has been ftyled the fecond inn of chancery. The time when it began to be inhabited by profeffors of the law is uncertain, but it undoubtedly was fo in the 32d Hen. VI.

Hall. The hall, which is a very fmall room, contains a few portraits of eminent law characters, and two bufts. The windows are likewife decorated with armorial bearings.

Society and Arms. The government of this inn is vefted in a principal and twelve ancients. The armorial enfigns are, party per pale, indented ermin and fable, a chevron frettee or and gules.

Counsel. Having thus defcribed the inns at which ftudents are called to the bar, with their appendages; it becomes neceffary to notice the office and rank of counfel. Of advocates, or (as they are generally called) counfel, there are two fpecies or degrees; barrifters and ferjeants. The former are in old books ftiled apprentices, *apprenticii ad legem*, being looked upon as merely learners, and not qualified to execute the full office of an advocate till they were of fixteen years ftanding; at which time they might be called to the eftate and degree of ferjeants, or *fervientes ad legem*. From both thefe degrees fome are ufually felected to be his majefty's counfel learned in the law; the two principal of whom are called his attorney, and folicitor-general. The firft *king's counfel*, under the degree of ferjeant, was Sir Francis Bacon, who was made fo *honoris caufa*, without either patent or fee; fo that the firft of the modern order (who are now the fworn fervants of the crown, with a fmall ftanding falary,) feems to have been Sir Francis North, afterwards lord-keeper of the great feal to Charles II. Thefe king's counfel anfwer in fome meafure to the advocates of the revenue, *advocati fifci*, among the Romans; for like them they muft not be employed in any caufe againft the crown, without fpecial licence*; but in the imperial law, except fome peculiar caufes, the fifcal advocates were not permitted to be at all engaged in private fuits. A cuftom has of late years prevailed of granting letters *patent of precedence* to fuch barrifters, as the crown thinks proper fo to honour; whereby they are entitled to the rank and pre-audience affigned in their refpective patents: fometimes next after the attorney-general, but ufually next after the king's counfel then being. The holders of thefe patents, as well as the queen's attorney and folicitor general, rank promifcuoufly with the king's counfel, and together with them fit within the bar of their refpective courts; but as they receive no falaries,

* Hence none of the king's counfel can publicly plead in court for a prifoner, or a defendant in a cri[illegible] a licence, which is rarely refufed; but an expence of about 9*l.* muft be incurred in obtaining it.

and

and are not ſworn, they are at liberty to be retained in cauſes againſt the crown. All other ſerjeants and barriſters indiſcriminately (except in the court of common pleas, where only ſerjeants are admitted) may take upon them the protection and defence of any ſuitors, whether plaintiff or defendant: who are therefore called their *clients*, like the dependants on the ancient Roman orators. Thoſe indeed practiſed *gratis*, for honour merely, or at moſt for the ſake of gaining influence: and ſo likewiſe it is eſtabliſhed in the courts in England, that counſel can maintain no action for his fees; which are merely honorary, and not given as ſalary or hire. In order to encourage due freedom of ſpeech in the lawful defence of their clients, and, at the ſame time, to give a check to unſeemly licentiouſneſs, it has been holden that a counſel is not anſwerable for any matter by him ſpoken, relative to the cauſe in hand, and ſuggeſted in his client's inſtructions; although it ſhould reflect upon the reputation of another, and even prove abſolutely groundleſs: but if he mentions an untruth of his own invention, or even upon inſtructions if it be impertinent to the cauſe in hand, he is then liable to an action from the party injured. And counſel guilty of deceit or colluſion are puniſhable by the ſtatute Weſtm. 1. 3 Edw. I. c. 28. with impriſonment for a year and a day, and perpetual ſilence in the courts. The latter part of the puniſhment, or more properly an entire excluſion from the bar, is ſtill ſometimes inflicted for groſs miſdemeanors in practice.

Serjeants. Serjeants at law, called in Latin "*narratores*," and in French "*countors*," are of very great antiquity, and by ſome authors the dignity is aſſerted to be prior to the conqueſt. They are expreſsly mentioned in a ſtatute of Edward I.; in the reign of Edward III. they were ſummoned to parliament, and ſat with the juſtices of both benches. They were ſpecially exempted from ſerving on trials of grand aſſize, except where there were no knights in the county, an evidence that they were eſteemed of an equal rank; and they precede, ſays Sir Edward Coke, "thoſe who ſit on an high bench in Weſtminſter Hall" (meaning the maſters in chancery.) In former times they were created with great pomp and ſolemnity, accompanied with many ceremonies, tedious, ridiculous, and expenſive. Even in modern times, the practice of proclaiming the appearance of a new ſerjeant in the court of common pleas by an exclamation from the chief juſtice, "I ſpy a brother," and a childiſh converſation in conſequence, is ſaid to have been retained; and the diſtribution of gold rings to all friends of the advocate, was continued till about the year 1790. At preſent a ſerjeant is created as formerly, by writ; and cannot receive that

dignity

dignity till he has been a barrister five years; they are bound by a solemn oath to do their duty to their clients; and by custom the judges of the courts at Westminster are always admitted into this venerable order, before they are advanced to the bench; the original of which was probably to qualify the *puisne* barons of the exchequer to become justices of assize according to the exigence of the statute of 14 Edw. III. c. 16. Serjeants could formerly only be created in term time; but on a recent occasion, some inconvenience having arisen from the death of a chief justice, whose place it was necessary immediately to supply, a statute passed, enabling the king at any time to call any barrister duly qualified to the degree of serjeant at law. In court, the judge being himself a serjeant, always addresses those of that rank by the title of brother, and they use the same style in speaking to each other. Serjeants alone can practise in the court of common pleas; but at the sittings at nisi prius, barristers may be employed.

Precedence. Pre-audience in the courts is reckoned of so much consequence, that it may not be amiss to subjoin a small table of the precedence which usually obtains among the practicers. 1. The king's premier serjeant, (so constituted by special patent.) 2. The king's ancient serjeant, or the eldest among the king's serjeants. 3. The king's advocate general. 4. The king's attorney general. 5. The king's solicitor general. 6. The king's serjeants. 7. The king's counsel, with the queen's attorney and solicitor. 8. Serjeants at law. 9. The recorder of London. 10. Advocates of the civil law. 11. Barristers. In the court of exchequer two of the most experienced barristers, called the *post-man* and the *tub-man*, (from the places in which they sit) have also a precedence in motions.

Serjeants' Inns. Besides the Inns of court and chancery, there have been from very remote antiquity other inns appropriated to the use of the judges of the king's bench, common pleas, barons of the exchequer, and serjeants at law. Two of these are still remaining, the one situate in Chancery-lane, the other in Fleet-street. A third stood in Holborn, called Scroop's Inn, but it has been long destroyed.

Serjeants' Inn, Chancery-lane. This Inn consists of two small courts, surrounded by the judges' chambers, which are spacious rooms. The principal entrance is from Chancery-lane, and fronts the hall: the second court communicates with Clifford's Inn, by means of a small passage. The buildings are modern, and the work of the last century: the only parts of them that merit notice are, the hall and the chapel. The ascent to the hall is by a handsome flight of stone steps and ballustrade. It is built of brick, with stone cornices, and ornamented in front

with

with a handsome pediment surmounted by a turret and clock. The inside is not large, but forms a well proportioned apartment; and the windows, like those of most of the other halls, are decorated with armorial bearings in stained glass. The chapel is a small neat edifice, with seats for the judges, but is no ways remarkable. This inn did not attain its present appellation of "Serjeant's Inn" till about the year 1484; previous to which it was called "Farringdon's Inn, in Chancellor's-lane;" and still earlier it was recognized as the tenement of John Skarle. In this inn the serjeants at law have a right to chambers as they become vacant; but their number is much greater than can be accommodated in so small a precinct. The judges do not reside in their chambers, but have clerks there, and attend themselves at proper times to transact business.

Serjeants' Inn, Fleet Street. This Inn retains its ancient name, but is at present little more than a mere private court, having been deserted by the judges on the buildings of the old inn falling to decay. It adjoins the north-east corner of the Temple, with which it has a communication by means of a narrow passage; but the principal entrance is from Fleet-street, where there are handsome iron gates, and was formerly a lodge where a porter was kept. The ancient inn having been burnt down in the fire of London; on the lease being renewed by the dean and chapter in 1670, the whole was rebuilt by a voluntary subscription of the serjeants; which subscription was to be repaid by a particular mode agreed on among themselves. The chapel, hall, and kitchen were erected with the overplus of a sum of money, deposited by seventeen new created serjeants, after deducting about 400*l*. for their feast. The whole inn has been again rebuilt, within these few years; and on the site of the ancient hall, (which was long used as a chapel,) the Amicable Society have lately erected an elegant building for the transaction of their business, which is a great ornament to the place. The arms of these two inns of judges and serjeants are appropriate; and described by heavenly bodies: 1. Mars, two galbes in saltire solis, bands jovis; 2. an ibis proper.

Judges. In treating on the superior courts of king's bench, common pleas, and exchequer, the judges who preside in them have occasionally been mentioned, but a few particulars remain to be noticed. The king himself, though intrusted with the whole executive power of the law, cannot sit in judgment in any court, but his justice and the laws must be administered according to the power committed to, and distributed among, his several courts of justice. In this distinct and separate existence of the judicial power, in a peculiar body of men, nominated in-

deed,

deed, but not removeable at pleasure, by the crown, consists one great preservative of the public liberty, which cannot subsist long in any state, unless the administration of common justice be, in some degree, separated both from the legislative and executive power. For this reason, the statute of 16 Chas. I c. 10. which abolished the court of star-chamber, removes all judicial power out of the hands of the king's privy council, who might be inclined to pronounce that for law which was most agreeable to the prince or his officers. It is also of the greatest importance to the law of England, and to the subject, that the power of the judge and jury should be kept distinct; that the judge should determine the law, and the jury the fact; nor can their office be confounded, without the confusion of law and destruction of justice. All judges must derive their authority from the crown, by some commission warranted by law: the judges at Westminster are all (except the chief justice of the king's bench, who is created by writ) appointed by patent, and formerly held their places only during the king's pleasure; but for the greater security of the liberty of the subject, the 12 and 13 W. III. c. 2. provided that their commissions should be in force during their good behaviour, nor could they be displaced but on the address of both houses of parliament. Still however their commissions become void in six months after the demise of the crown; but by statute 1 Geo. III. c. 23, enacted at the earnest recommendation of the king himself from the throne, the judges are continued in their offices during their good behaviour, and their full salaries are secured to them during the continuance of their commissions; his majesty having on that occasion patriotically declared, that "he looked upon the independence and uprightness of the judges, as essential to the impartial administration of justice, as one of the best securities of the rights and liberties of his subjects, and as most conducive to the honour of the crown." The judges are bound by oath to determine according to the known laws, and ancient customs of the realm; and their rule herein must be the judicial decisions and resolutions of other judges, and not their own arbitrary will and pleasure, or that of their prince. But although they are bound to judge by these rules and customs, they are freed from all prosecutions for any thing done in court arising from an error in judgment. Nor is a judge, constituted by the king, and thereby stamped with his approbation, and to whom alone it belongs to judge of his fitness, to be reflected on, censured, defamed, or vilified with respect to his ability, parts, fitness for his place, or in any other manner; for, if this were allowed, it would be impossible to preserve in the people

people that veneration for their perſons, and ſubmiſſion to their judgments, without which the laws cannot be executed with vigour and ſucceſs; and hence all ſcandalous reflections on the judges of Weſtminſter-hall are within the ſtatute of *ſcandalum magnatum*.

The ſalaries of the judges are: the chief juſtice of the king's bench, 5,500*l*.; the chief juſtice of the common pleas, and chief baron of the exchequer, 5,000*l*. each; and each of the puiſne judges and barons, 4,000*l*. After filling their ſtations fifteen years they may retire, and in that caſe, the king may grant penſions to the chief juſtice of the king's bench of 3,800*l*.; to the chief juſtice of the common pleas, and chief baron of the exchequer 3,300*l*. each, and to the other judges and barons 2,600*l*. each.

Other Courts. Thoſe already deſcribed are the principal courts for the trial of queſtions where the chief effect is compenſation for injury, or reſtoration of right; the tribunals which take cognizance of criminal matters alone will be ſubſequently conſidered. The court of parliament has already been treated of at large in the firſt volume, where it occupies a diſtinct ſection; the court of chivalry is alſo noticed in the ſame volume, page 492.; and at pages 178. and 179., as much mention as is neceſſary is made of the court of the ſteward of the king's houſehold, and the court, or board of green cloth. Various courts have been aboliſhed as uſeleſs or oppreſſive; ſuch are the courts of augmentations, firſt-fruits and tenths, now no longer neceſſary; and the courts of *high commiſſion* and *ſtar chamber*, which by their tyrannical proceedings diſgraced and incenſed the country. This latter court was of very ancient origin, but as new modelled by ſtat. 3 Hen. VII. c. 1., and 21 Hen. VIII. c. 20., conſiſted of divers lords ſpiritual and temporal, being privy counſellors, together with two judges of the courts of common law, without the intervention of any jury. Their juriſdiction extended legally over riots, perjury, miſbehaviour of ſheriffs, and other notorious miſdemeanors. Yet this was afterwards (as Lord Clarendon informs us) ſtretched "to the aſſerting of all proclamations and orders of ſtate; to "the vindicating of illegal commiſſions and grants of monopolies; holding for honourable that which pleaſed, and for "juſt that which profited, and becoming both a court of law "to determine civil rights, and a court of revenue to enrich "the treaſury: the council table by proclamations enjoining to "the people that which was not enjoined by the laws, and "prohibiting that which was not prohibited; and the ſtar-"chamber, which conſiſted of the ſame perſons in different "rooms, cenſuring the breach and diſobedience to thoſe pro-

"clamations by very great fines, imprisonments, and corporal "severities: so that any disrespect to any acts of state, or to "the persons of statesmen, was in no time more penal, and "the foundations of right never more in danger to be de- "stroyed." For these reasons it was abolished by 16 Chas. I. c. 10. to the general joy of the nation. From the just odium into which this tribunal had fallen before its dissolution, few memorials have reached us of its nature, jurisdiction, and practice; except such as, on account of its enormous oppression, are recorded in the histories of the times. There are however to be met with some reports of its proceedings in Dyer, Croke, Coke, and other reporters of that age, and some in manuscript; and there is in the British Museum (Harl. MSS. Vol. I. No. 1226.) a very full, methodical, and accurate account of the constitution and course of this court, compiled by William Hudson of Gray's Inn, an eminent practitioner in it. This account has been published in the second volume of Collectanea Juridica. A short account of the same court with copies of all its process may also be found in 18 Rymer's Fœdera 192. In the second volume of a collection of curious discourses by eminent antiquaries, published by Thomas Hearne, there is a paper by Mr. Tate, entitled *Camera Stellata*, or an explanation of the most famous court of Star Chamber, together with an account of the offences there punishable, the fees payable, and the orders for proceeding therein, which not only describes and explains, but vindicates and extols the principles and practice of this justly unpopular tribunal.

WESTMINSTER HALL. The superior courts are held in Westminster Hall. The royal palace at Westminster was built by Edward the Confessor, and many parts of the original structure still exist, though sunk into other uses. Succeeding monarchs added much to it. The great hall was built by William Rufus, or possibly rebuilt, as a great hall was always deemed a necessary appendage to a palace. The entrance from New Palace-yard was bounded on each side by towers, magnificently ornamented with numbers of statues in rows above each other, many of which are now lost: A mutilated figure of an armed man, supposed to have been one of these statues, was discovered under the exchequer stair-case in 1781. In this hall and contiguous rooms, Henry III. entertained six thousand poor men, women, and children, on new year's day, 1236. It became ruinous before the reign of Richard II. who rebuilt it in its present form in 1397; and in 1399 kept his Christmas in it with his characteristic magnificence. The cognizance of this unfortunate monarch, a white hart couchant under a tree, is still to be seen rudely carved in stone, as one of the ornaments surrounding the hall. Twenty-eight oxen,

oxen, three hundred ſheep, and fowls without number, were daily conſumed. His daily gueſts were ten thouſand. This room exceeds in dimenſion any in Europe which is not ſupported by pillars; its length is two hundred and ſeventy feet; the breadth ſeventy-four. Its height adds to its ſolemnity. The roof conſiſts chiefly of cheſnut wood, moſt curiouſly conſtructed, and of a fine ſpecies of Gothic. It is ſupported by thirteen Gothic ribs, of a noble dimenſion, ſpringing from the centre of each pier. It is in many places adorned with angels, ſupporting the arms of Richard II. and of Edward the Confeſſor. The ſtone moulding that runs round the hall, has likewiſe in many parts the device of Richard II.; the hart couchant under a tree. The whole roof, and the more ancient parts of the hall, are in the higheſt ſtate of preſervation. The ſky-lights and dormer-windows in the roof, are evidently modern additions, and rather interfere with the general ſimplicity; but the lights produced from them afford a brilliant variety of tints, diffuſing themſelves over the richly ornamented roof. At the upper end of the hall ſtand the courts of chancery and king's bench, to which there is an aſcent by an eaſy flight of ſteps. They are modern buildings, erected, it is ſaid, about the middle of the eighteenth century. On this ſpot Stowe tells us, "there was anciently a marble ſtone, of twelve feet in length, "and three in breadth; and alſo a marble chair, where the "kings of England formerly ſat at their dinners; and at other "ſolemn times, the lord chancellor. At this marble ſtone divers "matters of conſequence uſed to be tranſacted." The courts are ornamented with ſix whole length figures, finely decorated; moſt probably the effigies of ſome of our ancient kings, which formerly made a termination to the hall. On the north ſide of the hall is the court of common pleas; and at the right hand from the great entrance is a detached chamber for the court of exchequer.

Within the ſame building and communicating with Weſtminſter-hall, are the houſes of lords and commons, with their principal offices. Beſide theſe, there is the *court of requeſts*, a vaſt room modernized; at preſent a mere walking place. The outſide of the ſouth end ſhews the great antiquity of the building, having in it two great round arches, with zig-zag mouldings, the moſt ancient ſpecies of Engliſh architecture. The room in which the tremendous court of *ſtar chamber* was held ſtill remains, retaining its original name, but is no longer diſtinguiſhed by ſtars painted on the roof, from which it is erroneouſly ſuppoſed the court derived its title. The room now called the *painted chamber* is uſed as the place of conference between the lords and commons. It makes a very poor appearance, being hung with

with very ancient French or Arras tapestry, which, by the names worked over the figures, seems to relate to the Trojan war. The windows are of the ancient simple Gothic. On the north outside, beyond the windows, are many marks of recesses, groins, and arms, on the remains of some other room. Numbers of the other great apartments are still preserved on each side of the entrance into Westminster-hall, in the law court of exchequer, and adjacent, and the same in the money exchequer, and the court of the duchy of Lancaster; all which were parts of the ancient palace. At the foot of the stair-case is a round pillar, having on it the arms of John Stafford, lord treasurer from 1422 to 1424. On the opposite part are the arms of Ralph, Lord Botelar, of Sudley, treasurer of the exchequer in 1433.

Courts of Assize and Nisi Prius. Besides the regular administration of justice in the superior courts at Westminster, other courts are established for the trial of causes in every county in England, and they act as collateral auxiliaries to the courts at Westminster. From these, as has been observed, process issues at the suit of every person who is disposed to bring an action; but for the purpose of trying within the county where the interest arises, all the facts by which the dispute is to be determined, courts of assize, and nisi prius are established.

These are composed of two or more commissioners, who are twice in every year sent by the king's special commission all round the kingdom, except London and Middlesex, to try by juries of the respective counties the truth of such matters of fact as are then under dispute in the courts at Westminster. The courts of nisi prius in London and Middlesex are holden by the chief justices of the common law courts in and after every term; they are called sittings. Those for Middlesex were established by the legislature in the reign of Elizabeth. In ancient times all issues in actions brought in that county were tried at Westminster in the terms, at the bar of the court in which the action was instituted; but when the business of the courts increased, these trials were found so great an inconvenience, that it was enacted by 18 Eliz. c. 12. that the chief justice of the king's bench should be empowered to try within the term, or within four days after the end of it, all the issues joined in the courts of chancery and king's bench; and that the chief justice of the common pleas and the chief baron should try in like manner the issues joined in their respective courts. In the absence of any one of the chiefs, the same authority was given to two of the judges or barons of his court. The statute 12 Geo. I. c. 31. extended the time to eight days after term, and empowered one judge or baron to sit in the absence

ſence of the chief; and the 24 Geo. II. c. 18. has extended the time after term to fourteen days.

The judges of aſſize came into uſe in the room of the ancient juſtices in Eyre, who made their circuit round the kingdom once in ſeven years, for the purpoſe of trying cauſes; but the preſent juſtices of aſſize and *niſi prius* are more immediately derived from the ſtatute Weſtm. 2. 13 Edw. I. c. 30. which directs them to be aſſigned out of the king's ſworn juſtices, aſſociating to themſelves one or two diſcreet knights of each county. By ſtatute 27 Edw. I. c. 4. (explained by 12 Edw. II. c. 3.) aſſizes and inqueſts were allowed to be taken before any one juſtice of the court in which the plea was brought, aſſociating to him one knight or other approved man of the county. And, laſtly, by ſtatute 14 Edw. III. c. 16. inqueſts of *niſi prius* may be taken before any juſtice of either bench (though the plea be not depending in his own court) or before the chief baron of the exchequer, if he be a man of the law; or otherwiſe before the juſtices of aſſize, ſo that one of each juſtices be a judge of the king's bench or common pleas, or the king's ſerjeant ſworn.

Circuits. The judges uſually make their circuits in the vacations after Hilary and Trinity terms. The jealouſy of our anceſtors ordained, that no man of law ſhould be judge of aſſize in his own county, wherein he was born or inhabited, and this reſtriction was conſtrued to extend to every commiſſion of the judges; but it being found very inconvenient, the 12 Geo. II. c. 27. was enacted for the expreſs purpoſe of authorizing the commiſſioners of *oyer* and *terminer*, and gaol delivery, to execute their commiſſions in the criminal courts within the counties in which they were born, or in which they reſide. The judges upon their circuits now ſit by virtue of five ſeveral authorities. 1. The commiſſion of the peace. 2. A commiſſion of *oyer* and *terminer*. 3. A commiſſion of general gaol delivery. 4. A commiſſion of aſſize directed to the juſtices and ſerjeants therein named, to take (together with their aſſociates) aſſizes in the ſeveral counties; that is, to take the verdict of a peculiar ſpecies of jury, called an aſſize, and ſummoned for the trial of landed diſputes. 5. That of *niſi prius*, which is a conſequence of the commiſſion of aſſize, being annexed to the office of thoſe juſtices by the ſtatute of Weſtm. 2. 13 Edw. I. c. 30. and it empowers them to try all queſtions of fact, iſſuing out of the courts at Weſtminſter, that are then ripe for trial by jury. Theſe by the courſe of the courts are uſually appointed to be tried at Weſtminſter in ſome Eaſter or Michaelmas term, by a jury returned from the county wherein the cauſe of action ariſes; but with this proviſo, *niſi prius*, *unleſs*

unless before the day prefixed, the judges of assize come into the county in question. This they are sure to do in the vacation preceding each Easter and Michaelmas term, which saves much expense and trouble. These commissions are constantly accompanied by writs of *association*, in pursuance of the statutes of Edward I. and II. before mentioned; whereby certain persons (usually the clerk of assize and his subordinate officers) are directed to associate themselves with the justices and serjeants, and they are required to admit the said persons into their society, in order to take the assize, &c. that a sufficient supply of commissioners may never be wanting. But, to prevent the delay of justice by the absence of any of them, there is also issued of course a writ of *si non omnes*, directing, that if all cannot be present, any two of them (a justice or serjeant being one) may proceed to execute the commission.

These general circuits are six, comprising the whole kingdom of England, except those places which have already been mentioned as being entitled to separate jurisdictions. They severally comprise the following counties; and the assizes are held at the towns mentioned after their names. 1st. The *Home Circuit*, including *Hertfordshire*, the county town Hertford; *Essex*, Chelmsford; *Surry*, Kingston, in the spring, and in the summer, Guildford and Croydon alternately; *Sussex*, East Grinstead, in the spring, and in the summer, Horsham and Lewes alternately; and *Kent*, where the assizes are always at Maidstone. 2d. The *Midland Circuit*, in which are *Northamptonshire*, Northampton; *Rutlandshire*, Oakham; *Lincolnshire*, Lincoln; *Nottinghamshire*, Nottingham; *Derbyshire*, Derby; *Leicestershire*, Leicester; and *Warwickshire*, Coventry and Warwick. 3d. The *Norfolk Circuit*, comprising *Buckinghamshire*, Buckingham; *Bedfordshire*, Bedford; *Suffolk*, Bury St. Edmunds; *Huntingdonshire*, Huntingdon; *Cambridgeshire*, Cambridge; and *Norfolk*, Norwich. 4th. The *Oxford Circuit*, containing *Berkshire*, Reading; *Oxfordshire*, Oxford; *Herefordshire*, Hereford; *Shropshire*, Shrewsbury; *Gloucestershire*, Gloucester; *Monmouthshire*, Monmouth; *Staffordshire*, Stafford; and *Worcestershire*, Worcester. 5th. The *Northern Circuit*, having *Yorkshire*, York; *Durham*, Durham; *Northumberland*, Newcastle; *Cumberland*, Carlisle; *Westmoreland*, Appleby; and *Lancashire*, Lancaster. Durham, Northumberland, Cumberland and Westmoreland have assizes in the summer only, on account of the badness of the ways. The summer northern circuit is therefore called the long circuit, and the judges in travelling to its extremity and back to London, make a journey of 652 miles. 6th. The *Western Circuit*, in which are *Southampton*, Whichester; *Wiltshire*, Salisbury; *Cornwall*, Bodmin; *Devonshire*, Exeter; *Somersetshire*, Taunton, in spring, and

Wells

Wells and Bridgewater alternately, in summer; and an assize for the city and county of Bristol in summer only.

These circuits are supplied by the twelve judges, two being appointed to each. For which purpose, and to prevent any contention about choice, they all meet every Hilary and Trinity term at Serjeants' Inn, and the lord chief justice of the king's bench makes his election first; the chief justice of the common pleas chooses next; and he is followed by the lord chief baron of exchequer. Then the other judges choose according to seniority. After this choice amongst themselves, they wait on the king, who, at his pleasure, either confirms or alters their arrangement. In every Trinity term, the king also grants a warrant to the bishop of Durham, to issue commissions to the judges appointed to the circuit which includes that county, in the same manner as he gives his warrant to his judges for other counties, and in virtue of which their several commissions are issued. The senior or superior judge generally sits on the crown side, or for the trial of criminals, and the junior or inferior, on the nisi prius side, for the decision of cases of property.

Each circuit is attended by counsel; and it is a rule at the bar, that they who have elected one circuit do not, even if they have leisure, practise at another, unless on account of their great talents or reputation, they are brought there by a special retainer; and in that case, they plead only in the very causes wherein they are specially retained.

The officers belonging to the circuits are, the *clerk of the assize*, *associate*, *clerk of arraigns*, *clerk of indictments*, *judge's marshal*, *crier*, *clerk*, and *tipstaff*. The sheriff of each county, and his deputy attend the judges, and the coroner also attends to deliver in all inquisitions, &c. to the clerk of assize in court, and he is to return all writs of *venire*, *distringas*, and *habeas corpora*, where the sheriff is a party in the suit, which are specially directed to him for that purpose.

Of Tythings, Hundreds, and Counties. It has already been said at the beginning of this work, that the division of England into counties, and the further subdivisions of the land which have contributed so much to facilitate justice and preserve order, are generally ascribed to Alfred the Great. That prince, to prevent the rapines and disorders which prevailed in the realm, instituted tythings; so called from the Saxon, because ten freeholders, with their families, composed one. These all dwelt together, and were sureties, or free pledges to the king, for the good behaviour of each other; and if any offence was committed in their district, they were bound to have the offender

 forthcoming.

forthcoming. And therefore anciently no man was suffered to abide in England above forty days, unless he were enrolled in some tything or decennary. One of the principal inhabitants of the tything is annually appointed to preside over the rest, being called the tythingman, the headborough, and in some counties the borsholder, or boroughs-healder, being supposed the discreetest man in the borough, town, or tything. Tythings, towns, or vills, are of the same signification in law, and are said to have had each of them originally a church, and celebration of divine service, sacraments, and burials. As ten families of freeholders made up a town or tything, so ten tythings composed a superior division, called a hundred, as consisting of ten times ten families. The hundred is governed by a high constable or bailiff; and formerly there was regularly held in it the hundred court for the trial of causes, though now fallen into disuse. In some of the northern counties these hundreds are called wapentakes. An indefinite number of these hundreds makes up a county or shire. In some counties there is an intermediate division, between the shires and the hundreds, as lathes in Kent, and rapes in Sussex, each of them containing about three or four hundreds. These had formerly their lathe reeves and rape reeves, acting in subordination to the shire reeve. Where a county is divided into three of those intermediate jurisdictions, they are called tythings, which were formerly governed by a tything reeve. These tythings still subsist in the county of York, where, by an easy corruption, they are denominated ridings.

SHERIFFS. It seems that anciently the government of the county was by the king lodged in the earl or count, who was the immediate officer of the crown; and this high office was granted by the king at will, sometimes for life, and afterwards in fee. But, when it became too burdensome, and could not be commodiously executed by a person of so high rank and quality, it was thought necessary to constitute a person duly qualified to officiate in his stead, who hence is called in Latin *vicecomes*, and in English, sheriff, from *shire-reeve*, i. e. governor of the shire or county. He is likewise considered as bailiff to the crown; and his county, of which he has the care, and in which he is to execute the king's writs, is called the bailiwick. Although the sheriff is still called *vicecomes*, yet in all he does, all his authority is derived immediately, not from the earl, but from the king, who by his letters patent commits to him the guardianship of the county. He is therefore at this day considered as an officer of great antiquity, trust, and authority, having, according to Lord Coke, *triplicem custodiam*, viz. *vitæ justitiæ, vitæ legis, et vitæ reipublicæ*: *vitæ justitiæ*, to serve process, and to return

turn indifferent juries for the trial of men's lives, liberties, lands, and goods; *vitæ legis*, to execute proceſs and make execution, which is the life of the law; and *vitæ reipublicæ*, to keep the peace.

It was ordained by the ſtatute 28 Edw. I. c. 8. that the people ſhould have the election of ſheriffs in every ſhire, where the office is not of inheritance; for, anciently, in ſome counties the ſheriffs were hereditary, as it ſeems they were in Scotland until the ſtatute of 20 Geo. II. c. 43. and ſtill continue in the county of Weſtmoreland, of which the earl of Thanet is the hereditary ſheriff. The city of London too has the inheritance of the ſhrievalty of Middleſex by charter. This office may alſo deſcend to, and be executed by, a female; for Anne counteſs of Pembroke was hereditary ſheriff of Weſtmoreland, and exerciſed the office in perſon, ſitting at the aſſizes at Appleby on the bench with the judges. And although at this day the king has the ſole appointment of ſheriffs, except in counties palatine, and where there are *jura regalia*, yet he cannot apportion or divide it, that is, he cannot determine it in part, as for one town or one hundred; neither can he abridge the ſheriff of any thing incident or belonging to his office.

Qualification and Exemption. It is provided by ſeveral acts of parliament, that no man ſhall be ſheriff of any county unleſs he have in it ſufficient lands to anſwer the king and his people, in caſe of complaint againſt him; and that no one that is ſteward or bailiff to a great lord ſhall be made ſheriff, unleſs he be put forth of ſervice. The king having an intereſt in every ſubject, and a right to his ſervice, it is holden that no man can be exempt from the office of ſheriff, but by act of parliament, or letters patent. Excommunication was held to be no excuſe, becauſe the party might have removed that diſability; but a priſoner for debt is not bound. A man diſabled by a judgment in law is excuſed. Attornies are privileged under all circumſtances; and ſo by ſtatute 2 Geo. III. c. 20. are all perſons during the time they act as militia officers. No perſon can be placed or choſen in any office of mayor, ſheriff, or other office of magiſtracy, place, truſt, or employment, concerning the government of any city, corporation, borough, cinque-port, and their members, or other port-town, that ſhall not have, within one year next before ſuch choice, taken the ſacrament according to the rites of the church of England: and every ſuch perſon muſt take the oaths of allegiance and ſupremacy at the time when the oath for the due execution of the office ſhall be adminiſtered. And in default, ſuch choice ſhall be void. Proteſtant diſſenters who are exempted by the toleration act, 1 Will. & Mary, ſtat. 1. c. 18. from the

obligation

obligation of complying with the requisition of the corporation act, and who can plead their non-compliance as a reasonable and sufficient excuse, are not compellable to serve this office, nor of course to pay any fine for refusal.

Appointment and Oath. The high sheriff has his authority given him by two patents; by the one the king commits to him the custody of the county, and by the other, commands all other his subjects within that county to be aiding and assisting to him in all things belonging to his office. By the statute 9 Edw. st. 2. the chancellor, treasurer, and judges are to meet on the morrow of *All Souls*, being the third of November, every year, in the exchequer chamber, to nominate persons to be made sheriffs; but by 24 Geo. II. c. 48. sheriffs are to be appointed on the morrow of Saint Martin. And the manner is, the lord chancellor, treasurer, and other high officers, being of the privy council, together with the judges of both benches, and the barons of the exchequer, being assembled in the exchequer chamber, nominate three persons in every county, to be presented to the king, that he may prick one of them to be sheriff; but the king, by his prerogative, may make and appoint the sheriffs without this usual election or nomination in the exchequer, as is the daily practice on the death of any sheriff. When the king appoints a person sheriff, who is not one of the three nominated in the exchequer, he is called a *pocket sheriff*. It is probable that no compulsory instance of the appointment of a pocket sheriff ever occurred; the prerogative is ungracious, and whenever exercised, unless the occasion is manifest, the whole administration of justice throughout one county for a twelvemonth, if not corrupted, is certainly suspected. The sheriffs in the counties of Wales are nominated yearly by the lord president, council, and justices of Wales, and certified up by them, and after appointed and elected by the king as other sheriffs are.

Before he exercises any part of his office, and before his patent is made out, the sheriff is to give security in the king's remembrancer's office in the exchequer under pain of 100*l.* for the payment of his proffers, and all other profits of his sheriffwick; but these securities are never sued, unless there is a deficiency in the sheriff's effects. He also takes a particular oath of office, which is said to be by the ancient common law, and contains a concise enumeration of the nature and several branches of his office. There being, however, in this oath, some things which were thought too strict, it is now enacted by the 3 Geo. I. c. 15. that the following shall be taken by all high sheriffs, except those of Wales, and the counties palatine: "I will well and truly serve the king's majesty in the office of

"sheriff,

"sheriff; and promote his majesty's profit in all things that "belong to my office, as far as I legally can or may. I will "truly preserve the king's rights, and all that belongs to the "crown. I will not assent to decrease, lessen, or conceal the "king's rights, or the rights of his franchises; and where-"soever I shall have knowledge that the rights of the crown "are concealed or withdrawn, be it in lands, rents, franchises, "suits, or services, or in any other matter or thing, I will do "my utmost to make them be restored to the crown again; "and if I may not do it myself, I will certify and inform the "king thereof, or some of his judges. I will not respite or "delay to levy the king's debts for any gift, promise, reward, "or favour, where I may raise the same without great griev-"ance to the debtors. I will do right as well to poor as to "rich, in all things belonging to my office. I will do no "wrong to any man for any gift, reward, or promise, nor for "favour or hatred. I will disturb no man's right, and will "truly and faithfully acquit, at the exchequer, all those of "whom I shall receive any debts or duties belonging to the "crown. I will take nothing whereby the king may lose, or "whereby his right may be disturbed, injured, or delayed. I "will truly return, and truly serve all the king's writs, accord-"ing to the best of my skill and knowledge. I will take no "bailiffs into my service but such as I will answer for, and "will cause each of them to take such oaths as I do in what "belongs to their business and occupation. I will truly set "and return reasonable and due issues of them that be within "my bailiwick, according to their estate and circumstances; "and make due panels of persons able and sufficient, and not "suspected or procured, as is appointed by the statutes of this "realm. I have not sold, or let to farm, nor contracted for, "nor have I granted or promised for reward or benefit, nor "will I sell or let to farm, nor contract for, or grant for re-"ward or benefit, by myself, or any other person for me, or "for my use, directly or indirectly, my sheriffwick, or any "bailiwick thereof, or any office belonging thereunto, or the "profits of the same, to any person or persons whatsoever. I "will truly and diligently execute the good laws and statutes "of this realm, and in all things well and truly behave myself "in my office, for the honour of the king, and the good of his "subjects, and discharge the same according to the best of my "skill and power." A refusal of the oaths enjoined to be taken amounts to a refusal of the office; but if the sheriff is not in London, the oath may be taken by *dedimus potestatem*, directed to any two justices of the peace of the same county, one to be of the quorum, or to any other commissioners, or before one of the judges of assize for that county, or one of the masters in chancery, who, it is said, may, as well as the judge, administer such oath without any *dedimus*. The breach or violation of this oath, although an high offence, is not however punishable as perjury.

By stat. 25 Chas. II. c. 2. the sheriff must also, within six calendar months after his election, take and subscribe the oaths of allegiance, supremacy, and abjuration, in one of the courts at Westminster, or at the general or quarter-session of the place where he shall be or reside, between the hours of nine and twelve in the forenoon, and no other; and within three months after election, receive the sacrament, according to the rites of the church of England, in some public church on the Lord's day; and in the court where he takes the oaths of allegiance, &c. he must first deliver a certificate of having received the sacrament, under the hand of the minister and churchwarden, and then make proof thereof by two witnesses on oath; he must also, at the same time, make and subscribe the declaration against transubstantiation. But now, by 16 Geo. II. c. 30., the time is enlarged to six months after admittance and receiving the authority, and the not complying shall incur all the disabilities of 25 Chas. II. The sheriffs of Wales and Chester are not obliged to take these oaths, but must take the ancient accustomed oath, except certain words, obliging them to reside in their bailiwicks. Nor does the oath of office extend to the sheriffs of London and Middlesex, the county palatine of Durham, the county of Westmoreland, or to the sheriffs of any city or town being a county of itself, so as to prevent their placing in, or disposing of any of the offices of their under sheriffs, county-clerks, bailiffs, or other officers, or their continuance therein. After the sheriff has taken the oaths before-mentioned, then on the writ of discharge being delivered to his predecessor, the old sheriff, or his under-sheriff, at or before the next county court, the new sheriff must take over from the old one all his prisoners, which are in the gaol, by their names, and all his writs precisely by view, and by indenture to be made between them, in which the retiring sheriff must, at his peril, specify all the causes which he has against every prisoner, as the new sheriff is not responsible in any matter which is omitted. The ancient sheriff is not discharged, nor the new sheriff charged, till three things are done, viz. the patent to the new sheriff, the writ of discharge to the old sheriff, and the delivery of the prisoners by indenture to the new sheriff.

A sheriff cannot be elected knight of the shire for that county for which he is sheriff; and although he is, by virtue of his office, a conservator of the peace, yet it is enacted by the

1 Mar.

1 Mar. ft. 2. c. 8. that no perfon having the office of fheriff of any county, fhall exercife in that county, and during that period, the functions of juftice of the peace. By the 1 Hen. V. c. 4. it is alfo enacted, that no under-fheriff, fheriff's clerk, receiver, nor fheriff's bailiff, fhall be an attorney in any of the king's courts during the time that he is in office.

Jurisdiction and Duration of Authority. By the common law, the patents of fheriffs, like all other commiffions, determined by the death of the king; but now, by the 7 Will. and Mary, c. 27. and 1 Anne, ft. 1. c. 8. fuch commiffion fhall remain in full force for the fpace of fix months after fuch event, unlefs fuperfeded, or made void by the fucceffor. By the 14 Edw. III. c. 7. it is, however, enacted, that no fheriff, under-fheriff, nor fheriff's clerk, fhall abide in his office above one year, on penalty of two hundred pounds yearly; a pardon for fuch offence or forfeiture to be void; as are letters patent made to occupy fuch office above one year; and the perfon acting by force of them to be difabled ever after from being fheriff in any county in England. By the 1 Rich. II. c. 11. it is enacted, that none that has been fheriff of any county a year, fhall within the next two years be chofen again, if there be others fufficient; and by the 1 Hen. V. c. 4. it is enacted, that they that be bailiffs of fheriffs for one year, fhall be in no fuch office three years next following, except bailiffs of fheriffs who inherit their office. The claufe in the ftat. 4 Hen. IV. c. 5. obliging every fheriff to be dwelling within his bailiwick, is not now confidered as operative, and the claufe is left out of the oath; yet hence it is clear that a fheriff has no jurifdiction in any other county, nor can he do a judicial act, in which his perfonal prefence is required out of his county. It is held that he may do a minifterial act, as make a panel, or return a writ, out of his county; but if the fheriff be beyond fea, and make a panel or any return there, and fend it into England, it is not good, for he is an officer only in England. If on a *habeas corpus*, &c. the fheriff is commanded to carry a prifoner to a place out of his county, and in fo doing he is obliged to pafs through feveral counties, his authority continues; and if a prifoner efcapes into another county, the fheriff, or his officers, upon frefh fuit may take him again.

Duties. The powers and duties of the fheriff arife either as a judge, as keeper of the king's peace, as a minifterial officer of the fuperior courts of juftice, or as the king's bailiff. In his judicial capacity he is to hear and determine all caufes not exceeding forty fhillings value in his county court; and he has alfo a judicial power in divers other civil cafes. In a writ of rediffeifin, the fheriff acts as judge, as well as minifter; fo in inquiry

inquiry of waste, and admeasurement of pasture; when he executes his *judicial* authority, he must do it in person, and it is not sufficient by the under-sheriff, or other deputy. As the keeper of the king's peace, both by common and special commission, he is the first man in the county, and superior in rank to any nobleman. He may apprehend and bind in a recognizance, or commit to prison, all persons who break, or attempt to break the peace. He may, and is bound *ex officio* to pursue, and take all traitors, murderers, felons, and other misdoers, and commit them to gaol for safe custody. He is also to defend his county against any of the king's enemies; and for this purpose, as well as for keeping the peace, and pursuing felons, he may command all the people of his county to attend him; which is called the *posse comitatus*, or power of the county. This summons, every person above fifteen years old, and under the degree of a peer, is bound to attend, upon warning, under pain of fine and imprisonment. 2 Hen. V. c. 8. But although the sheriff is thus the principal conservator of the peace in his county, yet by the express directions of the great charter, cap. 17. he, together with the constable, coroner, and certain other officers of the king, are forbidden to hold any pleas of the crown, or, in other words, to try any criminal offence; for it would be highly unbecoming, that the executioners of justice should be also the judges; should impose, as well as levy, fines and amercements; should one day condemn a man to death, and personally execute him the next. Neither, as has been said before, may he act as an ordinary justice of the peace within his county, during the time he acts as sheriff. In his ministerial capacity, the sheriff is bound to execute and return all process issuing from the king's courts to him directed. In the commencement of civil causes he is to serve the writ, to arrest, and to take bail; when the cause requires trial, he must summon and return the jury; and when it is determined, he must see the judgment of the court carried into execution. In criminal matters, he also arrests and imprisons, returns the jury, has the custody of the delinquent, and executes the sentence of the court, though it extends to death itself. The ministerial office of sheriff consists in bailment of prisoners; in making replevin; in election of knights and burgesses for parliament, coroners and verderors; in attendance upon the judges, justices, &c.; in proclamation of statutes, and in keeping and collecting the rights and revenues of the king. As the king's bailiff, it is his business to preserve the rights of the king within his bailiwick; he must seize to the king's use all lands devolved to the crown by attainder or escheat; levy all fines and forfeitures; seize and keep all waifs, wrecks, estrays, and the like, unless they are granted

granted to ſome ſubject; and muſt alſo collect the king's rents within his bailiwick, if commanded by proceſs from the exchequer. As ſoon as he is made ſheriff, he is accountable to the king for all farms, rents, iſſues, and profits of the county, which run in account under the name of viſcontiels. But for the eſcheats of the green wax out of the exchequer, and ſome other matters, he is not chargeable. As writs and proceſs are directed to the ſheriff, neither he nor his officers are to diſpute the authority of the court out of which they iſſue, but, at their peril, truly to execute them as commanded, without favour, and with the utmoſt expedition and ſecrecy; but, on the other hand, he muſt not be guilty of oppreſſion, nor make uſe of other force or greater violence than the occaſion requires.

The ſheriff is an officer of that eminence, confidence, and charge, that he ought to have all right pertaining to his office, and ought to be favoured in law, before any private perſon.

Coroner. The coroner, *coronator*, is ſo called, becauſe he is principally engaged in pleas of the crown. In this light the lord chief juſtice of the king's bench is the principal coroner in the kingdom, and may (if he pleaſes) exerciſe the juriſdiction of a coroner in any part of the realm; but there are alſo particular coroners for every county of England; uſually four, but ſometimes ſix, and ſometimes ſeven. This office is of equal antiquity with that of ſheriff; and they were ordained together to keep the peace when the earls gave up the wardſhip of counties. The coroner is ſtill choſen by all the freeholders in the county court. For this purpoſe there is a writ at common law, *de coronatore eligendo*; and it was enacted by the ſtatute of Weſtm. 1. that none but lawful and diſcreet knights ſhould be choſen. There was an inſtance in the 5 Edward III. of a man being removed from the office, becauſe he was only a merchant; but it is now ſufficient if the perſon elected has lands enough to be made a knight, whether he is really knighted or not: for the coroner ought to have an eſtate ſufficient to maintain the dignity of his office, and anſwer any fines that may be ſet upon him for miſbehaviour; and if he has not enough to anſwer, his fine may be levied on the county, as the puniſhment for electing an inſufficient officer. Now indeed, through the neglect of gentlemen of property, the office is generally ſolicited for the ſake of emolument, coroners being allowed fees for their attendance by the ſtatute 3 Hen. VII. c. 1. The coroner is choſen for life; but may be removed, either by being made ſheriff, or choſen verderor, which are offices incompatible with the other; or by the king's writ, *de coronatore exonerando*, for a cauſe to be therein aſſigned, as that he is engaged in other buſineſs, is incapacitated by years or or ficknefs, has not a fufficient eftate, or lives in an inconvenient part of the county; and by the ftatute 25 Geo. II. c. 29. extortion, neglect, or mifbehaviour, are alfo made caufes of removal. The office and power of a coroner are alfo, like thofe of the fheriff, either judicial or minifterial, but principally judicial. This is in a great meafure afcertained by ftatute 4 Edw. I. *de officio coronatoris*; and confifts, firft, in inquiring, when any perfon is flain, or dies fuddenly, or in prifon, concerning the manner of his death, which muft be on view of the body; for if that is not found, the coroner cannot fit. He muft alfo fit at the very place where the death happened; and his inquiry is made by a jury from four, five, or fix of the neighbouring towns, over whom he is to prefide. If any be found guilty by this inqueft of murder, or other homicide, he is to commit them to prifon for further trial, and is alfo to inquire concerning their lands, goods, and chattels, which are forfeited thereby: but whether it be homicide or not, he muft inquire whether any deodand has accrued to the king, or the lord of the franchife, by the death; and muft certify the whole of this inquifition (under his own feal, and the feals of the jurors), together with the evidence thereon, to the court of king's bench, or the next affizes. Another branch of his office is to inquire concerning fhipwrecks, and certify whether wreck or not, and who is in poffeffion of the goods. Concerning treafure trove, he is alfo to inquire who were the finders, and where it is; and whether any one is fufpected of having found and concealed a treafure, whereupon he might be attached and held to bail, upon this fufpicion only. The minifterial office of the coroner is only as the fheriff's fubftitute; for when juft exception can be taken to the fheriff, for fufpicion of partiality; (as that he is interefted in the fuit, or of kindred to either plaintiff or defendant) the procefs muft then be awarded to the coroner, and he, inftead of the fheriff, muft execute the king's writs.

To execute his various duties, the fheriff has under him many inferior officers, viz. an under-fheriff, bailiffs, and gaolers; who, by 3 Geo. I. c. 15., muft neither buy, fell, nor farm their offices, on forfeiture of 500 *l*.

Under-Sheriffs. As the law, from neceffity, and in furtherance of juftice, allows the fheriff to make a deputy, it is fit that in all things in which the high fheriff's perfonal prefence is not required, the deputy fhould have the fame power with himfelf; and as by the nomination there is implicitly conferred on him a power of doing all fuch offices as the fheriff himfelf could execute, and which may be transferred by the law; it is likewife held, that the deputy's authority is by law fo equal with the

the principal's, that any condition, covenant, or other bargain to restrain it is void; and therefore it is now universally agreed that the under-sheriff may make bills of sale upon executions, assign bail-bonds, make returns to writs, and, in general, do every thing that the sheriff himself can do. He is appointed by deed, which is afterwards filed in the king's remembrancer's office in the exchequer. The high-sheriff, by law, is answerable for the conduct of his under-sheriff, yet he is not to be punished criminally for his acts, nor to be imprisoned, nor indicted for his misdemeanors. He may constitute and remove him at his will, even though by the deed he should declare him irrevocable; but by rules of the several courts, before the new sheriff returns any writ into chancery, the king's bench, common pleas, or exchequer, he ought to make and have an attorney, or deputy of record, there to receive all manner of writs and warrants to be delivered to them.

There are ancient laws, that no under-sheriff, or sheriff's clerk shall continue in office more than a year, or be a practising attorney; however wisely these laws may have been framed, there is reason at present to doubt their policy, for in the execution of so important an office, experience and knowledge are both highly requisite. The under-sheriff takes an oath detailing most of the duties of his office, and binding himself to execute them faithfully, and that he has not sold, or contracted for, or let to farm, nor granted or promised for reward or benefit, directly or indirectly, any bailiwick, or any other appointment belonging to his office. He must also take the oaths of allegiance, supremacy, and abjuration, receive the sacrament, and subscribe the declaration against transubstantiation, in the same manner as the high-sheriff, and within the same time.

Besides these oaths, the under-sheriff binds himself by an obligation, with sureties, and covenants with his superior to the following points:

1. To save the high-sheriff harmless.

2. To make the account in the exchequer, and procure the high-sheriff's discharge.

3. To return juries with the privity of the sheriff.

4. To execute no process of weight without the sheriff's privity.

5. To account to the sheriff and attend him.

6. To be ready to attend the sheriff.

7. For his good behaviour in his office.

8. To take or use no extortion. And,

9. To give attendance at the king's court.

BAILIFFS. The officers of the sheriff are of three kinds; first *bailiffs in fee*, or perpetual bailiffs, who have, by charter or prescription, the execution of writs within the guildable, secondly, *common bailiffs*, who are usually bound with sureties to the sheriff, in an obligation for the due execution of their office, and thence are called bound bailiffs; thirdly, *special bailiffs*, nominated by the plaintiff or his attorney, and appointed by the sheriff *pro hac vice*. Blackstone says, bailiffs or sheriff's officers, are either bailiffs of hundreds, or special bailiffs. Bailiffs of hundreds are officers appointed over those respective districts by the sheriffs to collect fines, to summon juries, to attend the judges and justices at the assizes and quarter sessions, and also to execute writs and process in the several hundreds; but as these are generally plain men, and not thoroughly skilful in this latter part of their office, that of serving writs and making arrests and executions, it is now usual to join special bailiffs with them; and these being, as already is mentioned, bound for the due execution of their office, the sheriff is answerable for all their misdemeanors, but he has recourse to their sureties for an indemnity. The sheriff's officer ought to execute his warrant with all speed and secrecy, and he is bound to pursue the effect of it in every behalf, otherwise it will not excuse him. A sworn and known officer, (be he sheriff, under-sheriff, bailiff, or serjeant) need not shew his warrant or writ when he comes to serve it upon any man's person or goods, although the party demand it; but a special bailiff, or other person, who is no sworn and known officer, must shew his authority or warrant, or the party may make resistance.

Arrest. Arrest, in common law, is the apprehending or restraining of one's person, in execution of the command of some court, or officer of justice. Arrest for debt is in two modes, the one on what is called *mesne process*, that is, where there is no judgment of a court against the party, but only an affidavit made by his creditor, that he owes him to the amount of 10*l.* at least; and from this the person arrested may be set at liberty on finding bail to the sheriff, as here after mentioned. The other arrest is on what is called *final process*, or where judgment has been obtained, and from this there is no discharge, but by payment of the money directed to be levied. An arrest must be, "by corporal seising or touching the defendant's body;" after which the bailiff may justify breaking open the house, in which he is, to take him: otherwise he has no such power, but must watch his opportunity to arrest him; for every man's house is his castle of defence and asylum, wherein he should suffer no violence. If a bailiff lays hold of one by the hand (whom he has a warrant to arrest) as he holds it out of the window, this is a sufficient taking to justify the breaking open the house to carry him away. A bailiff may also break open the door of a lodger, having first gained peace-

 able

able entrance at the outer door of the house. It is also to be observed, that the privilege of a man's house only extends to the owner, and will not protect any man that flies to it to escape the ordinary process of law, nor the goods of any person received into it to prevent lawful execution. Therefore, if the sheriff, having process against a stranger, desire to have the door opened, or to have the body of the party flying thither, if after such request, denial or refusal be made, the sheriff or his officers may lawfully break open the house, and execute the process. Where persons having authority to arrest or imprison, and, using proper means, are resisted, and the party making resistance is killed in the struggle, this homicide is justifiable; but, on the other hand, if the officer happen to be killed, it will be murder in all who take part in such resistance; for it is homicide committed in despite of the justice of the kingdom. The statute 29 Chas. II. c. 7. enacts, that on the Lord's day no writ or process shall be served or executed (except in cases of treason, felony, or breach of the peace), and persons arrested on that day may recover damages as if no writ or process had issued.

Privileged Places. No arrest ought to be made in the king's palace at Westminster, where his royal person resides, (except where the process issues out of the palace court) or in the king's presence, nor in any place where his justices are actually sitting. Formerly one of the greatest obstructions to public justice, both civil and criminal, was the number of pretended privileged places, especially in London and Southwark, where dishonest persons could shelter themselves from justice, under pretext of their being ancient palaces of the crown; such as White Friars, the Savoy, Salisbury-court, Ram-alley, Mitre-court, Fuller's-rents, Baldwin's gardens, Montague close, or the Minories, the Mint clink, and Deadman's place, within the hamlet of Wapping or Stepney. All these sanctuaries for iniquity are now demolished, and the opposing of any process in any of them is made highly penal by stat. 8 and 9 W. III. c. 27. 9 Geo. I. c. 28. and by 11 Geo. I. c. 22., which enacts that persons opposing the execution of any process in such pretended privileged places, or abusing any officer in his endeavours to execute his duty, so that he receives bodily hurt, shall be guilty of felony, and transported for seven years: and persons in disguise, joining in, or abetting any riot or tumult, on such account, or committing the same offences, shall be felons without benefit of clergy.

Privileged Persons. The persons by law privileged from arrest are, the king, the queen, whether regnant, consort, or dowager; all peers of the realm and parliament; peeresses by birth,

birth, and by marriage, until they lose their privileges by espousing a commoner; members of the lower house of parliament; embassadors and their servants, if *bona fide* retained; all these are absolutely and generally privileged, except the members of the house of commons, and their privilege is, by contrivance, rendered perpetual. To some other persons perpetual or temporary privilege is given. The king's domestic servants cannot be arrested without notice to the lord chamberlain; assistant officers of both houses of parliament down to the door-keepers, are privileged during the session, and until their return home; the clergy are protected while proceeding to and from church to perform divine service; judges and their necessary servants can in no case be arrested, but their clerks may; serjeants and barristers are not privileged; officers of the superior courts are; attornies have a limited privilege with respect to *mesne process*, but they may be taken in execution. The right of being exempted and freed from arrest by process of other courts, belongs to the lord chancellor, or keeper, and to all the masters, cursitors, ministers, and sworn clerks of the court of chancery, and to the menial servants of the chancellor or keeper, and of the ministers and officers. The clerk of the pells has privilege. Cursitor's clerk, auditor of the exchequer, and his servants, commissioners of the treasury, garter king of arms, receiver general of the revenues, clerk of the remembrancer, and an attorney of the exchequer, are intitled to privilege. The marshal of the King's Bench and warden of the Fleet are not to be arrested. Witnesses are protected in their necessary attendance, going to and returning from courts where they are called to give evidence; a bankrupt has his protection for forty-two days after actual surrender; soldiers and sailors, and persons in Wales and the counties palatine cannot be arrested, except in execution, unless the debt sworn to amounts to 20*l*. nor any other of his majesty's subjects, unless it amounts to 10*l*.

Persons arrested. For the protection of persons who are arrested against insult, fraud, and extortion, the stat. 32 Geo. II. c. 28. provides that no sheriff or sheriff's officer shall convey them to any tavern or public house, or to any house of their own (which are commonly called lock-up-houses, or by an expressive nick-name, spunging-houses) without their free consent; and the officers are not to carry the debtor to prison in less than twenty four hours after caption, unless he refuses to go to some other safe place of custody. The intent of this regulation is, that the unfortunate prisoner may not be made an object of gainful speculation on one hand, nor on the other, hurried to a common gaol, if he has reasonable hopes of procuring bail. The statute also

alſo contains ſtrict regulations for prevention of impoſition in charges for victuals and lodging, and the fair prices are directed to be publicly exhibited in the houſe of the bailiff.

If the perſon arreſted means to diſpute the juſtice of the plaintiff's claim, he is, by a late act of parliament framed by Lord Ellenborough, at liberty to pay into the hands of the ſheriff the ſum ſworn to, with a certain additional ſum for coſts, and give notice that he will defend the action, and in that caſe the plaintiff cannot, as he formerly could, demand the money depoſited, from the ſheriff, but muſt proceed in the cauſe. If the defendant procures bail to the ſheriff, they enter jointly with him into a bond with a penalty, double the amount of the debt ſworn to, that good bail ſhall be put in at the return of the writ; but if the debtor can neither pay nor depoſit the debt, nor find bail, he is conveyed to the gaol of the county in which he was arreſted, or he may, by writ of *habeas corpus*, be removed to the King's Bench, or the Fleet priſon; and in London and ſome other towns and cities, there are gaols ſet apart for the citizens, ſome of which have peculiar benefits. Of the proceedings ſubſequently taken by the plaintiff to compel the ſheriff to do his duty, or pay his demand, or upon aſſignment of the bail-bond; or of the meaſures purſued by the defendant to prevent theſe advantages, and of all other matters which ariſe in the courſe of a ſuit, it would be too technical here to treat.

Poundage. On levying an execution the ſheriff is entitled to poundage, or an allowance of one ſhilling in the pound up to 100*l*., and ſixpence in the pound on all monies after the firſt 100*l*. This ſum was formerly paid by the plaintiff, but by the act laſt mentioned it is to be levied on the defendant.

Escape. In either caſe of bailable, or final proceſs, if the defendant, after being taken, runs away, or is diſcharged from cuſtody without due bail, to the injury or delay of the plaintiff, it is termed an eſcape, and the ſheriff is liable to pay the debt and coſts, which he may recover from the negligent officer or his ſureties; but if a ſpecial bailiff is appointed at the requeſt of the plaintiff, the ſheriff is not anſwerable for his acts.

Gaolers. Gaolers are alſo ſervants of the ſheriff, and he muſt be reſponſible for their conduct. Their buſineſs is to keep ſafely all perſons committed to them by lawful warrant: and if they ſuffer any ſuch to eſcape, the ſheriff muſt anſwer it to the king, if a criminal matter; or, in a civil caſe, to the party injured. The abuſes of gaolers toward the unfortunate perſons in their cuſtody are alſo well reſtrained and guarded againſt by 32 Geo. II. c. 28.; and by ſtatute 14 Geo. III. c. 59. proviſions are made for better preſerving the health of priſoners, and preventing the gaol diſtemper.

Juries. As causes relating to property alone, and prosecutions for crimes are both tried by juries, it is intended in this place to treat of every kind of jury, the subject being equally connected with the description of courts which has been before given, and that of criminal courts which is immediately to follow.

Before this, the most usual kind of trial, is described, it may be proper to notice some others, which are only had in certain special and eccentrical cases; where the trial by the country, *per pais*, or by jury, would not be so proper or effectual. They are six: by record; by inspection or examination; by certificate; by witnesses; by wager of battel; and by wager of law.

Trial by Record. This trial is only used where a matter of record is pleaded in any action, as a fine, a judgment, or the like; and the opposite party pleads, that there is no such matter of record existing: upon this, issue is tendered and joined, and the party pleading the record has a day given him to bring it in, and proclamation is made in court for him "to bring "forth the record by him in pleading alleged, or else he "shall be condemned;" and, on his failure, his antagonist shall have judgment to recover. The trial therefore of this issue is merely by the record; for, as Sir Edward Coke observes, a record or enrolment is a monument of so high a nature, and imports in itself such absolute verity, that if it be pleaded that there is no such record, it shall not receive any trial by witness, jury, or otherwise, but only by itself. Thus titles of nobility, as whether earl or no earl, baron or no baron, shall be tried by the king's writ or patent only, which is matter of record. Also in case of an alien whether alien friend, or enemy, shall be tried by the league or treaty between his sovereign and ours; for every league or treaty is of record. And also, whether a manor be to be held in ancient demesne, or not, shall be tried by the record of *domesday* in the exchequer.

Inspection. Trial by inspection, or examination, is when in some point or issue, evidently the object of sense, the judges of the court decide the point on the testimony of their own senses; for in matters of such obvious determination, it is not thought necessary to summon a jury, who are properly called in to inform the conscience of the court, in respect of dubious facts: thus in some cases of age, death, and maihem, the court may decide by examination of the person; and in some relating to days and times by inspection of the almanac.

Certificate. The trial by certificate is allowed in cases where the evidence of the person certifying is the only proper criterion of the point in dispute. For, when the fact in question lies

lies out of the cognizance of the court, the judges muſt rely on the ſolemn averment or information of perſons in ſuch a ſtation, as affords them the moſt clear and competent knowledge of the truth, and to ſave trouble and circuity, permits the fact to be determined upon ſuch certificate merely. Of this mode of trial, many inſtances are given in old books, but few now remain; the principal is the mode of trying the cuſtom of the city of London by the certificate of the mayor and aldermen, delivered by the mouth of their recorder; but to this rule there is an exception, where the corporation of London is party, or intereſted; and there are other caſes.

Trial by Witnesses. The trial by witneſſes, *per teſtes*, without the intervention of a jury, is the only method of trial known to the civil law; it leaves the judge to form in his own breaſt his ſentence upon the credit of the witneſſes examined: but this trial is very rarely uſed in our law, which in almoſt every inſtance prefers the trial by jury. When, however, a widow brings a writ of dower, and the tenant pleads that the huſband is not dead; this being looked upon as a dilatory plea, is, for the ſake of favouring the widow, and for greater expedition, allowed to be tried by witneſſes examined before the judges; it is alſo uſed in ſome other caſes; and it is ſaid that in ſuch trials, the affirmative muſt be proved by two witneſſes at leaſt.

Wager of Battel. The trial by wager of battel is of great antiquity, but much diſuſed: though ſtill in force if the parties chuſe to abide by it. It ſeems to have owed its origin to the military ſpirit and ſuperſtition of our anceſtors, it being in the nature of an appeal to Providence, under an apprehenſion and hope (however preſumptuous and unwarrantable) that heaven would give the victory to him who had the right. This trial was introduced into England among other northern cuſtoms by William the Conqueror; but was only used in three caſes, one military, one criminal, and the third civil. The firſt in the court martial, or court of chivalry and honour; the ſecond in appeals of felony; and the third upon an iſſue joined in a writ of right, the laſt and moſt ſolemn decision of real property.

The laſt trial by battel that was waged in the court of common pleas at Weſtminſter (though there was one afterwards in the court of chivalry, in 1631; and another in the county palatine of Durham, in 1638,) was in the thirteenth year of Elizabeth, 1571, as reported by Sir James Dyer; and was held in Tothill-fields, Weſtminſter, to the great diſquietude of thoſe who were verſed in the law. The form is as follows.

When the tenant in a writ of right pleads the general iſſue, *viz.* that he has more right to hold, than the demandant has to recover; and offers to prove it by the body of his champion, which tender is accepted by the demandant; the tenant, in the first place, must produce his champion, who, by throwing down his glove as a gage or pledge, wages or stipulates battel with the champion of the demandant; and he, by taking up the gage, or glove, stipulates on his part to accept the challenge. The reason why it is waged by champions, and not by the parties themselves, in civil actions, is because, if any party to the suit dies, the suit must abate and be at an end for the present; and therefore no judgment could be given for the lands in question, if either of the parties were slain in battel; and also that no person might claim an exemption from this trial, as was allowed in criminal cases, where the battel was waged in person.

A piece of ground is then in due time set out, of sixty feet square, enclosed with lists, and on one side a court erected for the judges of the court of common pleas, who attend there in their scarlet robes; and also a bar is prepared for the learned serjeants at law. When the court sits, which ought to be by sun-rising, proclamation is made for the parties, and their champions; who are introduced by two knights, and are dressed in a coat of armour, with red sandals, bare-legged from the knee downwards, bare-headed, and with bare arms to the elbows. The weapons allowed them are only batons, or staves of an ell long, and a four-cornered leather target; so that death very seldom ensued in this civil combat. In the court military indeed they fought with sword and lance, as likewise in France only villeins fought with the buckler and baton, gentlemen armed at all points. When the champions, thus armed with batons, arrive within the lists or place of combat, the champion of the tenant takes his adversary by the hand, and makes oath that the tenements in dispute are not the right of the demandant; and the champion of the demandant, taking the other by the hand, swears in the same manner that they are; so that each champion is, or ought to be, thoroughly persuaded of the truth of the cause he fights for. Next an oath against sorcery and enchantment is to be taken by both the champions, in this, or a similar form: "Hear this, ye justices, that I have "this day neither eat, drunk, nor have upon me, neither bone, "stone, ne grass; nor any enchantment, sorcery, or witchcraft, "whereby the law of God may be abased, or the law of the "devil exalted. So help me God and his saints." The battel is thus begun, and the combatants are bound to fight till the stars appear in the evening: and, if the champion of the tenant can defend himself till the stars appear, the tenant shall

ſhall prevail in his cauſe; for it is ſufficient for him to maintain his ground, and make it a drawn battel, he being already in poſſeſſion; but, if victory declares itſelf for either party, for him is judgment finally given. This victory may ariſe from the death of either of the champions: which indeed has rarely happened; the whole ceremony, to ſay the truth, bearing a near reſemblance to certain rural athletic diverſions, which are probably derived from this original. Or victory is obtained, if either champion proves *recreant*, that is, yields, and pronounces the horrible word of *craven*; a word of diſgrace and obloquy, rather than of any determinate meaning. But a horrible word it indeed is to the vanquiſhed champion: ſince, as a puniſhment to him for forfeiting the land of his principal, by pronouncing that ſhameful word, he is condemned, as a recreant, *amittere liberam legem*, that is, to become infamous, and not be accounted *liber et legalis homo*; being ſuppoſed by the event to be proved forſworn, and therefore never to be put upon a jury, or admitted as a witneſs in any cauſe.

This is the form of trial by battel; a trial which the tenant, or defendant in a writ of right, has it in his election at this day to demand: and which was the only deciſion of ſuch writ of right after the conqueſt, till Henry II. by conſent of parliament introduced the *grand aſſize*, a peculiar ſpecies of trial by jury, in concurrence therewith; giving the tenant his choice of either the one or the other: this was juſtly conſidered a moſt noble improvement of the law.

Wager of Law. Our anceſtors, conſidering that in many caſes an innocent man of good credit might be overborne by a multitude of falſe witneſſes, eſtabliſhed this ſpecies of trial, by the oath of the defendant himſelf. He that waged, or gave ſecurity, to make his law, brought with him into court eleven of his neighbours, and then ſtanding at the end of the bar, was admoniſhed by the judges of the nature and danger of a falſe oath. And if he ſtill perſiſted, he was to repeat this or the like oath: "Hear this, ye juſtices, that I do not owe "unto Richard Jones the ſum of ten pounds, nor any penny "thereof, in manner and form as the ſaid Richard has declared "againſt me. So help me God." And thereupon his eleven neighbours or compurgators avowed upon their oaths, that they believed in their conſciences that he ſaid the truth. In England wager of law is never required; and is only admitted, where an action is brought upon ſuch matters as may be ſuppoſed to be privately tranſacted between the parties, and wherein the defendant may be preſumed to have made ſatisfaction without being able to prove it. Therefore it is only in actions of debt, upon ſimple contract, or for amercement, in actions of detinue, and of ac-

 count,

count, where the debt may have been paid, the goods reſtored, or the account balanced, without any evidence of either, that defendant is admitted to wage his law: it cannot be done when there is any ſpeciality (as a bond or deed) to charge the defendant, for that, if ſatisfied, would be cancelled; but when the debt grows by word only: nor does it lie in action of debt for arrears of an account, ſettled by auditors in a former action. And by ſuch wager of law (when admitted) the plaintiff is perpetually barred; for the law, in the ſimplicity of the ancient times, preſumed that no one would forſwear himſelf for any worldly thing. Wager of law however lies in a real action, where the tenant alleges he was not legally ſummoned to appear, as well as in mere perſonal contracts. There are many nice diſtinctions in the caſes where wager of law could, or could not, be admitted; the reſult of which in general is, that it ſhould never be allowed, but where the defendant bore a fair and unreproachable character; and it alſo was confined to ſuch caſes where a debt might be ſuppoſed to be diſcharged, or ſatisfaction made in private, without any witneſſes to atteſt it: and many other prudential reſtrictions accompanied this indulgence. But at length it was conſidered, that (even under all its reſtrictions) it threw too great a temptation in the way of indigent or profligate men; and therefore by degrees new remedies were deviſed, and new forms of action were introduced, wherein no defendant is at liberty to wage his law. So that now no plaintiff need at all apprehend any danger from the hardineſs of his debtor's conſcience, unleſs he voluntarily chuſes to rely on his veracity, by bringing an obſolete inſtead of a modern action; and wager of law is quite out of uſe, although not out of force. For this reaſon, when a new ſtatute inflicts a penalty, and gives an action of debt for recovering it, it is uſual to add, "in which no wager of law ſhall be allowed:" otherwiſe an hardy delinquent might eſcape any penalty, by ſwearing he had never incurred, or elſe had diſcharged it.

Trial by Jury. From theſe modes of deciding cauſes we return to the trial by jury; called alſo the trial *per pais*, or by the country; a trial that has been uſed time out of mind in this nation, and ſeems to have been coeval with its firſt civil government. Some authors have endeavoured to trace the origin of juries to the Britons, the firſt inhabitants of the iſland; but it is certain they were in uſe among the earlieſt Saxon coloniſts. Many aſcribe the invention of this, and ſome other pieces of juridical polity, to the ſuperior genius of Alfred the Great; to whom, on account of his having done much, it is uſual to attribute every thing; whereas the truth ſeems to be, that this tribunal was univerſally eſtabliſhed among the northern nations,

nations, and so interwoven with their very constitution, that the earliest accounts of the one give also some traces of the other. Its establishment, however, and use, in this island, of what date soever it be, though for a time greatly impaired and shaken by the introduction of the Norman trial by battel, was always so highly esteemed and valued by the people, that no conquest, no change of government, could ever prevail to abolish it. In *magna charta* it is more than once insisted on, as the principal bulwark of our liberties; but especially by chap. 29. that no freeman shall be hurt in either his person or property; "*nisi per legale judicium parium suorum vel per legem terræ*."

Trials by jury in civil causes, are of two kinds; *extraordinary* and *ordinary*.

The first species of extraordinary trial by jury is that of the grand assize, which was instituted as already mentioned, by Henry II. For this trial a writ *de magna assisa eligenda* is directed to the sheriff, to return four knights, who are to elect and chuse twelve others to be joined with them; and these together form the grand assize, or great jury to try the matter of right.

Another species of extraordinary juries, is that to try an *attaint*; which is a process commenced against a former jury; it is to consist of twenty-four of the best men in the county, who are called the grand jury in the attaint, to distinguish them from the first or petit jury; and these are to hear and try the goodness of the former verdict.

With respect to the ordinary trial by jury in civil cases, it takes place in this manner. When an action has proceeded so far that one party affirms a fact which the other denies, and both pray that it may be inquired of by the country, it is said that *issue is joined*, and the court, as matter of course, awards such process as in ancient times placed the cause in a situation to be tried at the bar of the court, but now it is generally tried, as already mentioned, at *nisi prius*. This process is in its form compulsory, and awarded against the jurors; it is called in the common pleas a writ of *habeas corpora juratorum*, and in the king's bench a *distringas*, commanding the sheriff to have their bodies, or to distrain them by their lands and goods, that they may appear on the day appointed. The entry therefore on the roll or record is, "that the jury is respited, through the defect "of the jurors, till the first day of the next term, then to ap-"pear at Westminster; *unless before that time* (*viz.* on a day "mentioned,) the justices of our lord the king, appoint-"ed to take assizes in that county, shall have come to "the place assigned for holding the assizes." And thereupon the writ commands the sheriff to have their bodies at

Weſtminſter on the ſaid firſt day of next term, or before the ſaid juſtices of aſſize, if before that time they come to the place appointed; *viz*. on the day aforeſaid. And as the judges are ſure to come and open the circuit commiſſions on the day mentioned in the writ, the ſheriff returns and ſummons this jury to appear at the aſſizes, and there the trial is had before the juſtices of aſſize and niſi prius.

When the general day of trials is fixed, the plaintiff or his attorney muſt bring down the record to the aſſizes, and enter it with the proper officers, in order to its being called on in courſe. If it be not ſo entered, it cannot be tried; therefore it is in the plaintiff's breaſt to delay any trial by not carrying down the record; unleſs the defendant, being fearful of ſuch neglect in the plaintiff, and willing to diſcharge himſelf from the action, will himſelf undertake to bring on the trial, giving proper notice to the plaintiff. This proceeding, from certain particulars in form, is called the trial by *proviſo*, but it is much diſuſed, ſince the ſtatute 14 Geo. II. c. 17. which enacts, that if, after iſſue joined, the cauſe is not carried down to be tried according to the courſe of the court, the plaintiff ſhall be eſteemed to be non-ſuited, and judgment ſhall be given for the defendant as in caſe of a nonſuit. If the plaintiff intends to try the cauſe, he is bound to give the defendant due notice; which, if he changes his mind, he muſt regularly countermand, or pay the coſts, occaſioned to the defendant, by his not proceeding to trial.

All previous proceedings having been regularly ſettled, the cauſe is called on in court. The record is then handed to the judge to peruſe, and obſerve the pleadings, and what iſſues the parties are to maintain and prove, while the jury is called and ſworn. To this end the ſheriff returns his compulſive proceſs, the writ of *habeas corpora*, or *diſtringas*, with the panel or jurors annexed, to the judges' officer in court. The jurors contained in the panel are either *ſpecial* or *common* jurors. Special juries were originally introduced in trials at bar, when the cauſes were of too great nicety for the diſcuſſion of ordinary freeholders; or where the ſheriff was ſuſpected of partiality, though not upon ſuch apparent cauſe as to warrant an exception to him. He is in ſuch caſes, upon motion in court on behalf of either party, and a rule granted thereupon, to attend the prothonotary or maſter, with his freeholders' book; and the officer is to take indifferently forty-eight of the principal freeholders in the preſence of the attornies on both ſides: who are each of them to ſtrike off twelve, and the remaining twenty-four are returned upon the panel. Special juries may be ſtruck on the trial of any iſſue, as well at the aſſizes as at bar; as well in indictments and informations for miſdemeanors,

meanors, as in civil actions; but there cannot be a special jury in cases of treason or felony, for the party must have the advantage of making twenty peremptory challenges in a prosecution for felony, and thirty-five in case of high treason. The party requiring the special jury also pays the extraordinary expence, unless the judge will certify (in pursuance of the statute 24 Geo. II. c. 18.) that the cause required it.

A *common jury* is one returned by the sheriff according to the directions of the statute 3 Geo. II. c. 25. which appoints, that the sheriff or officer shall not return a separate panel for every separate cause as formerly; but one and the same panel for every cause to be tried at the same assizes, containing not less than forty-eight, nor more than seventy-two jurors: and that their names being written on tickets, shall be put into a box or glass; and when each cause is called, twelve of these persons whose names shall be first drawn out of the box, shall be sworn upon the jury, unless absent, challenged, or excused; or unless a previous view of the messuages, lands, or place in question, shall have been thought necessary by the court: in which case six or more of the jurors, returned, to be agreed on by the parties, or named by a judge or other proper officer of the court, shall be appointed by special writ of *habeas corpora* or *distringas*, to have the matters in question shewn to them by two persons named in the writ; and then such of the jury as have had the view, or so many of them as appear, shall be sworn in on the inquest before any other jurors. These acts are well calculated to restrain any suspicion of partiality in the sheriff, or any tampering with the jurors when returned.

As the jurors appear, when called, they are sworn, unless challenged by either party. *Challenges* are of two sorts; to the array, and to the polls.

Challenges to the array are at once an exception to the whole panel in which the jury are arrayed or set in order by the sheriff in his return; and they may be made on account of partiality or some default of the sheriff, or his under officer who arrayed the panel.

Challenges to the polls *in capita*, are exceptions to particular jurors; and are reduced to four causes; 1st. *On the score of honour*; as, if a lord of parliament be impanelled on a jury, he may be challenged by either party, or he may challenge himself. 2d. *On account of defect*; as, if a foreigner be included in the panel. 3d. *For supposed bias or partiality*; which may be either a *principal challenge*, or *to the favour*. A *principal* challenge is such, where the cause assigned carries with it *prima facie* evident marks of suspicion, either of malice or favour: as, that a juror is of kin to either party within the ninth degree; that he has been

been arbitrator on either side; that he has an interest in the cause; that there is an action depending between him and the party; that he has taken money for his verdict; that he has formerly been a juror on the same cause; that he is the party's master, servant, counsellor, steward, or attorney, or of the same society or corporation with him: all these are principal causes of challenge; which, if true, cannot be over-ruled, for jurors must be above every exception. Challenges *to the favour*, are where the party has no principal challenge; but objects only some probable circumstances of suspicion, as acquaintance and the like; the validity of which must be left to the determination of the *triors*, whose office it is to decide whether the jury be favourable or unfavourable. The triors, in case the first man called be challenged, are two indifferent persons named by the court; and, if they try one man and find him indifferent, he is sworn; and then he and the two triors try the next; and, when another is found indifferent and sworn, the two triors are superseded, and the first two sworn on the jury try the rest. The 4th cause of challenge is *on account of crime;* which takes place when the intended juror has been guilty of some crime or misdemeanor, that affects his credit and renders him infamous: as for a conviction of treason, felony, perjury, or conspiracy; or if for some infamous offence he has received judgment of the pillory, tumbrel, or the like; or to be branded, whipt, or stigmatized; or if he is out-lawed or excommunicated, or has been attainted of false verdict, *præmunire*, or forgery; or lastly, if he has proved recreant when champion in the trial by battel, and thereby has lost his *liberam legem*. A juror may himself be examined on oath, with regard to such causes of challenge as are not to his dishonour or discredit; but not with regard to any crime, or any thing which tends to his disgrace or disadvantage.

Besides these challenges, which are exceptions against the fitness of jurors, and whereby they may be excluded from serving, there are also other causes to be made use of by the jurors themselves, which are matters of exemption; whereby their service is *excused* and not *excluded*. As by the statute West. 2. 13 Edw. I. c. 38. sick and decrepit persons, persons not commorant in the county, and men above seventy years old; and by statute of 7 and 8 Will. III. c. 32. infants under twenty-one. This exemption is also extended by divers statutes, customs, and charters to physicians, and other medical persons, counsel, attorneys, officers of the courts, and the like; who, all if impanelled, must shew their special exemption. Clergymen are also usually excused, out of favour and respect to their function: but, if they are seized of lands and tenements, they are in ſtrictneſs liable to be impanelled in reſpect of their lay fees, unleſs they are in the ſervice of the king or of ſome biſhop.

If by means of challenges or other cauſe, a ſufficient number of unexceptionable jurors does not appear at the trial, either party may pray a *tales*. A tales is a ſupply of ſuch men, as are ſummoned upon the firſt panel in order to make up the deficiency. For this purpoſe a writ of *decem tales, octo tales*, and the like, was uſed to be iſſued to the ſheriff at common law, and muſt be ſtill ſo done at a trial at bar, if the jurors make default. But at the aſſizes or *niſi prius*, by virtue of the ſtatute 35 Henry VIII. c. 6. and other ſubſequent ſtatutes, the judge is empowered, at the prayer of either party, to award a *tales de circumſtantibus* of perſons preſent in court, to be joined to the other jurors to try the cauſe; who are liable, however, to the ſame challenges as the principal jurors.

When a ſufficient number of perſons impanelled, or taleſmen appear, they are then ſeparately ſworn, well and truly to try the iſſues between the parties, and a true verdict to give according to the evidence, and hence they are denominated the jury, *jurata*, and jurors, *juratores*.

The jury are now ready to hear the merits; and, to fix their attention more cloſely to the facts which they are to try, the pleadings are opened to them by counſel on that ſide which holds the affirmative of the queſtion in iſſue. For the iſſue is ſaid to lie, and proof is always firſt required, upon that ſide which affirms the matter in queſtion. The opening counſel briefly informs them what has been tranſacted in the court above; the parties, the nature of the action, the declaration, the plea, replication, and other proceedings; and, laſtly, upon what point the iſſue is joined, which is there ſent down to be determined. Inſtead of which, formerly the whole record and proceſs of the pleadings was read to them in Engliſh by the court, and the matter in iſſue clearly explained to their capacities. The nature of the caſe, and the evidence intended to be produced, are next laid before them by counſel alſo on the ſame ſide: and, when their evidence is gone through, the advocate on the other ſide opens the adverſe caſe, and ſupports it by evidence; and then the party which began is heard by way of reply; but the reply is not allowed, except by the attorney-general, unleſs the defendant calls witneſſes.

When the evidence is gone through on both ſides, the judge, in the preſence of the parties, the counſel, and all others, ſums up the whole to the jury; omitting all ſuperfluous circumſtances, obſerving wherein the main queſtion and principal iſſue lies, ſtating what evidence had been given to ſupport it, with ſuch

ſuch remarks as he thinks neceſſary for their direction, and giving them his opinion in matters of law ariſing upon that evidence. The jury, after the proofs are ſummed up, unleſs the caſe is very clear, withdraw to conſider of their verdict: and, in order to avoid intemperance and cauſeleſs delay, are kept without meat, drink, fire, or candle, unleſs by permiſſion of the judge, till they are unanimous in their deciſion. When they are ſo agreed, they return; and, before they deliver their verdict, the plaintiff is bound to appear in court, by himſelf, attorney, or counſel, in order to anſwer the amercement to which, by the old law, he is liable, in caſe he fails in his ſuit, as a puniſhment for his falſe claim. The amercement is diſuſed, but the form ſtill continues; and if the plaintiff does not appear, no verdict can be given, but the plaintiff is ſaid to be *nonſuit*; therefore it is uſual for a plaintiff, when he or his counſel perceives that he has not given evidence ſufficient to maintain his iſſue, to be voluntarily nonſuited, or withdraw himſelf: whereupon the crier is ordered to call the plaintiff; and if neither he, nor any body for him, appears, he is nonſuited; the jurors are diſcharged, the action is at an end, and the defendant recovers his coſts. The reaſon of this practice is, that a nonſuit is more eligible for the plaintiff, than a verdict againſt him: for, after a nonſuit, which is only a default, he may commence the ſame ſuit again for the ſame cauſe of action; from which, after a verdict and judgment, he is for ever barred. If the plaintiff appears, the jury, by their foreman, deliver their verdict. When a verdict will carry all the coſts, and it is doubtful from the evidence for which party it will be given, it is a common practice for the judge to recommend, and the parties to conſent, that *a juror ſhould be withdrawn*, and thus no verdict is given, and each party pays his own coſts.

A verdict, is either privy, or public. A *privy verdict* is, when the judge has left or adjourned the court: and the jury, being agreed, in order to be delivered from their confinement, obtain leave to give their verdict privily to the judge out of court: this however is of no force, unleſs afterwards affirmed by a public verdict, given openly in court, wherein the jury may, if they pleaſe, vary from that which they had privately delivered. Thus the privy verdict is a mere nullity; and, as it allows time for the parties to tamper with the jury, is very ſeldom indulged; nor is it ever allowed in treaſon or felony. The public verdict alone is effectual and legal: in this the jury openly declare that they have found the iſſue for the plaintiff, or defendant; and if for the plaintiff, they aſſeſs his damages.

Some-

Sometimes, if there arises in the case any difficult matter of law, the jury, for the sake of better information, and to avoid the danger of having their verdict attainted, will find a *special verdict;* which is grounded on the statute Westm. 13 Edw. I. c. 30. In such a verdict, they state the naked facts, as they find them to be proved, and pray the advice of the court thereon; concluding conditionally, that if, upon the whole matter, the court shall be of opinion that the plaintiff had cause of action, they find for the plaintiff; if otherwise, for the defendant: this is entered at length on the record, and afterwards argued and determined in the court at Westminster, whence the issue came to be tried. Another method of finding a special verdict is, when the jury find generally for the plaintiff, but subject nevertheless to the opinion of the judge, or the court above, on a special case stated by the counsel on both sides with regard to a matter of law: which has this advantage over a special verdict, that it is attended with much less expence, and obtains a much speedier decision; the *postea*, or that writing indorsed on the record, which legally attests the fact of a verdict being found for either party, being stayed in the hands of the officer of *nisi prius*, till the question is determined; and the verdict is then entered for the plaintiff or defendant, as the case may happen. But in both these instances the jury may, if they think proper, take upon themselves to determine, at their own hazard, the complicated question of fact and law; and, without either special verdict or special case, may find absolutely either for the plaintiff or defendant.

When the jury have delivered in their verdict, and it is recorded in court, they are discharged. And so ends the trial by jury: a trial which, besides the other vast advantages, is also as expeditious and cheap, as it is convenient, equitable, and certain; for a commission out of chancery, or the civil law courts, for examining witnesses in one cause, will frequently last as long, and be full as expensive, as the trial of a hundred issues at *nisi prius;* and yet the fact cannot be determined by such commissioners, nor at all, till the depositions are published, and read at the hearing of the cause in court.

How much and how justly this mode of trial is favoured by the British nation need not here be displayed; but if it has so great an advantage over others in regulating civil property, it is evident that advantage is greatly heightened, when it is applied to criminal cases; since, in times of difficulty and danger, more is to be apprehended from the violence and partiality of judges, appointed by the crown, in suits between the king and the subject, than in disputes between individuals.

Our law has therefore wisely placed the strong and twofold barrier, of a presentment and trial by jury, between the liberties of the people and the prerogative of the crown. It was necessary to vest the executive power of the laws in the prince; but the founders of the English law have with excellent forecast contrived, that no man should be called to answer for any capital crime, unless on the preparatory accusation of a *grand jury*, consisting of twelve or more of his fellow subjects; and that the truth of every accusation, whether preferred in the shape of indictment, information, or appeal, should afterwards be confirmed by the unanimous suffrage of twelve of his equals and neighbours, indifferently chosen, and superior to all suspicion.

When a prisoner on his arraignment has pleaded not guilty, and for his trial has put himself upon the country, which country the jury are, the sheriff of the county must return a panel of jurors, free and lawful men of the neighbourhood; which is interpreted to be the county where the fact is committed. If the proceedings are before the court of King's-Bench, time is allowed, between the arraignment and the trial, for a jury to be impanelled, by writ of *venire facias*, to the sheriff, as in civil causes: and the trial, in case of a misdemeanor, is had at *nisi prius*, unless it be of such consequence as to merit a trial at bar; which is invariably had when the prisoner is tried for any capital offence. Before commissioners of oyer and terminer and jail delivery, the sheriff, by virtue of a general precept previously directed to him, returns to the court a panel of forty-eight jurors, to try all felons, who may be called on their trial at that session: and therefore it is there usual to try all felons immediately, or soon after their arraignment. But it is not customary, nor agreeable to the general course of proceedings, (unless by consent of parties, or where the defendant is actually in jail), to try persons indicted of smaller misdemeanors at the same court, in which they have pleaded not guilty, or traversed the indictment; they usually give security to the court, to appear at the next assizes or session, and then and there to try the traverse, giving notice to the prosecutor of the time.

When the trial is called on, the jurors are sworn as they appear, to the number of twelve.

Challenges may here be made, either on the part of the king, or of the prisoner; and either to the whole array, or to the separate polls, for the same reasons as in civil causes. Challenges on any of those accounts are stiled challenges for cause, which may be without limit both in criminal and civil trials; but in criminal cases, or, at least, in capital ones, there is is allowed to the prisoner, but not to the crown, an arbitrary and capricious species of challenge to a certain number of jurors, without shewing any cause at all; which is called a *peremptory challenge:* a provision full of that tenderness and humanity to prisoners, for which our English laws are justly famous. The king need not however assign his cause of challenge, till all the panel is gone through, and unless there cannot be a full jury without the persons so challenged; and, in that case, and not sooner, the king's counsel must shew the cause; otherwise the jury must be sworn. The peremptory challenges of the prisoner must, however, have some reasonable boundary; otherwise he might never be tried; and this is settled by the common law to be the number of thirty-five; or one less than three full juries. The peremptory challenge of a greater number was regarded as a proof that the prisoner had no intention to be tried at all; and therefore the law dealt with one, who so challenged and would not retract, as one who stood mute, or refused his trial; by sentencing him to the *peine forte et dure* in felony, and by attainting him in treason. This law still subsists in cases of treason; but by statute 22 Hen. VIII. c. 14. (which with regard to felonies stands unrepealed by 1 & 2 Philip and Mary, c. 10.), no person arraigned for felony can be admitted to make any more than twenty peremptory challenges. If he exceeded, the old opinion was, that judgment of *peine forte et dure* should be given, as where he challenged thirty-six at the common law: but the better opinion seems to be, that such challenge should only be disregarded and overruled.

If, by reason of challenges or the default of the jurors, a sufficient number cannot be had of the original panel, a *tales* may be awarded as in civil causes, till the number of twelve is sworn, "well and truly to try, and true deliverance make, "between our sovereign lord the king, and the prisoner "whom they have in charge; and a true verdict to give, ac- "cording to the evidence."

When the jury is sworn, if it be a cause of importance, the indictment is usually opened, and the evidence marshalled, examined, and inforced by the counsel for the crown or prosecution; but it is a settled rule at common law, that no counsel shall be allowed a prisoner on his trial, upon the general issue, in any capital crime, unless some point of law shall arise proper to be debated. This is apparently a defect in the administration of justice, and the judges themselves are so sensible of it, that they never scruple to allow a prisoner counsel to instruct him what questions to ask, or even to ask questions for him, with respect to matters of fact. And lest this indulgence should

ſhould be intercepted by ſuperior influence, the legiſlature has conferred particular advantages on perſons indicted for ſuch high treaſon as works a corruption of the blood, as will be noticed in an enſuing page.

When the evidence on both ſides is cloſed, and indeed when any evidence has been given, the jury cannot be diſcharged (unleſs in caſes of evident neceſſity) till they have given in their public verdict; they are to conſider of it, and deliver it in, with the ſame forms, as upon civil cauſes. The verdict cannot be privy, but the judges may adjourn, while the jury are withdrawn to confer, and return to receive it in open court. The verdict may be either general, guilty or not guilty; or ſpecial, ſetting forth all the circumſtances of the caſe, and praying the judgment of the court, whether, for inſtance, on the facts ſtated, it be murder, manſlaughter, or no crime at all. This is where they doubt the matter of law, and therefore chuſe to leave it to the determination of the court; though they have an unqueſtionable right of determining upon all the circumſtances, and finding a general verdict, if they think proper; but if their verdict is notoriouſly wrong, they may be puniſhed, and the verdict ſet aſide, by attaint at the ſuit of the king; but not at the ſuit of the priſoner. If the jury find the priſoner not guilty, he is then for ever diſcharged of the accuſation; except he be appealed of felony within the time limited by law; and on ſuch his acquittal, or on diſcharge for want of proſecution, he is immediately ſet at large, without payment of any fee to the jailor. But if the jury find him guilty, he is then ſaid to be convicted of the crime whereof he ſtands indicted. This conviction may accrue two ways; either by his confeſſing the offence and pleading guilty; or by his being found ſo by the verdict of his country.

When the offender is thus convicted, there are two collateral circumſtances that immediately ariſe: 1. On a conviction, (or even upon an acquittal, where there was a reaſonable ground to proſecute, and in fact a *bona fide* proſecution,) for any grand or petit larceny or other felony, the reaſonable expences of proſecution, and alſo, if the proſecutor be poor, a compenſation for his trouble and loſs of time, are by ſtatutes 25 Geo. II. c. 36. and 18 Geo. III. c. 19. to be allowed him out of the county ſtock, if he petitions the judge for that purpoſe: and by ſtatute 27 Geo. II. c. 3. explained by the ſame ſtatute 18 Geo. III. c. 19. all perſons appearing upon recognizance or *ſubpœna*, to give evidence, whether any indictment be preferred or no, and as well without conviction as with it, are entitled to be paid their charges, with a farther allowance (if poor) for their trouble and loſs of time. 2. On a conviction of larceny in particular,

cular, the profecutor obtains reftitution of his goods, by virtue of the ftatute 21 Hen. VIII. c. 11. For by the common law there was no reftitution on an indictment, becaufe it was the fuit of the king only; and therefore the party was obliged to bring an appeal of robbery, in order to recover his goods. But, it being confidered that the party profecuting the offender by indictment, deferves to the full as much encouragement as he who profecutes by appeal, this ftatute was made, which enacts, that if any perfon be convicted of larceny by the evidence of the party robbed, he fhall have full reftitution of his money, goods, and chattels, or the value of them, out of the offender's goods, if he has any, by a writ to be granted by the juftices. And the conftruction of this act having been in a great meafure conformable to the law of appeals, it has therefore in practice fuperfeded the ufe of appeals in larceny. It is now, in fact, ufual for the court, on the conviction of a felon, to order (without any writ) immediate reftitution of fuch goods as are produced, to be made to the feveral profecutors; or elfe, fecondly, without fuch writ of reftitution, the party may peaceably retake his goods, wherever he happens to find them, unlefs a new property in them is fairly acquired; or, laftly, if the felon is convicted and pardoned, or is allowed his clergy, the party robbed may bring his action of trover againft him for his goods; and recover a fatisfaction in damages.

Such action, however, will not lie before profecution; for fo felonies would be made up and healed: and alfo recaption is unlawful, if done with intention to fmother or compound the larceny; it then becoming the heinous offence of theft-bote.

It is not uncommon, however, when a perfon is convicted of a mifdemeanor, which principally and more immediately affects fome individual, as a battery, imprifonment, or the like, for the court to permit the defendant to fpeak with the profecutor, before any judgment is pronounced; and, if the profecutor declares himfelf fatisfied, to inflict a trivial punifhment. This is done to reimburfe the profecutor his expenfes, and make him fome private amends, without the trouble and circuity of a civil action.

CRIMINAL LAW.

Having thus given an outline of the eſtabliſhments for relief of the ſubject in caſes of property, and a general view of the mode of trial by jury, it remains to deſcribe the nature of offences againſt the well-being of ſociety, which are the objects of legal vengeance, with the courts which are formed, and the perſons who are empowered to adminiſter this moſt important office.

CRIMES AND MISDEMEANORS. A crime, or miſdemeanor, is an act committed, or omitted, in violation of a public law, either forbidding or commanding it. This general definition comprehends both crimes and miſdemeanors; which, properly ſpeaking, are ſynonymous terms; though, in common uſage, the word "crimes" is made to denote ſuch offences as are of a deeper and more atrocious dye; while ſmaller faults, and omiſſions of leſs conſequence, are compriſed under the gentler names of "miſdemeanors" only. The diſtinction of public wrongs from private, of crimes and miſdemeanors from civil injuries, it is ſaid, ſeems principally to conſiſt in this, that private wrongs, or civil injuries, are an infringement or privation of the civil rights which belong to individuals, conſidered merely as individuals; public wrongs, or crimes and miſdemeanors, are a breach and violation of the public rights and duties, due to the whole community, conſidered as a community in its ſocial aggregate capacity.

COURTS. Before the various crimes reſtricted by the law of England are deſcribed, it is propoſed to mention the courts which are empowered to take cognizance of them.

PARLIAMENT. The criminal juriſdiction of the high court of parliament has been already treated on at length.

COURT OF THE LORD HIGH STEWARD. The former authority, and decline of the office of lord high ſteward have already been noticed.

Since the office has ceaſed to be permanent, the court is alſo only occaſional, being inſtituted for the trial of peers indicted for treaſon or felony, or for miſpriſion of either. When ſuch an indictment is therefore found by a grand jury of freeholders in the king's bench, or at the aſſizes before the juſtices of oyer and terminer, it is removed, by a writ of *certiorari*, into the court of the lord high ſteward, which only has the power to determine it; a high ſteward is then nominated *pro hac vice* only, and it has always been cuſtomary, and is conſidered neceſſary, that he ſhould be a lord of parliament, as he elſe would

would be incapable of ſitting in judgment on a delinquent peer. The nobleman accuſed may plead a pardon before the court of king's bench, and the judges have power to allow it, in order to prevent the trouble of appointing an high ſteward, merely for the purpoſe of receiving ſuch plea. But he may not plead, in that inferior court, any other plea; as guilty, or not guilty, of the indictment: but only in this court of the high ſteward; becauſe, in conſequence of ſuch plea, it is impoſſible that judgment of death can be awarded againſt him. The king therefore in the commiſſion under the great ſeal, which creates a lord high ſteward, recites the indictment ſo found, and gives his grace power to receive and try it, according to the law and cuſtom of England. Then, when the indictment is regularly removed, by writ of *certiorari*, commanding the inferior court to certify it up to him, the lord high ſteward directs a precept to a ſerjeant at arms, to ſummon the lords to attend and try the indicted peer. This precept was formerly iſſued to ſummon only eighteen or twenty, ſelected from the body of peers: then the number came to be indefinite; and the cuſtom was, for the lord high ſteward to ſummon as many as he thought proper, (but of late years not leſs than twenty-three,) and that thoſe lords only ſhould ſit upon the trial. This ſyſtem threw a great power into the hands of the crown, and this its great officer, of ſelecting only ſuch peers as the then predominant party ſhould moſt approve of; and accordingly when the earl of Clarendon fell into diſgrace with Charles II. a deſign was formed to prorogue the parliament, in order to try him by a ſelect number of peers; it being doubted whether the whole houſe could be induced to comply with the views of the court. But now, by ſtatute 7 W. III. c. 3. upon all trials of peers for treaſon or miſpriſion, all the peers who have a right to ſit and vote in parliament muſt be ſummoned, at leaſt twenty-ſix days before, to appear and vote on the trial; and every lord appearing may vote, firſt taking the oaths of allegiance and ſupremacy, and ſubſcribing the declaration againſt popery. During the ſeſſion of parliament, the trial of an indicted peer is not properly in the court of the lord high ſteward, but before the court of our lord the king in parliament. It is true, a lord high ſteward is always appointed in that caſe to regulate and add weight to the proceedings: but he is rather in the nature of a ſpeaker *pro tempore*, or chairman of the court than the judge of it: for the collective body of the peers are the judges both of law and fact, and the high ſteward has a vote with the reſt, in right of his peerage. But in the court of the lord high steward, which is held in the recess of parliament, he is the sole judge of matters of law, as the lords triors are in matters of fact; and as they may not interfere with him in regulating the proceedings of the court, so he has no right to intermix with them in giving any vote on the trial. Therefore, on the conviction and attainder of a peer for murder in full parliament, it has been holden by the judges, that in case the day appointed in the judgment for execution should lapse before execution done, a new time of execution may be appointed by either the high court of parliament, during its sitting, though no high steward be existing; or, in the recess of parliament, by the king's bench, the record being removed into that court.

Court of King's Bench. This court, as already has been said, is divided into a crown side, and a plea side. On the crown side, or crown office, it takes cognizance of all criminal causes, from high treason down to the most trivial misdemeanor or breach of the peace. Into this court also indictments presented in inferior courts may be removed by writ of *certiorari*, and tried either at bar, or at *nisi prius*, by a jury of the county, out of which the indictment is brought. The judges of this court are the supreme coroners of the kingdom. And the court itself is the principal court of criminal jurisdiction, known to the laws of England. For this reason, the coming of the court of King's-Bench into any county, (as it was removed to Oxford, on account of the sickness in 1665,) at once absorbs and determines all former commissions of oyer and terminer, and general jail delivery.

Court of Chivalry. This was also a criminal court, when held before the lord high constable of England jointly, with the earl marshal, but it is now fallen into disuse.

Court of Admiralty. The high court of admiralty, held before the lord high admiral of England or his deputy, styled the judge of the admiralty, is not only a court of civil, but also of criminal jurisdiction. This court has cognizance of all crimes and offences committed either on the sea, or on the coasts, out of the body, or extent of any English county; and by statute 15 Ric. II. c. 3. of death and mayhem happening in great ships, being and hovering in the main stream below the bridges, which are then a sort of ports or havens; such as are the ports of London and Gloucester, though they lie at a great distance from the sea. But, as this court proceeded without jury, in a method much conformed to the civil law, the exercise of a criminal jurisdiction there was contrary to the genius of the law of England; in so much as

a man

a man might there be deprived of his life, by the opinion of a single judge, without the verdict of his peers. And, besides, as innocent persons might thus fall a sacrifice to the caprice of a single man, so gross offenders might, and did frequently, escape punishment: for the rule of the civil law is that no judgment of death can be given against offenders, without proof by two witnesses, or a confession of the fact by themselves. This was always a great offence to the English nation: and therefore in the eighth year of Henry VI., it was endeavoured to apply a remedy in parliament: which then miscarried for want of the royal assent. However, by the statute 28 Hen. VIII. c. 15. it is enacted, "that all felonies and robberies, &c. upon the sea, or in any haven, river, creek, or place, where the admiral or admirals have, or pretend to have, power, authority or jurisdiction, shall be inquired, tried, heard, determined, and judged, in such shires and places in the realm, as shall be limited by the king's commission to be directed for the same, in like form and condition, as if any such offences had been committed on the land; and such commissions shall be had under the king's great seal, directed to the admiral or admirals, or to his or their lieutenant, deputy or deputies, and to three or four such other substantial persons as shall be named or appointed by the lord chancellor of England, as need shall require, to hear and determine such offences after the common course of the law, used for felonies committed on the land. And such order, process, judgment, and execution shall be used against such persons, as against felons on the land; and such as shall be convicted of any such offence, by verdict, confession, or process, by authority of any such commission, shall suffer such pains of death, losses of lands, goods, and chattels, as if they had been attainted and convicted of such offence on the land; and also, that they shall be excluded from the benefit of the clergy." As this statute did not extend to accessaries, the defect was remedied by some subsequent acts. By 1 Anne, sess. 2. cap. 9. captains and mariners belonging to ships, and destroying the same at sea, are to be tried in such places as shall be limited by the king's commission, and according to 28 Hen. VIII. cap. 15.; and by 4 Geo. I. cap. 11. all persons, who shall commit any offence for which they ought to be adjudged pirates, felons, or robbers, by 11 & 12 Will. III. cap. 5. may be tried and judged for every such offence according to the form of 28 Hen. VIII. cap. 15. and shall be excluded from their clergy. Indictments for these offences are found by a grand jury, and afterwards tried by a petty jury. The judge of the admiralty still presides in this court, as the lord mayor is the prefident of the feffion of oyer and terminer in London.

COURTS OF OYER AND TERMINER AND GENERAL JAIL DELIVERY. Thefe courts are held before the king's commiffioners, among whom are ufually two judges of the courts at Weftminfter, twice in every year, in every county of the kingdom; except the four northern ones, where they are held only once, and London and Middlefex, wherein they are held eight times. It has already been obferved, that at what is ufually called the affizes, the judges fit by virtue of five feveral authorities. By virtue of the commiffion of affize and its attendant jurifdiction of nifi prius, the juftices exercife their power in civil caufes; they have alfo, by virtue of feveral ftatutes, a criminal jurifdiction in certain fpecial cafes. Their commiffion of the peace gives them authority over the juftices of the peace refiding in the county, who are bound by law to attend them, or elfe are liable to a fine; in order to return recognizances, &c. and to affift the judges in fuch matters as lie within their knowledge and jurifdiction, and in which fome of them have probably been concerned, by way of previous examiation. The fourth authority is the commiffion of oyer and terminer, to hear and determine all treafons, felonies, and mifdemeanors. This is directed to the judges and feveral others, or any two of them; but the judges, or ferjeants at law, only are of the quorum, fo that the reft cannot act without the prefence of one of them. The words of the commiffion are, "to inquire, hear, and determine:" fo that, by virtue of it, they can only proceed upon an indictment found at the fame affizes; for they muft firft inquire, by means of the grand jury or inqueft, before they are empowered to hear and determine by the help of the petit jury. Therefore they have befides, fifthly, a commiffion of general jail delivery; which empowers them to try and deliver every prifoner, who fhall be in the jail when they arrive at the circuit town, whenever or before whomfoever indicted, or for whatever crime committed. It was anciently the courfe to iffue fpecial writs of jail delivery for each particular prifoner, which were called the writs *de bono et malo*: but thefe being found inconvenient and oppreffive, a general commiffion for all the prifoners has long been eftablifhed in their ftead. Thus the jails are, in general, cleared, and all offenders tried, punifhed or delivered, twice in every year: a conftitution of fingular ufe and excellence. Sometimes, alfo, upon urgent occafions, the king iffues a fpecial or extraordinary commiffion of oyer and terminer, and jail delivery, confined to thofe offences which ftand in need of immediate inquiry and punifhment: upon which

which the courfe of proceeding is much the fame as on general and ordinary commiffions. Formerly it was held, in purfuance of the ftatutes 8 Ric. II. c. 2. and 33 Hen. VIII. c. 4. that no judge or other lawyer could act in the commiffion of oyer and terminer, or in that of jail delivery, within his own county, where he was born or inhabited; in like manner as they are prohibited from being judges of affize and determining civil caufes. But that local partiality, which the jealoufy of our anceftors was careful to prevent, being judged lefs likely to operate in the trial of crimes and mifdemeanors, than in matters of property and difputes between party and party, it was thought proper, by the ftatute 12 Geo. II. c. 27. to allow any man to be a juftice of oyer and terminer and general jail delivery within any county of England.

COURT OF GENERAL QUARTER SESSIONS OF THE PEACE. This court muft be held in every county once in every quarter of a year; which by a ftatute 2 Hen. V. c. 4. is appointed to be in the firft week after the Epiphany; the firft week after the clofe of Eafter; and in the week after the tranflation of St. Thomas the Martyr, or the feventh of July. It is held before two or more juftices of the peace, one of whom muft be of the quorum. The jurifdiction of this court, by ftatute 34 Edw. III. c. 1. extends to the trying and determining all felonies and trefpaffes whatfoever: though they feldom, if ever, try any greater offence than fmall felonies within the benefit of clergy; their commiffion providing, that, if any cafe of difficulty arifes, they fhall not proceed to judgment, but in the prefence of one of the juftices of the court of king's bench or common pleas, or one of the judges of affize; and therefore murders, and other capital felonies, are ufually remitted for a more folemn trial to the affizes. They cannot alfo try any new created offence, without exprefs power given them by the ftatute which creates it. But there are many offences, and particular matters, which, by particular ftatutes, belong properly to this jurifdiction, and ought to be profecuted in this court: as, the fmaller mifdemeanors, againft the public or common wealth, not amounting to felony; and efpecially offences relating to the game, highways, ale-houfes, baftard children, the fettlement and provifion for the poor, vagrants, fervants wages, apprentices, and popifh recufants. Some of thefe are proceeded upon by indictment; and others in a fummary way by motion and order thereupon; which order may, for the moft part, unlefs guarded againft by particular ftatutes, be removed into the court of king's bench, by writ of *certiorari facias*, and be there either quafhed or confirmed. The records or rolls of the feffions are committed to the custody of a special officer denominated the *custos rotulorum*. In most corporation towns there are quarter-sessions kept before justices of their own, within their respective limits: which have exactly the same authority as the general quarter-sessions of the county, except in a very few instances: one of the most considerable of which is the matter of appeals from orders of removal of the poor, which, though they be from the orders of corporation justices, must be to the sessions of the county, by statute 8 and 9 Will. III. c. 30. In both corporations and counties at large, there is sometimes kept a special or *petty session*, by a few justices, for dispatching smaller business in the neighbourhood between the times of the general sessions; as, for licensing ale-houses, passing the accounts of the parish officers, and the like.

THE SHERIFF'S TOURN. The sheriffs tourn or rotation, is a court of record, held twice every year within a month after Easter and Michaelmas, before the sheriff, in different parts of the county; being indeed only the turn of the sheriffs to keep a court-leet of the county, as the county court is the court baron: for out of this, for the ease of the sheriffs, was taken,

THE COURT-LEET, OR VIEW OF FRANKPLEDGE, which is a court of record, held once in the year, and not oftener, within a particular hundred, lordship, or manor, before the steward of the leet: being the king's court granted by charter to the lords of those hundreds or manors. Its original intent was to view the frank pledges, that is, the freemen within the liberty; who, according to the institution of the great Alfred, were all mutually pledges for the good behaviour of each other. Besides this, the preservation of the peace, and the chastisement of divers minute offences against the public good, are the objects both of the court-leet and the sheriffs tourn. All freeholders within the precinct are obliged to attend them, and all persons commorant therein; which commorancy consists in usually lying there: a regulation, which owes its original to the laws of Canute. But persons under twelve and above sixty years old, peers, clergymen, women, and the king's tenants in ancient demesne, are excused from attendance: all others being bound to appear upon the jury, if required, and make their due presentments. It was also anciently the custom to summon all the king's subjects, as they respectively grew to years of discretion and strength, to come to the court-leet, and there take the oath of allegiance to the king. The other general business of the leet and tourn, was to present by jury all crimes whatsoever that happened within their jurisdiction; and not only to present, but also to punish, all misdemeanors, as all trivial debts were

were recoverable in the court-baron, and county court: juſtice, in theſe minuter matters of both kinds, being brought home to the doors of every man by our ancient conſtitution. Theſe courts have, however, long been in a declining ſtate, their buſineſs having for the moſt part devolved on the ſeſſions.

COURT OF THE CORONERS. The court of the coroners is alſo a court of record, to inquire, when any one dies in priſon, or by a violent or ſudden death, by what manner he came to his end. And this can only be done on view of the body.

COURT OF THE CLERK OF THE MARKET. The court of the clerk of the market is incident to every fair and market in the kingdom, to puniſh miſdemeanors therein, as a court of *pie poudre* is to determine all diſputes relating to private or civil property. The object of this juriſdiction is principally the recognizance of weights and meaſures, to try whether they are according to the true ſtandard, or no; which ſtandard was anciently committed to the cuſtody of the biſhop, who appointed ſome clerk under him to inſpect abuſes, and hence this officer, though now uſually a layman, is called the *clerk* of the market. If they are not according to the ſtandard, then, beſides the puniſhment of the party by fine, the weights and meaſures themſelves ought to be burnt. This is the moſt inferior court of criminal juriſdiction in the kingdom.

COURTS OF THE ROYAL HOUSEHOLD. Theſe are two local courts eſtabliſhed by ſtatute, and although now never heard of, yet not aboliſhed. The firſt is the *court of the lord ſteward, treaſurer, or comptroller of the king's houſehold*, which was inſtituted by ſtatute 3 Hen. VII. c. 14., to inquire of felony by any of the king's ſworn ſervants, in the cheque roll of the houſehold, under the degree of a lord, in confederating, compaſſing, conſpiring, and imagining the death or deſtruction of the king, or any lord or other of his majeſty's privy-council, or the lord ſteward, treaſurer, or comptroller of the king's houſe. The inquiry, and trial thereupon, muſt be by a jury according to the courſe of the common law, conſiſting of twelve ſad men, (that is, ſober and diſcreet perſons) of the king's houſehold. The other is the court of the *lord ſteward* of the king's houſehold, or in his abſence, of the treaſurer, comptroller, and ſteward of the Marſhalſea, which was erected by 33 Hen. VIII. c 12., with a juriſdiction to inquire of, hear, and determine, all treaſons, miſpriſions of treaſon, murders, manſlaughters, bloodſhed, and other malicious ſtrikings, whereby blood is ſhed in, or within the limits, (that is within two hundred feet of the gate) of any of the palaces and houſes of the king, or any other houſe where he abides. The proceedings are alſo by a grand and petit jury, as at common law, taken out of officers and ſworn ſervants of the

the king's houſehold. The form and ſolemnity of the proceſs, particularly with regard to the execution of ſentence by cutting off the hand, which is part of the puniſhment for ſhedding blood in the king's court, are very minutely ſet forth in the ſaid ſtatute 33 Hen. VIII., and the ſeveral offices of the ſervants of the houſehold in and about ſuch execution are deſcribed, from the ſerjeant of the wood-yard, who furniſhes the chopping block, to the ſerjeant farrier, who brings hot irons to ſear the ſtump.

Court of the Universities. The chancellor's court has authority to determine all caſes of property, wherein a privileged perſon is one of the parties, except cauſes of freehold; and alſo all criminal offences or miſdemeanors under the degree of treaſon, felony, or mayhem. The trial of theſe latter offences is by a particular charter committed to the univerſity juriſdiction, the court of the lord high ſteward of the univerſity. If an indictment is found in any of the king's courts againſt a ſcholar or privileged perſon, he is to be tried before the high ſteward of the univerſity, or his deputy, who is to be nominated by the chancellor of the univerſity for the time being. But when his office is called into action, he muſt be approved by the lord high chancellor of England; and a ſpecial commiſſion under the great ſeal is given to him, and others, to try the indictment then depending, according to the law of the land and the privileges of the univerſity; but this can only be done when the cognizance is claimed by the vice-chancellor. If the offence be *inter minora crimina*, or a miſdemeanor only, it is tried in the chancellor's court by the ordinary judge; but if it be for treaſon, felony, or mayhem, it is then, and then only, to be determined before the lord high ſteward, under the king's ſpecial commiſſion. The proceſs of the trial is this: The high ſteward iſſues one precept to the ſheriff of the county, who returns a panel of eighteen freeholders; and another precept to the bedells of the univerſity, who return a panel of eighteen matriculated laymen, "*laicos privilegio univerſitatis gaudentes*:" and by a jury formed *de medietate*, half of freeholders, and half of matriculated perſons, is the indictment to be tried. And if it is neceſſary to award execution in conſequence of finding the party guilty, the ſheriff of the county muſt execute the univerſity proceſs; to which he is annually bound by oath.

Justices of the Peace. In aid of theſe courts ſubordinate magiſtrates are appointed under the name of juſtices of the peace. The common law has ever had a ſpecial care and regard for the conſervation of the peace; for peace is the very end and foundation of civil ſociety. And therefore, before the preſent conſtitution of juſtices was invented, there were peculiar

liar officers appointed by the common law for the maintenance of the public peace. Of thofe fome had, and ftill have, this power annexed to other offices which they hold; others had it merely by itfelf, and were thence named *cuftodes* or *confervatores pacis*. Thofe that were fo by virtue of office ftill continue; but the latter fort are fuperfeded by the modern juftices.

The king is, by his office and dignity royal, the principal confervator of the peace within all his dominions; and may give authority to any other to fee the peace kept, and to punifh fuch as break it; hence it is ufually called the king's peace. The lord chancellor or keeper, the lord treafurer, the lord high fteward of England, the lord marefchal, the lord high conftable of England, (when any fuch officers are in being) and all the juftices of the court of king's bench (by virtue of their offices), and the mafter of the rolls (by prefcription), are generally confervators of the peace throughout the whole kingdom, and may commit all breakers of it, or bind them in recognizances to keep it; the other judges are only fo in their own courts. The coroner is alfo a confervator of the peace within his own county; as is alfo the fheriff; and both of them may take a recognizance or fecurity for the peace. Conftables, tything-men, and the like, are alfo confervators of the peace within their own jurifdictions; and may apprehend all breakers of the peace, and commit them, till they find fureties for keeping it.

Thofe that were, without any office, fimply and merely confervators of the peace, either claimed that power by prefcription, or were bound to exercife it by the tenure of their lands: or, laftly, were chofen by the freeholders in full county court, before the fheriff; the writ for their election directing them to be chofen from among the moft honeft and powerful men in the county, for prefervation of the peace. But when Ifabel, the wife of Edward II., had contrived to depofe her hufband, by a forced refignation of the crown, and had fet up his fon, Edward III. in his place, this, being a thing then without example in England, it was feared would much alarm the people; efpecially as the old king was living, though hurried about from caftle to caftle, till at laft he met with an untimely death. To prevent, therefore, any rifings, or other difturbances of the peace, the new king fent writs to all the fheriffs in England, the form of which is preferved by Thomas Walfingham, giving a plaufible account of the manner of his obtaining the crown; namely, that it was done with the good liking of his father himfelf; commanding each fheriff that the peace be kept throughout his bailiwick, on pain and peril of difinheritance, and lofs of life and limb. In a few weeks after the date of thefe writs, it was ordained in parliament, that, for the better maintaining

maintaining and keeping the peace in every county, good men and lawful, which were no maintainers of evil, or barretors in the county, ſhould be aſſigned to keep the peace; and in this manner, and upon this occaſion, was the election of the conſervators of the peace taken from the people, and given to the king: Still they were only called conſervators, wardens, or keepers of the peace, till the ſtatute of Edward III. c. 1. gave them the power of trying felons; and they then acquired the more honourable appellation of juſtices.

These juſtices are appointed by the king's ſpecial commiſſion under the great ſeal, the form of which was ſettled by all the judges in 1590. It appoints them all jointly and ſeverally, to keep the peace, and any two or more of them to inquire of, and determine, felonies, and other miſdemeanors: in which number ſome particular juſtices, or one of them, are directed to be always included, and no buſineſs to be done without their preſence, the words of the commiſſion running thus, "*quorum* "*aliquem veſtrum*, A. B. C. D. &c., *unum eſſe volumus*;" whence each perſon ſo named is uſually called a juſtice of *quorum*. Formerly it was cuſtomary to appoint only a ſelect number of juſtices, eminent for their ſkill and diſcretion, to be of the quorum; but now the practice is to advance almoſt all to that dignity, naming them all over again in the quorum clauſe, except perhaps ſome one inconſiderable perſon for the ſake of propriety; and no exception is now allowable, for not expreſſing in the forms of warrants, &c. that the juſtices who iſſued them are of the quorum. When any juſtice intends to act under this commiſſion, he ſues out a writ of *dedimus poteſtatem*, from the clerk of the crown in chancery, empowering certain perſons therein named to adminiſter the uſual oaths to him; which, when he has taken, he is at liberty to act.

Touching the number and qualifications of theſe juſtices, it was ordained by ſtatute 18 Edw. III. c. 2., that two, or three, of the beſt reputation in each county, ſhall be aſſigned to be keepers of the peace; but theſe being found too few, it was provided by 34 Edward III. c. 1., that one lord, and three or four of the moſt worthy men, with ſome learned in the law, ſhould be made juſtices in every county. Afterwards the number of juſtices, through the ambition of private perſons, became ſo large, that it was thought neceſſary by ſtatute 12 Ric. II. c. 10., and 14 Ric. II. c. 11. to reſtrain them at firſt to ſix, and afterwards to eight only; but this rule is now diſregarded, and the cauſe ſeems to be, that the growing number of ſtatute laws, committed from time to time to the charge of juſtices of the peace, has occaſioned alſo (and very reaſonably) their increaſe to a larger number. As to their qualifi-

cations,

cations, the ſtatutes laſt cited direct that they ſhall be of the beſt reputation, and moſt worthy men in the county; and the 13 Ric. II. c. 7. orders them to be of the moſt ſufficient knights, eſquires, and gentlemen of the law; alſo by ſtatute 2 Hen. V. ſt. 1. c. 4., and ſt. 2. c. 1., they muſt be reſident in their ſeveral counties. At length, becauſe contrary to theſe ſtatutes, men of ſmall ſubſtance had crept into the commiſſion, whoſe poverty made them both covetous and contemptible, it was enacted by 18 Hen. VI. c. 11. that no juſtice ſhould be put into commiſſion, if he had not lands to the value of 20*l*. per annum; but, the rate of money being greatly altered ſince that time, it is enacted by 5 Geo. II. c. 18., that every juſtice, except as is therein excepted, ſhall have 100*l*. per annum, clear of all deductions; and, if he acts without ſuch qualification, he ſhall forfeit one hundred pounds. This qualification is almoſt equivalent to the 20*l*. per annum required in Henry the Sixth's time; and of this the juſtice muſt now make oath. Alſo it is provided by the act 5 Geo. II. that no practiſing attorney, ſolicitor, or proctor, ſhall be capable of acting as a juſtice of the peace.

As the office of theſe juſtices is conferred by the king, ſo it ſubſiſts only during his pleaſure; and is determinable, 1. By demiſe of the crown, that is, in ſix months after; but if the ſame juſtice is put in commiſſion by the ſucceſſor, he is not obliged to ſue out a new *dedimus*, or ſwear to his qualification afreſh: nor by reaſon of any new commiſſion, to take the oaths more than once in the ſame reign. 2. By expreſs writ under the great ſeal, diſcharging any particular perſon from being any longer a juſtice. 3. By ſuperſeding the commiſſion by writ of *ſuperſedeas*, which ſuſpends the power of all the juſtices, but does not totally deſtroy it, ſince it may be revived by another writ called a *procedendo*. 4. By a new commiſſion, which virtually, though ſilently, diſcharges all the former juſtices not included in it; for two commiſſions cannot ſubſiſt at once. 5. By acceſſion to the office of ſheriff or coroner; that is to ſay, he cannot act as a juſtice of the peace during the year he is ſheriff; but it is not equally clear that the election of a man as coroner diſqualifies him to be a juſtice. Formerly it was thought, that if a man was named in any commiſſion of the peace, and had afterwards a new dignity conferred on him, his office was determined, he no longer anſwering the deſcription of the commiſſion; but now it is provided that, notwithſtanding a new title of dignity, the juſtice on whom it is conferred ſhall ſtill continue a juſtice.

The power, office, and duty of a juſtice of peace depend

on his commiſſion, and on the ſeveral ſtatutes which have created objects of his juriſdiction. His commiſſion, firſt, empowers him ſingly to conſerve the peace, and thereby gives him all the power of the ancient conſervators at the common law, in ſuppreſſing riots and affrays, in taking ſecurities for the peace, and in apprehending and committing felons and other inferior criminals. It alſo empowers any two or more to hear and determine all felonies and other offences, which is the ground of their juriſdiction at ſeſſions, of which mention has been made.

When two or more juſtices are by ſtatute obliged to concur in any act, as the appointment of overſeers, and various others, both juſtices muſt be preſent and do the act together. As the poor laws, the revenue laws, and many other branches of the adminiſtration of juſtice have thrown a vaſt additional power as well as a great accumulation of buſineſs into the hands of theſe magiſtrates, it is uſual to allow an appeal from their ſummary proceeding to the general or quarter ſeſſions, where the caſe can be more ſolemnly argued, and ſometimes to the commiſſioners of the cuſtoms or exciſe. The power of a juſtice of the peace to convict an offender in a ſummary way, without a trial by jury, it is obſerved, is in reſtraint of common law, and in abundance of inſtances a tacit repeal of that famous clauſe in the great charter, that a man ſhall be tried by his equals; which alſo was the common law of the land, long before the great charter, even for time immemorial, beyond the date of hiſtories and records. Therefore generally nothing is preſumed in favour of this branch of the office of a juſtice; but the intendment will be againſt it; for which reaſon, where this ſpecial power is given to a juſtice by act of parliament, it muſt appear that he has ſtrictly purſued it; otherwiſe the common law will break in upon him, and level all his proceedings. So that where a trial by jury is diſpenſed with, yet he muſt proceed according to the courſe of the common law in trials by juries, and conſider himſelf only as conſtituted in the place both of judge and jury. Therefore there muſt be an information or charge againſt a perſon; then he muſt be ſummoned or have notice of ſuch charge, and an opportunity to make his defence; and the evidence againſt him muſt be ſuch as the common law approves of, unleſs the ſtatute ſpecially directs otherwiſe; then, if the perſon is found guilty, there muſt be a conviction, judgment, and execution, all according to the courſe of the common law, directed and influenced by the ſpecial authority given by ſtatute; and in concluſion, there muſt be a record of the whole proceedings, wherein the juſtice muſt ſet forth the particular manner and circumſtances, ſo as if if he ſhall be called to an account for the ſame by a ſuperior court, it may appear he has conformed to the law, and not exceeded the bounds preſcribed to his juriſdiction.

Lord-Lieutenant and Custos Rotulorum. The office of lord lieutenant is purely military, he being the principal perſon empowered to regulate the militia in his county; but to the appointment of lord lieutenant is commonly joined that of *cuſtos rotulorum*, in virtue of which he preſides over all the juſtices of the peace in the county, and new ones are in general put into commiſſion on his recommendation. He is nominated by the king's ſign manual.

Clerk of the Peace. By ſtatute 37 Hen. VIII. c. 1. and 1 Will. c. 21. the *cuſtos rotulorum* ſhall appoint an able and ſufficient perſon reſiding in the county or diviſion, to execute the office of clerk of the peace, by himſelf or his ſufficient deputy, (to be allowed of by the ſaid *cuſtos rotulorum*) and to take and receive the fees, profits, and perquiſites thereof, for ſo long time only as ſuch clerk of the peace ſhall well demean himſelf in his office. But the *cuſtos rotulorum* muſt not ſell the place of clerk of the peace, or directly or indirectly take any reward, or aſſurance of reward, fee, or profit, for ſuch appointment, on pain that the ſeller and buyer ſhall be diſabled to hold their reſpective places, and each forfeit double value of the thing given, to him who ſhall ſue. The clerk of the peace takes an oath that he has not gained his appointment by corruption, and thoſe of allegiance and ſupremacy. He draws ordinary indictments for felony, for which his fee is only two ſhillings, and if defective, he muſt prepare new ones gratis; he makes certain returns of fines, forfeitures, outlawries, convictions, and attaints, to the court of king's bench, and to the ſheriffs; and he delivers into the court of exchequer an account of all eſtreats, which he verifies on oath. He keeps a public office in the county, and his duties are very extenſive in all affairs tranſacted at the ſeſſions. Neither clerk of the peace, nor his deputy can act as ſolicitor, attorney, or agent, or ſue out any proceſs at any general or quarter ſeſſions, where he ſhall execute the office of the clerk of the peace or deputy, on pain of 50*l.* to him who ſhall ſue in twelve months, with treble coſts.

Constables. Conſtables are of two ſorts, high and petty. The former were firſt ordained by the ſtatute of Wincheſter; are appointed at the court-leets of the franchiſe or hundred over which they preſide, or, in default of that, by the juſtices at the quarter ſeſſions; and are removable by the ſame authority that appoints them. The petty conſtables are inferior officers in every town and pariſh, ſubordinate to the high conſta-

 ble

ble of the hundred, first instituted about the reign of Edward III. These petty constables have two offices united in them; the one ancient, the other modern. Their ancient office is that of headborough, tything-man, or borsholder; and these are as ancient as the time of Alfred; their more modern office is that of constable merely; which was appointed so lately as the reign of Edward III., in order to assist the high constable; and in general the ancient headboroughs, tythingmen, and borsholders, were made use of to serve as petty constables; though not so generally, but that in many places they still continue distinct officers. They are all chosen by the jury at the court-leet; or if no court-leet be held, are appointed by two justices of the peace.

Qualifications and Exemptions. No person is qualified to be a constable who is not an inhabitant of the place for which he is to serve; and every inhabitant may not be a fit person to be appointed to this office, for he ought to be of the abler sort of parishioners; and if a very ignorant or poor person is chosen, he may by law be discharged, and an abler appointed in his room. The persons exempt from serving the office of constable are, the president, commons, and fellows of the faculty of physicians and surgeons, in London; apothecaries in London, and within seven miles, being free of the company of apothecaries; and also those in the country who have served seven years apprenticeship; a sworn attorney, or other officer, of the courts at Westminster may have a writ of privilege for his discharge, by reason of his necessary attendance in those courts; and upon the like reasons, it is taken for granted, that practising barristers at law, and the servants of members of parliament, have the same privilege; an alderman of London, for the like reasons, is not compellable to be a constable; but it has been holden, that a captain of the king's guards, being presented to serve as constable, in pursuance of a custom in respect of his lands in a town, cannot claim this privilege, although he is bound by his office to personal attendance on the king; yet such office being of late institution, cannot prevail against an ancient custom. Yet if such an officer as before mentioned, or a gentleman of quality, who has no such office, or a practising physician, were chosen constable of a town which has sufficient persons besides to execute the office, and no special custom concerning it, perhaps he might be relieved by the king's bench; but it seems that even a custom cannot exempt fit persons from serving the office, where there are not others sufficient to execute it. These points seem not to be entirely settled; but no serjeant, corporal, nor private man, serving in the militia, is, during the time, liable to be a constable;

conſtable; every teacher or preacher in holy orders, or pretended holy orders, in a congregation tolerated by law, is, from the time of his ſubſcription and taking the oaths, exempted. As the office of a conſtable is wholly miniſterial, and no way judicial, it ſeems he may appoint a deputy to execute a warrant directed to him, when, by reaſon of ſickneſs, abſence, or for any other cauſe, he cannot do it himſelf; yet it does not ſeem to be ſettled, that a conſtable can make a deputy without ſome ſpecial reaſon; but by 1 Wm. c. 18. and 31 Geo. III. c. 32. perſons diſſenting from the church of England, and having ſcruples in regard of the oaths, or any other matter required to be done in reſpect of ſuch office, and alſo Roman Catholics, may execute it by a ſufficient deputy.

Duty. Every high and petty conſtable is, by the common law, a conſervator of the peace; and therefore if any man makes an affray or aſſault upon another in preſence of the conſtable, or threatens to kill, beats, or hurts another, or is in a fury ready to break the peace; the conſtable may commit him to the ſtocks, or other ſafe cuſtody for the preſent, and may afterward carry him before a juſtice, or to jail, until he find ſurety for the peace, which ſurety the conſtable himſelf may alſo take by obligation, to be ſealed and delivered to the king's uſe; and if the party will not find ſurety, the conſtable may impriſon him until he ſhall do it. But this is only where he perſonally ſees the affray; for he has no authority to bind over any man on the depoſition of another. The conſtable is the proper officer to a juſtice of the peace, and bound to execute his warrants; and therefore it has been reſolved, that where a ſtatute authorizes a juſtice to convict a man of a crime, and levy the penalty by warrant of diſtreſs, without ſaying to whom ſuch warrant ſhall be directed, or by whom it ſhall be executed, the conſtable is the proper officer to ſerve, and indictable for diſobeying. And by ſtatute 33 Geo. II. c. 55. two juſtices in ſpecial or petty ſeſſions may fine a conſtable or pariſh officer neglecting or refuſing to execute any lawful warrant in forty ſhillings, and for want of diſtreſs, commit him to the houſe of correction for ten days. The law protects conſtables in execution of their duty, and all perſons aſſiſting them, againſt malicious proſecutions. If the conſtable is aſſaulted in the execution of his office, he need not go back to the wall, as private perſons ought to do: and if in ſtriving together, he kills the aſſailant, it is no felony; but if the conſtable is killed, it is conſtrued premeditated murder.

Offences against Religion, Morality, and the Church Establishment. The offences included in this deſcription being for the moſt part the ſubjects of eccleſiaſtical animadverſion, have been already noticed, Vol. I. p. 416 et ſeqq. under the reſpective titles of *ſimony; blaſphemy and profaneneſs; apoſtacy; hereſy; impoſtures and pretended propheſies; witchcraft and ſorcery; and ſabbath-breaking*; and afterward in treating of the teſt acts, and the laws relative to diſſenters and papiſts. To what was there ſaid it is not neceſſary here to make any addition.

High Treason. This crime divides itſelf into two general heads; namely of offences immediately againſt the allegiance due to the king; and thoſe relating to the coin and bullion. The firſt of theſe diviſions is firſt to be noticed, and is moſt generally conſidered excluſively in ſpeaking of high treaſon.

In this ſenſe, high treaſon is defined to be a violation of the allegiance which is due from the ſubject to the king, as ſovereign lord and ſupreme magiſtrate of the ſtate. It is the greateſt crime againſt faith, duty, and human ſociety, and brings with it the moſt fatal dangers to the government, peace and happineſs of the nation; and therefore this offence, which includes felony, ſubjects thoſe who are convicted of it, to the greateſt ignominy and puniſhment. It is diſtinguiſhable from ſedition, which is now underſtood in a more general ſenſe, as extending to other offences, not capital, of like tendency, but without any actual deſign againſt the king in contemplation; ſuch as contempts againſt his perſon and government, riotous aſſemblies for political purpoſes and the like. But all ſuch contempts, though not amounting to high treaſon, are highly criminal, and puniſhable with fine, impriſonment, and ſometimes with the pillory. A ſecond offence of this ſort was, by a late temporary act, made puniſhable with tranſportation: but that ſtatute is expired.

Of Allegiance. Allegiance is that obedience and fidelity which every perſon, under the protection of the laws and government, owes, in return for that protection, to the perſon of the king, as ſupreme head of the ſtate, and diſpenſer of thoſe laws and that government. It is the tie which binds every ſubject to be true and faithful to his ſovereign liege lord the king, and truth and faith to bear of life and limb, and earthly honour; and not to know or hear of any ill intended him without defending him therefrom. This duty of allegiance alſo binds all perſons to ſerve the king faithfully and diligently in their ſeveral ſtations; to aſſiſt him with their advice when called upon; and to ſerve him in their perſons, if able, in defence of the realm, againſt rebels and foreign invaders: and they are indictable as for a high miſdemeanor for the wilful neglect or refuſal of any of theſe their bounden duties. The ſame fame duty obliges every fubject beyond fea to return on the king's letters for that purpofe, or to refrain from going abroad, on the king's pleafure fo expreffed, either by the writ of *ne exeat regnum*, or under the great or privy feal or fignet, or by proclamation; for the contempt of which he is indictable at common law, and his lands may be feized till his return. And inafmuch as the duties and obligations of the king towards his fubjects arife from the moment he is invefted with the regal character, and antecedent to his coronation oath, which is only a more folemn recognition of thofe inherent obligations; fo there is an original, implied, and virtual allegiance which the fubject owes to the fovereign, antecedent to any exprefs oath or engagement to that effect; for the breach of which, at an age of difcretion, he is amenable to juftice.

Allegiance is diftinguifhed into natural and local.

Natural Allegiance is that which is due from every man who is born a member of fociety. His birth in the ftate intitles him to peculiar privileges, which are, with great propriety, called his birth-right; and this being indefeafible, the allegiance arifing out of it is equally unalienable: it is due from him at all times and in all places; and hence the maxim, that no man can renounce his country. It is not in the power of any fubject to fhake off his allegiance, or transfer it to any foreign prince: nor can any foreign prince, by employing a Britifh fubject, diffolve the bond of allegiance between him and the crown. Allegiance is due as well from the hufband of a queen regnant to her, as from a queen confort to the king; and it is a high contempt at common law, to refufe the oath of allegiance, which all laymen above the age of twelve years are bound to take at the tourn or court-leet, and which has already been mentioned as an indifpenfable qualification for many fituations, ecclefiaftical, civil, and military.

Local Allegiance is that which is due from a foreigner during his refidence here; and is founded in the protection he enjoys for his own perfon, his family, and effects, during the time of that refidence. This allegiance ceafes whenever he withdraws with his family and effects; for his temporary protection being then at an end, the duty arifing from it alfo determines; but if he only go abroad himfelf, leaving his family and effects here, under the fame protection, the duty ftill continues, and if he commit treafon, he may be punifhed as a traitor: and this whether his own fovereign is at enmity, or at peace with ours; and if he aid even his own countrymen, in acts or purpofes of hoftility, while he is refident here, he may be dealt with in the fame manner. The cafe of an embaffador is not meant to be included in the foregoing obfervations: the exception,

 if

if any, is grounded on principles of policy, and not of justice; but an alien enemy not domiciled here, taken in avowed hostilities against the king or his government, is no traitor, though leagued with rebels; for he violates no trust or allegiance.

A prince or princess succeeding to the crown by descent, or by the previous designation of parliament, is, from the moment the title accrues, a king to all intents and purposes antecedent to the coronation, which does not confer but presupposes a right. But a titular king, as the husband of a queen regnant, is not within the law, but himself owes allegiance to the queen. It is also agreed that a king *de facto*, in the full and sole possession of the crown, is a king within the same statute of Edward III.; and that any other person out of possession is no such king, be his pretensions what they may.

WHAT ACTS AMOUNT TO HIGH TREASON, AND WHAT TO A LESS OFFENCE. The acts which amount to high treason are specified in several declaratory and enacting statutes. The first and principal of these is the 25 Edw. III. st. 5. c. 2. emphatically called the statute of treasons, because it reduced and settled all treasons, which were before very indefinite and often stretched by arbitrary constructions, to certain specific heads. It is thereby declared to be high treason, "when a man "does compass or imagine the death of the king, or of his "queen, or of their eldest son and heir; or if a man do violate "the king's companion, or the king's eldest daughter unmarried; or the wife of the king's eldest son and heir; or if a "man do levy war against the king in his realm, or be adherent "to his enemies in his realm, giving to them aid and comfort "in the realm or elsewhere; and thereof be proveably (*i. e.* upon "sufficient proof) attainted of open deed by the people of their "condition; and if a man counterfeit the king's great or privy "seal or his money; and if a man bring false money into this "realm, counterfeit to the money of England, as the money called Lushburgh, or other like to the said money of England, "knowing the money to be false, to merchandize or make payment, in deceit of the king and his people; and if a man "slay the chancellor, treasurer, or the king's justices of the "one bench or the other, justices in eyre, or justices of assize, "and all other justices assigned to hear and determine, being in "their places doing their offices." The statute afterwards proceeds to give this salutary caution, "that because many "other like cases of treason may happen in time to come, "which a man cannot think nor declare at this present time, it "is accorded, that if any other case supposed treason, which is "not above specified, does happen before any justices, the

"justices

" justices shall tarry, without any going to judgment of the " treason, till the cause be shewed and declared, before the " king and his parliament, whether it ought to be judged trea- " son or other felony."

This statute was reinforced and again made the only standard of treason by the 1 Mar. st. 1. c. 1., which abrogated all intermediate acts creating new treasons, or misprisions of treasons: but since that time, other treasons have been added by various statutes; of these it is only necessary to set forth the last in this place, reserving the rest for incidental mention. By statute 36 Geo. III. c. 7. " if any person, during the natural life of the " king, and until the end of the next session of parliament after " a demise of the crown, shall, within the realm or without, " compass, imagine, invent, devise, or intend death or destruc- " tion, or any bodily harm tending to death or destruction, " maim, or wounding, imprisonment or restraint, of the person " of the king, his heirs or successors, or to deprive or depose " him or them from the style, honour, or kingly name of the " imperial crown of this realm, or of any other of his majesty's " dominions or countries; or to levy war against his majesty, " his heirs or successors, within this realm, in order by force or " constraint to compel him or them to change his or their " measures or counsels, or in order to put any force or con- " straint upon, or to intimidate or overawe, both or either " houses of parliament; or to move or stir any foreigner or " stranger with force to invade this realm, or any other his " majesty's dominions or countries, under the obeisance of his " majesty, his heirs and successors; and such compassings, " imaginations, inventions, devices, or intentions, or any of " them, shall express, utter, or declare, by publishing any " printing or writing, or by any overt act or deed; being le- " gally convicted thereof, upon oaths of two lawful and credible " witnesses, upon trial; or otherwise convicted, or attainted by " due course of law, then every such offender shall be deemed, " declared, and adjudged to be a traitor." By s. 5. the benefit of the acts of the 7 W. III. c. 3. and 7 Anne, c. 11. as to the trial, is reserved.

By the act of union with Scotland, high treason, or misprision of treason in England, and none else, shall be high treason in Scotland. Such a provision was not necessary in the case of Ireland, which had the same general laws as Great Britain before its union with it; and therefore the eighth article of the union with Ireland only provides that all the laws in force, at the time of the union, in either country respectively, shall remain, unless afterwards altered.

On each of the heads of treason some few observations will be be made, but the whole fyftem of law is too large to be even abridged in this work.

Compaffing or Imagining the Death of the King. In this fpecies of treafon the old rule, which prevailed in all cafes of homicide, *quod voluntas reputabitur pro facto*, applies in its full extent. A mere imagination of the heart, if any open or overt act be done towards effectuating the defign, is deemed the fame degree of guilt as if carried into actual execution.

The firft fet of overt acts by which this degree of the crime is proved, is where the life of the fovereign is immediately and intentionally aimed at; the providing weapons, ammunition, or any other means of accomplifhing or procuring his death, in order to effectuate that intent, or the fending letters, or affembling for that purpofe, is evidence of high treafon under this branch of the ftatute. A bare confulting with others how to kill the king, though nothing elfe be done, and though the confpirators do not then determine upon any fcheme for that purpofe, or do not agree in their refolution, is an overt act of the fame treafon. If a perfon be prefent at only one fuch confultation, and conceal it, having had a previous knowledge of the defign of the meeting, it is evidence to be left to a jury of his affent to the defign, though he neither did nor faid any thing at fuch confultation; but if he had no fuch previous knowledge, as if he fell into the company by accident or upon fome indifferent occafion, a bare concealment without an exprefs affent is only mifprifion of treafon. If he be prefent at more than one fuch confultation, and do not diffent or make a difcovery, it is ftrong evidence of affent; and an affent to any overtures for that purpofe is a plain overt act of compaffing the king's death, in like manner as any advice, perfuafion, or command, to incite, encourage, or procure others to make an attempt againft his perfon.

The next head of overt acts of the fame fpecies of treafon relates to depofing or taking poffeffion of the king's perfon, which the common experience of all times and nations has fhewn to be the moft probable prelude to his death. And herefore it is held that the conftruction of this fpecies of treafon extends to every wilful and deliberate act or attempt whereby the king's perfon may probably be endangered, or fuch as cannot be executed without the apparent peril to him. Accordingly, entering into meafures for depofing or imprifoning him, or for forcibly taking his perfon into the power of the confpirators, or to compel him by force to yield to certain demands, or to remove evil counfellors, and all fuch other notorious acts, done or confpired to be done againft his perfon ſon or regal government, may be alleged as overt acts of compaſſing his death: they have a manifeſt tendency to that fatal iſſue.

Compaſſing the Death of the Queen or their eldeſt Son and Heir. The queen means the queen conſort or wife of the king, and extends to a wife *de facto* during the coverture, but after a divorce, though it be only *a menſâ et thoro*, ſhe is not within the ſtatute; nor is a queen dowager. Their eldeſt ſon and heir extends to a ſecond-born ſon, after the death of the elder, and the like of the reſt; and notwithſtanding the king ſhould have married a ſecond wife, and ſo the ſon ſhould not be *their* eldeſt ſon, but only the king's ſon. In like manner the eldeſt ſon of a queen regnant is within the act.

Violating the King's Companion, his eldeſt Daughter unmarried, or the Wife of his eldeſt Son and Heir. By the king's companion is meant his wife, that is, the queen conſort, during the marriage; but as the reaſon of the law was to guard the ſucceſſion of the crown from any ſuſpicion of baſtardy, to violate a queen dowager, or princeſs dowager, is no treaſon. On the ſame principle, the law extends to a ſecond daughter, the eldeſt being dead during the father's life; and this, whether there be any ſons or not; but the words of the ſtatute are not applicable to the eldeſt daughter, if a widow. In either caſe mentioned in the ſtatute, by "violation" is intended carnal knowledge, as well without force as with it; and this is high treaſon in both parties, if both conſent.

Levying War againſt the King in his Realm. Under this branch there muſt be an actual levying of war, and not barely a conſultation ſo to do; but the latter is made a diſtinct treaſon by the ſtat. 36 Geo. III. c. 7. during the king's life. Such war muſt alſo be levied againſt the king, and it muſt be in his realm. The levying war is either *expreſs* and *direct*, or *conſtructive*. Of the firſt ſort are all inſurrections againſt the perſon of the king, whether intended to dethrone, impriſon, or force him to alter his meaſures of government, or to remove evil counſellors from about him; but if, upon a ſudden quarrel, from ſome affront given or taken, and not as a cover for any traitorous deſign, a number of men ſhould riſe and drive the king's forces out of their quarters; though it would be a great miſdemeanor, and if death enſued, might be felony in the aſſailants; yet it would not be a treaſon; there being no intention againſt the king's perſon or government. It muſt in general be difficult in the beginning of inteſtine troubles to fix the period when oppoſition to the eſtabliſhed government ſhall be ſaid to wear the formidable appearance of inſurrection, and to conſtitute what, in the terms of the act, is called levying of war against the king. It is strictly, therefore, a question of fact to be tried by the jury under all the circumstances. Any assembly of persons, met for a treasonable purpose, armed and arrayed in a warlike manner, is *bellum levatum,* though not *percussum.* Inlisting and marching are sufficient overt acts, without coming to an actual engagement; in the same manner as cruising under an enemy's commission, though no act of express hostility be proved, is an adherence to the king's enemies. The military manner in which insurgents are assembled is not, however, so much the object of consideration, as their intent in assembling.

Holding a castle or fort against the king or his troops, if actual force is used to keep possession, is levying war; but a bare detainer, as by shutting the gates against the king or his troops, without any force from within, lord Hale conceives, will not amount to treason; but it may be fairly questioned, whether there are not many instances of constructive levying of war far short of the real guilt and consequences of such an act, and much less within the true meaning of the statute 25 Edw. III.

Joining with rebels, freely and voluntarily, in any act of rebellion, is levying war against the king; and this too, though the party was not privy to their intent; but it seems necessary in this case, either that the party joining with rebels, and ignorant of their intent at the time, should do some deliberate act toward the execution of their design, or else should be found to have aided and assisted those who did. If the joining with rebels is from fear of present death, and while the party is under actual force, such fear and compulsion will excuse him; but it is incumbent on the party setting up this defence to give satisfactory proof that the compulsion continued during all the time he staid with the rebels. It may perhaps be impossible to account for every day, week, or month; and therefore it may be sufficient to excuse him if he can prove an original force upon him, that he in earnest attempted to escape and was prevented, or that he was so narrowly watched, or the passes so guarded, that an attempt to escape or to refuse his assistance would have been attended with great difficulty and danger; and, if the circumstance will admit of it, that he quitted the service as soon as he could: so that, upon the whole, he may fairly be presumed to have continued amongst them against his will, though not constantly under an actual force or fear of immediate death. Such compulsion or fear, however, is no excuse for any other sort of treason than that of joining with rebels or enemies. So, sending money,

arms,

arms, ammunition, or other neceſſaries to rebels, will *primâ facie* make a man a traitor, though they ſhould be intercepted.

Conſtructive levying of war is in truth more directed againſt the government than the perſon of the king; though in legal conſtruction it is levying of war againſt the king himſelf. This is when an inſurrection is raiſed to reform ſome national grievance, to alter the eſtabliſhed law or religion, to puniſh magiſtrates, to effect innovation in a public concern, to obſtruct the execution of ſome general law by armed force, or for any other purpoſe which uſurps the government in matters of a public and general nature. Inſurrections of this nature, though not levelled directly againſt the perſon of the king, are yet an attack upon his regal office, and tend to diſſolve all government, ſociety, and order. The king is bound in duty to inforce the acts of the legiſlature and uphold their authority: any reſiſtance, therefore, to theſe muſt, in its conſequences, extend to the endangering of his perſon and government, by involving the ſtate in a general diſtraction; on which account this ſpecies of treaſon falls properly within the clauſe of levying war againſt the king. Of the ſame nature is an aſſembling together for the purpoſe of deſtroying all meeting-houſes or bawdy-houſes, under colour of reforming a public grievance; or an inſurrection to reduce by force the general price of victuals, to inhance the common rate of wages, to level all incloſures, to expel all foreigners, to releaſe all priſoners, or to reform by numbers or an armed force any real or imaginary grievance of a public and general nature, in which the inſurgents have no peculiar intereſt. Againſt ſuch inſurrections, magiſtrates, ſheriffs, and indeed all private perſons, may uſe force to ſuppreſs them without any ſpecial commiſſion, in the ſame manner as they may oppoſe foreign enemies coming hoſtilely into the kingdom. But where the object of the inſurrection is a matter of a private or local nature, affecting, or ſuppoſed to affect, only the parties aſſembled, or confined to particular perſons or diſtricts, it will not amount to high treaſon, although attended with the circumſtances of military parade uſually alleged in indictments on that head. As, if the riſing is only againſt a particular market, or to deſtroy particular incloſures, to remove a local nuiſance, to releaſe a particular priſoner, unleſs impriſoned for high treaſon, or even to oppoſe the execution of an act of parliament, if it only affects the diſtrict of the inſurgents; as in the caſe of a turnpike-act.

Adhering to the King's Enemies in his Realm, giving to them Aid and Comfort in the Realm or elſewhere. Beſide the ſtatute

tute 25 Edw. III. declaring these acts to be high treason, the 2 & 3 Ann. c. 20. provides, that if any officer or soldier shall, out of England or upon the sea, correspond with any rebel or enemy, or give them advice or intelligence, by letters, messages, signs, tokens, or otherwise, or shall treat or enter into any condition with them, without authority so to do, he shall be guilty of high treason. And, by the general mutiny acts for these and other like offences, the offender shall suffer death, or such other punishment as a court martial shall award.

By the term enemy, is always to be understood a foreign power owing no allegiance to the crown, and in a state of open hostility with us; though perhaps war may not have been regularly declared between the respective countries. Every species of aid or comfort, which, when given to a rebel within the realm, would make the subject guilty of levying war; if given to an enemy, whether within or without the realm, will make the party guilty of adhering to the king's enemies; though, in the case of giving aid to enemies within the realm, a subject might in some instances be brought within both branches of the act. It is also an adherence to the king's enemies if a subject makes war on the king's allies, engaged with him against the common enemy, though no act of hostility be committed against the king or his forces; for by this the enemy is strengthened and the king weakened. The same excuses of compulsion and necessity, which may be made for one who has joined or given aid to rebels or enemies within the realm, will also apply in the cases above alluded to; but the mere act of refusing personal assistance to the king, either against rebels or an invading enemy, amounts not to an adherence within the statute, though undoubtedly it is a high misdemeanor, and punishable by fine and imprisonment.

Entering into the service of any foreign state without the consent of the king, or contracting with it any other engagement which subjects the party to an influence or controul inconsistent with the allegiance due to our own sovereign, such as receiving a pension from a foreign prince without the leave of the king, is not high treason, but at common law a high misdemeanor, and punishable accordingly. Such also is the disobeying of the king's command to a subject abroad to return home; or his writ of *ne exeat regno* to a subject at home commanding his stay. This principle of the common law is inforced by several statutes, which, both by general and special prohibition, restrain the subjects of the British crown from entering into the service of foreign states.

Coun-

Counterfeiting the Seals. This crime includes the great and privy ſeals, and privy ſignet, and is, by ſtatute 7 Ann. c. 21. extended to the ſeals uſed in Scotland. On the demiſe of the king, though the office of the great ſeal expires, yet the ſame great ſeal continues to be the great ſeal of England, till another is made and delivered. Formerly public proclamation was made in caſe of a change of the ſeal, though now a memorandum only is entered on the cloſe rolls. But even after the making and delivery of a new ſeal, and the breaking of the old one, the counterfeiting of the latter, and applying it to an inſtrument of the date wherein it was in uſe, or to an inſtrument without date, is high treaſon. Although this is evidently a ſpecies of the *crimen falſi*, or forgery, and might naturally have been ſuppoſed to be governed by the ſame rules, yet the difference is conſiderable; for though the ſculpture of the inſtrument, which is in truth the great ſeal, be exactly counterfeited, yet if it be not uſed or applied to ſeal any thing, though intended for that purpoſe, the offence is not complete: but it ſeems there muſt be an impreſſion made in wax, in teſtimony of ſome writing; othewiſe it is no more than a mere intent or compaſſing to counterfeit the ſeal, and is only puniſhable as a high miſdemeanor. Again, it is ſaid that the affixing of the true great ſeal by the chancellor, or any caſual poſſeſſor of it, without warrant, or the affixing it to a wrong inſtrument knowingly, though a great miſpriſion, is no treaſon within the act of Edward III. (nor, by conſequence, within that of Mary); becauſe this is not a counterfeiting of the ſeal. For the ſame reaſon, the raſing of one manor out of a patent and inſerting another, or any artificial removing of the true writing and adding new matter; or even, it is ſaid, the taking off the wax impreſſed with the great ſeal from the true patent, and affixing it to a writing importing to be grant from the king, are none of them high treaſon, but only great miſpriſions. Splitting the ſeal and cloſing it again to a falſe patent is a counterfeiting, becauſe this is an alteration of the ſeal itſelf. And where the ſeal is ſubſtantially counterfeited, the adding or omitting of a crown, the leaving out words in the ſtyle, or adding others, or making any other minute variation in the counterfeit, which is often done purpoſely, and by way of eluding the law, will not alter the caſe. The diſparity, however, may be ſo great between the true and falſe ſeal, that it would not amount to a counterfeiting within the ſtatute, as, if it be evident to the view of every man's eye. Neither would it, if a man were to counterfeit the ſeal of one prince to a patent ſuppoſed to be granted in the time of another; or to the ſuppoſed patent of the ſame prince, after a new ſeal had been made

made and delivered; if the difference appear very legible and conspicuous; for at the time whereunto it relates there was no such great seal in being.

All aiders and consenters to the counterfeiting of the great or privy seal are within the act of Edward III.; and that of Mary extends to such in terms; but receivers or aiders after the fact are not within the words of either.

HIGH TREASON AGAINST THE KING'S OFFICERS. By the 25 Edw. III. "If a man slay the chancellor, treasurer, or the "king's justices of one bench or the other, justices in eyre, or "justices of assize, and all other justices assigned to hear and de-"termine, being in their places, doing their offices," it is declared high treason. By the 7 Ann. c. 21., to slay any of the lords of sessions, or justiciary of Scotland, in the exercise of their office, is high treason. The protection of the act is only during the times that these persons are in the actual execution of their respective offices; that is, sitting judicially in their places in the king's courts, where they usually, or by adjournment, sit in the administration of justice; for there they represent the king's person. Lord Hale extends it to the lord chancellor's house, when the seal is open there, and to the hearing of causes in his chamber, where, he says, use has sufficiently obtained to give it the style of *fesant son office*. The statute of Edward III. is also confined to the case of killing such officers, and extends not to a wounding or attempt to kill, unless death afterwards ensue from it. Yet the mere striking or assaulting them in the execution of their office is a great misprision, for which, in some cases of aggravation, the offender may lose his hand; but if many conspire to kill any such officer, and one actually accomplishes it, it seems treason in all.

HIGH TREASON IN RESPECT OF COIN. This subject is fully treated on in this volume, page 182.

There are other offences against allegiance, of which some do and some do not amount to high treason, and of the greater part of which sufficient mention has already been made. These are included in the obsolete regulations *with respect to papists, high treason, and other offences against the protestant succession*, many statutes relating to which have expired in consequence of the extinction of the pretender's family.

Seducing, or attempting to seduce, others from their Allegiance and Obedience to the Crown. In all cases falling within the legal notion of compassing the king's death, any attempt of this sort, though no act be done in consequence, will amount to high treason, and come within the statute 25 Ed. III.; but there are some other statutes relative to this matter, well worthy of particular notice.

notice. By the 23 Eliz. c. 1. "If any one ſhall have, or pre-
"tend to have, power, or ſhall by any means put in practice to
"abſolve, perſuade, or withdraw a ſubject from his natural
"obedience to the crown, or to withdraw him, *for that intent*,
"from the religion eſtabliſhed by the queen's authority within
"her dominions, to the Romiſh religion, or to move him to
"promiſe any obedience to any pretended authority of the ſee
"of Rome, or of any other prince, ſtate, or potentate, to be
"had or uſed within the queen's dominions, or ſhall do any
"overt act to that intent or purpoſe; or, if any perſon ſhall
"by any means be willingly abſolved or withdrawn as afore-
"ſaid, every ſuch perſon, his procurers, and counſellors, being
"lawfully convicted, ſhall ſuffer and forfeit as in caſes of high
"treaſon." It ſeems the bare pretending to ſuch a power, without any further endeavour to perſuade perſons from their allegiance, or the bare endeavour ſo to perſuade, without pretending to ſuch power, is within the act. By ſ. 3. of the ſame act, aiding or maintaining of ſuch offenders, knowing the ſame, or concealing any ſuch offence for twenty days after knowledge thereof, without diſcloſing the ſame to ſome juſtice of peace or other high officer, is made miſpriſion of treaſon. In later times, the ſame ſpecies of offence has taken another, and not a leſs perilous ſhape; and it has been found neceſſary to paſs an act for the better prevention and puniſhment of attempts to ſeduce individuals in the army and navy from their duty and allegiance; for which purpoſe the ſtat. 37 Geo. III. c. 70. has enacted, "That any perſon who ſhall maliciouſly and adviſedly
"endeavour to ſeduce any perſon ſerving in the king's forces,
"by ſea or land, from his duty and allegiance to his majeſty,
"or to incite or ſtir up any ſuch perſon to commit any act of
"mutiny, or to make or endeavour to make any mutinous
"aſſembly, or to commit any traitorous or mutinous practice
"whatſoever, ſhall, on conviction of ſuch offence, be ad-
"judged guilty of felony without benefit of clergy." And, by ſ. 2., any ſuch offence, whether committed in England, or on the high ſeas, may be tried before any court of oyer and terminer, or gaol delivery, for any county in England, as if the offence had been therein committed. Provided that no perſon tried and acquitted, or convicted under this act, ſhall be liable to be tried again for the ſame offence or fact, as high treaſon or miſpriſion of treaſon; nor ſhall this act prevent the trial of any perſon, as for high treaſon or miſpriſion of treaſon, who has not been tried for the ſame fact under this act.

Deſertion from the King's Forces. This offence, whether by land or ſea, in England or abroad, is by ſeveral ancient ſtatutes made felony without benefit of clergy. And the offence is made

made triable by the justices of every shire. These statutes are also levelled against some other inferior military offences, which are punishable as misdemeanors; but they are altogether fallen into disuse, as well on account of the manner of retaining soldiers therein referred to being no longer adopted, as because, since the annual acts for punishing mutiny and desertion, a more compendious and convenient system of military coercion has obtained. By the statute 1 Geo. c. 47. If any person (other than enlisted soldiers, who are already punishable by law for such offence) shall, in Great Britain, Ireland, Guernsey, or Jersey, persuade or procure any soldier to desert, he shall forfeit 40*l*. to be recovered by any informer; and if he has not property to that amount, or, from the heinous circumstances of the crime it shall be thought proper, the court before whom he is convicted shall imprison him not exceeding six months, and also adjudge him to stand in the pillory for one hour in some market town next adjoining to the place where the offence was committed. The prosecution must be commenced within six months after the offence.

Of Accomplices. It is generally said, that in high treason, whether at common law or by statute, there are no accessaries, but all are principals; that whatever will make a man accessary before or after in felony will make him a principal in treason, and that nothing less will. This is generally true, both with respect to new as well as old treasons, if taken with respect to the offence itself, or the offender after conviction; but there are certain exceptions and discriminations too minute to be introduced into this work. As it happens more frequently in trials for this than for any other offence, that acts of some of the conspirators, in the absence of the others, are given in evidence against them, it may be proper to notice one general rule on this point. When the connexion between the parties is once established, of which the court must in the first instance judge, then whatever is done in pursuance of that conspiracy by one of the conspirators, though unknown perhaps to the rest at the time, is to be considered as the act of all.

Trial. By the statute 1 & 2 Ph. & Mary, c. 10. "all trials "for any treason shall be had and used only according to the "due order and course of the common laws of the realm." This offence is triable therefore, like all others, in the county where it is committed, that is, where the overt acts charged in the indictment were done; but it is enough if one overt act be proved in that county. Treasons committed on the high seas are triable before the admiral, by commission under the great seal, by virtue of the 28 Hen. VIII. c. 15. which in this respect stands unrepealed by the 1 Mary, stat. 1. c. 1.

As to other treasons committed out of the realm, the statute 35 Hen. VIII. c. 2. enacts that they shall be inquired of, heard and determined before the king's bench, by jurors of the same shire where the court shall sit, or else before such commissioners and in such shire as shall be assigned by the king's commission, in like manner and form as if such treasons had been committed within the shire where they are inquired of. But the privilege of peerage is saved. A like provision is made with respect to Scotchmen, who, by the stat. 7 Ann. c. 21. are triable before commissioners in any shire, stewartry, or county of Great Britain, as shall be assigned by the crown for all treasons and misprisions of treasons committed out of the realm of Great Britain. One species of treason, namely, that of committing hostilities at sea, under colour of a foreign commission, or any other species of adherence to the king's enemies there, may be indicted and tried as piracy by virtue of the statutes 28 Hen. VIII. c. 15. 11 and 12 Will. c. 7. and 18 Geo. II. c. 30. There are instances in the books of trials in England for high treason committed by Irishmen in Ireland before the union; one of them is the case of an Irish peer, who objected without avail to the defect of trial by his peers. This has not passed without question: but, since the legislative incorporation of the two countries, these cases cannot be brought into precedent again.

By the statute 7 W. c. 3. "all and every person and persons "indicted for high treason, whereby any corruption of blood "may be made to them or their heirs, or for misprisions of such "treasons, shall be admitted to make their full defence by counsel; and the court before whom they are tried, or some judge "thereof, is required, immediately on his or their request, to "assign them such and so many counsel (not exceeding two) as "they may desire: to whom such counsel shall have free access "at all seasonable hours." And by 20 Geo. II. this privilege is extended to impeachments for treason, corrupting the blood, which had before been excepted generally from the benefit of the act of William. Each prisoner is entitled, under the statute of William, to have two counsel assigned him, though indicted jointly with others. The same act of William requires that the person or persons so indicted, "shall have a true copy of "the whole indictment (but not the names of the witnesses) "five days at least before trial, to advise with counsel thereupon, to plead and make their defence, his or their attorney "or agent requiring the same, and paying the officer his "reasonable fees for writing it, not exceeding five shillings for the copy of every such indictment. And every such "person shall have a copy of the panel of the jurors who are to "try him, duly returned by the sheriff, and delivered to him two

"days

" days at least before he shall be tried ;" but alteration has been made in some of these respects by the 7 Ann. c. 21. which enacts, that after the decease of the pretender, " when any " person is indicted for high treason, or misprision of treason, " a list of the witnesses who shall be produced on the trial for " proving the indictment, and of the jury, mentioning their " names, professions, and places of abode, shall be also given " at the same time that the copy of the indictment is delivered, " and that copies of all indictments for the offences aforesaid, " with such lists, shall be delivered to the party indicted *ten* " days before the trial, and in the presence of two or more " credible witnesses."

The operation of these acts, it is to be observed, is confined to such persons only as stand indicted for treasons, or misprisions, which work corruption of blood ; therefore the cases of petty treason, of treasons created by acts saving the corruption of blood, and of the treasons expressly excluded by the 13th section of the act, of counterfeiting the king's coin, the great seal, privy seal, sign manual, and privy signet, all stand upon the same foot as they did before the making of this act. The operation of the statute of William has been still further confirmed by a late act, which took its rise from the attempt of a wretched maniac of the name of Hadfield to assassinate his majesty, by firing a pistol at him in the theatre at Drury-lane. The reason of the statute, which is shortly hinted at in the preamble, is obvious : it was thought incongruous that greater privileges and indulgence should be allowed to a prisoner upon his trial, under a charge for assassinating or attempting the life of his sovereign, than if he had made the same attempt upon the life of any of his majesty's subjects. Upon this occasion the prisoner had the benefit of the statute of king William, and soon afterward, the legislature passed the stat. 40 Geo. III. c. 93. which enacts that in all cases of high treason, in compassing or imagining the death of the king, and of misprision of such treason, where the overt act or acts alleged in the indictment shall be the assassination or killing of the king, or any direct attempt against his life, or any direct attempt against his person, whereby his life may be endangered, or his person may suffer bodily harm, the person or persons charged with such offence shall and may be indicted, arraigned, tried and attainted in the same manner, and according to the same course and order of trial, in every respect, and upon the like evidence, as if such person or persons stood charged with murder : and none of the provisions contained in the acts of the 7 W. III. and 7 Ann. touching trials in cases of treason and misprision of treason, shall extend to any indictment for high treason or misprision, where the overt

 act

act or acts alleged, are such as aforesaid: but upon conviction, judgment is to be given, and execution done, as in other cases of high treason.

Evidence. The written evidence which may affect a prisoner indicted for treason is the subject of much learned discussion and many distinctions; but it is an essential requisite on the trial of this offence, that the treason charged in the indictment should be proved by two witnesses. It is, however, fully established that one witness to one overt act, and another to another of the same species of treason, are two sufficient witnesses within the statute of Edward. From that time the rule has prevailed. The statute 7 W. III. does not require that each overt act shall be proved by two witnesses, but only that the treason shall be so proved; and, by the express direction of that statute, either two witnesses to the same overt act, or one witness to one and another witness to another overt act of the same treason, that is of the same species of treason, are sufficient. But, if several overt acts are proved by different witnesses singly, they must relate to the same kind of treason, otherwise it is insufficient by the express provision of the statute 7 W. c. 3. which in this respect is only declaratory of what was the known rule of law before. And although the treason itself must be proved by two witnesses in the manner above specified; yet a collateral fact, not tending to the proof of the overt acts, may be proved by one witness only.

Judgment. The judgment in high treason for a man, in all cases except counterfeiting the coin, is to be drawn upon a hurdle to the place of execution, there to be hanged by the neck; to be cut down while he is alive, and his entrails to be taken out and burnt before his face; and his head to be cut off, and body quartered: and the head and quarters to be at the king's disposal. For women the judgment was always the same in high or petty treason, namely to be drawn to the place of execution, and there burnt alive: that is now altered to being drawn and hanged, by the statute 30 Geo. III. c. 48. but the forfeitures and corruptions of blood ensue as before the act; and further, women convicted as principals or accessaries before in petty treason, are made liable to the punishment inflicted by the statute 25 Geo. II. c. 37. on persons convicted of murder. In all cases of treason respecting the coin, whether newly created or not, and so in petty-treason, the judgment is only to be drawn on a hurdle and hanged. The sentence for counterfeiting the great or privy seal is the same as in other treasons. The consequences of a judgment and attainder in treason, are: 1. Corruption of blood to the party attaint; by which he can neither inherit nor transmit lands by descent to his heirs. 2. Loſs of dower to his wife. 3. Forſeiture to the king of all his lands, goods, and chattels: and this relates back to the time of the treaſon committed. 4. Execution. Without attainder, there is no forfeiture of lands, unleſs, ſays lord Hale, where the chief juſtice of the king's bench, as ſupreme coroner, in perſon, upon view of the body of one killed in open rebellion, records it, and returns the record into his own court; when both lands and goods are forfeited.

Misprision of Treason. Miſpriſion of treaſon is where a perſon knowing of a treaſon, but no party or conſenter to it, does not reveal it by a fair and full diſcloſure in convenient time to the king, or his privy council, or to ſome magiſtrate or perſon having authority to take the examination; and it is doubtful whether a declaration to any other than theſe is ſufficient. By the ſtat. 1 and 2 Ph. and M. c. 10. and other prior ſtatutes, ſuch a concealment or keeping ſecret of any high treaſon is now only a miſpriſion, though formerly it was deemed evidence of an aiding and abetting to the treaſon itſelf; but ſtill, under particular circumſtances, concealment may amount to evidence of aſſent to the treaſon, and ſo make the party a principal traitor. The knowledge muſt, however, be of the perſon of the offender, as well as of the deſign or offence, for a man cannot be ſaid to conceal that which he does not know.

Punishment. The puniſhment for miſpriſion of high treaſon is the loſs of the profits of lands during life, forfeiture of goods, and impriſonment during life: but miſpriſion of petty treaſon is only puniſhable by fine and impriſonment, as in caſe of miſpriſion of felony.

Homicide. Homicide, which is here uſed to denote the killing of a perſon by whatever means, is uſually treated of under the heads of murder, (of which petit treaſon is a more aggravated ſpecies,) *felo de ſe*, manſlaughter *per infortunium* or chance-medley, and homicide *ex neceſſitate*; which latter relates, either to the execution or advancement of juſtice, or to ſelf-defence. But as the ſhades between ſome of theſe are in many inſtances very faint, and as the difficulty in this branch of the law lies chiefly in diſcriminating between the one and the other, it is not judged neceſſary here to enter into all thoſe niceties which are laid down in larger treatiſes, but merely to deſcribe in a general way each mode of offence, with its uſual puniſhment.

Homicide is ſaid to be either *felonious*, *juſtifiable*, or *excuſable*.

Felonious homicide may be either againſt the life of another, or againſt a man's own life. The former is of two ſorts, *murder*, and *manſlaughter*.

Murder, in the ſenſe in which it is now underſtood, is the voluntarily

voluntarily killing any perſon under the king's peace, of malice *prepenſe* or afore-thought, either expreſs or implied by law. The ſenſe of the word *malice* is not confined to a particular ill will to the deceaſed, but is intended to denote an action flowing from a wicked and corrupt motive, a thing done *malo animo*, where the fact has been attended with ſuch circumſtances, as carry in them the plain indications of an heart regardleſs of ſocial duty, and fatally bent upon miſchief; and therefore malice is implied from any cruel act againſt another, however ſudden.

When this malice is exerted to the death of a maſter by his ſervant, or of a huſband by his wife, of an eccleſiaſtic ſuperior, by one owing obedience to him as ſuch, it takes the name of *petit treaſon*.

The groſſer inſtances of murder, where the depravity of the heart, or malice is apparent, form the *firſt* claſs of caſes under this head. 2. Where an officer, or one who aſſiſts in the advancement of juſtice where he lawfully may, is killed in the regular diſcharge of his duty. 3. Where a private man, lawfully interfering to prevent a breach of the peace, is oppoſed in ſuch his endeavour, and ſlain. 4. Where death happens incidentally in the proſecution of ſome other felony 5. Where it happens from other unlawful acts, of which death was the probable conſequence, done deliberately, and with intention of miſchief or great bodily harm to particular perſons, or of miſchief indiſcriminately, fall where it may; though the death enſue againſt, or beſide, the original intent of the party. 6. From deliberate duelling.

Clergy is taken away in all caſes of murder and petit treaſon from acceſſaries before, as well as principals; and lands and goods are forfeited; the forfeiture in ſuch caſe relating back to the ſtroke or other cauſe of death; but acceſſaries after the fact, either in petit treaſon or murder, are in no inſtance ouſted of clergy.

Manslaughter. Manſlaughter is principally diſtinguiſhable from murder in this, that although the act which occaſions the death be unlawful, or likely to be attended with bodily miſchief, yet the malice either expreſs or implied, which is the very eſſence of murder, is preſumed to be wanting in manſlaughter; and the act being imputed to the infirmity of human nature, the correction ordained for it is proportionably lenient. It follows that although there may be ſeveral principals, there cannot be any acceſſaries before to man-ſlaughter, becauſe it muſt be done without premeditation; but there may be acceſſaries after.

Punishment. The offence amounts to felony, but within benefit of clergy; and the offender is burned in the hand, and

 forfeits

forfeits all his goods and chattels. By ſtatute 19 Geo. III. c. 74, the burning in the hand may, in the diſcretion of the court, be changed to a moderate fine, but not to whipping; but this does not prevent the court from alſo adjudging the offender to be impriſoned for any term not exceeding a year.

The benefit of clergy is however taken away by the 1 Jas. I. c. 8. (commonly called the ſtatute of ſtabbing) in one ſpecies of killing, though done upon a ſudden provocation, namely, the offence of mortally ſtabbing another under certain circumſtances.

With reſpect to indictments for homicide on the high ſeas, before the admiralty ſeſſions, under the ſtat. 28 Hen. VIII. c. 15., inaſmuch as the marine law does not allow of clergy in any caſe, if the fact appeared upon the evidence to be no more than manſlaughter at common law, the priſoner was, prior to the ſtatute 39 Geo. III. c. 37., conſtantly directed to be acquitted. But now, by that act, perſons ſo tried, and found guilty of manſlaughter only, are intitled to clergy, and ſubject to puniſhment, as if they had committed the offence on land.

The caſes falling under the head of manſlaughter are either, 1ſt, where death enſues from actions in themſelves unlawful, but not proceeding from a malicious or felonious intention; 2dly, from actions in themſelves lawful, but done without due care and circumſpection for preventing miſchief; 3dly, where death enſues upon a ſudden combat or affray; or, 4thly, upon heat of blood from a reaſonable provocation given.

Suicide. The laſt kind of felonious homicide is that againſt a man's own life, which denominates the party ſlaying himſelf *felo de ſe*. This is where any one wilfully, or by any malicious act, cauſes his own death. The law regards this an heinous offence, and has ordained as ſevere a puniſhment for it as the nature of the caſe will admit of, namely, an ignominious burial in the high-way, with a ſtake driven through the body; and a forfeiture of all the offender's goods and chattels to the king. The uſual inſtances of this offence are either, 1ſt, where *felo de ſe* intended his own death; or, ſecondly, where he intended ſome other felony, in which he accidentally ſlew himſelf.

Justifiable Homicide. To make homicide juſtifiable, it muſt ariſe from an imperious duty preſcribed by the law, or be owing to ſome unavoidable neceſſity, induced by the act of the perſon killed, without any manner of fault in the party killing. In theſe caſes it is now clearly underſtood that the jury may acquit the priſoner generally, without obliging him, by a ſpecial finding of the matter, to purchaſe his pardon under the ſtatute of Glouceſter, c. 9.; and no forfeiture is incurred.

Excusable Homicide. Homicide is excuſable where the party

party killing is not altogether free from blame; but the necessity which renders it excusable may be said to be partly induced by his own act. And here the party seemed formerly not entitled to a verdict of acquittal, but the jury would find the facts specially, on which the court would bail the party, whose goods were forfeited at common law, to the next sessions or term; and upon certifying the record in chancery, a pardon issued of course under the statute of Gloucester, c. 9. to have them restored, without any application to the king, only paying for suing it out. Of late years, however, it has been more frequent, in cases even of excusable homicide, for the court to direct a verdict of acquittal.

The several descriptions of homicide referrable to either of the last two heads come next to be considered.

Homicide *ex necessitate*, which is of three sorts:

1. *In advancement of justice*, which is justifiable by *permission* of the law. This is, where persons having authority to arrest or imprison others, or to seize goods, or interfering to preserve the peace, and, using the proper means for that purpose, are resisted in so doing, and the party resisting is killed in the struggle; or where a felony has been committed, or a dangerous wound given, and the offender flies from justice, if in the pursuit the party flying be killed, the person killing is justified, provided the other could not be overtaken.

2. Homicide in *execution of justice;* which is justifiable by the command of the law. This is the carrying into execution the sentence of the law on malefactors condemned to death. Herein has been generally considered, 1st, How far the execution may vary from the sentence; 2dly, How far a want of jurisdiction in those who pass the judgment shall affect themselves, or those who carry such judgment into execution; 3dly, How far they are affected by the execution of an erroneous judgment; 4thly, To what extent a false witness is implicated.

3. Homicide in *defence of person or property* under certain circumstances of necessity. This is either justifiable by permission of the law, or only excusable. First, That necessity which justifies a man in killing another who comes to commit a known felony with force against his person, his habitation, or his property. In such cases, the injured party may repel force by force, and is not obliged to retreat, but may pursue his adversary in order to secure himself from danger. Secondly, That which only excuses him who kills another in his own defence upon a sudden combat, having first retreated as far as he could with safety, and with a view of declining the combat, before any mortal blow was given; and having no other possible, or at least probable method of escaping his own imme-

diate deſtruction or great bodily harm. This is denominated in legal phraſe, "*homicide ſe defendendo* upon chance-medley;" and here chance-medley is uſed in the proper ſenſe of the word. There is a third ſort of dire neceſſity, which is not induced by the fault of either party, where one of two innocent men muſt die for the other's preſervation: this has been holden by ſome to be *juſtifiable*; perhaps it may more properly be conſidered as *excuſable*.

The other kinds of homicide, not felonious, and by law deemed *excuſable*, are when the death happens by *miſadventure*, or by *chance-medley* uſually ſo called.

The ancient legal notion of homicide by chance-medley was, when death enſued from a combat between the parties on a ſudden quarrel; but it has ſince been frequently confounded with miſadventure or accident. Homicide by miſadventure is, when a man doing a lawful act, without any intention of bodily harm, and uſing proper precaution to prevent danger, unfortunately happens to kill another perſon. This is one ſpecies of excuſable homicide; but inaſmuch as no blame is imputable to the party, and ſuch an one ſeems more entitled to compaſſion than to cenſure, it ſeems to be now ſettled, whatever may have been formerly thought, that the jury, under the direction of the court, may acquit him generally, without putting him to purchaſe a pardon. The act upon which the death enſues muſt be lawful in itſelf; for if it be *malum in ſe*, the caſe will amount to felony, either murder or manſlaughter, according to the circumſtances. If it be merely *malum prohibitum*, as ſhooting at game by an unqualified perſon, that will not vary the degree of the offence. The uſual examples under this head are, 1ſt, Where death enſues from innocent recreations; 2dly, From moderate and lawful correction in *foro domeſtico*; 3dly, From acts lawful or indifferent in themſelves, done with proper and ordinary caution.

Theſe are the general outlines of the offences included under the term homicide; but they comprehend a vaſt variety of diſcriminations, ſome extremely minute, and ſome which were in their nature ſo doubtful as to leave the mind in perpetual indeciſion until ſettled by expreſs ſtatutes.

Indictment. In moſt caſes where juſtice requires that a man ſhould be put upon his trial for killing another, it is uſual (and proper if there be any doubt) to charge him in the indictment with murder; becauſe, in many inſtances, it is a complicated queſtion; and no injury can happen to the individual at all comparable to the evil example of a lax adminiſtration of juſtice: for the verdict and judgment will ſtill be adapted to the nature of the offence, ſuch as it appears

pears upon the evidence. Where a party is committed on ſuch a charge, he may be brought up by habeas corpus before the court of king's bench, and if the homicide appears to be either juſtifiable or excuſable, they will admit him to bail. Juſtices of peace ought not to bail in ſuch caſes; but ſhould commit till the next coming of the juſtices of gaol delivery. Even where the offence, if ſpecially preſented, would be ſhort of felony, the priſoner, if charged with murder, has this advantage, that an acquittal is a perpetual bar againſt any other indictment for the ſame death. On every charge of murder, the fact of killing being firſt proved, the law preſumes it to have been founded in malice until the contrary appear; and therefore all circumſtances alleged by way of juſtification, excuſe, or alleviation, muſt be proved by the priſoner, unleſs they ariſe out of the evidence produced againſt him. Upon the truth of theſe facts ſo alleged, the jury alone are to decide; but whether, taking them to be true, the homicide is juſtified, excuſed, or alleviated, is a matter of law upon which the jury ought to be guided by the direction of the court.

TRIAL. The general rule in this, as in other matters of criminal juriſprudence, is, that the offence muſt be inquired of and tried in the ſame county in which it was committed. But the ſtat. 33 Hen. VIII. c. 23. enacts, that upon examination before three of the council, treaſons, miſpriſions thereof, and murders committed in any place within the king's dominions, or without, may be inquired of, heard, and determined in any county where the king by his commiſſion of oyer and terminer ſhall appoint. If a perſon be ſtricken and die in one county and the body be found in another, it ſhall be removed into the firſt for the coroner of that county to take the inqueſt: Where the ſtroke and death are in different counties, the ſtat. 2 & 3 Edw. VI. c. 24. enacts, that the trial ſhall be in the county where the death happens.

Where a murder is committed in one county, and there are acceſſaries in another, an indictment found againſt ſuch acceſſaries in the county where the offence of the acceſſary was committed, is effectual in law; and the juſtices of gaol delivery or oyer and terminer, or two of them, are to write to the cuſtos rotulorum of the county where ſuch principal is attainted or convicted, to certify that fact; and on receipt of his certificate in writing under ſeal, the juſtices duly authorized may proceed upon the caſe of ſuch acceſſary, who is bound to anſwer upon arraignment, and abide the event.

By the ſtatute 26 Hen. VIII. c. 6., murders, and other felonies committed in Wales, may be tried in the next adjoining Engliſh county where the king's writ runs; which has been always construed to mean Salop, and not Chester. Appeals, however, must still be brought in the proper county. But supposing the stroke given in an English county, and the death in Wales, there seems to be some difficulty in ascertaining where the trial shall be.

It seems to have been a matter of great doubt, whether the killing of one who died at land of a wound received at sea could be inquired of at common law; but it is enacted by statute 2 Geo. II. c. 21., that where any person shall be feloniously stricken or poisoned upon the sea, or at any place out of England, and die of it in England; or where any person shall be so stricken or poisoned in England, and die upon the sea, or at any place out of England; in either case, an indictment found by the jurors of the county in which the death, stroke, or poisoning happened, shall be good in law against principals and accessaries.

Where both the stroke and death are at sea, or in a haven, river, creek, or place where the admiral has power, authority, or jurisdiction, the 28 Hen. VIII. c. 15. enacts that the offence shall be tried in such shire or place in the realm as shall be limited by the king's commission, directed to the admiral or his deputies, &c. and to three or four such other substantial persons as shall be appointed by the lord chancellor, to hear and determine such offences after the common course of the law. And where one standing on the shore shot at another standing in the sea, who afterwards died on board a ship, all the judges held that the trial must be in the admiralty court, and not at common law.

In regard to homicide committed in foreign parts, Lord Coke says, that if two of the king's subjects go over into a foreign realm and fight there, and the one kill the other, this may be heard and determined before the constable and marshal; relying principally on the stat. 13 Rich. II. c. 2., which says, that "to the constable it pertains to have conusance of contracts concerning deeds of arms, or of war, out of the realm, &c. which cannot be determined or discussed by the common law." But this seems always to have been a doubtful construction of that statute, and may probably be denied at this day, when that jurisdiction has fallen into disuse. The same may be said of the statute 1 Hen. IV. c. 14., which says, that all appeals for things done out of the realm shall be heard and determined before the same jurisdiction. But by stat. 33 Hen. VIII. c. 23. (which with respect to the trial of murder stands unrepealed by the stat. 1 & 2 Ph. & M. c. 10.) it is enacted "that if any person being examined before the king's council, or three of them, upon any treasons, misprisions of treasons, or murders, do confess

fess the same, or are vehemently suspected thereof by the said council upon such examination, the lord chancellor, by the king's command, shall send a commission of oyer and terminer under the great seal to such persons, and into such shires or places as shall be named and appointed, for the speedy trial of such offenders; which commissioners shall have power and authority to inquire, hear, and determine all such offences within the shires and places limited by their commission, by a jury returned by the sheriff, &c. in whatever other shire or place *within the king's dominions or without* such offences so examined were committed." "And no challenge for the shire or hundred (but for want of freehold) shall be allowed." This statute extends not to accessaries.

By 10 & 11 W. III. c. 25. murder and all other capital crimes in Newfoundland, and the isles thereto belonging, are triable in any county here, since when the acts of the 32 Geo. III. c. 46. and 33 Geo. III. c. 76. have enabled his majesty to erect courts of civil and criminal jurisdiction there, which are "to hold plea of all crimes and misdemeanors committed in Newfoundland, and on the islands and seas to which ships or vessels repair from Newfoundland, for carrying on the fishery, and on the banks of Newfoundland, in the same manner as plea is holden of such crimes and misdemeanors in England." These acts are continued by the 34 Geo. III. c. 44. and 35 Geo. III. c. 25.; but nothing appears therein to shew that the jurisdiction under the statute of King William is taken away.

Upon every indictment for petit treason or murder, the jury may negative the higher offence, and find their verdict for any lesser species of homicide. So the defendant in an appeal of murder may be found guilty of manslaughter only; and the appellant in that case shall not be nonsuited; and although it was formerly considered to be optional in the jury upon an appeal of murder, if the case appeared to be only manslaughter, to find accordingly, or to acquit the defendant altogether, yet it is now settled that they must find the manslaughter.

Appeals. The appeal here mentioned does not signify any complaint to a superior court of an injustice done by an inferior one, which is the general use of the word; but an original suit, at the time of its commencement. An appeal therefore, when thus spoken of, denotes an accusation by a private subject against another, for some heinous crime; demanding punishment on account of the particular injury suffered, rather than for the offence against the public. This method of prosecution is still in force; but very little in use, on account of the great nicety required in conducting it. This private process, for the punishment of public crimes, had probably its origin

in

in those times when a private pecuniary satisfaction, called a *weregild*, was constantly paid to the party injured, or his relations, to expiate enormous offences. As therefore, during the continuance of this custom, a process was certainly given, for recovering the weregild by the party to whom it was due; it seems that, when these offences by degrees grew no longer redeemable, the private process was still continued, in order to insure the infliction of punishment upon the offender, though the party injured was allowed no pecuniary compensation for the offence. An appeal of felony may be brought for crimes committed either against the parties themselves, or their relations. The crimes against the parties themselves are larceny, rape, and arson; and for these as well as for mayhem, the sufferers may institute this private process. The only crime against one's relation, for which an appeal can be brought, is that of killing him, by either murder or manslaughter; this, however, cannot be brought by every relation, but only by the wife for the death of her husband, or by the heir male for the death of his ancestor; which heirship was also confined, by an ordinance of Henry I. to the four nearest degrees of blood. It is given to the wife, on account of the loss of her husband: therefore, if she marries again, before or pending her appeal, it is lost and gone; or, if she marries after judgment, she shall not demand execution. The heir, as was said, must also be heir male, and such a one as was the next heir by the course of the common law, at the time of the killing of the ancestor. But this rule has three exceptions: 1. If the person killed leaves an innocent wife, she only, and not the heir, shall have the appeal: 2. If there be no wife, and the heir be accused of the murder, the person, who next to him would have been heir male, shall bring the appeal: 3. If the wife kills her husband, the heir may appeal her of the death. And by the statute of Gloucester, 6 Edw. I. c. 9. all appeals of death must be sued within a year and a day after the completion of the felony by the death of the party. These appeals may be brought previous to any indictment; and if the appellee be acquitted thereon, he cannot be afterwards indicted for the same offence. But if a man be acquitted on an indictment of murder, or found guilty, and pardoned by the king, still he ought not (in strictness) to go at large, but be imprisoned or let to bail till the year and day be past, by virtue of the statute 3 Hen. VII. c. 1. in order to be forthcoming to answer any appeal for the same felony, not having as yet been punished for it; though if he has been found guilty of manslaughter on an indictment, and has had the benefit of of clergy, and suffered the judgment of the law, he cannot afterwards be appealed. If the appellee be acquitted, the appellor (by virtue of the statute of Westminster 2. 13 Edw. I. c. 12.) shall suffer one year's imprisonment, and pay a fine to the king, besides restitution of damages to the party for the imprisonment and infamy which he has sustained: and if the appellor be incapable to make restitution, his abettors shall do it for him, and also be liable to imprisonment. If the appellee be found guilty, he shall suffer the same judgment, as if he had been convicted by indictment: but with this remarkable difference; that on an indictment, which is at the suit of the king, the king may pardon and remit the execution; on an appeal, which is at the suit of a private subject to make an atonement for the private wrong, the king can no more pardon it, than he can remit the damages recovered on an action of battery; and the ancient usage was, so late as the time of Henry IV. that all the relations of the slain should drag the appellee to the place of execution. However, the punishment of the offender may be remitted and discharged by the concurrence of all parties interested; and as the king by his pardon may frustrate an indictment, so the appellant by his release may discharge an appeal.

Judgment and Execution. The judgment in petit treason is the same as in the lower species of high treason, namely, to be drawn on a hurdle, and hanged until dead. It was formerly different in the case of women, who were adjudged to be drawn and burned; but this was altered by the 30 Geo. III. c. 48. which subjected them to the same judgment in all respects as men.

The judgment in murder was the same as in other cases of capital felony, namely, to be hanged by the neck until dead; but by 25 Geo. II. c. 37. all persons, found guilty of murder, are to be executed on the next day but one after sentence, unless it happens to be Sunday, and then on the Monday following. The body, if in Middlesex, or London, to be immediately conveyed to the Surgeons' Hall, or such other place as the Surgeons' Company shall appoint, and be dissected and anatomised. And in case the conviction is in any other county or place, the sentence is to be put in execution the next day but one, except it be Sunday, and the body delivered by the sheriff to such surgeon as the judge shall direct. And the sentence is pronounced in open court immediately after conviction (unless the court shall see reasonable cause for postponing it) expressing not only the usual judgment of death, but also the time appointed for the

execu-

execution, and the marks of infamy directed for the offender.

The judge may, for reasonable cause, stay execution; regard being always had to the true intent and purpose of the act: or he may appoint the body of any such criminal to be hung in chains; but in no case whatever the body shall be buried, until it has been anatomised. The act also directs that a murderer after conviction shall be confined in a separate cell, and no person but the gaoler or his servants shall have access to him, without licence under the hand of the judge or sheriff; but in case the judge shall stay execution, he may relax these restraints by licence in writing signed by him. Between sentence and execution, the convict is to be fed with bread and water only (except on receiving the sacrament, or necessaries administered medicinally by a professional man) under a penalty upon the gaoler of 20*l.* and imprisonment till it be paid, and forfeiture of his office. And if any person shall rescue, or attempt to rescue, out of prison, any person committed for, or found guilty of, murder, or going to execution; he shall be guilty of felony, without benefit of clergy. Also if any person after execution rescue or attempt to rescue the body out of the custody of the sheriff or his officers, or from the Company of Surgeons, or from the house of any surgeon, he shall be guilty of felony, and transported for seven years.

Maiming. A Mayhem or Maim, at common law, is such a bodily hurt as renders a man less able, in fighting, to defend himself, or annoy his adversary: but if the injury be such as disfigures him only, without diminishing his corporal ability, it does not fall within the crime of mayhem. Upon this distinction, the cutting off, disabling, or weakening a man's hand or finger, or striking out an eye, or fore tooth, or, as lord Coke adds, breaking his scull, are said to be maims; but the cutting off his ear, or nose, is not such at common law. But, in order to found an indictment, or appeal of mayhem, the act must be done maliciously; though it matters not how sudden the occasion.—All maims are said to be felony; because anciently the offender had judgment of the loss of the same member, &c. which he had occasioned to the sufferer; but now the only judgment, which remains at common law, is of fine and imprisonment; whence the offence seems to have been afterwards considered more in the nature of an aggravated trespass, and Lord Coke classes it as an offence "under all felonies deserving death, and above all other inferior offences."

But particular statutes have extended both the crime and the punishment. The 22 and 23 Chas. II. c. 1. is commonly called

called *the Coventry act*, from its having paſſed on occaſion of an aſſault made on Sir John Coventry in the ſtreet, and his noſe being ſlit by perſons who lay in wait for him, in revenge, as was ſuppoſed, for ſome obnoxious words uttered by him in parliament. It enacts that if any perſon ſhall, on purpoſe and of malice forethought, by laying in wait, unlawfully cut out or diſable the tongue, put out an eye, ſlit the noſe, cut off a noſe or lip, or cut off or diſable any limb or member of any ſubject, with intention, in ſo doing, to maim or disfigure him; the offender, his counſellors, aiders, and abettors, ſhall ſuffer death, as in caſes of felony, without benefit of clergy;" but not to work corruption of blood, forfeiture of dower, or of lands, or goods.

To bring an offender within the Coventry act, there muſt be proof of a deliberate and premeditated deſign to do to another a perſonal injury of the ſort deſcribed; and it muſt appear that the miſchief was done in the manner deſcribed therein, that is, on purpoſe and of malice aforethought, and by lying in wait for that purpoſe.

A moſt horrible practice, however, having prevailed among pickpockets and others, of lacerating thoſe who were the objects of depredation or reſentment, and the laws being found inadequate to reach and efficiently correct the evil, the legiſlature interfered, and by the 43 Geo. III. c. 58. (commonly called Lord Ellenborough's act) which recites, that, whereas divers cruel and barbarous outrages have been of late wickedly and wantonly committed upon the perſons of his majeſty's ſubjects, either with intent to murder, or to rob, or to maim, disfigure or diſable, or to do other grievous bodily harm to ſuch ſubjects; it is enacted, that if any perſon ſhall wilfully and maliciouſly ſtab or cut any of his majeſty's ſubjects, with intent to murder, rob, maim, disfigure, or diſable them, or to do ſome other grievous bodily harm, or to obſtruct, reſiſt, or prevent the lawful apprehenſion and detainer of the perſon ſo ſtabbing or cutting, or of any of his accomplices, for any offence, the perſon ſo offending, his counſellors, aiders, and abettors ſhall ſuffer death without benefit of clergy: provided, that if it appear on the trial, that ſuch act of ſtabbing or cutting were committed under ſuch circumſtances, as that if death had enſued therefrom, the ſame would not have amounted to murder, the perſon indicted ſhall be deemed not guilty of felony.

ASSAULTS WITH FELONIOUS, MALICIOUS, OR UNLAWFUL INTENT. An aſſault is any attempt or offer with force and violence to do a corporal hurt to another, whether from malice or wantonneſs; as by ſtriking at him, or even by holding up one's fiſt at him in a threatening or inſulting manner, or with

with ſuch other circumſtances as denote at the time an intention, coupled with a preſent ability, of uſing actual violence againſt his perſon; as by pointing a weapon at him within the reach of it. Where the injury is actually inflicted, it amounts to a battery, (which includes an aſſault,) and this, however ſmall it may be, as by ſpitting in a man's face, or any way touching him in anger without any lawful occaſion. But it is excuſed if the occaſion were merely accidental and undeſigned, or if it were lawful, and the party uſed no more force than was reaſonably neceſſary to accompliſh the purpoſe, as to defend himſelf againſt a prior aſſault, or to arreſt the other, or make him deſiſt from ſome wrongful act or endeavour: but to make this excuſe valid, the retaliation or other effort muſt not be exceſſive, and diſproportioned to the neceſſity, or the provocation received. Theſe offences are puniſhable by fine and impriſonment, and finding ſureties, or with other ignominious corporal penalties, ſuch as the pillory, where they are committed with any very atrocious deſign; as in the caſe of aſſaults with intent to murder, raviſh, or commit other felonies or high miſdemeanors.

Aſſaulting Privy Counſellors. The penalty of this offence is mentioned in this volume, p. 11.

Aſſaulting Members of Parliament. By 11 Hen. VI. c. 11. If any aſſault or affray be made to any lord ſpiritual or temporal, knight of the ſhire, citizen, or burgeſs, coming to, and attending the parliament, or to other counſel of the king by his commandment, proclamation ſhall be made three ſeveral days in the town where the offence was committed for the party to yield himſelf before the court of king's bench within a quarter of a year, or at the next day in the term then following; and if he do not, he is to be attainted of the ſaid deed, and pay double damages to the party grieved; to be taxed at the diſcretion of the judges, or by inqueſt if needful, and make fine and ranſom at the king's will. And if he appear, and is found guilty, he is to pay to the party grieved his double damages, and to be fined as before-mentioned.

Aſſaults in the King's Palace. The puniſhment of theſe is already deſcribed in ſpeaking of the court of the lord ſteward of the houſehold. See p. 569.

Aſſaults in Churches and Church-yards. Theſe may, if committed with the hands only, be puniſhed with excommunication, by ſtat. 5 and 6 Edw. VI. c. 4.; which further enacts, that "if any perſon ſhall maliciouſly ſtrike with, or draw any "weapon in any church or church-yard, or with intent to ſtrike, "he ſhall have one of his ears cut off; or if he have no ears, "then he ſhall be marked and burned in the cheek with a hot "iron, having the letter F therein as a fray-maker and fighter, "and ſtand *ipſo facto* excommunicated."

Aſſault

Assault with Intent to murder. The statute under which prosecutions of this sort are most frequently carried on, is the 9 Geo. I. c. 22. (commonly called the black act), which provides that if any person shall wilfully and maliciously shoot at another in any dwelling-house or other place; or shall forcibly rescue any person being lawfully in custody of any officer or other person for such offence; or shall, by gift or promise of money, or other reward, procure any subject to join him in any such unlawful act; he shall suffer death without benefit of clergy. It is not necessary in this case, as in some others to which the act applies, that the offender should have his face blacked, or be otherwise disguised. Malice being an essential ingredient in this offence; neither an accidental shooting, in the intemperance of passion, upon such a provocation as would in law reduce the homicide to manslaughter, is within the meaning of the statute: and although it is not necessary that any evil consequence should ensue, yet the shooting must be with a gun or other instrument, so loaded as to create danger of death, or maim; and it must be levelled at the party. This statute at once creating a new felony and making it capital, it must be so with all its consequences, and therefore every person present aiding and assisting must be a principal in the second degree.

Assault with Intent to rob. This offence at common law was only punishable as a misdemeanor; though by some it had been considered as felony, upon the mistaken maxim, *voluntas reputabitur pro facto*, but now by 7 Geo. II. c. 21. it is enacted, That if any person shall, with any offensive weapon, unlawfully and maliciously assault another; or by menaces, demand any money, goods, or chattels, with intent to rob; such offender shall be transported as a felon for seven years. And if the offender break gaol, or escape before such transportation, or shall return before the expiration of his term, he shall suffer death without benefit of clergy.

Assaults on Persons wrecked. By 26 Geo. II. c. 19. "If "any person shall beat, or wound, with intent to kill or destroy, "or shall otherwise wilfully obstruct the escape of any person "endeavouring to save his or her life from any ship or vessel in "distress, or which shall be wrecked, lost, stranded, or cast "on shore, in any part of his majesty's dominions, he shall be "deemed guilty of felony without benefit of clergy. And if "any sheriff or his deputy, justice of the peace, mayor, or other "magistrate, coroner, lord of the manor, commissioner of the "land-tax, chief or petty constable, or other peace officer, or "any custom-house, or excise officer, or other person lawfully "authorized, shall be assaulted, beaten and wounded, on ac- "count of the exercise of his duty, in or concerning the salvage

"or

"or preservation of any ship or vessel in distress, or of any ship, "goods or effects, stranded, wrecked, or cast on shore, "or lying under water in any of his majesty's dominions; the "offender, on conviction, at the assizes or general gaol delivery, "or at the quarter sessions, shall be transported for seven years."

Assaults by Mariners. The punishment of mariners preventing by violence their captain from defending his ship, is mentioned in this volume, p. 276.

Assault on Account of Gaming. By 9 Anne, c. 15. if any person shall assault and beat, or challenge or provoke to fight, any other person on account of money won by gaming, such person shall forfeit all his goods, chattels, and personal estate whatsoever, and be imprisoned in the county gaol for two years.

Assault with Intent to spoil Garments. By 6 Geo. I. c. 23. "If any person shall wilfully and maliciously assault another in the public streets or highways, with an intent to tear, spoil, cut, burn, or deface his garments or cloaths; the offender shall be guilty of felony, and liable to be transported for seven years. This statute was occasioned by the insolence of certain weavers and others, who, on the introduction of some Indian fashions prejudicial to their own manufactures, made it a practice to deface them either by open outrage, or by privily cutting, or casting *aqua fortis* in the streets upon such as wore them.

Assault with Intent to obstruct the free Passage of Grain. By 36 Geo. III. c. 9., "If any person shall wilfully and maliciously beat, wound, or use any other violence to or upon any one, with intent to deter or hinder him from buying corn or grain in any market, or other place within this kingdom; or unlawfully beat or wound the driver of any waggon, cart, or other carriage or horse, loaded with wheat, flour, meal, malt, or other grain, with intent to stop such wheat, &c., every such person, being convicted before two or more justices of the peace, or at the sessions, shall be sent to the common gaol or house of correction, to be kept to hard labour, not less than one, nor exceeding three months. And for a second offence transported for seven years. The same provisions were before enacted by the 11 Geo. II. c. 22., which is still in force; with this addition, that for the first offence the justices were also directed to adjudge the offender to be publicly whipped by the keeper of the gaol or house of correction, on the first convenient market day, at the market cross or place, between the hours of eleven and two. In both acts there is a provision, that no person punished by virtue thereof, shall be punished for the same offence by any other statute; but 36 Geo. III. declares, that nothing therein contained shall be deemed to abridge or take away any provision already made by law, or any part thereof, for the suppression or punishment of any offence mentioned in that act.

3 *Assaults*

Assaults on Master Wool-combers. By 12 Geo. I. c. 34. if any person shall assault or abuse any master wool-comber, or master weaver, or other person concerned in the woollen manufactures, for not complying with any illegal bye-laws, ordinances, rules, or orders, formed in unlawful clubs and societies; such offender being lawfully convicted, on any indictment found within twelve calendar months, shall be adjudged guilty of felony, and transported for seven years; and the like provisions are extended to combers of jersey and wool, frame work knitters, and weavers or makers of stockings, and to all persons whatsoever employed or concerned in any of the said manufactures.

False Imprisonment. This offence is most frequently the object of a civil action for a compensation in damages; that mode of it which relates to the arrest of ambassadors has been noticed in this volume, p. 52.

Kidnapping. The most aggravated species of false imprisonment is the stealing and carrying away, or secreting of any person, sometimes called kidnapping, which is an offence at common law, punishable by fine, imprisonment, and pillory. Of this nature is the offence pointed out by the 43 Eliz. c. 13., which, reciting that many subjects dwelling and inhabiting within the counties of Cumberland, Northumberland, Westmoreland, and the bishopric of Durham, had been taken, some from their houses, others in travelling, or otherwise, and carried out of the same counties, or to some other place within the same, as prisoners, and cruelly treated till they have been redeemed by great ransoms, enacts, that whoever shall, without good and lawful warrant and authority, take any of the queen's subjects against his or their wills, to ransom them, or to make a prey or spoil of his or their person or goods, upon deadly feud or otherwise; or whoever shall be privy, consenting, aiding, or assisting unto any such taking, detaining or carrying away of any such person or persons, prisoners as aforesaid, shall be adjudged felons, and suffer death without benefit of clergy, and shall forfeit as in case of felony.

The forcible abduction, or stealing and carrying away of any person, is greatly aggravated by sending them away from their own country into another, properly called kidnapping; though the punishment at common law is no more than fine, imprisonment, and pillory. By the habeas corpus act it is declared that no subject of this realm, being an inhabitant of the kingdom, shall be sent prisoner into Scotland, Ireland, Jersey, Guernsey, Tangier, or into ports, garrisons, islands, or places beyond the seas, within or without the king's dominions; that every such imprisonment is illegal; and any person so impri-

 soned

foned may maintain an action of falfe imprifonment againft thofe by whom he was imprifoned, fent prifoner, or tranfported, and againft all who framed, contrived, wrote, fealed, or counterfigned any warrant for fuch detainer, imprifonment, or tranfportation, or were advifing, aiding, or affifting in the fame, and the plaintiff in every fuch action fhall have treble cofts, befides damages; which fhall not be lefs than 500*l*. And the perfons convicted of fuch acts fhall be difabled to bear any office of truft or profit within the king's dominions; and fhall incur the pains, penalties, and forfeitures of a præmunire, and be incapable of pardon. No perfon can be tried or troubled for any offence againft the act unlefs within two years after the offence committed, or if the party grieved be in prifon, then within two years after the deceafe of the party imprifoned, or delivery out of prifon, which fhall firft happen.

Alfo by 11 and 12 W. and M. c. 7. if any mafter of a merchant fhip or veffel fhall during his being abroad force any man on fhore, or wilfully leave him behind, in any of his majefty's plantations or elfewhere, or fhall refufe to bring home with him again all fuch of the men whom he carried out with him, as are in a condition to return, when he fhall be ready to proceed on his homeward bound voyage; he fhall fuffer three months imprifonment without bail or mainprize.

Rape. This offence is felony without benefit of clergy by various ftatutes. If the object of it be under the age of ten years, her confent cannot be alleged in juftification; and if above ten, and under twelve, ftill, notwithftanding her confent, it is a high mifdemeanor; fo is an affault with intent to commit this crime, although the purpofe is not effected.

Forcible or Fraudulent Abduction, Marriage, or Defilement of Women of Substance. The 3 Henry VII. c. 2. reciting that "where women, as well maidens as "widows and wives, having fubftances, *fome* in goods moveable, "and fome in lands and tenements, and fome being heirs appa-"rent unto their anceftors, for the lucre of fuch fubftances be "oftentimes taken by mifdoers, contrary to their will, and "often married to fuch mifdoers, or to other by their affent, or "defiled," enacts, "that whatever perfon or perfons from "henceforth takes any woman, fo againft her will, unlawfully, "that is to fay, maid, widow, or wife; fuch taking, procuring, "and abetting to the fame, and alfo receiving wittingly the fame "woman fo taken againft her will, and knowing the fame, be "felony; and that fuch mifdoers, takers, procurators to the fame, "and receitors knowing the faid offence, in form aforefaid, be "adjudged principal felons." And the 39 Eliz. c. 9. takes away benefit of clergy from principals, procurers, and acceffaries before the

the fact. If a woman is forcibly taken in one county, and afterwards goes voluntarily into another county, and is there married or defiled with her own consent, the fact is not indictable in either: for the offence, which consists in the forcible taking and subsequent marriage or defilement, is not complete in either. But if the force continued upon her at all in the other county in which she was so taken, the offender may be indicted there; although the actual marriage or defilement afterwards took place with her own consent. It is held that a woman so taken away may be a witness against the man who has married her, but the practice has not been uniform; although the principle is settled; the testimony must be received with great caution.

By 4 and 5 Ph. and Mary, c. 8. if any person above the age of fourteen years shall unlawfully take or convey, or cause to be taken or conveyed, any maid or woman child unmarried, being within the age of sixteen years, out of or from the possession and against the will of her father, mother, or lawful guardian, such person shall suffer imprisonment for two years, or else pay such fine as shall be assessed by the court of star chamber; and "If any person or persons shall so take, or "cause to be taken away as aforesaid, and deflower any such "maid or woman child, or shall against the will, or unknowing of "or to the father if alive, or of the mother having the custody "or governance of such child if the father be dead, by secret letters, messages or otherwise, contract matrimony with any such "maiden or woman child; every such person shall suffer imprisonment for five years, or else shall pay such fine as shall be assessed "by the star chamber, a moiety to the crown, and the other "moiety to the parties grieved." By the 26 Geo. II. c. 33. the marriage is void; but the statute of Phil. and Mary is in force, and the court of king's bench has the powers which are given to the star chamber.

Polygamy or Bigamy is noticed in vol. I. p. 410.

Crime against Nature. This offence, of which it is horrible even to speak, is felony without benefit of clergy; accessaries before or after, are not deprived of clergy; but persons present aiding and assisting, are deemed principals.

Theft. The modes of theft punishable by law are subject to many nice distinctions, arising from an infinite variety of cases, and far too minute to be enumerated in this work.

Burglary. Burglary, which is derived from the German *burg*, a house, and *laron* or *latro* a thief, is a felony at common law, and is generally defined to be a breaking and entering the mansion house of another, in the night, with intent to commit some felony within the same, whether such intent be executed or not.

To perfect this crime, there must be *a breach* of the house

 made

made or procured by the act of the felon; and this either by construction of law, or by actual force. But although, generally speaking, every entry by a trespasser is a breaking in law, yet that is not sufficient in this case; for the words of the indictment are, feloniously and burglariously broke, &c. Therefore, if the door or window be left open, and the thief enter and take away the goods in the night, that will not constitute a burglary. Though it is otherwise if a thief enter by a chimney, because it is as much inclosed as the nature of the thing will admit of. To amount to a breaking within this branch of the definition, the entrance must be obtained either by fraud, conspiracy, threat, or force.

There must also be an entry, but if any part of the body, as a hand, or foot, be within the house, it is sufficient. The entry need not be at the same time as the breaking, provided both be in the night; therefore, if thieves break a hole in the house one night, and enter and commit felony on another, it is burglary.

The term *mansion* includes three distinct objects of burglary; 1. It may be committed, against the walls or gates of a walled town; 2. Against churches; and 3. Against private dwelling-houses. Every house for the dwelling and habitation of man is taken to be a mansion-house wherein burglary may be committed. Likewise a chamber or room, be it upper or lower, wherein any person inhabits or dwells, is a mansion-house in law. But no burglary can be committed by breaking into any inclosed ground, or into any booth or tent, though the owner lodge therein: but in case of robbery committed in these latter, a remedy is provided by the 5 & 6 Edw. VI. c. 9. The mansion not only includes the dwelling-house, but also the out-houses, such as barns, stables, cow-houses, dairy-houses and the like, if parcel of the messuage, though under the same roof, or contiguous.

Of *Inhabitancy* there must be some token, either by the present or at least by previous occupation of the owner, or some part of his family. However it is agreed by all, that a house wherein a man dwells but for part of the year, or a chamber in one of the inns of court, or a college, wherein a person usually lodges, may be called his dwelling house, whether any person were actually therein or not at the very time of the offence. Yet, where neither the owner nor any part of his family were in the house at the time of the breaking and entering, he must have quitted it with intent to return, in order to have it still considered as his mansion.

It is necessary to ascertain to whom the mansion belongs, and to state that with accuracy in the indictment: the rule on this

this subject is somewhat complex, but thus reduced by Mr. East from whose Treatise on Pleas of the Crown, most of the foregoing and many following observations are derived. Where the legal title to the whole mansion remains in the same person; there, if he inhabits it either by himself, his family, or servants, or even by his guests, the indictment must lay the offence to be committed against his mansion. And so it is although he let out apartments to inmates, who have a separate interest therein, if they have the same outer door or entrance into the mansion in common with himself; but if distinct families be in the exclusive occupation of the house, and have their ordinary residence or domicile there, without any interference on the part of the proper owner; or if they be only in possession of parts of the house as inmates to the owner, and have a distinct and separate entrance; then the offence of breaking, &c. their separate apartments must be laid to be done against the mansion-house of such occupiers respectively.

Burglary must be committed *in the night*. Anciently the day was accounted to begin only from sun rising, and to end immediately upon sun-set: but it is now generally agreed, that if there be day light enough begun or left either by the light of the sun or twilight, whereby the countenance of a person may be reasonably discerned, it is no burglary: but this does not extend to moon light; for then many midnight burglaries would go unpunished; and besides, the malignity of the offence does not so properly arise from its being done in the dark, as at the dead of the night, when all the creation except beasts of prey are at rest, when sleep has disarmed the owner, and rendered his castle defenceless.

The punishment of burglary is death without benefit of clergy; and by 5 Anne, c. 31. (which is principally levelled at the receivers of stolen goods,) any person who shall receive, harbour or conceal any burglars, &c. knowing them to be so, shall be taken as an accessary, and suffer death as a felon convict. A reward of 40*l*. and certificate of exemption from parish offices are given on the conviction of burglars by several statutes; and also a pardon to an offender out of prison discovering two or more accomplices.

Larceny and Robbery. The offence of feloniously taking the personal property of another is denominated either *larceny*, where the fact is accomplished secretly, or by surprise or fraud; or *robbery*, where accompanied by circumstances of violence, threat, or terror. These two offences, which in their nature are intimately connected, the first being includ-

 ed

ed in the other, are also in part blended together by the statute law. Simple larceny is defined to be, the wrongful or fraudulent taking and carrying away by any person of the mere personal goods of another, from any place, with a felonious intent to convert them to his (the taker's) own use, and make them his own property, without the consent of the owner.

There must be an actual taking, or severance of the thing, from the possession of the owner; for as every larceny includes a trespass: if the party be not guilty of a trespass in taking the goods, he cannot be guilty of felony in carrying them away. Hence it is that if the party obtain possession of the goods lawfully as upon a trust, for or on account of the owner, by which he acquires a kind of special property in them, he cannot afterwards be guilty of felony in converting them to his own use, unless by some new and distinct act of taking, as by severing part of the goods from the rest with intent to convert them to his own use, he determines the privity of the bailment, and the special property thereby conferred upon him. A bare charge of goods, such as that which is committed to a servant over the goods of his master, or a mere liberty to make use of a thing for a particular purpose, such as a guest at an inn has of the furniture, &c.; in as much as it does not in law convey even the possession of the goods, much less any special property in them, furnishes no objection to a charge of felony. In like manner, though the possession be delivered by the owner for a particular purpose, yet if it be obtained by any fraud it amounts to a tortious taking, in the same degree as if the party had taken it without any delivery at all from the owner. Though otherwise if the delivery be obtained on a trust without fraud. So a colourable gift, which in truth was extorted by fear, amounts to a taking and trespass in law; and has often been holden to constitute robbery, and this though the thing obtained were not originally in the contemplation of the robber, but received as the price of desisting from a felonious attempt of another kind. But the taking in all cases must be against or without the consent of the owner to constitute robbery or larceny. But although there must be a taking in fact from the actual or constructive possession of the owner, yet it need not be by the very hand of the party accused. For if he fraudulently procure another, who is himself innocent of any felonious intent, to take the goods for him, it will be the same as if he had taken them himself; and the taking must be charged to be by him. As if one procure an infant within the age of discretion to steal goods for him, or if by fraud or perjury he got possession of goods by legal process without colour of title.

The

The least removal of the thing taken from the place where it was before is a sufficient *carrying away*, though it be not quite carried off. If the thief once takes possession of the thing, the offence is complete, though he afterwards returns it, or lets it fall in struggling, and never takes it up again.

On the point by whom larceny may be committed, it is observed that the same excuses of insanity, idiocy, coverture, and infancy, which prevail in other cases of felony, will of course have place here. Jointenants or tenants in common of a chattel cannot be guilty of stealing the same from each other, because the property and possession is in both; but under some circumstances a man may be guilty of larceny in stealing his own goods, or of robbery in taking his own property from the person of another. So he may be an accessary after the fact to such larceny or robbery, by harbouring the thief or assisting his escape. For example; if a man delivers goods to another to keep for him, and then steals them, with intent to charge him with the value of them: this is felony in the person who steals, although he is the owner. So likewise, a man having delivered money to his servant to carry to some distant place, disguises himself, and robs the servant on the road with intent to charge the hundred; this is undoubtedly robbery. By the same rule the wife may steal the goods of her husband delivered for a limited purpose to another person; but a feme covert cannot commit larceny of her husband's goods from his own possession, because in law they are considered but as one person, and she has a kind of interest in them. On this account not even a stranger can commit larceny of such goods by the delivery of the wife, although he knew they were the husband's; but he may by taking the wife by force and against her will, together with the goods, by force of the statute. Neither can the wife commit larceny in the company of her husband; for it is deemed his coercion, and not her own voluntary act. Yet if she do it in his absence, and by his mere command, she is then punishable as if she were sole. And the husband, it is said, may be accessary to the wife in receiving her; though not the wife for receiving her husband.

For the prevention of larcenies by servants, and in aid of the common law on that point, several statutes have been made. That of the 33 Hen. VI. c. 1. provides against the dishonesty of those servants who on the death of their masters violently seize or spoil their property, that on information exhibited by the executors to the chancellor a writ may issue, commanding such servants to appear in the court of king's bench, to answer ſuch actions as the executors may bring againſt them, and if they do not appear, they may be attainted of felony. The ſtatute 21 Hen. VIII. c. 7. reciting the embezzlements and frauds committed by ſervants to whom property was intruſted by their maſters, enacts, that all ſuch ſervants (being of the age of eighteen and not apprentices) to whom any caſkets, jewels, money, goods, or chattels, by their maſters or miſtreſſes, ſhall be delivered to keep, if the ſervants go away with them with intent to ſteal them, or elſe being in the ſervice of their ſaid maſter or miſtreſs, without their aſſent or command, embezzle ſuch caſkets, &c. or otherwiſe convert them to their own uſe with purpoſe to ſteal them, if they are of the value of forty ſhillings, the offender ſhall be puniſhed as other felons are, by the courſe of the common law. After ſome alterations, repeals, and re-enactments, this ſtatute ſtill continues in force, and the offenders are deprived of clergy. It extends however only to ſuch as were ſervants to the owners of the goods, both at the time of the delivery and when they were ſtolen. This ſtatute however is but little reſorted to at this day; for, notwithſtanding the inference which might be drawn from it, it is a clear maxim of the common law, that where one has only the bare charge or cuſtody of the goods of another, the legal poſſeſſion remains in the owner, and the party may be guilty of treſpaſs and larceny in fraudulently converting them to his own uſe. Thus a butler may commit larceny of plate in his cuſtody, or a ſhepherd of ſheep. The ſame of a ſervant intruſted to ſell goods in a ſhop. This rule appears to hold univerſally in the caſe of ſervants, whoſe poſſeſſion of their maſter's goods by their delivery or permiſſion is the poſſeſſion of the maſter himſelf. Still as the common law and the ſtatute left ſome caſes unremedied, and ſome doubts unſatisfied, particularly in thoſe inſtances, where not received into the maſter's actual poſſeſſion before the taking by the ſervant; the declaratory ſtatute of the 39 Geo. III. c. 85. was framed, which enacts and declares, that if any ſervant, clerk, or any perſon employed in the capacity of a ſervant or clerk, to any perſon or body corporate or politic, ſhall, by virtue of ſuch employment, receive or take into his poſſeſſion any money, goods, bond, bill, note, banker's draft, or other valuable ſecurity, or effects, for or in the name or on the account of his maſter or employers, and ſhall fraudulently embezzle, ſecrete, or make away with the ſame, or any part thereof; every ſuch offender ſhall be deemed to have felonioufly ſtolen the ſame, although the property was no otherwiſe received into the poſſeſſion of ſuch ſervant or clerk; and every ſuch offender, his adviſer, procuror, aider, or abettor, ſhall be tranſported for any term not exceeding fourteen years.

The

The law againſt embezzlement by ſervants or clerks in the bank is mentioned in this volume, p. 165; that relative to perſons in the poſt office at p. 36; and by the ſtat. 24 Geo. II. c. 11. the ſervants of the South-ſea Company are ſubjected to the ſame penalties.

For the ſecurity of manufacturers, who are obliged to intruſt large quantities of raw materials to their ſervants or workmen, ſeveral proviſions are made. The moſt general is in the ſtatute 17 Geo. III. c. 56. by which perſons employed in the felt or hat, woollen, linen, fuſtian, cotton, iron, leather, fur, hemp, flax, mohair or ſilk manufactures, or in manufactures of thoſe materials mixed one with another, who ſhall purloin, embezzle, ſecrete, ſell, pawn, exchange, or otherwiſe unlawfully diſpoſe of any of the materials with which they are intruſted, whether wrought up or not, are puniſhable in a ſummary manner before two juſtices; who are directed for the firſt offence to commit the offender to the houſe of correction or other public priſon, there to be kept to hard labour not leſs than fourteen days, nor more than three months, and for any ſubſequent offence, not leſs than three months, nor more than ſix; and in either caſe may alſo in diſcretion order the party to be publicly whipped. And if any perſon ſhall buy, receive, accept, or take by way of gift, pawn, pledge, ſale, or exchange, or in any other manner, from any ſuch perſon, ſuch materials, &c. they ſhall, on like ſummary conviction, for the firſt offence forfeit not leſs than 20*l.* nor more than 40*l.* or on failure of payment ſhall be committed in like manner for not more than ſix, nor leſs than three months, or committed for three entire days, and once publicly whipped; for a ſecond offence to be committed till the quarter ſeſſions, and on conviction forfeit not more than 100*l.* nor leſs than 50*l.* or on failure of payment ſhall be committed to the houſe of correction, to hard labour, not more than ſix, nor leſs than three months, or for three entire days, and to be once publicly whipped. Selling, pawning, pledging, exchanging, or otherwiſe unlawfully diſpoſing of any of the ſaid materials, knowing them to have been embezzled, &c. ſubjects the offender to the ſame puniſhment as the principal.

The property of the plate glaſs manufactory is protected by a particular ſtatute, 13 Geo. III. c. 38. which enacts that if any perſon or perſons ſhall by day or night break into any houſe, ſhop, cellar, vault, or other place, or building, or by force enter into any houſe, &c belonging to the ſaid manufactory, or wherein the ſame ſhall be then carrying on, with intent to ſteal, cut, break, or otherwiſe deſtroy any glaſs, or plate glaſs, wrought or unwrought, or any materials, tools, or implements, uſed in, for, or about, the making thereof, or any goods

goods and wares belonging to the ſaid manufactory; or ſhall ſteal, or wilfully or maliciouſly cut, break, or otherwiſe deſtroy, any ſuch glaſs, materials, tools, or implements; every ſuch offender ſhall be tranſported not exceeding ſeven years. But the ſtat. 38 Geo. III. c. 17. (local and private acts) enables the court before whom any ſuch offender is tried, to adjudge him to ſuffer a leſs puniſhment.

Stealing woollen cloth or manufacture from the rack or tenters where it is put to dry, in the night time, is declared by 22 Chas. II. c. 5. to be felony without benefit of clergy; but the court has a power to ſentence the offender to tranſportation for ſeven years, and he muſt ſuffer capitally if he returns within the time. The 15 Geo. II. c. 27. gives power to juſtices of the peace, on complaint of ſuch offences, to iſſue ſearch warrants, and on diſcovery of the goods to apprehend the poſſeſſor; and if he cannot give a good account of his poſ-ſeſſing them, to make him pay treble their value or be im-priſoned. For the ſecond offence, both forfeiture and im-priſonment are incurred, and on a third offence the party is to be committed till the next aſſizes, or great ſeſſions, where he ſhall be tried; and if he ſhall not, by producing the party of whom he acquired the property or poſſeſſion of ſuch goods, or otherwiſe, prove to the ſatisfaction of the jury, that he lawfully obtained them, he ſhall be tranſported for ſeven years. But this act does not alter any former law in force for ſtealing or receiving ſuch cloth, woollen yarn or wool, except by laying the proof on the offen-der.

By 18 Geo. II. c. 27. every perſon who ſhall, by day or night, feloniouſly ſteal any linen, fuſtian, calico, cotton cloth, or cloth worked, woven, or made of any cotton or linen yarn mixed, or any thread, linen, or cotton tape, incle, filletting, laces, or any other linen, fuſtian, or cotton goods or wares, laid, placed, or expoſed to be printed, whitened, bowked, bleached, or dried, in any whitening or bleaching grounds, houſe, or other building, ground, or place, made uſe of by any calico printer, whitſter, crofter, bowker, or bleacher, to the value of ten ſhillings; or who ſhall aid or aſſiſt, or procure any other perſon to commit any ſuch offence; or who ſhall buy or receive any ſuch goods knowing them to be ſtolen, ſhall be deemed guilty of felony without benefit of clergy. But the court may, in-ſtead of giving judgment of death, order ſuch offender to be tranſported for fourteen years, but then breaking jail, or returning from tranſportation, before the term, is felony without clergy. Alſo the 4 Geo. III. c. 37. makes the breaking into any

any houſe, ſhop, or other place or building, with intent to ſteal, cut, or deſtroy, any linen, yarn, or cloth, &c. felony without benefit of clergy.

The ſtealing of any kind of military, naval, or ordnance ſtores or proviſions, to the value of twenty ſhillings, is made felony by the 31 Eliz. c. 4. and clergy is taken away by the 22 Chas. II. c. 5.; but the court may cauſe the offender to be tranſported for ſeven years. And although the ſtatute fixes the value to be ſtolen at twenty ſhillings, ſtill they who rob to a ſmaller amount may be indicted at the common law.

The ſtat. 3 and 4 W. and M. c. 9. enacts and declares, that if any perſon ſhall take away, with intent to ſteal, any chattel, bedding, or furniture, which by contract or agreement he is to uſe, or ſhall be let to him in any lodging; ſuch taking ſhall be adjudged larceny and felony; and the offender ſhall ſuffer as in caſe of felony. But it has been decided that an entire houſe let ready furniſhed is not within the proviſions of this act.

It is a common error to believe that it is no felony for one, reduced to extreme neceſſity, to take ſo much of another's victuals, as will ſave him from ſtarving; ſuch a caſe, ſtrongly and evidently apparent, might be a good ground for a recommendation to mercy, but no juſtification of felony.

Larceny muſt be committed of *goods* perſonal, and not of chattels real, or ſuch as are annexed to the freehold, unleſs in certain caſes provided for by ſtatute; for at common law it is merely a treſpaſs, and not a felony to take ſuch things. Therefore by the common law, no larceny can be committed of trees, graſs, hedges, ſtones or lead of a houſe, or the like; but when once they are ſevered from the freehold, either by the owner, or even by the thief himſelf, if there be an interval between his ſevering and taking them away, ſo that it cannot be conſidered as one continued act, it would then be felony. But ſeveral exceptions to the general rule have been made by ſtatute.

The 6 Geo. III. c. 36. enacts that every perſon who ſhall, in the night time, pluck up, dig up, break, ſpoil, or deſtroy, or carry away, any roots, ſhrubs, or plants, of the value of five ſhillings, being in any garden, nurſery, or other encloſed ground, ſhall be guilty of felony, and tranſported for ſeven years. And perſons abetting or aſſiſting, or who ſhall buy or receive ſuch roots or plants, of the value aforeſaid, knowing them to be ſtolen, ſhall be ſubject to the ſame puniſhment. By another ſtatute of the ſame ſeſſion, (c. 48.) every perſon who ſhall pluck up, cut, ſpoil, deſtroy, take, or carry away, any root or plant out of any fields, nurferies, gardens, or garden-grounds, or other cultivated lands; and fhall be convicted before one juftice of the peace, fhall forfeit for the firft offence not exceeding forty fhillings; for the fecond, not exceeding 5*l*.; and if convicted of a third offence fhall be tranfported for feven years. Larceny in refpect to other growing crops, as turnips, potatoes, cabbages, parfnips, peas, or carrots, fubjects the offender, on fummary conviction before a juftice of peace, to a fmall fine, or, in default, to imprifonment in the houfe of correction.

Statutes alfo provide exprefsly againft fome other modes of larceny.

By 6 Geo. III. c. 36. in the night time to lop, top, cut down, break, throw down, bark, burn, or otherwife fpoil or deftroy, or carry away any oak, beech, afh, elm, fir, chefnut, or afp timber tree, or other tree ftanding for timber, or likely to become timber, is felony and punifhable with tranfportation for feven years. Aiders and abbettors to be treated as the principals.

By ftatute of the fame feffion, c. 48. the fame or nearly the fame offences, in any of the king's forefts or chafes, fubject the offender, on conviction before one juftice of peace, for the firft offence to forfeit a fum not exceeding 20*l*.; for a fecond offence not exceeding 30*l*.; and for the third offence to be tranfported for feven years. For the purpofes of that act, oak, beech, chefnut, walnut, afh, elm, cedar, fir, afp, lime, fycamore, and birch trees, fhall be deemed timber trees; to which the 13 Geo. III. c. 33. adds poplar, alder, larch, maple, and hornbeam.

By 4 Geo. II. c. 32. every perfon who fhall fteal, rip, cut, or break, with intent to fteal, any lead, iron bar, iron gate, iron palifadoe, or iron rail whatfoever, being fixed to any dwelling-houfe, out-houfe, coach-houfe, ftable, or other building, or fixed in any garden, orchard, court-yard, fence or outlet, belonging to any houfe, or building, fhall be deemed guilty of felony; and may be tranfported for feven years; abettors and receivers the fame. The 21 Geo. III. c. 68. made to explain and amend the former, declares that they who fhall fteal, rip, cut, break, or remove with intent to fteal any copper, brafs, or bell-metal utenfil, or fixture, being fixed to any dwelling-houfe, out-houfe, or other building, ufed or occupied with, or belonging to, a dwelling-houfe or other building, or fixed in any garden, court-yard, or outlet belonging thereto, or any iron rails or fencing fet up or fixed in any fquare, court, or other place, fhall be in like manner tranfported for feven years, or kept in prifon to hard labour, not more than three years, nor lefs than

than one; and once at leaſt, but not more than thrice, publicly whipped. Abettors or receivers ſubject to the ſame puniſhment.

By 25 Geo. II. c. 10. breaking and entering by force into any black-lead mine, with intent to ſteal any wad, or black cawke, or black lead, or ſtealing any, although the entry was not by force: or aiding, abetting, or procuring any perſon to commit ſuch offence; is felony; puniſhable with one year's impriſonment and hard labour; public whipping; or tranſportation for ſeven years; breaking priſon, or returning before the expiration of the term, felony without clergy.

By 39 and 40 Geo. III. c. 77. any perſon ſtealing any coal, culm, or coak, wood, iron, ropes, or leather, not exceeding the value of five ſhillings, from any bank, yard, wharf, or other place, belonging to any manufacturer or coal dealer, or off or out of any boat, barge, waggon, cart, or other carriage; or ſtealing or embezzling any tools or implements uſed for cutting or getting coal, culm, or other minerals, not exceeding the value above mentioned, and being convicted before one juſtice of peace, is ſubjected to certain penalties, or impriſonment in lieu thereof, or until payment, but no other proſecution. And miners taking or removing iron ſtone or iron ore, with intent to defraud the proprietor, may on conviction before a juſtice of peace be impriſoned not exceeding three months.

As larceny cannot be committed of things real at common law, neither can it be committed of charters or other written aſſurances concerning the realty, becauſe they favour of the ſame nature; nor can it be committed even of the box or cheſt in which they are kept.

The ſame rule prevailed with reſpect to records, writs, and other proceſs of the courts of law and equity; but by 8 Hen. VI. c. 12. if any record, or parcel of the ſame, writ, return, panel, proceſs, or warrant of attorney, in the king's ſuperior courts, or in his treaſury, be ſtolen, withdrawn, or avoided by any clerk, or other perſon; ſo that any judgment be reverſed; ſuch offender, his procurers, counſellors, and abettors, being duly convicted by their own confeſſion, or by inqueſt, (half of which ſhall be of the men of any of the ſame courts (*i. e.* officers) and the other of other men, (*i. e.* of common jurors) ſhall be guilty of felony. And the inquiry ſhall be before the judges of the one or the other bench. Though acceſſaries before are only named in the ſtatute, yet there may be acceſſaries after by the general conſtruction of law. This ſtatute only extends to the courts expreſsly named, and to the court of chancery, ſo far only as it proceeds according to the courſe of the common law, And it does not extend to the judges; becauſe clerks are firſt named,

named, who are inferior to them. But judges in all cases, as well as others in cases not made felony by the above act, are by the stat. 8 Rich. II. c. 4. to pay a fine to the king, and make satisfaction to the party, for falsely entering pleas, or rasing rolls, or changing verdicts, to the disherison of any one.

In order to make the stealing of goods felony, they ought to have some worth in themselves, and not merely from their relation to some other thing: and therefore bonds, bills, notes, and other securities, which concern mere *choses in action*, were not the subjects of larceny at common law, as they were of no intrinsic value; but now, by 2 Geo. II. c. 25. it is enacted, "that if any person shall steal any "exchequer orders, or tallies, or other orders, intitling any "other person to any annuity, or share in any parliament-"ary fund, or any exchequer bills, bank-notes, south-sea "bonds, East-India bonds, dividend warrants, of the bank, "South-sea company, East India company, or any other "company, society, or corporation, bills of exchange, navy "bills or debentures, Goldsmith's notes for the payment of "money or other bonds, or warrants, bills or promissory notes, "for the payment of any money, being the property of "any other person, or of any corporation; notwithstanding "any of the said particulars are termed in law a *chose in* "*action*; shall be deemed guilty of felony of the same na-"ture, and in the same degree, and with or without the "benefit of clergy, in the same manner as it would have "been, if the offender had stolen any other goods of like "value with the money due on such orders, &c. or secur-"ed thereby, and remaining unsatisfied."

It is generally said that larceny cannot be committed of that wherein none have any determinate property, as of treasure-trove, waifs, &c. till seized. The same was said of wreck; but now the legislature have by a most just and humane statute, (26 Geo. II. c. 19.) protected property in this state against plunderers. Nor can larceny be committed of such animals in which there is no property, as of beasts that are *feræ naturæ*, and unreclaimed; such as deers, hares, and conies in a forest, chase, or warren; fish in an open river, or pond; old pigeons out of the house; or wild fowls at their natural liberty: although any person may have an exclusive right *ratione loci aut privilegii*, to take them if he can in those places. But if they are dead, reclaimed, and known to be so, or confined and may serve for food, it is otherwise even at common law. For of deer so inclosed in a park, which may be taken at pleasure; fish in a trunk or net, or as it should seem in any other inclosed place which is private

private property, and where they may be taken at the pleafure of the owner at any time; pheafants or partridges in a mew; young pigeons, or old ones when fhut up; young hawks in a neft, and even old ones, or falcons reclaimed and known by the party to be fo; larceny may be committed. The fame as to peacocks: fo of fwans marked and pinioned, or fwans unmarked, if tame, kept in a mote, pond, or private river: but if they range out of the royalty, it is no felony to take them though marked, becaufe it cannot be known that they belong to any perfon. Nor can larceny be committed of the eggs of thefe, or of hawks; becaufe the ftat. 11 Hen. VII. c. 17. has appointed a lefs punifhment, namely, fine and imprifonment. But the ftealing a ftock of bees, feems to be admitted to be felony.

By 1 Hen. VII. c. 7. the unlawful hunting in any foreft, park, or warren, being private property, in warlike array, by night or with painted faces, &c. was made felony. But the ufe of that ftatute, which feems principally to have been levelled at public difturbers of the peace, is fuperfeded by the more general law of the black act, 9 Geo. I. c. 22. whereby if any perfon armed with fword, fire-arms, or other offenfive weapons, and having his face blacked, or being otherwife difguifed, fhall appear in any foreft, chafe, park, paddock, or grounds inclofed, wherein any deer are ufually kept; or in any high road, open heath, common, or down; or fhall unlawfully hunt, wound, kill, deftroy, or fteal, any red or fallow deer; or rob any warren, or place where conies or hares are ufually kept; or fteal fifh out of any pond or river; or if any perfon, whether armed and difguifed, or not, fhall unlawfully hunt, wound, kill, deftroy, or fteal any red or fallow deer, fed or kept in any inclofed places in any of the king's forefts or chafes, or in any park, paddock, or grounds enclofed, where deer are ufually kept, or fhall forcibly refcue any perfon lawfully in cuftody for any of fuch offences, or fhall by gift or promife procure any to join in any fuch unlawful act; fuch offender fhall be guilty of felony without benefit of clergy. He may be tried in any county in England, but corruption of blood, &c. is faved. That part of the claufe which relates to hunting, killing, or ftealing red, or fallow deer, in any foreft, chafe, or inclofed place, where deer have been ufually kept, not being armed and difguifed, is repealed by 16 Geo. III. c. 30. which punifhes the firft offence with a pecuniary forfeiture, and a fecond with tranfportation for feven years. Although the ftatute only mentions red and fallow deer, yet the crofs breeds are within its provifions.

It has been doubted whether at common law, larceny can be committed

committed of fish in a pond; but by 5 Geo. III. c. 14. if any person enter into any park or paddock, fenced in or enclosed, or into any garden, orchard, or yard, belonging to any dwelling-house, through which any river or stream of water shall run, or wherein shall be any river, stream, pond, or other water; and shall steal or destroy any fish bred or kept in any such river, &c. or shall be aiding or assisting therein, or receive or buy any such fish, knowing them to be stolen, he shall, if indicted within six calendar months before any judge, or justices of jail delivery for the county, be transported for seven years. An offender discovering and convicting an accomplice is intitled to a pardon. If any person shall take, kill, or destroy, or attempt to take, kill, or destroy, any fish in any river or stream, pond, pool, or other water, not being in such places as before mentioned, but in any other inclosed ground, private property; he shall, on summary conviction, forfeit 5*l.* to the owner.

With respect to conies and hares, the general result of several statutes appears to be, that by 3 James I. c. 13. if a wrong doer shall hunt, drive out, take, or kill, any coney in the night time, in any inclosed ground kept for that purpose, which was such at the time of passing the act, or has become so since, by the king's licence, he may be prosecuted for the misdemeanor at the assizes or sessions. By the 22 and 23 Chas. II. c. 25. if he chase, take, or kill any coney, either by day or night, in any ground used for keeping conies, whether inclosed or not, he is liable to be convicted before a magistrate. The 5 Geo. III. c. 14. gives jurisdiction to the justices of oyer and terminer, and jail delivery, where the offence of *taking* or *killing* any coney is committed in the night in any ground usually appropriated to the keeping of them whether enclosed or not; and gives a discretionary power of transporting the offender. And if any such place where hares or conies are kept is robbed at any time, by any offender armed and disguised, it is made felony without benefit of clergy, by the black act.

But there are some animals, which, though they may be reclaimed, yet are considered of so base a nature that no larceny can be committed of them; such as bears, foxes, monkies, cats, ferrets and the like. And the same rule applied to dogs; but now, by statute 10 Geo. III. c. 18. the stealing of dogs is made punishable upon conviction before two justices, by forfeiture for the first offence of not less than 20*l.* nor more than 30*l.* with costs, and for default to be committed not less than six nor more than twelve calendar months. A renewed offence subjects the party to a fine not exceeding 50*l.* nor less than 30*l.* with costs; or to imprisonment not exceeding eighteen nor less than twelve months.

Of

Of domeſtic animals, ſuch as ſheep, oxen, horſes, and the like; or of domeſtic creatures which are fit for food, as hens, ducks, geeſe, turkeys, peacocks, &c.; and alſo of their eggs, larceny may be committed. Concerning ſome of theſe, particular proviſion has been made. By ſtatutes 1 Ed. VI. c. 12.; 2 & 3 Ed. VI. c. 33. the ſtealing of horſes, mares, geldings, foals, and fillies, is felony without clergy; and by 31 Eliz. c. 12. acceſſaries are in the ſame ſituation with principals. By 14 Geo. II. c. 6. to ſteal ſheep, or to kill them and take away parts, leaving the reſidue, is felony without clergy; and by 15 Geo. II. c. 34. the words *other cattle*, which had been uſed in the preceding act are declared, to extend to any bull, ox, ſteer, bullock, heifer, calf, and lamb, as well as ſheep, and to no other cattle whatſoever.

In order to prevent the trade of boiling horſe-fleſh from facilitating the practice of ſtealing cattle, the 26 Geo. III. c. 71. enacts, that no perſon ſhall keep any houſe or place for the purpoſe of ſlaughtering or killing any horſe, aſs, ox, ſheep, hog, goat, or other cattle which ſhall not be killed for butcher's meat, without firſt obtaining a licence at the general quarter ſeſſions for the county or place where the trade is to be carried on. The veſtries of pariſhes wherein ſuch ſlaughter-houſes are ſituate, are to appoint inſpectors, to whom the proprietors are to give notice in writing, containing an accurate deſcription of all cattle intended to be ſlaughtered, and of the time when. If the inſpector has reaſon to believe that any beaſt of which he has received notice is in a ſound or ſerviceable ſtate, or has been ſtolen or unlawfully obtained, he may prohibit the ſlaughtering for eight days, and advertiſe the circumſtances, twice or oftener in the newſpapers, and unleſs the owner of the animal ſhall ſatiſfactorily aſſure the inſpector that it was ſent to be killed with his conſent, the keeper of the houſe ſhall pay the expence of advertiſing. Perſons bringing cattle to be ſlaughtered, or bringing them already dead to be flayed, and not giving a ſatisfactory account of themſelves, and of the means by which they became poſſeſſed of the cattle, may be taken before a juſtice of peace and committed. Perſons uſing any ſuch ſlaughtering houſe without a licence, are to be tranſported for ſeven years. Thoſe who deſtroy, bury, or rub with corroſive matters any hides for the purpoſe of diſguiſing them; or offending againſt the act in any particular not expreſsly provided for, to be guilty of miſdemeanors, and puniſhed by fine, impriſonment, or corporal puniſhment. Perſons making falſe entries in any book, directed by the act to be kept, forfeit not more than twenty, nor leſs than ten pounds, or are to be committed to hard labour not exceeding three months nor leſs than one. They who lend any

 houſe,

houſe, barn, or place for ſuch ſlaughtering, without licence, are to be impriſoned for the like period; and witneſſes refuſing to attend juſtices forfeit ten pounds, or are committed for the like term.

It being felony to ſteal the animals themſelves, it is alſo felony to ſteal the product of them, though taken from them while living. Thus milking cows at paſture, and ſtealing the milk, was holden felony by all the judges. So, pulling the wool from the ſheep's backs is felony; it being underſtood in this, as in the other inſtance, that the fact is done fraudulently and feloniouſly, and not merely from wantonneſs or frolic; which muſt be collected from concurrent circumſtances, ſuch as the quantity taken, the uſe to which it is applied, the behaviour of the party, &c.

Such are the principal things in reſpect of which larceny may be committed.

The Place in which the offence is perpetrated is material, as many ſtatutes have been paſſed, more for the purpoſe of protecting particular places from being plundered, than of ſecuring any ſpecific property preſerved there: although attention muſt ſtill be paid, in ſome inſtances, to the general nature of the property taken. Larceny from the houſe is not diſtinguiſhed at common law from ſimple larceny, unleſs where it is accompanied with the circumſtance of breaking the houſe at night, when it falls under the deſcription of burglary. This offence may be effected, as well where the delivery of a thing out of the houſe is obtained by an artifice from any perſon therein at the time, as where the thief himſelf enters and takes it. In robbery and burglary the value is immaterial, for thoſe were capital offences before the ſtatute allowing clergy; and under different ſtatutes clergy is ouſted generally; but in all other caſes of larceny committed in a dwelling-houſe, where clergy is taken away, the value muſt exceed a ſhilling, or it is not a capital offence; and now, by various acts of parliament, the benefit of clergy is taken away from larcenies committed in a houſe in almoſt every inſtance. The multiplicity of thoſe proviſions creates ſome confuſion, but the general reſult is, that benefit of clergy is denied on the following domeſtic aggravations of larceny:

I. *In Larcenies above the value of 12d. committed,*

1. In a church or chapel, with or without violence or breaking.

2. In a booth or tent in a fair or market, in the day or night, by violence or breaking, the owner or ſome of

 his

his family being therein; though they need not be put in fear.

3. By robbing a dwelling-houſe in the day time, (which robbing implies a breaking;) any perſon being therein, though not put in fear.

4. In a dwelling-houſe, by day or night, without breaking, any perſon being therein and put in fear; which amounts in law to a robbery: and in both theſe laſt inſtances, acceſſaries before the fact are excluded clergy.

II. *In Larcenies to the value of 5s. committed,*

1. By breaking any dwelling-houſe, or any out-houſe, ſhop, or warehouſe, thereto belonging, in the day time, though no perſon be therein: which extends to aiders, abettors, and acceſſaries before the fact.

2. By privately ſtealing goods, wares, or merchandizes, in any ſhop, warehouſe, coach-houſe, or ſtable, by day or night; though the ſame be not broken open, and though no perſon be therein: which extends likewiſe to ſuch as aſſiſt, hire, or command the offence to be committed.

III. *In Larcenies to the value of 40s.*

In a dwelling houſe or its out-houſes, though not broken open, and whether any perſon be therein or not, unleſs committed by apprentices under the age of fifteen, againſt their maſters: this alſo extends to aiders and aſſiſters.

This abridged ſtatement is given by Mr. Eaſt as an index to a great number of ſtatutes, and a great variety of caſes which it would be tedious here to enumerate.

By the 24 Geo. II. c. 45. all perſons who ſhall feloniouſly ſteal any goods, wares, or merchandize, of the value of 40s. in any ſhip, barge, lighter, boat, or other veſſel or craft, on any navigable river, or in any port of entry or diſcharge, or in any creek belonging to ſuch river or port, or upon any wharf or quay adjacent; or who ſhall be preſent, aiding and aſſiſting in committing any ſuch offences, ſhall be excluded from the benefit of clergy. The penalty of plundering wrecks has already been mentioned.

The conſideration to whom THE PROPERTY in the things ſtolen belongs is very material. Some things are not the ſubject of property at all, or only ſo *ratione loci* or *privilegii*; and others are only ſuch *ſub modo*, that is, where ſome perſon has

 acquired

acquired a ſpecial dominion over them. But with reſpect to things which are the regular ſubjects of property, felony may be committed in ſtealing them, though the owner be not known; for the guilt of the thief is the ſame. He may therefore be charged in the indictment with having ſtolen the goods of a perſon to the jury unknown; or with having received goods ſtolen by a perſon unknown. And in ſuch caſe the king ſhall have the goods. But if the owner be really known, an indictment alleging the goods to be the property of a perſon unknown, would be improper; the priſoner muſt be diſcharged of that indictment, and tried upon a new one, for ſtealing the goods of the owner by name; and in the proſecutions for ſtealing the goods of a perſon unknown, ſome proof muſt be given ſufficient to raiſe a reaſonable preſumption that the taking was felonious or *invito domino*; for it is not enough that the priſoner is unable to give a good account how he came by the goods.

The EVIDENCE neceſſary to ſupport indictments for larceny, is beſt conſidered by adverting to the various modes of defence by which ſuch charges are palliated or denied.

1. *Denial of the Fact.* It may be laid down generally, that wherever the property of one man, which has been taken from him without his knowledge or conſent, is found upon another, it is incumbent on that other to prove how he came by it; otherwiſe the preſumption is, that he obtained it feloniouſly. This, like every other preſumption, is ſtrengthened, weakened, or rebutted by concomitant circumſtances, too numerous in the nature of the thing to be detailed. But the bare finding in one's poſſeſſion property of the ſame kind which another has loſt, unleſs that other can from marks or other circumſtances ſatisfy the jury of its identity, is not in general ſufficient evidence that the goods were feloniouſly obtained. Yet, where the fact is very recent, ſo as to afford reaſonable preſumption that the property could not have been acquired in any other manner, the court are warranted in concluding it is the ſame, unleſs the priſoner can prove the contrary. The confeſſion of the priſoner is often adduced in this caſe; but on this, as upon other occaſions, care muſt be taken to aſcertain, that ſuch confeſſion was not procured by promiſe or threat; as in ſuch caſes it ought not to be received.

2. *That the Goods were taken on a Claim of Right.* Goods may be ſo taken by the party's own immediate act, or by the act of the law through his means; but if it appear that a writ or proceſs is iſſued with the mere intent of gaining poſſeſſion

possession of the effects of another, without the least foundation for a claim, it is felony.

3. *By Mistake or Accident.* Analogous to the taking upon a claim of right, is the taking by mistake arising from heedlessness, or from mere accident; but in this case the mistake must be very apparent, and the conduct of the party free from all attempts to disguise, conceal, or clandestinely dispose of the property.

4. *On taking as a Trespasser, without Fraud.* The taking may amount only to a trespass, and the circumstances in such case must guide the judgment. As where a man takes another's goods openly before him or before other persons, otherwise than by apparent robbery; or having possessed himself of them, avows the fact before he is questioned.

5. *Finding.* Another defence is, that the goods were found. This is connected in great measure with the first mentioned mode of defence. It is the most trite excuse in cases of larceny, and in general the least founded. Still if the fact be so, it is no felony; although it may be attended with all those circumstances which usually prove a taking with a felonious intent; such as denying or secreting it.

6. *On a Possession by Delivery of a third Person.* It is a common mode of defence to state a delivery by a person unknown, and of whom no evidence is given: little or no reliance can consequently be had upon it. But this defence, however improbable, is entitled to consideration, since it is, if true, a valid defence.

7. The most comprehensive and most intricate line of defence is, *That the goods were delivered to the prisoner by or on behalf of the owner; or were taken with his consent or approbation.* For if it be proved that there was no trespass or felonious intent in taking the goods, no subsequent conversion of them can amount to felony. This defence involves, first, those cases where persons being previously apprised of an intention to commit a larceny, give facilities in order to detect and secure the thieves; the conviction or acquittal in these cases depends upon very minute circumstances. Second, where property is obtained with the consent of the owner, but extorted by threats of charging him with crimes; this is generally considered as robbery from the person. Third, cases where the inquiry is, whether the owner, in making the delivery, intended to part with the *property*, or only with the *possession* of the thing delivered; for if he parted with the *property* to the prisoner, by whatever fraudulent means he was induced to give the credit, it cannot be felony; but if the possession only was delivered, then it is materal to inquire whe-

ther the delivery was by way of charge, or as a general bailment, or for some special purpose. In this class are considered the cases of obtaining property by fraudulent appearances; by promises to return and pay for things delivered; by preconcerted fraudulent gaming; by ordering goods on promise to pay for them on delivery, and then retaining them without payment, and numerous other artifices by which money and goods are obtained. In this defence are also included the cases of those who, having got bills into their possession for the pretended purpose of discounting, keep or make away with them; of those who draw money or goods from the ignorant or credulous under pretext of finding valuable jewels or other things, in which the dupe supposes he is to share. In the consideration of this mode of defence, which applies also to a vast variety of other cases, the mode and intent of the delivery of the goods, or money alleged to be stolen, are often very material. The general result of the cases is, that if a person obtain the goods of another by a lawful delivery without fraud, although he afterwards convert them to his own use, he cannot be guilty of felony. As, if a tailor has cloth delivered to him to make clothes with; or a carrier receives goods to carry to a certain place; or a friend is intrusted with property to keep for the owner's use; which they afterwards severally embezzle. So if plate is delivered to a goldsmith to work or weigh, or as a deposit, his conversion of it will not be felony; but if such delivery is obtained by any fraud or falsehood with intent to steal, though under pretence of a hiring, or even a purchase; if in the latter case no credit was intended to be given, delivery in fact by the owner will not pass the legal possession, so as to save the party from the guilt of felony. But if the property were intended to pass by the delivery, there can be no felonious taking.

8. *Taking through necessity* is a common defence, but its want of validity has been noticed in a preceding page.

Larceny and Robbery from the Person. The crime of larceny from the person may be aggravated in two different manners. 1st. Where the thing is taken from the person *privately without the knowledge of the owner*; 2d. Where the person from whom it is taken is *put in fear* at the time, or the taking is accompanied with circumstances of *violence, threat, or terror*, which are sufficient grounds for presuming fear; in which case it assumes the denomination of robbery.

The first of these offences is derived from the stat. 8 Eliz. c. 4. which recites, that "whereas certain evil disposed persons, commonly called cut-purses or pick-purses, but indeed by the laws

laws of this land very felons and thieves, do confeder together, making among themselves as it were a brotherhood or fraternity of an art or mystery to live idly by the secret spoil of the good subjects of this realm; and as well at sermons and preachings of the word of God, and in places and times of doing service and common prayer, in churches, chapels, closets, and oratories, and not only there, but also in the prince's palace and presence, and at the places and courts of justice, and at the times of ministering of the laws in the same, and in fairs, markets, and other assemblies of the people, and at the time of doing execution, &c. do, without regard to any place, time, or person, &c. under the cloak of honesty by their outward apparent countenance and behaviour, subtily, privily, craftily, and feloniously, take the goods of divers subjects from their persons, by cutting and picking their purses, and other felonious slights and devices, &c." and enacts that no person indicted or appealed for feloniously taking of any money, goods, or chattels from the person of any other *privily without his knowledge*, in any place whatsoever; and thereupon found guilty, shall be admitted to benefit of clergy. The statute is confined to him who actually commits the fact, and extends not to accessaries before or after, nor even to those who are present aiding and abetting. Wherefore if there is an accomplice present, and it can not be told which of them took the goods, neither can be convicted of the capital part of the charge. There must be an actual taking from the person; taking in his presence is not sufficient, as it is in robbery. The stealing of notes, &c. is within the statute. The goods stolen must be above the value of 12d.; otherwise clergy is not ousted, as in robbery; for the statute was not intended to alter the nature of the crime, but only to exclude clergy where it was before necessary to procure the benefit of it.

Any sort of secret or sudden taking from the person, without putting him in fear, and without terror or open violence, seems within the act; though some small force be used by the thief to possess himself of the property; provided there be no resistance by the owner, or injury to his person; and the circumstances of the case shew that the thing was taken, not so much against, as without, his consent. But in no case where the property is obtained by any struggling or violence to the person, does the offence fall within this statute.

It was formerly holden that persons asleep or drunk were not within the protection of the act, which speaks of places of public resort and the like, where persons were supposed to

 use

use ordinary caution, and not expose themselves by carelessness or misbehaviour to these accidents. Yet subsequent cases solemnly considered have put a more enlarged construction upon the statute, so as to protect all persons at least who have not exposed themselves to such a loss by their own negligence or misbehaviour.

The indictment must lay the offence to have been done *privily without the knowledge* of the party, in exact pursuance of the words of the statute, otherwise the prisoner will be intitled to his clergy. And so he is if the value be not laid as well as proved to be above 12*d*. And in this, as in other aggravated larcenies, the prisoner may be acquitted of the capital part of the charge, and found guilty of simple larceny.

Robbery. The next species of aggravated larceny from the person, is robbery; which is a felonious taking of money or goods, to any value, from the person of another, or in his presence against his will, by violence or putting him in fear.

It is sufficient to oust clergy if the thing taken be of any value, though under 12*d*.; for the gist of the offence is the force and terror; but something must be taken; for an assault with intent to rob is an offence of a different and inferior nature.

In robbery it is sufficient if the property be taken in the presence of the owner; it need not be taken immediately from his person, so that there be violence to his person, or putting him in fear.

As to the sort of violence necessary to be proved, where the property is obtained in that manner, it is to be observed that no sudden taking of a thing unawares from the person, as by snatching any thing from the hand or head, is sufficient to constitute a robbery, unless some injury is done to the person, or unless there is some previous struggle for the possession of the property. Even if the pretence is lawful or indifferent, if the true intent is to steal, under the definition before given, and the possession is obtained by force and violence from the person of the owner, or in his presence, it amounts to robbery. This crime may also be constituted by putting in fear as well as by force; or perhaps in strictness, it may be said that fear will supply the place of force. Yet it is not necessary that actual fear should either be laid in the indictment, or strictly and precisely proved; provided the property be taken with such circumstances of violence or terror, or threatening by word or gesture, as would in common experience induce a man to part with it from an apprehension of personal danger; for the law,

law, *in odium ſpoliatoris*, will preſume fear where there appears to be ſo reaſonable a ground for it. If a man be knocked down without previous warning, and ſtripped of his property while ſenſeleſs, he can with no propriety be ſaid to be put in fear; and yet that would undoubtedly be robbery. So a colourable gift, which in truth was extorted by fear, amounts to a taking and treſpaſs in law. As if a perſon with a drawn ſword, or other circumſtances of terror indicating a felonious intent, beg alms of another, who gives it him through miſtruſt and apprehenſion of violence, the offence is the ſame notwithſtanding the pretence. So it is whether there were any weapon drawn or not; or whether it were an offenſive weapon; or whether the perſon aſſaulted delivered his money uponthe other's command; or afterwards gave it him upon his ceaſing to uſe force, and aſking it for alms; for the owner was put in fear by the aſſault, and there remained a reaſonable ground for its continuance. The ſame rule holds, although the thing taken were not really within the original contemplation of the robber, nor the object of his purſuit at the time. As where a man aſſaulted a woman with intent to commit a rape, but on her giving him money, took it, and being alarmed by perſons coming up, deſiſted from his original purpoſe and ran off. If a perſon by force or threats compels another to give him goods, and by way of colour obliges him to take, or if he offers, leſs than the value, it is robbery.

It is difficult to define exactly what the nature of the fear implied in this crime muſt be; but it is clear, that on the one hand, the fear is not confined to an apprehenſion of bodily injury; and on the other hand, it muſt be of ſuch a nature as in reaſon and common experience is likely to induce a perſon to part with his property againſt his will, and to put him as it were under a temporary ſuſpenſion of the power of exerciſing it, through the influence of the terror impreſſed; in which caſe fear ſupplies, as well in ſound reaſon, as in legal conſtruction, the place of force, or an actual taking by violence, or aſſault upon the perſon. Thus, therefore, the extorting of money by threats of future violence, of pulling down or burning a perſon's houſe, or charging him with an unnatural crime, have all been conſidered as robberies.

Grand and Petit Larceny, and their Punishment. In grand larceny, the value of the property taken muſt be above 12d. If it be only of that value, or under, it is but petit larceny: and in theſe proſecutions the valuation ought to be reaſonable; for when the ſtat. of Weſtm 2. c. 25. was made, ſilver was but 20*d*. an ounce. The nature of the offence is the

ſame

ſame in both; they are both felony, though they differ in the degrees of their puniſhment, and in ſome other particulars. At common law the judgment for grand larceny is of death, but the party may pray the benefit of his clergy, unleſs in caſes where he is ouſted by particular ſtatutes; and he ſhall alſo loſe his goods. In petit larceny, the offender was only ſubject to whipping, or other corporal puniſhment leſs than death, by which is now underſtood impriſonment: and in this caſe he alſo forfeits his goods on conviction. But in robbery, whatever be the value, the judgment is death. Beſide theſe, ſeveral other modes of puniſhment have been introduced by various ſtatutes. Perſons to whom clergy is allowed, may, for their further correction, be impriſoned for any time not exceeding a year, in the diſcretion of the court; or they may be burnt in the hand, or committed to the houſe of correction, for not leſs than ſix months, nor more than two years; or, inſtead of theſe, the juſtices may order them to be tranſported for ſeven years; or, inſtead of tranſportation for ſeven years, to hard labour on board the hulks for not leſs than one year nor more than five; but if the term of tranſportation was fourteen years, he may be placed on board the hulks for ſeven. Inſtead of burning in the hand, a moderate fine may be impoſed, or public or private whipping, not more than three times, may be ordered.

Accessaries. Though it is true that in larceny and robbery all thoſe who come to ſteal or rob are principals, although the fact may only be committed by one of them, and are ſubject to the ſame puniſhments; yet it is otherwiſe as to larcenies deprived of clergy under particular circumſtances, ſuch as the caſe of ſtealing privately from the perſon, under the ſtat. 8 Eliz. c. 4.; and the 39 Eliz. c. 15. for breaking and entering a houſe, &c. and ſtealing to the value of 5*s*.; [though in the latter caſe the deficiency is ſupplied by the ſtat. 3 & 4. W. & M. c. 9:] in which caſes the abettors at the fact are not excluded from clergy, but remain liable only to the penalties of ſimple larceny. In petit larceny there can be no acceſſaries either before or after, although it is felony; becauſe it is not ſuch as judgment of death ought by law to be paſſed upon it, but procurers and counſellors are principals, as in treſpaſs. With reſpect to grand larceny, the common law reſpecting acceſſaries ſtands upon the ſame footing as in other felonies.

Receivers of stolen Goods. At common law no receivers were acceſſaries but ſuch as received or harboured the thief himſelf: the receiving of the ſtolen goods only, did not

make

make a man acceſſary, without taking a reward to favour the felon's eſcape. If the owner received back his goods ſimply and without any agreement to favour the felon in his proſecution, it was lawful: but if he received them upon an agreement not to proſecute, or to proſecute faintly, it was called *theftbote*, and puniſhable by impriſonment and ranſom. But now by ſtatute 3 W & M. c. 9. if any perſon ſhall buy or receive any goods or chattels, knowing the ſame to be ſtolen, he ſhall be deemed, and incur the ſame puniſhment as, an acceſſary after the fact. The 5 Ann. c. 31. enacts to the ſame effect in general words. And by 4 Geo. I. c. 11. perſons convicted of receiving or buying goods, knowing them to be ſtolen, may be tranſported for fourteen years; but they muſt pray the benefit of the ſtatute, or they will be capitally convicted under that of Anne. Before theſe acts, the receiving of ſtolen goods was merely a miſdemeanor; but now the miſdemeanor is merged in the felony; and therefore a proſecution for a miſdemeanor only would be illegal and improper. This however is to be underſtood of thoſe caſes only where the principal can be come at, ſo as to give an opportunity of convicting the receiver as an acceſſary to the felony. For till the ſtat 1 Ann. the receiver could not be proſecuted or puniſhed at all before the principal thief was tried and convicted; on this account the receiver, who is generally the employer and patron of the thief, often eſcaped with impunity; by keeping the thief out of the way. To remedy this inconvenience, the ſtat. 1 Ann. ſt. 2. c. 9. enacts, that it ſhall be lawful to proſecute every perſon buying or receiving goods, knowing them to be ſtolen, as for a miſdemeanor; to be puniſhed by fine and impriſonment, although the principal felon be not before convicted, which ſhall exempt the offender from being puniſhed as acceſſary, if the principal ſhall be afterwards convicted; and by 5 Ann. c. 31. it is provided, that if any ſuch principal felon cannot be taken, yet it ſhall be lawful to proſecute the receiver, as for a miſdemeanor. Upon a conviction under the laſt mentioned clauſes of the ſtatutes of Anne as for a miſdemeanor, the puniſhment is by fine, impriſonment, or corporal puniſhment, at the diſcretion of the judge, as in caſes of miſdemeanors; but the 4 Geo. I. c. 11. which ſubjects receivers to tranſportation for fourteen years, does not extend to proſecutions under the ſtatutes of Anne for a miſdemeanor only; and where the principal is amenable to juſtice, the receiver ought ſtill to be proſecuted as an acceſſary to the felony, and not for a miſdemeanor only.

Theſe ſtatutes however left the law imperfect, for under that of 5th Anne, a receiver could not be convicted after the prin-

principal felon had been tried and executed; but the 22 Geo. III. enacts, that in all cafes whatfoever, where any goods or chattels (except lead, iron, copper, brafs, bell-metal, and folder) fhall have been felonioufly taken or ftolen; whether the offence of the principal fhall amount to grand larceny, or fome greater offence, or to petit larceny, only; (except where the perfon or perfons actually committing the felony fhall already have been convicted of grand larceny, or of fome greater offence; every perfon who fhall buy or receive any fuch goods and chattels, knowing them to have been ftolen, fhall be deemed guilty of a mifdemeanor, and punifhed by fine, imprifonment, or whipping, as the court of quarter feffions (who are thereby empowered to try fuch offender) or as any other court before whom he fhall be tried, fhall think fit; although the principal felon be not before convicted, and whether he is amenable to juftice or not. And in cafes where the felony actually committed fhall amount to grand larceny, or to fome greater offence, and where the perfon actually committing it fhall not before be convicted, fuch offender fhall be exempted from being punifhed as acceffary, if fuch principal felon or felons fhall be afterwards convicted. One juftice of the peace, on complaint made before him on oath, that there is reafon to fufpect that ftolen goods are knowingly concealed in any dwelling houfe, or other place, may, by warrant under his hand and feal, caufe every fuch place to be fearched in the day time; and the perfons knowingly concealing the ftolen goods, or in whofe cuftody they are found, being privy thereto; fhall be deemed guilty of a mifdemeanor, (and may be brought before a juftice of peace, and made amenable to anfwer the fame by warrant), and punifhed in the manner aforefaid. This not to repeal any former law for the punifhment of fuch offenders.

The legiflature has alfo made particular provifions in a variety of cafes againft receivers of certain ftolen goods. By 29 Geo. II. c. 30. every perfon who fhall buy or receive any lead, iron, copper, brafs, bell-metal, or folder, knowing the fame to be unlawfully come by; or fhall privately buy or receive any ftolen lead, iron, copper, brafs, bell-metal, or folder, by fuffering any door, window, or fhutter, to be left open, or unfaftened between fun-fetting and fun-rifing for that purpofe; or fhall, buy or receive the fame, or any of them, at any time, in any clandeftine manner, from any perfon whatfoever; fhall, being thereof convicted by due courfe of law, although the principal felon has not been convicted, be tranfported for fourteen years. By 21 Geo. III. c. 69. fimilar punifhment is extended to thofe who receive ftolen pewter pots, or any pewter in any form or fhape ſhape whatever, knowing the ſame to be ſtolen or unlawfully come by. So by 2 Geo. III. c. 28. buying or receiving any goods, ſtores, or things belonging to any ſhip or veſſel in the river Thames, knowing the ſame to be ſtolen or unlawfully come by. By 10 Geo. III. c. 48. every perſon who ſhall buy or receive any jewels, or gold or ſilver plate, or watches, knowing them to have been ſtolen by burglary, or feloniouſly taken by a robbery on the high way, ſhall be triable as well before as after conviction of the principal felon, whether he ſhall be in or out of cuſtody, and tranſported for fourteen years. And perſons indicted for theſe offences are by 39 and 40 Geo. III. to plead inſtanter, and not allowed time to traverſe, as is uſual in caſes of miſdemeanors.

As the laws againſt ſtealing *naval ſtores* are very ſtrict, ſo are thoſe againſt the embezzlement of them. By 9 and 10 William, c. 41. no perſons but thoſe authorized by contracting with the king's principal officers or commiſſioners of the navy, ordnance, or victualling office, for his majeſty's uſe, may mark any ſtores of war, or naval ſtores whatſoever, with the marks generally uſed to his ſtores, on pain of forfeiting the goods and 200*l.* one half to the king, the other to the informer. A ſimilar penalty attends thoſe, who are convicted on indictment of concealing ſuch goods, or having them found in their poſſeſſion; unleſs upon the trial they produce a certificate under the hand of three or more of the king's officers or commiſſioners of the navy, ordnance, or victuallers, expreſſing the numbers, quantities, or weights of ſuch goods as they ſhall then be indicted for, and the occaſion and reaſon of ſuch goods coming to their hands or poſſeſſion. The 9 Geo. I. c. 8. extends the ſame penalty to thoſe who have in their cuſtody timber and other articles ſimilarly marked. By the 17 Geo. II. c. 40. the juſtices have power to cauſe the offenders to be publicly whipped, and committed to ſome houſe of correction, or public workhouſe, to be kept to hard labour for three months. But by 39 and 40 Geo. III. c. 89. the ſelling and delivering, or receiving, or having in cuſtody and concealing ſuch ſtores, without a proper certificate, ſubjects the party to be tranſported for fourteen years. And the puniſhment of offenders againſt the ſtat. 9 and 10 Wm. c. 41. is increaſed by pillory, whipping, and impriſonment. They who wilfully and fraudulently deſtroy, beat out, deface, or eraſe wholly or in part, any mark whatſoever denoting the property of his majeſty, in or to any ſtores; or procure others ſo to do, for the purpoſe of concealing his majeſty's property in ſuch ſtores; are to be deemed guilty of felony, and tranſported for fourteen years. Perſons not tranſported for their firſt offence, committing a ſecond, are to be tranſported for fourteen years, and if they return, hanged. But in all cafes the court may mitigate, or commute fuch punifhment to pillory, public whipping, fine, or imprifonment, or by all, or any one, or more of fuch ways and means, as the court fhall think fit; one moiety of the fine (if any impofed) going to his majefty, and the other to the informer; and alfo to order fuch offender to be imprifoned until the fine is paid. Informers, in all cafes where fummary conviction is not given, receive 20*l*., over and above their fhare of penalties. Againft minor offences, feveral inferior penalties are denounced; and by the 39 and 40 Geo. III. feveral mifdemeanors are created, and a fummary jurifdiction given to principal officers or commiffioners of the navy, or juftices of the peace, with an appeal however to the quarter feffions; and the act does not prevent proceeding againft the parties as receivers of ftolen goods, provided they be not twice profecuted for the fame offence.

To prevent the influence which the impunity of receivers gave them over thieves, the ftat. 4 Geo. I. c. 11. enacts, that whenever any perfon takes money or reward, directly or indirectly, under pretence or on account of helping any perfon to any ftolen goods or chattels; every fuch perfon, unlefs he apprehends the felon, and caufes him to be brought to trial, and gives evidence againft him, fhall be guilty of felony, and fuffer according to the nature of the felony committed in ftealing the goods, as if he had himfelf ftolen them. And they who difcover, apprehend, and profecute to conviction fuch offenders are intitled to a reward of 40*l*. On this act the noted Jonathan Wild was convicted and executed; the principal felon being examined as a witnefs on the part of the crown.

For the fame purpofe another ftatute 25 Geo. II. c. 36. enacts, that any perfon publicly advertifing a reward, with "no queftions afked," for the return of things which have been ftolen or loft, or that fuch reward fhall be paid without feizing or making inquiry after the perfon producing the things ftolen or loft; or promifing or offering in any fuch public advertifement to return to any pawn-broker or other perfon any money fo paid or advanced by way of loan on fuch things, or any other fum of money for the return of them; and any perfon printing or publifhing fuch advertifement; fhall refpectively forfeit 50*l*. to any perfon who will fue for the fame.

TRIAL. The general rule in trials for larceny and robbery, as in other cafes, is that the offenders muft be tried in the fame county or jurifdiction wherein they were committed. In afcertaining which, it is neceffary to advert to two leading principles, from which certain deviations are exceptions.

1. The

1. The poffeffion of goods ftolen by the thief is a larceny in every county into which he carries them; becaufe the legal poffeffion ftill remaining in the true owner, every moment's continuance of the trefpafs and felony amounts to a new caption and afportation; and therefore if a man fteals goods in one county, and carries them into another, he may be indicted or appealed of larceny in the latter county; though he can be only charged with robbery in the county where the force or putting in fear was.

2. Where clergy is oufted on circumftances of aggravation, fuch circumftances muft *all* be proved to have happened within the county in which the offender is tried; otherwife, the fact of the larceny only being eftablifhed in that county, he will be intitled to clergy.

Restitution of Goods. There are feveral methods by which the party robbed, or whofe goods are ftolen, may have reftitution;

1. By an appeal of robbery, or larceny. This procefs is not particularly defcribed, as it is in a great meafure fuperfeded by the remedy next mentioned.

2. The ftat. 21 Hen. VIII. c. 11. firft gave reftitution upon an indictment; it enacts that if any felon do take away any money, goods, or chattels, from any of the king's fubjects, and thereof be found guilty by reafon of evidence given by the party fo robbed, or owner of the faid money, goods, or chattels, or by any other by their procurement; then the owner fhall be reftored to his property, and, as well the juftices of jail delivery, as other juftices before whom any fuch felon fhall fo be found guilty, have power to award writs of reftitution, in like manner as though the felon was attainted at the fuit of the party in appeal. The writ of reftitution has fallen into difufe; but upon the production of the goods at the trial, the court orders them to be reftored to the owner, without any inquiry as to frefh fuit; and if not reftored, he may maintain trover for them after conviction; and this notwithftanding a fale in market overt. But reftitution can only be had from the perfon in poffeffion of the goods at the time of, or after, the felon's attainder. Therfore if a party purchafe them *bona fide* in market overt, and fell them again before conviction, no action will lie againft him for the value, though notice were given to him not to fell.

3. By common law. The neceffity of profecuting and convicting or attainting the felon, in order to have reftitution, is only when the property is changed by fome intermediate act; as by the felon's waving it in his flight; the feizing of it by the king's officers under fufpicion of felony; or by the lord of the manor, or by a fale in market overt. For otherwife the owner may,

at

at common law, peaceably retake his goods wherever he may find them, without any writ of restitution; but if the owner take them back from the offender with intent to favour him, it is unlawful, and punishable with fine and imprisonment.

4. Special provision has been made for restitution in the instance of horse-stealing, by the 31 Eliz. c. 12. which requires certain entries to be made in the toller's books of the sale of horses in markets and fairs, and enacts, that if any horse shall be stolen, and after sold in any fair or market, and the same sale shall be used in all points and circumstances as aforesaid, that yet, nevertheless, the sale within six months next after the felony shall not take away the property of the owner from whom it was stolen, so as he, or some one for him, claim within six months, at or in the town or parish where the horse, &c. shall be found, before the mayor, or other head officer of a town corporate, or market town, or else before any justice of peace of that county near to the place, and so as proof be made within the next forty days, by two witnesses, before such head officer or justice, that the property was in the claimant, and was stolen from him; the party, his executors, or administrators, may then take again the horse, &c. upon payment, or offer to the party in possession, of so much money as he shall swear that he paid for the same *bona fide* without fraud or collusion.

5. Another method of obtaining, not indeed the very goods stolen, but a compensation for their value, is by suing the hundred wherein the robbery was committed, for neglecting to take the felon, which they are empowered to do by hue and cry. An hue (from *huer*, to shout) and cry, *hutesium et clamor*, is the old common law process of pursuing, with horn and with voice, all felons, and such as have dangerously wounded another. The principal statute, relative to this matter, is that of Winchester, 13 Edw. I. c. 1. & 4. which directs, that from thenceforth every country shall be so well kept, that immediately upon robberies and felonies committed, fresh suit shall be made from town to town, and from county to county; and that the hue and cry shall be raised upon the felons; and they that keep the town shall follow with hue and cry, with all the town and towns near; and so hue and cry shall be made from town to town, until they be taken and delivered to the sheriff. And if the county will not answer for the bodies of such offenders within the space of forty days, the inhabitants of the whole hundred where the robbery shall be done, with the franchises, being within precinct of the same, shall be answerable for the robberies and damages. But these statutes being thought oppressive, in subjecting the hundred to an action, notwithstanding its utmost exertions

exertions to apprehend the offender; and alſo to force the ſurrounding hundreds, as well as the party robbed, to contribute their aſſiſtance to attain the ends of public juſtice; it is enacted by the 27 Eliz. c. 18. That the inhabitants of every hundred wherein negligence, fault, or defect of purſuit and freſh ſuit, after hue and cry made, ſhall happen to be, ſhall anſwer and ſatisfy by the one moiety of the damages, which ſhall by force of the ſaid ſtatutes be recovered againſt the hundred in which the felony was committed. That no hue and cry ſhall be allowed as lawful, except the ſame be done and made by horſemen and footmen. That no perſon robbed ſhall maintain any action upon theſe ſtatutes, unleſs he ſhall, with as much convenient ſpeed as may be, give intelligence of the felony to ſome of the inhabitants of ſome town, village, or hamlet, near unto the place where ſuch robbery ſhall be committed; and alſo, firſt within twenty days next before ſuch action brought, be examined upon oath, before ſome juſtice of the peace of the county, inhabiting in the hundred where the robbery was committed, or near the ſame, whether he knew the felons or robbers, or any of them; and if upon ſuch examination it be confeſſed that he does know them, he ſhall, before action brought, enter into bond before the ſaid juſtice, effectually to proſecute the ſaid robbers by indictment or otherwiſe. But by 8 Geo. II. c. 16. no perſon ſhall, maintain any action upon the above recited ſtatutes, unleſs he ſhall, over and above the intelligence required to be given by the ſtatute of Elizabeth, give notice of the robbery committed on him to one of the conſtables of the hundred, or to ſome conſtable or officer of ſome town, pariſh, hamlet, village, or tithing, near unto the place where ſuch robbery ſhall happen, or ſhall leave notice in writing of ſuch robbery at the dwelling-houſe of ſuch conſtable or officer, deſcribing in ſuch notice the felon, or felons, and the time and place of the robbery: and ſhall alſo within the ſpace of twenty days next after the robbery committed, cauſe public notice to be given thereof in the London Gazette, therein likewiſe deſcribing the felon, or felons, and the time and place of ſuch robbery, together with the goods and effects whereof he was robbed; and ſhall alſo, before any ſuch action commenced, go before the chief clerk, ſecondary, or filazer of the county where the robbery happened, or the clerk of the pleas wherein ſuch action is intended to be brought, or their reſpective deputies, or before the ſheriff of the county where the robbery ſhall happen, and enter into a bond (gratis) to the high conſtable, who is authorized to ſupport or defend ſuch action of the hundred, in the penal ſum of 100*l.* with two ſufficient ſureties for ſecuring the due payment of his coſts in caſe he should be nonsuited, &c; and no hundred or franchise shall be chargeable by virtue of these statutes, if one or more of the felons be apprehended within forty days next after notice in the London Gazette. By 22 Geo. II. c. 24. no person shall recover against any hundred more than 200*l.* unless the person so robbed shall at the time of the robbery be together in company, and be in number two at least, to attest the truth of the same; nor by 30 Geo. II. c. 3.; and 4 Geo. III. c. 2. unless three persons be present, if the plaintiff is receiver of the land tax.

Rewards. In order further to encourage the apprehending of certain felons, rewards and immunities are bestowed by divers acts of parliament. The statute 4 & 5 W. & M. c. 8. enacts, that such as apprehend a highwayman, and prosecute him to conviction, shall receive a reward of 40*l.* from the public; to be paid to them (or, if killed in the endeavour to take him, their executors) by the sheriff of the county; besides the horse, furniture, arms, money, and other goods taken upon the person of such robber; with a reservation of the right of any person from whom the same may have been stolen; to which the stat. 8 Geo. II. c. 16. superadds 10*l.* to be paid by the hundred indemnified by such taking. By statutes 6 & 7 W. III. c. 17. and 15 Geo. II. c. 28. persons apprehending and convicting any offender against those statutes, respecting the coinage, shall (in case the offence be treason or felony) receive a reward of 40*l*; or 10*l.* if it only amount to counterfeiting the copper coin. By 10 & 11 W. III. c. 23. any person apprehending and prosecuting to conviction a felon guilty of burglary, house-breaking, horse-stealing, or private larceny, to the value of 5*s.* from any shop, warehouse, coach house, or stable, shall be excused from all parish offices; and by 5 Ann. c. 31. any person so apprehending and prosecuting a burglar, or felonious house-breaker, (or, if killed in the attempt, his executors,) shall be entitled to a reward of 40*l.* By 6 Geo. I. c. 23. persons discovering, apprehending, and prosecuting to conviction, any person taking reward for helping others to their stolen goods, shall be entitled to 40*l.* By 14 Geo. II. c. 6. explained by 15 Geo. II. c. 34. any person apprehending and prosecuting to conviction such as steal, or kill with intent to steal, any sheep or other cattle specified in the latter of the said acts, shall for every such conviction receive a reward of 10*l.* Lastly, by 16 Geo. II. c. 15. and 8 Geo. III. c. 15. persons discovering, apprehending, and convicting felons and others being found at large during the term for which they are ordered to be transported, shall receive a reward of twenty pounds.

Piracy.

Piracy. Next to the robberies already defcribed, Piracy would be confidered; but it is already treated of in this vol. p. 275.

Cheats. In forming a judgment who are cheats, it is neceffary to keep in mind the diftinction formerly noticed, whether the property, or only the poffeffion was parted with by the party deceived. If only the poffeffion was furrendered, it has already been fhewn to be a larceny, if the perfon who gains it with an intent to fteal, fulfils that intent by retaining or difpofing of the goods. If the abfolute property were intended to be paffed by the delivery, but fuch delivery were obtained by means of a *falfe token or pretence*, the cafe can only be reached in the firft inftance by a profecution for a cheat, either at common law, or by help of the ftat. 33 Hen. VIII. or in the inftance of a falfe pretence by the 30 Geo. II. Where indeed the poffeffion is honeftly obtained upon a contract or truft in the firft inftance, the fubfequent difhoneft converfion of it is no other than a breach of truft, for which the party injured has a civil remedy. To this there is an exception, where the privity of contract is determined; that is, where the property has been committed to a perfon for a limited time or ufe, and he, inftead of returning it according to his engagement, and the reafonable expectation of the owner, fells or makes away with it. The fraud or difhonefty, to become the fubject matter of a criminal charge at common law, muft be fuch as affects the public, fuch as is public in its nature, calculated to defraud numbers, to deceive the people in general, and againft which ordinary care or prudence is not fufficient to guard.

Cafes on this fubject are precifely regulated by two ftatutes; the firft is that of 33 Hen. VIII. c. 1. which enacts, that if any perfon falfely and deceitfully obtain any money, goods, or other things, by colour and means of any falfe token, or counterfeit letter made in any other man's name, he fhall, if convicted before the lord chancellor, or before the juftices of affize in their circuits, or juftices of the peace in their general feffions, or by action in any of the king's courts of record, fuffer imprifonment, pillory, or other corporal pain, except pains of death, as fhall be adjudged by the court, faving to the party grieved his civil remedy; and the juftices of affize, or two juftices of the peace, (one being of the quorum) may commit or bail offenders to the affizes or general feffions to anfwer the fame. A falfe "*privy token*" within the ftatute has generally been taken to denote fome real vifible mark or thing, as a key, a ring, &c.; a mere falfe affirmation or promife is certainly not fuch; and although *writings*, generally ſpeaking, may be conſidered as *tokens*, yet they muſt be ſuch as are made in the names of *third* perſons; whereby ſome additional credit may be gained to the party uſing them. The falſe token muſt be ſuch as is calculated to gain the party ſome additional credit and confidence beyond his own aſſertion, or that which is reſolvable into ſuch. This inquiry however is become leſs important from the following act.

In furtherance of the proviſions of the above ſtatute, it is further enacted by 30 Geo. II. c. 24. that all perſons who knowingly and deſignedly by falſe pretence or pretences ſhall obtain from any perſon money, goods, wares or merchandizes, with intent to cheat or defraud them of the ſame, ſhall be deemed offenders againſt law and the public peace; and the court before whom they ſhall be tried ſhall, on conviction, order them to be fined and impriſoned, or put in the pillory, or publickly whipped, or tranſported for the term of ſeven years. And any juſtice of peace, before whom ſuch perſon is brought, may commit or bail him, to anſwer the complaint at the next general or quarter ſeſſions, or next ſeſſions of oyer and terminer; and ſhall bind over the party complaining to proſecute in a reaſonable ſum not leſs than double the amount of the money or goods fraudulently obtained if they ſhall exceed 20*l.* in value; and the certiorari is taken away.

The term "*falſe pretences*" is of great latitude, and was uſed to protect the weaker part of mankind, becauſe all are not equally prudent: it ſeems difficult therefore to reſtrain the interpretation of it to ſuch falſe pretences only againſt which ordinary prudence cannot be ſuppoſed ſufficient to guard; but ſtill it may be a queſtion whether the ſtatute extends to every falſe pretence, either abſurd or irrational upon the face of it, or ſuch as the party has at the very time the means of detecting at hand; or whether the words which are general ſhall be conſtrued co-extenſively with the cheat actually effected by means of the falſe pretence uſed. Theſe may perhaps be matters proper for the conſideration of the jury, with the advice of the court.

There are various other proviſions by ſtatute for the puniſhment of particular kinds of frauds or cheats; ſuch as thoſe by goldſmiths, &c. in working up plate, embezzlements and frauds by ſervants, by officers of the bank, and of other public companies, by perſons in the poſt-office, by manufacturers, by lodgers, by perſons intruſted with the king's naval and military ſtores, and by thoſe intruſted with ſhips and goods at ſea. Frauds committed by bankrupts will be conſi-

2 dered

dered hereafter. Others it is ſufficient here barely to refer to, as the ſtat. 6 Geo. I. c. 18. againſt entering into public ſubſcriptions for certain ſchemes of commerce, &c. which is made indictable as a nuſance; and the ſtat. 37 Geo. III. c. 143. which gives a ſummary juriſdiction to juſtices of the peace in petty ſeſſions to puniſh retailers in whoſe poſſeſſion falſe weights and balances ſhall be found. Fraudulent conveyances are provided againſt by the 13 Eliz. c. 5. and by the 27 Eliz. c. 4.

At common law the puniſhment for a cheat is, as in other caſes of miſdemeanor, by fine, impriſonment, or, further, by infamous corporal pain in aggravated caſes. How this has been confirmed or extended by the two ſtatutes of Hen. VIII. and Geo. II. has been already ſhewn. And where goods have been obtained from another by mere fraud, the court has no power of awarding reſtitution on conviction of the offender, as in caſes of felony.

FORGERY. To *forge*, (a metaphorical expreſſion borrowed from the occupation of the ſmith), means, properly ſpeaking, no more than to *make* or *form*; but in law it is always taken in an evil ſenſe, and therefore *forgery* at common law denotes a *falſe* making, which includes every alteration of, or addition to, a true inſtrument; a making *malo animo*, of any written inſtrument for the purpoſe of fraud and deceit. This offence is puniſhable as a miſdemeanor at common law; but it has been enhanced in a variety of inſtances by different ſtatutes, upon which it is now moſt uſual to proſecute.

To conſtitute Forgery, the *intent* muſt be deceitful and fraudulent. The very *making*, with ſuch fraudulent intent and without lawful authority, of any inſtrument which at common law or by ſtatute is the ſubject of forgery, is of itſelf a ſufficient completion of the offence even before publication, and of conſequence before any actual injury ſuſtained: for though publication be the medium by which the intent is uſually made manifeſt, yet it may be proved as plainly by other evidence. And by the ſtatute law, the publication, with knowledge of the fact, is for the moſt part made a ſubſtantive offence. Forgery may even be committed by a party's making a falſe deed in his own name; as if he make a ſubſequent deed of feoffment, as of a date prior to a former deed of his own, conveying the ſame lands, thereby attempting to give the laſt an operation which in juſtice it ought not to have, in order to defraud his own feoffee. So, if a bill of exchange payable to A. or order get into the hands of another perſon of the same name with the payee, and such person, knowing that he is not the real payee in whose favour it was drawn, indorse it for the purpose of fraudulently possessing himself of the money, he is guilty of forgery. So, if one put off a note subscribed with his own name as the note of another, it is a false uttering and publishing within the statute. Making a fraudulent insertion, alteration, or erasure in any material part of a true instrument, although but in a letter, and even if it be afterwards executed by another person, he not knowing of the deceit; or the fraudulent application of a true signature to a false instrument, for which it was not intended, or *vice versa*; are as much forgeries, as if the whole instrument had been fabricated; for any such alteration gives it a new operation; as by altering the date of a bill of exchange after acceptance, whereby the payment was accelerated. The wilful insertion of a legacy in another's will unknown to him prior to and at the time of its execution is a forgery. But a bare nonfeasance or omission is said not to be such; as by omitting a legacy out of a will which one is directed to draw for another; unless, as some have holden, such omission makes a material alteration in other parts of the will. In all cases the thing made must be false; for certainly a man cannot be guilty of forgery merely by passing himself off for the person whose real signature appears, although for the purpose of fraud, and in concert with such real person; for there is no false making.

To what *instruments* the crime of forgery was applied at common law seems to have been very indistinctly marked. It was never doubted but that it extended to the falsification of records and other instruments of a public nature; as a parish register, a privy seal, a licence from the barons of the exchequer to compound a debt, a certificate of holy orders, a protection from a member of parliament, or the like. It is equally clear that it extended to private deeds or instruments under seal, but how far beyond these is somewhat doubtful.

But the various modes of forgery are amply provided against by a great variety of statutes, of which a brief mention will be made under certain heads.

1. *Records*. The stat. 8 Hen. VI. c. 12. provides against the stealing and avoiding any records, or any part of them, in any of the courts at Westminster, declaring such acts to be high misdemeanors. The word *avoid* is taken in a large sense, and includes rasing, clipping, or any other kind of avoiding: and not only any alteration of a record whereby the judgment is *reversed*, (by which is to be understood *annulled*) but also whereby it is so made void as to be reversible, is within the statute;

statute; and that, whether made before or after judgment, or whether or not afterwards amended by the court.

2. *Public Funds and Stocks of public Companies.* The statutes 8 Geo. I. c. 22. and 31 Geo. II. c. 22. protect from forgery all the public funds then or since established by the authority of parliament. The stat. 31 Geo. II. c. 22. and 4 Geo. III. c. 25. extend the same protection to the parliamentary funds or stocks of public companies, and the 8 Geo. I. c. 22. especially includes the South-Sea-Company, as the stat. 9 Geo. I. c. 12. and other acts especially include particular orders and public annuities. To these many others are added for the protection of various other chartered companies; as the British Plate-glass, and Globe Insurance; the objects of forgery are specified with great minuteness, and the offence is in all cases declared to be felony without benefit of clergy.

3. *Notes and other Securities of the Bank of England.* The laws respecting these are mentioned in this vol. p. 165.

4. *Stamps.* Stamps denoting the payment of certain duties are required by various acts of parliament to be affixed on a multiplicity of written or printed documents. And for the purpose of protecting the revenue from fraud, in counterfeiting, uttering, or vending the same knowingly, the respective acts always contain a clause declaring the forgery of them to be felony, without benefit of clergy. Another general provision in regard to offences against the stamp laws is in the stat. 12 Geo. III. c. 48. which enacts, that if any person shall write or engross either the whole, or any part of any writ, mandate, bond, affidavit, or other writing, matter, or thing whatsoever, in respect whereof any duty is or shall be payable on the whole, or any part of any piece of vellum, parchment, or paper, whereon there shall have been before written any other writ, bond, mandate, affidavit, or other matter or thing, in respect whereof any duty was or shall be payable as aforesaid, before such vellum, parchment, or paper shall have been again marked or stamped according to the said acts; or shall fraudulently erase or scrape out the name of any person, or any sum or date; or fraudulently cut, tear, or get off, any mark or stamp, from any piece of vellum, parchment, paper, playing cards, outside paper of any parcel or pack of playing cards, or any part thereof, with intent to use such stamp or mark for any other writing, the offender, and every person abetting or assisting him, shall be transported for a term not exceeding seven years. And if he escape, break prison, or return from transportation before the

expiration of his time, he ſhall ſuffer death as a felon, without benefit of clergy, and ſhall be tried for ſuch felony in the county where he is apprehended. But any fraudulent uſing of a legal ſtamp, which many of the abovementioned offences may be deemed to be, is made capital by ſubſequent ſtatutes, the 23 Geo. III. c. 58. and 27 Geo. III. c. 13.

Forging the ſtamps on gold or ſilver plate is by the 31 Geo. II. c. 32. made felony, without benefit of clergy; but the 38 Geo. III. c. 69. by which gold wares were allowed to be manufactured at a lower ſtandard than was before allowed, *viz.* at the ſtandard of eighteen, inſtead of twenty-two carats in a pound troy, enacts, that if any perſon ſhall forge, caſt, or counterfeit the mark or ſtamp, he ſhall be tranſported for ſeven years.

5. *Official Papers, Securities, and Documents.* Forging teſtimonials of ſoldiers or mariners; memorials of regiſtry of deeds and wills, and of bargains and ſales, in Yorkſhire and Middleſex; documents relating to ſuitors in chancery; Mediterranean paſſes; marriage regiſters and licences; ſeamen's letters of attorney, bills, tickets, certificates, aſſignments, laſt wills, and other powers or authorities; or certificates to obtain letters of adminiſtration to ſeamen, and other documents to receive wages; prefines; exchequer bills, orders, aſſignments; Iriſh debentures; lottery tickets or ſhares, or licences to keep lottery offices; and contracts for the redemption of the land-tax; are by various ſtatutes felonies without benefit of clergy. Forging franks of letters, felony puniſhed by tranſportation for ſeven years. Forging receipts for duties on legacies ſubjects the offender to a penalty of 500*l.*; forging the ſtamp is, like other ſtamps, a capital offence. Making or ſubſcribing falſe certificates of naval or military ſtores, ſo as unduly to authorize perſons to have them in their poſſeſſion, is a miſdemeanor puniſhable with a fine of 200*l.* and whipping and impriſonment.

6. *Private Papers, Securities, and Documents.* The 5 Eliz. c. 14. enacts, that if any perſon ſhall forge or make, or cauſe or willingly aſſent to be forged or made, any falſe deed, charter, or writing ſealed, court-roll, or the will of any perſon in writing, to the intent that the eſtate of freehold or inheritance of any perſon in any lands or hereditaments, freehold or copyhold, or their right, title, or intereſt in the ſame, may be moleſted, defeated, or charged; or ſhall pronounce, publiſh, or ſhew forth in evidence, any ſuch falſe and forged writing as true, knowing the ſame to be forged, he ſhall pay to the party

party grieved his double costs and damages, and be set upon the pillory in some open market town, or other open place, and there have both his ears cut off, and also his nostrils slit and cut, and seared with a hot iron, so as they may remain as a perpetual mark of his falsehood, and shall forfeit to the queen the whole issues and profits of his lands and tenements during his life, and shall suffer perpetual imprisonment. If the forgery affected only an estate or interest for a term of years, the offender was to forfeit to the party grieved his double costs and damages, and to be also set on the pillory, and to have one of his ears cut off, and also be imprisoned one year. Persons once convicted committing a second offence, were declared guilty of felony without benefit of clergy.

The above statute of Elizabeth has now nearly fallen into disuse since the passing of the 2 Geo. II. c. 25. which extends to all deeds and wills, upon which the prosecution is easier, and the punishment capital in the first instance. By this statute, which is made perpetual by 9 Geo. II. c. 18. if any person shall falsely make, forge, or counterfeit, or cause or procure to be falsely made, &c. or willingly act or assist in the false making, &c. any *deed, will, testament, bond, writing obligatory, bill of exchange, promissory note* for payment of money, *indorsement* or *assignment* of any bill of exchange or promissory note for payment of money, or any *acquittance* or *receipt* either for money or goods, with intent to defraud any person whatsoever, (and by stat. 31 Geo. II. c. 22. with intent to defraud any corporation whatsoever :) or shall *utter or publish* as true, any false, forged, or counterfeited deed, &c. with intent to defraud any person, (or corporation,) knowing the same to be false, forged, or counterfeited ; every such person shall be deemed guilty of felony without benefit of clergy. The stat. 7 Geo. II. c. 22. (made to supply the defects of the former act which it recites, and further that no punishment is inflicted by the said act on such as commit the offences thereinafter set forth), enacts, that if any person shall falsely make, alter, forge, or counterfeit; or cause or procure to be falsely made, &c.; or willingly act or assist in the false making, &c. any *acceptance of any bill of exchange*, or the *number* or *principal sum* of any *accountable receipt for any note, bill, or other security for payment of money, or delivery of goods*, with intent to defraud any person whatsoever, (and by stat. 18 Geo. III. c. 18. with intent to defraud any corporation,) or shall utter or publish as true any false, altered, forged, or counterfeited acceptance of any bill of exchange, or accountable receipt for any note, bill, or other security for payment of money, or warrant or order for payment of money or delivery of goods, with intention to defraud any person, (or corporation,) knowing

knowing the ſame to be falſe, altered, forged, or counterfeited, every ſuch perſon ſhall be deemed guilty of felony without benefit of clergy. In the ſtat. 7 Geo. II. there is no expreſs ſaving of corruption of blood, as in the others: and by the 2 Geo. II. c. 25. the act is not to extend to Scotland.

It is ſaid to be no way material whether a forged inſtrument is made in ſuch a manner as, were it true, it would be of any validity or not: but this muſt be underſtood, where the falſe inſtrument carries on the face of it the ſemblance of that for which it is counterfeited, and is not illegal in its very frame. Upon this ground it has been adjudged that the forgery of a protection in the name of one as being a member of parliament, who in truth was no member at the time, is as much an offence at common law as if he were ſo. In order to conſtitute forgery, it is not neceſſary there ſhould be a perfect reſemblance between the falſe inſtrument and that which is intended to be imitated: if they be ſo far alike that the deception is calculatted to impoſe upon perſons in general, it is ſufficient; though it would not impoſe on perſons having particular experience in ſuch matters. But though a ſimilarity to a common intent be ſufficient, yet it is neceſſary that the forged inſtrument ſhould in all eſſential parts have upon the face of it the ſimilitude of a true one; ſo that it be not radically defective and illegal in the very frame of it.

It is clear that the making of any falſe inſtrument which is the ſubject of forgery with a fraudulent intent, although in the name of a non-exiſting perſon, is as much a forgery as if it had been made in the name of one who was known to exiſt, and to whom credit was due. It makes no difference whether the making of the falſe inſtrument or ſignature be really neceſſary to the advantage ſo fraudulently attempted to be obtained by the party, or gain him any additional credit; it is ſufficient if it be made with ſuch fraudulent intent.

In trials for forgery, a conſideration which ſeems to have involved in it the greateſt difficulty is, how far perſonating the true man, or aſſuming a fictitious character at the time, will affect the offence. On this point the diſtinctions are extremely nice; but the following general principles are laid down. 1ſt, That if a perſon gives a note or other ſecurity as his own, and the credit thereupon be perſonal to himſelf, without any relation to another, his ſigning it with a fictitious name may indeed be a cheat, but will not amount to forgery; for in that caſe it is really the inſtrument of the party whoſe act it purports to be, and the creditor had no other ſecurity in view. But, 2dly. That if a note is given in the name of another perſon either really exiſting or repreſented ſo to be, and in that light it obtains

obtains a ſuperior credit, or induces a truſt which would not have been given to the party himſelf, it is then a falſe inſtrument, and puniſhable as forgery. 3dly. That the law would be the ſame, though the note or ſecurity were thus falſely ſubſcribed in the preſence of him who lent his money upon it, if the impoſtor and the party whoſe name is made uſe of were both ſtrangers to him; for then he could not know that ſuch impoſtor was not really the perſon whoſe name he aſſumed, and therefore the other would be equally deceived. But how far the firſt propoſition above laid down is to be taken in its utmoſt latitude, has been the ſubject of much difference of opinion.

PUBLISHING OR UTTERING. To pronounce or publiſh, ſays lord Coke, is when one, by words or writing, pronounces or publiſhes the inſtrument to any other as true. It extends, no doubt, to every other manner of exhibiting it as a true inſtrument; but in order to conſtitute ſuch an offence it muſt be done with knowledge of the forgery; which knowledge may come by the relation of another, as well as by the party's own obſervation. Such relation is not concluſive evidence of the fact of knowledge; it muſt be left to the jury upon the whole matter; for poſſibly there might be circumſtances which might invalidate or weaken the credit of the perſon relating it, or of his relation itſelf, though it afterwards appear to be true. This is an offence diſtinct from, though connected with, the act of falſe making, or forgery; and therefore it is the common practice to indict perſons who knowingly utter forged inſtruments as principals; and there may be acceſſaries before to ſuch offence.

ACCESSARIES. In forgery, it is laid down generally in the books that all are principals; and that whatever would make a man acceſſary before in felony, will make him a principal in forgery; but this, it is ſaid, muſt be underſtood of forgery at common law, and where it is conſidered only as a miſdemeanor.

INDICTMENT. It is eſſentially neceſſary to an indictment for forgery that the inſtrument alleged to be forged ſhould be ſet forth in words and figures; though there is no technical form of words for expreſſing that it is to be ſet forth. In ſetting forth, however, the tenor of an inſtrument, a mere literal variance will not vitiate the indictment. If any part of a true inſtrument be altered, the indictment may lay it to be a forgery of the whole inſtrument. It is a general rule applicable to this as to other offences, that an indictment on a ſtatute muſt in general ſet forth the charge in the very words of of the ſtatute deſcribing the offence; for equivalent words are not ſufficient.

Witnesses. It has been the uniform practice to reject every witneſs who is intereſted at the time of his examination, in ſetting aſide the inſtrument alleged to be forged, upon which, if genuine, he would be liable to be ſued. Incompetency ariſing from intereſt in the event of the verdict, where it really exiſts, extends to preclude the party from giving other evidence, as well as that of negativing the hand-writing which tends to prove the fact of the forgery. Therefore the executor of a perſon, whoſe promiſſory note had been forged, was rejected as a witneſs to prove what the priſoner ſaid to him when he tendered the note for payment. But if the party whoſe hand-writing is forged has no intereſt in invalidating the inſtrument in queſtion, there is no doubt but he is a competent witneſs: and ſome caſes appear to go the length of eſtabliſhing, that, being the beſt, he is the only witneſs, if living, to prove the forgery: but that is not confirmed by the current of authorities to ſuch an extent; though the teſtimony of ſuch an one, when diſintereſted, muſt doubtleſs be the moſt ſatisfactory of any, on the queſtion of his own hand-writing. And whatever might have been the intereſt of the party, in the tranſaction at firſt, there is no doubt, but if he be diveſted of ſuch intereſt, by releaſe, payment, or otherwiſe, at the time he is ready to be ſworn, it is no objection to his competency, whatever it may be, under certain circumſtances, to his credit. Therefore a releaſe from the holder of a promiſſory note to the ſuppoſed drawer in whoſe name it was forged, there being no other name on the note to whom the drawer could be liable, made him a competent witneſs to prove the forgery of his hand-writing upon an indictment againſt the priſoner, who had paſſed it off to ſuch holder without any indorſement. In Dr. Dodd's caſe, the earl of Cheſterfield, the ſuppoſed obligor of the forged bond, was admitted to diſprove his ſignature, on producing a releaſe from Fletcher, the ſuppoſed obligee.

Judgment, and its Consequences. In a variety of inſtances, which have been mentioned, the forgery of particular inſtruments has been made felony by ſtatutes, for the moſt part excluding the benefit of clergy. In all other caſes the offence muſt be taken to reſt in miſdemeanor, puniſhable at common law by fine, impriſonment, and ſuch other corporal puniſhment, as the court in their diſcretion ſhall award; and by ſtatute alſo with certain puniſhments of the ſame kind in particular inſtances, which have alſo been pointed out. One of the conſequences of any judgment for this offence is an incapacity

incapacity to be a witneſs, until reſtored to competency by the king's pardon under the great ſeal. The effect of the ſtat. 12 Geo. I. c. 29. with reſpect to attornies, ſolicitors, or law agents, has been mentioned.

Falsely personating Another. This offence, committed for the purpoſe of cheating another, by impoſing on him a falſe name or character, for the purpoſe of gaining either a new credit, or preventing detection, is in its nature nearly allied to forgery, with which it is uſually accompanied, to give it efficacy. They have been accordingly claſſed together by the legiſlature in various inſtances, with reſpect to perſonating the proprietors of government ſtocks, or the ſtocks of the different public companies; all which are made capital felonies. By referring to the terms of the different ſtatutes, it will be ſeen that the actual completion of the fraud, by the transfer of the ſtock, or the receipt of the dividends, is not neceſſary to conſtitute the offence; it is ſufficient if the offender falſely and deceitfully perſonates any true and real proprietor, *and thereby tranſfers*, or *endeavours to transfer*, the ſtock, or *receives*, or *endeavours to receive* the money; in which caſe he is, by the ſeveral acts, made guilty of felony without benefit of clergy. In theſe caſes, the real proprietor can be examined as a witneſs to prove the identity of the perſon intended to be defrauded. Perſonating ſailors, or out-penſioners at Greenwich hoſpital, with intent to receive their wages, prize money, or penſions, is alſo felony without clergy; but in theſe caſes, there muſt be ſome evidence to ſhew that there was ſuch a perſon of the name and character aſſumed, who was either entitled, or might, *primâ facie* at leaſt, be ſuppoſed to be entitled to receive on board ſuch a ſhip the wages, &c. attempted to be acquired.

By ſtat. 21 Jas. I. c. 26. all perſons who ſhall acknowledge or procure to be acknowledged, any fine, recovery, deed inrolled, ſtatute, recognizance, bail, or judgment, in the name of any other perſons not privy or conſenting to the ſame, ſhall be adjudged felons, without benefit of clergy; (ſaving corruption of blood and loſs of dower). The act does not extend to any judgment acknowledged by any attorney of record for any perſon againſt whom any ſuch judgment ſhall be given. This act extended only to proceedings in the courts themſelves: and therefore by ſtat. 4 W. and M. c. 4. the chief juſtices of the king's bench and common pleas, and the chief baron may reſpectively, together with one other judge of their reſpective courts, appoint commiſſioners (other than common attornies and ſolicitors) in every ſhire and county within England, Wales, &c. to take recognizances of ſpecial bail or bail pieces in actions and ſuits depending in their ſeveral courts. And any judge of of assize in his circuit is empowered to take such recognizances. Then any persons who shall, before any person so empowered, represent or personate any other, shall be adjudged felons, and suffer as felons. Under the act of James, it has been holden that the bare personating of bail before a judge at chambers, or the acknowledging thereof in another name, is no felony, unless the bail be filed; but only a misdemeanor.

In all other cases, not made felony by statute, the bare fact of personating another, though for the purpose of fraud, can in no instance amount to more than a cheat or misdemeanor at common law, and is punishable as such.

ARSON. Arson, which was felony at common law, and anciently punished with death, is described to be the malicious and voluntary burning the house of another. Many statutes have passed on this subject, most especially affecting the benefit of clergy; but the crime at this day rests principally on the 9 Geo. I. c. 22. commonly called the black act, which provides that if any person shall set fire to any house, barn, or out-house, or to any hovel, cock, mow, or stack of corn, straw, hay, or wood; or shall forcibly rescue any person being lawfully in custody for any such offence; or shall, by gift or promise of money or reward, procure any to join him in any such unlawful act; he shall be adjudged guilty of felony, without benefit of clergy; and offenders not surrendering on proclamation are also ousted of clergy. By the 9 Geo. III. c. 29. persons burning or setting fire to any mill are declared felons without benefit of clergy, but must be prosecuted within eighteen months. By further provision in the same statute, the offender may be required by order of the king in council to surrender within forty days, in default of which the court may award execution.

To constitute this offence there must be a malicious and voluntary burning; otherwise it is not felony, but only a trespass; and therefore no negligence or mischance amounts to it. As, if an unqualified person by shooting at game happen to set fire to the thatch of a house; or even if a man were shooting at the poultry of another, unless he meant to steal it, in which case, the first intent being felonious, the party must abide all the consequences. But by 6 Ann. c. 31. any servant *negligently* setting fire to a house or out-houses shall, on conviction before two justiqueences of the peace, forfeit 100*l*. or be sent to the house of correction for eighteen months. Further, it is necessary that the house, or some part of it, or some out-house, forming a parcel of it, though not contiguous, be burnt or set fire to; for the malicious burning of goods in the house does not amount to felony. The house must also, in a strict sense, be the house

house of another person, otherwise the offence is only a misdemeanor; but even the burning of a man's own house in a town, or so near to other houses as to create danger to them, is a great misdemeanor, and may be punished with fine and imprisonment, pillory and finding sureties.

Accessaries after, stand upon the same footing as in other felonies, and are not deprived of clergy by any statute, except after an order of the king in council, as above mentioned; in which case, after the time limited in the order is expired, such as conceal, aid, abet, or succour such offender, knowing him to have been so charged and required to surrender, are ousted of clergy. The *trial* may be in any county in England.

MALICIOUS AND FRAUDULENT MISCHIEF. Beside arson, many other offences may be classed under this head, some of which have already been mentioned, as mayhem, spoiling cloaths, and some modes of robbery; and others will form separate objects of consideration. In this division, however, some other malicious injuries will be noticed, as provided against by particular statutes, both local and general.

In the Northern Counties. By the 43 Eliz. c. 13. for restraining incursions, robberies, burning of towns and houses, in Cumberland, Northumberland, Westmorland, and Durham, and the imprisonment and cruel treating of the inhabitants, unless redeeming themselves by great ransoms, called *black mail*, it is enacted, that whosoever shall without lawful authority take any of the queen's subjects against their will, and carry them out of the said counties, or to any other place within any of the said counties, or detain, force, or imprison them to ransom them; or to make a prey or spoil of their persons; or goods, upon deadly feud or otherwise: or whosoever shall be privy, or assisting unto any such offence, or procure it to be committed; or whoever shall take, receive, or carry to the use of himself, or any other, money, corn, cattle, or other consideration, commonly called black mail, for the protecting or defending of him or them, or his or their lands or goods, from such thefts; or whosoever shall give any such money, &c. called black mail, for such protection; or shall wilfully burn, or aid, procure, or consent to the burning of any barn or stack of corn or grain, within any of the said counties or places, and shall be convicted at the assize or general sessions, shall be adjudged felons, without benefit of clergy. Authority is given to the court by a subsequent statute of the 18 Chas. II. c. 3. to execute or transport for life certain of those offenders, known in Northumberland by the name of moss troopers.

Burning Heath, &c. By 4 & 5 W. and M. c. 23. it is enacted, that no person, on any mountains, hills, heaths, moors, forests, chases, or other wastes, shall burn between the 2d February and 24th June, any ging, ling, heath, furze, gofs, or fern, upon pain of being committed to the house of correction, not exceeding one month, nor less than ten days, to be whipped and kept to hard labour. The 28 Geo. II. c. 19. rather limits than extends the objects of this offence, by omitting the word heath, and uses the words forests or chases only, instead of the more general words in the former act; but it gives a summary jurisdiction to one or more justices of the peace, and empowers them to inflict a penalty as well as to imprison.

By Hunters. By the 42 Geo. III. c. 107. if any person shall wilfully course, or hunt, or take in any slip, noose, toil, or snare, or kill, wound, or destroy, or shoot at, or otherwise attempt to kill, wound, or destroy, or shall carry away, any red or fallow deer, kept or being in the inclosed part of any forest, chase, purlieu, or ancient walk, or any inclosed park, paddock, wood, or other inclosed ground, wherein deer are, have been, or shall be usually kept, without the consent of the owner, or without being otherwise duly authorized, or shall be knowingly aiding, abetting, or assisting therein, he shall be deemed guilty of felony, and transported for seven years. The same offence in any uninclosed part subjects the offender to a penalty of 50*l.*; and if a keeper, or otherwise intrusted with the care or custody of deer, to 100*l.*, the second offence, to transportation for seven years.

By 16 Geo. III. c. 30. if any person carrying any gun, or other fire arms, or any sword, staff, or other offensive weapon, comes into any forest, chase, purlieu, or ancient walk, or into any inclosed park, paddock, wood, or other ground where deer are usually kept, be the same inclosed or not, with intent unlawfully to shoot at, course, or hunt, or to take in any slip, noose, toil, snare, or other engine, or to kill, wound, destroy, or take away, any red or fallow deer; it is lawful for every ranger, or keeper, or person intrusted with the care of such deer, to seize and take from him all such guns, fire-arms, slips, or other engines, and all dogs; and if any such person beats or wounds the ranger or keeper, his servants or assistants, or attempts to rescue any person in their lawful custody, he shall be adjudged guilty of felony, and transported for seven years.

GAME. Under this division may be ranked an offence constituted by a variety of acts of parliament; an offence, which the sportsmen of England seem to think of the highest import-

importance; and againſt which aſſociations have been formed all over the kingdom. It is the offence of deſtroying ſuch beaſts and fowls, as are ranked under the denomination of *game*: which, upon the old principle of the foreſt law, is a treſpaſs and offence in all perſons alike, who have not authority from the crown to kill game (which is royal property), by the grant of either a free warren, or at leaſt a manor of their own. The game laws have alſo inflicted additional puniſhments (chiefly pecuniary) on perſons guilty of this general offence, unleſs they are of the rank and fortune particularly ſpecified. All perſons, therefore, of what property or diſtinction ſoever, that kill game out of their own territories, or even upon their own eſtates, without the king's licence expreſſed by the grant of a franchiſe, are guilty of the firſt original offence, of encroaching on the royal prerogative; and thoſe who do ſo, without having ſuch rank or fortune as is generally called a *qualification*, are guilty not only of the original offence, but of the aggravations alſo, created by the ſtatutes. The *qualifications*, or more properly the *exemptions*, from the penalties inflicted by the ſtatute, are, 1. The having a freehold eſtate of 100*l.* per annum. 2. A leaſehold for ninety-nine years of 150*l.* per annum. 3. Being the ſon and heir apparent of an eſquire, or perſon of ſuperior degree. 4. Being the owner, or keeper of a foreſt, park, chaſe, or warren. For unqualified perſons tranſgreſſing theſe laws, by killing game, keeping engines for that purpoſe, or even having game in their cuſtody; or for perſons (however qualified) that kill game, or have it in poſſeſſion, at unſeaſonable times of the year, or unſeaſonable hours of the day or night, on Sundays, or on Chriſtmas-day, there are various penalties aſſigned, corporal and pecuniary, by different ſtatutes; on any of which, but only one at a time, the juſtices may convict in a ſummary way, or (in moſt of them) proſecutions may be carried on at the aſſizes. Theſe penalties conſiſt for the moſt part in ſeizures of guns, dogs, and other animals and engines, in ſearching for which extraordinary powers are given; in pecuniary fines, amounting in ſome caſes to 5*l.* for an offence; in impriſonment ſometimes for three months; and in whipping. By 28 Geo. II. c. 12. no perſon, however qualified to *kill*, may ſell or expoſe to ſale any game, on pain of like forfeiture as if he had no qualification. By the 25 Geo. III. c. 50. and 31 Geo. III. c. 21. every perſon, who ſhall go in purſuit of game without taking out a certificate from the clerk of the peace of the county or diſtrict where he reſides, ſhall forfeit 20*l.* The clerk of the peace ſhall receive for the certificate 3*s.* 4*d.*; and the certificate ſhall be in force from the day of its date till the first of July next following. And any person producing his certificate to another, who is in pursuit of game, may demand of him to shew his certificate, and if he does not, he may then demand of him his name and place of abode, which if he refuses to give, or gives a false name or place of residence, he shall forfeit 50*l.* The stamp on the certificate is 3*l.* 3*s.*; but it does not, as some erroneously suppose, amount to, or stand instead of a qualification.

In respect to timber and other trees, woods, coppices, &c. and other wood in general; roots, plants, &c. By 37 Hen. VIII. c. 6. persons wilfully barking any apple, pear, or other fruit trees, forfeit to the party aggrieved treble damages, and to the king 10*l.* And the 1 Geo. I. st. 2. c. 48. after providing, that if any person shall maliciously break down, cut up, pluck up, throw down, bark, or otherwise destroy, deface, or spoil any timber tree, fruit tree, or any other tree, the party injured shall recover damages against the inhabitants of the parish, village, &c. or place where such tree, &c. shall be so maliciously broken down, &c.; and reciting, that whereas divers woods, underwoods, and coppices, have been heretofore and lately set on fire, or burnt, to the great discouragement of planting; enacts and declares, that if any person shall maliciously set on fire or burn any wood, underwood, or coppice, or any part thereof, he shall be adjudged guilty of felony; and be liable to penalties and forfeitures as other felons.

Also the 6 Geo. I. c. 16. enacts, if any person shall, either by day or night, cut, take, destroy, break, throw down, bark, pluck up, burn, deface, spoil, or carry away, any woodsprings, or springs of wood, trees, poles, wood, tops of trees, underwoods, or coppice woods, thorns, or quicksets, without the consent of the owner, or of the persons chiefly intrusted with the care and custody thereof; or shall break down, throw down, level, or destroy any hedges, gates, posts, stiles, railings, walls, fences, dikes, ditches, banks, or other inclosures of such woods, wood-ground, parks, chases, or coppices, plantations, timber trees, fruit trees, or other trees, thorns, or quicksets, the party grieved shall recover damages against the parish, &c. in the same manner and form as for dikes and hedges overthrown by persons in the night, or at another season when they are supposed not to be espied, as is provided by the stat. 13 Edward I. st. 1. c. 46.; and further, that if any person or persons in a riotous, open, tumultuous, or in a secret and clandestine manner, commit nearly the same offences, two justices of the peace, or the justices in open sessions, upon complaint to them made by any inhabitant of the parish

parish or place, or of the owner of the property injured, may cause such offender or offenders to be apprehended, and hear and finally determine the offence; and if they convict any person or persons, they may inflict the penalties and punishments in the said act of the first of Geo. I. The 29 Geo. II. c. 36. which enables the proprietors of wastes, woods, and pastures, wherein any others have common of pasture, with the assent of the major part in number and value of the owners, &c. to inclose the same for the growth and preservation of timber or underwood, and gives an appeal in certain cases to the parties grieved, enacts, that if any person, after the time of appealing, shall either by day or by night unlawfully cut, take, destroy, break, throw down, bark, pluck up, burn, deface, spoil, or carry away, any trees growing within such inclosure, the owner shall have such remedy, satisfaction, and recompence from the inhabitants of the parishes, &c. or places adjoining to such inclosures, and recover such damages against them as is directed for dikes and hedges overthrown by the 13 Edw. I.; unless the offender or offenders shall be convicted of such offence within the space of six months. And any two justices of the peace of the county wherein the offence is committed, or the justices in sessions, upon complaint to them, may cause every such offender to be apprehended, and inflict the like penalty and punishment on them as is directed by the 6 Geo. I. c. 16. If any person shall unlawfully cut, take, destroy break, throw down, bark, pluck up, burn, deface, spoil, or carry away, any tree growing in any waste, wood, or pasture, in which any person, or body politic or corporate, has right of common, he may be in like manner convicted of such offence, and shall incur the like penalty.

By the black act also, any person, whether armed and disguised or not, who shall maliciously cut down, or otherwise destroy any trees planted in any avenue, or growing in any garden, orchard, or plantation, for ornament, shelter, or profit; or shall forcibly rescue any person in custody for such offence; or by gift or promise procure any to join him in any such unlawful act; shall be adjudged guilty of felony without benefit of clergy.

The 6 Geo. III. c. 36. provides for the preservation of timber, and timber-like trees, whether in forests, chases, and other open grounds, or in woods, plantations, or inclosed grounds, and against the plunder of nursery grounds, by enacting, that the breaking, spoiling, destroying, injuring, or carrying away any of them to the value of 5*s*. shall be deemed felony, and punished with transportation for seven years; and aiders, abettors, purchasers, and receivers are to be punished in in the ſame manner as the principals. Another act paſſed in the ſame ſeſſion directs, that perſons deſtroying or injuring trees in his majeſty's foreſts or chaſes, ſhall for the firſt offence forfeit 20*l.* and coſts, or be committed, not leſs than ſix nor more than twelve months; for the ſecond, forfeit 30*l.* and coſts, or be impriſoned not leſs than twelve nor more than eighteen months; and for a third offence, tranſported for ſeven years. The ſame ſtatute declares that all oak, beech, cheſnut, walnut, aſh, elm, cedar, fir, aſp, lime, ſycamore, and birch trees, ſhall be deemed timber trees within its meaning and proviſion. To which the ſtat. 13 Geo. III. c. 33. adds poplar, alder, larch, maple, and hornbeam. This ſecond act of the 6 Geo. III. and which is c. 48. alſo generally enacts, that every perſon who ſhall pluck up or cut, ſpoil or deſtroy, or take or carry away, any root, ſhrub, or plant, out of fields, nurſeries, gardens, or other cultivated lands, ſhall, on conviction before one juſtice of the peace, for the firſt offence forfeit not exceeding forty ſhillings, together with coſts; for the ſecond, not exceeding 5*l.* with coſts, and for the third, may be tranſported for ſeven years. Alſo perſons who ſhall go into woods, underwoods, or wood grounds, and there cut, lop, top, or ſpoil, ſplit down or damage, or otherwiſe deſtroy, any kind of wood or underwood, poles, ſticks of wood, green ſticks, or young trees, or carry or convey away the ſame, or ſhall have them in their cuſtody, and ſhall not give a ſatisfactory account how they came by them, ſhall, on like conviction, for the firſt offence forfeit not exceeding forty ſhillings with coſts; for the ſecond, not exceeding 5*l.* and coſts; and for the third, ſhall be deemed incorrigible rogues, and puniſhed as ſuch. It is remarked as an extraordinary circumſtance, that theſe two acts ſhould have paſſed in the ſame ſeſſion, enacting ſuch different proviſions on the ſame ſubject. And there are many other circumſtances in the ſtatutes above referred to, which render it evident that they were framed in haſte, and paſſed with ſome degree of negligence.

By 37 Hen. VIII. c. 6. if any perſon maliciouſly do burn, or cauſe to be burned, any heap of wood of any other perſon, prepared, cut, and felled, for making of coals, billets, or talwood, he ſhall not only forfeit unto the party grieved, treble damages, to be recovered by action of treſpaſs, but alſo ſhall forfeit to the king 10*l.* in the name of a fine.

Burning Wains or Carts laden with Goods. The laſt mentioned ſtatute ſubjects to the ſame puniſhment any perſon who ſhall maliciouſly burn any wain or cart laden with coals or other

other goods or merchandizes belonging to any other person.

Destroying Fences and Inclosures. Some provisions against the destruction of the fences of wood ground have been already adverted to in the stat. 6 Geo. I. c. 16. which refers to the remedy provided by the 13 Edw. I. st. 1. c. 46. This latter ordains, that where one having right to approve does then levy a dike or an hedge, and some by night, or at another season when they suppose not to be espied, do overthrow the hedge or dike, and it cannot be known by verdict of the assize or jury who did it, and men of the towns near will not indict such as be guilty of the fact, such towns shall be distrained to levy the hedge or dike at their own cost, and to yield damages. By 9 Geo. III. c. 29. if any person shall wilfully set fire to, burn, demolish, pull down, destroy, or damage, any fence erected or made for dividing or inclosing any common, waste, or other lands, in pursuance of any act of parliament, he may be transported for seven years. The prosecution to be commenced within eighteen months after the offence. By 16 Geo. III. c. 30. if any person shall pull down or destroy the pale or pales, or any part of the walls of any forest, chase, or other ground where red or fallow deer are kept, he shall forfeit 30*l.* on conviction before one justice of the peace, who, in case of non-payment, has power to commit. The prosecution must be commenced within twelve calendar months after the offence committed. Offenders of this description were also by the 5 Eliz. c. 21. subjected to treble damages to the party grieved, and to imprisonment for three months, and finding sureties for seven years.

Breaking down Mounds of Fish-ponds. The chief protection against this offence is in the black act, which declares, that if any person, whether armed and disguised, or not, shall maliciously break down the head or mound of any fish-pond, whereby the fish shall be lost or destroyed; or shall forcibly rescue any person in custody for such offence; or shall, by gift or promise of reward, procure any to join him in such unlawful act, he shall be guilty of felony without benefit of clergy. Clergy is also ousted from offenders not surrendering themselves upon proclamation; and from such as conceal, aid, abet, or succour them after the time expired for their surrender. And they may be tried in any county in England. The stats. 37 Hen. VIII. c. 6. and 5 Eliz. c. 21. have provided punishments for this offence, and they are not repealed; but as the black act is more effectual, it has superseded them in use.

Cutting Hop-binds. By 6 Geo. II. c. 37. this offence is felony without benefit of clergy; and by 10 Geo. II. c. 32. all the provisions in the black act, for bringing offenders and abettors to justice; making satisfaction to the parties injured; and encouragement of those who apprehend delinquents, are extended to this offence.

Obstructing the Passage of Grain. By 36 Geo. III. c. 9. it is enacted, that if any person shall beat, wound, or use any other violence, to deter or hinder others from buying corn, or grain, in any market or other place within the kingdom; or shall unlawfully stop or seize any wheat, flour, meal, malt, or other grain, in the way to or from any city, market town, or place in the kingdom; or shall break, cut, or destroy any waggon, cart, or other carriage, wherein any such wheat, or other grain, shall be loaded, or the harness of any horse drawing or carrying the same; or shall take off from any such carriage, or drive away, kill, or wound any such horse; or beat or wound the driver, with intent to stop such wheat, or other grain; or shall, by cutting off the sacks, or otherwise, scatter or throw it abroad, or take or carry away, destroy, spoil, or damage the same; all such persons, being convicted before any two justices of the peace of the county, wherein the offence shall be committed, or before the justices in open sessions (who are authorised summarily and finally to hear and determine the same), shall be sent to the common jail, or house of correction, to hard labour, not exceeding three months, nor less than one. If any such person shall offend a second time; or if any person, with intent to prevent or hinder any corn from being lawfully carried or removed from any place, shall pull down, throw down, or otherwise destroy, any storehouse, or granary, or other place in which such grain shall be kept, or enter such storehouse, or other place, and take and carry away any corn or grain; or shall throw abroad, or spoil the same, or any part thereof; or shall enter on board any ship or vessel, and take and carry away, cast, or throw out therefrom, or otherwise spoil or damage any corn or grain; he shall be adjudged guilty of felony, and transported for seven years. The 11 Geo. II. c. 22. still in force, which was levelled against offences of this description committed, as the title of the act states, with intent to hinder the exportation of corn, has the same provisions with slight variations, and with this further addition, that for the offences created by the first clause of that statute, the justices are also directed to adjudge the offender to be publicly whipped at the time and place before specified. By both acts a conditional remedy is given against the hundred.

Against Cattle. Provisions against maliciously killing, wounding, and injuring the cattle of others, were made by the statutes 38 Hen. VIII. c. 6. and 22 and 23 Chas. II. c. 37. but that most generally resorted to is the black act, which provides, that if if any perſon (whether armed or diſguiſed, or not) ſhall kill, maim, or wound any cattle; or forcibly reſcue perſons in cuſtody for ſuch offence; or by gift or promiſe procure any to join him in ſuch unlawful act; he ſhall be adjudged guilty of felony without benefit of clergy. Offenders not ſurrendering after order in council, and thoſe who after the time conceal or ſuccour them, are alſo felons without clergy. The trial may be in any county in England; and aiders and abettors at the fact are alſo ouſted of clergy. In order to bring an offender within this law, the malice muſt be directed againſt the owner of the cattle, and not merely againſt the animal itſelf.

Manufactures. The 22 Geo. III. c. 40. enacts, that if any perſon ſhall, by day or by night, break, or enter by force into any houſe or ſhop, with intent to cut or deſtroy any ſerge, or other woollen goods in the loom, or any tools employed in the making thereof; or ſhall cut or deſtroy any ſuch ſerges or woollen goods in the loom, or on the rack; or ſhall burn, cut, or deſtroy any rack on which any ſuch ſerges or other woollen goods are hanged to dry; or ſhall break or deſtroy any tools uſed in the making any ſuch ſerges or other woollen goods, not having the conſent of the owner ſo to do; every ſuch offender ſhall be guilty of felony without benefit of clergy. The ſame penalty, in terms varied according to the occaſion, is inflicted for offences with reſpect to velvet, wrought ſilk, or mixed with any other materials, and other ſilk manufacture, and with reſpect to linen or cotton, or linen and cotton mixed with any other materials, or other linen or cotton manufactures, together with the looms and all other implements uſed in manufacturing them. This act does not repeal one of the 4 Geo. III. c. 37. which declares, that if any perſon break into any place, with intent to ſteal, cut, or deſtroy, any linen yarn, or any linen cloth, or any manufacture of linen yarn, belonging to any manufactory, or the looms, tools, or implements uſed therein; or ſhall cut in pieces, or deſtroy any ſuch goods, either when expoſed to bleach or dry; he ſhall be judged guilty of felony without benefit of clergy.

By ſtat. 38 Geo. III. c. 17. for twenty-one years, from the 7th May, 1798, and to the end of the then next ſeſſion, if any perſon ſhall by day or night break into any place or building, belonging to the governor and company of the Britiſh caſt plate-glaſs manufactory, with intent to ſteal, out, break, or otherwiſe deſtroy any glaſs, wrought or unwrought, or any materials, tools, or implements, uſed in, for, or about the making thereof, or any goods or wares belonging to the ſaid manufactory; or ſhall ſteal or cut, break or deſtroy any ſuch glaſs, materials,

 tools,

tools, or implements; he ſhall be guilty of felony, and tranſported for ſeven years, or ſuffer a leſs puniſhment at the diſcretion of the court.

Highways. All nuiſances in highways are indictable at common law: and by the general highway act, 13 Geo. III. c. 78. the damaging of poſts, blocks, and great ſtones, ſet up to ſecure cauſeways, and of the banks which ſecure and defend the ſame, and the ſtones, bricks, or wood, fixed on the parapets or battlements of bridges; as alſo the pulling down, deſtroying, or defacing of mile ſtones or direction poſts, is made liable on conviction before a juſtice of the peace to a penalty not exceeding 5*l.* nor leſs than ten ſhillings; and in default of payment the offender is to be committed to the houſe of correction, there to be whipped and kept to hard labour not exceeding one calendar month nor leſs than ſeven days.

Turnpikes. By 13 Geo. III. c. 84. if any perſon ſhall, either by day or night, pull down, pluck up, throw down, level, or otherwiſe deſtroy any turnpike gate, poſt, rail, chain, bar, or other fence, ſet up, or erected, to prevent paſſengers from paſſing by without paying any toll; or any houſe erected for the uſe of any turnpike gate; or any crane, machine, or engine, made or erected on any turnpike road by authority of parliament, for weighing waggons, carts, or carriages; or ſhall forcibly reſcue any perſon in cuſtody for ſuch offence, he ſhall be adjudged guilty of felony, and tranſported for ſeven years, or committed to priſon for any term not exceeding three years, at the diſcretion of the court. Any indictment for ſuch offences may be tried in any adjacent county in England, and the hundred muſt make ſatisfaction.

Bridges. The malicious deſtruction or damaging of public bridges is, no doubt, puniſhable as a miſdemeanor, at common law, being a nuiſance to all the king's ſubjects; and the general highway act of the 13 Geo. III. c. 78. ſubjects to a penalty of 5*l.* on ſummary conviction before a juſtice of peace, and, in default of payment, to whipping, impriſonment, and hard labour, every perſon who ſhall break, damage, or throw down the ſtones, bricks, or wood fixed upon the parapets or battlements of bridges. In many inſtances the legiſlature has made the offence of deſtroying or damaging particular bridges felony; and in ſome, has ouſted ſuch offender from the benefit of clergy.

Mines and Engines. By 10 Geo. II. c. 32. if any perſon ſhall maliciouſly ſet on fire any mine, pit, or delph of coal, or cannel coal, he ſhall be adjudged guilty of felony without benefit of clergy; and all the proviſions made in the black act for bringing offenders to juſtice, and with reſpect to their aiders, and abettors,

abettors, and with refpect to the compenfation to the fufferers, are extended to this act.

The 13 Geo. II. c. 21. alfo enacts, that if any perfon fhall malicioufly divert water from any river, brook, water-courfe, channel, or land-flood, or convey water into any coal-work, mine, pit, or delph of coal, or into any fubterraneous cavities or paffages, or make any fubterraneous paffages, with defign to deftroy, or damage any coal work, &c. or fhall for that purpofe deftroy or obftruct any fough or fewer (which has been a fough or fewer in common for fifty years) made for draining any coal-work, &c.; or fhall attempt or continue any fuch mifchievous practice, or aid or affift therein, he fhall for every offence forfeit to the party aggrieved treble damages and full cofts, to be recovered in any of the courts at Weftminfter.

By 9 Geo. III. c. 29. if any perfon fhall burn, pull down, deftroy, or damage any engine, erected for draining water from collieries, or coal mines, or for drawing coals out of the fame, or for draining water from any mine of lead, tin, copper, or other mineral; or any bridge, waggon-way, or trunk, erected for conveying coals from any colliery or coal mine, or ftaith for depofiting the fame; or any bridge or waggon-way erected for conveying lead, tin, copper, or other mineral, from any fuch mine, or fhall caufe or procure the fame to be done, he fhall be adjudged guilty of felony, and the court may tranfport him for feven years. Profecutions muft be commenced in eighteen months after the fact. By 39 and 40 Geo. III. c. 77. if any perfon fhall pull down or fill up, any air-way, water-way, drain, pit, level, or fhaft; or damage or deftroy any rail-way, tram-road, or other road leading to or from any coal, or other mine-work; or if any perfon (not having or *bonâ fide* claiming a right to poffefs or work the fame refpectively) fhall unlawfully cut, dig, raife, take, or carry away any coal, culm, or other mineral, from any bed, band, vein, or mine, lying and being in wafte, open, or uninclofed lands; or fhall enter into any level, pit, or fhaft, with intent to take any coal, culm, or other mineral; or aid in fuch offence, he fhall be adjudged guilty of a mifdemeanor, and imprifoned not exceeding fix months. Profecutions to be commenced in nine months.

Sea-banks, and Banks of Rivers. By 6 Geo. II. c. 37. any perfon breaking down, or cutting down the bank of any river, or any fea-bank, whereby any lands fhall be overflowed or damaged, fhall be adjudged guilty of felony without benefit of clergy. And the regulations of the black act with refpect to bringing offenders to juftice, accomplices, &c. are extended to this offence. By the fame ftatute, if any perfon fhall cut off, draw up, or remove, and carry away any piles, chalk, or other

materials,

materials, driven into the ground, and ufed for the fecuring any marfh, or fea-walls or banks, in order to prevent the lands lying within the fame from being overflowed and damaged, it fhall be lawful for one or more juftices of the peace refiding near the place, to hear the complaint; and the offender upon conviction fhall forfeit 20*l*. or in default be committed to hard labour for fix months. By 19 Geo. II. c. 22. a fummary jurifdiction is given to one or more juftices of peace to inquire of, and determine certain offences againft the due prefervation of havens, roads, channels, and navigable rivers in England, by unloading rubbifh, &c. out of veffels within the fame, or fuffering old hulks to fink there, or not removing fuch as are ftranded.

Locks and other Works on navigable Rivers. The firft ftatute paffed on this fubject was the 1 Geo. II. c. 19. which reciting, that evil-difpofed perfons had deftroyed turnpike gates, &c. and had threatened the pulling down and deftroying of locks, fluices, and flood-gates; for preventing fuch practices, and for rendering the faid acts more effectual, enacts, that if any perfon fhall by day or night break down, &c. or otherwife deftroy any turnpike gate, &c. he fhall be fubject to certain corporal punifhment, upon conviction before two juftices of the peace, &c. Then by f. 2. if any fuch perfon fo convicted, fhall commit any of the offences aforefaid a fecond time; or, either by day or night, pull down or demolifh any houfe, erected for the fervice of any turnpike gate, &c. or wilfully and malicioufly break down or demolifh any lock, fluice, or flood-gate, erected by authority of parliament, *on any navigable river, for preferving or fecuring the navigation thereof*, and fhall be lawfully convicted of the fame refpectively upon indictment before any juftices of affize, oyer and terminer, or gaol delivery for the county, borough, or corporation where fuch offence fhall be committed; every fuch perfon fhall be adjudged guilty of felony, and may be tranfported for feven years. By 5 Geo. II. c. 33. fuch perfons returning from tranfportation, are guilty of felony without clergy; and by the 8 Geo. II. c. 20. the offence itfelf is made felony without benefit of clergy. By the fame act perfons malicioufly drawing up flood-gates, made for preferving the navigation, are fubject to imprifonment and hard labour for a month, upon a fummary conviction before two juftices of the peace.

Offenders in thefe cafes may be tried in any county in England; thofe out of prifon difcovering accomplices, are intitled to pardon, and parties injured may recover damages from the hundred.

Thefe general acts were fuffered to expire, and then were revived and made perpetual by the 27 Geo. II. c. 16; but the

4 Geo.

4 Geo. III. c. 12. enacts, that if any perſon ſhall break, throw down, damage, or deſtroy, any banks, flood-gates, ſluices, or other works; or open or draw up any flood-gate, or do any wilful hurt or miſchief to any ſuch navigation, ſo as to obſtruct, or prevent the carrying on, completing, ſupporting, or maintaining ſuch navigation; he ſhall be adjudged guilty of felony, and may be tranſported for ſeven years.

Drainage Works, &c. in particular Places. The injuries which may be done to theſe eſtabliſhments are provided againſt by various local ſtatutes, inflicting different penalties, from ſix months hard labour, to ſeven years tranſportation.

Weſt India Docks. By the 39 Geo. III. c. 69. it is enacted, that if any perſon ſhall ſet on fire any of the works to be made by virtue of this act, or any ſhip or veſſel lying in the ſaid canal, or the docks, or other works, he ſhall be adjudged guilty of felony without benefit of clergy. And if any perſon ſhall demoliſh, break down, cut or deſtroy, any of the ſaid works, or any veſſel lying in the ſaid canal, docks, or other works; he ſhall ſuffer fine, impriſonment, or tranſportation, at the diſcretion of the court before whom he is tried and convicted. In caſe any perſon ſhall cut, break, or deſtroy any rope, or other thing by which any ſhip or other veſſel in the ſaid canal, or docks, or in any place in the river Thames, between London-bridge and the mouth of the river Lea, ſhall be moored or faſtened, he ſhall for every offence forfeit not exceeding 10*l.*

King's Ships, Dock-yards, &c. The offence of embezzling the king's ſtores has been before treated of: and further, the ſtat. 12 Geo. III. c. 24. enacts, that if any perſon ſhall, either within this realm, or in any place thereunto belonging, ſet on fire, or burn, or otherwiſe deſtroy, or cauſe or aſſiſt in doing it, any of his majeſty's ſhips or veſſels of war, whether on float or building in any of his majeſty's dock-yards, or building or repairing in any private yards; or any of his majeſty's arſenals, magazines, dock-yards, rope-yards, victualling offices, or buildings thereto belonging; or any timber, or materials there; or any military, naval, or victualling ſtores, or other ammunition of war, or any place where the ſame are kept or depoſited; he ſhall be adjudged guilty of felony without benefit of clergy. The offender may be tried in any county, and the crime is alſo cognizable by a court-martial.

Private Ships, Wrecks, &c. Offences relating to theſe are deſcribed in this volume, p. 270.

Beſides the regulations there mentioned, it is provided by 2 Geo. III. c. 28. that if any perſon ſhall cut, damage, or ſpoil any cordage, cable, buoys, buoy-rope, head-faſt, or other faſt, fixed to any anchor or moorings belonging to any ſhip or veſſel

vessel at anchor or mooring in the river Thames, or any rope used for the purpose of mooring or rafting masts or timber; or shall be aiding or assisting therein; with an intent to steal the same; such person being convicted on the oath of two witnesses, shall be transported for seven years. Also, in case any person acting in the execution of any of the powers granted by this act, shall be obstructed therein; every person so obstructing, and all such as shall act in their assistance, on conviction at the general or quarter sessions of the county or city adjoining, shall be transported for seven years.

Also by 33 Geo. III. c. 67. (made perpetual by 41 Geo. III. c. 19.) if any seaman, keelman, caster, or ship carpenter, or other person, shall burn or set fire to any ship, keel, or other vessel, he shall be adjudged guilty of felony without benefit of clergy. And if any person shall destroy or damage any ship, keel, or other vessel, (otherwise than by fire,) he shall on conviction, either at a session of oyer and terminer, or at a general or quarter session of the peace, be transported, not exceeding fourteen years, nor less than seven. If these offences are committed at sea, they may be tried at an admiralty session; and prosecution must be commenced within twelve months.

Threatening Letters or Writings. The occasion and object of the laws in force against the offence of sending threatening letters and writings to others, are well explained in the preamble of the black act, which recites, that ill-designing and disorderly persons had, of late, associated themselves, &c. and had sent letters in fictitious names to several persons demanding venison, and money, and threatening some great violence, if such their unlawful demands should be refused, or if they should be interrupted in, or prosecuted for, such their wicked practices; and had actually done great damage to several persons, who had either refused to comply with such demands, or endeavoured to bring them to justice: and then enacts, that if any person, (whether armed and disguised, or not) shall knowingly send any letter without any name subscribed thereto, or signed with a fictitious name, demanding money, venison, or other valuable thing; or shall forcibly rescue any person in custody for such offence; or shall, by gift or promise, procure any to join him in any such unlawful act; he shall be adjudged guilty of felony without benefit of clergy. Such offenders not surrendering themselves when demanded by the king's proclamation, and making full confession of their accomplices, are also made guilty of felony without benefit of clergy. Persons who, after the time for such surrender expired, shall conceal, aid, abet, or succour any such offender, knowing him to have been so charged, and to have been required to surrender by such order, shall be guilty

guilty of felony without benefit of clergy. And such offences may be tried in any county of England.

The 27 Geo. II. c. 15. further enacts, that if any person shall knowingly send any letter without any name subscribed, or signed with a fictitious name or names, letter or letters, threatening to kill, or murder any of the king's subjects, or to burn their houses, barns, corn, hay, or straw, though nothing is demanded in such letter; or shall forcibly rescue any person in custody for the same; he shall be adjudged guilty of felony without benefit of clergy. Lastly, by 30 Geo. II. c. 24. all persons who shall knowingly send or deliver any letter or writing, with or without a name, or with a fictitious name or letter, threatening to accuse any person of any crime punishable by law with death, transportation, pillory, or any other infamous punishment, with a view or intent to extort or gain money or goods, shall be deemed offenders against law and the public peace, and be fined and imprisoned, or put in the pillory, or publicly whipped, or transported for seven years.

For protection of masters of manufactories, it is provided by 12 Geo. I. c. 34. that if any person shall write, or send any letter, or other writing or message, threatening any hurt or harm to any master-woolcomber, or master-weaver, or other person concerned in the *woollen manufacture*, or threatening to burn, pull down, or destroy any of their houses or out-houses, or to cut down or destroy any of their trees, or to maim or kill any of their cattle, for not complying with any demands, claims, or pretences of any workmen, or others employed by them, or for not conforming or submitting to any illegal bye laws, ordinances, rules or orders; any such offender, being convicted within twelve calendar months, shall be adjudged guilty of felony and transported for seven years. The 22 Geo. II. c. 27. extends these provisions to journeymen dyers, journeymen hot-pressers, and all other persons employed in the woollen manufactures, and also to journeymen, servants, workmen, and labourers, employed in the making of felts or hats, and in manufactures of silk, mohair, fur, hemp, flax, linen, cotton, fustian, iron, and leather, or any manufactures made up of wool, fur, hemp, flax, cotton, mohair, or silk, or of any of the said materials mixed one with another.

Riots. The *riotous assembling* of *twelve persons*, or more, and not dispersing upon proclamation, was made high treason by 3 and 4 Edw. VI. c. 5. when the king was a minor, and a change in religion to be effected: but that statute was repealed by 1 Mary, c. 1. though the prohibition was in substance re-enacted, with an inferior degree of punishment, by 1 Mary, st. 2. c. 12. which made the same offence a single felony. These

statutes

ſtatutes ſpecified and particularized the nature of the riots they were meant to ſuppreſs; as, for example, ſuch as were ſet on foot with intention to offer violence to the privy council, or to change the laws of the kingdom, or for certain other ſpecific purpoſes: in which caſes, if the perſons were commanded by proclamation to diſperſe, and they did not, it was felony, but within the benefit of clergy; and alſo the act indemnified the peace officers and their aſſiſtants, if death enſued from their endeavours to ſuppreſs ſuch riot. This act continued in force till the end of Elizabeth's reign, and then expired. From this period to the death of queen Anne, it was not revived: but, at the acceſſion of George the firſt, in order to ſupport the act of ſettlement, it was renewed and made perpetual, with large additions. For, whereas the former acts expreſsly defined and ſpecified what ſhould be accounted a riot, the 1 Geo. I. c. 5. enacts, generally, that if any twelve perſons are unlawfully aſſembled to the diſturbance of the peace, and any one juſtice of the peace, ſheriff, under ſheriff, or mayor of a town, ſhall think proper to command them by proclamation to diſperſe, if they contemn his orders and continue together for one hour afterwards, ſuch contempt ſhall be felony without benefit of clergy. The proclamation, or what is commonly called "reading the riot act," is in theſe words: "Our "ſovereign lord the king chargeth and commandeth all per-"ſons, being aſſembled, to diſperſe themſelves, and peaceably "to depart to their habitations or to their lawful buſineſs, "upon the pains contained in the act made in the firſt year "of king George, for preventing tumults and riotous aſſem-"blies. God ſave the king." If the reading of the proclamation is oppoſed by force, or the reader in any manner wilfully hindered, ſuch oppoſers and hinderers are felons without benefit of clergy: as are all perſons to whom ſuch proclamation ought to have been made, knowing of ſuch hindrance, and not diſperſing. The indemnifying clauſe, in caſe any of the mob are killed, is copied from the act of Mary; and, by a ſubſequent clauſe, if any of the perſons ſo riotouſly aſſembled, begin, even before proclamation, to pull down any church, chapel, meeting-houſe, dwelling-houſe, or outhouſes, they ſhall be felons without benefit of clergy. Perſons whoſe buildings are ſo demoliſhed may recover damages in an action againſt the hundred. And it was determined after the riots in 1780, that the owners of houſes might recover damages alſo for their furniture, or for any injury done to their property at the ſame time.

Beſide the powers given by theſe ſtatutes, the common law provided againſt tumultuary meetings in breach of the peace, denominating them, according to circumſtances, riots, routs, or unlawful aſſemblies.

A riot is a tumultuous diſturbance of the peace, by three perſons, or more, aſſembling together of their own authority, with an intent of mutually aſſiſting one another againſt any who ſhall oppoſe them in the execution of ſome enterprize of a private nature, and afterwards actually executing the ſame in a violent turbulent manner to the terror of the people, whether the act intended were of itſelf lawful or unlawful.

A rout is a diſturbance of the peace by perſons aſſembling to do a thing, which, if executed, would make them rioters, and actually making a motion to the execution thereof. But by ſome books the nature of a rout is confined to ſuch aſſemblies only as are occaſioned by ſome grievance common to all the company, as the incloſure of land where they all claim a right of common, &c. In general, it agrees with the deſcription of a riot, but that it may be a complete offence without the execution of the intended enterprize.

An unlawful aſſembly is ſaid to be a diſturbance of the peace by perſons barely aſſembling to do a thing, which, if it were executed, would make them rioters; but neither executing nor making a motion toward the execution of it. But this ſeems to be too narrow a definition; any meeting of great numbers of people with ſuch circumſtances of terror as cannot but endanger the public peace, and raiſe fears and jealouſies among the king's ſubjects, ſeems properly to be called an *unlawful aſſembly*; as where great numbers, complaining of a common grievance, meet together, armed in a warlike manner, in order to conſult on the moſt proper means for the recovery of their intereſts; for no one can foreſee what may be the reſult of ſuch meeting. Alſo an aſſembly of a man's friends for the defence of his perſon againſt thoſe who threaten to beat him, if he go to ſuch a market, &c. is unlawful; for he who is in fear of ſuch inſults muſt provide for his ſafety by demanding the ſurety of the peace againſt thoſe by whom he is threatened, and not make uſe of ſuch violent methods, which cannot but be attended with the danger of raiſing tumults and diſorders to the diſturbance of the public peace. Yet an aſſembly of a man's friends in his own houſe for defence againſt thoſe who threaten to make an unlawful entry, or to beat him therein, is indulged by law; for a man's houſe is looked upon as his caſtle. When perſons are thus unlawfully aſſembled to the number of twelve, the offence may be capital, but the puniſhment, when they do not exceed eleven, is by fine and impriſonment only. The ſame is the caſe in riots and routs by the common law; to to which the pillory in very enormous cases has been sometimes superadded. And by the stat. 13 Hen. IV. c. 7. any two justices, together with the sheriff or under sheriff of the county, may come with the *posse comitatus*, if need be, and suppress any such riot, assembly, or rout, arrest the rioters, and record upon the spot the nature and circumstances of the whole transaction; which record alone shall be a sufficient conviction of the offenders. In the interpretation of which statute it has been holden, that all persons, noblemen and others, except women, clergymen, persons decrepit, and infants under fifteen, are bound to attend the justices in suppressing a riot, upon pain of fine and imprisonment, and that any battery, wounding, or killing the rioters, that may happen in suppressing the riot, is justifiable.

By 33 Geo. III. c. 67. the assembly of seamen, keelmen, casters, and ship carpenters, to hinder or obstruct the loading or unloading, or the sailing or navigating of any ship, keel, or other vessel, or to deter, prevent, hinder, or obstruct any seaman, keelman, caster, or ship carpenter, from working at his lawful trade, is prohibited under penalty of imprisonment not exceeding twelve, nor less than six months. The punishment of a second offence is transportation, for not more than fourteen years, nor less than seven. The prosecutions are to commence within a year after the fact.

Assaults and Batteries. An *assault* is an attempt or offer, with force and violence, to do a corporal hurt to another; as by striking at him with or without a weapon, or presenting a gun at him at a distance to which the gun will carry, or pointing a pitchfork at him, standing within the reach of it, or by holding up one's fist at him, or by any other such like act done in an angry threatening manner: hence it clearly follows, that one charged with an assault and battery may be found guilty of the former, and yet acquitted of the latter. No words whatever can amount to an assault. Any injury, be it never so small, being actually done to the person of a man in an angry, revengeful, rude, or insolent manner, as by spitting in his face, or any way touching him in anger, or violently jostling him out of the way, is a battery in the eye of the law. The general punishment for assaults is by fine, but the party aggrieved has also an action, by which he may recover a compensation in damages; and there are express punishments by various statutes for different species of assaults, of which some account has already been given.

Affrays. The word *affray* is derived from the French word *effrayer*, to terrify, and, in a legal sense, is taken for a public offence to the terror of the people. There may be *an assault* which will not amount to *an affray*, as where it happens

5

pens in a private place, out of the hearing or feeing of any, except the parties concerned; no quarrelfome or threatening words whatfoever amount to an affray; and no one can juftify laying his hands on thofe who barely quarrel with angry words, without coming to blows; yet the conftable may, at the requeft of the party threatened, carry the perfon, who threatens to beat him, before a juftice, to find fureties. Affrays may be fuppreffed by any private perfon prefent, who is juftifiable in endeavouring to part the combatants, whatever confequence may enfue; but more efpecially the conftable, or other fimilar officer, however denominated, is bound to keep the peace; and to that purpofe, may break open doors to fupprefs an affray, or apprehend the affrayers; and may either carry them before a juftice, or imprifon them by his own authority for a convenient fpace till the heat is over; and may then perhaps alfo make them find fureties for the peace. The punifhment of common affrays is by fine and imprifonment; the meafure of which muft be regulated by the circumftances of the cafe: for, where there is any material aggravation, the punifhment proportionally increafes. Deliberately engaging in a duel, would be punifhed as an affray of the moft dangerous defcription; and affrays in a church, or church yard, are ftill more feverely confidered. In thofe places words, unaccompanied with acts, are fufficient to conftitute an offence; it being enacted by 5 and 6 Edw. VI. c. 4. that if any perfon fhall, by words only, quarrel, chide, or brawl, in a church, or church-yard, the ordinary fhall fufpend him, if a layman, *ab ingreffu ecclefiæ*, and, if a clerk in orders, from the miniftration of his office, during pleafure. And, if any perfon in fuch church, or church-yard, proceeds to fmite or lay violent hands upon another, he fhall be excommunicated *ipfo facto*; or if he ftrikes him with a weapon, or draws any weapon with intent to ftrike, he fhall, befide excommunication, being convicted by a jury, have one of his ears cut off; or having no ears, be branded with the letter F. on his cheek.

Riding or going armed. Riding or going armed with unufual or dangerous weapons is a fpecies of affray without actual violence or verbal threat, fince its direct effect is to terrify the people; it is confidered a crime againft the public peace, and is particularly prohibited by the ftatute of Northampton, 2 Edw. III. c. 3. upon pain of forfeiture of the arms, and imprifonment during the king's pleafure. A man cannot excufe the wearing fuch armour in public, by alleging that one threatened him, and that he wears it for the fafety of his perfon from his affault. No wearing of arms is within the meaning of this ftatute, unlefs accompanied with fuch circumſtances as are apt to terrify the people; and no perſon is within the intention of the ſaid ſtatute, who arms himſelf to ſuppreſs dangerous rioters, rebels, or enemies, and endeavours to ſuppreſs or reſiſt ſuch diſturbers of the peace or quiet of the realm.

FORCIBLE ENTRY AND DETAINER. By the common law a man diſſeiſed of any lands, or tenements (if he could not prevail by fair means), might lawfully regain poſſeſſion by force, unleſs he were put to a neceſſity of bringing his action, by having neglected to re-enter in due time. But this indulgence having been found by experience to be very prejudicial to the public peace, by giving an opportunity to powerful men, under the pretence of feigned titles, forcibly to eject their weaker neighbours, and alſo by force to retain their wrongful poſſeſſions, it was thought neceſſary, by many ſevere laws, to reſtrain all perſons from the uſe of ſuch violent methods of doing themſelves juſtice; therefore by the 5 Rich. II. ſt. 1. c. 8. all forcible entries are puniſhed with impriſonment and ranſom at the king's will; and by the ſeveral ſtatutes of 15 Rich. II. c. 2. 8 Hen. VI. c. 9. 31 Eliz. c. 11. and 21 Jas. I. c. 15. upon any forcible entry, or forcible detainer after peaceable entry, into any lands, or beneſices of the church, a juſtice of the peace, taking ſufficient power of the county, may go to the place, and there record the force upon his own view, as in caſe of riots; and upon ſuch conviction may commit the offender to jail, till he makes fine and ranſom to the king. And moreover the juſtices have power to ſummon a jury, to try the forcible entry or the detainer complained of; and, if the ſame be found by that jury, then, beſides the fine on the offender, the juſtices ſhall make reſtitution by the ſheriff of the poſſeſſion, without inquiring into the merits of the title; for the force is the only thing to be tried, puniſhed, and remedied by them; and the ſame may be done by indictment at the general ſeſſions. But this proviſion does not extend to ſuch as endeavour to maintain poſſeſſion by force, where they themſelves, or their anceſtors, have been in the peaceable enjoyment of the lands and tenements for three years immediately preceding.

SURETY FOR THE PEACE AND FOR GOOD BEHAVIOUR. As the laſt mentioned offences are chiefly conſidered as directed againſt the peace of the king's ſubjects, it may be proper in this place to give an account of the mode reſorted to for preventing them, by taking ſureties for the peace and for good behaviour. By the Saxon conſtitution theſe ſureties were always at hand, by means of Alfred's wiſe inſtitution of decennaries or frank pledges; wherein the whole neighbourhood or tithing

tithing of freemen were mutually pledges for each other's good behaviour. But this great and general fecurity being now fallen into difufe and neglected, there has fucceeded to it the method of making fufpected perfons find particular and fpecial fecurities for their future conduct: of which we find mention in the laws of Edward the Confeffor; "*tradat fidejuffores de pace et legalitate tuenda.*" This fecurity confifts in being bound, with one or more fureties, in a recognizance or obligation to the king, entered on record, and taken in fome court or by fome judicial officer, whereby the parties acknowledge themfelves to be indebted to the crown in the fum required, (for inftance, 100*l.*) with condition to be void, if the party fhall appear in court on fuch a day, and, in the mean time, fhall keep the peace, either generally, towards the king, and all his liege people; or particularly alfo, with regard to the perfon who craves the fecurity. Or, if it be for the good behaviour, then on condition that he fhall demean and behave himfelf well, (or be of good behaviour), either generally or fpecially, for the time therein limited, as for one or more years, or for life. This recognizance, if taken by a juftice of the peace, muft be certified to the next feffion, in purfuance of the ftat. 3 Hen. VII. c. 1.; and if the condition of fuch recognizance be broken, by any breach of the peace in one cafe, or any mifbehaviour in the other, the recognizance becomes forfeited or abfolute; and, being *eftreated* or extracted (taken out from among the other records) and fent up to the exchequer, the party and his fureties, having now become the king's abfolute debtors, are fued for the feveral fums in which they are refpectively bound. Any juftice of the peace, by virtue of his commiffion, or thofe who are *ex officio* confervators of the peace, may demand fuch fecurity according to their own difcretion; or it may be granted at the requeft of any fubject, upon due caufe fhewn, provided fuch demandant be under the king's protection; or, if the juftice is averfe to act, it may be granted by a mandatory writ, called *a fupplicavit*, a writ which is feldom ufed; for, when application is made to the fuperior courts, they ufually take the recognizances, under the ftat. 21 Jas. I. c. 8. A peer or peerefs cannot be bound over in any other place, than the court of king's-bench or chancery: though a juftice of the peace has power to require fureties of any other perfon, being *compos mentis*, even if he be a fellow juftice or other magiftrate. Wives may demand it againft their hufbands, or hufbands, if neceffary, againft their wives.

A recognizance may be difcharged, either by the demife of the king, to whom the recognizance is made, or by the

 death

death of the principal party bound thereby, if not before forfeited; or by order of the court, to which it is certified by the justices, (as the quarter sessions, assizes, or king's bench,) if they see sufficient cause: or in case he at whose request it was granted, if granted upon a private account, will release it, or does not make his appearance to pray that it may be continued.

Thus far what has been said is applicable to both species of recognizances, for the peace, and for the good behaviour; but as these securities are in some respects different, especially as to the cause of granting, or the means of forfeiting them, they are now to be considered separately.

And first, with respect to *sureties for the peace*. Any justice of the peace may, *ex officio*, bind to keep the peace, any person who, in his presence; makes any affray, or threatens to kill, or beat another; or those who contend together with hot and angry words; or go about with unusual weapons or attendance, to the terror of the people; and all such as he knows to be common barrators; and such as are brought before him by the constable for a breach of the peace in his presence: and all such persons, as having been before bound to the peace, have broken it, and forfeited their recognizances. Also, wherever any private man has just cause to fear that another will burn his house, or do him a corporal injury, by killing, imprisoning, or beating him; or that he will procure others so to do; he may demand surety of the peace against such person: and every justice of the peace is bound to grant it, if he who demands it will make oath, that he is actually under fear of death and bodily harm; and will shew that he has just cause to be so, by reason of the other's menaces, attempts, or having lain in wait for him; and will also further swear, that he does not require such surety out of malice or for mere vexation. This is called swearing the peace against another: and, if the party does not find such sureties, as the justice in his discretion shall require, he may immediately be committed till he does.

Such recognizance for keeping the peace, when given, may be forfeited by any actual violence, or even an assault, or menace, to the person of him who demanded it, if it be a special recognizance: or, if the recognizance be general, by any unlawful action whatsoever, that either is, or tends to a breach of the peace; or, more particularly, by any one of the many species of offences which were mentioned as crimes against the public peace, or by any private violence committed against any of his majesty's subjects. But a bare trespass upon the lands or goods of another, which is a ground for a civil action, unless

accompanied

accompanied with a wilful breach of the peace, is no forfeiture of the recognizance. Neither are mere reproachful words, as calling a man a knave or liar, any breach of the peace, so as to forfeit a recognizance, (being looked upon to be the effect of unmeaning heat and passion) unless they amount to a challenge to fight.

The *surety for good behaviour* includes security for the peace, and somewhat more. Justices are empowered by the 34 Edw. III. c. 1. to bind over to the good behaviour towards the king and the people, all them that *be not of good fame*, wherever they be found; to the intent that the people be not troubled or endamaged, nor the peace diminished, nor merchants and others, passing by the highways of the realm, be disturbed nor put in the peril which may happen by such offenders. Under the general words of this expression, that *be not of good fame*, it is holden, that a man may be bound to his good behaviour for causes of scandal against moral propriety, as well as against the peace, as for haunting bawdy-houses with women of bad fame; or for keeping such women in his own house; or for words tending to scandalize the government; or in abuse of the officers of justice, especially in the execution of their office. Thus also a justice may bind over all night-walkers, eaves-droppers, such as keep suspicious company, or are reputed to be pilferers or robbers, such as sleep in the day, and wake in the night, common drunkards, whoremasters, the putative fathers of bastards, cheats, idle vagabonds, and other persons, whose misbehaviour may reasonably bring them within the general words of the statute, as persons not of good fame: an expression, it must be owned, of so great a latitude, as leaves much to be determined by the discretion of the magistrate himself. But if he commits a man for want of sureties, he must express the cause with convenient certainty; and take care that such cause be a good one.

A recognizance for the good behaviour may be forfeited by all the same means, as one for the security of the peace; and also by some others. As, by going armed with unusual attendance, to the terror of the people; by speaking words tending to sedition; or by committing any of those acts of misbehaviour, which the recognizance was intended to prevent. But not by barely giving fresh cause of suspicion of that which perhaps may never actually happen: for, though it is just to compel suspected persons to give security to the public against misbehaviour that is apprehended; yet it would be hard, upon such suspicion, without the proof of any actual crime, to punish them as for a forfeiture of their recognizance.

NUISANCE. Nuisance, *nocumentum*, or annoyance, signifies

 any

any thing that works hurt, inconvenience, or damage. And nuisances are of two kinds; *public* or *common* nuisances, which affect the public, and are an annoyance to *all* the king's subjects; and private nuisances, which are defined to be any thing done to the hurt or annoyance of the lands, tenements, or hereditaments of another. In this place public or common nuisances alone will be treated of.

A common nuisance is an offence against the public, either by doing a thing which tends to the annoyance of all the king's subjects, or by neglecting to do a thing which the common good requires. Annoyances affecting particular persons only, are not punishable by a public prosecution, but are left to be redressed by private actions.

Under the extensive description of a nuisance, a great variety of offences are to be considered, and many of them are of sufficient moment to claim particular notice.

Nuisances with respect to High-ways. It is said there are three kinds of ways: a foot-way, which is called in Latin, *iter*; a pack and prime way, which is both a horse and foot-way, called in Latin *actus*; and a cart-way, which contains the other two, and also a way for carts, and is called in Latin *via* or *aditus*; and this is either common to all men, and then it is called, *via regia*; or belongs to some city or town, or privateperson, and then it is called *communis strata*. It seems that any one of these ways which is common to all the king's people, whether it lead directly to a market town, or only from town to town, may be properly called a high-way, and that any such cart-way may be called the king's high-way; and that a nuisance in any of them is punishable by indictment in the court-leet. And in books of the best authority, *a river* common to all men is called a high-way; but a street built upon a person's own ground is a dedication of the high-way so far only as the public has occasion for it, *viz.* for a right of passage, and is not to be understood as a transfer of the absolute possession of the soil.

By the common law, the general charge of repairing all high-ways lies on the occupiers of the lands in the parish wherein they are. And the 13 Geo. III. c. 78. at a length, and with a minuteness which cannot be transferred into this work, provides for the repair of high-ways by the appointment of commissioners, surveyors, and other proper officers, who are enabled to require from certain inhabitants of every parish the performance of necessary duties in respect to the reparation of ways, and to receive certain compositions or contributions from those who cannot perform them. Justices are also empowered to levy rates for extraordinary charges, and fines may be imposed for non-performance of the duty.

All

All injuries whatſoever to any high-way, as by digging a ditch, or making a hedge over thwart it, or laying logs of timber in it, or by doing any other act which will render it leſs commodious to the king's people, are public nuiſances at common law.

There is alſo a particular nuiſance created by ſtatute, namely the drawing of a travelling carriage with more than ſix horſes in length, the permitting which occaſioned the carrying of ſuch exceſſive loads in ſuch carriages, that the weight in many places rendered the roads impaſſable. On this ſubject the ſtatute already mentioned has provided, that no waggon, having the ſole or bottom of the fellies of the wheels of the breadth of nine inches, ſhall be drawn with more than eight horſes; and no cart, having the ſole of the fellies of the breadth of ſix inches, and rolling on each ſide a ſurface of nine inches, with more than five horſes; no waggon, having the ſole of the fellies of the breath of ſix inches, and rolling on each ſide a ſurface of nine inches, be drawn with more than ſeven horſes; and no ſuch waggon rolling a ſurface of ſix inches only ſhall be drawn with more than ſix horſes; no cart having the ſole of the fellies of the breadth of ſix inches ſhall be drawn with more than four horſes; no waggon having the ſole of the fellies of leſs breadth than ſix inches ſhall be drawn with more than five horſes; no cart having the ſole or bottom of the fellies of leſs breadth than ſix inches ſhall be drawn with more than three horſes upon high-ways, not being turnpike roads; under pain that the owner of ſuch waggon or cart reſpectively ſhall forfeit five pounds, and the driver, not being the owner, for every horſe or beaſt which ſhall be ſo drawing above the number limited, ten ſhillings to the uſe of the informer: but carriages moving upon wheels or rollers of the breadth of ſixteen inches on each ſide, with flat ſurfaces, are allowed to be drawn with any number of horſes, or other cattle. The proſecution is to be commenced before a juſtice within three days after the fact, and any action, within a month; and notice muſt be given to the owner or driver, on the very day that ſuch information or action is intended.

For the prevention of accidents by the careleſſneſs of drivers, and affording the means of bringing them to puniſhment for miſbehaviour, many excellent proviſions are made, ſuch as obliging the owner to inſcribe his name, with a certain number, on every cart, and directing the driver to be in ſuch a ſituation as to retain a proper command over the horſes; and not riding on the cart, or deſerting it; or by any negligence or miſbehaviour rendering likely, much leſs contributing to the injury of others. The offences in these respects are punished with fines to be recovered in a summary way before justices of the peace.

Nuisances in Turnpike Roads. The turnpike roads of England are placed under the management and direction of trustees, who are usually named and appointed by the respective acts of parliament, which are occasionally passed for the purpose of making, repairing, and sustaining such particular roads. But the powers of these statutes being confined to separate objects, it was thought expedient to pass some general laws which should apply in common to all trustees and turnpike roads throughout the kingdom. The chief statute on this subject is the 13 Geo. III. c. 84. which provides with great exactness for the appointment and qualification of trustees, the regulation of carriages, weighing engines, tolls, repairs, and many other particulars; and, with respect to nuisances, declares, that if the surveyor, or other person having the care of any turnpike road, shall knowingly suffer to be or remain, for four days in any part thereof, within ten feet on either side of the middle of such road, any posts, heaps of stones, rubbish, or earth, set up or raised on or above the surface of the said road, by which the passage may be obstructed or confined, except posts, blocks, stones, or banks of earth, fixed in the ground, or raised for securing horse or foot roads, or passages for water, and all direction posts and stones, such surveyor shall forfeit twenty shillings. If any person shall encroach, by making any hedge, ditch, or other fence, on any turnpike road, within the distance of thirty feet from the centre; or shall plough, harrow, or break up the soil of any land or ground, within fifteen feet; every person so offending shall forfeit forty shillings to the informer, and the trustees may compel him at his own expence to remove or remedy the nuisance. Persons damaging mile-stones, posts, blocks, banks, &c. forfeit not exceeding 5*l.* nor less than ten shillings, or for default of payment are committed to the house of correction, to be whipped and kept to hard labour not more than a month, nor less than seven days.

Nuisances with respect to Bridges. Of common right the charge of repairing all common bridges lies upon the county wherein they are, unless part be within a franchise, in which case it is said, that so much as is within the franchise shall be repaired by those of the franchise. A man is not bound to repair a new bridge built by himself for the common good; but the county is bound to repair it, if it become of public convenience. Those who are bound to repair bridges, must make them of such height and strength, as shall be answerable

ſwerable to the courſe of the water, whether it continue in the old channel, or make a new one; and they are not puniſhable as treſpaſſers for entering on any adjoining land for ſuch purpoſe, or for laying thereon the materials requiſite for ſuch repairs. Such is the proviſion made by common law; and by various ſtatutes, the juſtices in the county or place upon which the ſupport and reparation of the bridge lie, are enabled to take all proper meaſures for effecting thoſe objects, and for prevention of nuiſances and injuries.

Public Houses. The eſtabliſhment of houſes for the reception of travellers, or the reſort of perſons of every claſs, for honeſt purpoſes of buſineſs or pleaſure, is among the firſt conveniences of ſociety; but as no principle is ſo eaſily capable of perverſion to the moſt immoral and dangerous ends, as that which conſtitutes places of eaſy and promiſcuous reſort, ſo the regulation of public houſes is remarkably ſtrict, and abundant care is taken to prevent them from becoming nuiſances; or if they do degenerate into that character, to ſuppreſs them, and puniſh the proprietors.

By the common law, the keeper of an inn may be indicted and fined, as guilty of a public nuiſance, if he uſually harbours thieves or perſons of ſcandalous reputation, or ſuffers frequent diſorders in his houſe, or takes exorbitant prices, or ſets up a new inn in a place where there is no need of one, to the hindrance of other ancient and well governed inns, or keeps it in a place in reſpect of its ſituation wholly unfit for ſuch a purpoſe. But any perſon may lawfully ſet up a new inn, unleſs it be inconvenient to the public in ſome of the reſpects already noticed, and has no need of any licence from the king for this purpoſe, for the keeping of an inn is no franchiſe, but a lawful trade, open to every ſubject; but if an inn degenerates into an ale-houſe, by ſuffering diſorderly tippling, it ſhall be deemed as ſuch; and if one who keeps a common inn, refuſes either to receive a traveller as a gueſt into his houſe, or to find him victuals or lodging, upon his tendering a reaſonable price, he is not only liable to render damages for the injury, in an action on the caſe at the ſuit of the party grieved, but may alſo be indicted and fined, at the ſuit of the king. Alſo it is ſaid, that he may be compelled by the conſtable of the town to receive and entertain ſuch a perſon as his gueſt, and that it is no way material whether he have any ſign before his door or not, if he make it his common buſineſs to entertain paſſengers.

The ſtatutes 5 and 6 Edw. VI. c. 25., and 26 Geo. II. c. 31. provide that none ſhall be admitted or ſuffered to keep any common

mon

mon ale-houfe or tippling houfe, except. in fairs, but fuch as fhall be allowed in open feffions, or by two juftices of peace, whereof one to be of the *quorum*. The exception refpecting fairs is made from the neceffity of accommodating the perfons who refort to them, and therefore only allows the unlicenfed fale in the place where the common fair is held, and not in any private houfe which may be within the limits of the town for which it is kept. Houfes in public watering places, where they take in lodgers and boarders coming to ufe the waters during the feafon, and drefs their victuals, fupply them with ale, beer, and other liquors, and entertain their horfes at fo much per day, but fell to no other perfons, are not fuch public houfes as require to be licenfed.

By 26 Geo. II. c. 31. no licences fhall be granted but on the firft day of September, yearly, or within twenty days after; and fuch licence fhall be made for one year only, to commence on the twenty-ninth day of the faid September. The day and place for granting fuch licences is appointed by two or more of the juftices acting for the divifion where the perfon to be licenfed dwells, by a warrant under their hands and feals at leaft ten days before fuch meeting, directed to the high conftable of the divifion, requiring him to order the petty conftables to give notice to the inn-keepers and ale-houfe-keepers of the day and place. In Middlefex and Surry, by 32 Geo. III. c. 59. the juftices appoint at leaft fix, but not more than eight licenfing days; and in cities and corporations the ancient cuftoms with refpect to time are ftill followed.

No licence can be granted to any perfon not licenfed the preceding year, unlefs he produce at the general meeting of the juftices in September a certificate under the hands of the parfon, vicar, or curate, and the major part of the church-wardens and overfeers, or elfe of three or four refpectable and fubftantial houfeholders and inhabitants of the parifh or place where fuch ale-houfe is to be, fetting forth that fuch perfon is of good fame, and of fober life and converfation; and it fhall be mentioned in fuch licence that fuch certificate was produced; but this regulation does not extend to cities and corporations. If ale-houfe-keepers die or remove, &c. before the expiration of their licences, new ones may be granted to executors, or new tenants, till the next licenfing day, on entering perfonally into fuch recognizance, with fuch fureties as is directed in refpect to perfons to whom licences are to be originally granted. Licences muft be equally obtained by perfons keeping ale-houfes, or tippling-houfes, or felling wines, fpirituous liquors, or ftrong waters by retail; and all perfons felling quantities lefs than two gallons are

are retailers. Nor can a licence to ſell wine or ſpirituous liquors by retail be granted to any who have not alſo an ale or beer licence.

The recognizance above alluded to is required by the 26 Geo. II. c. 31. which directs, that upon granting a licence by juſtices of the peace to any perſon to keep an ale-houſe, inn, victualling houſe, or to ſell ale, beer, and other liquors by retail, every ſuch perſon ſhall enter into a recognizance to the king in the ſum of 10*l.*, with two ſufficient ſureties in 5*l.*, or one ſufficient ſurety in 10*l.* under the uſual condition of maintaining good order and rule within the ſame. Theſe recognizances are returned to the clerk of the peace, and delivered to the juſtices at their September meeting.

By the ſame act, any juſtice of the peace of any county or place, upon complaint or information that a licenſed perſon has committed any act whereby his recognizance may be forfeited, or the condition broken, may, by ſummons under his hand and ſeal, require ſuch perſon to appear at the next general or quarter ſeſſions of the peace, to anſwer to the matter of ſuch complaint; and alſo may bind the perſon making ſuch complaint to appear and give evidence, and the juſtices, in ſeſſion, may direct a jury to inquire of the miſdemeanor charged; and, if the perſon is found guilty, order the recognizance to be eſtreated; and the perſon offending is diſabled to ſell any ale, beer, or other liquor, for three years; and any licence granted him during ſuch term is void.

With reſpect to the keepers of unlicenſed houſes, it is enacted by 5 and 6 Edw. III. c. 25. that the juſtices of peace within every ſhire, city, or liberty, or two of them, may remove, diſcharge, and put away common ſelling of ale and beer in common ale-houſes and tippling-houſes. And it ſeems to have been the general opinion in the conſtruction of this clauſe, that an ale-houſe-keeper ſuppreſſed in purſuance of it cannot be licenſed again but in open ſeſſions. And by the ſame ſtatute, if any perſon not allowed by the juſtices, ſhall obſtinately keep a common ale-houſe, two juſtices may for every offence commit him to jail for three days; and before his deliverance he muſt enter into recognizance with two ſureties, not to keep any common ale-houſe, or ſell ale or beer. The 26 Geo. II. c. 31. adds a penalty of 10*l.* to be recovered before one juſtice, and applied to the uſe of the poor. For ſelling liquors without a licence there are alſo various penalties, ſome attended with, and ſome without impriſonment; and for prevention of extortion both with reſpect to gueſts and their cattle, ſome laws are enacted, but not ſtrictly regarded; nor would they perhaps in modern times produce the deſired effect.

The ſtatutes which moſt immediately tend to prevent what may

may properly be termed nuisances in public houses, are those which are levelled against tippling, drunkenness, and gaming in them. By 1 Jas. I. c. 9. and 4 Jas. I. c. 15. and 21 Jas. I. c. 7. and 1 Chas. I. c. 4., if any inn-keeper, victualler, or ale-house keeper, or any keeper of a tavern, &c. suffer any person to continue drinking or tippling, unless invited by any traveller, and accompanying him only during his necessary abode there; and except labouring and handicraft men, in cities and towns corporate, and market towns, upon the usual working days, for one hour at dinner time, to take their diet in an ale-house; and except labourers and workmen, who for the following of their work by the day or by the great, in any city, town, or village, shall, for the time of their continuing in work there, sojourn, lodge, or victual in any inn, &c.; or except for urgent and necessary occasions, to be allowed by two justices of the peace; that then every such inn-keeper, &c. shall forfeit ten shillings to the use of the poor. The penalty, in ordinary cases, to be levied by constables or church-wardens by warrant of distress, and in the universities by the governors, magistrates, justices of the peace, or other principal officers.

By 4 Jas. I. c. 5. and 21 Jas. I. c. 7. whoever shall be drunk, and within six months be convicted, either on an indictment at assizes or sessions, or court leet, or before any justice of peace, upon view or confession, or by oath of one witness, shall forfeit five shillings, to be paid within one week after conviction to the church-wardens of the parish, or levied by distress; and if the party is unable to pay, he is to be set in the stocks for six hours; and for a second offence, bound over to good behaviour with two sureties in 10*l*. A constable neglecting his duty in this matter forfeits ten shillings. By the same statutes, and the 1 Chas. I. c. 4. persons remaining beyond the time above described, tippling or drinking at any inn or public house, forfeit for each offence 3*s*. 4*d*., or may be set in the stocks four hours. These statutes do not abridge the ecclesiastical jurisdiction; but no offender can be punished in more ways than one; nor do they alter the jurisdictions, rights, privileges, or charters of the universities. Above all things, it is necessary to remember, that whatever crime or injury may be committed in a state of intoxication, the law considers that circumstance not as an excuse or extenuation, but as an original crime in itself, and an aggravation of that which arose out of it.

Ale-house keepers offending against these acts are for the space of three years next ensuing utterly disabled to keep any such ale-house.

With respect to gaming in public houses, the 30 Geo. II. c. 24. enacts, that if any person licensed to sell any sort of liquors

liquors ſhall knowingly ſuffer any gaming with cards, dice, draughts, ſhuffle-board, Miſſiſſippi, or billiard tables, ſkittles, nine-pins, or with any other implements of gaming, by any journeymen, labourers, ſervants, or apprentices; on conviction by confeſſion, or on the oath of one witneſs, before any juſtice of the county or place within ſix days after the offence committed, he ſhall forfeit forty ſhillings, and for every like offence afterwards 10*l*., to be levied by warrant of diſtreſs, and three-fourths thereof paid to the poor, and the other fourth to the informer; and if any ſuch perſons ſhall ſo game as aforeſaid, and complaint thereof ſhall be made on oath to a juſtice of the place, he may iſſue his warrant to a conſtable to apprehend and carry them before a juſtice of the county, and on conviction they ſhall forfeit from five to twenty ſhillings, or be committed to hard labour.

GAMING. The particular regulations with reſpect to gaming in public houſes lead to the conſideration of gaming in general. However uſual it may be to treat gaming as a crime, it is not ſo conſidered by the law; but, on the contrary, is permitted on every poſſible ſubject, except where it is accompanied with circumſtances repugnant to morality or public policy; or where, as in certain ſpecial caſes, it is reſtrained by poſitive ſtatutes. But on the other hand, the reſtrictions are ſo numerous, and the bad effects of diſregarding them ſo ſtriking and evident, both in a moral and political light, that all claſſes of men concur in reprobation of a practice which is at once the bane of proſperity, and the deſtruction of every virtue; which extinguiſhes honour, humanity, and ſocial affection, and levels all diſtinctions in ſociety, not by inſtructing and exalting the ignorant, the needy, and the humble, but by degrading the learned, the wealthy, and the honourable.

A *wager* or *bet* is defined to be a contract entered into without colour or fraud, between two or more perſons, for a good conſideration, and upon mutual promiſes to pay a ſtipulated ſum of money, or to deliver ſome other thing to each other, according as ſome prefixed and equally uncertain contingency ſhall happen, within the terms upon which the contract is made. Wagers which tend to violate the peace of ſociety, by exhibiting a third perſon, who is innocent, in a ridiculous and contemptible light, and to break in upon his private comfort and peace of mind, are void. Wagers alſo which conduce to the commiſſion of any criminal act, which are an incitement to immorality, or which are made upon a ſubject *contra bonos mores*, are void. And many contracts which are not againſt the principles of morality or public decency are ſtill void, as againſt the maxims of *ſound policy;* and therefore all wagers which in their nature tend to encourage evil and corrupt practices, repugnant

pugnant to the principles of juſtice and equity, and detrimental to the public good, are illegal; as, if a wager was laid with a judge upon the event of a cauſe depending before him; or even with one of the lords upon the event of an appeal; or if colourably made as a cover to conceal uſury, ſimony, or any other illegal practice.

The offence of keeping a gaming houſe is firſt noticed in the ſtatute 33 Hen. VIII. c. 9. which forbids all manner of perſons for gain, lucre, or living, to keep, have, hold, occupy, exerciſe, or maintain, any common-houſe, alley, or place of bowling, coyting, cloyſh-cayls, half-bowl, tennis, dicing-table, or carding, or any other manner of game prohibited by any ſtatute, under penalty of forty ſhillings a day; every perſon haunting ſuch places was to forfeit ſix ſhillings and eight-pence. This act was however chiefly levelled againſt offenders of the lower order; for it provides that every nobleman and other, having manors, lands, tenements, or other yearly profits, for term of life in his own right, or in his wife's right, to the yearly value of a hundred pounds or above, may command, appoint, or licenſe, his ſervants, or family of his houſe, to play within the precinct of his houſe or houſes, gardens, or orchards at cards, dice, tables, bowls, or tennis, as well among themſelves as others repairing to the ſame houſe or houſes; and that they ſo playing by command or licence as aforeſaid ſhall not incur any penalty. This diſtinction is however aboliſhed by ſucceeding ſtatutes, particularly 12 Geo. II. c. 28. and 18 Geo. II. c. 34. which prohibit all perſons from keeping houſes for playing at unlawful games, and annul the privilege of parliament in caſe of proſecution.

To prevent exceſſive and fraudulent gaming, the 16 Chas. II. c. 7. enacts, that if any perſon of any degree or quality whatſoever, by any fraud, cozenage, or unlawful device, in playing at or with cards, dice, tables, &c.; or by cock-fightings, horſe-races, dog-matches, foot-races, or other games; or by bearing a ſhare or part in the ſtakes, wagers, or adventures; or by betting on ſuch as play, act, ride, or run as aforeſaid, ſhall win, or obtain to himſelf or to any other, any money or other valuable thing, he ſhall *ipſo facto* forfeit and loſe treble the ſum or value won, half to the king, and half to the loſer, provided he proſecute for it within ſix months, or to any other perſon who will ſue within a year after the expiration of thoſe ſix months. The penalty may be recovered, with treble coſts, in any court at Weſtminſter.

The ſame ſtatute alſo directs, that if any perſon ſhall play or bet at any paſtime or game, (other than for ready money) and loſe any money or other thing, exceeding one hundred

hundred pounds, at any one time or meeting, upon ticket or credit, or otherwiſe, the party loſing ſhall not be bound or compellable to pay; but the contract and all judgments, recognizances, mortgages, bonds, bills, ſpecialties, and ſecurities, given for the ſame, or any part thereof, ſhall be utterly void; and the perſon winning ſhall forfeit treble the value, one moiety to the king and the other to ſuch perſon as ſhall proſecute or ſue within a year.

The 9 Anne, c. 14. proceeds much further, and declares, that all notes, bills, bonds, judgments, mortgages, or other ſecurities or conveyances, given or entered into, where the whole or any part of the conſideration ſhall be for money, or other valuable thing won by gaming or betting; or for the reimburſing or repaying any money knowingly lent or advanced for gaming or betting; or at the time and place of play, to any perſon gaming or betting, ſhall be void to all intents and purpoſes; and where ſuch mortgages, ſecurities, or conveyances, ſhall be of lands, tenements, or hereditaments, they ſhall enure to the ſole uſe and benefit of, and devolve upon, ſuch perſons as ſhould have, or be entitled to ſuch lands, tenements, or hereditaments, in caſe the grantors, or perſons encumbering, had been naturally dead, and as if ſuch mortgages, ſecurities, or other conveyances, had been made to the perſons ſo to be entitled after the deceaſe of the perſon incumbering; and all grants or conveyances for the preventing of ſuch lands, or hereditaments, from devolving upon ſuch perſons by the act intended to enjoy the ſame, ſhall be void. Any perſon, who ſhall at any time or ſitting, by playing or betting at cards, dice, tables, or other games, loſe in the whole the ſum or value of ten pounds, and ſhall pay or deliver the ſame, or any part thereof, the perſon loſing and paying ſhall be at liberty within three months to ſue for and recover the money or goods ſo loſt, or any part thereof, from the winner, with coſts of ſuit: and in caſe the perſon loſing ſhall not, within the time aforeſaid, really and *boná fide* ſue and with effect proſecute for the money or other thing loſt and paid, any other perſon may ſue for and recover the ſame, and treble the value with coſts; the one moiety to his own uſe and the other to the poor of the pariſh. The perſon ſued is alſo obliged to anſwer on oath to a bill filed for diſcovery of money won; and a perſon who makes diſcovery and repays, is indemnified againſt further proſecutions.

Any perſon winning by fraud, &c. above 10*l.* at one ſitting, and convicted thereof on indictment or information, forfeits five times the value, and ſhall be deemed infamous, and ſuffer ſuch corporal puniſhment as in caſes of wilful perjury. Two juſtices may alſo cauſe perſons who have no viſible eſtate, but do for the moſt part ſupport themſelves by gaming, to be brought before them, and they ſhall be committed until they find ſureties for their good behaviour for twelve months.

Alſo, by 18 Geo. II. c. 34. if any perſon ſhall win or loſe at play, or by betting, at any one time, the ſum or value of ten pounds, or within the ſpace of twenty-four hours the ſum or value of twenty pounds, ſuch perſons ſhall be liable to be indicted, and being convicted, fined five times the value of the ſum ſo won or loſt; which fine ſhall go to the poor of the pariſh.

Horſe-racing is a mode of gaming which it has been thought fit to encourage, as it tends to improve the breed of a moſt valuable animal; but exceſs and irregularity are reſtricted by the ſtats. 13 Geo. II. c. 19. and 24 Geo. III. c. 31. which require, that the horſes entered for any plate ſhall be the property of thoſe who enter them, on pain of forfeiture; that no plate ſhall be run for, of leſs value than 50*l.* on penalty of 200*l.*; and a penalty of 100*l.* is inflicted on thoſe, who ſhall make, print, publiſh, advertiſe, or proclaim any advertiſement, or notice of any plate, prize, ſum of money, or other thing, of leſs value than 50*l.* to be run for by any horſe, mare, or gelding.

On the laws againſt illegal gaming in *lotteries* ſome ſtatements and obſervations will be found at page 132 of this volume; it may be neceſſary to add, that by various ſtatutes from the 10th of William, to the 27th George III. various games, engines, and devices for playing by means of cards, dice, and other contrivances, are declared to be included in the term lotteries; and thoſe who open or keep them are accordingly ſubjected to a penalty of 500*l.*; one third to the king, another to the poor, and another to the informer. Perſons playing at them forfeit 20*l.* to be divided in like manner. Thoſe who print or publiſh any propoſals for ſuch illegal lottery are ſubject to a penalty of 100*l.* Perſons who ſet up any office or place, for making inſurances on marriages, births, chriſtenings; or under the denomination of ſales of gloves, fans, cards, numbers, or the queen's picture, for the improvement of ſmall ſums of money, or the like offices or places under the pretence of improving ſmall ſums of money, forfeit for every offence five hundred pounds, to be divided as aforeſaid; and perſons printing or publiſhing propoſals forfeit in like manner 100*l.* By 8 Geo. I. c. 2. every perſon who ſhall keep an office or place under the denomination of ſales of houſes, lands, advowſons, preſentations to livings, plate, jewels, ſhips, goods, or other things, for the improvement of ſmall ſums of money, or ſhall ſell or expoſe to ſale any houſes, lands, advowſons, preſentations to livings, plate, jewels, ſhips, goods, or other things, by way of lottery, or by lots, tickets, numbers, or figures; or ſhall make, print, advertiſe, or publiſh, or cauſe to be made, printed, advertiſed, or publiſhed, propoſals or ſchemes for advancing ſmall ſums of money by ſeveral perſons, amounting in the whole to large ſums, to be divided among them by the chances of the prizes in ſome public lottery or lotteries, eſtabliſhed or allowed by act of Parliament; or ſhall deliver out tickets to the perſons advancing ſuch ſums, to entitle them to a ſhare of the money ſo advanced, according to ſuch propoſals or ſchemes; or ſhall make, print, or publiſh, or cauſe to be made, printed, or publiſhed, any propoſal or ſcheme of the like kind or nature, under any denomination, name, or title whatſoever; and ſhall be thereof convicted upon the oath of one witneſs by two juſtices of the peace, he ſhall for every offence, over and above any former penalties inflicted by any former acts of parliament, forfeit five hundred pounds; but the perſon convicted may appeal to the ſeſſion. For default of payment he is committed to jail for twelve months, and further until payment. Perſons adventuring in ſuch ſales or ſchemes forfeit double the ſum contributed, with coſts.

Alſo by 9 Geo. I. c. 19. if any perſon ſhall, by virtue or colour of any authority from any foreign government, erect or keep any lottery, or undertaking in the nature of a lottery, under any denomination, or make, print, or publiſh, any propoſal or ſcheme for any ſuch lottery or undertaking, or ſell any tickets in any foreign lottery, he ſhall, on conviction before two juſtices, forfeit, over and above other penalties, 200*l*. to be levied by diſtreſs, and for want of effects remain in jail one year, and until the penalty be paid.

Theſe reſtrictions are extended and inforced by other ſtatutes of too great number and length to be here enumerated.

Of gaming in the public funds, as prohibited by the ſtatute againſt ſtock-jobbing, notice has been taken at p. 102 of this volume.

Disorderly Houses. A *Brothel* comes under the cognizance of the temporal law as a *common nuiſance*, not only in reſpect of its endangering the public peace, by drawing together diſſolute and debauched perſons; but alſo in reſpect of its apparent tendency to corrupt the manners of both ſexes, by ſuch an open profeſſion of lewdneſs. A *feme covert* is puniſhable for this offence as much as if ſhe were ſole. A lodger who keeps only a ſingle room for ſuch purpoſes is indictable for keeping a bawdy-houſe; but the bare ſolicitation of chaſtity is not indictable. Offenders of this kind are not only puniſhable with fine and impriſonment, but alſo with ſuch infamous puniſhment as to the court ſhall ſeem proper.

For encouragement of proſecution againſt perſons keeping bawdy-houſes, gaming-houſes, or other diſorderly houſes, it is enacted, that if any two inhabitants of any pariſh or place, paying ſcot, and bearing lot therein, do give notice in writing to any conſtable (or other peace officer of the like nature, where there is no conſtable) of ſuch pariſh or place, of any perſon keeping a bawdy-houſe, gaming-houſe, or any other diſorderly houſe, the conſtable ſhall forthwith go with ſuch inhabitants to a juſtice, and ſhall, upon their making oath that they believe the contents of ſuch notice to be true, and entering into a recognizance in the penal ſum of twenty pounds each to give or produce material evidence againſt ſuch perſon for ſuch offence, enter into a recognizance in the penal ſum of thirty pounds to proſecute with effect ſuch perſon for ſuch offence at the next general or quarter ſeſſions, or at the next aſſizes, as to the juſtice ſhall ſeem meet; and ſuch conſtable or other officer ſhall be allowed all the reaſonable expences of ſuch proſecution, to be aſcertained by any two juſtices, and be paid the ſame by the overſeers of the poor of ſuch pariſh or place; and in caſe ſuch perſon ſhall be convicted of ſuch offence, the overſeers ſhall forthwith pay the ſum of ten pounds to each of ſuch inhabitants, or on neglect or refuſal, forfeit double the ſum withheld. The juſtice may alſo bind over the perſon accuſed of keeping ſuch diſorderly houſe to appear at the ſeſſion, and to good behaviour in the mean time. The conſtable neglecting or refuſing to fulfil his duty forfeits 20*l*. to each inhabitant giving him notice.

An *unlicenſed place of public entertainment* is alſo ranked as a diſorderly houſe by the 25 Geo. II. c. 36., which provides that any houſe, room, garden, or place of public entertainment of the like kind, in, or within twenty miles of, London or Weſtminſter, without a licence had for that purpoſe, from the laſt preceding Michaelmas quarter ſeſſions, under the hands and ſeals of four or more of the juſtices there aſſembled, ſhall be deemed a diſorderly houſe; and any conſtable, or other perſon, being authorized by warrant under the hand and ſeal of one juſtice of the peace, may enter ſuch houſe, and ſeize every perſon found there, to be dealt with according to law. Every perſon keeping ſuch houſe, or place, without licence, ſhall forfeit one hundred

hundred pounds to him who will sue for the same; and on some conspicuous part of houses and places so licensed must be affixed in large capital letters the words, *Licensed, pursuant to act of parliament of the 25th king George II.*; and they must not be opened till five o'clock in the afternoon on pain of forfeiting the licence. This act does not extend to the theatres royal, nor to performances and public entertainments lawfully exercised and carried on by virtue of letters patent or licence of the crown, or of the lord chamberlain of his majesty's household.

STROLLING PLAYERS. By 10 Geo. II. c. 28. every person who shall for lucre, gain, or reward, act, represent, or perform, any interlude, tragedy, comedy, opera, play, farce, or other entertainment of the stage, or any part, or parts therein, (in case such person shall not have any legal settlement in the place where the same shall be acted) without authority by virtue of letters patent from his majesty, or licence from the lord chamberlain, shall be deemed a rogue and a vagabond, and liable and subject to all such penalties and punishments, and by such methods of conviction as are inflicted on, or appointed for, the punishment of rogues and vagabonds who shall be found wandering, begging, and misordering themselves. And every such player so performing, whether he has a legal settlement or not, is liable to a penalty of fifty pounds for every offence. This act also provided, that no person should be licensed to act plays in any place except in the city and liberties of Westminster, and in places where the king should be residing, and during such residence only; but the 28 Geo. III. enables the justices of the peace of any county, riding, or liberty, in general or quarter sessions assembled, to grant a licence to any person making application by petition, for the performance of dramatic pieces at any place within their jurisdictions, for any number of days not exceeding sixty, to commence within the next six months, and to be within the space of such four months as shall be specified in the said licence; so as there be only one licence in use at the same time within the jurisdiction so given, and so as such place be not within twenty miles of London, Westminster, or Edinburgh, or eight miles of any patent or licensed theatre, or ten miles of the residence of his majesty, or of any place within the same jurisdiction, at which, within six months preceding, a licence shall have been had and exercised, or within fourteen miles of either of the universities of Oxford and Cambridge, or within two miles of the outward limits of any city, town, or place, having peculiar jurisdiction; and so also as no such licence shall have been had and exercised at the same place, within eight months then next preceding. But no such licence can be granted to be exercised in any city, town, or place, having peculiar jurisdiction, unless proof shall be made that the majority of the justices acting for such peculiar jurisdiction have, at a public meeting, signed their consent and approbation to the said application, or unless an express condition shall be therein inserted, that the same shall not be valid and effectual until it shall have been approved by the majority of them at a meeting holden expressly for taking the same into consideration. And no such licence can be granted by the justices within any city, town, or place, unless notice shall have been given by the person applying, at least three weeks before the application, to the mayor, bailiff, or chief civil officer, of his intending to make it.

VAGRANTS. Under this general denomination are included three classes of persons, called, in strict language, idle and disorderly, rogues and vagabonds, and incorrigible rogues.

In the first class, that of *idle and disorderly persons*, are comprized, by (17 Geo. II. c. 5. which is intitled "an act to amend "and make more effectual the laws relating to rogues and vagabonds, and other idle and disorderly persons, and to houses "of correction;") all persons who threaten to run away and leave their wives and children to the parish; and all persons who shall unlawfully return to such parish or place from whence they have been legally removed by order of the justices of the peace, without bringing a certificate from the parish or place whereunto they belong; and also persons who, not having wherewith to maintain themselves, live idle, without employment, and refuse to work for the usual and common wages given to other labourers in the like work in the parishes or places where they then are; and also all persons going about from door to door, or placing themselves in the streets, highways, or passages, to beg or gather alms in the parishes or places where they dwell. And by 32 Geo. III. c. 45. it is enacted, that if it be made appear to any two justices that any poor person shall not use proper means to get employment, or, if he is able to work, by his neglect of work, or by spending his money in alehouses or places of bad repute, or in any other improper manner, shall not apply a proper portion of the money earned by him towards the maintenance of his wife and family, by which wilful default or neglect they, or any of them, shall become chargeable to their parish or township, he shall be considered as an idle and disorderly person.

Rogues and Vagabonds are by the same statute of Geo. II. thus described: It shall be lawful for any person to apprehend and carry before a justice of the peace any persons going about from door to door, or placing themselves in streets, highways, or passages, to beg or gather alms in the parishes or places where they

they dwell; and if they ſhall reſiſt, or eſcape from the perſon apprehending them, they ſhall be ſubject to puniſhment as rogues and vagabonds. All perſons going about as patent gatherers, or gatherers of alms, under pretence of loſs by fire, or other caſualty; or going about as collectors for priſons, jails, or hoſpitals; all fencers, and bear wards; all common players of interludes; and all perſons who ſhall for hire, gain, or reward, act, repreſent, or perform, or cauſe to be acted, repreſented, or performed, any entertainment of the ſtage, not being authoriſed by law; all minſtrels, jugglers, perſons pretending to be gypſies, or wandering in the habit or form of Egyptians, or pretending to have ſkill in phyſiognomy, palmiſtry, or like crafty ſcience, or pretending to tell fortunes, or uſing any ſubtil craft to deceive and impoſe on any of his majeſty's ſubjects, or playing or betting at any unlawful games or plays; and all perſons who run away and leave their wives or children, whereby they become chargeable to any pariſh or place; and all petty chapmen and pedlars, wandering abroad, not being duly licenſed or otherwiſe authoriſed by law; and all perſons wandering abroad, and lodging in ale-houſes, barns, out-houſes, or in the open air, not giving a good account of themſelves; and all perſons wandering abroad and begging, pretending to be ſoldiers, mariners, ſeafaring men, or pretending to go to work in harveſt; and all other perſons wandering abroad and begging. By the 23 Geo. III. c. 88. the deſcription is extended to any perſon who ſhall be apprehended, having upon him any picklock key, crow, jack, bit, or other implement, with an intent feloniouſly to break and enter into any houſe, or out-houſe, or ſhall have upon him any piſtol, hanger, cutlaſs, bludgeon, or other offenſive weapon, with intent feloniouſly to aſſault any perſon; or ſhall be found in or upon any dwelling houſe, or out-houſe, or in any incloſed yard or garden, or area belonging to any houſe, with intent to ſteal any goods. And alſo by 27 Geo. III. c. 1. to perſons dealing illegally in lottery tickets or ſhares, or in any other adventures dependant on the lottery. The 32 Geo. III. c. 53. recites, that divers ill-diſpoſed and ſuſpected perſons, and reputed thieves, frequent the avenues to places of public reſort, and the ſtreets and highways, with intent to commit felony; and although their evil purpoſes are ſufficiently manifeſt, the power of juſtices of the peace to demand of them ſureties for their good behaviour has not been of ſufficient effect, and therefore enacts, that any conſtable, headborough, patrole, or watchman, may apprehend ſuch perſons, and convey them before any juſtice of the peace; and if it ſhall appear that they are of evil fame, and reputed thieves, and they are not able to give a ſatisfactory account of themſelves, and it

 ſhall

ſhall alſo appear to the ſatisfaction of the juſtice, that there is juſt ground to believe they were in ſuch avenue, ſtreet, or highway, with ſuch intent as aforeſaid, they ſhall be deemed rogues and vagabonds, within the ſtatute 17 Geo. II. But if the ſuſpected perſons will enter into a recognizance with two ſureties, they may appeal to the next ſeſſion, and no puniſhment can be inflicted on them exceeding ſix months impriſonment and hard labour.

But the ſtat. of Geo. II. excepts from its operation ſoldiers having lawful certificates, and mariners duly licenſed, and perſons going abroad to work in the time of harveſt, having a certificate in writing, ſigned by the miniſter and one of the churchwardens, or chapel-wardens, or one of the overſeers of the poor of the pariſh, chapelry, or place, where they reſpectively inhabit.

Of *incorrigible Rogues*, one deſcription is taken from the 13 Geo. I. c. 33., where, under the denomination of end-gatherers, is noticed a claſs of perſons, who, under pretence of purchaſing or collecting the uſeleſs refuſe of woollen manufacture, committed various frauds and depredations; theſe are by ſeveral ſtatutes declared incorrigible rogues. In the ſame claſs, by the 17 Geo. II. c. 5., are included all perſons apprehended as rogues and vagabonds, and eſcaping from the perſons apprehending them, or refuſing to go before a juſtice of the peace, or to be examined upon oath before him, or refuſing to be conveyed by any paſs, or knowingly giving a falſe account of themſelves on ſuch examination, after warning; and all rogues or vagabonds who break or eſcape out of any houſe of correction before the expiration of their term; and all perſons who, after having been puniſhed as rogues and vagabonds, and diſcharged, ſhall again commit any of the ſaid offences.

By the act of Geo. II. any perſon may apprehend a vagrant begging in the place where he dwells; and in general any perſon may apprehend and convey to a juſtice or conſtable any vagrant. A conſtable neglecting his duty in this particular may be puniſhed; and if there is no conſtable, any other perſon, being charged by a juſtice of the peace ſo to do, who ſhall refuſe or neglect to uſe his beſt endeavours to apprehend or to carry ſuch offender before ſome juſtice, ſhall forfeit ten ſhillings to the uſe of the poor, to be levied by diſtreſs and ſale of the offender's goods.

A juſtice may order a reward of five ſhillings to be paid by the overſeer of the pariſh to him who ſhall apprehend any ſuch offender; and for apprehending a rogue or vagabond, whether by a conſtable or any other perſon, the juſtice may order the high conſtable to pay a reward of ten ſhillings, to be returned out of of the county rate; but these rewards are not to be paid unless such rogue or vagabond is punished.

The justices are also by the same statute of Geo. II. four times at least in every year, or oftener if necessary, to meet in their respective divisions, and by their warrant command the constables or other peace officers of every hundred, parish, town, and hamlet, who shall be assisted with sufficient men of the same places, to make a general privy search in one night, throughout their respective limits, for the finding and apprehending of rogues and vagabonds, whom they shall cause to be brought before any justice; and he is to inform himself by examination on oath of the persons apprehended, or of any other person, of their condition and circumstances, and of the parish or place where they were last legally settled, and transmit the substance in writing, subscribed or signed by the persons examined, to the next general or quarter sessions, to be filed and kept on record; and such justice is to order all the persons so apprehended to be publicly whipped, or sent to the house of correction, until the next general or quarter sessions, or for any less time. By another stat. 25 Geo. II. c. 36., the justice may examine not only as to settlement, but as to the means by which such parties get their living, and if they shall not make it appear to his satisfaction, that they have honest means of gaining their livelihood, or procure some responsible housekeeper to appear to their character, and give security for their appearance at some other day to be fixed for that purpose, to commit them to prison or the house of correction, for any time not exceeding six days; and in the mean time to order the overseers of the poor of the parish or place in which the persons were apprehended, to insert an advertisement in some public paper, describing them, and any thing or things found upon them, which they shall be suspected not to have come honestly by, and mentioning the place to which such person is committed, and specifying the time and place when and where such persons are to be again brought up to be re-examined; and if no information shall be then laid against them, they shall be discharged or otherwise dealt with according to law.

After vagrants have undergone the punishments directed by law, they are to be *passed*, by warrant under the hand and seal of a justice, to their legal settlement. The pass specifies how they are to be conveyed, whether by horse, cart, or on foot, and the rate of allowance to be made, which is settled at a general or quarter session. The pass is first given to the constable or other officer of the place where the vagrant is; he delivers the vagrant, with the pass and a duplicate of his examination, to the constable or other officer of the first town, parish, or place, in the next county, riding, division, corporation, or franchise, in the direct way to the place to which such persons are to be conveyed, taking his receipt for the same; and such constable, or other officer must, without delay, apply to some justice of the peace, who makes the like certificate as before, (*mutatis mutandis*) and delivers it to the constable; and so on to the journey's end. If there is reason to suspect that the pass is false or forged, the officers to whom the vagrant is delivered may carry him before a justice, and if the suspicion is well founded, he will be dealt with as an incorrigible rogue. The high constable pays the expence incurred to the petty constable, and receives it again from the treasurer of the county, out of the county rate. Every vagrant so passed, must previously have been publicly whipped, or committed to the house of correction for not less than seven days; nor can they be passed unless convicted of some act of vagrancy; but females are in no case to be whipped. And as it was found that the constables were negligent in conveying of vagrants, the stat. 32 Geo. III. directed that the justices at session might order all rogues and vagabonds to be passed by the master of the house of correction, or his servants. The parish or place to which such person is passed may set him to work, and if he refuses, they may carry him before a justice, to be sent to the house of correction to hard labour.

With respect to *Scotch vagrants*, the 17 Geo. II. c. 5. directs, that the constable or other officer of any parish or place within the counties of Cumberland, Northumberland, Durham, or town of Berwick-upon-Tweed, shall, upon any person being delivered to them by a pass and examination, whose place of legal settlement is in Scotland, deliver the said examination to the clerk of the peace for such county, and convey such person with the said pass into the next adjoining shire, or stewartry, or place in Scotland, and deliver him to some constable or other officer; and in case any such vagrant, after being so sent and conveyed into Scotland, shall be found wandering, begging, or misbehaving himself in England, he shall be deemed an incorrigible rogue, and punished accordingly.

Vagrants belonging to *Ireland*, *Man*, *Jersey*, *Guernsey*, or *Scilly*, when arrived at any sea-port in England or Wales whence a packet sails for any of those places, are to be conveyed across, in pursuance of a warrant under the hand and seal of a justice, for such price as shall have been fixed by the justices in session; and on refusal the master of the packet forfeits 5*l*.

Lunatic Vagrants are rather objects of the poor laws than of the criminal code; it is however provided in the general statute of Geo. II. that two or more justices of the peace, where such lunatic or mad person shall be found, may by warrant directed

rected to the constables, church-wardens, and overseers of the place, cause him to be apprehended, and kept safely locked up, and, if necessary, chained, in some secure place, within the county or precinct, if his last legal settlement was in any parish, or place, within such county or precinct; but if such settlement is not there, then he is to be sent to the place of his last legal settlement by a pass, and locked up or chained by warrant of two justices of the county or precinct to which he is so sent; and the reasonable charges of removing, keeping, maintaining, and curing him, are to be paid by order of two justices, directing the church-wardens or overseers where any of his goods, chattels, lands, or tenements shall be, to seize and sell so much of the goods, or receive so much of the rents of the lands and tenements as is necessary to pay the same; and to account for what is so seized, sold, or received, to the next quarter sessions: but if such person has not an estate to pay and satisfy the same, then such charges must be paid by the parish, or place to which he belongs, by order of two justices, directed to the churchwardens or overseers for that purpose.

With respect to *discharged convicts*, the 32 Geo. III. c. 45. enacts, that any of his majesty's judges at the assizes, and the justices at the general or quarter session, or any justice of the peace, may order any convict, upon his discharge from prison, to be conveyed by pass under hand and seal like other persons to be passed; and they may do the same by any person acquitted or discharged by proclamation or otherwise, stating in the pass the fact of discharge or acquittal; and the pass is to be given without any fee.

When vagrants are committed to the house of correction, and no settlement for them can be found, the justices at session may continue them in custody until they can place them out. And when vagrants who are committed to the house of correction, have any children above seven years old, the justices at session may order them to be placed out as servants or apprentices till the age of twenty-one, or any less time; and if the offender be afterward found with the same child he shall be deemed an incorrigible rogue. And if a woman wandering and begging, is delivered of a child, which is likely to become chargeable, the church-wardens and overseers may take her before a justice, who may commit her till the next session, when she may be ordered to be publicly whipped, and further imprisoned for six months; the church-wardens and overseers to be repaid their expences by the treasurer of the county, and the child, if a bastard, shall not be settled in the place where born, nor sent there for want of settlement; but

but the ſettlement of the mother ſhall be the ſettlement of the child.

The *puniſhment* of vagrants is in ſome caſes very ſevere. When an offender is committed by a juſtice to the houſe of correction, until the next general or quarter ſeſſions; and the juſtices at ſuch ſeſſions adjudge him a rogue, or vagabond, or an incorrigible rogue; they may order him to be detained in the houſe of correction to hard labour not exceeding two years, nor leſs than ſix months; and during the time of his confinement to be corrected by whipping in ſuch manner as they may think fit; and if ſuch perſon, being a male, is above the age of twelve years, they may ſend him to be employed in his majeſty's ſervice either by ſea or land. And in caſe any incorrigible rogue, ſo ordered to be detained and kept in the houſe of correction, ſhall before the expiration of the time break out, or ſhall offend again in like manner, he ſhall be deemed guilty of felony and tranſported for any term not exceeding ſeven years. Thoſe who knowingly harbour any rogue, vagabond, or incorrigible rogue, are ſubject to a penalty, not leſs than ten ſhillings, nor more than forty ſhillings, to be paid half to the informer, and half to the poor.

In the offences lately ſtated, malice againſt individuals does not form the principal point of conſideration, nor perhaps does it in the caſe of *neglecting quarantine*, which has been mentioned in this volume, page 277, and which is in ſome inſtances capital felony. The care to protect the public againſt the effects of careleſſneſs or ſelfiſhneſs which dictated thoſe laws, has alſo occaſioned various other regulations of a local, and ſome of a temporary nature, which it is not neceſſary here to enumerate.

Offences againſt the *revenue* form a conſiderable branch of the criminal and penal code. Some have been already noticed in a general way, as thoſe againſt the cuſtoms and exciſe, at pages 114 and 122; and the ſtamp duties, at page 123 of this volume. To enter into a minute detail would extend beyond all reaſonable bounds. One however muſt be noticed.

Owling. This offence, ſo called from its being uſually carried on in the night, is the offence of tranſporting wool or ſheep out of this kingdom, to the detriment of its ſtaple manufacture. It was forbidden at common law, and more particularly by various ſtatutes, which were all repealed by the 28 Geo. III. c. 38. and an infinite variety of regulations and reſtrictions upon the ſubject was conſolidated. This act is given almoſt at length in the fourth volume of Burn, tit.

tit. Woollen Manufacture, c. 2.; but as it contains nearly one hundred long clauses, it is impossible to give an adequate representation of it in an abridgment: the principal prohibitions are, that if any person shall send or receive any sheep, on board a ship or vessel, to be carried out of the kingdom, the sheep and vessel are both forfeited, and the person offending shall forfeit 3*l*. for every sheep, and suffer solitary imprisonment for three months. But wether sheep, by a licence from the collector of the customs, may be taken on board for the use of the ship's company. And every person, who shall export any wool or woollen articles slightly made up, so as easily to be reduced to wool again, or any fuller's earth, or tobacco-pipe-clay; and every carrier, ship-owner, commander, mariner, or other person, who shall knowingly assist in exporting, or in attempting to export these articles, shall forfeit three shillings for every pound weight, or the sum of 50*l*. in the whole, at the election of the prosecutor, and shall also suffer solitary imprisonment for three months. But wool may be carried coastwise upon being duly entered, and security being given, according to the directions of the statute, to the officer of the port whence the same shall be conveyed. And the owners of sheep, which are shorn within five miles of the sea, or within ten miles in Kent and Sussex, cannot remove the wool without giving notice to the officer of the nearest port as directed by statute.

Offences against trade are also restricted by law. Those of fraudulent bankruptcy, and fraudulent insolvency, will be considered in another division; and that of usury has been noticed at page 189 of this volume.

Seducing Artificers. To prevent the effect of those arts by which the kingdom might be deprived of some of its most valuable subjects, the legislature has provided several statutes against those who, by promises or solicitations, attempt to influence artificers to transport themselves to foreign countries. The 5 Geo. I. c. 27. enacts, that if any person shall contract with, entice, endeavour to persuade or solicit, any manufacturer or artificer of or in wool, iron, steel, brass, or any other metal; clock-maker, watch-maker, or any other artificer or manufacturer of Great Britain, to go out of this kingdom into any foreign country out of his majesty's dominions, he shall be fined any sum not exceeding one hundred pounds for the first offence, and imprisoned three months, and until such fine shall be paid; and if convicted a second time, fined at the discretion of the court, and imprisoned twelve months, and until such fine shall be paid. And if any of his majesty's subjects within this kingdom, being such artificer or manufacturer as aforesaid, shall go into any foreign country, to exercise or teach his

trade

trade or manufacture to foreigners; or in case any such subjects being in any such foreign country, shall not return into this realm within six months next after warning shall be given to him by the embassador, envoy, resident minister, or consul of the crown, or any person by him authorized, or by one of his majesty's secretaries of state, and from thenceforth continually inhabit and dwell within this realm; then every such person shall be incapable of taking any legacy that shall be devised to him, or of being an executor or administrator; and of taking any lands, tenements, or hereditaments, by descent, devise, or purchase; and forfeit all his lands, tenements, hereditaments, goods, and chattels to his majesty's use; and shall from thenceforth be, and be deemed an alien out of his majesty's protection. On complaint made upon oath before any justice of the peace, that any person is endeavouring to seduce or draw away any such manufacturer or artificer as aforesaid, the justice may send forth his warrant to bring the person before him; and if it shall appear that the party is guilty, the justice may bind him to appear at the next assizes, general jail delivery, or quarter sessions of the peace, with reasonable sureties for his appearance; or commit the person refusing surety to jail until the next assizes or quarter sessions; and in case any such artificer or manufacturer shall be convicted upon any indictment of any such promise or contract, or preparation to go abroad, he shall give such security not to depart, as the court shall think reasonable, and be imprisoned until such security shall be given.

By 23 George II. c. 13. the same offence with respect to any manufacturer, workman, or artificer of or in wool, mohair, cotton, or silk, or any of those materials mixed one with another, or in iron, steel, brass, or any other metal, or any clock-maker, watch-maker, or any other manufacturer, workman, or artificer in any other of the manufactures of Great Britain or Ireland of what nature or kind soever, and is punished with a forfeiture 500*l.* for every individual seduced or attempted so to be, and twelve months imprisonment; and for a second offence 1000*l.* and two years imprisonment. By the 22 Geo. III. c. 60. the seduction of any artificer or workman concerned or employed, or who shall have worked at or been employed in printing callicoes, cottons, muslins, or linens of any sort, or in making, or preparing any blocks, plates, engines, tools, or utensils for such manufacture, is punished in the same manner, and one half of the forfeiture is given to the king, the other to the informer. By 25 Geo. III. c. 67. those who contract with, entice, persuade, or endeavour to seduce and encourage any artificer or workman in the iron or

steel

steel manufactures; or persons employed in making or preparing any tools or utensils for such manufacture, to go out of Great Britain (except to Ireland) are subjected to the like penalties, which are to go, one half to the king, the other to such officer of the customs as shall sue and prosecute for the same, after deducting the charges of prosecution from the whole.

Exportation of Tools. Against the practice of exporting tools, so likely to be detrimental to the manufacturing interest, provision is made by the 23 Geo. II. c. 13.; the 14 Geo. III. c. 71; the 21 Geo. III. c. 37; the 22 Geo. III. c. 60. and the 25 Geo. III. c. 67. These statutes enact with great minuteness, that heavy penalties shall be imposed on those who export the tools employed in most of the manufactures of this kingdom; the penalty is, in most cases, forfeiture of the property, and a fine of 200*l.*; and every care is taken to restrain captains of ships from receiving such freight on board, and to prevent custom-house officers from allowing them to pass. The number and strictness of the acts shew how much importance the legislature has attached to this object.

Monopoly. A monopoly is an allowance by the king, to a particular person, or persons, of the sole buying, selling, making, working, or using of any thing, whereby the subject in general is restrained from the freedom of manufacturing or trading which he had before. Monopoly differs from *ingrossing* only in this, that monopoly is by patent from the king, and ingrossing by the act of the subject, between party and party. Monopolies had been carried to an enormous height during the time of Elizabeth, and were heavily complained of by Sir Edward Coke, in the beginning of the ensuing reign: but were in a great measure remedied by 21 Jas. I. c. 3. which declares them to be contrary to law, and void, (except as to patents, not exceeding the grant of fourteen years, to the authors of new inventions; and except also patents concerning printing, saltpetre, gunpowder, great ordnance, and shot;) and monopolists are punished with treble damages and double costs, to those whom they attempt to disturb; and, if they procure any action, brought against them for these damages, to be stayed by any extra-judicial order, other than of the court wherein it is brought, they incur the penalties of a *præmunire*.

Forestalling, Ingrossing, and Regrating. These were all offences at the common law; for it was considered that all endeavours to enhance the common price of any merchandize, and all kinds of practices which have an apparent tendency thereto, whether by spreading false rumours, or by buying things in a market before the accustomed hour, or by

buying

buying and felling again the fame thing in the fame market, or by any fuch like devices, are highly criminal; and all fuch acts anciently came under the general notion of foreftalling, which included all kinds of offences of this nature. *Foreftalling* was defcribed by ftat. 5 and 6 Edw. VI. c. 14. to be the buying or contracting for any merchandize or victual coming in the way to market; or diffuading perfons from bringing their goods or provifions there; or perfuading them to enhance the price, when there; any of which practices make the market dear to the fair trader. *Regrating* was defcribed by the fame ftatute to be the buying of corn, or other dead victual, in any market, and felling it again in the fame market, or within four miles of the place; for this alfo enchances the price of the provifions, as every fucceffive feller muft have fucceffive profit. *Ingroffing* was alfo defcribed to be the getting into one's poffeffion, or buying up large quantities of corn or other dead victuals with intent to fell them again. This muft of courfe be injurious to the public, by putting it into the power of one or two rich men to raife the price of provifions at their own difcretion. And fo the ingroffing of any other commodity, with an intent to fell it at an unreafonable price, is an offence indictable and finable at the common law. The general penalty for thefe three offences by the common law (for all the ftatutes concerning them were repealed by the 12 Geo. III. c. 71.) is, as in other minute mifdemeanors, difcretionary fine and imprifonment. The repeal of the ftatutes mifled many perfons into an opinion that the penalty of the law againft thefe offences was alfo abolifhed, but the court of king's bench decided otherwife, and in fome cafes inforced fevere punifhments.

Combinations to raise the Price of Victuals. The intent of the laws againft foreftalling, ingroffing, and regrating evidently is, to prevent the undue enhancement of the neceffaries of life. To this end many ftatutes ftill exift, enabling magiftrates to regulate the price of many commodities, not by any arbitrary ftandard of their own furmifing or inventing, but according to the evidence of facts and vifible ftate of the market. They alfo are empowered to exercife an infpection over thofe who fell certain commodities by weight and meafure, preventing the arts of fraud, and punifhing thofe who feek to enrich themfelves by difhonefty. Yet, as the vigilance of the moft upright magiftrates might be evaded by the efforts of many difhoneft individuals, combinations among victuallers or artificers, to raife the price of provifions, or any commodities, or the rate of labour, are in many cafes feverely punifhed by particular ftatutes; and in general, by 2 and 3 Edw. VI. c. 15.

c. 15. with the forfeiture of 10*l.* or twenty days imprisonment, with an allowance only of bread and water, for the first offence; 20*l.* or the pillory, for the second; and 40*l.* for the third, or else the pillory, loss of one ear, and perpetual infamy.

Many offences are committed in matters relating immediately to the administration of justice.

PERJURY. Perjury, by the common law, is said to be a wilful false oath, by one who, being lawfully required to depose the truth in any proceeding in a course of justice, swears absolutely in a matter of some consequence to the point in question, whether he be believed or not.

The perjury must be *wilful*; that is, the offence must be committed with some deliberation; for if, upon the whole circumstances of the case, it appears probable that it was owing rather to weakness than to perverseness, that it was occasioned by surprize, or inadvertency, or a mistake of the true state of the question, it will not amount to voluntary and corrupt perjury. False oaths, to fall within the denomination and punishment of perjury, must be taken before those who are intrusted with the administration of public justice, in relation to some matter before them in debate. And not only such persons are indictable for perjury, who take a false oath in a court of record, but also all those who forswear themselves in a matter judicially depending before any court of equity, or spiritual court, or any other lawful court, whether the proceedings therein be of record or not, or whether they concern the interest of the king or subject. Nor is the punishment confined to such oaths as are taken upon judicial proceedings, but extends to all such as any way tend to abuse the administration of justice. But no oath in a mere private matter, howsoever wilful or malicious it may be, is punishable as perjury in a criminal prosecution; for private injuries are left to be redressed by private actions; and upon this ground it has been holden, that a false oath taken by one upon the making of a bargain, that the thing sold is his own, is not punishable as perjury; nor does it extend to any promissory oaths; consequently no officer, public or private, who neglects to execute his office in pursuance of his oath, or acts contrary to the purport of it, is indictable for perjury in respect of such oath; yet his offence is highly aggravated by being contrary to his oath, and therefore he is liable to the severer fine on that account. No oath taken before persons acting merely in a private capacity, or before those who take upon them to administer oaths of a public nature, without legal authority for so doing, or before those who are authorized to administer some kind of oaths, but

but not thoſe which happen to be taken before them, or even before thoſe who take upon them to adminiſter juſtice by virtue of an authority ſeemingly colourable, but in truth unwarranted and merely void, can ever amount to perjuries in the eye of the law, becauſe they are of no force, but altogether idle. It is ſaid not to be eſſentially neceſſary that the fact ſworn ſhould be falſe; for howſoever the thing ſworn may happen to prove agreeable to the truth, yet if it were not known to be ſo by him who ſwears it, his offence is altogether as great as if it had been falſe, in as much as he wilfully ſwears, that he knows a thing to be true, which at the ſame time he knows nothing of, and impudently endeavours to perſuade thoſe before whom he ſwears to proceed upon the credit of a depoſition, which any ſtranger might make as well as he. It is alſo ſaid, that no oath ſhall amount to perjury unleſs it be ſworn abſolutely and directly; and therefore, that he who ſwears a thing according as he *thinks*, *remembers*, or *believes*, cannot in reſpect of ſuch an oath be found guilty; but perhaps this opinion is not altogether warranted, as it has, in ſeveral inſtances, been decided, that belief was to be conſidered as an abſolute term, and that an indictment might be ſupported upon it. If the oath for which a man is indicted of perjury, be wholly foreign from the purpoſe, or altogether immaterial, and neither any way pertinent to the matter in queſtion, nor tending to aggravate or extenuate the damages, nor likely to induce the jury to give a readier credit to the ſubſtantial part of the evidence, it cannot amount to perjury, becauſe it is merely idle and inſignificant.

SUBORNATION. Subornation of perjury is the offence of procuring another to take ſuch a falſe oath, as conſtitutes perjury in the principal.

The *puniſhment* of perjury and ſubornation, at common law, has been various. It was anciently death; afterwards baniſhment, or cutting out the tongue; then forfeiture of goods; and now is fine and impriſonment, and never more to be capable of bearing teſtimony. By the ſtat. 5 Eliz. c. 9. if the offender is proſecuted, it inflicts the penalty of perpetual infamy and a fine of 40*l*. on the ſuborner; and in default of payment, impriſonment for ſix months, and to ſtand with both ears nailed to the pillory. Perjury itſelf is thereby puniſhed with ſix months impriſonment, perpetual infamy, and a fine of 20*l*. or to have both ears nailed to the pillory; but the proſecution for the offence is uſually carried on at common law; eſpecially as, to the penalties before inflicted, the 2 Geo. II. c. 25. ſuperadds a power, for the court to order the offender

to

to be ſent to the houſe of correction for a term not exceeding ſeven years, or to be tranſported for the ſame period, and makes it felony without clergy to return or eſcape before the time is expired. Different acts of parliament alſo aſſign to various modes of perjury and ſubornation expreſs and peculiar puniſhments. Thus by 31 Geo. II. c. 10. taking or procuring any perſon to take a falſe oath for the purpoſe of obtaining the probate of a will, or letters of adminiſtration, in order to receive the pay or prize money of ſailors, is felony without clergy. By 28 Geo. II. c. 13. for the relief of inſolvent debtors; if any ſheriff or other officer perjure himſelf, in taking the oaths directed by the act, he ſhall forfeit 500*l*. And if the offence be committed by a priſoner or other perſon intending to take the benefit of the act, it is felony without clergy.

By the 23 Geo. II. c. 11. the juſtices of aſſize or *niſi prius*, or general gaol delivery, or any of the great ſeſſions of Wales, or of the counties palatine; are authoriſed (ſitting the court, or within twenty-four hours after) to direct any perſon examined as a witneſs upon any trial before them, to be proſecuted for perjury, in caſe there ſhall appear a reaſonable cauſe; and aſſign to the party injured, or other perſon undertaking ſuch proſecution, counſel who ſhall do their duty without any fee, gratuity, or reward. Such proſecution is alſo exempted from tax, or duty, and fees of court, and the clerk of the aſſize is ordered to give the proſecutor a certificate of the ſame, with the counſels' names, &c. And by 12 Geo. I. c. 29., if any perſon convicted of perjury, or ſubornation of perjury, ſhall act or practiſe as an attorney or ſolicitor, or agent, in any ſuit or action, in any court of law or equity, the judge or judges ſhall, upon complaint or information, examine the matter in a ſummary way in open court, and if it ſhall appear that the party has offended contrary to this act, ſhall cauſe him to be tranſported for ſeven years.

Barratry. Common barratry is the offence of frequently exciting and ſtirring up ſuits and quarrels, either at law, or otherwiſe. The puniſhment, in a common perſon, is by fine and impriſonment; but if the offender belongs to the profeſſion of the law, he may be diſabled from practiſing for the future. And indeed the 12 Geo. I. c. 29., places attornies and ſolicitors, convicted of barratry, on the ſame footing as thoſe who are guilty of perjury or ſubornation. To this head may alſo be referred the offence of ſuing another in the name of a fictitious plaintiff, either one not in being at all, or one who is ignorant of the ſuit; in the king's ſuperior courts it is, as a high contempt, to be puniſhed at their diſcretion; but in courts of a lower degree, where the authority of the judges is not

 equally

equally extenſive, it is directed by ſtatute 8 Eliz. c. 2. to be puniſhed by ſix months impriſonment, and treble damages to the party injured.

MAINTENANCE. Maintenance is an officious intermeddling in a ſuit that no way belongs to one, by maintaining or aſſiſting either party with money or otherwiſe, to proſecute or defend it. The puniſhment by common law is fine and impriſonment; and by ſtat. 32 Hen. VIII. c. 9., a forfeiture of 10*l.*; but a man may lawfully maintain the ſuit of his near kinſman, ſervant, or poor neighbour, out of charity and compaſſion.

CHAMPERTY. Champerty, *campi-partitio*, is a ſpecies of maintenance, and puniſhed in the ſame manner; being a bargain with a plaintiff or defendant, *campum partire*, to divide the land or other matter ſued for between them, if they prevail at law; whereupon the champertor is to carry on the party's ſuit at his own expence. In another ſenſe of the word, it ſignifies the purchaſing of a ſuit, or right of ſuing, a practice much abhorred by the law. Hitherto alſo muſt be referred the proviſion of the ſtatute 32 Hen. VIII. c. 9. that no one ſhall ſell or purchaſe any pretended right or title to land, unleſs the vendor has received the profits for one whole year before ſuch grant, or has been in actual poſſeſſion of the land, or of the reverſion or the remainder, on pain that both purchaſer and vendor ſhall each forfeit the value to the king and the proſecutor.

COMPOUNDING PENAL ACTIONS. By 18 Eliz. c. 5., if any perſon informing under pretence of any penal law, makes any compoſition without leave of the court, or takes any money or promiſe from the defendant to excuſe him, he ſhall forfeit 10*l.*, ſhall ſtand two hours upon the pillory, and ſhall be for ever diſabled to ſue on any popular or penal ſtatute.

EMBRACERY. Embracery is an attempt to influence a jury corruptly to one ſide by promiſes, perſuaſions, entreaties, money, entertainments, and the like. The puniſhment for the perſon embracing is by fine and impriſonment; and for the juror ſo embraced, if it be by taking money, perpetual infamy, impriſonment for a year, and forfeiture of the tenfold value. The falſe verdict of jurors, whether occaſioned by embracery or not, was anciently conſidered as criminal, and therefore exemplarily puniſhed by attaint.

BRIBERY. This offence, as applied to courts, is when a judge or other perſon concerned in the adminiſtration of juſtice takes any undue reward to influence his behaviour in his office. It is puniſhed, in inferior officers, with fine and impriſonment; and in thoſe who offer a bribe, though not taken, the ſame; but in judges, eſpecially the ſuperior ones, it has always been looked upon as a heinous offence, and the chief juſtice

justice Thorpe was hanged for it in the reign of Edward III. By a stat. 11 Hen. IV. all judges and officers of the king, convicted of bribery, shall forfeit treble the bribe, be punished at the king's will, and discharged from his service for ever. It has been held to be a misdemeanor to offer a sum of money to the first lord of the treasury, for the purpose of obtaining an office or appointment under government, by his interest and recommendation.

Neglect of Duty. The negligence of public officers intrusted with the administration of justice, as sheriffs, coroners, constables, and the like, makes the offender liable to be fined; and in very notorious cases will amount to a forfeiture of his office, if it be a beneficial one. Also the omitting to apprehend persons who offer stolen iron, lead, and other metals to sale, is a misdemeanor, and punished by a stated fine, or imprisonment, in pursuance of the statute 29 Geo. II. c. 30.

Extortion. Extortion is an abuse of public justice, which consists in any officer unlawfully taking by colour of his office, from any man, any money or thing of value, that is not due to him, or more than is due, or before it is due. The punishment is fine and imprisonment, and sometimes a forfeiture of the office.

Oppression. The oppression and tyrannical partiality of judges, justices, and other magistrates, in the administration, and under the colour of their office, when prosecuted, either by impeachment in parliament, or by information in the court of king's bench, (according to the rank of the offenders,) is severely punished with forfeiture of their offices, (either consequential or immediate,) fine, imprisonment, or other discretionary censure, regulated by the nature and aggravation of the offence committed.

Conspiracy. Conspirators, in the words of the statute 33 or more properly 21 Edw. I. "be they that do confeder "or bind themselves by oath, covenant or other alliance, "that every of them shall aid and bear the other, falsely "and maliciously to indict, or cause to indict, or falsely "to move and maintain pleas; and also such as cause "children within age to appeal men of felony, whereby "they are imprisoned and sore grieved; and such as retain "men in the country with liveries or fees for to maintain "their malicious enterprizes;" and this extends as well to the takers as to the givers; and to stewards and bailiffs of great lords, who by their seigniory, office, or power, undertake to bear or maintain quarrels, pleas, or debates, that concern other parties than such as touch the estate of their lords or themselves. From this definition it seems to follow, that

that not only thoſe who actually cauſe an innocent man to be indicted, and tried upon the indictment whereupon he he is lawfully acquitted, are conſpirators, but thoſe alſo who barely conſpire to indict a man falſely and maliciouſly, whether they do any act in proſecution of ſuch conſpiracy or not. Formerly the remedy was by writ of conſpiracy, but that is now diſuſed, and an action on the caſe is frequently brought for a malicious proſecution, in which it is incumbent on the plaintiff to ſhew that the original ſuit, whereſoever inſtituted, is at an end; for this purpoſe he muſt produce and prove a copy of the acquittal on record, the ſubſtance of the evidence, the charges of acquittal, and the circumſtances which ſhew that the proſecution was malicious and without probable cauſe. But if the proſecution was for a miſdemeanor, a copy of the record is not neceſſary to be granted by the court to found the action. The conſpirators may alſo be indicted at the ſuit of the king, and by the ancient common law, if they accuſed another of a matter which might touch his life, were to receive what is called the *villainous judgment*, that is, they were to loſe the freedom and franchiſe of the law, whereby they were diſabled to be put upon any jury, or to be ſworn as witneſſes, or even to appear in perſon in any of the king's courts; and alſo that their houſes, lands, and goods ſhould be ſeized into the king's hands, and their houſes and lands eſtreped and waſted, their trees rooted up and raſed, and their bodies impriſoned. In ſome books this is ſaid to have been the proper judgment upon every conviction of conſpiracy at the ſuit of the king, without any reſtrictions to ſuch as endangered the life of the party. There has been no inſtance of the villainous judgment ſince the reign of Edward III. The uſual mode of puniſhment at preſent is by pillory, fine, impriſonment, and ſurety for good behaviour. The offence is within the juriſdiction of the quarter ſeſſions; and on the motion in arreſt of judgment, the defendant muſt be perſonally preſent in court.

LIBELS. A libel is defined a malicious defamation, expreſſed either in printing or writing, or by ſigns, pictures, &c. tending either to blacken the memory of one who is dead, or the reputation of one who is alive, and thereby expoſing him to public hatred, contempt, and ridicule. It is termed *Libellus famoſus ſeu infamatoria ſcriptura*, and from its pernicious tendency has been held a public offence at common law; for men not being able to bear the having their errors expoſed to public view, were found by experience to revenge themſelves on thoſe who made ſport with their reputations; from whence aroſe duels and breaches of the peace; and hence written ſcandal has been held in the greateſt deteſtation, and has received the utmoſt diſcourage-

discouragement in the courts of justice. This species of defamation is usually termed *written scandal*, and hereby receives an aggravation, in that it is presumed to have been entered upon with coolness and deliberation, and to continue longer, and propagate wider and further, than any other scandal. But it is clearly agreed, that not only written or printed scandal comes within the notion of a libel, but it may be also applied to any defamation whatsoever, expressed either by signs or pictures; as, by fixing up a gallows at a man's door, or elsewhere; or by painting him in a shameful and ignominious manner, as, by exposing a man and his wife by a skimmington or riding, though a special custom is alleged for such practice. And not only charges of a flagrant nature, and which reflect a moral turpitude on the parties, are libellous, but also such as set him in a scurrilous, ignominious light; for these equally create ill blood, and provoke the parties to acts of revenge, and breaches of the peace. Libels on persons employed in a public capacity, are said to receive an aggravation, as they tend to scandalize the government, by reflecting on those who are intrusted with the administration of public affairs, which not only endangers the public peace, as all other libels do, by stirring up the parties immediately concerned in it to acts of revenge, but also have a direct tendency to breed in the people a dislike of their governors, and incline them to faction and sedition.

It is also agreed, that not only scandal expressed in an open and direct manner, but also such as is expressed in allegory and irony, amounts to a libel; and that the judges are to understand it in the same manner as others do, without any strained endeavours to find out loop-holes, or to palliate the offence, which in some measure would be to encourage scandal. It has also been resolved, that a defamatory writing, expressing only one or two letters of a name in such a manner that from what goes before, and follows after, it must needs be understood to signify such a person in the plain, obvious, and natural construction of the whole, and would be perfect nonsense if strained to any other meaning, is as properly a libel as if it had expressed the whole name at large; for it brings the utmost contempt upon the law, to suffer its justice to be eluded by such trifling evasions; and it is a ridiculous absurdity to say, that a writing which is understood by the meanest capacity, cannot possibly be understood by judge or jury. Obscene books are punishable as libels, and so are books reflecting upon christianity.

A person complaining of a libel, may bring his action for damages, or may indict, or move the court of king's bench for a criminal information. In the latter mode of proceeding, it is neceſſary, in order to induce the court to interpoſe its extraordinary juriſdiction, that the party ſhould ſtate in his affidavit, that the allegations complained of are falſe. In an indictment or criminal proſecution for a libel, the party cannot juſtify that the contents thereof are true, or that the perſon upon whom it is made had a bad reputation; ſince the greater appearance there is of truth in any malicious invective, ſo much the more provoking it is; for as lord Coke obſerves, in a ſettled ſtate of government the party grieved ought to complain for every injury done him, in the ordinary courſe of law, and not by any means to revenge himſelf by the odious courſe of libelling or otherwiſe. Alſo, it ſeems now ſettled, that no ſcandal in writing is any more juſtifiable in a civil action brought by the party to vindicate the injury done him, than in an indictment or information at the ſuit of the crown; for though, in actions for words, the law, through compaſſion, admits the truth of the charge to be pleaded as a juſtification, yet this tenderneſs is not to be extended to written ſcandal, in which the author acts with more coolneſs; and deliberation gives the ſcandal a more durable ſtamp, and propagates it wider and further; whereas in words, men often in a heat and paſſion ſay things which they are afterwards aſhamed of, and though they ſeem to act with deliberation, yet the ſcandal ſooner dies away and is forgotten; and therefore, from the greater degree of miſchief and malice attending the one than the other, though the law allows the party to juſtify in an action for words, yet it does not for written ſcandal; whence it follows, that the only favour truth affords in ſuch a caſe is, that it may be ſhewn in mitigation of damages in an action, and of the fine upon an indictment or information.

It had frequently been determined by the court of king's bench, that the only queſtions for the conſideration of the jury, in criminal proſecutions for libels, were the fact of publication, and the truth of the inuendos, that is, the truth of the meaning and ſenſe of the paſſages of the libel, as ſtated and averred in the record, and that the judge or court alone was competent to determine whether the ſubject of the publication was or was not a libel. But the legality of this doctrine having been much controverted, the 32 Geo. III. c. 60. was paſſed, intituled, "an "act to remove doubts reſpecting the functions of juries in "caſes of libels." It declares and enacts, that on every trial of an indictment or information for a libel, the jury may give a general verdict of guilty or not guilty, upon the whole matter in iſſue, and ſhall not be required or directed by the judge, to find the defendant guilty, merely on the proof of the publication of the paper charged to be a libel, and of the ſenſe aſcribed to it it in the record. But the ſtatute provides, that the judge may give his opinion to the jury reſpecting the matter in iſſue, and the jury may at their diſcretion, as in other caſes, find a ſpecial verdict, and the defendant, if convicted, may move the court, as before the ſtatute, in arreſt of judgment. But this ſtatute does not expreſs that the truth of the ſcandal ſhall be a defence, and is wholly ſilent as to actions of *ſcandalum magnatum*, or for a libel.

Every perſon convicted of a libel muſt be the contriver, procurer, or publiſher.

The puniſhment for a libel, if the defendant is convicted on an indictment or information, is by fine and corporal puniſhment, at the diſcretion of the court; and when a perſon is brought up to receive judgment for a libel, his conduct, ſubſequent to his conviction, may be taken into conſideration either by way of aggravation, or mitigation of the puniſhment.

Theſe are the chief offences for which the law of England has provided in the way of prevention or puniſhment. It remains only to give ſome account of various circumſtances incident to the condition, the trial, and the ſentence of malefactors.

ARRESTS. All perſons without diſtinction are equally liable to arreſt in all criminal caſes; but no man is to be arreſted, unleſs charged with ſuch a crime, as will at leaſt juſtify holding him to bail, when taken. In general, an arreſt may be made four ways: 1. By warrant. 2. By an officer without a warrant. 3. By a private perſon alſo without a warrant. 4. By hue and cry.

A *warrant* may be granted in extraordinary caſes by the privy council, or ſecretaries of ſtate; but ordinarily by juſtices of the peace; their power extends undoubtedly to all treaſons, felonies, and breaches of the peace; and alſo to all ſuch offences as they have power to puniſh by ſtatute. The warrant ought to be under the hand and ſeal of the juſtice, ſhould ſet forth the time and place of making, and the cauſe for which it is made, and ſhould be directed to the conſtable, or other peace officer, (or, it may be to any private perſon by name,) requiring him to bring the party either generally before *any* juſtice of the peace for the county, or only before the juſtice who granted it; the warrant in the latter caſe being called a *ſpecial* warrant. A *general* warrant to apprehend all perſons ſuſpected, without naming or particularly deſcribing any one in particular, is illegal and void for its uncertainty; and a warrant to apprehend all perſons guilty of a crime therein ſpecified, is no legal warrant. A warrant from the chief or other juſtice of the court of king's bench extends all over the kingdom: and is *teſted* or dated

England, not in any particular county. But the warrant of a justice of the peace in one county must be *backed*, that is, signed by a justice of the peace in another, before it can be executed there. And by 13 Geo. III. c. 31. any warrant for apprehending an English offender, who may have escaped into Scotland, and *vice versa*, may be indorsed and executed by the local magistrates, and the offender conveyed back to that part of the united kingdoms, in which such offence was committed.

Arrests by *officers, without warrant*, may be executed: 1. By a justice of the peace; who may himself apprehend, or cause to be apprehended, by word only, any person committing a felony or breach of the peace in his presence. 2. The sheriff; and, 3. The coroner, may apprehend any felon within the county without warrant. 4. The constable may without warrant arrest any one for a breach of the peace. And, in case of felony actually committed, or a dangerous wounding, whereby felony is like to ensue, he may upon probable suspicion arrest the felon; and for that purpose, is authorized (as upon a justice's warrant) to break open doors, and even to kill the felon if he cannot otherwise be taken; and, if he or his assistants be killed in attempting such arrests, it is murder in all concerned. 5. Watchmen, either those appointed by the statute of Winchester, 13 Edw. I. c. 4. to keep watch and ward in all towns, from sunsetting to sunrising, or such as are mere assistants to the constable, may *virtute officii* arrest all offenders, and particularly night-walkers, and commit them to custody until the morning.

Any private person (and *a fortiori* a peace officer) that is present when any felony is committed, is bound by the law to arrest the felon, on pain of fine and imprisonment, if he escapes through the negligence of the standers by; and they may justify breaking open doors upon following such felons; and if they *kill him*, provided he cannot otherwise be taken, it is justifiable; though, if *they are killed* in endeavouring to make such arrest, it is murder. Upon probable suspicion also, a private person may arrest the felon, or other person suspected; but he cannot justify breaking open doors to do it; and if either party kill the other in the attempt, it is manslaughter, and no more.

The hue and cry has already been mentioned.

COMMITMENT. The justice, before whom a prisoner is brought, is bound immediately to examine the circumstances of the crime alleged, and to take in writing the examination of the prisoner, and the information of those who bring him.

If

If upon this inquiry it manifestly appears, either tha such crime was committed, or that the suspicion entertained of the person was wholly groundless, it is lawful totally to discharge him; otherwise he must either be committed to prison or give bail.

Bail. Bail, in a criminal as in a civil case, signifies sureties for the defendant's appearance to answer the charge against him. To refuse or delay to bail any person bailable, is an offence against the liberty of the subject, in any magistrate by the common law, as well as by the statute of Westm. 3 Edw. I. c. 15. and the *habeas corpus* act, 31 Chas. II. c. 2.; and lest the intention of the law should be frustrated by the justices requiring bail to a greater amount than the nature of the case demands, it is expresly declared by statute 1 W. and M. st. 2. c. 1. that excessive bail ought not to be required; though what bail shall be called excessive must be left to the courts, on considering the circumstances of the case, to determine. On the other hand, if the magistrate takes insufficient bail, he is liable to be fined, if the criminal does not appear. Bail may be taken either in court, or in some particular cases by the sheriff, coroner, or other magistrate; but most usually by the justices of the peace. Regularly in all offences either against the common law or act of parliament, that are below felony, the offender ought to be admitted to bail, unless it be prohibited by some act of parliament. The prohibition to accept of bail or mainprize is inserted in several statutes where imprisonment is intended as a positive punishment for crimes, not as a cautionary measure to prevent escape, or as an alternative to countervail some fine or penalty which the person convicted is unable or unwilling to pay.

Hindering Arrests. It is an high offence to oppose one who lawfully endeavours to arrest another for treason or felony; some have said that the person who so opposes an arrest for treason, whereof he knows the party to have been guilty, is thereby guilty of the treason; and that he who so opposes an arrest for felony, is an accessary to the felony; but, if a person, knowing another to have been guilty of such a crime, barely receive him, and permit him to escape, without giving him any manner of advice, assistance or encouragement in it, as by directing how to do it in the safest manner, or furnishing him with money, provisions, or other necessaries, he is guilty of a high misdemeanor only, but no capital offence. The party himself who flies from such an arrest, is not thereby guilty of a capital offence, but only liable to forfeit his goods, when such flight is found against him by the jury on his trial.

Breaking

Breaking Prison. Breach of prifon by the offender himfelf, when committed for any caufe, was felony at the common law; or even confpiring to break it; but this feverity is mitigated by the ftatute *de frangentibus prifonam*, 1 Edw. II. which enacts, that no perfon fhall have judgment of life or member for breaking prifon, unlefs committed for fome capital offence; fo that to break prifon and efcape, when lawfully committed for any treafon or felony, remains ftill felony at the common law; and to break prifon, (whether it be the county jail, the ftocks, or other ufual place of fecurity,) when lawfully confined upon any other inferior charge, is ftill punifhable as a mifdemeanor by fine and imprifonment.

Escape. As all perfons are bound to fubmit themfelves to the judgment of the law, and to be ready to be juftified by it, whoever in any cafe refufes to undergo that imprifonment which the law thinks fit to put upon him, and frees himfelf by any artifice, before he is delivered by the courfe of law, is guilty of a high contempt, punifhable with fine and imprifonment. To conftitute an efcape, there muft be an actual arreft; and therefore if an officer having a warrant to arreft a man, fees him fhut up in a houfe, and challenges him as his prifoner, but never actually has him in his cuftody, and the party gets free, the officer cannot be charged with an efcape; arreft muft alfo be juftifiable; for a criminal matter; and its continuance at the time of the efcape grounded on that fatisfaction which the public juftice demands for fuch crime. It is an efcape, in fome cafes, to fuffer a prifoner to have greater liberty than by the law he ought to have; as to admit a perfon to bail, who by law ought not to be bailed, but to be kept in clofe cuftody; or to permit a prifoner to go out of the limits of a prifon, Wherever an officer, who has the cuftody of a prifoner, charged with, and guilty of, a capital offence, knowingly gives him his liberty with an intent to fave him either from his trial or execution, he is guilty of a voluntary efcape, and involved in the guilt of the fame crime with which the prifoner ftood charged. An officer making a frefh purfuit after a prifoner, who has efcaped through his negligence, may retake him at any time whether in the fame or in a different county. Negligent efcapes are punifhed by fine, and, if frequent, by lofs of office.

Nor is the offence of permitting an efcape limited to officers; for wherever any perfon has another lawfully in his cuftody, whether upon an arreft made by himfelf or another, he is guilty of an efcape if he fuffer him to go at large, before he has difcharged himfelf of him by delivering him over to fome other

other who by law ought to have the cuſtody of him; and therefore, if a private perſon arreſts another for ſuſpicion of felonys, and deliver him into the cuſtody of another private perſon, who receives and ſuffers him to go at large, it is ſaid that both are guilty of an eſcape; the firſt, becauſe he ſhould not have parted with him till he had delivered him into the hands of a public officer; the latter, becauſe, having charged himſelf with the cuſtody of a priſoner, he ought at his peril to have taken care of him. If the eſcape were voluntary, he is puniſhable in the ſame manner as an officer; and if negligent, he is puniſhable by fine and impriſonment.

RESCUE. Reſcue, or as it is ſpelt in law books, *Reſcous*, is the forcibly and knowingly freeing another from an arreſt or impriſonment, and it is generally the ſame offence in the ſtranger reſcuing, as it would have been in a jailor to have voluntarily permitted an eſcape. A reſcue therefore of one apprehended for felony, is felony; for treaſon, treaſon; and for a miſdemeanor, a miſdemeanor alſo. In theſe caſes, as in voluntary eſcapes, the principals muſt firſt be attainted or receive judgment before the reſcuer can be puniſhed: and for the ſame reaſon; becauſe perhaps in fact it may turn out that there has been no offence committed. By 11 Geo. II. c. 26. and 22 Geo. II. c. 40. if five or more perſons aſſemble to reſcue any retailers of ſpirituous liquors, or to aſſault the informers againſt them, it is felony, and ſubject to tranſportation for ſeven years. By 16 Geo. II. c. 31. to convey to any priſoner in cuſtody for treaſon or felony, any arms, inſtruments of eſcape, or diſguiſe, without the knowledge of the jailor, though no eſcape be attempted, or any way to aſſiſt ſuch priſoner to attempt an eſcape, though no eſcape be actually made, is felony, and ſubjects the offender to tranſportation for ſeven years; or if the priſoner be in cuſtody for petit larceny, or other inferior offence, or charged with a debt of 100*l*. it is then a miſdemeanor, puniſhable with fine and impriſonment; and by ſeveral ſpecial ſtatutes, to reſcue, or attempt to reſcue, any perſon committed for the offences enumerated in thoſe acts, is felony without benefit of clergy.

DURESS BY JAILORS. The conſiderate attention of the law toward thoſe who are confined for debt has already been noticed; and it is alſo to be obſerved that priſoners in criminal caſes, whether merely detained for ſafe cuſtody, or for puniſhment after trial, are alſo protected by the humanity of the law. To prevent abuſes by the extenſive power which is neceſſarily repoſed in jailors, it is enacted by 14 Edw. III. c. 10. that if any keeper of a priſon, or under-keeper, by too great dureſs of impriſonment, and by pain, make any priſoner become an appellor

appellor against his will, he is guilty of felony. And it is said to be no way material, whether the approvement is true or false, or whether the appellee be acquitted or condemned; but at common law this offence was esteemed a misprision only, unless the appellee were hanged by reason of the appeal. It has been determined that jailors, as well *de facto* as *de jure*, are liable to attachment for contempt of court, and to fine, imprisonment, and forfeiture of office for gross and palpable abuses; as in treating criminals with barbarity, extorting money, not making lawful deliverance, or suffering them to escape; and that if death ensues from their harsh treatment, it is felonious homicide. By 31 Chas. II. c. 2. if any person shall be committed to any prison, for any criminal offence, he shall not be removed unless by *habeas corpus*, or other legal writ: or where he is removed from one prison or place to another, within the same county, in order to his trial or discharge; or in case of sudden fire or infection, or other necessity; on pain that the person signing any warrant for such removal, and the person executing it, shall forfeit for the first offence 100*l.* and for the second 200*l.* to the party grieved. By 22 and 23 Chas. II. c. 20. the jailor shall not put, keep, or lodge prisoners for debt and felons together in one room or chamber; but they shall be kept and lodged separate and apart from one another in distinct rooms, on pain of forfeiting his office, and treble damages to the party grieved; and by 31 Geo. III. c. 46. as long as any person under sentence of transportation shall continue in the common jail, the jailor shall separate him, as far as conveniently may be, from every person in his custody, except prisoners convicted of felony. It is usual for the jailor to hamper a felon with irons to prevent his escape; and it is said that he is not punishable for keeping even a debtor in irons; but this can only be intended, where the officer has just reason to fear an escape; as where the prisoner is unruly, or makes any attempt to that purpose.

It is not intended here to enter into an account of all the forms used in bringing prisoners to trial; as the indictment, and subsequent proceedings; but merely to notice some peculiarities, which are of a less technical description.

Approver. A man is properly an approver, when being indicted of treason or felony, before competent judges, and in prison for the same, and capable of being an approver, he confesses the indictment, and is sworn to reveal all the treasons and felonies he knows, and then, before a coroner, enters his appeal against all who are partners with him in the crime in the indictment, being at the time of the appeal within the realm. The party thus appealed or accused, is called the

the *appellee*; the accuser is called in Latin, *probator*, in English, *prover* or *approver*. The exceptions which the appellee was entitled to take against the approver were very numerous, and the forms to be observed very strict; and it was purely in the discretion of the court to permit the appeal, or not. The admission of approvements has been long disused; for more mischief arose to good men by the false and malicious accusations of desperate villains, than benefit to the public by the discovery and conviction of real offenders. All the good that can be expected from this method of approvement is fully provided for in cases of coining, robbery, burglary, house-breaking, and larceny to the value of five shillings from shops, warehouses, stables and coach-houses, by various statutes, which enact, that if any such offender, being out of prison, shall discover two or more persons, who have committed the like offences, so as they may be convicted, he shall in case of burglary or housebreaking receive a reward of 40*l*. and in general be entitled to a pardon of all capital offences, except murder, and except all treasons, but coining. And if any such person, having feloniously stolen any lead, iron, or other metals, shall discover and convict two offenders of having illegally bought or received the same, he shall by virtue of the 29 Geo. II. c. 30. be pardoned for all such felonies committed before such discovery.

It has also been usual for the justices of the peace, by whom any persons charged with felony are committed to jail, to admit some one of their accomplices to become a witness (or, as it is generally termed, *king's evidence*) against his fellows; upon an implied confidence, which the judges of jail delivery have usually countenanced and adopted, that if such accomplice makes a full and complete discovery of that and of all other felonies to which he is examined by the magistrate, and afterwards gives his evidence without prevarication or fraud, he shall not himself be prosecuted for that or any other previous offence of the same degree. In the case of Mrs. Rudd, in which this subject is clearly and ably explained by lord Mansfield, and again by Mr. Justice Aston, in delivering the opinion of all the judges, it is laid down that no authority is given to a justice of the peace to pardon an offender, and to tell him he shall be a witness at all events against others; but where the evidence appears insufficient to convict two or more without the testimony of one of them, the magistrate may encourage a hope, that he who will behave fairly and disclose the whole truth, and bring the others to justice, shall himself escape punishment. This discretionary power exercised by the justices of peace is founded in practice only, and cannot controul the authority of the court of general jail delivery, and exempt, at all events, the accomplice from being prosecuted. A motion is always made to the judge for leave to admit an accomplice to be a witness; and unless he should see some particular reason for a contrary conduct, he will prefer the one to whom this encouragement has been given by the justice of peace. This admission to be a witness amounts to a promise of a recommendation to mercy, upon condition that the accomplice makes a full and fair disclosure of all the circumstances of the crime for which the other prisoners are tried, and in which he has been concerned in concert with them. Upon failure of his part of the condition, he forfeits all claim to protection; as upon a trial at York, before Mr. Justice Buller, where the accomplice who was admitted a witness, denied in his evidence all that he had before confessed, upon which the prisoner was acquitted; but the judge ordered an indictment to be preferred against this accomplice for the same crime, and upon his previous confession and other circumstances, he was convicted and executed.

On the arraignment of a prisoner, two incidents are worthy of notice; his standing mute, and his confessing the indictment.

Mute. Regularly a prisoner is said to stand mute, when, being arraigned for treason or felony, he either, 1. Makes no answer at all; or, 2. Answers foreign to the purpose, or with such matter as is not allowable, and will not answer otherwise; or, 3. Upon having pleaded not guilty, refuses to put himself upon the country. If he says nothing, the court ought, *ex officio*, to impanel a jury to inquire whether he stands obstinately mute, or whether he is dumb by the visitation of God? If the latter appears to be the case, the judges (who are to be of counsel for the prisoner, and to see that he has law and justice) shall proceed to the trial, and examine all points as if he had pleaded not guilty; but whether judgment of death can be given against such a prisoner, who has never pleaded, and can say nothing in arrest of judgment, is a point yet undetermined. If he is found to be obstinately mute, (which a prisoner has been held to be that has cut out his own tongue,) then if it be on an indictment of high treason, it is equivalent to a conviction, and he receives the same judgment and execution. And as in this, the highest crime, so also in the lowest species of felony, viz. in petit larceny, and in all misdemeanors, standing mute has always been equivalent to conviction; but upon appeals, or indictments for other felonies, or petit treason, the prisoner was not, by the ancient law, looked upon as convicted, so as to receive judgment for the felony; but should, for his obstinacy,

obſtinacy, have received the terrible ſentence of *penance*, or *peine forte et dure*. Before this was pronounced, the priſoner had not only three admonitions, but alſo a reſpite of a few hours, and the ſentence was diſtinctly read to him, that he might know his danger: and, after all, if he continued obſtinate, and his offence was clergyable, he had the benefit of his clergy allowed him, even though he was too ſtubborn to pray it; but, if the priſoner charged with a capital felony, continued ſtubbornly mute, the judgment was then given againſt him, without any diſtinction of ſex or degree. The penance was, that the priſoner be remanded to the priſon whence he came, and put into a low, dark chamber; and there be laid on his back, on the bare floor, naked, unleſs where decency forbids, that there be placed upon his body as great a weight of iron as he could bear, and more; that he have no ſuſtenance, ſave only, on the firſt day, three morſels of the worſt bread; and, on the ſecond day, three draughts of ſtanding water, that ſhould be neareſt to the priſon door; and in this ſituation this ſhould alternately be his daily diet, till he died, or (as anciently the judgment ran) till he anſwered. The chief end of this penance was to obtain eſcheats and forfeitures; for the law was, that by ſtanding mute, the judgment, and of courſe the corruption of the blood and eſcheat of the lands, were ſaved in felony and petit treaſon; though not the forfeiture of the goods. In high treaſon, as ſtanding mute is equivalent to a conviction, the ſame judgment, the ſame corruption of blood, and the ſame forfeitures always attended it, as in other caſes of conviction. Lately, to the honour of our laws, it is enacted by ſtat. 12 Geo. III. c. 20. that every perſon who, being arraigned for felony or piracy, ſhall ſtand mute, or not anſwer directly to the offence, ſhall be convicted of the ſame, and the ſame judgment and execution, with all their conſequences in every reſpect, ſhall be thereupon awarded, as if the perſon had been convicted by verdict or confeſſion of the crime.

Confession. Confeſſion is either expreſs or implied. An expreſs confeſſion is where a perſon directly acknowledges the crime with which he is charged; it may be received after the plea of "not guilty" recorded, notwithſtanding the repugnancy. Where a perſon upon his arraignment actually confeſſes himſelf guilty, or unadviſedly diſcloſes the ſpecial manner of the fact, on a ſuppoſition that it does not amount to felony, when in fact it does, yet the judges, upon probable circumſtances that ſuch confeſſion may proceed from fear, menace, or dureſs, or from weakneſs or ignorance, may refuſe to record it, and ſuffer the party to plead not guilty.

An

An implied confeffion is where a defendant, in a cafe not capital, does not directly own himfelf guilty, but in a manner admits it by yielding to the king's mercy; and defiring to fubmit to a fmall fine, in which cafe, if the court think fit to accept of fuch fubmiffion, and make an entry that the defendant threw himfelf on the king's grace, without putting him to a direct confeffion, or plea, the defendant is not eftopped from pleading *not guilty* to an action of the fame fact, as he is where the entry is that he confeffed the indictment.

No confeffion whatever, before final judgment, deprives the defendant of the privilege of taking exceptions in arreft of judgment to faults apparent in the record; for the judges muft *ex officio* take notice of all fuch faults; and any one, as *amicus curiæ*, may inform them of them.

The courfe of trial by jury has already been defcribed, but it may be proper to notice fome other modes anciently reforted to, and ftill often mentioned, though now utterly difufed.

ORDEAL. The trial of ordeal is of the higheft antiquity; it was peculiarly diftinguifhed by the appellation of *judicium dei*; and fometimes *vulgaris purgatio*, to diftinguifh it from the canonical purgation. It was of two forts, either *fire-ordeal*, or *water-ordeal*; the former being confined to perfons of higher rank, the latter to the common people. Both thefe might be performed by deputy; but the principal was to anfwer for the fuccefs of the trial; the deputy only venturing fome corporal pain, for hire, or perhaps for friendfhip. *Fire-ordeal* was performed either by taking up in the hand, unhurt, a piece of red hot iron, of one, two, or three pounds weight, or elfe by walking barefoot, and blindfold, over nine red-hot plough-fhares, laid lengthwife at unequal diftances: and if the party efcaped being hurt, he was adjudged innocent: but if it happened otherwife, as without collufion it ufually did, he was then condemned as guilty. *Water-ordeal* was performed, either by plunging the bare arm up to the elbow in boiling water, and efcaping unhurt, or by cafting the perfon fufpected into a river or pond of cold water; and, if he floated without any action of fwimming, it was deemed evidence of his guilt; but if he funk, he was acquitted.

CORSNED. Another fpecies of purgation, probably fprung from a prefumptuous abufe of revelation in the ages of dark fuperftition, was the *corfned* or morfel of execration; being a piece of cheefe or bread, of about an ounce in weight, which was confecrated with a form of exorcifm; defiring of the Almighty that it might caufe convulfions and palenefs, and find no paffage, if the man was really guilty; but might turn to health and

and nouriſhment, if he was innocent. This corſned was then given to the ſuſpected perſon, who at the ſame time alſo received the holy ſacrament. This cuſtom has long ſince been gradually aboliſhed, though the remembrance of it ſtill ſubſiſts in certain phraſes of abjuration retained among the common people; as, "I will take the ſacrament upon it;" or, "may "this morſel be my laſt," and the like.

Battel. The trial by battel may be demanded at the election of the appellee, in either an appeal or an approvement; and it is carried on with equal ſolemnity as that on a writ of right: but with this difference, that there each party might hire a champion, but here they muſt fight in their proper perſons. Therefore women, prieſts, and ſome others might counterplead and refuſe the wager of battel. The form and manner of combat are much the ſame as upon a writ of right; only the oaths of the two combatants are vaſtly more ſtriking and ſolemn. The appellee, when appealed of felony, pleads not guilty, and throws down his glove, and declares he will defend the ſame by his body: the appellant takes up the glove, and replies that he is ready to make good the appeal, body for body; thereupon the appellee, taking the book in his right hand, and in his left the right hand of his antagoniſt, ſwears to this effect: "Hear this, O man, whom I hold by the hand, who calleſt "thyſelf John by the name of baptiſm, that I, who call my"ſelf Thomas by name of baptiſm, did not feloniouſly mur"der thy father, William by name, nor am any way guilty of "the ſaid felony. So help me God, and the ſaints; and this "I will defend againſt thee, by my body, as this court ſhall "award." To which the appellant replies, holding the bible and his antagoniſt's hand in the ſame manner; "Hear this, "O man, whom I hold by the hand, who calleſt thyſelf "Thomas by the name of baptiſm, that thou art perjured; "and therefore perjured becauſe that thou feloniouſly didſt "murder my father, William by name. So help me God, and "the ſaints; and this I will prove againſt thee by my body, as "this court ſhall award." The battel is then to be fought with the ſame weapons, *viz.* batons, the ſame ſolemnity, and the ſame oath againſt amulets and ſorcery, that are uſed in the civil combat: and if the appellee be ſo far vanquiſhed that he cannot or will not fight any longer, he ſhall be adjudged to be hanged immediately; and then, as well as if he be killed in battel, providence is deemed to have determined in favour of the truth, and his blood ſhall be attainted; but if he kills the appellant, or can maintain the fight from ſunriſing, till the ſtars appear in the evening, he ſhall be acquitted. So alſo if the appellant becomes recreant, and pronounces the horrible word *craven*, he ſhall loſe his *liberam legem*, and become infamous; and the appellee ſhall recover his damages, and alſo be for ever quit, not only of the appeal, but for all indictments likewiſe for the ſame offence.

Copy of Record of Indictment. In caſes where the priſoner or defendant is acquitted by a jury, the court ſometimes grants him a copy of the record of his indictment and acquittal, as a foundation for a legal proceſs againſt the proſecutor; but this is frequently denied where there is any the leaſt probable cauſe to found ſuch proſecution upon. But an action on the caſe for a malicious proſecution may be founded upon an indictment, whereon no acquittal can be had; as, if it be rejected by the grand jury, or be *coram non judice*, or be inſufficiently drawn; for it is not the danger of the plaintiff, but the ſcandal, vexation, and expence, upon which his action is founded.

Clergy. The *privilegium clericale*, or, in common ſpeech, the *benefit of clergy*, had its origin from the pious regard paid by chriſtian princes to the church in its infant ſtate; and the ill uſe which the popiſh eccleſiaſtics ſoon made of that pious regard. The exemptions which they granted to the church were principally of two kinds: 1. Exemption of *places*, conſecrated to religious duties, from criminal arreſts, which was the foundation of ſanctuaries. 2. Exemption of the *perſons* of clergymen from criminal proceſs before the ſecular judge in a few particular caſes, which was the true original meaning of the *privilegium clericale*. Among their other encroachments the Romiſh clergy endeavoured to obtain a total exemption from the ſecular juriſdiction, but in this they failed; and although the ancient *privilegium clericale* was in *ſome* capital caſes, yet it was not *univerſally* allowed. In thoſe particular caſes, the biſhop or ordinary was uſed to demand his clerks to be remitted out of the king's courts, as ſoon as they were indicted: concerning the allowance of which demand there was for many years a great uncertainty; till at length it was finally ſettled in the reign of Henry VI. that the priſoner ſhould firſt be arraigned; and might either then claim his benefit of clergy, by way of declinatory plea; or, after conviction, by way of arreſting judgment. Originally the law was held, that no man ſhould be admitted to the privilege of clergy, but ſuch as had the clerical habit and tonſure; but in proceſs of time, a much wider and more comprehenſive criterion was eſtabliſhed, every one that could read being accounted a clerk, and allowed the benefit of clerkſhip. But when learning began to be more generally diſſeminated than

than formerly, it was found that as many laymen as divines were admitted to the privilege: and therefore by 4 Hen. VII. c. 13. a diſtinction was once more drawn between mere lay ſcholars and clerks that were really in orders; and, although it was thought reaſonable ſtill to mitigate the ſeverity of the law with regard to the former, yet they were not put upon the ſame footing with actual clergy; for the ſtatute directs, that no perſon once admitted to the benefit of clergy, ſhall be admitted thereto a ſecond time, unleſs he produces his orders; and in order to diſtinguiſh their perſons, all laymen who are allowed this privilege ſhall be burnt with a hot iron in the brawn of the left thumb. This diſtinction between learned laymen and real clerks in orders, was aboliſhed for a time by the ſtatutes 28 Hen. VIII. c. 1. and 32 Hen. VIII. c. 3. but is held to have been virtually reſtored by 1 Edw. VI. c. 12. which alſo enacts, that lords of parliament and peers of the realm, having place and voice in parliament, may have the benefit of their peerage equivalent to that of clergy, for the firſt offence, (although they cannot read, and without being burnt in the hand) for all offences then clergyable to commoners, and alſo for the crimes of houſe-breaking, high-way robbery, horſe-ſtealing, and robbing of churches. After clergy had been allowed, it was uſual for the ordinary to bring offenders to a new canonical trial, replete with abſurdity and groſs perjury; but this diſgraceful ſupplementary trial was aboliſhed by the 18 Eliz. c. 7. which directs, that after allowance of clergy and burning in the hand, the priſoner ſhall forthwith be enlarged, with proviſo, that the judge may, if he thinks fit, continue the offender in jail, for any time not exceeding a year. And thus the law continued, for above a century, unaltered; except only that the 21 Jac. I. c. 6. allowed that women convicted of ſimple larcenies under the value of ten ſhillings ſhould (not properly have the benefit of clergy, for they were not called upon to read, but) be burned in the hand, and whipped, ſet in the ſtocks, or impriſoned for any time not exceeding a year. And a ſimilar indulgence, by the ſtats. 3 and 4 W. and M. c. 9. and 4 and 5 W. and M. c. 24. was extended to women guilty of any clergyable felony whatever; who were allowed to claim once the benefit of the ſtatute, in the like manner as men might claim the benefit of clergy, and to be diſcharged upon being burned in the hand, and impriſoned any time not exceeding a year. The puniſhment of burning in the *hand* being found ineffectual, was alſo changed by 10 and 11 W. III. c. 23. into burning in the moſt viſible part of the left cheek, neareſt the noſe: but, ſuch an indelible ſtigma being found by experience to render offenders deſperate, this proviſion was re-

 pealed

pealed about ſeven years afterwards, by 5 Ann. c. 6. and, till that period, all women, all peers of parliament and peereſſes, and all male commoners who could read were diſcharged in all clergyable felonies; the males abſolutely, if clerks in orders; and other commoners, both male and female, upon branding; and peers and peereſſes without branding, for the firſt offence; yet all liable (excepting peers and peereſſes,) if the judge ſaw occaſion, to impriſonment not exceeding a year. And thoſe men who could not read, if under the degree of peerage, were hanged. Afterwards indeed it was conſidered, that education and learning were no extenuations of guilt, but quite the reverſe: and that, if the puniſhment of death for ſimple felony was too ſevere for thoſe who had been liberally inſtructed, it was, *a fortiori*, too ſevere for the ignorant alſo; and thereupon by the ſame ſtatute 5 Ann. c. 6. it was enacted, that the benefit of clergy ſhould be granted to all thoſe who were intitled to aſk it, without requiring them to read by way of conditional merit; but experience having ſhewn, that ſo univerſal a lenity was frequently inconvenient, and an encouragement to commit the lower degrees of felony; and that, although, capital puniſhments were too rigorous for theſe inferior offences, yet no puniſhment at all (or next to none) was as much too gentle; it was farther enacted by the ſame ſtatute, that when any perſon is convicted of any theft or larceny, and burnt in the hand for the ſame, according to the ancient law, he ſhall alſo at the diſcretion of the judge be ſentenced to the houſe of correction or public work-houſe, to hard labour in penitentiary houſes, and in ſome caſes to tranſportation. At this day the benefit of clergy is allowed to all clerks in orders, without branding, tranſportation, fine, or whipping, and this as often as they offend; but clergymen have no privilege in petty larcenies; they are liable to be whipped or tranſported like other perſons, though they are ſubject to no corporal puniſhment on being convicted of a grand larceny, or any clergyable felony. All lords of parliament, and peers of the realm having place and voice in parliament, by the ſtat. 1 Edw. VI. c. 12. (which is likewiſe held to extend to peereſſes,) ſhall be diſcharged in all clergyable and other felonies, provided for by the act, without any burning in the hand, or impriſonment, or other puniſhment; but this only for the firſt offence. Laſtly, all the commons of the realm, not in orders, whether male or female, are for the firſt offence diſcharged of the capital puniſhment of felonies within the benefit of clergy, upon being burnt in the hand, whipped, or fined, or ſuffering a diſcretionary impriſonment in the common jail, the houſe of correction, one of the penitentiary houſes, or in the places of labour for the benefit

of

of ſome navigation; or in caſes of larceny, upon being tranſported for ſeven years, if the court ſhall think proper. A layman, who has once had the benefit of clergy, may be precluded from obtaining it a ſecond time, by a counter plea on the part of the proſecution, averring the identity of the priſoner's perſon, and that he had before been allowed the benefit of his clergy, though the ſecond crime be quite different from the firſt; as, a perſon convicted of bigamy is liable to ſuffer death for a manſlaughter, or any other clergyable felony. The benefit of clergy is not allowed either in high treaſon, petit larceny, or in any mere miſdemeanors at common law; and therefore it may be laid down for a rule, that it was allowable only in petit treaſon and capital felonies, which for the moſt part became legally intitled to this indulgence by the ſtatute *de clero*, 25 Edw. III. ſt. 3. c. 4. But yet it was not allowed in all felonies whatſoever: for in ſome it was denied even in the common law, viz. *inſidiatio viarum*, or lying in wait for one on the high-way; *depopulatio agrorum*, or deſtroying and ravaging a country; and *combuſtio domorum*, or arſon; all which are a kind of hoſtile acts, and in ſome degree border upon treaſon. And further, all theſe identical crimes, together with petit treaſon, and many other acts of felony, are ouſted of clergy by particular acts of parliament, which have for the moſt part been mentioned. In general it may be obſerved, 1. That in all felonies, whether new created or by common law, clergy is now allowable, unleſs taken away by expreſs words of an act of parliament. 2. That where clergy is taken away from the principal, it is not of courſe taken away from the acceſſary, unleſs he be alſo particularly included in the words of the ſtatute. 3. That, when the benefit of clergy is taken away from the *offence*, (as in caſe of murder, robbery, and burglary,) a principal in the ſecond degree, being preſent, aiding and abetting the crime, is excluded from his clergy; but 4. That, where it is only taken away from the *perſon committing* the offence, (as in the caſe of ſtabbing, or committing larceny in a dwelling-houſe, or privately from the perſon,) his aiders and abettors are not excluded. The conſequences to the party of allowing him his clergy, excluſive of branding him, &c. are, 1. That by his conviction he forfeits all his goods to the king, which, being once veſted in the crown, ſhall not afterwards be reſtored to the offender. 2. That after conviction, and till he receives the judgment of the law, by branding, or ſome of its ſubſtitutes, or elſe is pardoned by the king, he is, to all intents and purpoſes, a felon, and ſubject to all the diſabilities and incidents of a felon. 3. That after burning or its ſubſtitute, or pardon, he is diſcharged for ever of that, and all other felonies before commit-

 ted

ted within the benefit of clergy; but not of felonies of which ſuch benefit is excluded, and this by ſtats. 8 Eliz. c. 4., and 18 Eliz. c. 7. 4. That by the burning or its ſubſtitute, or the pardon of it, he is reſtored to all capacities and credits, and the poſſeſſion of his lands, as if he had never been convicted. 5. That what is ſaid with regard to the advantages of commoners and laymen, ſubſequent to the burning in the hand, is equally applicable to all peers and clergymen, although never branded at all, or ſubjected to other puniſhment in its ſtead. For they have the ſame privileges, without any burning, or other ſubſtitute for it, which others are intitled to after it.

Imprisonment. The ordinary incidents attending impriſonments have been mentioned; when it is inflicted by way of puniſhment, the county jail is not always the place ſelected; but houſes of correction, work-houſes, or penitentiary houſes are frequently choſen. In forming the plan of theſe penitentiary houſes, the principal objects have been, by ſobriety, cleanlineſs, and medical aſſiſtance, by a regular ſeries of labour, by ſolitary confinement during the intervals of work, and by religious inſtruction, to preſerve and amend the health of the unhappy offenders, to inure them to habits of induſtry, to guard them from pernicious company, to accuſtom them to ſerious reflection, and to teach them both the principles and practice of every chriſtian and moral duty.

Burning in the Hand and Whipping. By the 19 Geo. III. c. 74. inſtead of burning in the hand, which was ſometimes too ſlight, and ſometimes too diſgraceful a puniſhment, the court in all clergyable felonies may impoſe a pecuniary fine, or, except in the caſe of manſlaughter, may order the offender to be once or oftener, but not more than thrice, either publicly or privately whipped; ſuch private whipping, to prevent colluſion or abuſe, to be inflicted in the preſence of two witneſſes; and in the caſe of female offenders, in the preſence of females only. Which fine or whipping ſhall have the ſame conſequences as burning in the hand; and the offender ſhall be equally liable to a ſubſequent detainer or impriſonment.

Fines. Fines and the term of impriſonment are often diſcretionary; for, whatever may be urged in favour of certain and equal puniſhments, it muſt be evident that equality in theſe reſpects would be the greateſt injuſtice; as ſome men would pay a fixed fine with contempt, and others would wreak their malice in defiance of an impriſonment, of which they knew the definite end. Courts are however prevented from inflicting exceſſive fines both by Magna Charta and the Bill of Rights.

Pillory. For ſome offences the puniſhment is to ſtand for a given time in and upon the pillory. This puniſhment was formerly

formerly attended with mutilations, as flitting the nofe, nailing down the ears, and burning with hot irons, but in the more mild adminiftration of juftice in modern days, fuch difgufting aggravations of pain are unheard of. The pillory is confidered as merely an exhibition of an offender, for the purpofe of rendering him notorious, and all means of giving him unneceffary pain, or exciting popular indignation, are cautioufly avoided. This lenity in the execution of fentence has contributed to humanize the people. They were ufed formerly to confider the pillory as intended to inflict every corporeal pain, fhort of death; and fhewed their readinefs to co-operate in the fpirit of the law, by pelting the criminal with miffiles of every kind, fo that fome have actually loft their lives by this lawlefs and misjudging violence. In later times, there are few inftances of perfons in the pillory being affaulted by the mob, and then only in cafes of the moft odious crimes; fuch indeed as reduce the confiderate and humane to the neceffity of deploring the violence of the people, without being able to commiferate the fufferers.

Stocks. Another place of expofure, which is reforted to without conviction before a court, for the punifhment of riotous, drunken, and diforderly perfons, common beggars and vagrants, is the ftocks, of which there is generally a pair in every parifh. In thefe the beadle or conftable, by order of a magiftrate, places fmall offenders, their ancles being received into holes made in boards placed for the purpofe, and the offender fitting there for the time prefcribed. Near to, or united with the ftocks, there is alfo a whipping poft, for the caftigation of thofe whom, on a fummary conviction for certain minor offences, a juftice is empowered fo to punifh.

Ducking Stool. Formerly, but not now-a-days, there was in every parifh, near a pond, an engine of correction called the trebucket, caftigatory, or *cucking* ftool, which in the Saxon language is faid to fignify the fcolding ftool, for the punifhment of common fcolds, who after conviction on indictment, might be fentenced to it. The name is frequently corrupted into *ducking* ftool, becaufe the refidue of the judgment is, that fhe who is fo placed therein is plunged in the water for her punifhment.

Transportation and the Hulks. From thefe inferior punifhments, thofe of a more folemn and affecting nature come next to be confidered. Tranfportation or exile is a fentence unknown to the common law of England; and where it is now inflicted, it is either by the choice of the criminal himfelf, in order to efcape capital punifhment, or it is impofed by the exprefs direction of fome act of parliament; for no power on earth, except the authority of parliament, can fend a fubject of England, not even a criminal, out of the land againft his will. The firft introduction of it into our laws was in the reign of Elizabeth; but it feems to have taken place more nearly as now practifed, about the time of the reftoration; and after the eftablifhment of Englifh colonies in America, it became in this country, as in all others which have had colonies, the moft common fentence of criminals. Several acts of parliament vefted in the king the power of tranfporting to America perfons convicted of divers offences, and of difpenfing with their tranfportation and allowing them to return, at his pleafure, which amounted to a pardon. But when America became independent, acts of the 19 Geo. III. c. 74. and 24 Geo. III. feff. 2. c. 56. empowered the courts, when any perfon fhould be convicted of grand or petit larceny, or any other crime for which he fhould be liable by law to be tranfported to America, to order him to be tranfported to any parts beyond the feas, or elfewhere, in like manner and for the fame term of years for which fuch perfon was liable to be tranfported to America.

By thefe acts too, penitentiary houfes, as already mentioned, were eftablifhed; and it was enacted, that where any *male perfon* fhall be lawfully convicted of grand larceny, or any other crime, except petty larceny, for which he fhall be liable to be tranfported to any parts beyond the feas for feven years, the court may inftead, order that fuch perfon, appearing to be of competent age, and free from any bodily infirmity, fhall be punifhed by being kept on board fhips, or veffels properly accommodated for fecurity, employment, and health; and by being employed in hard labour, in the raifing fand, foil, and gravel from, and cleanfing the river Thames, or any other navigable river, or any port, harbour, or haven, in England, fuch river, port, harbour, or haven, being previoufly approved and appointed for that purpofe by an order of privy council; or in any other fervice for the benefit of the navigation of the faid rivers, ports, harbours, or havens, or in any other public works, upon the banks or fhores of the fame, under the management and direction of fuch fuperintendant as fhall be appointed for the Thames by the juftices of Middlefex, and for other rivers, &c. by the juftices of the county where they are fituated, or of fuch counties adjoining the fame as the court fhall direct at their quarter feffion, for fuch term not lefs than one year, nor exceeding five years; or in cafe fuch offender fhall be liable to be tranfported for fourteen years, not exceeding feven years, as the court fhall think fit.

Still thefe regulations were infufficient to anfwer the required purpofes, until the 27 Geo. III. c. 2. which recited, that his

his majesty, by two several orders in council, had judged fit to declare and appoint the place to which certain offenders should be transported for the time or terms of their several sentences to be the eastern coast of New South Wales, or some one or other of the islands adjacent, and provided means for carrying those orders into effect.

In all cases of transportation, or sentence to the hulks, the party returning before his term is expired, or escaping from the hulks, and being at large, is guilty of felony, and suffers death without benefit of clergy.

ATTAINDER. When sentence of death is pronounced, the immediate inseparable consequence by the common law is attainder. He is no longer of any credit or reputation; he cannot be a witness in any court; neither is he capable of performing the functions of another man: for, by an anticipation of his punishment, he is already dead in law. This is after *judgment*: for there is a great difference between a man *convicted* and *attainted*; though they are frequently, through inaccuracy, confounded together. After conviction only a man is liable to none of these disabilities; but when judgment is once pronounced, both law and fact conspire to prove him completely guilty.

The consequences of attainder are forfeiture and corruption of blood.

FORFEITURE. Forfeiture is twofold; of real, and personal estates. First, as to real estates: by attainder in high treason, a man forfeits to the king all his lands and tenements of inheritance, whether fee-simple, or fee-tail, and all his rights of entry on lands and tenements, which he had at the time of the offence committed, or at any time afterwards, to be for ever vested in the crown: and also the profits of all lands and tenements, which he had in his own right for life or years, so long as such interest shall subsist. This forfeiture relates back to the time of the treason committed: so as to avoid all intermediate sales and incumbrances, but not those before the fact: and therefore a wife's jointure is not forfeitable for the treason of her husband; because settled upon her before the treason committed; but her dower is forfeited by the express provision of the 5 and 6 Edw. VI. c. 11: and yet the husband shall be tenant by the courtesy of the wife's lands, if the wife be attainted of treason: for that is not prohibited by the statute. But although, after attainder, the forfeiture relates back to the time of the treason committed, yet it does not take effect unless the attainder be had, of which it is one of the fruits: and therefore if a traitor dies before judgment pronounced, or is killed in open rebellion, or is hanged by martial law, it works

works no forfeiture of his lands: for he never was attainted of treason. But if the chief justice of the king's bench (the supreme coroner of all England) in person, upon view of the body of one killed in open rebellion, records it, and returns the record into his own court, both lands and goods shall be forfeited. At the time of the union, the crime of treason in Scotland was, by the Scots law, in many respects different from that of treason in England; and particularly in its consequences of forfeiture of intailed estates, which was more peculiarly English; yet it seemed necessary that a crime so nearly affecting government should, both in its essence and consequences, be put upon the same footing in both parts of the united kingdom. In new modelling these laws, the Scotch nation and the English house of commons struggled hard, partly to maintain, and partly to acquire a total immunity from forfeiture and corruption of blood: which the house of lords as firmly resisted. At length a compromise was agreed to, which is established by this statute, *viz.* that the same crimes, and no other, should be treason in Scotland that are so in England; and that the English forfeitures and corruption of blood should take place in Scotland till the death of the then Pretender, and then cease throughout the whole of Great Britain: the lords artfully proposing this temporary clause, in hopes (it is said) that the prudence of succeeding parliaments would make it perpetual. This has partly been done by the statute 17 Geo. II. c. 39. the operation of these indemnifying clauses being thereby still farther suspended, till the death of the sons of the Pretender.

In petit treason and felony, the offender also forfeits all his chattel interests absolutely, and the profits of all estates of freehold during life; and after his death, all his lands and tenements in fee simple (but not those in tail) to the crown, for a very short period of time: for the king shall have them for a year and a day, and may commit therein what waste he pleases; which is called the king's *year*, *day*, and *waste*. Formerly the king had only a liberty of committing waste on the lands of felons, by pulling down their houses, extirpating their gardens, ploughing their meadows, and cutting down their woods; but this tending greatly to the prejudice of the public, it was agreed in the reign of Henry I. in this kingdom, that the king should have the profits of the land for one year and a day, in lieu of the destruction he was otherwise at liberty to commit; and therefore *magna charta* provides that the king shall only hold such lands for a year and a day, and then restore them to the lord of the fee; without any mention made of waste. But the stat. 17 Edw. II. *de prærogativo regis*, seems to to suppose, that the king shall have his year, day, *and* waste: and not the year and day *instead of* waste. Which Sir Edward Coke (and the author of a mirror before him) very justly look upon as an incroachment, though a very ancient one, of the royal prerogative. This year, day, and waste, are now usually compounded for; but otherwise they regularly belong to the crown; and, after their expiration, the land would naturally descend to the heir, (as in gavel kind tenure it still does) did not its feodal quality intercept such descent, and give it, by way of escheat, to the lord. These forfeitures for felony do also arise only upon attainder; and therefore a *felo de se* forfeits no lands of inheritance or freehold, for he never is attainted as a felon. They likewise relate back to the time of the offence committed, as well as forfeitures for treason; so as to avoid all intermediate charges and conveyances.

The forfeiture of goods and chattels accrues in every one of the higher kinds of offence: in high treason or misprision thereof, petit treason, felonies of all sorts whether clergyable or not, self-murder or felony *de se*, petit larceny or standing mute, and the offences of striking, &c. in Westminster-Hall.

For *flight* also, on an accusation of treason, felony, or even petit larceny, whether the party be found guilty or acquitted, if the jury find the flight, the party shall forfeit his goods and chattels; for the very flight is an offence, carrying with it a strong presumption of guilt, and is at least an endeavour to elude justice: but the jury very seldom find the flight; forfeiture being looked upon, since the vast increase of personal property, as too large a penalty for an offence, to which a man is prompted by the desire of self-preservation.

There are some remarkable differences between the forfeiture of lands, and of goods and chattels.

1. Lands are forfeited upon attainder, and not before: goods and chattels are forfeited by conviction.

2. In outlawries for treason or felony, lands are forfeited only by the judgment: but the goods and chattels are forfeited by a man's being first put in the *exigent*, without staying till he is *quinto exactus*, or finally outlawed; for the secreting himself so long from justice is construed a flight in law.

3. The forfeiture of lands has relation to the time of the fact committed, so as to avoid all subsequent sales and incumbrances: but the forfeiture of goods and chattels has no relation backwards; so that those only which a man has at the time of conviction shall be forfeited. Therefore a traitor or felon may *bona fide* sell any of his chattels real or personal, for the sustenance of himself and family, between the fact and conviction: for personal property is of so fluctuating a nature, that it passes through many hands in a short time; and no buyer could

could be ſafe, if he were to return the goods which he had fairly bought, provided any of the prior vendors had committed a treaſon or felony. Yet if they be colluſively and not *bona fide* parted with, merely to defraud the crown, the law (and particularly the ſtat. 13 Eliz. c. 5.) will reach them; for they are all the while truly and ſubſtantially the goods of the offender; and as he, if acquitted, might recover them himſelf, as not parted with for a good conſideration; ſo in caſe he happens to be convicted, the law will recover them for the king.

Corruption of Blood. Corruption of Blood extends both upwards and downwards; ſo that an attainted perſon can neither inherit lands or other hereditaments from his anceſtors, nor retain thoſe he is already in poſſeſſion of, nor tranſmit them by deſcent to any heir; but they eſcheat the lord of the fee, ſubject to the king's ſuperior right of forfeiture: and the perſon attainted alſo obſtructs all deſcents to his poſterity, wherever they are obliged to derive a title through him to a remoter anceſtor.

Execution. The judgments on various offences have already been mentioned in treating of them. When a peer is convicted of high treaſon the ſentence on him is the ſame as on commoners, but it is uſual for the king to remit all parts of it except *beheading*. The judgment of death againſt a man or woman for felony has always been the ſame ſince the reign of Henry I. *viz.* that he or ſhe be hanged by the neck till dead; which in the roll is ſhortly entered thus, "*ſuſ. per coll.*" for *ſuſpendatur per collum*, let him be hanged by the neck. It may afford matter of ſpeculation, Blackſtone obſerves, that in civil cauſes there ſhould be ſuch a variety of writs of execution to recover a trifling debt, iſſued in the king's name, and under the ſeal of the court, without which the ſheriff cannot legally ſtir one ſtep; and yet that the execution of a man, the moſt important and terrible taſk of any, ſhould depend upon a marginal note. Upon this point Mr. Chriſtian gives the following judicious and ſatisfactory explanation: Though it be true that a marginal note in a calendar, ſigned by the judge, is the only warrant that the ſheriff has for the execution of a convict, yet it is made with more caution and ſolemnity than is repreſented by the learned commentator. At the end of the aſſizes, the clerk of aſſize makes out in writing four liſts of all the priſoners, with ſeparate columns, containing their crimes, verdicts, and ſentences, leaving a blank column, which the judge fills up oppoſite the names of the capital convicts by writing, *to be executed*, *reſpited*, or *reprieved*. Theſe four calendars, being firſt carefully compared together by the judge and the clerk of the aſſize, are ſigned by them, and one is given to the ſheriff, one to to the jailor, and the judge and the clerk of the aſſize each keep another. If the ſheriff receives afterwards no ſpecial order from the judge, he executes the judgment of the law in the uſual manner, agreeably to the directions of his calendar.

Execution ought not to be awarded into a different county from that wherein the party was tried and convicted, except only where a record of attainder is removed into the court of king's-bench, which may award the execution in the ſame county wherein it ſits; and where the priſoner is in the cuſtody of the marſhal of the king's-bench, the uſual place of execution is at Saint Thomas at Waterings, in the county of Surry. In all caſes, as well capital as otherwiſe, execution muſt be performed by the ſheriff or his deputy; whoſe warrant for ſo doing was anciently by precept under the hand and ſeal of the judge, as it is ſtill practiſed in the court of the lord high ſteward upon the execution of a peer, though in the court of the peers in parliament it is done by writ from the king. Afterwards it was eſtabliſhed that in caſe of life the judge may command execution to be done without any writ. In London, the Recorder, after reporting to the king in perſon, the caſe of the ſeveral priſoners, and receiving his royal pleaſure that the law muſt take its courſe, iſſues his warrant to the ſheriffs, directing them to do execution at the day and place aſſigned. If a man condemned come to life after he has been hanged, he ought to be hanged again; for the judgment is not executed till he is dead.

Reprieve. A reprieve, from *reprendre*, to take back, is the withdrawing of a ſentence for an interval of time, whereby the execution is ſuſpended. Every court which has power to award an execution, has alſo of common right a diſcretionary power of granting a reprieve; as where a perſon pleads a pardon defective in point of form, but ſufficiently ſhewing the king's intention of mercy; or where it is doubtful whether the offence be not included in a general ſtatute pardon; or whether, as it is laid in the indictment, it amounts to ſo high a crime as that with which the priſoner was charged. Judges continue to have this power after their commiſſion is determined; and by the 8 Geo. III. c. 15. a power is given to judges of aſſize to reprieve a priſoner for the purpoſe of obtaining a conditional pardon.

There are reprieves independently of grace, which ariſe from the neceſſity of law. If a woman quick with child is condemned either for treaſon or felony, ſhe may allege her being with child in order to get the execution reſpited, and thereupon the ſheriff or marſhal is commanded to take her into a private room, and to impanel a jury of matrons to

try

try and examine whether ſhe is quick with child or not; and if they find her quick with child, the execution is reſpited till her delivery; but this reſpite cannot be demanded more than once.

Another cauſe of regular reprieve is, if the offender become *non compos*, between the judgment and the award of execution: for regularly, though a man be *compos* when he commit a capital crime, yet if he becomes *non compos* after, he ſhall not be indicted; if after indictment, he ſhall not be convicted; if after conviction, he ſhall not receive judgment; if after judgment, he ſhall not be ordered for execution. The law in ſuch caſe knows not but he might have offered ſome reaſon, if in his ſenſes, to have ſtayed theſe reſpective proceedings. It is therefore an invariable rule, when any time intervenes between the attainder and the award of execution, to demand of the priſoner what he has to allege, why execution ſhould not be awarded againſt him; and if he appears to be inſane, the judge, in his diſcretion may, and ought, to reprieve him.

Pardon. The king may pardon all offences merely againſt the crown, or the public; excepting, that to preſerve the liberty of the ſubject, the committing any man to priſon out of the realm is by the *habeas corpus* act, 31 Chas. II. c. 2. made a *præmunire*, unpardonable even by the king. Nor can the king pardon where private juſtice is principally concerned in the proſecution of offenders. Neither can he pardon a common nuiſance while it remains unredreſſed, or ſo as to prevent an abatement of it, though afterwards he may remit the fine. Neither, laſtly, can the king pardon an offence againſt a popular or penal ſtatute, after information brought; for thereby the informer has acquired a private property in his part of the penalty. There is alſo a reſtriction of a peculiar nature, that affects the prerogative of pardoning, in caſe of parliamentary impeachments, viz. that the king's pardon cannot be *pleaded*, to any ſuch impeachment, ſo as to impede the inquiry, and ſtop the proſecution of great and notorious offenders; but after the impeachment has been ſolemnly heard and determined, it is not underſtood that the king's royal grace is further reſtrained or abridged.

As to the *manner* of pardoning: Firſt, it muſt be under the *great* ſeal. A warrant under the privy ſeal, or ſign manual, though it may be a ſufficient authority to admit the party to bail, in order to plead the king's pardon, when obtained in proper form, is not of itſelf a complete irrevocable pardon. Next, it is a general rule, that, wherever it may reaſonably be preſumed the king is deceived, the pardon is void. Therefore any ſuppreſſion of truth, or ſuggeſtion of falſehood, in a charter of pardon, will vitiate the whole, for the king was miſinformed. General words have alſo a very imperfect effect in pardons. A

 pardon

pardon of all felonies will not pardon a conviction or attainder of felony (for it is presumed the king knew not of these proceedings); but the conviction or attainder must be particularly mentioned; and a pardon of felonies will not include piracy, for that is no felony punishable at the common law. It is also enacted by 13 Rich. II. c. 1. that no pardon for treason, murder, or rape, shall be allowed, unless the offence be particularly specified therein; and particularly in murder, it shall be expressed whether it was committed by lying in wait, assault, or malice prepense. Pardons of murder were therefore always granted with a *non obstante* of the statute of King Richard, till the time of the revolution, when the doctrine of *non obstante* ceasing, it was doubted whether murder could be pardoned generally; but it was determined by the court of king's bench, that the king may pardon on an indictment of murder, as well as a subject may discharge an appeal. Under these and a few other restrictions, it is a general rule, that a pardon shall be taken most beneficially *for* the subject, and most strongly against the king.

A pardon may also be *conditional*, that is, the king may extend his mercy upon what terms he pleases; and may annex to his bounty a condition either precedent or subsequent, on the performance whereof the validity of the pardon will depend. But although the king may pardon conditionally, or remit part of the sentence of the law, he can in no case aggravate such sentence, or alter the terms of it by any fanciful commutation.

With regard to the manner of *allowing* pardons, it may be observed, that a pardon by act of parliament is more beneficial than by the king's charter; for a man is not bound to plead it, but the court must, *ex officio*, take notice of it; neither can he lose the benefit of it by his own *laches*, or negligence, as he may of the king's charter of pardon. The king's charter of pardon must be specially pleaded, and that at a proper time: for, if a man is indicted, and has a pardon in his pocket, and afterwards puts himself upon his trial by pleading the general issue, he has waived the benefit of such pardon; but, if a man avails himself thereof as soon as by course of law he may, a pardon may either be pleaded upon arraignment, or in arrest of judgment, or in bar of execution. Anciently, by 10 Edw. III. c. 2. no pardon of felony could be allowed unless the party found sureties for the good behaviour before the sheriff and coroners of the county; but that statute is repealed by 5 and 6 W. and M. c. 13, which, instead thereof, gives the judges of the court a discretionary power to bind the criminal, pleading such pardon, to his good behaviour, with two sureties, for any term not exceeding seven years.

Lastly,

Laſtly, the *effect* of pardon by the king, is to make the offender a new man; to acquit him of all corporal penalties and forfeitures annexed to that offence for which he obtains his pardon; and not ſo much to reſtore his former, as to give him a new, credit and capacity. But nothing can reſtore or purify the blood when once corrupted, if the pardon be not allowed till after attainder, but the high and tranſcendent power of parliament. Yet if a perſon attainted receives the king's pardon, and afterwards has a ſon, that ſon may be heir to his father.

Pardons (according to ſome theoriſts) ſhould be excluded in a perfect legiſlation, where puniſhments are mild but certain; for that the clemency of the prince ſeems a tacit diſapprobation of the laws; but the excluſion of pardons muſt neceſſarily introduce a very dangerous power in the judge or jury, that of conſtruing the criminal law by the ſpirit inſtead of the letter; or elſe it muſt be holden, what no man will ſeriouſly avow, that the ſituation and circumſtances of the offender, though they alter not the eſſence of the crime, ought to make no diſtinction in the puniſhment. In pure democracies there is no power of pardoning lodged in any member of the ſtate; but in monarchies the king acts in a ſuperior ſphere, and though he regulates the whole government as the firſt mover, yet he does not appear in any of the diſagreeable or invidious parts of it. Whenever the nation ſee him perſonally engaged, it is only in works of legiſlature, magnificence, or compaſſion. To him therefore the people look up as the fountain of nothing but bounty and grace; and theſe repeated acts of goodneſs, coming immediately from his own hand, endear the ſovereign to his ſubjects, and contribute more than any thing to root in their hearts that filial affection, and perſonal loyalty, which are the ſure eſtabliſhment of a prince.

END OF THE SECOND VOLUME.

Strahan and Preſton,
New-ſtreet-Square, London.

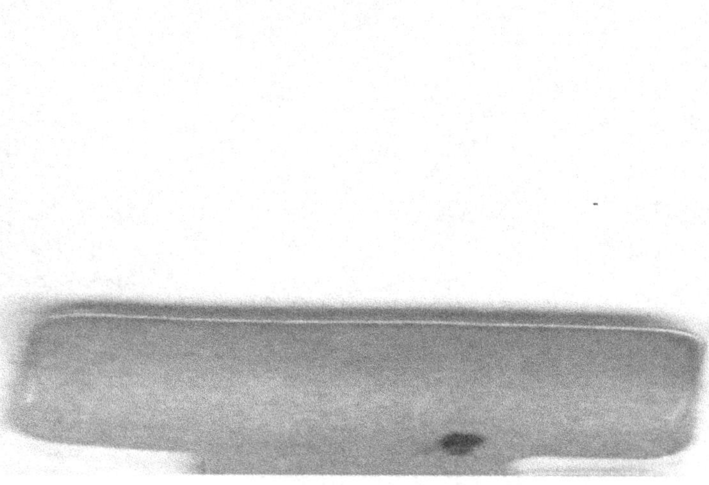

CPSIA information can be obtained
at www.ICGtesting.com
Printed in the USA
BVHW060224120819
555626BV00002B/262/P